HOME
MANAGEMENT

HOME MANAGEMENT

EDITED BY

Alison Barnes

Volume Two

GEORGE NEWNES LIMITED
15–17 LONG ACRE, LONDON, W.C.2

PRINTED AND BOUND IN ENGLAND BY
HAZELL WATSON AND VINEY LTD
AYLESBURY AND SLOUGH

CONTENTS

Volume Two

CONTENTS

CONTENTS

CONTENTS

CONTENTS

COLOUR ILLUSTRATIONS

Volume Two

COLOUR ILLUSTRATIONS

VOLUME TWO

A pleasant home in the spirit of the present, designed by Tayler and Green, FF.R.I.B.A.

THE HOME OF TODAY—
AND TOMORROW

What looks advanced and up to the minute now will be quite old-fashioned in twenty years' time

WE live in an age of revolution, and the most drastic changes of all are taking place in our homes.

A mere twenty years ago some of the labour-saving devices and ideas which we take entirely for granted had not even been tested. Think of the difference the quick-frozen foods have made to catering and budgeting, bringing out-of-season fruits, vegetables, meat, fish and poultry into the home in tip-top condition. Such foods are often of higher quality and may actually be a great deal fresher than the so-called "fresh" equivalents—

The house of the future, as seen by architects Alison and Peter Smithson, is built round a central patio garden. Fashions of the 1980's by Teddy Tinling

1

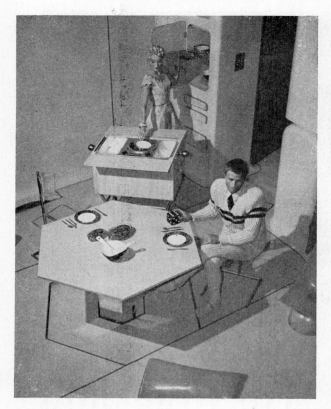

a modern roller instead of paint brushes. Wallpapers can be proofed against children's fingermarks; fabrics made waterproof, resistant to dirt and creasing, and have pleats woven into them during manufacture which will not come out, even during washing and drying. More and more materials are appearing which do not require ironing and which dry in a few minutes. When we travel, cook, scrub the floor, hang up our clothes or go for a picnic, we have cause to bless the name of Polythene, which makes unbreakable bottles and containers of all kinds, bowls, buckets, measuring jugs, protective bags large enough for a man's suit and small enough to keep a packet of sandwiches moist and fresh. We have plastic tablecloths that look like fine linen but only need wiping over with a damp cloth to restore them to absolute freshness, nylon undies and Terylene suits, skirts, trousers and net curtains, all of which dry in a few minutes; cellulose sponges and dish cloths and nylon pot scourers that never get smelly and unpleasant in use.

for the simple reason that they are produced specially for preserving and processed only when they are at their best.

Imagine the world of our grandmothers when turpentine and beeswax were laboriously mixed to make floor polish, when flies were commonplace everywhere and moths took a deadly toll of woollen goods each year. Today we have a dazzling array of soap and detergents to choose from, and there are polishes for every purpose, many of them giving a waterproof finish. The insecticides have effectively reduced the fly population, and modern ideas of hygiene forbid the exposure of food to dust and flies. There are chemicals which spell death to the clothes moth, and furnishing fabrics and woollen dress materials can be bought which have been specially treated to withstand the pest.

What a difference the introduction of quick-drying, easily applied, non-smelling plastic emulsion paints has made to the home decorator—and how much more quickly and easily the amateur works with

LOOK FIRST AT THE DESIGN

In fact, the problem has become, not "Where can we get what we want?" but "Which shall we choose out of this bewildering variety of goods?"

The modern housewife and her husband naturally want the best value for their money, to find their way through the maze of new developments in plastics and synthetic textiles and new treatments for traditional materials, to know something about the goods they are buying—and to survey the market before they finally embark on a purchase.

For those who are able to get to London, there is now the Design Centre at 28 Haymarket, S.W.1. Here British goods

The single thermostatically controlled water tap over the kitchen sink is foot operated and there is an electric waste-disposal unit in the kitchen of the future, with its waist-level fitments

selected for their good design by independent technical advisers to the Council of Industrial Design are on permanent exhibition on weekdays, including Saturdays, from 9.30 a.m. to 5.30 p.m.

The Design Centre provides a place where intending purchasers can browse and look. Nothing is sold here, but retail prices are either marked or available from the information desk and, whenever possible, the names of local stockists are given.

But the important thing is that, when you buy anything you have seen displayed at the Design Centre, you can rely on having chosen an article which will do its job efficiently, is well-made from good

3

materials and is a pleasure to use and look at—in a word, well designed. Nothing is displayed there that has not passed the critical scrutiny of the Council of Industrial Design, a completely independent body which is not beholden to any trade group or manufacturer. Whether it is a tea service or a dining set, a saucepan or a fireplace, a preliminary visit to the Design Centre is a valuable help.

Secondly, when in doubt about which of a number of competitive articles to buy, always go for one bearing the kite mark of the British Standards Institution. They are constantly testing and reporting fearlessly on products of all types. You can become an associate member and receive "Shopper's Guide" for 10s. a year, on application to the Consumer Advisory Council, The British Standards Institution, Orchard House, Orchard Street, London, W.1.

ATOMIC POWER IN THE HOME

Progress is literally taking place before our eyes. In the next twenty years even more astonishing changes will take place in the home. Today's modern houses will in a very few years look like period pieces.

Most important single factor will undoubtedly be the development of atomic power for peaceful uses, with its inevitable effect on living. In the not very remote future all newly built houses will be supplied cheaply and easily with central heating in winter, air conditioning in summer, and constant hot water all the year round from the nearest atomic power plant. There is no difficulty about this. For years the waste heat generated by Battersea Power Station has supplied hot water and central heating to several blocks of London flats in the neighbourhood. The surplus energy from the Harwell atomic plant also provides heating for the surrounding buildings.

When atomic power replaces coal, coke, electricity and gas as a means of domestic heating, there will be less smoke, dust and dirt in the atmosphere. This will help eliminate the dreaded "smog" which now hangs like a pall over many industrial areas, and will make housekeeping easier because everything will remain clean much longer. Think of furnishing fabrics already proofed against shrinkage, stains, moths, damp and spills, which do not get dirty because the air is always pure and fresh. In addition, electronic devices will extract every scrap of dirt and grain of dust from a room at the flick of a switch—the vacuum cleaner principle developed on a larger scale.

When the water supply runs through expanding, unbreakable pipes made of materials akin to Polythene, the annual English tragedy of burst pipes will be a thing of the past. When electrically operated refuse destructors auto-

The bath fills from the bottom at the required temperature and is automatically cleaned with a foamless detergent. Jets in the bathroom walls dispense warm air, and there is a combined shower and drier

matically dispose of all rubbish except perhaps cans and bottles, when house windows are made of glass through which you can see out but not in, when inside walls are movable and you can see who is at the front door without moving from the kitchen sink—then we shall really be on the road to labour-saving.

At a recent Daily Mail Ideal Home Exhibition two architects, Alison and Peter Smithson, showed their idea of what the home of the 1980's will be like. First point of interest is that the house is not set in its own garden, but contains a small patio within its walls. The roof is

Two pieces of electrical equipment destined to take a prominent place in the home of tomorrow. Kenwood's automatic Dishmaster washes, rinses twice and dries in a matter of minutes enough crockery for a meal for twelve people. The same firm's Wastemaster electrically disposes of all kitchen waste, no need for dustbins.

covered with aluminium foil which reflects the sun's rays, and outside walls are soundproof and fireproof, the outer casing faced with aluminium foil. Heating, which comes chiefly from the floor, is supplied from the nearest atomic power station. Warmest room in the house is the bathroom, with its combined shower and drier unit, an infra-red lamp in the domed ceiling and jets dispensing either water or warm air, according to taste. The bath fills from the bottom at whatever temperature is required and has an automatic rinsing system which swills it down with a foamless detergent.

Air conditioning ensures that all smells are mechanically extracted, particularly in the kitchen, and that dust infiltration is also practically non-existent. There is a portable electro-static dust collector that works on its own, attracting dust and retaining it on easily replaceable paper sheets.

The rooms lead into one another like the compartments of a cave, and folding doors, which normally disappear inside wall fittings, can be used if greater privacy is required. All the rooms are of different size, height and shape, the highest being the living room, which faces south across the patio; the lowest the bedroom. The tilt of the roof over the bathroom allows the sunlight into the patio and the high living room.

Warm Air to Welcome You

At the kitchen sink there is a single thermostatically controlled water tap capable of delivering water at any temperature from cold to boiling at the touch of the foot, and an electric waste disposal unit. Near the dressing-room wash basin, which can be filled with rain water from a butt in the garden, is a paper towel dispenser with a small electric incinerator.

One of the most delightful touches about this house is the protective screen of warm air which comes into operation the moment the front door is opened. Having welcomed the chilly arrival, the warm air is extracted again through a grill in the floor —taking with it any dust from the visitor's shoes.

At a flick of the control panel, a portion of the living-room floor rises to become a dining- or coffee-table and lighting can be raised or lowered on dimmers. The external telephone for both loudspeaking and receiving, also records messages that come through while you are out and the built-in combined colour T.V. and radio looks like a frosted-glass panel in one wall. A loudspeaker telephone system also enables the front door to be opened electrically from either kitchen or hall, while tradesmen can leave packages in appropriate hatches outside the front door.

All the kitchen fittings are above waist level and nearly all equipment is built in. Scraps as well as dirty crockery, cutlery, etc., are fed into the dish-washer, which disposes of all rubbish, including bones, and washes and dries too. There are two ovens at eye level—one a conventional electric model, the other a super high-fre-quency cooker for high-speed work, which can cook a 3 lb. roast in less than 15 minutes or heat up the latest frozen foods in their aluminium foil or plastic packs in seconds. Instead of boiling rings, thermostatically controlled electric saucepans and frypans are used. These are made of titanium, because foods and fats cannot adhere to its extra smooth hard surface and a hot-water rinse will therefore clean them thoroughly.

Latest addition to the foods kept in the refrigerator is wrapped bread, which will keep fresh for days. But raw meat, milk, butter and fresh fish no longer require to be stored in a "fridge" in our house of the future. The secret is this: before being packed in airtight plastic containers, all these perishable foods are bombarded with gamma rays, an atomic pile by-product, which kills all bacteria. Thus they can safely be kept indefinitely at any temperature and have only to be transferred to the refrigerator when the packing has been removed.

Milk that won't Sour—and Shell-less Eggs

By the time these predictions have become fact, fresh vegetables will be bought packed and prepared ready for cooking, milk will only have to be delivered once a week and gamma-ray treated eggs will reach the kitchen minus their shells, packed in individual plastic sachets, either whole or the yolks and whites separately.

Whether we should really enjoy living in a home with no movable furniture except a sprinkling of polyaster chairs, sleeping in an island bed between nylon sheets, bathing in a circular bath, dressing in Teddy Tinling's idea of a smart space-suit, remains to be seen; but there is no doubt that many of the practical notions incorporated in the house of the future will improve the art of home-making still further.

Meanwhile, most of us have to go on making do with what we have. It might be exciting and romantic to move, as a young bride, into this architects' day-dream of a home of the future. We know for a fact that it can be stimulating and challenging to make something comfortable out of an inconvenient cottage, a too small flat or a rambling old barn of a house. . . .

WHAT MAKES A HOME

Some people call it "a woman's touch." It brings to life the best work of interior decorators—as in this welcoming living room designed for the Council of Industrial Design by Robert and Margery Westmore

A HAPPY home is easy to recognise and appreciate. It is the one to which husband and children hurry at the end of the day. They bring their friends there, knowing they will always be welcomed. Rest and relaxation are encouraged, yet everyone is proudly conscious of having a personal stake in a family enterprise.

To create a home like that and keep it running smoothly and happily is a major operation, requiring the varied arts and skills of an expert home-maker with her heart very much in the job. For architects and interior decorators can only build and furnish premises; they never yet brought to life a true home. That is woman's work. She has been doing it ever since prehistoric woman succeeded in making a very passable home for her family in a cave with nothing but a few skins to furnish it. Modern woman carries on the tradition.

The difference is that she has a bewildering variety of furnishings, modern equipment and labour-saving devices to choose from and a great deal of expert advice to guide her.

All this has made home-making easier and more fun, if a great deal more expensive. Anyhow, these days a woman quite often runs her home and a full-time job, brings up her children and manages to be a very real companion to her husband—without even neglecting friends or dropping outside interests. Any woman who is going to live a full life in at least three dimensions at once must obviously spare herself as much as possible by planning her routine sensibly and taking practical advantage of the best (though not necessarily *all*) labour-saving devices.

Not that the happiest homes are the most elaborately furnished or those full of new

7

WHAT MAKES A HOME

The great thing is never to confuse the business of furnishing a house (however exciting it may be) with the art of home-making. Naturally, the choice of colours, furnishings, everything, from carpets to cups and saucers, is important to the whole family. They should be bought with an eye to good design, quality and workmanship. But the chattels must never take priority over the people, whose happiness alone will turn a house into a home.

Two more views of the flat planned by the Westmores for a couple with two sons. Left, the dining end of the living room. The lounging end seen on the previous page has a folding workbasket for mother and shelves for the family's books, plants and ornaments. Below, the kitchen is in white with working surfaces topped with pale grey plastic and patterned curtains

gadgets. They are certainly not where the woman of the house wears herself out polishing and cleaning quite unnecessarily and out of sheer excess of house pride. Freshly laundered curtains and loose covers or new paint look lovely—but they are far too heavy a price to pay for a mother without a smile, who is too tired to play with the youngsters. And any sensible husband would rather come home to a happy, welcoming wife, even in an untidy room, than a worn-out, bad-tempered woman in a setting that looks like a furniture showroom. Women who make domestic slaves of themselves only end up with a permanent sense of grievance and usually make their families miserable with their constant exhortations to "be careful of the new carpet" or "mind the paint."

Within reason, it is not selfish extravagance to buy an expensive piece of household equipment if it gives the home-maker more time with her husband and children.

8

A pleasantly masculine study-bedroom for a musical 12-year-old and his brother, 16, a budding physicist. Gaily patterned curtains contrast with grey walls and carpet and green divan covers

Pink is the colour of the carpet and glazed divan top in the parents' bedroom, with its lime green striped curtains, a brilliant panel of pink, green and dark grey wallpaper behind the bed and black and white accents on the furniture

All furniture in the flat shown on these pages supplied by Williams' Furniture Galleries, Kilburn High Road, London

ROOMS WITH PERSONALITY

*Planning a home is a wonderful opportunity to
be bold and adventurous with colour and ideas
—and so express yourself in your surroundings*

IN the exciting business of planning a
home, two factors bulk large: the now
almost unlimited choice of furniture, textiles and so on—against limited spending
power. Naturally the two must be made
compatible if a dream home is to become
reality. And this is not only possible, but
reasonably easy too.

The underlying essential is a useful
grasp of basic principles—in planning
colour schemes, choosing loose covers and
curtains and floor treatments to provide a
harmonious whole that is also the right
background for the function of each room.

The living room, for instance, is the most
used, the background to social and family
life. Therefore, visually its need is to suggest the serenity and comfort that offers a
silent welcome to guests, while functionally
it is adaptable to family needs without
chaos reigning. This is all that need be said
at this point, as individual rooms, their
colour schemes and furniture are discussed
in detail in the following chapters. Here we
shall keep to fundamentals that will help
you to plan and spend without disappointing results.

It is an excellent plan, before you do any
spending at all, to make plenty of paper
and pencil notes. Jot down a room's
colour scheme first, with the amount of
paint, distemper or wallpaper you will
need, and the approximate price (see
Estimating Your Materials, p. 18). Take
window measurements carefully for the
amount of curtaining needed; calculate the
cost at, say, 5s. 11d. or 6s. 11d. a yard as a
guide to how much you can allow for this
item. Bear in mind accessories such as
lampshades, and whether the budget for the
whole room will allow these to be bought
ready-made or made at home. Floor treatment may call for expenditure on wood
stain and rugs, a small carpet, or perhaps
the laying of a composition tile floor or all-
over carpeting; whatever your choice, note
it down—colour, quantity and approximate
price. Under "oddments," allow for items
in the nature of pelmet boards, paint
brushes or rollers, scrapers and so on.

These estimates are essential for begin-
ner-planners as a guide to just how far a
given sum of money will go and where
adjustments in expenditure must be made;
once complete, they become useful shopping lists you can carry around with you,
without the nagging fear that you may be
over-spending.

THE COLOUR QUESTION

There is no need to play safe and have
cream walls throughout because "anything
goes with cream." Maybe it does in
theory; in practice it can be as dreary as the
chestnut-haired woman who always dresses
in brown. And too often these "safe"
cream walls draw about them all manner
of patterns and colours, simply because
"anything goes with cream." Such a room
is nondescript and has no background
value.

So adventure! Choose a basic *colour*,
adding further colour in lighter and darker
shades of the basic, plus one contrast. This
is a safe beginner's plan from which you
can diverge as you gain confidence. And
to help your choice of main colour, keep
two points in mind: (*a*) the room's aspect;
(*b*) its proportions. For colour can do quite
a lot to both.

Aspect

The room that gets strong sunlight needs
a cool colour—a pale green with a hint of
yellow in it, for example; avoid the too-
favourite *eau de Nil*, that pale blue-green
that looks cold even in sunlight. Certain
shades of blue are good; a pale, clear china

**Showing what can be done with contrasting wallpapers—the recesses are "brought forward"
by the trellis pattern paper. Vertical stripes on the other walls—in red and grey—add height.
Both are Crown wallpapers**

blue or the misty blue of a May sky are examples. Wild-rose pink is restful and too delicate a shade to look hot in sunlight.

A room that is for the most part of the day in shade needs a colour that is light with a certain brilliance to it. A mixture of white and canary yellow can produce this effect; a straight primrose yellow or a white base mixed to a pale but glowing apricot are two more examples for brightening a darkish room.

Proportions

In general this should be remembered: the darker the colouring on walls and ceiling, the smaller the room will look; in reverse, the lighter the colouring the greater the sense of space.

Smooth, matt surfaces are best for a small room. Rough-cast, stippled or other decorative surfaces detract from the size. The soft sheen of a good wall paint is an advantage in a darkish room.

Get away, when possible, from the white ceiling. In rooms low to average height, it draws attention to the low ceiling, in loftier, larger rooms it presents a cold white expanse that too quickly becomes dull grey with dust—particularly in towns—and produces a depressingly heavy note. The wall colour can safely be carried up over the ceiling; a little paler if you like, but be wary of having it darker—the effect may be that of a weight on your head. Contrast colour ceiling can be fun.

Again, as a general principle and when possible, keep walls of rooms up to eight feet in height free from dados, picture rails and friezes if you are aiming at producing the maximum effect of height. Rooms higher than this can safely have height-cutting horizontal lines introduced.

Colour—and You

There is a last point, and an important one, to talk about here, and that is the psychological effect of colour. Some people react to certain colours either well or badly. Therefore in working quarters such as the kitchen, den or study, a centre of relaxation such as the sitting room, or a playroom, and again in the bedroom, certain colours may be better than others. Many people, for example, find blue a restful colour and might incorporate a blue wall or ceiling in the sitting room—conversely, others find it depressing. Cool yellow-green, clinical all-white or a lively combination of red and white may appeal to the differing temperaments of housewives in their kitchens; old rose may act as a soothing agent in a bedroom; many find a single deep-red lampshade a focal point with a calming effect. This is, of course, a highly individual matter, but one to be considered carefully, even if you have only a vague predilection for a certain shade. It may make the difference between complete enjoyment in a finished room effect and an uneasy sense that you have not quite achieved what you want.

THE QUESTION OF PATTERN

So far, we have been considering plain colours only; now we turn to patterns. Here a tremendously exciting field opens up, for designs are legion and imaginative, providing an infinite variety of choice. There are, of course, hazards, but again certain basic principles will save you from unsatisfactory shopping.

Mixing Patterns

There are several types of basic pattern: (a) floral; (b) striped; (c) spotted effect—that is, solid rounds, open circles, stars, diamonds or any small conventional design dotted over the fabric as the only ornament; (d) pictorial; (e) geometric—squares, cubes, oblongs, rectangles, diagonal lines and so on. There are variations, of course, on all these themes, but if you think of a pattern in terms of a type, it becomes much easier, as you make your initial plans, to compare it in your mind's eye with another type, and judge whether or not the two mix.

In this instance, when you are finding your feet in room planning, it is better to play safe and decide on obvious (but no less effective) pattern mixing—for example, floral fabrics if you have a floral carpet; striped drapes if furniture upholstery is striped or carries a traditional design—such as Jacobean or *fleur de Lys*, or a spot. Plain, spotted and striped fabrics mix most pleasantly.

Pattern can be introduced into wall and ceiling treatments as well as fabrics. Choice in wallpaper design is wonderfully varied. You can give your room a spotted or striped ceiling paper, or have a heaven of stars. With a decorative ceiling, plain walls give the best effect and fabrics can pick up the ceiling motif.

A complete and lovely room scheme can very often be planned round a single object. For example, a newly-married couple may number among their gifts a lounge chair, perhaps a carpet or rug or an eye-pleasing table or standard lamp complete with shade, even a picture. Around the colouring and design of one of these can be built the colour scheme of the whole room—the basic plain colour chosen to blend with the given object, and further colour and pattern chosen to enhance or contrast with it.

Pattern mixing, when you have gained confidence, can be taken beyond these simple effects, although they are invariably the most successful, and for beginner planners the best means of spending a small budget unwastefully.

INDIVIDUAL COLOUR SCHEMES

Now we can "ice the cake" and consider individual colour schemes for different rooms, carrying out simple plain and pattern ideas.

The best way to start planning a room scheme is to choose a basic colour, add lighter and darker shades of it, and one contrast. Here it is useful to introduce the colour wheel as a safe and interesting way of choosing either contrasting or harmonising colours. As you know, the primary colours are: (1) Red; (2) Blue; (3) Yellow. The secondary colours are: (a) Violet (made by mixing red and blue); (b) Orange (made by mixing red and yellow); (c) Green (made by mixing blue and yellow). Then come six intermediary colours—those lying between the primaries and secondaries. These again break up into many gradations of colour. To pick contrasts, choose any two colours lying opposite each other on the wheel; for harmonising shades, choose those lying next to each other.

The many gradations of greys and browns come from mixing the third primary with those producing the secondary colours. For example, if primary blue is added to secondary orange (from yellow and red), a brown results. Greys and browns can safely be introduced, and the colour schemes that follow will help to illustrate these points. There are in every case alternatives—for a light room and a dark one. In the main, colours only are given, but where wallpaper can be suggested, this has been done.

We start with some schemes for hall and stairs: too often these areas are neglected. But when you think that they are the first to meet the eye on opening the front door, the logical conclusion is to give them a pleasant, welcoming look.

HALL, STAIRS, LANDING

Scheme 1 (where there is plenty of light)
Walls—Sea green.
Ceiling—As walls.
Woodwork—Several shades deeper.
Doors—Sea green.
Floor—Flame red.
Stair covering—Green to match woodwork.
Curtains—Patterned: picking up red and green with black and/or grey.

Scheme 2 (inclined to be dark)
Walls—Ivory.
Ceiling—As walls.
Woodwork—Primrose yellow.
Doors—Ivory or primrose.
Floor—Orange yellow.
Stair covering—Dark grey.
Curtains—Patterned: orange yellow, pale grey on ivory.

LIVING ROOM

Scheme 3 (light)
Walls—Briar rose.
Ceiling—As walls.
Woodwork—Grey with a hint of pink.
Floor or carpet—Old rose carpet, patterned grey/lilac shades.
Curtains—Plain: lilac pink.
Loose covers or upholstery—Elephant grey.
Cushion covers—Lilac shades.
Lampshades—Briar pink.

Scheme 4 (dark)
Walls—Pale lime yellow.
Ceiling—As walls.
Woodwork—White.
Floor or carpet—Plain: deep yellow-green.

A pleasing effect created by contrast—the shining mahogany unit with doors veneered in glowing Brazilian rosewood, the matching oval table and the soft off-white carpet, the dark tub chairs and slotted mahogany wall bench. Furniture designed for Hille of London Ltd. by Robin Day

Curtains—Patterned: lime ground, amethyst predominating.

Loose covers or upholstery—As curtains.

Cushion covers—Plain: picking up curtain colours.

Lampshades—Off-white.

DINING RECESS

As a part of a whole room the decoration here needs a little careful thought. You may prefer it to carry the same colour as the main room, but it can be effective in a contrast colour or contrast treatment—that is, if walls are plain distemper or paint in the main room, the dining recess could be papered and *vice versa*. We can follow out this idea with the two living room schemes, 3 and 4:

Scheme 5 (light, to go with living room, Scheme 3)

Walls—Delft blue.

Ceiling—As walls.

Woodwork—Grey (matching Scheme 3).

Floor or carpet—Old rose, plain.

A hall with a gay welcome—the Crown wallpaper is pale grey on brown, ceiling pale blue (for extra height and light), woodwork white and floor coverings bright red

Curtains—Plain: blue to match walls, or Patterned: blue ground, pink and grey.

Scheme 6 (dark, to go with living room, Scheme 4)

Walls—White wallpaper patterned with pale yellow-green predominating, and touch of grey.

Ceiling—Lime yellow (as Scheme 4).

Woodwork—White.

Floor or carpet—Deep amethyst or as Scheme 4.

Curtains—Plain: to match green in paper.

DINING ROOM

Scheme 7 (light)

Walls—Champagne.

Ceiling—As walls.

Woodwork—Old gold.

Floor or carpet—Warm brown.

Curtains—Patterned: Georgian green, rust, golden yellow, brown.

Scheme 8 (dark)

Walls—Clear primrose.

Ceiling—As walls.

Woodwork—A little deeper than walls.

Floor or carpet—Blackberry.

Curtains—Patterned: blackberry, yellow, grey.

BEDROOM

Decorative ceilings and one wall, or part of a wall, can be pleasant to look at, and there is no fear of tiring of a design in a room where, mainly, one is asleep.

Scheme 9 (light)

Walls—Pale cool green matched to—

Ceiling.—Pale green paper decorated with tiny pink flowers.

Woodwork—Matching green.

Floor or carpet—Deep blue-green.

Curtains—Patterned: picking up colour and pattern of ceiling paper.

Bedcover—To blend with carpet.

Lampshades—Pale rose pink.

Scheme 10 (dark)

Walls—Ivory paper with pink button quilted paper behind bed.

Ceiling—Ivory.

Woodwork—Ivory.

Floor or carpet—Honey.

Here's an unusual bedroom idea—a favourite picture highlighted on a contrast wall behind the beds. Only pattern is introduced by Vantona Consort bedcovers in coral pink and white—two on the beds and one made into matching curtains

Curtains—Patterned: honey/pink on ivory.

Bedcover—Sunlight yellow.

Lampshades—Pink to match quilted paper.

CHILD'S ROOM OR NURSERY

Delightful papers, many of them washable, are available to make rooms for children very much their own. Too much pattern is worrying even to young eyes, but one or two walls can be fun.

Scheme 11 (light)

Walls—One or two walls in cream continental design paper, remaining walls cream.

Ceiling—Cream.

Woodwork—Deep green picked from paper.

Floor or carpet—To match woodwork.

Bed or cot cover—Paler green.

Lampshades—Cream with green trims.

Scheme 12 (dark)

Walls—One wall of "First Impressions" children's paper with white or pink ground.

Ceiling—White or pink.

Woodwork—Deep rose pink.

Floor or carpet—Matching rose pink.

Bed or cot cover—Pale pink.

Lampshades—Pale pink/rose trims.

BATHROOM

Here again, washable papers and a change from the mundane green/white or green/yellow of bathroom décor can create a livelier impression.

Scheme 13 (light)

Walls—Pale green plastic paint with matching green fish-patterned paper on one wall or as a surround at bath level.

Ceiling—As walls.

Floor—Coral or deep green.

Curtains—Green plastic to match walls.

Accessories—Green and coral.

Scheme 14 (dark)

Walls—White plastic paint.

Ceiling—White washable paper stubbed scarlet stars.

Floor—Scarlet.

Curtains—Scarlet terry towelling with white motif.

Accessories—Primrose.

NOTE: The alternatives, "floor or carpet," are given in all cases because coloured linoleum tiles, thermoplastic and P.V.C. tiles and rubber flooring may be chosen for all types of room in preference to carpeting (see All about Floors).

ROOMS WITH A DIFFERENCE

The foregoing schemes, as they suggest colours for light and dark aspects, can be applied to most rooms, large or small. One or two exceptions, however, must be mentioned before finishing with room schemes.

The Bed-sitter

In a combination room of this kind the best plan is to consider it in its main theme —as a living room—and plan its colour scheme accordingly.

The High Long Room

This may be met with in a flat converted from an old house. Here you can plan a ceiling darker than the walls because you can afford to bring the height down. (This applies to any shape of high room.) Wallpapers are helpful too, and you could use a clearly defined striped ceiling paper, with the stripes set *across* the length of the room to break it: again, have walls and ceiling plain, and a small but bold patterned paper on the end wall. If the room is large as well as high and long, much can be done to proportion it with patterned wallpaper panels, bordered all round and set at intervals on a plain ground; such a job is best carried out professionally.

Cottage Rooms

Where these are around 6 ft. in height, pattern should be introduced *most* cautiously. Narrow vertical stripes are good for walls because they create the illusion of height. On the whole, pale clear colours and wall paints that produce a slight sheen are best for space promoting, particularly if walls and ceilings are broken by dark beams.

CHOOSING COLOURS— OTHER METHODS

Many people find it easier to decide on a colour scheme if they can first see it in reality, instead of trying to visualise it in the mind's eye. Here are some simple ways of experimenting with colour schemes.

Flowers

If you can find man-mixed colours to match flower colours—which is quite possible—you have a tremendous range of colour combinations from which to choose. And Nature never makes an error in mixing her colours. Think of the violet-blue pansy. The centre is a pale yellow; the deep violet-blue surrounding it is the correct colour contrast if you check with the colour wheel; and within the pansy face are graduated shades. A bed of mixed wallflowers gives plenty of choice for a scheme based on the clear creamy yellow of the palest variety. The right shades of deeper yellow, the glowing red-rusts through to the velvety red-browns are all there to inspire a room scheme. Flower colours offer an endless variety.

Fabrics

A whole room scheme may be built round a piece of furniture, a picture or a vase—or even a patterned fabric the design and colouring of which appeal to you. Well-known makes of furnishing fabrics are designed by artists, so that again there are no errors of judgment in the combination of colours. The background colour of the fabric can safely be used for walls and ceiling, the remaining colours being picked out for curtains, upholstery and so on.

The British Colour Council is an institution to which many enthusiastic amateur home planners owe thanks without knowing it. Set up to co-ordinate colour and design, the B.C.C. has many manufacturers of paint, furniture, fabrics, wallpaper, linoleum and so on as members. The public benefit by the prolific choice of colours and furnishing designs, and the fact that developments in home decoration and planning are quickly reflected in the materials available for amateur homemakers.

For domestic colour schemers, the British Colour Council's *Dictionary of Colours for Interior Decoration* is available for consulting in many Public Libraries and good furnishing stores. This is a work consulted by professional colour-planners, and for amateurs it is a safe, stimulating and absorbing guide.

COLOUR MAGIC IN YOUR HOME

*Two leading
designers
present ideas
you can
easily copy*

ABOVE, Olive Hammond makes a rather dark attic bedroom cheerful with clear, clean colours. Walls are painted plain lemon except for certain surfaces papered in matching stripes. Woodwork is broken white, curtains and cushions scarlet, and a few touches of black give sharpness to the scheme. Right, John Lawrence's clever idea—a panelled door looks effective in bright red (or any other strong colour) with mouldings painted white or pastel. Paints are by Blundell's; in the attic room Lemon Pammastic was used and, for the woodwork, Broken White Pammel.

COLOUR SCHEMING

1. *Harmonies of muted green with red in curtains and wallpaper for warmth and contrast in a living room*

2. *The sharp contrast of turquoise and yellow inspires this scheme. Brown and terracotta give it mellow warmth*

3. *A bold scheme with strong blues and red set against tones of grey and dead white paintwork*

4. *A simple scheme for a bedroom in pink, grey and white with touches of blue-green to offset the pink*

5. *Grey carpet and wall form a background for the vivid combination of red with shades of lime green and lemon yellow*

Showing you how to use different tones of the same colour—and how to introduce contrast to bring variety and vitality to your rooms

by ROGER SMITHELLS

6

7 A cool blue and white room planned for a sunny aspect. Mahogany furniture and a bedspread patterned in terracotta provide a note of warmth

7

6. *This bedroom was inspired by the blue-mauve-pink colour range of the petunia. The green of the leaves appears in the lamp*

HERE you see the principles of colour scheming applied to four living rooms, four bedrooms, and a kitchen and bathroom. Layout of the living rooms and bedrooms is identical, but their character and appearance are transformed by different combinations of harmonies, contrasts and tones.

It is the same in the "working rooms" of the house. Bright colours in the bathroom cheer you on a winter morning. This is a small room so, if you use patterns, choose small designs.

Kitchens grow more colourful every year. Those which face north or are poorly lighted need warm colours and light tones. If the kitchen fitments are white, use rich colours for the walls. If the fitments are coloured, choose a contrasting wall colour. For the sake of cleanliness, use light tones with a washable finish.

There may be a scheme here to suit your room or, better still, they may start you planning original schemes of your own.

8

8. *Mushroom walls are in gentle contrast to the turquoise and green of this scheme, but it needs red accents*

9. *Kitchen with black and white floor, walls in two greys, gay tomato red paintwork and yellow ceiling to bring in sunshine*

10. *The all-white bathroom is a thing of the past; a placid scheme in blue and sea-green, with daffodil yellow curtains*

9

10

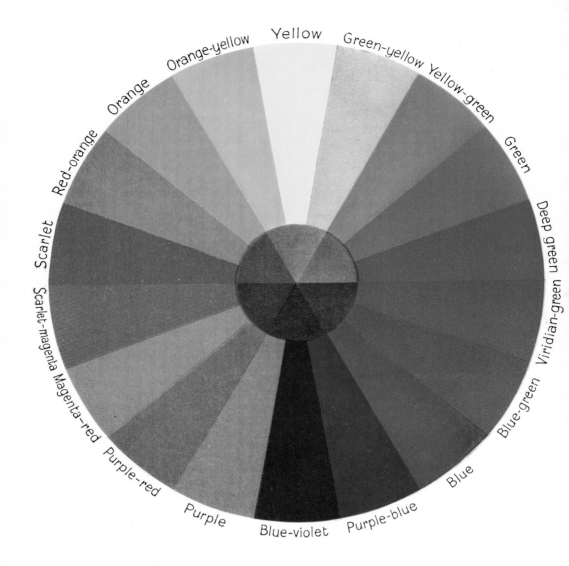

HOW TO USE THE COLOUR WHEEL

The colour wheel shown here provides a useful check-point when you are planning your colour schemes. Colours immediately opposite one another in the wheel are contrasts; adjacent colours are harmonies. Thus the direct contrast of red is green, its harmonies scarlet-magenta and red-orange.

So, if you are planning a blue room and want to know what other colours to include, the colour wheel shows you that for harmony you need purple or greenish blue, and for contrasting warmth you should add touches of red-orange.

The rooms on the two preceding pages show how different tones of the same colour can be used and contrasting colours introduced to give variety and vitality to the schemes. Use the wheel to put your own colour scheme ideas to the test.

DECORATING TO PLAN

Tackle the job in the right way from the start—budgeting your costs, raw materials and time

Be realistic, too, about the time which each job is likely to take. Brushing on the last coat of paint and hanging the exciting new wallpaper may be the most fun, but if you want to feel really proud of the result, be prepared to spend a lot of time on pre-liminaries.

HOME decorating has become the favourite week-end hobby, a grand one because a couple can enjoy it together. You feel specially proud of a room you have decorated yourselves and it is a big economy, too.

Successful decorating takes time. Don't spoil the fun—or the effort—by trying to rush it, or to cram more into one week-end than you can really manage. And don't start at all until you have made A PLAN.

First, decide how much of your home you are going to redecorate, and plan your colour scheme accordingly. If, for example, your carpets, curtains, chair covers and paintwork are to remain as they are, then your new wall and ceiling colours must go with them.

Remember, too much pattern is restless and confusing; too many plain surfaces may be dull. Distribute the patterned surfaces so that there are plain surfaces to show them off. Floral patterns and abstract designs, such as checks, stripes and spots, can be used happily together; but beware of combining period and modern florals.

You will find some useful tips on colour planning in the pages immediately preceding this.

BUDGET FIRST

Even if you are doing all the work yourselves, the cost of tools and raw materials may be greater than you expect. The way to avoid unpleasant shocks and keep down your costs is to make a realistic estimate of the quantities of materials needed.

Do not buy your materials until you are ready to use them. This will spread the cost and avoid unnecessary stocks.

IMPORTANT PRELIMINARIES

You may have to give a whole week-end to washing down paintwork, patching up plaster, scraping off old wallpaper and preparing a good surface before you can make a start on the actual decorating. This is time well spent.

You are probably going to live with your new scheme for years, so don't be discouraged if it takes longer than you expect to do the job.

You may have a room where the furnishings and decorations are still in good condition, but where the general effect is dull and disappointing. You do not want to redecorate completely, but you want to do *something* to bring the room to life.

BE BOLD!

A small change may make a big difference. A coloured ceiling, one wall or part of a wall covered with a lively new wallpaper, a touch of bright colour on the edges of bookshelves or on the window and door frames may work miracles.

You can work out all sorts of ideas of this kind and these are jobs which *can* be quickly done.

Finally, don't be *afraid* of colour. It is quite natural, if you are a beginner, to feel nervous about planning a daring colour scheme. It *may* be all right, you feel, but what if it turns out to be *awful*?

Don't let this feeling get you down. Study the schemes in our pages and in good furnishing showrooms and exhibitions; decide what you like and take the plunge.

HOW TO ESTIMATE YOUR MATERIALS

*Work out exact quantities needed in advance and you
won't run out of paint with the job half done—
or have trouble matching up your colours later on*

OIL PAINT

FINISHING coats usually cover about 9 or 10 sq. yd. to the pint, undercoats slightly more. Remember to double the amount of undercoating if you are going to use two coats. Buy plenty of turpentine substitute when you buy your paint—you will need at least a pint.

To find out the area of the walls, multiply the length by the height, and subtract the area of doors, windows, fireplace and skirting board if they are to be painted a different colour. Add 25 per cent. to the first undercoat area if it is going on plaster, which is porous.

When measuring woodwork, assume an average door and frame to measure 7 ft. by 4 ft. and you will have enough paint for mouldings and edges.

Similarly, you should count the area of a window with many glazing bars as one expanse, measured from side to side of the frame. If panes are large and without glazing bars, deduct 25 per cent. from this area.

Add a good inch to the measured surface of the skirting if the top edge is moulded.

DISTEMPER AND EMULSION PAINT

Distemper will cover about $5\frac{1}{2}$ sq. yd. to the pound, plastic emulsion paint 40–60 sq. yd. a gallon.

Measure the floor to discover the area of the ceiling, and add space above picture rail for the total ceiling measurement.

If you are using a light colour on a dark surface, you may need several coats. If you are using a similar colour, one coat of distemper or two of emulsion paint may be sufficient. Absorbency of plaster affects the amount for first coat.

WALLPAPER

Wallpaper is usually sold in $11\frac{1}{2}$-yd. "pieces," 22 in. wide, untrimmed. To estimate how much paper you need, find out how many times 22 in. goes into the distance round the walls.

Start at the right-hand side of the window, using a piece of string cut to the right length.

At a corner, the strip should turn only $\frac{1}{2}$ in. on to the next wall. Make a note of the amount of paper that will have to be trimmed off its width, and continue measuring your 22-in. spaces from a point $\frac{1}{2}$ in. from the corner.

When you come to a low obstruction like a fireplace, count the strips that will have to be cut to fit round the sides as complete strips, but make a note of the length of short strips above the fireplace, or above and below a window.

At doors or narrower features, count the left-hand strip as complete, and start measuring again from the right-hand edge of the door, having noted the area of the space left above the door.

Now add up the number of full-length strips. Add 6 in. to the length of each for waste, and see how many come from a "piece" of wallpaper.

Next, compare the notes you have made of the areas not covered by complete strips with the left-over pieces of wallpaper. These can be used around windows, doors and fireplaces, leaving enough for odd corners.

There may also be enough to replace any damaged strips.

If you choose a large-patterned paper, you will have to allow extra wastage, for each length may have to be staggered so that the pattern matches at the joins.

Estimate as above, and the dealer will tell you how much more you should allow.

PREPARING THE WALLS

The success of all your cleverest colour planning and home decorating depends entirely upon the care with which you first prepare the surface

BEFORE you start, make sure that faults such as peeling wallpaper or crumbling distemper are not due to dampness caused by structural defects and, if they are, have them attended to.

Ideally, old wallpaper should always be removed, but if it is in good condition, untorn, and showing no signs of peeling, it is usually safe to paint or paper over it.

Brush it well to remove dust and, if you are going to paint it, test a small corner to make sure that the colours will not run.

Damaged or peeling paper must be removed completely. If you paint on top of it, scars will show on the final surface. Don't try to scrape dry paper, but soak it thoroughly. Start at one corner and work from bottom to top.

You will have to go over the walls several times before the paste is softened. Test a top corner, and if the paper is loosening, help it with a stripping knife, dribbling water behind the loosening paper with a sponge.

Try to remove large pieces of paper bodily and, if there are any stubborn patches, soak them and go back to them later.

FILL IN CRACKS

When the paper is off, wash the walls over with clean water, and look carefully for any cracks or holes.

Scratch out any loose plaster, and fill the places with Keene's cement or a patent filler. First wet the surface of the fault so that the filling will stick to it. For small faults, a putty knife or a broad kitchen knife should be used

Best for holding wet filler for cracks is a "hawk." You can make your own from a 9-in. square of wood screwed to a short piece of broomstick (above)

—or even your thumb—but large breaks in the plaster may need a plasterer's trowel. Fillings should stand slightly above the surface so that they can be levelled with glasspaper when dry.

Having filled and glasspapered all faults, brush the walls, and if at all rough, rub them lightly with 0 glasspaper.

WHEN TO "SIZE"

Plaster is porous, and if the walls are to be papered, painted or distempered, they must be sized. Size can be applied with any wide brush and dries quickly. Size must not be used if plastic emulsion paint is to follow.

Walls and ceilings painted with the cheaper types of distemper must be scrubbed with hot water and a hard brush to bare the plaster before any new finish can be put on. Holes and cracks must be filled. Oil-bound distemper, however, is fairly stable, when it has been well cleaned with plain water.

STRIPPING

Patches of peeling oil-bound distemper must be stripped with an abrasive block or glasspaper. Bubbling may indicate a damp wall, and this should be investigated before any new finish is applied.

Kitchen and bathroom walls with a glossy finish provide a good surface for fresh oil paint, but for little else. It is difficult to remove paint from plaster entirely, and paper or distemper rarely give good results when applied on top of glossy paint. Many coats of good-quality plastic emulsion paint are the most practical way of solving the problem.

To remove old wallpaper, test a top corner with a stripping knife

19

THE TOOLS FOR THE JOB

FOR PREPARING THE WALLS
You will need
A putty knife
Abrasive block
Stripping knife
Scrubbing brush
Glasspaper
A bucket
Sponge
Filler or Keene's cement
Size and a brush
Plasterer's small trowel

FOR PAINTING OR DISTEMPERING WALLS AND CEILINGS
You will need
A roller with tray
    or
A large flat wall brush
A small paint brush
A clean mixing bucket, if
    distemper is being used
Clean rag

FOR WALLPAPERING
You will need
Paste brush
Scissors
A plumbline
Paperhanger's brush
A damp cloth or sponge
Paste
A clean bucket
Steps
Pencil or coloured chalk
String
A dry cloth
A long table

FOR PAINTING WOODWORK
You will need
Dusting brush
Abrasive block
Putty knife, Stripping knife
One 2-inch paint brush
One 1-inch paint brush
Bucket, Scrubbing brush
Sugar soap
Rags or sponge
Glasspaper
Turpentine
A cheap metal shield for
    doing windows, etc.

DECORATOR'S TIPS

Stripping wallpaper is easier and quicker—and causes less damage to the plaster—if you use Quickstryp, which gets at the paste behind the paper.

Polycell is a cellulose paste which cannot stain the most delicate wallpaper even when you get some accidentally on the front surface—can be used for sizing too.

For washing down and mopping up, use a Spontex household sponge, a short-handled Quick-mop for ceilings.

Free new brushes from dust and loose hairs by working the bristles on the palm of your hand for a few minutes; restore old brushes with Strypit.

To keep your hands free of paint, wrap newspaper round the handle of the brush and change the paper as soon as it gets messy.

Decorating with Roger Smithells

HOW TO HANG WALLPAPER

It need not be a difficult job, if you tackle it together with a plumbline and follow these tips

START by making a perfectly vertical line, either at the right-hand side of the main window or at the centre of the mantelpiece.

Attach your plumbline or weighted string to the top of the wall and let it drop so that the weight is just above the floor. Rub the string with coloured chalk and, holding the bottom firmly, pull it a few inches from the wall; let it snap back, the chalk will mark the wall. This line is the left-hand edge of the first piece of paper you hang.

Have the blank margins of the wallpaper trimmed in the shop.

Cut one roll of trimmed paper into lengths several inches longer than the height of the wall, making sure that the pattern will match up at the edges. Lay them face down one on top of the other on the table.

PASTING

Mix your paste, and paste the top piece, brushing along the middle and then towards the edges. When you have pasted one end, fold it back, paste side to paste side, slide the paper over the end of the table and paste the other end. Fold it similarly but don't crease folds.

Pick up the paper by the top corners, taking care not to tear it; mount the steps and unfold one end. Place the edge against the line you have drawn, allowing the paper to overlap 3 inches at the top of the wall.

Fix the top end by smoothing lightly with the hand and make one stroke down the middle of the paper with your paper-hanger's brush or clothes brush. Then brush towards the sides.

Next, unfold and brush the bottom half in the same way.

To trim the overlapping ends press the paper into the angle between wall and ceiling or picture rail with the tip of the scissors. Pull the top few inches of paper away from the wall and cut along the crease.

Brush the paper back thoroughly. Repeat at bottom.

PAPERING ROUND DOORS

When you come to a door or window, hang a strip on the side from which you are working, creasing and cutting it to fit round the window as at picture rail and skirting board. Continue from other side with a full-length strip, leaving space above until later.

At corners, fold and cut the paper to a width which will turn $\frac{1}{2}$ in. round the corner. Convex corners should be overlapped slightly, concave corners joined edge to edge. Use the plumbline to make sure that the next strip is vertical. Do areas above doors and windows last.

If you are using a heavy paper, the joins should be pressed with a boxwood roller or an old castor when each piece has been up for 10 or 15 minutes.

Paper ceiling before walls.

Remove whitewash by hard scrubbing, but paper, if it is not greasy or torn, can be left.

Hang the first piece parallel with the shortest wall. The pasted paper should be folded concertina-wise and supported in your left hand with a spare roll. Work away from the light.

HOW TO USE
WALL PAINTS

Put on the quick-drying, sponge-able plastic emulsion paints the quick way—with a roller

THERE are various kinds of paints for walls and ceilings. Oil-bound water paint can be lightly washed and makes a good surface for any walls which are not exposed to grease. But in bathrooms and kitchens it absorbs steam and has to be re-newed often.

Water paint (not oil-bound) is only suit-able for ceilings or walls which will not be touched.

Distemper or water paint can be applied with a roller or wide brush. Protect the floor with dust-sheets or newspaper.

Work across a ceiling in 1-ft. strips, mov-ing towards the window and not parallel to it. Paint a wall in yard-square patches.

Paint quickly, never letting the edge of the area you are working dry out. Dis-temper must be put on with criss-cross strokes, and avoid making straight edges with the brush. Keep the bristles in almost constant contact with the surface, working the distemper well into the plaster.

Do not swing the brush, slapping the surface with the bristles—this makes splashes and an uneven surface. Make sure all the surface is covered. Distemper cannot be touched up once it dries. Wipe drips with a damp cloth before they harden.

PLASTIC EMULSION PAINT

Plastic emulsion paint forms a continu-ous skin which is water resistant, and can be washed. It is dearer than distemper, but longer lasting.

The best way to apply emulsion paint is with a roller (good ones are obtainable from Woolworths).

Buy the best-quality paint, but a moder-ately priced roller is satisfactory. If a special tray is not sold with the roller, a baking tin will serve. Pour some paint into the tray (which should be slightly tilted to make a pool at one end), work the roller in it, then distribute the paint evenly by rolling on the dry part of the tin until the roller is charged but not dripping.

Start rolling at the top left-hand corner of one wall. Generally it is best to get the paint on with short, firm strokes, then smooth these out with long sweeps. A brush will be needed for edges and corners.

NO SIZE

Plaster walls must not be sized when using emulsion paint. Instead, well dilute the first coat with water. The number of coats you will have to use depends on the surface and on the quality of the paint— the better the paint, the fewer the coats.

As emulsion paint dries in about 1 hour, you can start the second coat almost as soon as you have finished the first. If you find you have left gaps or if touching up is needed, you will not have to re-do a whole wall for, unlike distemper, patches of emulsion paint will not show up when dry.

Because emulsion paint dries so quickly, make sure that none hardens in your brushes or roller; wipe up splashes im-mediately and touch up patches as you go.

If you stop work for a time, leave the brushes in a bucket of water to keep them from drying. When you have finished, rinse immediately under the tap and then wash them with warm water and soap.

Dry all brushes and rollers before stor-ing them away.

HOW TO PAINT
WOODWORK

Be sure the surface is good, smooth and absolutely clean before you begin —and be generous with the undercoats

PREPARING THE SURFACE

TO achieve a good result, clean the surface thoroughly. If the oil paint is in good condition, a scrubbing with sugar soap is enough. An abrasive block will smooth the surface.

Work from the bottom upwards and rinse thoroughly. Wipe the surface with a dry sponge or rag.

If the old paint is badly blistered or cracked, you may have to clean it off entirely. Professionals use a blowlamp, but equally good results can be obtained with an electric paint stripper.

Work systematically, raising the softened paint with a broad scraper. Finish by rubbing with number one glasspaper.

A chemical paint remover also gives good results. Follow the maker's instructions carefully. Make sure no active remover is left to mar the new paint.

TOUCHING UP

When the surface is clean, look carefully for cracks, dents or screw-holes and fill them with plastic wood or a patent filler. When dry, rub the fillings level with glasspaper and dab on a little undercoating.

Rub down when hard. Bare wood should also have a touch of undercoating, and knots should be sealed with knotting to stop resin staining the paint.

Unless the new paint is the same colour as the old and the surface perfect, apply an undercoat before the top coat.

If the new finish is of a different colour from the old, two undercoats will be necessary to prevent the old colour from showing through. Stir the paint well (it will be easier if you stand the tin upside down overnight) and apply as carefully as glossy paint.

Allow each coat to dry for at least 12 hours. If the surface shows brushmarks, rub lightly with glasspaper when it is hard. Brush off all the dust before you start the next coat.

AVOIDING BRUSHMARKS

Stir the paint thoroughly and apply generously, but not so thickly that it shows brushmarks or forms "runs." Dip the brush no more than halfway up the bristles and wipe off all surplus paint on the inside of the can.

When painting woodwork, brush first in the direction of the grain; on a wall or other large expanse put the paint on with vertical strokes, doing about 2 sq. ft. at a time. Smooth the first strokes by brushing across them and finish by painting in the direction in which you started, adding no more paint and using only the tips of the bristles. A 2-in. brush is best for wide areas.

For window and door frames a 1-in. brush is the most useful width. If the walls are to be papered, paint $\frac{1}{2}$ in. of wall round the woodwork. Clean the brushes by working them about in "turps." Leave the soiled turps standing overnight and pour it off for further use.

If the whole job is finished, wash the brushes out finally in warm, soapy water and, when quite clean and dry, store them, laid flat.

PROFESSIONAL IDEAS

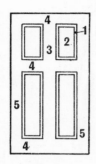

It's quicker, easier and far more efficient to do the job as the experts do after years of experience

Paint the sections of a panelled door in the order shown to avoid brush marks. Wield the brush up and down, except on Section 4, for the top, centre and bottom panels

To paper round light switches (above), first mark the centre of the switch on the paper, then draw it away from the wall. Cut a star shape radiating from the point marked, press the paper back, draw round projection with scissors and trim off superfluous paper. To keep wallpaper or paint off switches, wrap a strip of transparent tape round them, then remove when the job is done (above left)

Copy the professionals and hold your paint brush with a pencil grip (right). Change occasionally to an overhand grip when your hand gets tired. Don't apply paint with a heavy hand

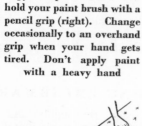

As you unroll each piece of wallpaper (left), draw it gently, face upwards, over the edge of the table and the curl of the paper will be straightened out

Knock a ring of nails into the top of the stepladder to hold your can of emulsion paint or distemper firmly in position. It will save you many a spill!

Suspend your paintbrush in a jar of water overnight and it will not dry up. Make a small hole near the top of the handle and pass a piece of wire or a nail through this to support it on the rim of the jar (right)

Stretch a wire across the paint or distemper bucket (right), and wipe surplus off your brush before applying to walls or ceiling. And don't forget, when painting straight from the can, to wipe the brush on the inside so that you don't get dribbles running down to the floor

Bathroom walls that run with condensed steam can be "treated" at home with Seculate, an effective anti-condensation compound. Used like ordinary paint, it is made in sixteen colours. You'll need a gallon for 30 square yards

PICK-ME-UPS
FOR TIRED ROOMS

No time to redecorate right through, so try a coloured ceiling, one wall with a gay wallpaper, a touch of colour somewhere . . .

They don't take long, any of them, but what a difference!

New life for a dull kitchen. Paint the wall behind the shelves a brilliant contrasting colour—in a washable paint

Turn a dull corner into a decorative feature. Paper or paint a fireside recess in gay colour, then fit shelves for ornaments

Colour the tiles on that old fire surround with heatproof paint. Add gold size to undercoat and paint will not flake

Gay bedhead. Hide the dirty mark on a plain wall with a panel of pretty wallpaper to contrast in tone or colour

Excitement for a too-quiet room. Paper the chimney breast in a gay pattern. So little paper—and time—required. You could do it in an evening

Modern unit furniture of this type can be built up gradually as your home expands.
Designed by Minty of Oxford

FIRST FURNITURE

Buy the real essentials when you first set up home—then go on adding to them as funds permit

THE question of how to spend the furniture money is a big one for a young couple or, indeed, anyone setting up home these days. The best solution is to agree on essentials, keeping comfort in mind, and put off buying the complementary items till later. A number of furniture designers are blessedly unit conscious, offering equipment that can be added to as funds grow, and most are well aware of the need for good contemporary design and pieces in proportion to room sizes; "dual-purpose" is another excellent idea and finds expression in essential items. "Combination pieces" are also well worth considering in the early stages of furnishing. So, the hunt is on! Now to the minimum needs of two principal rooms first.

LIVING ROOM

Chairs are a primary consideration: money is well spent on the good branded makes and you can choose from a wide range of shapes with foam rubber, rubberised hair and various types of sprung seats. (For the pros and cons of different types of chair, see For Sitting in Comfort.)

The three-piece suite still has its uses, representing seating for four or five, but its purchase is usually prohibited by the price tag. Comfort yourselves with the thought that single chairs are more manœuvrable, more interesting because different designs can be chosen, and more fun because colouring and design of upholstery can be judiciously varied. Start with a minimum of three, costing approximately, say, £15, £12 and £10, sizing according to the three bears is quite a good plan. One to take a man comfortably, one for the woman of the house and the third might well be a unit type that, later, can be added to in duplicate or triplicate and used together as a settee or as separates: alternately, the third might be the tub type of armchair with stick back that can also do duty at the dining table.

Tables.—Plan for one to begin with—long, low and adaptable; costing around £6, about 2 ft. 6 in. long, 15 in. wide and 18 in. high, it can stand against a wall to hold flowers, ash tray and so on; it can be brought forward for tea and it can be provided with a removable padded cushion to stand in as extra seating. Later, you might add extra small tables, a nest of tables or trolley-cum-stand for television according to needs and preference.

Cupboards, Bookshelves.—A necessity in a living room is space for storing sewing materials, cards and games and books. Here, unit or sectional pieces offer excellent beginnings. Choose, for example, at around £16 a cupboard with matching bookcase to one side of it or on top.

Later, extra cupboard space or bookcases can be added, and, as funds allow, a matching writing desk. All such pieces are designed to fit together or stand alone, and you have the pleasure of rearrangement as and when you wish.

You may, of course, have recesses on either side of the fireplace. In this case it would be worth having shelves and cupboards built in by a local carpenter, and this would cost considerably less.

Lighting Fittings.—Table and standard lamps usually figure among wedding presents, and one or both is essential to the comfort of any room. A separate chapter deals in detail with adequate lighting for different rooms, but it may not be possible on a small budget to install all you need at once. The best compromise is a standard lamp with an adjustable head, and on a long flex so that it can be moved easily to wherever it is needed most. Allow about £6 for this item.

Approximate Cost.—Three chairs, £37; table, £6; combined bookcase/cupboard, £16; standard lamp, £6; total: £65.

BEDROOM

Bedstead.—This is the first essential and worth the largest share of the room's budget. Be prepared to spend between £25 and £30 on this item and it will last a lifetime with little maintenance under normal conditions. Choice of mattress, of course, is an individual matter, but there is a considerable range from which to choose. For those who like twin beds, the mattresses can be different to suit the user. Such a firm as The London Bedding Centre, 13 Brompton Road, Knightsbridge, London, S.W.3, is always ready to advise, on the premises or

One of your first three armchairs might be this low-slung one in two shades of corduroy—pine green and honey is a lovely scheme. Treat yourself later to the streamlined magazine rack or one of the fabric "pictures" by Pamela Smith. All from Liberty's, London

by letter, and can supply a number of well-known makes.

Later, you can add a headboard combination piece that includes bedside cupboards and/or shelves, or separate cupboards. (See also Bedtime Story.)

Dressing Table, Chest of Drawers.—These two might well be a combination piece. Look for the type the "top drawer" of which pulls out to disclose a lift-up mirror and plenty of space for two people's brushes and toilet needs. Such a piece costs about £19.

Alternately, consider a low chest of three drawers, about 2 ft. 5 in. in height with mirror above or long mirror to one side. A good chest can be bought for around £15 and combined with a mirror from the wedding presents. Later a feminine dressing table could be added, leaving the chest for male occupation.

Wardrobe.—Money will not have to be spent on hanging space if built-in cupboards already exist. If not, any recesses can be utilised in this way, and costs may be less than the outlay on a wardrobe. However, if this item must be faced, it is an essential, and a reliable double wardrobe with clear hanging space would cost about £25.

Chairs.—One at least will be needed, and here is suggested a do-it-yourself job on these lines: hunt around junk shops for a sound wooden kitchen-type chair at about 7s. 6d. Scrub in hot detergent soapsuds, rinse and dry. Rub down with medium sandpaper and enamel in a shade to tone with the wall colour. When dry, make a shaped, padded seat cushion covered with the curtain fabric. Total cost about 12s. Later, a more interesting type of chair can be added and/or a dressing-table stool, or long stool across the foot of the bed.

Lighting Fittings.—Here again a portable standard with adjustable head, at around £6, is the best buy. In an average-sized bedroom it can be moved between bed and dressing table as needed. When funds allow, you will want to consider separate lighting for these two points.

Approximate Cost.—Bed, £30; dressing-table combination, £19; wardrobe, £25; chair, 12s.; standard lamp, £6; total: £80 12s.

OTHER ROOMS

Dining Room or Recess

Table.—The extending type offers the greatest use, allowing seating for from two to six people as occasion demands. Such a table could be bought at a price between £15 and £20.

Chairs.—Two are essential, four are necessary if you don't want to limit entertaining too much when you start housekeeping. The Windsor type of all-wooden dining chair, at around 50s. each, provides pleasing, simple design and the greatest economy. Later, host and hostess armchairs can be added and slim padded cushions made for all, if these are not supplied with the chairs in the first place.

Sideboard.—If all cutlery, cloths and so on can be housed in the kitchen, a trolley can well take the place of a sideboard as a serving table,

The problem of the spare bed is cleverly solved by Greaves & Thomas' studio couch, which can be made up into one double or two single beds, according to requirements

The cost of a really good bed is always money well spent. This Myers Divan has a sponge-clean headboard. Over this you can slip your own material to match your bedspread if you wish

apart from its extreme usefulness in fetching and carrying. Allow about £6 for a well-made type of useful size.

A sideboard, however, may have to be considered an essential and about £25 allowed for one of good simple design incorporating cupboard and drawer space.

Approximate Cost.—Table, £15; four chairs, £10; trolley, £6, *or* sideboard, £25. Total: £31 or £50.

Spare Bedroom

The same essentials are needed here as in the main bedroom and, naturally enough, this is a room that must take its turn after the principal rooms have been provided with the minimum needs.

The Spare Bed

One possible answer to the question of the overnight guest is a bed-settee. Small houses, flats and "two rooms with use of kit." have created a need for such a piece, and manufacturers have used skill and imagination in their design.

Prices range from approximately £23 to over £50, but there are these advantages: any type of bed-settee will give you a two- or three-seater couch by day, so that you could start with this and one easy chair. There are also those designs that, while acting as a settee and emergency guest bed in the living room, can be moved up to the spare bedroom, as a permanent bed or beds, when funds permit the furnishing of that room and the filling of the gap left in the living room. There are enough types of bed-settee—transformable into single, twin or small or large double beds—to meet all needs, particularly those starting out in a bed-sitting room.

Bathroom

Essential furnishings are a seat and some receptacle for soiled linen. The two can be combined in one unit if the clothes' bin is the stool type with hinged cork-topped lid that does duty as a seat. You may have to allow for a towel rail if this fixture is not already in place. Allow about £5 for bathroom equipment.

29

You can furnish a modern dining room—or dining recess—by degrees, starting with a table like this in natural oak, adding the sideboard and more chairs later. Furniture by Meredew Design Group

Hall

A coat rack, umbrella stand and shelf, or small table with drawer for telephone and directories have to be considered. The trellis type of metal coat-hanger studded with coloured knobs is a lively modern note; holders for umbrellas can be picked up reasonably in junk shops; old shell cases may sound grim, but given a coat of enamel or a covering of brilliant wallpaper, their background is soon forgotten. A local carpenter would fix a telephone shelf for a few shillings. Allow about £3 for furnishings on these lines.

All the furniture mentioned could cost less—or more—and is chosen to represent the sort of medium-priced pieces made by reputable firms that assure durability as well as excellent contemporary design.

GOOD BUYING

It is not possible for the layman to know exactly all the points of sound manufacture in household goods, constructively or otherwise—at least, it would take a lifetime to learn. Fortunately, there is help for all shoppers. The question of shoddy goods is one that has had much constructive attention given to it.

Consider the British Standards Institution; it has already done a tremendous amount to standardise quality in many goods and introduce symbols that lead the shopper direct to such goods. The B.S.I. "Kite" symbol means that any commodity bearing it has been manufactured under the inspection of the Institution. It can be found on many items of furniture; beds and bedding, for instance. The Institution Specification Number is another great help; if, for example, you are having electric wall plugs and sockets fitted bearing the symbols "B.S. 546" and "B.S. 1363," these assure you that the manufacturer has undertaken to conform to the requirements of the published British Standard. There are over 1,800 British Standards, covering a wide range of consumer goods; whatever the mark, you may take it for granted the item concerned will be dependable, well made of good materials.

Again you can safely buy *household appliances and accessories* bearing the

Guarantee Seal of the Good Housekeeping Institute and *textiles* covered by the Seal of the Lux Washability Bureau, because this signifies that they have passed rigorous washing tests. *Carpets* bearing the label of the Federation of British Carpet Manufacturers can be relied on to be British, made by a reputable firm and to give value for money; *linoleum* made by a member of The Linoleum Manufacturers' Association is real linoleum of sound quality.

Let it be said at once that there is no implication here that goods not showing these labels are to be avoided. These safe-buying signs are quoted simply as guides for shoppers who like to have the judgment of experts to support their own.

Buying by Name—and Otherwise

Branded names that have become household words naturally mean safe investment of money.

There are times, however, when a piece of furniture or a particular fabric, perhaps, is " just what you want," but the maker's name is unknown and there is no other guide to its goodness or otherwise. Then you must ask questions:

Of Fabrics.—If it is called only by a made-up name, ask what kind of fabric it

Photo: Crown Wallpapers

Put a panel of French Walnut Lincrusta on the wall and mount on it a contemporary metal coat rack with multi-coloured knobs. An old metal umbrella stand is papered

Every item of your first furniture should serve at least two purposes—like this three-way-stool by Len Ltd., Maidstone, which can be a coffee table, upholstered stool or footstool extension to a chair. The top is reversible—rubberised hair upholstery on one side, polished wood on the other

is—it may be one of the synthetics such as nylon, Terylene, Orlon, a rayon or pure fabric containing synthetic threads. Whatever it is, ask how it should be washed and ironed or if it should be dry-cleaned only. Other important questions are—(*a*) Will it shrink? (*b*) Will it fade in the sun? (*c*) Are the colours fast? (*d*) Is it crease-resisting? If you cannot get satisfactory answers, much the wisest plan is to leave it alone.

Of Furniture.—Your best defence is to buy from a store with a sound reputation. *They* will know the name and repute of the branded goods and they may have their own workrooms and make excellent incidental pieces, often most reasonably. A reputable firm is most unlikely to risk its good name by selling poor quality.

A WARM WELCOME IN YOUR HOME

*If it is properly winterproofed, you will eat, sleep, work,
play, cook, wash and even dress in draught-free comfort*

A HOUSE can only be truly said to be warm and welcoming if it is winterproof from foundation to chimney pots. Those who live in it must be able not only to sit round the fire in comfort, but also to eat, sleep, work, play, cook, wash and (this is the acid test) dress and undress in an atmosphere of cosy warmth.

In winterproofing a house it is not only the degree of comfort that matters; the ease and economy with which it can be maintained is equally important. Comfort is hardly worth while if it costs more than one can afford in time, energy and money.

Winter discomforts cannot be placed in order of importance, because they are all dependent on each other. One cannot afford to neglect any of them. Here we deal with all aspects of the subject, from the right type of fire to warm a certain room—to leaking roofs and damp walls.

What is *adequate heating*? This seems a simple enough question, but it is not an easy one to answer, since a room that is warm to one person may be chilly to another. A room that is too warm and lacking in ventilation can be almost, if not quite, as uncomfortable as one that is cold and draughty.

Various Temperatures

No hard-and-fast rules can be laid down regarding the degree of warmth for maximum comfort. Obviously, this varies according to the age and health of the occupants of the house, and to their various occupations. Elderly people, invalids and babies, who move about very little, need a comparatively high room temperature; older children and adults, who lead a reasonably active life, require lower temperatures. So for complete comfort in most homes it is ideal to have rooms at various temperatures.

The dining room should be well heated at meal times. Unless old people or babies use the sitting room during

The approach to this modern house is always dry. A porch
protects the door from wind and rain; concrete path and steps
are properly drained

the morning, it can be left cool until the afternoon or early evening, when it should be a comfortable and even temperature. The kitchen should be cool in comparison with the living rooms, but there must be some form of heating, independent of the cooker, if no solid fuel appliance is used.

Although, from the point of view of heating, the hall, staircase and landing are the most important parts of the house, they are usually the most neglected. If they are cold and draughty, the whole house is certain to be uncomfortable.

Bedrooms need warmth in the mornings and evenings, but remember that warm air rises and if the ground floor is adequately warmed, the first floor will not be chilly even without independent heating during the day.

Bathrooms and lavatories should be kept warm. Too often they are left with windows open and no kind of heating whatever. This means extreme discomfort and, probably, frozen water pipes and cistern at some time during a severe winter.

An idea originally developed for wartime aircraft, Mhoglas elements are made from glass fibre into attractive panels. The heat is so evenly distributed that it can safely be touched even by a child

Warm All Over

A winterproofed house is warm all over so that every corner of every room can be used, and even the passages and hall are warm enough for children to play in. This state of affairs cannot be achieved with open fires alone—even if there is a fire in every room. Some form of auxiliary or background heating is essential.

If central heating is out of the question, there are now scores of different appliances, most of them portable, which can be used to supplement the coal fire. Among others, oil-filled electric radiators, oil-burning radiators, electric and gas convector heaters, fan heaters (which blow air through a hot element and can be used for cooling in summer) and high-level reflector heaters for bathrooms.

Before considering new heating appliances, reduce draughts to the minimum. Burning fuel to heat the outside air, which is what draughts really are, is just sheer waste of time and money. Once the draughts are reduced, the next step is to deal with the problem of the size of the chimney opening.

In normal circumstances, one and a half air changes per hour are necessary in a living room, which means about 2,500 cu. ft. of air passing through each hour. Where a normal open fire is used with an unregulated chimney opening, the volume of air passing through each hour can be about 7,000–9,000 cu. ft. This air will be drawn in cold from other cooler parts of the house, and from outside, through badly fitting doors and windows. It will be warmed as it passes through the heated room, drawing the warmth from furnishings and people on its way to the chimney, up which it returns unhindered to the outside world. Burning more fuel by increasing the size of the fire simply increases the air flow, and the occupants of the room remain nearly as cold as before.

The efficiency of a standard fireplace can be increased by fitting a throat restrictor, obtainable from ironmongers and quite simple to install. It may be possible to accommodate a free-standing convector These are complete units with their own fire giving both radiant and convected heat.

throat restrictors. They are easy to install in most fireplace surrounds and do not become landlord's fixtures.

A continuous-burning open fire may prove a satisfactory and inexpensive method of providing adequate warmth where there is a standard fireplace. This type of fire will burn all kinds of fuel for ten hours without attention and can be fitted into a tiled surround without structural alterations. A throat restrictor will reduce the amount of heat lost up the chimney and minimise draughts due to air circulating in the room.

Another alternative is the openable heating stove supplying convected warm air throughout the room and now obtainable with thermostatic control so that it will burn for hours without attention. These are particularly suitable for people out all day who want to come in to a warm home in the evenings.

Where there is an old-fashioned large fireplace it is usually possible to close the chimney, leaving a small opening to which a free-standing fire or an open-closable stove can be connected.

Draughts

It is impossible to eliminate draughts completely unless one also eliminates the open fire. There are, however, two ways of tackling this problem: either to ensure that the air, which is drawn across the room and up the chimney, is already warm, or to supply the fire with air it needs by bringing in its own supply from outside.

The first solution involves thorough draught-proofing, with metal strip, of all external doors and windows, so that air drawn into the room comes from the hall, passages or adjoining rooms which, if the house is properly winterproofed, will be warm. If the fireplace is on an external wall, the other solution is to have an air brick inserted as near to the fire as possible. The fire then takes its air supply direct from outside rather than from the other side of the room.

There are hearth-level fires that draw in the air for combustion from outside and thus reduce draughts to a minimum, but, as they require a depth of at least 14 in. for the ash container below floor level, they are only suitable for ground floor rooms.

An Inner Door

If there is room in the hall, an inner door, glazed to admit light, will eliminate most of the cold air which penetrates into the house every time the front door is opened. In summer, the outer door can be left open during the day.

The old-fashioned folding draught screen is still as effective as it was a hundred years ago, when the Victorians loved to decorate it with coloured pictures and prints which were stuck on and then varnished over. A better selection of prints is now available, and magnificent screens can be made.

Better Insulation

Cold is the greatest enemy of winter comfort. It can be kept at bay by building innumerable and large fires, but it is cheaper to have insulators installed, as the better the insulation, the less fire is needed.

In the ordinary brick-and-tile house, about one-third of the heat produced by fires, etc., is lost through the external walls; one-quarter is lost through the windows and doors; one-quarter through the roof, and the remaining sixth through the ground floor. It is rather expensive to improve the insulation value of existing walls as it means replastering and redecorating at least, but matters can be helped by double-glazing the bigger windows on the north or east side of the house. Heavy curtains are also effective, as well as being cheaper than double glass. The ground-floor insulation can be improved by carpets—especially if a good underfelt is used. Paper for covering cracks in boards helps to prevent draughts on the floor. But by far the most rewarding result comes from dealing with the roof.

Tackling the Roof

The simplest and easiest method is to buy insulating material such as mineral wool or glass silk, which is supplied in the form of thin mattresses and can be unrolled over the upstair ceilings. They need no fixing, and if the roof space is accessible, the job can be done without professional help. The results have to be experienced to be believed. These materials can also be obtained in narrow rolls to fit between joists.

Aluminium foil is another effective form of insulation, and yet another is vermiculite, which is obtained loose, in bags, to spread between the joists yourself.

Fires, Flues and Fuels

The smoky chimney is still a regular winter problem (we will deal with this separately later), for no builder or architect can guarantee that a flue, even in a new house, will not smoke. If the cause of the trouble is down-draught, there are one or two types of chimney pots or cowls which will definitely cure it.

Other remedies for smoky fires are to restrict the throat at the bottom of the flue and to insert an air brick in the external wall near the fire.

Slow-combustion stoves can sometimes cause trouble because of condensation of flue gases in the chimney. This may result in the staining of the chimney breast and even decomposition of the mortar in the brickwork of the flue, which is sometimes caused by burning damp fuel or wet kitchen refuse. One way of preventing this is to burn the stove at full heat occasionally, in order to warm the flue up and dry out moisture.

Designed on the balanced flue principle, this gas space heater draws air from outside and must be fitted on an outside wall.   Cowper Penfold & Co. Ltd.

Smokeless fuels are a great advance on the ordinary sooty coal. There are several types, and though they may be a trifle more expensive to buy, they produce more heat and create much less dirt.

Gas ignition eliminates the bother of chopping sticks, collecting newspapers and blowing with bellows. A firescreen which catches sparks is a wise precaution.

The airing and drying of damp clothing, sheets and so on is often a problem in winter. The old-fashioned drying rack suspended from the kitchen ceiling is not a practical solution in small modern houses. Low-powered gas or electric heaters are invaluable for inexpensive heating of existing cupboards.

Electricity can make great contributions to winter comfort, supplying power as well

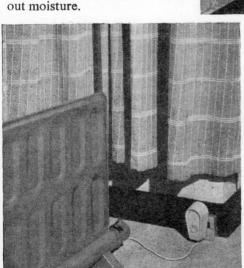

Here's a clever economy idea—by using the Pullin Plug-Stat in place of a normal electric plug, you can regulate the room temperature thermostatically by simply setting the switch

as lighting and heat. A time switch is now on the market which can be used to switch on or off any electrical device of up to two-kilowatt capacity at any predetermined time. It can be set to turn the fire on half an hour before one returns from the office or to turn it off after one has got into bed. It can also be set to turn on the radio in the morning or to boil a kettle.

Another inexpensive, useful control is a thermostat to fit on to any electric fire. There are two types. One has a plug between the wall plug and the one fitted to the flex of the fire and a thermostat which hangs on the wall and is connected by flex to the plug. The other type incorporates the special plug and thermostat in one unit. Both control the current, switching it on and off according to fluctuations of room temperature so that an even warmth is maintained, the thermostat being set to the temperature required.

Simple Heating Rules for Greater Comfort

If an existing open fire is inadequate, try fitting a throat restrictor to decrease

The Walmer convector gas fire provides a cosy glow at your feet, while gentle currents of convected heat circulate right round the room, bringing it to a uniform temperature. (Bratt Colbran Ltd.)

the air flow; use a radiant gas, electric or oil fire for intermittent use, or use a gas, electric or oil convector heater for continuous day and night burning. Placed under a window, it cuts down draughts.

Do not poke the fire or use wood mixed with coal or coke to increase the rate of burning, as this wastes the coal.

Dining Rooms

DO use a convector heater to give moderate continual background warmth and supplement it with a radiant fire at meal-times.

Central heating radiators are no longer ugly dust traps. This Hurseal oil-filled electric panel fits flush to the wall and blends with a modern room

Halls, Stairs and Landings

DO provide adequate warmth to avoid draughts in well-heated living rooms—
- (*a*) by convector or panel electric heater;
- (*b*) by gas or oil convector heater;
- (*c*) by one or more radiators run from an existing solid-fuel boiler which provides surplus hot water. This possibility needs careful investigation, in every case by an expert.

Bedrooms

DO provide quick heating night and morning by electric or gas radiant fires. One

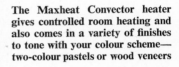

The Maxheat Convector heater gives controlled room heating and also comes in a variety of finishes to tone with your colour scheme— two-colour pastels or wood veneers

The Spark Screen (left): Steel mesh curtains worked by chain and pulley to draw across open fire against the danger of flying sparks. Fitted by Froys

Two contemporary electric heaters provide background and occasional heating in this room—the radiator is a Dimplex permanently oil-filled model and the portable fire a Dimplex infra-red

portable fire could be used for bedroom and dining room.

Sickrooms

DO ensure even, continuous warmth day and night. A room thermostat and special plug are available at low cost for automatic control of any electric radiant fire.

Nurseries

DON'T use radiant fires unless fixed and enclosed with an adequate guard or fitted out of a child's reach on the wall. DO use an electric or gas panel or convector heater. DO put in a small window ventilator to give ventilation without draughts in cold weather.

**Thick, well-fitted curtains and under-sill radiators combine to winterproof this bedroom
both cosily and artistically against the coldest weather**

DO provide a small portable radiant fire for use during babies' feeding and bath times, but it must not be left unattended.

DO provide adequate clothes drying and airing facilities.

Kitchens

DO provide space heating where there is no solid-fuel appliance to give enough. An electric or gas panel or radiant heater can be fitted on the wall, or a convector heater can stand on the floor.

DON'T use a portable radiant fire.

Bathrooms and Lavatories

DON'T on any account use electric radiant fires because of the danger of electricity in contact with water.

DO warm them with electric, gas or oil convector heaters or electric panels.

Solid-fuel Fires

DO make up a good fire. Adding small quantities of coal frequently is extravagant and gives no comfort. When the fire is burning well, bank the back with slack or small coal and leave it alone. Peat blocks burn well and economically under the slack behind the coal in a large fireplace.

DON'T use wood mixed with any kind of coal or coke.

DON'T poke the fire except when it needs making up, then free the bars of all ash.

DO adjust the under-fire draught by the control supplied.

DO control the flow of air over the fire by restricting the chimney throat.

DO use a gas poker for igniting, if possible.

DO ensure speedy, sure lighting with special firelighters. Tarred-paper lighters or an absorbent brick block soaked in paraffin are both efficient.

Electric Fires

DON'T use one in an open fireplace without blocking the chimney.

DON'T use radiant types in kitchens, bathrooms, lavatories or nurseries.

DO provide a long-enough flex for portable fires.

DON'T run flexes under carpets or through doors where friction causes damage and potential danger.

Chimneys

DON'T fit a gas fire, boiler or an open-closable stove without checking ventilation in the chimney. An air brick can be used to prevent damage by excess damp.

CONSERVING HEAT

Thermal insulation means insulation against loss of heat, and the simplest example is a pullover or cardigan. It keeps body heat from radiating away too quickly and insulates one against cold draughts. The same kind of thing can be done for the house, and there are two main advantages to be gained. One is freedom from heat losses in the plumbing system, the other is the avoidance of wasted heat in the rooms. Similar kinds of material are used for both applications, the principle being the same.

A considerable portion of the heat generated by fires or radiators in an average house is lost through the walls and roof, and of this wasted heat, most passes through the roof. Even if the roof is close-boarded under the tiles, you will find that there are large gaps round the eaves which readily allow warm air to escape.

Designed specially for bedrooms and small rooms, the panel gas fire fits flush to the wall and takes little space. "Lutello" by Bratt Colbran Ltd.

Nursery heating must be adequate—and safe. The Radiation Wenlock panel-type gas fire fits flush to the wall at any height and is fitted with regulation fireguard

Cresta's simple, inexpensive reflector fire can be switched to half load, has a fireguard that hinges up for cleaning the reflector, then clicks back firmly into place for absolute safety

The most effective method is to stop the warmth escaping through the ceilings of the upper floors. It is not practicable to do this entirely, but for a modest outlay you can stop half the waste heat coming through the ceiling by using one or other of the various forms of thermal insulating materials. In bungalows the effect is most noticeable because most of the lost heat passes through the ceilings.

Materials available can be divided into three classes as follows:

Fibrous materials may be had in the form of glass wool or mineral wool made up in either strip or blanket form, or as loose material.

Granulated materials are used as "loose fills."

Metal foil is used as a wrapping or covering material. It differs from the other types in that it exploits the principle of reflecting heat from a polished surface.

Fibrous materials made up in blanket form may be laid between the ceiling joists, or across them. The blankets are of glass or mineral wool and are usually 1-in. thick. They can be obtained in greater thicknesses, which give better insulation, but are accordingly higher in price. When laid *across* the joists, the strips should overlap each other at the edges for about 3 in. They

should also be allowed to sag a little between the joists so that you can clearly see where to tread. Clout nails driven through the blankets into the joists here and there will prevent the strips being kicked up, though this is only necessary in the immediate vicinity of the water tank and pipes.

As an alternative measure, you can use "loose fill" insulation packed between the ceiling joists. Typical materials are glass or mineral wool packed loosely about 2 in. deep, or else vermiculite or mica chips poured between the joists and levelled off 2 in. deep. All these materials are delivered in bags, usually weighing 28 or 56 lb. each.

Perfectly safe for bathrooms and nurseries, the Universal fan convector by Baker stands on the floor or, by means of a clip fastener, hangs on the wall

Aluminium foil can be laid across the joists, with about 3 in. overlap between the edges of the strips, or it can be lightly crumpled and laid between them. A better method is really a combination of the two, using crumpled foil between the joists with the top material, consisting of kraft paper, sandwiched between two sheets of foil laid crosswise. The "sandwich" type material has one "flat" face and the other corrugated, and when used the flat side should be uppermost.

Pipe Lagging

Pipes are "lagged," or covered with thermal insulation material to prevent loss of heat from the water they contain. This

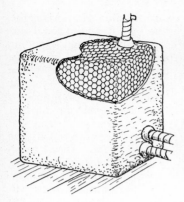

Both hot and cold water tanks (left) should be lagged with a prefabricated insulating jacket but do *not* lag the ceiling under the tank

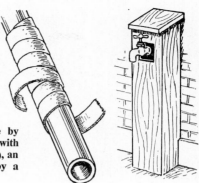

(Right) Lagging a pipe by wrapping spirally round with hair-felt strips; (far right), an outdoor tap protected by a box structure

guards against winter freezing of cold water supplies or wasted heat radiation from hot water pipes.

The usual method is to wrap the pipes spirally with glass wool, mineral wool or hair-felt strips. The strips should overlap at the edges and be secured at intervals with string ties. Bends or corners should have a double wrapping, using a short length of material wrapped and tied into the bend before the main lagging is put on.

Particular attention should be given to sections of the piping which are exposed to draughts, an example being the feed pipe from the cold tank to the toilet cistern. In many cases, this runs across the ceiling rafters to a corner of the roof, then down through the eaves and into the lavatory. The bend at the eaves is the part most susceptible to freezing and, again in many cases, the most difficult to reach. To cater for this situation, pack glass or mineral wool "loose-fill" into the corner and as closely round the pipe as possible. The object is to block up any crevices through which icy draughts may blow on the pipe.

Another type of pipe insulation consists of glass wool "pipes" known as rigid sections, which are split lengthwise and hinged along one joint. They are placed on the pipes and secured with wire ties or metal bands which are supplied with them. The sections are 3 ft. long and are produced to fit all pipe sizes from $\frac{1}{2}$-in. bore up to, and including, 12-in. bore. The thickness of the insulation—that is, the "wall" of the section—is in sizes from $\frac{1}{2}$ in. up to 2 in. Corners or bends are negotiated by cutting V-shaped notches out of the section, which can then be bent to shape and secured with extra wire ties.

Tank Lagging

Hot or cold water tanks or cylinders are lagged for the same reason as pipes, and you can use a prefabricated insulating jacket, make up a jacket from a thermal insulating blanket or build a hardboard

To stop house warmth escaping through the ceilings, special glass silk is fitted between the floor joists of the loft. British Hermeseal Ltd.

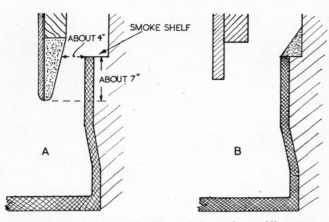

Section views of two fireplaces. A is good, providing two barriers against down-draught; B has a throat funnelled downwards and will smoke

box structure right round the tank to contain "loose-fill" material. Where a cold water tank situated in the loft is concerned, it is most important to *avoid* lagging the ceiling *under* the tank. If this happens, the small amount of warmth normally coming through the ceiling will not keep the water temperature above freezing. Where the box and "loose-fill" construction is used, it will be necessary to ensure that there are no crevices through which the granulated type materials, in particular, can seep under the tank. The top should be covered with an insulating blanket—just laid in position on a wooden cover so that both can be removed to give access to the ball valve.

SMOKY CHIMNEYS

The three principal causes of smoky chimneys are incorrect design of the fireplace or flue, down-draught or obstruction inside the chimney and insufficient ventilation in the room.

The first is the most general cause, and Figs. *A* and *B* show a section view of two fireplaces, illustrating good and bad design. In sketch *A*, air heated by the fire is expanded, thus reducing its density and causing it to rise into the throat of the fireplace. The throat is funnel-shaped, which makes the speed of the warm air increase so that it "shoots" into the flue, past the horizontal smoke shelf. Cold air entering the room flows to the fireplace and helps to push the heated air, and the smoke carried with it,

into the flue. Providing the flue is unobstructed and reasonably straight, the air and smoke should travel up and away from the chimney without difficulty. Important design features to note are the rounded entrance to the throat under the fireplace lintel, the funnelled or tapered shape of the throat and its dimensions, and the horizontal smoke shelf.

In the fireplace shown in sketch *B,* the air heated by the fire expands and rises behind the fireplace lintel, but instead of being accelerated, its speed is considerably reduced by the squared-off recess behind the lintel. To add to the problem, the sloped-off back to the throat acts as a funnel pointing in the downward direction (which, in certain circumstances, accelerates the speed of cold air sinking down the flue) and blows the warm air and smoke into the room.

Down-draught

Such a condition is known as "down-draught" and may be caused by a variety of circumstances, including the height of the chimney stack with respect to the roof of the house and neighbouring buildings, the pitch of your own or neighbour's roof, the aspect of the house, etc.

What happens is that air, for one reason or another, is forced or drawn down the chimney and, in turn, carries the smoke with it. If the throat of the fireplace is "funnelled" downwards, as in sketch *B,* the speed of the air is increased by the "funnel" and a considerable amount of smoke may be blown into the room. On the other hand, the correct design shown at *A* provides two barriers against down-draught. First, the smoke shelf constitutes a *cul-de-sac* to the downward stream of air and, secondly, the shape of the throat is designed to produce a speedy *upward* thrust of air. The combination of these two features almost always ensures freedom from smoke troubles, providing there are no external complications as already mentioned.

It follows that down-draught is an individual problem requiring individual attention and it would be foolish, indeed, to attempt to prescribe a universal remedy. Chimney pots or cowls cure the trouble in most cases, and at least one manufacturer guarantees his products and backs the guarantee with an advisory service if the appliance does not solve the problem. For all but the mildest cases, the best thing to do is to obtain expert "on-the-spot" advice and perhaps avoid a good deal of expense on "trial and error" methods.

Before leaving the subject of smoky fires, we must consider the room ventilation. It is very rare for a room to be so closely shut against ventilation that it will cause smoking at the fireplace, but it may well be the source of the trouble when a fire persistently does not "draw" properly. A good solution to this problem is to have an "air-brick," or ventilator, inserted in an external wall close to the fireplace to provide a supply of air to the fire itself. Inside the room the ventilator can be finished with a decorative grille, and these can be had embodying means of adjusting the air flow as required.

HOT WATER

Hot water in a never-failing supply is of the utmost importance for winter comfort and, indeed, all the year round. If your hot-water supply is inadequate or inefficient, there are simple and inexpensive ways to improve it.

A water softener for the household water supply eliminates scale, and portable models are now obtainable quite cheaply. "Micromet" granules in a mono-metal basket used in the cold water storage tank reduce scaling.

However hot the water may be when it leaves the boiler, it will run cold from the taps if it has to heat too many rooms and corridors on the way.

Hot water pipes, tank or cylinder must be well lagged. Most prefabricated lagging has sections that can be opened to heat the airing cupboard. If all the heat is needed in the water, lag the tank heavily and use a low-powered heater for the cupboard.

Heating water by solid fuel is the cheapest method—gas or electric heating costs twice as much—but using a solid-fuel boiler with no thermostatic control involves many difficulties.

For Solid Fuel Boilers

DO try to obtain the fuel best suited to the boiler. Manufacturers of appliances will advise on this question. Reputable coal merchants do their best to provide the right fuel when customers are insistent.

DO use anthracite when you can get it, mixing it with coke. Equal proportions of both give the best results, but very little anthracite keeps coke burning well.

DO experiment with damper positions, particularly when using coke. It is usually possible to find the right draught to keep the fuel burning. Coke always needs more draught than anthracite or coal.

DO see that a coke fire is glowing red before refuelling. When the fire is low, add only a little fuel at a time.

DO empty the ashpan regularly, and remove all ash from the bars.

DO have the boiler chimney swept regularly if rubbish is burnt on the fire.

DO fit a thermometer to indicate water temperatures on a boiler without thermostatic control.

DON'T roar the fire with the bottom

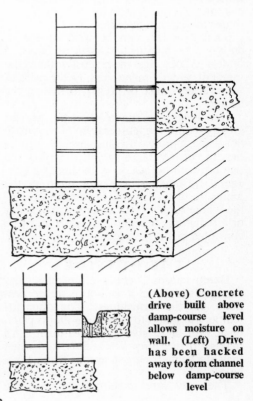

(Above) Concrete drive built above damp-course level allows moisture on wall. (Left) Drive has been hacked away to form channel below damp-course level

damper left wide open. This wastes fuel by sending the heat up the chimney, creates clinkers and burns out fire-bars.

DON'T burn large quantities of kitchen waste on the boiler. It damps the fire down, cools the water, uses fuel for combustion and creates soot.

Gas and Electric Water Heating

Gas circulators or electric immersion heaters are usually regarded as alternatives to solid-fuel boilers for summer use, but can also be used in conjunction with them. They are available when the fire burns sluggishly, for quick heating when the boiler has gone out and for topping up water temperature. A gas circulator should be fitted near the storage tank with a special flow and return, and a valve in the existing hot water pipe to cut out the loop to the boiler in the summer. An electric immersion heater should be fitted by the local electricity authority—wrong fitting and inadequate lagging will produce high bills and low water temperature.

A 30–60-gallon storage cylinder can be heated by an immersion heater or a gas circulator. A small cylinder can be placed under the draining board.

Such cylinders can be used independently or in conjunction with an existing boiler. They are more costly than the methods already mentioned, as the price of the cylinder must be added to that of the heater.

One long pipe run to a single tap can greatly reduce the temperature of the whole hot water supply. In this case, it may be best to cut out this pipe and to supply the one tap with hot water by means of a storage or instantaneous heater fitted to the mains, instead of raising the temperature of the whole supply with an immersion heater or circulator. A reliable plumber must be consulted before such an alteration is made.

THE OUTSIDE

Damp causes a chilly atmosphere and damages the fabric of the house, the decorations and the furnishings. Too often attempts are made to disguise a damp patch on a wall or to give local treatment. All makeshift measures are useless, and while they are being tried out serious trouble can be caused.

The only sure remedy is to trace the cause of the damp and tackle it at the source.

Damp may get into a building in all sorts of ways, owing to defective damp courses, flashings, aprons, valleys, eaves-gutters, down-pipes, gullies, pointing, by lack of ventilation due to blocked vents or air-bricks, by broken or missing slates, by tiles or weatherboards, or by porous walls, condensation, etc. Often a single patch of damp may be due to several causes. It is sometimes impossible to decide exactly what is causing a damp patch on a wall or ceiling without pulling part of the house down to discover where the damp is coming from.

Generally speaking, it is most dangerous for an amateur to attempt to cure an outbreak of damp himself, for unless he diagnoses the cause correctly he may give the patient the wrong medicine. For instance, if a wall is damp owing to a defective damp course and a waterproofing liquid is applied to the outside in the belief that the wall is porous, the condition will be made very much worse, for the damp will only be able to escape into the house.

The amateur should therefore confine himself to seeing that gutters are in order, that the damp course has not been "short-circuited," and that there are no obvious cracks in the wall or roof, missing slates or tiles.

Gutters

Overflowing gutters are usually caused by an accumulation of dirt, leaves, birds'-nests or blocked-up down-pipes. Clearing the gutters is a straightforward job, while blockages in down-pipes can usually be removed with a long piece of rattan or chair cane. As an alternative, use a long osier if you cannot get rattan cane. Both are usually obtainable from handicraft stores.

Another cause of an overflowing gutter may be a broken bracket which allows the gutter to sag. Gutter brackets can be bought at builders' merchants. When fixing the new bracket, lift the gutter to its original position and support it with a 6-in. nail knocked into the facing-board. Pour some water into the gutter to check that it is not too high, and adjust its level by bending the nail up or down. When correct, screw the bracket close under the gutter and pull out the nail.

The diagram on this page shows how lengths of guttering are joined together with screws and nuts, and how a mastic compound is used to make the joints watertight. The gutter rests in brackets screwed to the facing-boards under the eaves. Leaking at the gutter joints may be caused by a broken mastic seal or a loose fixing screw. Tightening the screw or fitting new washers may solve the problem, but if the mastic seal is leaking, the gutter section should be taken right off and the joints recaulked.

The nuts on the fixing screws are usually rusted tight, but can often be freed by brushing on a little penetrating oil, which should be left for an hour or so in order to loosen the rust. Failing this, cut off the screw by hacksawing through the lead washer and the stem of the screw itself. Scrape the old mastic from each end of the length of guttering, also from the ends of the guttering still in position.

A tube of special sealing putty (not ordinary putty) is excellent for caulking the gutter joints prior to assembling them. Two "strips" of the putty are used in each joint. The length of gutter is then put into position and secured with the screw and nut. Two lead washers are fitted to each screw, one above and the other below the gutter.

Faulty Damp Course

A faulty damp course, unless rectified, may lead to dry-rot attack in the floor timbers. The dampness usually appears at skirting level and spreads upwards and outwards. In most cases of this kind the damp course is actually quite sound, but has been "bridged" in some way; for example, by the earth of a flower-bed being piled against the wall, by a cement rendering, or a concrete path or drive. The latter situation is illustrated in the diagram on page 43, showing a concrete drive which has been built up just above damp-course level, thus allowing surface

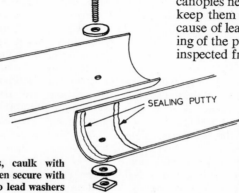

To avoid gutter leaks, caulk with special sealing putty, then secure with screws and nuts and two lead washers

SEALING PUTTY

moisture to creep up the wall. To rectify the trouble, the drive has been hacked away and the final stage will be to form a small cement channel against the wall and below damp-course level, as shown in section view in the small sketch. The channel will either lead into an existing gully, or have drain holes formed every couple of feet by driving a wooden stake through the wet cement as soon as it is laid. After an hour the stakes are carefully pulled out so that there is no chance of them becoming "set" in the concrete.

Leaking Roofs

It is possible to treat a leaking flat roof—lead or zinc—with a bituminous waterproofing compound, obtainable from any builders' merchant. The roof is cleaned and washed over with plain water. When it is dry, the compound is spread evenly over the roof, taking particular care to cover joints in the metal. This treatment, however, should be regarded merely as a stopgap and must be repeated at frequent intervals to remain effective.

If the damp persists and does not appear to have been caused by any of the above-named faults, it is wise to call in either a local builder or an architect, or, in a difficult case, an expert firm of waterproofers. There are one or two firms who will investigate, diagnose and prescribe treatment for any outbreak of damp for a nominal fee and, if necessary, carry out the treatment with their own expert staff.

There are also firms who specialise in curing roof defects, and will undertake to render almost any roof watertight, guaranteeing their results.

Glass roofs to conservatories or canopies need periodic attention to keep them watertight. The usual cause of leaks is drying and cracking of the putty, and this should be inspected from time to time.

Modern sealing compounds are excellent for jobs such as this, as they are specially made to resist movement due to expansion and contraction or vibration. Normal putty dries hard after a time and is fractured by movement, whereas modern sealing putties remain plastic under a self-forming hard "skin" and are unaffected by expansion or vibration movement.

Doors and Windows

There are all sorts of reasons why doors and windows jam or stick, the most frequent cause being moisture penetration due to a perished or cracked paint film. The only lasting cure in such cases is to allow the wood to dry out as much as possible, recramp and secure the joints and, if necessary, plane away the wood at the "tight" part and repaint to prevent a recurrence of the trouble.

Another quite common cause, though seldom suspected, is swelling of the wood in the hinge recesses, particularly if they have not been painted. If doors or windows are allowed to bang about in high winds, the hinges take considerable punishment and it is quite easy for them to be strained in their recesses. Once the normal contact between the back of the hinge and the wood is broken in this way, moisture can usually penetrate and, of course, cause the wood to swell. The hinge then starts to rust, the gap becomes more capable of absorbing moisture and a vicious circle is started which results in the hinge being gradually pushed out of the recess. The opposite side of the door or window soon begins to jam, and if one planes the edge and forgets to paint it properly afterwards, the bare wood offers even greater possibilities for swelling and jamming.

The best remedy for swollen hinge recesses is to pare them back to their correct depth and give them a heavy coat of priming, which should be well brushed in. Aluminium wood primer is the best material for this and, in fact, for all kinds of exterior wood painting.

Rattling doors and windows are a great source of draughts. Loose or worn catches, lock shoots or striking plates are frequent causes of rattles and draughts, and you may well find that replacement of such parts cures the trouble by pulling the door or window close into the jamb or recess when it is shut.

Draught-excluders are effective and long-lasting. The metal-type excluders are well known, but there is a tendency for them to be used incorrectly, with the result that the door or window sometimes needs a strong man to shut it.

The strip is nailed in position while it is flat, and, following this, a wheeled tool or a screwdriver is run along the "crease" in the strip, causing the back edge to rise. Very little pressure is needed to do this, and if the edge is raised too far by using too much pressure along the crease, the door or window will surely jam. It is almost impossible to take out the crease without spoiling the strip, so the axiom *gently does it* may save you annoyance and expense.

Doors are a nuisance if they are hinged on the wrong side, and an uncomfortable, draughty living room may sometimes be transformed merely by rehanging the door to deflect draughts in a different direction. This job should be done by a carpenter but should not be expensive.

Worn locks also cause rattling. Usually the fault is due to the bolt being worn, and the best cure is to renew it. Another common cause of looseness, where cranked bolts are concerned, is the absence of a metal plate on the door frame. This plate contains a hole for the end of the bolt to enter, the wood being bored out behind it. If the plate is not fitted, wear soon takes place in the wood and the bolt gets slack. Replacement plates can be obtained from most ironmongers, and can easily be fitted in the correct position by shooting the bolt into the hole in the plate, and then screwing it to the door frame.

Condensation

Kitchens are notorious places for condensation troubles, particularly in winter when the windows are closed. Much of this trouble can be avoided by providing extra ventilation, but it must be easily controlled. One good way to do this is to have a ventilator fitted in one of the normally "closed" window panes. Most glass merchants or builders' stockists can show a variety of them (one firm alone makes six different types), and you should have no difficulty in getting one fitted into an existing window. It may be necessary to take out the pane and have the ventilator fitted at the shop; alternatively, it is not too expensive to buy a new pane for the average kitchen window and have the ventilator fitted into it.

Cheerful in front but draughts at the back! See (left) how an old-fashioned grate draws every draught of cold air from defective doors and windows towards the fire —past and round the unhappy person sitting in front.

Right, still cheerful in front, but no draughts now! With a modern restricted-throat fire, the amount of air allowed up the chimney is controllable. All other air in the room is heated and circulated, the flow of air being reduced by more than three-quarters. You can be warm without sitting in the fireplace.

The Hurseal "Hurdapta" convector open fire is a complete free-standing unit that will fit into almost any fireplace, top and side grilles being detachable to alter the shape and size. Its restricted throat saves loss of heat up the chimney

NO MORE UNDER-DOOR GALES

For the many homes where inside doors do not fit well enough to keep out draughts, there is an automatic draught excluder. The Auto-Seal (seen below) consists of a flexible, non-metal blade that rises clear when you open the door and lowers to a perfect draught-proof seal when closed.

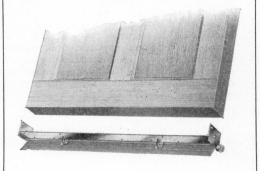

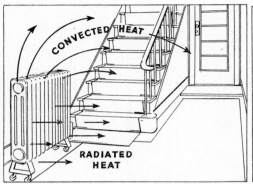

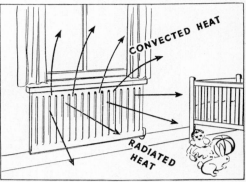

THE trouble with the old-fashioned open fireplace is that you usually only manage to toast your feet, while the rest of you is chilled by the current of cold air, often more than 9,000 cubic feet an hour, which goes to feed the hungry chimney.

Modern convector open fires of the adaptor type have a restricted throat which reduces the flow of air to little more than 2,000 cubic feet an hour, just enough for room ventilation. By preventing waste of heat up the chimney, as much as 50 per cent. fuel saving may be effected.

A heater that provides the warmth just where you want it, safely out of reach of children— the Radisil infra-red instant heater has no exposed element, is cheap to run

KEEP OUT WINDOW DRAUGHTS

Weatherproofing is now within the scope of the home handyman and woman. Even metal windows can be sealed quickly and easily with Stick-a-Seal self-adhesive plastic foam weather strip. No nails, screws or special adhesives are needed to apply it to the window frames. You simply unroll it and press it firmly into position with the fingers, as shown right.

NOTE TO THE HOUSEPROUD: A small square of Stick-a-Seal on the bottom of an ornament will prevent it scratching polished furniture.

HEATING THE HOME

No aspect of home-making is of greater importance to the health
and happiness of the whole family than adequate warmth

A house with lights on and a warm, friendly atmosphere always bids the traveller welcome
and makes the worker feel glad to return at night

WE, in the U.K., have tended to be conservative in our methods of home heating, but of recent years the high cost of fuel, smoke pollution and the need to save labour have brought forth various inventions and adaptations of systems already used in other parts of the world.

The idea of whole-house warming, instead of the heating of individual rooms as required, is finding increasing favour. In existing houses a complete central heating installation is often quite practicable and with new buildings whole-house warming may prove more economic in every respect. It also ensures a much higher level of comfort and much less work and dirt.

You may decide on full central heating extending to the whole house and of such a standard that supplementary heating is not normally required anywhere; or, where money is limited, on partial central heating in one or two main rooms and the hall. Partial central heating can also be used to provide all-over-the-house background warmth at a lower temperature (say 50° F.) with a higher temperature 55°–58° F.) in the living-room.

Consideration must be given to the choice of boiler, fuel and type of radiator. Radiators should be positioned with the object of providing a uniform temperature. A favourite position is under the window to counteract cold draughts, but in this case the radiator should be the full width of the window.

Panel-type wall radiators are the neatest and easiest to keep clean. Skirting heating is becoming increasingly popular and is made to look exactly like skirting board. It is made in two forms—the radiant type containing two pipes, through which hot water circulates; and the convector variety, which also emits hot air through grilles at the top. Rather more expensive to instal than conventional radiators, skirting heating gives a very even distribution of heat and is virtually invisible, being painted to match the skirting to which it is fixed.

PLANNING HEATING WITH THE BUILDING

To be most successful, heating for a new house should be planned along with the building. In fact, it can be said that the architect will often design round the system proposed, in consultation, of course, with the builder and other technicians. This is because many whole-house warming systems form the central core of a house and because they also make the currently favoured "open" planning, where rooms are not so rigidly divided as in the past, extremely practical.

WHOLE-HOUSE WARMING BY DUCTED AIR

The "Radiation" System

A system that has had some years of practical test operates by means of a unit built into a central insulated recess. Cold air is drawn in through ducts, passed through the unit which contains a furnace operated by solid fuel or oil—or, alternatively, a specially designed gas burner, with a heat exchanger—and is then given out as warmed air into the various rooms of the house. Control is fully automatic, with a thermostat regulating the rate of burning and a further thermostat in the living room. When more heat is called for, an electric fan is automatically switched on and warmed air is conveyed to the rooms until the required temperature is attained. At this point, the fan switches off and the furnace "idles" or the gas goes down, leaving only the pilot light.

Temperatures of individual rooms can be varied by opening or closing the hot air register. If, as is usual, a rather lower whole-house temperature is preferred at night (say, 55° F.), it will take only about half an hour to raise the temperature to 60° F. in the morning. A further increase to evening sitting-room-comfort temperatures of 65°–67° F. takes only 30–40 minutes.

The unit, usually sited in utility room or kitchen, is small and compact and normally contains a hot-water cylinder for supplying, from the same heat source, hot water to sink, basin and bath. In the summer the unit will supply cooled instead of warmed air if required. Provision for gas or electric summer water heating is usually included.

Efficiency and cost of operating the unit depend to a certain extent upon the kind of fuel used. Solid fuel (smokeless or not) is cheapest, but means fuelling twice in the twenty-four hours with anthracite, coal or similar dense fuel, and from twice to four times in the same period with coke. Clearing the fuel bed is a simple matter, since a shaking grate for removal of ash, stones, etc., is provided. Some work and dust cannot, however, be avoided. Space heating with solid fuel is at the rate of 35,000 B.T.U. (British Thermal Units) per hour, enough for full heating for a small house of 1,000 sq. ft. The unit also supplies ample domestic hot water.

With oil, fed by gravity through small copper piping from a large storage tank usually situated outside the house, the amount of heat generated is slightly more (40,000 B.T.U.), so that 1,500 sq. ft. of floor space can be heated. The same applies to gas. With both these fuels, work involved is negligible and they are appreciably cleaner than solid fuel. Cost is slightly higher for oil and rather more again for gas. In all cases running costs should compare very favourably indeed with those of other heating systems.

Although the radiation ducted air system is particularly applicable to the small family house, two units can be installed to service a much larger one. Building in the unit in a 1,500 sq. ft. house is estimated to cost from £300–£400. Such a house, however, would need no fireplaces, nor room chimneys, which would considerably cut costs in other directions.

The Weatherfoil System

A somewhat similar type of heating unit supplying *background* warmth to the small house (1,000–1,500 sq. ft.) also circulates warmed air through grilles. The Weatherfoil unit, which rather resembles a large-scale car radiator, is installed in a central shaft passing through the core of the house. Alongside the box stands an oil, gas or solid fuel boiler to supply the power. Again, a thermostatically controlled electric fan acts as booster.

Domestic hot water is also supplied by the unit, the cylinder being inside the central shaft in the airing cupboard section on the first floor. Again it is essential that the house and heating are planned, before building begins, as one integral whole. In one specially designed small house (family of two adults and one child) the installation cost under £200. Running costs again compare very favourably with other heating methods.

WHOLE-HOUSE WARMING BY HEAT PUMP

The heat pump which, by extracting heat from the air, cools a larder, provides a small refrigerating unit and at the same time heats domestic hot water, has been on the market for some time.

Whole-house warming by means of a heat pump has also proved successful.

The heat pump "machine," run by a 3-kw. motor, either heats air which can be passed through ducts to warm the rooms, in a similar way to the methods already described, or warms water which is passed through coils laid in the floor or ceiling. In either case, domestic hot-water heating is incorporated and running costs are very economic.

The installation is automatic, dependent on the operation of the thermostats, and completely clean and trouble free.

The Crane Cavendish, above, operates well with modern small-pipe forced circulation heating systems and is therefore good for conversions

The Ideal Classic Elite, left, a thermostatically controlled, easily operated solid fuel boiler, gives central heating plus domestic hot water

CENTRAL HEATING BY INDEPENDENT BOILER

While whole-house warming by ducted air has much to commend it to those who are able to have a house designed and built, central heating by the more conventional method of hot-water radiators has a good deal in its favour. The initial installation may prove rather more expensive, owing to the cost of the radiators themselves, but it is both well tried and very flexible, boilers being obtainable to give almost any heat output desired.

Although building in with the house is always most economic, a conventional central heating system of this kind can be fitted into an existing house. Conversions naturally vary a great deal in cost according to the original plan of the house and the work involved. Once fitted, however, full central heating is likely to provide more economically *an equivalent amount of heat* than any system of individual room heating. It must be realised, however, when comparing costs, that since only part of a non-centrally heated house is normally heated at one time, actual fuel bills may be smaller in the latter case.

What makes a Good System?

The efficiency, and hence the running costs, of any system of central heating by means of an independent boiler and hot-water radiators will depend upon:
(1) the heat-conversion efficiency of the boiler,
(2) the placing and length of the pipe run and the lagging or insulating of hot-water cylinder and pipes.

Solid smokeless fuel is cheapest for a boiler, and nowadays it is possible to obtain up to 80 per cent. efficiency (i.e. four-fifths of the fuel used is converted into heat) with the very best appliances, compared with 30–40 per cent. only a few years ago; 70 per cent. efficiency is considered good.

Thermostatic Control

Boiler efficiency depends partly on the fuel and the way it is fed to the fire but largely on the intrinsic design. Thermostatic control, now fitted to a number of small boilers as well as to the larger, completely automatic ones, means that the draught is controlled without manual manipulation. Because more draught is applied, and hence the fire boosted, *immediately* hot water is drawn from the boiler or the surface temperature falls, the response is much swifter than if dampers had to be opened by hand. This does add to the boiler's efficiency as well as, of course, saving trouble, but it is not, as already stated, the only factor that contributes.

What "Boiler Output" means

Before shopping for a boiler, the amount of heating required should be determined. According to its size and power and sometimes the frequency with which it is re-fuelled, a boiler will service so many square feet of radiation surface, including unlagged pipes. Sometimes the maker's explanatory leaflets give this. It may range from a few square feet (enough for a single small radiator) to several hundred (providing enough radiators adequately to warm a fair-sized house). More often, however, only the British Thermal Units (B.T.U.) rating is given.

An efficient small boiler with a 30,000 B.T.U. rating should service up to about 80 sq. ft. of radiation surface, including unlagged pipes, as well as supplying a 30-gallon hot-water cylinder (large enough for a *small* family).

A boiler giving 60,000 B.T.U. output would be necessary to supply full central heating (5–6 radiators) for a reasonable-sized 3–4 bedroom house. These figures can only be very approximate, for much depends upon aspect and height of rooms, the amount of draughts and the temperatures required, as well as on economical placing of pipes, adequate lagging and so forth.

Though in general the more heating required, the more powerful the boiler necessary, more frequent refuelling can, within limits, increase the output of all except automatically fuelled types. For a small house it is to-day possible to get moderately priced thermostatically controlled coke-burning boilers that need refuelling, under average conditions, only twice in the twenty-four hours. These are of a reasonable size for the housewife to cope with herself. Price depends mainly on power, measured by B.T.U. output, but it is also advisable to check the thermal efficiency, i.e. the heat conversion rate. It is usually rather higher in the more expensive designs, which will be correspondingly more economic in operation.

Gravity-feed Automatic Boilers

For a larger installation, gravity-feed automatic boilers are the most labour saving and satisfactory. These vary in details of design, but all have a high combustion efficiency. Ash formed by the burning of the fuel is fused into a clinker which is removed once in twenty-four hours, when refuelling is done. This is the

Specially designed to fit into a small space, the Potterton Diplomat 31 gas boiler has all controls, including automatic pump for use with small bore systems, inside

The Kayenco Popular gas boiler provides a complete hot-water service, is fully automatic with fingertip control, has a smart modern appearance to grace any kitchen

only attention necessary. Rate of burning is controlled by thermostat—in some cases the draught being aided by a small electric fan, in others controlled by a low voltage electric magnet damper.

Most models use anthracite of a special small type. As this fuel is much denser than coke, the boiler does not need to be so large to accommodate the necessary fuel. When refuelling is done by a woman, this is a real advantage, as lifting a hod to a height of over 4 ft. takes a certain amount

of effort. Smallest boiler made in this class has a rating of 35,000 B.T.U., but 80,000 is a popular size for the medium to medium-large house. Initially these boilers cost about twice as much as non-automatic ones that need more frequent refuelling, but they are very economic in fuel consumption owing to their high thermal efficiency.

Oil-fired Independent Boilers

Although the modern gravity-feed automatic boilers are both economic and particularly labour-saving in relation to any other kind of solid-fuel heating equipment, they do have certain disadvantages. Fuelling has to be done manually, even though it only means pouring in a hodful of fuel once in twenty-four hours. There is no cleaning out of ash, with the inevitable dust, but the clinker has to be removed, also once in twenty-four hours, though it takes only a moment or two.

It is in overcoming these drawbacks that the oil-fired boiler scores.

Once the controls have been set and regulated, oil is fed in as automatically as

No stoking, clinkering, fuel to carry or ashes to clear with the Nu-way Home-Fire Burner, using oil. Easily installed in any suitable small independent boiler

electricity. There are no anxieties about getting supplies and the quality of fuel oil is consistent and dependable. With one type of oil burner (the least expensive, vaporising kind used for smaller boilers), cleaning is necessary once a fortnight only. This is estimated to be a ten-minute job. The more costly, fully automatic burners need no cleaning other than one or two service visits a year. The dirt and dust, inseparable in a greater or lesser degree from all solid-fuel-burning apparatus, are completely absent from both types.

Principal argument against the oil-fired boiler is that of expense. Running costs, though a lot cheaper than for electric heating and a good deal less than for gas-firing, are only slightly higher, or even comparable with those of solid fuel. *But* initial installation, or conversion of existing solid-fuel boiler, when suitable, is far from cheap. The cost of fuel bunkers or other storage facilities must be added, together

with the necessary piping from the tank, probably another £100, with builder's work. The actual central-heating installation (hot-water cylinder, piping, radiators, etc.) is additional with solid-fuel and oil-fired boilers.

In actual fact, buying a boiler suitable for oil firing and a separate oil burner is recommended by many heating consultants as being a good deal more economical, and as efficient, as having a specially designed cabinet unit. Advantages of the latter are the neater appearance and the completely silent working.

Conversion of Solid-fuel Boiler to Oil Firing

In many cases it is possible satisfactorily to convert an existing solid-fuel boiler to oil-firing. There is a most efficient oil-conversion unit that can be inserted with the minimum of trouble into almost any old or new solid-fuel stove already used for hot water or central heating. There are two sizes, one for heating a 25–30-gallon tank, the other for a 40–50-gallon tank.

"Vaporising" and "Pressure Jet" Types of Burner

Cheapest types of domestic oil burner for firing an independent boiler are those that vaporise the oil. These are suitable for small systems servicing 5–6 radiators and hot-water supply (60,000 B.T.U. output). They are usually fitted with a small electrically driven blower to assist draught. There is thermostatic control and the flame goes down to a tiny one when the boiler is idling. This is the kind needing cleaning once a fortnight. Equally suitable for conversion are the fully automatic pressure jet types of burner which are usually fitted, in addition, with push-button control. The flame goes right out when the boiler is idling. They are completely trouble-free, needing no cleaning by the householder whatsoever. Made mainly for the larger house system, they cost from about twice as much, according to size, as the vaporising kind.

Safety Checks on Oil-fired Boilers

Fuel oil does not ignite until vaporised, so that the fire risk is actually less than with an open fire. All burners have provision for stopping the flow of oil in the event of breakage of the oil burner connection. In addition, a fusible link, to control a valve and shut off oil supply in case of emergency, can be fitted as an optional extra at the cost of a few pounds. The oil pipe from tank to burner must be absolutely leakproof, and only the oil specified, which will have the correct flashpoint, must be used. This last is looked after by the oil companies and, providing the appropriate oil is ordered, there is nothing for the householder to worry about.

Cost of oil, known as domestic or heating fuel oil, but sometimes as gas oil, is around 1s. 6d. a gallon, according to delivery zone and the quantity ordered. It is most economical to order 500 gallons at a time.

Cheapest zones are nearest the big refineries. On the whole, fuel oil, as compared with solid fuel, is cheaper in the south than in the north of England. Suppliers, in addition to the big petrol companies, include a number of the larger coal merchants. Some of these offer a very helpful advisory service to intending users. One firm, supplying the London area and the Home Counties, has a showroom where various types of oil burner with appropriate boilers are installed and where a knowledgeable consultant will give helpful advice.

Background House Warming by Oil-burning Warmed-air Circulators

For large houses with a big central hall

Pither's Studio Stove will heat 2,000 cubic feet. Larger stoves in the Pither range burn anthracite beans or peas, give 80 per cent. efficiency burning at slow draught, supply hot water and/or radiators

with a fireplace, background house warming can be simply and economically provided by the installation of a special type of flued, warmed-air circulator burning fuel oil. Resembling a large closed stove in appearance, this operates by the heat exchanger method and has an automatic but non-electric draught control.

Very little attention is required. A smallish model, burning about $2\frac{1}{2}$ pints of oil per hour at "high," and only a quarter of that at "low," has a maximum output of 32,000 B.T.U. per hour. Other larger types give a total circulating and radiant heat of 50,000 B.T.U., which is estimated by the makers as sufficient to heat 16,000 cu. ft. of floor space.

Domestic fuel oil is usually burned, though the small model can be operated on paraffin (which is more expensive) if preferred. A service tank holding some 6 gallons can be fixed to the side, but a more labour-saving method is to couple up the heater with an outside tank of some 150-gallons capacity, so that the heater is gravity-fed.

WHOLE-HOUSE WARMING BY THE SMALL PIPE SYSTEM

This system is applicable to small and medium-sized houses or bungalows with floor areas up to about 1,500 square feet, i.e. a three- or sometimes four-bedroom house. It can be operated with solid fuel, oil- or gas-fired boilers.

This is how it works: the hot water is forced through $\frac{1}{2}$-in. or $\frac{3}{8}$-in. copper piping by means of a small electric pump and

The Neofire provides domestic hot water, feeds two radiators and a towel rail, gives continuous burning fire if hood is used. (Ideal Boiler Co., Hull)

pliances. These are open fires, stoves or sometimes cookers designed to provide some space heating in rooms other than the one in which they are installed. Their big advantage is that they do this comparatively cheaply. Heat is utilised that would otherwise be wasted, and the additional firing necessary is a good deal less than would be required for a separate appliance. In addition, there is often a saving of labour as one fire only has to be tended instead of two or more.

the boiler is thermostatically controlled. The pipes, being so small and unobtrusive, can very easily be concealed, run through quite small holes drilled in walls, painted to match skirting boards, etc. and in the case of installation in existing premises, floor boards do not have to be taken up or decorations disturbed.

The greatest advantage of the system is its low cost of installation, owing to the absence of structural work and the price of both pump and control is usually more than offset by saving in pipes, radiators and labour, compared with other central heating systems. It is also more economical to operate than a gravity system, because no heat gets wasted in the roof and very little from the surface of the small pipes. But to obtain the best combination of fuel economy, efficiency and unobtrusive appearance, the design and layout should be carried out only by a contractor, architect or engineer who has studied the special design characteristics of the system.

PARTIAL HOUSE WARMING

When, by reason of expense or for preference, central heating proper is not installed, there is much to be said for the increasingly popular method of partial house warming by multiple or double-duty ap-

Background Warmth from a Sitting-room Back Boiler

The most usual method of getting secondary warmth from one appliance is through a back boiler. This can be supplied with many types of modern open fire and also to open-close stoves. The boiler usually services a 30-gallon hot-water cylinder for domestic hot water and one, two or even three radiators. As with small independent boilers, the whole output could be used to heat a larger hot-water cylinder of, say, 40 or even 60 gallons or, if hot water is produced by other means, the whole output can be used for radiator heating.

Coal can be burned but with coke, the overall efficiency—room heating plus hot water output—is at least 50 per cent. and may be higher. Such fires can be run very slowly in summer with the boiler damper open so as to concentrate on hot water production and minimise heat output in the room.

Some free standing convector fires with restricted throats and a number of openable stoves also have boilers large enough to heat a radiator or two as well as hot water.

Background Warmth from Cooker

There are many efficient solid-fuel, continuous-burning, insulated cookers that provide ample domestic hot water, as well as full cooking facilities and some space heating in the kitchen. One or two models are made with extra powerful boilers that will, in addition, service a couple of radiators as well.

The essential point is that the whole installation should be made at one time and only those cookers which are specifically sold as capable of heating radiators should be asked to do it. Fuel consumption will naturally increase somewhat when radiators are being served, as a bigger fire must be maintained. From this it follows that in households where a lot of cooking is done regularly, demanding a big fire fairly continuously, the cooker designed to heat a couple of radiators will prove an economic choice.

Background Warmth by Convected Air from Open Fire

An increasing number of modern open fires are so designed that, instead of being set solidly into the brickwork of the stack, they are surrounded at the back and sides by a narrow air space. Heat normally lost is returned as warmed air by such a convector fire, either directly into the room, or it may be ducted to an adjoining ground floor room or one above. These inset convector fires are best fitted during construction of a house but can be installed in existing property.

Both convector and non-convector fires may have a built-in back boiler for supplying hot water or radiators, although the space heating direct from the fire is then somewhat reduced. Some non-convector fires have an extra large boiler capable of feeding two or three small radiators in addition to providing normal domestic hot water. In summer, domestic hot water only can be provided without undue room heating.

Full Space Heating from Cooker

One cooker-water-heater is designed to heat *to full winter comfort standard*, 350 sq. ft. of floor space. By the heat-exchanger method (see Whole-House Warming, p. 50), a flow of thermo-statically controlled warmed air is ducted to an adjoining room or rooms. This improves on the other systems of partial house warming already described in that a greater degree of warmth can be given out and it is thermostatically controlled. This particular appliance, which also supplies full cooking and hot-water facilities for up to eight people, should be planned for when the house is being built. It could be fitted into some existing houses, but considerable builders' work would probably be needed.

ROOM HEATING

To-day the individual room can be efficiently heated by a fixed or portable heater. There is also a wide choice of different fuels—solid fuel (coke, anthracite, manufactured smokeless fuels and coal); oil (paraffin); gas, both mains and bottled supplies; and electricity. All methods have their good points and drawbacks.

Solid fuel is cheapest and is specially good for continuous heating. Paraffin

A thermostatically controlled boiler, the Agamatic, will run up to four radiators and provide an ample supply of domestic hot water for a small house

Excellent for installing in old-fashioned fireplaces, the Haddon is a continuous burning fire with gas ignition, obtainable with low grate for an existing back boiler. (Allied Ironfounders)

comes next on grounds of expense and gives a remarkably good return in heat whether used for continuous or intermittent heating. Gas and electricity are the highest priced, but for short-period heating can work out more economically than solid fuel. Though modern appliances are a vast improvement on older types, solid fuel still involves most work and causes an appreciable amount of dust. Electricity is the cleanest of all fuels, with no fumes or odour and no waste. Its advantages in these respects sometimes out-balance the fact that in most circumstances it is the most costly.

Solid-fuel Room Heating

All solid-fuel appliances have to be fixed, since they need a chimney outlet. Some types of stove and continuous-burning open fire are self-contained units and can be slid into any standard fireplace opening and easily fixed in position. This kind of appliance becomes a tenant's fixture when installed by him and can be moved as required. Those that are built in become landlord's fixtures, whoever supplied them in the first place.

Size of Heater

First essential when choosing a heating appliance, is to get one big enough and

for this purpose it is important to know the cubic capacity of the room to be heated (easily obtained by multiplying the length by the width by the height). For a room of up to 1,750 cubic feet, a 16-in. continuous-burning fire is recommended. Space heating appliances come in different sizes capable of heating rooms of up to 5,000 cubic feet. Remember, it is better to have a fire that is too big for the room and let it burn at a slow economical rate for most of the time, than one only just big enough that has to be burned at maximum to keep up the desired temperature.

The Restrictable Throat Fire

Although to-day's open fires are considerably more efficient than their predecessors, much of the heat generated does inevitably escape up the chimney. Even the most up-to-date continuous-burning open fire, with its accurate air control, is the least efficient of modern solid fuel appliances. Giving about 15 per cent. greater efficiency is the free standing convector fire, which is easily installed in most fireplaces, comes in a wide range and does not become the landlord's property.

The Sunken Grate Fire

A method of reducing the over ventilation and draughts which lower a fire's efficiency is to draw the necessary air from under the floor. Installation costs of these hearth-level fires are high, because of the structural alterations involved and they are only practicable in ground floor rooms, owing to the depth of the ash container. Good points are that the heat is radiated from floor level and that the large-capacity ash box usually needs emptying once a week only.

Built-in Gas Ignition

All types of modern open fire can have built-in gas ignition at a very small extra

The Radiation Parkray room heater projects only 7 in. on to the hearth, has clear glass doors that can be opened—or you can see the fire even when they are shut

A grate on roller bearings (left), so that the fire can be shaken from underneath without disturbing the top is a feature of the continuous burning Rola-Fyre by Smith & Wellstood

A highly efficient convector unit, the Sofono Mk. II fire will heat 2,600 cubic feet by radiation and convection, or convected air can be ducted to another room

cost (under 10s.). Where mains gas is available, this undoubtedly saves labour, as it obviates the need for paper and wood when laying the fire and speeds up lighting.

Openable Stoves

In terms of efficiency, the good openable stove is superior to even the best open fire. Advantages are their comparative cleanliness (in the best designs, riddling is done without opening the stove at all, as with a modern boiler) and the fact that, properly managed and with the cor-

A door that slides up into a panel enables the fire to be seen in the Otto range of continuous burning stoves (above), with a shaking grate for dust-free riddling. (Allied Ironfounders)

The Beutesse is an entirely closed stove with shaking bottom grate, and is refuelled through the top cover. Economical on fuel and highly efficient. (Smith & Wellstood)

rect fuel, they can be lit in the autumn and kept going throughout the winter without being let out.

Their main drawback in many people's eyes is that they lack the charm of the open fire. To counteract this, manufacturers have produced a variety of models with doors that fold right back, or slide up or down out of sight, to give a really clear view of the fire itself.

Closed Stoves

The closed, slow-combustion stove is the most economical and efficient solid-fuel appliance. It is particularly suitable where a large area has to be heated and where a cheery focal point is not specially wanted. Although smokeless fuels are usually the most satisfactory, many closed stoves will burn any type of fuel at a low rate of consumption.

Room Heating by Oil (Paraffin)

While all solid-fuel and many gas heaters require a flue to carry away the combustion waste products, a paraffin stove of quite substantial heating capacity is self-contained and can therefore stand anywhere in a room or be used where there is no chimney. For this reason, paraffin heaters are usually classed as portables, athough the more powerful ones weighing about 25 lb. empty, do involve some effort in moving from room to room.

As with solid-fuel stoves and fires, the modern trend is towards increased efficiency—i.e. more of the fuel burned is converted to usable heat coupled with greater cleanliness. The up-to-date oil stoves involve much less work than older types and, though the more efficient appliances are higher priced initially, they are cheaper to run. The specially refined grades of paraffin—"pink" and "blue"—now obtainable cause less smoke and smell than the cruder oils of the past, so that to-day an efficient type of oil heater will live up to the makers' claims of being odourless and labour-saving.

Needing least attention—they can safely be left burning overnight or even longer—and particularly economical to run, are the modern convector heaters. In these, the burner and tank are enclosed within a stove-enamelled cabinet with grilles or heat deflectors from which the warmed air is dispersed. In appearance they closely resemble gas or electric convectors, but have the additional advantage of being entirely without "strings"—i.e. flex or tubing.

Most of these oil convectors have a capacity of 1 gallon, on which they will burn anything from 40–45 hours with a heat output of approximately 3,400 B.T.U.s per hour, roughly the equivalent of 1 kilowatt. Some can have the flame regulated, so that they will give out up to 5,500 B.T.U.s per hour and burn for about 25 hours to the gallon. Slower-burning convectors (60 hours to the gallon),

There is an Esse stove, either open or closed, for every need. The one above was made for a block of council flats, but the Esse 450 is very similar. (Smith & Wellstood)

useful for background heating, and smaller capacity ones are also made.

For quick, concentrated warmth, a powerful radiant heater will give best results. There are also good-looking contemporary oil space heaters that combine radiant and convected heat with portability and which really glow red and warm, just like a real fire, for 30 hours on one gallon of fuel. An even more ingenious oil heater comes with its own cooking trivet stored in the back; when required for boiling or frying, you simply take it out and hang it from the top rail of the guard.

A small and truly portable but quite powerful type of heater works on the pressure principle embodied in the familiar primus stove. Typical of this class is the bowl-fire radiator, cream enamelled and with carrying hook and handle. Forty-eight hours' heating is available from approximately ¾ gallon of paraffin.

The less expensive, more ordinary radiant oil heaters (more attractive versions of the familiar "oil stove") may have yellow or blue flame burners.

For bathroom heating, where electricity may be dangerous unless special precautions are taken, and gas inconvenient, the fully enclosed cabinet oil convector is specially satisfactory.

Many safety features have been laid down in order to reduce the danger of accident in using oil appliances. So, when buying a domestic paraffin-heating appliance, particularly of the radiant drip-feed variety, look for a label bearing the

British Standard (B.S. 3300) and be sure to read the manufacturers' warning against carrying a heater when alight, on the need for adequate ventilation, on protection from draughts, against the use of petrol and against placing the appliance where it can be knocked over. Appliances bearing the British Standard have been tested in draughts up to 17 or 18 m.p.h. in a wind tunnel, their fuel tanks are made of corrosion-resistant materials and they have some provision for fixing to the floor or wall to prevent them overturning.

Gas Radiant and Convector Heaters

As a fuel for space heating, mains gas comes into a midway category. Once it is connected, it flows into the appliance at the turn of a tap, but is not completely labour-saving, as some darkening of the walls and some dust are associated with its use. Extremely flexible—the heat may be regulated instantly at the turn of a tap—giving a quick build-up of warmth. The moment it is no longer needed, you turn it out. Modern gas room heaters usually

For continuous or intermittent heating, the Aladdinique convector heater (above) is light in construction and easily portable. Maximum consumption, 27 hours per gallon of paraffin

A streamlined contemporary oil heater, the LEOglow Mk. VII, has a patent burner, highly polished reflector— and cooking trivet tucked away in the back

A bowl fire that burns paraffin under pressure, the Bialaddin (left) may be tilted as required and gives intense radiant heat. Ideal for studies, bath rooms, spare bedrooms, etc.

Warm air circulates into the living room through the top louvres and is also fed to the dining room; the lower louvre is the air intake. The Halcyon Selective Heater provides rapid room heating very cheaply

Both radiant and convected warm air are provided by this good looking Main 268 Radiant Convector gas fire, above, designed for medium-sized rooms

combine radiant and convected heat and have automatic ignition and, often, controls giving as many as three heat positions. It is estimated that these modern appliances make 4 therms of gas do the work that called for 5 or more in the older types of fire.

Then there is a wide range of gas background heaters for keeping the chill out of halls and passages. These include radiator-type convectors of smart appearance, neat little ones to fix on a wall and the "balanced flue" convector that has to be fixed on an outside wall and which works on the principle of drawing cold air in from outside, warming it and releasing it into the house.

Really portable gas heaters are now on the market too. You just pick them up when you go into another room and plug in wherever there is a gas point.

More costly than solid fuel or paraffin, though in some circumstances just as economical, mains gas usually works out rather cheaper than electricity, though individual use may alter the case. Bottled gas needs special appliances and an adjacent container. This makes it more expensive, but in country districts without electricity it is a tremendous boon.

giving off both radiant heat and warm air which circulates quickly round the room, and the reflector type with a rod-shaped element throwing out radiant heat in one direction according to the shape of the polished reflector. Radiant fires range from the small portable bowl shape to the decorative "coal effect" variety, with imitation coals lit by a flickering lamp.

An interesting new development in radiant heating is the infra-red type of heater, fixed at high level to shine down on the space to be heated. The elements are sheathed in tubes, so this kind of heater is safe, even in damp atmospheres, and particularly useful, therefore, for bathrooms and kitchens. Fire and accident risks are virtually eliminated with these high-level heaters.

In addition to fires, there are two distinct classes of heater whose function is chiefly all-over room warming and background heating.

Size of Heater for the Room

To choose the right size of heater, a rough and ready guide is that a 10–12 cu. ft. per hour consumption appliance is desirable for a small sitting room (say $10 \times 10 \times 8$ ft. high). It would not need to be full on all the time, but this power will warm up a room of this size reasonably quickly. For other rooms (bed or dining), a less powerful heater would be sufficient: 6–8 cu. ft. per hour per 100 cu. ft. of floor space is a good average.

The actual power of a heater is only an approximate guide to its performance. For instance, radiant heat is increased by a highly polished reflector, and the internal design of a convector determines its total efficiency.

Room Heating by Electricity

For cleanliness and utter simplicity of operation, electric heating has no rival. No flues are necessary, whatever the size and power of the heater. Electricity also offers the most diversified choice of heating equipment.

Radiant fires are of the fire bar type

Convector Heaters

There are three main types of convector heaters and air warmers, some of which are fitted with built-in thermostats and all of which can now be fitted with time switch control, enabling them to be switched on automatically at a pre-set time, say, half an hour before getting-up time or an hour before you expect to reach home.

1. The enclosed type, where the heat is given off from the surface, such as radiators fixed or portable and filled with oil heated by electricity, and tubular heaters which have a loading of 60 watts per foot

A basket fitted with "logs" which give the friendly glow and movement of real firelight, the decorative Berrylog, left, is powered by electricity

For quick warming, "Four-ten," an inexpensive electric pedestal fire (below), has a chromium-plated reflector specially designed to project a beam of heat where wanted. (Electroway Heaters Ltd.)

and are specially suitable for background warmth in halls, passages and large rooms, also for airing cupboards. These tubular heaters now come in attractive colours and finishes.

2. Convector heaters, both built-in and portable, which have vents to permit the air heated by the elements to circulate freely through the room.

3. Fan heaters in which a fan blows air over the heating elements. Separate switches operate the fan and heating elements, so that these can be used for heating in winter and cooling in summer.

Tubular heaters, with a 2-in. diameter heavy-gauge steel tube completely enclosing a heating element are specially useful for fixing in awkward-to-warm or draughty spots, such as under a window or in corridors. They can be mounted singly or in banks of up to 4–6. They heat up in a very short time and the surface temperature is always less than that of boiling water, making them very safe. A thermostat can be incorporated in the installation so that the heat may be maintained at any desired temperature automatically. This can effect a substantial saving in current.

Convector cabinets, which take various forms and shapes, contain a heating element with an inlet for cold air at the

Compact, light and almost noiseless, the Baker Mayhurst is a fan heater with three temperature settings and can also be used for cooling in summer

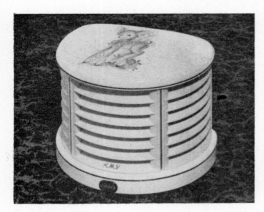

Safe even for tiny children, the H.M.V. Berkeley Fan Heater has push-button controls, two fan speeds and two heat settings, coming in various colours, including a nursery transfer

An electric wall fire with wood trim and reeded surround—the "Belford" even provides you with a little mantelshelf. (Allied Ironfounders)

good selection of comparatively small models that are true portables. Many have an incorporated thermostat, which adds a couple of pounds to initial price but reduces running costs. Whether they are thermostat or switch controlled, convector heaters cost more initially than most electric fires of comparable power, but in the long run are usually more economical in operation.

Electric radiators look exactly like those used in ordinary central-heating systems, but are fitted with an enclosed and insulated heating element so that each radiator is completely self-contained. They take some little while to heat up, but also retain their heat for some time after the current is switched off. The surface never gets too hot to touch safely.

Apart from waterless models, the most popular are oil-filled ones. They need no topping up and are not liable to damage by frost. Wall and floor mountings are available, or the smaller kinds, both in panel or column form, can be obtained as portables, with or without castors. Thermostatic con-

bottom and an outlet for warmed air at the top. Some have an incorporated fan; others rely on their method of construction to draw in the cold air and emit it again as circulating currents of warmed air. Heating up is rapid (though it will take a little while for the warm air to raise the temperature of the room) and, as with the tubular heaters, the outside of the cabinet does not get too hot to the touch. They are particularly safe in nurseries or where there are old people.

Some designs are meant for building in, others come into the transportable class in that they can be moved but are too big and heavy to lift easily. There is also a

You can warm rooms without ugly pipes and radiators, by means of the Isopad electrically heated carpet underlay, placed between carpet and felt

For background heating, an oil-filled radiator, obtainable in panel or column type, is excellent. (Dimplex)

trol is usually incorporated or provision made for a wall-type thermostat to be used in conjunction. Initially rather expensive, these oil-filled radiators are safe, long lasting, efficient and economical in use.

Radiant convectors, as the name implies, are convector heaters, usually in the form of medium-sized, easily portable cabinets with a radiant rod element incorporated. Either or both elements can be switched on at once, so that the heater can be used to warm up a small area quickly, for background warming, or both at once.

Low-temperature Radiant Heaters

These usually take the form of a cast-

Two forms of heating, combined for use together or separately. The convector circulates warm air throughout the room, the radiants provide instant direct warmth. (Morphy Richards Ltd.)

iron, steel, glass or plastic panel, into which the element is fused. These can be built into walls, skirtings or ceilings, or mounted (often in the form of a decorative screen) as portables. In new houses, where heating is planned with the building, low-temperature radiant heating consisting of grids of heating wires can be incorporated in the wall, ceiling or floor construction.

Low-temperature radiant heaters vary considerably according to make and type. Some warm up quickly, others take longer, while the surface temperatures differ, too. The common feature that makes this form of heating very attractive is that most of the heat is given off as widely distributed low-temperature radiation. The rest is convected. High-temperature radiation usually means a narrowish fierce beam of heat. With the low-temperature panel, the heat is spread over a much larger area, but one still enjoys the glow associated with all forms of radiant heating.

Electric Floor Warming

This is becoming increasingly popular in domestic as well as commercial buildings and blocks of flats. Special heating wires or cables are embedded in a concrete floor which, with the fabric of the building, is heated up at night when power at "off-peak rates" is available (particulars from your local Electricity Board). The stored-up heat is discharged during the day. Obviously this is more suited for installation during building, but electric floor warming can be installed in existing property where a suitable layer of concrete can be laid over a solid floor.

Another method of floor heating is a heated underlay which goes under the carpet. This works on the principle of the electric blanket.

Bathroom Heating by Electricity

It is most dangerous to use any kind of portable electric heater in a bathroom. Electrically heated towel rails must be fixed to floor or wall and properly earthed by a qualified electrician. The switch should be outside the bathroom door. For heating proper, a reflector or infra-red fire fixed high on the wall, out of reach and with a cord switch or switch outside the door is the best choice.

How to Determine the "Loading" necessary

For living rooms, a rather more powerful fire is desirable than elsewhere in the house. This allows for reasonably quick warming up. Once the room is warmed, the fire can be switched down, if not thermostatically controlled. On this basis, a small room $10 \times 10 \times 8$ ft. high, should have a $1\frac{1}{2}$-k.w. fire, and one 15×16

Here's an attractive new idea—a fan heater that is actually part of a table, the Tabulair has two-heat and thermostatic control

$\times$ 8 ft. high, a 3-k.w. size. Elsewhere in the house 1 k.w. per 1,000 cu. ft. of room space is the usual estimate.

Types of Heater Appropriate

For living rooms: a reflector-type fire, plus tubular or skirting heaters or a convector, or (singly) a low-temperature panel heater, or, least expensive initially, a fire-bar fire.

For dining rooms: some form of convection heating is usually advised. With precautions, this is also a good choice for the nursery, though an infra-red fire installed high on the wall out of reach is an alternative. This last is also recommended for bathrooms.

For occasional bedroom warmth: a reflector fire. For an always - warm room: tubular heaters or a convector.

A modern kitchen with the latest in heating—a high-level infra-red heater above the window and an oil-filled electric towel rail, both by Dimplex

ALL ABOUT FLOORS

*Give your rooms the right kind of flooring for their purpose
and you have laid the foundation of warmth and comfort*

Wood block floors and Oriental rugs create a pleasant atmosphere of spaciousness in this modern
combined-living-dining-room

THE floor collects more dust and dirt
than any other surface of a room, and
gets more wear. A flooring which is un-
suited to its purpose—such as a kitchen
floor which stains when anything is spilt
on it—is a constant source of worry to a
house-proud housewife and adds enormously to her labours.

A hall floor, especially in a country
house, must be easily cleaned and hard
wearing, and not show every footmark. A
kitchen floor must be non-absorbent and
resistant to spots of fat, oil, hot water and
weak acids—and it has to stand more wear
than any other floor in the house. A cloakroom floor must be hygienic and waterproof, and a sitting-room floor warm, quiet
and easy to maintain in immaculate condition.

Stair carpets or coverings take a great
deal of buffeting. A bathroom floor in a
family house should be waterproof and
hygienic, but a good carpet is quite practical, provided there is heating to dry it if it
gets damp. A bedroom floor gets very

little wear—softness and warmth are all-
important, but it should have a surface
which neither collects nor disseminates
fluff. A nursery floor should be easy to
clean and non-absorbent, but not cold or
unsympathetic in appearance.

This chapter aims to help you solve
some common flooring problems, both
practical and decorative.

TAKE YOUR CHOICE

There are now so many floorings and
floor coverings on the market that it is not
possible to describe each one. The more
important ones have therefore been
grouped under collective headings, and
those qualities common to the group are
described.

Prices vary widely according to the size
and complexity of the job and the place
where it is to be done. Generally speaking,
the larger the area and the simpler the
shape, the lower will be the price per
square yard.

TO LAY A CORK FLOOR: FIRST REMOVE OLD FLOOR

Then fill cracks and holes and, if floor is of wood, cover with Armstrong's Paper Felt before fixing Armstrong's Cork Tiles. Find centre of two opposite walls, run chalk line between them and mark its centre

Now, using a carpenter's square, strike a second line through the centre point—or, alternatively, you can use one of the tiles as a right angle, the object being to divide the room into four quarters

Asphalt and Mastic

Natural bituminous material or coal-tar pitch mixed with limestone, grit, etc.

Laying.—As these floors are laid in a hot, molten state and special plant is needed to melt them, they are more economical for use in large areas than small. Laid by experts only, on rough concrete, thereby saving cost of preparatory treatment with cement.

Properties. — Warm, quiet, durable, easily cleaned, impervious to damp, but may be slippery if over-polished.

Colours.—Black, red, dark brown.

Where to Use. — Specially valuable where rising damp is anticipated, but not in kitchens, since oil and grease have damaging effects.

Clay Tiles

Include quarry tiles, vitreous tiles and encaustic tiles. Made of pressed burnt clay, 4 in., 6 in. and 9 in. square, thickness according to size.

Laying.—Bedded in cement mortar on concrete base by experts.

Qualities. — Easily washed, hygienic, very durable, but cold.

Colours.—Quarry tiles are usually buff, red, brown. Vitreous and encaustic tiles are made in many colours.

Where to Use.—Wherever dirt and mud are likely to be brought into the house; window ledges.

Composition

Jointless flooring, made of Magnesite, wood flour and silica, etc.

Laying.—Applied in plastic form by craftsmen or specialist firms, preferably on concrete sub-floor. Can be laid on existing brick and tile floors and, if special precautions are taken, on wood floors.

Properties.—Warm, quiet.

Colours.—Red, buff, black, brown.

Where to Use.—All rooms.

Concrete

Ordinary cement concrete is usually unsatisfactory for home use, because it makes dust. Chemicals can be added to the mix to prevent this, or it can be ground and polished, or painted with a special paint (life about one year or more). Granolithic cement contains granite chips and is very hard, but may also make dust.

Laying.—Laid as a wet mix by experts.

Properties.—Durable but cold.

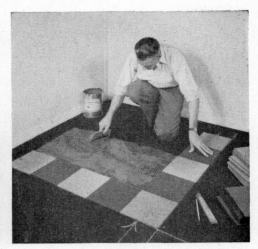

COVERINGS AND SCRUB . . .

Along the chalked lines lay rows of uncemented tiles from the centre to one side wall and one end wall (above, light and dark tiles are used to make instructions clearer, the real ones are light golden brown $\frac{3}{16}$ in. thick)

Fix the uncemented tiles lightly in position with two pins. Using spreader provided, spread along pinned tiles (top right) sufficient adhesive cement (there is one for concrete and one for wood floors) for about ten tiles. Start from centre and lay ten tiles, driving a pin home into centre and corners

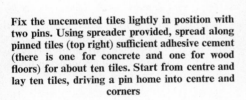

Remove uncemented pinned tiles and continue until whole floor is covered except borders. Flush with the wall chalk edge of last tile, place new tile face down, one edge against wall, the other across chalked tile. Flex slightly and snap tile against chalk edge (right centre). Cut along chalk line on border tile, fit against wall, repeat all round till whole border is tiled

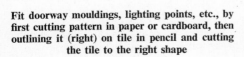

Fit doorway mouldings, lighting points, etc., by first cutting pattern in paper or cardboard, then outlining it (right) on tile in pencil and cutting the tile to the right shape

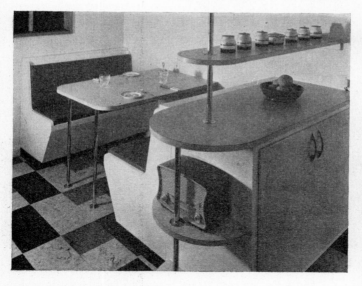

Rubber tiles in ruby red, blue and pearl grey make a colourful and practical floor in this kitchen with dining section by Froys of Hammersmith

Laying.—Can be laid on any sound, smooth sub-floor. If laid on solid concrete ground floor, a damp-proof membrane is advisable. Tongued and grooved tiles can be laid by a competent handyman.

Properties.— Resilient, warm, quiet, durable, non-slip, insulating. May be dented by heavy furniture.

Colours.—Normally grey, but coloured pigments may be used to give several tints.

Concrete Tiles

Made of cement mixed with various substances—marble, quartz, etc.—in normal tile sizes.

Laying.—As for clay tiles.

Properties.—Durable, easily cleaned but cold.

Colours.—Many.

Where to Use.—Cloakrooms, halls, as for clay tiles.

Cork Compound

Cork pieces supplied in bags to be mixed with cement.

Laying.—Laid by experts. Can be laid on existing stone, brick or concrete floors, or on new concrete, when it is laid before surface concrete has set.

Properties. — Quiet, resilient, warm, waterproof.

Colours.—Red, orange, green, brown, buff.

Where to Use.—All rooms on ground floor.

Cork Tiles

Natural granulated cork and resin. Supplied in tiles $\frac{5}{16}$ in. thick with tongued and grooved edges, $\frac{3}{16}$ in. thick with square edges only. Size 12×12 in., 36×12 in., 36×6 in. Skirtings curved to the flooring are available.

Colours.—Natural cork colour, light or dark.

Where to Use.—All rooms, but sealer needed in kitchens or bathrooms.

Linoleum

Cork and oxidised linseed oil on a backing of jute or, in some qualities, bitumenised felt. Supplied in rolls, squares or tiles.

Laying.—Preferably stuck down with special adhesive. Can be done by handyman (see p. 77). Felt paper underlay recommended when laying on wooden floors. Concrete floors must be dry.

Properties.—Thicker gauges very durable if professionally laid, quiet, resilient, non-absorbent.

Colours.—Plain, flecked, marbled, inlaid, almost any colour except white. Some grades have surface printed in colours.

Where to Use.—All rooms, particularly bathrooms and kitchens.

Plastic Sheet

A very thin skin of plastic with smooth or grained surface on a felt backing.

Laying.—Laid like a carpet.

Properties.—Resilient, quiet, long wearing, easily cleaned.

Colours.—Many.

Where to Use.—Hall, stairs, kitchen, bathroom.

Rubber Latex

A jointless floor made of cork sawdust or marble, combined with rubber Latex or a rubbery synthetic resin. Supplied in bags for mixing with water.

Laying.—Laid in semi-liquid state to thickness of about ¼ in., and then trowelled to give plain surface or polished to give mottled or *terrazzo* finish. Some makers claim that their products can be laid by a handyman, but most need expert treatment. Can be laid on any firm floor—brick, flagstones, wood or concrete.

Properties.—Resilience can be varied to suit requirements. Non-slip, resistant to grease, dustless, durable.

Colours.—Sometimes only buff, red, brown, but can be tinted to match any colour sample.

Where to Use.—All rooms.

Rubber

In sheets or tiles, ⅛ in. or ¼ in. thick.

Laying.—Can be laid by handyman on any smooth level base.

Properties. — Non-absorbent, resilient, quiet. Oil and grease spots should be wiped away quickly or they may cause damage.

Colours.—Almost unlimited.

Where to Use.—Halls, bathrooms, lavatories, nurseries.

Slate Flags

Natural material in sizes and thicknesses as quarried.

Laying.—On solid concrete base with waterproof membrane incorporated.

Qualities.—Durable, attractive, but cold.

Colours.—Natural.

Where to Use.—Halls, loggias.

Thermoplastic Tiles

Made of thermoplastic binder with asbestos fibres, fillers and pigments, in tiles ⅛ in. or 3⁄16 in. thick, 6 in., 9 in, and 12 in. square.

Laying.—Bedded in special adhesive on any firm, level floor by experts.

Properties.—Durable, non-slip, easy to clean, but rather cold. Affected by grease and fats.

Colours.—All colours, plain and marbled. Dark colours are cheaper.

Thermoplastic tiles in grey and black for a lounge opening straight out on to the garden in a new house

Where to Use.—All rooms, particularly those on ground floor.

Vinyl Tiles and Sheet

Similar to thermoplastic tiles, but with P.V.C. binder. Made in 9-in. and 12-in. squares, $\frac{1}{16}$ in. and $\frac{1}{8}$ in. thick. Certain makers supply sheets 36 in. wide. Some tiles have thin cork backing.

Laying.—Bedded in suitable adhesive on any level floor by experts. Paper-felt underlay recommended for wood floors.

Properties.—Flexible and resistant to grease. Durable, hygienic, non-slip, easy to clean.

Colours.—Unlimited range, plain and flecked.

Where to Use.—Kitchens, bathrooms and all other rooms, especially where hard wear is expected.

Wood Boarding

Softwood boarding usually 1 in. nominal thickness, with tongued and grooved edges.

Laying.—Nailed to wood joists or to battens in solid concrete floors. Spacing of supports according to thickness of boards.

Properties.—Warm, fairly durable, but

Specially designed for the nursery, schoolroom or kitchen, Accoflex tiles in vinyl-asbestos have a smooth surface and good resistance to oils, fats and grease

liable to rot and woodworm, and apt to expand and contract.

Colour.—Colour of wood used, or can be stained.

Where to Use.—Everywhere, but needs linoleum or similar covering in kitchens and bathrooms, and carpets and rugs in sitting rooms, mainly to deaden natural resonance.

Wood Block

Small pieces of hardwood, $\frac{3}{4}$ in. or 1 in. thick.

Laying.—Bedded in mastic on concrete floors.

Properties.—Warm, fairly quiet, durable and attractive.

Colours.—Natural colourings according to type of wood; maple, beech, oak, mahogany and various African hardwoods are used.

Where to Use.—Everywhere on ground floor except in bathrooms, kitchens and lavatories.

Wood Mosaic

Small hardwood blocks about $4\frac{1}{2} \times \frac{7}{8} \times \frac{3}{8}$ in. thick made up into squares. One manufacturer supplies the material in 18-in. squares on paper backing.

Laying.—Laid in bitumen by experts on any sound, level floor.

Properties.—As for wood block.

Colours.—Various woods, which can be used together to form contrasting colours.

Where to Use.—All rooms, except kitchen and bathroom.

Wood Parquet

Thin pieces of wood or plywood $\frac{1}{4}$ in. or $\frac{3}{8}$ in. thick.

Laying.—Pinned and usually glued to existing level wood floors, either over entire floor or as surround to carpet. Paper-felt underlay is advised to prevent movement of floor affecting parquet. Normally an expert's job, but some types can be laid by a competent handyman.

Qualities.—Warm, durable, attractive appearance, hygienic.

Colours.—Natural woods.

Where to Use.—All rooms, except kitchen and bathroom.

Wood Parquet Floorboards

Normal parquet bonded in the factory to

For the hall of a lovely old seventeenth-century farmhouse, rush matting is both practical and in keeping with the period

tongued and grooved soft-wood boarding.

Laying.—As for ordinary floorboards.

Properties.—Long wearing, luxurious appearance, warm.

Colours.—Various woods, mostly beech and oak.

Where to Use.—All rooms, except kitchen and bathroom.

Wood Strip

Similar to wood block, but in long strips which may be tongued and grooved. Also in ¼-in. thickness for laying like parquet on top of boarded floors.

Laying.—Laid on joists for suspended floors, or on battens let into surface concrete, or bedded in mastic on concrete.

Properties.—As for wood block.

Colours.—As for wood block.

Where to Use.—Everywhere on ground and first floors except in kitchens and bathrooms.

Wood Veneer Tiles

A thin wood veneer on a resin-bonded sand base.

Laying.—On cement and sand mix. Laid by experts. Suitable for new floors only.

Properties.—Warm, durable, resistant to moisture.

Colours.—Light or dark hardwoods.

Where to Use.—All rooms on ground floor.

Wood Chipboard

Tiles of various types and shapes made of wood chips or sawdust, with cement or resin binders.

Laying.—Some are laid in cement, some

in bitumen, on new concrete floors, by experts. Skirtings curved to the flooring available with some types.

Properties.—Hard wearing, warm.

Colours.—Natural wood colours, rather like cork. Also black and green in some types.

Plywood, Hardboard

Sheets of various sizes and thicknesses, with or without veneered surface.

Laying.—Nailed and/or glued to existing smooth, level wood floors. Can be done by handyman.

Qualities.—Warm.

Colours.—Natural woods, and can be stained.

Where to Use.—All rooms, except bathroom or kitchen.

ESTIMATING

Unless the floor is to be covered with a plain or close-patterned material, a scale drawing should be prepared, from which the amount of material needed can be assessed.

To make the drawing, buy some squared (or graph) paper and then measure the length and breadth of the room. If you can arrange each individual square to equal 3 in. measurement on the floor, this is a convenient scale, especially for tiles, which are usually 6 in., 9 in. or 12 in. square.

The next thing to check is the squareness of the walls, as this has a considerable bearing on laying any type of floor. For example, measurements taken across each end of the room may not agree, and this indicates a wall out of true. Examine the run of the floorboards to see which wall is affected. You will probably find that a narrow tapered "filler" board has been placed next to this wall, or the plaster thickness is not constant and the skirting is not parallel with the floorboards. If so, this discrepancy should be shown on your scale plan.

Carpet, Felt, Linoleum, Sheet Materials

Use your scale plan, remembering to allow for the repeat in the pattern if it is necessary to match perfectly.

Tiles or Blocks

Here the scale plan is also used to design the pattern you are going to follow, and the first step is to mark two lines across the floor which intersect exactly in the centre. From this point outwards you should mark in the tiles or blocks, colouring with crayon or poster paints so that you have a design which you can easily follow.

The position and design of border strips or tiles are also marked on the plan, from which you will be able to count how many tiles of the various colours you will need, as well as the total length of border strip, where this is to be used.

Always take your scale plan to the shop, where the salesman will give you his estimate of the amount needed, which you can then check with your own. Buy carpet in the most economical width, of course —the scale plan will decide this.

The table on the right shows the conventional width, sizes and quantities in which most flooring materials are sold, although the one you choose may be slightly different.

MATERIAL	Width or quantity in which sold
Linoleum	6 ft. wide. Sold by the sq. yard (90 ft. per roll)
P.V.C.	Tiles: 9, 12 and 24 in. square. Sheet: 36 in. wide. Sold by the yard. Feature strips: 1 in. and 1¼ in. wide.
Rubber	Tiles: 9, 12 and 18 in. square. Sheet: 36 in. wide. Sold by the yard. Slabs: 6 ft. and 3 ft. Tiled sheet: 6 ft. wide.
Cork	Tiles: 6, 9 and 12 in. square. Strip: 36 in. by 6 or 12 in. wide. Coved Skirting: 36 in. by 4 in. high.
Thermoplastic Tiles	Tiles: 9 and 12 in. square. Border strips: 24 in. by 1 in. to 5½ in. wide, multiples of ½ in.
Parquet Faced Boards	7 ft. to 7 ft. 10½ in. long by 6 in. wide.
Wood Blocks	8–12 in. long by 2½– 2⅞ in. wide by ¾–1 in. thick.
Wood Parquet	8–12 in. long by 2½–3 in. wide by ¼ in. thick. Lengths 2½–3 in. wide.
Chipboard	8 ft. by 4 ft. by ½ in. or ¾ in. thick.
Carpet	Strip: 18, 27 and 36 in. wide. A few firms make wider widths. Sold by the yard, and in squares.
Carpet Underfelt	54 in. wide. Sold by the yard.
Rubber Underlay	36 and 54 in. wide. Sold by the yard.
Trowelled-on Plastics	4 to 8 sq. yd. per tin; also in bags.
Floor Paint	30 to 50 sq. yd. per gallon.
Floor Lacquer	10 sq. yd. per litre.

Linoleum in a plain, clear colour is ideal for all-over flooring in the nursery bedroom of this charming modern cottage

LAYING LINOLEUM

Laying linoleum is not too difficult a job for a handy housewife, especially if her husband will help, but for a first attempt it is a mistake to choose a tiny space —such as a microscopic bathroom or doll-sized front hall—especially if it contains several doors. A small job sounds easy but is not, because there is so little room to manipulate the heavy linoleum. It is better to start on a straight passage or a medium-sized room with few or no recesses.

Avoid Patterns

Linoleum of a definite pattern creates matching problems. So for a first attempt try to choose a plain, jaspé or moiré. These need no matching and save both work and yardage, but jaspé (a fine, irregular self-stripe) and moiré (a watered effect) must run the same way everywhere; they cannot be turned at right angles.

To estimate the quantity required, measure the *greatest* length and width of your room and multiply one by the other. Thus if your space measures 12 ft. by 9 ft. (which is 4 yd. by 3 yd.) you will need 4×3 =12 sq. yd. If the linoleum is 2 yd. wide (a normal width), you will need 6 yd. Re-member when considering price that this is reckoned by the *square* yard. The 72-in. width contains *two* square yards and will be charged for accordingly.

If the linoleum is only 60 in. wide, reckoning quantity is more complicated. In this case it is best to give the shopman your floor measurements and ask him to cut off the right amount.

If possible, never lay linoleum in bitter, frosty weather, especially in an unheated room, for cold makes it liable to crack easily. If you *must* lay it then, keep it for a day or two first in a warm place.

You will need a really sharp linoleum knife with a curved blade (photograph on next page); ironmongers stock them. Have ready a steel or metal-edged ruler, prefer-ably 24 in. long, and a piece of tailor's chalk (from a haberdashery counter).

Prepare the Floor

Linoleum can only be laid successfully on a floor which is clean, dry and perfectly smooth. Wash a wood floor long enough beforehand for it to dry thoroughly. Nail down any loose floorboards and hammer down or extract all projecting nails or bits of old linoleum. A concrete floor should

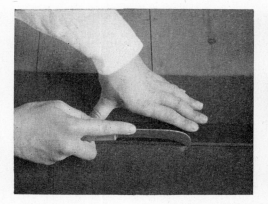

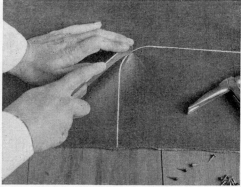

How to cut linoleum along a straight line (above), knife moving right up to steel ruler

How to use the knife for cutting linoleum on a curve (above), with blade slanted outwards

Bending over scored linoleum (left) to break it in two along scored edges

be well swept to remove its dust, but do not try to *wash* this dust away.

When re-laying a small area, such as a toilet, try to remove the old linoleum carefully in one piece and use it as a pattern for cutting the new. In this way you will save a lot of work and get an exact fit round the toilet pedestal. In a larger room, where the old linoleum is in several pieces, try to use similarly as patterns those parts which fit round the hearth, window recesses or awkward mouldings. Any portions worn away completely, such as in a doorway, must have extra allowed for the missing bit when re-cutting.

Practise Cutting

There is a right way of cutting linoleum. Practise this on some unwanted bit of the old floor covering before cutting into your new roll. All cutting lines should first be marked with chalk.

If the line is straight, lay your metal ruler exactly along it, holding it firmly in place with your left hand (photograph top left). Grip the knife handle in the right hand, with the fore-finger extended along the blade-top. Then, keeping the knife to the ruler edge all the way,

score firmly along the chalk line. Do this more than once if necessary, till the linoleum thickness is cut half through. Then bend the scored edges over outwards, right side uppermost, until they break in two (as shown in the photograph on the left). If required, cleanly cut apart the canvas base on the underside with scissors or knife.

A ruler cannot be used when scoring a curved line. Work as shown in top right-hand photograph, steadying the blade by pressing on it near the curved end. Keep the knife upright when cutting; if tilted, the edges will slant and not fit closely together. You may need a slanted edge to fit a sloped-off corner in a modern room—but take care it slants the right way.

Linoleum is usually laid *across* the boards on a wood floor and running the long way of the room on concrete, unless the short way considerably economises yardage. Cut each length with an inch or so to spare, to allow for any small inaccuracies in measuring. Make sure that the door has enough clearance to move smoothly over the linoleum. Some unfortunate people covered their floor, went out, and then could not get in again because the door jammed. They had to have its bottom edge slightly shaved off.

In old houses there are often ornamental mouldings at windows and doors which are impossible to fit accurately if cut direct in the linoleum. Take a pattern first in tough but flexible brown paper. Lay this paper on the linoleum with plenty to spare where the moulding will be and mark the paper surface clearly "Right Side." Then chalk on the linoleum round its overlapped edges. Place the paper to the moulding, with several inches of it standing upright against the wall. With scissors, slash these vertical edges downwards to fit the paper exactly round all curves and into any crevices.

Allow for Stretching

Be *most* careful, before cutting the linoleum, to lay the pattern, right side up, exactly into its chalked lines. When cutting linoleum to a complicated outline, you will often find that a pair of saw-toothed kitchen scissors do it more easily than the knife, though this will blunt them rather badly.

Linoleum laid on wood floors and not cemented down always stretches a little. So fit it accurately only at doors, for their free working. At other edges let it bulge a little for a week or two. Then, when stretching is complete, close-trim all edges to fit. Linoleum well fitted on a wood floor should not need nailing down except along a doorway join.

Linoleum on Concrete

Many post-war houses have concrete floors, on which you have to fix the linoleum with an adhesive. If so, cut the linoleum to fit exactly without trimming allowances. Buy a special linoleum cement (there are a number on the market) and use it according to the accompanying instructions.

CARPETS AND HOW TO CHOOSE THEM

Do you want a carpet to last for the rest of your life?

A good-quality wool carpet will do this —there are carpets still in use which were made 150 years ago—provided it is well looked after and escapes serious accidents. The moth danger need no longer be a serious one, since many of the best wool carpets on the market are specially treated to protect them against damage by both the common clothes moth and carpet beetle grubs. However, long life is not always an advantage, especially when the carpet is brightly coloured, or patterned in a "fashionable" style, for the colour will seriously restrict freedom of choice when it comes to redecorating, and the pattern will become "dated" long before the carpet is worn out.

A stair carpet in a dark colour contrasts well with white paint. Note the clever way it is fitted from wall to wall, right across without painted borders

As a background for fine dining-room furniture, there is nothing to compare with a plain fitted carpet like the one above, laid with seams running away from the window

Even the best carpets fade a little and wear thin in places, while the main body is still in good condition. It is then bound to look a little shabby for the last few years of its life. It can be dyed, of course, but that is not the same thing as having a new carpet.

If you want a plain or lightly patterned carpet of quiet colour, it may pay you to get an expensive one; but if you want a "smart" carpet, in a bright "fashion" colour, there is something to be said for choosing a cheap one and replacing it when it begins to wear.

Do you want a fitted carpet or a square?

A fitted carpet makes a room seem bigger and more comfortable. It is also warmer and enables you to clean the whole floor in one operation with sweeper or vacuum, without having to polish any surrounds. Its disadvantages are that it cannot be turned or moved about when it begins to wear, that it cannot, without considerable expense and wastage, be moved to another house or to another room; that there is an awkward little gap round the edges which collects dust and fluff, and offers ideal breeding conditions for moths.

It also costs more, not only because the area of carpet is greater, but because it has to be specially made up and fitted—with the pattern matching and the pile inclining away from the light. A square, which can be obtained in one piece up to a maximum width of 21 ft., can be turned four times to equalise wear, and a rectangle can be turned twice. A seamless square is also stronger than a made-up carpet.

Is luxurious appearance and "feel" more important than good wearing and lasting qualities?

In a bedroom a soft, deep pile will last for years, for the wear to which it is subjected is light and there is no mud or grit to work its way into the fibres and destroy them; but the same carpet in the hall of a country cottage will wear out much more quickly. For hard wear, a short, dense pile gives the best results, and if a cushioned "feel" is wanted it should be achieved by means of a thick underfelt.

Patterned or plain?

Though this is largely a matter of taste, there are practical considerations to be taken into account. A pattern limits the

Chintz patterned carpet softens the lines of contemporary furniture by Hille. The rose-spattered Alcosto design is in non-crush textured wool pile

choice of other decorations, but small stains and burns may be hidden or at least partially camouflaged by a pattern.

Carpets made from very tightly twisted yarn, known as non-crush carpets, have a curly, springy pile which does not show pressure marks. Two-tone carpets, which, as the name implies, have a pattern in two tones of the same colour, are excellent at concealing marks of all kinds. Sculptured or embossed carpets are also good, but the pattern is achieved by leaving gaps in the pile, and these gaps are apt to harbour dust—and moths. Another effective type of carpet has a pattern of

Footmarks do not show on the Alcosto Axminster with its non-crush textured wool pile. These two traditional designs come in lovely pastel colours and are made into squares in seven sizes

textures, sometimes using uncut or looped pile with ordinary pile. Looped pile has the disadvantage that dogs and cats are apt to catch their claws in the loops and pull them out, so that the carpet looks as if it were sprouting.

Formal carpet patterns vary between the riotous motifs and glowing colours of old Eastern rugs (the glow being due to the many slight variations in each colour), to the soldierly rows of dots and stars on contemporary carpets. A pattern with a heavily accented border makes a room look much smaller, specially when the carpet square is itself surrounded by a contrasting border of stained boards or parquet.

Equally at home in lounge or bedroom, a charming modern carpet design of white scrolls on mid-green

Perhaps the safest choice is to have a plain carpet of subdued or neutral colouring, with bright patterned rugs at the points which receive most wear—by the door, in front of the fire, and beside any piece of furniture which is frequently used.

Remember, when choosing your colour, that a very dark carpet shows up dust and fluff, and a very pale one shows dirt and stains. An exception in the latter case is a carpet with a deep and uneven pile such as one finds in hand-made Indian carpets, which even when off-white in colour seem to "wear clean." It is well to remember that a coloured carpet looks much brighter when it is laid.

How much can you afford to spend?

A fitted pile carpet of fair quality for a medium-sized room will cost up to £50, plus underfelt, making up and laying (though some firms will perform this service free). This makes it by far the most expensive item in the average room.

One can economise, when building a new house, by omitting a normal floor finish and laying a fitted carpet with a bitu-

minised underlay direct on the solid concrete. But in an existing house, if one cannot afford a good pile carpet, it is wise to consider the merits of some of the many substitutes now available.

Haircord, made principally from cowhair, is a hardwearing and not unattractive alternative. It is very easy to keep clean, and its hardness and lack of resilience can be reduced by using a good underfelt, which will also prolong its life. It is made in many colours and a few simple patterns and stripes, and makes a good background for coloured rugs.

Felt of very dense quality is comfortable and good-looking for bedrooms, but it may fade and show spillmarks. As, however, it is the same colour all the way through, it does not show wear. It is apt to stretch out of shape unless it is fitted wall to wall. It can be obtained in a wide and exciting range of colours.

Needleloom carpet, a type of felt with a rubber backing, is cheaper and saves money in other ways, too, because it needs no underfelt and no binding or sewing. It has been laid successfully direct on solid concrete floors in a new house, but its life is much shorter than that of a pile carpet. A good range of colours is made, and some types have a slight surface texture.

Fibre or sisal matting is useful in hall or dining room and goes very well with simple cottage furniture. It is made in a limited range of colours, most of which are very bright, and a few patterns. Dust and dirt pass right through it and can easily be collected up when the matting is lifted, especially if newspaper is laid underneath.

Rush matting, which is imported from Holland, has the same characteristic of allowing dust to pass through, and is suitable for similar situations. It is quiet and comfortable to walk on.

There are a number of other new carpet-substitutes, most of them with a foam-rubber backing, but it is too early yet to assess their wearing qualities. Many of them have attractive textures.

LAYING FITTED CARPET AND FELT

Carpets should always be laid on as level a surface as possible. Loose floor-boards, electric flex between carpet and floor and other irregularities cause wear which should be avoided. It is always better to use an underfelt, and paper laid beneath an underfelt is an excellent protection against dust blown up by draughts between floorboards.

Laying a carpet is a straightforward job but it must be carefully done to achieve professional - looking results. Binding the cut edges used to be the most difficult task, but in recent years a textile adhesive has been produced which makes this easy.

Essential tools are a lino knife (kept as sharp as possible), a straight-edge (steel is preferable—otherwise wood), a rule or steel measuring tape and a carpet stretcher. You can make the carpet stretcher, shown in the diagram, at home.

The spikes are 3-in. wire nails driven into the end of the tool, the heads are then cut off and the nails filed to a

Fine grade worsted yarns with 124 tufts to the inch make this Uskaba Wilton seamless square from the Carpet Manufacturing Co. Ltd., Kidderminster. (Furniture by Hille)

A carpet stretcher is essential for laying fitted carpets. Make one at home—the spikes are 3-in. nails filed to points

point. To use it, stand with one foot outside the carpet, the other on it, and about 6 in. from the edge. Put the tool close beside your foot on the carpet and press down so that the points penetrate the carpet base but do not stick in the floor. Now press against the stretcher with the side of your foot to pull the carpet taut while an assistant nails it down. Do not use a stretcher for felt as it may tear it.

Always cut the carpet from the back, and, as far as possible, make the cuts along the warp or weft strands of the base. If you have to cut a curve, do it in a series of tiny right-angled cuts rather than slicing diagonally through the base of the strands. The pile of the carpet will even out the little "steps" cut in the edge.

Use a special textile adhesive for joining the various strips together and also to prevent cut edges from fraying. These edges should be treated as soon as they are cut by applying the adhesive along the inside of the edge to approximately half-way up the pile from the back.

To pin the strips together, take them in pairs and lay them side by side, face down on the floor, with the edges to be jointed close together. Stretch each length and temporarily tack each to the floor at about 8-in. intervals between the tacks, which should be about 3 in. from the joint. (This is to keep the strips taut while the joint is made.)

Run a blunt knife between the jointing

Furniture feet do more damage to carpets than human ones, so stand them in Armstrong's Furniture Rests

edges to push the pile downwards, then cut a strip of upholstery webbing about 3–4 in. wide to the length of the joint. Apply a generous coat of adhesive to a width of 1½ or 2 in. either side of the joint and about 3 ft. long. While it is still wet, press the webbing over the joint and hammer it down firmly, taking care to see that the edges adhere closely. Fold back the excess webbing and repeat the process in stages of not more than 3 ft. at a time. When the job is completed, allow the adhesive 30 minutes to dry before removing the temporary fixing tacks. When the carpet has been jointed together, turn it over and arrange in position. Stretch it midway along the length of the strips and fix down with carpet nails. Do the same across the width and then work outwards in exactly the same way.

LAYING A STAIR CARPET

Remember the lie of the pile must flow from top to bottom. Felt pads the full width of the carpet should be laid first, covering not only the top but also the edge of each step.

Roll up the carpet and begin at the top of the stairs, fixing the end down with three carpet nails.

The straight run of the stairs is perfectly easy to handle, but you may have difficulty if there is a bend. The problem is how to handle the slack at the narrow end. First get the carpet in place and hold it with the stair rod or carpet clips, next grasp the loop of carpet and draw it forward so that you

have a double fold. You can then arrange the carpet so that the top fold is parallel and close to the tread of the stairs. Lift this fold back, but retain the position of the carpet and nail the sides to the riser (back of the step). Then put in another nail at the centre. The top fold is then brought forward and nailed to the riser close under the tread or stair nosing.

CARE OF CARPETS

Hints about New Carpets

"Fluffing" is a characteristic of all new carpets. Do not brush the fluff away too vigorously, but give the pile time to settle. It is wise not to use either vacuum cleaner, sweeper or brush more than is absolutely necessary on a new carpet. Odd loose ends should be cut off. Loops "pulled" in a Brussels type of carpet should be drawn back into place by lifting the loops on each side to take up the slack.

Stair carpet should always be laid with extra inches top and bottom so that it can be moved up or down to spread the wear. It should be moved about twice in the first six months and subsequently at least twice a year.

Wear and Tear

Animals, grit, deep cutting furniture castors, crêpe or rubber-soled shoes and metal heel-tips are a carpet's worst enemies, so do try to protect yours from all these. It pays to fit your furniture with the new type of circular furniture rests which

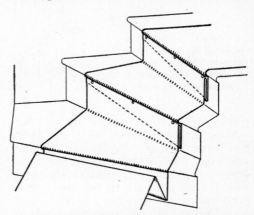

How to turn the corners when laying stair carpet. Always start at the top, fixing the end with three nails

not only prevent marks, but enable you to move the furniture round easily and so distribute the wear the carpet receives.

Watching television can be a wear hazard too, especially if the members of the family always sit in the same chairs in the same places, probably lying back with the heels of their shoes deeply embedded in the carpet. Small rugs under the feet and at other strategic points in the room, where the wear is hardest, will take care of this.

Cleaning the Carpet

Moths find safe harbourage for their eggs in the carpet and felt fluff that accumulates in cracks between floorboards. Turn back the carpet and felt and vacuum clean the boards, thoroughly loosening fluff, if necessary, with a skewer. This may be sufficient cleaning, but boards may need scrubbing with a good disinfectant soap, which helps to discourage moths. Rinse them well and leave exposed until dry.

Vacuum clean both sides of the underfelt. If there is sign of moth, and if the felt is not too big, give it a sunning in the garden while cleaning the boards. Treat the carpet in the same way, but beware of exposing it to strong sunlight, which may fade colours.

If you have no vacuum cleaner, hang carpets, rugs and underfelts over a line in the garden and brush and beat both sides thoroughly. Large, heavy carpets can be spread on the lawn for cleaning the pile. Pile and colours of the carpet can be freshened by drawing it right side downwards over slightly damp grass.

Stain Removal

Many stains on floor coverings are ordinary soil from shoes and can be washed out. Obstinate stains are usually caused by spills of food or drink and by grease, and must be removed individually

Small rugs can be shampooed successfully by scrubbing gently with a solution of good soapless detergent and warm water. Rinse well to wash out suds completely

When removing grease marks, surround the stain with a roll of clean white rag to prevent the grease from spreading to a larger area when it becomes wet. Grease can also sometimes be removed by ironing over a piece of blotting paper

Clean the surface of a large carpet with suds of soapless detergent applied with a rag. This does not make the carpet thoroughly wet. Rinse really well

before the whole surface is shampooed.

Treat stains from drinks with a mild detergent solution. Apply the liquid with a clean, white non-fluffy rag, working from the outer edge of the mark towards the centre. When the stain is clean, rinse well with clear warm water.

The same treatment may prove successful in removing some food stains, but as these are fixed with grease, a good grease solvent usually has a better effect. Use any reliable spirit cleaner applied in the same way as the detergent solution. When the stain is clean, rinse the area with fresh spirit applied with a clean rag.

If a stain remains when the grease has been removed, it is probably caused by a vegetable dye from the food, which can only be removed with a bleaching agent. A mild solution of hydrogen peroxide (1 part hydrogen peroxide in 4 parts water) can be used on wool pile and on fast colours in the same way as ammonia solution. There is risk that the treatment may affect the dyes in the carpet and it should therefore be tried first on an inconspicuous corner.

Grease marks can usually be removed with a good spirit grease solvent applied in the same way as detergent solution, but if the pile is deep and thick several treatments may be necessary. Before starting work, place a pad of absorbent fabric under the stained area to absorb any grease that soaks down through the canvas backing. To prevent this grease spreading, surround the stain with a roll of cotton wool or clean white rag.

Apply the spirit liberally from the outer edge of the stain towards the centre. Rinse thoroughly with fresh spirit and clean rag. Wait until the carpet is quite dry before repeating the treatment. Often the mark is unnoticeable while the wool is damp but reappears when dry: this is because partially dissolved grease near the bottom of the pile works up to the surface as the spirit dries out. Repeat until marks disappear.

(For treatment of other stains on carpets, see chapter on Stain Removal.)

Shampooing

This is not necessary every year, and is not advisable unless colours are dull through dirt. Often carpets get dirty more quickly when they have been thoroughly wetted by shampooing. Sponging lightly may be sufficient. For this use 2 tablespoonfuls vinegar in 1½ pints tepid water, followed by rubbing with a cloth wrung out in clear warm water. A week solution of ammonia may be used in the same way. Sponging with suds of any soapless detergent prepared in warm water is equally effective.

If thorough shampooing is necessary, the carpet must be taken up and hung on a line or spread in a yard. Brush it with a mild solution of soapless detergent in warm water, used freely. Rinse thoroughly with plenty of clear warm water. Rub as dry as possible with a non-fluffy white rag and leave hanging out of doors, if possible, to dry.

On no account put furniture back on the carpet until it is dry.

Thorough shampooing of large carpets is hard, tedious work and drying presents problems. Cleaning can be done satisfactorily and quickly by most reputable dry-cleaning firms.

Black Lines on Carpets

These appear when there are gaps between floorboards. Vacuum cleaning accentuates them, because the suction draws dust through from below the boards. The marks can usually be removed by shampooing. To prevent them recurring, seal the cracks with wide strips of adhesive brown paper or cover the whole floor with lining paper designed for use under carpets and obtainable from furnishing stores.

Cleaning Haircord

Haircord carpets are easy to wash and can be treated either with soap or soapless detergent whipped to thick suds in warm water. Apply the suds to the carpet with a cloth or a soft brush. Clean a small area at a time and rinse with a cloth wrung out of tepid water. Avoid making the carpet very wet and overlap each area when washing to avoid a water mark.

Do not wash the carpet on the floor over an underfelt. The underfelt will probably get wet and is likely to stain the haircord. The best plan is to move the carpet into a yard or sling it over a line before starting work. Allow it to dry outside, if possible, and do not replace it on the felt until it is dry. If shampooing must be done indoors, remove the felt and sweep the floor thoroughly under the carpet.

CHOSEN FOR SITTING IN COMFORT

Chairs and settees should be chosen to fit the shape and size of their occupants as well as their surroundings

Beautifully warm and draught-free, a wing chair (above) with tension sprung seat and back, foam rubber seat cushion, from Heal's, London

Specially designed for a woman, Minty's "Malvern" (right) has low arms, short seat and high concave back—ideal for restful sewing or knitting

EASY CHAIRS

AFTER the bed, an easy chair is perhaps the most important furniture purchase for a home. Correctly chosen, it will make an important contribution to comfort and relaxation for many years to come. On the other hand, a chair that does not really "fit" can be nothing but a rather unwieldy piece of furniture representing a large outlay of cash.

The Question of Shape

Support, not softness, matters most. It is a mistake to buy a chair when feeling tired and ready to flop on anything that looks inviting. One needs to sit down critically, move around in the chair and see whether the small of the back is supported. One's head should feel comfortable and legs reach easily to the ground without any cutting of the thigh. This should be checked when sitting well back.

Ideally, an easy chair should be chosen by its future occupant. A long-legged man, for example, wants a deeper seat than his shorter wife. Many chairs to-day are made with alternative seat depths, the shallower ones being designated ladies' models. The angle of the back is equally important. In very general terms, as the back slopes back, so should the seat slope from front to back. This seat slope is also affected by height from ground and the front to back measurement. Height of *back* is also governed by the proportions of the seat.

The only safe rules are: to take time in choosing and to test out the comfort in all the particulars mentioned above *when sitting in one's normal attitude*. This can be very important to the woman purchaser. Because of its appearance of luxury, the temptation is often to buy a chair in which, to be at ease, one has to lean well back and lounge. If, in actual fact, one spends most time sitting fairly upright to sew or read, such a chair will not prove a success.

What makes Good Upholstery?

To-day there are two main types of easy chair. The first have wooden arms and legs, with or without upholstered arm-pads. The back frame is often wooden, too, either with upholstered front or deep cushion. The second kind of chair, usually larger overall, is completely upholstered.

Show-wood chairs, as the first type are known, are becoming increasingly popular. They are less bulky, easier to move and more in proportion with to-day's smaller rooms. Also, they bring better quality upholstery within the reach of the average purse. In a fully upholstered chair, the fabric cover may easily account for two-thirds of the cost. This means that, unless a fairly substantial price is paid, the quality of the unseen upholstery cannot be of a satisfactorily high quality. Show-wood chairs, in contrast, use a comparatively small amount of covering. This means that very good fabrics and upholstery are obtainable for the price of an indifferent all-over-stuffed chair.

Types of Springing

Upholstery consists essentially of springing and padding. Springs may be *coil*, usually in "coil units" of a number of springs, *tension* or *serpentine* (also known as *zigzag*). These last, used largely in backs or for stool seats, generally run rather lighter and cheaper than the other two kinds. Coil springs are not better than tension ones, or vice versa. There are variations, in type and quality, of both. Suitability to purpose or personal choice determines which is chosen. Coil springs take up more depth and are used mainly in seats and for seat cushions. Tension springs, which should be covered with fabric or plastic, are excellent for backs as well as seats. Usually, but not invariably, tension sprung seats have loose cushions which may be coil sprung or of latex foam.

Padding or Stuffing

Except in the best hand-sprung chairs, a layer of lint is the usual covering for coil springs. The stuffing used with tension

The back of a settee shows when it is pulled up to the fire—the Ernest Race model (above) looks good from all angles

For perfect relaxation sit in the Greaves & Thomas "Bodiline" chair (left). Your body finds its own level and you feel just as if you are floating in air

A suite that changes shape to fit you. Press-stud the head cushions at the nape of the neck for upright sitting, lower them for lounging. Minty's "Henley" is in foam rubber for comfort

The modern tub chair (right), designed by Robin Day from Hille of London Ltd., would be at home in any room in the house—and is delightfully comfortable, too

them very suitable for to-day's style of manufacture. Labour represents a very big item of the costings, so the use of labour-saving standardised units or factory-made parts means better value to the customer.

Hand-sprung Chairs

Nothing has come to supersede the hand-sprung chair, where each coil spring is individually fastened, but it does cost a lot. The big advantage of hand-springing is that springs of different strength can be used according to the amount of pressure they are likely to take. Also, when in time a spring does "go," it can be replaced. With the coil unit a complete new unit is necessary. Hand-sprung chairs are still upholstered in curled hair which can be packed to give the degree of resilience required. Loose, down-filled cushions are considered the correct finish to these aristocratic chairs, but they need plumping up and some people therefore prefer latex foam ones.

springs is mainly rubberised hair or latex foam. Both are good in their way. Latex foam is very luxurious-feeling. For some tastes it may be too soft and yielding, though according to the amount of air-cells incorporated it will be soft or very soft. There is nothing to go wrong; air circulates through it freely, so that it never gets too hot and it will not lose its shape. Rubberised hair, comfortable but rather firmer, should also give trouble-free service. Both this and latex foam come in slabs that are flexible and easy to cut to shape, making

SETTEES

The three-piece suite with identical chairs and settee is less popular than in the past, but settees nearly always have easy chairs designed to go with them. Alternatively, a separate settee, merely linked to the rest of the furnishings by fabric or colouring, is just as correct and attractive.

The Settee for a Purpose

If you buy a settee on its own merits, instead of as part of a suite, you are much more likely to get the right shape and type. Unlike an easy chair, a couch will probably be used by a number of different people and for various purposes.

In the home where guests are frequent and conversation or televiewing is usual, a rather straight-backed style, with not too deep a seat, will prove most successful. It can be without arms, and then at a pinch will seat more people, though this reduces its comfort when only one or two really want to relax. The armless settee, or one with fairly low arms, is also a good choice for frequent daytime naps.

When a settee is wanted mainly for luxurious relaxation, the lower, deep-seated kind with very soft cushions is a natural choice, though for sewing or anything needing concentration, rather firmer additional cushions will be required to prop the occupant to a straighter position. The most generally useful models are a cross between the extra-deep and the modern tele-bench types.

Choosing for Appearance

Unless the room is big, and has a feeling of space, a good rule is to avoid anything too massive and deep from back to front, which always looks much bulkier in the home than in a showroom. Consider carefully the line of the back as well as the appearance of the front and side, for this will be noticeable when the settee is drawn up to the fire.

UPHOLSTERY FABRICS

Quality in Coverings

A firm texture and close weave are essential. Specially woven, pure wool upholstery fabrics give extremely good service, but the rather less expensive wool and cotton mixtures can be very satisfactory, too.

Moquettes, with a cut or uncut wool pile, should stand up to exacting wear. Tapestries and tweeds, though less sturdy, are also good if the quality is right. For an elegant drawing-room, brocades, preferably of silk rather than rayon on account of its wearing qualities, and cotton mixture, or furnishing velvets, look more in keeping. High fabric costs have largely put an end to the former custom of having chairs upholstered in lining with specially fitted loose covers of linen, chintz or damask. When this is done, however, or when a set of loose covers is ordered, spending a pound or two extra on having the material preshrunk before making up will prove a long-term economy.

Here are the chief points to look for when choosing furnishing fabrics, drawn up by Mr. E. Minty, whose Oxford firm has been designing and manufacturing upholstered furniture since 1870.

Tests of Quality

First, when you are shown a swatch of upholstery squares, remember that in the finished chair the material will look lighter than in the sample piece. This is because it stretches slightly when fitted.

It is important to watch the stretch. Pull your sample square from top to bottom to see if the weave opens to reveal the backing. If it does, reject it or, after a time, your chairs will look threadbare.

Then take the two opposite corners of the square and pull diagonally, both ways. If it stretches too much, it will soon look baggy. If it has too little elasticity, it will not "give" as the chair settles, and will soon become a bad fit.

Next, to test its density, hold the sample up to the light. The less daylight shining through the better, because it means the cloth is closely woven, has substance and should wear well. If the material feels stiff, it may be because it contains too much dressing.

The choice between cottons and wools is difficult. Close-weave cottons, for instance, wear well, are not susceptible to moths and are tougher than wool. On the other hand, wool cloths do not show the grease and dirt so readily, they clean well, look warmer and, particularly in the case of the latest deep-textured cloths, wear magnificently.

When choosing an upholstery fabric, hold the sample up to the light to see if it is closely woven (below). Then stretch it (right), and don't buy if it opens to reveal the backing

Photographs taken in the Minty Showrooms

Next, pull it diagonally to test its elasticity (above). If you have children or pets, choose smooth surfaces and informal designs in light and shade that will hide marks. Remember that a fabric always looks lighter on the chair than in the sample

If you like hard-wearing moquettes—and these are now available in colours and designs to suit all contemporary tastes—remember a wool-pile moquette is better than one with a cotton pile. However, beware uncut moquettes and tufted wool fabrics if you have a pet in the house, for the loops are apt to pull out under animals' claws.

And the ideal fabric? "In my opinion," says Mr. Minty, "a combination of wool, cotton and rayon, of which there are many designs."

Where there are children or pets in the home, smooth-surfaced repps, tightly woven tapestries or tough moquettes are the most practical—but watch those claws and sharply pointed toys in case they catch and tear the loops in the fabric. It is worth remembering, too, that a mixture of light and shade in an informal rather than a regular design will disguise the odd ink or paint spot, and hide the traces of muddy paws.

OCCASIONAL CHAIRS

This kind of chair comes halfway between the traditional "easy" and the ordinary "dining" chair and is particularly practical. It should be light enough for moving around, as it frequently does duty in more than one room, and fairly small, but both lower and bigger in the seat than an upright chair. Good makes usually have tension or serpentine springing for seat and back,

An occasional chair with laminated frame in walnut, mahogany, elm or sycamore from E. Kahn

often with a loose seat cushion, either coil sprung or of latex foam. This type of chair may have a wooden frame and arms, or be of the armless variety with no wooden frame visible. Most people find an arm rest more comfortable for relaxed sitting, but for sewing, knitting, pouring out tea, etc., the armless chair is preferable. "Nursing" chairs, for a mother with a baby on her lap, are simple armless occasional chairs with a decided backwards slope to the seat.

Dining Chairs

These should be chosen in relation to the table, not only for

No seating problems with Q-Stak stacking chairs. In three wood and four coloured plastic finishes, by Robin Day from Hille of London Ltd.

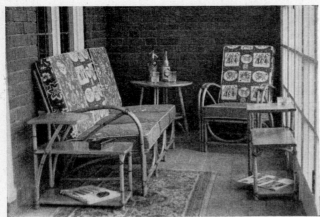

INDOORS OR OUT

The furniture that is equally at home in the garden, on the balcony, or in the lounge — and ideal for TV.

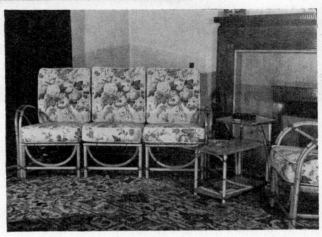

Made from selected ash with foam rubber or spring interior upholstery, these Lustycraft easy chairs can be used alone or grouped to make a settee. Obtainable with zip-fastened covers for easy cleaning, they have matching occasional tables and dining chairs

style but for size. Tables vary in height and a too low or too high chair can be very uncomfortable. In modern chairs depth of seat does not vary a great deal, but overall depth and the angle of the back do. Chairs with a straight back set roughly at right angles to the seat suit most people. Ladder or stick backs, if set at about the same angle, are also good.

Unless the seat slopes slightly to meet it, curved back chairs lack the necessary support. The contemporary moulded or laminated chairs with back and seat all in one can be very comfortable. Arms on dining chairs are best avoided, especially if the chairs are bought independently of the table, for they may make it impossible to draw the chair right up to the table.

Some people still favour the old custom of having two armed dining chairs for the host and hostess; others find the arms most inconvenient for carving or serving. So the choice is one of personal taste.

Desk or Work Chairs

These are more upholstered and deeper in the seat than dining chairs, but, like them, they are best chosen in relation to the desk or table at which they are to be used. Again, arms are best avoided unless the "fit" is right. Support for the back is essential, and for this reason a hard chair can prove more successful than an easier-seeming one of the wrong shape. To cushion the seat, a separate latex foam cushion may be added, so long as it does not make the seat too high, one of the worst sins against comfort in a chair.

A central lighting fixture should be low enough to throw the light up over the whole ceiling area

LIGHTING UP

Health, efficiency and good eyesight depend on correct lighting at home as well as at work

MOST of us spend a large part of our waking hours in artificial light, so this aspect of furnishing must be considered from the scientific as well as the æsthetic viewpoint. The right light can make all the difference to the atmosphere of a room —and even more to the health of those who live and work there.

A great deal of research has gone into the relationship of lighting to working efficiency, good eyesight and general health. Certain standards have been arrived at which provide a guide to the best choice of lighting without strain to the eyes.

A central lighting fixture, for instance, should be so shaded that the light is thrown up over the whole area of ceiling as evenly as possible. The makers of Mazda lamps have it worked out in inches. Therefore it should be hung fairly low, but not

less than 84 in. from the floor. Their estimate for the height of a standard lamp is 58 in. from floor to bulb-holder, and for a table lamp, 15 in. Have an overhead bed-light 30 in. above the surface of the bed and a bedside light 20 in. above.

Then there is the question of the amount of light, or number of bulbs, necessary to illuminate a room adequately. The following table shows the requirements in a central ceiling fitment for various sized rooms:

Room Area 120 sq. ft.

1	200 watt bulb(s) in a		one-light fitting		
2	100 ,,	,,	,, ,, two	,,	,,
3	75 ,,	,,	,, ,, three	,,	,,
4	60 ,,	,,	,, ,, four	,,	,,

Room Area 180 sq. ft.

2	150 watt bulb(s) in a		two-light fitting		
3	100 ,,	,,	,, ,, three	,,	,,
4	75 ,,	,,	,, ,, four	,,	,,

Room Area 240 *sq. ft.*
2 200 watt bulb(s) in a two-light fitting
3 150 „ „ „ „ three „ „
4 100 „ „ „ „ four „ „

Room Area 360 *sq. ft.*
3 200 watt bulb(s) in a three-light fitting
4 150 „ „ „ „ four „ „

For an area of 360 sq. ft. or over, the central lighting is better spread over two smaller fittings rather than one large one.

A reasonably accurate room measurement can be taken by pacing out length and breadth and multiplying the two together.

The Light for the Job

Apart from adequate wattage in the central fixture to give general lighting to the room, it is important to have the right lights for different purposes in each room.

Reading.—A standard or table lamp is best placed so that the light falls over the shoulder on to the print, 15 in. to the left and 26 in. back at right angles. Use a 150-watt bulb in a standard, a 100-watt bulb in a table lamp.

Sewing.—Placing of table or standard lamp is important, and either should be set 15 in. to the left of the work and 12 in. back at right angles. A 150-watt lamp is advisable or one of 200 watts for close fine work.

Writing. — A 100-watt bulb in a table lamp, placed to the left and 12 in. back from front edge of table, avoids shadow-casting from pen or pencil and gives an efficient light.

Dressing - table Lighting.—Two 60-watt lamps give an adequate, even distribution of light over the face if placed at equal distances; as a guide, Mazda advise a distance of 36 in. between lamps on either side of a mirror 24 in. wide or less.

A modern floor standard with red and white shade provides good light for reading and adds to the simple contemporary decorative scheme.
Council of Industrial Design

A kitchen, being a workroom, needs light of a high overall intensity. The Philips "Gearless" system, above, combines fluorescent and tungsten filament lamps and does not throw shadows

Bed Lighting. — Overhead lamps (containing 60-watt bulbs) should be placed on the wall at a point 6 in. in from the outer corner of the bedhead and, as already noted, 30 in. above the surface of the bed. For reading in bed, choose a 100-watt bulb in a bedside lamp placed 22 in. away from the book and 16 in. back at right angles.

This emphasis is placed on the correct position of lights because research has proved that a single glaring light causes severe eye strain. The right strength and proper diffusion of light prevents both eye and nerve strain, taut muscles and stooped shoulders. Children's eyesight, in particular, should be protected in this way when they are doing homework.

There is a right and a wrong way to read. Left, wrong, with light shining into the eyes, book aslant. Above, correct, with a good light shining over right shoulder

has itself a diffusing effect. Any thicker type of semi-opaque, totally enveloping shade should be used with clear lamps.

The type of bulb with a coiled coil filament gives up to 20 per cent. more light for the same amount of current than a straight coil filament one.

Fluorescent lamps give much more light for equivalent current consumption, are obtainable in a choice of colours, and are equally ideal for kitchen and workbench or for concealed lighting in living-rooms.

Types of Bulb

It is not enough simply to go into a shop and buy a bulb. The difference the right kind for the job can make to lighting efficiency amply repays a little study of the subject.

In the Mazda range, for example, their "Silverlight" lamps diffuse glare to such an extent that they need only be screened with a light shade.

Pearl lamps should be used when fully covered by a thin semi-opaque shade that

Lighting the Dark Spots

Correct lighting is important in all rooms. It is an absolute essential for the danger spots that exist in many homes. The staircase always needs clear lighting from top to bottom operated by two-way switches. Bottom, middle and top of stairs should all be clearly visible: some staircases, because of their slope, may need an extra light in the middle. A fluorescent

Older people need more light than younger ones. A 100-watt lamp with directional shade gives a good light for mother's fine embroidery; daughter can read comfortably with less

tube may well be the answer, but expert advice should be taken if there is a problem here.

Cellar staircases and semi-spiral flights are often found in old houses and cottages. A cellar staircase invariably needs a good light at the bottom and a light-coloured covering on the stairs to reflect it. If there is a light outside the entrance to a cellar, see that it is high and strong enough to cast light down the stairs to join that coming up from the bottom light.

In cottages the semi-spiral flight, sometimes shut off from the ground floor by a door, or the flight leading up out of a room, are almost bound to need mid-way wall lighting plus the safety of two-way switches top and bottom.

Large dark cupboards or

Both photographs and the one on page 94 by Philips Electrical Ltd.

Widespread, even lighting is right for a garage. A portable hand lamp—of the approved safety type—is needed for detail work inside a motor engine

An oil table lamp of good modern design that gives a clear, steady light even in the strongest draught. A "Bialaddin" Pressure Lantern

way with clear hot water and rub dry. Keep the metal cap dry, remembering always that water and electricity are dangerously opposed.

Gas Lights

When renewing mantles on vertical or inverted burners, brush away all dust and fluff with camel-hair or similar soft-bristle brush, and remove all fragments of old mantle from the burner. Before fitting the new mantle, light the gas to check that it is burning blue. If the flame is yellow or yellow tinged, adjust to blue by turning the screw controlling the gas supply. Fix the new mantle, checking first whether its container carries any special instructions for fixing. The flame from a correctly adjusted jet should just fill the mantle.

Oil Lamps

To give the best light, these should be filled daily to the stated capacity and, to avoid smell, any spilt paraffin should be wiped off the metal with a clean cloth. Once or twice a week trim the wick. Turn it up level with the top of the central tube; wipe away charred fragments, cut off any loose threads and gently pat level all round. Replace a cracked or broken chimney at once or this may interfere with the draught and a poor light will result. Clean burners at regular intervals, using warm soda water and a stiff brush. Oil lamps with incandescent mantles should be cleaned and operated according to the maker's instructions.

Shades

Paper Shades.—Dust or brush regularly Occasionally clean with artist's eraser.

Parchment.—Wipe with a cloth wrung out of tepid water containing a teaspoonful of vinegar to each pint. Rinse in the same way, using one level teaspoonful of soda dissolved in a pint of water. When white and cream parchment shades become discoloured by the heat from the lamp,

larders with only indirect light from outside may be lit by the automatic type of battery light that switches on with the opening of the door.

The outside light over the front door is not only welcoming, but helps to prevent accidents, particularly if an uneven path and steps have to be negotiated. The Local Authority should be consulted first about lighting restrictions before installing any outside lights.

CARE OF FITTINGS

Good lighting fixtures of any kind need the benefit of regular cleaning. It is a shock sometimes to realise how much dust can collect on bulbs, shades and so on.

Electric Light Bulbs

Always handle gently, dust daily and, when necessary, wipe with a cloth wrung out of hot soapy water. Rinse in the same

they should be replaced by new ones.

Buckram.—Clean regularly with the small brush attachment of the vacuum cleaner.

Plastic.—Wipe with a cloth wrung out of a warm soapy lather. Rinse with clean water and leave to dry slowly.

Glass.—Wash in hot soapy water. Rinse in hot water and rub dry while hot.

Fabric.—Fabric shades are usually of silk or cotton. If the frame is rust-proof, they may be sponged with warm soapy water and rinsed in the same way with clear warm water. Dry them quickly in a warm place. If the frame is not guaranteed rust-proof or if the fabric is stuck, not sewn, in position, sponge with a spirit grease solvent. Treat a small area at a time and rinse immediately with a clean cloth and spirit, or send the shade to a reputable dry-cleaning firm.

Lamp shielded by diffusing glass gives a wide angle of illumination on desk or table. Merchant Adventurers Ltd.

Left, a contemporary table lamp with fabric shade held on by elastic, easily removable. From Wireworms

Other Parts

As well as spending the necessary time daily on bulbs, shades, chimneys, etc., spare some time weekly for bulb holders, flex and plugs. Brush out the inside of each holder and the pin-holes in plugs with an artist's brush. Run a duster up and down flex. Electrical contacts must be kept clean for best results, while dust engrained in the cotton or silk covering of flex causes it to fray. Any sign of rust on metal parts should be rubbed off gently with an emery board or paper.

LAMPS AND SHADES TO MAKE

Artistic lighting adds charm and warmth to a room and expresses your personality

Drum Shade (above) looks charming in spotted white plastic over plain yellow, edged top and bottom with frills

You can make the three-legged lamp and its shade (right). The half-shade (below) is satin, velvet trimmed

to the first one, trim edges. Repeat with yellow plastic.

Place lining round frame, allowing ½ in. to turn in at top and bottom. Pin firmly in position and sew by hand. Treat the spotted plastic in the same way. Cut both edges to ¼ in. and fold the turning up on the outside of frame.

Make a box-pleat frill for the top of the spotted plastic, 1½ in. deep and finished length 37 in.; machine along the centre of the strip. Make a second frill for the bottom of the shade. Sew each frill into position, then paint a thin gold line over the stitches.

THERE is nothing like an unusual lamp or a new and colourful shade to bring a fresh note of gaiety and add a smart touch to your rooms. Here are some charming ideas that are quite simple and quick to copy . . . and great fun to do.

DRUM SHADE

Materials required.—Drum frame 8 in. deep; ½ yd. white spotted plastic; ½ yd. plain yellow plastic (for lining); white tape; cream and gold paint.

To make.—Paint frame struts, and when dry bind top and bottom of frame with tape. Cut one straight piece of spotted plastic 37 in. by 9 in. and an identical piece in yellow. Machine side seam of spotted plastic so that it will fit *exactly* round frame. Make a second row of stitches close

TABLE LAMP

Materials required for three-legged lamp (opposite page).—Frame; parchment; red bias binding; 1 hardwood ball 1½ in. diameter; 3 hardwood balls 1 in. diameter; dowelling, 2 ft. 3 in. by ⅜ in.; an electric socket; 2 yd. flex; 1 plug; glue; paint.

Tools required. — Handsaw; drill; ⅜ in. and ¾ in. drill bits.

To assemble.—Drill holes in balls, making sure the three legs enter the large ball at correct angle. Glue a 9-in. length of dowelling into each of the three leg holes. Cut the top of lampstand flat to mount electric socket. Paint legs white and balls red.

To make shade. Cut a paper pattern to fit frame. Then cut parchment. Use Sellotape to attach parchment to the frame temporarily and glue bias binding around top and bottom. Tiddlywinks can be used for the spots. Glue on to the parchment.

VELVET-EDGED HALF SHADE

(bottom illustration opposite page)

Materials required. — 1 frame; ½ yd. primrose velvet; ½ yd. oyster satin; 1 yd. narrow gold ribbon.

To make.—Fold satin into a triangle, cut along fold. Pin material on to outside of frame. Cut round shape of frame, allowing 1 in. overlap. Sew in position, trim close to stitches.

Even this elegant contemporary wall standard lamp is within the scope of any enthusiastic handyman—or woman—and so is the coolie shade with the pleated under-shade

Cut velvet on the cross, pin to inside of frame, stitch in position, making stitches invisible. Trim material round bottom close to stitches. Cut sides, allowing for double turning, stitch in place.

Cut velvet at top 2 in. above frame. Drape into a scallop by drawing up each end with gold ribbon, turning under the raw edges. Attach a small decorative "tail" at each side of outer edge of frame.

Cut a strip of velvet on the cross, 2 in. deep by 31 in. long. Make a neat hem. Drape velvet round shape of frame, gathering in as shown in the photograph. Stitch in position.

PLEATED SHADES

Paper or parchment is best for this kind of shade. It should be an inch or so wider than the frame's depth, to allow a slight overlap top and bottom. Amount of material required is three times the widest circumference of the frame. (A shade 12 in. round the bottom and 8 in. at the top would therefore need 36 in. or one yard.)

Fold material, previously pencil-marked, into pleats of required size, on a flat surface, pressing firmly with a strip of wood, then working material backwards and forwards to make pleats crisp. When whole shade is pleated, punch holes through centre of pleats in position required near top and bottom. Thread cords through holes, fit shade on to frame, draw cords tight and tie.

For a good fit, make small semicircular nicks in the inside folds of the pleats just below the punched holes to hold the shade firmly to the rings of the frame. The easiest way to make these nicks is with a punch, using only half of its cutting edge.

HOW TO MAKE A WALL STANDARD

Materials required.—Brass tubing, 6 ft. 6 in. $\frac{1}{2}$ in. in diameter; 2 hardwood balls, 2 in. in diameter; 2 hardwood balls, $1\frac{1}{2}$ in. in diameter; 2 wooden wheels, 3 in. in diameter; an electric socket; 3 yd. flex; 1 plug.

Tools required.—A drill or brace; $\frac{1}{2}$ in. centre bit and $\frac{1}{4}$ in. drill bit.

Bend the tube by pressing one end on the ground and bearing on it about 3 ft. along, to get a smooth curve. Drill at F, $\frac{1}{4}$ in. holes in wheels to fix to wall. Drill $\frac{1}{2}$ in. hole in two balls as D and in last ball at A and C. Drill $\frac{1}{4}$ in. hole at B for wire. Screw wheels to balls D, with screws E, and assemble.

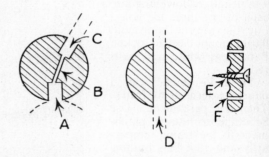

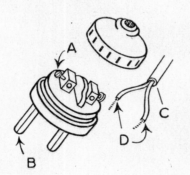

HOW TO WIRE THE PLUG

Most plugs are similar inside to those shown in our diagram. To fix a light plug, remove cap and thread on to wire. Trim wire covering back as shown at C, making sure that the inner insulation is not cut through with the outer cover. Trim back neatly at D and roll wire ends to avoid any fraying. Loosen screws A but do not remove. Put one wire in each brass boss, in opposite directions. Tighten the screws, replace cap. Make sure prongs B are providing a good grip when plugged in. If loose, insert knife blade in each and lever to open slightly.

HOW TO FIX A CABLE SWITCH

When you fix a cable switch, make sure that the wires are separated by a distance equal to the length of the switch and that one wire only is trimmed. Slide half of switch casing up wire past this position. Insert bared wires into appropriate holes and tighten screws. Slide second half of casing up and assemble.

LOOSE-COVER LAMPSHADES FOR QUICK CHANGES

FABRIC lampshades have an unfortunate habit of getting dirty, thus raising the question: to try to wash them on the frame or take them to pieces? Neither is very satisfactory. Now, to solve the problem, come "Formashayd" loose-cover lampshades with collapsible frames (for easy packing) and fabric covers and trims that just slip easily on and off for washing or replacement. They are obtainable in a wide range of shapes, including Milk Churn, Coolie Hat, Bell, and in a charming variety of materials to go with most colour schemes, from G. & S. Wright Ltd., Mill Road, Dewsbury, Yorks.

Just a flick of the switch and one table lamp (above) with 60-watt bulb gives bright reading light, medium for ordinary use, dim for TV, or low for the nursery. The Baker Regulite

Left, the "Formashayd" range of shapes—Milk Churn, large and small, Coolie Hat and Bell. Above, a Coolie Hat is fitted on to an upturned Milk Churn to give a charmingly diffused light

BEDTIME STORY

"Oh sleep! it is a gentle thing, beloved from pole to pole"
—and very largely dependent on a comfortable bed

Three-quarters of bed comfort is in the pillow. Put your shoulder in, not under it. Downland pillows in Haworth harlequin cases

BETWEEN the feet of your bedstead and the quilt lie a number of items, including bed spring, mattress and all the bedclothes. The needs of the sleeper have never had so much attention paid to them before, both from a health and æsthetic point of view. Different types of mattress, fillings for pillows and mattresses, new fabrics used for bedclothes, between them make up the bedtime story.

BEDSTEAD

The modern base on which the mattress rests is a matter of spiral springs, slung between an iron or wooden frame, each row of springs supported by a crossbar

bolted to the frame. In effect, this type of spring keeps the spine straight because it gives only at pressure points, shoulders and hips, without sagging between them and dropping the spine in an unrestful curve.

Such a base may be bought plain—that is, without upholstery—or upholstered, when it is generally known as a box spring, the sides and top of which are covered with ticking, a specially firm fabric of cotton or linen, or a mixture of the two.

A box spring is made either with a firm edge or a cane edge. In the former, the springs are built into a solid wooden frame, usually about 8 or 9 in. deep, the padding over the top of the springs slightly overlapping the edges of the frame. In a cane-edged box spring the sides are flexible, giving a rather more resilient base for a mattress than a spring with a firm edge.

In the majority, wooden legs or castors are fitted to box springs to become popular divans. These can be bought with or without headboards, and in most cases when a headboard is included it is detachable.

The old-fashioned type of bed spring—

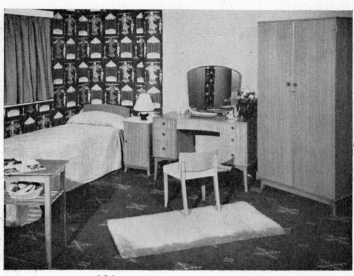

A charming bedroom for a 'teen-ager, the suite is in eucalyptus wood, one wall brightly papered. William Perring of Kensington, London

TRANSFORMATION SCENES FOR DULL ROOMS

An attic bedroom with sloping ceiling (above) acquires new charm and character. Between the built-in cupboard and drawers a little table is fixed, daintily curtained and with a Victorian mirror on the wall. Note how the alcove is papered a delicate shade in contrast with the brightly striped paper on the sloping roof.

Contrasting
walls and
gay surprises
in unexpected
corners give
a house
character

If you have some favourite ornaments or plants, why not display them in the corner beside the door of your bedroom or drawing-room? The small corner shelves, right, take up the minimum of space, look charming painted different shades or against one wall papered differently from the rest of the room. For a traditional room, the corner fitment, above, is ideal, painted to match the room's woodwork or in a contrasting colour.

COLOUR FOR SWEET REPOSE...

1. Pretty and romantic, these perfect honeymoon sheets are embroidered with lovers' knots on coloured borders. Ever-wear "Marie Antoinette."

2. In a gay choice of colours, plain hem-stitched sheets and pillow cases in Irish linen or rayon.

3. Coloured cotton bed linen embroidered in the same colour on a contrasting white border.

4. White towels gaily sprigged in yellow, lilac or pink to match the sheets pictured opposite (E), by Horrockses.

5. A wavy satin band on coloured cotton sheets with appliqué trimming.

6. Coloured spots and matching border on white cotton sheets in a lovely array of shades.

7. Candy striped gingham edges on white sheets and pillow cases, in pink, blue, green and lemon. Barlow & Jones.

8. To tone or contrast with coloured sheets, Lan-air-cel cellular blankets come in ten glorious shades, including wine, dark blue and all the pastels.

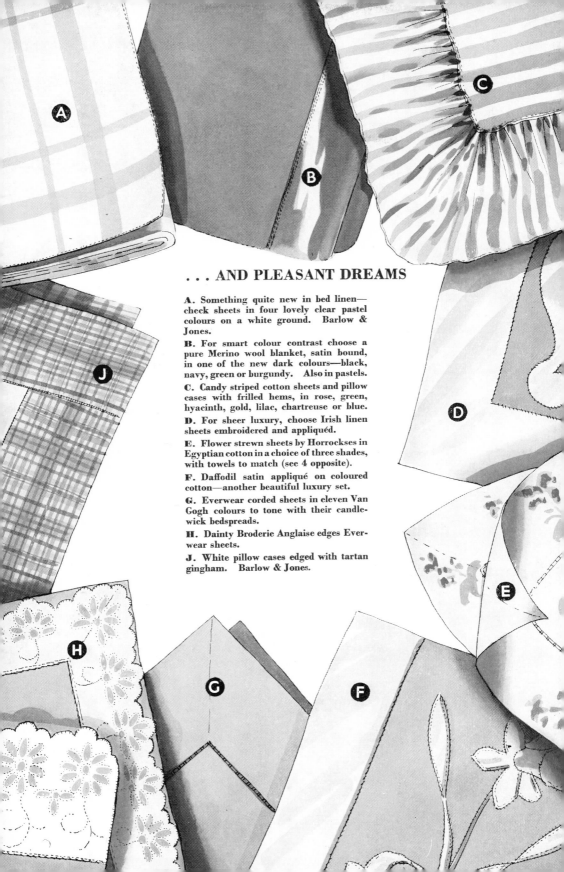

. . . AND PLEASANT DREAMS

A. Something quite new in bed linen—check sheets in four lovely clear pastel colours on a white ground. Barlow & Jones.

B. For smart colour contrast choose a pure Merino wool blanket, satin bound, in one of the new dark colours—black, navy, green or burgundy. Also in pastels.

C. Candy striped cotton sheets and pillow cases with frilled hems, in rose, green, hyacinth, gold, lilac, chartreuse or blue.

D. For sheer luxury, choose Irish linen sheets embroidered and appliquéd.

E. Flower strewn sheets by Horrockses in Egyptian cotton in a choice of three shades, with towels to match (see 4 opposite).

F. Daffodil satin appliqué on coloured cotton—another beautiful luxury set.

G. Everwear corded sheets in eleven Van Gogh colours to tone with their candlewick bedspreads.

H. Dainty Broderie Anglaise edges Everwear sheets.

J. White pillow cases edged with tartan gingham. Barlow & Jones.

PUTTING UP THE UNEXPECTED GUEST

Three clever ways of conjuring an extra bed out of nowhere—and making it comfortable

Couchette (right) is a comfortably capacious chair with plenty of space for two. With no trouble at all, it opens into a ready-made bed with luxurious spring interior mattress, Latex upholstered and covered in attractive tapestries or moquettes.

Left, the Studio Couch looks perfectly at home in a lounge. Headboard and fitment in straight grained walnut veneer, covers in a wide choice of contemporary materials —and the cushion cover unzips to reveal the pillow inside.

Here is the perfect idea for a home where sons or daughters are always bringing young friends home unexpectedly for the night or the weekend. The Two-into-one-Bunk—a double-decker bunk or twin single beds, in solid beech with mesh springs, easily fixed together, sturdy and secure, with two safety rails and a good firm ladder for the top-bunk-sleeper to ascend in comfort and safety. A winner for the playroom.

All these and many other two-in-one furniture ideas are to be found at Harrods

that of coiled or linked wire mesh—is fast passing out of usage because it is anatomically unsound. But where good beds still exist with this type of spring, they can be modernised by the addition of box springs. These can rest on top of the existing frames or, if this would make the bed too high when the top mattress is added, the spring can be made to fit inside the existing frame, with an outer flange which rests on the frame.

Above, a lovely bedspread of scrollwork design in tiny tuft candlewick, the housecoat in baby chenille tufting. Both Everwear Candlewick, setting and furniture by Maples

A new reversible woven cotton bedcover (left) has a flower and check design, is dark on pale colour one side, reversed the other. Vantona "Cromer" in 4 colours

To contrast with the maroon and white wall, below, soft coral pink bedcovers, with curtains and pillow covers made from an extra bedcover to match. Vantona Consort Clove Hitch design

MATTRESS

Choice in this item comes under three heads: (a) spring interior; (b) filled, without springs; (c) rubber.

Spring Interior

Until quite recently this type of mattress was beyond the purse of most people. Now it is possible to buy one at a suitable price down, or on deferred terms. This kind of mattress on top

The Staples "Skidivan" (above) is easy to move, because of its broad skid feet which are tucked out of the way underneath, and does less damage to carpets

of a box spring gives a truly excellent bed.

Two types of spring are used, the pocket spring and the open spring. When the former is used for an interior unit, the unit consists of a large number of small cylindrical springs each encased in a cotton or jute pocket, all linked or stitched together to keep their position. In an open spring unit, each spring is a double cone type—that is, it looks like an hour-glass—and each row of springs is joined with spiral wire to hold their position.

Next comes padding for top, bottom and sides of the spring unit, followed by the outer covering of ticking or other suitable material. The paddings used may be washed flock, curled hair, cotton felt, coir (coconut fibre) or sisal fibres and woollen flock, to mention only a few.

The cost of your mattress depends on all these items, their quality and the quantities used. They can vary tremendously, but if you spend your money on a mattress bearing the British Standards Institution's kite mark and number, you are buying good quality in every respect. British Standards exist for minimum requirements in the production of sound mattresses, pillows and bolsters, the fillings of which also measure up to a British Standard of cleanliness. You can also safely spend on a well-known branded name—"Beautyrest," "Relyon," "Sleepeezee," "Slumberland," "Somnus" are a few. All good furniture stores stock a representative selection. If you know how you like to sleep, you can choose firm, medium or soft sleeping with the help of a trained salesman who knows his stock. Good mattresses are tested for average weight, but a heavily built man or woman can easily buy a mattress with a heavier spring.

Filled Mattresses without Springs

The best known stuffings are hair and kapok, but a number of other fillings are used.

Among them is *washed flock,* made up of shredded woven, knitted and felted fabrics already used; it is warm and resilient when containing a high percentage of wool.

Woollen flock is made up of new cloth, blankets or carpets, and is generally nearly all pure wool, making an excellent filling.

Coir fibre is an inexpensive, clean and sterile filling. When added to hair, it makes a stuffing almost as good as hair, but cheaper.

Sheep's wool, after treatment, is light and warm and keeps its resilience for a long time. It can also absorb moisture to a great extent without becoming damp itself.

Kapok is a downy vegetable fibre, very light, buoyant and waterproof, and most useful for asthmatics allergic to animal fibres.

Goose and duck feathers are the best for mattresses, as they contain a certain amount of down.

These non-spring mattresses are made in three ways: (i) with a set-in border all round between top and bottom of mattress, and tufted or buttoned to hold filling in position; (ii) with no border (sometimes called a French overlay), though the corners may be turned in to give a "squared" look—they are also tufted or buttoned; (iii) with or without border and with no tufting or buttoning—these are thin and light, usually stuffed with feathers or fine wool flock and stitched into several sections, either crosswise or lengthwise. They are good for giving extra warmth and softness on top of an existing mattress, and a daily shake keeps them fluffy.

Again, many of these kinds of mattress conform to British Standards of quality.

Rubber Mattresses

Latex Foam is a familiar household phrase, and the Latex Foam mattress is the newest development in bed comfort. Such a mattress need not be turned, is dustless and in every way hygienic, and needs no maintenance. But for full comfort in winter, have a thin wool under-blanket between it and the sheet if it is not upholstered.

The newest type of Latex Foam mattress is electrically heated. Special insulation makes it perfectly safe and you can bask in low, medium or high heat, with the control switch under your pillow.

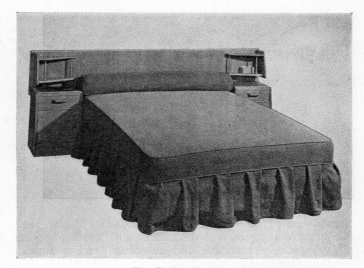

The G-plan Continental headboard (above) provides cupboard, drawer and shelf space, and is obtainable to fit a single or double divan

Special Shapes and Sizes

Despite the variety of mattresses and beds now available, there are occasions

Myers' luxurious Vogue 55 divan (below) has a Matchmaker headboard. You change the covering (right) to match curtains, bedcover, sheets—or cover it with leather, woven raffia, white nylon fur, an embroidered tapestry panel or what you will

when one of a special size or shape is needed, perhaps to fit into an awkward alcove or turn a tiny room into a guest-room. One reliable bedding firm, whose goods are all made entirely by hand, is Friendly Rest, the South London Bedding Centre, 132 Plumstead High Street, London, S.E.18, who undertake to make a mattress to any size or shape, provided they are supplied with a template.

They have made a divan set 7 ft. by 4 ft. 6 in., a

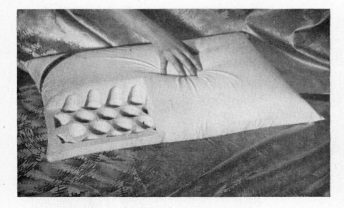

A pillow that gives perfect comfort, yet makes no dust or fluff—ideal for sufferers from asthma or hay fever and very hygienic—Dunlopillo Latex Foam

circular bed 7 ft. in diameter, mattresses in the shape of triangles, with the corners cut off or specially rounded, and complete window seats. They also make a pallet mattress filled with Tropal for people who feel the cold in bed and for sufferers from rheumatic complaints.

Care of Mattresses

The secret of keeping a soft wool or hair-filled mattress in good condition is to turn it regularly—one day from head to foot and the next day from side to side. During the first few months of its life, daily turning is essential. After that, it should be enough to turn it every two or three days.

The Spring Centre mattress is heavier and more difficult to turn than the soft type and, fortunately, does not need turning so often.

Whatever the type of mattress, it is important always to strip the bed immediately upon getting up and leave as long as convenient before making, to give the filling time to expand after being compressed all night.

A mattress should be given an occasional dose of sunshine. Stand it on edge in front of an open window, then brush with a stiff brush or clean with a vacuum cleaner, especially under the tufts or buttons, where moths like to breed. Once a year, at least, the mattress should be taken out of doors, laid on a dust sheet and given a good beating both sides with a cane or carpet beater, or cleaned with a vacuum cleaner.

It is not generally realised how much dust is absorbed by all mattresses. This dust is part of the air which passes through the mattress while it breathes. It is therefore strongly recommended that every mattress should be kept, if possible, in a loose washing cover. Calico sheeting is the best, but old sheets, or old curtains or printed cotton or linen, or, in fact, any washable fabric, will do just as well.

Moths are particularly fond of mattresses because the filling provides an unending supply of food for grubs. Mattresses should therefore be inspected often (especially during summer months or if not in constant use), turned regularly, kept well brushed and, once every three months or so, sprayed with liquid D.D.T. Latex foam is, however moth and grub resistant.

If a mattress becomes badly infested with moth, send it to a bedding specialist to be stoved at a high temperature, which kills all the grubs and the eggs.

PILLOWS AND BOLSTERS

Here again there is as much variety of filling as there is for mattresses.

Down, the undercoating of duck, goose or swan, makes a bubble-light, soft pillow, while a mixture of down and feather, in varying proportions, makes a light but rather firmer pillow.

Crimped Terylene floss is one of the newest additions to pillow fillings, giving a light resilient pillow with the merit of quick drying after washing.

Other types of comfortable pillows are filled with kapok, hair and wool flock, or you can choose a Latex Foam pillow, made in varying densities. Hair and foam pillows are firm but not hard: wool flock and kapok make lighter and softer pillows.

A good down, or down and feather pillow, should weigh about $2\frac{1}{2}$ lb. in the most usual size of 18 in. by 27 in., and it should stand up straight and keep its shape when held up in one hand on one of the short sides. This is a simple test you can try before buying a pillow. Other fillings should weigh about 3 lb.

Bolsters running the width of the bed are less and less used, one reason being the increasing difficulty in buying bolster cases. The under-pillow is more convenient and gives greater scope for individual preference in height and firmness. The Downland Bedding Company make a pocketed bolster, known as the "WEJ," to support the pillow at the correct sleeping angle. It is wedge-shaped, the soft feather filling being divided into three compartments to retain its shape and prevent the feathers from all slipping into one corner. This type of bolster takes a normal pillow-case despite its unusual shape.

Once again British Standards can be applied to the manufacture of pillows and bolsters.

When you buy a pillow, hold it up in one hand. If it remains upright, like this Downland "Cirrus," it will be light and full, soft and resilient, as a good pillow should be

To give the correct sleeping angle, the Downland WEJ bolster is sloped from 4 in. at the top to almost nothing, is pocketed inside to keep the feathers in place. Curtains by Rosebank

Cellular wool blankets are even lighter, and allow air to circulate while still keeping you warm. They look rather like intricate crochet work in most attractive patterns.

The blue-grey type of blanket, rather heavier than normal blankets, is usually cheaper, but very good value for emergency bedding, under-blankets or camping.

Popular for under-sheets for rheumaticky people or invalids, or for lightweight summer warmth, are flannelette sheets. Lightly woven and raised to a delightful soft, fluffy

BLANKETS

The household word here is "Witney," indicating pure wool or union (wool mixture) fabric. Whether Witney-made or otherwise, a good wool blanket is never heavy because its warmth is in its lightness. The fluffy pile may be light or dense, but should always feel soft in the hand.

finish, they wear excellently. Vantona Blansheets are a good make to look for, and good furnishing stores usually sell their own type of blanket-sheet.

Of course, there is no need to buy white or white-with-coloured-borders blankets to-day. You can be as gay as you like, choosing from pale pink through to burgundy, leaf green to forest green, and so on. And the difference in price is so little that the added lift to one's spirits fully compensates.

On Choosing and Caring for Blankets

Salient points to look for when choosing a blanket are these:

(1) Handle it for softness. It should be soft and yielding, yet springy, with no slimy, unpleasant feel.

(2) Test its weight by lifting it up and weighing it in your arms. It should be warm but not heavy.

(3) Study the finish: see if the blanket is well raised, with a good rich "cover" which makes it difficult to see the actual blanket texture underneath. Beware of over-raised blankets which, although attractive, will wear badly because the pile will quickly shed.

(4) Make sure that blankets are of adequate size for the beds on which they are to be used. Many are too narrow and/or too short for comfort, especially if used with a thick spring interior mattress. It is always advisable to measure the bed before purchasing blankets—taking careful note not only of the full length and width, but also of the *thickness* of the mattress. It pays to buy a larger blanket than is absolutely necessary, rather than a smaller one. For most single beds, choose a blanket 70 in. by 100 in. and for a double bed a blanket 90 in. by 100 in. Do *not* let a salesman put you off with a single-size blanket that is only 90 in. long; single sizes are obtainable in the full 100-in. length if you insist.

With reasonable care, a good blanket should last literally a lifetime. Remember, however, that it is made entirely or partly of wool, and wool will not stand up to maltreatment in washing. The safest way is to send blankets to one of the manufacturers who operate a cleaning service and who know the best methods to use.

The Dormy Blanket Cleaning Service, Hallcroft Works, Retford, Notts., will clean and re-bind and/or re-dye wool or part-wool blankets *of any make,* including cellular types, but not cotton, flannelette and similar varieties. Cost is 7s. 6d. per blanket.

If, however, blankets are washed at home, this is the correct procedure:

(1) Soak in cold water for 5 minutes, then add warm (body temperature) water.

(2) Using good-quality soap flakes or a *mild* detergent (in the quantities prescribed by the makers), press blanket up and down until the dirt is removed. Do *not* rub or twist. If using a washing machine, wash for 2 or 3 minutes, one blanket at a time.

(3) Rinse three or four times in clean, soft water at body temperature. Remove surplus moisture by squeezing gently or by wringer adjusted to *low* pressure.

(4) Hang lengthwise to dry so that water drips from sides, not ends. If possible, two clothes-lines about 3 ft. apart should be used. While drying, ease gently to shape and shake lightly to keep fluffy. Whilst still damp, brush lengthwise with fairly hard brush to straighten pile. When quite dry, spread on table and ease blanket to its correct shape, again brushing lengthwise.

(5) Iron satin binding with warm iron, but do not iron the blanket itself.

NOTE: Really hot water, too much soap and strenuous treatment are all very bad for blankets. Never attempt to re-dye one at home.

SHEETS AND PILLOW-CASES

There is a wonderful variety in fabrics from which to choose: plain cotton, Egyptian cotton, rather coarse and off-white in tone; union, a fabric containing a mixture of two or more of the following: jute, linen, hemp, cotton; twill, a diagonally woven cotton; cotton in cellular weave; percale, a finely woven cotton with a slight glaze; linen; rayon and nylon. Linen and nylon are the most expensive, but linen is

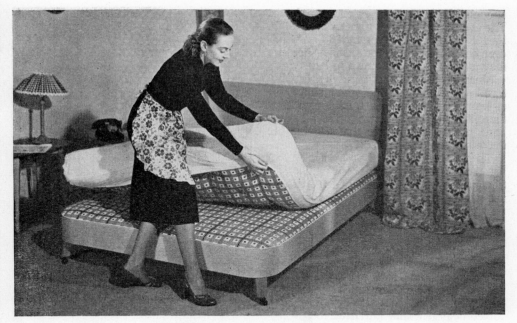

Top sheets that can't come adrift, because they have corners shaped at one end, are in the range of fitted sheets in ten sizes by Barlow & Jones

beautiful, nylon can be speedily washed and dried at home and both have very long-wearing qualities. Plain or pastel sheets with fitted ends are gaining in popularity and are made in a variety of sizes.

The trend for colour and pattern in sheets and pillow-cases is an exciting and stimulating change from all white. Advantages are many: a coloured sheet and pillow-case do not develop that drab, tired look after a few days, and the bed linen now blends in with the scheme of the whole room.

So you can run riot with plain colours ranging from pale to deep tones, contrasting with or matching coloured blankets; possibly dark colours for the men, pastels for young girls and teenagers, and flattering, deeper-than-pastels for the older woman.

And then pattern: delicate flower sprays scattered all over sheets and pillow-cases; candy-striped sheets with the stripes repeated in frills round white pillow-cases; harlequin diamonds on white; coloured sets with deep white borders polka-dotted in contrast shades; pastel colours with double corded edges in white or white em-

broidery round the edge—these are a few examples, and new ones keep appearing.

Buying and Care of Sheets and Pillow-cases

Always ask to see new sheets or pillow-cases *out* of the packet before buying them. And here are a few simple tests you can apply in the shop to bed linen:

First, stretch between your hands and hold it up to the light. It should be closely woven, free from knots, loose threads and puckers, with a smooth, flat finish and very little "fuzz." Next, rub two parts of the sheet or pillow-case together: if there is a fine powder left on your hands, there is too much filling in the material, which will wash out at the first laundering and leave the sheet limp. Then study the selvedge, which should be closely woven with a tape-like firmness; and the hem, which should be evenly stitched with reinforced corners, and no puckers.

As when choosing blankets, always measure the length, width and thickness of the mattress before buying sheets. Then allow at least 8 in. for tucking in at both sides and top and bottom; this gives enough blanket turn-over for top sheets. The average double bed needs a sheet 90 in. by 108 in., a single 70 in. by 108 in. Children can usually use shorter sheets because they tend to sleep low down in bed.

Measure your pillows carefully, too, before buying pillow-cases, which should be at least 1 in. wider and 2 in. longer than the pillow. Cases that are too small make hard pillows, and those that are too big make sloppy-looking beds.

To get the best out of your sheets, protect the tuck-in of the under one with a mattress pad over the springs of the bed and use an under-blanket, both for extra warmth and smoothness.

Always go over bed linen for tears and rips before you wash it or send it to the laundry; washing increases the rent. If you wash at home, soak in cold water first, preferably overnight. Rub well-stirred soap or dissolved detergent suds into extra soiled parts before washing. Rinse twice and wipe the clothes line before hanging out sheets. Fold evenly to avoid wrinkles when putting through a wringer; shake pillow-cases flat before wringing.

Fold sheets and pillow-cases until ready to iron, then open

Luxurious candlewick bedspread in five-tone floral motif, with flower and scroll design

Topper, an unusual bedspread with a scalloped sweep edge and poplin frilled dust ruffle

out, sprinkle lightly and evenly with warm water and iron with a fairly hot iron, doing pillow-cases from the edge inwards and taking care to fold sheets differently at alternate washings to prevent folds from wearing thin.

QUILTS AND BEDSPREADS

Here again variety is wide, and there is hardly a fabric that is

Designed from an old Colonial pattern, Richmond Rose has a flower and leaf motif stitched by hand and a knotted fringe. All three bedspreads from the Everwear Candlewick range

Satin squares with candle-wick tufting worked over them—a charming and unusual design in Ever-wear Candlewick

Cotton is used in a variety of weaves and weights, fast colours and contemporary designs for bedspreads of the simple throw-over type. In the Vantona range, for example, there are enough delightful modern designs to enable one easily to pick the right spread to complement a modern décor.

not used for the overall covering of our beds.

Candlewick has gained a firm place for bedspreads, and those with rounded corners are a new and good idea. The white cotton honeycomb spread of old has changed to a wool honeycomb spread in modern colours, doing double duty as an additional blanket. American style valanced bedspreads are neat without a too rigidly tailored look.

The much decorated, plumped-up quilt or eiderdown is losing favour a little to the thinner and less elaborate quilt. Many delightful kinds are made now in glazed chintz and cambric, patterned and stitched simply in squared or curved design. And many such quilts have matching frilled spreads.

Heavy rayon crêpe and satin in glowing colours are used for lovely sets of plain throw-type spreads and stitched quilt.

Ideal complement to contemporary furniture, the reversible woven cotton bedcover in spot design is "Malvern" from Vantona, and comes in blue, green, cherry and bronze

And Egyptian cotton spreads should not be forgotten for cheapness, good-wearing qualities and their brilliant heartening colourings.

On Buying and Caring for a Quilt

Be sure, when choosing a quilt, to examine the filling, which should go right to the corners, and see that the outer panels are not too wide. About 7½ in. is the ideal, but they should never be more than 9 in. wide.

When you get a quilt home, it should be opened at once and left in a warm room for a few hours to restore its buoyancy. Always put it on top of all the other bedclothes (never under a blanket) and do not put anything on it—that includes sitting and putting a suitcase down on it! It is not advisable to try to wash a quilt, which should be sent to a reputable firm of dry cleaners, when dirty or stained.

Laundering Candlewick

Candlewick, well-known for its practical, hard-wearing qualities and now so popular a material for bedspreads, dressing-gowns and soft furnishings, can safely be laundered at home provided the following basic rules are carefully followed.

Use a rich lather of the weekly wash powder (soap or detergent) in warm water, and squeeze but do not rub the material. Rinse twice in warm water, then squeeze

out moisture, shake well and pull gently into shape. Never wring too vigorously by hand or put through a mechanical wringer, as this bends and twists the pile. Hang out of doors, if possible, in a strong breeze to dry, shaking at frequent intervals to bring up the pile. Never iron or you will flatten the pile; the vigorous shaking takes the place of ironing.

The loose fluff which comes away from new candlewick material will disappear after one wash, which will bring the material up like new again.

THE END OF THE STORY

In passing, all the coloured bedwear mentioned is made to launder well and keep its colour.

When bringing a bedroom up to date, these reminders may prove helpful.

Good furniture shops, or a mail order firm such as the Witney Blanket Co. Ltd., of Witney, Oxon, will remake a wool or hair mattress into an interior spring mattress, reconditioning the filling and re-upholstering.

Many stores sell loose covers for eiderdowns and quilts, and will also re-cover and recondition them.

It is often a good idea to buy an extra bedcover and use it for making matching curtains and loose covers for pillows. See also chapters on Making and Re-covering an Eiderdown.

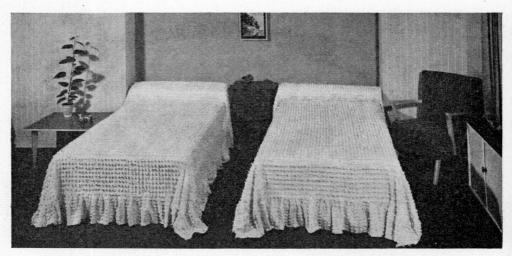

Delightfully fresh in turquoise, lime, shell pink, honey and white, these Vantona Candytuft bedcovers are easily washed and made with tufts woven into the cloth

CONSTANT HOT WATER

Comparing the various methods of supplying the bath,
toilet basins and kitchen sink all day and every day

NEXT to a good cooking stove, there is little doubt that an on-tap supply of really hot water makes the biggest contribution to domestic efficiency and comfort.

When an installation is under consideration, various points should be weighed up. Is cheapness or a minimum of work the more important? Is hot water wanted throughout the day or does the demand come at definite times only, say morning and night? Are any auxiliary services, such as an airing cupboard, wanted from the installation?

METHODS OF WATER HEATING

Piped hot water can be supplied by means of a back boiler on a space heating or cooking appliance, or by an independent boiler or other heater. Back boilers are described in the chapter on Heating the Home. Here, therefore, we are concerned with independent heaters whose sole job is to supply hot water.

All the water-heating appliances consist essentially of a heater of some kind and a container or containers for the water. The water may be heated:

(*a*) in one container or boiler and then pass up into a storage tank or cylinder from which it is drawn off;

(*b*) in the actual storage chamber by a heater installed in it, or

(*c*) in the process of flowing along from the mains or a cold cistern to the hot tap to be drawn off.

Most **boilers** heated by solid fuel supply domestic hot water and will also heat two or three radiators. There are gas- and oil-fired ones, usually for large systems. With **storage heaters,** electricity is the most usual fuel, in which case the immersion heater is installed directly in the storage container.

Some storage heaters employ gas, and both gas and electricity are used for **instantaneous heaters.**

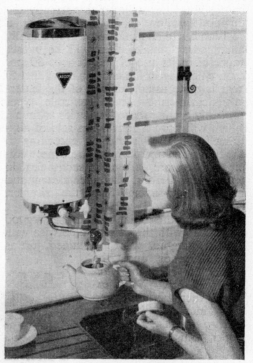

No need for a kettle for tea-making; boiling water is available in under a minute with the Ascot 509. Turn the dial and hot or warm water is obtained in ample quantities. Can be wall-mounted or stand on a window-sill

All these methods of water heating have advantages and drawbacks, making one more practical in some circumstances, another in others.

SOLID FUEL

Solid fuel is cheaper than gas or electricity, but it may be less economic for water heating than appears at first sight. This would probably apply when hot water is not required all day but only at specific times, and when the total amount is not very large. Solid fuel boilers, even of the cleaner, better-insulated types, do require fuelling and emptying, and they certainly cause more dirt in the room in which they are installed than either gas or electric heaters.

However, for the average small family with the housewife at home all day, a small solid fuel independent boiler, supplying a 30-gallon (or 40-gallon for a family above four, or when fairly heavy demands are made) hot-water cylinder is normally the thriftiest proposition. When choosing, a decision has to be made between an initially fairly cheap model that will be rather wasteful in its use of fuel (about 30 per cent. efficiency in the conversion of fuel to heat is quite usual), or one of the better-insulated, thermostatically controlled types probably costing more than twice as much, which will have a conversion rate of anything from 50–70 per cent., according to the insulation and design. These more efficient boilers are both more economical in their use of fuel and also much cleaner and more labour-saving than the simpler, cheaper ones.

Although the choice of boiler has a good deal to do with the ease or otherwise with which piping-hot water is obtained, just as much depends upon the layout of the whole *hot-water system*. Water expands when it is heated and rises into the hot-water storage tank from the boiler. This starts up a cir-culation which continues so long as there is a difference in temperature between the water in the boiler and in the tank.

The hottest water is always at the top, so the "flow" pipe leaves the boiler at the top and enters the tank near its top. The "return" pipe carrying the colder water back to the boiler for heating leaves the tank and enters the boiler nearer the bottom. Thus, in order that the system may work, the hot-water tank at its lowest point must be above the top of the boiler. In addition, the piping should be as compact as possible, otherwise there will be too long a delay before the water reaches its destination and the hot water will cool on its journey. To obviate this, lagging the flow pipes is recommended, and it is also wise to lag the hot-water storage vessel to some extent.

ELECTRICITY

Electricity is in some areas the most expensive *fuel*, but all the current consumed goes to heating the water (i.e. 100 per cent. heat conversion efficiency). It is also possible to regulate the amount actually heated much more closely than in the case of a solid fuel boiler. Thus, providing the installation is suitable and intelligently used, an electrical hot-water system need not, in appropriate circumstances, cost more than a solid fuel one.

In the average family household a **combined solid fuel and electric** system works out most profitably. In the winter the boiler is used, the "waste" heat from it being acceptable in warming to some extent the room in which it is situated, and also perhaps the bathroom and an airing cupboard. For summer use, when the boiler's extra warmth (not to mention the dirt associated with it) becomes a liability, an immersion heater, generally thermostatically

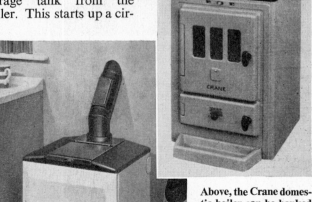

Above, the Crane domestic boiler can be banked with coke and left for 14-16 hrs., to supply hot water or heat radiators

The Radiation Nautilus 55, left, is thermostatically controlled will heat 70 to 80 sq. ft. of radiator area as well as providing constant hot water

You can heat any quantity of water, from a cupful to a gallon, to any temperature you like, from warm to boiling with a Creda Corvette (left)—and watch it boil too!

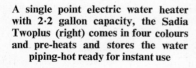

A single point electric water heater with 2·2 gallon capacity, the Sadia Twoplus (right) comes in four colours and pre-heats and stores the water piping-hot ready for instant use

controlled and fixed to the inside of the water storage tank or cylinder, is used instead. When extra hot water is required in winter, the immersion heater can be switched on as a "booster."

Immersion heaters are comparatively inexpensive and fitting is simple, though it must be done correctly. For economic operation effective lagging is essential. Most economical is the Dual Immersion Heater. No larger than an ordinary one, it has two switches and provides a double service—quick small supplies of hot water when switched to the "sink" position, and ample amounts for bathing when the "bath" switch is turned on. So little cur-

rent is consumed by the sink elements, which has its own thermostatic control, that it can be left on all the time.

The "Series" System

An alternative method for combined solid-fuel-electric heating is to have an electric pressure heater of the two-in-one type (see over) incorporated into the existing system. With a new installation, this heater is used as the storage vessel in the solid fuel circuit and is connected to the boiler. In the case of an existing installation, the pressure heater acts as an additional hot-water storage container. In warm

117

Smart to look at, the right size to go under a draining board, the 20-gallon Creda Centrepoint electric water heater (above) requires no flues

To supplement hot water supplies, a small 1½-gallon electric storage sink heater provides ample water for washing up and occasional use. Berry Electric in four colours

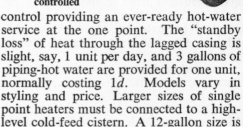

weather, it alone is used. In winter, water from the boiler passes through it to be further heated if necessary.

An All-Electric System is best serviced by a factory-made, self-contained thermal storage heater (or heaters). There is a wide range available in each of two main types: single point and multi point. All are thermostatically controlled and insulated to a high degree of efficiency, so that the glossy exterior casing is always cold when the water inside is scalding hot.

Single Point (non-pressure) heaters are designed to service one outlet (sink, basin, washing machine, etc.) only. The small sizes (1½ to 3 gallon), suitable for a sink or basin, are screwed to the wall, usually above the outlet point, and can be connected direct to the water main. The 1½-gallon size usually heats from cold to 160° F. (scalding hot) in 40 minutes; the 3-gallon size in 1 hour. These can be left switched on continuously, the thermostatic

A dual immersion heater, the Twimerser by Hotpoint: two separate elements mounted on one head, thermostatically controlled

control providing an ever-ready hot-water service at the one point. The "standby loss" of heat through the lagged casing is slight, say, 1 unit per day, and 3 gallons of piping-hot water are provided for one unit, normally costing 1d. Models vary in styling and price. Larger sizes of single point heaters must be connected to a high-level cold-feed cistern. A 12-gallon size is needed to supply a bath.

Multi Point (pressure) heaters are designed for use when hot water may be wanted from more than one tap at a time. These are fed from a ball valve cistern fixed some distance above, in order to provide the necessary head of water, and not direct from the cold supply. This kind should be fitted as close as possible to the most-used tap, usually that at the sink. Smaller sizes are usually fixed to the wall (wall mounting), but those from 20 gallons capacity upwards may be designed to stand on the floor. Capacities range from 5 gallons upwards, with loadings of from $1\frac{1}{2}$–3 k.w.

An increasingly popular type of pressure heater is the **"twin" or dual element** version. Made with a flat base to stand on the floor (under the kitchen draining board is practical for the most-used 20-gallon size); these come in 20–40 gallon capacities. The advantage lies in having the heating elements in two separate tanks. The top, 500- to 1,000-watt element is kept on, so as to provide about 6 gallons of piping-hot water always ready for use. The lower heater, generally $2\frac{1}{2}$ k.w., comes into action when a foot switch at the bottom of the heater is turned on. This brings the remainder of the water up to full heat for baths or laundry work. Both heaters are thermostatically controlled, but with the top heater only operating for most of the

The 3-gallon Creda Crusader water heater can be connected direct to the cold water main and will give 6 gallons of piping-hot water per hour, switching on and off automatically

Tucked neatly away under the draining board is a Two-in-One electric storage water heater by G.E.C. which serves bath and kitchen sink

119

time, the amount of hot water in store is lessened so that running costs are reduced, too. Initial cost is rather higher than with a single element multi point heater.

In some circumstances, particularly in a bungalow or flat, **a cistern type pressure heater** (single or multi point) is advisable. This has its own feed system, a small cistern holding only a gallon or two, contained in the casing. It may be connected direct to the cold-water main and must always be fitted above the level of the taps it supplies. Thus, in a two-storey house with upstairs bathroom, the heater must be fixed in the bathroom, not the kitchen.

Although storage heaters are generally recommended for domestic installation, **a single point instantaneous type** is available, giving 2–4 pints of boiling water per minute. Working is automatic.

Before making a decision as to a specific heater, it is advisable to have a qualified electrical engineer inspect the premises and discuss the kind of service wanted. The Electricity Boards are happy to give estimates and suggestions without obligation.

GAS

Gas is considerably more expensive than solid fuel, and slightly cheaper, as a rule, than electricity. Under some conditions, a gas water-heating system, owing to the flexibility of the output, may not work out appreciably more expensive than a solid fuel one. Whether it will prove less costly than electric water heating will again depend upon circumstances, including the initial cost and local rates for both fuels. Heaters should normally be professionally serviced about twice a year and all except small single point ones require a flue venting to the outside air.

Bottled gas provides a wonderful service to the country dweller not on the mains (gas or electric), but works out more expensive than mains gas or electricity. Most gas water heaters have bottled gas versions.

Solid Fuel plus Gas Systems

Gas water heating is not usually linked with solid fuel in the way that an electric immersion heater is installed in the hot-water storage tank, although a **circulator** can be fitted to a solid fuel circuit to take the place of the boiler or to be used in conjunction with it. If it has an economy valve, small quantities of water can be heated by setting a dial. A new type of "injector" circulator is fitted like an immersion heater but on the outside of the storage tank and connected through a small hole drilled in the tank. Most usual is to install a separate **instantaneous** gas heater to be used in summer, or when the solid fuel boiler is not functioning.

An All-Gas System is efficiently operated by self-contained, factory-made thermostatically controlled heaters of either the instantaneous or the storage type. The former are the most generally popular. They take up comparatively little room and, since the water is heated immediately before being drawn off, there is no "standby loss," although a small pilot flame must be kept burning the whole time. On the other hand, to be satisfactory, the instantaneous type must have adequate water pressure. Where this is lacking, as sometimes in flats on higher floors, or in country districts where there is no mains water, a storage type is a better proposition.

Single Point Instantaneous Heaters to service sink or basin, etc., are best fixed immediately above and are normally supplied direct from the water main. Flue equipment is not usually necessary. Around $\frac{1}{2}$ gallon can usually be raised 80° F., and there is one which gives boiling water in less than one minute. **A storage heater** of roughly similar overall size heats 2 gallons from cold in about $\frac{1}{2}$ hour and then automatically regulates the gas so that the water is kept piping hot.

For large single point installations there is the **instantaneous bath water heater,** with a long swivel spout to serve an adjacent basin, which will raise around $1\frac{1}{4}$ gallons 100° per minute. Water supply from the main. Flue pipe *must* be fitted.

Multi Point Instantaneous Pressure Heaters to service sink, basin and bath have the output connected to the pipes serving the hot-water taps. The cold-water inlet may be served by a cistern in the roof or direct from the main. Heaters of this kind do not function at full efficiency if the outlets are more than 20 ft. away. The best position for the heater is normally close to the kitchen sink. Approved type of flue outlet to the outside air is essential.

Multi Point Storage Heaters are extremely efficient and make a specially good choice for a rather bigger household or where a large amount of hot water—say, for baths—is required to be drawn at once. Heating coils for a linen cupboard or a hot towel rail can be run from the system (which is not possible with an instantane-ous heater). This does, however, put up costs, and a linen cupboard serviced by a small electric tubular heater and a separate gas-heated towel rail might well prove more economical. Cold-water inlet is served by a roof cistern, and an approved flue is essential. Where flueing facilities are inadequate, as in many converted houses or blocks of flats, a specially de-signed multi-point on the balanced-flue system is the best solution. This type of heater must be fitted to an outside wall, from which a brick is removed and a ter-minal inserted. Through this, air is drawn in and the products of combustion dis-charged. It can be installed under the draining board.

An alternative for a large house is a gas-fired boiler with a separate hot-water storage cylinder (as with a solid fuel boiler). First-class lagging of the cylinder and of exposed pipes is essential.

IMPORTANT NOTE

Whatever heating method is used, the price of the appliance does not represent the total initial outlay. When a *complete hot-water system* is required, *installation and all the necessary plumbing may often cost a good deal more*. Always get quali-fied advice and *estimates*. Local Gas and Electricity Boards are easiest to consult.

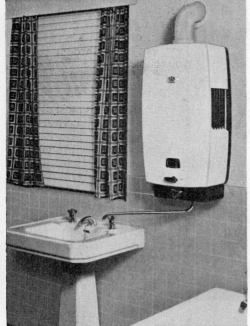

A versatile instantan-eous gas water heater, the Main Triton (above) operates as single or dual point in the bathroom, or multi-point serving kitchen sink, bath, and wash-basin

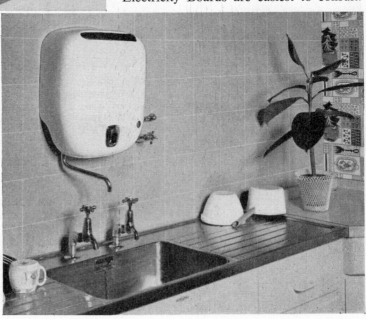

The Radiation New World Speedlyn (right) gas storage sink heater has a capacity of 1½ gal-lons of hot water, which it can deliver in three-quarters of a minute. Press the push-button regulo and the water re-heats in 6 to 7 minutes

GOOD-LOOKING BATHROOMS

Whether you are choosing fixtures for a new house or just buying new towels or curtains, the choice is wide and exciting

Peach-coloured fixtures look charming with a floor of green marble rubber tiles and walls papered in green and peach (the paper specially treated against condensation), with accents in black. This and the two schemes opposite by Froys, Hammersmith

FIXTURES

If you are building your house and can choose your fixtures and fittings, or if you are having an inconvenient bathroom refitted, your choice is wide.

Baths

Their size varies most usefully. For purposes of conversion—say, an old cottage without a bathroom or a fifty-year-old house into flats, where space available for a bathroom is limited—you can choose one with an overall length of 4 ft. 6 in. You can go even smaller and install a sit-down bath with an overall length of 3 ft. 6 in. They can be sat in comfortably since the interior is chair-shaped; and they make bathing possible in otherwise too restricted spaces. Incidentally, such a bath is helpful for elderly people, who often find it a strain getting in and out of a full-length bath.

At the other end of the scale, the limit in bath lengths is just over 6 ft. Approximately 5 ft. 6 in. is a comfortable average between the small and the large sizes, the average width being 2 ft. 4 in.

Bath shapes have changed. It would be difficult now to buy the curved edge, rounded-end type of bath that stands on ornamental feet looking rather naked. The modern bath is designed to be boxed in, and much nicer it looks too. Other excellent improvements seen at Froy's showrooms include baths with strong handles let into the sides, a practical safety measure for getting in and out: and a bath with a drop front and a handle opposite, again making it safe and easy to use. Then there is the elegant "Neo-Classic" model made

WHAT a blessing that bathrooms are now, in the main, reasonably sized, capable of being heated adequately and made to look beautiful. It is still fun to come across the vast Victorian bathroom, with minute fireplace, closet discreetly disguised as a chair and austere marble-fronted bath—so long as you do not have to use it. Æsthetic and material comfort are easy to combine to-day; in one way or another, the bathroom can become as much "a lovesome thing" as the poet's garden.

all in one piece with a rounded end. This can be supplied for a right- or left-hand angle and is at present a top-price fixture.

Plastic has come into its own for panelling round the bath, and it can be applied at a slope when boxing-in the long front, so that toe space is available. Specially shaped metal end brackets make this possible, and it is a distinct advantage when getting into the bath; other panels are designed with a moulded toe space.

Hand Basins

Design here is also varied and sizes accommodating. With limited space, you can choose an angle basin, to fit into a corner, measuring as little as $17\frac{1}{2}$ in. across at the widest point, and 10 in. from back to front. They are made with bowed or straight fronts.

Rectangular basins start at approximately 14 in. wide by 10 in. and go up to over 30 in. wide by over 20 in. from back to front. A popular size is approximately 25 in. wide by 18 in. from back to front. Some basins have bowed fronts, some have a slight but graceful curve to the front, others have squared-off corners and others again have stepped fronts. There is a choice between earthenware and vitreous china basins, the

latter having the better wearing qualities.

You can choose between a pedestal base, square or round metal legs, or brackets for holding the basin in position.

Lavatory Pans

The term to use here is "suite," as this

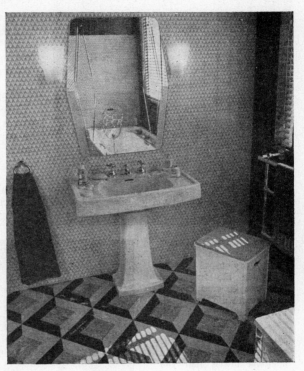

An attractive metal ring towel-holder is a feature of the bathroom (above) in primrose and black. Two walls are tiled in grey, yellow and white, the others in black, the floor covered in rubber with a raised box effect in off-white, grey and black. Bath, etc., are primrose

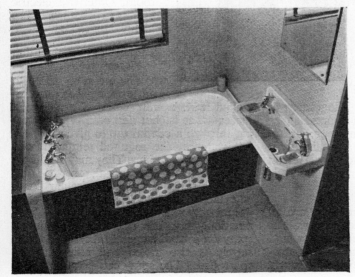

A small budget bathroom (left) specially designed for a small space. Bath (4 ft. 6 in. × 2 ft. $2\frac{1}{2}$ in.) and bijou basin are white glazed earthenware and the bath is built in with a black glazed panel

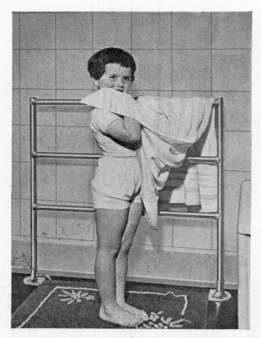

colours available, and also a neutral—a soft grey holding the merest hint of blue.

Where bath, hand and lavatory basins are all being installed at one time, they can, of course, be supplied to match, not only in colour but in overall design.

FITTINGS

In this sphere you can choose good ideas to add to the pleasure and efficiency of an existing bathroom, as well as adding all the finishing touches to a new bathroom.

Heating

Given a good house water-heating system, a metal towel rail can be run off the supply on the same principle as a hot-water radiator. This is often adequate heating in a small bathroom; for a larger space, towel rails can be bought that include a centre radiator panel. A visit to gas or electricity showroom will produce variations using either of these fuels, and there are also excellent oil-burning heater-cum-towel rail units. The bogy of an electric fire in the bathroom is no bogy **provided** it is (*a*) high-level; (*b*) installed by a reputable electrician, and (*c*) controlled by a switch outside the room or a pull-cord switch inside the room. Otherwise, electric fittings in a bathroom are highly dangerous.

There is nothing more comforting than a thick, warm, dry towel always ready in the bathroom. You can be sure of that luxury with a Hurseal oil-filled electric towel rail, above

So gay and up to the minute are these colourful Vantona towels that you could use them as beach mats or stoles. A variety of colourings, lemon, rust and moss green, all on white

includes the pan and the method by which it is cleared. The latter can be either (*a*) syphonic, when the cistern is directly above the pan and is operated by press-button or push-down lever; or (*b*) flushing, when the cistern is a certain height above the pan and operated by a chain puller.

Colours

Baths, basins and lavatory pans are all now made in standard colours as well as white. Shades of blue, green, yellow and pink vary with the different manufacturers. There are some perfectly lovely

Showers and Combination Pieces

These can be added to an existing bath or installed with a new bath. Combination pieces—that is, hot and cold taps operating through a central tap to give a flow of hot water at the required temperature—come in many designs. They may be simple and streamlined, hexagonal, or with hot- and cold-water taps set in circular bases and the central tap in the shape of a dolphin or other ornamental piece. Combination pieces can also include a shower spray on a flexible metal tube. The water supply is also mixed and independently controlled. The spray can be supplied to rest on hooks above the taps, or it can be attached to a vertical rail fixed to the wall above the bath in such a way that it may be slid up and down to provide a shower from various heights. It is detachable from the rail if needed for use when sitting in the bath.

When taps need renewing, there are excellent types available. "Supataps" are suspended over bath and basin on graceful curved arms. They have the great advantage that they can be re-washered without turning off the water at the main, a valve at the top of the tap cutting off the water while the washer is renewed. Where space behind the taps is cramped, "Easy-Reach" taps are shaped at an angle so that they lean forward and away from the wall. Other taps are shaped with long spouts pointing slightly upwards for easy cleaning, and others again are cone-shaped with press-button action, and hexagonal.

Earthenware and vitreous china soap holders can be supplied in varying sizes recessed or semi-recessed for letting into walls, and they can include a strong hand-grip as part of the fitment. Similar fitments are available for toilet rolls, and all are made in white or colours.

Lavatory seats which look shabby and dingy can be renewed with black or coloured seat and lid combinations in light, strong plastic. They may be plain, or mottled with a mother-of-pearl effect.

ACCESSORIES

Here lies the greatest choice of colour and design.

Towels and Bath Mats

These are no longer plain, but gay, hilarious, brilliant or soft-toned. Imagination has run riot and to good purpose, for

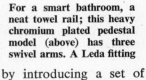

For a smart bathroom, a neat towel rail; this heavy chromium plated pedestal model (above) has three swivel arms. A Leda fitting

by introducing a set of contemporary towels, any bathroom can be given a fresh lease of life. You can have pink elephants on a black bath mat, or white footprints on a rose mat. The Queen of Diamonds (or any other Court card) may grace your bath towel, which, if you prefer, can be gently flower-strewn or robustly designed and coloured with geometric figures. Also included are candlewick tufted, coloured mats for in front of the lavatory basin and matching covers for the lid. Bath mats, too, come in this medium. Guest towels are prettier than they have ever been, and linen roller towelling is lifted right out of its rut of single-stripe border into a realm of moss

An adjustable overhead shower, complete with wall rail by Froys of Hammersmith

roses, Greek key pattern and many other designs drifting down its borders.

When buying a bath towel, hold it up to the light to make sure the background is closely woven. A good absorbent towel has a moderately (but not too) springy pile. If you can persuade the salesman to let you, it is a good plan to test a towel's absorbency in a saucer of water on the counter in the shop. When buying new towels, aim to have at least 8 hand towels, half a dozen bath towels, not fewer than 4 smooth guest towels, a couple of bath mats (and one more in the linen cupboard as a replacement), plus at least one razor cloth (drying razors ruins towels). Two bath mats in constant use are really an economy, doubling the chances of finding a dry one. Hand towels should be at least 20 by 40 in., and bath towels 40 by 70 in. for a man and 30 by 53 in. for a woman.

Incidentally, terry towelling by the yard does not make good bath towels; it is of a lighter weight, suitable for curtaining, beach coats, etc.

Always remember to mend towels before laundering and to wash them *before* they get really dirty. The best method is to soak in cold water for a few hours, then wash in hot soapy (or detergent) suds, rinse twice, dry in the open air, if possible, and shake to raise the pile Never iron towels and do not boil coloured ones.

Clean towels should be put away at the bottom of the pile so that the same ones do not get all the wear.

Curtains and Blinds

Terry towelling can be bought by the yard, in plain colours and in patterns, and various widths. It makes excellent bathroom curtains; so do glazed chintz and washable plastic fabric. For the bathroom that gets brilliant sun or is overlooked, the old-time Venetian blind in modern mood is a delightful compromise between drawing the curtains or installing frosted glass. These can be made-to-measure and are easily installed.

The Smaller Items

Contemporary design combines delicate, smooth line with full usefulness. Toothbrush and glass holders, glass shelves, wall towel rails, soap holders for across the bath, are designed to be wholly useful. Masque bathroom fittings are one example of good design and ingenuity; all are made to fit over special wall plates so that no

Gone are the days when white was the colour for the bathroom! Choose a tufted bath mat by Everwear Candlewick—soft, hard-wearing and easily washable—in turquoise, Italian pink, gold, royal, green or black with a white design (above)

Step lightly from your bath—on to a mat covered with elegant swans (left). This bath mat is in the famous Swan design by Osman, with towels available to match

screws show. Bath racks combine steel and polythene for long wear and lasting looks, or you can choose enamelled metal or un-adorned metal, polished and rustless. You can have elegant metal rings sunk into the wall to hold towels. The lavatory brush is now of rubber, hygienically encased in a polythene holder, or a shaped bristle brush can hang in a coloured metal holder to preserve its bristles when not in use.

Bathroom Furniture

Mirrors and cupboards are essential. It is possible to buy a useful-sized cupboard of which the door is lined *inside* with mirror; this can be swung into position to get the best light. Another type of mirror tilts to get the right position for light. Frameless mirrors are best for bathrooms, and

For sheer luxury and beauty, why not a Dolphin tap, beautifully made by Froys and adaptable for any bath?

all shapes and sizes can be bought. It is well worth having strip lighting at either side or over the top of the mirror. Cupboards can also be bought with interior strip lighting and mirror glass on the outside of the door. Wooden cupboards are preferable to metal, but they should be well enamelled to withstand damp.

Where space permits, twin cupboards, one on either side of the hand basin, could be built-in to provide plenty of storage space.

DECORATION

Floor

Floor coverings have been dealt with in "All About Floors," but for convenience points are summarised here. Cork tiles are highly recommended; like rubber and thermoplastic tiles, they are warm and easily kept clean. Linoleum is popular but needs careful laying and time to settle before fastening down. An alternative is linoleum tiles, which can be fixed straight away with adhesive.

For a bathroom window that is overlooked, Sunway Venetian Blinds provide privacy without destroying the modern appearance. Curtains may be in glazed chintz or one of the many pretty plastic materials

Walls and Ceiling

For these you can have any effect you want through the medium of tiles, washable wallpapers, prepared panelling or the right paint.

Vitrolite and glazed tiles are prepared for bathroom use, specially in heated bathrooms. There are lovely colours to choose from in either plain or mottled effects.

Wallpapers designed for bathroom use are moisture-resistant and come in fascinating designs. They have the advantage also of being washable if accidents happen.

Specially prepared panelling can be used as splashbacks, wall panels or for any other decorative purpose. It is thin and can be edged with wooden beading, which should be given a coat of enamel.

Walls and ceiling are best treated with the anti-condensation facilities of rubberised paint, when this means of decoration is preferred.

In all these products a wide range of colour is available, and in most cases the items mentioned can be applied by the amateur. For information about wall tiling, see chapter, "Tile Your Own Walls."

Upkeep

There are one or two points on special care worth noting. For example, the yellowish stain that sometimes appears on baths is often caused by the action of bath salts. If the bath is washed with a paste cleanser immediately after use, and cleaned

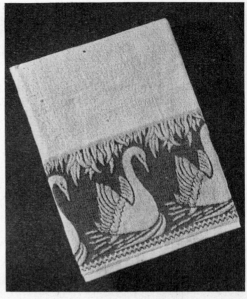

A companion to the charming bathmat on page 126, Osman's famous Swan design also appears on matching bath towels from Harvey Nichols

weekly with paraffin on a piece of old blanket, the surface should remain flawless. Some bath suppliers sell a specially prepared cleanser.

Use scouring powder or detergent suds sparingly on washable paints and wallpapers; simply wipe with a warm, damp cloth.

Three pink elephants march, trunk to tail, across a black or white bathmat, which serves equally well as a play rug. It is in Jacquard woven cotton, exclusive to Harvey Nichols, obtainable also with black elephants on white and vice versa

CUSHIONED IN WOOL

*Gay and simple to make—
and so inexpensive !*

A LL you need is a piece of curtain net, some wool and a bodkin. The original cushion was 15 in. by 13 in. in bright yellow double knitting wool scattered with 13 white flowers on each side and trimmed with white cotton cord all round the edge. Against the rich background of a purple chair, the little lemon cushion made an ideal contrast.

Making this cushion gives you enormous scope. You can use any kind of curtain net (so here's that chance to use up your odd scraps), and you can adjust the thickness of the wool to the size of holes to be filled in. And, of course, you can choose any colour scheme you like.

Starting at the right-hand side of your material, darn the wool in and out of the holes in the curtain net, leaving 1 in. of spare wool at either end. When you have finished filling the cushion, turn it inside out and stitch up the seams. Sew on cord, frilling or a fringe in the same or perhaps a gay contrasting colour. The white daisies on the cushion shown here were worked in lazy-daisy stitch. Centres are yellow.

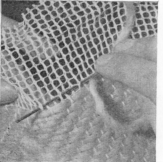

Thirteen white flowers in lazy-daisy stitch scattered on a cushion made of bright yellow double knitting wool — what could be gayer ?

Close-up of stitch (left): pick up one square, miss next two. Stitch can be varied according to thickness of mesh

★　★　★　★　★　★　★　★　★　★　★　★　★　★

PLASTIC BREAKFAST SET

Materials : ½ yd. each of patterned plastic, clear plastic and plain material for interlining. 3 yd. braid.

Make an envelope-shaped paper pattern for napkin bag. Cut out in all three materials. Cut out tray mat. Put interlining between clear and patterned plastic, and sew together, patterned plastic outside, turning in edges. Finish off by putting braid round edges.

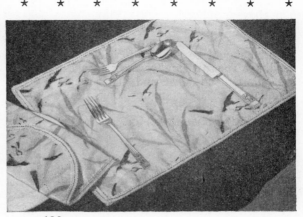

CURTAIN AND PELMET MAKING

*You can give your rooms a new lease of life and a
different character with artistic window treatments*

CURTAIN-MAKING in general is fairly
simple but, as with other simple things,
complete success depends on attention to
detail and, in this case, on careful measuring and cutting.

Measuring the Windows

If possible, take measurements with a
yardstick. This does away with the need to
stand on a chair or ladder to reach the top
of a high window and is more accurate than
a tape measure, which is apt to slip or
stretch. A substitute can be made by pinning a tape measure to a broom handle
with drawing pins.

Write down each measurement—preferably in a note book which can be kept for
future reference and thus save remeasuring
when more new curtains are needed.

When measuring for the width of side
curtains, remember to measure the wall-space to be covered at each side and not
only the glass.

**For adequate fullness, curtains which
are to be drawn should be from one and a
quarter to one and a half times the width
of the space they have to cover.**

Glass curtains should be one and three-quarters to twice the width of the glass.

Sill-length curtains should finish an inch
or two below the actual window.

Floor-length curtains should end about
6 in. above the floor.

Having decided the length, consult the
following table to see how much extra
material should be allowed for hems and
headings. The smaller allowances given are
for shorter curtains and light-weight
materials, the larger are for long, heavy
curtains. Shrinkage (which may average $1\frac{1}{2}$
in. per yard) is not allowed for.

Unlined Curtains

Floor length, with top heading.	.	9 in.
Floor length, without heading .	.	6–8 in.
Sill length, with top heading .	.	4–7 in.
Sill length, without top heading	.	3–5 in.

Lined Curtains

The actual fabric (any length) .	.	4–6 in.
Lining material (any length)		3–5 in.

Transparent Glass Curtains

Long, with top hem	.	3–5 in.
Long (for French window) with top and bottom headings and casings	.	7–8 in.
Short, with 1-in. heading . .	.	4–5 in.
Short, with 1-in. heading and casing	.	5–6 in.
Short, with casing	.	3–4 in.
Short, with casing and bound bottom edge	.	$2\frac{1}{2}$–3 in.

Dainty voile or nylon frilled curtains go
charmingly with these Venetian Vogue
Sunway blinds and a modern furnishing style

NOTE: Allowances given are per curtain or curtain width, *not per pair*, and except in the last example include bottom hem or (for lined curtains) turn-up.

UNLINED CURTAINS

Unlined curtains usually have to stand up to a good deal of laundering, and if the material to be used is at all likely to shrink, this must be allowed for, either by making the curtains extra long or in one of the following ways:

(1) By making an extra deep hem which can be let down after washing.
(2) By making an extra deep hem and then hand-sewing a tuck on the wrong side. This does not show from the front and is easy to let down.
(3) By making a tuck on the right side the same depth as the hem, if possible, and an inch or two above it.

Cutting Out

If a thread can be drawn easily in the material, this is the best way of ensuring a straight lower edge. Mark the required length with pins on both selvedges and check the measurements very carefully. Fold the material across from pin to pin, or draw another thread, and cut.

Making-up

When more than one width of material is used, this joining should be done first and the seams pressed. Selvedges should be joined with a plain seam the width of the selvedge, slashed (Fig. 1) before seaming.

Join a cut edge and a selvedge with a flat-fell seam (Fig. 2). Stitch a plain seam with wide turnings, press both turnings the same way and trim off the under one as closely as possible. Make a narrow single

Floor length curtains and a matching fringed pelmet make these windows look larger and bring a note of warmth and luxury to the room

turn in the wide turning, tack down flat over and concealing the narrow one and from the right side stitch along the tacking. Press well.

If a half-width is joined to a whole width the seam should be arranged to come on the side nearer the wall.

Top with Casing

If a pelmet or frill is being used, the curtain top is finished with a simple casing—i.e. an ordinary hem deep enough to take the rod or wire (allowing for shrinkage if necessary).

Casing and Heading

Curtains to be hung without pelmet or frill are finished with a casing and heading

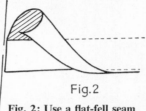

Fig. 1

Fig. 1: When joining two widths, slash selvedges and join with a plain seam

(Fig. 3). The top of the *casing* is the top of the curtain's measured length.

Top without Heading

Turn down $\frac{1}{2}$ in. material on to the wrong side along the top of the curtain. A $\frac{1}{4}$ in. below the fold, place Rufflette tape, an inch or two longer than the curtain width, and stitch right along its upper and lower edges—avoiding the double line of cord threaded through the tape.

Heading with Rufflette Tape instead of Casing

One inch is an average depth for a heading Mark where the actual top of the curtain should come (minus heading), then crease and fold on to the wrong side enough material to make a heading of the required depth. Finish with Rufflette tape as already described.

Extra Deep Heading

A heading of $1\frac{1}{2}$–2 in. is sometimes used to conceal an ugly fitment. To prevent sagging, run several rows of machine stitching, about $\frac{1}{2}$ in. apart, right across the width, through both thicknesses of material, or insert a strip of canvas.

Bottom Hem

This should be done last. Measure the exact length (from the middle of the Rufflette tape, if this has been used), mark with pins, fold along pinned line and make a double hem in the usual way, overcasting at each end.

If light-weight curtains are likely to blow

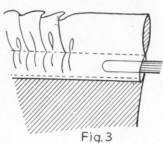

Fig. 2

Fig. 2: Use a flat-fell seam to join a cut edge and a selvedge

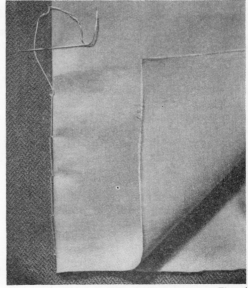

Fig. 3

Fig. 3: Curtain top with casing and heading

about at a casement window, weighted tape (obtainable from haberdashery departments) can be inserted through the bottom hem (with washable material, one end should be left open so that the tape can be easily taken out).

Draw up the Rufflette cords until the curtain is the required width, knot the ends and tuck them in, but do *not* cut them off.

Side Edges

Selvedges are left plain in most curtains, but if they "draw" at all they should be cut off. The sides should then either be narrowly hemmed, faced with matching bias tape or 1-in. bias strips, or bound. A contrasting binding may be used to give a decorative finish.

Hanging

Curtains finished with Rufflette tape can be hung either on rods or on a special runway, a metal rail with ring attachments which slide along. These rails can also be obtained

Fig. 4

Fig. 4: Locking a lined curtain—catch lining to curtain with tiny buttonhole stitches

with side cords, by means of which the curtains can be easily drawn, without tugging at the material. Rufflette hooks are slipped into the special tape (no sewing is needed) and put through the rings.

LINED CURTAINS

When measuring and cutting lined curtains, make the linings 1 in. shorter than the curtains.

If the two materials are simply stitched together on the wrong side and then reversed, the curtains will not hang well. The correct method of "locking" the two materials is slower, as most of the work must be done by hand, but it does ensure good-looking curtains and is well worth the extra effort. On very large curtains two people can work at the same time, and in any case a large table, or two tables put together, make for easier working.

If more than one width of material is being used, these seams should be joined first (as already described for unlined curtains).

Locking

Spread the curtain out quite flat with the lining on top of it, wrong sides touching. Smooth out very carefully and, when all wrinkles have disappeared, fold the lining material back lengthwise one-third of its width (leaving the curtain material flat). With matching thread, catch the lining to the curtain with tiny, very loose, buttonhole stitches 4 in. apart (Fig. 4).

Fold the lining material back in the same way one-third of

its width from the other side and lock again.

Curtains made from one or one and a half widths require two lockings.

Curtains made from two widths need an extra locking in the exact centre, which should be done first, by folding the lining material in half.

With a hot iron, turn in and press 1 in. of material down each side of curtain, and turn up and press the necessary depth along the bottom edge.

Open out the lining material again and turn in the sides to face the curtain sides, so that the lining finishes $\frac{1}{2}$ in. inside the curtain. Slip-stitch the two materials together, using long stitches (see Fig. 5). Finish the bottom hem in the same way, with the lining material 1 in. inside the curtain.

Top Finish

From the finished lower edge, measure upwards to the required length and turn down curtain and lining together on to the wrong side. Sew on Rufflette tape (as for top of unlined curtains).

If large rings are needed, strong braid should be used instead of the Rufflette tape, and the rings sewn on to this at 3-in. intervals. For very heavy curtains, each ring should be sewn in two places.

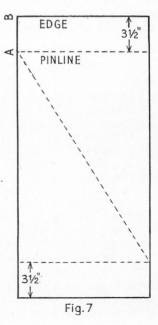

YES NO

Fig. 6

Fig. 5: Slip-stitch material and lining together at sides

Fig. 6: To hem a glass curtain (above), make the first turn the full depth of hem

Fig. 7: Waterfall glass curtains (right): lay material flat, mark depth of heading and casing, then mark a diagonal

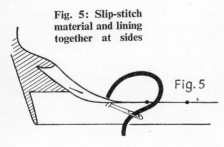

Fig. 5

Fig. 7

TRANSPARENT GLASS CURTAINS

Glass curtains are made in the same way as other unlined curtains but, because they are made of transparent material, there are a few special points to notice.

If a join must be made to give the required width (one and three-quarters to twice the width of the space to be covered), a very narrow French seam should be used.

To avoid joins it is sometimes possible when making short curtains to use the material the wrong way—with selvedges top and bottom. (The lower edge should be hemmed up or the curtain will not hang well.)

Ready-frilled material can also be used in this way, and the frill across the bottom weights the curtain nicely. The top frill should be hemmed down to half its width.

Finishing Top and Bottom

Glass curtains are finished at the top with a casing and heading (as for unlined curtains), the rod or wire being inserted through the casing.

At French windows it is necessary to secure the glass curtains at top and bottom, so both ends of the curtain are finished in the same way. Otherwise a plain ½-in. hem is used at the bottom, with the first turn the full depth of the hem (so that there is no untidy edge to show against the light when the curtain is hung—Fig. 6).

Cross-over Frilled Glass Curtains

When calculating the amount of material needed for this type of curtain, allow:

(1) One and a half times the glass width for each curtain.
(2) Two and a half inches for top and bottom finishes.
(3) Three to six inches (according to height of window) for looping.
(4) For frills (unless ready frilled material is used), sufficient material to provide 3-in. wide strips (cut straight across from selvedge to selvedge) which, when joined, will be one and a half times the length of one side and the lower edge of each curtain.

To make the frills, join lengths with tiny French seams and stitch very narrow hems along one edge. Fold a narrow single turn along the other edge of the frill and mark it with pins placed 18 in. apart. Mark the curtain edge with pins 12 in. apart. Gather up each 18-in. frill section on a separate thread, and draw up to fit the 12-in. section on the curtain. Join curtain and frill with a French seam.

Place the curtains one on top of the other, with frills facing, measure from the hem up to the required length, fold down both curtains together, and stitch hem deep enough to take rod or wire.

To loop up the curtains, coloured cords, strips of curtain material or ribbon can be used with curtain rings at both ends to attach to cup hooks on the window frame.

Waterfall Glass Curtains

Curtains of this type are suitable for a squarish window. They are made by cutting a length of material in half diagonally, and reversible material *must* be used.

In estimating the amount of material needed, add to the curtain length allowance for two top headings and casings. The width of the material should be seven-eighths of the width of the window.

Lay the material out flat, mark with pins the required depth for heading and casing *at both ends*, and run a diagonal line of tacking from one pin to the opposite one (see Fig. 7).

Place bias binding, with edges just touching, along each side of this line and seam each into place. Cut the fabric through the diagonal line between the two bindings, and from A to B in diagram, cut straight up.

Put the two curtains together, one reversed, to give a triangular space between them, join in the centre along straight edges with a flat fell seam, then make heading and casing in the usual way (see Fig. 3).

PELMETS

Pelmet-making is one of the easiest jobs in home upholstery, but it is not a particularly quick one because all the work, except the joining of seams, must be done by hand.

The depth and design chosen must depend on the shape and size of the window, and to a certain extent on the room's furnishings. Generally a simple, strip pelmet is best for a small window and in a room with contemporary furnishings. Very

CURTAIN AND PELMET MAKING

Softest pastel-tinted drapes inside the heavier curtains give the charming window on the right an illusion of constant sunshine

Both rooms furnished by Chippendale Workshops

Contemporary patterned fabric in brown and sage green on cream calls for trimly tailored curtains and a plain pelmet (below). Note the double-duty desk and dressing table in bird's-eye maple

large, tall windows can stand more elaborate designs. A special case is the round-topped type of window found in some of the older Victorian houses. For this it is best to have the pelmet board well above the top of the window frame with the lower edge of the pelmet exactly following the curve of the window top.

Most pelmets are covered in the same material as the curtains, but if the curtains are strongly patterned a plain pelmet in one of the main colours of the pattern is effective.

Making a Pattern

Paper patterns can sometimes be bought, but as windows vary so much, it is generally more satisfactory to make them. A roll of kitchen paper is useful for this, and saves pasting smaller sheets together.

Measure the window with a yardstick. The pelmet must be long enough to stretch across the

Fig. 8: To join buckram, overlap the two edges and secure them with a zigzag stab-stitch, using a strong needle and thread

(3) Lining of a cheap material such as casement cloth or sateen.

Upholstery buckram, 36 in. wide, can be bought from the furnishing departments of big stores. As a long shallow strip nowhere more than 18 in. in width is required for a pelmet, it is economical to make two pelmets at once. Otherwise, buy half the length of buckram, plus an inch or two for an overlapping join.

This also applies to surface and lining materials, but several inches will be needed for turnings on these two layers, and this plan will not work for a pelmet which is anywhere more than 15 in. deep if the material is less than 36 in. wide, as velvets and cretonnes often are.

As a rough guide, a pelmet 2 yd. long and 15 in. deep (at its deepest point) will require 1 yd. of buckram and 1 yd. each of 48 in. or 36 in. surface and lining material.

Cutting Out

If the buckram has to be joined, do this first. Cut it in half lengthwise and overlap two short edges by 1 in., taking care to keep an unbroken straight line along the top. Make the join with a large zigzag stabbing-stitch (Fig. 8), using a strong needle and thread, NOT cotton.

Place the paper pattern on the buckram, with its centre front edge to the buckram join, and pin into place with drawing pins or slip-on paper clips. Mark out with tailor's chalk (Fig. 9) and cut along the chalked line (no turnings are needed).

If centre front joins have to be made in the surface and lining materials, these should be machined and pressed well before cutting out.

Fold both the materials along the joins, place the centre front of the pattern to the folded edge and cut out both materials roughly, with about 2 in. turnings all round (Fig. 10).

Making Up

Lay the cut-out material wrong side uppermost, and if it is at all creased iron it smooth.

entire width of the window (or pair of windows if these are close together) and round the thickness of the pelmet board or rail to which it will be fixed, so as to touch the wall on either side. This usually means adding 7 or 8 in. to the actual window width.

Simple pelmet designs can be drawn easily on paper. To mark out a curved design, draw round part of a large circular tray, or a round or oval dish.

As a rough guide, a straight strip pelmet should be from 6 to 12 in. deep; on a shaped one, the drop ends or deepest point of the design should be from 12 to 18 in. deep and the shallower parts from 8 to 12 in. It is a good idea to cut the pattern on the deep side and try it against the window. The depth can be adjusted by cutting along the straight top edge.

In a pelmet with drop ends, these deeper parts should fall over wall or woodwork so that the light is not obscured.

Materials Required

Pelmets are made in three layers:
(1) Surface material (matching or contrasting with curtains).
(2) A stiff interlining of yellow-brown upholstery buckram (dress buckram and other stiffish materials are NOT suitable).

Drawing-pin the cut-out buckram on to it, with the material turnings projecting on all sides and the pins at least 2 in. away from the buckram edges.

Upholstery buckram (and no other kind) is stiffened with glue, and a mixture of damp and heat will make it stick to the material.

Have ready a damp sponge and a hot iron. Damp the buckram edges all round to a depth of about 2 in., then quickly iron down the material turnings on to the buckram (Fig. 11). At corners and along curves slash the turnings so that they will fold over and stick down flatly. (Two people can work at this, one damping and the other pressing.)

The pelmet should not be left long in this stage. As soon as possible, place the lining, right side uppermost, over the buckram and fold in turnings all round to make it slightly smaller than the pelmet. Slip-stitch to the ironed-down surface material, using a longer slip-stitch than in dressmaking (Fig. 12).

The lower edge can be finished with a matching pelmet fringe, sewn on from the right side with a line of running stitches along both the top and bottom of the un-fringed heading. When turning corners, mitre the braid neatly and flatly; round curves, pleat it slightly so that it lies smoothly. If liked, a matching braid may be sewn along the straight top edge of the pelmet.

Large pelmets in big rooms are some-times trimmed with more braid sewn in patterns above the fringe. This should be stab-stitched in place through surface material and buckram *before* the lining is sewn in. In small rooms, however, pelmets are usually better without this additional trimming.

Special Materials

(1) *Rayon:* Some types of rayon shrivel if damp heat is applied to them, so the gluing method cannot be used with these.

If using a rayon material, test a small piece first to see if it will stand sufficient heat to release the glue from the buckram. If it will not, the material must be tacked to the buckram with stab-stitches before the lining is put on. Make very small stitches on the right side so that they will not show when the pelmet is hung. (If a fringe is added this will cover the stitches.)

Should the rayon be at all flimsy, either pad the edges of the buckram with strips of calico or spread a layer of domette over the buckram before laying on the material, to prevent the hard edges from wearing through the rayon.

Fig. 9: Place the paper pattern on the buckram, pin or clip down, mark the outline with tailor's chalk and cut; no turnings are needed

137

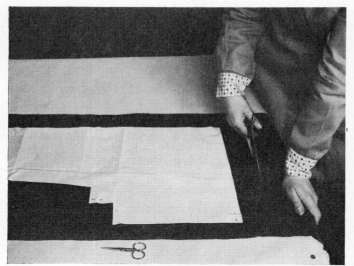

Mark the exact centre of the board and the centre of the pelmet. Starting at this centre point, and working outwards to each side, nail or drawing-pin the top edges of the pelmet to the front thickness of wood.

Alternatively, a metal pelmet rail can be used. In this case the top edge of the lining should be finished with Rufflette tape as already described for curtains.

NOTE: If a plastic pelmet is to be hung

Fig. 10: Cut out surface material and bring roughly to shape with 2-in. turnings on all edges

Fig. 11: Upholstery buckram is stiffened with glue, so iron surface material turnings down on to the damped buckram edges and it will stick firmly

(2) *Plastic:* The advantage of a plastic pelmet is that it can be sponged over when soiled, but as this material will not stand ironing the gluing method cannot be used.

The most satisfactory method is to use plastic material for both surface and lining. Cut both, without turnings, to the exact pattern size, place the buckram between them and tack round the edges. Neaten and finish all round with a binding of braid doubled over the edges and stab-stitched into place.

Fixing Pelmets

Fix above the window frame, on brackets, a narrow wooden board or shelf 3 in. or 4 in. wide.

from a rail it must be lined with ordinary material and not plastic.

VALANCE FRILLS

For certain windows and certain rooms —particularly the low-ceilinged cottage type—valance frills are preferable to the more formal pelmets. They are nearly always made of the same material as the curtains, and are very easy to make, being really just miniature curtains. Valances generally vary from 3 to 12 in. in depth, depending on the size and type of window. It is advisable first to cut a strip of paper of what seems a suitable depth, pin it in position, and adjust its depth before making a final decision.

Quantity of Material

For a gathered frill allow one and a half times the finished length.

For a box-pleated frill allow two and a half times the finished length.

The frill strips should be cut straight across the width from selvedge to selvedge. Each must be the required depth, plus 3 to 5 in. for top heading and bottom hem. (The deeper the finished frill, the deeper the heading and hem required. For a 4-in. frill allow 3-in. turnings; for a 12-in. frill allow 5-in. turnings.)

Making a Gathered Valance

Measure and cut out frill strips as carefully as for curtains (see p. 131). Join strips (selvedge edges) with plain $\frac{1}{2}$-in. seams and press turnings flat, one each way. Hem the lower edge and fold down a heading ($\frac{3}{4}$ in. to $1\frac{1}{2}$ in. in depth, according to depth of valance), and finish with Rufflette tape.

If the valance is to be fixed to a pelmet board, make a casing below the heading

Fig. 13: Making a box-pleated valance frill. Each tuck is pinned into a pleat with one of its folds touching the pins $\frac{3}{4}$ in. away

(see Curtains), run a tape through, gather it to the required length and drawing-pin the valance to the pelmet board.

Box-pleated Valance Frill

In a slightly more formal room, a box-pleated valance looks better than a gathered one.

Join the widths, press seams open and hem along the lower edge.

Starting 1 in. from one end of the length, mark out with pins along the top of the frill these three measurements, repeating them all along in the same order:

(1) $\frac{3}{4}$ in.; (2) 3 in.; (3) $1\frac{1}{2}$ in.

Afterwards measure and pin identically along the bottom edge.

NOTE: If the valance is a deep one the pleats should be larger. The distances between pins should be 1 in., 4 in. and 2 in.

Pin each 3-in. space as a wide tuck; then spread it out flat into a box pleat, making sure that one of its folds just touches the pins, at top and bottom, which mark off the neighbouring $\frac{3}{4}$-in. space (Fig. 13).

Pin each pleat in place, top and bottom, and tack down. Remove pins and press.

Fold down and stitch the top heading and finish off either with Rufflette tape or plain curtain braid, according to whether a metal rail or pelmet board is used.

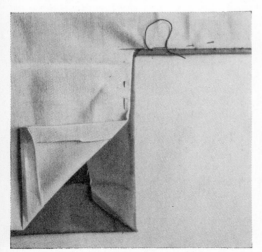

Fig. 12: Fold the lining turnings slightly inside the pelmet outline and slip-stitch them to the ironed-down surface turnings

139

MAKING LOOSE COVERS

A new look for your chairs or sofas—and all your own work

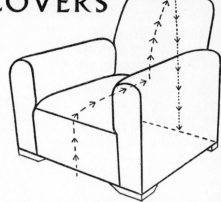

Fig. 1. The arrowed line shows how to make the first measurement for estimating the material needed to cover a chair

LOOSE COVER making is not really such a formidable undertaking, but for a first attempt it is wise if possible to choose a simple chair and either a plain material or one with a small all-over pattern.

In most cases, 31-in. material cuts more economically than 48–54 in. As a very rough guide an easy chair, without frills or loose cushion, will take about $7\frac{1}{2}$–$9\frac{1}{2}$ yd. of 31-in. material and a modern two- or three-cushion settee about 15–25 yd.

Material Required

To estimate the amount of material needed:

(1) Measure from the ground up the front of the chair, across the seat, well down into the crevice between seat and back, up the inside back, over and down the outside back to the ground (see fig. 1). Write down this measurement.

(2) Push the tape measure into the crevice between seat and arm, measure up the inside of the arm, over and down the outside of the arm to the ground.

NOTE: If the arm is curved, follow the curve with the tape-measure; do not just measure straight down to the ground.

Double this arm measurement and add to measurement (1).

(3) If the chair has a loose cushion, measure for this separately. If 31-in. material is being used, measure the cushion's length, double this measurement and allow 3 in. for turnings. If 48–54-in. material is used, measure the cushion's breadth. If this is less than half the width of the material, one cushion length of material will be enough. In either case the thickness strip can be cut from left-overs.

All seams, except those which tuck into the seat, should be piped—not only for the sake of appearance but also to ensure a longer life for the cover—with fine white piping cord. The cord must be boiled for 5 minutes and thoroughly dried before use.

Have ready a tape measure, a piece of tailor's chalk, a large pair of cutting-out scissors and a good supply of pins. Small upholstery skewers, which can sometimes be bought at arts and crafts shops, are useful for holding the material to the chair during cutting, but are not essential.

The cutting-out is done on the chair, using doubled material for half of each part except the arm. One arm is fitted and cut out in two thicknesses of material (as for the sleeves of a dress).

Using chalk (it will brush off afterwards) or by pinning on a piece of fine piping cord, mark the *exact* halfway line down the outside and inside back of the chair, across the seat and down to the ground.

Cutting-out

The cutting is done in four stages:

(1) *Inside Back.*—Double the material lengthwise, wrong side out, and place one end on the inside back of the chair with the fold on the halfway line and the cut end projecting 1 in. at the top (see fig. 2). Fix in position with skewers or pins, tuck the material 4 in. to 6 in. into the crevice between seat and back and, allowing ample turnings, cut off. Cut the material extending at the side to the chair's shape, allowing 1-in. turnings and tucking well into the crevice between arm and back.

Leave the cut material pinned in position on the chair.

(2) *Seat.*—Place doubled material, with fold on halfway line, on the seat and tuck

in well (*a*) between seat and back, (*b*) between seat and arm. Pin down and cut to shape.

If the front edge of the seat is straight, or almost so, the collar (depth piece) can be cut in one with the seat piece. Pin an inch-wide tuck along the front edge (to allow for piping later), let the material fall to the collar depth and cut off with 2-in. turning (1-in. if the cover is to be finished with a frill).

For a curved seat cut seat and collar pieces separately, shaping carefully and allowing 1-in. turnings everywhere except on the tuck-ins.

(3) *Arms.*—Place two widths of material together, right sides touching, tuck well down into crevice and cut inside and outside arm pieces separately, so that the seam will come along the outer edge of the arm (see Fig. 3). Shape carefully when cutting, and slash round the top where the arm joins the back.

If the arm is rounded, with a roll-under, pin up darts in the top part of the outside arm to make a neat fit.

(4) *Outside Back.* — Place doubled material with folded edge to the halfway line, pin in position, and cut. If the top has a roll-under, pin up darts to fit.

One half of the chair is now covered. With tailor's chalk,

Fig. 2 (below). Preparing to cut out the cover. Material, doubled lengthwise, is placed on inside back, projecting one inch above the top

mark all the seam lines over the pins. Trim all turnings to an even $\frac{3}{4}$ in. and notch at intervals through all thicknesses.

Testing the Fit

Remove the cover and pin the two sides together on the wrong side, matching notches. Put the cover on the chair *right side out*. If slight alterations are needed, mark these with pins.

When taking off the cover, plan for a placket by unpinning one back seam from the bottom upwards until the cover comes off easily. Mark this point with a crosswise pin. (For some chairs no placket is needed; others may need two.)

Piping

The piping must be prepared before the cover can be put together.

From the spare material cut strips $1\frac{1}{2}$ in. wide on the true bias. This can be obtained by placing a straight crosswise thread of the material exactly against a selvedge or a straight lengthwise edge (as in Fig. 4). The diagonal fold thus formed is the true bias. Cut the fold open (see Fig. 5) and cut the first strip with this line as one of its edges, making it as long as the material will allow.

Cut more strips, parallel to the first, and join them together to the required length.

Strips must be joined on a straight thread of the material, i.e. slanting across the strip.

Fig. 3 (left). Cutting the arm pieces from two widths of material, right sides touching. The seam comes along the outer edge

Fig. 4 (below). How to cut piping strips on a true bias—place a straight crosswise thread exactly against a selvedge

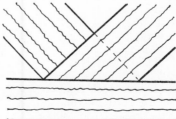

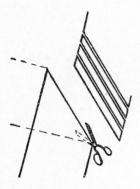

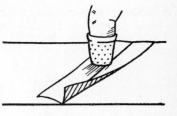

Fig. 5 (left). For bias strips cut the fold open and cut the first strip with this line as one edge

Fig. 6 (below). Joining bias strips: start the upper a seam's width farther on than the lower one

Fig. 7 (above). Finally, the seams are opened out flat and pressed with a thimble

Start the upper strip a seam's width farther on than the lower one (Fig. 6). Open the seams out flat and press well with a thimble (Fig. 7).

Fold the prepared strips over the piping cord, pin and tack them together as close to the cord as possible.

Making-up

Make-up the cover in the following order:

(1) Join seat and collar pieces.
(2) Join inside and outside arm pieces.
(3) Join inside and outside back.
(4) Join together seat, arms and back.

A special method of seaming and piping is used for loose covers. To join, say, the seat and collar, lay the prepared piping along the front edge of the seat piece with the cord lying inwards and the raw edges of the cord-covering exactly over the raw edges of the seat piece. Pin the cord in place all along. Place over this piped edge the edge of the collar, right side downwards, and roughly overcast all four edges together (Fig. 8).

At corners and on curves slash the turnings almost, but not quite, to the piping cord when overcasting. They will then lie flat.

Machine the hem very close to the cord without actually stitching through it.

If the machine has a piping foot, this can be used. If not, work right up to the cord by running the presser foot of

the machine along the top of the cord itself, so that the needle travels along almost touching it.

Awkward corners, such as the junction of arm and back pieces, cannot be satisfactorily machined and should be finished by hand, using strong backstitching.

Placket

On the placket seam, stitch as far as the opening and leave hanging enough piping to reach to the foot of the cover. Tack this piping down the turned-in placket edge on the front piece of the cover. Face this edge with a straight $2\frac{1}{2}$-in. wide strip of self-material. (If the placket is curved or slanted, use a bias strip.)

Machine one edge of the facing to the piped cover edge, right sides touching, fold over the piping to the wrong side of the placket and press flat. Tack and machine, from the right side, along the tacking.

If the material is wide enough, it may be possible to finish the under edge of the placket with a hem which when finished should underlap a good inch beneath the piped placket edge. Otherwise, or if the placket line is out of the straight, an added wrap is needed. Cut a 3-in wide strip 1 in. longer than the placket. Lay one edge to the placket edge, right sides touching, with a spare $\frac{1}{2}$ in. at the top tucked in. Seam, then double the wrap in half lengthwise, enclosing all raw edges and projecting well beyond the seam. Fold in the free raw edge and

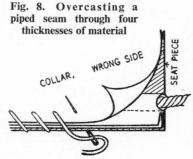

Fig. 8. Overcasting a piped seam through four thicknesses of material

COLLAR. WRONG SIDE SEAT PIECE

stitch down over the first seam (Fig. 9).

Sew on press studs 2 in. apart, but put hooks and eyes at points where there is a special pull, such as the top and bottom and where the arm joins the back.

Cover for Loose Cushion

Cut two pieces the size and shape of the cushion, allowing ¾-in. turnings all round.

If the cushion is wider at the front than the back and has sloping side seams, make a careful paper pattern from the cushion itself and cut out from this.

For the depth piece cut a strip long enough to go right round the cushion plus a 2-in. turning, and wide enough to allow ¾-in. turnings on both long edges. This strip

Fig. 9. Most loose covers need a placket, which is finished as above

The depth of the frill will depend on the type of chair, but generally a gathered frill should not be more, and a box-pleated one not less, than 5 in. deep when finished.

Gathered Frill

Cut enough straight strips across the width of the material to give the required length, allowing 1-in. turnings. Join together and press seams out flat.

With pins, divide the bottom edge of the cover into equal convenient lengths (say, quarters). Divide the frill in the same way and gather each section on a separate thread, leaving the threads hanging and knotted at the ends.

Draw up each thread until the gathers fit the

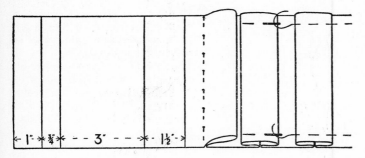

may have to be joined in several places. Join with plain seams and ½-in. turnings. Press turnings out flat.

Pipe (see p. 141) and machine the seams, joining the strip to the top and underside.

Leave most of the back edge of boxing strip and underside open, with the piping stitched along one edge only. Seam up the ends of the strip, insert the cushion, and slip-stitch the unpiped to the piped edge.

Frilled Covers

Certain types of smaller chair look better with frilled covers. To estimate the amount of extra material required, after taking the usual measurements (see p. 140), measure right round the base of the chair. Allow one and a half times this measurement for a gathered frill and two and a half times for a box-pleated one.

Fig. 10 (above). Stages in the making of a box-pleated frill. Two needles are used to tack the pleats top and bottom at exact distances apart

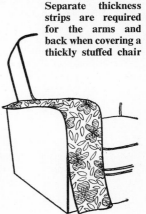

Fig. 11 (below). Separate thickness strips are required for the arms and back when covering a thickly stuffed chair

corresponding section of the cover. Hem the lower edge of the frill.

Join the cover and frill, through the gathers, with a piped seam (see p. 141). If the cover has a placket the frill should begin on one side of it and end at the other.

Box-pleated Frill

Cut straight strips of material, as for gathered frill, join up and press seams. Hem along one edge (allowing for plackets).

Put a pin 1 in. from one end of the

Flower patterned material with contrasting piping was used for the cover of this large, straight-armed easy chair of modern design

A wing chair, of the type shown on the right, can be successfully covered, provided you pin and chalk the material to fit the curved sides

material and, measuring from this pin, mark the frill right round, top and bottom, with pins spaced *exactly* the following distances apart: (1) $\frac{3}{4}$ in., (2) 3 in., (3) $1\frac{1}{2}$ in.

Thread two needles with long tacking cotton. Pin up each 3-in. space, right round the frill, as a wide tuck. Spread each tuck out flat (Fig. 10) into a box-pleat so that the pin touches the pin at the end of the adjacent 3-in. space. Pin down each pleat top and bottom, then tack (using two needles).

Press the pleats, using a hot iron, and first a cloth wrung out in warm water and then a dry cloth. Take out pins while pressing and finally remove tackings.

Join frill to cover with a piped seam (see p. 141).

SPECIAL SHAPES

The general principle is the same for all loose covers, but certain chairs need slight modifications. For instance, the type shown in Fig. 11 requires separate thickness strips (*a*) between inside and outside back, and (*b*) between inside and outside arms.

Open Armchair

To estimate the amount of material required to make a cover for a chair with plain wooden, unstuffed arms, measure:

(1) From floor up, across seat, up back, over and down to floor.
(2) Depth and width of upholstered part along outside of chair below the arm.

To the sum of these two measurements add $\frac{1}{4}$ yd. for turnings and $\frac{1}{4}$ yd. for piping.

Cut and fit pieces for inside and outside back, seat and collar (as described on p. 141). Across the width of the material cut strips the width and depth of the "side collars" (i.e. the pieces between the front collar and the lower part of the back). Cut both at the same time, in double material.

Make up as described on p. 142. Seam front edges of side-collar strips one to each end of the front collar. Finish top edges of side strips with piping and facing (as described for upper edge of placket on p. 142). Hem or face the back side-edge to fasten with hooks and bar eyes on to the lower part of the back placket. The hem round the lower edge of the cover should continue along the side strips.

If the side edges of the seat piece are selvedges they can be tucked in as they are; otherwise narrow hems will be necessary.

Armless Easy Chair

An armless chair is not difficult to loose-cover and takes very little material. The chair in photograph A (overall dimensions, height 32 in., width $19\frac{1}{2}$ in., depth front to back 21 in.) required only $2\frac{3}{4}$ yd. 31-in. wide. For covering a chair of this size in 48-in. fabric allow about $1\frac{3}{4}$ yd. Also needed are 4 yd. of medium white piping cord and about $\frac{1}{4}$ yd. of press-fastener tape.

When cutting, allow these turnings: 4–5

Photo: Gordon McLeish

BACKGROUND FOR ADVENTUROUS LIVING

It's gay . . . it's stimulating . . . it's original . . . a modern décor for a living room built round a brilliant red carpet. That fascinating striped effect, with the white diamonds, is created by the use of normal and hard twist pile in different heights. In striking contrast, a Calypso chair in black and yellow, pot plants growing in a jardinière and the useful magazine rack are all strictly contemporary. From Bowman Bros.

The secret of successful furnishing is the clever blending of fabrics, carpet and furniture. The study, above, is mellow with highly polished wood, warm red carpet; the heraldic curtains in "Tournament" design introduce a note of gaiety.

Above, the plain Tri-tone carpet and the patterned curtains in shrink-resisting "Grottos" are closely blended, with a dash of contrast in the moulded plastic upholstered chair: "Rondo."

Bright blue Rondo chair and mahogany corner cupboard, left, look their best against a light background of curtains in "Magnolia Twig" and a plain carpet.

Below, upholstery matched to the main colour in the printed "Helix" curtains, with speckled carpet as a closely related contrast, produces an elegant, sophisticated look.

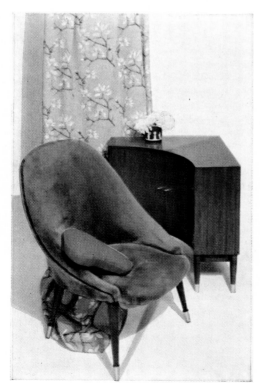

All these room settings show Greaves & Thomas furniture; Rivington carpets; "Moygashel" rgtd. furnishing fabrics containing Courtauld's fibres.

in. on the tuck-in edges between seat and back, 1 in. on all other seams, and 1½ in. along the lower edges of border and outside back.

In general, cut in doubled material laid to a halfway dividing line (photograph A) as described earlier. But if the fabric is plain or all-over patterned, do not fold the 31-in. width (or a half-width of 48-in. stuff) exactly in half. If you do there will be useless narrow strips left along each selvedge. Instead, fold over only enough to cover the chair width plus turnings. If you cut thus the two back pieces and the seat, you will have left a long uncut strip for the seat border.

Striped or vertically patterned material should be matched at the top back join and on inside back and seat.

Start with the inside back. Cut this, as in photograph A, high enough to fold over the top thickness of the back and wide enough to fold round its side thickness, to meet the outside back piece. Fit the top corner snugly by pinning a slanting dart, which eliminates the surplus triangle of stuff here. Push the stuff right down into the seat crevice before cutting it off (photograph B), and do the same with the back seat edge when cutting this.

It is convenient to shape the border next.

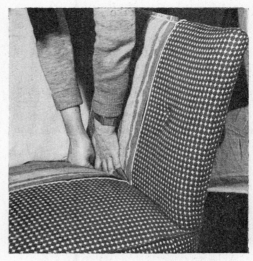

Photo B: Seat piece cut; tucking inside back and seat edges right down between the back and seat

But before cutting off the single strip long enough for this, cut out roughly with ample turnings the outside back piece and put it aside. Double the border strip, place its fold to the centre-front seat depth and take it right round the front corner and along the side to the lower part of the outside back. Be careful to keep the straight thread (and the stripes if using striped material) level along the *bottom* border edge. This type of chair seat slopes downwards from centre to sides and back, so the top border line must necessarily be on the slant, as in photograph C.

If the border itself slopes inwards, a dart or vertical seam at the front corner will be needed to fit it here. Afterwards cut the outside back piece. Notch all pieces in the usual way.

Make about 4 yd. bias strips for piping (see p. 141) from left-overs. Stitch the back darts and the corner darts or seams in the border and press well. Assemble as already described, piping the seams of the two back pieces and that connecting seat and border. Turn up all bottom edges in a 1-in. hem, so that the cover reaches just to the base of the chair framework (photographs D and E). To keep the cover from riding up in use, run a long tape through this hem, to be tied tightly round one back leg and its ends tucked up out of sight.

A press-fastener tape placket is very

Photo A: To cover an armless chair, the halfway line is marked and inside back piece cut with dart pinned at top corner

quick and easy to make down the lower part of one back seam (though chairs of some shapes may need a longer opening or one down *each* side). The turn-back in photograph E shows some of this handy tape, bought already studded with firmly fixed "poppers." Continue the piping, tacked only down the upper placket edge. Overlap the under edge about 1 in. on to the outside back (photograph E) and at that point make a single right-side turn. Pin the two halves of the tape together at the top, to keep their stud halves coinciding exactly. Then stitch or hand-hem the tape down each placket half to cover all raw edges and make a firm, neat fastening.

SETTEES AND SOFAS

A loose cover for a settee is made in exactly the same way as already described for an armchair. To estimate the material required, measure as for chair but double

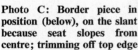

Photo D: The finished cover (right) looks smart, trim and tidy and easily comes off for laundering

Photo C: Border piece in position (below), on the slant because seat slopes from centre; trimming off top edge

or treble measurement (1) according to width of material and length of settee, and allow ½ yd. extra for piping. When joining the widths, try to ensure that the seams will be as inconspicuous as possible.

Victorian Sofa

For this type of sofa, 31-in. material is usually the most economical. To estimate the amount of material required, three measurements are needed:

(1) From seat crevice over arm and down to floor (following arm curve carefully).
(2) Back (if upholstered) from seat crevice up over inside back and down outside to floor.
(3) Seat length from crevice between arm and seat.

Add these three measurements together and estimate for collar, arm scrolls and frill.

Cutting-out.—Because these sofas are not symmetrical the whole of each piece must be cut in one thickness only.

The pieces required are:

(1) Seat.
(2) Collar.
(3) Inside arm.
(4) Outside arm.
(5) Front and back arm scrolls.
(6) Frill.

If the back is upholstered, inside and outside back pieces will also be needed.

The scrolls should go down to the frill and should not be cut short by the collar.

Avoid a conspicuous join in the seat if possible by using a length of material along the seat with selvedges along back and front. Plan the back and collar piece in the same way.

Lay the material on the sofa for cutting *right* side uppermost and pin the pieces together on the *right* side. After notching, re-pin as ordinary wrong-side seams.

To keep the exact shape of the scrolls, first chalk the lines on the right side of the material, then tack over the chalk lines with contrasting thread.

Make the placket (see p. 142) in the seam joining the outside arm and back pieces.

Divan Covers

When measuring to estimate the amount of material required, the divan should be made up with an average number of bed-clothes.

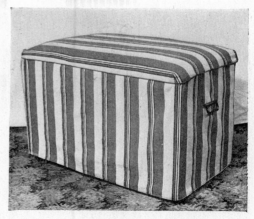

Photo F: Tailored cover in striped material for a box ottoman. Note the slots for the handles neatly placed

Pin up the cover on the wrong side and try it on the made-up divan to test the fit.

If a frill is needed, make a box-pleated one, as described on p. 143.

Box-Ottoman Covers

These often consist merely of a top piece with gathered frill (see p. 143) reaching the floor. The frill should be joined to the top by a piped seam (see p. 141).

A fitted cover uses less material than the frilled type. Stripes, as in photograph F, are particularly effective in this style, and with slots for the handles the ottoman can be lifted without removing the cover.

For an ottoman the size illustrated (31 in. by 18 in. by 21 in. high) you will require: $1\frac{3}{4}$ yd. of 48-in. wide plain or all-over patterned material; $\frac{1}{4}$ yd. contrasting fabric for piping and slots; 3 yd. white medium piping cord; and $\frac{1}{2}$ yd. of press-fastener type. Striped material needs $2\frac{1}{4}$ yd. the same width, but out of this, if wished, you can get enough for piping and slots.

Cut the lid piece first, with the stripes running lengthwise. If the lid is padded for a seat, as in the photograph, the piece must be large enough to cover this rather domed shape down to the top of the box, plus $\frac{3}{4}$-in. turnings on all edges. For an unpadded top, allow the lid size with the same turnings.

Cut two entire widths from selvedge to selvedge for the all-round border, making them 2 in. deeper than the box depth without lid. To make the border long enough

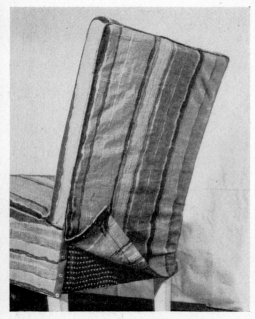

Photo E: The armless chair cover has a placket in one of its back seams for good fitting and a neat finish

A divan standing a little way off the floor may need a frilled cover, but for a low one the cover should be quite plain and made in only two pieces: (1) the top, (2) the collar, joined together with a piped seam (see p. 141), using extra thick piping cord.

Cut the top piece without a join, allowing $\frac{3}{4}$-in. turnings on all edges, and make the collar piece long enough (joining it if necessary) to go right round the frame and $1\frac{1}{2}$ in. to 2 in. deeper than the finished depth.

Photo G: Prepared press-fastener tape is used to provide a neat finish to the placket on the box ottoman cover. Raw edges are bound with matching tape or overcast

With drawing pins fix the border in position round the ottoman sides, so that its hem just clears the floor all round and the two ends meet at one back corner with a small overlap. Feeling through the border, carefully mark with pins on each end the position and length of the handle slot. Remember when doing this that the slot must be at the level, not of the handles as they hang down, but of their fixture points.

On no account cut the slits now. When you are sure the pins are accurately placed, unfasten the border from the box and carefully mark the slit positions and lengths, either in ink (with a ball-point pen) or in tacking, before removing the pins.

The slots are merely extra large bound buttonholes, made in a firm fabric matching the main stripe. Make them now exactly as for dressmaker's bound buttonholes.

Fit the top piece to the padded lid by putting it on wrong side out and pinning a fitting dart at each corner. Tack and stitch these darts from the edge inwards, tapering them away to a mere thread. Press them well, leaving the fold uncut. Make enough piping to encircle the lid, lay it along all edges of the lid piece and tack in place.

to encircle the box plus 2 in., you will also need part of the piece left on the width after cutting the top. Seam the border strips into one long piece, matching the stripes at the seams as accurately as possible to keep the pattern unbroken. Tack (do not stitch) a $\frac{1}{2}$-in. hem along the bottom edge of the whole border.

Don't be afraid to mix period and contemporary furniture—matching loose covers bring this Victorian sofa and modern armchair into complete harmony

A box-pleated frill looks effective on this divan cover with its matching curtains and cushion in vertical stripes. Horizontal built-in fitment, designed by David Griew for Chippendale Workshops, combines chest of drawers, bookcase and bedside table

Put the piped top back on the lid, inside out, accurately fitted on at the corners and with the stripes running straight. Place the border, also inside out, in position, with the handles through the slots, and pin the border turnings to the piped top turnings all round. Take care that the border hangs straight and unstrained everywhere and that the slots are not pulled out of position.

Remove the cover. First tack, then stitch top and border together, leaving the overlap placket edges projecting. Try on the cover right side out and note if the bottom hem is level all round. If not, adjust it where necessary and stitch it. Finish the placket edges with press-stud tape as already described for the chair cover and shown in photograph G. Overcast all raw edges or bind them with tape.

GENERAL HINTS

To save frequent washing of whole chair covers, "collar and cuff sets" can be made to protect the parts of the cover which get most quickly soiled—the inside top of the back and the arms.

The "collar" should fit over the top back and come down inside to the neck of the occupant.

The loose cover can be used as a pattern for this. Pipings and seams on the "collar" should be in the same places as on the cover. Hem lower edges.

"Cuffs" are made in the same way, to cover the front corners of the arms.

Repairs

If a small piece of material is required for patching, a strip 2 in. or 3 in. wide can be cut from the tuck-in between seat and back and replaced by an oddment of other material.

When a long stretch of piping is worn so that the white cord shows through, new piping must be inserted (see p. 141), but if only a small piece is rubbed, cut a 1½-in. bias strip 1 in. longer than the worn piece. Fold in each end, then fold one long edge in singly and hem it down to the cover just below the piping cord. Bring the strip over to cover the cord and hem down as close to the seam as possible.

CUSHIONS AND CUSHION COVERS

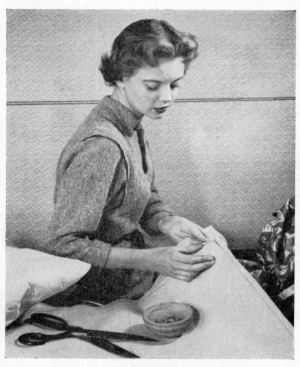

For a professional finish the seams of the cushion cover should slope slightly downward at the corners

When there is no time—or cash—to redecorate, you can always strike a new note with some gay cushion covers

N EW cushions or cushion covers can do a surprising amount to give fresh life to a room. As the modern trend is towards small, firm cushions in place of the larger, floppy ones, they can be quickly and inexpensively made. It is now possible to buy cushion pads, ready for covering, in a wide range of sizes and shapes, including small bolsters and neck rests, but for those who want to make their own, here is the correct method:

Cushion Making

Cushions can be filled with (*a*) kapok, (*b*) feathers or (*c*) Latex foam crumb, but whichever filling is used, a foundation case, under the cover, is necessary. With kapok or Latex foam crumb, any material can be used—unbleached calico, casement cloth, or parts of an old dress or curtain—but with feathers special down-proofed material or pillow ticking well rubbed over with beeswax on the wrong side is essential.

Kapok is usually sold in 1-lb. bags, and for an average cushion (say 17–20 in. square) this quantity is ample.

Foundation Covers for Kapok or Latex Foam Filling

Having decided what size you want to make your cushion, cut out the squares, allowing $\frac{1}{2}$-in. turnings all round. Make certain that both pieces are cut on the straight thread of the material, with accurate right-angle corners, but before stitching the two pieces together, take a pair of large, sharp scissors and, beginning about 3 in. from each corner and working towards the corner, slice off just a fraction of an inch of the edge so that there is a very slight downward slope towards each corner. This is a trade tip and much improves the look of the finished cushion.

Place the two pieces of material together, right sides touching and, beginning 2 in. from a corner, stitch all round, leaving $\frac{1}{2}$-in. turnings, to 2 in. beyond the last corner. Turn cover right side out, fill with kapok or Latex foam crumb, putting in a little at a time, turn in single turnings along the open edges and slip-stitch or overcast firmly together.

Filling with Feathers

Using down-proofed material (preferably down-proof cambric), make a foundation cover as for kapok filling, and either machine the seams or back-stitch closely by hand, afterwards overcasting all turnings to prevent leakage of feathers.

Open the top edge of the bag of down

very carefully, without disturbing the feathers, place the foundation cover over the opening, and tack it on to the bag of down (pleating up if one opening is larger than the other), then gently push the feathers from the bag into the cover. Do not fill too tightly—a down pillow should be soft.

After filling, sew up the opening very firmly and closely. Overcasting is best, but if you use slip-stitching, see that the slips are short and the stitches close together.

Cushion Covers

When making outer cushion covers, cut the two squares of material 1 in. longer each way than the foundation cover and slant off corners as already described for foundation covers.

The two pieces should either be piped together, or finished with mock self-piping. For piping instructions, see Loose Covers, p. 141. If contrasting piping is wanted, ready-prepared bias binding can be used. For self-piping, prepare strips as described on p. 141.

Mock self-piping is simply a French seam reversed so that the finished seam sticks out a little on the right side. Place the two squares of material together, right sides inwards touching each other. Seam together all round, leaving most of the fourth side open. Trim the turnings narrowly, turn the cover right side out, press seams and stitch again so as to enclose the turnings.

Cushion Cover Placket

If a cushion cover is likely to need frequent washing, it is best to finish one side with a placket and fastenings.

To make the placket, using self material or something as nearly matching it as possible, cut two straight strips, each 1 in. longer than the opening in the cushion cover. One strip should be $2\frac{1}{2}$ in., the other $1\frac{1}{2}$ in. wide.

Double the wider strip lengthwise, turn in its edge at each end to face, and stitch round the two ends and the fold. Fold in single turns to face along the remaining long edge. Sandwich between these turns the unpiped raw edge of the cushion opening and stitch in place from the right side. Face the piped edge of the opening by laying the narrower strip to it, stitching cover,

piping and strip together. Then fold down the strip on the wrong side as a facing and stitch down again along its other (turned-in) long edge. Make the ends of the two placket halves exactly the same length and cross-stitch these ends neatly together (see Fig. 1). At 2-in. intervals sew hooks to the piped facing and corresponding bar eyes to the unpiped side, arranging them so that, when the placket is closed, its under edge lies exactly along the inner edge of the piping. Fig. 2 shows a neat placket.

Boxed Oblong or Square Cushion Covers

Boxed cushions should always be filled with kapok or Latex foam and not down, for a firmer cushion better suited to this tailored type. A useful average size is 15–16 in. square, with a boxing strip of 3 in. (these measurements include $\frac{1}{2}$-in. turnings on all edges), for which you will need $\frac{3}{4}$ yd. of 36-in. material or $\frac{1}{2}$ yd. of double-width material. All the edges of a boxed cushion

When inserting down filling, the cushion cover is tacked on to the bag of down to prevent the feathers from flying about

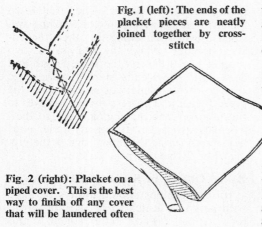

Fig. 1 (left): The ends of the plracket pieces are neatly joined together by cross-stitch

Fig. 2 (right): Placket on a piped cover. This is the best way to finish off any cover that will be laundered often

cover should be piped or bound in self or contrasting colour.

Cut out two squares or oblongs of the required size, but do not shave off the corners as suggested for an ordinary cushion cover. Next, cut out a straight boxing strip long enough to go right round the square or oblong top with 1 in. over. (Joins can be made in this strip if it is necessary to economise material. They should be pressed flat before the cover is made up.)

If the cover is to be piped, prepare piping and make up the cover as described for ordinary cushions, except that the edges of both upper and under surfaces are piped and the boxing strip is inserted between them. After seaming is in place, join the ends of the strip together with a neat vertical seam, making this somewhere along a side (where the opening comes) and not at a corner. Leave enough of the strip and under surface open to insert the cushion and make a placket as already described.

For bound edges, make up the cover in the usual way but stitch all seams on the *right* side, as if starting a French seam. Then neaten and decorate in one operation by trimming the seam turnings to an even $\frac{1}{4}$-in. width, doubling and tacking contrasting binding over them and stitching it on with matching cotton, both sides at once.

CHAIR PADS AND SQUABS

Sometimes a wooden chair or stool needs a flat cushion, either to give it a little extra height, to soften the hard surface, or merely to introduce a note of colour. Cushions of this type, which are made to be sat upon, are always known as pads, and their making varies slightly from that of ordinary cushions.

No foundation cover is needed for a pad, because the filling is made of material which can be lifted out in one piece when required. The correct stuffing is layers of some thick material cut to the exact size and shape, and sewn together so that they cannot shift in wear. The best filling is three or four layers of underlay carpet felt (six to eight layers if the cushion is boxed) or Latex foam sheet, which is specially clean and hygienic. Other satisfactory materials are old (but not too thin) blanket, especially Army blanket, travelling rug or cheap terry towelling.

A pad should fit the seat it is to cover exactly, following its curves and being indented to fit round the uprights of the chair back, if these exist, where they join the seat, so first make a paper pattern. Place kitchen paper or newspaper on the seat, hold it down with a weight and cut accurately all round the seat.

Use the paper pattern to cut out the filling layers, cutting exactly to the pattern. Place layers one on top of the other, quite flat, then tack, taking large stitches, first all round the edge and then across and across in several directions so that the layers cannot ruck up in wear.

Pads usually consist of top and underside only. Cut these from the paper pattern, allowing $\frac{1}{2}$-in. turnings on all edges. If a very thick pad is needed, the cover may be boxed, but this is not advisable if the seat is at all complicated in shape. Boxing for a pad should not be more than 2 in. wide, including turnings.

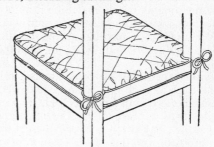

Fig. 3. Seat pad for a chair without arms. Tapes to tie round the uprights are sewn on at the two back corners

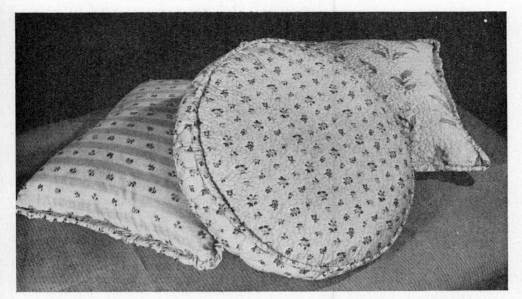

Ruched piping, made by cutting piping strips 1½ times the finished length, is a pleasing finish
for these sprigged covers in Rosebank chintz, used over ready-made Downland pads

Pipe and make up an ordinary pad cover as described for a square cushion cover or a boxed one (see p. 151), except that the *whole* of the edge which will go to the back of the chair (or one short end if the cover is for an oblong stool) should be left open for filling. If the cover is of washable material, finish this back edge with a placket (see p. 151) so that it is asily slipped on and off for laundering. On a boxed pad cover, the placket or opening should come between the boxing strip and the underside.

Place the padding flatly inside the cover, so that it fits everywhere, then sew up the open edge or fasten the placket.

A pad for a chair which has arms, even of the open kind, will usually stay in place of its own accord, but if the chair is armless, sew tapes to the two back corners of the pad and tie it on to the uprights of the back (see Fig. 3). For a stool, put tapes at diagonally opposite corners of the pad and tie round the legs.

Chairback Pads

An oblong head-rest for a wooden-backed chair can be made in the same way as an ordinary pad, but without a piped edging. After inserting the filling and closing the opening, secure the filling to the back half of the cover with a few stitches, as nearly invisible as possible, so that the filling cannot double up when the pad is hanging on the chair.

The pad can be secured to the chair with tape loops sewn on to the top corners of the pad and hung over the top posts of the chair back, or with a length of elastic from one top corner to the other.

Squabs

A squab is a very firm, mattress-like cushion used for a window-seat or for a wooden chair when extra height is necessary.

To make a squab you will need, as well as unbleached calico for the inner case and decorative material for the outer (but not detachable) cover, a mattress needle, leather tufts, rugging for stuffing (all these can be bought at an upholsterer's or from the soft furnishings department of any large store) and strong, fine string.

Cut a paper pattern the exact size of the seat for which the squab is wanted, and from this cut out four pieces (two for the inner case and two for the outer) with ½-in. turnings on all edges. Cut four boxing strips for the inner case, each 3 in. wide (including turnings) and as long as one side or end of the squab plus 1 in.

Place the pattern on the shaped inner case pieces and mark the actual seam lines in pencil round it. Pin the boxing strips into place between the top and bottom pieces, and exactly at each corner tack the boxing strip seams, straight and vertical. Then stitch these short seams, without unpinning them from top and bottom pieces more than just enough to get the stitching clear. Now tack the strips between top and bottom, over the pins, exactly along the pencil lines. When a corner is reached in this tacking, unpick the strip seam just to the depth of the turning and also slash the turning of the main piece to the same depth. Thus you will get good right-angle corners, which are important in a squab.

Leave most of the lower back edge of a chair-seat squab, or one end of a window-seat one, open for stuffing. Pick over the rugging, a little at a time, to break up any lumps and remove loose dust, then stuff the calico case as hard and tight as possible, putting in the rugging in handfuls and pushing it up well. Do not stint the stuffing and make sure that the corners are hard and tight. Sew up the opening firmly, then beat the squab with a carpet beater or stick so that it is flat and even all over.

The outer case is made in exactly the same way as the inner case, except that the seams are piped (see p. 141). If the squab is for a chair seat, tapes (to tie round the uprights of the chair back) should be stitched in with the upper seam at two back corners. Draw the outer case over the squab, fitting it exactly everywhere, and sew up the opening.

For tufting, first mark out on the squab, on both top and under side, where the tufts are to come. They should be about 6 in. apart and in rows also 6 in. apart. Alternate the dots in the rows so that each comes half-way between and below those in the previous line.

Thread a mattress needle with string and thrust it through from the top of the squab, at a pencil dot, to the corresponding dot on the underside. Re-insert it from the under side towards the top $\frac{1}{2}$ in. away from where it came through (see Fig. 4). As the needle is pointed at both ends, it is usually easier to make the return stab with the eye end. Pull the needle through on the top and, while there is still a loop of string left on the under side, slip a tuft under it. Then pull the string really tight so that it indents the under surface a little. The tuft is to give something strong to pull against and to prevent the string from cutting the cover.

On the top side, when first putting the needle through, leave only a short end of string sticking out. Put a tuft under this, knot the end and tie the string in the needle firmly together over the tuft and cut off with quite short ends. Tuft all the pencil marks in the same way, and the squab is ready for use (see Fig 5).

If it is essential that the squab should have a detachable cover, tufted through the inner case only, make the outer piped case as described above, leaving the whole of one side open. Insert the squab and sew up.

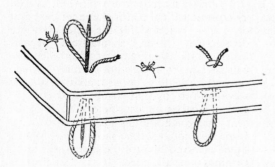

Fig. 4 (above): Fine string and a mattress needle, pointed at both ends, are used for tufting. The return stab is made with the eye end of needle

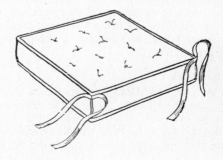

Fig. 5 (below): Completed squab for a chair without arms. The corner tapes are stitched in with the piping

THE ABC OF CURTAIN HANGING

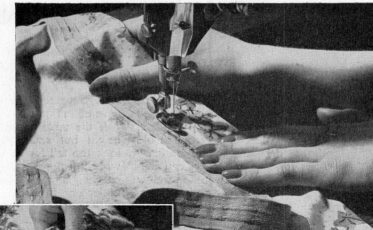

Right: turn down curtain top to the depth of heading required (usually $1\frac{1}{2}$ in.), place Rufflette tape in position and sew along top and bottom

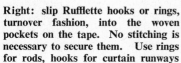

Left: knot the drawcords at one end, and pleat the curtain to required width by drawing up cords from the other end. Do not cut off surplus cord (it will be needed when the curtain is flattened for washing); knot and tuck surplus into heading

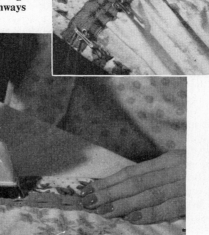

Right: slip Rufflette hooks or rings, turnover fashion, into the woven pockets on the tape. No stitching is necessary to secure them. Use rings for rods, hooks for curtain runways

For washing and ironing, slip out hooks or rings (left), untie drawcords, and pull curtains out flat. They are quickly gathered again by pulling up the drawcords

FRILLS FOR YOUR DRESSING TABLE

They add a sweetly feminine touch to a dainty kidney table or
transform an old piece of furniture into a thing of beauty

WHEN it is necessary to be economical with both space and money, a frilled dressing table can often work wonders. The foundation can be made from an old table or washstand—either the ordinary oblong shape or a corner one—or can consist merely of a shelf fixed over the window sill or to a convenient wall. Another space-saving idea is to buy a triangular clothes-hanging fitment already fitted with curtain rods and rings. One of these, fixed at dressing-table height and provided with correspondingly brief curtains, is ideal for a tiny bedroom. Kidney-shaped tables can be bought in white wood, and these always look well with frilled draperies, but they are relatively expensive.

There are various ways of treating the table-top. For easy cleaning, laminated plastic is best, or a sheet of heavy glass. If glass is used, a piece of the frill material should be placed under it unless the top is in very good condition and well painted or polished. An alternative method is to cover the top with the same material as the frills, either making the drapery all in one piece, with the frills attached, or making the top piece separately with a thickness border just deep enough to cover the frill tops.

If one side of the table is to stand against a wall, it is not essential to have frills along the back—an ungathered strip about 6 in. deep can be used instead. The advantage of having frills all round, even in this case, is that they can be reversed and will thus last longer.

When estimating the amount of material required, allow $1\frac{1}{2}$ times the measurement right round the table for a fairly substantial material such as cretonne; twice round for thinner materials, such as dress cottons; and $2\frac{1}{2}$ times round for thin materials such as organdie, curtain net or nylon.

The frills should be cut straight across the material from selvedge to selvedge. Having calculated how many of these widths will be necessary, add 2 in. to each strip for hem and turnings and allow

enough material for the top if this is to be covered in fabric.

If the table you are using is of normal height but small measurements, it may look too tall for its size. In this case you will get a prettier effect and cut the apparent height by using a double frill—the under one from the table-top to the floor and the one over it hanging from the top to from one-third to half the distance down.

If the table has a front drawer, arrange for two separate frills which meet at the centre front and can be easily pulled clear of the drawer when necessary, or give a knee-hole effect by placing the frills one on each side of the drawer.

Making the Frills

Cut out the necessary number of strips, allowing turnings suggested above, and seam selvedges together with good turnings (nicking these diagonally if the selvedges are tight and inclined to draw). Press the seams well, one turn-in each way. If joining widths without selvedge edges, a French seam is usually best.

Edges which are to meet in front, or to give a knee-hole effect, should be finished with narrow hems.

Screw two cuphooks into the back of the table just under its top rim and provide a wire spring rod which can be stretched round just under the rim, out of sight, from one hook to the other. Make a hem (casing) along the top of the frills deep enough to take the wire comfortably (about $\frac{1}{2}$ in.). Thread the wire through the casing, fix in position and then turn up a bottom hem on the frills so that they just clear the ground. Stitch and press this hem.

For double frills, join widths for both frills separately and make a hem round the shorter one. Place the shorter frill on top of the longer one and fold both top edges together into the top casing, so that one wire will take them both. Fix frills on to table and then turn up the bottom hem of the longer frill so that it just clears the floor.

To make frills attached to table top, cut widths for the frills and join them as described above. Cut a piece of matching material the size of the table-top with $\frac{3}{4}$-in. turnings all round. This is joined to the frill with a piping which follows the table edge exactly all round. The piping can either be of matching material or a contrast (in which case bias tape can be used). For piping instructions, see p. 141.

Dividing the Fullness

Gather the upper edge of the frill to fit the table-top piece. To make certain that the fullness is equally divided all round, first find the total number of inches right round your table-top. Thus, if the table is 30 in. long by 16 in. wide, $30 + 16 + 30 + 16$ gives a right-round measurement of 92 in. Divide this into four equal lengths of 23 in. each and mark these off with pins round the table-top edge. They will not come just at corners, but this does not matter.

Now, by folding in half and then in half again, divide the top edge of the frills also into four equal portions and mark also with pins. They will, of course, be much longer than the table-top divisions. If they are too long for each section to be gathered on one thread, it may be necessary to pin both table-top piece and frill in six equal divisions instead of four.

Gather each marked portion of the frill on a separate thread, leaving this loose and knotted at both ends for later adjustment. When all are gathered, tack the prepared piping round the table-top piece, raw edges facing outwards and flush with its raw edges. Draw up each gathering thread so that its section of the frill fits the corre-

Contemporary fabric by David Whitehead makes a charming "skirt" for an oak-faced kidney dressing table with triple mirror. The stool has Dunlopillo padded top, black metal legs. From William Perring of Kensington, London

sponding section of the top piece, tack in position, then stitch as close to the piping cord as possible.

When an all-in-one cover is to be knee-holed in front to accommodate a front drawer, leave the necessary space between the gathered portions and neaten the piped edge between them with a wrong-side facing.

Any scraps of material left over from dressing-table frills can be used to cover a stool to match or even a little lampshade to stand on the table.

157

MAKING A FITTED BEDSPREAD

With a made-to-measure cover, finished either with
a flounce or pleats, your bed will always look tidy

FITTED bedspreads can be made in various styles to suit the furnishing of the bedroom.

Use light-weight material for gathered or circular frill, medium-weight or heavy fabric for tailoring or pleating. Heavy fabric is best made with top and sides separate. Any fabric chosen should be guaranteed washable and "non-shrink." Otherwise buy a vat-dyed fabric with a close weave.

Before making up unguaranteed fabric, wash and iron a small piece, measuring before and after, to estimate the shrinkage per yard. If shrinkage is noticeable, allow extra material when cutting the bedspread and launder each piece before making up.

Many fabrics are sold quilted and plain, so that it is possible to buy quilted fabric for the top, and plain for the sides.

COVERING PILLOWS

Covering for pillows can be arranged in several ways with:

Gussets.—Stitch a triangular gusset at each side of the head of the bedspread between top and sides, with the wide end of each triangle to the end of the bedspread. The widest edge of each triangle should equal depth of pillows, plus ½-in. turnings on each side. The side of the gusset attached to the flounce must be cut straight along selvedge threads.

Wrap-over.—Allow extra length at top of bedspread to wrap round pillows. This extension piece must measure two and a half times width and depth of pillows, plus hem and turnings. Cut two straight pieces of the same length for ends, the width measuring depth of pillows plus hem with turnings, seam allowance and 2 in. tuck-in. Stitch a narrow hem round one end and side of each piece, and stitch one piece to each side of the extension with a flat seam. Hem the remaining end of each piece when finishing top.

Pillow-cases.—Make separate cases for each pillow. The bedspread can then be made to fit flat over the mattress from top to bottom. This is the simplest method, but uses more material.

BEDSPREAD WITH GATHERED FLOUNCE

The Top.—If possible, choose material wide enough to cover top of bed, allowing ½-in. turnings on either side. Measure length of mattress plus ½-in. turnings for bottom and 1½ in. for turnings and hem at top. Allow extra required for gussets, wrap-over or pillow-cases.

When narrow material is used, remember to allow for matching pattern when joining a figured fabric. Stitch the extra width in two pieces down each side so that two seams run down the top of the bedspread, equidistant from the centre. These seams can be flat or finished with piping. Neaten turnings by folding rough edges on to wrong side, and stitching close to the fold. Stitch in gussets, or side pieces of wrap-over.

The Gathered Flounce

Fabric Required.—Length: for a full flounce allow twice the total measurement of the edges of sides and bottom of the bedspread top; for medium fullness, one and three-quarter times. Depth: measure from top of mattress to floor, add about 2 in. for hem and ½-in. turnings top and bottom.

Cutting.—Cut strips of required depth so that selvedge edge runs up and down and weft along the flounce.

Making Up.—Cut off selvedge edges and stitch pieces together with flat seams. Neaten edges as already described. Turn in and stitch narrow hems at each end. Turn up bottom hem with ½-in. turnings and hand-stitch. Stitch-mark ½-in. turnings along top edge. Gather top with two rows of stitching, working first row along stitch-marking and second row a quarter of an inch below.

For Piping.—Cut 1½-wide strips of fabric on the cross, and stitch them together

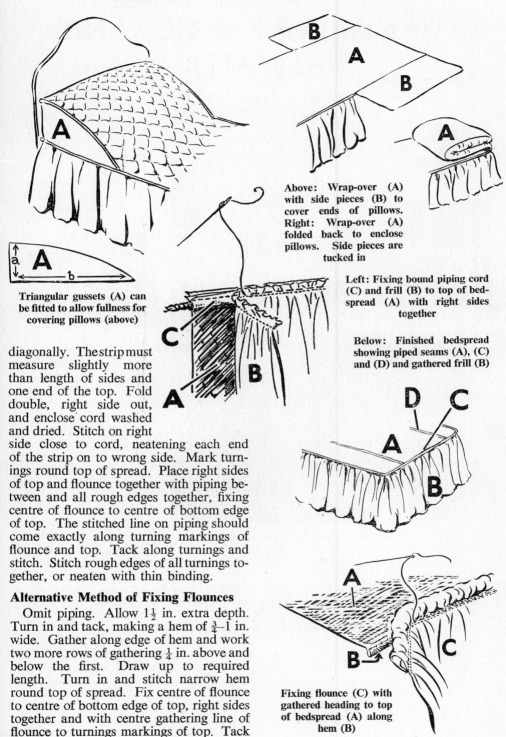

Triangular gussets (A) can be fitted to allow fullness for covering pillows (above)

Above: Wrap-over (A) with side pieces (B) to cover ends of pillows. Right: Wrap-over (A) folded back to enclose pillows. Side pieces are tucked in

Left: Fixing bound piping cord (C) and frill (B) to top of bedspread (A) with right sides together

Below: Finished bedspread showing piped seams (A), (C) and (D) and gathered frill (B)

diagonally. The strip must measure slightly more than length of sides and one end of the top. Fold double, right side out, and enclose cord washed and dried. Stitch on right side close to cord, neatening each end of the strip on to wrong side. Mark turnings round top of spread. Place right sides of top and flounce together with piping between and all rough edges together, fixing centre of flounce to centre of bottom edge of top. The stitched line on piping should come exactly along turning markings of flounce and top. Tack along turnings and stitch. Stitch rough edges of all turnings together, or neaten with thin binding.

Alternative Method of Fixing Flounces

Omit piping. Allow $1\frac{1}{2}$ in. extra depth. Turn in and tack, making a hem of $\frac{3}{4}$–1 in. wide. Gather along edge of hem and work two more rows of gathering $\frac{1}{4}$ in. above and below the first. Draw up to required length. Turn in and stitch narrow hem round top of spread. Fix centre of flounce to centre of bottom edge of top, right sides together and with centre gathering line of flounce to turnings markings of top. Tack and stitch together.

Fixing flounce (C) with gathered heading to top of bedspread (A) along hem (B)

159

FURNISHING FABRICS AND WALLPAPERS

From the wealth of modern design available, anyone can create an individual scheme unlikely to be seen anywhere else

Past and present in harmony—Crown wallpaper in pale yellow-green with gold motifs, Adam pelmet mouldings in Anaglypta painted gold, curtains in deep rose velour

recently a tremendous swing-over to wallpaper, now that the amateur decorator has mastered the art of applying this type of wall covering.

MODERN WALLPAPER

There is, of course, nothing new about this, and wallpaper has been manufactured in England for several hundred years. The revolution came, over a century ago, when a machine was invented capable of printing paper successfully, where previously it had been hand-printed. This didn't oust hand-printed papers entirely, but enlarged scope and output to meet the steadily increasing demand. To-day there is a tremendous choice of machine-printed wallpapers, reasonably priced, with a smaller output of hand-printed and more expensive papers for special work where lesser quantities are needed.

Wallpaper Finishes

In the manufacture of wallpaper to-day, almost any effect is possible, as is constantly being proved by the new finishes produced to meet contemporary tastes and needs.

What are known as textured papers maintain a steady popularity. You can choose a wallpaper giving the effect of linen, tweed, or the coarsely woven hessian;

TO all who are interested in home-making, there is no greater exhilaration than that of plannning new room schemes. Interior decoration, if not as changeable as feminine fashion, is quite as stimulating. It as surely has its trends, though blessedly these are subtler and more elastic, and a room newly decorated one year is not necessarily out of date the next.

The trend of room fashion gently changes with the new developments in fabric and wall treatments and their colour and design. There has, for instance, been

For those who find the unrelieved lines and functional design of modern furniture too stark for their liking, a charming traditional rose-spattered Alcosto carpet (left) softens the effect. It does not show footmarks, is luxuriously resilient and, being square, can be turned round occasionally to spread the wear.

Photos: Gordon McLeish

A MATTER OF TASTE...

"*I like to be new and different*"

his up-to-the-minute bed-
om has blue and white
eck linoleum on the floor
nd a matching headboard
u can make yourself. You
ed a 2 × 2 in. deal frame
ith 3 × ½ in. mahogany
rip edges; the linoleum is
ounted on hardboard. It
an be free standing or fixed
the wall. Furniture in
camore and the hand-
ainted box pyjama cases,
om Bowman Bros., London.

ne smart way of planning
room scheme is to start
ith the floor covering and
ork round that, whether it
carpet, lino, tiles or what
ou will. Here are two
ttractive examples—a sit-
ing room (above) and (right)
a bedroom.

The Italian influence—an elegant hall, left, has one wall papered in Palladio hand-printed "Sicilian Lion", the other in stripes from the Crown range, both in white and gold. A grey and black star is inset into the white linoleum, Madonna blue velvet curtains introduce a dash of colour.

Below, three very different floral treatments, all in Morton Sundour fabrics. 1. Stuart, a Jacobean design, in colourings taken from Queen Anne embroideries. 2. Trollius, named after one of the blooms in the colourful garlands of flowers and leaves. 3. Orchid, with the lovely Catleya finely drawn on a variety of grounds. In each case there is a wide choice of colourings.

another one will resemble heavy damask, and almost feel like it; another will have the look of quilted satin. If you want the appearance of leather, wood grain, rough cast or trowelled plaster, marble or stone, there is a wallpaper simulating these surfaces. Progress in machinery and the introduction of the embossing machine have made it possible to develop the many and interesting effects of these high and low relief surfaces.

Again the finish of wallpaper varies according to the printing process. Papers printed on engraved rollers have their colours prepared by a method different from that used for surface printing. Many of these papers are found in pattern books for halls, staircase walls and bathrooms, because this method of printing resists humidity and moisture.

A distinct advantage to-day are the surfaces devised for certain wallpapers that render them washable without imparting the hard, bright glaze of varnish. For nurseries, bathrooms, kitchens, cupboard lining, these are admirable and appropriately designed for these specialised purposes.

Wallpaper pieces, or the rolls as we know them, are approximately 21 in. wide. Each machine-printed roll is $11\frac{1}{2}$ yd. long, and each hand-printed roll measures 12 yd. in length.

The Breadth of Design

The thought behind present design is lively and versatile, and the impetus is, and always has been, that of current tastes, interests and events. Just as, long ago, the first importations of new woods and foreign goods, and the rise of furniture craftsmen with their individual styles, became factors in the design of those periods, we can trace the standards of to-day in contemporary design. There is a vigour and directness that typifies this age, with its emphasis on speed and its lack of "frills."

There is the direct influence of children and young people, who have considerably greater interest taken in their welfare now than ever before; a host of wallpaper designs cater specially for them in their different age groups.

The kitchen is no longer the servants' domain, but the housewife's workroom. And as such, the artist has been inspired to cater accordingly; wallpapers for kitchens are varied enough for any woman to choose a decoration that meets her needs and reflects her personality.

The trend for creating a feeling of outdoor living indoors has given rise to novelty papers, resembling bricks, wattle fencing, or bamboos, possibly inspired by the popularity of green pot plants in wall holders, pedestal troughs and so on, for indoor decoration.

But despite all these modern influences a vast storehouse of beautiful designs of former eras remains to delight us. Just as Adam fireplaces, Hepplewhite chairs and other period pieces, are treasured

An original cork-faced wallcovering called Cortex, imported from Spain, is in green, the curtains in blue floral Sanderlin fabric, carpet turquoise.
From Sanderson

Sophisticated floral paper—black roses on yellow and white—for a chimney breast, above, the fireplace covered with hardboard decorated with marble wallpaper. Both Crown papers

possessions to-day, so are the traditional designs of wallpapers and fabrics, and, wisely, the manufacturers preserve the old in new textures and new weaves. Florals, stripes, Adam ornamentation and Jacobean motifs are some of the older forms of design that never lose favour.

OTHER WALL COVERINGS

A further step in the embossing process is that which produces Lincrusta, in squares to allow for the much deeper relief. New effects and colours have been added, and Lincrusta tiles introduced. These come now in black, pink, pale blue and green, in addition to the white and cream tiles previously available.

Rollywood is a fascinating Scandinavian wall covering that can be hung on most surfaces to give interesting effects. It consists of thin strips of wood veneer, approximately $\frac{1}{4}$ in. wide, plaited together with strong cotton thread. Aspen, walnut, pine and mahogany are some of the woods used, and it can be bought in any length of either 4 ft. or 8 ft. width.

Jute canvas is specially treated to make

Lintex, a washable cotton-backed, plastic-fortified wall fabric in black and white is smart and practical for a kitchen above, with bright pineapple design paper in the breakfast corner. Crown

Below, an Italian style dining room has walls in white marble paper from the Crown range, black and white linoleum tiles, Dorice Tubular Furniture in black metal and plastic, simulating marble trimmed mauve-pink roses, touches of gold

"Canotex" wall covering a truly contemporary part of interior decoration, and it is supplied in modern colours. It is hardwearing, has a waterproof backing, and so can be brushed or scrubbed. There are many uses in the home for these few examples of the simple yet sophisticated trend in contemporary design.

A curtain in white Vetrona marquisette—the fabric made of glass—is used as a room divider in a pleasant contemporary show flat, right, furnished by Frederick Restall

Trellis design of ivy leaves (below) gives an outdoor feeling to an odd corner. Other walls are in green and white texture pattern paper. Crown

Although not for walls, Anaglypta should be mentioned here, as a further example of bold relief material. Again, it is made in squares and mainly in period style, for use on ceilings. One that has quite a modern look absorbs echo by the nature of its design, and the room with this ceiling is quiet.

FURNISHING FABRICS

Here again there is the same range of design and finish as in the wallpaper field, and again the printing processes are similar. The large selection of medium-priced fabrics are roller-printed and those that are

One of Sanderson's beautiful hand-painted Chinese panels, left, in shades of blue and green, with pleated pale blue-green silk on side walls, blue carpet

The light filters through Vetrona, the fabric made of glass, which is ideal for bedroom curtains. Those right are hand screen-printed with sword grass on a white ground

screen-printed include the more expensive ranges.

Sanderson fabrics and wallpapers are designed to co-relate, and at their magnificent London showrooms, where you can browse around to your heart's content, it is possible to plan a whole colour scheme—paintwork, paper and soft furnishings—and see them together before making the final choice.

In London, both Heal and Liberty have a constantly changing range of exclusive contemporary fabrics by leading designers.

Types of Fabric

Cotton, linen, rayon, wool, Terylene and even glass are used for furnishing fabrics, often in combinations. Lurex, a metallic thread, is added to cotton and woollen fabrics. Terylene makes particularly good net curtaining, which washes easily, drip-dries in no time and does not shrink or pull out of shape.

Vetrona, made of 100 per cent. glass filament, is a furnishing fabric that comes in many weaves and colours, including prints. Its great advantage is that it filters and re-

flects the light and so produces fascinating decorative effects. And, being made of glass, it is proof against moth, damp, smoke, fire, stains, fading and shrinking.

Another exciting fabric is called Lyfflon. With the authentic look and feel of the most luxurious velvet, it is non-absorbent and therefore resistant to all forms of stains because liquids and loose dirt simply stay on the surface without soaking in and only have to be wiped off with a damp cloth. Colours like pale lilac, lime and even white are perfectly practical in Lyfflon.

Whatever fabric you choose, take note of the finish and whether it is guaranteed against shrinkage, stretching and creasing, if it's proof against fading, stains and moths.

MODERN WEAVES

Below, two fabrics by modern designers, from Heal and Son Ltd., London—left, Crescendo by Giorgio Bay, an Italian student of architecture, and, right, Peony by Maj Nilsson, a Swedish girl who won first prize in a wallpaper competition

Above, Teasie by Jane Daniels, from Heal and Son Ltd., in a choice of eight colourways. Jane Daniels, who first intended to be a dentist, specialises in designs based on plant form and growth, lives in a cottage in the country

The contemporary design, above, machine-printed in black and white on kingfisher blue textured cotton, with its casual scribbly treatment, is characteristic of Rosebank fabrics

Left, an upholstery or curtain fabric woven with a white and black striped design on a pale rust ground. Also available in other colourways.
A Rosebank fabric

TRADITIONAL PATTERNS

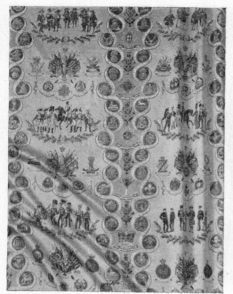

The Queen's Colours, above, designed by Philip Stockford, is gay with soldiers in period uniforms, banners and badges inscribed with regimental nicknames. Rosebank

Versailles, above, is a traditional heavy-weight cretonne roller printed in a variety of flower colours. Designed by George Willis, from Liberty of London

Left, the ever popular large floral from Rose-bank—ovals of white lilies and coloured foliage machine-printed on reversible textured cotton

Above, Sanderson's Rose Colonnade by Giorgio Cipriani, is in fourteen colourings in muted shades on heavy cotton or Terylene-cotton sheer

A design to make your mouth water—lemons, grapes, pears and foliage, heavy and luxuriant, grow on this vertically striped Rosebank Cubaleen in lovely colourings, including yellow-green and white on a black ground

CONTEMPORARY DESIGNS

Above, Estate, a modern design by Gio Ponti, a leading Italian architect, in green, gold, blue and red on white cotton and rayon mixture. Sanderson

Right, the liveliest fabric possible for a nursery is called Block Party. An exclusive Sanderson reproduction of an American original, in a choice of three dramatic colourings on cotton

Below, delightfully escapist is Rosebank's foliage design on textured cotton in lime, flame or hyacinth blue over-etched with black

Aptly named Big City, the ultra-modern Sanderson fabric, above, with its bold design of skyscrapers, comes in cinnamon, midnight blue and granite heavy cotton

Below, The Bait, another Sanderson American reproduction is of Christopher Marlowe's poem, "The Passionate Shepherd to his love," in black on white Everglazed chintz

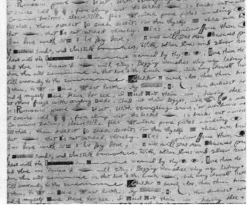

MAKE YOUR OWN EIDERDOWN

*And you will be sure of a lighter, warmer and more luxurious
one for your money, whatever quality filling you use*

THE main purpose of an eiderdown is to give the maximum of warmth with the minimum of weight, and because the lighter the filling the more expensive it is, you will have more luxury for your money if you make your own.

For the Filling

Various grades of filling can be bought all good drapers and stores, but the more expensive fillings may have to be ordered specially for you. In case of difficulty, write direct to The Downland Bedding Company, Ltd., Kirkby Trading Estate, Liverpool.

The following chart shows the quantities of the different types of filling needed for single-bed or double-bed eiderdowns:

For size: Eiderdown	Fine Duck Down	Grey Feathery Down	Down and Feather	Feather and Down	Common Feather
Single 6 ft. × 4 ft.	1¾ lb.	2¼ lb.	3 lb.	3½ lb	4½ lb.
Double 6 ft. × 5 ft.	2¼ lb.	3 lb.	3½ lb,	4 lb.	5 lb.

in pound bags. The most luxurious of all —Fine Duck Down—is more than five times as expensive as the cheapest—Common Feather, at 5s. a pound—but you will need more than twice the quantity of the cheaper filling.

Feather and Down and Common Feather are both easily obtainable from

The Inner Cover

An inner cover of down-proofed cambric is necessary with all fillings except the finest down, and even then a specially down-proofed material, such as Cubaleen, must be used for the eiderdown cover itself, otherwise the filling will push through. You can buy this attractive material in two widths, 36 in. and 50 in., but it is not proofed sufficiently to resist feathers. Down - proofed cambric can be purchased at drapers—width 48 in.

The Outer Cover

This is usually made from rayon taffeta, which is a strong and to a certain extent dust-resistant material. When estimating the material required, allow for ruching if this kind of edging is intended. Measure your combined edges. If you are

A home-made eiderdown can look just as professional as a bought one if you carefully follow the instructions for making

PAST AND PRESENT IN HARMONY

Showing how cherished pieces of antique furniture can be perfectly at home in contemporary settings

The Regency pedestal table and sturdy Windsor chair have been in the family for years, yet fit perfectly into this room with its contrasting walls in white distemper and tan-and-white stripes and the tweed-covered armchairs

IN nearly every home there is at least one cherished item of old furniture; not necessarily a genuine or valuable antique, but a period piece that has been in the family for a generation or two and for which someone has a sentimental affection. Perhaps in your house there are several such relics of the past. You wouldn't part with them for the world but, because of their presence, you feel you will never be able to go in for modern decorations and contemporary styles. In actual fact, you can quite easily have the best of both worlds in furnishing, because good design has a happy knack of going well with good design, whatever the period, as these four pages are specially designed to prove.

All the photographs were taken with the approval of the Council of Industrial Design, showing how one or more beautiful piece of antique furniture can blend perfectly into an up-to-date background and look at home alongside contemporary furnishings.

Two centuries keep company

A fine eighteenth-century tallboy (above) keeps good company with some very modern pieces—a beech and mahogany trolley, an oddly shaped occasional table, a deep chair covered in yellow and a simple contemporary lamp. Furniture by Liberty, London

Below, a bachelor girl's flat in the mid-twentieth century style—spacious, comfortable, functional. But the touch of distinction, the mark of personality, is given by the beautiful period dressing table and mirror and the dignified old grandfather clock

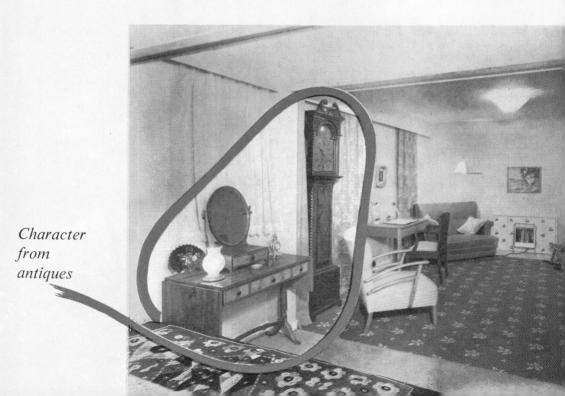

Character from antiques

*New
light
on an
old
bureau*

A fine old bureau-bookcase (above) looks quite at home beside a modern standard lamp and Gordon Russell's contemporary rosewood and mahogany sideboard. Black and white check covers the armchair, the wallpaper is blue and gold, the rug white

The Regency home (below) in London of a modern architect has two rooms opened into one, the chimney breasts blocked out with bookcases. The lovely ornate gilt mirror and clock contrast strikingly with the owner's own design for a steel and glass table, the built-in cupboards and the chairs by H. K. and Ernest Race

*Regency
background
to steel
and
glass
furniture*

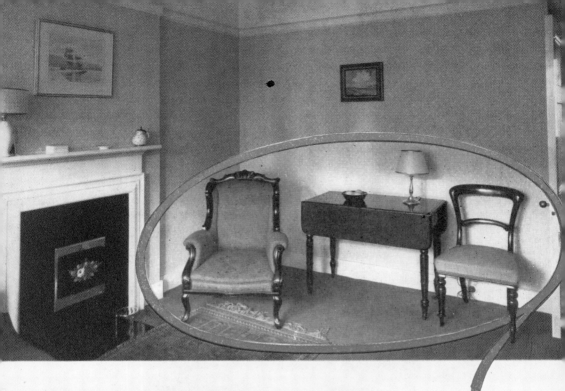

Don't despise Victorian !

This kind of Victorian furniture is still to be found in abundance, is practical, comfortable and solidly made. Put it in a contemporary setting, as above, with walls papered in a white fleur-de-lis design on grey, white paintwork and the minimum of ornament— and it can look delightful

The charm of strong contrast

Here the family heirloom is an unusual antique clock standing on a quaint old table. Lovely with the Victorian atmosphere echoed in the Venetian blind, the boot rack converted to a plant stand—and, in contrast, the modern chair, tables and fabrics. Liberty furniture

Choose a design that is not too complex, mark and stitch it first on the cambric inner cover, then pin it through to the right side of the outer covering and stitch

making a 6 ft. by 4 ft. eiderdown, this will be 20 ft. You will need approximately one and a half times this—30 ft. or 10 yd.—for the ruching. The strips should be 2½ in. wide. You need about ⅔ yd. of 36 in. wide or ½ yd. of 50 in.

NOTE: Make your eiderdown cover ½ in. smaller all round than the eiderdown inside. It fits better this way.

Making the Eiderdown

(1) Mark the design on the cambric inner cover, marking on the right side.

(2) Carefully fill the cover. To prevent the feathers flying about, pin the bag opening in the cambric cover and transfer the contents to the cover with a shake. Sew the opening with double thread.

(3) See that the filling is evenly distributed before beginning to stitch it into position. Stitch carefully, with close running stitches, or back stitches, along the pattern of your design. The inner eiderdown is now finished.

(4) Join up the strips for ruching. Fold them over piping cord, securing firmly at the beginning with a few strong stitches. Gather the folded strip over the piping cord, pulling up as you go. Pin the ruching to one piece of taffeta, on the right side, edge to edge, having ample cording at the corners. Make sure that each edge is rounded. When it is in position right round the piece, cut the cord and blind-pin the other side of the cover over the ruching, right sides together. Leave one of the narrow sides open to insert the eiderdown. Tack the other three sides firmly, then machine.

Turn the cover right side out, put in the eiderdown, Blind-stitch the open end of the cover, then lay the eiderdown flat on the table, push the corners and edges well into the edges of the cover, pin right round the border, pinning through so that both sides of cover and the eiderdown inside coincide. Feel for the stitched pattern on your eiderdown inside, and pin through here to hold cover and eiderdown together. Stitch along these lines.

RE-COVERING AN EIDERDOWN

This practical repair job is not beyond anybody who can
either use a sewing machine or work neat hand back-stitch

RE-COVERING an eiderdown is costly when done professionally, but can quite simply be done at home by anyone who knows how to use a sewing machine or how to work neat hand back-stitch. Accuracy and patience are necessary, since the job is a long one and the stitching must be exact, particularly if the design is at all elaborate.

An eiderdown covered in good-quality material will give many years' wear and should wash or clean satisfactorily. To provide variety in furnishing, it is a good plan to cover the two sides of the eiderdown in different materials, to match two sets of curtains. This presents no greater difficulties than using one fabric for the whole cover.

Preparation

If there is an inner lining, remove the top cover. Wash the eiderdown in tepid, soapy water or use a mild solution of soapless detergent, squeezing the feathers and fabric gently to remove dirt. Rinse in several waters and hang, out of doors if possible, to dry. Do not pass through the wringer, as the pressure of the rollers may break feathers, though it will not damage good down.

Cutting New Cover

Choose light-weight, closely-woven fabric. If the old covering is not featherproof, the new one must be; or an interlining of light-weight, featherproof cambric can be used under any light furnishing fabric. Suitable fabrics for the outer covering are feather-proof sateen, made in a wide range of colours, permanently glazed fine cotton in colourful patterns or plain colours, or rayon furnishing taffeta.

Measuring

Measure length and width of the eiderdown, allowing $\frac{1}{2}$-in. turnings on all sides, $\frac{1}{2}$-in. turnings on seams, fullness needed for feathers and extra for matching patterned fabric.

Amount of Fabric

For a single eiderdown, allow two lengths of 36-in. material, plus $1\frac{1}{2}$ yd. for a frill. Wider material will cut wastefully.

For a double eiderdown, allow four lengths of 36-in. material, plus 2 yd. for frill *or* three lengths of 48–50-in. material, from which there will be trimmings over for a frill.

Seaming

When covering a double eiderdown, measure two lengths of material for each side. Use one length down centre, cut the second length in two and join with flat seams to either side of the first to give the width required. Press seams flat with a warm iron. Mark centre of one side of new cover and pin to centre of eiderdown down the whole length. Pin cover along lines of stitching, working out from centre, and then work along pins with stitch-marking. Remove pins and cut stitch-marking.

Place the two sides of new cover with right sides together and pin firmly. Stitch-mark the pattern on to second side and cut through stitching. Mark in pattern on both sides of cover with tacking stitches. Tack the two pieces, right sides together, along the turnings, round three sides, leaving one end open.

If the edge is to be finished with bound cord or a frill, it must be inserted between the two pieces of fabric before tacking. Place frill or cord towards the centre and raw edges to edges of covering fabric. Pin and tack along turnings, fixing to one side only of open end. Machine-stitch along tacking.

Turn cover on to wrong side. Pin seam of closed end to end of eiderdown, placing pins on right side. Turn cover back on right side to first line of tack markings. Pin both sides of cover along tack markings to first line of stitching on eiderdown with pins on outside. Continue pinning out along each row of tacking to stitching of eiderdown, gradually turning cover back on to the right side. Turn in the raw edge of the open end and pin along stitching of frill. Tack and then hem neatly by hand. Tack-stitch right through eider-down and both sides of cover along all pinned lines. Remove pins and machine-stitch or hand back-stitch along all tackings. Remove tackings.

To Prepare Bound Cord

Cut crossway strips of fabric to measure the length of the four sides of the eiderdown, plus $\frac{1}{4}$-in. turnings at both ends of each strip. Seam the strips together with flat seams and join the two ends. Place piping cord on wrong side of centre of strip. Fold edges of strip together and tack close to cord to enclose it. When fixed in position, machine-stitch close to cord.

To Prepare Frill

Cut crossway strips, 2-in. wide, from both materials used for the double-sided eiderdown, having enough of each colour to measure twice the total length of the four edges of the eiderdown. Stitch the strips together as for binding. Place the two pieces right sides together and stitch along one side, allowing $\frac{1}{4}$-in. turnings. Stitch the two ends to-gether with a flat seam on the wrong side. Press seam open with turnings together. Turn on to right side, fold along seam and press. Stitch close to rough edges along second side. Gather by hand or pleat by machine along raw edges to the length of sides of eiderdown.

Alternatively, an eiderdown re-covered in a patterned fabric may have a frill of plain material picking up one of the colours in the print; or one covered in two plain colours to tone with differ-ent room schemes would look charming with a spotted or floral frill.

This shows how to pin the frill between the edges of the cover. Bound cord is fixed in the same way

Pinning the last row of tacking on the cover to the stitching of the eiderdown

The cover can be in two colours to blend with different colour schemes. The frill hides the second colour

HOW TO MAKE RUGS

Your feet sink luxuriously into these hand-made Turkish Pile
and Stitched Pile rugs, which are fun to make and remarkably
hard-wearing

MAKING your own rugs is a fascinating hobby and pile rugs made by the "Turkey" method are the most hard-wearing of all, with a rich deep pile which is most luxurious to walk on; they clean beautifully too. The basic idea is a surface of short lengths of wool knotted double over the threads of the canvas; these knots hold the wool firmly in position so that they never come out. The following instructions explain the method, which is very simple and quick to do.

TURKEY PILE RUGS

Materials Required

Patons Turkey Rug Wool, Turkey Check Canvas and a latch hook. A 27 × 54 in.

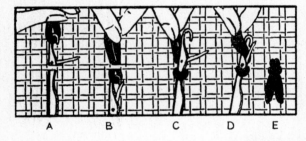

rug takes 1¾ yards of 27-in canvas. This will give the length of 24 blue squares required for the design, plus a minimum of 2 in. to turn across each end. A corresponding amount for turning should be allowed in other sizes. *Count off the number of squares required and turn over the surplus before beginning the design.*

Cutting the Wool

Use a Patwin Cutter or a Turkey Rug Gauge; either will cut the wool to the correct length of 2¾ in.

Making the Knot

FIRST METHOD: Insert the hook under the double weft (widthways) thread of canvas. Place wool on hook and double it equally; on this depends the evenness of the pile (A). Pull hook and wool until the latter is halfway through the hole. The latch will automatically close and make it easy for you to draw the wool through (B). Now push hook forward through the loop until the wool is behind the latch (C). Turn point of hook to the right and place the cut ends of wool into the crook (D). Pull hook through loop, bringing the cut ends with it. Give a slight pull to make the knot firm (E).

SECOND METHOD: Pile worked by this method lies the opposite way from that worked by the first method. Two people can work on the same rug, starting at opposite ends and working to the middle, one using the first and the other the second method. The completed pile will all lie in the same direction. One person alone

Making the knot—the first method is shown step by step, A to E, in the diagram left; the second method, for pile lying the opposite way, is shown below

can, by this method, work over empty canvas with the pile in front; by the first method the empty canvas is in front. Greater care is necessary to keep the pile even; the wool *must* be doubled equally on the hook:

1. Place wool, doubled equally on shaft of hook. Insert hook under the double

thread of canvas with hook turned to left. 2. Twist cut ends of loop *behind* the latch and across *under* the hook. 3. Pull hook through loop, bringing cut ends with it. 4. Give a slight pull to make the knot firm.

Working the Pile Fabric

Double the spare canvas upwards across the width at the starting edge. Work knots through the double thickness to give a neat,

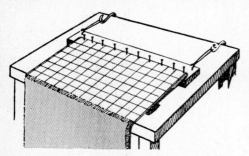

The simple and easily made frame, above, holds the unworked canvas firmly in position during the working of the rug

strong edge. Oval and semicircular rugs cannot be worked in this way; they require binding. Work from left to right in rows across the width of the canvas for both rectangular and semicircular rugs. Do not work separate blocks of pattern in colour.

Holding the Canvas of a Partly-worked Rug

Rugmakers using the First Method of making the knot, already described, will find the simple frame illustrated here worth making. It consists of a stout piece of wood about $\frac{3}{4}$ to 1 in. thick, 3 to 4 in. wide and slightly longer than the width of the canvas. Drive in a row of 2-in. nails at regular intervals, leaving about $1\frac{1}{2}$ in. of their length protruding. Screw in a cup hook at each end as shown in the diagram. Stretch a loop of string from each cup hook to a double hook which is hooked on to the table edge. This hook can be made or bought and should be padded with rag during use to prevent damage. The unworked canvas can be slipped on over the row of nails which will hold it firmly without damaging it.

Binding the selvedges with a firm plaited effect along the edge

As the pile is completed it is quite easy to remove the canvas from time to time and re-spike it in a fresh position.

Finishing

To make the surface even, clip any long ends with scissors. Wipe over with damp cloth to remove fluff.

Binding Stitch—Rectangular Rugs

Overcast with a matching shade the two ends worked through double canvas. Bind the selvedges with the stitch shown in the diagram. Hold rug wrong side towards you; work from left to right over the selvedge into the first row of holes. Insert needle, threaded with rug wool, into first hole and bring it towards you, leaving an end of about 3 in. to be darned in later. Work forward from 1st to 4th hole, then back to 2nd, and forward to fifth (movement shown in diagram), 3rd to 6th and so on.

This gives two stitches into every hole of the canvas and a firm plaited effect along the edge. Use the shade predominant at the edge or in the main background. It takes 3 oz. Patons Turkey Rug Wool to bind a 27 × 54 in. rug.

Binding Semicircular, Circular and Oval Rugs

Cut away surplus canvas from the finished rug but leave a margin of about $1\frac{3}{4}$ in. Turn this to the back. Choose a matching carpet braid, 2 in. wide, and stitch it round the outer edge, as close as possible to the pile, using linen thread. Pin down the inner edge of the braid, making flat pleats on the curves where necessary, and then stitch it. The straight edge of a semicircular rug can be oversewn with the binding stitch above. After sewing, press the braid under a damp cloth with a hot iron.

HOW TO MAKE A PILE RUG BY STITCHING

Two methods are described here of making pile rugs by stitching a series of loops on to a Turkey Check Canvas and then cutting through them to form the pile. Both methods produce a shorter pile than the Turkey Pile method.

Materials Required

Patons Turkey Rug Wool or Patons Pastella in the following quantities: Turkey Check Canvas; a blunt-ended rug needle; a Short Pile Gauge, which is a narrow slip of wood about $\frac{3}{8}$ in. wide.

Shape	Size	PATONS TURKEY R.W.		PATONS PASTELLA	
		Turkey Pile	Short Pile	Turkey Pile	Short Pile
Rectangular	27 × 54 in.	7¼ lb.	5¾ lb.	5 lb.	3¾ lb.
Rectangular	36 × 70 in.	11¾ lb.	9 lb.	8¼ lb.	6¼ lb.
Semicircular	27 × 54 in.	6 lb.	4¾ lb.	4¼ lb.	3¼ lb.
Semicircular	36 × 70 in.	9¼ lb.	7¼ lb.	6½ lb.	4¾ lb.
Oval	27 × 54 in.	6¼ lb.	4¾ lb.	4¼ lb.	3¼ lb.
Slip Mat	14 × 30 in.	2 lb.	1¾ lb.	1½ lb.	1¼ lb.
Staircarpet, per yard	18 in. wide	3 lb.	2¼ lb.	2 lb.*	1½ lb.*
Staircarpet, per yard	22 in. wide	4 lb.	3¼ lb.	3 lb.*	2 lb. 1 oz.*
Staircarpet, per yard	27 in. wide	4 lb. 13 oz.	3¾ lb.	3 lb. 6 oz.*	2½ lb.*
Body Carpet, per yard	36 in. wide	6 lb.	4 lb. 10 oz.	4¼ lb.	3 lb. 2 oz.

* Though weights of wool are given for stair carpet in Pastella, the Pastella shade range is not suitable for most stair carpets.

Short Pile Method

Lay the canvas on the table and weight it so that the row to be worked lies exactly along the edge. Thread the needle with a length of wool and start on the first row of the pattern, beginning in the bottom left-hand corner and working in rows from left to right on the double weft threads of the canvas (see diagrams below).

(1) Insert needle under the lower of the two double threads of canvas, draw wool through, and leave a free end as long as the width of the gauge.

(2) Hold free end firm and insert needle under upper thread, so that the wool lies to the right of the needle. Draw wool through.

(3) Lay gauge on canvas. Pass wool under and over gauge and insert needle under lower thread as in (1), but with wool to left of needle. Draw it through.

(4) Draw wool through and insert needle under upper thread as for (1), with wool to right of needle as in diagram. These two stitches make a firm knot from the left side of which, when the loop is cut, come two ends forming one unit or square of the design. Repeat these stitches all along the row, working the various colours as called for by the design. When changing colours, cut the end of wool in use to the same length as the loops.

(5) On reaching the end of the gauge, slip

The Short Pile method of making a rug by stitching shown in five simple stages, with the canvas lying flat on the table and weighted so that the row to be worked lies along the edge

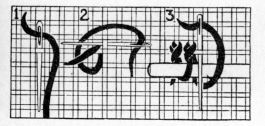

it out and cut completed loops with scissors.

Surrey Stitch (diagram above)

(1) Insert needle through one double thread of the canvas with the long end hanging to the right; pull needle through, leaving short end of wool.
(2) Hold end of wool with thumb of left hand and make a stitch through the lengthwise double thread. Pull needle through and give a downward tug to tighten the knot.
(3) Lay wooden gauge in position on top of wool and repeat movements in (1) and (2). Withdraw gauge and cut loops as work progresses.

Finishing

Rub over the completed pile fabric with the hands to remove loose fluff. Trim any long ends with scissors. Finish off the edges with the binding stitch, or with binding as described for Turkey Pile rugs.

Cross-stitch

The diagram just above for this basic stitch is self-explanatory. A cross is made over each intersection of the canvas. The stitch should be made in two movements: (1) push the needle through to the back of the canvas, and (2) pull needle through to front. The diagram shows the needle making the stitch in one movement only, but this is merely to show the two points between which the wool passes.

RAINY DAY RUG

An attractive opportunity for using up oddments of Turkey Rug Wool

Size: 27 × 56 in. without fringe.

Materials: 60 in. of Turkey Check Canvas, 27 in. wide; a blunt-ended Short Pile needle; 3 lb. Patons Turkey Rug Wool (the original used 1¼ lb. Bottle Green 947 and 1¾ lb. brightly coloured oddments).

The decorative Rainy Day rug is gaily striped in contemporary design and made in simple herringbone stitch, using up oddments of rug wool

How to Work the Rainy Day Rug

Turn 2 in. across each short end of the canvas and press them flat. As the rug is stitched *lengthways*, the first and last stitches of each row are worked through the double canvas. Thread the needle with about 36 in. of wool in any bright colour and run it in and out of the canvas for a few stitches before starting the first stitch of the first band of double herringbone. The stitch diagram shows how this is done in two journeys down the canvas over the first three *lengthways* double threads. On the second journey work a contrasting shade on top of the first row, filling in the spaces. Next work a band of double back-stitch over one double-thread in Bottle Green. Work alternate bands of double herring-bone and double back-stitch until the opposite selvedge is reached. Vary colours of double herringbone bands according to the wool you have available; keep the bands of double back-stitch in Bottle Green throughout. Work the binding stitch described on page 173 over the selvedge edges; cut the remaining wool into 8-in. lengths and knot them with a crochet hook into the folded ends to make a fringe.

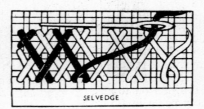

SELVEDGE

Reprinted from Rugcraft *by permission of Rugcraft Ltd.*

AQUAMARINE RUG

Turkey rugs may have intricate-looking patterned designs or be quite plain and in keeping with simpler modern furniture.

The design here really falls into both these camps, as it is simple enough for the plainest setting, yet the graceful, flowing design makes it an interesting design to do.

It is worked solidly by the "Turkey" method already described in a main shade of pretty moonstone blue or soft mastic fawn, with spots and lines in the contrasting colours from diagram opposite.

Aquamarine, a charming Turkey rug, looks lovely in moonstone blue or soft mastic fawn with spots and lines in contrasting colours. **Turn to next page for working diagram of this rug**

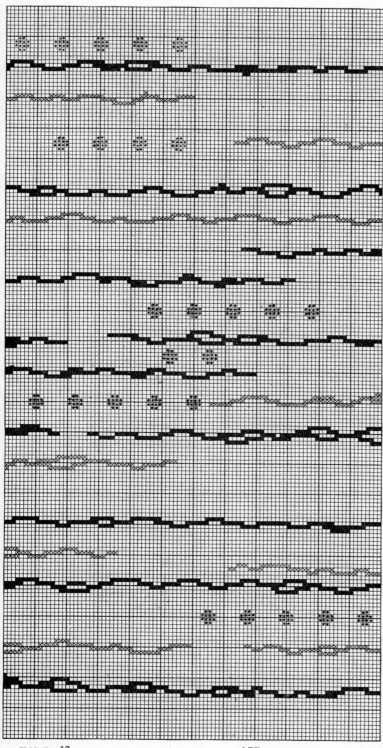

AQUAMARINE 27 × 54 IN.

This rectangular rug is illustrated on the previous page and the chart above shows the whole of the design. 1¼ yards of Turkey Check Canvas 27 in. wide will be required and Patons Turkey Rug Wool as follows:

FIRST SCHEME		
Moonstone	955	6¾ lb.
Dark Brown	942	½ lb.
Drab	901	¼ lb.
Cream	50	¼ lb.
		Total 7¾ lb.

KEY
☐ ■ ☒ ⊡

SECOND SCHEME	
Mastic	940
Dark Brown	942
Dark Rust	911
Cream	50

1

2

3

4

FIVE ENTICING PICTURES FOR A
FRAME UP!

That special snap you took, those interesting postcards,
some favourite prints, all find their way on to your walls

5

HOW TO MOUNT THE PICTURES

THE pictures photographed on this page show you how attractive you can make a display of inexpensive prints—or you can use enlargements of your favourite holiday snapshots.

No. 1.—A postcard reproduction of a painting by Utrillo is mounted on a dull pink background, after the original white border has been removed, and framed in natural polished light wood.

No. 2.—A reproduction of a wood engraving by Thomas Bewick is mounted on black paper, which is cut back to within ⅛ in. of the picture, then mounted on yellow card double the height and width of the print, and framed in black.

No. 3.—A reproduction of a black-and-white Whistler etching has a thin white border, is mounted on dark red and has a mahogany-coloured frame.

No. 4.—A small reproduction of French tapestry is cut out, leaving a thin white border, mounted on bright red book-binding linen, and framed in two shades of grey.

No. 5.—Three fashion prints are first mounted on a lavender card, then on white, cream and gold paper backed by thick strawboard and placed in a frame painted grey, lavender and white.

Choose your own favourite pictures for framing, then group them together as the charming focal point of a room—or up the stairs.

Materials Required. — Rule, steel straight-edge, cutting board, sharp knife, thick strawboard, rubber solution, coloured cards, patterned wallpapers, fancy wrapping papers, box papers, book-binding linen, according to taste, and a roll of gum strip.

Cut coloured card, fancy paper or linen to fit frame and fix to strawboard backing. Cut picture to size and mark its position on the mount, placing it slightly above centre. Marked area and the back of the picture should be lightly coated with solution. Then, when really tacky, stick together. Be careful that you do not cover beyond the surface to be stuck down.

Pieces of gum strip and a few panel pins at the back of the frame will hold the glass, mount and strawboard in position.

HOW TO MAKE AND FINISH THE FRAMES

Even the most inexperienced carpenter can tackle this job with flying colours.

Materials Required. —Mitre box and small tenon saw for cutting corners of frames as shown in Fig 3; casein glue; thin, strong cord; eight small wooden blocks 1 in. by $\frac{1}{2}$ in. by $\frac{1}{2}$ in.; $\frac{5}{8}$-in. panel pins; sandpaper; glass cut to size; wax; paint or stain; 12-in. ruler.

Types of Frame Moulding.—Fig. 1 shows sections of the most common types of simple mouldings you can buy ready made. You can also get decorated ones of the same proportions.

FIG 1

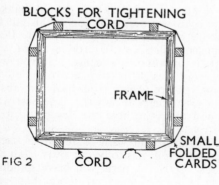

BLOCKS FOR TIGHTENING CORD

FRAME

FIG 2   CORD

SMALL FOLDED CARDS

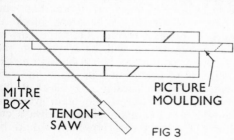

MITRE BOX

TENON SAW

PICTURE MOULDING

FIG 3

To mitre corners, cut moulding into lengths about 1 in. longer than sizes required. Mark out exact position of mitres on both ends of each length of moulding, and cut at 45 degrees on the mitre box with tenon saw—see Fig. 3.

Assemble frame without glue at first, to make sure the corners are at right angles. Put casein glue on each mitre and then assemble frame on a clean, flat surface.

Tie the cord around the frame, protecting each corner with a small piece of folded card—as in Fig. 2.

Slide the wooden blocks between the cord and the frame, one on each side of the corners to tighten the cord; they hold the frame together until the glue has set. A $\frac{5}{8}$-in. panel pin in each corner makes an extra safeguard, particularly with a heavy frame.

Cut a pattern about $\frac{1}{16}$ in. smaller in width and length than the space in the frame, and have glass cut to this size.

You should be able to get the various materials at your local hardware store.

To give a highly polished finish to your natural wood frame, use a good furniture polish. Apply tan boot polish twice for a mahogany stain.

PRINT YOUR OWN FABRICS

Even a child will quickly learn the technique of lino-printing,
described here by L. K. Donat, with designs by Jessie Renton

LINO-BLOCK printing is a modern development of the much older art of printing with wooden blocks. It is a simple technique which can be easily learned by anybody, including children, and which is particularly suitable for contemporary furnishings.

The tools needed are few and cheap, and are obtainable at most art and handicraft shops. Small pieces of linoleum for the blocks can be bought at any furnishing shop. It must be plain brown lino ¼ in. thick with a smooth surface. Cork lino is not suitable. You will need a sharp knife with a point, a handle for the lino cutter and three or more cutting blades, called gouges, which are obtainable in various shapes. To begin with, a V-gouge is required for cutting thin lines, a U-shaped gouge No. 10 for bigger spaces, and another, No. 8, for cutting away larger pieces of the background, will be sufficient.

You will also want a piece of wood or hardboard for holding down the block while printing. An even better way is to cut the hardboard to the same size as the block

A charming repetitive design for a cushion cover very much in the spirit of contemporary furnishings

and glue it on to its back. Very small lino-block patterns can be nailed or glued on to a cotton reel for handy printing. A wooden mallet or an ordinary hammer covered with a soft pad is used for beating the block when printing. A piece of glass, or a tile, is needed for mixing and thinning the coloured inks; a palette or kitchen knife; a rubber roller as sold for photographic purposes; a bottle of turpentine; a rag for cleaning up after printing; and oil colour specially prepared for printing on fabrics. This, as well as the thinning oil, can be bought in various-sized tubes.

Most Suitable Fabrics

The most suitable fabrics for lino-printing are: cottons, linen, silk and even thin wool, but rayon is less suitable. As most materials contain some dressing when new, they should be washed before they are used for printing. As the oil paints are specially prepared, they will wash very well and even mild detergents will not harm them—but it is better not to send them to the laundry.

The table on which you are going to print must be covered with an old blanket or rug for softness. On top of this put an oilcloth or thick layers of newspaper. If no table is available, use an ironing board.

It is important to realise that you will get your design in reverse, from left to right, except where you have an absolutely symmetrical pattern. The best way to test this is to hold the design up to a mirror.

Whatever you want to retain in background colour has to be cut away from the block. Only the parts you leave standing will print in colour. If more than one colour is wanted, a separate block is needed for each colour. Only the part of the design which will be wanted in the particular colour will be cut on each block. This has to correspond in shape and size with the original design. To check it, put one block on top of the other where it should fit. The main block is always cut first. The beginner, however, would be

The shapes of leaves, fruit and flowers will all suggest designs. The most effective are bold and simple like the pattern on the cloth (left) and the curtain border (right)

well advised to print in one colour only.

After having drawn the design on paper, prepare a lino-block of the right size to fit it To cut this from a larger piece of lino, mark the size with a pencil and score along the lines with a sharp-pointed knife. Do not try to cut through the lino but only make a cut through the surface. Bend back the lino along this cut. It will break easily and only the canvas at the back will need cutting.

It is much easier, especially in cold weather, to work on lino which has been slightly warmed in front of a fire. The right angle for using the lino-cutting tool will soon be found by practice. If it is held at too great an angle to the surface of the lino, the gouge will cut too deeply. If the angle is too shallow, the tool will slip. Try to work always in small sections, working from corner to centre. Cut the outline with the V-gouge, guiding this with the forefinger. Hold the block with the other hand *behind* your tool to avoid cutting your fingers.

If you want to cut curved lines, keep the tool in the right hand almost still and move the block with the left hand towards the tool. This makes a rounder line than you could achieve otherwise.

The patterns shown here demonstrate the effectiveness of bold and simple design. It will be easy to make up your own patterns and much more rewarding than copying somebody else's. The shapes of leaves, fruit and flowers alone will offer you an inexhaustible variety of design.

When using lino print in a repetitive pattern, it is advisable to work out the arrangement of the pattern first because, here again, an almost unlimited variety of effects can be produced by using the same pattern in various positions.

When your design is ready and cut, take a proof on a piece of paper before printing on to the fabric. Sometimes a design can be improved by adding or taking away part of the pattern.

A little printing ink is squeezed out on to the tile. A drop of thinner is added and, with the knife, worked into the ink. This is spread out with the roller until an even consistency is achieved. Using the roller, transfer the ink to the block. Never use the ink too thickly or the thin lines will clog.

Getting a Clear Print

On the material, spread out ready for printing on your working table, mark the size of the block with a pencil to help spacing. It will be found most convenient to work from left to right. Place the block on to the material, holding it down firmly with a piece of wood or hardboard, if this has not been fixed to the block previously. Hold the block in position with your left hand and strike the back four or five times sharply with the hammer.

Carefully raise the block to avoid smudging. After having rolled ink on it once more, make the next impression in the same way. Continue until the whole pattern is finished. As the inks dry very quickly, it is necessary to clean the block, roller and tile immediately with a rag moistened with turpentine. Hang up the work and let it dry overnight.

A frill of brown linen makes hinged doors on this home-made sideboard on which gay china can be effectively displayed

FURNISHING ON A SHOESTRING

A new sideboard for the lounge and a dainty dressing table for the spare room at very little cost

The other side of the tape is tacked or glued on to the wooden arms with the press fasteners corresponding.

A small cupboard knob screwed to the centre of each arm will enable the "doors" to be opened easily. Unless the bookcase has a solid back, narrow strips of wood or beading are glued along the backs of the shelves.

THE SIDEBOARD

THE sideboard sketched above was made from a small bookcase, two orange boxes and some dark-brown linen. The boxes were first rubbed down with emery paper, then screwed firmly together side by side. The insides were painted, but could equally well have been lined with wallpaper.

Next, hinge an arm of wood about 2 in. wide to the top outer sides of the boxes, the unhinged ends meeting in the centre.

A strip of linen (or cretonne) is then gathered to fit on to the two sides of the boxes and to run along the two arms of wood making the sideboard doors. The top of material is given a tacked hem of 1¾ in. and upholstery tape containing large press fasteners sewn along the base of hem.

THE DRESSING TABLE

The dressing table is made in very much the same way, but choose one of the dainty chintzes, furnishing satins or brocades for the frill. The table consists of two orange boxes and a length of strong glass (or painted wood) about 4 ft. long and wide enough to cover the box tops. The boxes are not fixed together, but stand at each

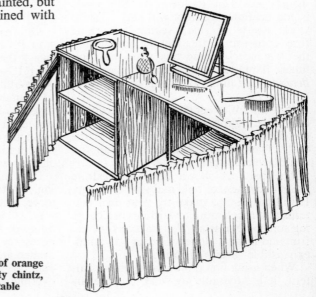

A sheet of glass on top of a couple of orange boxes, with a gathered frill of pretty chintz, and you have a dainty dressing table

182

end of the glass, supporting it. They are prepared in the same way as for the sideboard and lined with pretty wallpaper. Unless the sides are fairly thick and strong, you will have to reinforce the side that takes the long hinges needed to support the arms, which are just about twice the length of the sideboard ones, or it can have doors just across the boxes, leaving the centre open.

The tops and the sides facing inwards are covered with material, attached with drawing pins for easy removal. The frill is made as for the sideboard, extending right round the outer side as well as along the front and must be really full. The minimum length along the top edge should be at least 2 yd., so about 1½ yd. of 36-in. material is needed for each arm.

The frill is put on with press-stud tape, as for the sideboard, and the top should come slightly above the edge of the dressing-table top.

Two more bright ideas for newly-weds with little money to spend—a bedroom (or bathroom) rug and cushion knitted in dishcloth yarn and candlewick

THE STRIPED RUG AND CUSHION

Soft furnishings to make from the cheapest possible material—dishcloth yarn.

The Rug

Knitting tension.—5 stitches to 2 in. in width. *Materials.*—1 pair of needles size 0; 1 lb. thick dishcloth yarn. The coloured stripes are introduced by working some of the rows in contrasting candlewick, which has fast colours—quantities according to width of stripes. *Measurements.*—Length, 31 in. Width, 18 in.

To Make

Cast on 45 stitches loosely. **1st row:** Knit. **2nd row:** Purl. **3rd row:** Knit. **4th row:** Work in loop stitch as follows: Insert needle into first stitch as if for a knit stitch. Place first finger of left hand behind needles at this point. Wind wool

twice in anti-clockwise direction round both this finger and top of inserted needle. Then pass wool upwards again and round this needle's point as for a knit stitch. Draw loops through and slip them on to left-hand needle. Knit them together. As this loop stitch is completed, pull down loops with left hand in order to tighten up work.

These four rows make the pattern. Repeat this pattern until rug measures about 31 in., and finish with three stocking-stitch rows. Cast off.

Making Up

Back rug with hessian, inserting, if possible, a piece of old carpet between the two thicknesses for extra stiffness. Remember to remove this carpet interlining when the rug is washed.

The Cushion

Materials.—1½ lb. dishcloth yarn for two sides, ¾ lb. for one only. Candlewick in colours for stripes. *Measurements.*—20 in. × 20 in.

To Make

Cast on 50 stitches. Work exactly as for rug, finishing with the three rows of stocking stitch. If both sides of the cushion are knitted, sew three edges together and insert sliding fastener in fourth. Otherwise a coloured material can be used for the cushion back.

MADE FROM BAMBOO

Three delightful little presents you can make for your own home
—or somebody else's—in an hour or two

To make the opposite corner unit, pass the wire through the second set of canes, starting at the top. Knot the wire securely at the end.

Knot the second length of the wire. Interweave the loose ends of cane to form the other two corners, and thread with wire as before. Cover the exposed wire with raffia, using blanket-stitch for an inch at the beginning and end, and simply binding in between. Buttonhole round the ring with raffia, and cover the wire knots with raffia.

UMBRELLA STAND

Materials required: 16 bamboo canes, 24 in. long.

Cane, 11 in. long.

5 yd. strong flexible wire. 1 small oblong baking tin. Raffia.

Bend 3 yd. wire in half and twist at the bend to form loop with which to attach stand to wall. Continue to twist for 1½ in., then place a cane between wires and twist again about nine times before adding another cane. Continue until 15 canes are wired into position. Cut away the end of one piece of wire, and with the other end make a loop to match the first one, doubling back to finish with last twist (this procedure is shown in detail in the diagram left).

Without making end loops, and using remaining wire, wire

HANGING BASKET

Materials required: 2 lengths single bell-wire, 2 yd. long.

1 ring for hanging.

Raffia.

Cane cut to following sizes: 4 pieces of 9 in., 4 of 8½ in., 4 of 8 in., 4 of 7½ in., 4 of 7 in., 4 of 6½ in., 4 of 6 in., 4 of 5½ in., 4 of 5 in.

Drill a hole ½ in. from each end through all the pieces of cane. Knot an end of one piece of wire securely, so that it cannot slip through the hole, and thread it through two pieces of cane of each measurement, starting at 5 in., and ending with the 9 in. This makes one corner unit.

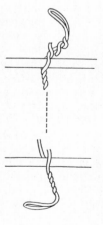

canes together about 6 in. from the other end, leaving about $\frac{1}{2}$ in. between each so that they fan out. Bind the wire with raffia. When necessary, knot the raffia and bind in the loose ends.

Place 24-in. cane level with top wire and bind in position beside wire loops. Bind 11-in. piece to outside canes at level of lower wire.

Place the baking tin so that it is held in place by the lower cross-bar and makes a drip tray.

BOOK-RACK

Materials required: 2 pieces of cane 24 in. long; 2 pieces 12 in. long; 4 pieces 10 in. long; 40 pieces 8 in. long.

4 pieces strong, flexible wire, each $1\frac{1}{2}$ in. long, 1 piece 22 in. long.

Raffia.

4 pencil-eraser rubber tips.

Drill holes 2 in. from one end of each 10-in. piece of cane; 1 in. from one end of each 8-in. piece, 2 in. from each end of each 12-in. piece and 1 in. from each end of 24-in. piece.

Thread wire through two 10-in. pieces, then through the 8-in. pieces, then through remaining 10-in. pieces. Twist the ends of wire over bamboo and bind with raffia. Bind the other ends of the cane alternately to 24-in. bars with raffia.

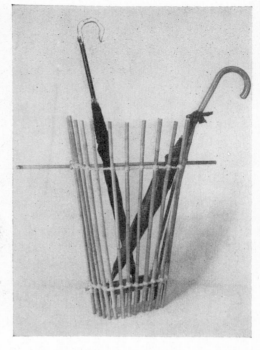

Rest the 12-in. bar across the top of side bars and secure with short wires through holes. Bind with raffia to cover the wire.

To prevent scratching furniture, put pencil-eraser rubber tips over ends of canes forming feet. With a strip of wood, or better still, a long oblong meat tin or enamel dish inside to support flower-pots, this rack can also be used as a plant-stand.

An excellent addition to a modern sitting room, this bamboo rack can be used either for books or magazines, will stand on floor or table

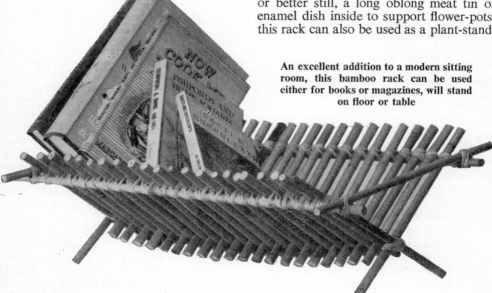

CHRISTMAS PARTY DECORATIONS

Simple directions for making these amusing novelties for entertaining either adults or children, devised by Joan Wickes

THE CHRISTMAS LOG (above)

Materials required.—1 log (of the long, round variety about 1 foot long). 3 or 4 fir cones. Holly. 2 candles. Cotton wool. Red ribbon. Glue. Small piece of yellow and small piece of red felt or paper.

Method.—Try to find a log which stands firmly on its side. If this is impossible, saw off a thin layer on the under side or strip off some of the bark to ensure a steady base.

Scoop out a long, narrow trough in the centre of the log, leaving about two inches untouched at each end. This need not be very accurate or neat, as the decorations can easily be arranged to cover any roughness. Hammer and chisel do the job well in a matter of 10 minutes.

Fix the candles at one end with glue and pad round with cotton wool. Also wedge in a small branch of holly behind the candles, making sure, of course, that, when the candles are lit, the holly is not in the path of the flame. Fill in the remainder of the trough with fir cones, holly and cotton wool. Arrange one piece of holly to hang over the side of the log and tie a piece of red ribbon on to this.

The little owl is easily assembled from two fir cones. Cut the pointed end off each. Stick the two cones together with glue, the face being the rounded end of one cone. Decorate with eyes of yellow felt with black centres and a nose of red felt, glued on. Tie a ribbon "scarf" round his neck and make a hat from any coloured piece of paper.

186

MOCK CHRISTMAS CAKE (right)

Materials required.—Large round tin with lid. Silver cake base. White paint. Small crackers. Cake frill and ribbon. Cotton wool. 2 candles. Cake decorations. Christmas string. Glue.

Method.—Paint the tin white and allow to dry. Stand the tin on the cake base and stick the small crackers round the base. Tie the frill and ribbon round the tin. For mock icing tie a long strip of cotton wool at equal distances (approximately 1 in. apart) with festive string. Glue the "icing" round the top rim of the tin. Decorate the top with the cake decorations, candles, etc., and glue firmly in place. Place the gifts inside the tin.

Apart from the painting of the tin, the "cake" is easily assembled in half an hour, and looks very realistic.

A delightfully original table centre for the Christmas tea-table. The top is lifted to reveal gifts for all the family

FESTIVE BOTTLE TOP (left)

Materials required.—Green felt or crêpe paper. 2 quarto sheets of stiff paper. Small piece of red felt or paper for tub. Glue. Miniature Christmas tree decorations, silver paper, etc.

Method.—The tree can be made any size, according to the height of the bottle it is to decorate.

From the two sheets of stiff paper draw and cut A and B (identical). Place A and B on the green felt, draw round the edges and cut out. Repeat. Take the two A's, place together with the paper pattern in the middle and stick all firmly together. Fold down the centre. Repeat again with the two B's. Firmly glue one folded half of A to one half of B.

The size of the tub is governed by the neck of the bottle, and should fit it snugly over the neck. Cut out tub (C) and join sides. Slip the tree into the tub and pad with a little cotton wool. Stick or stitch on cracker charms and fancy shapes cut from silver paper.

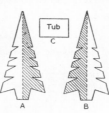

The little diagrams (right) show how to cut out the tree and tub for the gay bottle top (above)—an ideal present for Father

187

A charming "fancy dress" to cover up a gift—the Snow House would be nice for Mother

SANTA'S BOOT
(below)

Materials required.—Cardboard. Black and red felt or crêpe paper. Glue. Ribbon. Cotton wool.

Method. — Using patterns shown in diagrams below, cut out the sole of the boot A from the cardboard. Cut out B, C, D and E from the black felt. Stick A on to C, the end of C coming under the sole to form the back of the boot. Stitch B right round the sole to form the sides of the boot. D, curved and stitched to B and C, forms the leg of the boot. E forms the top of the boot and the tongue, and is easily stitched into place on B and D. Cut out a strip of red felt, F, and stitch round the top of the leg of the boot. Add a bow of ribbon on top of the tongue and the boot is complete.

Stick firmly to a cardboard base covered with cotton wool and fill with gifts.

THE SNOW HOUSE (above)

The actual size is governed by the size of the gift to be concealed in the stalk.

Materials required.—3 sheets of thick quarto paper or thin card. Fawn felt. Small pieces of coloured felt or paper. Cotton wool. Various decorations. Glue.

Method.—From diagram below of Toadstool top, cut A from the thin card; cut

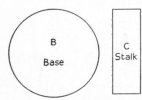
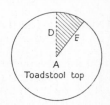

along D to the centre; overlap D to E and stick firmly with glue. Smear A with glue and cover with cotton wool. This now forms the shape of the toadstool top. Cut out the base B, smear with glue and cover with cotton wool. Cut C from the fawn felt and stick pattern and felt together. Bend round and stitch to form cylinder. Glue C to base. Add door and window in coloured felt, snowman, robin, tree and any other decorations available. The toadstool top is lifted and the gift found hidden in the stalk.

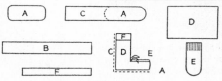

The boot can be made in any size. The paper patterns (left) are in proportion and can be enlarged accordingly

For every gift on the party table a little figure to hide it—here are the Snowman, concealing
Tom's present, and Father Christmas with Jane's hidden under his robes

THE SNOWMAN (above)

The size of the snowman depends on the size of the gift to be covered.

Materials required.—Thin white card. Cotton wool. Black and red felt or crêpe paper. Glue. Newspaper.

Method.—Using diagram below, cut A from the white card. Fold along the line C and cut along the dotted lines. Stitch D and E together to form cylinder. Dab the outside with glue and cover carefully with cotton wool. Cut out B, which fits the top of the cylinder, stick in place and cover with cotton wool. For the head, roll a piece of newspaper into a ball, smear with glue and cover with cotton wool. Stick head to body. Cut out gloves, boots, buttons, eyes and eyebrows in black felt or paper and stick into place. Add nose, mouth and scarf in red and add black top hat, easily made of black felt.

FATHER CHRISTMAS (above)

Materials required.—2 sheets of thin cardboard. Scarlet felt, or crêpe paper. Small piece of pink and of black felt, or crêpe paper. Cotton wool. Glue. Red cotton.

Method.—Using diagrams below, cut out A in cardboard, place on scarlet felt and cut out. Stick the pattern and felt together. Bend A round and stitch D to E with red cotton. The body is now formed. Cut C from the pink felt or crêpe paper, add eyes (black), nose and mouth (red) and stick in place with glue. Bend F and G, about 1 in from the top, round the scarlet conical body. Stick on cotton wool hair, beard and moustache.

Cut B from cardboard, place on red felt and cut two identical pieces. Stick one piece on each side of pattern B. Curl the cone round and stitch at appropriate height. Glue buttons and gloves of black in place and trim gown with cotton wool.

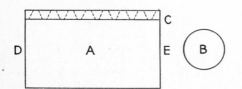

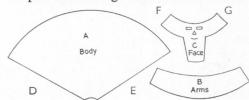

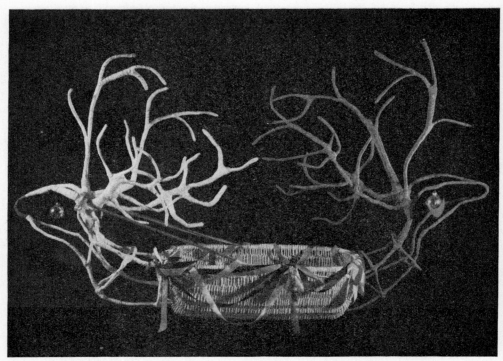

Both reindeer are made of wire: Rudolf, on the left, being covered in white silk, friend, on the right, with red—and in the middle is a basket for the party gifts and crackers

MEET RUDOLF–AND FRIEND

What more suitable to the festive season than a pair of tame
reindeer to deliver the gifts?   And they are simple to make

RUDOLF is, of course, the one with the red nose, and he is rather less elegant than friend because he was made first, and you improve with practice. The overall length is 6 ft. 6 in. from nose-tip to nose-tip, and the antlers themselves are about 2 ft. 6 in. high. They are quite simple to make and, apart from the actual materials (wire, cotton wool and fabric), all you need is patience and a fair amount of time.

1½–2 yd. of 36-in. wide cheap white silk will make Rudolf and the same amount of red is required for friend. One could, however, use up any remnants from dressmaking.

The reindeer's antlers are made from a strong but easy-to-bend wire; the face and neck of a very strong tough wire with sufficient strength to support the antlers. If you do not possess a suitable basket, you could make a simple one of wire.

There are four sets of antlers, each of which is composed of a double branch, and these double branches are bent all in one piece. You should leave a good 2 ft. spare wire at each end for attaching to the head shape.

Having made the wire shapes, you will find it necessary to add stiffeners of the strong wire, as shown in the diagram, to keep the antlers rigid. For ease of handling, wrap the antlers before attaching them to the head, binding them first with cotton wool, and then with long strips of bias-cut fabric, about 1½ in. wide. If you bind as for a bandage, there is no need to sew on each new piece, but the end of each previous piece should be secured with a few firm stitches to prevent the material from slipping.

The next step is to fix the head and neck to the basket, which is done quite simply (though it needs strong hands) by pushing the ends of the wire through convenient holes, bending them up and lashing with a single twist of soft wire. Then attach the antlers to the head by twisting the spare 2 ft. of soft wire you left for this purpose round and round the strong wire. When you have two sets of antlers and two head outlines fixed at one end of the basket, join them at the nose (string will do for this) and then across the top of the head between the antlers with soft wire. Use soft wire also for forming the ring stiffeners round the neck, taking one turn as tightly as you can round each of the four pieces of wire which make the neck outline.

When the heads are rigidly fixed, complete the wrapping with cotton wool and fabric. The eyes are simply coloured Christmas balls—a gold one for Rudolf and a silver one for friend.

A Christmas tree can be made in the same way, using a large bough culled from the garden, binding it first with cotton wool and then quite haphazardly with a variety of fabrics. The result is very colourful and most effective.

You can either bind such a tree with plain materials in scarlet, green and white to go with Christmas decorations, or in more unusual colours to go with your room scheme—or better still, you can use some of everything available in your "pieces bag," including prints, plains, stripes, spots of all the colours in the rainbow. Children love these gay trees and will help to decorate them.

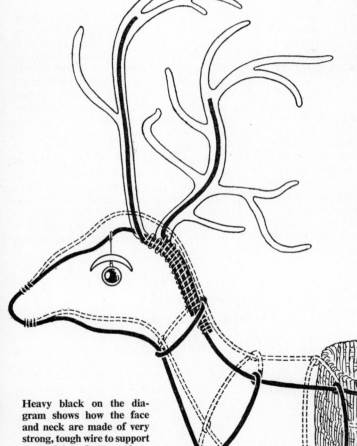

Heavy black on the diagram shows how the face and neck are made of very strong, tough wire to support the weight of the antlers; stiffeners of the strong wire are used to keep the antler rigid; also how antlers are attached to head by twisting soft wire round and round

PARTY GAMES

*A variety of light-hearted suggestions for keeping your guests entertained,
assuming they are grown-up. If not, see chapter on "Children's Parties"*

HELLO, hosts and hostesses! If you plan to have lots of fun at your parties, you will almost certainly prepare for a games session. The following suggestions have been collected from known "winners" and are offered to help you choose a programme to suit all comers and rooms of all sizes.

ICE-BREAKERS

It's rarely that all guests already know each other: some of these games will quickly get strangers talking and fill in the awkward time when guests are arriving and you have to hover between front door and party room.

What's Your Number?

Prepare a small numbered card for each man guest and a similar card for each woman; put the men's into one box and the women's into another. As each guest arrives, he or she picks a number at random from the correct box. Tell them they are to fill in the next few minutes asking each other, "What's your number?" When a pair meet they are to say, "Hello, how are you?" They will probably do this in unison, laugh—and go on from there.

Odd or Even

Hand each arrival six dried beans, peas, buttons or anything convenient to hold. Their instructions are to put a few into a clenched hand and go about asking, "Odd or even?", holding out their fist. All challenged must make a guess. If it is right, they claim the beans offered; if wrong, they hand over an equivalent number. If a guest loses all his beans, he still carries on, his empty clenched hand counting as "even." Allow the last guest to mingle in play for a minute or two, then ask all to count up their beans—and declare the holder of the most the winner.

Taking Particulars

Give each arriving guest paper and pencil and instructions that, until the gong goes (or some signal), they are to write down the name, address and occupation of as many guests as possible. By the time you have welcomed the last guest and allowed them a few minutes to join in, a complete thaw should have taken place.

After the ice-breakers, team games are a good idea for consolidating the thaw. First some ideas for pairing the guests when necessary:
(1) Send the men out of the room, number each woman consecutively from one upwards. Each man comes in in turn, calls a number and claims his lady.
(2) Hand a slip of card, face down, to each guest. Each card should bear a single word that has a well-known complement—e.g. Salmon and Cucumber; Knife and Fork; Darby and Joan; and so on. At a given signal, all read out the words and pair up.
(3) Possible for the room with a screen big enough to hide all the girls behind it. Once hidden, give each girl a small ball of string. She holds the free end and at a given signal all balls are thrown over the screen. Each man catches a ball and claims the girl on the other end.

TEAM GAMES

Now for games:

Walking on Hot Bricks

Guests are paired into teams of one man and one girl, and the pairs line up at one end of the room. Each girl is given two "bricks" to stand on—these should be fairly thick blocks of newspaper, or bundles of magazines (securely fastened together with sticky tape) measuring about 9 in. by 12 in. At the starting signal, each man kneels and moves forward one of his partner's bricks and she must step on to it. Then the other brick is moved, and so on, until one team arrives at the finishing line at the other end of the room. If a girl comes off a brick, she and her partner must go back to the beginning. Sounds easy, but just try it—and have a prize for the winning team.

Picking up Nuts

Place your guests in two mixed teams facing each other. At the top of each team, stand a dish of nuts (Brazils or walnuts preferably) on a chair, the number of nuts to equal the number of players. Each player crosses his hands at the wrist, and at the word "Go" the one by each chair picks up a nut with his near-hand, passes it into his other hand and from there to the player beside him. He in turn passes the nut through both his hands and on to the player beside him, and so on down the line to the last player, who drops the nut into a waiting empty plate on a chair. The pace is quick because the first players no sooner part with a nut than they pick up the next and send that down the line—but a dropped nut must go back to the beginning again—and lots of laughter is provoked by the awkward handling of the nuts, for the hands must remain crossed throughout play. The team first to transfer all their nuts from one end to the other wins.

All Tied Up

An hilarious game for a moment when everyone is at full steam. Pair up the guests into man-girl partnerships, and one by one put each pair through their paces. First, tie his right wrist to her left wrist—or *vice versa*—and then give them a job to do with their free hands only—wrapping up a parcel and tying it with string; threading a needle and tacking down a hem on a piece of material; folding sheets of paper and putting them into envelopes, and so on. Only the ambidextrous will find this easy.

Somebody always dries up—or says something that creates great amusement—when playing Association of Ideas

Jewellers

Pair up the men and girls and range the men in a line at one end of the room, partners standing by. Give each man a needle and length of thread, and set a row of saucers at the opposite end of the room, one for each girl and each with twelve beads on it. On the "Go" sign, the men must immediately start to thread their needles. The moment one succeeds, his partner hops on one foot *or* the other (no changing) to her saucer, picks up two beads and *runs* back to her partner. He threads the beads and she hops away for two more—the first couple to thread their twelve beads and tie in a necklace round the girl's neck wins the race.

Answer the Question

A good one this as a breather between more active games. Prepare beforehand a list of questions that can be answered simply by "yes" or "no." Also prepare two large sheets of paper with "yes" on one and "no" on the other. At the time of the game, pin these to one wall with a space between in which the question-master stands. Divide the party into two mixed teams some distance away. At the "Ready," a player from each team stands out, you call a question and the two players run to the "yes" or "no" sign. The player first reaching the right sign wins a point for his team. This is usually a popular game, so have plenty of questions to cover two or three rounds if necessary.

Passing the Penny

A variation of *Picking up Nuts*, for which the players may be seated in two mixed teams facing each other. Hands are clenched and held out, backs up. The top player in each team is provided with a penny placed on the back of his outside hand. The "Go" signal is given, and the penny must be slid on to the first player's other hand, from there to the near-hand of the second player, who transfers it to his other hand and from there to the third player, and so on down the row. A dropped penny is sent back to the first player to start again and, of course, the team that first gets its penny to the end of the line wins.

Fashion Plates

Man-girl partnerships again, but all the girls have to do is to stand still and not giggle too much. Group all in a circle. Place in the centre of the circle a large bundle of newspapers and a large box of pins and give each man a pair of scissors. Start them off, and each man must contrive a dress for his lady, using his scissors, the pins and the newspapers. Allow about 20 minutes, then judge the winner—maybe there's a Hartnell among you.

PAPER AND PENCIL IDEAS

These are always popular both among guests and with hosts and hostesses whose space is too limited for other games.

From A to Z

Print the letters of the alphabet on small squares of card and hide each letter somewhere in the party room. Make a list as you go along of each letter and its hiding place. Give each guest a pencil and a paper with the alphabet printed down one side. They then hunt for the letters, as unobtrusively as possible, and write down each hiding place against the appropriate letter on their lists. Set a time limit and award a prize to the best hunter.

Spot the Ad.

Prepare beforehand a large sheet of brown paper and on it stick a dozen or more advertisement symbols from newspapers and magazines. Choose illustrations as well as catch phrases well known as a whole advert.—but not so easy to distinguish in part only. Drawing-pin the paper to the wall at the time of play, set a time limit and award the prize to the player with the most correct.

A Variation.—For a party where all guests are known to have gardens, a collection of illustrations cut from flower seed packets could be displayed, numbered, and the guests asked to write down the name of each flower against its number on his paper.

Opposites

Prepare a list beforehand of at least 24 words, each of which has an exact opposite. for example: black (white); large (small); sour (sweet); tall (short). Guests are to write down the opposites as you call the words—and imperceptibly quicken your pace until they are frantically scribbling, and thinking.

Anagrams

Again on a large sheet of paper print clearly six or more sets of jumbled words—say, one set of four flower names, the letters of each well mixed up; another set of four makes of car; birds; planets; composers—choice of subject is wide and can be varied to suit your guests. Set a period of time in which the words are to be unjumbled and reward the winner.

Telegrams

A quiet sitting-down game in which the players are given a word—it could be "Telegram"—and this they write on their papers: within a given time they are to compile a telegram using each letter of the word as the initial letter of each word in their telegram. The letters should be used

To play Pass the Matches, the outer cover of an ordinary match box is put on the first player's nose and has to be passed from nose to nose, without help from hands, right down the line

consecutively, and when the time is up the results are handed round so that no player holds his own, and then read out one by one.

ALL TOGETHER GAMES

Here are some alternatives to team games which can be played by a large or small number and will provide much hilarity:

Musical Supper

Beforehand prepare a parcel of a small, hard bar of chocolate, wrapping it in numerous layers of paper and tying each layer with string. To play, seat the guests in a circle on the floor and put a plate, a knife and a fork in the centre. Music plays, and the parcel is quickly passed from hand to hand round the circle. Whoever holds it when the music stops must start undoing string and wrapping, but passes it on in whatever state it is when the music restarts. The player who finally reaches the chocolate has to earn his supper by putting it on the plate and eating it in full view of the assembled company with the knife and fork and with no help from his hands.

Crossword Clues

There are so many crossword puzzlers about that this game should appeal. Prepare beforehand a list of trick clues, the answer to each being an animal or bird or flower—whatever you like—hidden in the clue. Here are some examples:

1. Only grown in the *last er*a. (Aster)
2. Travel to Ba*li on* this animal. (Lion)
3. After the cant*er I ca*me back. (Erica)
4. Did the la*st one chat*ter too much? (Stonechat)

With players seated in a ring, read out the first clue to player No. 1. Allow a few seconds and, if no answer is forthcoming, pass on to player No. 2, and so on. Count the correct answers from each player and award a prize to the one who gets the most.

The Letter is . . .

Another word game that provides several bright minutes and suits all ages. Arm yourself with a dictionary against dispute, group the players in a circle and then start play by calling out a letter and pointing to a guest. He or she must immediately reply with a dictionary word beginning with that letter. The one next to him clockwise follows instantly with another word of the same letter, and so on round the circle. Bar proper names and foreign words, and eliminate all who default in this way, stumble or just can't think of a word immediately. Change the letter after each round and play for a set time or until all but one are eliminated.

Handcraft Exhibition

Children or adults can equally enjoy this piece of entertainment, and laughs and surprises are certain. Collect as many simple craft materials as possible beforehand and have them handy on a convenient table, covered with a cloth. Some suggestions are: bundles of pipe cleaners; sticks of coloured modelling clay or wax; coloured pencils and drawing paper; packets of gummed, coloured paper squares; crêpe paper; scissors; pins, and a reel or two of florist's wire. At a given moment, whip off the cloth and tell the party that each is to produce some piece of handcraft, using as many as they like or can utilise of the materials available. If they are in merry mood, and particularly if unskilled in these artistic pursuits, the results will be equally so.

Smiles

Of course, you *won't* have a dull moment at your party, but there might come that pause when, quite suddenly, everyone is quiet. To avoid any danger of the pause lengthening, say something like this: "Now, please, all keep poker faces while I throw someone a smile. Whoever gets it, wears it for a second and then throws it to someone else." Say your piece with a Buster Keaton face yourself, then catch someone's eye, suddenly grin at them, wipe the grin off your face with your hand, bunching it up as though the grin were inside, and make a throwing movement to the person you grinned at; he or she must instantly grin, wipe it off and throw it at someone else. The poker faces won't last ten seconds and you can then introduce another game, say:

Association of Ideas

Start by saying clearly a single word—for instance, "gin"—and point at one of the guests. He or she must at once answer with another word suggested by your word—possible "sling" or "cocktail" or "trap"—and point to a third guest, and so you go on. It's fun and not as easy as it seems—someone is almost bound to dry up. If they do, they should shake their heads and point to another player as quickly as possible.

Tongue-twister

Certain to produce howls of laughter, introduce this round game when everyone is mellow and ready to sit after an active game. Range them in a rough circle and then repeat the first of the following tongue-twisters. The one next you clockwise repeats it, and so on round the circle back to you. They will probably think that's that and it's a bit dull, but you repeat the first once more and add the second, and request each guest to do the same. By the time you produce the third they'll be sitting up and getting a grip on themselves—and if anyone stays the course, award him or her a worthwhile prize.

Here's the complete list of twelve:

(1) One Oxford ox opening oysters.
(2) Two teetotallers totally tired trying to trot to Tradbury.
(3) Three tall tigers tippling tenpenny tea.
(4) Four fat friars fanning fainting flies.
(5) Five flippant Frenchmen foolishly fishing for flies.
(6) Six sportsmen shooting snipe.

(7) Seven Severn salmon swallowing shrimps.

(8) Eight ecclesiastics eagerly examining Europe.

(9) Nine noblemen nibbling nonpareil.

(10) Ten tinkering tinkers tinkering ten tin tinder boxes with ten tenpenny tin tacks.

(11) Eleven elephants elegantly equipped.

(12) Twelve teachers travelling Turkey trying to teach topography.

I went to Paris

An ever-popular favourite this, and not so tricky as Tongue-twisters. Sit in a rough circle, and begin by saying to your next-door neighbour, "I went to Paris." His reply is, "And what did you buy there?" To which you respond, "A Dior model"— for example. He, or she, then turns to his neighbour, saying, "I went to Paris," and on being asked in his turn what he bought there, repeats the first purchase and adds one of his own, and so on: any player who forgets a purchase drops out.

THE END OF THE PARTY

No good party should be allowed to drag itself out at the end, but if guests have had a happy time and are tired, they reach the point of feeling they ought to go, yet linger on; they will be grateful for a winding-off motif—and so will you.

Some suggestions, then, are a special good-night dance if you have the room—one family I know, whose parties are very popular, always end up with Sir Roger de Coverley; another idea to finish the party is to have a prize-giving, presenting the prizes to all who have won games through the evening. Choose someone to present the prizes who can turn on some witty patter while doing so.

Otherwise, choose a good moment to bring in a steaming bowl of punch or a tureen of soup with an appetising aroma. Once they have finished their helping, it is easy for all to say their "thank-you's"— and depart with warm thoughts of a grand party.

Pencil and paper games, such as Telegrams or the old favourite, Consequences, are ideal where space is limited, or it is important to keep noise down to a minimum

A flower group in a period setting emphasising, by its shape, the line of the books. The container is a lustre bowl

FLOWER ARRANGEMENT

How to grow, choose, arrange and make the best of
fresh or dried flowers, foliage and leaves in the home

By BETTY MASSINGHAM, *author of the Penguin Handbook of Flower Arrangement*

FLOWER arrangement as we know it is of comparatively recent origin in this country. About a hundred years ago the Victorians feverishly put as many flowers as possible into as many containers as were available. There were, in consequence, vases for sideboard decorations, for the drawing room, for the dinner table and for halls and staircase landings. That was the day of the flower-filled épergne and the Wardian case full of ferns. Edward Sayers, writing in the *American Flower Garden Companion* in 1838, says that it is "now an almost universal practice to have cut flowers in rooms as natural orna-ments." But before this period in history there is very little evidence of anything which could be described as widespread in-terest in flower arrangement.

The profusion of the Victorians gave place to a most welcome restraint towards the end of the century, perhaps partly due to the wise counsels of Gertrude Jekyll and William Robinson and to the influence of William Morris. His famous golden rule: "Have nothing in your house that you do not know to be useful or believe to be beau-tiful," must have caused some anxiety in the hearts of many housewives.

There was even, during the years 1896–7, a series of articles published in the *Studio* magazine on the art of Japanese floral decoration, showing the use of a very few flowers, sometimes alone and sometimes with foliage. It was emphasised that the whole character of the plant must be shown. "The loveliest buds and blos-soms torn from their stems and crushed together in a mass . . . convey to the Japanese mind no idea of floral art or beauty," stated the author. A great change was taking place in ideas about flower ar-rangement, and this brings us to the current style in floral decoration.

Fortunate people with gardens—even small ones—can, with careful planning, supply themselves throughout the year with flowers and foliage for indoor decoration. Of course, their needs must not be on too large a scale, but an average house does not generally involve the use of vast supplies of material, particularly if there is also a small greenhouse. This can be a great boon, producing more exotic blooms when they might not be available otherwise in the garden, and would be expensive to buy in the shops. A greenhouse will also foster geraniums, which can be brought into the house for cutting throughout the winter, and provide a most valuable touch of colour with other flowers or with foliage.

GROWING THE FLOWERS

When making suggestions for the garden, with flower arrangement in mind, it is useful to include flowering shrubs and plants with attractive leaves as well as flowers. It is difficult, in a short space, to give a complete list of ideas, but I would like to mention a few which come to mind as being particularly useful.

Flowers

Acanthus. Tall, purple-white flower spike, with dark green elegant leaves. Flowers useful for drying.

Astrantia. Green and white flowers, light, graceful. Continue flowering — no trouble to grow. Most useful.

Bouncing Bet. Rather like pink gypsophila, but slightly bigger flowers, producing a less fussy effect in an arrangement.

Chinese lanterns (Physalis). Good colouring for autumn and winter. Easy to grow. Dry well.

Clematis. Great variety of colours and sizes, and flowering times. Wonderfully useful for arrangement.

Delphinium. All varieties of blue and white. Most useful for drying.

Eremurus. Very tall, digni-

fied flower spikes. Rather slow to get established, with fleshy roots which damage easily. Good for big arrangements.

Everlasting Pea. White or pinky-mauve. Either provides a quantity of flowers with attractive foliage and curving stems.

Fennel. Very fine, tall, yellow flower heads. Decorative, easy to grow, feathery foliage.

Globe artichoke. Most dramatic, flower heads purple and green. Flowers dry well, turning golden brown. Leaves very beautiful in shape and texture.

Globe thistle. Tall, blue-grey flowers like round thistles. Good for decoration and dry quite well.

Hop. Sprays of green flowers in graceful curves. Very pretty colour. Last well.

Honesty. Purple flowers, green seed pods and dried silver pods are all useful for flower arrangement.

Iris. Almost all colours available at some time or other during the year. Most valuable flowers and foliage.

Jasmine. Both summer and winter jasmine are assets—the clear yellow flowers

The use of foliage with a few flowers is a well-known economy for the autumn. A few polyantha roses with sprays of green and white tradescantia are arranged together here

of the winter jasmine being particularly welcome when there is very little in the garden.

Larkspur. Great variety of colours. Very useful for drying for the winter.

London pride. One of the most attractive smaller flowers for decoration. A great asset. Pale pink and white.

Love-in-a-mist. Both the blue and white are pretty and useful, particularly the white. The seed heads dry in most exciting colours.

Love-lies-bleeding (Amaranthus). Dramatic festoons of dark red or pale green.

Mignonette. Most charming flower, in a soft green and reddish-brown colour. Lasts very well.

Peony. Invaluable in any of its colours. Sometimes slow in flowering. Does not like to be moved. One or two add distinction to a group.

Rose. Almost any variety and any colour are quite indispensable for flower arrangement.

Sea holly (Eryngium). Decorative soft blue small thistle flower. Lasts very well.

Solomon's seal. Graceful stems with clear green leaves and, underneath, small white flowers edged with green.

Sweet rocket. Cottage garden flowers—very charming in pale lilac and white.

Verbascum. Tall, greyish spikes with yellow flower and grey velvet leaves.

Shrubs

Berberis. Clusters of bright yellow flowers, followed later by berries. Very useful foliage.

Ceanothus. Small blue flowers on long, spreading branches.

Escallonia. Small pink and white flowers on thin, curving branches.

Guelder rose. Tall shrub bearing white clusters of flowers which are a soft green before opening.

Hydrangea. Variety of coloured flowers, with handsome leaves. Some of the flowers dry well.

Pieris floribunda. Clusters of flowers, rather like suspended lilies of the valley, with green fan-like leaves.

Philadelphus. Sweet-smelling, pure white flowers with yellow stamens.

Privet. Cream-white flowers on dark green foliage, later producing green and then black berries.

Plants with Useful Foliage

Berberis, camellia, globe artichoke, golden privet, iris, ivy, lavender, lavender cotton, magnolia, purple sprouting broccoli, rosemary, Solomon's seal, Stachys lanata, summer jasmine, verbascum.

To these lists it might be helpful to add a short one for the benefit of those without a garden who have room for a tub, a window box, or a small bed of soil in a back yard. They might grow honeysuckle, jasmine, clematis, hydrangea, geranium, rosemary, everlasting pea, fig, and certain climbing roses.

BUYING THE FLOWERS

Before setting out to buy flowers for arrangement, it is helpful to have a scheme in mind of colour and shape. There may be something left from the vase to be replaced which, if combined with the right material, will go a long way towards making the new group. Then there is the very real problem of flowers usually being sold in bunches of one dozen, or even half a dozen. Sometimes one needs a variety of colours and a contrast of shape, and it would be nice to walk round a shop buying one from this bunch, and two from another. This seems to be a difficulty which can only be overcome by a good deal of thought and, sometimes, persistence. If the florist is imaginative and helpful, she will often allow three of one kind of flower to be taken from a bunch, particularly if she sees that you are really interested in a special colour scheme. Otherwise, one has to depend on bunches of the same flowers in mixed colours; asters, anemones, polyanthus, larkspur, and sometimes gladioli.

It is useful, too, to have in mind some idea of the lasting properties of certain flowers. This can best be gained by personal experience, but there are a few flowers which may generally be depended on to last well.

Long-lasting.—London pride, agapanthus, love-lies-bleeding, montbretia, gladioli, Michaelmas daisy, chrysanthemum, Shasta daisy, godetia, mignonette, marguerite, freesia and Corsican hellebore.

Among flowers which are known to fade quickly there are lupins, phlox, mimosa (in the fluffy state), and poppies.

WITH A BACKGROUND OF LIGHT

An upper window of frosted glass gives extra light in a rather dark room. This is lit artificially at night and provides an excellent background for a group of flowers, showing up the material in outline and emphasising the contrast in foliage. This is a spring arrangement with rosemary, eucalyptus, pieris, tulips, guelder rose and budding lilac.

HARMONY WITH FURNISHINGS

The importance of harmony with the setting cannot be over-emphasised. These spring flowers (above) in an oblong porcelain basket, follow the line of the picture above them and the little cabinet on which they stand. They must not conceal or be out of proportion with the painting.

ON THE STAIRS

A wall bracket on a staircase (left) provides a useful position for flowers. It usually means that they are out of the way, but in a good situation to be seen. They should have a certain amount of clear wall space round them, so that they show up well.

SPRING FLOWERS

Spring flowers particularly ask for space and air in arrangement. They last much better when they are not crushed into a vase close together, and certainly show off their beauty better when they have a chance to be seen separately. A glass vase gives a clear view of the fresh green stems.

MARIGOLDS AND FOLIAGE

Garden ragwort foliage used with marigolds (right). Softer contrasting colour reduces the harsh orange of the marigolds, and the grey and off-white of garden ragwort leaves makes an especially good background. The container is a white porcelain Victorian shell mounted on grey porcelain.

AN UNUSUAL ARRANGEMENT OF DRIED FLOWERS

A large group of dried flowers can make an economical and an attractive decoration for a room, hall or landing. It can consist chiefly of garden flowers, or wild flowers and seedheads, or be a mixture of both. It can be produced in almost any colour scheme to combine or contrast with the furnishings. The group photographed includes acanthus flowers, hydrangea heads, sumach, leek seedheads, great reeds, buddleia and grasses. All this material will last from one year to another with very little loss of colour if it is packed away carefully in the spring.

The most important aspect of buying flowers is to be sure to choose a reliable florist. Even if slightly more expensive, it is a hundred times worth it, though a good florist is not necessarily an expensive one. I have bought white carnations threepence cheaper per bloom in the West End of London than in the East End on the same day. A good florist will take trouble with a colour scheme or with suggestions. If some of her flowers are not quite fresh from the market, she will tell you so and offer them to you a little cheaper. She will never over-persuade you, or make you feel you should buy something because you have given her trouble. Such a florist is worth looking for —and they are to be found.

CONTAINERS

The right container can make a great difference to an arrangement, and some-times the most unlikely receptacles for holding water provide the most exciting vases for flowers. They may be made of porcelain, glass, pewter, copper, stone-ware, or even wood or basketwork with a tin inside to hold the water   Shape and colour are the important points to look for, and as long as these are right for the par-ticular flowers to be arranged, absolutely anything may be suitable.

The *shape* of a container will decide whether it is to be a large arrangement or a small one, holding many flowers or only a few. It will also decide whether it is to be a spreading arrangement or a compact one. A wide-necked vase will obviously take more flowers than a tall, narrow one, and a shallow bowl will take short flowers better than heavy branches. The *colour* of the container is important because of the flowers to go into it and the furnishings surrounding it. Very few flowers show up as well in a busily design-covered vase as they do in a plain, soft-coloured one. Brilliantly painted patterns on containers are apt to pall after a time—unlike a quiet, subdued design.

Victorian vases of porcelain and coloured glass can be most exciting and dramatic to use, and there is still quite a good supply awaiting those with the time to hunt for them on market stalls and junk shops, but they take time to find. Late Victorian jardinières make most at-tractive containers for large arrangements, and are usually suitably fitted with a zinc lining. An early Staffordshire teapot, hav-ing lost its lid, was a most attractive shape to use for a spreading arrangement, and a glass decanter, having similarly lost its stopper, proved to be an excellent shape for tall branches.

Baskets of all kinds—trugs, strawberry punnets, small rush baskets and large In-dian baskets with lids and handles—all can make original and economical containers. They need only a glass cooking dish inside for the water, which can be concealed completely by the flowers.

Kitchen dishes provide another unending source of supply. It is quite unnecessary to spend very much money on a collection of containers, when there is all the iron-ware in the kitchen cupboard to draw upon. Flat baking dishes, gravy boats, vegetable dishes and soup tureens all make interesting and unusual foundations for an arrangement.

Apart from these, there is available to-day a wonderful selection of contemporary containers of all kinds. A vase for flowers is at last considered as important as a tea-pot, and made in as many different designs and colours to suit varying tastes.

GENERAL PRINCIPLES OF ARRANGING FLOWERS

Having either grown or bought the flowers, and chosen a container in which to arrange them, it is now important to think a little about the design of the ar-rangement itself, and to discuss rules which it may be necessary to follow. After all, when learning music one has to learn scales, and when studying a language, to learn the verbs. Much the same applies to flower arrangement. Neither the scales in music nor the verbs in a foreign language impede freedom in either playing the piano or speaking in French or German. They act as a guide, as a basis for everything else. The rules of flower arrangement, too, should be simple and few, so that, once learned, they are remembered almost sub-consciously and become the foundation of a personal style.

Here, very simply, are a few basic rules:
(1) The stalks of the flowers and foliage must come from a central point, and

off the flowers and leaves, not to draw attention to the arranger.

These are simple, uncomplicated rules, which will come so naturally after a time as not to need thinking about. Like most rules, they should sometimes be broken. At all costs, they must not be misused to encourage stereotyped results. For flower arrangement should be expressive and characteristic of individual taste, which has to be developed independently and can never be culled from books.

not cross each other, so giving the effect, as far as possible, that the flowers are still growing.

(2) An uneven number of flowers used in a small arrangement usually gives a happier result than an even number.

(3) The stalks should be cut in different lengths, so that all the flower heads do not form one solid line.

(4) The height of the arrangement should be one and a half times the height of the container, except where a wide base gives added balance, and the arrangement is a spreading one.

(5) Heavy flowers should not generally be used towards the edge of a group. They should be grouped towards the centre, with smaller ones to the outside, and never in a straight line one above another.

(6) Each flower should be seen separately, as far as possible. Overcrowding is a bad mistake, as it means the flowers are not seen to their best advantage.

(7) The general effect, when the arrangement is finished, should be as natural as possible. There should be no need to contort branches into peculiar shapes, or to strive after an artificial grouping. A dramatic effect can sometimes be interesting, but generally tends to look contrived and affected. The main object, after all, is to show

DOING THE FLOWERS

Time is one of the most important factors in home management, and flower arrangement need not take up a lot of time, provided everything required is ready to hand and you have some kind of method.

Whether the flowers come from the garden or a shop, it is always wise to give them a long, deep drink before arranging them. While they are enjoying their cool bucket of water, one can be doing other things in the house, and then have everything ready to start.

The choice of container depends very much on the flowers to be arranged and their position in the room. Having selected the suitable vase, you may well find that it requires a good washing or dusting. After that place the vase in position in the room.

In the vase cupboard (one shelf in a cupboard will do if there is not much space available) it is useful to keep the gardening scissors and a dust-sheet, the piece of wire mesh or whatever you prefer to hold the flowers in place, and a small teapot or jug with a long spout. The dust-sheet will protect polished floors or furniture. If it is a good-sized one which can be spread out on the floor, the flowers can also be laid out on it so that you can see exactly what material there is to work with. These are small items, but they all help to save time and make the actual work much easier.

If, for any reason, it is not possible to arrange the flowers in position in the room, it is important to do them at the same eye-level somewhere else. For instance, if they are finally to stand on the top of a book-case or a corner cupboard and one arranges them standing by the kitchen table, looking down into them, they will look quite different—and probably not very effective—when transferred to their higher position.

The vase should be three-quarters full of water before the flowers are arranged, and then filled right up to the brim when they are all in place. This gives them the longest drink possible. The teapot is used for filling up the vase without disturbing the flowers. Adding a little water to the vase is better than changing it completely, which would disturb the arrangement.

COLOUR SCHEMES AND FURNISHING SCHEMES

Colour plays a tremendously important part, but is so much a matter of opinion that one can only make sugges-tions and leave the rest to personal taste and experi-ment. Then, too, a colour often looks different when it is put close to another one. For instance, a clear yellow daisy arranged with a blue delphinium takes on a different shade of yellow from one that is arranged with an orange marigold. Both may be equally effective, but the final tone of yellow will be different.

Two contrasting shapes and colours of foliage used to-gether without flowers—the fern is light and a clear green, the creeper bronze and rather heavy

There are, however, a few guiding prin-ciples to consider when thinking of colour schemes.

First, there is the question of warmth and coolness. A room which has sunlight pouring into it may require quite a dif-ferent colour scheme from one with a north aspect. White, green, blue and mauve are all cool colours and would be effective in a sunny room, but the warmer colours of red, yellow, orange, pink, brown and deep purple might all be wiser selections for a cold room. Apart from this question of warmth, there are, of course, the furnish-ings to consider.

It is sometimes more subtle to bring out a less obvious colour in the flowers—per-haps matching something striking in a painting, or the stripe in a chair cover, or the material of a lamp shade—than to have blue flowers in a room which is mainly furnished in blue, or orange and yellow in a yellow room. Sometimes it is interesting to introduce an entirely new colour through the flowers.

For example, picture a scheme in olive green with touches of Chinese red—olive walls, paintwork and carpet with, perhaps, the red introduced in a cushion or a piece of porcelain. Rather than have an un-successful matching of the red, it might be interesting to introduce cream or white flowers, or even a soft pink, with dark green foliage.

In a dining room with dark oak furniture, white walls, and blue and white curtains and chair covers, a touch of red might be a welcome introduction, particularly if it appears elsewhere in a small quantity in the room. (Most reds are possible to match—there is usually a geranium available or two or three carnations which will be enough for the purpose—but Chinese red is a difficult shade.) In a room I know, with grey walls, yellow curtains and chairs upholstered in grey material with a yellow pattern, there is a painting over the fireplace of a girl with a blue ribbon in her hair. I have seen the blue ribbon caught by a certain colour of delphinium and cornflower; the effect was more discreet than the more obvious yellow.

Flowers can be worked out in different shades of one colour; they can be in a variety of colours; they can also provide contrast. When using different shades of one colour, it is important to remember to include in the group the lightest and darkest tones possible. In a mauve group consisting of purple leek heads, cerise gladioli and blue agapanthus, there were also some pale mauve-pink carnations and some deep purple zinnias. If only the one central shade is used, say, blue-mauve, the effect will be flat—rather like the countryside on a cloudy day. But with the light and dark shades, one gets the effect of sun and shadow and so reaps the full benefit from the colour.

In a bowl of mixed colours almost any shades and tones can be used together, but the deeper colours should always be arranged towards the centre, the lighter ones towards the outside of the group. Again, a variety of colours of one depth is apt to be insipid. Light and dark flowers should be mixed together.

Contrasting colours must be selected with care to produce the best results. One colour often sets off another, and to get the best effect, both contrasting shades must be the right tone. In a mixed arrangement of green honesty seedpods and deep red peonies, the green had a certain amount of blue in it, and the red of the peonies could not, on any account, be a pink-red. A true deep red was needed to be effective.

FOLIAGE AND LEAVES

Foliage arrangements have been an important part of flower decoration in Japan for many hundreds of years. The Japanese often make groups of leaves—with one of the leaves acting as the flower by its contrast of shape or colour—and call them flower arrangements. The leaves and stems of a plant are just as important to them as the bud or flower. We in the

---

YOUR CUT FLOWERS WILL LAST IF YOU . . .

Plunge them right up to their necks in fresh cold water for an hour as soon as you get them home. If they are very long-stemmed, wrap the blooms and upper part of the stems carefully in newspaper so that the weight doesn't bend the stems.

Cut the ends of the stalks, whatever kind they are.

Crush the stalks quite brutally with a hammer, or slit them up from the ends for 2 or 3 inches, if they are hard-wooded varieties, such as chrysanthemums.

Put them into vases that are nice and wide at the base and don't crowd the stems at the point where they should be drinking.

Remove most of the lower leaves or they will make the water stale.

Add fresh water every day so that the vases are always as full as possible. Do this with a long-spouted kettle or teapot so as not to disturb the flower arrangement.

Plunge tired-looking anemones into a bowl of really hot water—it revives them immediately.

A small dried flower group of mixed colours (above) arranged in a strawberry punnet. This includes gnaphalium, helichrysum, corn, sea lavender and globe thistle. Any colour scheme may be worked out according to taste

The beauty of wild clematis seed heads is shown off in silhouette (right). Nothing could be more simple or economical, and the container is an old glass scent bottle bought quite cheaply because it had no cork

West are not yet altogether accustomed to this idea, the demand being chiefly for what is described as "a touch of colour." So many people do not regard green as a colour and are inclined to think of it only as a very useful background.

The use of foliage can, however, be highly decorative and also an economy. An arrangement consisting of different shapes and shades of leaves and branches will often last for some time without replenishment, and can be most exciting if there is enough contrast of shape and colour. Varying from pale yellow, through all the tones of green to a deep olive colour, leaves provide as much variety as a bowl of mixed flowers. In the country the cost may be nothing at all; and with only a small town garden, it is still possible to find leaves which contrast well and so make interesting arrangements.

A few suggestions for contrasting foliage used together are:

(a) small-leaved cotoneaster with laurel;
(b) globe artichoke leaves, giant horse-radish leaves;
(c) ivy with escallonia branches;
(d) sea buckthorn branches with lungwort leaves;
(e) periwinkle with hollyhock leaves;
(f) golden privet with fig leaves or castor-oil plant leaves;
(g) summer jasmine with broom.

Some of the most suitable containers for foliage arrangements are kitchen dishes or baskets.

DRIED FLOWERS

There are many exciting discoveries to be made in the use of dried—not artificial —flowers. Here, again, is an economy measure. Once the flowers are collected, dried and arranged, they will last well without any further replenishment throughout the most difficult of the winter months. They should be taken down when the first spring branches begin to come in, as the competition would be unfair. There is nothing, after all, to compare with the first flowers of the year and dried flowers, which have been useful through the winter, should not be expected to do their duty any longer.

The colours of dried flowers, seed heads and grasses are necessarily softer and more subtle than the colours of fresh flowers. Very beautiful colour schemes are possible, but they are usually subdued rather than vivid. This is a good thing since a dried flower group will last for at least three months, and would become very tiring if it were too bright or garish.

There are various flowers and seed heads which dry without any trouble at all: others are more capricious. Some can be hung upside down in a normal room temperature, while others must have the heat of an average airing cupboard. Some flowers dry while standing in water; others must be kept free from all damp. Many seed heads dry on their plants and only have to be cut off when they are ready. To find exactly which treatment applies to which flower is, more than anything else, a matter for individual experiment. Sometimes what dries one year will not dry another under what seem to be exactly the same conditions. So much depends on the temperature at the time

A dried arrangement for a small table—poppy heads, iris seed heads, corn and iris fœtidissima, all cut very short indeed

of cutting, the state of the flowers and, finally, the method you decide to adopt to dry them.

Among the most generally successful for drying are: globe thistle, sea holly, orange lanterns, helichrysum, anaphalis, gnaphalium, larkspur, delphinium, golden rod. These all seem to dry best when hung in a slightly warm temperature—not too hot, or some of the colour will go. Hydrangeas, which dry well, in a great variety of beautiful colours, should be dried while still in water. Globe artichoke flowers are magnificent, and also dry off while standing in water. Bulrushes, nipplewort, bur-reed, teasels and giant reeds all dry well: they seem to prefer to be hung in bunches in an ordinary temperature. The seed heads of love-in-a-mist, poppies, iris, etc., are most successful; the poppies like a gentle heat at a certain stage, but the other two usually dry on the plant.

Dried flowers are sometimes more difficult than fresh ones to keep steady in an arrangement, as there are no leaves on the stems to act as anchorage. If wire mesh is used, it is advisable to get the smallest mesh and crumple up the wire into a fairly tight foundation. The stalks will then remain in position without slipping about. If it is difficult, in a low, flat arrangement, to conceal the wire netting, a thin layer of green moss will make an attractive background.

IN HARMONY WITH THE SETTING

In a recent talk to the Royal Horticultural Society the lecturer emphasised two points about a perfect garden: first, that it should look as natural as possible; second, that it should seem to merge into the surrounding countryside and appear to be a part of it.

It seems to me that these two principles

An idea for a large dried arrangement. This group is composed mostly from wild grasses and seed heads, will combine with any colour scheme, and will last for weeks. To show off well, it should stand against a plain background

apply in exactly the same way to flower arrangement. Harmony should apply just as much to the house as to the garden. Natural arrangements, based on simple rules, will harmonise with their surroundings; they will also form an integral part of the furnishing scheme.

A flower arrangement is something more than just an arrangement of flowers. It must harmonise with the setting and be complementary to the interior.

Think of the flowers in your rooms as an essential part of the furnishings of your home—not just as a separate bowl with no relation to its surroundings, and your flower decoration will really fulfil its purpose.

Perhaps the last word of all should be a plea for simplicity. As Gertrude Jekyll, that great gardener, says: "In all matters of decoration . . . one of the first and wholesomest laws is that of restraint and moderation." Let this be our watchword.

PLANTS FOR THE HOUSE

*You can have something green
and growing indoors, however
little space there is available*

ALTHOUGH many house plants
thrive with very little care, most
of them need some attention weekly
and, in many instances, more often.
This includes watering, cleaning, re-
potting, and in some cases feeding.

Watering.—It is not possible to
give definite rules for the frequency
of watering, but in general the state
of the soil in the pot will be a good
guide. It should not be allowed to
become dry and powdery before
being watered: on the other hand,
over-watering is even more dangerous. Except in the case of a few
plants, such as the spiræa and marguerite, the pot should not be allowed to stand permanently in
water. Good drainage in the pots (a
piece of broken pot or a few stones
at the bottom) is a great help in
keeping plants moist but not too wet.

In general, plants need watering
much more frequently in summer
than in winter. If, in this respect,
one treats them rather like human beings,
one will not go far wrong. They lose
moisture in just the same way in the hot
weather. Probably two or three waterings
a week will be required in summer. The
pots may occasionally be submerged temporarily in a basin of water, but must be
allowed to drain properly afterwards before
being returned to any outer pot or receptacle. Always use water with the chill off it.

Plants in small pots require more frequent watering than those in larger pots
and any surplus should be emptied away.

Cleaning. — Plants live and breathe
through the pores in their leaves. They
must not, therefore, be allowed to get
clogged up with dust and other substances
in the air. Plants such as ferns, ivies,
aspidistras, palms and others with green
leaves require regular cleaning, as they

A good place for pot plants is at the side of a window
where they are protected equally from intense sunlight
and cold, and are well away from radiators and fires

tend to pick up a great deal of dust. A
spray is ideal, but a damp rag or sponge
makes a perfectly adequate substitute.
Here again warm (not hot) water should
be used. They must be gently dried after
cleaning.

Potting.—Soil for house plants should
be light. Peaty soil with plenty of fibre and
an equal amount of leaf mould, with half
the quantity of sharp sand, is ideal.

Re-potting.—Careful watch must be kept
to see that plants do not become pot-
bound, i.e. that the roots do not come out
of the pot. As soon as you see any sign of
this, re-pot carefully, selecting a considerably larger pot to allow for further growth
and filling with the best earth you can
obtain, if necessary taking the advice of a
nursery or florist about the advisability of
adding some feeding substance. Water

thoroughly after re-potting.

Feeding.—Most pot plants do not need feeding, certainly not frequently. Here again it is advisable, if possible, to take expert advice as to the best type of "food" for the particular plant.

Situation.—It is most important to keep plants out of draughts and away from gas fires and the warm air from radiators. Many plants, if put in a very sunny window, get scorched and the leaves turn yellow and gradually fall off. On the other hand, most plants like plenty of light. They will tend to be drawn to the light and the pots must be turned in order to keep them straight and upright.

Pruning.—Branching, climbing or trailing varieties of house plants should be pruned, preferably in spring. Newly potted plants should be allowed time to settle down first.

CHOICE OF PLANTS

The choice of plants is a highly individual matter, but the following are some suggestions:

Climbing Plants

Ivies (many varieties are available in the shops), Canary Creeper, Convolvulus, Nasturtiums, Philodendron scandens, Ivy Leaf Geraniums, Cup and Saucer Vine, Bougainvillæa.

These may be grown in various ways. One of the most popular methods is in hanging wicker baskets, which can be bought or made by a clever member of the household. Small pieces of trellis may be arranged in a corner of a room and the plants trained up, the pots standing in containers attached to the trellis or in a trough underneath it. Hanging baskets in a porch are most attractive and can be kept replenished and changed all the year round.

Non-climbing Plants

Here the choice is even more varied, but some that may be mentioned are:

Azaleas, Zinnias, Polyanthus, Lilies, Lily of the Valley, Spiræa, Marguerites, St. Paulia (African Violet), Saxifrage (Mother of Thousands), Fuchsia, Solanum (Winter Cherry), Dwarf Sweet Peas, Lobelia, Hydrangeas, Geraniums, Carnations, Chrysanthemums, Genista, Cyclamens, Primulas, Shrimp Plant, Ericas, Mind-your-own-Business (a delightful creeper which certainly does nothing of the kind).

From these, you can plan a complete rotation from January to December.

With the help of a large flat bowl, some earth and a few stones, two or three small rock plants picked up in a market or begged from a country-dwelling friend, you can make a little garden which will provide endless pleasure and decoration throughout the year. For instance, Mother of Thousands combined with one or two small ferns, a primrose and a polyanthus or primula, will provide a gay substitute for a full-sized garden.

Cacti

There are many varieties of cacti, and a collection of them can provide a great deal of enjoyment. They should be watered during the summer, but left dry in the winter and then gradually watered again in the spring.

Plants you can grow from Seed

An orange, lemon or grapefruit pip will provide you with a beautifully glossy green

Cissus antarctica, with its beautiful, profuse foliage, looks lovely growing in a handled beaker. It is equally at home with period or modern furnishings

A fine specimen of Ficus elastica (the rubber plant) with Hedera helix Chicago, a hardy creeper, rioting around its base

plant all the year round. Peach, plum and cherry stones, acorns and horse chestnuts also grow into amusing plants. These should all be planted in pots, with a piece of pot or stones in the bottom, filled with good soil and watered and tended as already given under general directions.

The following are uncommon flowers suitable for indoor cultivation from seed:

Impatiens, Holstii Hybrids.—This is a beautiful plant which has an abundance of coloured flowers. If sown early, it will flower the first year. It is half hardy and can also be used for outdoor bedding.

Nomocharis Mairei.—A member of the lily family, this comes from Western China. Bulbs grown from seed the first year. Ultimately, it grows to about 18 inches high, bearing beautifully coloured flowers.

Streptocarpus (Cape Primrose).—This has very large blooms in a variety of colours and may be grown to flower all the year round.

Mimosa Pudica (The Sensitive Plant).—Ornamental foliage which shrinks and folds up when touched.

Cuphea (Mexican Cigar Plant).—Flowers the whole year round, bearing bright scarlet blooms.

The Shoo-Fly Plant.—A peculiar house pot plant which blooms in 60 days from seed. It is said that flies will not stay in a room where it grows; the reason is obscure as it has no smell at all. Apart from this, it is particularly valuable as a winter bloomer, the blossoms being large, cup-shaped and of a lovely light blue colour with a white centre.

The Weather Plant.—If the leaves stand upward, the sky will be cloudless; if they stand out straight, changeable weather is indicated. When the leaves hang downwards, rain may be expected. It has bright yellow flowers, followed by crimson pods with black and red seeds, used for making beads.

Angels Trumpet.—A magnificent indoor and garden plant, it blooms in the house in winter or out of doors in summer. Beautiful pure white trumpet-shaped flowers as fragrant as jasmine. Of compact growth with large tropical leaves.

Rose Seed.—Plants grown from these seeds are literally covered with small roses. They are hardy and can be planted into the open ground after being raised indoors in a seed box. Frost will not hurt them, but for the first year it is advisable to protect them with a little hay or leaves. Ideal as a house plant until about three years old, when they became too large and should be placed in the open.

The Golden Tassel.—Flowers profusely with bright yellow blooms, which have long ornamental stamens. Grows about 9/10 inches high. This is an annual.

Seeds for all these are obtainable from: Miss Kathleen Hunter, Wheal Frances, Callestick, Truro, Cornwall.

FOLIAGE PLANTS

The more exotic and unusual plants have become popular for home decoration in recent years, and many of the most fashionable are foliage plants cultivated, not for flowers, but entirely for the beauty of their leaves.

Among those which can successfully be grown in the house are:

A windowsill gay with pot plants. From left to right: Ficus radicans, Rhoicissus rhomboidea, Hedera helix variegata, Hedera helix Chicago, Cissus antarctica, Philodendron scandens. In the hanging pot: Ficus pumila. On the table: Saintpaulia.

Climbing Plants

Flowering.—Passiflora Cœrulea, Plumbago Capensis, Hoya Carnosa, Jasminum Plyanthemum, Amaryllis, Nerine Bowdenii, Vallotta Purpurea (Scarborough Lily).

Non-flowering. — Hedera Helix Chicago, Rhoicissus Rhomboidea, Golden Tradescantia, Silver Tradescantia, Ficus Radicans Variegata, Scindapsus Aureus, Hedera Canariensis Fol. Var., Cissus Antarctica, Commelina, Fittonia Argyrœurea, Sanchezia, Oplismenus.

Non-climbing Plants

Flowering.—Acacia Armata, Anthurium Andreanum, Belleperome Guttata, Bilbergia Nutans, Clivias Miniata Improved, Echeveria.

Non-flowering. — Monstera Deliciosa, Ficus Decora, Ficus Radicans Variegata, Sansevieria Trifasciata Laurentii, Begonia Rex, Carex Japonica, Cissus Rhombefolia, Ficus Elastica, Asparagus Plumosus, Bromelias, Eurya Latifolia, Jacaranda Mimosæfolia, Maranta Kerchoviana, Philodendron Scandens, Acer.

There are many ways of growing the above, one of the most attractive being in indoor window boxes.

The Coraline pot or trough is particularly good for climbers, as it has extra thick sides, open in texture, facilitating storage of moisture and making drainage holes unnecessary. The pot has a stem-shaped cane to hold the plant in position without tying. These are available filled with various plants from Stuart Low & Co. (Enfield) Ltd., Royal Nurseries, Bush Hill Park, Enfield, Middlesex.

Here is a brief guide to the commoner varieties, drawn up to help the new indoor gardener to start a collection.

Scindapsus Aureus.—Has dark green leaves streaked with yellow. Likes semi-shade except in the depth of winter, when it needs all possible light. Likes to be moist but will acclimatise itself to room conditions. Marble Queen, another variety of Scindapsus, has silver streaks but grows more slowly.

Hedera Canariensis Fol. Var.—Grows more slowly than the green ivy. Likes to be kept fairly moist. An occasional wash or spray will prevent leaves going yellow.

Cissus Antarctica.—Roots should be kept moist when actively growing. Does not need much light. Can be trained and pruned to any desired shape. Very hardy.

Hedera Helix Chicago.—Very easy to grow. Likes to be moist but never wet. Makes quick growth, often in fits and starts. When in active growth, requires

★ ★ ★ ★ ★ ★ OUTDOOR PLANTS ★ ★ ★ ★ ★ ★ ★

THE PENGUIN GOURDS (often known as "Arctic Snowbirds").—The gourd resembles a penguin in shape. When ripe, they are painted and mounted on a wooden base with cotton-wool around to represent snow. Most unusual and, when artistically done, find a ready sale, especially at fêtes and bazaars.

THE CHINESE WOOLFLOWER.—Plants grow to 3 t. high, the blooms starting early with a central head, round and globular, which often reaches 2 ft. in circumference. Scores of branches are thrown out, each bearing a ball of scarlet wool. All these branches support numerous laterals of bloom, mixed with fresh green foliage, so that the plant looks like an immense bouquet in the ground.

THE BIRD PLANT.—Has pretty flowers of pale yellow with purplish spots. Its seeds have a very distinctive appearance, with a long curved horn which splits into two parts as they ripen and harden. Very effective in combination with Penguin Gourds, they can be painted to represent canaries, blue jays, robins, etc., and mounted on a piece of sandpaper are a distinct novelty.

THE BIRD OF PARADISE PLANT.—The flower is a rich golden yellow, measuring $2\frac{1}{4}$ inches across and produced in very large trusses. The long incurved stamens and pistils, which spread out in fan-like form, are bright crimson. The foliage is also highly decorative.

A charming variety of plants: Variegated bougainvillea, Cissus rhombefolia, variegated and Chicago Ivy, Cissus Antarctica, Holnis self-branching Ivy and Philodendron Cordatum

Below: Ficus pumila, Cissus Antarctica, Hedera helix Chicago. In the centre: Tradescantia and Hedera helix Chicago. On the ledge: Monstera deliciosa, Ficus radicans, Sansevieria trifasciata

leaves. Good climber or trailer, very hardy.

Ficus Decora.—Likes rich soil and constant feeding once the pot is full of roots. Keep away from sunlight, moist but not wet. Very hardy.

Philodendron Scandens.—Heart-shaped leaves, medium green. Good trailer or climber. Likes a dark position and to be kept moist.

Ficus Pumila.—Small leaved plant from China. Must be kept thoroughly moist. Climbs well because it throws out many small suckers of great clinging capacity. Can also be grown as a bushy plant by taking off the tips of all the growing shoots about 6 in. from top of pot.

Sansevieria Trifasciata Laurentii.—Slow grower. Must be kept dry almost to desert conditions. If over-watered, plants will rot and fall over at base. Thrives on little light. Does not need re-potting for a considerable time. Could exist on watering only once a month.

Bulbs

See p. 216 for a separate chapter on Growing Bulbs in Fibre, including choice of suitable varieties and the care and planting of bulbs.

more water, which should be reduced when it is not growing. Does not like direct sun. Leaves should be washed or sprayed occasionally.

Rhoicissus Rhomboidea. — Can stand heat, dryness and a fair amount of light. Keep moist but not wet, or it will shed its

*All plants shown in this chapter grown by Thomas Rochford & Son Ltd., Broxbourne Herts.,
and photographed by Violet Stevenson*

KEEPING THE HOUSE COOL

*Homes, like people, need to put on summer
clothes for comfort when the weather warms up*

by GLADYS MANN

THERE is nothing more refreshing in
summer than to walk into a cool, airy
house and escape from the heat and glare
outside. Just as we change our own clothes
from winter to summer, we should change
our homes into summer dress—and this
does not only mean stopping fires and turning off central heating.

A house that *looks* cool also *feels* cool.
Start your campaign by removing from
your rooms everything that has been put
there for warmth in winter. Heavy curtains and pelmets should be replaced by
cool-looking prints and chintzes; chairs and
settees given loose covers in the same
materials or plain to tone. The colours that
give the effect of coolness are ice blue, pale
green, pale yellow and, of course, white.
Avoid violent reds, spicy pinks, purple
(though mauve is good with pale green)
and vivid orange. Velvet cushions should
be re-covered in silk or cotton material.

Leave parquet floors bare, apart from an
occasional mat or rug. Move the furniture
away from the fire and have the seating
arangement facing the garden or the window. Fill the fireplace with growing plants,
and, if possible, have a miniature aquarium
set in some eye-catching corner. There is
nothing so cool and restful as the sight of
green water and fish swimming in leisurely
fashion.

Keeping out the Sun

During the hottest part of the day, the
sun must be kept out of the rooms. For
this, venetian blinds are excellent. The
windows can be opened and the blinds
pulled down and adjusted so that the required amount of light and air comes in.
Modern venetian blinds are a great improvement on their Edwardian forebears.
They are easy to operate and to keep clean,
and are made in lovely pastel shades to
match individual colour schemes.

Outside, blinds and awnings in gay
stripes create a Continental atmosphere.
Used on windows leading to a roof garden,
they give an added illusion of space.
These, too, can be adjusted according to
the slant of the sun. It is as well, when
having sun blinds fitted, to have a matching curtain for the door. This saves paint
blistering and flaking, and, especially
where there are glass panels to the door,
keeps the hall cool.

Another way to keep rooms cool, yet
airy, is by means of ventilators set into the
windows. Hand-operated ones can be adjusted by a cord. Electric ventilators extract stale air and admit cooled fresh air
without draughts.

The Hot Kitchen

The room where, perhaps, the heat is
felt most is the kitchen. Unfortunately,
many kitchens have a southerly aspect—or
a pantry facing south. As soon as the
sun shines, this becomes a hot-air cupboard.

If this is the case, it may be possible to
plant a quick-growing bush to protect the
pantry. Failing that, have some sort of permanent shade erected on the sunny side.
Some air, however, must be allowed in the
pantry. At least part of the window should
be of metal gauze or perforated zinc, ensuring an air-draught all the time. Small
electric fans are ideal for the pantry.
When it is very hot, a piece of sacking or
coarse blanket-cloth, soaked in cold water
and hung dripping wet over the window,
will work wonders. The cloth should be re-soaked several times a day.

In the kitchen, an air-extractor or electric window fan is almost a necessity, and
any window that catches the sun should
have an outside blind or shade. The newest type of portable fan, which can be
placed near the stove or on the table, has
rubber blades, is small and elegantly designed and almost noiseless in action.

Plastic curtains are cool-looking and are
really better than cotton in the kitchen in
summer. They are easy to sponge down
when they become sticky and damp.

Cook by Fridge

One of the most heating things in any house, especially on hot days, is cooking. In summer, try making your refrigerator "cook" for you, rather than your stove. It is cooler to cook in the morning or evening, and while on the job prepare more than you need. Extra food can always be stored in the refrigerator. If you heat the kitchen only once a day, you will help to keep the house cool. See that jellied foods are available in the refrigerator, and long cool drinks for people who may arrive hot and tired.

Below, a portable fan by G.E.C. with rubber blades, can be placed near the cooking stove or on the table to cool a hot kitchen

Above, a window air-extractor fan keeps a kitchen fresh and cool. Cooking smells are eliminated. The Xpelair fan has a regulator providing four different speeds.

Heat causes flies to come out, though in these days of D.D.T. insecticides, the old summer fly pest is almost a thing of the past. Daily room spraying is a good habit in summer, even if flies are not visible. Insecticides kill eggs and grubs as well. Alternatively, an insecticidal lacquer can be painted on window ledges and doors—or wherever flies and other pests can get in. This will make them pest-repellent for eighteen months to two years and it can be used both indoors and out.

Though you may not feel inclined to keep the hot water supply going all the time, remember that tepid baths are more refreshing than cold ones and hot water is needed for washing and washing-up even on the hottest day. If heating the water makes the kitchen unbearable, do it late at night.

GROWING BULBS IN FIBRE

*The secrets of success are—choose the best bulbs and fibre,
give ample depth in bowls, provide light, air and water*

by J. S. DAKERS, A.H., R.H.S.

GROWING bulbs in bowls of fibre is something that every member of the family can do. It requires neither greenhouse nor garden, can be carried out in a room and is neither exacting nor difficult, though there are certain well-defined rules which must be followed.

The first thing to remember is that one is dealing with living things and any wrong or casual treatment will result in poor quality of flowers (if any) or even in complete failure. In other words, the developing bulb and its root system must be kept in mind and the essentials of plant life must always be available; in this case, water, air, light and cleanliness.

Secondly, good-quality materials must be used—first class bulbs, extra good fibre and bowls which allow reasonable space for the roots to develop. The third important point is that there must be some sort of time-table, though it is seldom a very rigid one.

There are many things in which bulbs can be grown besides bowls which are specially made for this purpose. Old soup tureens, vegetable dishes, bronze and copper vases, plastic ware and the ordinary flower pot or earthenware pan could be used. The only thing against pots or pans with drainage holes in the base is that they must have saucers or tins underneath while in the house.

Ideal Depth

The ordinary bulb bowl, having no holes in it, is therefore more useful and generally much more in keeping with the room and its furniture. Beware of shallow bowls, for they are seldom serviceable and certainly not as satisfying to the root system of the bulbs. The ideal depth of the rooting area is 3 in., though $2\frac{1}{2}$ in. is enough for some of the smaller and dwarf-growing bulbs, such as crocus, scilla, chionodoxa, snowdrop, muscari, miniature narcissus and winter aconite.

Any receptacle deeper than 3 in. can, of course, be used, for there is nothing against this extra rooting area, so long as one remembers that watering could easily be overdone where a larger bulk of fibre is used. The main point is to avoid the shallow pan.

There are many materials in which bulbs can be grown, but here I am dealing with fibre only, and its quality is of vital importance. Always buy the best fibre from a reliable source, specially mixed and blended with other things for this particular work. Bulb fibre is a mixture of horticultural peat and coconut fibre with some oyster shell and crushed charcoal added. If purchased dry, its colour should be light brown. If sold by weight, buy it dry and not wet, or you will be paying for water.

Soak the Fibre

Having bought the fibre, it is very important to soak it well. If bulbs are planted in fibre which is not wet, it is very difficult to moisten afterwards. When fibre is bought in loosely made bags, the best way to soak it is to put the whole bag into a tub of water and leave it there until the whole of the bulk is saturated. Then turn it out of the bag, drain and partly dry it. Loosen it by turning two or three times, and when it gets to the stage where it can be handled without sticking to the fingers, it can be considered ready for use.

At this stage the bowls, fibre and, most important, the bulbs themselves should be ready. Here I want to emphasise the importance of quality. If you are going to spend money, time and labour on this type of cultivation, it pays to buy the best bulbs. Cheap ones or those bought in bulk at the end of the planting season are seldom any use indoors, so never begrudge the extra pence for a good bulb. The bud which will ultimately give you the flower you anticipate is already formed and ready to begin its development.

The procedure of filling the bowls and

planting is very simple, but when the basal layers of fibre are placed in the bowl they must not be pressed too hard, especially if the fibre is on the wet side. You may have seen bulbs force themselves upward and out of the fibre as they started to grow. This happens when the strong roots growing from the bulb cannot easily push their way into the fibre, and so they push the bulb upwards. This should not occur if the top layers are made very firm when the bulbs are planted and the lower ones left just normally pressed.

Before planting, one must decide whether the surface of the bowl shall be mounded up above the rim or whether it shall be level and just below the rim. If the former, there will be more fibre in the bowl, which is all to the good, but watering will have to be done more carefully.

Fill the bowl about half-way with fibre and then place the bulbs in position. When the bulbs are covered, their noses should be visible when the fibre between them has been made quite firm. One or two trials will soon show you the right depth. Most bulbs can be planted almost touching each other. Nothing spoils a bowl of flowers more than a skimped appearance due to not having enough bulbs.

Photo: Carters Tested Seeds Ltd.

John Evelyn, with broad white perianth and a large apricot-orange cup. It grows well in fibre

When to Plant

The actual planting season begins in early September and goes on until November. The first to go in will be those required for Christmas blooming—"prepared' hyacinths, early narcissi, snowdrops, winter aconite, certain bulbous irises and early tulips—these being followed by the later flowering bulbs of all kinds.

Having filled the bowls, pressed the surface and finished off the fibre in a tidy manner, stand the bowls on a level surface and water them. This settles the fibre and also ensures that from the start it is nicely moist all through.

Now comes the question of where these bowls are to stand during the period of root-making. The answer is—*outdoors*. Find a level spot well out of everyone's way, place them close together and cover with 4 or 5 in. of old ashes. By so doing, one is really only following Nature's method of starting the growing bulb in cool conditions. To give any bulb warmth at this stage will mean failure. Covering with these old weathered ashes (or soil, peat, sand or leaf-mould) will also ensure that the bulbs do not rise upwards, the very

Early tulip Ibis, rose-pink with silvery sheen. An excellent
variety for bowls

into the half-light for a fort-night, when the foliage will have turned green. The more light they have the better, but keep the bulbs still as cold as possible. It is the patient grower who is most likely to achieve outstanding success.

Once out of the plunge bed of ashes, the vital thing is to avoid the fibre drying out. If it does, the roots may suffer and die. The best way to water all bowls is to immerse the whole thing in water, allow it to remain for a time, lift out and stand the bowl on its side so that superfluous water can drain away. Bowls watered in this way will remain moist for a good time, though no one can say for just how long, so the grower must watch for the first appearance of dryness on the surface.

Give them Light

Give ample light at this stage and turn the bowl round quite frequently, otherwise the foliage will be drawn towards the light and the result will be lop-sided flowers and foliage.

Watch for the moment when the buds are seen just leaving the nose of the bulb, for this is the moment when it is permissible to move the bowl into a warm room. If they are taken into warmth too soon, the result may be too much weak foliage and "papery" dried-up buds.

At this stage of development, support must be considered. For daffodils and narcissi the simple method is to place four thin hazel sticks around the side of the pot, sloping these slightly outward, and tie them round with soft green twine or wool, making sure the sticks are long enough for a second encircling tie as the foliage develops.

Tulip foliage will not require support but the flower stem may, and a thin piece

weight of the covering keeping them down.

If it is not possible to put the bulbs outside, then the next best place is the coldest room or shed you have, and it is not essential for the bowls to be in the dark. The one place to avoid is the warm, airless cupboard.

Keep them Cool

Those covered with ashes should be allowed to remain for six weeks if planted in September and five weeks for the October planting. After this period, take a bowl or two out and examine them. If the growth has started and is an inch or so long, the bowls must be taken out and put

of wire pushed into the fibre or bulb with the stem tied to this is ideal. Early tulips should not require it. The same method of wires or very thin sticks can be used for the hyacinth—the spike of flower only needing support.

Bulbs to Choose

To make the flowers last in full beauty for as long as possible, avoid very hot rooms or positions near a radiator or stove. At this time air and light are just as important as they are all through the season of growth.

Summing up, bulb-growing in bowls demands the best fibre and bulbs, ample depth in the bowls, light and air, careful watering and a certain amount of patience. Given these, anyone should achieve success.

Here follows a list of subjects which can be grown with no other facilities than are generally found in the normal home.

Narcissus and Daffodil. — Some of the most rewarding of all bowl-grown bulbs. Paper-white and Soleil d'Or will come into bloom before or by Christmas in cool conditions. Follow them by such well-known sorts as Cragford, Spring Glory, Carlton, King Alfred, Halvose, Fortune and a whole host of others. In all good bulb catalogues the varieties useful for bowls are listed in their flowering sequence.

Tulips.—These are divided into sections—Early Flowering Singles, Early Flowering Doubles, Triumph, Mendel, Darwin, Parrot and May flowering groups. Again one must study catalogues, but the order in which I have placed them shows the sequence of blooming.

Hyacinths. — Choose those known as the "pre-cooled" or "prepared" hyacinths for early blooming as well as those smaller-flowered types known as Roman or Italian. They may be followed by all the named sorts, of which there are now almost every colour. The patient grower who keeps hyacinths in the cool

until the flower is well out of the bulb will score the most success.

Crocus.—These are easy but hate artificial warmth in any form, so keep them outdoors until late January. The result will surprise you.

Iris.—The bulbous irises are also excellent if one keeps them cool and gives ample light. The best of the early flowering sorts are *I. tingitana, I. imperator* and the Spanish and Dutch sorts, notably the lovely blue Wedgwood. The miniature irises must not be given *any* warmth.

Many other bulbs can, of course, be grown in this way, such as Winter Aconite, Snowdrop, Chionodoxa, Scilla, Fritillaria, Jonquil and, for those with experience, Lachenalia, Ranunculus, Ixia and certain Anemones.

Halvose, a delightful bunch-flowered narcissus, with a rich red crown and strong yellow perianth

HOW TO MAKE A
WINDOW-GARDEN

You can grow flowers in infinite variety,
herbs or even salads on a city window-sill

JUST any old box won't do for a window-garden. If it is the wrong shape, it might fall off the sill and injure someone on the pavement below. So start with a bar of iron across the sill, screwed into the wall at each side. Then make your box to fit. Raise it on tiles to allow the air to circulate beneath, and the drainage holes to work.

Anyone can make a window-box; it is the simplest form of carpentry and, even if the corners and edges are a bit rough, the paint will cover that. Study the facings of the house before painting. If red brick, green or white are the best colours; but if the house is of grey stone, scarlet or deep blue will add a welcome note of gaiety and colour.

When the paint is dry, cover the bottom

Photo: "Amateur Gardening"

Anything taller than these daffodils would block the view from the window and keep the light from the room

of the box with broken brick or rubble. Then fill up with compost, which is stocked at all nursery shops for that purpose. Leave 2 in. clear at the top, otherwise the drips from watering will annoy people passing below; and when planting or working with the soil, use a small trowel to do the job neatly without spilling earth. If the boxes are correctly sited, they can provide real pleasure gardens all the year round.

Siting is the real secret of window-gardening. Before planting anything, the question should be asked: Which way does the window face?

This is important, because planning depends on aspect. Bulbs such as the crocus will grow in boxes facing north or east, but the coloured Italian hyacinths, charming in blue, pink and pale yellow when they flower, do better facing south. Yellow winter aconite, and a gorgeous show of anemone fulgens, can be produced facing south or west; but under no circumstances should the boxes be filled with wallflowers, which simply can't help shrivelling in the winds and draughts. The very sight of them makes the winter seem long.

Avoid Tall Flowers

When the bulbs have flowered, they can be taken out and stored. Then the soil can be turned over with the trowel, and replanted for the summer. For north aspects choose London pride, calendula, Canterbury bell, foxglove, creeping jenny, or the "Lilliput" nasturtiums—those dainty little flowers which produce themselves in great profusion to a height of only 6 in.

This matter of height is important too, for window-gardens with tall occupants block the view. They keep the light out of the room as well, and that is why ivy-leafed geraniums, which hang so beautifully over the side, are so much in demand.

If your window faces east, there is no need to be discouraged. Marigolds will grow well there and fulfil a double purpose.

The plant is a herb and the petals can be used *dried*, for infusion in soups. Or they are delicious and sleep-inducing with hot milk. Stocks, violas and pansies all grow well, too, on eastern window-sills, and the night-scented stock (*M. tristis*), though weedy and drab in appearance, can be slipped in to fill the room with scent on a still summer evening.

South- and west-sited window-gardens will grow almost anything. Geraniums and lobelias make a glorious show, and clever house-wives can have nasturtiums in profusion and make sauce with the flowers. Afterwards they can gather the seeds and pickle them for use instead of capers.

Photo: *"Amateur Gardening"*

Many flat-dwellers have balconies where flowers can be grown in a really large box—or even an old sink

Endless are the uses of window-gardens. You can have a herb garden with borage, camomile and marigolds, or you may grow the drabber-looking chives and parsley. You can cultivate lettuce and even tomatoes, if these are trained to grow up the wall at each side so as not to interfere with the light of the room.

Indeed, adventure is the very spirit of window-gardening. Instead of using soil, the boxes can be filled with knobby bits of stone to give a rock-garden effect; and then planted like a Dresden china picture. Aubrietias, pink double-daisies and other rock plants will flourish in these circumstances.

Water even when it Rains

Nothing will grow in a window-garden without regular watering, and even when the rain is pouring down outside, that is not a substitute. The eaves of some houses overhang greatly, so in the wettest weather a window-garden can be as dry as a bone. So feel the soil each day, to make sure that it is moist and that the drainage system is working properly. Use the water-can carefully, to avoid annoyance to people below.

All plants dislike draughts, and window-gardens catch cold, so when the window is wide open, remember to shut the doors.

The expense of continually buying new plants can be avoided by using a "Home Seed Raiser." This enables the soil to be heated by electric current; moisture is controlled by a "wick" drawing water from the trough at the side, and the result is the beginning of fine healthy salads in the middle of winter. Later on, the space can be used for raising flowers from seed.

Cacti should not be planted in window-boxes. They are natives of warm climates and do much better in pots, which can be taken indoors in cold weather. A large amount of sandy soil is not necessary for cacti, so the pots may be small for the size of the plants, and in the summer these can be put out on the boxes, where they give a fine effect with a background of flowers. But cacti, if they are to flower well the following year, need heat in the autumn when they are ripening their wood, so they are better indoors. And during the winter they need no watering.

Many flats and houses have balconies, and builders are often glad to get rid of the old-fashioned stone sinks. On the balcony you can make a *sunk* garden out of a sink, providing the bottom is well drained in exactly the same way as for the window-gardens. The taller plants, such as roses or chrysanthemums, can be grown in a sink, or you can make a miniature pond in it with a water-lily and goldfish.

GROWING WITH LIGHT

*Decorative lamps to illuminate your rooms—and at the same time
make your plants grow*

NOT so long ago the fashion for indoor plants was confined to an aspidistra in the parlour window. Not very decorative perhaps, but this foliage plant, with its broad taper leaves, stood up to a lot of punishment and made a brave showing—if anyone took the trouble to look at it.

It was so common that nobody *did* look.

To-day, when indoor plants are high fashion and are often cultivated with lighting effects, it would be impossible *not* to look at them because they strike the eye instantly. Such plants as anthurium, azalea, balsam, begonia, cactus, fuchsia, myrtle, oxalia and a host of others can now be nurtured inside the house, and trained to look their best under electric lamps, which also help with their cultivation.

How our grandmothers would have

"Solar" is a table lamp fitting in white with a gay yellow shade and three plant holders in pale blue and white stripes

"Latin," a Siemens Fleurlite Fitting, has a red, black and white contemporary shade, a green base and white stem

gasped at this new form of interior decoration. All they could do to give a room a new look was to move the furniture around, but to-day we can make our homes sparkle with light and colour by a touch.

This is a delightful development, particularly for those who have no outside gardens. The technique is quite simple. Keeping the soil moderately dry, the pot containing the established plant is placed within a larger pot, and the space between the two pots is then filled with moist garden peat or moss. Thus the soil around the roots of the plant dries out slowly over a period of about a week; *and when water is required to revive it to further activity, this is applied to the outside circle of peat or moss.*

No plant, either inside or outside, will grow well with too little or too much moisture, and it is well to remember that

These Fleurlite wall fittings lend themselves particularly well to the cultivation of trailing plants such as ivies. (Above) "Chelsea" is in Wedgwood blue with black and red buckram shades. (Right) "Oslo" is in white, with a yellow shade and blue and white striped plant holders

professional gardeners feel the base with their hands before they attempt to water at all.

By this means a varied collection of flowering, trailing and foliage plants (about which the nurserymen are prepared to give friendly advice) can be trained to grow at a slow rate with the aid of floral lighting. No window light is necessary. Ingeniously graded lamps, including wall brackets as well as floor and table fixtures, can change the atmosphere of a room by one flick of a switch.

The electric bulbs are known by the scientific names—"mercury vapour discharge" and a "tungsten filament lamp"—but do not be discouraged by that.

This delightful hobby, called "growing with light," originated with the increased interest in interior decoration. It introduces a new beauty to the home, but could in time do more than that. It might introduce quite a new form of gardening, in which exotic plants such as orchids (some varieties of which are fairly hardy) and, of course, cactus, could be successfully propagated.

What an opportunity for the growing of ferns! They, too, like aspidistras, were once popular for indoor decoration—and very handsome some of them looked—but are seldom seen now. By means of floral lighting, varieties of fern hitherto only available for those with heated greenhouses could be cultivated.

You can change the "mood" of a sitting-room, or bedroom for that matter, merely by means of a switch. The mood may be drowsy and restful, if the weather outside is depressing; or you can change over to a bright and cheerful summer atmosphere.

There is no end to the possibilities of this new culture. In the same way as a garden, it can express personality.

PERIOD FURNITURE

The characteristics to look for in the beautiful hand-made pieces of by-gone times

IN the vocabulary of furnishing the terms "antique," "period," and "traditional" tend to be used rather loosely. **Antique**, according to generally recognised custom, can be applied to anything more than one hundred years old. **Period** usually means in the style of one of the recognised epochs or schools of furniture design, dating roughly from early seventeenth to the early nineteenth centuries. Even twenty-five years ago, good furniture design was deemed to have ended with the Regency period (*circa* 1800–1830), but early Victorian styles now qualify as antiques and are admitted under the "period" banner.

All period furniture is not, however, antique. Reproductions of the designs of earlier epochs have always been, and still are, being made. A few of these are very good, a number mediocre, and perhaps even more no better than travesties of the originals. Such furniture may be labelled "reproduction"—for example, "Jacobean repro," "Queen Anne," "Chippendale"—but is frequently just referred to as period or traditional without any further qualification. **Traditional**, in its broadest sense, is applied to everything not obviously in the contemporary or modern idiom.

CHARACTERISTICS OF THE VARIOUS FURNITURE PERIODS

Jacobean (1603–1688)

Outside of museums and of the great country houses, scarcely any furniture earlier than this period survives. This is partly due to sheer age, but also to the fact that before the seventeenth century there was comparatively little in common use.

Onwards from the end of the preceding reign of Elizabeth an increasing number of new houses were built for merchants and others of the prosperous middle class and furniture was accordingly required for them. Made mainly of English oak, this early Jacobean furniture is sturdy, simple in shape and scaled to fit the low-ceilinged rooms of the time.

The chairs are high in the seat, for, to keep feet off the draughty floors, footstools were much used. These seats are usually of wood and the chairs themselves are rather square-looking with slightly bulbous turned legs. Tables are rectangular, with low cross rails or stretchers between the legs. Chests of drawers and sideboards, as we know them, were not made. Instead, there are chests with top lids, dressers, cupboards and the court cupboard made in two tiers with the top half slightly recessed. Another characteristic piece was the joint stool. This is largely reproduced to-day for use as a small occasional table or seating stool. Although the shape of early seventeenth-century furniture is simple, most surfaces are richly carved.

A two-tiered Jacobean oak court cupboard, ornamented with fleur-de-lys and shield, bearing the date 1607

Cromwellian (1649–1660)

About the middle of the century fashion changed, rather more drastically than it might otherwise have done, when Cromwell and his Roundheads came to power. Decoration was abhorrent to the Puritans, so carving disappeared. Comfort, however, did not suffer and the wooden seats and backs of chairs were largely superseded by leather ones fixed to the frame by dome-headed studs.

Carolean (1660–1689)

With the Restoration in 1660 came another drastic change. Not only did decoration in every form come in again, but velvet, brocade and petit point upholstery on chair backs and seats are characteristic; so is a heavy fringe finish. A frequent decorative motif is the crown. The graceful barley sugar twist gives a lighter air to legs and stretcher rails. Gateleg tables are usually associated with this period. Oak was no longer the favourite wood but was rivalled by walnut.

William and Mary (1689–1702)

When James II, after a brief reign of three years, fled to France and his daughter Mary and her Dutch husband came to the throne, fashion turned again to the Continent for inspiration. In general, everything became softer and more gracious-looking, curves taking the place of rectangular lines. Inlay is more characteristic than carving, especially in the Dutch marquetry style. Chairs of this period have high, straight backs, as did the Stuart ones, but they are less angular in appearance. Scroll-shaped stretchers to both chairs and tables are another identifying feature.

Queen Anne (1702–1714)

With the eighteenth century a simple elegance comes into design. Mahogany from abroad begins to rival English walnut. The first signs of the borrowing from the Chinese which was to prove so important an influence during the next hundred years are to be seen in the lacquered decoration on some Queen Anne cabinets and also in the ball and claw legs. The simpler cabriole legs are also typical—for instance, on the beautiful small kneehole tables which make such attractive writing desks.

Curved backs are a characteristic of the

An oak joint stool of the mid-seventeenth century, with knobbed and ringed legs, at the Victoria and Albert Museum

chairs, which are often ornamented by a carved cockle shell. The stretcher between the chair legs has largely disappeared. Small Queen Anne chests of drawers have fine proportions, without the unwieldiness of some later styles, as have the early tallboys (double chests with the top half somewhat set back).

Georgian (1714–1800)

Furniture designed during the rest of the century, in the reigns of the first three Georges, is in tune with the simple yet beautiful domestic architecture of the time. It was principally made of mahogany and has in common fine, dignified proportions, a flowing outline and detail demanding skilled craftsmanship. In such a long period of time, however, there were naturally changes of fashion and of emphasis. These were intensified because of the brilliance of some of the designers who worked during the epoch and who have given their names to styles they themselves originated.

Chippendale (1745–1780)

First and probably the greatest of the master cabinet makers and designers was

Thomas Chippendale of Worcester, who came to London and had a shop in St. Martin's Lane. His influence extended far beyond his immediate customers, because he published a book of original furniture designs which became the textbook of craftsmen all over the country. This first appeared in 1754. He had a wonderfully fertile brain and superb technique, and created furniture in the grand manner worthy of the magnificent homes of the nobility.

He used mahogany almost entirely, and enriched it with

A magnificent carved mahogany bookcase attributed to Thomas Chippendale, who created furniture in the grand manner worthy of the splendid homes of the nobility

Robert Adam paid as much attention to designing furniture as houses—the chair (left) is one of his, to be seen at the Victoria and Albert Museum

carving needing the most skilful execution, often in intricate designs of ribands or in pierced ladder-back effects. The shaped, rectangular backs of his handsome chairs are joined directly to the seat. Back legs are usually straight, the front ones often of cabriole or ball-and-claw type, except in the Chinese Chippendale, where open fret rectangular carving is used. Seats are sometimes bow-fronted. Small, elegant "pie-crust" tables and others with little fretwork galleries, huge "breakfront" (the centre section slightly deeper than those at the sides) bookcases with glazed doors, cabriole-legged tables that were sometimes fitted dressing tables that were sometimes transformed into bureaux — all these, in many variations, are "Chippendale," but no sideboards. A Chippendale style sideboard may embody features associated with the designer's work, but it cannot be genuine.

Hepplewhite (1760–1790)

The Prince of Wales, later the Prince Regent and then George IV, was the leader of high society when George Hepplewhite, who followed Chippendale, was creating his charming and quietly distinguished furniture. Quite naturally, therefore, the Prince of Wales' feathers often appeared in the carving. In various forms they appear in chair backs, as do interlacing hearts and shields. These backs are usually separated from the seat by a rail an inch or so above it. Hepplewhite legs are straight and square with spade feet, and the general effect is rather less overwhelming and formal than that of Chippendale chairs.

Hepplewhite sideboards are exceptionally fine, satinwood often being allied with mahogany. A characteristic and much copied style is bow or serpentine fronted with six square, spade-footed legs and concave corners. There are small cupboards each end and a centre drawer, but no back. A pedestal type of sideboard with a broad single drawer, set at a rather lower level, between the two cupboards and with a small low back behind the centre section only, is another variation. Drawer and cupboard handles usually take the form of simple brass rings. The typical dining table of the period is oval, with simple tripod supports at each end.

Robert Adam (1758–1792)

The fashionable domestic architect, Robert Adam, in partnership with his

brother James, designed whole interiors, as well as the noble houses themselves, for his wealthy clients. Although he did not make it himself, he paid as much attention to the furniture as to the panelling or decoration of a fireplace. All his designs were classic in inspiration, using for decoration all the motifs associated with Greek art. His swags, stylised wreaths, garlands and urns, and also the painted masks and figures of birds and animals, have a somewhat cold elegance. Painted decoration was used instead of inlay, and sometimes fine Wedgwood medallions are incorporated. Side tables, long and narrow, or of the graceful semicircular console type, designed to be placed flat against a wall, are characteristic.

Sheraton (1790–1810)

Much lighter and often on a smaller scale than all the rather massive early and mid-Georgian furniture, Sheraton pieces are yet, owing to their fine balance, surprisingly strong. Thomas Sheraton,

The Prince of Wales' feathers often appear in the charming and quietly distinguished furniture of Hepplewhite, as in the chair (left)

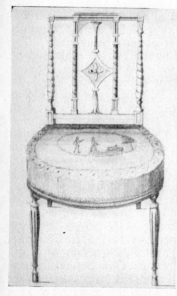

A typically pretty and delicate drawing-room chair from Sheraton's Drawing Book, 1791–4 (above). They often have lyre- or urn-shaped open backs

The motifs of Greek art inspired much of Robert Adam's work. Right, is a typical long narrow side table, carved and gilt, dated 1765

Photo: "Country Life"

like Chippendale, was a master cabinet maker who published a famous book of furniture designs.

The general feeling of Sheraton furniture is not unlike that of Hepplewhite, except for the use of a great deal of satinwood inlay, often in shell motifs and fine lines, but only occasionally restrained carving.

The pretty and delicate chairs often have lyre- or urn-shaped open backs, or sometimes the backs consist of effectively simple, crossed, open uprights. These are more often rectangular in outline and lower than Hepplewhite style ones, which are frequently curved. Dining tables, oval shaped, have tapered legs, sometimes reeded. The inlaid sideboards resemble Hepplewhite ones in general outline, though details differ. A brass rail at the back for a curtain is sometimes incorporated. Many small pieces, cupboards, bureaux, fitted dressing tables, have the unmistakable Sheraton handwriting, but unfortunately there have been many bad copies in which a slight distortion of the proportions and detail has destroyed the delicate charm.

Regency (1810–1837)

Like the Prince Regent himself, during the actual years of the Regency and when he was on the throne, Regency furniture inclines to be florid. There is a certain likeness between late Georgian of the Adams' and Sheraton schools and Regency, but the restraint has gone. Curves are everywhere, and there is a profusion of decoration. Following Nelson's victory of the Nile, an Egyptian flavour is discernible. Sphinxes and other winged animals appear in carving, and particularly in the metal decoration that is so typical. Feet of the circular, centre-column dining and occasional tables, for instance, are often brass shod in the form of a sphinx's claws. Narrow ormolu galleries and backs to side tables and marble tops are also a feature.

William IV and Early Victorian (1830–1850)

The general shapes of much of the furniture made in this period resemble fairly closely the Regency styles, but the line is often blurred and thickened. Regency may border on the vulgar in its elaboration but it possesses real elegance. By 1840 this characteristic has largely gone, carving has lost definition and is becoming over-heavy. On the other hand, workmanship is superb, veneers are exquisitely worked and the quality of the wood first class.

Rosewood continues fashionable as well as mahogany. Narrow brass inlays are still used, but the sphinxes and so forth have vanished. There is a good deal of pleasant "parlour" furniture, designed for ladies' informal sitting rooms rather than formal drawing rooms. Bow-legged, open-backed chairs, not too big or heavy, and often with needlework seats, work boxes set on the top of shaped columns, games tables, also set on a column that splays out into a broad foot, have a definite charm. Some of the small chiffoniers (a type of small sideboard) are also attractive.

Country Made and Country Styled Period Furniture

In furniture, as in everything else, there are various qualities and classes of workmanship, and of styling. This is particularly true with genuine period furniture which was, of course, hand made. The fashionable London cabinet makers, who made for the well-to-do nobility, turned out a very different type of work from the country-town craftsmen, whose customers were the local gentry or the better-off middle-class. Their designs were simplified and usually rather behind the times. They used local woods as much or more than the imported mahogany.

This explains why much of the antique period furniture to be bought to-day, outside of the exclusive antique dealers, does not conform to the book, as it were. It has the general feeling of the period, and even some characteristics of the great cabinet makers' designs, in just the same way as a dress made from a "Dior design" pattern will repeat, in modified form, current Dior features, but it could not be mistaken for a couturier model.

Country made, as it is usually called, Georgian furniture, for instance, may often be of oak, walnut or fruit wood, and wooden seats to chairs are common. Carving is much simplified.

Furniture of this class can often be picked up at country auctions or in the smaller antique shops. If there is a set of chairs, for instance, prices are likely to be quite high, even if the workmanship and condition are not first class, but the single chair, or the small table, is often less expensive than a modern equivalent.

Country style furniture has its own traditions, born of the local countryside in which it was made. It was not an adaptation of the prevalent London fashion. Simple, sturdy Windsor chairs, ladder-back chairs, wheel-back chairs are examples. Often the proportions and workmanship are very satisfying indeed. The spool or spindle used in spinning is another motif used, usually to decorate the back of a variation of the ladder-back chair. Seats are most often of wood but sometimes of rush. Oak, beech and chestnut are most popular woods, but elm, ash and yew are not uncommon.

Photo : " Country Life "

USING PERIOD FURNITURE

There are no hard and fast rules on how to introduce antiques into the home, but it is easier not to mix early Jacobean with eighteenth century, as the feeling of the periods is so different. On the other hand, both can be used in conjunction with carefully chosen modern furniture to excellent effect. If possible, there should be some unifying feature, such as curved (or rectangular) lines. The scale of all pieces should be similar, too, and in proportion to the room. A huge eighteenth-century library bookcase would clearly be out of keeping in a small drawing room.

Nelson's victory of the Nile made Egyptian styles popular — like the occasional table (above), with brass gallery, gilt and carved support

A fine example of simple, sturdy country-style furniture is the Windsor chair (left), in yew with an elm seat, date about 1770, at the Victoria and Albert Museum

Country style furniture can look very well in contemporary schemes, and a single piece of Queen Anne, Chippendale or Regency will become a focus round which the rest of the furnishing scheme can be built. On the other hand, too much would be overwhelming except in rather grand rooms. Hepplewhite is perfect for a dining room that need not be very large, and Sheraton blends beautifully into a quite modest sitting room.

Prices of period furniture depend upon current fashion as well as on its rarity and quality. All genuine seventeenth-century and Queen Anne furniture in decent condition is getting scarce and prices are scaled accordingly. With later eighteenth-century work, a great deal depends upon the quality. Country made pieces are the best buy for those of moderate means. Regency is now fashionable and so is often inflated in price. Early Victorian, if chosen with a good eye and discrimination, can be an excellent proposition. See colour plates for how to recognise the various periods.

ANTIQUE COLLECTING ON A SMALL SCALE

Some hints for the home-lover of modest means

THERE is only one sensible way for the unknowledgeable to set about collecting antiques of any kind. It is to acquire only what one likes personally and what will fit into a furnishing scheme or give pleasure when displayed. Obviously, purchases should, at least to start with, be kept well within one's means.

Luckily, there is plenty of scope for those who appreciate the handmade furniture, accessories and knick-knacks of the past but who cannot afford to spend much.

In furniture proper, country made or country style individual items are the best proposition. In addition to the single or, sometimes, pairs of wooden-seated or similar upright chairs that can often be acquired for a pound or two each, a useful item is the small oval or circular "loo" table. This has a graceful centre pedestal on which the top swivels so that it can be folded down flat against it. These Georgian-type tables, appearing in oak and fruitwood as well as mahogany, are useful in a sitting room and also by the side of the bed. Price depends very largely upon condition, but ranges from a couple of pounds upwards.

Early nineteenth-century games and work tables are rapidly increasing in price, but quite a pleasant, though not exceptional, one should not cost more than £10, and sometimes less. The workmanship will be good and, if the condition is also satisfactory, this may well work out cheaper than a modern equivalent.

Toilet mirrors are very desirable if they are of eighteenth- or early nineteenth-century vintage. One would be lucky to get anything really attractive for less than £10; many cost more. On the other hand, if condition is satisfactory, this may well be cheaper than a contemporary design mirror. Eighteenth-century firescreens, usually with silk needlework panels, are fairly common and not unduly expensive, but are sometimes more difficult to fit usefully into a room than one thinks.

Chests of drawers on which to stand the mirrors may be expensive. In general, anything earlier than late Georgian will not be cheap, and bow-fronted and small chests always cost a good deal more proportionately than larger and flat-fronted ones. Tallboys, except occasionally rather late-period, unwieldy specimens, are rarely cheap, but a late Georgian or early Victorian gentleman's wardrobe with beautifully veneered mahogany panels to the doors and fine solid workmanship can often be acquired for the price of a modern machine-made hanging wardrobe.

Amongst furnishing accessories the Regency and Victorian fitted boxes offer a large and pleasant field to the amateur collector. There is a big variety of work boxes, games boxes, plain empty boxes, folding table desks and, of course, tea caddies. Amongst these last, the smaller ones, going back to early Georgian times, can be quite costly, but larger mid-nineteenth-century caddies can still be acquired for two or three pounds or less. Other boxes are usually even less expensive, though good examples, with completely fitted interiors, will fetch more. Fitted apothecaries' cabinets or medicine chest boxes, and boxes containing decanters are rather rarer. Workmanship of Victorian examples is often superb.

Prints and Engravings

Coloured prints, and even black and white engravings, can be very attractive so long as the margins are clean and not badly discoloured. Some are genuine collectors' pieces and therefore beyond the amateur. Hand-coloured prints are usually more modestly priced than those printed in colour. Into the former category come fashion and flower plates (the older the better, as a rule) and also some of birds, though these are harder to find and usually dearer. Original early nineteenth-century theatrical prints of the twopence coloured variety have a charm of their own. Tinsel pictures, which are hand decorated and enriched versions, are more interesting but are sought after and not cheap.

Samplers and needlework pictures are not difficult to find. Here quality is everything. Early date, fine workmanship and good condition put up the price, but there are still opportunities for those content with less good examples. All old needlework has possibilities, even men's and women's costumes (eighteenth and nineteenth centuries), though the latter may be difficult to put to good use.

China to-day usually fetches good prices, and in this field some knowledge is really essential for buying anything other than oddments, such as single soup tureens and vegetable dishes (mainly nineteenth and

Photo : " Country Life "

Above, an early nineteenth-century worktable of cala-mander wood with adjustable writing board, brass gallery and inlaid chessboard

Eighteenth- and nine-teenth-century toilet mirrors are most desirable. Above is a walnut one in square frame, standing on two tiers of drawers and with fluted scroll feet. About 1735

Boxes of all kinds are good collectors' pieces. The one below is veneered and banded with tulip and rosewood, with brass handles. About 1790

letter trays to card cases — that can be picked us for shillings, and look very effective in a cabinet or other display.

Tunbridge ware, made from tiny wood mosaics (inkwells, pen trays, paper knives), is worth looking out for, so are fine examples of beadwork (markers, pin-cushions, purses). Cases of wax fruit and pictures made from seaweed, hair work, coral and shells have become fashionable, though good examples are not very easy to find. These, used with

late eighteenth century) for use as flower bowls, and single dessert or dinner plates for their decorative value. A part dinner service can sometimes be acquired reasonably but only of a fairly pedestrian kind. Mason's Ironstone, however, is attractively decorated and not usually expensive

As time goes on, even the bric-à-brac of the past acquires charm. There are countless small objects—from inkwells and

skill, can add a piquant touch to a modern décor, but unless the buyer has a definite idea of where they will be used they may turn out less worthwhile than they seem. Late Victorian and Edwardian examples of "seaside" shellwork (marine views, mirrors and boxes) are less desirable and can come into the junk class, though sometimes their gaiety of appearance makes up for lack of artistic merit.

China soup tureen in Mecklenburg pattern, made in 1763 and copied exactly in 1893 by Copeland-Spode for King George V and Queen Mary

KNOW YOUR CHINA

How to recognise the genuine antique from marks used by the famous old potteries

SPODE *1*

Spode *2*

Spode *3*

4

JOSIAH SPODE purchased the Stoke potteries in 1776.

His earliest productions bear the name "Spode" impressed, as Figs. 1 and 2 or, on the finer china, painted in red or gold as Fig. 3.

It was at this time that willow-pattern plates were being made, and in addition to the more usual blue ones, Spode printed some in black which are much prized by collectors, but the word Spode must be impressed on them.

When Josiah Spode died in 1797 his son, Josiah Spode the second, continued the business. He was the most successful potter of his day, and produced a new ironstone ware which was marked "Spodes New Fayence," as Fig. 4.

After the second Josiah Spode's death in 1827, his cousin took over the works, but when he too died, the firm passed into the hands of the Copelands and the name Spode practically disappeared.

OLD DERBY

The earliest Derby mark was used in 1750, when Duesbury and Heath, as the company was at first known, used the letter D with the date in gold (Fig. 1). The better-known marks are the crown and the D (Fig. 2), in blue or purple, of the Crown Derby period which began in 1773. The crossed batons and six dots in puce, blue, gold or red (Fig. 3), introduced about 1782, were alleged to be a challenge to all other factories except three, those of Sèvres, Dresden and Berlin.

The Duesburys controlled the factory until 1815, when Robert Bloor took it over. He used the old Crown Derby mark until 1830, when he introduced his own mark (Fig. 4). Until this time the marks had been pencilled on, now they were printed. The factory continued under various names until it closed in 1870. The Royal Crown Derby Porcelain Co. Ltd. of to-day traces its origin back to this firm.

OLD WORCESTER

The Worcester Porcelain Company was founded by Dr. Wall in 1751. Early productions were based on Chinese models, and the first marks used were the letter W or a crescent in blue, as Fig. 1, or variations of Chinese characters, as Fig. 2.

Some of the best creations were produced between 1764, when some of the Chelsea artists moved to Worcester, and 1776, when Dr. Wall died.

In 1783 Thomas Flight took over the factory, and the marks used were as Figs. 3 and 4. When Martin Barr joined the firm in 1793 it became as Fig. 5.

Mr. Chamberlain, head of the decorating department during Dr. Wall's time, established a factory of his own, using the marks shown in Figs. 6 and 7. In 1840 the two factories were amalgamated under him.

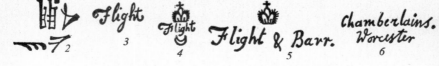

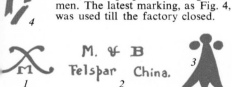

WEDGWOOD

Josiah Wedgwood discovered Jasper, the familiar ware with the coloured background and raised white ornamentation, in 1774, and used it for his famous Portland Vase, a copy of the original glass vase made in the third century and found in a tomb near Rome. During the years 1759 to 1769 pieces were marked as Fig. 1, probably the earliest mark. In 1762 he presented Queen Charlotte with a breakfast service for which he received the title "Potter to Her Majesty." This "Queen's Ware," an ivory or cream earthenware, has been a staple product ever since. In 1769 he went into partnership with Thomas Bentley and the mark was changed to Fig. 2. The stamp, Fig. 3, is found on basalt, granite and Etruscan, but never on Jasper vases. The mark on "Queen's Ware" to-day is as Fig. 4, and that on bone china, discontinued from 1816 to 1878, is as Fig. 5.

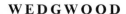

BOW

Bow, or "New Canton," was founded in 1730. In 1744 Edward Heylyn and Thomas Frye took out a patent for a new material considered to be better than imported china-ware.

Frye's two daughters assisted him in the painting of the Bow figures.

The marks are confusing, and experts do not agree about them, but those shown here are to be found on china from the factory.

The B (Fig. 1) and the bow (Fig. 2) explain themselves.

Fig. 3 shows the mark to be found on a sporting figure, and it is thought that the dagger was introduced from the City of London arms, both proprietors being freemen. The latest marking, as Fig. 4, was used till the factory closed.

WEDGWOOD
MADE IN
ENGLAND

WEDGWOOD
BONE CHINA
MADE IN
ENGLAND

MINTON

Bone china was made at the Minton factories at Stoke-on-Trent from the end of the eighteenth century. While some authorities agree that its manufacture was abandoned until 1821, others maintain that its production was uninterrupted. The mark shown in Fig. 1 was used from about 1800. Thomas Minton was the founder.

On his death in 1836, Herbert Minton, a son, took control, John Boyle became a partner and the mark of the factory was M. & B. in some form or other (Fig. 2).

Between 1850 and 1862 the ermine mark, Fig. 3, was found on pieces painted by hand, and in 1868 the mark in Fig. 4, a variation of which is used to-day, came into use.

SALOPIAN

In 1750 Thomas Turner first made porcelain, and his famous dark-blue china at the Coalport factory in Shropshire, where the "Willow Pattern," copied by so many firms, was first made. The marks on Caughly ware are, on some pieces, a crescent (Fig. 1), on others a C (Fig. 2), and markings as Fig. 3 are also of this period. The mark used at the beginning of the nineteenth century was as Fig. 4, but in 1820 the factories at Swansea and Nantgarw were incorporated and their initials form the mark, Fig. 5.

CHELSEA

The earliest mark on Chelsea china was on a milk jug. It was a triangle and the date, 1745, scratched on under the glaze.

After this an anchor is usually included, the earliest design (Fig. 1) being embossed in red about 1750.

From this date until 1765 anchors (Figs. 2 and 3) were used, the better specimens being marked in gold, others in blue or red. The double anchor (Fig. 4) was used only on very high-class pieces.

In 1769 William Duesbury, of the Derby factory, bought the Chelsea works. The marks of Derby and Chelsea were amalgamated (Figs. 5 and 6) and used until 1784, when the Chelsea works were pulled down.

HOW TO RECOGNISE ANTIQUE

PERIODS	TUDOR	STUART		RESTORATION	
STYLE	ELIZABETHAN 1558–1603	JACOBEAN 1603–1649	CROMWELLIAN 1649–1660	CAROLEAN 1660–1689	WILLIAM andMARY 1689–1702
WOODS	OAK			WALNUT	
	1570 1580 1590 1600 1610 1620 1630 1640 1650 1660 1670 1680 1690 1700				

CHAIR LEGS

CHAIR BACKS

CARVING AND ORNAMENT

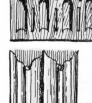

METAL WORK

FURNITURE by H. DALTON CLIFFORD

Q. ANNE		GEORGIAN				VICTORIAN		
QUEEN ANNE	EARLY GEORGIAN	CHIPPEN- DALE	ADAM	HEPPLE- WHITE	SHERATON	FRENCH EMPIRE	REGENCY	EARLY VICTORIAN
1702–1714	1714–1745	1745–1780	1758–1792	1760–1790	1790–1810	1793–1830	1810–1837	1837–1850

WALNUT				MAHOGANY					SATINWOOD					
1700	1710	1720	1730	1740	1750	1760	1770	1780	1790	1800	1810	1820	1830	1840	1850

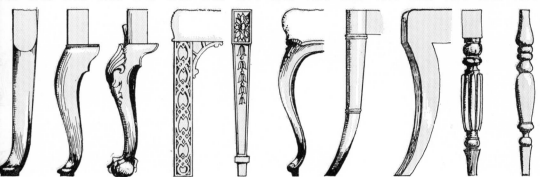

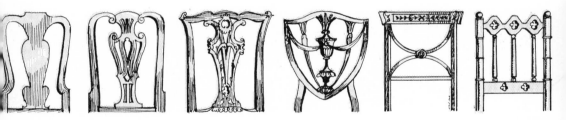

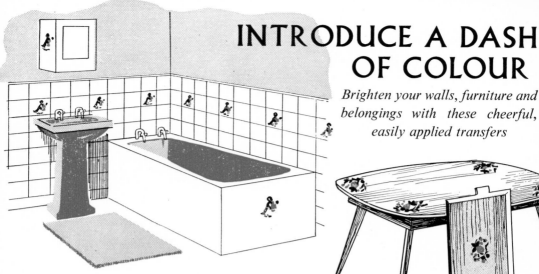

INTRODUCE A DASH OF COLOUR

Brighten your walls, furniture and belongings with these cheerful, easily applied transfers

Transform your bathroom with a row of funny little ducks marching out from under the shower, their towels tucked over their wings

Every home-maker has said at some time, "If only I could introduce a touch of colour there." Well, you can—without paint and in a matter of seconds —so easily that even a child can do it perfectly. Decorettes, a new form of transfer decoration, are washable, resistant to wear and as simple to put on as a postage stamp. In a few minutes you can create a variety of charming hand-painted effects on walls, furniture and belongings. All you need to apply the transfers is water, and there are well over a hundred designs, from floral patterns to animals and toys.

Strawberries, cherries, plums and pears (see design, top right of opposite page) add a cheerful note to a coffee table and matching tray (above)

The merry little elephants (all six are shown in detail on the opposite page) dance hilariously around a child's bedhead and one decorates a drinking mug (left)

Decorated canisters and storage jars for the kitchen are expensive to buy. These (below) are easily made for a few pence: just collect tins and jars the right shape and size, paint them with undercoating and a couple of coats of enamel paint—then finish with transfers like the little bunches of cherries (left)

Here's an idea for families—a different transfer design for each member of the household and all his belongings identified with it

The funny little duck (above) looks just as cute on the end of a cot, the backs of hair brushes, the door of the toy cupboard or a nursery lampshade, as he does (opposite) on the bathroom tiles

The bibulous pink elephants (right) are great fun stuck on to the sides of party tumblers, dinner mats or a cocktail tray, where they act as a timely (if humorous) warning

Dip Decorette in warm water for 20 seconds. Remove, leave one minute

Slide design off backing paper face up onto surface to be decorated

Smooth design firmly down with dry cloth and allow time to dry thoroughly

233

HOW DO YOU VIEW?

You and your family can sit huddled uncomfortably round the set and damage your eyes—or, with a little clever planning, you can watch TV in comfort and ease. It's up to you

A number of small, easily movable chairs are far more convenient than the conventional three-piece suite, when you may want to seat extra viewers for the evening

Here's an idea for a music unit which houses radio, TV, gramophone and records. Facing it —in perfect position for viewing or listening—is a long padded wall bench.

TELEVISION has changed the buying and planning habits of home-makers out of all recognition. The large three-piece suites that used to be found in most living-rooms have given way recently to practical, smaller, more comfortable and more easily adaptable seating arrangements. This is in many respects an advantage; certainly there are more small chairs on the market that really fit different human shapes, and more homes now seem to have room for the un-expected guest to sit really comfortably.

Since the TV set has obviously moved into our homes for good, the next thing is to arrange matters so that you can be comfortable while viewing. You need small, well-designed chairs or benches, and be sure there are enough for your whole family or friends. Three-piece units which will divide into separate chairs, or can be put together to form a long sofa, are a practical buy. Built-in, padded wall benches are also practical. But whatever kind of seating accommodation you choose, it must be the right height for your set, or, alternatively, the set must be the right height for the chairs (it really depends which you buy first)—about eye-level.

This is important, because watching pro-grammes, looking either steeply up or down, is bad for both the eyes and the body posture. Eye specialists agree, how-ever, TV need not harm or strain the eyes, provided you sit squarely in front of the screen and avoid trying to view from the side of the room at awkward angles.

There is no need to "black out" the room with heavy curtains, closed doors and lights off. On the contrary, a reason-able supply of fresh air will prevent you from getting drowsy and tired from lack of oxygen. As to the lighting, the eye special-ists say no direct glare to reflect on the screen, but not complete darkness, either; rather a gentle diffused light in the room.

And here is a tip particularly valuable for the children—do try to take an interval in an evening's viewing to rest the eyes.

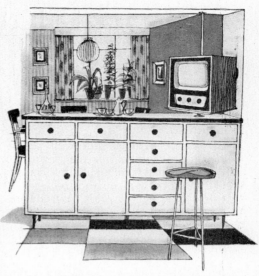

If you have a wall with a 2-ft. storage space behind, you can have your TV built in and concealed behind a sliding picture

With a swivel base for the TV set, viewing is possible from either side of the partition—from lounging or dining part of the living room

TRY ARRANGING YOUR ROOMS LIKE THIS:

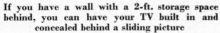

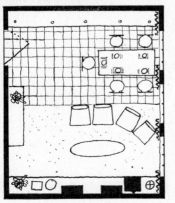

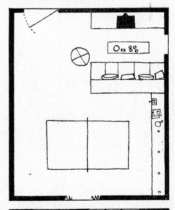

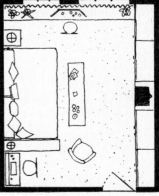

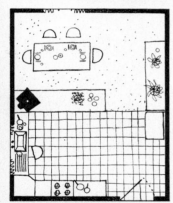

Mount your swivel-based set between kitchen and dining room (see diagram left). This way you can cook while you view and later eat and still see the programmes

Here's a well-planned sports room for the children (right), with ping-pong table at one end, space for all sports equipment, and a viewing corner, with a long low sofa and lots of cushions square in front of the TV set

Enjoy your after-dinner coffee sitting, comfortably relaxed, around a low television table, in easy chairs regrouped for comfort and convenience (left)

When you have a big party of guests coming in for a special programme, try seating them in a row on a divan turned sideways (right): it's comfortable, and everybody gets a good straight view

ETIQUETTE

*There is a right way of meeting most social obligations—
and it is usually the common-sense as well as the correct one*

AGNES MIALL *gives the advice.*　　　　NICOLAS BENTLEY *drew the pictures*

Introductions

ALL social life must start with people meeting each other for the first time. So it is very important that introductions should be properly made and received. If you are a little nervous about introducing and being introduced, here are some broad rules to guide you.

First, when making people known to each other:

(1) *Pronounce both names clearly, so that they are distinctly heard and remembered by those introduced.* Make quite sure *you* know both names correctly. If you are uncertain of the name of someone you yourself only met, perhaps, a few minutes ago, say quite frankly and simply: "I wonder if I've got your name quite right? Is it Harris or Parrish?" Or: "Let's see, your name is . . . ?"—expectant pause—during which the name will be given.

(2) *Get the order right. When presenting him to her, put his name first; when making known Miss to Mrs., mention Miss first. When introducing two un-married women, or two married women, or two men to each other, give the name of the younger of the pair first.* Thus: "Mr. Jay, I would like you to meet Miss Kay. Mr. Jay—Miss Kay." Or: "My dear, may I introduce Miss Dee to you? Miss Dee—Mrs. Lee."

(3) *Give each person some clue to the identity of the other, in addition to the name, or refer to some interest they share which will set them chatting easily.* Thus: "My cousin, Mr. Jay—my college friend, Miss Kay." Or: "I think you're both great card players." It is especially important to give such "clues" if, after making the introduction, you cannot start conversation going between them. The hostess at a large party, for example, must hurry off to welcome other guests or make further introductions.

Memorise these three rules and introductions will soon be easy to you and helpful to your friends. Like all rules, they have a few exceptions. For example, introduce a girl to a man, not the other way round, if the man is much more important than she is. But in nine cases out of ten the rules will carry you happily through.

Here are three basic rules for those who are *being* introduced:

(1) *Listen carefully to the other person's name and try to remember it.* But if you fail to do so, take an early opportunity of admitting this gracefully and getting the information again. *Smile, and bow or shake hands as the occasion demands, and say "How do you do."* You *both* say this simultaneously, or nearly so. It is not a question or an enquiry after your health and requires no answer. Do not reply: "Quite well, thank you" or say "Pleased to meet you."

(2) *A man should rise when introduced to a lady.* If out of doors, he raises his hat, or should he be hatless, makes an equivalent gesture of courtesy. *A young woman should rise when presented to an older woman.* Often both parties to the introduction rise, but the lady in the first case or the older woman in the second may correctly remain seated if she wishes.

Are you going to worry over whether to bow or shake hands? Then don't, for it really isn't very important. In general, when being formally introduced at a function to someone of whom you know nothing, a bow is best. On informal occasions, in a private house, when you are meeting someone you have already heard talked about, a handshake comes more naturally. When in doubt, if other introductions precede yours, do what the others do. The one thing you must *not* do is to ignore a proffered hand. Even if a bow would be more correct and the other person mistakenly expects to shake hands, do so at once rather than show up the error or appear stand-offish.

(3) *After the "How do you do's," start conversation at once,* about the weather or the common link suggested by your introducer.

Introductions by Letter

Someone you know is going to another town and you would like her to meet some friends of yours who live there. Or you yourself will be settling in a strange place where you know no one, but where there are friends of yours.

Owing to distance, no personal making known is possible in these cases, but a letter of introduction does the trick.

If writing such a letter to friends, be sure that the person you are introducing is someone you know something about and is likely to be congenial. Hesitate before giving a letter of introduction, out of mistaken kindness, to someone picked up by chance, say, on a day's outing, or who is awkward, bad-mannered or a crashing bore. It simply isn't fair to your friends.

Let us suppose you wish to introduce that nice Mr. A, whom you know all about, to Mr. and Mrs. B, people you know in the town in which he is taking up a new job. Write to Mrs. B, telling her who Mr. A is, something about him and how long you have known him and the reason why he is settling in their neighbourhood. Tell Mrs. B also, as you would in a personal introduction, of any interests Mr. A may share with the B's. End something like this: "I feel that he could have no happier start in your town than by knowing you both from the outset, and I shall be most grateful for any kindness you are able to show him."

Put the letter in an *unsealed* envelope addressed to Mrs. B. It is left open so that Mr. A may know what you have said about him—so take care that it is nothing tactless or uncomplimentary. Should you have anything private to tell them, write a second letter to them direct, posting it to

When introduced to a lady,
a gentleman raises his hat

arrive before Mr. A presents the unsealed letter.

Mr. A, having read your introductory letter if he wishes, should then seal it and either post it to the B's or drop it through their letter-box on arrival. Etiquette requires that within a day or two the B's should get in touch with Mr. A and invite him to visit them. When they have thus met him, they will probably introduce him to others, and so help him to make friends in his new surroundings.

Mr. A must not fail to write you a letter of thanks, telling you of the hospitality he has received from your friends. Mrs. B should also let you know that she has honoured your introduction.

Answering Invitations

There are other letters besides introductory ones which offer pitfalls to the inexperienced: for instance, answering letters of invitation.

Here etiquette is stern. You may put off again and again replying to chatty letters from friends, but you *must* answer invitations promptly. Whether you are asked to stay with friends, to a wedding, party, lunch or friendly evening, your reply should be sent within 48 hours. Why? Because your host or hostess has arrangements to make for that function, whatever it is, and how can these be settled or catering embarked on until it is known who, and how many people, are coming?

If for a good reason you are unable

to accept or decline very promptly, you should write or phone at once explaining why. "I'm not quite sure yet if my exam. will be that day," or "With Mother ill, I can't make any plans for the moment." Then add something like this: "If you don't mind my leaving it open for a day or two, I will write again as soon as I know." And you must *do* so—write again definitely, I mean.

To put off answering a dull invitation, in case something more exciting may turn up for the same date, is quite inexcusable. So is accepting and then telephoning at the last minute some excuse for not coming, because a more thrilling "date" has come along. In social life one just has to take the risk of occasionally being bored at a dull party or missing a later one which one would have preferred.

How you reply to an invitation is just as important as *when* you do. The rule is that you should reply in the same form as that in which you are invited. If you receive a formal card in the third person: "Mrs. S requests the pleasure of Miss T's company . . ." you write back "Miss T thanks Mrs. S for her kind invitation for—[date] —and has much pleasure in accepting," or "much regrets she is unable to accept owing to—[previous engagement, illness or other reason]."

If, on the contrary, the invitation begins: "Dear Jenny, I'm throwing a little party next Thursday and do hope you can come," then you answer in the same friendly, informal style. But it is incorrect to telephone in reply to a written invitation, unless your friend suggests in her letter that you should do this.

When accepting an invitation to stay, say just when you may be expected. It is very annoying to prepare lunch for a guest, who then casually turns up at tea-time. Your hostess may suggest the time of day she prefers. In that case, agree to that time if possible when accepting the invitation. If you *have* to arrive at some other hour, state this clearly with the reason why and with apologies for any inconvenience caused.

After staying with people even for one night, the guest must send what is known as a "bread-and-butter" letter within two days of the visit. The fact that she has already thanked her hosts warmly before

leaving does not excuse the guest from sending this letter. In it you express thanks for the hospitality received and say how much you have enjoyed yourself. Some very well-mannered people also write after having been entertained to dinner, but in these days of scant leisure this is not a general practice.

Letters of Condolence

No one likes writing these, but it is ill-bred to shirk this comfort-giving duty. Write quickly, while the grief is very recent or the illness still in progress and sympathy is therefore most needed. But if you do not happen to hear of a death until two or three weeks afterwards, still write, explaining why you have not sent your condolence earlier.

What to write? Imagine yourself the sick or bereaved person and you will not find it difficult to express your sympathy sincerely and kindly. In the case of an illness, wish the patient a speedy recovery; if you know her well and are within range, ask if she would like you to visit her in hospital. When writing of a death, hope that the end came peacefully and without pain unless you know for certain that this was not the case. Express your sense of the heavy loss your friend has suffered, offer any help you can give and say something in praise of the dead and of what you felt for him or her. Of course, all these things may not be appropriate in a particular case. You must word what you say tactfully to fit circumstances.

Modes of Address

If you need to know the correct ways of writing to outstanding people, such as your M.P., clergyman, a peer or bishop, go to your local public library and ask the librarian where you can find this information. Rules about British titles are too complicated to give here; in any case, few of us are called upon to write often to title-holders. But in the most humdrum daily life little points about how to address certain people are bound to crop up.

Medical men, for instance. When speaking to a physician, you call him Doctor Zed, and when writing you start your letter: "Dear Doctor Zed," *not* "Dear Doctor," without the name. It is incorrect to speak of him to others merely as "Doctor"

Say: "The Doctor" or "Doctor Zed." Strictly speaking, the correct form for the envelope is "X. Y. Zed, Esq., M.D.," with his initials and medical degrees. But it is becoming more and more usual to write the simpler "Dr. X. Y. Zed."

A surgeon is *not* a doctor and is always called and referred to as *Mr.* So-and-So. Notice how unfailingly the staff do this in hospital. Letters are addressed: "A. B. So-and-So, Esq.," with the surgical degree, such as F.R.C.S. (Fellow of the Royal College of Surgeons) after the name.

In the Royal Navy, Sub-Lieutenants and Lieutenants are both addressed socially in speech as Mr., but envelopes should be addressed to Henry Drake, Esq., R.N., and Lieut. Blake, R.N., respectively. In the Army, both Second Lieutenants and Lieutenants are spoken of as "Mr." and written to as "Esq.," followed by the name of their regiment. In the Royal Air Force, Pilot Officers and Flying Officers are both called "Mr." and written to as "Esq., R.A.F." Officers, from the rank of Lieutenant Commander (Navy), Captain (Army) and Flight-Lieutenant (R.A.F.) upwards are spoken of and written to by their rank.

What about the Vicar of your parish? Some people, you will notice, call him "Vicar," instead of Mr. Smith, and begin letters with "My dear Vicar." This is suitable only when you know him quite well, especially in his parochial capacity. It is perfectly correct to speak and start letters to him as Mr. Smith, and always the safest plan when in doubt.

One thing you must *not* do—address an envelope to "Rev. Smith." The title Reverend must be followed by initials or Christian name—"Rev. John Smith" or "Rev. J. T. Smith." It is equally incorrect to call him "Rev." when speaking to him or to refer to him as such. *Not* "I saw Rev. Smith [or worse still, 'the Reverend'] to-day," but "I saw Mr. Smith" or "the Vicar." Rev., like Esq., is a title for envelopes and printed matter only.

If you don't know how to address a bishop . . .

Two in a Restaurant

There are certain conventions of behaviour expected when lunching or dining in a restaurant or hotel, particularly when a woman is with her husband or a girl is invited out by her boy.

In a good-class restaurant, the head waiter will allot a table to arriving patrons or show them to the one which the man may have booked beforehand. The lady follows directly behind the waiter, her escort coming after her, since the spaces between tables do not permit of their walking side by side. The man sits only when his companion has chosen the seat she prefers and is comfortably settled in it.

The chief thing she must remember, apart, of course, from the usual good table manners, is that her escort is her host as much as though they were having a meal in his own home. He therefore gives all instructions to the waiter, who is, so to speak, his employee. You, as the guest, must therefore ask him, not the waiter, for anything you want. Not: "Waiter, some more bread, please," from you, but instead: "Do you think I might have some more bread, Harry?" Whereupon Harry says, "Of course," summons the waiter and himself gives the order: "Another roll for the lady, please."

Similarly, at the start of the meal, although you may each have a menu to consult, you tell Harry, not the waiter, what you would like from it, or better still, if you are inexperienced, leave him to do the choosing.

When leaving after the meal, the guest should take no more interest in the size of the bill or the paying of it than a visitor at home would do in what the meal had cost. The lady goes out first, walks a few paces beyond the pay-desk, and waits casually for her escort till he has paid the bill and rejoined her. This public disinterest in the cost of the meal is correct even when a woman is dining with her husband and they have agreed beforehand

239

exactly how much will be spent. Good manners require that the man should appear to the world as the protector and provider of the lady he escorts.

Of course you will thank him prettily for his hospitality and say how much you enjoyed your lunch or dinner in his company —again, even if he is your husband.

Telephone Manners

You should be just as careful to show good manners on the telephone as anywhere else. When you get a wrong number, an angry exclamation and a loud banging down of the receiver are quite unjustified. You wouldn't treat a friend so. Then why a stranger who can't see who you are? Instead, apologise for the trouble unwittingly caused.

At busy times be brief in your calls. Others may be waiting to use the line. The time for long, cosy chats about nothing in particular is at slack hours, say on Sunday morning or latish (but not bed-timeish) in the evening.

Try to smile while telephoning as you would when talking face to face. The other person doesn't see your smile, but it permeates your voice and manner, giving charm and courtesy to the conversation. Try not to telephone when angry or upset, for these emotions get through.

Be sparing in going to a neighbour's premises and asking to use the telephone, and never fail to pay for calls so made. If you don't know the cost of a call the operator can tell you. It is often the most tactful plan to leave the amount on the table beside the instrument. If a friend in need has "borrowed" your telephone, try to leave him or her alone in the room; the call may be private.

Paper and pencil should be kept beside the instrument and all unfamiliar names, numbers or messages received should be written down at once.

Flying Etiquette

When travelling by air for the first time, you will have added confidence if you know the few special points of etiquette which have now become customary on aeroplane journeys.

Obey all starting or arriving regulations (lighted indicators or the air-line staff inform you of these) promptly and willingly.

They are for the safety of everyone, and include not smoking until given permission to do so. If you do not know how to fasten your safety belt, you will be shown. The rear seats may not be occupied till the 'plane is airborne but, if you wish to sit in them, inform the steward or stewardess and you will be able to do so a little later if they are not already booked.

A booking is not made for a flight unless there is a seat available, so there is no need to hustle to the front when called to board the 'plane. If you join the 'plane at an intermediate point—say at Bordeaux, which is roughly halfway between London and Madrid—the through passengers who have alighted there first take their former seats and you can then choose any one which is still vacant.

According to the length of the journey, refreshments or a meal, or both, are provided free of charge during the flight. The only beverages included gratis are a cup of tea or coffee. But drinks of all kinds, and also cigarettes, can be ordered at low (because duty-free) rates, either with or between meals. As in a train dining car, you receive a bill for these towards the end of the flight and, when paying this, you also tip the steward or air hostess in the usual way (see Notes on Tipping, page 242).

On arrival at the airport terminal, you also tip the uniformed employee who will call you a taxi. It is not necessary or customary to give anything to those who handle your luggage at the points where it is examined by the Customs, or to the girls who escort you from waiting room to 'plane and vice versa. They are paid adequately by the company on a non-tipping basis.

Hostess and Guest

When inviting someone to stay in the house, whether for a week-end or longer, word the invitation *definitely*, especially to people whom you don't yet know very well. "Can you come for the week-end, from lunch-time on Saturday, July 2nd, until Monday morning?" Otherwise a guest with plenty of leisure may interpret a week-end as lasting from Friday until Tuesday, and arrive accordingly.

It is courteous, whenever possible, to meet the guest at the station or other point of arrival. The guest-room should be ready, looking its best, with a few flowers in it. And if someone else is turning out to make room, even for a week-end visitor, try to clear at least *one* peg and one small drawer for use. Even if the bed is made up with what you consider ample covers, lay a spare one nearby. People so often feel much colder in a strange bed than in their own.

If it suits you better to bring breakfast up on a tray next morning, so that you have a clear field downstairs, say so frankly. And in cold weather provide heat in the bedroom.

Find the happy medium between making such a detailed time-table for your guest that she feels harassed and dominated and drifting along without

In cold weather, provide heat in your guest's bedroom . . .

any plans at all, so that she is plain bored. And don't be too tired or busy to enjoy her company. Far better have simpler meals, or say matter-of-factly: "I know you won't mind helping me wash up, so that we can go out while it's sunny."

A guest should be cheerful, tidy, adaptable, easily interested and amused and self-providing, bringing her own hot-water bottle in winter and not always running to her hostess for a needle, safety-pin or postage stamp. Guests who "can't" eat this and don't like that (without any valid health reason) are unpopular and a trial. So are those who never lift a finger to help a busy hostess. You should make your bed as a matter of course and lend a hand willingly with other household tasks.

If you cannot return the hospitality, send presents next Christmas to your hostess or the children, invite her to a restaurant lunch or the pictures when she is in your neighbourhood, or something like that.

Calling and Card-leaving

Before the First World War all married ladies (as they were called then) had their monthly afternoon when they were "At Home" to any friends who cared to call. With this ceremonial visiting went the ritual of leaving cards.

Between the wars, perhaps because many married women were out all day working, calling and card-leaving vanished from our social life. But to-day they have been revived in one quarter at least — among Service officers and their wives living at Service Stations.

To start with, remember that the new arrival never takes the lead, but waits for those already established in the station to issue a welcome, which they do by calling and leaving cards.

So, if you are the newcomer, be prepared for visitors and don't be caught at calling hour (about 3.30 to 4.30 p.m., though it may vary) in your oldest frock or shampooing your hair. Also, as you must return the calls, order your visiting cards (and your husband's) beforehand.

Strictly speaking, visiting cards should be engraved, not printed; this means having a plate made with your name and style on it. A good stationer will undertake this. In the old days cards also bore their owner's address. But this meant having the plate altered when there was a change of address. So it is quite usual for Service people, who may not stay very long anywhere, to have only their names on their cards and to write in themselves their current address and telephone number.

Names on cards are always formal—not Mary Green or Mrs. Mary Green, but Mrs. H. R. Green (using your husband's, not your own initials). Thus your card indicates whose wife you are. Your husband's cards, which are rather smaller than yours, give his Service rank.

Ladies who have called leave cards in the hall as they go out, so there should be a small table near the door, with a bowl or little tray on it to receive them.

A first call on a newcomer is usually brief. The caller has come merely to introduce herself and to give you a formal welcome. She may stay only ten or fifteen minutes. So do not delay her by bustling round to get tea; though, if you are having yours when she arrives, you will naturally offer her some.

There is no need to "hug the house" in case someone arrives. Should you be out, the caller will leave cards or call again. Within the next day or two you must return the call, or if she only left cards, then do the same. Always, as a newcomer, follow the old resident's lead.

Now comes the question of what cards to leave. The principle is this: for card-leaving purposes a husband and wife are considered as one. In theory, Major and Mrs. Black call on Captain and Mrs. Green. In practice, the wives make and receive the calls on behalf of their husbands as well as themselves. The cards left therefore represent the absent men as well as the present women.

Thus, Mrs. Black calling on the new arrival Mrs. Green, leaves *two* of Major Black's cards (in theory, one each for Captain and Mrs. Green) and one of her own (for the absent Captain). Thus each married couple has "called" (by card or in person) on the other couple. Should either lady be unmarried or widowed, one card is omitted. So a widow calling on a married woman leaves two of her own cards (the second for her hostesses's husband) only. If a widow or spinster receives a visit from a wife, the caller leaves one each of her own and one of her husband's cards.

Teen-age girls may have their name printed or written in under their mother's, the name being prefixed by Miss unless the girl is titled. If such a girl calls without her mother, she crosses out her mother's name on the card, leaving only her own.

It must be understood that the rules given above are for *first* calls only. A woman then leaves her own card, even though she has called in person, so that her hostess may have a record of her style, name and address for reference. These are known when later calls are made, so the visitor then leaves only two of her husband's cards, none of her own.

A newcomer will find it helpful to write down in a special notebook the name of each caller, the date of the call, about how long it lasted, and the date (after making it) of her own return call. Then she will know just when and how to proceed.

Tipping

Unfortunately tipping is not an exact science and, as the value of money is continually changing, precise figures tend to go out of date.

Remember that habit makes tipping easier. In time you get to know almost instinctively the right amount to give. Till you acquire that "sixth sense," it is often wise to ask advice in advance from someone more experienced. Men are usually much surer about tipping than women.

Tips are customarily given to those who wait on you or give you some form of service which is personal to you. Thus you tip the taxi-man, who goes wherever you want, but not the bus conductor who conveys folk in general to a fixed destination. You tip the girl who sets your hair but not the one who serves all-comers in a shop. People to be tipped include waiters and waitresses (with their sea and air counterparts, stewards and stewardesses), station and hotel porters, chambermaids, taxi-drivers, car-park and cloakroom attendants, hairdressing assistants, caddies at golf courses, and so on.

A useful basic guide to tipping is: 10 per cent. (2s. in the £1) of your bill. This is a *minimum* tip on all bills of, say, 5s. or over. It needs adding to on many occasions, and it is not even a basic guide to sums under 5s. If you are charged a shilling for tea you can't possibly leave 1½d. (roughly 10 per cent.); 3d. (25 per cent.) would be correct. On most other small amounts (say, a modest meal costing 3s. 6d.), 6d. is, to-day, the minimum tip.

The percentage guide is, however, of most lasting value, because it increases with the charges.

Taxi-drivers by custom are tipped on a higher rate than most other people—about 25 per cent. (one-quarter) on a small amount, diminishing gradually to from 20 to 15 per cent. as the charge rises.

When on holiday it is neither necessary nor correct to tip the whole hotel staff, whether they serve you or not. If you drink nothing but water and prefer walking up and down stairs to travelling by lift, neither the wine waiter nor the liftman will expect to be remembered. Again, at a smart restaurant or theatre the commissionaire is very much on view, but one tips only for service rendered. If, on a rainy night, he brings his umbrella to keep you dry between car and door or calls a taxi for you, you would then, of course, tip him, increasing the sum if taxis are scarce and it takes him some time to find one.

With these exceptions, 10 per cent. of the bill is usually adequate for *routine* service, and is as much as most people can afford. Don't be afraid of being thought mean when you are really correct. People who give lavish tips often do so from nervousness, inexperience, a desire to show off, or because they are "spoilt children" expecting priority of attention. A pleasant expression of thanks: "We *have* enjoyed being looked after so well . . ." with a smile may be as welcome as the tip. All should thank when tipping and learn to bestow their generosity with charm and appreciation.

A minimum sum suffices for routine, grudging or inefficient service. In fact, some people make it a rule to give less than the minimum to show their displeasure at incivility or poor attention. They are quite right in that large tips are not payment, but a reward for extra trouble and willingness.

The hotel management will probably charge extra for breakfast in bed, but you should also tip the chambermaid who brings it rather more than you would have done otherwise. You would give her still more if she pressed a creased frock for you.

In an hotel (or on a cruise) your percentage for tips must be divided among various people. Suppose the bill for a married couple for a fortnight is £40. If the hotel likes a weekly settlement, you still do all the tipping when leaving. Ten per cent. is liberal rather than minimum on a sum this size and works out at £4; you could spend rather less without being mean. Of the £4, give the dining-room waiter or waitress about half (£2), the chambermaid a quarter (£1), and the remaining staff, hall-porter and perhaps liftman and/or page, the last quarter (£1) between them. Of this the porter gets the lion's share.

With a larger staff each does less for you, so you split the proportion among them. If, for instance, there are both day and night porters, divide the amount between them.

There are certain tips that cannot be reckoned as a percentage on a bill. Below are given the amounts suitable at the time (1956) when this is written. One cannot guarantee them further, but if they alter it is certain to be up, not down.

Attendant (*cloakroom*).—Use of toilet, washbasin and mirror, 6d. In a grander place, where cosmetics are provided and used, 9d. to 1s.

Attendant (*car-park*).—According to length of time the vehicle is parked, from 3d. for a bicycle to 1s. for a car.

Tips are customarily given to those who wait on you . . .

If a fixed charge is made either in cloakroom or car-park, do not tip except for some special extra attention.

Golf Caddie.—2s. to 2s. 6d. per round (in addition to his fee).

Finally, there are a few people whom you should *never* tip. Proprietors, for example; they are working for themselves and are presumably making a sufficient profit. Tip the waiter but not the restaurant-keeper; the girl who perms your hair but not the manageress who runs the establishment.

A member of a club, or any guest she invites there, should not tip any of the staff. They are paid on a "no tips" basis. Members, however, usually contribute liberally towards staff Christmas gifts. If, however, you stay in a friend's house where there are servants, tip them when you leave on the basis of hotel staff.

YOUR PUBLIC SERVICES

*The U.K. is justly proud of its official guardians of health
and welfare—and every family should know how they work*

Milk samples are constantly being subjected to laboratory tests.
Thus quality and cleanliness are ensured

is a complete survey of the
year's work and progress
by all concerned in the
maintenance, and better-
ing, of your health.

The M.O.H. has many
responsibilities: the care of
the aged; tracing to its
source, and checking, the
spread of infection immediately a notifiable disease or
case of food poisoning is
reported by a doctor; constant work and campaign-
ing for hygiene in food
handling, and regular
checks on various drugs,
foodstuffs, milk, ice cream
and water. In the case of
county councils, as local
health authorities, there are
the additional tasks of providing health services: district and school nurses, mid-
wives and health visitors,

WHEREVER you live in the U.K., there
exists—rather regrettably little known
or thought about by most people—a highly
efficient network of local specialists vigil-
antly guarding the health and welfare of
your family. To know something about
them enables you to make the best possible
use of the facilities they provide—and
should also encourage you to give them all
possible help and support in their valuable
work. A general heading under which
much of this activity comes, is "Public
Health."

HEALTH

Whatever form of local government ad-
ministers the affairs of your community,
rural or urban district council, county, or
non-county borough, the Medical Officer of
Health heads the department concerned
with personal and environmental health
and hygiene. He receives regular reports,
and each year sums up in an Annual Report, which he presents to his Council. This

maternity and child welfare clinics, ambulance and hospital car services, and so on.

The Sanitary Inspector

Most of the Sanitary Inspector's work
closely affects commodities in daily domestic use.

Meat. Sanitary Inspectors check on
slaughterhouses, wholesale manufacturers,
retail butchers and sausage manufacturers,
meat cooking premises (meat pies, hams,
meat cakes and so on), according to the
number and kind of such premises registered with their respective councils.

They attend the slaughterhouses at the
time of slaughtering and examine carcases,
condemning all or part of those that are in
any way unsound. Many visits of inspection are also paid to the various other
premises mentioned; thus a close watch is
kept on the soundness of the food and the
conditions in which it is prepared.

Milk. Both distributors and dairies are
registered with their local council, and con-

stant inspection of premises, and testing of milk samples is undertaken each year. Licences are granted to dairymen to designate milk as "sterilised," pasteurised" or "tuberculin tested" only after it has passed the required tests. You can be sure then that not only milk, but pasteurising plant, bottle-washing machinery, bottles, and all equipment is maintained at a sound standard.

Poultry, eggs, groceries, confectionery, fruit and vegetables, fish and canned foods (including imported foodstuffs), whether sold by shops, stores or markets, are regularly inspected and unsound goods condemned.

In a recent Annual Report by the Medical Officer of Health to a large county borough, it is recorded that a total weight of 122 tons, 4 cwt., 68 lb. of food was condemned as unfit for human consumption during the year. The fact that this kind of scrupulous attention to the food we eat is going on all the time, all over the country, should bring comfort and reassurance to

In the abattoir a carcase is examined and condemned as unfit for human consumption. Meat is carefully inspected at all stages

all conscientious housewives.

Under the Food and Drugs Act, 1938, Inspectors take large numbers of samples for analysis. It may be ground almonds or aspirin tablets, ice cream, iodine, oranges or sulphur tablets, but if results are not satisfactory, suitable action is taken.

Food and Hygiene

As part of the campaign for clean handling of food, canteens, bakehouses, restaurants and food shops are regularly inspected, and every effort made to persuade those responsible to introduce hygienic methods of preparing, serving and handling food.

The Public Analyst

His services are called on by the county councils. Facilities available to district councils are offered by the Public Health Laboratories,

A water sample is taken from one of the Metropolitan Water Board's tanks at Walton, Surrey. The Board supplies Greater London with about 350,000,000 gallons of water a day and these same laboratories are also used by the county councils. They operate all over the country, essentially for bacteriological investigations. Their part in promoting sound public health is the valuable aid they give to medical officers and sanitary inspectors acting on behalf of medical officers.

Immediately a case of food poisoning or infectious disease is reported, the M.O.H. or Sanitary Inspector investigates to trace the source of infection and advises on means to prevent its spread. Analysis of specimens is more often than not a means of tracing infection to its source, especially in the case of food poisoning, and where a Public Analyst is not available, a Public Health Laboratory will be.

In this way M.O.s and Sanitary Inspectors have ready facilities, not only for the detecting of infection, but for the guarding of health generally, for they call on their analysts to test milk samples, those taken under the Food and Drugs Act, doubtful commodities set aside during inspections of shops, etc.

The Waterworks Engineer

The testing of water is carried out regularly and an analysis made. Where a waterworks engineer does not operate, a sanitary inspector will be responsible for water tests, or water samples will be sent for testing to the nearest Public Health Laboratory.

Rodent Operator is the title of a man whose work is of tremendous importance in the pattern of public health. His job is the survey of a given area for infestation by rats and mice, and the provision of suitable treatment. Any one survey will include sewers, refuse tips or sewage disposal works, open spaces or banks likely to harbour rodents, local authority properties, private dwellings (if called on by the occupier, or in answer to a complaint) and business premises.

This work has another good side, for in hunting rats, the operator may discover defective sewers or drains and so prevent later trouble.

So much for the unremitting work being done to protect our health. There is another branch of protection—these officials, working on an all-the-year-round basis, guard the housewife's pocket.

Inspectors of Weights and Measures

Routine checking of scales, at the time they are made, as well as all the time they are in use, is a big part of the work. It goes beyond this, however, to the checking of the weight of foodstuffs and the measure of liquids. The baker, milkman, coalman, on their rounds can expect to be stopped, and the weight or measure of their goods checked by an inspector.

After checking scales in wholesale and retail shops, barrows and market stalls, an inspector will usually follow up by checking weight of merchandise.

So much food is pre-packed now that it is not weighed in the presence of the housewife, and although by law most of it must be marked with its weight, the inspector weighs it just the same.

In his rounds he meets with some discrepancies, and these bring forth a warning and helpful advice. But if both are ignored, prosecution follows, particularly in the serious matters of falsely describing food and those concerned with weight.

The Housewife is the important person on the reverse side of this picture.

To her, Medical Officers and all concerned make a strong appeal for co-operation, particularly in the care of, and handling of food; by herself and by those with whom she deals in shops and restaurants (see also chapters on Home Precautions Against Food Poisoning).

It is significant that against the hundreds of tests made in a year on suspect food, by one council's health officials, only twenty-one individual complaints were investigated concerning unsatisfactory food and dirty milk bottles. Several of these resulted in prosecutions.

Yet another Medical Officer, referring to a case of food poisoning (caused by a trifle, infected by a cut finger, and left overnight in an unsuitable temperature), regretted that few homes had refrigerators although many displayed TV aerials.

The public health officials are approachable people. They can be called on with legitimate complaints, and something will be done. They can be called on to spread the wisdom of co-operative public health

A food inspector stops a milk roundsman in the street (right) and takes a sample for testing

Chief duty of the Water Boards throughout the U.K. is to keep the taps running, supplying millions of homes with pure, wholesome water

by giving talks to clubs and organisations; and there is much to interest the thinking man and woman in the facts that a Medical Officer of Health and his skilled staff can give.

WATER BOARDS

The Minister of Health has extensive powers over the distribution of water supplies either through Boards or District Councils. Although you will no doubt deal with a plumber where water installation and repairs are concerned, you may also like to know that, in emergency (say a burst tank or pipe), you can call the "Service" telephone number of your Board, day or night, for a plumber if you cannot get hold of your own. If there is a great delay in getting your own man for the replacement of washers even, a Board plumber can be called, and some Boards will also replace ball valves. If you are not entirely satisfied with a plumbing installation or its fitting, you can get expert advice by calling at the Chief Engineer's office. There is no charge for this. Charges for repairs are competitive, based on time and material.

Your Board will always turn off the stop-cock beyond your house boundary, if you notify them when you go away in winter, say, and want to empty tanks and cisterns. And in passing, if you don't know the whereabouts of the main stop-cock in the house, get a plumber to show you and label it—you can then at once turn off the water when a burst occurs.

Your Water Board, once it has supplied pure and wholesome water has, in effect, done its job. But beyond that, every Board issues bylaws governing the prevention of waste, undue consumption, etc., for the guidance of plumbers. Therefore the advice given and repairs carried out by a reputable plumber constitute an indirect advisory service from your Water Board.

As a matter of interest, there are local Acts still remaining that lay down maximum water rates. An application can be made to the Minister of Health for their revision, decrease or increase, by a company, local authority or by twenty consumers.

SANITARY SERVICES

Association of ideas couples "drains" with "Sanitary Inspector," and certainly if you are a tenant with cause for complaint about drainage, and your landlord takes no notice of your appeals, you should let him know you mean to inform the sanitary authorities. This usually does the trick, for sanitary inspectors are thorough, and may find other matters wrong, apart from the drains. But if even this approach to your landlord fails, then write or call on the Sanitary Inspector for your area—he is to be found in the offices of the local District Council (Urban or Rural), County Borough Council or, in London, Metropolitan Borough Council. His powers are extensive and something will be done.

The sanitary authorities deal with all of what are known as "statutory nuisances." These might be, to quote the Public Health Act, 1936—"any premises in such a state as to be prejudicial to health or a nuisance"; in fact, a statutory nuisance might be a rubbish dump; dust or other deposit from manufacture; foul water from a pond, ditch and so on; indeed, anything producing conditions prejudicial to health or a nuisance.

House Refuse.—There is no obligation on a sanitary authority to remove refuse; it may resolve to do so or the Minister of Health may require it to do so. Once the decision is made, the authority is bound to make the necessary arrangements for removal. It is up to you to notify the authority if this service is not carried out and you know that it is available.

You can make arrangements with your sanitary authority for a special collection of rubbish; for example, if you have moved into a new house and there is building débris to be cleared, or into a house in which the outgoing tenants have left a mass of litter. There will be a reasonable charge for this service, but it is often abundantly worth it.

POLICE

"Telephone for Police, Fire or Ambulance"—all very nice and reassuring. But most people hope they will never have to and seldom go any deeper into the various public services available.

The citizen is obliged by law to help the police. On the other hand, there are many ways in which the police give constant help to the individual under the heading of "Extraneous Duties." You may, for instance, be stranded on your way home,

The collection of home refuse by the dustman is the responsibility of the local authority under the direction of the Medical Officer of Health

Night and day the police guard the peace—
and also provide many personal services for the
people about which little is known

As well as putting out fires, the fire brigade
deals with chimneys that catch alight and often
rescues man or beast from heights

unable to get back that night, no 'phone at home and someone waiting anxiously. Get in touch with the police and arrangements will be made with your own police for a constable to deliver a reassuring message in person.

Again, you may be stranded, this time financially—lost wallet or handbag, perhaps. Find the nearest police station or police house and explain the circumstances. They will ring through to your home police and a constable will be sent to your home, or to someone whom you know will provide the necessary money to get you back. This is handed to the policeman, who then sends through the O.K. to the station where you are waiting and they advance you the money, recovering it from your home police.

These are only two instances of many; there is the case of a personal friend into whose sitting room water poured one Sunday during a storm. She rang the police, they rang a plumber and a temporary repair was made in a very short time.

It is perhaps more difficult for the citizen to cultivate the idea of helping the police. People are often shy of offering amateur help to the professional. The police are, however, trained to sort the wheat from the chaff, so if you have any suspicions of anybody or anything seemingly unlawful, do report it. You may see someone behaving oddly, you might see a window open in a house you know to be shut up and empty. Whatever it is, if instinct warns you it is suspicious, inform a policeman or report to a police station. You will certainly not be rebuffed and an investigation will be made.

FIRE BRIGADE

Apart from their normal task of putting out fire, preventing its spread and carrying out any rescue work involved, firemen can be called out for several other purposes. It happens that both people and animals get trapped through an accident other than fire or, through some misadventure, get up to a dangerous height and cannot get down. It is then quite in order to call the fire brigade to the rescue.

If your house gets flooded, you can call the brigade and they will bring equipment to pump out the water. You may, in the first instance, call the police and they will call in the fire service, and it is quite likely that, if the policeman comes along as well, he will help to mop up.

A chimney on fire is not an uncommon cause of a call on the fire brigade, and they will come and deal with it. Two points arise here: (a) chimneys should be swept regularly to avoid this danger; (b) although you pay nothing to the fire brigade for this service, an old law still prevails in some country districts whereby the police can fine a householder whose negligence has caused a chimney fire.

Before we leave this subject, remember you may be liable to prosecution for using an unguarded electric fire in a room where children play, if an accident happens. It is not possible now to buy a new electric fire that is not fitted with an approved safety guard, but many people still have old ones.

Another service of the Fire Brigade, fortunately not too often required, is that of supplying water where normal supplies have failed. And, although not affecting the home, there is an invaluable fire prevention advisory service available for the planners of industrial, commercial and public buildings.

AMBULANCE

The ambulance service is now part of the personal health services administered by county councils and county borough councils and the London County Council as local health authorities. It is their duty to provide an adequate ambulance service for the following specific purposes: (a) *accident cases* at home, in the streets or wherever they occur; (b) *sudden illness* in the street, public places (cinema, shops, etc.) or places of employment; (c) *urgent illness* at home, if a doctor certifies the necessity and arranges for admission to hospital; (d) *maternity cases* (i) where an expectant mother has booked a hospital bed (she will be given full instructions by the hospital for calling the ambulance), (ii) for emergency cases in the street or public places, (iii) in cases where it becomes necessary to remove a mother to hospital for the birth of her baby, provided doctor or midwife makes the arrangements.

The ambulance may be called by private, public or police telephone in the case of (a), (b) and (d) (i) and (ii). A doctor makes the call in the case of (c), and doctor or midwife in the case of (d) (iii). There are no charges for these statutory ambulance services.

Ambulance services are usually hard-pressed, and it may not always be possible to get one for what is termed a "non-essential" purpose outside the statutory purposes. If, for instance, someone at home has to go to a convalescent home, or to hospital for an X-ray or periodic treatment and they are not too fit, or move with difficulty, you can call the ambulance service and they will probably refer you to the St. John or Red Cross ambulance depot. But in this case you should be prepared to pay a fee based on distance and the number of attendants needed for the patient.

TELEPHONE

A surprising number of those living alone are unaware that the telephone exchange (even where it is automatic) will call them in the morning if they need to be up betimes to catch an early train or keep a particularly early appointment. Where an exchange has a night staff you can be called any time during the 24 hours. Cost is the price of the call.

The personal call has more to it than merely assuring that you speak to one particular person: you can name a substitute as well; or you can arrange to speak only if two named persons are both available at one particular number; or you can arrange for a person not on the telephone to be brought to a neighbour's telephone (provided you know the neighbour has given consent). The charges for this, apart from the cost of the call, are: midnight to 6 p.m. and 10.30 p.m. to midnight, 1s. 6d.: 6 p.m. to 10.30 p.m., 9d.

Information about ships, their position and time of arrival can be had from any post office coast station. You can telephone through or send a reply-paid telegram. The charge is 1s. in addition to cost of telegram and reply (six words) or the cost of the 'phone call.

It costs a call only to know what the day's weather will be, either locally or in various parts of the British Isles. In London, dial WEA 2211 for local London weather; for other information call the Meteorological Office, Victory House—HOLborn 3434—and ask for the "Forecast Office." A full list of Meteorological Offices that may be called is given in *The Post Office Guide*. A copy is usually available in most post offices, or may be bought for 2*s*. 6*d*. The *Guide* is a mine of information and remarkably good value.

ELECTRICITY BOARDS

Electricity distribution undertakings are now grouped under twelve Area Boards in England and Wales and three in Scotland, each appointed by the Minister of Fuel and Power. What concerns the consumer, who may have wishes to state concerning charges and facilities, is the Consultative Council for the Area Board; the members of this are appointed from among members of local authorities and those representative of consumers. Approach the Secretary of the Council in writing or through the Councillor who represents your area on District, County or Borough Council. The address and telephone number of your Board's Consultative Council will be given in the telephone directory.

Also in the directory, under your Board, note the "Service" number; through this you can arrange for repairs to be done or for advice on installation.

Service engineers can be called at any time in the 24 hours for blown fuses, other repairs or failure of any sort. On the whole, servicing is free of charge, but where negligence is apparent a charge may be made. Payment must be made for replacements.

At your nearest showroom, specialists in every branch of electrical engineering are available for consultation. All apparatus sold through the showroom carries a one-year guarantee and has been thoroughly tested for safety and efficiency.

Hire purchase terms can also be arranged and instalments, or any extra charges, are included on your quarterly account.

If you buy a cooker, you will receive a call from a woman adviser a day or two later to enquire if all is well. If you are not entirely satisfied with cooking results, a demonstrator will call and undertake actual cooking, so that you can go through the process with her and ask questions.

In cases of extreme emergency—suppose your electric washing machine breaks

When a sick person must travel by train, British Railways provide special facilities. Here a stretcher is passed through the invalid window in one of B.R.'s all-steel coaches

down as you start the family wash—it may be possible for the showroom to lend you a machine while your own is repaired.

If anything happens to the outside supply (from which your house current comes), it will be quickly detected and put right as promptly as possible.

GAS BOARDS

These work to the same pattern as the Electricity Boards, and if there is not already a Consultative Council for your Board, there will be.

Your local showroom has much to offer, and the person to approach is the Home Service Adviser. There are already over 400, and the number is increasing. This helpful expert will answer questions, demonstrate appliances of all kinds, help you with problems of kitchen planning, all free of charge.

Service engineers are available day or night, so if you have a loose tap on cooker or heater, a pipe joint that needs tightening, etc., call the "Service" number in the telephone directory and the fault will have attention, usually quite quickly. Actual servicing is free, but replacements (radiants for fires, cooker parts, taps and so on) are chargeable and will be included in your account for gas consumption; so, too, can items you buy new through the showroom on hire purchase terms.

BRITISH RAILWAYS

No need to worry about what would happen if you were taken ill and to hospital while away from home. The hospital authorities in conjunction with B.R. have an efficient, smoothly working scheme. When you can be moved, an ambulance takes you to the nearest main line station and a fast train. You are transferred to a reserved compartment and a nurse goes with you to the station nearest your home. Here you are met by another ambulance and are taken to a hospital in your own locality. The scheme is part of the National Health Service and free of charge.

It may be necessary to send your child alone on a train journey. This is a recognised service, to be arranged with the stationmaster at your end. He notifies the guard, and your son or daughter becomes the guard's responsibility until he personally hands over his charge to someone meeting the child. You should be sure that the child knows, or has in writing, his home address and telephone number, and the name, address and 'phone number of those to whom he is travelling, in case whoever is meeting him fails to appear and enquiries have to be made. If that happens, the child passes to the care of the stationmaster until his sponsor arrives. Age limits are elastic and there is no charge.

Many large main line stations have wheel chairs available for those in need of them to get from train to car or taxi, and a porter can be asked for the use of one; again, no charge. There is always a First Aid Station with a nurse on duty at large stations; a first aid kit and a trained member of the station staff at smaller stations.

You can send parcels by train, often a great advantage when time is a factor and the normal postal service would take too long. Make up the parcel securely, address clearly and take it to your station. Here it is weighed and you pay the necessary amount. It then goes off by the next train and at the journey's end it may be: (a) met and taken away as soon as it is cleared, a few minutes only; (b) kept at the station until called for, or (c) delivered to the addressee by van—whichever you arrange when sending it off. Cost depends on weight and mileage; as an approximate example, a 7-lb. parcel travelling between 30 and 50 miles would cost about 2s. 2d.

If you have arranged to meet someone at a station and cannot get there, ring the stationmaster's office and every effort will be made to find the person and give them the message. The railways do urge you, however, to try and give a definite means of identification ; the loudspeaker, where there is one, is used only as a last resort because, acoustically, it is not necessarily helpful, and in the first instance a messenger is sent to look for your friend.

AIR TRAVEL

Any travel agency or airways booking office is the starting-off point for tickets, reservations and full information.

Here you may like to know what a ticket for a long distance journey covers. In addition to your own transport and free baggage allowance (approximately 66 lb. First Class, 44 lb. Tourist Class), the fare includes accommodation at night stops, all meals and gratuities in the air and on the ground between departure and arrival. On First Class trips, wines and spirits are free and a cabin bag is provided to hold your overnight necessities. Drinks are paid for by passengers on Tourist Class trips and cabin bags are not provided.

Much is done for children. They can safely travel alone, well looked after, from the age of seven upwards. Younger, they must be accompanied and you should provide all their needs. Even so, some aircraft are provided with cots and supplies of napkins, and all carry the food and liquid needs of babies on a normal mixed diet. Facilities are available for sterilising feeding bottles, and arrangements can be made for special baby foods to be carried.

The steward has medicines for minor ailments of children and adults; he or she has some practical knowledge of nursing, and in general is a highly trained person, expected, and able, to meet any emergency on a flight.

Domestic pets may travel with you in the hold in crates conforming to R.S.P.C.A. standards. If there is not space on the passenger plane, animals are sent by freighter plane and, in either case, every care is taken of them. A passenger with impaired sight and dependent on a guide dog is excepted, and the dog travels with him in the cabin.

Excess baggage can also be carried if space permits, and this is chargeable.

No gratuities are allowed to ground or air crews or to servants at hotels *en route*.

If you look on the back of your demand note for the General Rate you will see that this rate covers the cost of, among other things, police, fire service and ambulance service (included in Public Health). No charges

are incurred if you make use of these services except, of course, if they are wilfully misused. A District Council may be the authority for your water supply, and in this case the water rate will be included in the general rate. The cost of sanitary services is also included, and if you are good at figures you can see how much money is needed for each service and how your rate per £ is estimated to help meet the cost.

Further Information

All these services and others (with the exception of the telephone, railways and airways) form the work of Local Government, and there are various ways in which you can enquire into, or have action taken on, any service in which you are interested. Your local councillor on either district or county council is the person most easily reached, and a good councillor is always ready to attend to those who support him.

Citizens' Advice Bureaux are able to answer questions on local government services, and more and more councils are setting up information offices where anyone may seek information on all the social services available.

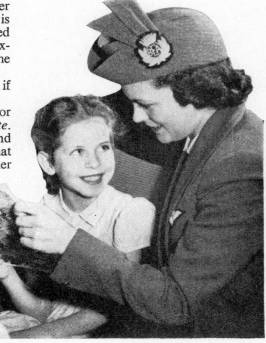

Children can safely travel unaccompanied by air. Right, a B.E.A. hostess entertains a young passenger in a Viscount

Photographs in this chapter: B.E.A., British Railways and British official photographs — Crown copyright reserved

WHAT MAKES A BALANCED DIET

How to translate the five chief nutrients into meals for a family

by DR. MARY LYMINGTON

THERE is a tendency in "civilised" countries and modern times to regard food as merely the excuse for a pleasant social occasion or for personal indulgence.

It is, however, most important that we should not forget the real function of food —to refuel and repair the body. The primary responsibility of the housewife is, indeed, to see that her family get a well-balanced diet.

Good balance is achieved only when the five chief nutrients are taken regularly in the correct proportions. If the balance gets upset, the result is malnutrition, as in the case of a child with rickets due to Vitamin D and calcium starvation, or a 'teenager who gets too fat owing to an excess of starch in the diet.

Food is composed of the following five nutrients:

(1) *Carbohydrates*, which provide the body with energy and, if unused, may be stored in the body tissues.
(2) *Fats*, which also provide energy and form body fat.
(3) *Proteins*, for growth and repair of body tissues.
(4) *Minerals*, which help in growth and repair, and are particularly important because of their function in regulating body processes. They include salt, calcium, phosphate, iron, iodine and a trace of copper.
(5) *Vitamins*, which have all kinds of important effects in regulating different processes.

What is a Normal Diet?

A diet for people trying neither to gain nor lose weight should contain 1 part protein to 1 part fat to 4 parts carbohydrates, calculated by weight.

The energy value of food is measured in terms of heat units called calories, a calorie being the amount of heat needed to raise the temperature of 1,000 grams of water by one degree Centigrade, from 15° to 16°. Obviously, the quantity of food a person requires depends very largely upon his expenditure of energy. In other words, a miner working hard below ground all day needs a great deal more nourishment than a lady of leisure, while a growing boy or girl in the 'teens requires more than a busy housewife because of the demands of physical development and growth.

As can be seen from the table shown opposite, a child from the age of ten up needs as many calories as an average adult, while from fourteen, the requirements of a boy or girl are *above* that of the average grown-up.

Where to Find the Nutrients

In order to produce a well-balanced diet, it is essential to know which of the common foods contain which of the nutrients. Many do, of course, contain more than one. Brown bread, for instance, is a source of protein as well as of carbohydrate, and milk contains some of practically everything needed in a diet. Listed opposite are the main sources of the five nutrients.

BALANCED DIET

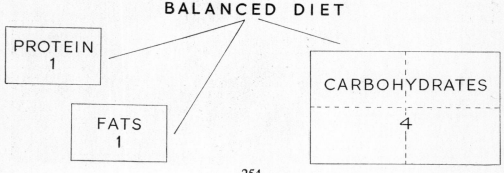

PROTEIN 1

FATS 1

CARBOHYDRATES 4

WHAT MAKES A BALANCED DIET

As a rough guide, these are the approximate food require-ments per day of people leading different kinds of life

CALORIES	1,000	1,250	1,500	2,150	2,550	2,700	2,800	2,900	3,000
Children : 1–2 years	☆								
2–3 years		☆							
3–6 years			☆						
8–10 years				☆					
10–12 years					☆				
12–14 years								☆	
Girls : 14–18 years							☆————		☆
Boys : 14–18 years									☆ to 3,400
Man doing hard manual work								4,000	
Man doing light work									☆
Woman doing hard work									☆
Woman doing light work (housewife)						☆			

A man and woman of approximately equal size doing equal work require the same number of calories

Carbohydrates

Sugar, syrup, flour, oatmeal, jam, raisins, dates, currants, white bread, pota-toes and, to a lesser degree, all fruits and vegetables.

Fats

Butter, margarine, lard, dripping, olive oil, nuts, bacon, cheese, fat meat, herring, egg, milk, canned salmon.

Proteins

There are two sources of protein:
(1) *Animal or First-class Protein*, found in all kinds of meat, game, poultry, fish (including shellfish), milk, cheese and eggs.

(2) *Vegetable or Second-class Protein.* The richest source is nuts, followed by dried peas and beans (though their pro-tein value is reduced by the necessary process of soaking), and then fresh peas and beans and certain root vege-tables. Potatoes contain more protein than carrots or turnips.

Minerals

The daily amount of *salts* required by

an average person is more than accounted for by the common foods included in a normal diet and the salt added in cooking or taken at table. *Calcium*, essential for the formation of teeth and bones and therefore particularly important for expectant mothers and children, is found chiefly in milk, cheese and milk products, to a lesser degree in sardines and tinned salmon, bread and green vegetables. *Iron*, a deficiency of which produces anæmia, is found particularly in liver, kidneys, corned beef.

Vitamins

Vitamin A (essential to a child's growth, and also for good sight, healthy skin, bones and teeth, and for protection against infection) is found in animal foods, such as liver, dairy produce and eggs and in green and yellow vegetables (carrots). Halibut- and cod-liver oil are the two most concentrated sources.

The *Vitamin B* group has many subdivisions, including *Vitamin B₁* and *Riboflavine*, both of which contribute to the body's effective use of energy foods, help to maintain the muscular and nervous systems, and prevent undue fatigue. They are chiefly found in dried brewers' yeast, liver, wheatgerm; Vitamin B₁ also in peanuts, bacon, oatmeal, peas and beans, Riboflavine in milk and eggs. There is also in the Vitamin B group, *Nicotinic Acid*, a deficiency of which produces skin troubles, digestive upsets and mental symptoms. Main sources are meat extract, dried brewers' yeast, liver, kidney, meat and fish, wheatgerm. The other B vitamins, too numerous to describe in detail, are found chiefly in yeast, liver, cereals and pulses, some in green leafy vegetables.

Vitamin C (Ascorbic Acid) occurs mainly in fresh fruit and vegetables, but at least half is destroyed by cooking, even when the best possible methods are used. If Vitamin C is not contained in sufficient quantity in a diet, children's growth is checked, the gums and mouth are susceptible to infection, healing (of wounds) is slowed down and eventually scurvy results. Richest sources of Vitamin C are blackcurrants, then oranges, lemons, grapefruit and rose hips (which may be taken in the form of syrup).

Vitamin D is essential to good bone formation (and therefore of special importance to infants, children and expectant mothers); a deficiency leads to rickets. Our chief sources of Vitamin D are (*a*) foods such as cod-liver oil, sardines, herrings, canned salmon, margarine, and (*b*) sunlight on the skin.

Vitamin E, thought to affect fertility, is found chiefly in milk and wheatgerm; *Vitamin K*, which enables the blood to clot, in cabbage and green peas.

Value of Certain Foods

The chart opposite shows how many of the common items of a normal diet contain several of the essential nutrients and thus help the natural balance.

Notice the foods rich in all the essential components, particularly milk and, to a lesser degree, chocolate—and the value of eggs and certain fish. Try to build your family's menus around them, always bearing in mind the necessity for variety in stimulating the appetite. Although food fads should not be encouraged, particularly in children, there are some people who just cannot take milk, others with their own pet dislikes. For them, the problem is to find suitable alternatives. Children who will not drink milk or eat milk puddings will often take it in savoury form—turned into a tasty cheese sauce, for example, or as a white sauce served with fish or vegetables. They may also eat cheese and butter, which between them provide the next best thing to milk (see also chapter on Children's Meals).

Here is a specimen diet which provides good balance between all the components and upon which you can base your own menu planning:

BREAKFAST
Cereal or porridge and milk or fruit
Bacon, egg, fish, etc.
Toast and marmalade
Tea or coffee

LUNCH
Meat, fish, egg or cheese,
with salad or cooked vegetable
Pudding or fruit
Tea or coffee

TEA
(if desired)
A large tea meal usually results in too

BALANCED DIET SHEET
VALUE OF SOME FOODSTUFFS

	PROTEIN	FAT	CARBO-HYDRATE	SALTS	VITAMINS
MILK	+	+	+	} Phosphate and Calcium	A and D
BUTTER	—	+	—		A and D
MARGARINE	—	+	—		+
CHEESE	+	+	—	} Iron, Phosphate and Calcium	A and B
CHOCOLATE	+	+	+		
COCOA	+	+	+		
EGG	+	+	—	Iron and Phosphate	
SUGAR	—	—	+	—	
GOLDEN SYRUP	—	—	+	Iron	
HONEY	— (small amounts)	—	+	—	
JAM	+	—	+	Iron	
MARMALADE	+	—	+	Iron	
BREAD	+	+ (small amounts)	+	} Iron and Phosphate	B
BISCUITS	+	+	+		
FLOUR	+	+	+		
MEAT	+	+	—	—	sometimes B
BLOATER	+	+	—	} Iron and Phosphate, some Calcium	
KIPPER	+	+	—		
HERRING	+	+	—		
SALMON	+	+	—		
COD	+	—	—		(Cod) B
HADDOCK	+	—	—		
VEGETABLES	+	—	+	+ all salts	+ especially A and C
APPLE, GRAPES, ORANGE	+ (small amounts)	—	+	—	C
BANANA	+	—	+	—	A

much starchy food, particularly in the case of the sedentary worker, who may, as a result, suffer from indigestion or tend to put on weight. Most people will be satisfied with a cup of tea and a slice of cake or two or three biscuits.

DINNER
Soup
Meat, fish, egg or cheese, with vegetables or salad
Pudding or fruit
Cheese   Tea or coffee

BEDTIME
(optional)

Drink of some kind, preferably made with milk

The lunch and dinner menus are interchangeable according to circumstances. Generally speaking, children and old people should have their main meal at midday and a light supper; sedentary workers, on the other hand, are better with a big meal at night since it is bad to sit all the afternoon with a full tummy.

NOTE: *Liquids* should be taken, if possible, between meals, and their importance must on no account be overlooked. The need of the body for water is second in importance only to its need for air. *At least* 1½ *pints* of water or other fluid should be drunk every day; more if possible. Bear in mind that, if too little is drunk, dehydration occurs, whereas if too much is drunk, the body gets rid of the excess quite easily through the kidneys. So it is better to drink *more* than the daily minimum requirement than less. (This does not, of course, apply to alcoholic drinks.)

Effect of Cooking

The process of cooking nearly always directly improves the nutritional value of food, as well as improving its flavour and making it generally more attractive and appetising. The one great exception is Vitamin C, which is very easily destroyed by heat and a high proportion of which is invariably lost in the preparation of food for the table (see chapter on The Effect of Cooking and Storage on Vitamins).

When potatoes are peeled and then boiled, the loss of Vitamin C is 50 per cent.; when they are fried, 30 per cent. But bake them in their skins and the loss is reduced to 20 per cent., boil them in their skins and it is only 15 per cent.

Green vegetables lose more when they are put into cold water and then brought to the boil than when they are plunged into boiling water.

The best way to avoid this inevitable loss of Vitamin C in cooking is (1) to eat the vegetables raw in the form of salads, and (2) to cook them so that the loss is reduced to the absolute minimum. Essential cooking rules are:

(1) Choose absolutely fresh vegetables (long storage also destroys Vitamin C).

(2) Peel them as thinly as possible or, better still, cook in their skins.

(3) Prepare at the last minute, just before cooking.

(4) Take care not to overcook them.

(5) Cook in a saucepan with a tight-fitting lid and in the smallest quantity of fast-boiling salted water, just enough to prevent them from burning.

(6) Never use bicarbonate of soda.

(7) Serve immediately

Balancing a Baby's Diet

Though milk is the nearest approach to a complete food (and a number of adults, conducting a scientific test, have successfully lived on nothing else for some time and gone about their daily work), it is deficient in Vitamin C and iron, and does not contain sufficient Vitamins A and D for a growing child. Hence the necessity to supplement a baby's diet of cows' milk with orange juice or rose-hip syrup (for Vitamin C), cod-liver oil (for Vitamins A and D) and to start sieved greens and lightly cooked eggs at an early age. Both these contain iron, and eggs are rich in animal protein and Vitamins A and D.

Feeding Schoolchildren

As has already been shown, schoolchildren are growing so fast and using up so much energy that their calorie requirements are higher than those of their parents—as is proved by their large appetites. Their great need is for protein, calcium, Vitamins A, D and C, all in the most concentrated form available. The best source of all these is milk. Cheese, meat, eggs, fruit and green vegetables are also essential; and bread and home-made cakes (which contain fat, sugar, milk and eggs) will supply extra calories. The same principles apply to a suitable diet for adolescents, who should take plenty of milk and proteins.

A family who live on a well-balanced diet start off with a sound foundation of good health. But do remember that "calories" are merely terms of measurement, to help you assess the food values of certain commodities, not to be discussed over every meal; and that mealtimes should be pleasant, peaceful family occasions, not exercises in advanced dietetics. Food does people good in direct proportion to how much they enjoy it.

SLIMMING WITH SAFETY

*Why we put on weight, the dangers of
obesity and a practical plan for healthy
and gradual reduction*

SINCE the slim figure has established
itself as the æsthetic ideal of modern
woman, much interest has centred on the
problem of the putting on of fat and for the
most part this interest has served the cause
of health and fitness. Long-continued overweight can have serious repercussions
upon all the systems of the body. Surplus
fat is a burden upon all the tissues and organs, and statistics of Life Assurance Companies show that mortality rates rise
steadily in proportion to the extent to
which people are overweight.

There are still many men and women
who accept increasing bulk with deplorable
complacency, but they are a decreasing
number. Obesity is a great handicap in the
ceaseless competition of modern life.

A definition of obesity is difficult to give,
for, while gross fatness is obvious, the insidious spreading of adipose tissue renders
the frontier between normality and ab-
normality hard to detect. It is unfortunately the case that most people find themselves well in the toils of obesity before they
awaken to the significant fact. Authorities
have elaborated weight tables according to
height and age and, although there is some
divergence of opinion, they are for the most
part reliable as guides. Naturally, there are
individual variations, especially in so far as
people differ in the compactness and weight
of their bones. But a good rule is that
adults, say over thirty-five years of age,
should not vary much in their weight until
middle age, when, after a *slight* temporary
increase, there should be a slight decline in
the elderly age period.

It is said with a good deal of truth that
most men and women over forty are too
fat. Again, it is usually agreed by doctors
that there is some advantage in a slight
degree of overweight in individuals under
thirty-five. A small excess of fat seems to
constitute a protection against infectious
diseases which are the main causes of
death in the early decades. It is equally
agreed that there is an advantage in slight
underweight after middle life, when degen-
erative diseases of the heart, blood vessels
and kidneys take the prime place in the
mortality figures.

It is the abdominal wall which suffers
first. Fat develops between the muscle
fibres, and these most important muscles

TABLE OF AVERAGE WEIGHTS OF WOMEN

HEIGHT ►	4'8"	4'9"	4'10"	4'11"	5'0"	5'1"	5'2"	5'3"	5'4"	5'5"	5'6"	5'7"	5'8"	5'9"	5'10"	5'11"	6'0"
AGE 20	7.8	7.10	7.12	8.0	8.2	8.4	8.7	8.10	8.13	9.2	9.6	9.10	10.0	10.3	10.7	10.11	11.2
25	7.11	7.13	8.1	8.3	8.5	8.7	8.9	8.12	9.2	9.5	9.9	9.13	10.3	10.7	10.11	11.0	11.4
30	8.0	8.2	8.4	8.6	8.8	8.10	8.12	9.1	9.5	9.8	9.12	10.2	10.6	10.10	11.0	11 3	11.7
35	8.3	8.5	8.7	8.9	8.11	8.13	9.1	9.4	9.8	9.12	10.2	10.6	10.10	11.0	11.3	11.6	11.9
40	8.7	8.9	8.11	8.13	9.1	9.3	9.6	9.9	9.12	10.2	10.6	10.10	11.0	11.4	11.7	11.10	11.13
45	8.10	8.12	9.0	9.2	9.4	9.6	9.9	9.12	10.1	10.5	10.9	10.13	11.3	11.7	11.10	12.0	12.3
50	8.13	9.1	9.3	9.5	9.7	9.9	9.12	10.1	10.4	10.8	10.12	11.2	11.7	11.11	12.1	12.5	12.8
55	8.13	9.1	9.3	9.5	9.7	9.9	9.12	10.1	10.4	10.8	10.13	11.4	11.9	11.13	12.3	12.6	12.9

ALL WEIGHTS IN STONES AND POUNDS

are weakened and become ineffectual. Later, fat accumulates within the abdomen and further impedes organic activity. Briefly, the results are constipation, dyspepsia, liverishness, a tendency to gall stones, piles and a general lowering of vitality.

But the pathology of obesity does not stop there. A grave penalty of overweight is diabetes, which has a notoriously high incidence among the corpulent. Apart from the formation of fat round the heart, the heart muscle has extra labour to perform in maintaining a more extensive blood circulation. This in time leads to high blood pressure, hardening of the arteries and kidney inefficiency. Further, owing to the debilitated state of the heart muscle, the obese patient is a bad surgical risk. Overweight also produces adverse mechanical effects upon the skeletal tissues, the bones and joints.

All fat people eventually develop bad postures. They become round-shouldered, while the hip and knee joints creak under the strain. Osteo-arthritis is nearly always accompanied by obesity. The arches of the feet give way and this occasions much pain and distress.

Cause of Obesity

The fundamental cause of overweight is an excess of food intake over the body's requirements. Overweight is mainly the result of over-eating. Yet it is a remarkable physiological phenomenon how the healthy body maintains constancy in weight over long periods, in spite of great variations in food intake and in physical activity.

It is similar to the maintenance of body temperature under widely varying conditions. We know that the gourmand does not necessarily become obese and that the abstemious in food may remain plump. It is generally agreed that most of us eat more than our calorie requirements, but the excess in the normal person may not be absorbed or is easily dissipated. If it were not so, obesity would be a universal malady. We do not know all the factors which enter into the mechanism for regulating body weight, but there is the important factor of endocrine balance.

Our gland endowment to a large extent determines the rate at which our vital activities are carried out, whether the body furnace shall burn brightly or smoulder slowly.

These two factors, excess of food intake and the endocrine balance, are responsible then for overweight, but so far as *treatment* is concerned (except where there is obvious endocrine disturbance) *dieting* is the recognised, and, if properly carried out, the efficacious method.

It is often thought that hard exercise is a weight reducer, but when it is realised that an average person would consume only 60 extra calories by walking a mile (and that this often increases appetite), it can be understood that it would require very arduous and sustained muscular work to reduce weight effectively. The practical procedure, therefore, is the adoption of a rationally constructed *sub*-calorie diet. Drastic methods such as purgation by salts, the production of severe sweating by Turkish baths, starvation diets, and the use of thyroid extracts and other drugs have had their vogue: their effects are likely to be short-lived and they are often most harmful to health.

Dietetic Control

In constructing a reducing dietary, the most important factor is the total *calorific value* of the diet. A calorie is the unit of food energy. There are three main kinds of food, carbohydrates (starches and sugar), protein (meats), and fat; and 1 gram of carbohydrate produces 4 calories, 1 gram of protein 4 calories, and 1 gram of fat 9 calories. Hence, if we know the composition of any food, we can calculate simply the calorie value of any given quantity: e.g. $3\frac{1}{2}$ oz. (half a glass) of milk contains 5 grams of carbohydrate, $3\frac{1}{2}$ grams of protein and $3\frac{1}{2}$ grams of fat. Therefore the total calorie value is $65\frac{1}{2}$. The daily calorie requirements of a healthy adult vary with the nature of the activities, from about 2,000 for a sedentary worker to 3,000 for a heavy manual worker, some variation being allowed for physique.

For reduction to the desired weight, it is recommended that a dietary of 1,000–2,000 *calories* should be adopted. It is generally considered unsafe to adopt a dietary of less than 1,000 calories unless the person is under medical supervision and confined to bed. A very low calorie

diet may lead to faintness, weakness and irritability, with an unduly rapid loss of weight. The ideal is a steady and progressive loss of weight amounting to *two or three pounds* each week.

The next factor to consider is the proportion of the basic foodstuffs, the carbohydrates, proteins and fats. Since it is usually an excessive consumption of starchy and sugary foods which leads to overweight, it is obvious that such foods should be restricted as far as possible in reducing diets. But excessive curtailment can lead to feelings of faintness, weakness and headache, so that not less than 100–130 grams of carbohydrate should be taken each day. The greater part of this should be taken in the form of fruit and green vegetables, for these give bulk to the diet and are low in calorie content. Moreover, they give a feeling of satiety and provide the roughage which prevents constipation, which low

The following are foods to be avoided:

Sugar, sweets, jams, cakes, pastries, scones, thick soups and sauces made with flour and butter, fried foods, cream, fat meat and bacon, pork, duck and goose, nuts, sweet wines, beers and stouts, fruits canned in syrup, peas, beans, parsnips and beetroot

It is well to remember that toast is not less fattening than bread and that no foods are "slimming" foods

calorie diets may otherwise tend to produce.

With regard to fat, as the body calls upon its own reserves, this item can be reduced to a minimum. Some reducing diets exclude fats as such, only such fat being permitted which is inseparable from such foods as meat. Thus the daily intake may be as low as 20 grams. But extreme reduction of fats makes the diet unpalatable and would require the addition of the fat-soluble vitamins to maintain health. It is therefore considered that 40–50 grams of fat per day should be provided.

As protein is stimulating to the vital processes (metabolism), it is sometimes given in large quantities, but as this means a higher calorie intake and an unbalancing of the diet, it is not recommended. On the other hand, too low a protein intake will cause excessive destruction of tissue protein and will disturb the chemical balance of the body. Some 60–80 grams of protein is considered the best amount. It is not deemed wise to restrict fluids in a reducing diet, except for alcohol and sweetened drinks, but salt and salty foods are to be avoided.

Methods of Dieting

Those who would reduce, as already indicated, should aim at remaining on a dietary of 1,000–1,200 calories until such time as they have reached their ideal weight. Assuming a moderate degree of overweight, this should take from roughly four to six weeks. Thereafter, they should cautiously increase their dietary selectively to about 1,500–1,800 calories, carefully watching their weight. All the good will be undone if they return to their old diet, especially in those who tend to put on weight easily. Life for them becomes a series of "diet cures," and this is bad for health and morale.

It is possible progressively to reduce the amount of food per day by 50–100 calories and so reach the desired 1,000–1,200, and some may prefer to accustom themselves gradually to the low dietary in this way. But most people are anxious to achieve results as quickly as possible. Needless to say, this will involve a certain self-discipline and a degree of conscientiousness for success. The first few days may be difficult, but once these are over, it should not

prove unduly difficult to maintain the regime.

If one wishes to tackle a slimming diet in a strictly scientific way, then it is necessary to obtain scales and to weigh all the foodstuffs. Actually, this is not essential, provided the prescribed dietaries are followed intelligently and the approximate quantities are adhered to.

The following is a reducing dietary of 1,200 calories, containing 116 grams of carbohydrate, 70 grams of protein and 52 grams of fat.

BREAKFAST

One orange or half a grapefruit sweetened with saccharin NOT sugar
Tea or coffee with milk from ration *
One egg or one ounce of cold lean ham or tongue
One ounce of bread (equivalent of one thin slice) and quarter-ounce of butter (one small pat)

DINNER

Clear soup
Two to three ounces of lean meat, chicken, or white fish
A large helping of vegetables, excepting potatoes, dried peas, beans or lentils
Fresh salad (lettuce, cabbage, without oil or cream dressing)
Three-quarters of an ounce of cheese
Half an ounce (half-slice) of bread, or two plain biscuits
Fresh fruit, except bananas or plums
Coffee with milk from ration *

TEA

Tea with milk from ration * sweetened with saccharin, NOT sugar
Bread, one and a half ounces (one and a half slices)
Tomato, lettuce or cress for sandwiches
Quarter-ounce butter (small pat)

SUPPER

Clear soup
Three ounces (cooked weight) of fish, or egg, or one ounce lean meat
Vegetable salad and fruit as at dinner
Bread, half an ounce, or piece of crisp-bread
Milk from ration * for coffee, or for custard, using egg from breakfast

* RATIONS FOR DAY

Butter, three-quarters of
an ounce
Milk, half a pint
NO sugar

The free foods which can be taken by
those feeling hungry between meals
while dieting

It should be noted
that most fresh fruits,
green vegetables, meat
extracts and clear soups,
tea and coffee without
milk can be taken freely,
so that those who ex-
perience hunger between meals can find
comfort by taking such foods.

There it is then—a typical weight reducing dietary which can lend itself to a
great many variations to avoid a depressing
monotony. It is not a difficult dietary to
prepare and it is not expensive.

Here is a six days' guide:

EVERY DAY
BREAKFAST

Orange or half a grapefruit; one egg,
boiled, poached or scrambled; or one
ounce lean ham, or two ounces white
fish, baked or steamed, or one kipper or
one herring; one piece crispbread or
one thin slice of bread or toast; half
an ounce sugarless marmalade; tea or
coffee with milk, from **ration of half a
pint per day;** and butter from **three-
quarter ounce ration per day.***

FIRST DAY
DINNER

Tomato juice
One and half ounces lean grilled bacon,
tomato and cauliflower
Three starch-reduced rolls or slices with
butter from ration *
One apple
Coffee or tea with milk from ration *

SUPPER

Orange juice
One lean grilled chop,
celery and sprouts
One piece crispbread with
butter from ration *
One fresh pear with three
tablespoonfuls junket

SECOND DAY
DINNER

Clear soup
Two ounces lean meat,
cabbage and carrots
Fruit salad (orange,
apple, grapes)
One slice bread with
butter from ration *
Coffee or tea

SUPPER

Tomato juice
Three ounces steamed fish with lemon
juice and celery
Three ounces stewed apricots
Two starch-reduced rolls or slices with
butter from ration *
Three tablespoonfuls cornflour mould

THIRD DAY
DINNER

Half a grapefruit
Two ounces braised rabbit, cabbage and
carrots
One piece crispbread and butter from
ration *
Stewed rhubarb with tablespoonful rice
pudding
Coffee or tea

SUPPER

Clear soup
Two ounces lean roast meat with cauli-
flower
One slice fresh pineapple with three table-
spoonfuls junket
One slice bread with butter from ration *

FOURTH DAY
DINNER

Vegetable broth (unthickened)
Two ounces grated cheese with lettuce,
watercress and tomato
Three starch-reduced rolls or slices
with butter from ration *
One orange
Tea or coffee

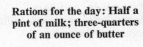

**Rations for the day: Half a
pint of milk; three-quarters
of an ounce of butter**

SUPPER

Lobster or crab salad

Stewed apples with three tablespoonfuls cornflour mould

One piece crispbread with butter from ration * and a small portion of cheese

FIFTH DAY

DINNER

Orange juice

One poached egg with spinach

Three starch-reduced rolls or slices with butter from ration *

Three ounces stewed apricots with three tablespoonfuls sago pudding

Coffee or tea

SUPPER

Clear soup

Three ounces haddock (steamed), tomato and lettuce

One slice bread and butter from ration * and small portion of cheese

One apple

SIXTH DAY

DINNER

Half a grapefruit

Two ounces cold lean meat with salad (lettuce, watercress, tomato)

Two starch-reduced rolls or slices with

butter from ration * and small portion of cheese

Coffee or tea

SUPPER

Tomato juice

Two ounces lean grilled ham, tomatoes and spinach

Two starch-reduced rolls or slices with butter from ration *

Two and a half ounces figs with three tablespoonfuls custard

Finally, it must be again emphasised that successful dieting demands some special knowledge along with a reasonable self-discipline. Failure to achieve results nearly always arises from a loss of interest and enthusiasm, or from disappointment that the desired loss of weight is not achieved sufficiently rapidly. Patience is required, but the restoration of the body to its normal weight will assuredly improve the health of mind as well as body, and increase the joy of living.

FOOD TABLES

These tables show the number of calories given by convenient quantities of the common foodstuffs and their approximate content of carbohydrate, protein and fat. Reference to these tables will enable a person to diet with a considerable degree of accuracy.

Carbohydrate

CEREALS

	Oz.	Calories	C.	P.	F.
Arrowroot, uncooked	$\frac{1}{2}$	61$\frac{1}{2}$	15	0	0
Bread, average, white	1	74	15	3	0
Bread, average, brown	1	68	15	1$\frac{1}{2}$	0
Corn Flakes	$\frac{1}{2}$	45	10	1	0
Macaroni, boiled	2	58$\frac{1}{2}$	10	2	1
Oatmeal, raw	$\frac{1}{2}$	68	10	2	2
Rice, uncooked	$\frac{1}{2}$	51	12$\frac{1}{2}$	0	0
Sago, uncooked	$\frac{1}{2}$	51	12$\frac{1}{2}$	0	0

SUGARY FOODS

Chocolate, average, milk	$\frac{1}{2}$	84	7$\frac{1}{2}$	1	5
Chocolate, average, plain	$\frac{1}{2}$	62	7$\frac{1}{2}$	1	3
Golden Syrup, as purchased	$\frac{1}{2}$	51	12$\frac{1}{2}$	0	0
Honey, as purchased	$\frac{1}{2}$	51	12$\frac{1}{2}$	0	0
Jam, average	$\frac{1}{4}$	20$\frac{1}{2}$	5	0	0
Marmalade, ordinary	$\frac{1}{2}$	51	12$\frac{1}{2}$	0	0
Marmalade, sugarless, reliable make		Negligible			
Sugar, one large lump	$\frac{1}{2}$	20$\frac{1}{2}$	5	0	0

Carbohydrate (*continued*)

MILK

	Oz.	Calories	C.	P.	F.
Buttermilk	$3\frac{1}{2}$	42	5	3	1
Milk, fresh	$\begin{cases} 1 \\ 3\frac{1}{2} \end{cases}$	19 / 67	$1\frac{1}{2}$ / 5	1 / $3\frac{1}{2}$	1 / $3\frac{1}{2}$
Milk, skimmed	$3\frac{1}{2}$	$41\frac{1}{2}$	5	4	$\frac{1}{2}$
Milk, condensed unsweetened	1	61	5	3	3
Milk, dried	$\frac{1}{2}$	67	5	$3\frac{1}{2}$	$3\frac{1}{2}$

FRUIT AND NUTS

	Oz.	Calories	C.	P.	F.
Apple, with skin	2	$20\frac{1}{2}$	5	0	0
Apricots, fresh, with stones	3	25	5	1	0
Banana, average size	3	$61\frac{1}{2}$	15	0	0
Figs, green, raw	2	26	5	1	0
Grapefruit, with skin	6	22	5	$\frac{1}{2}$	0
Grapes, fresh	1	20	5	0	0
Melon, edible part	$3\frac{1}{2}$	23	5	1	0
Nuts, almond	$\frac{1}{2}$	78	$\frac{1}{2}$	3	7
Nuts, brazil	$\frac{1}{2}$	86	$\frac{1}{2}$	2	8
Nuts, chestnut	$\frac{1}{2}$	68	5	3	4
Nuts, walnut	$\frac{1}{2}$	74	$\frac{1}{2}$	2	7
Olives	1	$46\frac{1}{2}$	0	0	5
Peaches, fresh, with stones	$2\frac{1}{4}$	$22\frac{1}{2}$	5	$\frac{1}{2}$	0
Pears, fresh, with skin	3	27	6	$\frac{1}{2}$	0
Pineapple, fresh, edible part	$1\frac{1}{2}$	$20\frac{1}{2}$	5	0	0
Plums, ripe, Victoria (with stones)	2	$20\frac{1}{2}$	5	0	0
Rhubarb		Negligible			

VEGETABLES

	Oz.	Calories	C.	P.	F.
Asparagus, fresh, boiled (edible part)	8	16	$2\frac{1}{2}$	$7\frac{1}{2}$	0
Beans, broad	$2\frac{1}{2}$	33	5	3	0
Beans, butter	2	56	10	4	0
Beans, haricot	2	56	10	4	0
Beans, french	8	16	$2\frac{1}{2}$	$1\frac{1}{2}$	0
Beans, scarlet runner		Negligible			
Beetroot, boiled once	$1\frac{3}{4}$	25	5	1	0
Brussels sprouts ⎫ Cabbage, spring ⎬ Cabbage, winter ⎭		May be considered negligible			
Carrots, boiled once	4	23	5	$\frac{1}{2}$	0
Cauliflower ⎫ Celery, raw ⎬ Celery, baked ⎪ Cress ⎭		May be considered negligible			
Cucumber, raw, without skin	5	14	$2\frac{1}{2}$	1	0
Cucumber, boiled	6	11	$2\frac{1}{2}$	0	0
Lettuce, raw		Negligible			
Mushrooms		Negligible			
Onions, boiled once	$3\frac{1}{2}$	14	$2\frac{1}{2}$	$\frac{1}{2}$	0
Peas, boiled once, green, fresh	2	70	14	2	$\frac{1}{2}$
Peas, tinned, green	2	57	10	4	0
Peas, green, dried	2	57	10	4	0
Potato, raw or boiled once	1	$22\frac{1}{2}$	5	$\frac{1}{2}$	0
Spinach, boiled once	6	46	$2\frac{1}{2}$	9	0
Tomatoes, raw, cooked or tinned	4	20	3	1	0
Watercress, raw	1	Negligible			

	Protein Oz.	Calories	C.	P.	F.
Cheese	½	50–70 varies roughly			
Eggs, one average whole egg	—	76	—	6	5½

FISH	Oz.	Calories	C.	P.	F.
Cod, boiled	3	61	0	15	0
Crab, edible part	2	58	0	10	2
Haddock, boiled	3	82	0	20	0
Halibut, boiled	1½	58	0	10	2
Herring, fresh	2	112	0	10	8
Kipper, boiled	1½	76	0	10	4
Mackerel, boiled	3	114	0	15	6
Plaice, steamed	2	50	0	10	1
Salmon, boiled	3	142	0	15	9
Skate, boiled	2	50	0	10	1
Turbot, cooked	3	60	0	15	0
Whiting, steamed	2	41	0	10	0

MEAT	Oz.	Calories	C.	P.	F.
Bacon, fat, fried	1	160	0	5	15
Bacon, lean	1½	220	0	10	20
Beef, average roast	2	201	0	15	15
Beef, roast lean	2	87	0	15	3
Ham, boiled, lean only	1½	94	0	10	6
Kidneys, cooked	2	87	0	15	3
Lamb, roast	3	175	0	20	10
Liver, cooked	2	141	0	15	9
Mutton, roast	2	168	0	15	12
Mutton chop, lean, grilled	2	224	0	20	16
Pork, roast	2	229	0	15	18
Rabbit, stewed	2	89	0	15	3
Sweetbreads, cooked	1½	78	0	10	4
Tongue, ox, tinned	1½	162	0	10	13
Veal, roast	2	156	0	20	8

POULTRY AND GAME	Oz.	Calories	C.	P.	F.
Chicken, roast or boiled	2	103	0	15	4½
Duck, roast or boiled	1½	134	0	10	10
Goose, roast	2	173	0	15	12
Turkey, roast	2	89	0	15	3

FATS	Oz.	Calories	F.
Bacon	½	116	12½
Beef fat	½	116	12½
Butter	½	116	12½
Cream, average	1	46½	5
Dripping	½	139½	15
Lard	½	139½	15
Margarine	½	116	12½
Suet	½	139½	15

ROUTINE FOR PUTTING ON WEIGHT

Plenty of rest and exercise, a good diet of fattening foods and no worries—those are the essentials

PUTTING on weight is very much more difficult than taking it off. Even those few extra pounds which can make all the difference to the appearance, comfort and, no doubt, general health, can be quite a problem.

Before embarking on a diet, it is always advisable to seek the advice of your own doctor. This is particularly important if there has been a sudden or prolonged loss of weight for no good reason and without affecting normal appetite. Where loss of weight is the result of an illness or operation, it is usually quite quickly and easily regained after recovery. The routine to be described in this chapter will help in such cases, subject to the approval of your own doctor.

We are concerned here chiefly with that large army of men and women who are anxious to put on weight but who are the thin type by nature. Such people are born worriers, with excitable and energetic natures and over-active bowels, whose food does not remain in the intestines long enough to be properly absorbed.

Essential in the fattening process are:

Italian actress Pier Angeli gets through a huge plate of ice cream—an excellent fattening food

(1) **Keep calm and stop worrying.** That is obviously a counsel of perfection to those who easily get worked up, but it *can* be achieved by cultivating outside interests that take your mind away from the source of anxiety (it may be professional, domestic, financial, or all three).

(2) **Take plenty of rest.** A minimum of between 8 and 9 hours in bed at night, plus between 10 and 30 minutes after every meal.

(3) **Avoid rushing about, but take regular exercise.** On no account jump up immediately after a meal; take life at a leisurely pace. Strenuous games are good if you really enjoy them, because they create appetite; so does any form of outdoor exercise, however mild.

(4) **Eat well and regularly, and concentrate on the fattening foods** (list follows). But be careful not to stuff between meals or you will defeat the whole object and be unable to eat your main meals, which are far more important. You must also avoid *over*-eating, with the inevitable danger of indigestion and biliousness. Aim at three good meals a day, plus any extras (such as sweets, etc.) which you really fancy and a hot, preferably milk, drink last thing at night. The housewife should take as many meals out as she conveniently can because she will not have the worry of preparing them.

(5) **Cut down your smoking.** It diminishes the appetite, so, if you must smoke at all, only after meals, please.

FATTENING FOODS

Sugar, sweets, jam, marmalade, fruits in syrup, treacle, honey, Golden Syrup.

Cakes, scones, pastry, cereals, bread, biscuits, puddings.

Thickened soups and gravies, sauces made from flour, butter and/or milk.

Fried foods, cream, salad dressings, butter, dripping.

Pork, duck, goose. All fat meat and bacon. Tinned fish in oil.

Sweet wines, beer, stout, spirits, sweet aerated waters.

Dried fruits. Bananas, grapes, plums.

Potatoes, peas, dried beans, parsnips, beetroot.

Cod-liver oil, Virol, olive oil.

Salt with food.

Foods with very little fattening value

Meat extracts. Marmite. Clear soups. Gelatine. Egg-white.

Green vegetables and salads. Vinegar. Tea. Coffee.

SPECIMEN DIET FOR PUTTING ON WEIGHT

Minimum: 1 pint of milk per day

On waking: Cup of tea, preferably with milk and sugar.

Breakfast: Cereal or porridge with milk and sugar or honey or syrup.
Bacon, egg, fish, etc.
Toast, butter and marmalade.
Coffee or tea.

11 a.m.: Coffee, cocoa or milk and a biscuit, or try this cocktail: One teaspoonful Spanish olive oil sandwiched between layers of orange juice in a wineglass. You can increase the quantity of olive oil gradually.

Lunch: Thick soup, if liked (if this makes it impossible to eat main course, substitute tomato or orange juice as an appetiser instead).
Meat, fish, game, poultry, etc.—both *fat and lean*. Serve with gravy, roast or fried potatoes and a green vegetable or salad with plenty of oily or cream dressing.
Pudding and/or cheese, butter and biscuits. Coffee.

Tea: Tea with cake or bread and butter or banana sandwich.

Dinner: Thick soup (see Lunch).
Fish, meat or poultry, with gravy, at least one vegetable from list of Fattening Foods; one green vegetable or salad with cream or oil dressing.
Steamed or boiled pudding or milk pudding or ice cream.
Cheese with bread or biscuits and butter. Coffee.

NOTE: Cocktails, wines, etc., may be taken as desired and obtainable. Stout or beer is good.

Bedtime: A hot drink, preferably containing milk.

Instead of rushing about just after eating, lie back in bed and enjoy your breakfast in leisurely fashion if you really want to put on weight

THE EFFECT OF COOKING AND STORAGE ON VITAMINS

*Information supplied by the Medical Director of
the Nutrition Information Service, Vitamins Ltd.*

SINCE we eat much of our food cooked, either in the home or before purchase, it is important to know whether we can do anything, by choice of method, to prevent loss of vitamins.

Methods of cooking are many and various: food may be cooked dry, in fat, in water or in steam; it may be exposed to air or enclosed in a pressure cooker; it may be cooked at high or low temperatures for short or long periods, and it may have been subject to some form of processing before cooking.

It is small wonder, therefore, that there is great variation in the nutritive value of foods as presented at the table.

Until recently, little research had been done on this subject, but by now we know a good deal about the effects of various cooking methods on vitamin retention.

MEAT

Meats are the chief sources of the vitamin B_2 group, riboflavine and nicotinic acid, and only to a lesser extent are they sources of vitamin B_1.

Riboflavine and nicotinic acid are relatively stable, and losses are usually less than 15 per cent. by roasting, grilling, frying, braising or stewing. Vitamin B_1 is more readily lost, especially by slow cooking. In stewing, as much as 50 per cent. may be lost, and 42–64 per cent. by roasting. But since meats are not the best sources of vitamin B_1 in any case, this is not as important as it might otherwise be.

Vitamin A is present in very high concentration in liver, and there is some, though less, in kidney, but this vitamin is not water soluble and is not reduced in amount by cooking.

EGGS

The chief vitamins of eggs are A, D and riboflavine. There is little B_1 or nicotinic acid and no vitamin C. Vitamins A and D are stable to cooking, but 10–15 per cent. of riboflavine may be lost when eggs are cooked either alone or as baked custard.

CEREALS

These are our chief sources of vitamins B_1, B_6 and E. Some contain also some nicotinic acid, and riboflavine is present only in small amounts.

Since most cereals are eaten cooked and some prepared foods are subjected to high temperatures, it is important to know what the effects are.

Vitamin B_1 is lost by oxidation. Hence in bread, less is retained in the crust than in the crumb, and toasting causes further loss. Any cereals browned throughout, like biscuits, or much charred, cannot be relied on to contain vitamin B_1. The use of baking powder, sodium bicarbonate and sour milk, unless used in excessive quantities in the baking of buns and cakes, seems to make no difference in the retention of vitamin B_1.

VEGETABLES AND FRUIT

Vegetables are the main sources of vitamin C and carotene, and, since vitamin C is one of the least stable of all vitamins, every possible measure should be taken to prevent loss.

Experiments have been done on the effects of various methods of cooking on the vitamin C content of a number of different vegetables. These included carrots, beets, potatoes, peas and leafy vegetables, such as cabbage, broccoli and spinach.

The retention of the vitamin was found to depend more on the method of cooking than on the type of vegetable, but there were wide variations from sample to sample. In general, it can be said that most vitamin is retained by pressure cooking and least when a large amount of water is used.

Vitamin C retention	Per cent. of fresh value
Pressure cooking	60–90 per cent.
Little water only	50–85 per cent.
Water to cover	40–70 per cent.

Storage after Cooking

Cooked vegetables rapidly lose their vitamin C if they are kept for the next day's meals. New potatoes cooked in their jackets retain their vitamin C well, but, if peeled, half the vitamin C may be lost by the next day. The type of utensil used for cooking—i.e. enamel, stainless steel, aluminium, glass—seems to make no difference.

Blackcurrants

Blackcurrants contain very large quanties of vitamin C, but the season for fresh fruit is short, so it is important to know the effects of preserving.

Very little vitamin C is lost by bottling, but much passes into the juice, which should always be used. There is progressive loss during storage. The best conditions are: low temperature, protection from light, and the use of glass or metal rather than plastic covers.

Jams

The following figures have been published:

Retention of ascorbic acid in:

	Freshly made	After 1 year storage
Blackcurrant jam	70 per cent.	30 per cent.
Gooseberry jam	66 per cent.	28 per cent.
Strawberry jam	55 per cent.	17 per cent.

THE STATE OF FOOD WHEN PUT INTO STORAGE

Some foods, such as hard fruits (apples and pears), root vegetables (potatoes, carrots, parsnips) and cereals (rice), are commonly stored for several months without special treatment; others are treated first, either by drying, salting, pickling, heat sterilisation or freezing, and are stored in special containers or sealed in tins or glass jars.

The vitamin content of the food when eaten depends on its state when put into storage and the conditions under which it is stored. The following are important factors for consideration: length of storage, temperature, access of light and air and moisture, both within the food and in its surroundings.

Vitamins, and especially water-soluble vitamins, occur within the living cells of plants. As long as the cells remain intact, the vitamin content is little changed, but mechanical damage as caused by bruising or cutting, or loss of water as caused by wilting, allows considerable deterioration.

Dried grass, finely divided, is now widely used by farmers as a source of vitamin A activity, and may lose as much as 40–50 per cent. of its potency during storage; or more if allowed to wilt before storage. Even so, it is a better source of carotene than hay. Vegetables and fruits which are little damaged by packing and handling hold their vitamins better than the more delicate varieties. As an example, cabbage bears the stress of transport better than spinach.

Vitamin C, being readily oxidised, is the vitamin most easily lost and the one about which most information is available.

Cabbage left whole and stored in the open but protected from rain loses very little ascorbic acid in a week and only about one-third of its content when stored for a month at room temperature.

On the other hand, minced or finely cut cabbage may lose much of its ascorbic acid in a matter of minutes.

Spinach, which wilts quickly, may lose 40 per cent. of its ascorbic acid in a day and nearly 80 per cent. in two days.

Asparagus may lose 80 per cent. in four days, from wilting.

Fruit similarly loses its ascorbic acid by cell damage. Apples and pears, when bruised, lose much of their ascorbic acid.

These examples show how important it is: (a) to handle all fresh foods so as to **avoid cell damage** and (b) to **prevent wilting.**

STORAGE

Foods stored in the home without special containers—e.g. fresh fruits and vegetables, bread and cereals, cheese—may lose some of their vitamins. The most vulnerable is vitamin C, then the B complex, and, to a lesser extent, vitamin A.

The chart opposite provides data on

EFFECT OF COOKING AND STORAGE ON VITAMINS

	Fresh	1st day	2nd day	3rd day	4th day	5th day	6th day	7th day	Conditions
Blackcurrants . .	50 mg./oz.			45 mg./oz.	42 mg./oz.				Room temperature
Broccoli tops .	49				37		30		Room temperature
Brussels sprouts .	38				34				
Cauliflower . .	24						17		
Cabbage . .	14						13 11		0°–3° C. 20° C.
Spinach . .	14						13 2		0°–3° C. 20° C.
Asparagus . .	3	2·5			0·5				20° C.
Peas . . .	3						3 1·5		0°–3° C. 20° C.

vitamin C losses in fruits and vegetables kept for short periods.

Green vegetables exposed to the air at ordinary temperatures may lose as much as half their vitamin C in a day and almost four-fifths in 2 days, but if fresh uncut cabbage is wrapped and kept at refrigeration temperature, it will retain its vitamin C for several weeks. Other green vegetables packed in ice retain their original vitamin C content for as long as 5 days, and tomatoes retain 90 per cent. when kept in a refrigerator for a week.

Root-type vegetables kept in a cool cellar retain their vitamin C well during the winter.

Potatoes, parsnips, onions and carrots contain relatively little of the vitamin but, as the quantities eaten are greater, they do contribute some vitamin C to the total amount consumed, and if these vegetables are taken in quantity, the amount is by no means negligible.

Vegetables are, in general, better stored at low temperatures, and where the texture is hard, vitamin retention is better. Potatoes, parsnips and carrots, for example, lose less during storage than do onions or celery. Onions lose from 50–80 per cent. in three months, while with potatoes the loss is progressive up to 50 per cent. or 60 per cent. in six months.

Fruits and vegetables are not good sources of the B vitamins. The small quantities of riboflavine present are not much changed with storage, but there is commonly a loss of 10–20 per cent. of vitamin B_1. The riboflavine of bread and rolls is protected by wrapping, even with translucent waxed paper.

Cereals are better sources of the B vitamins, and here freedom from moisture is important.

Bread, which contains about 50 per cent. of moisture, is usually kept only for a matter of days, but rice, oatmeal, pearl barley and packeted cereals may be stored for months. Although it is not customary to keep cereals indefinitely, Bemax, with a moisture content of about 5 per cent., will retain its vitamin B_1 without appreciable loss for many years, samples over twenty years old being as potent as those of contemporary manufacture.

Cheese, a food with a relatively low vitamin B_1 content, retains it well, only about 12 per cent. being lost in three months and 25 per cent. in six months.

PRESERVATION

The commonest process for the preservation of foods is **canning**, with which can be included **bottling**.

Exclusion of air is more efficient from canned than bottled foods, and this helps in the retention of vitamin C, which is lost by oxidation. Access of light is also prevented by canning.

Carotene and **vitamin A** remain relatively stable during both canning and subsequent storage, unless this is prolonged unduly. There is also little loss of vitamin D. This latter is important, since individuals other than infants may obtain their major supplies of vitamin D from canned fish such as herring and sardines.

Of the **B vitamins**, riboflavine and nicotinic acid are well retained in meat, fish and milk, but, during the prolonged heating needed for sterilisation, as much as 70 per cent. of vitamin B_1 may be lost. Little further loss occurs during storage, only up to 10 per cent. at refrigeration temperature, and up to 20 per cent. during one year at ordinary room temperature.

Vitamin C may be destroyed by the preliminary blanching of vegetables, but little is lost by the process of canning. From 30–50 per cent. may pass into the liquid portion of the contents. Even at relatively high room temperatures, the losses in fruit juices and sliced fruits are in most cases under 25 per cent.

The addition of ascorbic acid in not more than 0·2 per cent. of the weight of fruit stabilises the colour of canned fruit without affecting texture or flavour, and is retained for long periods in 30–60 per cent. sugar syrup.

CANNING

Non-acid foods, such as beans, peas, spinach and corn, retain only about half their original vitamins C and B; oranges and tomatoes much more. Fresh oranges vary widely, but canning losses in the juice are negligible.

Canned foods are best kept in a cool, dry place. It has been shown that storage at 50° F. causes only 5–15 per cent. loss of vitamin C, but at 80° F. this is increased to 20–35 per cent.

FREEZING

Freezing is looked upon as the most modern method of food preservation, although as early as 1865 slow freezing of fish and poultry was introduced, closely followed by the freezing of meat. Meat and fish preserved by this method lose little, if any, of their nutritive value after storage for long periods. During thawing, however, there is a tendency, particularly in the case of beef, to lose juices which will contain water-soluble proteins, minerals and vitamins.

The development of the quick method of freezing in 1929 has provided the most effective method for the preservation of vitamins in foods. Loss of water-soluble vitamins occurs during the preliminary processes; this is higher in vegetables than in fruits, fish, meat and poultry, since vegetables are subjected to blanching to destroy the oxidative enzymes. The storage temperature of foods preserved by these methods is of the utmost importance—28° C. being considered the maximum temperature for the effective retention of vitamins. Storage at −19° C. results in loss of one-third of the vitamin C in strawberries and beans. If the temperature is allowed to fluctuate between −19° C. and −17° C., loss is even greater, reaching 66 per cent. in strawberries and 8 per cent. in beans.

"Quick frozen" foods do not readily lose vitamins on thawing, but fruits allowed to stand for 12 hours at room temperatures lose a considerable amount of vitamin C.

SALTING

Salting, on the other hand, is the oldest method of food preservation and is still in use both domestically and commercially, either alone for the preservation of vegetables, or combined with saltpetre or smoking for the curing of meats and fish.

The domestic preservation of vegetables, such as beans, by packing in jars with salt is very destructive to vitamins. Little or no vitamin C can be expected to remain after 3 months' storage, and 47–80 per cent. of the original vitamin A is lost.

272

VITAMINS PRESERVED		VITAMINS DESTROYED	
	More vitamin B₁ in crumb than crust. Bemax retains it for years.		Any cereals toasted, browned or charred lose vitamin B.
	Pressure-cooking vegetables is the method retaining most vitamins.		Least vitamins are preserved when vegetables cooked in much water.
	Fresh uncut wrapped cabbage in a fridge retains vitamin C for weeks.		Green vegetables exposed to the air lose half their vitamin C in a day.
	Tomatoes retain 90 per cent. vitamin C in a refrigerator for a week.	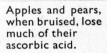	Apples and pears, when bruised, lose much of their ascorbic acid.
	Quick-frozen foods do not readily lose vitamins on thawing.	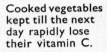	Cooked vegetables kept till the next day rapidly lose their vitamin C.
	Cured hams contain a high percentage of their original vitamins.		Packing beans in jars with salt is very destructive of vitamins.
	Canned fish retains vitamins A and D; fruits most of their vitamin C.	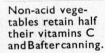	Non-acid vegetables retain half their vitamins C and B after canning.

More vitamin B₁ in crumb than crust. Bemax retains it for years.

CURING

Curing and corning of meat are effective methods for the retention of the B vitamins. Hams prepared commercially by being placed in pickling solution for 12 days and then being smoked for 18 hours have been shown to contain 73 per cent. of their original aneurine, 92 per cent. of their riboflavine and 84 per cent. of their nicotinic acid. Corned beef retains 20–52 per cent. of its aneurine and 90–100 per cent. of its riboflavine. The nitrites and nitrates of cured meat rapidly destroy the vitamin C in vegetables when cooked with them in such dishes as stews.

PRESERVES

The making of jams is an effective method of preserving fruit without much loss of vitamin C, since the vitamin is resistant to the heat treatment of jam boiling. Commercially prepared jams which contain 30–40 per cent. of fruit may be said to contain approximately 30–40 per cent. of the vitamin originally present in the fruit from which they were made. The use of sugar for jam making is the most profitable way of using the amounts available when these are restricted.

PICKLES

Pickling is another method used both commercially and domestically for the storage of vegetables and fruits. The acetic acid present in vinegar penetrates the cells of vegetables immersed in it, particularly if these are sliced, and causes rapid oxidation of the vitamin C. Green walnuts are a very good source of vitamin C and when made into chutney at home retain 94 per cent.; when prepared commercially, the chutney retains only 40 per cent. of the vitamin C. Sauerkraut, which is prepared by fermenting cabbage, contains approximately the same amount of vitamin C as fresh cabbage, during and immediately after the fermentation process. Storage, however, results in rapid loss of the vitamin.

CHEESE

The manufacture of cheese is a method of converting surplus milk into a form in which it can be stored, to provide an excellent source of protein and calcium. Freshly made cheese contains 25–33 per cent. of the riboflavine, 9 per cent. of the aneurine and 85 per cent. of the vitamin A of the milk from which it is made. During the ripening process, the vitamin A remains stable, but further loss of 43–73 per cent. aneurine occurs. Riboflavine appears to increase in the surface layers of the cheese,

probably owing to synthesis by micro-organisms.

To summarise:

(1) Vegetables and fruit should be as fresh as possible when used either for cooking or preserving.
(2) If storage is necessary, they should be kept in as cool a place as possible.
(3) In cooking, the least quantity of water that is practicable should be used. Cooking should be rapid and for the shortest possible time.
(4) Vegetables should not be cooked one day for use the next.
(5) It should be noted that figures quoted in tables of vitamin values frequently refer to fruits and vegetables as freshly collected and may need considerable modification when used for calculations of the vitamin content of diets as eaten.

HIGH CALORIE DIETS

Increased physical activity, at work or play, demands extra intake

Information supplied by the Medical Director of the Nutrition Information Service, Vitamins Ltd.

THE body does not distinguish between work and play. Increased physical activity, whether as a farm labourer or a mountaineer, a despatch rider or a fast swimmer, demands an extra intake of all the nutrients concerned in muscular activity.

All sorts of mistaken ideas are still current regarding the kind of food needed. It is said that high protein meals containing plenty of meat are necessary for strength and athletic achievement. In the animal world the elephant, though moving slowly, can pull down a tree, and the deer achieves a speed of 30 m.p.h., both on vegetarian diets. In man, provided the total protein intake is adequate in quality and quantity, there does not appear to be any need for additional amounts. Calories are needed in amounts increasing with the degree of muscular effort, and it has been shown that carbohydrate is the most satisfactory way of supplying the bulk of these extra calories. Excess fat may reduce muscular efficiency by loss of energy during its conversion.

The British Medical Association (Committee on Nutrition) gives six grades of activity for men and five for women as follows:

	Calories Men	Women
0. No work, almost basal (e.g. lying in bed) . .	1,750	1,500
1. Sedentary work and little travelling . . .	2,250	2,000
2. Light work and travelling	2,750	2,250
3. Medium work and travelling	3,000	2,500
4 Heavy work and travelling	3,500	3,000
5. Very heavy work and travelling	4,250	3,750
6. Extremely heavy work and travelling . . .	5,000	—

There is thus a 2–3-fold variation between the lowest and the highest calorie intake. In general, there is not such a wide variation in the size of the human stomach, and the weight of the food eaten varies from about 3½–5 lb. daily.

Hunger is experienced when the stomach is empty, satiety when it is relatively full, regardless of the calories available from the stomach contents. The problem is therefore to give the body the nutrients it needs in the bulk which it finds comfortable.

THE SIGNIFICANCE OF BULK

Individuals whose need for calories is low, must consume relatively bulky foods like green vegetables and fruits, whilst those whose need for calories is high must eat more highly concentrated foods of small bulk, e.g. chocolate or bread. The diagrams here show the relative weights of examples of foods, all of which supply 100 calories.

People doing heavy physical work or strenuous forms of athletics will need all the calories they can get without overloading the stomach with excess bulk. It may be necessary for some meals to contain relatively large amounts of fat. It has been recommended by the National Research Council (U.S.A.) that for those whose energy requirements are less than 3,000 calories daily, 20–25 per cent. of total calories should be supplied by fat, and for those with greater requirements 30–35 per cent. should be derived from fat.

Physical efficiency is lowest before breakfast and highest about an hour after meals.

TO SUPPLY 100 CALORIES YOU NEED

1. ¾ oz. butter, bacon or chocolate.

2. 1 oz. cereal, sugar or sardines.

3. 1½ oz. bread, beans or meat.

4. 2 oz. egg, herring or prunes.

5. 4–6 oz. potato, milk, banana or fish.

6. Right: 10–16 oz. apple, orange, onion or carrot.

7. Below: 20–25 oz. cabbage or tomato.

8. Over 30 oz. lettuce.

There is evidence that for heavy work and activity in cold or hot environments or at high altitudes, small frequent meals are better than larger ones at intervals.

EFFECT OF GLUCOSE

Glucose has long been looked upon as the best source of energy. Experiments show that there is no change in performance following the administration of a large dose of glucose. The liver and muscles of healthy adults contain glycogen ready for immediate breakdown. This process is hastened by the output of adrenaline in anticipation of approaching effort and for short sprints. The event is over before glucose or any other sugar taken just before the start can be absorbed and circulated to the muscles going into action.

THE DIET OF EXPLORERS

Men exploring new regions, whether polar or at high altitudes, have to carry heavy loads and at the same time be able to withstand extreme cold. They aim at reducing the weight of food to be carried to 2 lb. or less for each day's supply, but require a calorie intake of 4,000–5,000. This is achieved by carrying dehydrated or relatively dry foods to which water can be added when meals are prepared. A typical ration consists of dried meat or pemmican, biscuits, cereals, chocolate, dried vegetables and fruits, dried egg and dried milk.

Pemmican was originally made by Red Indians from dried buffalo or caribou meat made into cakes with fat. British pemmican is a modification in which beef is used.

An Actual Example used in Arctic Exploration

Food	Weight oz.	Calories
Pemmican	8	1,304
Butter	4	920
Milk chocolate	2	326
Fruit and nut chocolate	2	290
Sugar	4	464
Oats	3	357
Pea flour	1½	156
Biscuits	2	276
Bemax	1	104
Raisins	1	80
Cocoa/milk	1½	177
	30 oz.	4,454

PROTECTIVE FACTORS

Explorers have learned that the provision of calories in small bulk is not the only or even the most important consideration. The diet must be fully protective, and this means an adequate supply of good protein and all the necessary vitamins and minerals. The example given contains the necessary protein and factors of the vitamin B group, but is clearly short of vitamins A and C. On the expedition during which this was used, vitamin tablets were taken to compensate for these deficiencies.

In hot climates or during heavy work in a hot humid atmosphere, extra salt and vitamin C are needed.

For all athletes and heavy workers it is not sufficient to increase the intake of calories to the required amount. Extra calories will require extra B complex vitamins, particularly vitamin B_1, to effect their complete metabolism.

High Calorie Meals which can be carried by heavy workers or those engaged in outdoor activities

Calories

(1) 8 buttered dry biscuits
    2 oz. cheese
    2 hard-boiled eggs
    2 oz. chocolate   1,275

(2) 6 oz. corned beef
    4 slices bread and butter/margarine
    4 digestive biscuits   1,275

(3) 4 fried sausages
    2 slices bread and butter/margarine
    2 oz. stoned dates   1,140

(4) Pork pie
    2 oz. nuts and raisins
    4 buttered biscuits   1,100

The nutritive value of all these meals can be improved by the addition of tomatoes, oranges, etc., if these can be carried. If not, care must be taken to include in the breakfast or evening meal a good source of vitamin C. It is probably easier to ensure an adequate intake of the vitamin B complex, vitamin A and calcium either at breakfast or the evening meal eaten on returning. The appropriate quantities are provided by ½ pint of milk and 1 oz. Bemax.

SHOPPING TO ADVANTAGE

*How to buy economically and how to choose
fruit and vegetables that are really fresh*

LET it be a comforting thought to all new housewives that even those of long experience can sometimes fall down on food purchases. Certainly there is much for the beginner to learn about wise buying of food; all the different cuts of meat, varieties of fish, fruit, vegetables and dry goods, and whether or not they are as fresh as they should be, in season or out of it.

To graduate as a good food shopper, over whom no salesman can pull a fast one, you will need to "pass" in three aspects of the job: knowing (*a*) what you want; (*b*) the right price for the goods and for your housekeeping budget; and (*c*) whether what you buy is fresh or not.

You can, and should, take your time over (*a*). It is not possible to learn all the cuts of meat and kinds of fish until you have cooked and tried different recipes for some little time. Included in the Meat and Fish chapters of this book there is plenty to guide you initially. Seek advice on the shops with the best reputation and shop

there. Goods may cost a penny or two more, but this is not lack of economy when it ensures quality and freshness. Also you can ask for advice, and get it. You may learn a lot from experienced shopkeepers.

Turning now to (*b*) price, and (*c*) freshness, you need to gain knowledge on these aspects as quickly as possible. Once you have memorised the average prices of meat, fish, fruit and vegetables, and which prices suit your budget best, you can shop by price, asking for something at so much.

The radio and some newspapers give weekly food bulletins for the housewife. If you note these down for two or three weeks, you can make yourself a useful guide to average prices.

CHOOSING VEGETABLES

(See also Fruit and Vegetable Recognition Chart in colour five pages farther on.)

Artichokes (Globe).—When you cut the stems they should be white and moist, leaves should be very firm.

Artichokes (Jerusalem). — Should be hard. They quickly soften if kept.

Asparagus.—Sticks should be straight and stiff, tips close packed, no leaf sprouts.

Aubergines.—Stems should be firmly fixed to skins, deep violet-purple in colour. Pips and pulp creamy, free from blemishes.

Beetroots.—These must be firm and skins absolutely whole and undamaged, otherwise they will "bleed" in cooking.

Broad Beans.—Buy when young and pale apple green; indigestible when large.

Broccoli.—Stalks should be short and crisp.

Brussels Sprouts.—Best when small and tightly closed.

Cabbage.—Hearts should be firm and closely packed. Watch out for holes which may indicate caterpillars inside.

Carrots.—Buy firm and bright coloured with no splits and only a tiny circle of green at the top.

Cauliflower.—Leaves should be crisp and green, flower white, closely packed and unblemished.

Celeriac.—Choose these small and hard.

Celery.—Small, closely packed heads.

Chestnuts.—Skins tightly filled.

Chicory.—See that leaves are crisp and silvery and heads tightly packed.

Corn on the Cob to be fresh should be greenish, turning golden.

Cucumber must be firm with a shiny green skin.

French Beans.—These should be a soft, clear green, plump with a smooth skin.

Kale or Turnip Tops.—Buy if crisp and bright coloured.

Kohl Rabi.—Should be firm, medium-sized and unblemished.

Leeks.—Choose snowy-white and small.

Lettuce should be bought only when crisp and with a faint shine on the leaves.

Marrows should look like sausage-shaped balloons, lightly polished, and very firm.

Mushrooms are heavy when fresh and the underside pinkish brown.

Parsnips are at their best after frost.

Peas (Green).—The pods should be a good green without blemish, juicy when pressed, not too tightly packed.

Potatoes.—The point here is to ask for a floury kind (Arran, British Queen and Epicure are some) for plain boiled and mashed potato dishes; a waxy kind (Sharp's Express, King Edward and Gladstone when small) for frying and sauté potatoes, because they do not readily absorb fat.

Runner Beans.—Pods should be bright green and fine textured, and they should snap sharply when bent in two.

Salsify should be firm and unblemished.

Sea Kale should be crisp and creamy white.

Spinach.—This is fresh when the leaves are straight and lightly glossed.

Swedes and Turnips, like all roots, should be firm with undamaged skins.

Tomatoes.—Buy when firm and of a uniform redness and without blemish.

FRUITS

On the whole, fruits are easier to choose well than other perishables. Colour should always be good and skins undamaged. Oranges and lemons particularly should have brightly coloured, clean skins, and should be soft when squeezed, to be juicy.

Bananas should be firm with clear, soft yellow skins and only light touches of brown; too much brown may mean pulpy patches under the skin. Feel the stem end of a pear; it should be just soft to be ready to eat. Soft fruits should *not* be soft when bought. They should hold their shape well, be true coloured and dry. Strawberries should look lightly polished. To test if a pineapple is ripe, lightly pull out one of the green leaves, which should come out quite easily.

ECONOMICAL BUYING

This may sound ironic these days when prices remain high for most of the year, but you can still beat the price rises if you time your bulk shopping wisely.

Canned goods are one of the most helpful items, and a wise plan is to lay in a small stock of fruit and vegetables in the summer for use in winter. The same can be done with dried fruits, which should be washed at the time of purchase, thoroughly dried and stored in clean storage cans in a cool, dry place.

Egg prices are very variable, but whenever they drop a little, buy as many extra as you can afford and preserve them. Date them all in pencil so that you use them in rotation.

EXOTIC FRUITS

Introducing some lesser-known delicacies and how to serve them, by LILIAN K. DONAT

A selection specially photographed at Shearn's of London: at the back, a Pineapple; in front and just to the left, an Avocado Pear; far left, a Custard Apple. Next to it, the pale smooth fruit, seen also sliced on the plate, is an Ortanique, with several Passion Fruit to its right and, far right, an Ugli. The little things in front are Lychees

EXOTIC fruit, so new to many of us, is now to be bought in the shops, and such delicacies as pineapples, custard apples, avocado pears, persimmons and pomegranates are to be seen on the barrows in street markets.

Some of these, which I have tried myself, are exciting to eat. The **Avocado Pear** (wrongly called Alligator Pear by some people) is a native of Mexico, but now grows in the West Indies, Madeira, and parts of the U.S.A. It does not really taste like a fruit and is served as a first course or savoury. You cut it in half, remove the large stone and then spoon out the soft pulp and eat it as it is, or add salt and white pepper, lemon, lime juice or French dressing. This fruit is rich in oil and Vitamin B and grows very well indoors when planted in a large pot and given plenty of light. The large, laurel-shaped leaves make it an interesting plant, suitable for modern interiors.

Cape Gooseberries, or Cape Golden Berries, originally came from tropical America. In India, where they also grow, they are called Brazil Cherries. As the name indicates, they are now grown also in South Africa. In France, where they are very popular, they are called Physalis or Coqueret. This fruit is eaten without its covering, and its acid flavour is very refreshing. It is also most suitable for fruit cheese, prepared in the same way as quince or damson cheese.

When I saw **Custard Apples** for the first time, I admired the green, quilted-looking skin, but when I tasted them, I realised that my palate had met with a new experience. They are creamy and sweet, and deliciously flavoured. They, too, are spooned out, and taste wonderful with a little cream and brown sugar.

Lychees are another exciting fruit: the thin, prickly shell is removed and a moist, white fruit remains, tasting like a cross between a large, skinless grape and a gooseberry. The kernel is comparatively large and has to be discarded. Lychees, which originally came from China, are now quite

279

extensively cultivated in the West Indies, South Africa and the Philippines.

The best fruit, according to many connoisseurs, is the **Mango,** eaten when really fresh. It is imported from the West Indies and Malaya. The Mango is a versatile fruit, used when still unripe as an addition to salads. There are also curries whose main ingredient is the Mango. It is pickled with salt, oil and chillies, used in jellies and preserves, boiled with milk and sugar to make Mango Fool, and also used dried.

One day I saw a large green cone at the fruiterer's, and when I heard that this was the **Monstera Deliciosa,** I had to try it out. This fruit has to lie in a sunny place until its skin—or, better, its shell—bursts. It has a most puzzling and unusual flavour, like a banana and pineapple mixture. The only disadvantage is that the black, rather prickly seeds are slightly irritating to the tongue. In Mexico, where this plant grows as a climber, people are so used to it that they do not notice the seeds at all.

Passionfruit (or Grenadilla) is a fruit similar to the Pomegranate. The moist pulp, which is full of pips, should be scooped out with a teaspoon. It is greatly improved when served with a mixture of cream, sherry and sugar.

The small, olive-like fruit of the date plum, called **Persimmon,** grows wild in Japan and the southern parts of America. It needs frost to turn the sour, unripe fruit into a sweet and soft dessert fruit. The wood from the date plum tree, which is related to the ebony, is a very strong timber used for many purposes.

One of the earliest fruits imported into Europe is the **Pomegranate.** It is the size of an orange and has pockets, full of soft and slightly acid grains, though almost seedless varieties are now grown in Spain and Tunisia. It is a refreshing fruit, but has very little flavour.

Ugli fruit looks like a grapefruit gone wrong. It is one of the most palatable citrus fruits and very popular in the U.S.A., where it is called Tangelo. It can be eaten like an orange or used for the same purposes—i.e. in fruit salads, for flavouring, etc. It is extensively grown in Jamaica.

A reddish fruit, looking like an outsize Victoria plum, is called **Winepods,** or Tree Tomato. It comes from Madeira, and though the first impression is disappointing, the taste for this fruit can be acquired. The skin has a bitter flavour and the juicy pulp is bitter-sweet.

QUICK GLACÉ FRUIT

Glacé Fruits are very expensive to buy, and the usual process of making them is fairly complicated and laborious. However, there is a simplified version which tastes good, its only disadvantage being that it has to be eaten the same or the next day, before the covering dissolves.

Preparations can begin the previous day. The fruit must be stoned, marzipan for stuffing can be either made or bought and, if canned fruit is used, it should be drained overnight.

You will need the following ingredients: Various kinds of fruit, such as white and black grapes, large prunes, dates, figs, orange slices, etc. *For stuffing:* Nuts or almonds, marzipan. *For glacé icing:* 2 lb. sugar, preferably lump, 2 tablespoonfuls vinegar, ¾ pint and 5 tablespoonfuls water. Thin wooden skewers or toothpicks for dipping the fruit. Oil or melted butter for greasing plates.

When using marzipan, add a few drops of edible colour and half the amount of icing sugar in weight (to ½ lb. marzipan add ¼ lb. sugar). Form marzipan into small sausages, the size of a prune or date stone, and insert it so that it shows. Grease baking sheets or plates with either oil or melted butter and dip the ends of toothpicks or skewers in fat. Pour water and vinegar over sugar and let it stand for ½ hour. Bring to the boil, and boil briskly until the sugar thermometer shows 310° F. If no thermometer is available, dip a wooden skewer into cold water, then into the boiling syrup and back into cold water. Break off sugar, which should be brittle. If it draws a thread, it is not yet ready.

Insert greased end of skewer into fruit and dip into syrup, let drip for a moment and put fruit on greased sheet or plate.

Remove toothpicks or skewers as soon as the fruit dries (in a few minutes). Put each fruit into a paper case before serving.

As the sugar darkens quickly, it is advisable to dip the light-coloured fruits first and the darker ones later. This quantity of sugar will be sufficient for about five dozen fruits.

Apple goes with all kinds of pork, including sausages

Cranberry sauce, the American accompaniment to roast turkey

Horseradish adds zest to roast beef and Yorkshire pudding

Mint sauce, made with sugar and vinegar, with roast lamb

Sage and onion, the perfect stuffing for roast duck

Cucumber, refreshing contrast to the richness of salmon

WHAT GOES WITH WHAT

There are certain flavours that complement one another and are served together

With oysters, a squeeze of lemon and brown bread and butter

Crisp celery brings out the flavour of cheese—so does an apple

With melon serve castor sugar and a little ground ginger

Milk puddings — particularly junket—taste better with nutmeg

Corn on the cob and asparagus both need plenty of melted butter

Boiled mutton is never insipid if served with caper sauce

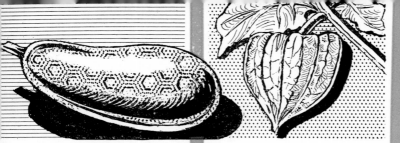

Monstera resembles green cucumber 8–10 in. long; separates easily into segments when ripe

Cape Gooseberry, a cherry-like fruit from South Africa, makes wonderful jam or fruit cheese

Custard Apple has sweet flesh o "custard-like" texture when ripe Eat halved with spoon and suga

FRUIT AND VEGETABLE RECOGNITION CHART

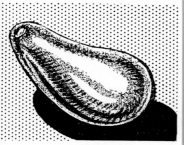

Avocado Pear, large and green; flesh should yield to a very slight pressure when really ripe

Lychees are walnut-sized with sweet translucent pulp and large hard kernel in russet husk

Mango—very juicy, of rich flavour with large slippery ston —not easy to eat elegantly

Pomegranate—roll and squeeze to break up interior pockets, cut off top and pour out the juice

Persimmons look like orange tomatoes, sweet, juicy, and mellow. Halve and eat with spoon

Pawpaw resembles green pear shaped melon with small seed in centre and has fleshy pulp

Pumpkin, a gourd with several varieties; its chief use is cooked in the form of Pumpkin Pie

Guava—a tropical fruit more used for making a delicious sweet jelly than for eating fresh

Quince, an old-fashioned garden fruit, makes delicious jelly also adds flavour to apple dishes

Globe (or Green) Artichoke—
eaten raw or cooked—pull out
the leaves and dip in dressing

Jerusalem Artichoke, a tuberous
root, is eaten peeled and cooked.
Used also for soups and purée

Aubergine (or Egg Plant) has
deep purple skin, soft flesh.
Serve cooked and/or stuffed

FRUIT AND VEGETABLE RECOGNITION CHART

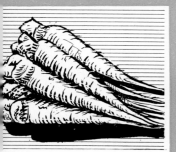

Salsify (or Vegetable Oyster) has
tapering root full of a most
unusual oyster-flavoured juice

Endive—much used on the Continent instead of lettuce for salads,
but may sometimes be tough

Curly Endive has pleasantly
pungent flavour, grows in thick
heads. Good as salad ingredient

Corn Salad (or Lamb's Lettuce),
much used in France as salad,
is slightly bitter like spinach

Capsicum or Sweet Peppers may
be red, green or yellow, in various shapes. Excellent stuffed

Celeriac, a variety of celery with
turnip-shaped root. Boil till tender and serve cold with dressing

Kohl Rabi, sometimes also
called the cabbage turnip, may
be white, green or purple

Sweet Potato is the tuber of a
climbing plant popular in North,
South and Central America

Garlic, a bulb with a pungent
taste, divided into cloves—gives
subtle flavour if used discreetly

A. *Tarragon.*   B. *Mint.*   C. *Bay leaves.*   D. *Chervil.*
E. *Fennel.*   F. *Parsley.*   G. *Marjoram.*
H. *Chives.*   I. *Sorrel.*   J. *Sage.*   K. *Thyme.*   L. *Garlic.*

HERBS FOR THE HOUSE

Use them every day in your cooking —and grow them as close to the kitchen door as possible

The blossom, berries and leaves of the elder are all valuable

IT is exciting to plan an intensive culture garden from which you can harvest something all the time as the French do. They grow herbs for daily use in the kitchen all the year round; and they plant them as near the kitchen door as possible.

We are inclined to sow our parsley, or our mint and sage, with vegetables which may be some distance away. The result is that we grow herbs every bit as well as the French but, when it comes to using them in bad weather, the effort of picking may be too much. For culinary purposes, therefore, plan the herb garden at least within sight of the kitchen window so that its cheerful inhabitants may be always reminding you of their very useful presence.

This sort of herb garden may be of any size, and even with poor soil it can be very profitable. One of the best we have seen was made in a derelict hen-run after it had been painfully cleared of a heavy crop of weeds. It contained an elder tree, said to be the mother of all herbs, and what an amazing number of uses the elder blossom has! Put in a jug of water, it softens the water and gives a delicious perfume. The water is also very good for the complexion; and if you pour a pint of boiling water on two heads of elder blossom, brew this for 20 minutes, and drink half a tumblerful on going to bed, you have a fine drink for curing a cold and making you sleep.

The Invaluable Elder

Elder-bushes were always found beside the kitchen window in old cottage gardens, to keep away flies. The leaves were also tied in bunches to the heads of horses in hot weather, for the same purpose.

Elder flowers, when used with gooseberries in jams or cordials, impart a delicious flavouring of Muscat grapes. And for a genial summer drink a syrup may be made with equal weights of gooseberries and sugar dissolved in a gill of water, and a few heads of elder flower for each 1 lb. of the liquor. You tie them in muslin and add when the liquid is nearly boiling. Take them out when the flavour is right, before straining the syrup.

Frenchwomen use elder blossom in this manner, and if they have not got a bush in their gardens they go out and find some in the hedgerows. Anyone can follow this excellent example, for our woods are full of elders.

Plan for Beauty

Drabness should have no place in a herb garden. Make a round bed in the centre encircled by bricks or stones (or, in a new garden, the inevitable rubble discarded by the builders), and in this plant what is known as "the sun's herb"—i.e. common or garden pot **marigolds.** They are lovely to look at, and their dried petals infused in hot milk can be used in cooking instead of saffron. The flowers may be dried for the flavouring of soups.

To this centre bed, add some old English **borage**, whose bright blue flowers are so beloved of bees. The leaves of borage, picked fresh, can be used in long summer drinks, especially those made with ginger ale, and a claret cup is incomplete without them.

Borage is a hardy, native plant which thrives in poor, even stony, soil. It is a tall plant, strong in growth, and should therefore be sown in April or May, and when the seedlings come up, thinned to about 18 in. apart.

The path around this centre bed can be

planted with **camomile,** which can be mown like grass in the autumn, but provides in high summer a lovely, pungent fragrance. On a hot day you want to roll on a camomile path, so intoxicating is the scent. But again we can be practical and dry its blossoms for storage in tins to make comforting winter infusions.

These three herbs—marigold, borage and camomile—will provide beauty in plenty for the centre bed, but with the purely culinary herbs, to be used every day in the kitchen, a long bed, handy to reach, is maybe preferable.

Angelica is also a native, but fussy in comparison with its neighbours. Germination of the seed can be slow and irregular, but it is worth persevering with, and the best results are obtained by placing the seed in sand and keeping it moist for several weeks before sowing. When it does take a hold, it is sturdy enough, and the leaves and stalks can be blanched and eaten as celery, or boiled with meat and fish.

Herbalists value angelica's curative properties, and it is said to have been given by an angel to a monk, to save his flock from the plague.

In this long bed can be grown **sweet marjoram.** It is a hardy perennial, and can be sown in April in the open. The plants should be allowed about 10 in. each way, and the aromatic leaves are used both green and when dried for flavouring. It is also regarded as a tonic and a cure for flatulence or indigestion.

Chives are useful additions to this long bed. They are used as a mild substitute for onions in salads or in soups; and the plant will grow freely in any soil.

It may be grown from seeds sown in April or May, but propagation is also affected by division of the roots, bunches of which can be obtained cheaply at the nurseries. This saves time, and once your chives are in they maintain a continuous growth of young and tender shoots, which should be cut regularly in succession, whether wanted for the table or not.

To this long bed we would add **sage, parsley** and **thyme.** Sage, because it can also be raised with the minimum of trouble, again from propagated plants. It can be cut in June and in August, and dried in the sunshine on newspapers, to be stocked in the store cupboard for flavouring purposes in soups and savouries.

Parsley, because it must be always at hand. It is indispensable to every kitchen, and the lesson for the cultivator is that it should have plenty of room. It is a rich, handsome crop which, unlike so many other herbs, requires well-cultivated soil. To keep the household well supplied, sowings should be made in April, May and June; it can be grown as an edging, but at intervals it becomes coarse and should be cut over. It will go on throughout the winter if protected by some straw. In gathering, take only about two young leaves from each plant.

There is an old country saying, "If parsley grows well in your garden, the woman wears the pants," which is a compliment to housewives who insist on having plenty of it, no matter what the male members of the household may say. The herb can be dried in the same way as the others, but requires a much higher temperature in a hot oven, and when really crisp should be rubbed down or it will reabsorb water again and become like rubber.

The common thyme, like parsley, makes an effective edging; it is an aromatic herb in constant demand for the house. Seedlings are easily raised from sowings in April, or the plant can be grown from division of the roots in spring. **Lemon thyme,** on the other hand, is propagated entirely by division of the roots, and not from seed. For flavouring, many good housewives prefer it to lemon.

Plant a little **bay** tree, which is also a traditional occupant of every good herb garden. Its leaves, according to ancient legend, "resist all evils old Satan can do to man, and no danger can touch the place where a bay tree grows." In addition, they are extremely useful for flavouring soused herrings, soups and stews.

Balm also has superstitious associations, and the oil distilled from its leaves when dried alleviates fever. They are used for making tea, and wine as well; the plant is a perennial herb and can be grown as an annual from seed.

Tarragon, another aromatic herb, is used for a variety of purposes, but mainly for imparting its powerful flavour to vinegar. It is best propagated from divisions in March or April. Not so hardy, perhaps, and a cloche will help it along in the early spring to resist frost. It is worth a lot of bother because the green leaves are invaluable for salads, while the dried ones will flavour almost anything.

Cheese of the Seven Herbs

At this point, having described how to grow and use some of the herbal ingredients, we must supply the recipe for a dish called "The Cheese of the Seven Herbs," which gave the old monks much inspiration and peace.

Take 4 oz. of grated cheese, 2 tablespoonfuls top of milk, some pepper and salt, 3 oz. margarine and 2 tablespoonfuls of finely minced chives, tarragon, chervil, sage, thyme, parsley and pot marjoram.

Put all into a double

Lavender, stitched up in a bag and tucked under the pillow, induces sleep—but is better grown as a hedge (right) than in the herb garden

Mint (below), of which there are many varieties, requires a bed to itself or it will upset the whole balance of your other culinary herbs

Photos: Amateur Gardening

saucepan over gentle heat and stir until the mixture becomes a pale green colour. Then turn it into pots and, when cold, use for spreading.

Chervil is used for salads, garnishings and every kind of culinary purpose. Few herbs are in such constant request in the best kitchens.

To secure a regular supply of chervil leaves, small successional sowings are the best, all the way through from spring till autumn, with plenty of watering in dry weather; and for winter use the seed can be sown in boxes if brought indoors.

Herb growers who introduce **Mint** to the beds where other culinary herbs have been planted are sorry afterwards.

An Invader Herb

Mint is a swashbuckler, an aggressive invader, who must be watched and disciplined or he will upset the balance of the others, and may mess up your herb garden. He should have a bed to himself, for he is invasive and will be all over the place in no time unless firmly dealt with.

Here the builders' rubble will come in, or bricks if not available, and this material should be dug in about a foot round the mint bed to confine his activities.

But, having done all this, you have some very decorative clumps. Apple mint grows to about 4 ft. and, according to the epicures, its leaves make the best mint sauce.

Photo: Amateur Gardening

In the centre of the herb garden plant marigolds —their dried petals infused in hot milk can be used instead of saffron, the dried flowers for flavouring soups

There are many other varieties too— lemon mint, spearmint, peppermint and eau de Cologne mint, all providing fresh green leaves for sauces, or for storage purposes when dried.

Fresh plants of mint may be raised from cuttings taken about the end of September, and commercial growers usually start a new plantation each year. If the aggressive roots remain in the same plot year after year, the leaves become small and the roots as wiry as nettles.

Other Culinary Herbs

Lavender, too, should not be introduced to the herb beds for the same reason; it grows to a height of 2 ft. and absorbs all the sunshine. Propagated from cuttings, it looks better as a hedge, and the crop is invaluable if stitched up in little bags for the clothes cupboards and chests-of-drawers. Tucked under the pillow, a lavender bag induces sleep.

Good cooks are for ever experimenting with herbs, or trying variations of the *bouquet garni* used in so many forms of cooking. The chopped leaves of **Fennel,** for instance, make a delicious change from parsley in white sauce. This is another hardy perennial, with elegant feathery foliage, and the stems may be blanched like celery and boiled as a vegetable. Sow in drills 18 in. apart in April or May, and then thin out the plants to about 15 in. apart. The seeds are sometimes used for flavouring.

The same applies to **Purslane,** which thrives best in a very sunny position; the leaves may be eaten as a vegetable or raw in a salad.

Rampion, on the other hand, likes a shady place. Both the roots and leaves are used in winter salads.

Sorrel can be served as a separate dish, or mingled with spinach; in soups, sauces and salads it is very useful. To keep the bed free from weeds is the only attention necessary, except that the plants should be removed in September to another position or they will become coarse.

Caraway, a 3-ft. biennial, produces seeds for flavouring cakes and eating with baked apples; and **Garlic,** if you like it, is easily grown.

All these are worth a place in the herb garden, but there are innumerable others to be found in the nurserymen's lists.

Herbs in Window Boxes

The smaller herb plants do well in window boxes, and are rewarding to flat-dwellers or those who have not a garden with their houses.

Certain basic principles, however, must be observed. The boxes should be at least 9 in. deep, and painted both inside and out to keep the wood weatherproof. Holes must be bored through the bottom to permit drainage; and the box itself raised above the sill on buttresses of wood placed underneath. Also allow the box to tilt slightly towards the window, and attach it by strong nails to the wall for security; otherwise accidents might happen to people in the street below.

Nurserymen stock excellent composts for window boxes, but to prevent the soil becoming waterlogged a layer of broken bricks or cinders should be placed at the bottom.

The plants selected—this applies to both herbs and flowers—depend on the windows themselves. Tall plants keep too much light out of the room. Those window boxes facing north are the most difficult to fill, but chives, garlic, sage and thyme will grow anywhere.

For window boxes with a south aspect more colour may be introduced by planting marigolds, borage and the ever-needful (and very beautiful) parsley.

Boxes facing east are rather a problem, but tarragon, sage and marjoram will not be easily defeated.

All window-box herbs should be kept well watered, for the eaves of the roof often shelter them from rain. If the window is kept wide open for hours at the bottom, producing draughts, even the hardiest of plants will wither and die.

Bitter Herbs

Finally we come to an entirely different family of herbs, known as the "bitter herbs," which are used for medical purposes but require considerable knowledge in their preparation if they are to be of any value.

Wormwood, indeed, is the symbol of bitterness, but until recently it was grown in many cottage gardens as a cure for all ills. It takes up a lot of room, and although the flower is beautiful, it has no fragrance. Moths hate it in a wardrobe.

Mugwort, one of the commonest wayside weeds, produces a wholesome spring tonic, and it is used in flavouring brandy, but there is no need to have it in the garden.

Southernwood, mixed with salad oil, was for centuries thought to be a cure for baldness. People also kept it in their prayer-books, with balm and mint, because of its pleasant scent.

Even the **Woad,** used by the ancient Britons for staining and tattooing themselves, has a beautiful and decorative flower.

There is no end to the list. During the wars people grew **foxglove, valerian, belladonna** and other herbs that could not be obtained from abroad and were urgently required by the hospitals; but when the emergency passed, it was evident that medical herb farming was a highly scientific occupation not suitable for private gardens, and better in the hands of experts. But what was proved beyond all doubt is that soil and climatic conditions in the U.K. are every bit as good for herb growing as those of Germany and the Balkans.

Nowadays herbs for the house are grown in every utility garden, partly, perhaps, because the making and care of a herb garden is a cure for depression and melancholy. There is no doubt whatever about that; there is something about a herb garden that goes with prayers and deep faith, for among the fragrant plants cheerfulness is born. And appetite; try it and see!

To remind you to make full use of culinary herbs, they are painted on this charming Irish linen glass cloth, obtainable in pink, turquoise, blue, maroon and orange

THE KITCHEN STORE CUPBOARD

Herbs, spices, flavourings, colourings and decorations are just as important to good cookery as the basic ingredients

THERE are a number of things, apart from basics like tea and flour, which everyone ought to keep in their kitchen. They crop up, as apparently minor ingredients, in countless recipes, but they are important. They are as vital, in their way, as the contents of a sewing basket, and a cook will need them to work on the basic materials. If you have not got them at hand, you must either forgo the dish you intended to make, or make it imperfectly.

Herbs

Chief of these are the cooking herbs. Most recipes for stews, and things cooked in a pot, demand a "bouquet garni," which is nothing more than a bunch of herbs. Generally it consists of 3 or 4 sprigs of parsley, a sprig of thyme and a bay leaf, but some dishes require rosemary, chives, cummin, mint, sage, sorrel, fennel or marjoram, and all these should be kept. In the summer many of them can be grown in the garden or, in the city, in flower pots or a window box on the kitchen sill (see chapter on Grow Your Own Herbs). Fresh herbs are best, but out of season they can be bought dried. As well as the individual plants, it is useful to keep a packet of mixed herbs for omelets, etc.

Garlic is another essential. It comes in roots like a very small onion and, although supposed to be foreign to British palates, it is widely used in good cooking everywhere.

Spices

Next come the spices. Paprika, cinnamon, ginger, mixed spice, black peppercorns, curry powder, Cayenne, cloves, mustard, nutmeg, chillies, mace and allspice. Like the herbs and garlic, all these, except the curry, can be kept indefinitely, either in the neat matched jars with coloured tops which are everywhere available or, equally well, in the screw-topped bottles in which many liquids are sold.

NOTE: Allspice is known in some places as Jamaica pepper or pimento.

Sauces and flavourings are necessary too. Gravy browning, beef extract, horseradish, chutney, pickles and the favourite family sauce. Tomato purée (in tins or tubes), celery salt and always some cheese for cooking.

Olives are useful, and capers, gherkins and anchovies. There should be a bottle of olive oil and of vinegar, and with these, as with curry powder, it is best to stick to a chosen brand because strengths and flavours vary a lot.

Finally, before turning to sweeter things, there should be a bottle of cheap red cooking wine, and a bottle of dry cider which can often be used when the recipe calls for a white wine.

WHAT GOES INTO CAKES AND SWEETS

Cake- and sweet-making is an important part of good cookery, particularly to those who have children, and it is a good idea to devote one corner, however small, of the kitchen to the ingredients that may be needed at one time or another, for sponges or fruit cakes, fudge or peppermint creams. Perhaps you have a corner in your grocery cupboard or store-room, or, failing this, why not invest in one of those wonderful expanding contraptions which have a number of baskets made of enamelled wire on legs? It will sit or hang literally anywhere.

Basic Needs

Now for the stores required:

Flour—plain is essential; self-raising highly desirable; wholemeal a slight "extra," but it makes wonderful scones. Baking powder and cornflour, which is used in many cake and biscuit recipes and also for fillings.

Bicarbonate of soda has its place in many scone and other recipes, and cream of tartar is often wanted for scones, too, and also for some toffees and sweets.

Oatmeal is obtainable — fine, medium and coarse. Usually the fine is required for biscuits and similar baking. Ground rice is wanted in such things as Sand Cake.

Sugars: castor, for light cakes; granulated for heavier cakes, puddings and many sweets; Demerara or Barbados (sometimes called "pieces") for fruit cakes, gingerbread and toffee; icing, for sweets and decorative purposes.

Condensed and evaporated milk should be available for sweet-making. Golden Syrup and treacle are useful for sweetening purposes and essential for such things as gingerbread. Jam and marmalade.

Dried fruits: currants, raisins, sultanas, peel (preferably ready chopped), prunes, dried apricots.

Other fruits: glacé cherries (tend to get sticky if kept too long) and canned fruits, such as pineapple.

Nuts: almonds, walnuts (cheaper in the long run to buy these shelled), ground almonds, desiccated coconut (which does not keep well for long periods).

NOTE: Hazelnuts make an excellent nutty flavouring for a cake if put through a Mouli-mincer.

Flavourings

Always buy a good brand of essence. It is cheaper in the long run than those of poor quality, which invariably taste horrible.

Vanilla pods give a very delicate flavour if you are using liquid in which they can first be soaked. They can be dried off after

A DOZEN LEADING QUESTIONS . . .

1. What is a bouquet garni?
2. Is sorrel a herb?
3. For what do you use mixed herbs?
4. What does garlic look like?
5. Know another name for allspice?
6. How long can you keep nutmeg?
7. Does curry powder last?
8. What can you use instead of white wine in cooking?
9. Which kind of sugar for fruit cakes?
10. Can you use vanilla pods a second time?
11. What gives yellow colouring?
12. How do you tint icing a pale pink?

use, ready for the next time.

Lemon: fresh lemon juice can now be bought and many people prefer it to the essence. Fresh lemon peel, finely grated and/or the juice of the lemon is, of course, excellent.

Almond essence.

Coffee flavouring: one of the coffee powders may be used in preference to the bottled liquid.

Powdered chocolate or cocoa: do not buy in large quantities as it quickly gets stale. Block cooking chocolate is also required sometimes. Incidentally, an excellent flavour results if you melt chocolate in black coffee instead of water.

Colourings

Cochineal colours from pale pink to deep red, depending on the quantity used. Saffron for yellow. There are also other vegetable colourings for special purposes.

Decorations

Most professional results are often achieved with decorations, and it is fun to add, as and when you can, to your jar or tin of "pretties," angelica for flower stalks, silver balls, violet and/or rose petals (crystallised), mimosa balls (available in several colours), hundreds and thousands, chocolate vermicelli. Marzipan also is useful for making your own decorations.

Always keep in stock a box of birthday cake candles with suitable holders. Father Christmas, a robin, snowmen and lots more will ultimately find their way into your collection. Clean them properly after use, and they will last for years.

ENGLISH COUNTIES

*Some traditional recipes from all over England,
compiled by Whitbread & Co. Ltd.*

BEDFORDSHIRE

Apple Florentine Pie (an 18th-century Christmas dish)

4 *good cooking apples*	*Grated lemon peel*
Short pastry (see	*2 tablespoonfuls*
Pastry Chapter)	*sugar*

For the hot spiced ale

1 *pint ale*	*A little nutmeg and*
1 *tablespoonful sugar*	*cinnamon*
	1 *clove*

Core the apples, wash them and place in a deep pie dish. Put sugar over them and lemon peel, and cover with short pastry. Bake in a moderate oven for 30 minutes. Remove the pastry, pour the spiced ale over, cut pastry into required pieces and put back on the dish. Serve hot.

Spiced Ale.—Heat the ale very gently with the spices and sugar. Do not let it boil. It used to be served in a very large pewter dish.

Catherine Cakes (or Kattern Cakes)

So-called after Catherine of Aragon, the Queen who used to live at Ampthill Castle. Ampthill was a favourite lace-making district, and Catherine was very interested in it. Catherine Cakes were specially made for November 25th, St. Catherine's Day.

2 *lb. dough (see*	2 *oz. sugar*
Bread Chapter)	*A few caraway seeds*
1 *egg*	2 *oz. butter*

Dough made with yeast, as for bread. Knead well with butter, caraway seeds, sugar and egg. Leave to rise in a warm place for 2 hours. Place on floured baking tin and bake in a moderate oven for 2–3 hours.

BERKSHIRE

Bacon Pudding

1 *lb. flour*	6 *oz. suet*
6 *oz. fat bacon*	2 *onions*
A little sage	*Salt and pepper*

Make a stiff paste with flour, shredded suet and water. Roll out ½ in. thick. Cover with bacon and chopped onions mixed with sage and seasoning. Roll up pastry and secure at both ends, wrap up in cloth and boil for 2 hours.

Poor Knights of Windsor

8 *slices of bread* ½ *in.*	*A little butter or lard*
thick	*A little jam, sugar*
A little white wine or	*or cinnamon*
milk and sugar	

Put white wine or milk and sugar into a dish; dip the bread in it on both sides. Then fry bread gently, on both sides, in a little hot fat. Dish up on a hot plate and spread a little jam or sugar or cinnamon over it.

BUCKINGHAMSHIRE

Stokenchurch Pie

1 *lb. flour*	1½ *lb. meat (any*
8 *oz. lard*	*cooked meat or*
4 *oz. macaroni*	*scrag)*
A little stock	3 *hard-boiled eggs*
	A little salt

Mince the meat and add to a little thickened stock. Boil the macaroni in salt water until tender, cut up and mix with meat. Cut up the eggs in quarters. Make a good pastry with flour and lard (see Pastry chapter), roll out and line a well-greased tin. Put in half the meat, the eggs, and then the rest of the meat on top. Cover with pastry. Make a hole in the centre, decorate the top with bits of pastry, and brush over with milk. Bake in a hot oven for 30 minutes.

Old Bucks Custom for Baking a Joint of Beef

Use brown sugar for sprinkling instead of salt; the result is extra rich gravy and a fine flavour to the beef.

CAMBRIDGESHIRE

Cambridge Sauce

Cambridge sauce is similar to mayonnaise, served cold with cold dishes. The ingredients are oil and vinegar, yolks of hard-boiled eggs, tarragon, chives, chervil and a little cayenne.

CHESHIRE

Cheshire Pork Pie

Pork
Salt, pepper and nut-
meg to taste
Shortcrust pastry
A little white wine or cider
Apples
Sugar
A little butter

Layers of pork and apples seasoned with salt, pepper, nutmeg and sugar. Add a little white wine or cider and a little butter on top. Cover with pastry and bake in a moderate oven for 45 minutes.

Chester Pudding

4 oz. breadcrumbs
4 oz. flour
4 oz. shredded suet
4 oz. black currant jam
2 oz. castor sugar
A little bicarbonate of soda
A little milk
A little salt

Mix flour, breadcrumbs, suet, salt and sugar. Make a well in the centre and put in the jam; warm the milk, add the bicarbonate of soda to it and pour over the jam. Mix everything together. Place in a well-greased basin or mould and steam for 3 hours. Serve with black currant jam sauce.

Flummery

The name is now applied to any starch jelly made from cereals, wheat flour, rice, sago, etc. It used to apply to oatmeal only, eaten with honey, wine, sack, claret, strong beer, ale or milk. It is like porridge, but when the oats are cooked, they are passed through a sieve, sugar is added and orange flower water. It is then put into shallow dishes and served with one of the beverages mentioned above.

A tea-time treat with happy holiday memories—
Cornish Splits with jam and cream inside

CORNWALL

Cornish Pasty (or Hoggan)

The great distinction between the Cornish pasty and any other kind of pasty is that the ingredients are raw, not previously cooked remains. The pasty is joined at the side, but the Cornish hoggin is joined at the top.

½ lb. flour — *Water to make fine*
3 oz. dripping or lard — *dough—about 1 gill*
Pinch of salt

For the filling

½ lb. beef steak — *¼ lb. calf's liver*
2 uncooked potatoes — *1 large onion*
1 medium-sized turnip — *1 large or 2 small*
Pepper and salt — *carrots*
A little egg-white

Time to bake.— 1 hour; at first in a good oven to raise the pastry, and then in a moderate oven to cook the meat and vegetables.

Roll out the dough fairly thin, cut in squares. Chop the steak and liver finely, mix together and season. Peel or scrape, and slice the potato, onion, turnip and carrot. Mix and season the vegetables. Put a layer of vegetables on half of each square of pastry and some of the chopped meat on top. Brush the edges of the pastry with egg-white, fold the plain half over the meat and pinch the edges well together. Bake as above.

NOTE: It is important to close the edges neatly and closely so that no steam escapes, and to use uncooked meat and vegetables. The contents cook in their own juices, so after the first few minutes require a very moderate oven The amounts given make 2 large or 3 medium pasties.

It has been said that Cornishwomen put everything into a pasty. Variations include:

Apple Pasty

Peel apples, slice thinly and lightly sprinkle with brown sugar. In summer time blackberries are usually mixed with the apple.

Chicken Pasty

The chicken is cut up into small pieces.

Eggy Pasty

Bacon cut in dice, parsley and one or two eggs, according to size of pasty required.

Herb Pasty

Pastry	Parsley
Chopped shallots	Bits, a North Cornish
Cut-up spinach	herb (optional)
1 egg	Slices of bacon

Prepare pastry as for pasties. Take equal quantities of parsley, finely chopped shallots, bits, spinach, some finely cut slices of bacon and a well-beaten egg. Pour boiling water over the herbs, leave to stand a little, squeeze all moisture out of the herbs. Mix all together except the egg, and put into the pastry. Before quite closing it, add the egg, finish pinching and bake in quick oven.

Jam Pasty

These are usually made smaller than a savoury pasty and any kind of jam may be used.

Mackerel Pasty

Allow one or two mackerel to each pasty and clean and boil them in the usual way; remove skin and bones and lay on pastry. Fill up with washed parsley and add pepper and salt. Finish as above.

Parsley Pasty

These are made with parsley and lamb or mutton.

Pork Pasty

Fresh pork and potatoes, flavoured with onion, sage or thyme.

Rabitty Pasty

Use fleshy part of rabbit, cut up fairly small, in the same way as other meat.

Cornish Splits

1 lb. flour	1 oz. butter
½ oz. yeast	½ oz. castor sugar
½ pint tepid milk	1 teaspoonful salt

Cream yeast and sugar until liquid, then add milk; sieve the flour and salt into a basin. Melt the butter; add milk and salt with the butter to the flour and mix into a smooth dough. Let the dough rise in a cool place for 45 minutes. Then shape into round balls and bake in a floured baking tin in a hot oven for 15–20 minutes. Split them, cover with butter and serve hot, or let them get cold and serve with jam and cream or Golden Syrup.

Eel Pie

Eels	Handful of currants
Suet pastry to cover	A little butter
	Sweet herbs

Cut the eels into 2-in. lengths, place them in a pie dish, add sweet seasoning, a handful of currants and a little butter, cover with suet pastry and bake in a moderate oven for about 40 minutes.

Heavy Cake

1½ lb. flour	A little grated lemon
4 oz. beef dripping	peel
2 dessertspoonfuls	4 oz. butter
sugar	12 oz. currants
1 teaspoonful salt	

Mix butter and dripping roughly into the flour. Mix in the other ingredients, add a little water and make into a stiff dough. Roll out on a board, then roll it up again and put aside for 1–2 hours. Roll out again. Cut across with a knife. Bake for 20–30 minutes in a fairly hot oven.

Saffron Cakes

1 lb. 2 oz. flour	2 oz. mixed peel
4 oz. butter	3 oz. sugar
4 oz. lard	Pinch of saffron
½ oz. yeast	A little milk and salt
	Pinch of nutmeg

Mix the ingredients together well, add the yeast, leave till the dough rises and bake in a moderate oven for 50–60 minutes.

Star-gazy Pie

6 herrings, mackerel	3 or 4 eggs or cream
or pilchards	A little pepper and
Tarragon vinegar	salt
Pastry	A little parsley
Breadcrumbs	A little fat
	2 uncooked potatoes

Clean and bone the fish well, and season with salt, pepper and chopped parsley. Do not cut off heads. Place in a pie dish lined with fat and breadcrumbs, with heads facing inwards. Pour the eggs beaten in Tarragon vinegar, or cream over them. Put a pastry over the dish (with potatoes as for pasties), leaving a hole in the middle for the heads of the fish to stick out. Bake for about 1 hour in a moderate oven. Place parsley into the mouths of the fish before serving.

CUMBERLAND

Almond Pudding

2 oz. butter	4 oz. rice flour
2 eggs	2 tablespoonfuls ·
2 oz. castor sugar	ground almond
Raspberry jam	Short pastry (see
	Pastry Chapter)

Line 3 saucers with short pastry and prick with a fork. Spread a thin layer of raspberry jam over them. Cream butter and sugar, add eggs, and work in rice flour and almonds. Spread over jam, bake in a moderate oven for 30 minutes. Serve hot

Clipping-time Pudding

8 oz. rice	3 oz. sugar
Beef marrow bones	4 oz. currants
4 oz. stoned raisins	A little cinnamon
1 pint milk	1 egg
	A little salt

Blanch the rice in a little salt water, cook slowly in milk, then add cinnamon and sugar, and boil for a while longer until the rice is tender. Beat the egg and add, with currants and raisins, and stir well together. Then add the marrow cut in small pieces. Bake for 20 minutes in a moderate oven.

Sandcake

2 oz. butter	A little lemon essence
4 oz. cornflour	4 oz. castor sugar
1 teaspoonful baking	1 oz. plain flour
powder	2 eggs, lightly beaten

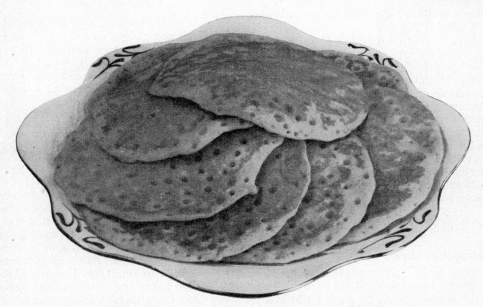

Pikelets come from Durham and are eaten piping hot and spread lavishly with butter

Cream butter and sugar, add lemon essence, eggs, cornflour, plain flour and baking powder. Mix well and bake in a moderate oven in a well-greased and lined tin.

Vanilla Jelly

2 tablespoonfuls sugar
½ oz. powdered gelatine
1 pint milk
2 eggs
A little vanilla essence

Warm the milk and add egg-yolks beaten with sugar and vanilla essence. Stir over gentle heat until creamy; pour into basin. Dissolve the gelatine in a little water. Add to the milk and pour in the beaten egg-whites. Pour into wetted mould and leave to set. Turn out and serve cold.

DERBYSHIRE

Bakewell Tart

2 eggs
4 oz. butter
8 oz. sugar
8 oz. jam
Puff pastry (see Pastry Chapter)

Line a patty tin with pastry. Cover with a layer of jam. Melt the butter, and stir eggs and sugar into it. Beat well together. Place a thick layer on the jam-covered pastry. Bake until delicately brown in a moderate oven.

Steamed Batter Pudding (a speciality of Duffield)

3 eggs
1 pint milk
A little salt
3 tablespoonfuls flour
1 oz. butter

Mix flour with sufficient milk to moisten it, add more milk very gently, stirring all the time. Melt the butter, and stir into the mixture; add salt, beat in the eggs and stir well. Pour into a well-greased pudding basin, seal tightly, place in boiling water and move the basin about for 1 minute to prevent the flour from dropping to the bottom. Boil for 1 hour and 35 minutes. Serve with fruit, jam or wine sauce.

DEVONSHIRE

Devonshire Cream

Pour fresh milk (straight from the cow, bottled milk is no good for it) into a large shallow pan. Leave to stand for at least 6 hours until the cream has risen to the top.

Heat the milk very, very slowly (on no account must it boil) for 1 hour. Do not skim the cream off the milk until it is quite cold, preferably the next day.

Devon Flats

8 oz. Devonshire cream
1 egg
A little milk
1 lb. flour
8 oz. sugar

Rub the cream into the flour, beat the egg in and add the sugar. Mix well and make into a smooth dough with milk. Roll out very thinly on a board and cut into rounds. Sprinkle with a little sugar and bake in a hot oven for 10 minutes.

Junket

1 pint milk
A little rum or brandy
A little sugar
1 large teaspoonful essence of rennet

The milk should be "blood" warm. Mix sugar, milk, rum and rennet, in that order; stir well, then leave to set and do not disturb. Use a pretty dish for making the junket, or individual small pudding dishes.

Squab Pie

1 lb. neck of mutton chops
1 onion
Ground allspice
¼ pint gravy or water
2 lb. sour apples
Short pastry to cover (see Pastry Chapter)
Pepper and salt

Fill a pie dish with a layer of chops and slices of onion and peeled and cored apples. Season well and repeat until the dish is full. Pour in gravy or water and cover with pastry. Bake for 2 hours in moderate oven. Squab is also the name given to a young pigeon, weighing just under 1 lb.

Sally Lunns

1½ pints milk
4 oz. butter
2 oz. lump sugar
A little castor sugar
1 oz. yeast
2 lb. flour
Cream

Make a thick batter with 1 pint of warm milk, yeast, flour and a little sugar. Cover and leave to rise in a warm place for 2 hours. Add lump sugar dissolved in ¼ pint warm milk. Rub butter into a little of the flour. Mix with the batter and knead lightly; leave to stand for ½ hour. Make into round cakes and place on tins. When they have risen, bake in a hot oven for 30 minutes. Split and spread with cream.

Widecombe Fair: Spiced Ale and Gingerbread

For the gingerbread
5 oz. butter
1 teaspoonful ginger
6 oz. sugar
6 oz. flour
6 oz. treacle

Rub butter into flour, and add sugar and ginger. Warm the treacle and mix in well. Drop small pieces on a well-greased tin and bake in a moderate oven for 30–40 minutes.

For the spiced ale
1 quart ale
A little mixed spice
1 teaspoonful nutmeg
4 cloves
2 apples
1 teaspoonful sugar

Heat the ale very slowly until very hot, but on no account must it boil. Cut up the apples in slices and add all ingredients. Stir well, strain and serve hot with a slice of apple floating in the glass or tankard.

DORSET

Roast Cygnets

Cygnets (young swans) used to be served at official banquets as far back as the fourteenth century. Cygnets are still eaten once a year at the Vintners' Hall in the City of London, in the traditional manner, covered with a flour-and-water paste.

Stuff the cygnet, trussed the same way as a goose, with minced rump steak well seasoned with grated nutmeg, salt and pepper and finely chopped onions. Sew up, cover the bird with greased paper and roast for about 2 hours, according to size, basting frequently. Serve with gravy and port wine sauce. In former days the birds were wrapped up in a flour-and-water paste and roasted for 4 hours.

DURHAM

Buckwheat Cakes

1 teaspoonful brewer's yeast	A little salt
Buckwheat meal	3 pints warm water
	A little butter

Eccles Cakes, a famous Lancashire delicacy that can easily be made at home

Mix the yeast with water in a basin and stir in buckwheat meal to make a good batter, add salt, cover the basin and let it stand in a warm place to rise. When full of bubbles, pour a spoonful of the batter into a buttered frying pan and cook as for pancakes. Butter the cakes while hot and serve.

Pikelets

8 oz. flour	A little bicarbonate of soda
Buttermilk or sour milk to mix	A little salt
1½ oz. sugar	Lard for frying

Mix flour, sugar and salt. Make a well in the centre and pour in enough buttermilk to make a nice batter. Add bicarbonate of soda, dissolved in a little water. Beat the batter well and fry on a girdle or frying pan in a little lard until golden brown on both sides. Spread with butter and serve hot.

Stanhope Firelighters

4 oz. sugar	4 oz. oats
4 oz. margarine	

Mix all ingredients together and put in a dripping tin. Bake for 30 minutes in a moderate oven. When done, cut into squares.

ESSEX

Epping Sausages

1 lb. pork	1 lb. suet
A little sage, thyme, savoury marjoram, lemon, nutmeg	Pepper and salt 1 egg

Mince the pork and shred the suet. Mix all the ingredients together. Make into shape of sausages and fry or grill.

Samphire Pickle

Samphire is common on rocks along the coast (not in the north of England or Scotland). It has fleshy leaves, yellow flowers, and a resinous taste.

1 pint samphire	A few elder buds (or nasturtium seeds)
A few peppercorns	A little salt
A little horseradish	
½ pint cider	½ pint vinegar

Wash the samphire and elder buds, and place in a jar with peppercorns and horseradish and pour boiling vinegar and cider (or wine or water) over them with a little salt. Put the jar into a warm oven for 1 hour to infuse. Seal and store.

GLOUCESTER

Cheese-and-Ale

8 oz. Gloucester cheese	½ pint ale A little mustard
Brown bread	

Cut some Gloucester cheese into thin flakes. Place in a fireproof dish. Spread some mustard over the cheese and cover with ale. Cook in the oven until the cheese is dissolved. Make some toast with thick slices of brown bread, and moisten with hot ale. Pour the cheese over the toast and serve very hot.

Gingerbread Husbands

Figures of men made of gingerbread pressed into wooden moulds, baked and gilded.

HAMPSHIRE

Isle of Wight Doughnuts

2 oz. butter	Pinch of salt
½ oz. yeast	1 lb. flour
Lard	2 eggs
Raspberry jam	1 oz. castor sugar
1½ gills of warm milk	

Mix flour, salt and sugar, and divide into two basins. Rub butter into one, yeast and milk into the other. Let batter mixture rise for ½ hour, then mix both together and beat in the eggs. Let the batter stand for 1 hour to rise. Knead and make into 24 round balls; make a hole and put a little jam in the centre of each. Close up securely. Leave to stand for a little on a floured tin to prove. Drop into a deep bath of boiling fat and fry until a golden brown; then roll in castor sugar.

Friar's Omelet

6 good cooking apples	3 oz. butter
2 oz. sugar	4 egg-yolks
Grated lemon rind	Cloves or nutmeg to flavour
4 oz. breadcrumbs	

Bake the apples till tender. Scrape out the pulp. Cream butter and sugar, add lemon rind, pulp and grated cloves or nutmeg. Grease a pie dish and sprinkle with breadcrumbs. Beat the yolks into the apple in the pie dish, pour the mixture over, cover with breadcrumbs, put small pats of butter on top and bake in a moderate oven for 1½ hours till firm and set.

Hampshire Drops

4 oz. flour	4 oz. castor sugar
1 egg	4 oz. cornflour
4 oz. butter	A little baking powder
A little jam	

Beat butter and sugar until creamy, add egg and beat well, then mix in the other ingredients except jam. Put in teaspoonfuls on a greased tin. Put two together, when all are baked, with a little jam in the middle. They take 10 minutes to bake in a moderate oven.

Mothering Sunday Wafers

2 tablespoonfuls cream	2 tablespoonfuls sugar
2 tablespoonfuls flour	1 tablespoonful orange flower water

Beat all together for 30 minutes, spread very thinly on a flat greased tin, about 6 in. diameter. Bake in a hot oven. Roll over a stick as soon as they are a light golden colour. They are very crisp when dry, and are served with jelly.

HEREFORDSHIRE

Love in Disguise

A calf's heart	4 oz. breadcrumbs
2 tablespoonfuls shredded suet	2 oz. minced ham
	4 or 5 slices of fat bacon
A little mustard	
2 teaspoonfuls chopped parsley	1 teaspoonful marjoram
A little lemon rind	Salt and pepper
1 oz. broken-up vermicelli	Gravy made with tomatoes
	1 egg

294

Cook the vermicelli, drain and leave to get cold; remove all the pipes from the inside of the calf's heart, wash and put in cold water for 1 hour. Make a stuffing from breadcrumbs, suet, a little of the egg, herbs, mustard, salt and pepper, ham and lemon rind. Dry the calf's heart, fill it with the stuffing, wrap the bacon round it and fasten with small skewers. Wrap up in greaseproof paper and cover with fat. Bake in a baking tin for 1½ hours. Remove the paper and brush over with egg-yolk. Then roll in breadcrumbs mixed with vermicelli. Put back in the tin and bake in the oven till nicely browned. Serve with tomato gravy.

HERTFORDSHIRE

Pope Lady Cakes

1 lb. flour	A little baking
12 oz. butter	powder
2 oz. cornstarch	Lemon or almond
1 lb. sugar	extract or rose
16 egg-whites	water

Cream butter and sugar with 8 egg-whites. Sift flour, cornstarch and baking powder, and add to mixture. Beat the remaining egg-whites very stiff and fold in gently. Add the flavouring. Grease two baking tins, pour in the mixture and bake in a slow oven for about 1½ hours.

HUNTINGDONSHIRE

Huntingdon Pudding

8 oz. flour	1 egg
3 oz. castor sugar	A little baking
5 oz. suet	powder
1 pint gooseberries	¼ pint milk

Mix the flour and shredded suet, add sugar, baking powder and gooseberries. Stir well. Beat up the egg in milk, and add to the mixture gradually. Steam in a greased basin for 3 hours and serve with Golden Syrup.

KENT

Huffkins

1 lb. flour (plain)
2½ gills warm milk
   and water
1 teaspoonful sugar
1 oz. compressed yeast
½ teaspoonful salt
1 oz. lard

Warm the mixing bowl. Sift flour and salt, and rub in the lard. Cream yeast and sugar in another basin. Add milk and water. Then pour into the flour and make a light dough. Stand in a warm place for 1 hour to rise. Knead well. Then divide into three oval cakes about ½ in. thick. Make a hole in the middle. Flour the cakes and place on a warm tin. Leave in a warm place to prove until well risen. Bake in a hot oven for about 10–20 minutes, according to size. Take out and wrap the cakes in a warm cloth until cool. This will keep the crust soft and tender.

Kentish Cheese Pasties

1 lb. flour	Cayenne pepper and
4 oz. lard	salt to taste
4 oz. butter	12 oz. cheese, cut in
1 egg	very thin flakes,
	mixed with butter

Make some flaky pastry (see Pastry chapter) with flour, butter and lard. Roll out very thin on a board and cut into circles the size of a saucer. Put a tablespoonful of the cheese in the centre and sprinkle with salt and Cayenne pepper. Moisten the edges of the pasties and fold up. Brush over with beaten egg. Bake in a hot oven for about 15–20 minutes and serve hot.

Oast Cakes

1 lb. flour	2 oz. sugar
4 oz. lard	A little lemon juice
6 oz. currants	1 teaspoonful baking
A little salt	powder
A little water to mix	Lard for frying

Lancashire's traditional Hot Pot is a nourishing and tasty dish for a cold wintry day

Mix dry ingredients and rub in the lard, add currants. Make a light dough with a little water and add lemon juice. Shape the dough into small pieces and roll out on a board. Fry in lard until golden brown. Serve hot.

Twice Laid

Codfish
A little milk
Salt and pepper
A little fat
Mashed potatoes
1 egg
Breadcrumbs

Divide the remains of codfish or cold salt fish into flakes. Mix in twice as much mashed potatoes. Add a little milk. Season with salt and pepper and make into balls. Dip into the egg, roll in breadcrumbs and fry in fat until brown.

LANCASHIRE

Eccles Cakes

Shortcrust pastry (see Pastry Chapter)
A little nutmeg
4 oz. currants
1 oz. ground almonds
4 oz. Golden Syrup
A little lemon juice
1 oz. ground coconut

Line some patty pans with shortcrust, put in each a layer of syrup, then currants, spice, lemon juice, coconut and almonds. Cover with pastry. Roll over with the pin very gently. Bake in a moderate oven for about 30 minutes.

Brawn

1 pig's head
1 tongue
1 heart
A little lemon rind, cloves, mace, pepper and salt
¼ pint vinegar

Simmer the meat very gently in a saucepan with enough water to cover. When tender, remove the bones and cut the meat into small pieces. Return to the water, add seasoning and vinegar. Boil up once and pour into a mould and leave to set in a cool place. Turn out when cold.

Lancashire Hot Pot

2 lb. mutton chops
2 lb. potatoes
8 oz. mushrooms
2 oz. ham (or bacon)
3 sheep's kidneys
Cayenne pepper and salt to season
1 lb. onions
2 oz. butter
½ pint stock (or water)

Cut the kidneys, peel and slice the onions and potatoes, and chop the ham. Place a layer of chops in a casserole, then the kidneys, mushrooms, ham, onions and potatoes, and season every layer; the last layer must be potatoes. Pour over the stock and put little pieces of butter on top. Cover the casserole and cook *very* slowly for about 3 hours. Take the lid off and brown the top before serving.

Manchester Pudding

Shortcrust pastry (see Pastry Chapter)
2 oz. butter
1 oz. castor sugar
Rind of 1 lemon
Jam (stoneless)
2 eggs
1 tablespoonful brandy
½ pint milk
2 oz. breadcrumbs

Boil the lemon rind in milk and pour over the breadcrumbs. Take the rind out and beat in the egg-yolks after 5 minutes with butter, sugar and brandy. Line a pie dish with pastry and spread some jam over it. Cover with the breadcrumbs mixture and bake in a moderate oven for 45 minutes. Whip the egg-whites with some castor sugar and lay over the dish. Return to the oven for 1 minute to set. Serve cold.

Parkin

1½ lb. oatmeal
8 oz. brown sugar
1 lb. treacle
1 teaspoonful ground ginger
8 oz. butter
1 teaspoonful allspice

Mix the dry ingredients. Heat treacle and butter; add to the dry mixture and leave to stand overnight. Place in a well-greased shallow baking tin and bake in a moderate oven for about 2 hours. It is done when the parkin springs back when touched.

Potted Shrimps

1 pint shrimps
1 blade ground mace
A little ground nutmeg
4 oz. butter
A little Cayenne pepper

Only the freshest shrimps should be used. Melt the butter, add seasoning and shelled shrimps. Heat through gently, but do not boil. Pour into small pots and eat when cold.

Tripe and Onions

1 lb. tripe
½ pint water
2 onions
½ pint milk
A little flour
Salt and pepper

Wash the tripe well, cut into square pieces and bring to the boil in water. Throw the water away and add water and milk, chopped onions, salt and pepper. Thicken with flour, after having boiled the tripe for a good 3 hours, by stirring it in with a little milk. Bring to the boil again and serve.

From Grantham, Lincolnshire, comes the unusual White Gingerbread (above), which is baked very pale. Below, Parkin from Lancashire

off after a short while; leave for 24 hours. By that time the husks should have burst and the wheat set to a thick jelly. This process is to "cree" or stew the wheat, and is then called "frumenty wheat." It can be eaten as a breakfast food with milk and sugar, or with eggs beaten in with it, or as a sweet with fruit and cream.

Melton Mowbray Pie

2 lb. pork cut in small
  dice
1½ lb. flour
1 egg
1 lb. lard
A little milk and
  water mixed
Salt and pepper to
  taste

Rub half the quantity of lard into the flour with a little salt. Boil the rest of the lard with the milk and water. When boiling, pour half over the flour and stir well, then add the egg (beaten well) and pour over the rest of the liquid. Knead the mixture and leave to stand for a few minutes. Line a mould or tin, and put in the pork with a little pepper and salt and a little water. Roll out the rest of the pastry and cover the top of the pie and decorate the edge. Brush over with a little egg and bake for 2 hours, starting with a very hot oven and reducing the heat. Make a stock of the bones and trimmings of the meat until it jells. Pour into a hole in the centre of the pie with a funnel when lukewarm. Serve cold.

LEICESTERSHIRE

Bosworth Jumbels

8 oz. flour	6 oz. butter
1 lb. sugar	1 large egg

Beat the sugar and butter, and stir in the egg. Add flour and mix thoroughly. Shape pieces of the mixture into the form of an S and place on a hot greased tin. Bake in a moderate oven until brown.

This recipe is said to have been picked up on the battlefield of Bosworth, having been dropped by Richard III's cook.

Frumety (see also under Lincolnshire)

Wash wheat. Place in a stone jar and fill with three times the wheat's measure of water. Put in a hot oven, but turn the oven

LINCOLNSHIRE

Apple Pudding

9 apples	2 eggs
½ lemon	Puff pastry (see
2 oz. Demerara sugar	Pastry Chapter)
A little cinnamon	8 oz. butter
Cloves and nutmeg	

297

Peel, core and slice the apples. Stew in a little water until soft, add cloves, nutmeg and cinnamon. Pass through a sieve and mix in butter, egg-yolks, one egg-white and sugar; add lemon juice and mix well together. Line a pie dish with puff pastry, decorate the edges and pour in the mixture. Bake in a moderate oven for 20 minutes.

Frumenty (see also Leicestershire)

1 quart frumenty	Sugar to sweeten
wheat	1 quart milk
2 oz. raisins	A little nutmeg
A little flour	

Boil the frumenty wheat in milk for about 15 minutes, add the other ingredients and when it begins to thicken, stir in a little flour made into a cream with a little milk. Boil up and serve.

Grantham Gingerbread (White)

8 oz. flour	A little baking
4 oz. sugar	powder
1 oz. ground ginger	4 oz. butter
1 egg	

Cream butter and sugar, beat in egg-yolk, add flour, baking powder and ginger. Whip the egg-white and fold into the mixture. Bake on a greased paper in a moderate oven for 30–40 minutes, but keep pale in colour.

Mock Goose

| Sage and onion | Leg of pork |
| stuffing | |

Parboil the pork. Take off skin and bone. Fill the void with the stuffing. Press into the shape of a goose and roast until golden brown. Serve with apple sauce and brown gravy.

LONDON

Chelsea Buns

12 oz. flour	¼ oz. yeast
4 oz. sugar	4 oz. butter
1 lemon	2 eggs
A little milk	

Warm the milk and add the yeast creamed with a little sugar. Rub half the butter into the flour and add half the sugar. Beat in the eggs and yeast, a little lemon rind and juice and leave to rise in a warm place for about 2 hours. Knead the dough and roll out on a board about ¼ in. thick. Spread the other half of butter and sugar over the dough. Fold in three, roll out

again into a square. Roll up the dough and cut into thick slices. Leave to stand for about 20 minutes to prove. Bake in a moderate oven for 20 minutes.

Johnny Cakes (or London Buns)

2 lb. flour	1 oz. candied orange
4 oz. castor sugar	peel
1 pint milk	1 egg
1 oz. yeast	3 oz. butter

Sift flour and sugar into a basin. Melt butter in a saucepan and add milk. Dissolve the yeast in the milk. Pour into centre of the flour, mix well; add finely cut orange peel. Leave the dough to rise in a warm place for about 2 hours. Knead and make into 24 round buns. Place on a greased baking sheet and let them prove. Bake in a hot oven for 30 minutes. Brush over with a little egg and sugar mixed, to glaze the buns.

MONMOUTHSHIRE

Backstone Cakes (Baxton, Bakestone)

| 8 oz. flour | Cream to mix |
| 2 oz. butter | |

Rub the butter into the flour and make into a stiff paste with cream. Roll out very thin and cut into small rounds. Bake on a backstone or girdle; turn once or twice until lightly browned. Split, butter and serve hot.

Treacle Posset

2 pints ale	2 teaspoonfuls grated
4 oz. treacle	nutmeg
1 pint milk	

Heat the ale and melt the treacle in milk and mix together. Add nutmeg and serve very hot.

NORFOLK

Biffins

Take some Norfolk biffins (red-cheeked apples), choosing the clearest without any blemishes, lay them on clean straw on baking wire and cover well with some more straw. Set them in a very slow oven for about 4 or 5 hours. Draw them out and press them very gently, so as not to burst the skins. Put back in the oven for another hour, and press again. Rub them over with clarified sugar when cold. These are the dried biffins sold in Norwich.

Norfolk and Suffolk are the counties for dumplings, which are either eaten as a separate dish or added to a stew

Dumplings

1 lb. flour	1 teaspoonful castor
¼ pint hot water	sugar
½ oz yeast	A little milk

Cream yeast and sugar. Pour milk and water over the yeast. Put flour into a basin and pour milk and yeast into it, making a well in the centre. Mix well and allow to rise for about 2 hours. Knead the dough well and form into dumplings. Allow these to stand for 10 minutes. Have ready a saucepan with boiling water, throw in the dumplings and boil for 20 minutes. Serve hot with a little melted butter and a sprinkling of sugar, or omit the sugar when preparing the dumplings and serve hot with meat and gravy.

Pork Cheese (Brawn)

A hock of salt pork	Pepper and sage to season

Stand the hock in cold water for 12 hours. Place in a saucepan with enough water to cover. Boil until the meat comes off the bone. Lift out and remove the bones. Put the bones back into the saucepan and simmer. Rub a little pepper into the meat and add finely chopped sage. Cut up the meat very finely. Strain the stock over the meat (there should be ½ pint left). Pour into wetted basin. Turn out when cold.

NORTHAMPTONSHIRE

Cheese Cakes

Some short or flaky pastry (see Pastry Chapter)	A little grated nutmeg
	2 oz. currants
	1 egg
1 oz. butter	1 pint sour milk
1½ oz. sugar	A little grated lemon rind
A little almond essence	

Stir butter, egg and sugar in a saucepan over a low fire until thick; do not allow to boil. Boil the sour milk until it separates into curds and whey. Strain off the curd, press well. Add it to the mixture when cold, with currants, spice, flavourings. Line some patty pans with pastry, fill them with the mixture and bake in a hot oven for about 10 minutes. Cheese cakes and frumenty were eaten at sheep-shearing.

Fig Pudding

8 oz. dried figs	A little salt
2 eggs	4 oz. flour
4 oz. sugar	6 oz. grated suet
	½ pint milk

Chop the figs and mix with suet, flour, salt and sugar. Beat eggs and add. Make into a dough with milk, place in a greased pudding basin and steam for 3½ hours.

Dried figs were sold in quantities for fig pudding on Fig (Palm) Sunday.

Seed Cake

1 lb. flour	1 lb. butter
1 lb. sugar	8 eggs
2 oz. caraway seeds	1 grated nutmeg

Separate the egg-yolks from the whites. Beat the butter to a cream, add the sugar, and then beat the egg-whites and add, beat the egg-yolks and add. Beat in the flour, spice and seeds, turn into a greased cake-tin and bake in a hot oven for 1½ hours.

Seed cake was eaten at sheep-shearing.

Venison Pasty

1 lb. venison	A few herbs
½ pint port wine	Pie crust (see
Salt and pepper to	Pastry Chapter)
taste	Redcurrant sauce
2 onions	

Chop the meat and onions very fine. Boil for 3 hours, add port wine, herbs and seasoning, and simmer until the meat is quite tender. Strain the meat and put in a pie, when cold, and add as much of the gravy as desired. Bake in a moderate oven for 1 hour. Serve hot or cold, with redcurrant sauce.

NORTHUMBERLAND

Felton Spice Loaf

4 oz. butter	A little milk
2 eggs	4 oz. sugar
2 oz. ground almonds	8 oz. currants
4 oz. plain flour	2 oz. shredded peel
4 oz. self-raising flour	

Sieve almonds and flour. Mix peel and currants in a separate basin. Cream butter and sugar, and add eggs, beating all the time. Add flour and milk, then mix in the fruit. Turn into a well-greased dripping tin and spread level. Bake in a fairly hot oven for about 30 minutes, turning the heat down half-way through.

Pan Haggerty

1 lb. potatoes	Pepper and salt
A little dripping	8 oz. onions
4 oz. grated cheese	

Peel potatoes and onions, cut in very thin slices and dry the potatoes in a cloth. Make the dripping hot in a pan, put in a layer of potatoes, then of onions, then cheese and another layer of potatoes. Season each layer with pepper and salt. Fry gently until nearly cooked through, then either turn in the pan or brown the haggerty under the grill.

Pickled Salmon

Salmon	A little mace, cloves,
Vinegar	pepper and salt
	White wine

Boil the salmon in salt water, sufficient to cover. Drain off the liquor when cooked and place the salmon in a deep dish, pour over it equal quantities of the liquor, vinegar and white wine, seasoned with a little mace, pepper and some cloves. Leave to stand in a cool place until next day. Warm the salmon in the liquor and serve hot.

Singin' Hinnies

Singin' Hinnies get their name from the fact that they are so rich that they sing and sizzle while they cook.

1 lb. flour	½ teaspoonful cream
½ teaspoonful bicar-	of tartar
bonate of soda	6 oz. currants
4 oz. lard	A little mutton fat
A little milk	4 oz. butter
A little salt	

Rub the lard and butter into the flour. Add the cream of tartar, bicarbonate and salt. Add the currants. Make into a stiff dough with the milk. Shape into a round and roll out to ½-in. thickness. Rub the girdle with a little mutton fat. Place the cake on it and cook until the underside is brown. Turn carefully with a palette knife. Turn again when cooked, to have it quite hot. Cut into pieces, split, butter and serve hot.

Snails

Snails are best from spring to autumn.

Drop them into boiling salt water and boil for 30 minutes. Take off the shells and cut away the hard bits. Put the meat into a fireproof dish with a little butter, garlic, pepper, salt and chopped parsley. Cover, and bake in a hot oven for 10 minutes. Serve with brown bread and butter and lemon.

Snails used to be the traditional fare at the Glassmakers' Feast.

NOTTINGHAMSHIRE

Cowslip Vinegar

2 *pints cowslip "pips"* 1 *pint white wine*
Soda water   *vinegar*
Brandy   *Lump sugar*

Gather the cowslips on a dry day. Pick all the flower "pips" from the stalks. Put them into a basin. Pour on white wine vinegar and leave to stand in a cool place for 3 days to infuse. Wet a piece of muslin with vinegar and strain the liquor from the pips into a stone jar; add 1 lb. lump sugar to every pint of liquor. Stir until the sugar is dissolved. Cover the jar, set in a saucepan of boiling water and boil for 1 hour. Add 1 wineglassful of brandy to each pint. Bottle when cold and seal the corks. Dilute with soda water as a cooling drink.

Pork Pie

4 *lb. pork*
4 *oz. suet*
8 *oz. butter*
Salt, pepper and sage
  to taste
8 *oz. lard*
4 *lb. flour*
Stock for the gravy
  made from 2 pig's
  feet and 1 pint water

Rub fats into flour and knead into a stiff dough with water. Roll out 1 in. thick and line a greased tin with it. Cut up the pork very fine, put into the tin and season. Pour stock from the pig's feet over it (this will jelly when cold). Cover the pie, but leave a little opening. Bake in a moderate oven for 2½ hours. When cool, add more stock through the opening. Serve cold.

OXFORDSHIRE

Banbury Apple Pie

5 *good-sized cooking*
  apples
3 *oz. sugar*
4 *oz. currants*
Shortcrust *(see*
  Pastry Chapter)
2 *oz. candied peel*
3 *oz. butter*
A little ground ginger
  and cinnamon
A little milk

Peel and slice the apples. Place a layer in a greased pie dish, then the chopped peel, spices and currants. Pour a little melted butter on top. Place another layer of apples and chopped peel over it. Boil ½ pint of water, melt some sugar in it and pour over the apples. Cover with short pastry and bake for 30 minutes in a moderate oven. Glaze with a little sugar and milk.

Brasenose Ale

6 *quarts of ale*   Sugar
Nutmeg and cloves   6 *roast apples*

Heat the ale, season with nutmeg and cloves, add sugar to taste and float the apples in it.

This is served in Brasenose College hall, in an enormous silver tankard, after dinner on Shrove Tuesday.

Tripe and Onions, as cooked in Lancashire—long and slowly in milk

Carrot Pudding

2 lb. carrots	2 tablespoonfuls flour
1 egg	A little butter
A little milk	Salt and pepper

Boil the carrots until soft, then mash. Melt butter and brown the flour in it, add milk and seasoning, and mix well. Add egg-yolk and carrots. Beat the egg-white and fold into the mixture. Put in a greased pudding basin, tie up and steam for 15 minutes. Turn out, pour a little melted butter over it and serve hot.

Oxford Pudding

6 apricots	2 egg-whites
A little cream	Puff pastry (see
Sugar to taste	Pastry Chapter)
4 eggs	

Steam the apricots until tender. Cut up and add a little sugar to taste. When cold, beat in the whole eggs and cream. Butter a pie dish and line with puff pastry. Place the mixture over it and bake for about 30 minutes in a hot oven; turn the oven down for the last 15 minutes. Beat up the 2 egg-whites, add a little sugar and place over the dish. Bake in a hot oven for 10 minutes.

RUTLAND

Plum Shuttles or Valentine Buns

Buns of an oval shape like a weaver's shuttle, carried round on Valentine's Day. They have currants and caraway seeds.

SHROPSHIRE

Fidget Pie

1 lb. potatoes	8 oz. onions
8 oz. bacon or ham	Pepper and salt to
½ pint stock	taste
Sugar or Golden	Shortcrust to cover
Syrup to taste	(see Pastry Chapter)
1 lb. apples	

Peel and slice the potatoes, apples and onions. Cut the ham or bacon into small pieces. Place a layer of the potatoes in the bottom of the dish, then the bacon and apples (add sugar or Golden Syrup if sour). Repeat until the dish is quite full. Season each layer with a little salt and pepper, and sprinkle with onions. Pour the stock over it all. Cover the dish with the shortcrust and bake for 1½ hours in a moderate oven.

Shrewsbury Biscuits (see also Biscuits chapter)

4 oz. butter	1 egg
A little baking powder	8 oz. flour
4 oz. sugar	

Beat the butter to a cream, add sugar, beaten egg, baking powder and flour. Mix well and roll out on a board to ¼ in. thickness. Cut into rounds and prick. Bake in a moderate oven. Sprinkle sugar over them while still hot.

Shrewsbury Cakes

8 oz. butter	8 oz. castor sugar
¼ gill cream	½ lemon
1 egg	8 oz. flour

Cream butter and sugar, add the egg, then the flour, grated lemon rind and juice and, lastly, the cream. Turn out on a board and knead well. Leave to stand for ½ hour. Roll out thinly, cut into small rounds and place on a greased baking sheet. Bake in a moderate oven for about 10 minutes. Sometimes a little sherry, rose water, caraway seeds or nutmeg are added.

SOMERSET

Bath Buns

1 lb. flour	A few caraway seeds
4 oz. butter	½ oz. yeast
2 oz. crushed lump	3 oz. castor sugar
sugar	3 eggs
2 oz. sultanas	3 oz. candied peel
	1 gill milk

Cream the yeast with a little sugar, add milk, strain into half the flour and mix well. Leave to stand until risen. Rub butter into other half of the flour, and add sultanas, castor sugar, candied peel and yeast mixture. Beat in the eggs well and leave to rise again. Form into 12 rocky buns, sprinkle with crushed lump sugar and caraway seeds. Let them "prove," and bake in a moderate oven for about 15 minutes.

Plovers' Eggs

Plovers' eggs are a great April delicacy. They should be semi-hard-boiled by simmering gently for 5 minutes. It is, however, now legally forbidden to take all the eggs from the nests. Each nest always has four eggs; only two eggs should ever be taken from each nest at a time; the hen then lays another and the process is repeated. This has the indirect result of giving the young plover a better start in life, since the last batch of four eggs will hatch out in May when the weather is milder. Gulls' eggs are very similar to, and are often sold in place of, plovers' eggs.

Singin' Hinnies hail from Northumberland and get their name because they are so rich they sizzle as they cook

STAFFORDSHIRE
Whip Syllabub

½ gill brandy
½ gill sweet wine
¼ lb. sugar
1½ pints cream
1 lemon (juice and
    grated rind)

Whisk all the ingredients well, take off the froth as it rises and put on a sieve. Fill some custard dishes with the mixture and cover with froth.

Yeomanry Pudding

4 eggs (4 yolks, 2 whites)
Some raspberry jam
1 oz. ground almonds
8 oz. butter   Rich pastry to cover
8 oz. castor sugar   (see Pastry Chapter)

Grease a pie dish and line with some of the pastry. Spread a layer of jam over the bottom of the dish. Beat the yolks and whites together. Cream the butter, and add sugar, almonds and beaten eggs. Pour over the jam and bake in a hot oven for a little, then reduce heat and bake for about 50 minutes.

SUFFOLK
Almond Pudding

4 oz. ground almonds   2 egg-whites
¼ pint cream   2 oz. castor sugar
4 egg-yolks   A little rose or orange
1½ oz. breadcrumbs   water
    A little butter

Warm the cream and pour over the breadcrumbs, stir in sugar, almonds and flavouring. Beat up egg-yolks and egg-whites. Mix well with the other mixture and place in a pie dish. Put a little butter on the top and bake in a moderate oven for 30 minutes.

Suffolk Dumplings

Dough made with yeast and milk as for bread (see Bread chapter) left to rise 1 hour in a warm place. Make into balls the size of an apple. Throw in boiling water and boil for 20 minutes. Test by sticking a fork into the dumplings; if it comes out clean, they are done. Serve immediately with gravy, butter or meat.

SURREY
Maids of Honour Cakes

These cakes are said to derive their name from Queen Elizabeth's maids of honour when she lived at Richmond Place. The recipe is taken from a cooking manuscript of the period.

4 oz. butter   Grated rind of 1
1 oz. sugar   lemon
½ pint milk   2 tablespoonfuls
3 eggs   breadcrumbs
2 oz. ground almonds   Puff pastry (see
             Pastry Chapter)

Boil the milk with breadcrumbs, and let the mixture stand for a few minutes; then add butter, sugar, almonds and lemon rind. Beat in the eggs, one at a time; line some patty pans with puff pastry and place the mixture in them. Bake in a hot oven until they are golden brown.

SUSSEX
Arundel Mullets

Mullet   2 onions
A little lemon juice   Salt and pepper to
2 wineglassfuls red   taste
  wine   A bunch of sweet
A little nutmeg   herbs
    A few anchovies

Boil the mullet very gently in salt water for about 15 minutes. Pour away half the water and keep the fish warm. Add the wine, with finely chopped onions and the other ingredients, and cook gently until done. Serve the fish in a shallow dish and pour the sauce over. Shrimp or oyster sauce may be used as well. Mullet is also very good fried in butter and served with lemon and anchovies

Chiddingly Hot Pot

1 lb. beef	8 oz. celery
8 oz. olives	A little tarragon
A little allspice	vinegar
1 lb. potatoes	A little malt vinegar
A few cloves and	1 lb. onions or
black peppercorns	shallots

Place a layer of chopped onions on the bottom of a large casserole dish with chopped olives and celery. Put thin slices of beef over them and sprinkle with spices and vinegars. Cut potatoes into thin slices and place over the meat with some more chopped olives. Repeat until all the ingredients are used up. Pour enough water into the casserole nearly to cover. Cook in a low oven for about 3–4 hours according to quantities used. The vinegar renders additional salt unnecessary.

Ifield Vicarage Hog's Pudding

1 lb. pork	A little allspice
A little baking powder	1 lb. currants
1½ lb. flour	Some sausage skins
	1 lb. lard

Cut the meat into small pieces and put on to boil gently for about 1 hour. Mix the flour and baking powder with the meat, currants and spice, and rub in the lard. Fill sausage skins and tie up in bunches. Prick the sausages with a fork and drop into boiling water. Boil them for 1½ hours. Take out and hang up to dry. They will snap when broken in two. Hog's pudding is usually the size of an egg and irregular in shape, and is generally eaten as a savoury, either hot or cold.

Lardy Johns

4 oz. flour	A few currants
A little baking powder	2 teaspoonfuls sugar
2 oz. lard	

Rub all the ingredients together and make into a stiff dough with a little water. Roll out thinly and cut into squares. Bake for 10 minutes in a hot oven.

Sussex Blanket Pudding

12 oz. flour	2 eggs
A little pepper and	12 oz. suet
salt	8 oz. breadcrumbs
	A little milk

Mix dry ingredients together and fold in the eggs. Make into a light dough with a little milk. Roll out and spread one of the fillings (see below) over the dough. Roll up in a floured cloth and boil for 2–3 hours.

Fillings.—(1) Liver and bacon, minced, with parsley and onion; (2) sausage meat; (3) any scraps of minced meat.

Sweet fillings.—(1) Jam or Golden Syrup; (2) mincemeat; (3) chopped apples, a little butter, and orange marmalade or quince jam; (4) finely chopped peel, currants, raisins and sugar.

Sussex Heavies

2 breakfastcupfuls flour	1 teacupful milk soured with the
1 oz. castor sugar	juice of half a
2 oz. currants	lemon
2 oz. lard	

Rub lard into flour, add sugar and currants and make into a stiff pastry with soured milk. Roll out on a board to 1-in. thickness, cut into small rounds, brush over with a little soured milk, place in a moderate oven and bake for 15 minutes.

WARWICKSHIRE
Baked Apples and Caraway Comfits

1 tablespoonful icing sugar	1 tablespoonful caraway seeds
6 baking apples	A little gum arabic
A little starch	

Clean and core the apples, place in a pie dish and bake in the usual way. Clarify the sugar. Dissolve the gum arabic in a little hot water. Put a sixth part of the sugar, starch and gum in a small saucepan, boil the mixture and add the caraway seeds. Add a little more gum and stir the pan until the seeds are dry. Take the comfits out of the pan and place in a sieve. Repeat the process 5 times, cleaning out the pan each time. Dry the caraway comfits in a low oven. Sprinkle over the baked apples.

Crayfish and Bacon Savoury

3 freshly boiled crayfish	A little salt and pepper
6 pieces of buttered toast	6 rashers of bacon

Cut the bacon into small pieces and fry gently in a frying pan. Cut up the crayfish into small pieces and add to the bacon when there is enough fat in the pan for them not to stick. Fry for a few minutes, season, pour on to hot buttered toast.

WESTMORLAND

Easter-ledge, Dandelion or Nettle Pudding

Easter-ledge leaves (Persicaria)
1 egg
A little butter
Pepper and salt to taste
Boiled barley

Take young Easter-ledge leaves, or nettle. Wash, drop into boiling water and cook for about 20 minutes. Strain and chop. Add a little boiled barley, hard-boil the egg, chop up and add to the leaves with a little butter and pepper and salt. Put the mixture into the saucepan and heat through, turn into a pudding basin and press well down; then turn out on a plate and serve with meat.

WILTSHIRE

Devizes Pie

A few slices of cold calf's head, cold lamb, calf's brains, tongue and bacon
Pastry to cover (see Pastry chapter)
3 hard-boiled eggs
Spice
Cayenne pepper and salt to taste
Gravy

Season the meat and place in a pie dish in layers with the eggs cut in rings. Fill the dish with a rich clear gravy, made from the calf's head. Cover the pie with pastry and bake in a moderate oven for about 1 hour. Turn into a dish when cold. Garnish the edge with parsley and serve.

YORKSHIRE

Doncaster Butterscotch

1 lb. brown sugar
6 oz. butter
½ pint milk
A little cream of tartar

Melt the sugar in milk over a low heat, add butter and cream of tartar. Boil until a little dropped into cold water hardens. Pour into greased tins and leave to set.

Solomon Gundy

6 herrings
A few capers, mushrooms and pickled oysters
1 large apple
4 oz. anchovies
Peel of 2 lemons
1 onion, shredded

Boil the herrings as gently as possible. Take the fish from the bone, without removing head and tail. Do not break the bones. Shred and mix the herring meat with anchovies, apple, onion and a little grated lemon peel. Lay the mixture over each of the bones in the shape of a herring. Garnish with lemon peel, capers, mushrooms and pickled oysters.

Yorkshire Pudding (see Puddings chapter)

ISLE OF MAN

Sollaghan (served on Christmas Day)

Put some oatmeal in a pan over a low heat and stir until crisp and dry. Then skim the top of the stock pot on to it and stir well. Eat with pepper and salt.

Maids of Honour come from Richmond, Surrey, and were named after the first Queen Elizabeth's ladies when she lived at Richmond Palace

SCOTLAND

*Many a world-famous dish, from haggis to porridge,
hails from North of the Border*

SOUPS

Cock-a-Leekie Soup (for 10)

2–3 *bunches of leeks*	5 *quarts of stock*
1 *boiling fowl*	*Seasoning*

Wash the leeks well (if old, scald them in boiling water). Take off the roots and part of the heads, and cut them into 1-in. lengths. Put half the quantity into a pot with the stock and the fowl and simmer gently for ½ hour. Add the remaining leeks and simmer for 3–4 hours. Skim carefully and season to taste. Before serving, carve the fowl, place the pieces in tureen or plates and pour the soup over.

Hare Soup

1 *hare*	4 *peppercorns*
3 *carrots*	1 *stick celery, or* 1
½ *turnip*	*teaspoonful celery*
4 *onions*	*salt*
Small bunch thyme	*Butter for frying*
and parsley	*Flour*

After the hare has been skinned, cleaned and cut up, put into a basin of cold water for a few minutes. Then take the pieces out, dip in flour and fry in butter. The blood should have been retained. Add to the water in the basin and strain in with the meat; stir till it boils. Season and simmer for 6–8 hours, adding the vegetables about 2 hours before the cooking is done. Take out the back when cooked and save for cutting in dice when the soup is served. If not thick enough, add a little flour and butter thickening.

FISH

Baked Stuffed Haddock

1 *large fresh haddock*	1 *teaspoonful*
3 *oz. breadcrumbs*	*chopped parsley (or*
1 *oz. chopped suet*	*other herbs if*
Pepper and salt	*preferred)*
A little milk	

Mix the breadcrumbs, suet and seasoning well together with a little milk. Wipe the fish, cut off fins, scrape a little to remove scales. Wipe the inside with a moistened cloth dipped in salt. Stuff and fix with a skewer or by sewing, which can be easily undone after cooking.

Sprinkle with breadcrumbs and put small bits of suet or butter on top. Bake in moderate oven for 25–30 minutes. Serve with egg or brown sauce (see Sauces).

Fillets of haddock may also be stuffed in this way, rolled up and cooked in casserole or a pie dish for 20–25 minutes.

Baked White Fish

Brill and halibut are the usual fish used in this recipe, but haddock, monkfish and cod are also very tasty done this way.

Cut the fish in neat pieces and place flat in a pie dish. Sprinkle freely with soft breadcrumbs seasoned with salt, pepper, chopped parsley and grated nutmeg to taste. Just cover with milk, and place on each piece of fish a small piece of butter. Bake in a quick oven until nicely browned —about 15 minutes. A little grated cheese may be added on top, if liked.

Fish Custard (for 2)

¼ *lb. filleted white*	1 *egg*
fish	*Salt and pepper*
½ *pint milk*	*Nutmeg if liked*
A little flour	

Cut the fish into neat pieces and dip in seasoned flour. A little nutmeg, if liked, much improves the seasoning. Place in a greased pie dish. Beat the egg, add milk, pour over the fish and bake carefully in a moderate oven until nicely browned and set.

Fried Trout

Mushrooms	*Trout*
Truffles (if available)	*Salt*
Tomato sauce	*Pepper*
Egg and breadcrumbs	

Prepare a stuffing of well-minced mushrooms, truffles, salt and pepper. Clean and empty trout, allowing one per person. Fill with stuffing. Sew the fish up and

Herrings fried in oatmeal, garnished with lemon and parsley, are good for breakfast or supper and full of nourishment

cook gently in Court Bouillon, made as under. Leave to get cold, drain well, dip in beaten egg-yolk and breadcrumbs. Fry and serve with tomato sauce.

Court Bouillon.—Water, salt, pepper, carrots, onion, thyme, bay leaf, clove, vinegar, white wine (or half wine, half water). The fish must be entirely covered whilst cooking.

Haddock Cases

1 *smoked haddock*	1 *gill thick cream*
(cooked)	1 *oz. butter*
A little Cayenne	*Bread*
pepper	1 *egg-white*

Pound the butter and cooked haddock. Pass through a sieve. Add the cream and flavour with pepper. Beat to a rich purée. Meanwhile, prepare some tiny cases of fried bread. Fill with the mixture and cover them with stiffly whipped egg-white. Bake in a slow oven till the white is crisp and pale brown in colour.

Herrings Fried in Oatmeal

Wash and clean herrings in usual way. Roll well in fine oatmeal and fry in boiling fat from which the smoke is rising.

Partan (Crab) Pie

Take the meat from the claws and body of the crab. Then clean the shell thoroughly. Season the crab meat with salt, white pepper and nutmeg, adding some pieces of fresh butter and breadcrumbs. You may add to it also a wineglassful of vinegar, seasoned, if liked, with a little mustard. Alternatively, salad oil can be substituted for the butter. Then return the crab meat to the shell and brown under the grill.

Pickled Herrings

Herrings	*Mace*
Pepper and salt	*Butter*
1 *bay leaf*	*Vinegar*

Wash the required number of herrings in cold water and a little salt, remove the heads and tails, split them down the back and take out the backbones: then dry well in a cloth, sprinkle with a little pepper and salt, and lay on each herring a piece of butter the size of a filbert. Then roll the herring up, beginning at the head, and place in a dish with the bay leaf and mace and vinegar to cover. Cook in a slow oven for 1 hour or until done.

307

Scotch Potatoes

Bake some large potatoes in their jackets (one or more for each person), break them in half with a fork and scoop out the insides and beat up in a bowl with plenty of margarine, salt, pepper, a little anchovy or Worcester sauce, and some chopped cooked fish. Stuff the potato shells with the mixture. Sprinkle each one generously with grated cheese, dot with margarine and brown under grill.

Whiting in the Scots Way

Choose small fish if you can, and be sure they are quite fresh. Then rub them in flour until it adheres. They should, traditionally, be fried in butter, but the best cooking fat may have to suffice. Sauté them very slowly—they should *not* be dry or coloured. Mince some parsley and chives (or small green onions) very finely; put them into some good broth with 2 tablespoonfuls of top of the milk, mix well together and pour over the whiting before they are quite cooked. Move the fish about gently so as not to break them until they are done. A simple method, but great care is required in the frying.

MEAT DISHES

Beef Soufflé (for 2–3)

½ lb. lean roast beef	3 egg-yolks
Pepper	4 egg-whites
Salt	Shallot

For the sauce

1 oz. butter	1 teacupful beef gravy
½ tablespoonful flour	Worcester or anchovy
1 tablespoonful	sauce
mushroom ketchup	Pepper and salt

To make the sauce.—Melt the butter, add flour and cook for 1 minute. Stir in gravy, ketchup and sauce, and add pepper and salt. Boil until it thickens.

Mince and pound the beef with the sauce, season well with pepper and salt. Add the egg-yolks. Put through a sieve and mix in chopped shallot to taste. Fold in lightly the stiffly beaten egg-whites. Pour into a soufflé dish, lay a paper over the top to prevent burning, and bake for 20 minutes.

Galantine or Bassamore (for 5–6)

2 lb. fillet of veal	Breadcrumbs
½ lb. ham	Pepper, salt, nutmeg
3 egg-yolks	A pinch of mace
2 egg-whites	Grated rind of 1
1 little cream	lemon

Chop all but the eggs and cream very finely. Mix with eggs and cream. Tie up in a cloth and boil for 1½ hours. Glaze (see chapter on French cookery) and serve cold.

Haggis

Sheep's bag and pluck	½ teaspoonful
½ lb. minced suet	powdered herbs
½ lb. oatmeal	Pepper and salt to
4 small onions	taste

Wash bag in cold water, scrape and clean well. Leave in cold water with salt overnight. Wash the pluck. Put it into a pan of boiling water with a tablespoonful of salt. Boil for 2 hours, letting the windpipe hang out of the saucepan. When cold, cut off the windpipe, grate half the liver, mince the heart, lights, suet and onions very small. Add the oatmeal, which has been toasted to a golden brown, the pepper, salt, herbs and a cupful of the liquor in which the pluck was boiled. Mix well, fill the bag rather more than half with the mixture, and sew it up. Place in a saucepan of boiling water and boil for 3 hours, pricking it occasionally to keep it from bursting.

Quenelles

Equal quantities fresh	Butter
or cooked meat	1 well-beaten egg
and breadcrumbs	A little cream
soaked in milk	Seasoning

Pound well in a mortar the meat, breadcrumbs and butter. Add the other ingredients and mix to a firm paste. Pound all well again. Pass through a fine sieve. Shape with a large spoon, or put in small moulds. Poach in a pan of hot water for 10 minutes.

Scotch Collops (for 4–5)

2 lb. tender side of a	1 slice bread, grated
round of beef	1 apple, minced
Pepper and salt	1 small onion, minced

Mix bread, apple and onion. Beat the beef with a rolling pin, then cut it in pieces. Rub the saucepan with beef suet, put a layer of the beef in the bottom. Shake some of the bread, apple and onion mixture over it, also pepper and salt. Then put another layer of beef and another layer of bread, apple and onion. Continue with alternate layers, cover with a lid and cook in a slow oven till done

Sheep's Head

1 sheep's head	Parsley
2 tablespoonfuls pearl	Thyme
barley (or rice)	Bay leaf
2 onions	10 peppercorns
2 small carrots	Salt
1 small turnip	Pepper

Cut the head in half, remove the brains, wash them and put them into cold water with a little salt. Wash the head in several waters, carefully remove any splintered bones and soak in salt and water for 1 hour. Put it in a saucepan and cover with cold water. Bring to the boil, pour away water and refill with fresh water. Add parsley, thyme, bay leaf and peppercorns. Season with salt and pepper. Boil up and skim well. The head must be cooked slowly for approximately 3 hours; 1½ hours before serving, add the vegetables (sliced) and barley (or rice). The liquor in which the head is boiled must be retained for the sauce.

Sauce for sheep's head

1½ oz. butter	1½ oz. flour
Brains	Seasoning

Remove skin and fibre from brains. Tie them in muslin and boil for 10–15 minutes in the liquor in which the head was cooked. Chop coarsely. Heat the butter, add flour, stir over flame for 2 or 3 minutes. Add ¾ pint liquor from the sheep's head. Simmer for 10 minutes. Add brains. Season to taste.

Serve the head garnished with parsley, carrots and other vegetables and masked with the sauce.

Sheep's Head Mould

A good-sized sheep's	Hard-boiled egg
head, scalded	Pepper and salt

Boil the head till the meat leaves the bones easily. Remove from heat and leave until cold. Boil down the liquid to a pint. Cut the meat up in small pieces. Slice the tongue. Line the bottom of a bowl with sliced hard-boiled egg, then a layer of meat. season well with black pepper and salt, and, as you fill up, pour the liquid over. Leave standing in a cool place all night to set. Turn out.

Pickled or "soused" herrings, eaten either hot or cold, are very popular in Scotland

Sheep's Head Pie

1 sheep's head	2 or 3 eggs (hard-boiled)
Ham or bacon (cooked)	Pepper, salt, mixed spice
Short pastry	

Wash the head thoroughly and boil till the bones shake out. Strain the stock from the head and cut slices of ham or bacon. Cut the meat from the head in small pieces and put layers in a pie dish alternately with the ham or bacon and eggs. Season with pepper, salt and spice. Pour in the stock and cover with a good short pastry. Bake for ¾ hour in a hot oven.

GAME

Grouse Soufflé

Cold grouse	1 tablespoonful meat glaze, dissolved in a little stock
Two handfuls boiled rice	
1 oz. butter	Seasoning
3 eggs	

Remove the meat from the bones of the grouse, pound well with the rice, butter and glaze, season well and rub all through a wire sieve. Mix in the egg-yolks, then add the whites beaten very stiff. Steam gently for 1 hour and serve with brown sauce.

To Cook Tough Blackgame, etc.

Remove the meat from the breast, leaving the skin. Pound well with a very little butter. Put back on the bird, shaping it to the correct shape. Cover with the skin and cook as usual.

To Cook Old Game (Game Mould)

Prepare the bird for cooking as usual. Then cut off the legs at the knees, and the wings at the pinions. Rub the bird inside and out with 2–4 oz. butter, according to size of bird. Add a small pinch of pepper and salt. Put the bird in a pie dish with plenty of good gravy. Fill up with water. Turn another pie dish over the first. Put the whole into a slow oven and stew for 3 hours. Then add a very little gelatine to set the gravy. Leave until quite cold. Turn out on to a meat dish. It will have set into a Game Mould.

PUDDINGS

Baked or Boiled Carrot Pudding (for 4–5)

½ lb. breadcrumbs	¼ lb. currants
4 oz. suet	3 oz. sugar
¼ lb. raisins (stoned)	3 eggs
¾ lb. carrots	Milk
Nutmeg	

Boil carrots until tender enough to mash to a pulp. Add the remaining ingredients and moisten with sufficient milk to make a thick batter. If the pudding is to be boiled, put the mixture into a greased basin, tie down with a cloth and boil for 2½ hours. If to be baked, put it into a pie dish and bake for about 1 hour. Turn out on a dish and dredge with castor sugar.

Potato Pudding (for 4–5)

1 lb. old potatoes, boiled and mashed	3 eggs
	¼ lb. sugar
2 oz. butter	Brandy or sherry (optional)
1 doz. sweet almonds	
1 tablespoonful cream	

Mix all the ingredients well. A glass of either brandy or sherry is a great improvement but is not essential. Turn mixture into pie dish and bake for 1 hour in a moderate oven.

Red Grout

1¾ lb. juice of currants	¼ oz. minced bitter almonds
1½ pints water	½ lb. sago
½ oz. minced sweet almonds	½ oz. cinnamon
	Sugar to taste

Put all the ingredients except the sago into a saucepan and bring to the boil, then add the sago (which has first been well rinsed in cold water). Boil for ¼ hour, stirring frequently. Turn the mixture into moulds or cups rinsed with cold water and leave to get cold. Turn out and serve with cream and sugar.

Snow Cheese

1 pint cream	Wineglassful sherry
Juice of 2 lemons	Sugar to taste

Mix cream, lemon juice, sherry and sugar. Beat well until quite thick. Put into a cloth and leave to drain overnight, when it will be ready to serve.

Sweet Potato Soufflé (for 3–4)

3 oz. potatoes (boiled and put through a sieve)	3 oz. butter
	3 eggs
	Juice of 2 lemons
3 oz. castor sugar	Jam or apple purée

Put the potatoes, lemon juice, sugar and butter into a basin and whip them together with a fork until they are creamy. Separate the yolks of the eggs from the whites and stir them in. Butter a soufflé dish and bake mixture in it for 10 minutes. Remove and put a layer of jam or apples on the top. Whip the whites of the eggs with a little castor sugar until quite stiff. Place on the

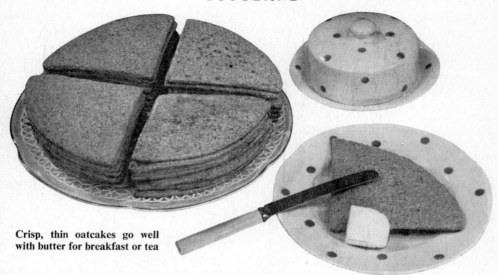

Crisp, thin oatcakes go well with butter for breakfast or tea

top, return to the oven and bake until the meringue is firm and light brown in colour.

CAKES AND SCONES

Brandy Wafers

2 oz. syrup	1¾ oz. sugar
1¾ oz. flour	½ teaspoonful lemon
½ teaspoonful ground	rind
ginger	½ teaspoonful brandy
	2 oz butter

Melt butter, syrup and sugar in a saucepan. Stir in flour, ginger, lemon rind and brandy. Mix well. Drop in small teaspoonfuls on a greased tin. Bake 5–10 minutes in hot oven. Roll quickly round a wooden roller.

Drop Scones (1)

6 tablespoonfuls flour	½ teaspoonful cream
1 tablespoonful sugar	of tartar
½ teaspoonful	2 eggs
bicarbonate of soda	4 teacupfuls of milk

Beat the eggs and milk together. Sieve the dry ingredients, and add egg and milk. Grease the girdle and, when hot, drop on about a tablespoonful for each scone. Turn with a knife when done, and cook the other side.

Drop Scones (2)

6 teacupfuls flour	3 tablespoonfuls
2 teaspoonfuls	sugar
bicarbonate of soda	Buttermilk (sour or
1 teaspoonful cream	fresh milk may be
of tartar	substituted)

Sieve flour, soda, cream of tartar and sugar. Mix to a stiff batter with the buttermilk. Grease the girdle and, when hot, drop about a tablespoonful for each scone. Turn with a knife when done and cook on the other side.

Girdle Cakes

½ lb. flour	½ lb. butter or mar-
Salt	garine
	Milk

Sieve the flour with a little salt. Rub in the butter or margarine and mix to a stiff dough with the milk. Roll out to ¼ in. thick. Cut in small rounds. Grease girdle (a heavy frying pan will do instead if no girdle is available) and, when hot, put the cakes on. When cooked on one side, turn. They should be served very hot, split and buttered.

Girdle Scones

2½ breakfastcupfuls	Pinch of salt
flour	1 oz. butter
1 teaspoonful cream	1 teaspoonful Golden
of tartar	Syrup
1 teaspoonful	Buttermilk (sour or
bicarbonate of soda	fresh milk may be
	substituted)

Sieve the flour, cream of tartar, soda and salt. Rub in the butter. Add the syrup and mix to a soft consistency with buttermilk or milk. Turn out on a floured board and roll quickly. Cut into shapes. Grease and heat a girdle (or heavy frying pan) and bake scones on both sides. Cooking time: 10 minutes.

Oatcakes

2 *large breakfastcupfuls fine oatmeal*
A pinch of bicarbonate of soda
A pinch of salt
1 *tablespoonful fresh lard or beef dripping*
1 *teacupful hot water*

Put meal in large bowl, adding soda and salt. Rub in the dripping or lard. Mix with the water to pastry consistency. Roll out on pastry board well dusted with oatmeal. Cut in rounds or squares and cook on a hot girdle.

Petticoat Tails

This is an old Scotch recipe.

6 *oz. butter*   1 *lb. flour*
6 *oz. sugar*   *A little water*
                    Castor sugar

Rub butter and sugar into the flour. Add water and work to a smooth dough. Divide into two. Roll into two round cakes about the size of a large dinner plate. Cut a round from the centre of each with a cutter 4 in. in diameter. Then cut the outside of each into eight pieces. Prick the tops, dust over with castor sugar and bake in a moderate oven for ½ hour. Lay the rounds on separate plates, with eight petticoats round each.

Plum Cake

2 *oz. currants*   1 *teaspoonful*
2 *oz. raisins*   *bicarbonate of soda*
4 *oz. brown sugar*   2 *large teacupfuls*
4 *oz. butter or mar-*   *milk*
  garine   2 *teaspoonfuls mixed*
8 *oz. flour*   *spice*
2 *oz. peel*

Wash fruit. Mince raisins. Chop peel. Dissolve soda in milk and add spice. Cream fat and sugar until soft. Sieve flour, add fruit and peel, and stir into fat mixture alternately with milk. The mixture must be very moist. Add further milk if necessary. Bake in a very hot oven for 1¼ hours, reducing heat slightly after 30 minutes.

Plain Scones (1)

1 *pint milk*   *Flour*
            Pinch of salt

Bring the milk to the boil and then sprinkle in sufficient flour to make the mixture the consistency of thick porridge. Add a little salt. Remove from pan and roll out on a well-floured board, fairly thin. Cut into rounds and cook on a well-greased girdle or thick frying pan until brown. Turn, and cook on the other side.

Plain Scones (2)

1 *lb. flour*   3 *teaspoonfuls baking*
1 *oz. butter or mar-*   *powder*
  garine   *A little salt*
            Milk

Sieve the flour, salt and baking powder. Rub in butter. Mix to a light dough with milk. Roll out on a floured board and cut with round or fancy cutter. Bake in a hot oven.

NOTE: It is always easy to see if scones are cooked. Pick one out, pull gently, and if it parts in the middle it is done.

Potato Scones (1)

1 *lb. flour*   ½ *oz. butter*
½ *teaspoonful baking*   *Pinch of salt*
  soda   *Buttermilk (sour or*
3 *potatoes, cooked*   *fresh milk may be*
  and mashed   *substituted)*

Sieve the flour into a basin, add the mashed potatoes, soda and salt. Rub in butter and mix well with buttermilk or milk. Roll out thin, cut into rounds and place on a hot, greased girdle (or thick frying pan). Turn when brown and cook on other side. Serve hot.

Potato Scones (2)

½ *lb. flour*   3 *oz butter*
6 *oz. mashed potatoes*   *A little water*

Rub the butter into the sieved flour. Add the potatoes. Mix with a little water. Roll out on a floured board about 1 in. thick, or thinner, as preferred. Cut into rounds and bake in a hot oven.

Potato Scones (3)

1 *pint mashed*   ½ *teaspoonful salt*
  potatoes   1 *tablespoonful butter*
1 *teaspoonful baking*   2 *tablespoonfuls flour*
  powder   *Water to mix*

Sieve flour, salt and baking powder. Rub in butter and add potatoes. Mix with a little water. Roll out on a floured board to ¼ in. in thickness, cut into rounds and bake in a hot oven. Split and butter.

Shortbread (1)

1 *lb. flour*   ½ *lb. fresh butter*
            4 *oz. castor sugar*

Mix the flour and sugar. Work in the butter. Divide the dough in half. Knead it into two rounds. Nick round the edges with thumb and prick with fork. Divide the rounds in four and bake in a moderate oven.

Shortbread (2)

> 1 lb. butter (prefer-
> ably half fresh and
> half salt)
> 1¼ lb. flour
> 6 oz. sugar
> 4 oz. rice flour

Beat the butter to a cream. Mix in flours and sugar. Knead into rounds. Nick round the edges with thumb and prick with fork. Mark each round in four divisions and bake in a moderate oven. The shortbread may be ornamented with orange peel before baking if desired.

NOTE: Margarine may be substituted for butter, but for shortbread butter is infinitely better.

Soda Scones

> ½ lb. flour (sieved)
> ½ teaspoonful salt
> ½ teaspoonful baking
> soda
> ½ teaspoonful cream
> of tartar [1]
> Pinch of sugar
> Nut of butter
> Milk to mix

[1]Sour milk makes a very light mixture. If using sour milk, add very little cream of tartar.

Sieve all dry ingredients, rub in butter, add enough milk to make a stiff dough (the right consistency leaves the bowl clean when you turn it out). Roll out very lightly and cut into rounds, or leave in one large round and cut in triangles. Bake in a very hot oven. *The oven can scarcely be too hot for scones, which should cook in 5–10 minutes.*

Parkins (1)

1 lb. oatmeal	1 lb. flour
12 oz. syrup	½ lb. lard
½ lb. sugar	6 teaspoonfuls
6 teaspoonfuls ginger	cinnamon
3 teaspoonfuls baking	3 teaspoonfuls mixed
soda	spice
	2 eggs

Sieve all the dry ingredients together

Drop Scones, one of the many varieties for which Scotland is famous, are cooked on a girdle

thoroughly. Rub in fat. Melt sugar and syrup, and mix with dry ingredients and fat. Beat eggs and add. Roll into small balls in dry oatmeal and bake in a slow oven until brown.

Parkins (2)

1 lb. oatmeal	½ lb. sugar
5 oz. lard	1 lb. flour
1 oz. bicarbonate of	1 lb. syrup
soda	Almond essence
Egg	Almonds

Sieve dry ingredients. Rub in fat. Melt sugar and syrup, and mix in. Add almond essence and a little milk. Roll into small balls, set well apart on a well-buttered sheet. Brush over with egg. Put half an almond (blanched) on top of each and bake in a very cool oven for about ½ hour.

BEVERAGES

Atholl Brose

1 *lb. honey*	1½ *pints whisky*

About a cupful of cold water

Put honey in a basin. Add sufficient cold water to dissolve it. Stir with a silver spoon and, when honey and water are well mixed, add the whisky by degrees. Stir briskly till a froth begins to rise. Bottle, and keep tightly corked.

Highland Bitters

This is a very old recipe.

1¾ *oz. gentian root*	¼ *oz. camomile flower*
½ *oz. bitter orange*	¼ *oz. cinnamon stick*
peel	½ *oz. cloves (whole)*
1 *oz. coriander seed*	*Whisky*

Bruise the coriander seed, camomile flower, cinnamon stick, cloves, gentian root and bitter orange peel. Cut the root and peel in small pieces. Add as much whisky as desired. Leave to soak for about 10 days. Strain off. Put more whisky on. The ingredients are sufficient for two bottles of whisky at a time, and may be used a number of times.

Rowanberry Liqueur

1 *pint brandy*	1 *pint syrup*

1 *handful picked rowanberries*

Dry the berries until they shrivel. Place in the brandy and leave for a week or 10 days. Strain and mix with an equal quantity of thick, very clear, syrup, made with loaf sugar in a brass pan.

MISCELLANEOUS

Aberdeen Toast

4 *oatcakes*	2 *egg-yolks*
Blouter paste	1 *oz. butter*
1 *egg-white*	*Cayenne pepper*

Make the oatcakes quite hot. Melt the butter, add the eggs, the bloater paste and Cayenne. Stir till thick. Pile on hot oatcakes, sprinkle with browned crumbs and serve at once.

Bignon's Sauce for Cold Lamb

Take equal quantities of capers, parsley, chives, gherkins and tarragon. Mince all very finely. Mix. Season with pepper, salt and cayenne, and put into a jar with tarragon vinegar. When required, add plenty of finely minced chervil, a little French mustard and salad oil to taste.

Oatmeal Porridge (for 4)

4–5 *handfuls oatmeal*	2 *pints boiling water*

Into 2 pints boiling water sift a handful of oatmeal through the fingers of the left hand, stirring all the time with a wooden spoon. Repeat this until the porridge is fairly thick. About 4 or 5 handfuls to this quantity of water. Draw the pan to the side of the fire or put on a low flame, preferably with an asbestos mat underneath. Add salt, put the lid on and cook steadily for about 1 hour, stirring well at intervals.

Rowan Jelly

Gather the berries just as they are on the point of ripening. Rinse in water and put them in a jelly pan with enough water to cover. Boil till the berries are soft. Strain the liquor through a jelly bag and return it to the fire. Add 1 lb. of loaf sugar to every pint of juice and boil rapidly for ½ hour, simmering carefully. Test on a saucer for setting and, when ready, bottle in warm jars and cover immediately with air-tight tops.

Scotch Marmalade (Thick)

2 *lb. bitter oranges*	9 *lb. sugar*
and 2 sweet oranges	2 *lemons*
6 *pints water*	

Wipe the fruit with a damp cloth and pare the yellow rind thinly off 3 or 4 of the oranges. Cut it with scissors into fine shreds and soak in a little of the water.

Peel the fruit, taking off all white pith. Quarter and cut the fruit up finely, removing pips. Soak the pulp for 24 hours in the water, also the pips tied in a muslin bag. Put the shreds and the pulp into a preserving pan. Squeeze the liquid from the pips and throw the pips away. Boil slowly for ¾ hour.

Remove from the fire, add the sugar, and boil until a little will set on a plate—about ½ hour. Skim and put into jars.

Sugar Tablet

2 *lb. sugar*	¼ *lb. butter*
3 *cupfuls water*	*Flavouring to taste*

Dissolve the sugar in the water. Add the butter, but do not boil as fast as for toffee. Test in cold water, and when a little rolls into a soft ball, take it off. Add flavouring to taste. Stir quickly with a spoon. It will begin to solidify round the edge. Scrape this off repeatedly and keep stirring until it is all of a soft, creamy consistency. Pour into a buttered slab or tin. Leave until set, then cut.

WALES

Welsh Rarebit is not by any means the only national dish; most of these recipes are by courtesy of the Whitbread Library

Bara-Brith (the national bun loaf of Wales) with yeast (makes 2 loaves).

(There are 60 varieties of bread, buns, etc., in the Welsh-English dictionary, all starting with Bara, meaning eat, sustenance.)

½ oz. yeast	1 heaped teaspoonful
4 oz. sugar	mixed spice
½ pint and 4 table-	1 large egg
spoonfuls milk (or	4 oz. sultanas
milk and water)	4 oz. raisins
1½ lb. flour	4 oz. currants
½ level teaspoonful	1 oz. chopped
salt	candied peel
2 oz. margarine	

Glaze

1 heaped tablespoon-	2 tablespoonfuls
ful brown sugar	water
A squeeze of lemon juice (optional)	

Cream the yeast and sugar together. Heat the milk until just lukewarm, and blend with the yeast. Sieve the flour, salt, and mixed spice together into a warmed basin. Make a well in the centre and pour in the yeast mixture. Stir, cover with a damp cloth, and set in a warm place for 30 minutes to rise (the bars over the cooker are very suitable when the oven is on, or when the heat is low on top).

Melt the margarine gently, add to the risen yeast mixture, stir in, sprinkle with flour, and knead for 3 minutes. Again cover with a damp cloth, and leave for a further 30 minutes in a warm place to rise. Beat the egg, add to the dough, mix in, knead well, then stir in the fruit and peel. Turn the mixture on to a floured board, divide in half, mould each into an oblong, and place in two 2-lb. bread tins, well brushed inside with melted margarine. Leave to prove in a warm place until the

Bara-Brith, the national bun loaf of Wales, right, and Huish Cake are two characteristic national dishes. Made and photographed specially by the Stork Margarine Cookery Service

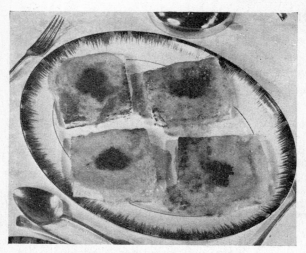

A real Welsh Rarebit, served lightly brown, contains ale in its ingredients

the eggs and beat the yolks into the creamed mixture. Add flour and ground rice sieved together. Beat the egg-whites stiff and add them and the yolks (well beaten) and caraway seeds. Stir well, place in a 7-in. greased baking tin and bake in a moderate oven for about 1 hour 10 minutes.

Leek Porridge

Wash, skim and trim the leeks and put on to boil in a little cold water. When done, cut the leeks into thin slices and place in porridge or soup plates, pouring a little of the water over them. Serve with toast cut into fingers.

Welsh Mutton Cowl (for 4)

1½ lb. scrag or best
   end neck of mutton
Piece of turnip

Parsley	Bunch of leeks
2 oz. pearl barley	1½ pints of cold water
Carrot	Salt and pepper to
Potatoes	taste

Wash and joint the meat and put it into a saucepan with the cold water. Bring to the boil quickly and skim the top. Add whole potatoes, diced carrot and turnip, pepper and salt, and pearl barley. Chop the parsley finely. Wash the leeks well in salted water, and cut them into rings, discarding the green part unless they are very young. Add parsley and leeks to meat and simmer for 1½ hours. Serve at once without thickening while the leeks are almost crisp, in small bowls with bread cut into dice.

Snowdon Pudding (for 4)

8 oz. suet	Grated rind of 2
6 eggs	lemons
Pinch of salt	4 oz. stoneless raisins
6 oz. lemon mar-	1½ oz. rice or corn-
malade	flour
8 oz. breadcrumbs	6 oz. brown sugar

Butter a quart mould or basin thickly and ornament with raisins. Mix all the dry ingredients together, beat the eggs and add to the mixture. Pour into the basin carefully, tie up and boil for 1½ hours. Serve with wine sauce.

Wine Sauce

Rind of ½ lemon	1 oz. butter
Water	1½ wineglassfuls
½ teaspoonful flour	sherry, madeira or
1½ oz. sugar	white wine

dough is even with the rim, with a nicely domed centre. Bake side by side on the middle shelf of a hot oven for 15 minutes. Turn the heat down to moderate and bake for 30–35 minutes longer until golden brown and firm. Cool on a wire tray.

To make the glaze, place the ingredients all together in a pan, stir until the sugar is dissolved, and boil for 1–2 minutes, but do not allow to caramelise. Cool a little, and brush evenly over the tops of the loaves. Leave until set before cutting. (Halve all ingredients for one loaf.)

Boiled Salted Duck

1 duck	1 lb. onions
A little butter, flour	Salt and pepper
and milk	

Salt the duck the day before. Put in a saucepan with enough water to cover and simmer for 1½ hours. Make onion sauce by boiling the onions in milk and water with salt and pepper, melting the butter in another saucepan, stirring in flour and gradually adding boiled milk and onions. Dish up the duck and pour the sauce over it.

Huish Cake

4 oz. ground rice (or	4 oz. margarine
semolina)	4 oz. flour
8 oz. castor sugar	4 eggs
	A few caraway seeds

Cream margarine and sugar. Separate

Boil sugar and lemon rind in a wine-glassful of water for about 15 minutes. Remove lemon peel and stir in butter into which flour has been kneaded. Add the wine, stir, and serve when quite hot.

Spiced Beef

10 or 12 lb. silverside of beef   8 oz. salt
2 oz. black pepper   2 oz. saltpetre
   2 oz. allspice

Rub the saltpetre into the beef and leave for 24 hours. Then rub the other ingredients in, having mixed them well previously. Put the beef into an earthenware pan and leave there for a fortnight, turning it every day. Put it into a clean pan, pour melted suet over it and cover the top of the pan with a paste made from flour and water. Bake in a very slow oven for 12 hours. Then place the meat between two plates and put a weight over it. The meat should be eaten cold and will keep for some time.

Welsh Pikelets

8 oz. flour   1 teaspoonful bicarbonate of soda
A little lard
½ gill boiling water   2 oz. castor sugar
4 oz. buttermilk   Pinch of salt

Mix flour, salt and sugar into a thick batter with buttermilk. Dissolve bicarbonate of soda in boiling water and add to the mixture. Take a tablespoonful of the batter at a time and fry on both sides in a little hot lard. Serve hot and buttered.

Welsh Rarebit (for 2)

4 oz. grated cheese   1 oz. butter
2 large tablespoonfuls ale   Pepper, salt and mustard to taste
2 slices toast

Put the ale into a saucepan and melt the cheese in it slowly. Add the pepper, salt and mustard, and the butter. When thoroughly hot, pour the mixture on the freshly made toast, place under a grill until lightly browned and serve.

COOKERY AT HOME AND ABROAD

IRELAND

Good eating has for long been associated with the Emerald Isle. Recipes compiled from the Whitbread Library

Colcannon (for 4)

1 lb. boiled cold potatoes   8 oz. boiled cabbage
2 oz. bacon fat   Salt and pepper to taste
1 onion

Mash the potatoes. Chop the onion fine and fry gently in the bacon fat. Add the potatoes and cabbage, season, mix well together and turn into a greased pudding basin. Reheat in the oven, turn out on a dish and serve.

Hunter's Pie (for 6)

6 mutton chops   2 dozen potatoes
A little butter   Pepper and salt to taste
A little gravy

Braise the chops. Boil and mash the potatoes and add pepper and salt. Butter a large pie dish, line with potatoes, put in the chops and cover with the remaining potatoes and bake in a moderate oven for 30 minutes. Cut a hole in the top and pour in the gravy (made by thickening the water in which the chops were cooked).

Irish Apple Baskets (for 4–6)

Filling

1 lb. cooking apples   Pinch of nutmeg, mixed spice or cinnamon, or 1–2 heaped tablespoonfuls sultanas or stoned raisins
3 heaped tablespoonfuls sugar
3 tablespoonfuls water
½ oz. margarine

Short pastry

6 oz. flour   3 dessertspoonfuls cold water, milk or water, and castor sugar to coat
Pinch of salt
3 oz. margarine

Turn on the oven heat, and set to fairly hot.

Peel, core, and slice the apples, and place in a saucepan with the other ingredients. Simmer gently until soft, and mash smoothly with a fork. Cool.

Make short pastry (see Pastry chapter),

using the ingredients listed, roll out thinly, cut into rounds, and line 9–12 bun tins. Using the scraps of pastry to make narrow strips, put in the apple filling and arrange the strips in star or lattice patterns over the apples. Brush with milk or water, sprinkle with castor sugar, and bake for 20–25 minutes in a pre-heated oven on the second shelf from the top. Serve either hot or cold. (Makes 9–12 tartlets, according to size.)

Irish Cheesecakes

4 oz. sweet almonds
3 oz. sugar
A little rose-water
2 oz. butter
Pastry as for Irish Apple Baskets
A little lemon juice and grated lemon peel
3 bitter almonds
3 eggs

Blanch and chop the almonds very fine. Mix in the rose-water. Beat the eggs and add with melted butter, lemon peel, juice and sugar. Line 12 patty pans with pastry and fill with the mixture. Bake in a hot oven for about 15 minutes.

Irish Delight (for 4)

1½ oz. cornflour
2 eggs
A little vanilla essence
3 oz. breadcrumbs
1½ pints milk
A little fat
1 dessertspoonful castor sugar

Mix the cornflour to a smooth paste with a little of the milk. Bring the rest of the milk to the boil and stir gently into the cornflour, boil for 10 minutes, stirring all the time. Add the vanilla and sugar, and pour into a shallow flat tin or dish. When quite cold, cut into oblong slices, dip in beaten egg, roll in breadcrumbs and fry a golden brown in a little hot fat. Salt, pepper and grated cheese can be used in stead of sugar and vanilla.

Irish Soda Cake

1 lb. plain flour
1 rounded teaspoonful cream of tartar
1 rounded teaspoonful bicarbonate of soda
1 level teaspoonful salt
4 oz. margarine
4 oz. sugar
4 oz. sultanas, or stoned raisins
2 oz. mixed chopped peel
½ pint and 6 tablespoonfuls sour milk.

Turn on the oven heat, and set to fairly hot. Brush a 7-in. cake tin all round inside with melted margarine. Sieve the flour, cream of tartar, bicarbonate of soda, and salt together into a mixing bowl. Cut the margarine into pieces, add, and rub in until the mixture looks crumbly. Stir in the sugar, fruit, and peel. Add the milk and mix with a knife to a fairly soft dough. Turn out on to a well-floured board, sprinkle with flour, knead very lightly, and form into a round. Put into the prepared tin; press out with the knuckles to the sides; mark a cross, or squares, etc., on the top with a knife, and bake for 1 hour on the middle shelf of the prepared oven. Turn the heat down to moderate and bake for a further half-hour.

NOTE: 2 heaped tablespoonfuls caraway seed may be used instead of fruit.

If bicarbonate of soda and cream of tartar are not available, use 4 heaped teaspoonfuls baking powder instead.

If sour milk is not available, use ½ pint and 5 tablespoonfuls fresh milk and 1 tablespoonful vinegar, mixed together, and if necessary, heated very gently until the milk curdles. Cool before using.

Irish Pancakes

4 eggs
1½ oz. butter
A little grated nutmeg
⅛ pint cream
3 oz. plain flour
A little castor sugar

Beat 2 egg-whites with 4 yolks and mix in the cream, slightly warmed. Then add melted butter, mix to a smooth batter with flour and add nutmeg. Fry the pancakes in a little butter. They should be very thin. Roll, sprinkle with a little sugar and serve hot.

Irish Stew, made from scrag or neck of mutton with onions and potatoes, needs to simmer slowly

Irish Apple Baskets and Irish Soda Cake are two favourite tea-time recipes from Ireland, here seen tested and photographed by the Stork Margarine Cookery Service

Irish Stew (for 6)

2 lb. scrag or neck of mutton	½ pint water
1 lb. onions	Pepper and salt to taste
3 lb. potatoes	

Cut the meat into neat pieces, slice the potatoes and the onions and put into a good saucepan, the meat first, then the potatoes and onions, sprinkling each layer with pepper and salt. Repeat, then pour on the water and simmer for 3 hours.

Pig's Face

Half a pig's head   Cabbage

Singe off all the hair from the head and soak in a basin of water for 12 hours. Wash well and boil in cold water, allowing 25 minutes for each pound. When cooked, lay the head on one side, score the skin and grill a golden brown in front of an open fire or in the oven. Cabbage should be put all round the pig's face to garnish and the liquor in which the head was boiled served as soup.

Potato and Apple Cake (for 4–6)

6 good-sized mashed potatoes	1½ lb. flour
8 oz. dripping	6 good-sized apples
	3 oz. sugar

Rub dripping into flour, mix with potatoes into a stiff dough and roll out on a board about ½ in. thick. Grease a fireproof dish and line with some of the pastry. Cover with peeled, cored and sliced apples and sprinkle with sugar. Cover with another layer of pastry, and then apples and pastry again. Bake in a moderate oven for 1 hour. Serve hot.

Potato Cakes

6 boiled potatoes	2 tablespoonfuls flour
Butter	
A little salt	

Mash the potatoes, and add the salt and sufficient flour to make into stiff dough. Roll out on the board ½ in. thick, cut into squares and bake on a griddle. Split and butter immediately and serve hot.

★   **TO DISCOVER THE REAL POSSIBILITIES OF THE POTATO, TRY IRISH COOKERY**   ★

ELIZABETHAN RECIPES

Authentic traditional fare from the days of Good Queen Bess,
as served in the Elizabethan Room at the Gore Hotel, London

Lobster Pie

MAKE a good crust, boil two lobsters, take out the tails, cut them in two, take out the gut, cut each tail in four pieces, and lay them in the dish. Take the bodies, bruise them well with the claws and pick out all the rest of the meat. Chop it all together, season it with pepper, salt and about two or three teaspoonfuls of vinegar, melt half a pound of butter, stir all together, with the crumb part of a bread roll rubbed in a small, clean cloth, lay it over the tails, put on your pastry cover, and bake in a slow oven.

Artichoke Pie

Boil your artichokes well, then take the bottoms from the leaves, and season them with a little beaten mace, and put to them a pretty quantity of butter, lay a layer in the bottom, then lay in the artichokes, sprinkle them with a little salt, put some sugar over them, put in grated pieces of marrow rolled in egg-yolks, then put in a few gooseberries or grapes, and lay upon it large mace and dates stoned, some yolks of hard-boiled eggs, lettuce stalks, and citron (lemon), cover it with butter, and when it is baked, put in scalded white wine and shake it together and serve it up.

Syllabub

Take a pint of canary or white wine, a pint of raspberry juice, a sprig of rosemary, a nutmeg quartered, the juice of a lemon, and some of the peel with sugar, put these together in a pot all night and cover them. In the morning take a pint and a half of cream, and a pint and a half of new milk. Then take out the lemon peel, rosemary and nutmeg, and squirt your milk and cream into the pot. With a wooden cow, fold at the corners. (The nearest modern equivalent of a wooden cow is a grooved wooden butter pat; the proper thing is to turn out the mixture and fold it in at the edges with the pat, but this part of the recipe can be omitted without damage to the resulting dish.)

Peacock

Roast a peacock exactly as you would any other bird of the same size, then place it on the mounted model.

Sturgeon

Cook a centre cut of sturgeon in the same way as salmon, boiling or grilling it.

Roast Swan

Roast a swan just as you would any other bird of the same size and weight.

Hare in Coffin

First remove the head, legs and tail from a hare. The body may either be roast whole, minced or turned into a paté and then encased in pastry, leaving openings for the insertion of head, tail and legs. Bake.

Colour page (top) shows a sucking pig, boar's head, centre cut of sturgeon garnished, lobster pie, a peacock with tail erect and a roast swan. In the lower picture, syllabub is seen in small wooden bowls

Photographs taken by McCall's of New York

A TYPICAL FEAST AS IN THE DAYS OF THE FIRST QUEEN ELIZABETH

MINCE PIES

Previously cooked, put to warm 1.10.

SAUSAGES and BACON

Put on to grill 1.15, turn after 5 minutes.

VEGETABLE

Put celery on 12.50. Brussels sprouts 1.5.

PUDDING

Pre-cooked, put on to steam in saucepan of boiling water 11.15.

GIBLETS for GRAVY

Put on to simmer 11 a.m. Make gravy 1.15.

TURKEY

Put stuffed turkey into pre-heated oven 9 a.m.

POTATOES

Put in to roast round turkey 12 noon (previously boiled for 5 minutes).

COOKING PLAN FOR CHRISTMAS DINNER AT 1.30

The only way to cook the Christmas feast for a family and still enjoy it yourself, without feeling worn-out and harassed, is to do as much of the preparing as you can beforehand and, on Christmas morning, work to a schedule. Here we have timed the whole operation for you, based on a meal to be served at 1.30. It is 1.5 and the housewife in our picture is making her bread sauce; she put on the onion to infuse at 9 a.m.

PLANNING THE
CHRISTMAS DINNER

It should be done with the precision and advance preparation of a
military operation—if the cook is going to enjoy it too

WIFE, mother, sister, whoever does the Christmas catering, must be able to enjoy herself with the others, without giving too much time to the stove and the kitchen. A strict timetable is the best answer, both beforehand as well as on the day itself.

ORDERING

All the extra items needed for Christmas cooking should be thought of well ahead. First, sit down and choose your recipes for cake, puddings and mincemeat, and list the ingredients you will need for all these items. Start at the beginning of November and lay in these stocks during the month.

Help yourself when it comes to cooking, by washing all dried fruit as you buy it. Mop it in a clean towel, and spread out on kitchen paper over wire trays to dry off. Store in airtight tins.

At the appointed time, the bird, vegetables and trimmings are on the table and the most festive meal of the year can begin

At the beginning of December, make a preliminary decision on the kind of bird you would like, and start enquiries as to price and availability. As soon as your final decision is made, and the bird ordered, list the accessories you will need for it—bacon, sausages, kind of stuffing, vegetables — and quantities, according to the weight of the bird and number of people for Christmas dinner. If you have groceries, bread and vegetables delivered, mark on your list the day on which you must order all these items for delivery in time for the holiday.

If you shop personally, you will not want to be carrying extra heavy loads, so buy bread (for stuffing and bread sauce) four days before Christmas Eve, vegetables the day before, and sausages, bacon and any other garnishes on Christmas Eve. Spread potato buying over the other days of Christmas week, as the total weight needed will be the heaviest.

At the beginning of Christmas week, order the joint you are likely to need to help over the rest of the holiday, and also the fresh bread for the whole holiday period. If collecting this yourself, do so as late as possible on Christmas Eve.

Spread the buying of soft drinks, wines and spirits needed over the month of December, aiming at having your supply complete by the beginning of Christmas week.

Flour cannot be kept too long, but if you have cool, dry storage space, you can get in your quantity a fortnight ahead.

COOKING BEFOREHAND

Mincemeat, puddings and cake can all be made a matter of weeks before the festive holiday.

Mincemeat.—When this contains wine or spirits, it can be made in early November, as soon as you have all the necessary ingredients. Otherwise, make it two or three weeks before Christmas Day.

Puddings.—These may be made one month before needed.

The Cake.—Make the cake itself one month beforehand. When quite cold, wrap in greaseproof paper and store.

The Almond Paste should be put on the cake at least one week before Christmas, and must be left for two or three days at least to dry out completely before the white icing is put on.

The Icing and Decoration.—Accomplish this task two or three days ahead.

JOBS FOR THE 24th

Try to get all shopping done as early as possible, leaving you free to carry out the following preparations:

Make mince pies, also make a batch of pastry and store in a tin or in the refrigerator. This will be useful for making additional mince pies or other sweet or savoury pastry items over the holiday.

Make stuffing, and prepare and stuff the bird (but do not put in sausage meat). Put the bird ready in its tin to go in the oven the next day.

Make the necessary quantity of breadcrumbs ready for the bread sauce; and, if hard sauce is on the menu for the pudding, make this.

Prepare sausages for the bird, rind the bacon and do all vegetable preparation.

See that the pudding is in order, ready for reheating the next day.

CHRISTMAS DAY

Aim at a definite time for the meal. The housewife in the colour photograph is happy over her careful schedule for dinner at 1.30 p.m., which is worked out as follows:

8.45 a.m.—Preheat oven. Add sausage meat stuffing to the turkey.

9 a.m.—Put turkey in oven, baste half-hourly. Put the onion to infuse in the milk for bread sauce.

10 a.m.—Lay table and put wines ready. If a white sauce is preferred to a hard sauce for the pudding, make it now and put to heat when you dish up the pudding.

11 a.m.—Put giblets to simmer for gravy.

11.15 a.m.—Pudding on to reheat in saucepan of boiling water.

11.30 a.m.—Potatoes on to boil for 5 minutes.

12 noon.—Potatoes round turkey to roast.

12.50 p.m.—Celery on now, if on menu.

1.5 p.m.—Sprouts on to boil. Finish the bread sauce and keep hot.

1.10 p.m.—Mince pies to warm.

1.15 p.m.—Sausage and bacon on to grill, turn after 5 minutes. Put potatoes to pan roast if they cannot be cooked round turkey. Make gravy and dish up turkey and vegetables.

Pudding should be left on a pin-point of gas while first course is being eaten, and dished while one or two of the diners clear away the first course.

CATERING HINTS

*How much for how many—and
how to tell the good from the bad*

Ice Cream Brandy Punch (above) is a party winner. Left, an economy idea: when grilling, line the pan with Mirap aluminium foil—its shiny surface reflects the heat, speeds cooking and protects the pan from grease

IN the initial stages of housekeeping it is a little difficult to know how much to buy of this and that commodity, especially the perishables.

Here is an approximate guide: allow 4–6 oz. of meat or fish per person, including active children; 4 oz. vegetables and 2–3 medium-sized potatoes; when soup starts the meal, allow two-thirds of a soup *cup* per person of thick soup, rather more of thinner soups.

For sweet courses, reckon that a pint pudding basin (steamed puddings) or a pint dish (trifle, rice pudding, etc.) will serve four.

For such items as dressed crabs, allow one large one for four persons, a medium one for three; in the case of small fish such as sprats, allow about 1 lb. for three people. Salmon is a rich, solid fish, so allow a little less.

Catering for Large Numbers.—Allowing for waste and loss of weight in cooking, a 12-lb. turkey will serve about 14 people; the same weight of goose serves about 10 people; one good-sized, plump duck, or two smaller ones, will serve 6–7 people. Reckon on a joint of 10 lb. for about 12 persons.

Larger Numbers: Party Items.—Allow 1 pint of ice cream for about 7 people; 3 sandwiches, 3–4 cocktail sausages, 2 pastry savouries per person. Sweets are most easily managed served in individual glasses or dishes—about half-full, for at a party

both children and adults are inclined to eat a little of a fair variety of eatables, rather than a lot of one kind.

Here is a very good party recipe:

Ice Cream Brandy Punch

1 *family brick vanilla* 1 *pint milk*
  ice cream 1 *egg (optional)*
  ½ gill brandy

Add ice cream, cut into small pieces, to other ingredients in a large mixing bowl, whisk till frothy. Serve from a punch bowl. Makes 6 to 8 glasses.

HOME GOODNESS TESTS

There is always a certain amount of worry about mushrooms. If you have any doubt at all, put a real silver spoon or coin in the pan. If it turns black, the mushrooms are dangerous.

Eggs too are sometimes unknown quantities, but here are some tests: put the doubtful one into a bowl of water when it will (*a*) sink to the bottom if fresh; (*b*) rise slightly, broad end up, if two or three weeks old; (*c*) come to the surface or above it if really stale. You can apply a further test by holding the egg against a strong light. If it looks unclouded, it is fresh; if it is bad, it will look dark-coloured

Among dry goods, flour and floury items are not always good keepers. If you feel uncertain of them, grasp a handful and squeeze for half a minute. If the substance is pure, it will hold its shape; if not, it will break up and fall.

JEWISH

Some typical dishes selected from a rich and varied tradition

by FLORENCE GREENBERG, *author of "The Jewish Chronicle Cookery Book" and*
"Florence Greenberg's Cookery Book"

JEWISH cookery characteristics are derived from two main sources—religious tradition and the wanderings of the Jewish people.

Traditional Jewish laws impose bans on the consumption of animals that do not chew the cud and have cloven hooves, such as pigs and rabbits, and on sea food that does not have fins and scales, such as shellfish. Scavengers, birds of prey, and hindquarter meat are also forbidden. Indeed, because consumption of blood is not allowed, all animals must be slaughtered by a "shochet," a man specially trained to kill them by severing the jugular vein, a method which permits the maximum flow of blood. All blood remaining on the meat is removed by the housewife by the process of soaking in cold water and salting, known as Koshering. Finally, traditional religious laws state that milk and meat must not be cooked together, nor, generally speaking, consumed at the same meal.

As a result, Jewish housewives are limited in the foods they may utilise for cooking, and the limitation has often been magnified in the past by the privations and poverty that the Jews have suffered in their wanderings in many countries of the world. Thus prevented from gaining variety by using different kinds of food, the Jewish housewife developed the art of cooking the same foods differently. It is, perhaps, because Kosher meat was not always available that she developed particular ability in preparing fish dishes and in chopping the fish, as in "Gefillte Fish," to make the food go farther when it was in short supply.

Many dishes prepared by Jewish housewives are derived from the countries in which their forebears sojourned. Thus, for example, it was in Spain and Portugal that they learned to fry fish in oil, in Germany

that they learned to make sweet and sour stews, and in Russia that they learned to make blintzes and borsch.

At the same time there has grown up a specifically Jewish tradition in which particular dishes are associated with particular festivals. For Jews, each festival, including the Sabbath, lasts from sunset to sunset and the festive meal is taken on the eve of the holy-day to usher it in.

On the Sabbath eve it is customary to eat cold fried fish or gefillte fish. And because on the Sabbath all work, including the lighting of a fire, is forbidden, a special stew called "Cholent" is prepared before sunset on Friday, then left simmering in a very cool oven until midday dinner the following day.

On New Year's Eve (which falls in the autumn, according to the Jewish calendar) honey cake and apples dipped in honey are consumed, to signify the hope of a sweet and fruitful year to come. At Tabernacles, the harvest festival, stuffed cabbage leaves, sweet and sour, are traditional. The Feast of Purim commemorates the exposure by the Jew Mordecai of the conspirator Haman, and "Haman Taschen," a three-cornered bun said to represent the "asslike" ears of the rogue, are eaten. At Shevouoth, celebration of the gleaning of the firstfruits, cheese dishes, especially blintzes, are the festive fare.

During the Festival of Passover, when Jews commemorate the liberation of their ancestors from Egyptian bondage, only unleavened bread may be eaten, as a reminder that the Israelites left in such a hurry that they had no time to leaven their bread, which they baked on their backs as they went. From the injunction to use only unleavened flour during this festival has arisen a whole galaxy of special

One of the dishes customarily eaten on the Sabbath eve is cold fried fish

recipes, some examples of which are given here.

In the course of the following pages it has been possible to give a few samples only from a rich and varied tradition. But I think that those who taste will find them good.

PASSOVER DISHES

Almond Biscuits

6 oz. fine motza meal	3 oz. castor sugar
4 oz. margarine	1 egg
Almond essence	Chopped almonds

Cream the margarine and sugar. Reserve a little of the egg-white to brush over the top of the biscuits, beat up remainder and add to the creamed margarine together with the motza meal, flavour with almond essence and knead thoroughly. Press on to a greased baking sheet to a thickness of about ¼ in., brush over with white of egg and sprinkle with chopped almonds. Bake in a moderately hot oven till lightly browned—about 20 minutes. Cut into squares or fingers, then remove from tin and cool on a cake tray.

Wafer Biscuits

1 oz. potato flour	2 oz. margarine
1 oz. fine motza meal	1 egg
2 oz. castor sugar	Vanilla essence

Melt the margarine, but do not let it boil.

Whip the egg and sugar till light and frothy, add the melted margarine and a few drops of essence of vanilla, whisk again, then stir in the meal and potato flour.

Grease some baking-tins very thoroughly with cooking fat and put on teaspoonfuls of the mixture, with a good space between each, as they spread considerably. Bake in a hot oven till set and the edges lightly browned. Remove from tins immediately and cool on a cake tray.

Savoury Balls for Soup or Stew (Motzakleis) (for 4–5)

1 motza	Fine meal
1 small onion	Seasoning (pepper,
1 egg	salt and ginger)
1 oz. chicken fat	

Soak the motza in cold water till soft, then drain and squeeze dry. Put in a basin and beat up with a fork. Chop the onion finely (there should be about 1 tablespoonful) and fry in the fat till lightly browned, then add it to the soaked motza together with the fat in which it was fried, season with salt, pepper and ginger, add the beaten egg and sufficient fine meal to bind the mixture. Roll into tiny balls and coat with fine meal. Drop into fast-boiling soup or stew, and after 2 minutes reduce the heat and simmer for 20 minutes.

These are best made in advance and left

for a few hours in a cool place or re-frigerator before cooking.

Steamed Fruit Pudding (for 4–5)

6 oz. dried fruit	2 oz. brown sugar
1 oz. chopped peel	2 motzas
3 oz. shredded suet	½ teaspoonful mixed
2 tablespoonfuls	spice
motza meal	2 eggs

Soak the motzas in cold water till soft, drain in a colander and press out all moisture, then put in a mixing bowl and beat up with a fork. Add the remaining ingredients and mix thoroughly. Turn into a greased basin and steam for 2–2½ hours.

This pudding can also be baked. Turn the mixture into a greased baking dish and bake about 1 hour in a moderate oven.

Apple Charlotte (for 5–6)

6 oz. medium motza	3 oz. margarine
meal	2 oz. sultanas
1½ lb. apples	Sugar
4 tablespoonfuls	¼ lemon
water	

Peel the apples and cut into small pieces. Rub 2½ oz. margarine into the meal and add 2 tablespoonfuls of sugar. Grease a baking dish and put in one-third of the meal, cover with half the apples, sprinkle with sugar, sultanas, grated lemon rind and juice. Repeat the layers and pour over the water. Put the remaining meal on top, sprinkle with sugar and dot with remaining margarine. Bake in a moderate oven 1–1¼ hours.

Stuffed Chremslach (for 4–5)

2 motzas	¼ teaspoonful cinna-
2 oz. motza meal	mon
1 oz. sugar	Fruit filling
1 egg.	Cooking fat for
	frying

Soak the motzas in cold water till soft, drain, squeeze dry and beat up with a fork. Add the meal, beaten egg, sugar and cin-namon, and mix thoroughly. Form into small flat oval shapes, cover half with the fruit filling and place another on top. Shape neatly, coat with motza meal and fry a golden brown on both sides in hot fat. Serve hot, sprinkled with sugar.

Fruit Filling.—Mix together 6 oz. dried fruit, 1 oz. sugar, ¼ teaspoonful cinnamon and 2 teaspoonfuls lemon juice.

OTHER DISHES

Bream with Sweet and Sour Sauce (for 4–5)

2 lb. bream	Salt
1 small onion	1 oz. sultanas
1 bay leaf	1 oz. sugar
4 tablespoonfuls	2 oz. margarine
vinegar	1½ oz. flour
Pepper	

Cut the fish into convenient-sized pieces for serving, place in a saucepan with the sliced onion and bay leaf, sprinkle with salt and pepper, and pour over sufficient hot water to cover. Put the lid on the pan and simmer gently until the fish is cooked— about 15 minutes. Then remove the bay leaf and lift fish on to a serving dish.

Melt the margarine, stir in the flour, then gradually add ¾ pint of the liquor in which the fish was cooked and the vinegar, stir till boiling, add the sugar and sultanas, season with salt and pepper, and simmer for 5 minutes. Pour over the fish and serve either hot or cold.

The amount of vinegar and sugar can be varied according to taste.

Cod or haddock can be cooked in the same way.

Fried Fish (for 5–6)

2–3 lb. fish	Frying oil
2–3 oz. flour	Parsley
2 eggs	Salt

Any kind of fish can be used. Small fish can be fried whole, larger ones can be fil-leted or cut into steaks.

Wash the fish, put it in a bowl, sprinkle with salt and leave for 15 minutes, then dry thoroughly. Coat the pieces of fish with flour seasoned with salt, then with beaten egg. Heat sufficient frying oil in a frying pan to half-cover the fish and, when really hot, fry the fish a golden brown, first on one side, then the other. Drain thor-oughly on soft paper and serve cold, garnished with parsley.

Gefillte Fish (for 5–6)

2–2½ lb. fish (bream,	2 sticks of celery
cod or haddock)	1 tablespoonful
2 eggs	chopped parsley
2 onions	1½ pints water
1 large carrot	Fresh breadcrumbs
Salt and pepper	

Remove the skin and bones from the fish and put them in a saucepan with one cut-up onion, the celery and a small piece of carrot, pour over the water and season with salt and pepper. Cover and simmer gently for ½ hour, then strain.

Put the fish and remaining onion through the mincing machine, add the parsley and beaten eggs to the minced fish and sufficient fresh breadcrumbs to bind, season with salt and pepper. With floured hands, roll into balls. Slice the carrot, add to the fish stock and bring to the boil, then lay in it the fish balls, cover and simmer very gently for 1 hour. Lift the balls on to a serving dish and place a slice of carrot on top of each. Spoon over a little of the fish stock and serve cold, when the stock should have set in a jelly.

Cholent (for 5–6)

This is the traditional dish served on the Sabbath when a hot meal is required. It is prepared on Friday and cooked till midday dinner the following day.

2 lb. fat brisket or short rib of beef	Dumpling
½ lb. butter beans	1 onion
2 lb. medium-size potatoes	1 oz. sugar
	Salt and pepper
	Water

Use a short-handled saucepan with a tightly fitting lid, or a large casserole.

Peel the potatoes and leave them whole. Put the beans in the bottom of the pan, add the chopped onion and half the potatoes. Place the meat and dumpling on top and fill up with remaining potatoes. Season each layer with salt and pepper, sprinkle over the sugar and pour over sufficient boiling water to cover. Place greaseproof paper over the top before putting on the lid. Place in a very slow oven till required the following day.

For the dumpling

4 oz. flour	1 large potato
1 small onion	2 teaspoonfuls
1 oz. suet or raw chicken fat	chopped parsley
	Salt and pepper

Peel and grate the potato and onion, chop the suet or chicken fat finely, mix all ingredients, seasoning with salt and pepper, then form into a roll.

Calves' Feet with Prunes and Chestnuts (for 4–5)

2 calves' feet	1 small onion
½ lb. prunes	2 sticks celery
½ lb. chestnuts	2 or 3 olives
2 tablespoonfuls sherry	Stock or water
	Salt, pepper, paprika

Soak the prunes in cold water overnight. Boil the chestnuts for 15 minutes, then remove outer and inner skins. Cut up the onion and celery. Joint the calves' feet and put them in a stewpan with sufficient stock or water to cover well. Season with salt, pepper and ½ teaspoonful of paprika, cover and cook very gently for 2 hours.

Gefillte fish is one of the best known of Jewish dishes. Minced fish is made into balls which are then boiled, decorated with carrot and served cold

Then add the prunes, chestnuts, onion and celery and continue to cook gently for another hour. Before serving, add the sherry and the chopped olives.

Stuffed Cabbage Leaves, sweet and sour
(Holishkes) (for 4–6)

¾ lb. raw minced beef	1 oz. sugar
1 teacupful cooked rice	Cabbage leaves
	½ pint water
1 tablespoonful grated onion	2 oz. sultanas
2 tablespoonfuls concentrated tomato purée	2 tablespoonfuls vinegar
	Salt and pepper

Use a white cabbage. Remove twelve of the largest leaves, place them in a bowl, cover with boiling water, leave for 2 or 3 minutes, then drain, dry with a cloth and cut away the tough stem ends. Mix the meat and rice, add the grated onion and ½ teaspoonful of tomato purée, and season with salt and pepper. Put a portion in the centre of each cabbage leaf, fold over the sides, roll up like a parcel and fasten with thread. Line a large saucepan with a few more scalded leaves and place the rolls close together on top. Pour over the tomato purée and water, add the vinegar, sugar and sultanas. Cover, and cook over a very gentle heat for 2 hours. If the liquid boils away, add a little more water.

If preferred, these can be cooked in a covered casserole in a slow oven.

Poppy Seed Buns (Haman Taschen)

1 lb. flour	½ oz. yeast
2 oz. castor sugar	2 oz margarine
½ pint milk	1 egg
Poppy-seed filling	Honey

Cream the yeast with a teaspoonful of sugar. Melt the margarine in the milk and, when just lukewarm, pour it on to the creamed yeast. Sieve the flour with a pinch of salt into a warmed basin, make a well in the centre and pour in the yeast mixture, gradually work in the flour from the sides and knead to a smooth dough. Cover and leave in a warm place to rise for 1½–2 hours, then add the sugar and beaten egg, and knead thoroughly

Roll out the dough ¼ in. thick and cut into 4-in. squares. Put a heaped teaspoonful of the filling in the centre of each and fold across into triangles, pressing edges well together and folding them under. Place well apart on greased baking tins and leave in a warm place to rise for 1 hour,

then brush the tops lightly with warm honey and bake in a moderate oven till golden brown—about 20 minutes.

Poppy-seed filling

1 teacupful ground poppy seeds	1 oz. sugar
	2 oz. margarine
1 teacupful milk or water	2 tablespoonfuls honey
1 oz chopped peel	1 oz. sultanas
1 oz. chopped nuts	

Put all ingredients into a saucepan, bring to the boil and cook over a gentle heat until the liquid is absorbed, keeping it well stirred.

Filled Pancakes (Cheese blintzes) (for 4–5)

4 oz. flour	2 eggs
¼ pint milk	6–8 oz. curd cheese
¼ pint water	Grated lemon rind
1 teaspoonful sugar	Salt
Fat for frying	

Add the sugar and a little grated lemon rind to the cheese. Make a smooth batter with the flour, eggs, milk and water, adding salt to taste.

Grease a heated omelette pan with cooking fat and pour in just sufficient batter to cover the bottom of the pan with a very thin layer. Cook over a moderate heat until the pancake is firm, frying on one side only, then invert on to a clean cloth, cooked side uppermost, and fry remaining batter in the same way. Put a little of the cheese in the centre of each and fold over in the shape of an envelope. Fry a golden brown on both sides.

Purim Fritters (Fritlach) (for 5–6)

2 eggs	Flour
3 tablespoonfuls oil	Castor sugar
Oil for frying	

Beat up the eggs, stir in the oil, then mix in enough flour to make a soft dough. Knead very thoroughly, break off small pieces and roll out wafer thin into circles about 8 in. across, then cut each into four sections. Leave for an hour or longer till quite dry, then fry in hot oil a very light brown. Drain and sprinkle with castor sugar. These need careful handling, as they break very easily.

Apple Steffon (for 5–6)

1½ lb. apples	10 oz. flour
2 oz. currants	1 teaspoonful baking powder
1 oz. chopped peel	
1 oz. margarine	Brown sugar
Pinch of salt	Cinnamon
Cold water	½ lemon
4 oz. shredded suet	

Lockschen Pudding is made with either noodles or spaghetti and sultanas

Sieve flour, baking powder and salt, add the suet and water to make a soft dough.

Spread the margarine thickly over the bottom and sides of a 2-pint pudding basin, then sprinkle liberally with brown sugar.

Roll out three-quarters of the pastry ⅓ in. thick and line the basin with it. Peel, core and cut up the apples, put half in the lined basin, sprinkle over the peel, currants, grated rind and juice of half a lemon, and dust of cinnamon and sugar to taste, then add the remaining apples, a little more sugar and pour over ½ teacupful of cold water. Cover with remaining pastry, twist a greased paper over the top and bake in a moderate oven about 1¼ hours.

Stuffed Monkey

6 oz. flour	½ teaspoonful
4 oz. margarine	cinnamon
4 oz. soft brown	1 egg
sugar	Filling

Sieve the flour and cinnamon, rub in the margarine, add the yolk of the egg and the sugar, and knead to a pliable dough. Roll out the paste into two rounds to fit an 8-in. shallow cake tin (about 2 in. deep). Grease the tin and put in one round, spread with the filling and cover with the other round. Brush over with white of egg and bake in a moderate oven about 30 minutes. Cool in the tin.

For the filling

2 oz. chopped peel	2 oz. ground almonds
1½ oz. margarine	1 oz. castor sugar
1 egg-yolk	

Melt margarine, mix all ingredients.

Honey Cake (Lekach)

½ lb. honey	½ teaspoonful mixed
12 oz. flour	spice
4 oz. castor sugar	½ teaspoonful
2 eggs	bicarbonate of soda
¼ pint warm water	3 tablespoonfuls
1 teaspoonful ground	cooking oil
ginger	Shredded almonds

Grease a shallow cake tin about 9 in. across. Sieve the flour, ginger, spice and bicarbonate of soda, warm the honey. Beat the eggs and sugar till light and frothy, add the oil and warmed honey, then the dry ingredients alternately with the water and mix to a smooth batter. Turn into greased tin, sprinkle with shredded almonds and bake about 1 hour in a moderate oven.

Lockschen Pudding (for 4–5)

1 pint cooked noodles	2 oz. sugar
or spaghetti	2 oz. margarine
4 oz. sultanas	¼ teaspoonful
1 oz. chopped peel	cinnamon
2 eggs	

Melt the margarine, beat eggs lightly. Mix all ingredients. Turn into a greased baking dish and bake in a moderate oven about 40 minutes.

329

FRANCE

*The paradise of the gourmet, where every housewife
brings a touch of true inspiration to her cooking*

Some recipes, classical and regional, of specialities served à l'Ecu de France,
London, and compiled by EUGÈNE HERBODEAU

THE pre-eminence of French cookery derives from the four duchies or provinces, each as delectable as the rest, into which the culinary realm is divided. These are:

First, *La Haute Cuisine*, the aristocracy of the Art, the triumph of our great chefs, our renowned practitioners, who have set up, for every country in the civilised world to follow, a model and exemplar of cookery in perfection.

Then, *La Cuisine Bourgeoise*, that home or family cooking which is the pride and glory of the first-rate cooks and the housewives of France.

Next, *La Cuisine Impromptue*, that is to say, "unpremeditated," "pot luck," none the less exquisite for being spontaneous, "the perfume and suppliance of a minute."

And finally, *La Cuisine Régionale*, which epitomises, so to speak, the taste, the character, the individuality of each separate French province.

Of the four schools of French cookery, it is the regional school which, from the nature of the case, has hitherto been the least widely known. And judging by the success of l'Ecu de France, London, where g e n u i n e French regional dishes are served, the English public appreciate the merits of this method of cooking, the distinctive characteristic of which is its delightful originality.

In addition to our Regional Recipes, we have also included a number of Classical Dishes and Fonds which, we venture to think, every housewife who takes a pride in her table will be glad to have for reference. We mean no disrespect to Classical Cookery when we say, as we do without hesitation, that in the Regional Cookery the soul and expression of typical French cooking is really and most completely to be found.

A chef in the Dordogne department of France prepares one
of the famous specialities of the region

One sure way to recapture happy memories of a holiday in Paris, with its gay cafés, is to try making some of the French dishes in this chapter

(In the following recipes the quantities have been reduced, as far as possible, to come within the scope of ordinary households. One or two, including the Fonds, have had to remain unchanged. If they were made with smaller quantities of the various ingredients, they would, due to the long cooking, simply reduce themselves to nothing.—EDITOR.)

The White Fonds

8 lb. knuckle of veal	1 stick of celery
1½ lb. fowl	1 oz. parsley stalks
12 oz. carrots	1 sprig of thyme
6 oz. onions	1 bay leaf
1 small leek	4 quarts water
½ oz. salt	

Break the veal knuckles into small pieces and put them into a casserole or stock pot with the fowl. Cover with water and add salt. Simmer gently. Remove the scum carefully as it forms. Add the vegetables. Boil for 4 hours, strain through a cloth. Keep in cool place for use when required.

Clear Fonds of Veal

6 lb. veal shoulder and knuckle	6 oz. onions
4½ lb. crushed veal bones	1½ oz. parsley stalks
12 oz. carrots	1 bay leaf
	1 sprig thyme
	4 quarts water
½ oz. salt	

Put meat and bones into the oven until browned, then place in a casserole or stock pot with the carrots and add seasonings; put the lid on and simmer for 15 minutes. Add the water, little by little, and bring to boiling point, skimming carefully. Add rest of vegetables and boil slowly for 6 hours. Strain through a cloth.

Thickened Veal Fonds

3½ pints veal fonds   ½ oz. arrowroot

Boil the veal fonds until reduced to 1 pint. Mix the arrowroot with a few spoonfuls of cold fonds until smooth. Add to the reduced fonds and boil for 1 minute. Strain through muslin.

Meat Jelly

2 lb. knuckle of veal	1 oz. leek
2 lb. veal bones	1 stick celery
1¾ lb. lean beef	1 bouquet garni (bay
1 calf's foot, boned	leaf, parsley stalks,
and scalded	sprig chervil, sprig
3 oz. fresh bacon rind	tarragon, thyme)
3 oz. carrots	4 quarts water
3 oz. onions	1 egg-white

Put the knuckle, bones, calf's foot and 1 lb. lean beef with vegetables, bouquet garni, bacon rind and water in a stock pot. Bring slowly to the boil, skim carefully, and simmer for 6–8 hours. Pour through a strainer, and carefully take off the fat.

Put in a stew pan the remaining ¾ lb. minced lean beef and the egg-white. Pour the fonds on the minced meat and stir with a whisk. Bring slowly to boiling point, whisking all the time. Simmer for 15 minutes and strain.

Preparation of Glazes

Glazes are concentrated extracts of meat, poultry, game or fish, reduced to the consistency of jelly.

The fonds intended to be reduced to glaze require the use of very fresh meat and a slow and regular cooking. Great care must be taken to get perfectly transparent glazes. A large proportion of bones and meats rich in gelatinous elements, such as knuckles of veal, are indispensable. Season with great discretion, especially as regards salt. Beware of reducing the fonds too much and so destroying the delicacy of their flavour. The glaze should have the consistency of a thick syrup with a sound and clean savour, free from any bitter taste.

Court Bouillon for Fish

1 quart water	1 oz. parsley stalks
1 quart white wine	1 sprig thyme
¾ lb. carrots and	½ bay leaf
onions, cut in	1 oz. salt
round slices	¼ oz. peppercorns

Mix the liquids and seasonings in a stock pot and boil slowly.

Put the fish into cold court bouillon if whole, or into hot court bouillon if sliced. In both cases cook very slowly, simmering, not boiling.

Souse (Marinade)

4 oz. carrots	1 bay leaf
4 oz. onions	1 sprig thyme
1½ oz. shallots	2 cloves
1 oz. celery	A few peppercorns
2 cloves of garlic	2 pints white wine
3 parsley stalks	1 pint vinegar
½ pint olive oil	

Mince the carrots, onions and shallots. Put them all together, with the flavourings, into a vessel and pour in the wine, vinegar and oil. Keep in a cool place.

The meat must be seasoned with salt and pepper before being soused. This souse can be boiled, but then all vegetables and spices should be covered in oil first before adding wine and vinegar. Boil slowly for 25 minutes and let it cool before pouring it over the meat in the vessel.

SAVOURY BUTTERS

Anchovy

Pound 2 oz. fillets of best anchovy, well washed and dried; add ¼ lb. butter. Continue pounding together and pass through fine sieve.

Maître d'Hôtel

Cream ¼ lb. butter and blend with a tablespoonful of chopped parsley and the juice of ½ lemon. Season with salt and pepper.

Colbert

Same process as for Maître d'Hôtel butter, to which is added ½ teaspoonful of chopped tarragon and 1 tablespoonful of dissolved chicken glaze.

Escargot

6 oz. butter	2 teaspoonfuls
½ oz. minced shallot	chopped parsley
½ crushed clove of	1 ground peppercorn
garlic	¼ oz. salt

Mix well and keep in a cool place.

SAUCES

Les Roux

2 oz. butter	2¼ oz. flour

Melt the butter, sprinkle in the flour, and stir over low heat until it has become a flaxen colour. To have it a deeper colour, cook a little longer until it becomes hazel brown. If a roux is to be used for a Béchamel sauce, great care must be taken that it does not get coloured at all.

In order to make a sauce, add to the roux 2 pints of liquid, either clear veal fonds for a velouté or milk for a Béchamel.

Le Velouté

2½ oz. roux blond   1¼ pints white stock

Dilute the roux with the white stock. Stir while bringing to the boil, then boil steadily for ½ hour. Skim carefully. Strain with tammy and stir until cold.

Tomato Sauce (La sauce tomate)

1¼ oz. streaky bacon,   ¾ pint white stock
  cut in dice   Small sprig thyme
3¼ lb. fresh tomatoes   ¼ bay leaf
2 oz. diced carrots   ½ clove garlic
1¼ oz. onions   ¼ oz. salt
1¼ oz. flour   ¼ oz. sugar
          Pinch of pepper

Fry the bacon lightly in a casserole. Add carrots and onions, sliced. Fry gently and add the flour. Cook until lightly browned. Add the tomatoes, which should be crushed, the stock, herbs, garlic, salt, sugar and pepper. Bring to the boil while stirring, cover the casserole and cook slowly in the oven for ¾ hour. Pass through a strainer.

White Sauce (La sauce Béchamelle)

2½ oz. white roux
1 pint milk
½ small onion, minced
1 teaspoonful salt
1 small sprig of
  thyme
1 pinch of mignonette
  pepper

Mix the white roux with the milk, brought to boiling point. Stir until it reaches the boil. Add seasoning and cook very slowly for 30 minutes. Pass through tammy.

La Sauce Bordelaise

½ gill red wine
1 tablespoonful
  chopped shallots
2 oz. beef marrow
1½ gills thick veal
  fonds
A pinch of mignonette
  pepper

Add shallots and pepper to red wine and reduce to half. Add the veal fonds and simmer for about 30 minutes. Strain and add the marrow, previously poached in boiling water and cut in dice.

La Sauce Hollandaise

2 egg-yolks   6 oz. butter
        Lemon juice

Put in a casserole or bowl 2 tablespoonfuls of water and the egg-yolks. Melt the butter separately in advance. Place the casserole or bowl over a pan of boiling water, add the butter and whip lightly. From time to time add a little water to make the sauce light. Season and add a few drops of lemon juice. Pass through tammy.

Mayonnaise

3 egg-yolks   ½ teaspoonful salt
⅞ pint of olive oil   ¾ tablespoonful
Pinch of white   vinegar or lemon
  pepper   juice

Whip the egg-yolks with salt, pepper and a few drops of lemon juice. Add the oil drop by drop to begin with, then as a

The French housewife has an abundance of foods to choose from and likes to buy her fish, vegetables, meat and fruits from the market

333

thin trickle; from time to time break into the body of sauce with a dash of vinegar.

Add 3 tablespoonfuls of boiling water to ensure the cohesion of the sauce and prevent its disintegration.

La Sauce Béarnaise

6 tablespoonfuls vinegar	1 teaspoonful chervil
2 tablespoonfuls chopped shallot	Pinch of mignonette pepper
½ oz. tarragon	Pinch of salt
	3 egg-yolks
¼ lb. butter	

Put into a casserole the chopped shallots, tarragon crushed, the chervil, pepper, salt and vinegar, and reduce to two-thirds. Leave for a few minutes to cool, then add the egg-yolks. Place the sauce on a low fire with the butter and whip gently until it thickens. Pass through a tammy and add 1 teaspoonful of chopped tarragon and ½ teaspoonful of chopped chervil.

CLASSICAL SOUPS

Le Pot au Feu

3½ lb. beef	1 leek
1 knuckle veal	½ stalk of celery
1½ lb. fowl	Small sprig of thyme
1 oz. salt	1 bay leaf
2 large carrots	1 small onion with
1 large turnip	clove stuck into it
1 clove of garlic	

Cover the meat in cold water. Bring slowly to boiling point and skim thoroughly. Add vegetables and herbs. Simmer slowly and evenly for 6 hours. Skim the fat off, strain, and season to taste. This stock can not only be used for soup, but it will be the basis of numerous sauces.

Potato Soup (Potage parmentier) (for 8)

1½ lb. potatoes	1 gill cream
3 whites of leeks	3 pints stock
3½ oz. butter	

Chop the leeks and cook in butter. Add potatoes, peeled and cut in large pieces. Cover with stock and bring to boil rapidly. Simmer until vegetables are tender. Whisk into a purée and pass through tammy. Reheat, adding finally butter and cream.

NOTE: This purée is the basis of numerous soups, such as:

Watercress Soup

Add to the purée ¼ lb. leaves of watercress cooked 5 minutes in salted water.

Potage Santé

Add to the purée ¼ lb. sorrel chopped finely and cooked in butter.

Lettuce Soup

Scald the lettuce in salted water, and then put it under cold water. Chop finely and cook in butter. Add to the purée.

Potage à la Reine (for 6–8)

1 3-lb. fowl	3 egg-yolks
2½ pints stock	½ lb. butter
¼ lb. rice	1 gill cream

Cook the fowl in the stock until tender. Remove the fowl. Add rice and cook thoroughly. Bone fowl, retain the breast in fillets. Pound the rest of the flesh, then add the cooked rice and continue to pound into a fine purée. Pass through tammy, diluting with stock. Replace on fire and bring to boil. Withdraw from fire and add butter, cream and well-beaten egg-yolks. Garnish the soup with the breast cut into very small dice. Season to taste.

Green Pea Soup (Potage St. Germain) (for 6)

1 pint large shelled green peas	1 lettuce
	1 green top of leek
Cream and butter	

Cook in salted water the peas, lettuce and leek chopped finely. Strain in colander and retain the stock. Pound in mortar to reduce to a purée and pass through tammy. Dilute with the stock and bring to boiling point. Remove from the fire and add about ½ oz. butter and a little cream.

For a garnish, add a few whole peas previously boiled in water, a few leaves of chervil and small croûtons of bread fried in butter and served separately.

Potage Bonne Femme (for 8–10)

5 whites of leeks	½ oz. salt
1 lb. potatoes	2½ oz. butter
2 quarts tepid water	

Chop leeks and cook in butter. Add the water, potatoes and salt, and cook gently. Before serving, add the butter. Serve with small rounds of toasted bread.

Consommé à la Minute (for 6)

2 lb. beef with all fat removed, and hashed	2½ pints cold water
	Salt to taste

Place meat and water in a casserole and bring very slowly to boiling point. Skim thoroughly. Add salt. After boiling slowly for another 10 minutes, pass through a fine cloth.

Another Method. — Bring the water to the boil with a little salt. Add a stick of celery, a grated carrot, a small chopped onion and a sprig of chervil.

After a few minutes of boiling, add the meat.

Boil very slowly for 10 minutes and pass through a wet cloth.

Lobster Soup (Bisque de homard) (for 8)

  2 *lb. small lobsters*
  2 *oz. carrots*
  2 *oz. onions*
  1 *sprig thyme*
  1 *small bay leaf*
  Few sprigs of parsley
  5 *oz. fresh butter*
  5 *oz. rice*
  1 *small glass brandy*
  1 *gill white wine*
  2½ *pints of stock*
  ½ *oz. salt*
  ½ *gill cream*
  Pepper

Cut the carrots and onions into small dice and brown in butter. Remove the shells from the lobsters, well washed and cut up in small pieces, and chop the flesh finely. Season with salt and a little freshly ground pepper. Add the herbs, brandy and the white wine. Cover with ½ pint of stock and cook for 15 minutes.

Cook separately the rice with the remainder of stock. Add all ingredients and the cooked rice, and pass the whole through tammy. Dilute this purée with ⅛ pint of stock, ⅛ pint of cream, and add the butter. Correct seasoning, adding a pinch of Cayenne pepper.

Only in Marseilles can you obtain all the varied ingredients needed for the authentic Bouillabaisse, including many kinds of shell fish and other sea food

FISH DISHES

Stewed Eels Meusienne (La matelote d'anguille Meusienne) (Nancy)

The Matelote Lorraine is made with carp, pike, large and small barbel or, failing that, eel. Cut the fish in pieces and put in a casserole with salt, pepper, bay leaf, thyme, a minced onion, parsley, 2 cloves, and cover with white or rosé wine. Put on a brisk fire until cooked, remove the fish and keep it warm; strain the stock and pour it over small browned onions and mushrooms; bind this roux with two egg-yolks (no flour) and 3 or 4 tablespoonfuls of cream, whipping it gently without letting it boil; then, in what remains of the stock, warm up the fish on a hot fire; place it in a deep dish upon slices of toasted bread, and pour the whole of the stock over it.

Fillets of Pike in White Butter (Le brochet de Loire au beurre blanc) (Tours)

The pike can be boiled in a court bouillon (see p. 332) or else baked in the oven on a bed of carrots, onions, parsley, thyme, bay leaf, peppercorns, a spray of fennel and moistened with a glass of good white Anjou wine. Once cooked and drained, cover with melted butter, sprinkle with chopped parsley and serve at once.

Beurre Blanc (White Butter) (for 6)

2 tablespoonfuls white vinegar	1 chopped shallot 6 oz. fresh butter
Salt and pepper	

Reduce to half the vinegar with the chopped shallot, salt and pepper; before the reduction is complete, and while still over a hot fire, add 2 oz. butter. When it begins to bubble, remove the saucepan from the fire and add, in small quantities, remainder of butter, shaking the pan constantly without whipping.

Pike cooked in Chablis (Le brochet des settons rôti au Chablis) (Dijon)

Thickly butter a flat gratin dish; sprinkle over it 2 or 3 finely cut shallots; moisten with ½ pint Chablis wine and add 2 or 3 crushed tomatoes. Cut and clean the pike, season with salt and pepper, and place in the middle of the dish. Put in a hot oven, baste every 5 minutes. After cooking for 25–30 minutes it should be well browned.

Serve on a long dish, garnished with slices of lemon and chopped parsley placed round the fish. Add to the sauce about 2 oz. butter. Beat in without boiling. Pass through a sieve and pour over the pike.

Le Saumon Braisé au Vin du Rhin (Strasbourg) (for 4–6)

1 lb. fresh salmon	Sprig of thyme,
½ bottle of Sylvaner	parsley and chervil
1 carrot	1 bay leaf
1 onion	Salt and pepper
2 oz. butter	Cream and lemon juice

Cut the carrot and onion into slices and fry slightly in a casserole. Add the seasoning and Sylvaner. Place the salmon in the casserole and braise in the oven. When cooked, skin and dress on the serving dish. Reduce the sauce slightly, add 2 tablespoonfuls of cream, a tablespoonful of lemon juice and bind with Hollandaise sauce (see p. 333). Cover the fish with the sauce, and garnish with a few mushrooms, pieces of puff pastry and slices of truffle.

Le Sole au plat à la Rochellaise (Bordeaux)

Cover the soles in dry white wine, with chopped shallots, mushrooms cut in small pieces and crushed tomatoes; season strongly with salt, pepper and paprika.

Poach on a low fire for about 10 minutes. When cooked, drain and keep them warm. Add to the sauce half a glass of white vinegar and some cream and reduce. Add Hollandaise sauce (see p. 333) and heat slightly on a corner of the fire. Garnish with shelled shrimps; add lemon juice in suitable quantity to flavour.

Cover the soles with this sauce, brown under the grill and place a large slice of truffle on each sole before serving.

Les Filets de Sole à la façon du pêcheur Cauchois (Rouen) (for 6)

12 good-sized sole fillets	2 glasses well-flavoured stock
2 carrots and an equal amount of parsley root	2 oz. butter Juice of 1 lemon
2 sticks of celery	1 tablespoonful chopped parsley
6 mushrooms	Few small heads of
2 glasses of white wine	blanched mushrooms
Few shelled shrimps	

Chop into dice the carrots, parsley root, and celery, and blanch well. Chop the mushrooms and keep them aside. Put the fillets of sole in a well-buttered pan, add the wine, stock, carrots, parsley root, celery and mushrooms. Place over a hot fire and bring to the boil. When cooked, remove fillets and arrange them on a dish diagonally. Drain the vegetables and arrange around the dish.

Stir the sauce and cook gently until it reduces and thickens. Remove from the fire and add butter, lemon juice, chopped parsley, small heads of mushrooms and shelled shrimps. Cover the fish with the sauce and serve very hot.

Le Turbotin Braisé au Champagne Brut (Rheims) (for 6–8)

1 chicken turbot	Parsley
1 bottle Brut Champagne	Cream 4 oz. butter
¼ lb. shallots	Juice of 1 lemon
2 onions	Few braised mushrooms
Chervil	

Slice the onions and shallots, and add chervil and parsley to form a bed in a casserole. Add champagne. Butter the turbot and place in the casserole. Braise in a moderate oven, basting frequently.

When cooked, strain and place on the serving dish. Reduce the liquor, add butter, juice of a lemon and a little cream. Place over the fish a few braised mushrooms and pour the sauce over it.

COOKERY AT HOME AND ABROAD

TWO DISHES FROM ITALY

Selected by P. G. Leoni of Leoni's Quo Vadis Restaurant, London

SUPREME DE VOLAILLE YOLANDA (above). Cut white meat from breast of a chicken with the wing bone, beat out flat. Pass through flour, beaten egg, and grated Parmesan cheese. Fry in oil until golden, arrange three spears of asparagus on top, sprinkle with grated cheese, add a walnut of butter and grill for a few minutes.

CANETON NOEMI (FROID) (below). Prepare a roast duck and serve cold with this sauce: Sieve contents of a small tin of tunny fish. Add 3 tablespoonfuls each of mayonnaise and cream and enough tomato ketchup to tint pink. Mix, season with pepper and salt. Mask the duck with cold sauce, decorate with a border of cherries. Garnish with triangles of chopped cooked tomatoes, aubergines, courgettes bound with mayonnaise and covered with sauce and gelatine.

COOKERY AT HOME AND ABROAD

NORWAY

Typical Scandinavian cold table (above): Ham, sliced thin and rolled with lettuce; roast lamb, also rolled; Italian salad; beetroot; salami with cauliflower; egg and tomato boats with cucumber; mixed vegetable plate—and to finish with, a whole gorgonzola cheese with biscuits

POLAND

Chlodnik is a Polish cold soup (right). Its rich red colouring comes from the beetroot it contains. It is served chilled with fresh cucumber, lettuce, etc., and sour cream added at the last moment. Served hot with different accompaniments, this soup is the famous Barszcz

Homard à l'Américaine
(Classical Modern) (for 6)

1 *lobster (about 2 lb.)*
4 *tablespoonfuls*
  olive oil
2 *tablespoonfuls*
  butter
5 *tablespoonfuls*
  brandy
4 *oz. butter*
1 *gill dry white wine*
2 *chopped shallots*
6 *peeled, pipped,*
  chopped tomatoes
1 *clove garlic*
Pinch of parsley
½ *lemon*
Salt and pepper
Chopped parsley and chervil

Split the lobster down the middle. Remove the pocket at the top of the head. Put on one side the creamy part which will be found at the side of the pocket, crush with a fork on a plate and mix in a spoonful of butter. Remove the claws, crack the shell to remove the meat after it is boiled; cut each half of the lobster in three pieces; season with salt and pepper.

Heat the oil with a tablespoonful of butter. Place the pieces of lobster in the boiling sauce. Toss over the fire until they take on a bright red colour; sprinkle in the brandy and wine; add the shallots, garlic, tomatoes and parsley; cover the saucepan, cook for 20 minutes.

Place the pieces in a deep dish; mix with the liquid the creamy part removed from the pocket at the top of the head. Keep warm, without cooking, and add in small pieces the ¼ lb. butter and the lemon juice. Sprinkle with parsley and chervil finely chopped.

The culinary art goes really gay—a roast is intricately and beautifully decorated with a flower design by a Paris chef

MEAT AND POULTRY

Braising (L'estouffade) (Classical) (for 6)

2 *lb. ribs of beef*   ½ *oz. salt*
½ *lb. lean bacon*   *Pinch of pepper*
3 *medium-sized*   ½ *lb. mushrooms*
  onions   1 *quart red wine*
1 *clove garlic*   1 *quart veal fonds*
1 *bouquet garni*   *Butter*

Cut the beef in small squares of about 4 oz. Cut the bacon in large dice. Blanch, fry and drain it. In the same fat, fry lightly the pieces of beef and the onions cut in quarters. Drain the fat and pour in the red wine and the veal fonds thickened. Add the garlic crushed, the bouquet garni, salt and pepper, and cook in a covered saucepan in a slow oven for 4 hours. Add the bacon and the mushrooms fried in butter. Remove any fat from the sauce and simmer for another 30 minutes.

Truffles (Le filet de bœuf à la Sarladaise)
(Périgueux) (for 12)

4 *lb. fillet of beef*   *Truffles*

For the marinade

½ *bottle white wine*   1 *tablespoonful*
2 *tablespoonfuls*   *chopped thyme*
  brandy   *Bay leaf*
Sliced onion   *Clove of garlic*
1 *tablespoonful*   *Salt and pepper*
  chopped parsley

Lard the beef and stick with truffles. Souse it overnight in the marinade. Remove the fillet and place the marinade on one side. Cover the fillet well with butter and roast, basting frequently with the marinade mixture. Remove the fillet, which should be blood-red when cut. Use the remainder of the marinade to drain the dish and obtain a thick, well-flavoured gravy. Serve with potatoes and truffles cut into rounds and sautéd in butter. Serve the gravy separately.

Stewed Oxtail (La queue de bœuf en hochepot à la façon du Cambrésis) (Amiens) (for 5)

1 oxtail	Salt and pepper
2 boned calves' feet	10 small chipolata
Carrots, onions,	sausages
thyme, bay leaf,	1 lettuce
garlic	Dry white wine and
Bacon rinds	stock
Few mushroom tops	

Slice the carrots and onions and add thyme, bay leaf, and garlic to form a bed in a casserole. Joint the oxtail and place the pieces on the bed of vegetables. Add bacon rinds, boned calves' feet, and leave in the oven for ½ hour. Steep all the pieces in dry white wine and stock mixed. Season with salt and pepper, cover with a buttered paper and cook for 4 hours in a gentle oven.

When the pieces are cooked, remove them into a sauté pan, skim the sauce well and strain. Cut the bacon rinds in coarse shreds and put them back with blanched mushroom tops, braised carrots, chipolata sausages, small onions and lettuce braised in butter. Simmer for ½ hour.

Serve very hot with baked potatoes.

Leg of Lamb with Vegetables (La gasconnade de fins-gigots aux légumes nouveaux) (Bayonne) (for 8)

Thickly butter a nice plump leg of lamb, graft a good clove of garlic in the knuckle and roast on a flat dish. Brown on the dish a few small slightly smoked lardons (strips of fat bacon) and cook in a slow heat, basting frequently.

Separately, sauté in a pan a few chopped shallots, with very finely cut celery. Prepare carrots and turnips, 2 pints of green peas, a few tops of mushrooms and small spring onions, and sauté in butter. When this garnish becomes mellow and light brown, add it to the leg a short while before serving.

Serve the meat, which must be pink under the knife.

Rinse the meat dish with a dash of Madeira and a few tablespoonfuls of white fonds (see p. 331). Simmer for a few moments. Sprinkle with chopped parsley.

Poulet à la Crème (Classical) (for 6)

1 3-lb. chicken	2 egg-yolks
6 small onions, peeled	2 oz. butter
2 cloves of garlic	Bouquet garni
1 oz. lean bacon	1 glass of very dry
1 pint fresh cream	white wine

Into a casserole put the butter, the bacon diced and blanched, the onions, bouquet garni and garlic. Melt on a low fire. Put in the chicken cut in pieces, salt, and stir with a wooden spoon so that nothing sticks to the bottom of the casserole. Cook until a light brown. Put the casserole on a very low fire. Cover and cook for 20 minutes. Remove the pieces of chicken and keep them warm; drain off all the grease. Add the glass of white wine and reduce.

In the meantime, mix the yolks with the cream and add this to the mixture in the casserole, stirring all the time, but do not let it boil again. Add the portions of chicken to the sauce, warm it up, and season.

La Poulet Sauté comme à Chambéry (Grenoble)

1 tender chicken	Few lardons (strips
2 oz. butter	of fat bacon)
½ pint Chambéry	½ lb. artichokes
vermouth	¼ pint cream
Few small mush-	Paprika
rooms	Chopped parsley

Cut the chicken in pieces and brown in the butter. Add the Chambéry vermouth, small tops of mushrooms, lardons, artichokes blanched and cut in four, cream, and a dash of paprika. Continue cooking for about 20 minutes.

Serve the chicken; season and complete the sauce with a few spoonfuls of cream. Serve very hot with a sprinkling of chopped parsley.

A dish to make a hostess famous in a night—Pancakes in the French manner, flavoured with brandy

La Poularde Sautée à la Nantaise (Nantes)

1 *young chicken*	1 *glass white*
1 *onion, minced*	*Muscadet wine*
1 *carrot, minced*	*Vinegar*
2 *oz. butter*	1 *shallot, chopped*
Bouquet garni	*Hollandaise sauce*
Salt, pepper and	*(see p. 333)*
paprika	

For the garnish

Mushrooms	*Carrots*
Small onions	*Artichokes*

Put into a casserole the onion, carrot, bouquet garni, salt and pepper, butter and chicken. Cook over a moderate fire for a few minutes, add the wine, dash of vinegar, and continue cooking for 30–40 minutes, according to size of the chicken. Place the chicken in an earthenware dish.

To the juice remaining in the casserole add the chopped shallot and reduce strongly. Add vinegar to taste, and increase with the Hollandaise sauce. As a garnish, add mushrooms cut in quarters, small onions, carrots cut in four, and a dice of artichoke bottoms, all blanched. Season to taste, use paprika lightly, in order that the sauce may retain a golden tint; cover the chicken with the sauce and garnish.

Sprinkle with finely chopped herbs.

Le Poulet Sauté à la manière des Vignerons Tourangeaux (Tours)

Brown in good butter a handful of small onions, a generous helping of small leeks cut in strips, lardons (strips of bacon), small heads of mushrooms and crushed tomatoes. When this garnish has taken a good colour, add a bottle of Vouvray, a tablespoonful of cream; season with salt, pepper and paprika. In a separate pan cook in butter some quarters of chicken and, when nicely coloured, simmer with the sauce until quite cooked. If necessary, finish the binding with double cream. Just before serving, sprinkle with chopped parsley and serve very hot.

La Fricassée du Poulet à l'ancienne
(Classical) (for 6–8)

1 *4-lb. chicken*	½ *gill stock*
2 *oz. butter*	½ *gill cream*
½ *lb. small onions*	3 *egg-yolks*
½ *lb. white mush-*	2 *tablespoonfuls flour*
rooms	*Bouquet garni*
Lemon juice, salt and pepper	

Cut the chicken in pieces, season with salt and pepper; fry lightly with the butter in a pan without browning. Sprinkle in the flour. Cook for a few minutes without browning. Pour in the stock and cook for 15 minutes. Drain out the pieces of chicken and place in a fresh pan, adding the onions partly cooked and the raw mushrooms. Pour over all the sauce passed through a pointed strainer. Add the bouquet garni and cook very slowly for about 40 minutes. At the last moment, give body to the sauce with the yolks mixed with the cream and a little lemon juice.

Le Caneton farci et mijoté à l'ancienne mode de Provence (Marseilles)

1 duckling	A few stoned green
Périgueux or Brown	olives
Sauces (see Sauces	¼ lb. artichoke
Chapter)	bottoms
Madeira	Tops of mushrooms

For the stuffing

½ lb. streaky bacon	Egg-yolk
Duckling liver	20 black olives
2 or 3 chopped onions	20 white mushrooms
½ teaspoonful fried	Few Jamaica peppers
shallot	Truffles
Pepper and salt	Armagnac

To make the stuffing.—Boil the bacon until almost cooked, then mince finely. Add the liver, chopped onions, shallot, salt and pepper and mix well. Bind with the egg-yolk. Stone the olives and chop with the mushrooms, Jamaica peppers, and mix with the hash. Add a few dice of truffles, moisten with a good dash of Armagnac.

Stuff the duckling with this, 24 hours before cooking. Braise, adding a rich Périgueux sauce well moistened with Madeira, quarters of artichoke bottoms, tops of mushrooms, and a few stoned green olives. Allow 20 minutes per lb. for cooking.

Jugged Hare (Classical) (for 6–8)

1 4-lb. hare	7 oz. streaky bacon
20 small peeled	cut into dice and
onions	blanched
5 crushed cloves of	Bouquet garni
garlic	4 oz. butter
5 minced shallots	3 tablespoonfuls flour
2½ pints red wine	1 glass brandy
Salt and pepper	

Skin and clean the hare, taking care to collect all the blood, and the liver. Carve the hare into equal portions of 1½–2 oz. each. Place the butter in a sauté pan and lightly brown the bacon. Drain and spread on a plate. In the same butter, brown the small onions, drain, and keep on one side with the bacon.

Season the hare with salt and pepper, place in the pan and brown on a quick fire. Add the shallots, garlic and the flour. Cook for a few moments, add the wine and brandy, bring to the boil, skim, add the bouquet garni, the bacon and the small onions. Cover, and cook on a slow fire.

Chop the liver finely, mix with the blood and, when the hare is cooked, blend the sauce with this mixture but do not allow it to boil.

Le Civet de Lièvre de Diane de Château-morand (Belley) (for 6–8)

1 hare	¼ pint stock
1 oz. fat pork	1 tablespoonful
2½ oz. butter	olive oil
1 oz. flour	¼ pint good red wine

For the marinade

1 wineglassful	2 onions
wine vinegar	Pepper and salt
½ wineglassful	Thyme
olive oil	

Skin and gut the hare, carefully preserving the blood and the liver. Place the hare in a tureen large enough to hold it whole, pour over it the vinegar and olive oil. Season with pepper, salt and thyme, and 1 onion cut in rounds. Turn the hare frequently in this marinade and leave for 12 hours at least before cooking.

Chop together the onion and pork, cut the hare in pieces and cook the whole in butter for 20 minutes, when the flesh will have taken on a white-grey colour and exuded its moisture. Sprinkle with the flour and cook slowly for 25 minutes, stirring frequently. Pour in the stock and red wine. Add seasoning and cook for another 35 minutes.

Pound the black liver to a fine purée and dilute with the marinade after removing the onion and thyme. Mix the blood with it and pass through a sieve. Pour the whole preparation over the hare 5 minutes before serving, and bring to the boil. Try the sauce and, if it is insipid, season with a dash of vinegar. Finish by adding a tablespoonful of olive oil.

This can be made on the eve of the day when it is to be eaten, as it is better when warmed up. Its succulence depends on the quality of the hare and on the quantity of blood gathered; the colour of the ragoût must be like chocolate boiled in water. (*After Lucien Tendret.*)

Rice Pilaw (Pilaff de riz)

9 *oz. Patna rice*	1 *tablespoonful*
4 *oz. butter*	*chopped onion*
1 *pint stock*	*Pinch of salt*

Cook the onion in 2 oz. butter in a casserole until golden brown. Mix in the rice with a wooden spoon until it is well blended with hot butter and add salt. Have boiling stock ready and pour over it. Cover the casserole with a tight-fitting lid and put it in the oven for 18 minutes. When

In Brittany they wear their colourful national costumes (above) to serve their famous regional dishes

A Soufflé (right) is not an extravagant or a difficult dish to make—and what a thrill when it comes out of the oven looking like that

Artichokes à la Greque

15 *small artichokes*
1¾ *pints water*
¼ *pint olive oil*
⅓ *oz. salt*
Juice of 3 lemons
Sprig of thyme
1 *bay leaf*
Few whole pepper-corns
1 *stick of celery*

Soufflé by Creda. All other photographs in this chapter: French Government Tourist Office

Trim the artichokes, cut into four, remove fibrous part, blanch in boiling water with lemon juice, strain and cool. Boil together all the other ingredients, which will constitute a marinade. Cook the artichokes in the marinade. Take the pan off the fire and let them cool down in the marinade. This same marinade may be used for cauliflowers, small onions, leeks, squash, celery, etc.

cooked, mix in quickly 2 oz. butter in small pieces.

CLASSICAL PASTRY RECIPES

Short Pastry (La pâte à foncer)

1 *lb. flour*	½ *oz. salt*
10 *oz. butter*	1 *egg*
2 *oz. sugar*	¼ *pint water*

Cream the butter, spread the flour in a circle, making a well. Mix the butter with the sugar, egg and salt, and place in the middle, incorporating flour and water. Do not knead, but beat and shape into a ball, and keep in a cool place.

Noodles (La pâte à nouilles)

1 lb. flour	5 egg-yolks
4 whole eggs	½ oz. salt

Mix the flour and salt with the eggs. Knead several times to obtain a well-mixed paste, and let it rest for 1 hour. Cut it in long thin strips, and lightly dry, spread over a cloth.

Poach the noodles for 10–12 minutes.

Pancakes (La pâte à crêpes) (for 6–8)

½ lb. flour	1¾ pints milk
3 oz. sugar	1 glass of brandy
Pinch of salt	2 tablespoonfuls of
6 eggs	orange flower water

Put the flour, sugar and salt in a bowl and add the eggs. Mix until smooth and thin out with the milk. Add the brandy and orange flower water at the last moment before cooking.

Batter (La pâte à frire)

¼ lb. flour	½ pint lukewarm
Pinch of salt	water
2 tablespoonfuls	2 egg-whites
olive oil	

Place all except the egg-whites in a bowl. Mix well without working the paste. Just before using, add the egg-whites whipped to a snow.

Les Madeleines

5 eggs	½ teaspoonful
½ lb. castor sugar	lemon-flavoured
½ lb. clarified butter	sugar
7 oz. flour	Pinch of salt

Mix in a bowl the sugar, salt and 2 eggs. Whip the mixture until it is quite white. Add the other 3 eggs, one at a time, always whipping. When the mixture is a stiff froth, add alternately the flour, passed through a sieve, and the clarified butter, folding it carefully into the mixture. Put the mixture into special tins of "madeleine" shape and cook in a moderately hot oven.

Le Soufflé (for 4)

1 gill milk	1 oz. potato flour
2 oz. sugar	3 egg-yolks
Pinch of salt	½ oz. butter
4 egg-whites	

Mix the flour with 2 tablespoonfuls of cold milk. Boil the rest of the milk with the sugar and salt, and pour over the flour paste. Cook the mixture for 2 minutes and, while still stirring, remove from the fire and add the egg-yolks and the butter. Mix well and add suitable flavouring to taste. At the last moment, add the whites whipped to a stiff froth. Cook in a moderate oven.

Custard (La crème Anglaise) (for 4)

1 pint milk	4 oz. sugar
½ pod vanilla	8 egg-yolks

Boil the milk with the vanilla; whisk the egg-yolks and sugar and pour the milk over them. Cook this cream over the fire, stirring constantly until nearly boiling.

To keep this mixture a really creamy texture, add, if liked, ½ oz. of arrowroot to the yolks when beating.

Fritters (Les beignets soufflés) (for 6–8)

½ pint water	¼ oz. sugar
1¾ oz. butter	4 eggs
Pinch of salt	6 oz. flour

Put into a saucepan the water, butter, salt and sugar, and bring to the boil. Shake in the flour, previously passed through a sieve. Work it into a paste until it forms a thick cream and will easily leave the sides. Remove from the fire and add the eggs one by one, continuing to knead the paste. Flavour to taste with lemon, vanilla, etc.

To cook.—Place in moderately heated fat, pieces of the paste the size of a walnut. Heat gradually until a golden brown. Remove and drain. Sprinkle with soft sugar.

Soufflé Surprise du Château Trompette à Bordeaux (Bordeaux) (for 6–8)

5 egg-yolks	1 lb. castor sugar
8 egg-whites	

Whisk the egg-yolks and castor sugar until thick and creamy. Whip separately the egg-whites until stiff and mix all together, using a butter pat.

Set out in a silver dish, finger-biscuits steeped in a liqueur (preferably Grand Marnier). Cover with a vanilla ice. Pour out the egg mixture in a tall heap. Smooth with the butter-pat to give it a regular shape, and decorate.

Glaze in a hot oven for 2 or 3 minutes. Serve at once. Flame.

To flame.—Place over it 2 or 3 egg-shells containing the liqueur. Set fire to it and shake the shells so that the burning liqueur runs over the sides of the soufflé.

RESTAURANT FRENCH

A handy guide to some of the French terms you may find
on the menu and with which you may not be quite familiar

Abricot: Apricot.

À la carte: Indicates choice of any dish shown.

Aloyau de bœuf: Beef, sirloin of.

Ananas: Pineapple.

Anchois: Anchovy.

Anguille: Eel.

Asperges: Asparagus.

Bœuf: Beef.

Bombe: A moulded ice cream, probably including a richer ice cream, fruit and nuts.

Bouchées: Very small patties of puff paste with savoury fillings.

Café au lait: Coffee, white.

Café noir: Coffee, black.

Canapés: Small savouries; various shapes of fried or toasted bread with savoury toppings.

Canard rôti: Duck, roast.

Canard sauvage: Duck, wild.

Carrelet: Plaice.

Champignons: Mushrooms.

Chaudfroid: A sauce, of which Béchamel is the base, for masking cold, cooked meats. A cold entrée.

Chou-fleur: Cauliflower.

Consommé: Clear meat soup, served hot, or cold and jellied.

Consommé de volaille: Chicken soup.

Côte de bœuf rôtie: Beef, roast of.

Côtelettes d'Agneau: Lamb cutlets.

Crêpes: Pancakes.

Entrecôte: A steak cut from the sirloin.

Entrée: A hot or cold side dish.

Entremets douceurs: Sweets.

Escalopes: Thin steaks cut from fillet or leg of veal, usually egg and bread-crumbed and lightly cooked in sauté pan.

Faisan: Pheasant.

Foie-gras: A savoury paste of goose liver and herbs served with thin toast.

Fraises: Strawberries.

Framboises: Raspberries.

Fricandeau: Fillet of veal, larded and braised.

Fromage: Cheese.

Fruits confits: Preserved fruits.

Gigot de mouton: Leg of mutton.

Haricots verts: French beans.

Hollandaise: Well-known sauce of which butter is the base.

Homard: Lobster.

Jambon: Ham.

Légumes: Vegetables.

Lièvre en casserole: Hare, jugged.

Maître d'hôtel: Well-known garnish of chopped parsley pounded with butter, seasoned with salt, pepper and lemon juice.

Maquereau: Mackerel.

Marrons glacés: Chestnuts, glazed.

Mornay: Well-known sauce, Béchamel base with finely grated Gruyère or Parmesan cheese added.

Navarin: Haricot mutton.

Nouilles: Noodles.

Oie rôtie: Goose, roast.

Oignons: Onions.

Pêche: Peach.

Perdrix: Partridge.

Petits pois: Green peas.

Poire: Pear.

Poisson: Fish.

Pommes-de-terre: Potatoes.

Potage: Soup.

Potage lyonnais: Onion soup.

Potage parmentier: Potato soup.

Poulet rôti: Chicken, roast.

Poussin: Baby chicken.

Prunes: Plums.

Purée de lentilles: Lentil soup.

Ragoût: Meat stew.

Raisins: Grapes.

Ris de veau: Sweetbreads.

Rognons: Kidneys.

Saumon: Salmon.

Selle de mouton: Saddle of mutton.

Soufflé: A very light egg dish, sweet or savoury.

Table d'hôte: A set meal, usually consisting of Soup or Hors d'œuvres; Meat or Fish; Sweet or Biscuits and Cheese.

Tête de veau: Calf's head.

Tournedos: Small, thinly sliced fillets of beef.

Veau: Veal.

SWITZERLAND

Some typically simple peasant dishes described by the proprietors of Maison Suisse and Bartholdi's Restaurant and Stores, London

THEY eat well in Switzerland. The Swiss as a nation are interested in good food and their fare is distinguished by a glorious variety—not surprisingly, when one considers the geography of the country. The best dishes of three neighbouring lands go to make up those wonderful meals which impress the tourists in Switzerland. But the cuisine in the hotels is too international to be characteristic. The dishes given here, often very simple and peasant in origin, are those found in the homes of the Swiss people—in town homes as well as in remote mountain châlets. They represent the traditional fare of Switzerland, influenced by French cuisine in the south-western region, Italian in the southern, and German in the northern and eastern parts.

The geographical position of a region, the Swiss dairy produce—the plentiful milk, butter, eggs and well-known cheeses, such as Gruyère, Emmenthaler, Appenzeller and Vacherin—and the mountain air (whetting the appetite!) determine the type —and quantity—of the food.

The famous **Fondue** is a truly Swiss national cheese dish, made all over the country and particularly in the French-speaking parts.

It is a fine dish to return to on a cold winter's night, and its method of serving and consumption is very much a family, domestic affair.

To make it, the Swiss housewife allows about 6 oz. of Gruyère or Emmenthaler cheese and a wineglassful of white wine (preferably a dry wine) for each member of her family. She rubs garlic around the inside of an iron pot or fireproof earthenware dish or heavy saucepan, and puts in a piece of butter to keep the cheese from sticking. She then adds the cheese, grated, with half the quantity of wine, and puts it on a very low heat to melt and come to the boil, stirring it constantly. After about 20 minutes, she adds the rest of the wine. It should now have a batter-like consistency.

Meanwhile the family has gathered round the table, each member armed with a piece of bread impaled on a fork (preferably French bread with a strong crust). The housewife puts the pot or dish on the table over a spirit flame to keep the cheese at boiling point, with just a bubble now and then working up. The family then gets to work. Each member dips his or her piece of bread in the dish, twisting the fork to wind the strands of cheese safely round the bread—and then just eats it off the fork, dipping in more bread until the pot is empty. That is all—except that Kirsch should be drunk with it. In some districts a liqueur glass of Kirsch is added to the pot, but this is frowned on elsewhere as confusing the flavours. No other course to the meal is needed—the *fondue* is enough to satisfy any appetite.

There are several variations. Some people, for instance, add onions, cut into large pieces, to the pot, and some add a little cornflour. Strong-flavoured local cheeses are often used, and gherkins eaten with the *fondue*. Cider can be used instead of wine.

Raclette is another favourite cheese dish of great simplicity—to make a snack meal. A slab of Gruyère is held against the fire or put under the grill. As the cheese melts it is scraped off with a knife, put on a plate, and eaten with crusty bread and gherkins.

Dishes from the Northern and Eastern Regions

These dishes are made everywhere, but are mainly characteristic of the German-speaking areas (the larger part of Switzerland).

Bernerplatte is a well-known Swiss dish

turnips, *Sauerkraut*, potatoes. . . . A little of the meat liquor is served also.

Rippli is smoked and salted loin of pork cooked on a layer of *Sauerkraut*. To make this for 4 persons, put about 1½ lb. of *Sauerkraut* and 2 lb. of pork in a big saucepan, with just enough water not to have to throw any away at the end. Simmer until the meat is ready and

With appetites whetted by the mountain air, visitors to Switzerland enjoy a meal served by waiters on skates. Below, a typical home scene—serving the famous Fondue is a very domestic affair

Photos: Swiss National Tourist Office and Swiss Federal Railways

Everyone comes to the table armed with a piece of bread impaled on a fork—and dips in the Fondue that bubbles merrily in a fireproof bowl over a lighted spirit lamp

only a little juice left. Potatoes are sometimes cooked in the same saucepan.

Speck und Bohnen is another popular dish in Swiss homes. Fry onions in a big pan, add runner beans and toss them in the fat, then add a piece of bacon and water to cover it. Simmer until the bacon is cooked.

Sausages of all kinds and smoked ham are much in evidence. Among the sausages, **Cervelat** is a favourite, composed of beef and pork. The Swiss take the skin off, cut it into very thin slices and serve it with "heaps of onions," sliced and dressed with oil and vinegar.

—and an elaborate one when it appears in its full glory. It consists of an assortment of boiled meats, served hot. As many as ten kinds of meat can be used—fresh beef, salt beef, streaky bacon, tongue, Frankfürter and other boiled sausages, perhaps a piece of boiled calf's head, and so on. With this noble array a variety of vegetables is served—cabbage, celery, leeks,

Bratwurst, a veal sausage made with milk, is fried and eaten with a salad—perhaps a cabbage salad (white cabbage shredded very finely and dressed with oil and vinegar). And it may be accompanied by *roesti*.

Roesti is a simple dish, found everywhere in Switzerland. To prepare this, boil potatoes in their jackets, peel and let them go cold before using. Then slice or shred them. Fry some sliced onions in shallow fat, add the potatoes, and fry to a golden brown. This must be done quickly and the *roesti* served as soon as ready. If the potatoes are shredded, it can be turned out like a pancake. This is eaten with a meat dish or on its own. Swiss farmers like it for breakfast.

Knoepfli is a favourite dish in Swiss homes. For this, make a thick dough with ½ lb. of plain flour, two eggs, milk and salt. It must be well beaten. Let it stand for an hour or so, if possible. Have a large saucepan ready with boiling salted water. Put some of the dough on a small board and, from this, cut thin strips straight into the water. Do small quantities at a time. When the strips come to the top (after about 2 minutes), they are cooked. Put them into a dish with grated cheese on top and melted butter or breadcrumbs fried in butter.

Dishes from the Southern and Western Regions

Swiss dishes from these parts naturally show French and Italian influences. Spaghetti and other *pasta* are used a great deal.

Croûton au Fromage.—Make a pancake batter with milk and egg. Cut pieces of Emmenthaler cheese about 1 in. square and ¼ in. thick. Put them into the batter and lift them out again, well coated, with the help of two forks. Fry them in deep fat.

The following is a popular variation of the Italian **Gnocchi,** using potatoes, which give lightness to the dish.

Mix ½ lb. of flour with ½ lb. of boiled and mashed potatoes; make into a paste with two beaten eggs and a little milk. Roll it out, then roll it up and cut it on the slant into pieces about the size of a nut. Press each piece with a fork into a cockleshell shape. Then let them dry for a time,

with a little flour sprinkled under and over them. Drop them into a pan of boiling salted water, and boil for about 20 minutes. Lift them out and cook in butter until golden. Serve with a sauce made with chopped onion, garlic and well-fried tomatoes, and sprinkle with grated Parmesan cheese.

Ricotta is found in the Ticino district. After cheese is made, the residue is treated to produce a curd. This curd, when fresh, is beaten up with eggs, salt and pepper, and fried in butter.

The Italian **Polenta** is made in Switzerland as follows: Boil maize flour in a copper pan of boiling salted water for about 20 minutes to make a stiff paste. Work a piece of butter into it. Let it cool, then cut it up and sauté in butter, or serve as it is with a brown sauce. Or press the *polenta* into buttered moulds lined with plenty of grated cheese. Turn out and eat with meat dishes.

Morilles.—Mushrooms are a favourite food in Switzerland, and people climb the slopes gathering them. Here is a dish popular in Lausanne and Geneva, using the wild mushrooms, *morilles* (obtainable in tins in the U.K.). Sauté the mushrooms in butter with chopped shallots, according to taste, and a very little garlic. Add fresh cream, salt and pepper, and simmer. Add a little butter when cooked. Dish up and keep hot. Thicken the sauce with cornflour and pour over. This is served as a separate dish. The ordinary field mushrooms are also cooked in this way, but *morilles* give a finer flavour.

Soup is a very regular feature of Swiss fare, but there is none specifically Swiss. Vegetable soup with a meat base is the most common.

Similarly, the sweets, cakes and pastries which delight the visitors in the hotels are mostly French and Austrian in origin. Switzerland does not even claim the familiar "Swiss Roll." (This is said to have been invented by a Swiss chef.) In Swiss homes, cheese and fruit tend to take the place of a sweet course.

The celebrated Swiss black cherry jam is, however, a national speciality and is exported as such. The fruit is kept whole in the syrup. It is served at breakfast.

Italian table-ware, hand-painted by Mancioli, in olive green and black on white, from Bentall's

ITALY

Where cooking is infinitely varied and even spaghetti is served differently in each province

"*A TAVOLA non s'invec-chia*"—"at table one does not grow old." This is an old Italian proverb which is also a most appropriate one. In Italy a good deal of time is spent at the table, and the preparation of good food is a natural pride of every Italian housewife.

Italian cooking is most varied. Each region—indeed, each province—has its own specialities, and even dishes which might loosely be termed national vary considerably from place to place. Thus, when talking of Italian cooking, we must visualise a whole series of regional cuisines rather than, as in most other countries, a mass of national dishes with here and there a leavening of local specialities.

Spaghetti—most popular and best known of all Italian dishes—is a case in point. In Bologna it would be served with a rich sauce of minced meat and mushrooms, whereas in Naples it would be eaten with a thin watery sauce or perhaps with *vongole*. These are small Mediterranean shell-fish something like cockles.

Vegetables play an important part in the Italian menu. These, when in season, are plentiful, varied and cheap. Not only are they cooked in a great variety of ways, they are also used raw in salads with olive oil,

vinegar or lemon juice, salt and pepper. In this way they are usually eaten as an *antipasto*—hors d'œuvres. The most popular are perhaps sweet peppers or capsicums—yellow, red and green—but celery, fennel, globe artichokes and cardoons are among the vegetables eaten in this way. Green salads, too, are served every day in most households. Potatoes are not as popular as they are in the U.K., and certainly do not appear at every meal. They are used fairly extensively in soups and gnocchi, but only occasionally as a vegetable.

Italy, being an agricultural country, produces a great variety of cheeses. Because of this, cheese is used as a condiment in a large number of dishes. In Southern Italy, Peccorino cheese, made from goats' milk, and Mozzarella, a soft creamy cheese made of buffalo milk, are very popular. Northern Italy, and especially the Lombardy plain, produces lovely cheese in great variety—Gorgonzola, Parmesan, Bel Paese, Fontina, Stracchino, Mascarpone are just a few of the most popular and have become world famous.

Puddings are hardly ever served. A meal usually ends with fresh fruit, which is varied, plentiful and cheap. Particularly delicious are the famous *pesche di vigna*—

large, luscious peaches grown between rows of grape vines—but there are also figs, both mauve and white, dripping with syrup, apricots, cherries, Palermo blood oranges from Sicily, walnuts from Sorrento, to mention only a few.

Margarine and dripping are rarely used. Instead, the Italian housewife turns to butter, olive oil and, in Southern Italy, lard.

Italy also produces wines in great variety, both red and white, among which Chianti, Barbaresco, Barolo, Asti spumante and Marsala are perhaps the best known.

HORS D'ŒUVRES (Antipasto)

One of the most popular ways of beginning a meal is with a large dish of *affettato*, which consists of thin slices of mixed salami, cooked and raw, such as Coppa (salted loin of pork), Mortadella and Parma Ham. This is a delicious specially cured unsmoked ham, which is sliced very thinly and eaten with fresh figs or iced melon.

Tunny Salad (Insalata di tonno)

1 *can tunny fish*	1 *Spanish onion*
Olive oil	*Vinegar*
Salt and pepper	*Parsley (optional)*

Break tunny fish into small pieces and add finely sliced onion. Mix with olive oil, vinegar, salt and pepper. A little chopped parsley can be added, but this is optional.

Poached Eggs with Green Sauce (Uova in camicia con salsa verde)

1 *egg per person*	1 *small tomato*
2 *fillets of anchovies*	½ *clove of garlic*
1 *small onion*	*Olive oil*
Salt and pepper	*Parsley*
1 *tablespoonful vinegar*	

Poach the eggs in salted water to which the vinegar has been added, drain well, and when cold cover with the following sauce: Chop very finely the parsley, tomato, anchovy fillets, garlic and onion, put into a basin and mix with olive oil, vinegar, salt and pepper. The sauce should be quite thick, so plenty of parsley must be used.

Calf's Head Salad (Insalata di testina di vitello)

½ *calf's head*	2 *onions*
1 *clove of garlic*	2 *carrots*
1 *bay leaf*	1 *stick of celery*
Olive oil	*Vinegar*
Salt, pepper and	*A little dry mustard*
peppercorns	*Lettuce*
Chopped parsley	

Wash the calf's head thoroughly, put into a saucepan, cover with cold water and bring to the boil. Skim well, add celery, carrots, one onion, garlic, salt, peppercorns and bay leaf. Boil again. Lower heat and cook slowly until tender. Allow to cool slightly, then cut into small pieces, add a finely sliced Spanish onion and a tablespoonful of chopped parsley and cover with a salad dressing of olive oil, vinegar, dry mustard, salt and pepper.

One of the many variations of the famous savoury, Pizza, specially made at Forte's

Each province of Italy has its own particular Fritto Misto. In Florence it is cooked in olive oil, in Milan in butter—but it always contains a variety of ingredients

Sliced Tomatoes with Anchovies (Pomidori affettate con acciughe)

3 *large firm tomatoes*   *Lettuce*
Vinegar   *Fillets of anchovies*
Pepper   *Olive oil*
         Chopped parsley

Cut the tomatoes into fairly thin slices and place on a dish lined with lettuce leaves. On each slice place a rolled fillet of anchovy, then pour on a salad dressing of olive oil, vinegar, pepper, and sprinkle with chopped parsley. A little salt can be added, but be sparing with it as the anchovies are salty.

SOUPS (Minestre)

Minestrone (for 6)

This is the best known and most popular of all Italian soups and, although it is really a speciality of Milan, it is eaten all over Italy. It can be made either with stock or water, and served either hot or ice cold.

4 oz. butter or haricot beans (previously soaked for at least 12 hours)	2 large carrots
	3 potatoes
	1 onion
2 celery stalks	2 oz. streaky un-smoked bacon
2 oz. French beans (cut into small pieces)	1 clove of garlic (optional)
½ small white cabbage	3 pints water (or stock)
1 oz. butter or olive oil	2 oz. rice (or cut macaroni)
Grated Parmesan cheese	Bay leaf
	Salt to taste

Chop the bacon and garlic very finely and put into a saucepan with the butter or olive oil, add the chopped onion and fry together lightly. Next, add all the other vegetables, except the cabbage, cut up small and toss them in the saucepan; add water or stock, bay leaf and salt to taste and bring to the boil; add shredded cabbage, simmer for another hour, add either rice or macaroni, according to taste, and cook until tender. Serve piping hot or ice cold, with a sprinkling of grated Parmesan cheese.

Fish Soup (Zuppa di pesce) (for 5-6)

¼ lb. turbot (cut near the head)	2 tablespoonfuls olive oil
¼ lb. rock salmon	1 wineglass white wine
¼ lb. mackerel	
1 medium-sized red mullet	½ teaspoonful chopped garlic
12 prawns	4 peeled and crushed tomatoes
1 celery heart	
½ teaspoonful chopped parsley	Pinch of saffron
1 onion	Salt and pepper
A little thyme, sweet basil and a bay leaf	Slices of French bread (either toasted or fried in olive oil)
2½ pints water	

Put olive oil into a fairly large saucepan and lightly fry the onion, garlic and bay leaf, add turbot, mackerel and rock salmon, cut in pieces, prawns and chopped celery and cook briskly for a few minutes. Next, add the wine and let it reduce for a few minutes on a strong heat, then add the red mullet, cut into pieces, tomatoes, salt and pepper, cover and simmer for 5 minutes. Pour in the boiling water, add a pinch of saffron and boil briskly for about 10 minutes. Lastly, add the parsley, thyme and sweet basil. Put slices of fried bread in individual soup plates and pour the hot soup over them.

Married Soup (Miniestra maritata) (for 4)

For this soup a good chicken or meat stock is needed.

1 egg	2 tablespoonfuls grated Parmesan cheese
2 tablespoonfuls fresh white bread-crumbs	
2 pints of good stock	2 tablespoonfuls cream
Salt and pepper	

Beat egg in basin, add to it the cheese, breadcrumbs, cream, a little salt and pepper, and mix together thoroughly. Bring stock to the boil, add a little to the mixture, stir well, return to saucepan, bring to the boil again and serve.

This is a very good nourishing soup and very simple to make.

FISH (Pesce)

Baked Fish (Pesce al forno)

Bream lends itself well to this special way of preparing fish as it is a nice white "meaty" fish, but other white fish, such as halibut, turbot, etc., can be used.

1 large bream (about 2 lb.)	A little flour
1 tablespoonful chopped capers	2 tablespoonfuls fresh breadcrumbs
2 fillets of anchovy (finely chopped)	3 tablespoonfuls chopped parsley
6 tablespoonfuls olive oil	1 clove of garlic (finely chopped)
	Salt and pepper

Fillet and skin the fish, coat with flour, salt and pepper, and place on a fireproof dish. Mix all the chopped ingredients with a little olive oil, cover the fish with this mixture, pour the rest of the olive oil on top and bake in a slow oven for about 1 hour.

Red Mullet as eaten in Leghorn (Triglie alla Livornese)

1 red mullet per person	Pinch of thyme
	2 cloves of garlic
Olive oil	1 tablespoonful chopped parsley
Peeled and chopped tomatoes	A little chopped onion
Bay leaf	Flour, salt and pepper

Scrape the mullet and pull out its gills, wash, and dry well in a cloth. Rub the fish in flour seasoned with salt and pepper, and fry in olive oil. When cooked, place care-

Ravioli served as a main dish. They can also be boiled in stock and served as soup

fully on a fireproof dish and keep warm while preparing the sauce. Put 2 tablespoonfuls of olive oil in a saucepan and, when warm, add the onion, finely chopped garlic, parsley, bay leaf, with salt and pepper and thyme. Lastly, add the tomatoes and cook for about 20 minutes. Pour over fish and serve at once.

Fried Scampi (Scampi fritti)

Take as many scampi (or Dublin Bay prawns) as needed, wash and dry thoroughly in a cloth. Toss in flour and fry in fairly deep smoking-hot olive oil. Serve with quarters of lemon or mayonnaise.

Mayonnaise

1 egg-yolk	Juice of half a lemon
Salt, pepper, dried mustard and vinegar to taste	1 teacupful olive oil or refined tea-seed oil

Place the yolk in a basin and break with a hand whisk or fork; add lemon juice and a good pinch of salt. Stir together before adding oil, drop by drop, beating steadily. When all the oil has been added, the mayonnaise should be of a nice thick consistency. Add vinegar, etc., to taste.

MEAT (Le Carni)

Braised Beef (Manzo stuffato)

NOTE: This dish needs a thick solid piece of meat of at least 3 lb.—preferably more.

A nice thick piece of lean beef	2 tablespoonfuls olive oil
4 mushrooms	2 carrots
1 clove of garlic	1 onion
1 glass dry red wine	4 peeled and chopped tomatoes
1 tablespoonful Italian tomato paste	1 stick of celery
Salt and pepper	Bay leaf
A little water	

Put the oil into a saucepan that will just take the meat but is not too large. When the oil is warm, put in the chopped onion and garlic, then add the meat, well seasoned with salt and pepper, and fry it on all sides, turning round continually for about 10 minutes. Pour in the wine and let it reduce by cooking uncovered on a fairly strong heat. Add all the other ingredients, including the finely chopped mushrooms and about half a teacupful of water, and cover tightly. Cook slowly, allowing about 35 minutes per lb. of meat.

When meat is cooked, remove from saucepan and keep in a warm place. Next, take out the vegetables, pass them through a fine wire sieve and return them to the sauce remaining in the saucepan, stirring well. If the sauce seems a little thin, reduce it by boiling quickly for a few moments with the lid off. Slice the meat thickly, place on a large dish, pour the sauce on top and serve with a border of creamed potatoes.

Cutlets Milanese (Costolette alla Milanese)

1 *cutlet per person*	*Butter*
(cut from best end)	*Fresh breadcrumbs*
Flour	*Egg*
Salt and pepper	*Lemon*

Beat and trim the cutlets, season them and coat with flour. Dip into well-beaten egg and, lastly, coat with fresh breadcrumbs, patting well so that the breadcrumbs stick to the egg. Put butter into a frying pan and, when hot, add the cutlets. Fry well on both sides, then place on a dish. Put another piece of butter in the pan and, when foaming, pour over cutlets and serve them still sizzling. Quarters of lemon and sauté potatoes should be served with the cutlets.

Fritto Misto (for 4–6)

Each province of Italy has its own particular Fritto Misto. The difference is in the fat used for cooking, as the basic ingredients are usually the same. In Florence, for instance, it is cooked in deep olive oil, in Milan it is cooked in butter. The following is the Milanese recipe:

1 *set of calf's brains*	6 *slices of calves'*
6 *thin slices of veal*	*kidney*
6 *small sausages*	6 *pieces of cooked*
6 *slices of tomato*	*cauliflower*
2 *oz. butter, or more*	*Egg, flour and fresh*
if necessary	*breadcrumbs*
6 *slices of calves' liver*	*Lemon to garnish*

Soak and wash the brains in cold water and cut into six pieces. Coat the brains and cauliflower, with flour, egg and breadcrumbs, prick the sausages, and coat all the other ingredients in flour only. Put about 2 oz. butter in a frying-pan and, when hot, cook all the ingredients carefully, taking care not to break them. Add more butter if necessary. Place on a very hot dish, pour foaming butter on top and serve with quarters of lemon.

Fried Red Peppers (Peperonata) (for 4)

(Red, yellow or green peppers can be used, but the yellow or red are usually much meatier.)

4 *large peppers*	3 *tomatoes*
2 *onions*	*Olive oil*
Salt and pepper	

Wash the peppers and cut into strips about 1 in. wide. Put 2 tablespoonfuls of olive oil into a large frying pan and, when warm, add the finely chopped onions. Cook until golden, then add peppers, peeled and crushed tomatoes, salt and, if capsicums are sweet, a little pepper. Cover the pan and cook slowly for about 35–40 minutes, stirring frequently to prevent sticking.

Peas with Garlic and Ham (Piselli alla toscana) (for 4)

8 *tablespoonfuls fresh*	1 *clove of garlic*
or quick-frozen	*(chopped)*
peas	2 *tablespoonfuls*
1 *slice unsmoked lean*	*olive oil*
bacon cut into	3 *tablespoonfuls cold*
small pieces	*water*
Pinch of sugar	*Pinch of salt*

Put all the ingredients into a small saucepan, bring to the boil, cover and cook slowly for about 25 minutes, or until peas are cooked. The time, of course, will depend on the quality of the peas, which really should be young and tender.

Potatoes with Rosemary (Patate al Rosmarino)

Potatoes	*Rosemary*
Olive oil	*Salt*

Cut the potatoes into any desired shape. (Many people like to make them into little balls with a special gadget which can be bought at any good kitchen equipment shop.) Put the olive oil into a frying pan and, when hot, add potatoes. Add salt while cooking and scatter enough rosemary over them to give a good flavour. Cook until potatoes are golden brown and soft, and serve piping hot.

Ravioli with Tomato Sauce (Ravioli al sugo)

There are several methods of making ravioli. The following is a practical and good recipe.

For the paste:

3 *eggs*	8 *heaped tablespoon-*
½ *teaspoonful of salt*	*fuls plain flour*

For the filling:

A little cooked
  chicken
½ calf's brain
1 egg
2 tablespoonfuls stock
1 oz. butter
2 slices lean ham
1 bay leaf

½ small onion
2 heaped tablespoon-
  fuls grated
  Parmesan cheese
2 tablespoonfuls
  cooked chopped
  spinach
Salt and pepper

Make a dough with the flour, eggs and salt. Knead firmly on a floured board until smooth and even. Let the dough stand covered with a cloth for about 30 minutes, then cut in half and roll out into two thin sheets. This takes a little time, but the results are well worth the effort.

For the filling.—Soak and wash the brain in cold water, drain and dry. Slice the onion and fry it lightly in the butter, add ham, brains, chicken, bay leaf, spinach salt, pepper and stock, and cook gently for about 30 minutes. Remove the bay leaf and pass the mixture through a fine mincer, place it in a basin, add the egg-yolk and Parmesan cheese, season to taste and mix well into a thick paste.

With a plain round cutter, 2½–3 in. in diameter, cut the paste into rounds. Place about ½ teaspoonful of stuffing on each round, damp edges with a little beaten white of egg and fold over, pressing edges firmly together so that ravioli do not open while cooking. Boil for about 20 minutes, or longer if liked very soft, in a large saucepan of boiling water. Drain well, serve with either tomato or Bolognese sauce (see page 354) and sprinkle grated Parmesan cheese on top.

Ravioli are also good as a soup. Just boil them in a good stock and serve about 6 per person floating in a bowl of hot stock.

Risotto Milanese
(for 4)

6 tablespoonfuls
  Italian rice
1 oz. butter
3 tablespoonfuls
  grated Parmesan
  cheese
1 small onion
1 oz. beef marrow
  fat
2 pints good chicken
  stock
Pinch of saffron
Salt and pepper

Melt the marrow fat and add chopped onion. When onion is cooked to a golden brown, add rice and saffron, stir well and gradually add stock. Simmer for about 20 minutes, or longer if you like it very soft, stirring often to prevent rice from sticking. Add butter, seasoning and cheese, stir well and leave covered for a few minutes before serving.

Risotto with Mushrooms (Risotto con funghi) (for 4)

6 tablespoonfuls
  Italian rice
2 oz. butter
2 oz. sliced mush-
  rooms

3 tablespoonfuls
  grated Parmesan
  cheese
2 pints good stock
1 small onion

Put 1 oz. butter in a saucepan and, when warm, add the finely chopped onion. Fry lightly, then add sliced mushrooms and mix well together. Wash and dry the rice thoroughly and add to the saucepan. Stir well and add boiling stock. Simmer for about 20 minutes or until all the stock has been absorbed by the rice. Reduce the heat, add the rest of the butter and grated cheese, stir well, cover and leave for a few minutes before serving.

Rice with Peas (Riso e piselli) (for 4)

6 tablespoonfuls
  Italian rice
2 oz. butter
3 tablespoonfuls
  grated Parmesan
  cheese

Small onion
4 tablespoonfuls new
  peas
2 pints good stock
Salt and pepper

Proceed as for Risotto with Mushrooms, adding peas just after stock so that they will retain their colour.

Spaghetti with Tomato Sauce (Spaghetti al pomidoro) (for 4)

1 lb. long spaghetti
1 tablespoonful
  Italian tomato paste
1 oz. butter
1 clove of garlic
Grated Parmesan
  cheese
2 tablespoonfuls stock
8 oz. Italian peeled
  tomatoes
2 tablespoonfuls
  olive oil
1 small onion
1 bay leaf
Salt and pepper

Chop the onion and garlic very finely and

COOK'S TIP

TO FRY WITHOUT SPLASHING—

dry all foods thoroughly before putting them into the hot fat. It's water that causes the spluttering.

fry to a light golden brown in a small saucepan with the olive oil. Add bay leaf, tomatoes, tomato paste, salt and pepper, and stock. Bring to the boil and cook very slowly for about 30 minutes. Meanwhile, cook the spaghetti (left long and *not* cut into small pieces) in a large saucepan of boiling salted water for about 20 minutes. Drain well, put on a hot dish, add butter and sauce, and mix well. Sprinkle with a good portion of grated Parmesan cheese and serve very hot.

Spaghetti Bolognese (Spaghetti alla Bolognese)

To make a Bolognese sauce, the method is the same as in the previous recipe, but before adding tomatoes, add 4 oz. peeled and chopped mushrooms and about 6 oz. lean minced beef, preferably fillet.

Stuffed Peppers or Capsicums (Pepperoni ripieni) (for 4)

4 *large red or yellow*	*Salt and pepper*
capsicums	1 *aubergine*
2 *slices white bread*	1 *tablespoonful*
soaked in milk	*capers*
¼ *lb. black olives*	4 *fillets of anchovy*
Olive oil	

Wash, dry and remove stalks and seeds from capsicums, taking care not to break them. Peel and cut aubergine into small slices or pieces and fry in about 2 tablespoonfuls of olive oil, add salt and pepper, cover saucepan and cook over a low heat until tender, stirring now and again to prevent sticking. Leave to cool. Squeeze the bread free from milk and put into a basin, add chopped capers, anchovies, stoned olives, salt and pepper and the aubergine, and mix well together. Stuff the capsicums with the mixture, place in a fireproof dish, pour on top about 2 tablespoonfuls of olive oil and cook in a moderate oven for about 1 hour. They can be eaten either hot or cold.

Tagliatelle with Bolognese Sauce (Tagliatelle alla Bolognese) (for 4)

3 *eggs*	8 *heaped tablespoon-*
¼ *teaspoonful salt*	*fuls plain flour*

Put flour and salt in a bowl, make a well in the centre and break in eggs. Mix together thoroughly, then knead on a floured board until smooth and even. Cover with a cloth and let the dough rest for about 30 minutes. Cut into two and roll into sheets,

the thinner the better. Again let the sheets rest on a floured board until they dry a little, then fold over several times (as a newspaper would be folded). With a sharp knife, cut into thin strips about ⅛ in. wide. (The width is a matter of taste. Some people like their noodles cut into much thicker strips.) Shake the strips well and leave on a floured board until needed.

Boil in a large saucepan of salted water as for spaghetti, drain well and serve with a Bolognese sauce (see previous column).

SWEETS (Dolci)

Rich Shortcrust Tart (Tarta di pasta frolla)

6 *oz. butter*	½ *lb. plain flour*
4 *oz. castor sugar*	1 *egg*
Grated rind of a lemon	

Put all the ingredients, including the lemon rind, in a bowl and knead into a smooth dough. Put on a floured board and roll out to about ¼ in. thickness. Well grease a tart tin with butter, sprinkle with flour, and line with the pastry.

In Italy, either jam or cooked fruit is put in the tart and strips of pastry about ¼ in. wide are laid crossways on top, the whole being then brushed with beaten egg and baked in a fairly hot oven for about 1 hour.

If fruit is used, it is usual to slice either apples or ripe pears rather thinly and put into a frying pan with about 1 oz. melted butter. Sugar to taste, and cover until cooked. It is advisable to stir now and again to prevent fruit from sticking. If liked, a thin slice of lemon or orange peel can be added to flavour the fruit. Allow fruit to cool before putting it on the pastry.

Stuffed Peaches (Pesche ripiene)

Sponge cake	*Marsala wine, sherry*
Chopped almonds and	*or liqueur*
whole almonds	2 *whole peaches cut*
2 *oz. ground almonds*	*in half*
Raspberry jam	1 *egg-yolk*
2 *oz. castor sugar*	

Cut 4 rounds of sponge about ¼ in. thick with a fancy cutter. Spread with hot sieved jam, roll in chopped almonds, place on a plate and put half a peach on each piece of cake. Mix together the ground almonds, sugar, egg-yolk and wine or liqueur, put mixture into a forcing bag and fill the halved peaches, then put a whole blanched almond in the centre of each. Pour on top

Among the most popular ways of serving spaghetti in Italy are with Tomato or Bolognese Sauce

a sauce made from sieved jam diluted with water and flavoured with wine or liqueur.

Zabaglione al Marsala

2 egg-yolks	4 tablespoonfuls
2 teaspoonfuls castor	Marsala wine
sugar	

Put all the ingredients into the top part of a double saucepan, beat well with a whisk and place over the bottom part of the saucepan, which should be half-full of boiling water. Continue beating, without stopping, until the mixture becomes creamy and frothy, taking care not to let it curdle. Serve in individual glasses, with sponge fingers.

SAVOURIES

Pizza

There are several kinds of Pizza, but this is the most popular and best known all over Italy:

Bread dough, flaky or	5 tablespoonfuls
unsweetened short	olive oil
pastry	¼ lb. black olives
6 fillets of anchovies	3 skinned and seeded
¼ lb. Bel Paese or	tomatoes
Mozzarella cheese	1 clove garlic
1 teaspoonful oregano	(chopped)

NOTE: Oregano is a very popular herb in Italy and is always used in Pizza.

Well grease a round tart tin with olive oil and line with a thin layer of one of the pastries suggested. Stone the olives, cut in pieces and place neatly in a straight line across the tart. Do the same with the tomatoes, cheese and anchovies until the whole tart is covered, varying the colours so that the pizza looks really attractive when cooked. Pour on the rest of the olive oil, sprinkle with chopped garlic and oregano and bake in a moderate oven for about 40 minutes. It should be eaten hot, although some people like it cold.

Mozzarella in Carozza

NOTE: Mozzarella is a fresh cream cheese made from buffalo milk.

Thin slices of bread	A little flour
Beaten egg	Deep olive oil for
Thin slices of	frying
Mozzarella	Cocktail sticks

Cut the bread and mozzarella into squares of about 2 inches, put together alternate layers of bread and cheese to make a thick sandwich, beginning and ending with bread (3 squares of bread and 2 of cheese is the usual size), and hold together with wooden cocktail sticks. Dip in flour, then in beaten egg and fry in deep oil. Serve very hot—straight out of the pan.

SPAIN

*Rich, colourful and highly seasoned, Spanish food
makes you think of hot golden sunshine*

Described by G. NEGRI, *of Martinez Spanish Restaurant, London*

YOU really need the climate of Spain to enjoy Spanish cookery in all its rich, colourful and highly seasoned glory.

Like all European countries, it has borrowed a little from the French, but, nevertheless, Spanish cookery remains highly individual. Because butter is expensive, nearly everything is cooked in oil and the (to us) most unlikely ingredients are used together. Chicken, shellfish and rice combine with a number of vegetables to create the famous national dish, Paella.

In Spain, sweet dishes are seldom made, and the most popular sweet course is Turron, a kind of very sweet nougat.

Arroz à la Valenciana (Paella) (for 4)

2 *teacupfuls rice*	1 *small chicken*
1 *small cooked lobster*	6 *teacupfuls chicken*
1 *dozen mussels*	*broth*
¼ *lb. Chorizo*	*A handful of shelled*
(Spanish sausage)	*peas*
½ *small packet*	*A smaller handful of*
shredded saffron	*pimentoes*
(or a pinch of	¼ *pint best oil for*
powdered saffron)	*frying*
Salt and pepper	

Cut chicken into pieces. Make the oil very hot and cook the raw rice in it until it becomes a golden colour. Add the cubed chicken and cook until that too turns golden, then in turn the peas, the sliced sausage, the sliced pimentoes, lobster, mussels and, finally, the chicken broth, stirring well. Season with salt and pepper, and add saffron. Simmer all together for 25 minutes, when the rice should have absorbed all the liquid.

The Spanish housewife makes infinite variations on this theme, using eels and veal, for instance, instead of lobster and chicken, but the important thing is the mixture of meat, fish and rice.

NOTE: Spanish sausage (Chorizo) is not easy to find in the U.K., but can sometimes be bought in continental shops, particularly in London's Soho. It is smaller than salami, about 5 in. long, and a deep red colour from the pimentoes it contains.

Spanish Omelet

As served in Spain, this is a very simple dish. Just fry in oil a few diced cold boiled potatoes and a little onion chopped fine, then pour in the lightly beaten eggs and make the omelet in the usual way (see Egg Dishes), the only difference being that a Spanish omelet is served flat, instead of folded in two, and is usually finished off under the grill.

As served at Martinez Restaurant, London.—Diced cold boiled potatoes, finely sliced onion; chopped pimentoes and tomatoes are added to the eggs before the omelet is made in the usual way—and served flat, not folded.

Huevos à la Flamença

Put a thin slice of ham into a well-buttered or oiled individual chafing dish or casserole, add a few cooked peas, two or three thin slices of Chorizo (Spanish sausage), some chopped tomatoes and pimentoes, and then break one or two eggs on top. Put under a hot grill, or into a quick oven, until the eggs set, when the dish is ready for serving.

If serving Huevos à la Flamença before the main course, one egg per person is sufficient; if it is the main dish, use two eggs each.

Sole (Lenguado) Alfonso

Cook the sole in butter as for Sole Meunière (see chapter on Entertaining) and serve with finely chopped tomato and onion fried in oil and lightly fried sliced bananas.

Cocido (for 4)

This is the national dish and is served all over Spain, particularly on Sundays.

Paella, the famous Spanish national dish, in which chicken, shellfish and rice are mixed with a number of vegetables. The Spanish housewife makes many variations on this theme

1 *small boiling*	1 *small cabbage*
chicken	1–2 *lb. boiling beef*
½ *lb. potatoes*	1 *lb. pork*
½ *lb. Spanish chick*	2 *or* 3 *Spanish*
peas	*sausages*

Boil separately the chicken, the meats, the potatoes, cabbage, chick peas (previously soaked) until all are done. Dish up on one large dish and keep hot.

Serve the broth first, thickened with rice or vermicelli, and the meat as a separate main course with the vegetables. Many Spaniards like oil and vinegar or tomato sauce with the meat.

Fabada (for 4)

4 *pork chops*	*Olive oil for frying*
2 *large slices cooked*	1 *lb. haricot beans*
ham	4 *slices black pudding*
4 *slices Spanish*	*Garlic*
sausage	*Tomato sauce*

Heat the olive oil in a pan with just a touch of garlic. Remove the garlic, then quickly fry the pork chops until they are golden on both sides. Boil the haricot beans (previously soaked overnight) and put them into a deep casserole, moisten with a little tomato sauce (made from fresh tomatoes, *not* bottled, then add the chops, ham, black pudding and sausage. Cover and cook in a moderate oven for about 15 minutes.

Fish Soup

There are various Spanish fish soups very much like the Bouillabaisse of Marseilles. What kind of fish goes into them depends on what is caught in the locality, but they can be made with practically any good mixture of white and shellfish, such as Red Mullet, Mussels and Turbot, plus some good fish stock. First wash and cut up the fish, then fry it gently in boiling oil till golden. Add fish stock and a touch of saffron. Serve with croûtons.

Andalusian Gaspacho (for 6)

Pound 3 cloves of garlic, with salt and green pepper to taste, in a mortar, then gradually add a handful of crumbled dry bread and after that, a little at a time, olive oil, stirring continuously until the bread has dissolved. Add two skinned tomatoes, vinegar to taste and sufficient water for six plates. Chill in the refrigerator and serve ice cold, garnished with cubes of cucumber and bread.

Huevos à la Cubana, eggs fried in deep fat and served with fried bananas on a bed of onions and rice

Trout in Oil

Fry the trout in olive oil with some herbs and finely sliced onion, until it is 90 per cent. cooked. Then dish it up and cover it with vinegar and leave for 4 or 5 days. At the end of that time it will be delicious for hors d'œuvres.

Asparagus with Egg and Cheese

Boil the asparagus in the usual way (till tender), put into a flat dish, pour over some melted butter, then add a generous sprinkling of grated cheese and a fried egg per person. Put under a hot grill to melt the cheese. (Alternatively, raw eggs may be dropped on to the layer of grated cheese and set under the grill.)

Globe Artichokes à l'Espagnole

Boil the artichokes till tender with a little lemon juice to preserve their colour. Strain and dry, then separate the leaves and fill with a mixture of grated cheese and breadcrumbs, salt and pepper. When the cavities have been well filled, close the leaves again, put the artichokes into a casserole with a little oil in the bottom, cover and cook gently over a very low flame for about 10 minutes (or until the cheese melts inside the leaves).

Gaspacho as served in Majorca (for 10)

5 green peppers	2 medium-sized fresh cucumbers
7 or 8 large tomatoes (seeded)	1 clove garlic
4 oz. bread with the crusts on, soaked in water	3 tablespoonfuls best white vinegar
3 tablespoonfuls olive oil	1 tablespoonful mayonnaise
4 medium-sized onions	1 teacupful cold water
	Salt to taste

Pound the garlic and peppers in a mortar. Mince the other solids into a large bowl, then add the rest of the ingredients, mix well and strain through a cloth or fine strainer. Put the liquid in the refrigerator to chill. Serve the soup very cold, accompanied by separate little dishes of sliced green peppers, cucumbers, tomatoes, raw onion and toasted bread.

Garlic Soup

1 thin slice of bread per person	Stock
1 clove garlic	Oil for frying
	Salt and pepper to taste

Fry the garlic in the oil, then remove it and put in the bread and seasoning. Cover with the hot stock, bring to the boil, boil for a minute or two, then serve.

Garlic soup is improved out of all recognition with this addition: Drop one raw egg per person into the boiling soup, sprinkle generously with grated cheese and put under a very hot grill just long enough to set the egg and melt the cheese.

Chick Pea Salad

Soak the chick peas for 24 hours, boil for 10 minutes before salting—if you put the salt in sooner, the peas will not absorb it—and simmer gently till tender. When cold, mix with finely sliced onion, add a fairly hot and vinegary French dressing an hour before serving. (This is an excellent way of using up left-over cooked chick peas.)

Tunny Salad

Thoroughly mix together a shredded lettuce, some flaked tunny fish and a shredded onion. Dress with oil and vinegar and seasoning.

Eggs Otero

For each person bake one good-sized potato in its jacket until soft. Split each potato in half lengthwise, scoop out the contents, mix with peeled shrimps, Béchamel sauce (see Sauces chapter), salt and pepper and an egg per person, then put back into the skins, sprinkle with grated cheese and brown under a hot grill for a minute or two (or until the cheese melts nicely).

Bacalao à la Vizcaina (for 6–8)

The traditional Dry Salt Cod served on Good Friday.

1 salt cod	Ordinary ground
1 oz. bread	pepper
10 oz. tomatoes	Chopped parsley
3 Spanish red peppers	2 oz. flour
1 clove garlic	7 oz. olive oil
Ground Spanish red	10 oz. onions
pepper	Salt

Soak the fish for 24 hours, then remove the bones and cut in pieces 1½ in. × 3 in. Dip in flour and fry in oil. Place in a baking pan with the bread, cut up and fried, on top. Thinly slice and fry the onions in the oil and, when golden brown, add the garlic, chopped very finely, the chopped parsley, Spanish peppers and peeled, chopped tomatoes. Season with salt and pepper. Pour this sauce over the cod, garnish with a few strips of Spanish pepper and cook in the oven for 30 minutes.

Bacalao Omelet

To use up left-over Bacalao, make an ordinary soft plain omelet and warm the Bacalao with a little cream. When the omelet is done, fold the Bacalao mixture into the middle, before folding it over. Top with grated cheese, putting the omelet under the hot grill for a minute or two to melt the cheese.

Huevos à la Cubana

Into very hot deep oil drop the eggs, one at a time, so that they cook like poached eggs, forming a coating of white. Dish them up on to a bed of plain boiled rice. Sauté in a little oil some very finely chopped onion and the faintest trace of garlic. Top the rice with this and some fried bananas.

Suprème Hortelana—fried breast of chicken with young vegetables—is another favourite dish on the menu at Martinez Restaurant

PORTUGAL

*Monday is the national wash-day here too, and everyone eats Boiled Salt
Cod for midday dinner to save a lot of cooking*

by JOAN CROFT DE MOURA

PORTUGUESE cookery has much in common with Spanish, but it is generally simpler, less exotic and exaggerated. Nearly everything is cooked in oil, which is used both for frying and baking; food is seldom served boiled. All the meats are marinaded, even steaks and chops, for a few minutes, and all fat removed from the meat. Soup, usually a thick vegetable soup, is generally served at lunch and dinner, often followed by fish, meat, an egg dish and fresh fruit. In the north, the soup comes *after* the fish and meat courses.

The average Portuguese housewife has no packaged cereals, jams or canned goods in her store cupboard. Milk in Portugal is not good. Meat is not abundant, with the exception of pork, which is plentiful, most families in the country, even the poorest, owning a pig. Those who live on the coast eat plenty of fresh fish, including grilled sardines (which taste much better than the canned variety), but inland, with the exception of large towns, the only fish available is dried salt codfish, which is therefore much used.

Eggs are cheap and plentiful, so the Portuguese housewife uses them lavishly, thinking nothing of using eight eggs for a cake. Favourite dishes are eggs fried in oil, scrambled eggs and omelets.

Every meal ends with fresh raw fruit, which is eaten in tremendous quantities all day and every day, as dessert and between meals. There are oranges in winter, and in summer sixty or seventy kinds of grapes to choose from, as well as water-melons and all the other summer fruits. Vegetables, which are much the same as those available in the U.K., are usually served with oil and vinegar. The Portuguese eat a lot of bread—and cook with it, too—but not much butter, which is very expensive. If they do have jam, they do not spread it on bread and butter, but eat it by itself in a spoon; cheese (mostly made from goats' milk) is also eaten alone.

Boiled Salt Codfish

This is the national Portuguese dish, which you will find served all over the country on Mondays when housewives are too busy with their washing for much cooking. Everybody eats codfish, from the poorest peasant to the Duke of Palmela. Soak the codfish overnight. Boil it with onions and potatoes, and serve hot with oil and vinegar.

Braised Tunny

Tunny fish	Cream
A little lemon juice	Fillets of anchovies
Slices of fat bacon	Mixed vegetables
Herbs and spices as	Port wine
liked	Mashed sorrel
	1 egg-yolk

Interlard a slice of tunny with fillets of anchovies, the quantity depending on individual taste. Boil in salted water to which some lemon juice has been added. After a few minutes, place the tunny in a flat pan on a bed of vegetables and slices of fat bacon. Cover with equal parts of port wine and the liquid in which the fish was boiled. Simmer for 45 minutes with herbs and spices as liked. Place the tunny on a purée of fresh cream, egg-yolk and mashed sorrel. Skim the fat off the stock and make demi-glacé sauce (see Sauces chapter) reduced to the consistency of thick syrup and pour it over the tunny. Serve hot.

Caldeirada a Fragateira de Lisboa (for 6–8)

2 lb. fish (mullet, bass, hake, eel, sole, red mullet or skate)	1 lobster
	A few shrimps, mussels or cockles
3 onions	3 tomatoes
3 pints water.	Sprig of parsley
Juice of ½ lemon	Wineglassful of port wine
Salt and pepper	
Coriander	Clove of garlic
Bay leaves	Olive oil for frying

Remove heads and bones from fish and

Sweet Rice (right) patterned with cinnamon is the Portuguese version of rice pudding. On the left are Coconut and Almond Balls, and, above, Golden Threads

make them into a stock by simmering slowly for 30 minutes in the water and wine, with one finely minced onion, parsley and bay leaves, salt and pepper. Stir, and remove froth as it rises. Put through a fine sieve, then pour into an earthenware cocotte with 2 sliced onions, a clove of garlic (mashed), the tomatoes (with pips removed), and a little coriander. Bring to the boil, and boil for 10 minutes. Then put in the fish and shellfish, and boil again for 15 minutes. Serve hot with sippets fried in olive oil.

Codfish Cakes (Pasteis de bacalhau)

Equal quantities of dried salt cod and mashed boiled potatoes
1 or 2 eggs
Olive oil for frying

Soak the cod overnight in cold water. Next day, boil it, then shred it as finely as possible. Prepare an equal quantity of very well mashed boiled potatoes, mix with the fish, binding with one or two egg-yolks and mixing thoroughly. Beat the egg-whites till stiff and fold them into the fish mixture. Drop tablespoonfuls of the mixture into very deep frying fat (preferably olive oil) and fry to a light golden brown. Serve with a crisp green salad and black olives. These fish cakes, which should be the shape of the spoon, are equally good eaten hot or cold.

Left-over Fish

Left-over salt codfish can be flaked, and added, with a little fried onion and chopped black olives, to scrambled eggs. Or flake the fish into a casserole, slice some boiled potatoes, onions and olives, and bake in the oven with a little oil.

Liver Slices (Iscas a Portuguesa)

Slice the liver very thinly, marinade overnight in white wine vinegar with garlic, bay leaf and a few peppercorns. Fry the liver very quickly in a little lard in a frying pan (preferably of earthenware).

361

Into the remainder of the lard pour a little of the vinegar with the garlic and bay leaf, boil quickly to reduce and pour over liver. Serve at once with sliced boiled or fried potatoes.

Pork Roast in White Wine

Marinade a loin of pork overnight in white wine, with garlic, salt and bay leaves, having first removed all the fat. (In Portugal pork is not served with crackling.) Next day, place plenty of pork fat on the joint and roast it. Bake little potatoes in their jackets until they are soft, then squash them up and finish them off in the pan with the pork, so that they absorb the gravy. Serve with lemon juice and sugar mixed.

Alternatively, the pork may be served with baked apples and chestnuts. For this, first boil and skin the chestnuts, then bake them and the apples (cut in halves) in the meat tin with the pork.

Sauté de Veau au vin de port (for 4)

2 lb. veal	1 tablespoonful lard
½ glass of port wine	A little flour
¾ pint hot water	Seasoning

Cut the veal into strips about 1½ in. long. Melt the lard in a cocotte and fry the meat in it to a golden brown, turning it on all sides. Remove the fat, sprinkle a little flour over the meat and fry till brown; then add water. Season. Leave to simmer for 1 hour, watching that the gravy does not catch or become too thick. Add the port wine ½ hour before serving.

Almond Pudding à la Portugaise

6 oz. almonds (whole)	6 oz. sugar
3 eggs	Wineglassful of port
1 pint milk	wine

Soak the almonds in a mixture of boiling milk, sugar and a small glass of port wine, red or white; stir carefully and add the beaten egg-yolks and then the whites. Put the mixture into a mould in which you have previously melted some sugar to a caramel, and steam. Cool and serve with cream flavoured with vanilla.

Coconut and Almond Balls (Bolas de Coco e Amendoa)

These are made in three parts:

(1)	8 oz. ground almonds	3 egg-yolks 8 oz. sugar
(2)	4 oz. chocolate 4 oz. ground almonds	4 oz. sugar A little water
(3)	4 oz. shredded coconut	3 egg-yolks 4 oz. sugar

(1) Boil sugar with a little water, stir in ground almonds and egg-yolks, mix well, and leave to cool.

(2) Grate the chocolate, add sugar and mix with a little water, then add ground almonds and knead well.

(3) Mix the coconut with the sugar, add egg-yolks and knead well.

Take a little of each mixture, in the order given above, form into cigar shape and press well together, using a little syrup or egg-white to make them stick. Roll in castor sugar.

Golden Threads (Fios de Ovos)

5 or 6 egg-yolks	½ lb. sugar
A little port or Madeira	Glacé cherries (for decoration)
Cream (optional)	Water (about ¾ pint)

Break up the egg-yolks with a fork and strain through a fine sieve. Heat the sugar in a frying pan with sufficient water to make a fairly liquid syrup. Keep the flame low so that the syrup is very hot but not boiling. Pipe egg-yolk through an icing bag into the syrup, making long threads. Leave threads in syrup for 3 or 4 minutes, then lift out with a fork and pile on a dish. When cold, pour a little port or Maderia on top and decorate with glacé cherries. Serve with cream if liked. Golden Threads can also be used for decorating other sweets.

Sweet Clouds (Nuvens or Farofias)

Make a boiled or steamed (not baked) custard with several egg-yolks and plenty of sugar. Beat the egg-whites till stiff. Drop spoonfuls of them into boiling milk. They will poach quite quickly. Remove from milk and drain. Serve the custard cold in individual cups and cap with the poached whites.

Sweet Rice (Arroz Doce)

This is the Portuguese version of rice pudding.

1 cupful rice	2 or 3 egg-yolks
2 cupfuls milk	A little lemon peel or
Cinnamon	vanilla pod

Bring the rice, milk and lemon peel or vanilla very slowly to the boil and cook gently till the rice is quite soft. Then stir in, little by little, the egg-yolks, stirring till it thickens. After the eggs have been added, the mixture must not boil. Pour into a flat dish to cool; sprinkle with cinnamon in a criss-cross pattern.

THE NETHERLANDS

*The Dutch have many delicious ways of cooking
and serving vegetables, usually with spices*

Compiled by MIA VAN DEN BERG

**Asparagus with hard-boiled eggs, melted butter and grated nutmeg, is served
elegantly garnished as a main dish**

THE Dutch like to eat well, and they do eat well every day of the week.

The Dutch housewife takes pride and pleasure in preparing meals of great variety, using to full advantage the abundance of inexpensive but high quality food —dairy products, vegetables and meat— that Holland produces.

Yet the Dutch menu is, as an everyday rule, simple, straightforward and easy to prepare. It does full justice to the food values, such as mineral salts and vitamins, and takes little time to prepare.

It is customary to have one main cooked meal a day, mostly in the evening. Breakfast consists usually of cheese, an egg, bread and tea; lunch of bread with cold meat and coffee; and tea of a cup of tea and a biscuit. The evening meal is therefore a substantial one, beginning with soup, followed by meat, vegetables and potatoes, and ending with a sweet. At each course the helpings are hearty.

Vegetables in Holland can all be bought cleaned and cut up ready for cooking. Even the smallest greengrocers have machinery to do this, and it is a tremendous boon to the busy housewife and especially the businesswoman who also runs her own home. You pay a few cents more to have the vegetables prepared, but even potatoes can be peeled while you wait.

Most of the vegetables are steamed in plenty of butter and very little water, and flavoured with spices, nutmeg being a favourite.

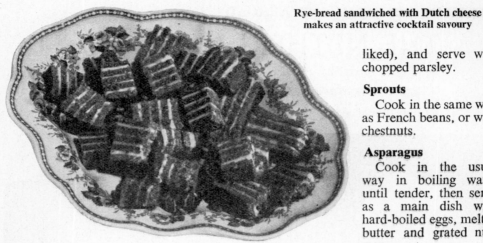

Rye-bread sandwiched with Dutch cheese makes an attractive cocktail savoury

NOTE: Dutch rusks and Dutch dried vegetables for soup are obtainable from many continental shops and the provision departments of large stores.

VEGETABLE COOKERY

At the main meal it is usual to serve two or three different vegetables and perhaps lettuce with a French dressing into which a hard-boiled egg has been grated. The following are characteristic methods of cooking and serving ordinary vegetables.

French Beans

Wash and string the beans, leaving them whole. Put into a *very* little fast-boiling water and cook till just tender but *not* mushy. Drain. Put a good big pat of butter or margarine into the bottom of the pan, melt over a medium flame, put back the beans and simmer in the butter for 2 or 3 minutes, shaking the pan to prevent them from sticking. Serve with grated nutmeg.

Cauliflower

Boil in the usual way until tender, and serve with a white or cheese sauce and grated nutmeg.

Young Green Peas

Cook in the same way as French beans, in butter, and serve with chopped parsley.

Carrots

Cook in the same way as French beans, with a little sugar added to the butter (if liked), and serve with chopped parsley.

Sprouts

Cook in the same way as French beans, or with chestnuts.

Asparagus

Cook in the usual way in boiling water until tender, then serve as a main dish with hard-boiled eggs, melted butter and grated nutmeg.

Red Cabbage

Wash and cut up the cabbage and plunge into a *small* quantity of fast-boiling water, with 2 or 3 cloves and 1 grated apple, a dash of vinegar and sugar to taste. Cook until the cabbage is tender but still reasonably crisp. Drain well, simmer with pat of butter and thicken with cornflour.

Hot Beetroot is a delicious dish which is very popular in Holland. Cooked beetroot is sliced, then gently heated in a little water, with a dash of vinegar, salt, sugar and 1 or 2 cloves. Simmer with a pat of butter.

Endive

Cook in the same way as French beans and serve with white sauce and nutmeg.

Mashed Potatoes

Using a wooden spoon, mash boiled potatoes to a really smooth cream with milk and butter, beating in a little nutmeg at the last minute.

Spinach (Spinazie) (for 4)

4 lb. spinach	3 or 4 Dutch rusks
2 eggs	Some stale bread
Salt	1 oz. margarine

Wash and clean the spinach, add a pinch of salt and cook in a little hot water, with the lid on the pan, for 5–10 minutes. Drain thoroughly and chop. Add the margarine and finely crushed Dutch rusks, and simmer for another 5 minutes. Boil the eggs hard, shell and divide them in quarters. Fry strips of bread in margarine until golden brown.

Serve the spinach with the egg and fried bread-strips on top.

MEAT DISHES

Vegetable Soup with Small Meat-balls
(Groentesoep met balletjes) (for 4–6)

2 pints stock (or water with 4–5 meat cubes)	½ lb. minced meat
	Dutch dried
Milk and bread-crumbs	vegetables for soup
	2 oz. vermicelli
	Salt and pepper

Boil the stock (or water with meat cubes) for about 5 minutes, add dried vegetables and salt to taste, boil for about 15 minutes. Meanwhile, mix minced meat with bread-crumbs and milk, add salt and pepper to taste, and form the mixture into small meat-balls the size of marbles. Add meat-balls to the boiling soup, cook for 15 minutes, add vermicelli and boil slowly for 15 more minutes.

Hotchpot with Stewing Steak or Pork
(Hutspot met klapstuk) (for 4–6)

1 lb. fat stewing steak or Pork	1 lb. onions
	2 oz. fat
3 lb. carrots	1½ pints water
4 lb. potatoes	Salt

Wash meat and add water and salt. Bring to the boil and simmer for about 2 hours. Peel and mince carrots and add them. In ½ hour, add peeled potatoes and chopped onions and simmer for ½ hour more until the vegetables are very tender. By this time the water should have evaporated completely. Take out the meat, mash the vegetables with a wooden spoon, add fat and serve.

Veal Escallops with Bacon and Minced Meat (Blinde vinken) (for 4)

4 thinly cut veal escallops (about 3 oz. each)	4 oz. butter
	Salt and pepper
	1 egg
4 oz. minced meat	Breadcrumbs
4 rashers bacon	

Rub salt and pepper into both sides of the veal escallops. Put one rasher of bacon

Two stages in the preparation of Veal Escallops with Bacon and Minced Meat—right, the stuffing is put on the escallops ; left, they are rolled up and tied for cooking

on top of each escallop. Mix the minced meat with the egg and some breadcrumbs until smooth, adding pepper and salt to taste.

Divide the minced meat between the escallops, roll them round it, tying together with a piece of thread around each little roll. Fry the "blinde vinken" quickly in butter until golden brown, then put on a low flame, add some water and simmer for about ½ hour.

Cut the threads and serve very hot.

Calf's Tongue in White Sauce, Runner Beans, Haricot Beans and Potato Croquettes (Tong in zure saus, snijbonen, witte bonen en kleine aardappel-croquetjes) (for 4)

1 calf's tongue (about 1 lb.)	Margarine, milk, breadcrumbs
2 oz. butter or margarine	1 beaten egg
1 oz. flour	Salt, onion, carrot, parsley, herbs
Salt, vinegar or lemon juice	1 pint water
½ lb. haricot beans	1 lb. runner beans
	2 lb. potatoes
Deep frying fat	

Clean the tongue and boil for about 1½ hours in water with a pinch of salt, onion,

Cinnamon Bread Turnovers are a delicious, inexpensive and quickly prepared sweet

carrot and herbs. Skin the tongue, cut into thick slices and cover with a sauce made as follows.

For the sauce.—Melt the butter, stir in the flour and then the water, stirring all the time. Finally, add vinegar or lemon juice to taste. Boil runner beans and haricot beans (soaked beforehand for 12 hours) separately until tender. Boil potatoes, mash with margarine and milk and make them into small croquettes, cover with breadcrumbs, beaten egg and again with breadcrumbs, and fry in deep fat until golden brown. Serve everything piping hot.

Dutch Steak, Peas, Carrots, French Beans, Sprouts and Fried Potatoes (Hollandse biefstuk, erwtjes, worteljes, princessebonen, spruitjes en gebakken aardappelen) (for 4)

2 lb. tender round steak (1½ in. thick)	2 tablespoonfuls vinegar
1 teaspoonful pepper	¼ lb. butter or margarine
½ to 1 cupful water	(for frying)
1 lb. peas	or packets of frozen vegetables
1 lb. carrots	
1 lb. French beans	
1 lb. sprouts	
Parsley	2 lb. potatoes
Pats of butter or margarine	Salt

Pound the meat on both sides and cube it. Mix vinegar with salt and pepper and rub this on both sides of steak. Leave for ½ hour. Fry steaks just before serving. Brown butter or margarine in heavy frying pan, place steaks in pan and fry for about 1 minute each side—or a little longer if you prefer them well done—moving them backwards and forwards continually. Add hot water to the fat in the pan and serve this in gravy boat.

Boil the vegetables separately in a very little water, add a pinch of salt. Drain, and simmer with a pat of butter or margarine. Cut the potatoes in flat slices and fry in ample butter or margarine. Sprinkle chopped parsley over peas and carrots, and serve everything on a flat dish piping hot.

HOT CHEESE DISHES

Cabbage and Dutch Cheese (for 4)

1 large cabbage	½ lb. Dutch Gouda or Edam cheese
Salt	
Breadcrumbs	Butter

Clean the cabbage. Cut the outer leaves off very carefully and boil them in water

To serve with cocktails, these little Cheese Puffs are made of choux pastry with a delicious savory filling of butter and cheese

with a pinch of salt until they are nearly cooked. Drain the cabbage leaves and roll a piece of Dutch cheese, about ½ in. thick and 3 in. long, into each cabbage leaf. Put these into a greased fireproof dish, cover with breadcrumbs and pats of butter, and put the dish in a fairly hot oven until golden brown.

Spinach with Dutch Cheese (for 4)

2 oz. grated Dutch Gouda or Edam cheese	2 lb. spinach (or 1 lb. canned chopped spinach)
4 tablespoonfuls milk	4 eggs
2 oz. butter	Pepper and salt

Clean the spinach (if fresh) and cook in little or no water and a pinch of salt until done. Chop, add salt and butter to taste and keep warm. Beat the eggs with a pinch of salt and pepper, add milk, fry four small omelets made from the mixture. Cover each omelet with spinach, roll it up and put into a greased fireproof dish. Cover with grated cheese and leave the dish in a moderately hot oven for 2 minutes.

SWEET DISHES

Cinnamon Bread Turnovers (Wentelteefjes) (for 4)

8 slices stale bread	½ pint milk
2 oz. sugar	1 teaspoonful ground cinnamon
Margarine for frying	
Pinch of salt	1 egg

Beat the egg with 1 oz. sugar, pinch of salt and some cinnamon. Soak the bread in a mixture of milk and the beaten egg until the slices are quite soft. Fry in a shallow pan in margarine until golden brown on both sides. Sprinkle with the remainder of the sugar and cinnamon.

Dutch Rusks with Currant Sauce (Beschuit met bessensap) (for 4–6)

12 Dutch rusks	1 pint red currant juice (or diluted red currant jelly
1 pint water	
½ lb. sugar	
1 piece spiced cinnamon	1 tablespoonful cornflour
Peel of 1 lemon	

Soak the rusks, each one separately, in half the red currant juice in a large dish.

Slowly heat the rest of the juice with the sugar, water, cinnamon and peel. Mix the cornflour with a little water and add this to the hot juice when almost boiling. Keep on stirring and let the sauce boil for several minutes. Then pour over the rusks in a dish and serve hot or cold.

Butter Cake (Boterkoek)

1 *egg*	*Salt*
½ *lb. butter or*	½ *lb. flour*
margarine	½ *lb. Demerara sugar*
Grated lemon rind	

Beat the egg, saving some of it in a separate dish. Cut butter or margarine into small pieces and add with flour, sugar, pinch of salt and, if desired, grated lemon rind, to the egg.

Put into a greased 8-in. or 9-in. cake tin. Cover the top with the remainder of the egg. Bake the butter cake for 45–60 minutes in a fairly hot oven until light brown. Cool before serving.

COLD DISHES—COCKTAIL SAVOURIES

Rye-bread and Dutch Cheese

1 *packet "Pumpernickel" rye-bread*
1 *packet Dutch cream cheese (or a mixture of butter and grated Dutch Gouda or Edam cheese in equal quantities*

Put a thick layer of Dutch cream cheese, or cheese mixture, in between three or four slices of rye-bread. Cut into thin strips, then into squares, and you have a cocktail savoury which looks interesting and tastes even better.

(It is easier to cut the squares after the rye-bread with the cheese filling has been in the refrigerator for about 1 hour.)

Cheese Puffs (enough for 25–30 puffs)

4½ *tablespoonfuls*	1 *oz. butter or*
water	*margarine*
Pinch of salt	1 *oz. flour*
1 *egg*	

For the filling

4 *oz. Dutch Edam or*	4 *oz. butter or*
Gouda cheese	*margarine*
French mustard to taste	

Bring the water, margarine and salt to the boil, then add all the flour at once, stir for a short while until the mixture sticks together and remove from heat. Add, still away from heat, the egg and beat into the mixture. This will take some time. With

two teaspoons, form into small balls the size of marbles and put them on a greased baking tin, about 1–2 in. apart. Bake in a hot oven for 10–15 minutes. Do *not* open the oven door during the first 10 minutes or the puffs will go flat.

Filling.—Put the butter or margarine in a warm place for a while and add the grated cheese. Flavour with a pinch of salt and some French mustard to taste, and stir well.

Cut the puffs open at the top and fill them with the cheese and butter mixture, close them again, or top them with some grated cheese.

Cheese Fritters

1 *oz. margarine*	1 *oz. flour*
2 *oz. water*	1 *egg*
2 *oz. old Dutch cheese, grated*	*Pinch of salt*

Bring water, margarine and salt to the boil, then add all the flour at once, stir for a while until the mixture sticks together, then remove from the heat. Add the egg and grated cheese and mix thoroughly. Put the mixture into a piping bag; from it drop small quantities into hot deep fat, and fry very quickly until golden brown.

Cheese Biscuits

6 *oz. flour*	4 *oz. butter*
4 *oz. grated Dutch Gouda or Edam cheese*	*Pepper and salt*
	1 *egg-yolk*

Mix the flour with the butter and nearly all the grated cheese, add salt and pepper to taste. Roll out the dough about ¼ in. thick, cut into 2-in. squares, or into biscuit shapes. Cover the biscuits with egg-yolk, sprinkle the remainder of the grated cheese over them, and bake for about 10 minutes in a fairly hot oven.

Asparagus Tips in Bread

Cut very thin slices of white or brown bread and butter, cover with grated Dutch Gouda or Edam cheese. Roll each slice of bread round an asparagus tip and fix with a cocktail stick.

Tomatoes filled with Cheese and Butter

Cut each tomato into the shape of a basket by cutting two sections away at the top. Remove the seeds. Fill tomatoes with a mixture of butter and grated Dutch Gouda or Edam cheese. Sprinkle some chopped parsley on top.

RUSSIA

Exciting foods full of unexpected flavours and strange contrasts are a legacy of the Czars

Niki, who serves dishes à la Russe at
Chez Luba Restaurant, London, describes
some of his specialities below

FOR a typical Russian main meal, begin with Bortsch, served with Piroschki or Blinys and caviare washed down with vodka, follow that by Chicken Kieff, and finish with Sernik, a pancake stuffed with sour cream and sultanas. Unusual, yes, but delicious. . . .

Bortsch (for 4)

2 onions	½ cabbage
1 leek	6 uncooked beetroots
1 stick celery	2 oz. margarine
Clove of garlic	Bay leaf
Dried mushrooms	Thyme
Lemon juice	4 oz. uncooked lean
1 carrot	pork or beef

Shred the onion, leek, celery, carrot, cabbage and five of the beets very fine, and sauté them in a covered pan in the margarine for 10–15 minutes. Add 2 quarts of cold water, bring to the boil and simmer gently for 20 minutes. Then add the bay leaf, garlic, thyme, three or four little pieces of dried mushroom and the meat cut up small. Cook for 20–25 minutes. By this time the Bortsch will have lost its colour so, just before serving, shred the last beetroot, previously boiled by itself, sprinkle it lavishly with lemon juice and drop it into the soup to restore the colour. After this the Bortsch must not be brought to the boil again. It is now ready to serve and is a good deep red. It should be accompanied by Piroschki, which is served in Russia instead of bread.

Piroschki (for 4)

About 2 oz. each of cooked lean beef and veal	1 hard-boiled egg
	1 onion
	4 oz. puff pastry
2 oz. margarine	Sage, parsley, salt
1 teaspoonful cream	and pepper to taste

Mince the meat. Chop the onion finely and fry till golden in margarine. Add the meat, sage, parsley, salt and pepper, the shredded hard-boiled egg and the cream, and mix thoroughly but do not cook any more. Roll out your puff pastry and fill it with the prepared stuffing like a large sausage roll. Cut the roll into four slices (one for each person), brush with egg and bake in a moderate oven for 15–20 minutes. Serve hot with Bortsch.

Russian Pancakes (Blinys)

2 oz. buckwheat flour	¼ oz. yeast
4 oz. white flour	Pinch of salt
1 egg	1 gill of milk

If buckwheat flour cannot be obtained, white flour can be used.

Warm the milk slightly. Put the yeast in the warmed milk and leave for 10 minutes. Put the flour and salt in a basin, add the egg, the milk and yeast, and make a thick pancake mixture. Then fry like ordinary pancakes in a small pan. Keep them in the oven, hot and dry, till served.

Blinys are best served with smoked salmon and caviare, but some people like them with sour cream.

Chicken Kieff (for 2)

1 chicken	2 oz. butter
2 oz. mushrooms	Clarified butter for
Egg and breadcrumbs	frying
Salt and pepper	

This is an extravagant dish. As only the breast of the chicken is used, you need one bird for every two people, but it's worth it!

First carefully remove the two breasts from the chicken, cutting the meat away from the carcase with a very sharp knife and leaving only the top of the wing bone attached. Next, slice a little thin fillet, about 4 in. long and 2 in. wide, off the inside of the breast and put this aside. Then run a sharp knife into the flesh of the breast and right round it to make a little envelope. Now take the little fillet and wrap it firmly round a rectangle of butter (about 1 oz.). Put this inside the opening in the "envelope," together with the chopped mushrooms and salt and pepper and close firmly.

Sprinkle the stuffed breast with flour, dip first in egg and then breadcrumbs and fry in very hot clarified butter for about 5 minutes or until golden brown. It is advisable to test the hot clarified butter by dropping in a piece of raw potato; if it quickly fries into a perfect chip, the temperature is right for the chicken.

Having used the breasts of chicken, what do you do with the rest of the bird or birds? Here is the solution.

Forschmak Dragomiroff

Boil the chicken legs for 15 minutes. Remove all the skin and meat from the bones. Dice it, add equal quantity of diced cooked ham and half the quantity of diced mushrooms. Mix this into a plain white sauce to which has been added either the yolk of one egg or grated cheese to taste. Top with grated cheese and bake in a fireproof dish for 15 minutes. Serve with baked rice.

Baked Rice

4 oz. margarine	Bay leaf
1 cupful washed rice	Teaspoonful salt
Garlic to taste	2 cupfuls chicken
Pepper	stock or water
1 onion	

Fry the chopped onion in the margarine till golden. Add the rice and fry with the onion for about 5 minutes or until quite dry, stirring to prevent it sticking to the pan. Then add 2 cupfuls of chicken stock or water, the bay leaf, salt, pepper and a touch of garlic; bring to the boil, then cook in the oven for 15–18 minutes. Remove from the oven and stand on one side for at least 10 minutes, being careful not to shake it, or the rice will not dry thoroughly and may be sticky.

Zrazy à la Nelson (for 4)

1 lb. fillet steak	1 teaspoonful tomato
2 medium onions	purée
1 oz. flour	4 small tomatoes
4 oz. margarine	4 or 5 mushrooms
½ pint stock or water	1 teaspoonful cream
Parsley	Croûtons

Fillet steak *must* be used for this dish. Cut it about ½ in. thick into circles approximately 1 in. in diameter, grill or fry according to taste. Meanwhile, fry some croûtons in deep fat and place the steaks on top of these, then cover the whole with the following sauce.

Fry chopped onions in margarine till golden, add flour to make a roux. Add a teaspoonful of tomato purée and enough stock or water to make the sauce a creamy consistency. Fry four or five mushrooms separately and add these to the sauce, with a little gravy browning to darken the colour and the cream to make it richer.

When this sauce has been poured over the steaks, top each one with a blanched and lightly fried tomato and a sprinkling of fresh parsley.

Sole à la Russe

This consists of a fillet of sole cut into tiny fingers, floured, rolled in egg-yolk and breadcrumbs, then fried in deep fat and served on a doyley with lemon.

Sernik

For the pancakes

4 oz. flour	1 egg
½ pint milk	Pinch of salt

For the filling

4 oz. sour milk (made	Icing sugar
from about 1½	Pinch of cinnamon
pints)	1 level dessertspoon-
1 oz. sultanas	ful sugar
Grated rind of	Squeeze lemon juice
1 lemon	Pinch of salt
1 dessertspoonful	1 egg-white
cream	2 oz. butter for frying

Make an ordinary pancake batter (see Puddings chapter) and fry one good-sized pancake for each person. For the filling, leave about 1½ pints of milk in a really warm atmosphere for 24 hours, till it begins to separate, then pour it into a muslin bag and leave to drip; this will provide approximately 4 oz. of sour milk cheese, but the amount varies with the quality of the milk. (The cream cheese sold at delicatessens for cooking purposes can be used but is not so good.) Mix all the filling ingredients together, using a wooden spoon, and the egg-white to bind them. Place some of the mixture on half of each pancake, fold over, seal the edges with egg-yolk to close like an envelope. Fry in butter for 2–3 minutes until golden, then turn over and do the other side. Sprinkle with icing sugar and serve, either as a first or last course.

Chicken Kieff is an extravagant dish, using one whole breast of chicken per person, but it's worth it

Potato Cakes

> 2 medium potatoes
> Salt and pepper
> 1 egg
> Olive oil for frying

Peel and shred the potatoes finely, add salt and pepper, half the egg-yolk and all the white, and stir together. Fry the mixture, dropping it in little dollops off a spoon into hot, half-deep olive oil, for about 5 minutes until golden brown and crispy. Serve hot with sour cream, jam or marmalade, according to individual taste.

Sernik—pancakes with a filling of sour milk cheese—are served either first or last

Turbot Caucasien

1 thick cutlet of turbot per person	8 oz. margarine or olive oil
1 onion	Clove of garlic
Chopped mushrooms	Paprika to taste

Skin, flour and fry the cutlets in the margarine or oil. Meanwhile, chop the onion into half-rings and fry separately until golden. Add the chopped mushrooms, garlic and paprika to the onion. Cover and fry for about 10–15 minutes. Pour over the cooked fish and serve hot or cold—preferably cold.

Russian Herring Salad

Cut cooked turnip, carrot, peas and pimento into little squares in equal quantities, mix with salt and pepper and a home-made mayonnaise, flavoured with lemon juice, tomato ketchup or Worcester sauce. Top with slices of herring fillet (obtainable from delicatessens) and decorate with lemon and parsley.

Beetroot as a Vegetable

For this dish you must boil your own beetroots, adding lemon juice to keep the colour, then mince finely. Fry two or three little pieces of pork or a rasher of bacon cut up small, add the minced beetroot and a dessertspoonful of white sauce, lemon juice or vinegar to taste, and serve hot.

HUNGARY

*Paprika lends a distinctive flavour and a bright
red hue to soups, meat and fish dishes*

Recipes by L. RODESINO, *Chef de Cuisine, Hungaria Restaurant, London*

BRILLIANT red dishes, coloured and distinctively flavoured with paprika, are typical of Hungarian cookery. Paprika, which is not hot like Cayenne, goes into Hungarian soups, fish and meat dishes, and gives its name to one of Hungary's two most famous national dishes: Chicken Paprika. The other, of course, is Goulash.

Yellow Split Pea Soup

4 *oz. dried yellow split peas*	3 *oz. lard*
1 *onion, finely chopped and fried in lard*	1 *piece of lean smoked pork*
	A little cream, salt and pepper
1 *tablespoonful flour*	

Wash the dried peas well and soak overnight in cold water. Drain; add fresh cold water; bring to boil; skim; add the smoked pork and cook till very tender. Melt lard; add flour and cook, stirring till it becomes a yellow colour. Remove from fire and mix gradually with stock and peas. Boil and strain. Boil again; add salt and pepper to taste, the chopped onion, the meat from the pork cut into small dice and a little cream. Serve with fried croûtons.

Carpe à la Racz

This excellent recipe for Carp can be used for any salt- or fresh-water fish, other countries not being as abundantly supplied with fresh-water fish as Hungary.

1 *medium-sized carp*	*A little chopped garlic*
2 *oz. lard*	1 *coffeecupful sour cream*, 1 *teaspoonful flour (well mixed together)*
2 *oz. diced bacon, partly fried*	
3 *tomatoes (quartered), not skinned*	
2 *green pimentoes, cut in squares*	3 *cooked potatoes cut in thick slices*
1 *dessertspoonful paprika*	¼ *lb. finely sliced onions*
	Salt

Scale and clean the carp. Remove head. Divide in two, lengthwise; cut each side in three. Salt and leave to stand for 30 minutes. Fry onions in lard to a golden colour; add paprika and garlic and stir; pour in two cupfuls of water; bring to boil.

Lay pieces of fish in shallow saucepan; place tomatoes, pimentoes, potatoes, bacon and paprika on top; cover with the prepared mixture; bring to boil and finish cooking in moderate oven for about 10 minutes.

Remove from oven, pour in gradually the flour and cream; mix by shaking the saucepan while bringing it to the boil; add salt, if needed, and simmer for a few minutes.

Stuffed Pimentoes

Stuffing for 6 fresh pimentoes

¾ *lb. chopped pork*	*Freshly ground peppers*
1 *small chopped onion*	*Garlic (very little)*
2 *tablespoonfuls cooked rice*	*Salt*
	Lard for frying
1 *egg*	

For the sauce

1 *oz. flour*	1½ *pints water or stock*
1 *oz. lard*	
1 *dessertspoonful sugar*	*Salt and pepper*
	1 *cupful tomato purée*

Fry onion lightly in lard; add garlic and rice and mix well with meat, egg, salt and peppers. Open pimentoes from the stalk side; remove seeds and dip the pimentoes in boiling water for 1 minute. When cold, stuff with the mixture.

For sauce, heat lard; add flour and fry without browning; add water or stock and tomato purée. Season with salt, pepper and sugar, and mix. Bring to boil; add pimentoes and cook for 30 minutes.

Veal Goulash (for 4)

1 *lb. stewing veal*	1 *dessertspoonful tomato purée*
1 *dessertspoonful paprika*	
6 *oz. chopped onions*	1 *green pimento (shredded) if available*
3 *oz. lard*	
1 *clove garlic (chopped)*	2 *tomatoes (cut in quarters)*
1 *tablespoonful flour*	

Cut meat into cubes and wash well. Fry onions in lard till they begin to brown; stir

Veal Goulash, one of Hungary's most famous national dishes, is flavoured with paprika and can be served with spaghetti, rice or potatoes

in paprika; add 1 cupful of water, garlic, meat and tomato purée. Bring to boil and stew slowly with lid on till tender, adding a little water during cooking if necessary.

When cooked, sprinkle the flour on the meat and stir; add more water to cover; bring to boil and simmer for a few minutes, adding the pimentoes and the tomatoes.

Serve with spaghetti, rice or potatoes.

Chicken Paprika

2 2-lb. chickens	¼ pint milk, ¼ pint.
2 oz. lard	cream, 1 tablespoon-
1 medium onion	ful flour (mixed
(chopped)	well together)
Salt	1 oz. paprika
¼ lb. tomatoes	1 pimento
1 cupful water	(if available)

Remove legs from chickens, split breasts into two, removing all small bones. Fry the onion in the lard until it begins to brown, stir in paprika, add water, salt and the chickens. Bring to the boil and cook with lid on until tender (about 20–30 minutes). Add a little water during cooking if necessary. Add the tomatoes and pimento during the last five minutes. When cooked, pour in the mixture of milk, cream and flour, stir while bringing to the boil and simmer for a few minutes. Add salt if required and serve with rice, spaghetti or boiled potatoes.

Cherry Strudel

1 lb. flour	¼ lb. sugar
1 egg	Lard
3 lb. cherries (stoned)	Dried breadcrumbs
Cinnamon powder	

Make a fairly soft dough with flour, egg and tepid water; work it and beat it till it comes clean off the table; lay it on floured board; cover with serviette and leave for 1½ hours. Place dough on a well-floured large cloth; pull and stretch it carefully in all directions until it is very thin and transparent. Trim off odd pieces outside the cloth. Spread on the top breadcrumbs, cherries, sugar and cinnamon powder, and sprinkle with melted lard. Lift the two corners of the cloth and roll till completely folded. Lay the rolled pastry on buttered pastry tray; brush with melted lard and cook in moderate oven for about 20 minutes.

Cut into portions and sprinkle with sugar.

GREECE

*Traditional Greek Dishes
as served at the White
Tower Restaurant, London*

To prepare the aubergine for Aubergine Imam Bayeldi the vegetable is peeled thinly in strips, leaving three or four of the strips on, above, and then slit with a knife to take the stuffing, right. Below, the finished dish

Dolmades are made with vegetable leaves—vine, cabbage or lettuce—stuffed with minced raw meat and previously cooked rice well seasoned with herbs, then cooked very slowly in a little stock in a casserole in the oven until tender but not disintegrating. Pimentoes and baby marrows are also treated in the same way. Do

GREEK cookery owes its inspiration to many lands, the strongest single influence being that of the Ottoman Empire. Stewy dishes are popular and there is an interesting method of cooking vegetables, not separately in water but with the meat they are to accompany, and usually "dolmadised." That delicious, mouth-watering word simply means stuffed, but in a very special way.

not skin pimentoes, but remove pips. Baby marrows should be partly skinned (for method, see Aubergine Imam Bayeldi and pictures on this page) if they are on the large side, and the pips removed.

This dish is served hot. A variation, consisting of vine (or cabbage or lettuce) leaves stuffed with rice and herbs only, without meat, makes a delicious hors d'œuvre and should then be served cold.

*Stuffed vine leaves, lamb grilled on a skewer, a gourmet's dream soup—
the Greeks have a word—and a recipe for them all*

Shashlik, a famous dish in all the Balkan countries, consists of small pieces of lamb, with various accompaniments, grilled over a charcoal fire and served with boiled rice

Taramosalata

This is a delicious Pâté of Smoked Cod's Roe which is easily and quickly made by adding chopped parsley, lemon juice, breadcrumbs and olive oil until it is a soft consistency for spreading. Serve hot on buttered toast.

Aubergine Imam Bayeldi
(for 4)

This dish, which is a stuffed aubergine, got its name because a famous Imam, a great gourmet but exceedingly greedy, ate so much of it that he "bayeldied," i.e. fainted away!

4 *medium (or 2 large) aubergines*
1 *clove of garlic*   *Olive oil for frying*
4 *onions*   *4 tomatoes*

To prepare your aubergine, remove the hard stalky end, then peel it fairly thinly lengthwise, in strips, leaving three or four strips of the skin on. This prevents the aubergine from falling to pieces during cooking. Finally, make about half a dozen lengthwise slits right through to the centre (see photos opposite). Now gently fry the aubergine in olive oil till golden. In another pan, fry to a golden brown the finely chopped onions, tomatoes and garlic (you need about twice as much as required to stuff the aubergine). Fill the slits with half this stuffing, lay the aubergines in a neat row in a casserole and pour the remainder of the stuffing over them. Bake slowly in a moderate oven until the onion is thoroughly done and the aubergine feels soft but still holds together. Leave to cool and serve cold with baked beans or cold stewed French Haricots Blancs.

NOTE: If using one large aubergine between two, always divide it lengthwise. This is because the thin stalky end has less goodness and flavour, and thus you equally divide the good and the not-so-good.

375

Fish Flaki

This is usually made with mackerel, but other fish could be used. It is baked in the oven for about an hour, smothered with sliced tomatoes, onions and garlic which have first been fried to a golden brown in olive oil. Can be served hot, but is even better cold.

Potage Avgolemono (for 4)

This is the Greek national soup, expensive but worth it.

1 *small to medium boiling chicken*	3 (*or, if possible, 5*) *new-laid eggs*
½ *lb. Patna rice*	*Lemon juice*

Boil the chicken very slowly, until it is practically falling to pieces, with the rice. Beat the eggs in a large bowl with the lemon juice, then, when the chicken broth is ready, begin to pour it into the bowl *very* slowly—the tiniest quantity at a time— without stopping beating for a moment. (Obviously, this is much easier if there are two of you in the kitchen.) When the quantity in the bowl is about double that of the original beaten eggs, pour it back into the broth, mix together and serve. Be sure to have a peppermill filled with black pepper on the table, as this is essential to bring out the full flavour of the soup. Or you can do as they do in some parts of Greece and serve with a little cinnamon sprinkled on top.

Fonds d'Artichaut à la Polita (for 4)

4 *globe artichokes*	½ *lb. green peas or*
1 *lemon*	*French beans*
½ *lb. young carrots*	*Olive oil and lemon*
½ *lb. young pickling onions*	*juice for dressing*

Always, when preparing an artichoke, squeeze lemon generously over it to keep it white; otherwise the artichoke, the knife and your hands will all blacken rapidly. Boil the base of the artichoke with the remains of the lemon (lime will not do) and cook until soft. Meanwhile, boil baby carrots, young pickling onions, green peas or young French beans (you need something green and the red of the carrots to make this otherwise colourless dish look appetising). Arrange round the artichokes and serve cold, garnished with a dressing of olive oil and lemon juice to taste.

Mussaka (for 4)

4 *medium aubergines*	*Mixed spice, garlic,*
Olive oil for frying	*onions and bay*
¾ *lb. minced beef*	*leaves to season*

For the sauce

1 *oz. flour*	4 *oz. grated*
2 *oz. butter*	*Parmesan cheese*
	½ *pint milk*

This pie, made with layers of aubergines and minced meat, is a famous Greek national dish. First, peel the aubergines and slice them, removing all the skin, then fry in olive oil until pale golden in colour. At the same time, fry minced beef, well seasoned, also in olive oil. Put aubergines and meat in alternate layers in a casserole, cover with a rich cheese sauce and bake in the oven for about an hour. Serve hot.

Shashlik is a very famous dish in all the Balkan countries and consists of little pieces of lamb grilled on a skewer, with various accompaniments, over a charcoal fire.

Choose lean lamb, cut it into small neat squares and marinade it in olive oil with bay leaves, onion and lemon juice. Skewer the meat squares through their centres, alternately with slices of tomato and onion, small rashers of bacon and mushrooms. Grill (preferably over a charcoal fire) very fast in intense heat, turning the skewers frequently, until the lamb is done. Sprinkle with chopped parsley and serve on a bed of boiled rice.

Loukmades (for 4)

6 *oz. flour*	*Cinnamon, castor*
½ *teaspoonful yeast*	*sugar and honey*
Olive oil for frying	*for garnish*

Mix thoroughly well together the flour, water and a very little yeast and leave to stand. This must be done in the morning if you wish to make the Loukmades that evening. Make a little olive oil really hot in a frying pan. Then, with your bare hand, take a small handful of the dough, close your fist tightly so that a little squeezes through your first finger. With a teaspoon dipped in water, nip off a tiny little blob of the dough no bigger than a small fried potato. Drop it into the hot olive oil and fry on both sides until golden brown in colour and swollen and puffy. They should swell up but be "full of nothing." Sprinkle with cinnamon and castor sugar and serve hot with honey.

POLAND

Here is a cuisine that avoids dullness, displays imagination, tastes excellent—and makes even cabbage seem exciting

by HALINA WUDZKA

IT is not generally realised how deeply Polish literature and art were influenced by the romantic period in English literature at the beginning of the nineteenth century. This, indeed, is regarded as the classical period in Poland's literature and it owes its origin directly to Byron, Wordsworth and their contemporaries, just as Chopin's music owed so much to the influence of John Field.

Ever since then there has been a streak of romanticism in the Polish national character, and so Polish cooking is, in its own way, romantic too. It successfully avoids dullness, it displays imagination and it tastes excellent. Good restaurants in prewar Warsaw were among the best in Europe, and Polish sausages were the best on the Continent.

In addition to the good restaurants, the dairies or "milk shops" were a feature of Warsaw. These were little places with perhaps half a dozen small tables where one could drink a glass of hot or cold milk or get the most popular snack, "set milk with potatoes." This was fresh-set sour milk (not yoghourt) set in individual bowls and cooled or chilled, accompanied by a plateful of hot boiled potatoes with crisply fried onions sprinkled on the top. It was eaten with a spoon, alternate mouthfuls of the milk and the potatoes.

Try some of the Polish recipes and discover what an exciting thing, for in-

stance, cabbage can be—a vegetable not generally regarded as likely to stir up strong emotions.

Polish Beetroot Soup (Barszcz)

2–3 *pints clear beef stock or freshly made beef bouillon*	1 *bay leaf*
1 *grated raw beetroot*	1 *or 2 beetroot, cooked, peeled, cut into thin strips like noodles*
½ *teaspoonful vinegar or lemon juice*	½ *lb. tomatoes*
1 *tablespoonful butter*	½ *cupful flour*
Salt and pepper	

For beef bouillon.—1½ lb. beef, 1 carrot, 1 onion, a bouquet garni, cooked together and skimmed clear.

Cook the tomatoes separately in 3 tablespoonfuls of water until soft, then rub through a sieve. Add the tomato purée, the cooked beetroot and the vinegar or lemon

Chicken Cutlets may be topped with a fried egg and served with potatoes, mushrooms and new peas, or eaten cold as a picnic dish

377

juice to the stock or bouillon, and bind the soup by slightly browning the flour in the butter and gradually adding a little of the broth until it is smooth and thin, then.stirring into the soup. Simmer gently for at least 1½ hours, adding salt and pepper to taste and a bay leaf. Just before serving, colour with grated raw beetroot and bring just to the boil; if cooked any longer, the colour will fade. Serve with finely chopped dill (or fennel) or parsley and sour cream; these are usually served in side dishes so that each person can suit his individual taste. For variation, small Frankfurter-type sausages or little cubes of ham may also be added to the soup.

Polish Cold Soup (Chlodnik)

Prepare beetroot soup as above. When ready, add 1 or 2 cupfuls of diced boiled beef (from the freshly made beef bouillon), some diced ham or Frankfurters, or both, some diced fresh cucumber, a couple of sliced radishes, a little shredded tender lettuce or spinach or sorrel and a cupful of sharp cider or red wine. Chill thoroughly. Just before serving, add at least ¼ pint sour cream.

Dressed Herring

1 *herring, salted or cured in brine*	*Vinegar, olive oil and black pepper*
Milk	*Onions*

Soak herring for at least 24 hours in milk; drain; cut off head and tail; scrape off skin; remove all bones.

Cut across in ¾-in. strips, lay them on a flat dish, keeping the shape of the fish, and make it more attractive by appropriately placing the head and tail. At least 1 hour before serving, cover with a dressing of 1 part vinegar to 2 parts olive oil and a good sprinkle of pepper, preferably black.

Serve surrounded with onions, either raw mild onions cut in thin slices or rings, or onion salad.

To make onion salad.—Slice 3 or 4 onions in thin rings, parboil for a few minutes until they become transparent, drain well and, while still warm, mix with basic dressing: ½ teaspoonful salt, ¼ teaspoonful pepper, ½ teaspoonful mustard, 2 tablespoonfuls vinegar (preferably malt vinegar), 2 tablespoonfuls olive oil.

Stuffed Herring

1 *herring, salted or cured in brine*	
½ *lb. cooking apples, raw, peeled and cored*	*Cold boiled potatoes, of bulk equal to the quantity of apples*

Begin as for dressed herring, again keeping aside the head and tail. After removing all bones, put the herring, apple and potatoes twice through a fine mincer to ensure that it is finely minced, then mix with a dressing as for dressed herring, adding salt to taste.

Serve on a flat dish, making the mixture into the shape of a fish (with a fork) and adding the head and tail. Surround with raw onion rings or onion salad, as already described.

Meat and Cabbage (Bigos) (for 4)

1–2 *lb. fresh cabbage or Sauerkraut, and approximately the same quantity of ham or gammon cut in small chunks or salt pork or bacon*	
A *few pieces of smoked sausage*	1 *or 2 Frankfurter sausages cut in pieces*
A *few pieces of garlic sausage*	*Bacon or pork fat*
Salt and pepper	1 *wineglassful red wine*
2 *tablespoonfuls flour*	
Several sliced onions	

Finely shred the cabbage or Sauerkraut, cover it with water and bring to the boil, then drain thoroughly, to remove any traces of bitterness. Add the meat, sausage and sliced onions to the prepared cabbage, season well with salt and pepper, add a little water and simmer very gently for at least 1 hour, adding a little more water if necessary but only just enough to keep it moist. When the cabbage and onions are thoroughly cooked and tender, make a gravy separately by melting some bacon or pork fat, stirring into it the flour and browning slightly, then adding a little water. Pour this over the meat and cabbage, and at the last minute add the wine. Heat, but do not cook any longer. Serve at once.

This dish may be served with boiled potatoes and should be accompanied by a good red wine and rye bread.

Chicken Cutlets (Pożarski)

1 *boiling fowl*	*Milk*
Flour or fine bread-crumbs and butter for frying	1–2 *cupfuls white bread and 1 or 2 eggs, according to size of fowl*
Salt and pepper to taste	

Photographs of Polish food taken at the Polish Air Force Club, London

There are many ways of cooking Stuffed White Cabbage. Sour cream or sour cream cheese and rye bread are served with most main dishes

Remove skin and mince finely all the white meat from a boiling fowl. Add the bread soaked in milk and mince again. Season with salt and pepper. Mix well with the eggs, lightly beaten, and shape into small flat cakes about 1 in. thick. Coat with flour or egg and breadcrumbs and fry in butter, quickly browning the outside first, then cooking slowly to keep the cutlets juicy while cooking right through. Serve hot with mashed potatoes, carrots, little peas, button mushrooms, asparagus tips; or eat cold with salad as a picnic dish. A fried egg may be served on each cutlet, if liked.

Pirogi

Pirogi are a mainstay of Polish and Russian home cooking. They are a kind of small turnover, boiled in water, with various fillings, both sweet and savoury.

For the dough

12 oz. plain flour	1 egg
A knob of fat	Salt

Make a not too soft dough, knead well and roll out to $\frac{1}{8}$ in. in thickness. Cut into rounds, about $2\frac{1}{2}$ in. diameter, and put a teaspoonful of filling in the middle of each. Close them up very firmly—this is essential, otherwise the filling will cook out—and boil for 3 minutes in salted water.

These are some popular fillings:

Sour Milk Cheese Filling

$\frac{1}{2}$ lb. sour milk cheese	Butter or margarine
$\frac{1}{2}$ lb. boiled potatoes	1 oz. Danish blue
1 tablespoonful	cheese
semolina	Salt and pepper to
1 small onion	taste

Fry the chopped onion in butter or margarine until golden brown, then add all the other ingredients and mix together very thoroughly.

Serve with chopped onions fried in butter or margarine until golden brown.

Morella Cherry Filling (a summer dish)

Stone the cherries and put 3 or 4 on each round of dough. When the Pirogi are cooked, brush them over with melted butter and serve cold with yoghourt poured on top and plenty of sugar.

Curds or Curd Cheese mixed with an egg to a smooth paste and very slightly salted. When Pirogi are cooked, brush generously with melted butter, serve hot with sour cream and sugar or sugar mixed with nutmeg or cinnamon to taste.

Polish Roast Chicken

One small chicken or Poussin per person is stuffed with breadcrumbs and plenty of chopped dill bound with a beaten egg, or simply with branches or sprigs of dill. Roast in butter, basting frequently. Make gravy in the roasting pan by lightly browning a little flour and adding sour cream at the last minute and just heating through. Serve with fresh cucumber salad and new potatoes.

"Selyanka" Meat and Cabbage

Approximately 1 lb. of various meats: bacon or gammon or ham; smoked and well-spiced pork sausage or garlic sausage or ham sausage	*1 or 2 lb. Sauerkraut, squeezed dry of its liquid*
	1 or 2 lb. onions, sliced
	Garlic
	Cooking fat and olive oil
Breadcrumbs and/or grated cheese	*Salt and pepper*

Fry the meats, cut in small strips, very gently until well done in a large frying pan, then remove to a good-sized mixing bowl. There should be plenty of fat left in the pan. Add cooking fat (or good dripping), if necessary, and a dash of olive oil, and fry the onions, gently, until transparent; also a whole bud of garlic, which should then be removed. When the onions are done, take them out of the frying pan and add to the meat. Then fry the drained Sauerkraut, stirring constantly until well browned, and adding more fat as required to prevent sticking or burning. Season well with salt and pepper. Mix all the ingredients thoroughly, put into ovenproof dish, sprinkle the top with breadcrumbs and/or grated cheese. Before baking, add about a teacupful of boiling water (or perhaps a little more), so that the cabbage is quite moist. Bake in the oven until brown. Serve with boiled potatoes.

Tripe à la Polonaise (Flaki) (for 3–4)

1 lb. tripe	*3 oz. butter*
2 oz. flour	*A little ground ginger,*
2 carrots	*nutmeg, cloves, salt,*
2 sticks celery	*pepper and*
A little more than 2 quarts stock	*Cayenne to taste*
	1 onion
Mixed herbs	

Clean the tripe and wash several times, then blanch in boiling salted water, wash again in cold water, then put into boiling water and simmer very slowly for 5–6 hours. Take out and cut into narrow strips like noodles. Melt the butter, stir in the flour and brown it, then make a roux with a little of the stock. Add this to the stock with the sliced vegetables, herbs, seasoning and spices. Bring to the boil and simmer for 20 minutes. Add the tripe, cover and simmer until all is tender.

NOTE: As a rule the sauce is only lightly spiced, this dish always being served in Warsaw accompanied by a whole array of little separate dishes containing an assortment of spices from which one helps oneself, according to taste. The spices should include mixed herbs, ground ginger, grated nutmeg, red pepper, chopped marjoram, grated cheese, salt, and black pepper in a mill.

Cabbage Pie

Line a deep baking dish with pastry or yeast dough. Scald a white cabbage for a minute or two, drain, cut up in 1-in. squares, mix with a lightly beaten egg, season with salt and pepper, and fill the baking dish with these ingredients. Cover the cabbage with a lid or plate to keep in the steam and prevent it from browning, and bake in a moderate oven until tender. Serve very hot, adding several knobs of butter at the last minute so that they just melt on top.

Mushrooms with Eggs

This very popular Polish dish can be made either with fresh mushrooms or—this is well worth trying—with dried ones. Dried mushrooms from Italy can now be bought by the ounce in many shops.

½ lb. mushrooms	*2 oz. butter*
5–6 tablespoonfuls fresh-set sour milk	*1 tablespoonful semolina*
1 medium-sized onion, chopped	*Fried eggs as required*
Salt and pepper	

Wash, but do not peel, the mushrooms and slice them finely. Fry the onion in the butter until transparent, then add the mushrooms and fry together for 1 minute. Add water to cover and simmer for ½ hour, add semolina and sour milk, salt and pepper to taste and serve with fried eggs.

If dried mushrooms are used, wash them and let them soak for a few hours in warm water, then proceed as above, cooking in the water in which they were soaked.

Stuffed White Cabbage (A dish from East Poland, sometimes called Golubtsy or Little Pigeons)

1 *lb. minced beef (raw)*
1 *tablespoonful rice*
1 *large white cabbage*
1 *medium-sized onion, finely chopped*
Salt and pepper
Finely chopped mushrooms

Babka is a famous national cake, always made in a fluted tin like a jelly mould and lightly iced

For the gravy

1 *oz. dripping*   1 *oz. flour*
1 *tablespoonful*   1 *tablespoonful*
Golden Syrup   *vinegar*
1 *medium-sized onion*   *Salt*
          ½ *pint stock or water*

Peel off the outer leaves of the cabbage, cut off the protruding parts of the stalks and plunge into boiling water for 1 minute to make them pliable. Mix all the other ingredients together and put 1 tablespoonful in each leaf, fold up neatly and tie with string. Pack tightly into a fireproof dish. *For the gravy.*—Cut up the onion and fry it in the dripping until golden brown, add flour and fry until flour is brown too, then add boiling water or stock, Golden Syrup, vinegar and salt, and boil for a few minutes. When smooth, pour over the stuffed leaves and put into a slow oven. Cook until the leaves are dark brown on one side, then turn them over and brown the other side. This dish should simmer in the oven for several hours—in fact, it improves considerably if it is cooked on two successive days, as the slowly roasted cabbage leaves give a distinctive flavour.

Babka

A cake with a texture between a fine-grained Angel Cake and a porous Sponge Cake.

1½ *lb. flour, well sifted*
6 *egg-yolks*
1 *cupful melted butter*
1¼ *to* 1½ *oz. yeast, dissolved in* ½ *cupful warm milk*
Pinch of salt, handful of sultanas, teaspoonful vanilla flavouring
2 *to* 3 *tablespoonfuls white icing, a little rum or lemon juice*
¾ *cupful sugar*

Beat egg-yolks thoroughly, mix well with melted warm (not hot) butter, add yeast dissolved in milk, mix thoroughly, add flour, beat well, put into warm place to rise for ½ to ¾ of an hour. Add sugar, salt, flavouring and sultanas, and knead or beat again, the longer the better, until dough shows bubbles and no longer adheres to the hands. Let it rise again in a warm place, and be sure always to cover it and protect it from draughts, for 1½ to 2 hours. Knead or beat for another 10 minutes, put into greased baking tin shaped like a jelly mould, filling only one-quarter to one-third, let it rise again till tin is about three-quarters full. Bake in hot oven for about an hour.

While still warm, spread over the top a little white icing, flavoured with a few drops of rum or lemon juice, letting it trickle down the sides.

AUSTRIA

*From Vienna comes a cuisine that is good and gay, with
a sublime disregard for slimming rules*

by Camilla Kapralik

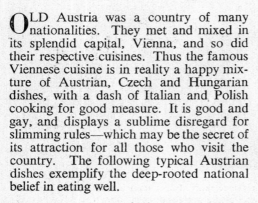

OLD Austria was a country of many nationalities. They met and mixed in its splendid capital, Vienna, and so did their respective cuisines. Thus the famous Viennese cuisine is in reality a happy mixture of Austrian, Czech and Hungarian dishes, with a dash of Italian and Polish cooking for good measure. It is good and gay, and displays a sublime disregard for slimming rules—which may be the secret of its attraction for all those who visit the country. The following typical Austrian dishes exemplify the deep-rooted national belief in eating well.

Beef Broth with Liver Dumplings (for 4)

The centrepiece of the Austrian middle-class family's regular midday meal on weekdays is boiled beef, with vegetables or horseradish sauce, preceded by a beef broth, sometimes with vermicelli, etc., in it, but more often with liver dumplings.

For the broth

1½ lb. beef (prefer-	1 onion
ably chuck steak)	Peppercorns
Parsley	A few sticks of celery

Boil the beef slowly in salted water with the other ingredients. When the meat is tender, strain off the soup and cook the dumplings in it.

For the dumplings

¼ lb. calf's liver	1 clove of garlic,
1 calf's milt (spleen)	crushed (optional)
1 crisp roll (or bread)	1 oz. dripping
1 egg	White breadcrumbs
Pinch of salt	

Cream the fat and salt, mix in the egg, soak the roll or bread in water and squeeze out all the liquid. Mince the liver and milt, and mix with the other ingredients, add about 2 tablespoonfuls of breadcrumbs, and let the mixture stand for a while. It should be of such a consistency that it can be formed into little dumplings. Boil for about 5 minutes in the broth.

Beef Gulasch (for 4)

Although of Hungarian origin, the Austrian version is a great favourite.

1½ lb. beef (prefer-	1–2 oz. beef dripping
ably back-rib)	or lard
½ lb. onions	1 heaped teaspoonful
½ teaspoonful paprika	flour
(not red pepper)	½ teaspoonful cara-
Salt to taste	way seeds

Chop the onions finely and fry in the fat in a heavy saucepan until they are a rich golden brown. Cut the meat into 1-in. squares and add it, with all the other ingredients, to the onions, and fry, stirring frequently, until the flour is dark brown. Cover with a lid and simmer until the juice is extracted from the meat. When all the liquid has evaporated (this is a critical moment; if left too long the meat will burn), add a little water and continue to simmer until the meat is tender. Serve with boiled potatoes.

Veal Gulasch

This is made in the same way as Beef Gulasch, using stewing veal in place of the beef, one ripe tomato instead of the caraway seeds and omitting the flour when frying. The onions should be fried only to a pale golden colour. Stir 1 teaspoonful of flour into about half a bottle of yoghourt, or top of the milk with a few drops of lemon juice, until quite smooth and free from lumps, and when the meat is tender add this to the gravy and let it simmer for a while.

Weiner Schnitzel (for 4)

This is the favourite Austrian Sunday dinner dish and, when served cold, is also popular for picnics.

4 slices of leg of veal	Breadcrumbs and
or pork	flour
Pinch of paprika	2 tablespoonfuls milk
Lard for frying	2 eggs
Salt	

Note: To make authentic Schnitzel, as

eaten in Vienna, here are three important rules:

(1) Prepare the breadcrumbs yourself—bought o n e s will not do! Buy two French loaves and put them in a very cool oven until they are quite dry but not brown, then grate them and finally rub them through a sieve.

(2) Use lard for frying, NOT dripping or any fat that has been used before.

(3) Do not let the meat stand for any length of time after it has been coated, as the bread-crumbs will become soaked and the schnitzels will not crisp. Prepare the second piece of meat while the first is frying.

Beat out the meat until it is ⅓-in. thick and salt slightly on both sides. Mix the eggs with the milk, paprika and salt. Roll the meat in flour, shake off surplus, then dip in the egg mixture, drip off any excess, coat with bread-crumbs, dabbing the crumbs on lightly and shaking off the surplus. (Make sure that all the meat is evenly covered with all the ingredients.) Get the lard smoking hot in a heavy pan and deep-fry the schnitzels. Serve with potatoes and slices of lemon but, please, NOT with tomato sauce and macaroni.

Spring chicken (*poussin*) prepared in the same way, but fried more slowly, makes another famous Austrian dish, and so does fish—carp being a particular favourite.

In summer it is the thing to serve Weiner Schnitzel with new potatoes tossed in butter and finely chopped parsley and a cucumber salad.

Cucumber Salad

Slice the cucumber very thinly, salt and cover it for ¼ hour, then squeeze out the liquid. Make a dressing of French vinegar,

To be really extravagant, serve Stuffed Rumpsteak with puff-pastry crescents, or vol-au-vents filled with creamy potatoes and diced ham

diluted to taste, a pinch of sugar and a pinch of pepper, and pour it over the cucumber. If liked, a little olive oil may be added and a small piece of crushed garlic.

Boiled Ham, Sauerkraut and Dumplings
(Geselchtes, kraut und knödel) (for 4)

1½ lb. bacon (gammon or shoulder)	½ teaspoonful sugar
2 bay leaves	1 or 2 cloves
Sauerkraut	½ teaspoonful caraway seeds
1 large raw potato	

NOTE: Very good tinned sauerkraut—either Dutch or Israeli—is obtainable in the U.K.

Simmer the bacon until tender, with the sugar, bay leaves and cloves. Simmer separately the sauerkraut with the caraway seeds for ½ hour, then grate the raw potato into it and simmer for another ½ hour.

For the dumplings

1 *French loaf*	2 *oz. dripping or*
1 *egg*	*margarine*
½ *teaspoonful salt*	¼ *pint milk*
4 *tablespoonfuls plain flour*	

Cut the bread into small cubes and pour over it the melted fat. Mix together the egg, milk and salt, add to the bread and leave for at least 1 hour, stirring occasionally. Add the flour, mix thoroughly, form into four balls, roll them in flour and boil for 10 minutes in salted water.

NOTE: Roast pork is also served in Austria with sauerkraut and dumplings. When roasting pork, the Austrians add an onion and sprinkle the joint generously with caraway seeds, which gives it a distinctive flavour.

Stuffed Rump Steak (for 4)

2 *oz. dripping or lard*	4 *good-sized rump*
¼ *lb. onions*	*steaks*
8 *fillets of anchovy*	4 *bacon rashers*
1 *oz. capers*	½ *bottle Yoghourt*
1 *teaspoonful French*	1 *or 2 pickled cucum-*
mustard	*bers (not gherkins)*
½ *teaspoonful paprika*	*Flour*

Beat the steak to ⅓-in. thickness, sprinkle with paprika, spread with finely chopped anchovy, capers and mustard. Put the bacon rashers into boiling water for a minute or two, then put one on each steak and add half or quarter of a pickled cucumber, according to size, roll up and tie with white sewing cotton. Chop the onions and fry in the dripping or lard until golden brown. Roll the meat in flour and fry with onions until a rich brown on all sides, then proceed as for Beef Gulasch (page 382). When the meat is tender, add half a bottle of yoghourt with 1 teaspoonful flour and simmer for 20 minutes. Remove cotton and serve with boiled potatoes or, if you want to be really extravagant, with pastry crescents or vol-au-vents filled with creamed potatoes and diced ham.

Minced Meat Fritters (for 4)

1 *lb. beef (topside)*
1 *crisp roll (or white bread)*
Breadcrumbs
1 *clove garlic, crushed*
½-*lb. pork*
1 *egg*
Salt and pepper
Lard for frying

Mince the raw meat (or get the butcher to do it for you). Soak the bread in water, then press out all the liquid and add the egg, garlic, salt and pepper and mix together very thoroughly, adding 1 tablespoonful of breadcrumbs. Form the mixture into oblong fritters, dip them in breadcrumbs and fry in medium deep fat (preferably lard) until a rich brown on both sides. Serve with mashed potatoes, potato salad, pickled cucumbers or cucumber salad.

Minced meat fritters are in the luxury class made this way, as served in Vienna

Viennese Guglhupf, a typical Austrian delicacy, is delicious served with coffee or chocolate topped with sweetened whipped cream

Lights and Heart with Dumplings (Beuschl mit knödeln) (for 4)

This competes in popularity with Gulasch.

1 *set of calf's (or*	1 *onion*
pig's) lights with	*A few peppercorns*
the heart or 2 *hearts*	1 *clove of garlic*
A sprig of thyme	1 *tablespoonful*
2 *sticks of celery*	*French vinegar*

For the gravy

1 *oz. flour*	1 *oz. dripping*
Meat broth as required	

Cook all the ingredients together until tender, then leave to cool (preferably over-night). Make a fairly thick gravy, using the flour fried in dripping until golden brown, and some of the broth in which the meat was cooked. Bring to the boil, stirring all the time, then add the finely sliced meat and reheat, but do not boil. Serve with slices of lemon.

This dish is also served with bread dumplings (see boiled ham, sauerkraut and dumplings, as above).

SWEET DISHES

Dough made with yeast is typically Austrian and is used in many different ways. It is made as follows:

12 *oz. plain flour*	*A pinch of grated*
1 *oz. yeast*	*lemon rind*
4 *oz. butter or mar-*	2 *egg-yolks*
garine	½ *pint milk (approx.)*
3 *oz. castor sugar*	

Warm the milk, pour off one-third and add to it 1 teaspoonful sugar and the yeast, cover and put in a warm place to rise. Work the butter or margarine into the flour (as for short pastry), add egg-yolks, sugar, lemon rind, risen yeast and—slowly—the rest of the milk, to make a fairly soft dough. Beat with a wooden spoon until it no longer sticks, is quite smooth and shows little bubbles. Cover it up and keep in a warm place until it has risen to twice its size.

This yeast dough is the basis for the following sweet dishes and cakes:

(a) Viennese Guglhupf (the famous tea-time cake)

Before the dough has risen, add 1 oz. sultanas. Grease a fluted baking tin (special Guglhupf tins can be bought in big cities) thickly with melted butter or margarine and let it cool, then sprinkle the sides of the tin with thinly sliced blanched almonds. Fill the tin with the dough and leave covered in a warm place until the dough has risen to double its original size, Bake for $\frac{3}{4}$ hour in a cool oven until golden brown, turn out on to a plate and, while still hot, sprinkle freely with vanilla sugar.

This Guglhupf is served with coffee or chocolate, topped with sweetened whipped cream.

Vanilla Sugar

Place a vanilla pod, cut into two or three pieces, in a screw-top jar full of icing sugar. In about 10 days the sugar is delicately flavoured.

(b) Steam Noodles

Sprinkle a warmed pastry board with flour and place the dough on it in table-spoonfuls. Make a small well in the centre of each little piece of dough and fill with $\frac{1}{2}$ teaspoonful plum jam mixed with grated lemon rind and a pinch of cinnamon. Fold the dough over the jam and close tightly. Put into a well-greased oven-glass dish and grease each bun on the sides or they will stick together. Leave in a warm place until risen to double size, bake in a cool oven for about 30 minutes, then, before the buns begin to show any colour, sprinkle them with about $\frac{1}{4}$ pint boiling water, and keep them in the oven for about 20 minutes longer. The buns should not have any colour. Serve hot with melted butter and ground walnuts mixed with vanilla sugar (see above).

NOTE: A pure jam should be used. Jams made with special pectin preparations may start to run and so spoil the dough.

(c) Viennese Buns (Wiener buchteln)

These are made in exactly the same way as Steam Noodles, but filled with any jam you fancy and baked, without adding water, until they are a golden brown. While still hot, sprinkle with vanilla sugar. They are served at tea-time or as a sweet dish after a main meal.

(d) Viennese Sparrows (Wiener spatzen)

After the dough has risen, cut off pieces with a tablespoon and drop into a frying pan containing deep hot lard. Fry until golden brown on both sides, then put on to blotting paper for a minute or two, sprinkle with vanilla sugar and serve hot with raspberry jam.

NOTE: If a tablespoonful of rum is mixed with the dough for this recipe, it will absorb less fat.

Apfelstrudel

To make an Apfelstrudel (the real thing) you need a fairly large table, say about 2 ft. 6 in. by 3 ft. 6 in. Also, as flour in the U.K. is completely different from flour in Austria, I would strongly suggest using McDougall's self-raising flour, with which I personally have obtained the best results.

For the dough

12 oz. flour	2 oz. lard

Use lukewarm water to make a soft dough which must be kneaded until it shows little bubbles. Now warm a bowl, cover the dough with it and let it stand for $\frac{1}{2}$ hour.

For the filling

2 lb. cooking apples (Bramleys or Blenheims, peeled and sliced)	5 oz. breadcrumbs
	Lemon juice
	4 oz. castor sugar
	6 oz. margarine
A pinch of cinnamon	3 oz. sultanas

Fry the breadcrumbs in 2 oz. margarine until golden brown, melt the rest of the margarine. When all the ingredients have been prepared, put a cloth on the table and sprinkle it with flour, then pull out the dough on the cloth until it is nearly as thin as tissue paper. Cut off the thick edges, sprinkle with the 4 oz. melted margarine, put the sliced apples and sultanas on only a quarter part of the dough along the wide side of the table, and sprinkle the apples with lemon juice. Scatter the breadcrumbs and the sugar mixed with cinnamon all over the dough. Pick up the ends of the table-cloth and, by moving the cloth, roll the strudel up very tightly. Grease all over with melted margarine, put on a greased baking-tin and bake in a moderate oven for about 1 hour until golden. Immediately it comes out of the oven, cut it in pieces, put on a plate and sprinkle with vanilla sugar.

NOTE: The pulling out of the dough needs practice. Do not be discouraged if you do not succeed the first time—try again.

Viennese Chocolate Cake

6 oz. sugar	6 oz. ground plain
3 oz. margarine	chocolate
1½ oz. breadcrumbs	6 eggs
3 oz. ground almonds or cobnuts	A dash of rum

Cream the margarine with the sugar and the egg-yolks, add breadcrumbs, rum, almonds or cobnuts (ground with their skins), chocolate and, finally, the stiffly beaten egg-whites. Put the mixture into a loose-bottomed cake tin well greased with butter and lightly covered with breadcrumbs (shake off the surplus). Bake in a cool oven for about ¾ hour. When cold, split and fill with the following cream:

4 oz. chocolate	3½ oz. margarine or
4 oz. sugar	butter
1–2 tablespoonfuls	1 egg-yolk
rum	

Melt the chocolate with a little water and leave to cool. Cream the butter or margarine with the sugar and egg, and add the chocolate and rum. Cover the cake with chocolate icing (see Icings chapter).

Emperor's Omelet (Kaiserschmarrn)

3 oz. plain flour	4 oz. castor sugar
3 oz. margarine	1 oz. sultanas
Milk (about ¼ pint)	¼ pint whipped cream
3 eggs	A pinch of salt

Mix the flour to a thin paste with the milk, add the egg-yolks, sugar and salt, Whip the egg-whites very stiffly and mix into the paste very carefully. Add the whipped cream. Put the margarine in a baking tin and let it get hot, pour in the mixture and cook in a moderate oven until golden brown, then pull to little pieces with two forks (if not quite done, put back into the oven for a few minutes) and add the sultanas, sprinkle with vanilla sugar and serve with stewed plums.

Linzer Torte

6 oz. sugar	6 oz. margarine
6 oz. breadcrumbs	6 oz. ground almonds
1 egg (whole)	1 egg-white
½ teaspoonful mixed	Grated lemon rind
ground spice	Strawberry jam

Make a dough, using all ingredients except egg-white and jam, and put three-quarters of it into a baking tin with a loose bottom. Moisten the 1-in.-thick dough with the egg-white. Make the rest of the dough into long thin strips and with these make a rim round the bottom layer of dough and a lattice-work pattern on top. Paint with white of egg. Bake in a cool oven until well browned, then fill the spaces with strawberry jam.

Another famous national sweet dish is Linzer Torte, a lattice-patterned tart tasting of almonds and topped with strawberry jam

GERMANY

Where the food reflects the national character and good rye bread is plentiful

IT has been said that a nation's cuisine reflects that nation's basic characteristics. Germany is a country of many tribes, and just as north Germans differ from Rhinelanders and Bavarians, so does their way of cooking. Food in north Germany is rather stern and robust, in the south it is more akin to the rich Austrian fare.

Good bread, and plenty of it, is an essential part of a German meal. Praise is due to the quality of German bread, especially to the dark grey rye bread which can be bought in the U.K. This is wholesome and an excellent help to digestion. The pumpernickel type of bread is also worth trying; it is delicious with butter and cheese.

Visitors to Germany will probably have come across some of the following dishes.

Cold Cherry Soup (for 4–5)

2 lb. black cherries	½ lb. sugar
1½ pints water	Cinnamon
Cloves	1 egg-white
Cornflour	

Stone the cherries and cook in water with the sugar and spices; thicken with cornflour. Pour into soup bowls and leave to cool. When cold, put in the centre of each bowl a blob of slightly sweetened whipped egg-white.

Pea Soup with Sausage (for 4)

½ lb. dried peas	Frankfurters (or other
1 oz. dripping	continental cooking
1 tablespoonful flour	sausages)
Water or stock	

Soak the peas (the wrinkled green variety are the best available in the U.K.) for about 12 hours, boil in water or stock until quite tender, pass through a sieve and add sufficient stock or water to make four helpings. Fry the flour in the dripping until golden brown, add to the liquid and simmer for about ½ hour. Before serving, add some continental cooking sausage or Frankfurter cut in small pieces. Serve with small cubes of fried bread. This is a very tasty, substantial and nourishing dish.

Herring Salad (for 4)

3 salted herrings	Yoghourt
A little vinegar	1 sprig of thyme
1 bay leaf	A pinch of sugar
1 onion (cut into thin rings)	½ teaspoonful French mustard

Soak the herrings in water for 48 hours, changing the water once or twice, then bone the fish and cut into small pieces. Cook the onion in the vinegar, diluted to taste, with the herbs and sugar. When cold, add the yoghourt and mustard, and pour over the herrings. Leave to stand for 2 days, then serve with potatoes boiled in their jackets.

Stuffed Herrings

Pickled herrings	Vegetable salad
1 apple	Mayonnaise
Pickled cucumber	Tomatoes
Parsley	

Pickled herrings can be bought in jars. Remove them from the brine and drip dry, then split open and stuff with a mixture of vegetable salad, mayonnaise and sliced apple. Serve garnished with cucumber, tomatoes and parsley.

Macaroni with Boiled Bacon (for 4)

½ lb. macaroni or noodles (real egg noodles are the most suitable)	4 tablespoonfuls yoghourt
	½ lb. cooked bacon
	2 oz. margarine
3 eggs	Breadcrumbs

Cook macaroni or noodles in boiling salted water until tender, and rinse in cold water. Separate the egg-yolks from the whites, and cream the margarine with the yolks. Mix with the cold macaroni or noodles, chopped bacon and yoghourt. Add the very stiffly whipped egg-whites. Grease a fireproof dish, sprinkle with breadcrumbs, pour in the mixture and bake in a moderate oven until golden brown. Serve with lettuce, white cabbage salad

Pickled herrings, stuffed with mixed vegetable salad and garnished with
cucumber, tomato and parsley

dressed with vinegar and oil, or with a rich tomato sauce.

Boiled Chicken with Lemon Sauce and Rice

1 *boiling fowl*
2 *sticks of celery*
Lemon juice
Rice
1 *or* 2 *cloves*

Parsley
White sauce
1 *small onion*
1 *egg-yolk*
Peppercorns

Boil the chicken with the onion, peppercorns, celery and parsley until tender. Serve with white sauce, to which lemon juice and egg-yolk have been added.

Rice is boiled in the chicken broth, in the proportion of 1 teacupful of rice to 2 teacupfuls of broth. Add the onion, whole, with the cloves stuck firmly in it, and cook in a slow oven until tender.

Reibe Kuchen (Potato pancakes)

1 lb. potatoes	Salt and pepper
3 tablespoonfuls plain	1 egg
flour	1 onion (optional)
Oil for frying	

Grate the raw potatoes and let them drip off; mix in the egg, flour and salt and pepper, and grated onion (if liked). Make into thin fritters and fry, preferably in oil, until golden brown on both sides.

Hackbraten (Minced meat loaf with savoury sauce) (for 5—6)

1½ lb. raw beef (top rib)	Breadcrumbs
	¼ lb. pork
2 eggs	2 oz. white bread
Salt and pepper	1 medium-sized onion
2 hard-boiled eggs for stuffing	1 oz. dripping

For the sauce
2 oz. capers
About 4 tablespoonfuls of sour cream or
yoghourt   Four

Soak the bread in water, then squeeze out all the liquid. Mince the raw beef and mix it very thoroughly with the eggs and soaked bread; add salt and pepper to taste. Form into an oblong loaf, with the hard-boiled eggs in the middle and completely covered by meat. Roll in breadcrumbs and put into a roasting tin with a little dripping and the onion, peeled and cut in half. Roast for about 1½ hours, then add the capers, sour cream and a little flour for thickening. Keep in the oven for another ½ hour. Serve with very creamy mashed potatoes.

Cheese Cake

Short pastry	¼ lb. sour-milk cheese
2 oz. margarine	4 oz. castor sugar
3 egg-yolks	2 oz. sultanas
Grated lemon rind	½ teaspoonful baking
Blanched almonds	powder

Line a loose-bottom sponge cake tin with the pastry. Cream the margarine with the sugar and the egg-yolks, add the cheese, baking powder, sultanas and lemon rind. Put this mixture on the pastry, sprinkle with thinly sliced blanched almonds and bake in a moderate oven until golden brown.

Pancakes with Asparagus

10 oz. plain flour	3 eggs
Milk	Salt and parsley
Asparagus	Margarine

Wash, peel and trim the asparagus, and braise until tender in margarine and water with finely chopped parsley and salt. Meanwhile, make pancakes (see Puddings and Sweets) wrap sticks of asparagus in

One of the most typical of all German dishes—Frankfurters are served hot with sauerkraut and boiled potatoes or cold with potato salad

Whole pears served in a dish
of chocolate sauce

them, and serve hot. Put a
slice of beetroot on each pancake
and fix with a cocktail stick.

Cold Rice with Rhubarb Jelly
(for 4)

> 2 teacupfuls rice
> 5 teacupfuls milk
> Pinch of salt
> 6 oz. sugar
> ½ vanilla pod
> 1½ lb. red rhubarb
> ½ pint water
> ½ lb. sugar
> Cinnamon
> 1 oz. gelatine
> 1 orange
>
> For decoration
> 1 tablespoonful straw-
> berry or raspberry
> jam
> Whipped cream

Cook the rice in the milk with
the sugar and vanilla pod. Remove the vanilla pod and press
half the rice into a mould, rinsed
out with cold water. Leave until
quite cold. Cut the orange in half
and carefully scoop out the fruit,
taking care not to cut the skin.
Cook the rhubarb with sugar and

A party sweet, Cold Rice with Rhubarb Jelly set in orange
skins and decorated with whipped cream

391

cinnamon until tender, then pass through a sieve, dissolve the gelatine in the hot liquid, fill the orange skins, and leave to set. When the remaining jelly is nearly set, put it on top of the rice in the mould and leave to set. Press the remainder of the rice firmly down on top of the jelly and turn on to a plate. Cut the jelly-filled orange into thin slices, cut each slice in half and place round the foot of the mould. Mix the jam with the cream and pipe a decoration on the top.

Kirschenblotzer (Cherry soufflé)

3 oz. butter	2 oz. sugar
4 eggs	6 oz. flour
Black cherries and sugar	Cream

Stone the cherries, sprinkle well with sugar and leave to stand. Cream the butter, add sugar and egg-yolks and then the flour, gradually, and some fresh cream. When well mixed, add stiffly-beaten egg-whites. (The mixture must not be too hard.) Prepare a soufflé dish and fill with alternate layers of mixture and cherries, beginning and ending with the mixture. Cook in a moderate oven for about 1 hour.

NOTE: If desired, 2 stiffly-beaten, sweetened, egg-whites can be put on top of the soufflé 15 minutes before serving.

Marmorkuchen (Marble cake)

14 oz. flour	1 teaspoonful baking powder
8 oz. sugar	
3 tablespoonfuls cocoa or chocolate powder	4 eggs
	Small cupful of warm milk
6 oz. butter	

Beat butter and sugar to a cream, add egg-yolks gradually, then flour and baking powder. Lastly, add the milk and the well-beaten egg-whites. Divide the mixture in half, and add to one half the cocoa or chocolate powder. Fill cake tin with alternate layers of plain and chocolate mixture and bake in a hot oven for 1 hour.

Chocolate Cream with Pears

¾ pint milk	1 oz. cornflour
2 tablespoonfuls cocoa or chocolate powder	2 oz. sugar
	1 egg
	Cream
Vanilla essence	Pears

Heat the milk, sugar and vanilla essence, and stir in cocoa or chocolate powder. When boiling, add cornflour (previously mixed to a paste with a little milk) and,

lastly, egg-yolk. Place in a dish to cool. Place pears on top (drained tinned ones will do if fresh are not available), decorate with glacé cherries and piped whipped cream.

Schnee Eier (Snow eggs)

½ pint milk	2 egg-whites
2 tablespoonfuls sugar	Thick custard

Beat the egg-whites with sugar until very stiff. Heat the milk in a shallow pan and, when boiling, put in the egg-whites, shaping with a tablespoon to look like eggs. Leave for a few minutes, turn once, then take out and place round the custard in a shallow bowl.

Apple Soufflé

1 lb. cooking apples	2 eggs
4 oz. sugar	4 oz. flour

Peel and core the apples, cut into thin slices and place in a soufflé dish. Beat eggs and sugar together, add flour, and mix well. (If too stiff, use a little milk, or another egg.) Pour over apples and bake slowly in a moderate oven for about 1 hour.

Rote Grütze (Red sago mould)

1 lb. red-currants and raspberries (or red-currants only)	6 oz. sugar
	2 oz. sago

Place fruit in pan with sufficient water to stew. Cook very slowly to preserve flavour. Drain off the fruit juice, add sugar to it and bring to the boil. Stir in sago and cook until tender. Place in prepared mould, leave to cool, and serve with fresh cream or custard.

Sandkuchen (Sand cake)

6 eggs, and their weight in flour, sugar and butter

Beat eggs and sugar to a cream. Add flour gradually, then the butter. Bake in a moderate oven for about ¾ hour.

Creamed Potatoes

Steam the required amount of potatoes, then peel them and leave to cool. Cut into fairly thick slices. Make half a pint of white sauce, using 1 oz. margarine, 1 oz. flour, and add the potatoes to it. (More milk can be added if needed.) Chopped parsley should be added just before serving.

NOTE: This dish is generally eaten without a second vegetable; lettuce or beetroot make good additions—suitable for meat without gravy.

NORWAY

*In the land of the midnight sun, where the climate is
cold, they eat lots of fish caught around their coasts and
cook it in many interesting ways*

NORWEGIANS lead a very active life in a very cold climate. The Norwegian housewife therefore provides sustaining though plain meals, and since the sea lies all about her, she relies on fish as a staple item of diet, cooking and preparing it in many different ways, preserving, smoking and pickling the fish harvest in even greater variety than her Danish and Swedish neighbours.

Norwegians like their fish to be really fresh, so the housewife buys it alive from tanks in the fishmarket. She broils, bakes or fries it by itself, mixes it with vegetables and also makes fish soups and puddings. Cauliflower with shrimps, garnished with a cream sauce, is a delicious and favourite dish.

Smoked meat is popular, smoked mutton and reindeer in particular, and smoked reindeer tongues are a great luxury. Meat is usually served in "made up" dishes, and very often in aspic.

In the autumn there is plentiful game, and roast ptarmigan is a national delicacy. Poultry, too, is popular and chicken (*kylling*) is often served roast with a cream sauce. Duck stuffed with prunes is another Norwegian speciality.

Although Norway has to import fruit and green vegetables to balance her diet, the housewife has plentiful supplies of potatoes, root vegetables and many berries. She uses quantities of potatoes at each meal, and serves her vegetables with a cream sauce. Salads she dresses with sour cream and garnishes with chopped dill or parsley.

Like most Scandinavian housewives, she uses dairy produce and grain for nourishing and filling dishes. Oats, barley and rye are baked into thin bread wafers called "Flatbröd," while milk soup with barley groats is the prelude to many a country family's main meal.

Fruit soups are popular for dessert as well as the usual Scandinavian berry puddings and pies. Often the meal ends without a sweet dish, and then sometimes there will be waffles served with the coffee or a delicious nut coffee layer cake.

Fish Soup (for 4)

1 *tablespoonful butter*	*Chopped chives and salt*
1½ *pints fish stock*	2 *tablespoonfuls wheat flour*
½ *pint milk*	½ *gill sour cream*
1 *egg*	

To make the stock

Skin and bones of fish	1 *large teaspoonful salt to each quart of water*
Water	

Put the skin and bones into a saucepan with enough cold salted water to cover them. Cook very slowly, with the lid on, for ½ hour and skim carefully. Take out bones and strain the stock.

Lapskaus, or Norwegian Stew, is made from a mixture of beef and pork, served with a crisp salad or mashed turnips

To make the soup.—Put butter and flour in a pan and stir until well mixed. Add stock, then milk, a little at a time, stirring continually, and bring to the boil after each addition of liquid. Boil for 5–10 minutes and salt to taste. Beat the egg and cream in the tureen and pour on the soup, stirring steadily. Add chives. This is often garnished with small fishballs.

Exquisite Fishballs (Fiskeballer) (for 4)

1 lb. fresh haddock
1 dessertspoonful potato flour
½ gill cream
2 teaspoonfuls salt
¼ teaspoonful mace
¾ pint milk

Scrape the fish and rinse several times in cold water. (Always scrape from tail to head.) Dry well and fillet. Skin and take away membrane and bones, rub with salt until fillets are leathery. Stir well for about 10 minutes in a basin with potato flour and mace. Mix in the cream and milk, cold, one tablespoonful at a time, doubling the quantity when half the cream and milk has been used, and stirring all the time. This paste can be used for:

Fishballs.—Form into small balls, using a spoon dipped into cold water, put into boiling fish stock and cook gently for about 5–10 minutes.

Pudding and timbales.—Put the paste into a tin, or into timbale moulds, greased with melted butter. Stand the tin in a larger pan half-filled with boiling water and cook in a moderate oven. Cook timbales for 20 minutes, pudding ¾–1 hour. The water must not boil hard enough for the pudding to rise too high. Serve with shrimp sauce (see Sauces chapter).

Herring Salad (Sildesalat) (for 4—6)

10 salt herrings
¾ lb. boiled potatoes
½ lb. pickled beetroot
6 oz. apples
A thin slice of onion
2 oz. pickled gherkin
4 tablespoonfuls vinegar
2 tablespoonfuls water
1 oz. sugar
½ pint cream (whipped)
1 sliced hard-boiled egg
Pepper to taste
Parsley

Clean the fish, removing the heads, and soak overnight in cold water. Drain, skin and fillet, then dice the fillets, potatoes, beetroot, apple, onion and gherkin and mix thoroughly. Blend vinegar, sugar and water well, season with pepper and add, stirring gently. Add the whipped cream.

Rinse a mould in cold water, put the mixture in and chill in the refrigerator. Turn out of the mould to serve, garnish with the egg and chopped parsley. To be really Norwegian, this dish should be eaten with sour cream.

Salad Dressing (Römmesalat)

¾ pint sour cream
¼ oz. sugar
2 teaspoonfuls vinegar

Mix the ingredients together, adding the vinegar by drops. When smooth, use for dressing on lettuce.

Duck with Prune Stuffing (for 4–6)

1 *duck (3–5 lb.)*
White pepper
2 *teaspoonfuls salt*

For the stuffing

5 *peeled and sliced apples*
10–15 *prunes*

For the sauce

3 *tablespoonfuls flour*
1 *gill cream*
Blackcurrant juice if liked
3½ *gills gravy*

Prepare and season the duck as usual. Stuff with the fruits, sew up, and roast in oven for 1¾–2½ hours.

Skim the fat from the gravy, add a little water and stir in flour to thicken. Add the cream and, if liked, a little blackcurrant juice. Serve with fried potatoes and more cooked prunes and apples.

Norwegian Stew (Lapskaus) (for 4–5)

¾ lb. diced raw beef
½ lb. diced fresh pork
½ teaspoonful pepper
2 lb. raw potatoes
1 onion
Salt

Cover raw beef and fresh pork with water and boil slowly for ½ hour. Peel and cut the potatoes in pieces, add to the meat, together with sliced onion and pepper. Simmer for another ½ hour, or until tender. Add salt if desired. Serve with a crisp salad, boiled carrots or mashed turnips.

Ptarmigan with Brown Sauce (for 4)

2 *ptarmigan*
2 *tablespoonfuls butter*
2 *oz. lard*
1 *gill water*
¾ pint milk
1 *teaspoonful salt*

For the sauce

1 *tablespoonful butter*
3½ *gills gravy*
2 *tablespoonfuls flour*
1 *gill sour cream*

Clean the birds well in water, dry carefully. Cut lard into thin strips, slit the breast skin and put lard on both sides of the

A delicious cold buffet dish—finely sliced salami surrounds a cauliflower, cooked whole and garnished with hard-boiled egg, gherkin and beetroot

breastbones, then put skin back in place. Tie wings and legs together. Melt the butter in a warm pan until golden, put birds and the entrails into pan together with boiling milk and water and a little salt. Cook the birds gently in the oven until tender (1½–2 hours), basting them frequently. K e e p warm, and use the gravy from the pan for the sauce.

Brown Sauce.—Stir butter and flour in warm pan until light brown. Pour in gravy, little by little. Stir well and bring to the boil. Add cream and boil for 5–10 minutes. Salt to taste. Chop entrails and hearts up small and put into the sauce.

Loganberries with Rice (Tyttebaer med ris)

1 lb. cold boiled rice	½ pint whipped cream
1 quart loganberries	1½ oz. sugar (omit if
(or 8 oz. jam)	jam is used)

Place a layer of rice in a round baking-dish, then a thin layer of jam or loganberries and a little sugar, and so on alternately, ending with a top layer of berries. Whip the cream with sugar and spread on top. Chill and serve.

NOTE: This recipe is equally suitable for raspberries.

Waffles (Vafler)

4 eggs	½ lb. flour
2 oz. sugar	1 pint sour cream

Beat the eggs, sugar, flour and cream together until light. Cook in waffle irons in the usual way. Often eaten with coffee for breakfast.

Norwegian Dessert-cake (Dessertkake)

Weigh 3 boiled potatoes and take the same weight in butter and flour. Rub butter well into the flour and mash the pota-toes. Mix together, then put into the refrigerator for ½ hour or until thoroughly chilled. Roll out very thinly, cut into circles, using a saucer or small plate, and bake in a slow oven until light brown. Sandwich with jam, preferably rhubarb, and top with whipped cream.

The Prince's Cake (Fyrstekake)

3½ oz. butter	7 oz. flour
1 egg-yolk	2–3 tablespoonfuls
3½ oz. sugar	water
1½ teaspoonfuls baking powder	

For the filling

5½ oz. almonds	5½ oz. icing sugar
½ teaspoonful vanilla	½ teaspoonful carda-
essence	mom
½ oz. baking powder	3 egg-whites

Grease a round tin with butter. Cream sugar and butter until white, add egg-yolk and water. Sift in flour and baking powder, and mix well. Leave in a cold place.

Scald, blanch and dry almonds, and mix with the icing sugar, spice and baking powder. Beat egg-whites until stiff and add, with essence, to almond mixture.

Roll out the cake dough and put two-thirds into the tin, making it about ½ in. higher at the edge. Spread the filling all over it, then cut the remaining dough into ½-in. strips and put them on in check pattern. Brush strips with beaten egg and bake in a moderate oven until it rises nicely, is golden brown and the filling a little leathery.

SWEDEN

*A land of modern design
and up-to-date equipment
where the favourite dishes
are traditional*

BOTH Swedish kitchens and Swedish cooking have changed considerably since the Second World War. Modern domestic equipment and time-saving methods, largely of American origin, have brought the Swedish housewife much precious leisure time. Deep frozen foods, such as meat, fish and vegetables, are available in almost every country shop all over Sweden. But in spite of modern methods, traditional and local customs are still observed in most Swedish homes.

Most famous dish of all—known, indeed, all over the world—is the Swedish Smörgåsbord, a rich variety of hot and cold dishes, sometimes amounting to thirty different kinds. This Smörgåsbord is set out on a special table and everybody is invited to serve themselves as often as they like—or can! This is a practical expedient, since no plate is large enough for more than samples at one time of bread, butter, cheeses, different kinds of ham and sauces, omelets, meatballs, crabfish, salads and, most important, the herring dishes, the fish being served in various ways—in vinegar, with leeks and spices, salted, smoked, fried, and in marinade.

Fish does, in fact, play an important part in the Swedish diet, and the herring is a basic food. Although it can always be bought fresh, the Swedes are extremely fond of eating fish pickled and smoked. Dried cod, called "lutfisk," is served traditionally at Christmas. Its flavour is unusual, perhaps, to the outsider, since it has been soaked for over three weeks in a mixture of wood-ash, lime and soda.

Shellfish is also popular and is excellent in Sweden. From August 8th, when the crayfish season is in full swing, crayfish suppers are a great attraction all over the country, and special table linen, decorated with crayfish designs, is used. It is an old custom to drink a glass of schnapps with every claw—and you are expected to eat at least ten crayfish.

The climate doubtless makes the Swedes great meat-consumers. The meat is nowadays extremely good, and for Sunday dinner you will often find either a so-called "Slottsstek" (Steak of the Castle) or a steak of veal. But for everyday, joints are cooked and served with various sauces and spices (dill mutton and collops, for example).

Salads have become more and more popular now that vegetables are available throughout the year, even in the far north. Consequently, potatoes are no longer the mainstay of the household as in the old days. Vegetables are often served as a stew, a relic of the time when they were scarce and so had to be made into a substantial main dish.

Milk and cheese (also Filbunke, or sour milk) are nearly always on the table, but there are also soups made from vegetables, fruit and milk. Many of the sweet dishes are made of fruit and berries. Puddings, pancakes and lots of sweet cakes are also served, usually with jam. A typical Swedish jam is made from "lingon," a Nordic kind of cranberry.

Swedish housewives like to bake at home, chiefly white sweet bread and the famous "Seven Assorted Cakes" for their coffee. Another type of everyday bread is the famous "knäckebröd," once baked at home in bulk and strung on a pole near the ceiling. Very good for the teeth and the

Ideal both for cooking and serving Swedish dishes, colourful Rorstrand ovenware is obtainable in the U.K.

digestion, highly recommended for children and served at school breakfasts, this bread has become an important Swedish export. It is found all over the world as "Rye-King."

No chapter on Swedish cooking would be complete without a mention of the Swedish Pea Soup, the "Arter med fläsk," which is served every Thursday in almost every Swedish home, including the Royal Palace. The soup is accompanied by a glass of hot Swedish punch and always followed by pancakes. Similarly, Fettisdagsbullar is the dessert served on Shrove Tuesday. It is rather like cream buns filled with whipped cream and marzipan, and eaten in a soup-plate with hot milk flavoured with cinnamon.

Christmas is, of course, the time for traditional dishes in Sweden as elsewhere. The main meal is usually served in the kitchen, already decorated, at midday on Christmas Eve. This consists of Smörgåsbord, with special extra dishes. To start with, there is the "Doppigrytan," a simple,

symbolic ceremony in which various types of bread, such as Limpa (sour) and Vörtbörd (sweet), are dipped into the decorated copper pot full of stock in which the traditional ham and pork sausages have been boiled. At this meal everyone serves himself. Dishes typical of Sweden as a whole include ham, up to five different kinds of sausages, meatballs, brown beans, red cabbage, salads. A pig's head is smoked and decorated, a memory of pagan times. Later in the day there is a Christmas coffee

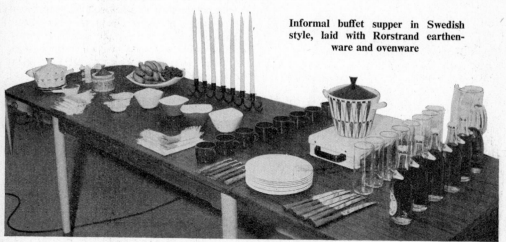

Informal buffet supper in Swedish style, laid with Rorstrand earthenware and ovenware

table with cakes and biscuits of different kinds, such as Peppercakes and bread shaped into figures.

Later on in the afternoon there is a sit-down meal with Lutfisk, Christmas porridge (Risgrynsgröt), and then many families start all over again with Christmas Smörgåsbord!

SMÖRGÅSBORD

Anyone wishing to cook in the Swedish way will, of course, start with Smörgåsbord, a few suggestions for which are:

1. Cut hard-boiled eggs in half and arrange strips of anchovy fillets across them.
2. Slice cold roast beef wafer thin. Decorate each slice with a whirl of mayonnaise or horseradish cream, or, alternatively, roll a slice of cooked ham round a stick of asparagus.
3. Cut very thin slices from the cold joint. Garnish with sliced gherkins or cucumber. If you are using veal, make the gravy into a jelly and use to garnish, decorating with parsley.
4. Cover halves of hard-boiled eggs with mayonnaise. Surround with cooked shrimps and garnish with parsley.
5. Arrange three or four different kinds of cheese, each in a small glass dish, garnished with radishes, parsley or chopped chives.
6, On a bed of lettuce arrange sliced tomatoes, cold rice flavoured with chopped pimento and slices of hard-boiled egg. Garnish with olive.

No Smörgåsbord would be complete without these two special herring dishes:

The Glazier's Herring (Glasmästarsill)

2 lb. salted herrings
2¼ coffee cupfuls sugar
¼ carrot
A piece of gherkin (salted if available, otherwise pickled)
2 teaspoonfuls whole Jamaica pepper
1 pint vinegar dressing (made of ⅓ vinegar and ⅔ water)
4 leeks (red)
½ horseradish

Skin the herrings without removing the bone and soak them in water overnight. Mix the dressing with the sugar, and warm, then chill it. Dry the herrings on paper, cut them in pieces straight across the big bone, and put in a pot with pounded pepper and the vegetables cut in thin slices between the layers. Cover with the dressing and

leave for at least 3 hours (it can be left for a week).

Another delicious hot fish dish on the Smörgåsbord is:

Mr. Janson's Temptation (Janson's frestelse)

5–6 raw potatoes
2–2½ gills cream
1 tablespoonful margarine or butter
2 leeks
6–8 anchovies
Breadcrumbs

Cut the potatoes in fine strips, the leeks into thin slices and fillet the anchovies. Into a buttered fireproof dish, put layers of potatoes, then anchovy, then leek and so on, ending with potatoes. Pour on the cream and, if possible, some of the juice from the anchovies. Dot with pieces of margarine and sprinkle breadcrumbs on top. Cook in a moderate oven until the potatoes are tender (about 45 minutes).

Instead of anchovy you can use 4–6 smoked herrings.

OTHER DISHES

Swedish Pea Soup (Arter med fläsk) (for 4)

½ lb. split peas
1½ quarts water
1 leek or onion (or ginger if preferred)
Salt to taste
1 lb. pork (fresh or slightly salted)
Sweet marjoram

Wash the peas and soak them overnight in salted water. Cook them in the same water, together with marjoram and onion, bringing them quickly to the boil and skimming off the shells as they float to the top. When all shells have been removed, add the pork and season. Cover the pan and simmer gently until both pork and peas are tender. Remove the pork, slice it and place on a dish. Pour the soup into individual bowls and serve with the sliced pork and mustard. The pork can also be cut in cubes and served in the soup.

Nettle Soup (for 4)

3 pints very young nettles
A few sprigs of chive, chervil or fennel seed
Poached or hard-boiled eggs
2 oz. butter
3½ pints rich stock
3½ oz. flour
Pepper and salt

Clean and rinse the nettles well. Plunge them into boiling salted water and simmer for 15 minutes. Drain, rinse in cold water and drain again. Chop finely together with the chives, chervil or fennel seed. Sprinkle

For gracious dining, a Rorstrand porcelain dinner service, "Ice Crystal," patterned in misty blue-grey on white, with salt and pepper pots in cobalt blue

with flour. Heat in melted butter, add stock gradually, stirring all the time. Simmer with lid on for ¾ hour. Skim well and season. Serve with hard-boiled eggs cut into sections, or poached eggs.

NOTE: The nettles are picked in the spring. They can be dried in the open air and stored in paper bags so that it is possible to have nettle soup all the year round. Alternatively, spinach may be used instead of nettles.

Mashed Turnips (Rotmos) (for 4)

1 lb. turnips	½ gill cream or 2 oz.
1 lb. potatoes	butter
1 pint stock (prefer-	1 rounded teaspoonful
ably made from	sugar
shank pork)	Salt and pepper

Wash, peel and cube turnips and potatoes. Cook turnips in stock for ½ hour, add potatoes and cook until soft (about 20 minutes). Drain and mash, adding cream or butter and seasoning. Beat until quite smooth. Serve with the pork shank, or salt beef, or sausages.

Swedish Hash (Pytt i panna) (for 4)

1 lb. left-over cold	2 medium-sized
meat	onions
1 lb. cold boiled	2 oz. butter
potatoes	Salt and pepper
4 fried eggs	Chopped parsley

Dice the meat and potatoes and chop the onions. Using half the butter, fry the onions until golden brown. In the remaining butter, fry first the potatoes and then the meat until both are nicely browned. Mix with the onions and add the seasoning. Arrange on a hot dish and garnish with chopped parsley. Serve with fried eggs, similarly garnished, placed on top of the hash.

Meatballs (Köttbullar) (for 4)

1 lb. finely minced	2 medium-sized
meat (¾ lb. beef	onions
and ¼ lb. pork)	1½ oz. butter
1 oz. breadcrumbs	Salt and pepper to
½ pint milk	taste
1 egg	A little cream
½ oz. flour	

Soak the breadcrumbs in milk. Add the meat, the grated onion, raw egg, salt and pepper, and mix thoroughly. Shape balls in the left hand with a spoon and fry them in butter. Keep hot. Whip up the butter with a little water and make into a gravy with the flour. Season the gravy to taste and, if too thick, add a little cream. Serve with boiled potatoes and sliced gherkin and cranberry jam. (Instead of potatoes, cooked marcaroni can be served.)

Stuffed Herrings (Sill i krappock) (for 4)

4 large fresh herrings	6 oz. each chopped
2 oz butter.	parsley, chives and
2 teaspoonfuls salt	onions
1 tablespoonful lemon	Waxed paper
juice	

Slit the underside of each fish, remove bones and intestines, and wash well under running cold water. Dry, and sprinkle with salt. Stuff with a mixture of parsley, chives, onion and lemon juice. Put each fish in buttered waxed paper, each piece large enough to form an envelope for one fish. Cook on a baking sheet in a moderately hot oven for 10—15 minutes. Serve, still in their paper envelopes, with boiled potatoes.

NOTE: Trout may also be cooked in this way.

Baked Eel (Ungstekt äl) (for 4)

1 fat eel (about 2 lb.	1 egg
weight)	3 oz. breadcrumbs
2 oz. butter	Juice of ½ lemon
	Salt and pepper

Loosen the skin round the eel's neck with a sharp knife and draw off with a piece of cloth held in the hand. Remove the head and backbone, split open and clean thoroughly, taking care not to pierce the flesh. Dry, then rub with salt and lemon juice, and brush with beaten egg and sprinkle with seasoned breadcrumbs. Place in a well-buttered baking dish or fireproof oven dish and dot with remaining butter. Bake in a hot oven, basting frequently and adding a little hot water if needed, for about 40 minutes. Serve hot, with boiled potatoes, or cold, with salad.

Swedish Brown Beans with Pork (for 4)

12 oz. brown beans	1 tablespoonful
2½ pints water	Golden Syrup
2 saltspoonfuls vinegar	Pinch of salt

Rinse the beans, put into cold water, bring to the boil and simmer until tender (about 3 hours), adding hot water occasionally if necessary. When cooked, add syrup, vinegar and a pinch of salt. Serve with fried bacon or pork.

Swedish Christmas Porridge (Julgröt) (for 4)

1 teacupful Carolina	3½ oz. butter
rice	½ pint cream
1¼ pints water	1 teaspoonful salt
1 tablespoonful sugar	

Rinse the rice, cook in boiling water until soft and strain. Add the butter and the cream whipped stiffly. Reheat the porridge, but do not let it boil. Add salt and sugar, and serve with cold milk.

NOTE: An almond is always hidden in the porridge. The person who finds it will be the first to get married!

Steak of the Castle (Slottsstek—a typical Swedish Sunday dish)

2 lb. rump steak	2 teaspoonfuls salt
2 oz. butter	8 grains of Jamaica
1 bay leaf	pepper
1 red leek	8 grains of white
3 anchovies	pepper
2 tablespoonfuls	1 tablespoonful
cream	vinegar
Water	½ tablespoonful syrup
2 tablespoonfuls flour	

Roast the meat in a braising pan until it is brown on the outside, add all the other ingredients and cook in the oven until done (about 2 hours).

Berry Cream (for 4)

1 quart mixed berries	1 pint water
1 oz. potato flour	5 oz. sugar

Wash the berries. Bring the water to the boil, add the berries and the sugar, and boil for several minutes. Mix the potato flour with a little cold water, stir in with the fruit and bring the mixture to the boil. Serve cold, with cream or milk.

Sour Milk (Filbunke) (for 4)

2 tablespoonfuls sour	Sugar, cinnamon and
cream	ginger to taste
1 pint fresh milk	

Spread the sour cream in the bottom of a bowl and add the milk. Cover the bowl and leave in a warm place until the milk becomes thick as custard. Then chill and serve with sugar, ginger and cinnamon.

Swedish Peppercakes (225 cakes)

3½ oz. white sugar	5½ oz. butter
3½ oz. Demerara	3 teaspoonfuls cinna-
sugar	mon
½ teaspoonful cloves	½ teaspoonful
1 gill thick cream	cardamon
Bicarbonate of soda	1 lb. 3 oz. flour
7½ oz. syrup	

Beat together the two sugars, the syrup, butter and the powdered spices for about 15 minutes. Whip the cream and add. Finally, add the flour mixed with the bicarbonate of soda, keeping back a little of the flour for rolling. Knead the dough well and leave for 24 hours (well covered), then knead again. Roll it out thin and cut with fancy cutters. Bake in a hot oven for 8–10 minutes.

A typical dish of Smørrebrød, fish, meat, eggs and vegetables all appetisingly
arranged on slices of thickly buttered rye bread

COOKERY AT HOME AND ABROAD

DENMARK

The home of Smørrebrød—open sandwiches
in infinite variety—is full of good ideas for
home entertaining

THE Danes do enjoy food, have immense appetites and take their meals seriously. The Danish housewife is extremely house-proud, most particularly of her kitchen, and can draw on plentiful supplies of homegrown dairy produce, meat and fresh fish.

"Smørrebrød," the traditional open sandwich, is perhaps the best known of all Danish dishes, and forms the midday meal for children and the majority of workers. Generally, these tasty snacks, each almost a meal in itself, are made on a foundation of rye bread, the butter smeared on thickly and the filling so generous that it hangs over the edges. With the midday "smørrebrød" the children drink milk. Grown-ups usually prefer Danish beer.

The evening meal is taken at six o'clock, sometimes earlier, as soon as all the family have arrived home. The first course is often a fruit soup, a typical Danish speciality, or one of the sustaining beer-flavoured gruels that taste a great deal more pleasant than they sound. The main course is usually a meat dish.

The Danes love entertaining in their homes, and no housewife feels that time spent on preparation and decoration is wasted. As a result, the food is beautifully served and appetisingly garnished, the tables laid with fine china and silverware and massed with flowers and candles.

As in most countries, entertaining reaches its peak at Christmas. At six o'clock comes the traditional Christmas Eve dinner, which begins with a sweet rice pudding, continues with roast goose stuffed with prunes and apples, served with stewed red cabbage and caramel potatoes, and finishes with a sweet red-berry pudding. After that, one is served with coffee and

Christmas biscuits, home-baked and in infinite variety, not to mention cherry brandy, a favourite drink with the Danes, which invariably follows.

Beer and Bread Soup (Øllebrød) (for 4)

10 *oz. rye bread*	1 *stick cinnamon*
1 *gill water*	(¾ *in. long by* ½ *in.*
2 *pint bottles pale ale*	*thick, approx.*)
Lemon peel	2½ *oz. sugar*

Cut bread into small dice and soak for 12 hours in water and one bottle of ale. Then simmer for 20 minutes, rub through a sieve and cook the purée with the cinnamon over slow heat, thinning gradually with the second bottle of ale. Add the lemon peel and sugar and serve in soup plates with whipped cream.

NOTE: This dish is served in Denmark as a porridge in the morning, as a soup to start a meal, as a sweet or supper dish.

Giblet Soup (Kraasesuppe) (for 4)

1–2 *sets of giblets*	3 *small apples*
3 *carrots*	2 *or 3 prunes*
2 *small sticks of*	½ *oz. sugar*
celery	1 *tablespoonful*
1 *leek*	*vinegar*
Salt to taste	

Soak the prunes overnight. Slice the carrots and apples into small pieces. Wash the giblets thoroughly, cover with cold salted water and bring gradually to the boil. Skim, and simmer for 30 minutes. Add the vegetables and fruit, and simmer until quite tender. Add sugar and vinegar, and serve hot with Flour Dumplings. Alternatively, thicken the soup with 3 tablespoonfuls cream and an egg-yolk.

Flour Dumplings (for 4)

2 *oz. butter*	2 *eggs*
2 *oz. flour*	*Pinch of salt and*
¼ *pint boiling water*	*cardamom*

Melt butter and stir flour into it. When well mixed, add boiling water and stir until the mixture comes away from the sides of the pan. Leave to cool. Add egg-yolks, salt and cardamom, and finally the egg-whites, beaten stiff. Form into small balls, drop into boiling salted water or soup and cook for 5–10 minutes. Lift out the dumplings, using a perforated ladle. Serve with meat or fruit soups.

Copenhagen Codfish

The Danes have an unsurpassed reputation for fish cookery, and in Copenhagen restaurants it is usual to offer four or five different sauces with each dish. Copenhagen Codfish can be served with one of the four milky sauces suggested below.

½ *lb. raw cod fillet*	1 *rounded tea-*
(*skin removed*)	*spoonful chopped*
1 *oz. breadcrumbs*	*parsley*
2 *oz. suet*	1–2 *tablespoonfuls*
1 *egg*	*lemon juice*
¼ *gill milk*	(*strained*)
Pepper and salt	*Parsley for decora-*
Flour	*tion*

Shred cod finely; chop suet with about 1 teaspoonful of flour (this makes chopping easier). Mix all ingredients well together to a dropping consistency. Season well.

Turn mixture into a greased pudding bowl, cover with pudding cloth or greaseproof paper, and steam gently for ¾ to 1 hour. Turn out and coat with either Dutch Cream, Anchovy, Egg or Shrimp Sauce.

Dutch Cream Sauce: Cook ½ pint of white sauce slightly, add one raw egg-yolk and stir over a moderate heat till the yolk thickens. Do not boil. Add a few drops of lemon juice and vinegar to give a sharp flavour.

For Anchovy, Egg and Shrimp Sauces, see Sauces chapter.

Minced Fish (Fiskefars) (for 4)

2½ *lb. cod (middle*	¼ *pint cream*
cut) to give about	1 *oz. potato flour*
1½ *lb. fish when*	1 *oz. butter*
skin and bones are	*Salt and pepper to*
removed	*taste*
Breadcrumbs	1 *egg-white*

Remove skin and bones from the fish, and mince finely three or four times at least. Add flour, and mix with the egg-white and cream. Season, and put in a tin buttered and spread with breadcrumbs. Stand this tin inside another one containing boiling water and cook in a moderate oven for ¾ hour, or until it is a nice golden brown.

Egg and Bacon Cake (Aeggekage) (for 4)

8 *rashers streaky*	1 *oz. flour*
Danish bacon	1 *oz. butter*
4 *eggs*	*Salt and pepper to*
¼ *pint milk*	*taste*
Chopped parsley or chives	

Fry or grill the bacon rashers and keep hot. Beat the eggs, flour and milk together, seasoning with salt and pepper. Melt butter in a heated omelet pan, pour in the mixture and cook quickly until nearly set, shaking the pan from time to time. Turn on to a hot dish, place the cooked bacon on top and garnish with chopped parsley or chives.

Cucumber Salad (easily digested)

Cut cucumber into paper-thin slices, put into a shallow bowl or soup plate with plenty of salt, cover with a plate and put a really heavy object (such as an iron) on top. This helps to squeeze the juice out of the cucumber. Leave for an hour, then put cucumber into a clean cloth and squeeze hard to get out the rest of the water. Serve in a glass bowl in ¾ cupful vinegar with ¼ cupful water and a tablespoonful of salt. Sprinkle with black pepper.

Herring Salad (Siddesalat) (for 4)

2 *soused herrings*	2 *tablespoonfuls*
3 *large cooked pota-*	*olive oil*
toes	2 *tablespoonfuls*
1 *cooked beetroot*	*vinegar*
1 *pickled cucumber*	*Salt and pepper to*
2 *dessert apples*	*taste*
2 *hard-boiled eggs*	*Chopped parsley*

Flake the fish, or cut them into small pieces. Dice the potatoes, beetroot and cucumber. Core apples, but do not peel them. Cut them into pieces. Blend the oil and vinegar together in a large bowl, add the other ingredients and the seasoning. Mix thoroughly. Serve in a glass dish or wooden salad bowl, garnished with sliced hard-boiled eggs and chopped parsley.

Caramel Potatoes
(Brunede kartofler) (for 4)

1½ *lb. potatoes*
2 *oz. sugar*
2 *oz. butter*

Wash, boil and peel the potatoes. Cut them into pieces. Melt the sugar in a pan, add the butter and heat until light brown. Rinse the potatoes in cold water, then dip them in the caramel mixture, thoroughly coating each piece. Serve hot.

Fruit Jelly (Rødgrod med fløde)

1 *lb. berries (equal*	1 *pint water*
parts strawberries,	4½ *oz. sugar*
currants and black-	1½–2 *oz. potato flour*
berries, or red-	*to every quart of*
currants, rasp-	*juice*
berries and cherries	
are good mixtures)	

Wash the berries and remove stalks. Cook them in the water until they are soft. Press through a fine sieve. Measure the juice before you put it back into the saucepan and add the sugar, Mix as much flour as you need with cold juice and stir thoroughly in the saucepan. Cook until thickened. Pour it into a glass bowl and sprinkle with sugar to prevent the formation of skin. Serve hot or cold with cream, garnishing with chopped almonds.

Peasant Girl with Veil (Bondepige med slor) (for 4)

8 *oz. rye-bread-*	2 *oz. butter*
crumbs	1½ *lb. cooking apples*
3 *oz. brown sugar*	2 *oz. grated chocolate*
Lemon juice and	¼ *pint double cream*
sugar to taste	*(whipped)*

Mix the crumbs and sugar together and fry in the butter until crisp. Peel, core and cut up the apples, and cook them until soft in a very little water with a good squeeze of lemon juice and sugar to taste. Into a glass dish put alternate layers of the fried crumb

Cheese is eaten at breakfast-time in Denmark with rolls or rye bread and milk or coffee

mixture and apple pulp, finishing with a layer of crumbs. When the pudding is quite cold, spread the whipped cream on top and sprinkle with grated chocolate.

SMØRREBRØD

These open sandwiches provide infinite scope for the housewife's originality in devising mixtures that both look and taste delicious. They also enable left-overs to be used up. Here are a few popular varieties:

Sunrise at Bornholm (Solopgang paa Bornholm)

In the middle a raw egg-yolk, with pieces of smoked herring (previously boned) in a circle round it, then another circle of chopped beetroot (cooked and in marinade) and another of chopped leek. Finally, sprinkle the sandwich with capers.

Shrimps in the Crush (Reier i traengsel)

Pile a lot of shrimps high on the bread and sprinkle over them a little Jamaica pepper mixed with white pepper.

The Vet's Nightsnack (Dyrlaegens natmad)

On the buttered bread put a thick slice of foie gras with a slice of salt beef on top.

Hans Christian Andersen's Sandwich

On a thickly buttered slice of bread put a rasher of crisp grilled bacon, then a thick slice of raw tomato and one of liver sausage with a pat of horseradish cream and/or a little meat jelly.

Fillets of Plaice with Remoulade

Fillets of plaice, rolled in egg and breadcrumbs, are fried in butter and served hot on slices of rye or white bread with a remoulade sauce garnish. (Remoulade is a mayonnaise flavoured with chopped parsley, fennel and tarragon leaves, shallots and made mustard. See Salads chapter for method.)

Cod Roe Salad

Boil the roe in salted water for about 30 minutes, depending on size. Leave in water to cool, then skin and pass through a sieve. Add lemon juice, a little curry powder and other spices according to taste. Spread on buttered bread and garnish with slices of lemon and cress.

Meat Salad

This is a good way of using up left-overs of cooked meat. Remove fat and cut meat into small squares and cover with mayonnaise to which are added some diced gherkins or cucumber. Pile on well-buttered bread.

Salami

On a thick slice of buttered bread put a slice of salami sausage, then a thick slice of tomato and a slice of hard-boiled egg, with an olive or a dab of tomato ketchup on top.

Another very popular sandwich is just a slice of salami on a slice of thickly buttered bread, but its name is poetic—"The Roskilde Turnpike."

DANISH CHRISTMAS BISCUITS

These small cakes are extensively served at Christmas-time in Denmark, and made in large quantities ready for the festive season's entertaining.

Brown Cakes (Brune Kager)

1 lb. black treacle	¼ lb. butter
½ oz. ground cinnamon	½ lb. brown sugar
	⅙ oz. ground cloves
1 teaspoonful bicarbonate of soda	½ oz. ground ginger
	1½ lb. flour

A little grated orange peel
For decoration
Blanched almonds and candied peel

Heat together in a strong pan the treacle, sugar, butter, cloves, cinnamon, ginger and orange peel and, when hot, add the bicarbonate of soda. Remove from the stove and stir in the flour. Leave the dough for 3 or 4 days, then roll it out very thin, using a little flour if it sticks. Cut into oblong cakes, place on a greased baking sheet, decorate with almonds and candied peel, and bake in a brisk oven until brown and crisp.

Flead Cakes (Klejner)

3 eggs	1½ lb. flour
5 oz. sugar	¼ lb. butter
½ pint cream	A little cardamom
A little grated lemon rind	Lard for frying

First, stir together the eggs, sugar, butter (just slightly warmed), cardamom and lemon rind, then work in the cream and flour. Roll the dough out very thin and cut into strips. Make an incision in the middle of each strip and draw one end

The Danes like elegant table-settings. Here the national colours have been cleverly used, red mats set-off by white china, napkins and candles

through. Heat the lard in a strong, deep pan until very hot, drop in the biscuits and cook to a nice brown colour, then spread them on brown paper to drain. Next day, place in a cake tin, where they will keep fresh for a long time.

Jewish Cakes (Jodekager)

1 lb. flour	½ teaspoonful salt of
10 oz. sugar	hartshorn
A little grated lemon	1 egg
rind	A small glass of
¾ lb. butter	Danish Akvavit

For decoration
Sugar, chopped almonds and pounded vanilla

Mix all the ingredients together and roll out the dough very thinly. Cut into small rounds with a biscuit cutter or wineglass, place close together on a baking sheet, brush over with beaten egg, then sprinkle with sugar, vanilla and almonds. Bake in a quick oven until light brown.

Peppernuts (Pebernodder)

4 eggs	1 teaspoonful salt of
2 teaspoonfuls grated	hartshorn
lemon peel	Small equal quantities
A little lemon juice	of cardamom and
1 lb. flour	ground ginger
10 oz. sugar	

Beat the eggs well and with them mix the sugar, cardamom, ginger, lemon peel and salt of hartshorn diluted in water and a little lemon juice. Work in the flour and form into thin sticks. Roll into balls and bake in a hot oven.

Vanilla Rings (Vaniljhekranse)

1 lb. flour	½ lb. sugar
¾ lb. butter	1 egg
1 vanilla pod	¼ lb. almonds

Blanch and peel the almonds and chop them up finely, then work all the ingredients together to a firm dough. Make into long thin rolls, cut off 4-in. lengths, form into rings. Bake in a hot oven until light brown.

BELGIUM

A country of nine provinces, each with its own customs, folklore and traditional dishes

described by FLEUR VAN ACKER

BELGIUM is divided into nine Provinces, partly Flemish, partly Walloon, and each with its own characteristics, customs, folklore and traditional dishes. On the coast is *West Flanders*, the capital of which is Bruges. Here, every year on the first Monday after May 3rd, the traditional Procession of the Holy Blood passes through the main streets. This ceremony dates back to the twelfth century when, after the Second Crusade, Derrick d'Alsace brought back a few drops of the holy blood from the Holy Land. The traditional dish served on this day is roast veal and spinach, while no visitor ever leaves Bruges without some of the famous "Nœuds de Bruges."

Spinach

1 lb. spinach per person	1 egg-yolk
Pepper and salt	1 oz. butter, dripping or margarine
	Nutmeg

Remove stalks from spinach, wash thoroughly and put into a colander to drain for a few minutes. Rinse out a saucepan with water, but do not dry it, and put in the spinach. Cover, and bring to the boil. When boiling, remove lid and boil until tender. Pour spinach into a colander and leave to drain for about 5 minutes, then rub through the colander and return to saucepan, adding fat and seasoning. Heat, stirring all the time, and immediately before serving stir in the egg-yolk.

Nœuds de Bruges

½ lb. flour	¼ lb. butter
¼ lb. dark brown sugar	Salt
	½ pint water

Sieve the flour into a basin, add salt, sugar and mix well. Melt the butter in the water, leave to cool and, when just lukewarm, pour into the centre of the flour mixture. Mix lightly to a stiff consistency, then, on a floured pastry board, roll out to ½-in. thickness and leave for 1 hour.

Next, divide the dough into four pieces, and each piece into ten. Roll the pieces in brown sugar and shape either into figures of eight or little bows. Put them—½ in. apart—on a buttered baking tin, flatten out slightly and sprinkle with brown sugar. Leave overnight and cook in a very hot oven until the sugar has turned to caramel (about 20 minutes). Cool on a wire tray or on greaseproof paper.

All along the coast during the summer months, the Blessing of the Sea takes place, starting at Ostend on the first Sunday after June 29th (Saints Peter and Paul, Patron Saints) and ending at Zeebrugge at the end of August. Two dishes invariably eaten during this period are "Tomates aux Crevettes" and "Croquettes aux Crevettes." Both are delicious and frequently served at public dinners.

Tomatoes with Shrimps (Tomates aux Crevettes)

To serve as an hors d'œuvre, allow for each person:

2 firm, medium-sized tomatoes	3 oz. fresh shelled shrimps
1 tablespoonful mayonnaise	Seasoning and lemon Chives or parsley
Lettuce	for decoration

Wash the tomatoes and wipe them dry. Cut off the tops and scoop out the pulp with a teaspoon, taking care not to split the tomatoes. Sprinkle the insides with salt and pepper, then turn them upside down and leave. Add 1 tablespoonful of mayonnaise to the shrimps, mix well, and put into the tomato cases. Squeeze a few drops of lemon over the filling and replace the tomato tops. Decorate with chopped chives or sprigs of parsley and, if liked, serve on a bed of lettuce.

East Flanders.—The capital is Ghent, a town with many attractions for the tourist,

The Province of Hainault is famous for the Carnival de Binche, when the men wear costumes with humps and bells and dance through the streets

The Procession of the Holy Blood passes through the streets of Bruges (below). The traditional dish is roast veal with spinach

Most striking are the curled ostrich feather hats worn at the Carnival de Binche, when Onion Soup is served in restaurants and beer-houses

Photographs: Belgian Marine Railways, Tourism

including the famous Van Eyck paintings in the Cathedral of St. Bavon (Sint Baafs), medieval streets and buildings, among which is the Petit-Beguinage Notre Dame, founded in 1234, and museums. July 21st, when Ghent holds its Kermesse (Gentse Feeste), is also the Belgian National Day, and feasting continues for three days with music and dancing in the streets. The main attraction is on the Place d'Armes, or Kouter, where dancing goes on all night.

The dish served everywhere at this time is Waterzooi—chicken in hot broth.

Waterzooi (for 4)

Foundation (Broth)

2 lb. chicken giblets
1 large knuckle of veal
1 large head of celery
1 leek
A few chicken heads, necks and feet (well-washed)
A few carrots

Photo: Robelus, by courtesy of the Belgian State Tourist Office

All along the coast in summer the Blessing of the Sea takes place, and the dish popularly eaten is Tomatoes with Shrimps

1 saltspoonful pepper
4 pints cold water
1 slice of bread, 1 in. thick
2 doz. parsley roots

Chicken

1 fair-sized chicken or 2 spring chickens
1 teaspoonful salt
4 oz. butter
1 pint stock or boiling water
Chopped parsley

Put all the broth ingredients into a deep saucepan, bring to the boil and simmer until all are tender, then pass through a colander.

Melt the butter in a saucepan and, when very hot, put in the chicken, turn it so that it is lightly fried on all sides, but do not let it get brown. Add stock (or water) and salt, and boil gently until tender. When ready, add the foundation and serve. Chopped parsley can be added before serving and the chicken can be cut up if desired.

Fresh cream, bread and butter, and pieces of lemon should be handed round with this dish.

Tarte au Riz Liegeoise

This is the great speciality of the *Province of Liege* and is served with coffee between 3.30 and 5 p.m.

About 8 oz. short or flaky pastry
1½ pints milk
6 oz. sugar
1 tablespoonful cornflour
¼ lb. rice
Pinch of salt
Pinch of cinnamon
3 eggs

Roll out the pastry to ¼-in thickness and line a tart tin with it. Wash the rice well, drain it and bring to the boil in the milk with salt, stirring with a wooden spoon. When boiling, add cinnamon and sugar and cook for ½ hour or until tender (and the rice must be *really* tender). With a little milk mix the cornflour to a smooth paste, add the whisked egg-yolks, pour into the rice and continue stirring until it thickens, then remove from heat and add the whipped egg-whites. Pour evenly on to the pastry, brush over with beaten egg and sugar, and cook in a hot oven until golden brown (about $\frac{1}{2}$ hour). When cool, sprinkle icing sugar on top.

Gâteau de Verviers

This is a kind of bun-loaf.

    2¼ lb. flour
    ½ lb. butter or
      margarine
    1 tablespoonful castor
      sugar
    2 oz. yeast
    ½ lb. candy (or
      small pieces of
      lump) sugar
    4 eggs
    1 teaspoonful salt
    1 pint water
    Pinch of cinnamon

These little brown biscuits in animal shapes and iced are called Speculaus, and belong to the Feast of St. Nicholas. Tea service is Royal Doulton's "Desert Showers" in teal green on a cream background, from the Civil Service Stores

Make these ingredients into a smooth paste and leave for 1 hour, to rise, in a very warm place, adding the lumps of sugar when ready. Divide into two or four pieces and place on buttered baking sheets or tins. Bake in a warm oven, as for bread.

The Province of Hainault is famous for the Carnival de Binche, which is held on Shrove Tuesday (Mardi Gras). All the men of the town join in this, wearing a special costume which has humps and bells both front and back. They wear clogs and carry wicker baskets full of oranges which they throw or hand to the spectators. But most striking are their hats, made of curled ostrich feathers and more than 3 ft. high. The men also perform a dance, shaking the bells in rhythm to the strains of a brass band.

A special soup is served in all the restaurants and beer-houses during the Carnival Season:

Soupe à l'Onion (for 6)

4 pints stock	2 lb. onions
2 oz. butter, mar-garine or dripping	1 lb. potatoes
	1 bay leaf
2 oz. Gruyère and Parmesan cheese mixed	Seasoning
	Fried bread

Cut $\frac{3}{4}$ lb. onions into thin slices and cook in the butter, margarine or dripping, until very pale golden brown, then add 1 pint of stock and bring to the boil slowly. Simmer until tender, taking care that they do not break up too much. In another saucepan, boil the potatoes and the rest of the onions with the bay leaf and 2 pints of stock. When tender, put through a hair sieve, return to saucepan, add the onions and remainder of the stock, season and bring to the boil. When serving, add to each plate or bowl a round of fried bread, and top with grated cheese. This is a delicious and very nourishing soup.

Belgian Ardennes.—The chief specialities in this Province are dishes using wild boar, venison, hare and rabbit. One that is extremely popular.

Rabbit with Prunes (Lapin aux Pruneaux)
(for 6)

1 rabbit	2 oz. butter
Small piece of un-salted pork fat (2 in. square)	¼ lb. finely chopped onions
Sprig of thyme	2 bay leaves
1 teaspoonful corn-flour	¼ lb. prunes
	1 wineglassful red wine or ⅓ wine-glassful vinegar

Cut the rabbit into fair-sized pieces, wash, dry thoroughly and dust lightly with flour. Melt the butter and let it get brown, then put in the pork fat. Brown in it the pieces of rabbit until they are dark brown on all sides (but take care not to let them burn). Take out the rabbit and put in the onions and brown them, stirring all the time. Return the rabbit to the pan, add ½ pint water, herbs and seasoning, bring to the boil and simmer for ½ hour before adding prunes. Continue simmering until the rabbit is tender (but the pieces should still be whole). Some people put the sauce in which the rabbit was cooked through a hair sieve, but others prefer to leave the pieces of onion and prune as they are. The sauce should be thickened with cornflour and a wineglass of red wine or a ½ wineglass vinegar added just before serving.

NOTE: If wild rabbit, or hare, is used, it should first be left overnight in a marinade made from one-third wine vinegar and two-thirds wine, well seasoned.

Tarte au Fromage Blanc

This is served either as a dessert or at 5 o'clock coffee, and is a favourite in the Walloon country.

Flaky pastry	2 tablespoonfuls
2 oz. sugar	melted butter
½ oz. flour	Pinch of salt
Fresh cottage cheese	2 eggs

Roll out the pastry and line an open tart tin with it. Separate the egg-yolks from the whites, put aside the whites and mix all the other ingredients together, then whip the whites stiffly and add them, stirring well. Fill the tart with the mixture and bake in a hot oven. When cooked, sprinkle with sugar and return to oven for 1–2 minutes until the sugar is nicely browned.

Limbourg.—Every seventh year on the Sunday before the Assumption, the Marian procession of the Virgin Jesse takes place in Hasselt, the capital of Limbourg. Great crowds flock to the town and there is much feasting when, among the many excellent dishes served, there is always a large Vol au Vent.

Vol au Vent (for 4)

2 pints stock (or water)	Juice of 1 lemon
	½ boiling fowl
1 small pigeon (duck is sometimes used)	1 small knuckle of veal
2 oz. forcemeat (pork and veal)	¼ lb. sweetbreads
	2 egg-yolks
Seasoning	

Flaky or puff pastry vol au vent case the size of a 2-lb. cake tin

Soak the sweetbreads in milk for 12 hours. Bring the stock or water to the boil, put in the meat and poultry and boil until almost tender, then add the sweetbreads and continue boiling until tender. Remove all the meat from the broth and cut it into fair-sized pieces, taking away any skin, bone and gristle.

Make very tiny balls of forcemeat, drop them into the boiling broth for about 1 second, and then add them to the meat.

Make a roux, using broth instead of milk, add lemon juice, season to taste and bring to the boil. Stir in the beaten egg-yolks and remove immediately from the fire. Stir in all the meat and pour into the pastry case. Decorate with parsley and serve piping hot. Mushrooms can be added.

Saint Nicholas (December 6th).—By tradition this is the children's day and a school holiday. The good Saint rides through the night in a sledge drawn by reindeer and visits every home, bringing sweetmeats and presents, among which is always the traditional "Speculaus." This is a kind of dark brown biscuit (looking like a ginger biscuit), decorated with white and pink sugar and cut into various shapes —horses, elephants, clowns, milkmaids and even St. Nicholas himself. These biscuits measure anything from 3 in. to 1 yd. in length. When they are more than ½ yd. long, they are tied down on to a piece of wood covered with white paper. They should be made about a week, or even longer, before they are needed, and kept in a tin or in a very dry place.

Speculaus

1 lb. plain flour	1 oz. ground cinnamon
6 oz. fresh butter or margarine	½ teaspoonful baking powder
Pinch of salt	Water to mix
6 oz. dark brown sugar	

Mix the dry ingredients together, knead in the butter and enough water to make a pliable dough. Roll out and leave for 1–2 days. Place on a lightly floured pastry board and roll out to ½–1-in. thickness, according to size and depth required, and cut in fancy shapes. (These can be bought in the U.K. as well as on the Continent.) Put on a baking sheet and bake in a fairly hot oven until an even golden colour. Cool on a wire tray and, when quite cold, store in an airtight tin—they improve in flavour with keeping. Decorate with white and pink icing sugar.

Namur.—There has recently been a revival of a Fête Folklorique called "Le combat des Echasseurs" (The Battle of the Stiltrunners) which dates back to a visit made by Napoleon I. There are two Stilt Societies, the Melans and the Avresses, exclusive to Namur. They wear special outfits in the colours of their societies and are perched on stilts also in the societies' colours. In the "battle" each society tries to dislodge its opponents from its stilts, and there is a prize for the winners. A special dish is served at this time, but it has become so popular that it can often be obtained at other times as well.

Meuse Fish in Jelly (Poisson de Meuse à l'Escaveche)

Fish	Butter and a little
Onions	olive oil for frying
1 lemon	

For the sauce

| ⅔ white vinegar to ⅓ water | 1 teaspoonful salt |
| A few cloves and peppercorns | A few sheets of gelatine, broken into small pieces |

Fry the fish in butter and olive oil until deep brown, but not broken up or burnt. Place in a fairly deep earthenware dish and put on top thinly sliced onion and slices of peeled lemon. Prepare the sauce by boiling all the ingredients together. Boil for 2–3 minutes and pour immediately over the fish. Leave for a few days in a cool place before serving. Bread and butter is always served with this dish.

Province of Brabant.—Brussels, the capital of Belgium, is also the capital of this Province. Here there has now been revived the famous Omegang, a procession including the Town Magistrates, surrounded

One of the most popular dishes throughout Belgium is Chicons à la Portugaise—chicory in cheese and tomato sauce with eggs. Specially photographed in a Pyrex dish, with ovenware and cruets in yellow and grey Denby Dovedale from the Civil Service Stores

by all their colourfully dressed attendants, military detachments and decorated wagons depicting the Legend of St. Michele and St. Gudule, patron saints of Brussels, and other legendary and historical subjects. Thousands of people flock to the capital to see the procession, and the favourite dish at this time is Sweetbreads in Madeira Sauce (Schoesels au Madère).

Sweetbreads in Madeira Sauce (for 4–6)

2 ox sweetbreads	½ lb. breast of veal
1 lb. onions	1 kidney (ox)
½ lb. lamb (lean)	1 glass of beer
Butter for frying	1 wineglass vinegar
Sprig of thyme	2 bay leaves
2 parsley roots	Salt, pepper and nut-
½ lb. mushrooms	meg
2 wineglasses Madeira	1 dessertspoonful
Minced pork and veal	cornflour
1 oxtail	A few lumps of sugar

Cut the onions into thin rounds and brown them in butter in a saucepan, then add the oxtail, cut into small pieces, and brown. Cover the pan and simmer for about 1 hour, then add the veal, sweetbreads, kidney and lamb all cut into medium-sized pieces. Add the beer, sugar, herbs, vinegar and seasoning, cover and simmer for 2 hours. Make the pork and veal into small meatballs, clean and slice the mushrooms and add to the other ingredients. Mix the cornflour to a smooth paste with the Madeira and, when all ingredients are tender (about 2½–3 hours altogether), remove herbs and add cornflour mixture, stirring it in very lightly and taking care not to break up the pieces. Serve with boiled or mashed potatoes.

From October until the end of March, Brussels chicory (Witloof) is served all over Belgium, both in the home and in the restaurants, either raw or cooked in various ways.

Chicons à la Portugaise

1 lb. Brussels chicory	1 oz. flour
(Witloof)	2 oz. grated Gruyère
1 oz. butter	cheese
1 oz. tomato purée	1 large cupful milk
Seasoning	Juice of ½ lemon

Boil the chicory for 20 minutes in salted water with the lemon juice. Pour into a colander, rinse under the cold tap and leave to drain. Meanwhile, make a white sauce with the butter, flour, milk and seasoning, bring to the boil, then add the cheese and stir until it has melted. Dilute the tomato purée with a little water and add to the sauce, then bring to the boil. Arrange the chicory on a dish and pour the sauce on top, covering completely. Garnish with halved hard-boiled eggs and chopped parsley.

Chicory in Melted Butter

Cook and drain chicory (see Vegetables chapter). Melt butter or margarine in a frying pan. When it is golden brown, put in the heads of chicory and brown them on all sides, then arrange them on a dish, pour on the melted butter and sprinkle with chopped parsley.

Province of Antwerp.—This Province has two special dishes—Asparagus and Eels in Sorrel. Malines is famous for its asparagus, which is exported all over the Continent.

Asperges à la Flamande

1 bundle asparagus	Chopped parsley
White sauce	Hard-boiled eggs

Wash the asparagus, cut off coarse end of stalks (about 1 in.) and place in salted water in a large saucepan (a special tray which hangs from the side of the saucepan can be used). Bring to the boil and boil until tender (about 15–20 minutes). Take out asparagus, keeping the water for sauce, place on a long dish and garnish with halved hard-boiled eggs and parsley. Make a white sauce, using half milk and half asparagus water, and either serve separately or pour over half the asparagus.

Eels in Sorrel (Anguilles au Vert)

This dish can be eaten all the year round and many restaurants in Antwerp are famous for it.

2 lb. eels	¼ lb. sorrel
A little parsley	A few small onions
Sage	2 oz. melted butter
Juice of 1 lemon	Pepper and salt
1 teaspoonful corn-	1 egg-yolk
flour	

Chop up finely the sorrel, parsley, onions and sage, put into saucepan with the butter and simmer. Cut the eels into medium-sized pieces and add, with the lemon juice, pepper and salt and cook for 10 minutes. Before serving, bind the sauce with the cornflour and egg-yolk.

INDIA

Described by J. R. Mody,
*proprietor of Jamshid
Restaurant, London*

*All kinds of spices are much used—but there are
many other dishes besides curry !*

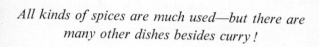

From top down-
wards: dried French
beans, yellow lentils,
almonds, dried peas,
green lentils

THERE are three main characteristics of Indian cookery, which does *not* consist entirely of curries.

(1) Everything contains spices of one kind or another.

(2) Rice is extensively used.

(3) The basis of most dishes is ghee or clarified butter

Ghee can sometimes be obtained in the U.K., but it is very simple to make. Boil the butter over a very gentle heat, constantly skimming off the froth as it rises to the top, for between 1 hour and 1½ hours, then strain it. The resulting fat is less solid and easier to use for cooking than butter, and will keep for about 6 to 9 months.

How to cook Rice

Fill the largest available pan with water to within an inch of the top and bring to the boil. When boiling really vigorously, add the rice and boil for 10–12 minutes. After 10 minutes, examine a few grains, pressing between finger and thumb, to see if they are done. Strain rice in a colander and pour plenty of cold water over it. Then reheat dry in a moderate oven for about 10 minutes. The rice should then be perfect and ready to serve.

Lamb Curry (for 4)

1 lb. lean lamb (pref- erably leg)	¼ lb. ghee or cooking fat
4 green chillies	3 tablespoonfuls curry paste
4 large onions	
2 cloves of garlic	1½ pints stock
Salt to taste	

Chop the onions finely and fry till golden brown in the ghee. Add the garlic (crushed) and the chillies (sliced), and cook for a few minutes. Add the curry paste and allow to simmer for 10 minutes,

413

making sure there is enough fat in the pan to prevent the onions from burning—they must remain golden brown. Wash meat, cut into 1-in. squares, put into the mixture and cook for 10 minutes. Add the stock and cook slowly over a gentle heat until the gravy is thick and the meat tender (about 1¼ hours), adding salt to taste.

Curry Powder needs to be as freshly roasted and ground as coffee, so it should be bought only in small quantities at a time. If it is then carefully kept in a tin, it should last for 2 to 3 months. A good curry paste which contains oil will last 4 or 5 months.

Curried Eggs (for 4)

6 hard-boiled eggs	1 dessertspoonful
1 oz. curry powder or paste	tamarind
½ fresh coconut	¼ lb. ghee or cooking fat
2 cloves of garlic	2 medium onions
½ teaspoonful cinnamon powder	Salt to taste

Soak the tamarind in half a cupful of warm water, stand for 15 minutes, then squeeze through muslin. Pour boiling water over grated coconut and let it stand for 15 minutes, then squeeze that through muslin. Chop onions and fry in the ghee till golden, adding crushed garlic, curry powder or paste, stirring all the time, then add the cinnamon, coconut milk, tamarind water and salt. Simmer until the mixture thickens. Drop in the eggs, and bring slowly to the boil. Serve with boiled rice.

Straw Potatoes and Chicken (Sali moorgi) (Parsee speciality) (for 4)

1 medium roasting chicken	1 pint cooking oil
	Salt to taste
1 lb. peeled potatoes	A piece of fresh ginger or ½ teaspoonful ginger powder
4 cloves of garlic	
1 medium onion	
1 tablespoonful ghee or cooking fat	

Wash, clean and cut the chicken into convenient joints. Crush the ginger and garlic together and rub the mixture over the chicken, then leave it for 1 hour. Cut the potatoes into thin straws, sprinkle them with salt and leave. Slice the onion thinly and fry in the ghee. When golden, add the chicken and fry lightly; then 5 teacupfuls of water and salt to taste, and cook on a low heat until the chicken is tender and only a cupful of gravy remains. Then fry the potato straws in very hot oil (they should be cream-coloured and very crisp). Dish up the chicken and cover with the potato straws. This is an excellent dish for children because, unlike nearly all Indian dishes, it contains no spices.

Fish Curry (for 4)

6 medium cutlets of turbot or halibut	3 dessertspoonfuls vinegar
3 medium onions	Juice of 2 lemons
7 green chillies	4 tablespoonfuls cooking oil
5 cloves of garlic	
1 teaspoonful turmeric powder	1 tablespoonful flour
2 cupfuls coconut milk	A piece of fresh ginger or ½ teaspoonful ginger powder
1 dessertspoonful brown sugar	

Wash and salt the fish. Chop onions and chillies and crush garlic. Fry onions in oil till golden, add chillies, garlic and ginger (ground, if in the piece), turmeric and flour. Keep on low heat for 5 minutes, stirring all the time. Add coconut milk and boil gently for 10 minutes. Add fish, simmer gently until cooked. Mix vinegar, lemon juice and sugar together, and pour over fish. Keep on low heat until the liquid thickens.

Vegetable Curry (Mixed vegetable salad) (for 4)

3 medium potatoes	¼ teaspoonful mustard
1 large aubergine	¼ teaspoonful fenugreek seeds
1 small cauliflower	
3 large onions	1 small piece cassia
1 parsnip	½ level teaspoonful cummin grey powder
5 cloves of garlic	
1 heaped tablespoonful grated coconut	½ level teaspoonful turmeric powder
1 level teaspoonful chilli powder	Juice of 1 lemon
2 tablespoonfuls ghee	1 level teaspoonful chopped parsley
3 green chillies	
Salt to taste	1 small piece fresh ginger
½ level teaspoonful coriander powder	

Slice onions, chop chillies, crush ginger and garlic, fenugreek and cassia. Cut all the other vegetables into small pieces and boil till tender. Fry onions in ghee till golden, add mustard, fenugreek and cassia, stirring all the time. When it bubbles, add the rest of the spices, chopped parsley, ginger and coconut. Stir over low heat for 5 minutes, add all the vegetables, more salt if needed, and mix together, adding a little water if required. Simmer for 10–15 minutes. Add lemon juice and remove from heat.

Dhal (for 4)

¼ lb. red lentils	½ teaspoonful
2 small onions	coriander powder
¼ lb. tomatoes	½ teaspoonful cummin
2 green chillies	grey powder
¼ teaspoonful	Salt to taste
turmeric	3 oz. ghee or cooking
1 teaspoonful chilli	fat
powder	

Chop chillies, tomatoes and onions. Wash lentils, put them in a pan with 1½ pints of cold water, the turmeric and salt, and cook for ½ hour on medium heat, when they should have absorbed all the liquid. Meanwhile, fry the onions till golden, add chillies, spices and tomatoes, and mix well with the lentils. Add small cupful of water and bring to the boil. Stir continuously and remove from heat when well mixed and of the required thickness (it should be about the consistency of thick soup). Pour over boiled rice. Alternatively, it may be cooked until very thick, like paste, and eaten with chapatis.

Chapatis (Indian bread) are with dhal and rice the staple diet.

1 oz. ghee	1 lb. atta (Indian
Pinch of salt	wheat flour)

Rub the ghee into the atta and salt, and mix to a stiff dough with a little warm water. Leave for ½ hour, then knead well with a little warm water to a fairly soft dough. Divide into ten equal-sized balls, roll each one out thinly into a circle about 6 in. in diameter. Get a griddle plate very hot, then drop the chapati on to it, moving it round until it puffs up but does not turn brown. Turn over and cook on the other side—about 1 minute each side. Finally, put the chapati over a bare gas flame for a second till it puffs up like a balloon, repeating on the reverse side. Serve hot or cold with the main dish. In India, chapatis are eaten with vegetable dishes or a dry meat dish, but not with rice.

Savoury Biscuits (Pappadams)

These are bought in tins and cooked by bringing plenty of oil to the boil in a deep frying pan. When the oil is smoking, slide in the pappadams, one at a time, turning

A curry, hot and spicy, as made in India and Pakistan, often served with Chapatis (Indian bread), which are eaten with everything except rice

Sali moorgi, or Straw Potatoes with Chicken—an excellent Indian dish for children because it is one of the few that contain no spices

them instantaneously and removing them—all in a split second. Drain them, preferably vertically. Serve cold as a cocktail savoury.

Capsicums

These vegetables are obtainable fresh in the U.K., usually between July and the end of October.

1 lb. capsicums	½ teaspoonful chilli
2 onions	powder
½ lb. fresh peas	¼ teaspoonful
½ teaspoonful	coriander powder
turmeric powder	¼ teaspoonful cummin
3 tablespoonfuls	grey
cooking oil	Salt to taste

Wash and cut tops from capsicums. Then cut them lengthwise into four or six pieces each. Slice onions and fry in oil till golden. Cook peas separately, add them with capsicums, salt and spices, cover and simmer on low heat, stirring occasionally, for about 15 minutes. Serve as a side dish with meat or with dhal and chapatis.

Finally a sweet dish:

Barfi (for 4)

2 pints milk	Juice of 2 lemons
1 oz. blanched	2 oz. ground almonds
almonds	1 lb. granulated sugar
2 teaspoonfuls vanilla	1 tablespoonful
essence	butter

Boil the milk, then add the lemon juice as required to curdle it. Tie up in muslin till all the liquid has run out, then pass the "curds" through a sieve. Put into a pan with the vanilla, sugar, ground almonds and butter over a low flame, stirring all the time and taking great care that it does not burn. It is ready when, on tilting the pan towards you, the mixture comes clear away from the bottom. Butter a dish and spread the mixture about ½ in. thick. Slice and very lightly fry the blanched almonds and decorate the top of the mixture with them. Cool, shape into diamonds and cut.

* * * * * *

NOTE ON SUPPLIES: All spices used throughout this chapter, also cereals such as atta (Indian wheat flour), pappadams, etc., are obtainable from Jamshid's Spice Box, 19 Old Brompton Road, London, S.W.7.

PAKISTAN

*Rice is a staple item of daily diet, and the housewife really
knows how to cook it perfectly*

Compiled exclusively by the BEGAM AHMAD ALI KHAN

PAKISTAN is largely a Muslim country, so our foods are mainly Middle Eastern, with the addition of the spices used so much in India.

Wheat and rice are the staple items of our daily diet, and the three spices most used in our dishes are turmeric, coriander and chilli powder. We vary our flavours by using more of one or less of another and sometimes leaving out one of the three. All three spices—and also cummin grey, which we use in cooking nearly all our vegetables—can be obtained in London (from Selfridges Ltd., Oxford Street; Lal Jolly, 60c, Guilford Street, W.C.1, and Jamshid's Spice Box, 19 Old Brompton Road, S.W.7).

RICE DISHES

On Choosing Rice

European housewives often ask how they can tell a good rice from an inferior one. We test the quality by cooking a number of samples in little muslin bags, but the chief point to look for in uncooked rice is a long, thin grain. Patna rice, now easily obtainable, is quite a good average quality and much better than the little roundish grains. Do not be put off by rice of a darker colour. It usually means that it is older and should be better than the very white varieties.

To Prepare Boiled Rice (1st method)

Soak for about 2 hours or less (this applies to Patna rice, but the time varies according to the quality of the rice). Boil in plenty of salted water in a large pan until, when you take out a grain to test it, it feels almost but not quite soft. Strain. Pour cold water over the rice, shake well to get out the water, return to the pan, which must be tightly covered by a well-fitting lid (a little butter melted in the pan before the rice is put back will prevent it from sticking), and cook for about 20 minutes over a low heat.

To Prepare Rice (2nd method)

Soak the rice for about 2 hours. Fry an onion till lightly coloured in about 2 oz. fat, add the rice and double the quantity of warm water (two teacupfuls of water to one teacupful of rice), and cook fast for 10 minutes, then simmer for 20–30 minutes or until the rice grain is tender when pressed between finger and thumb and the rice is dry.

Lamb Pullao (for 4)

1 *lb. rice*	4 *oz. butter or cooking fat*
1 *lb. lamb*	
	½ *lb. onions*

Soak the rice for about 2 hours. Fry sliced onions until golden brown, add the lamb, cut into small pieces, and about ½ pint water and cook until tender and almost dry. Put in the rice, twice as much water and cook as for rice—2nd method—given above.

Chicken Pullao (for 6)

Medium-sized boiling fowl	½ *teaspoonful saffron*
	¼ *lb. butter or cooking fat*
1¼ *lb. rice*	
	1 *bottle yoghourt*

Boil the chicken in a little water until tender enough to break easily into joints. Break into convenient pieces, put in a bowl, spread thickly with yoghourt and leave for about 2 hours so that the yoghourt is absorbed.

Prepare the saffron by placing it under the grill for 1 minute so that it becomes dry and crisp, powder it with the fingers, then pour over it a tablespoonful of boiling water and leave it to dissolve.

Prepare the rice by the 1st method given above, but before returning it to the pan melt the butter with ¼ cupful of water, then take out half for use later on. Strain the cooked rice and place half in a saucepan, put the chicken on top and then the remainder of the rice mixed with the saffron. Cover with a tight-fitting lid, cook fast for 7 minutes, add the remaining water and butter, and cook slowly for another 15 minutes.

Curry (for 4)

1 lb. lean stewing lamb or mutton	Potatoes
1 onion	1 teaspoonful turmeric
¼ lb. butter or cooking fat	2 teaspoonfuls coriander
Chilli powder to taste	

Fry the chopped onion in the fat until golden, add the spices and a little water gradually, stirring all the time to get the full flavour out of the spices. Add the meat, washed and cut into small pieces, and enough water to cover. Simmer slowly for 1 hour, or 1½ hours (depending on the quality of the meat), and, when tender, add sliced potatoes and continue simmering until they are cooked. (This curry should not be very dry.)

Marrow, turnips, peas, etc., can be used instead of potatoes. If using spinach or tomatoes, cook until nearly all the water has disappeared.

SWEETS

Halva (made from carrots) (for 4)

1 lb. carrots	1 pint milk
Sugar to taste	Seedless raisins or chopped almonds
2–3 cardamoms	
½ lb. butter	

Peel, wash and finely grate the carrots. Melt the butter and put into it 2 or 3 cardamoms and the carrots, and cook gently with the lid on until all the butter has been absorbed. Add the milk and simmer on a medium heat, stirring occasionally, until all the milk has dried up and the butter begins to show again at the bottom of the pan (the mixture should be the consistency of rice pudding), add sugar and chopped almonds or seedless raisins, according to taste. Serve either hot or cold.

Gujrela (for 4)

½ lb. carrots	Almonds, pistachios and angelica for decoration
1 pint milk	
1 tablespoonful rice	
Sugar to taste	

Peel, wash and grate the carrots, cook with the rice in a pint of milk slowly until thick. Add sugar, decorate and serve ice-cold.

COOKING VEGETABLES

In Pakistan we cook all the vegetables in butter flavoured with cummin grey, usually two or three vegetables being cooked together. To cook 1 lb. potatoes, melt 2 oz. butter or cooking fat with ½ teaspoonful cummin grey. When the cummin grey is golden brown, put in the sliced potatoes, salt and pepper, ½ cupful of water and cook over a low heat for about 10 minutes with the lid on—or until the potatoes are a little soft—add sliced tomatoes and cook for another 5 minutes. Beans, peas or spinach may be cooked with the potatoes.

SAVOURIES, Etc.

Pouri

4 oz. white self-raising or wholemeal flour	½ oz. butter or cooking fat
Salt	Fat for frying

Shred the fat into the flour, add salt, then, with a little water, mix to the consistency of pastry. Divide into six equal portions, roll each out thinly into a circle about the size of a coffee saucer and fry in hot deep fat until it turns golden brown and becomes puffy.

Paratha

4 oz. plain flour	Butter for "spreading" and frying
2 oz. butter or lard for dough	
	Salt

Make a dough with the flour, butter or lard, salt and a little water, divide into four equal portions and roll each out into an oval. Spread lightly, or brush over, with butter, then fold over one long side of the oval, brush over with butter and roll, fold over the other side, brush with butter and roll again (the dough is now the shape of a rolled pancake); fold up one narrow end half-way, brush with butter, roll, then fold over the other end so that you have a small square. Roll this out thinly, still keeping it square, prick in two or three places with a fork; then fry in a very little butter until golden brown and like a pancake. Repeat with the other three portions.

Samosas

These are stuffed savoury pouri filled either with a meat or vegetable stuffing.

For the pouri

4 oz. white self-raising flour	1 oz. butter or cooking fat

A typical meal as served in India or Pakistan. The main dish (right) is Chicken Pullao, with Samosas (left) and Halva just behind as a sweet

For a meat filling

½ lb. minced meat
1 medium onion
Chilli powder to taste
Fat for frying
¼ teaspoonful turmeric
½ teaspoonful coriander

For a vegetable filling

½ lb. potatoes
½ teaspoonful cummin grey
Salt and chilli powder
1 oz. butter or cooking fat
1 teaspoonful lemon juice

Make the pouri as already described, roll out into circles and cut each circle in half. Fold the half-circle across in half again, and stick the two halves of the straight side together by damping with water, thus forming a cone shape.

The filling.—If using meat, fry the chopped onion till golden brown, add turmeric, coriander and chilli powder to taste, stirring all the time. Add the meat and cook slowly for about 20 minutes.

For the vegetable filling, peel and slice potatoes into tiny pieces about the size of large peas, cook in melted butter or cooking fat with cummin grey, salt and chilli powder until golden brown, adding lemon juice.

Fill the little cones with the mixture, fastening their tops by damping and pressing edges together. Fry in deep fat until golden brown. Serve hot as an afternoon tea dish or with cocktails.

Pakoras (Cocktail or teatime snacks)

4 oz. Gram flour (Basan Atta)
Chilli powder to taste
½ teaspoonful cummin grey
Fat for frying
1 cupful water
Pinch of salt
Spinach or lettuce leaves or potatoes sliced as for chips

Make a batter, using the flour, chilli powder, salt, cummin grey and water, and beating well. Take separate leaves of spinach or lettuce, or a slice of potato, dip in the batter and fry in deep, very hot fat. Serve piping hot, with chilli sauce if desired.

CHINA

Compiled by T. W. Chen Hsu from the classical Chinese cuisine of the Great Wall Restaurant, London

Snow on the Meadow, like all Chinese dishes, can be eaten with chopsticks or spoon and fork. A knife never comes to a Chinese table

IN Chinese cookery, rice is used extensively, so are chicken, pork and eggs, but Chop Suey, so often served as a national dish, is never seen in China. Spices and herbs are not used, the only strong flavours being garlic and onion. At least four or five dishes are always served at the same time and all the food can be eaten either with chopsticks or a spoon and fork. A knife never comes to a Chinese table, because everything is cut up beforehand.

The following is the kind of meal that would be served to guests in China:

First: *Hors d'œuvres*, a number of different dishes arranged daintily around a plate and including, for instance, chopped roast pork; Soochow fish; chicken gizzard stewed in soya sauce; bean sprout salad with sweet-sour sauce; sweet and sour cucumber; tea-flavoured eggs.

Second: *Four Hot Dishes*, such as fried lobster or other sea foods.

Third: *Two Dessert Dishes*, one sweet, such as Snow on the Meadow; one savoury, such as Bao-Tse (Steamed Meat Buns).

Fourth: *Four Stewed Dishes*, a whole stewed duck or chicken; stewed beef; a vegetable dish; stewed fish, the fish always being eaten last. This served with plenty of boiled rice.

And, finally, tea to drink.

The reason for the four courses goes far back into Chinese history when it was the custom to give the whole day to entertaining a friend. When entertaining was telescoped into a few hours, all the meals for the day were served at once and in the right order. Thus the hors d'œuvres represent the cold first meal or breakfast; the four hot dishes, lunch; the dessert, afternoon tea, and the four stewed dishes with rice, the evening meal.

The following recipes have been specially chosen because they are all made from ingredients obtainable in the U.K. Chinese mushrooms (which are quite different from British ones—black all over and bigger) are obtainable dried, by the ounce; bamboo shoots, sweet lychees and water chestnuts in tins; green Chinese beans by the pound and Chinese vermicelli by the bundle, from Oriental shops, such as Jamshid's Spice Box, 19 Old Brompton Road, London, S.W.7; Lal Jolly, 60c Guilford Street, London, W.C.1, or the Hong Kong Emporium, 53 Rupert Street, London, W.1.

NOTE: Bean shoots can be grown in any kitchen. Scatter a pound of green Chinese beans on a large piece of flannel, cover with a second piece of flannel and sprinkle gently with water every day. The shoots will begin to appear in about ten days in winter, four or five days in summer weather, and will go on shooting.

Shallow Frying

Most Chinese frying is "shallow-frying,"

The Chinese serve several dishes at once. Here, from left to right, are Steamed Meat Buns, Sweet and Sour Pork and mixed vegetables

which means that only a very little fat is used, just to grease the pan (as for frying pancakes), which must be very hot, with a little water added as required. In China, soya bean or peanut oil is chiefly used, but the best substitute easily obtainable outside China is tea-seed oil.

Three Sisters Soup (for 4)

The three sisters are Chicken, Chinese Mushrooms and Bamboo Shoots.

1 quart chicken broth	Salt to taste
4 pieces of dried mushroom	1 oz. bamboo shoots Breast of one chicken

Slice the bamboo shoots, dried Chinese mushrooms and breast of chicken very fine, and drop into the boiling chicken broth. Cook gently for about 3 minutes and serve—in little round bowls (not soup plates) if you want to be really Chinese.

Dan Jiao (Stuffed Egg Rolls) Soup

For soup

Stewing meat	A bundle of Chinese
½ lb. fresh watercress	vermicelli

For dan jiao

4 eggs	Oil or fat
¼ lb meat (pork or veal)	½ oz. spring onion Salt to taste

Beat up the eggs and add a pinch of salt.

For the stuffing, mince the meat and cut the onion into tiny bits; mix them together and add salt to taste.

Rub the oil or fat on a hot ladle, place over a low flame, so that a thin film of fat forms on the ladle's surface, and pour in half a tablespoonful of egg. Shake the ladle so that the egg forms a circle and immediately put on to it a little of the stuffing mixture. Fold the circle carefully in two, close it up and turn it over, and one dan jiao is thus formed. Repeat the process. 4 eggs make roughly 30 rolls.

For the soup, soak vermicelli in boiling water for 10 minutes, cut into lengths of 6–8 in.; boil the meat on a low flame for 1 hour, then add vermicelli.

Put the dan jiao and watercress into the soup and simmer for 1 minute. It will then be ready for serving.

Sliced Chicken

1 clove of garlic	½ lb. white meat of
¼ lb. mushrooms	chicken (uncooked)
A little cornflour	¼ lb. French beans
1 medium onion	Oil for frying
Cooking sherry to taste	

Slice chicken into thin pieces and mix it

in the cornflour, made into a paste with a little water, to prevent the pieces sticking together. Slit the beans in halves and cut them into inch-long pieces. Skin the mushrooms and cut into pieces the same size as the chicken slices. Slice the onion in the same way.

Fry the crushed garlic in hot oil and shallow-fry it with the onion until just cooked. Add salt to taste. Then shallow-fry the French beans and mushrooms. When cooked, dish up. Wipe the pan with a clean cloth or use a fresh pan. Put in some fat or oil and shallow-fry the chicken slices until they are almost cooked. Add other ingredients and a little cooking sherry, and stir the whole thing until the chicken slices are fully cooked.

To Cook Rice

4 *teacupfuls rice*	6 *teacupfuls of water*

Experiment is advisable. Those who prefer soft rice may, for instance, add a little more water.

Wash the rice thoroughly four or five times, then put in a pan with the cold water. Bring quickly to the boil and cook gently for a further 20 minutes, when the rice will be ready to serve.

Fried Rice with Ham and Egg

5 *teacupfuls of rice*	2 *eggs*
(*cooked as above*)	1 *oz. spring onion*
2 *oz. ham*	*Lard or oil for frying*
	Salt to taste

Cut the ham and spring onion into tiny pieces. Beat the eggs, and add salt to taste. Put some lard or tea-seed oil in a frying pan and fry the rice for about 5 minutes. Scramble the egg in a similar way in another frying pan for about 2 minutes. Mix the cooked egg and chopped ham with the rice and fry again for about 3 minutes.

Sweet and Sour Pork

½ *lb. pork (or veal)*	1 *egg*
2 *tablespoonfuls self-*	*Fat for deep frying*
raising flour	

For the sauce

1 *teacupful vinegar*	2 *tablespoonfuls oil*
1 *desertspoonful*	1 *sliced tomato and*
cornflour	*some boiled green*
A clove of garlic	*peas*
6 *tablespoonfuls sugar*	

Cut the pork into pieces (half-domino size). Beat the egg and mix with flour. Dip the pieces of meat into this batter and fry in deep fat until brown. Serve hot with the sauce made as follows:

Mix the cornflour with the vinegar and sugar in half a cupful of water. Fry the crushed garlic in hot oil, add the cornflour and boil the mixture. Add the sliced tomato and simmer for 3 minutes. Lastly, add the boiled green peas.

Fried Lobster

Cut cooked lobster into domino-sized pieces, dip in batter (made from 1 egg and 2 tablespoonfuls self-raising flour as above) and deep-fry until golden.

Meat Balls

These are made from minced raw pork mixed with a little celery and onion to taste and minced very fine. Add salt and shape into balls, sprinkle with flour, dip in batter (made from 1 egg and 2 tablespoonfuls self-raising flour) and deep-fry until golden. Serve with sweet and sour sauce (see under recipe for Sweet and Sour Pork).

Mixed Vegetables

Use any or all of the following: onion, leek, Chinese mushroom (this should be included if possible), tomato, bean sprouts (or bamboo shoots or water chestnuts), celery, green peppers, spring greens.

Wash and clean all the vegetables, then slice them up into very thin strips and shallow-fry them all in very little oil in a hot pan. Add a little water and simmer for 5 minutes. The dish is then ready to serve in its own juice.

NOTE: This dish can be served as Vegetable Chop Suey.

Tea-flavoured Eggs

Hard-boil the required number of eggs, remove the shells and stand them in a bowl, covered in tea and a little salt for ½ hour. They will be chocolate-coloured and slightly flavoured with tea.

Snow on the Meadow

1 *large packet frozen*	2 *or 3 egg-whites*
green peas	*Plenty of lard for*
6 *tablespoonfuls*	*frying*
castor sugar	

Cook the peas in the usual way in boiling salted water until tender, then put them through a mincer and mix in the sugar. Melt a large knob of lard (about 2 oz.) in a very hot pan and fry the minced peas for 10 minutes. Put on to a plate, keep hot and top with stiffly beaten cold egg-white

Chopped vegetables and prawns are included in this salad. On the right are delicately flavoured lychees, often served as a dessert, either fresh or canned

Steamed Meat Buns (Steamed bao-tse)

For the pastry

1 *lb. self-raising flour*	1 *oz. yeast*
1 *teaspoonful sugar*	*Water to mix*

For the filling

Minced raw pork	*Soya bean sauce*
1 *minced spring onion*	*Salt to taste*

Dissolve yeast in a teacupful of warm water. Stir thoroughly, then mix with the flour and sugar into a dough. Leave for 10 minutes, then roll out and cut into circles about 2½ in. in diameter. Put about half a tablespoonful of filling into the centre of each circle, wrap the edges over the meat and leave for 20 minutes. Steam for 20 minutes.

Stewed Duck or Chicken

(This is a very popular dish in Southern China.) First remove *all* the bones from the bird (including the wing ones), stuff with a mixture of minced chestnuts, mushrooms, chopped ham and boiled rice, and stew in a very little water and about 3 tablespoonfuls of soya bean sauce for about 3 hours. Serve with rice. It can be done, though no *so* well, with a duck or chicken that still has its bones.

General Hints

As a dessert course at a Chinese meal, serve either preserved ginger or lychees, which can be bought in tins and are absolutely delicious with a flavour all their own. Bamboo shoots may be served as a separate vegetable—finely sliced and shallow-fried in oil with a little water added. Soya sauce is served with practically all meat, fish and vegetable dishes and with rice. Like the bean sprouts, it is full of vitamins.

INDONESIA

by S. F. RUNTUWENE

*No meal is complete without lots of rice and at least
one savoury dish fiery with chillies*

THE chief characteristics of Indonesian cooking are the extensive use of rice and the fact that most dishes contain chillies and are therefore very hot.

A typical Indonesian main meal consists of rice with four subsidiary dishes—one containing chicken or meat, one fish, one vegetables, and the fourth very hot and spicy, called Sambel. After that, fresh fruit is eaten and sometimes a savoury. But whatever else is served at a meal, the rice is of the greatest importance and is eaten first.

To Cook Rice—Indonesian Style

Allow 1 lb. of Patna rice for 4 people.

Put the rice into a pan and cover it with cold water to a depth equal to two joints of the middle finger. Bring to the boil, stir once to prevent it sticking to the bottom, then cover and cook slowly for ½ hour or until the grains feel soft. Strain and serve.

Yellow Rice (Nasi kuning) (for 4)

1 lb. Patna rice	1 teaspoonful tur-
1½ pints coconut milk	meric powder
(or milk)	½ teaspoonful salt

Decoration

2 eggs	Red chillies
1 onion	Black soya beans
Celery leaf	½ cucumber
Carrots or radishes	

Bring to the boil the coconut milk (made by soaking for 15 minutes and squashing well half a grated fresh coconut or ½ lb. desiccated coconut with 6 of 7 tablespoonfuls of water, then passing through a sieve), add the rice and seasonings, cook until milk is absorbed, stirring to prevent burning; leave on a low heat for about 5 minutes. Finish by steaming the rice until cooked. Make an omelette with the eggs, cut it into strips and use for decoration with the other ingredients listed above. Serve with roast chicken.

FISH DISHES

Pindang Serani (for 4)

2 mackerel	¼ teaspoonful tur-
5 red chillies	meric powder
5 green chillies	1 teaspoonful ground
1 bay leaf	ginger
Salt	Lemon juice
1 onion	Margarine or oil for
3 cloves of garlic	frying

Slice the onion, garlic and chillies. Fry a golden brown, and add salt, turmeric powder, ginger and bay leaf. Add 6 teacupfuls of water and bring to the boil. Wash and clean the fish, add with the lemon juice and cook gently for about 5 minutes until the fish is cooked but not falling to pieces.

NOTE: This dish is vastly improved if made 2 or 3 days beforehand and the fish left to soak in the liquid until required. If this is done, an aluminium pan must NOT be used.

Pickled Fish (for 4)

2 mackerel or whiting	3 cloves of garlic
1 onion	2 almonds
½ pint frying oil	1½ teaspoonfuls sugar
1 teaspoonful tur-	6 red chillies
meric powder	½ pint vinegar
Salt	8 shallots or spring
½ pint water	onions

Wash and clean the fish, mix with salt and a little vinegar, and fry a golden brown in the oil. Put dry seasonings, garlic and onion through a mincer. Fry for about 2 minutes. Add water and vinegar. Bring to the boil. Add shallots or spring onions, sliced chillies and fried fish. Continue to cook for a few minutes.

Roast Fish (for 4)

2 mackerel	6 red chillies
½ lemon	¼ teaspoonful ground
1 tablespoonful mar-	ginger
garine	Salt

Clean and wash the fish. Chop the chillies finely, add ginger, salt and lemon juice. Melt margarine, add the fish and seasoning. Slowly simmer until cooked.

MEAT AND POULTRY DISHES

Orak-Arik (for 4)

½ lb. cabbage
Breast of 1 chicken
Margarine
½ teaspoonful pepper
Celery leaves
5 shallots
2 eggs
Sugar and salt to taste

Chop the shallots, mix with pepper and fry in margarine. Add sliced chicken, celery leaves and mashed cabbage. Beat the eggs and pour into the mixture; add salt and sugar and cook for about 5 minutes, or until cabbage is sufficiently cooked. Serve with fried onions.

Abon (for 4)

1 lb. beef
½ pint oil
2 cloves of garlic
1 teaspoonful lemon
  juice
Salt and sugar to taste

Cook the beef in ½ pint

At the main meal rice is accompanied by subsidiary dishes containing chicken or meat, fish and vegetables, as well as a spicy Sambel

of water until it is so soft that it falls apart in strings. Chop garlic fine, mix with salt, sugar, lemon juice and the meat and leave for about 5 minutes. Heat the frying oil and fry the beef mixture until a golden brown. Eat with rice.

Nasi Gurih Ajam (for 4)

1 lb. rice	4 teaspoonfuls coco-
1 onion (or 10	nut milk (made
shallots)	from 2 lb. coco-
1 bay leaf	nut. See Yellow
1 young chicken	Rice recipe)
Salt	

Decorations

¼ lb. cabbage finely shredded, cucumber, omelet (1 egg) cut into strips, young celery leaves, radishes.

Wash the rice. Clean the chicken and cut in pieces. Put half of the rice into a stewpan with chicken, sliced onion (or shallots), bay leaf and salt. Put the rest of the rice on top, pour coconut milk over the rice and chicken and bring to the boil. When boiling, stir and mix everything well together. Continue cooking over a low heat for about 40 minutes. Garnish with decorations listed above.

Liver Dish (Sambel goreng ati) (for 4)

1 lb. liver	3 cloves of garlic
2 tomatoes	½ lb. desiccated
½ teaspoonful	coconut
paprika powder	1 teaspoonful chilli
½ lb. fresh green peas	powder
2 tablespoonfuls	2 tablespoonfuls
sliced onion	margarine
2 bay leaves	

Cut the liver into squares of about 1 in. Slice the garlic and fry with the onion, chilli powder and paprika powder. Add the liver, the bay leaves, and then the tomatoes and peas. Place the lid on the pan and switch to a low heat. Stir occasionally and, when nearly cooked, add 1 teacupful of coconut milk (made from ½ lb. desiccated coconut, see Yellow Rice recipe). Continue to cook until the liver is ready, stirring constantly to prevent curdling.

Roast Meat Balls (for 4)

1 egg	½ clove of garlic
4 potatoes	½ lb. minced meat
1½ tablespoonfuls	1 onion
margarine	¼ teaspoonful ground
3 tablespoonfuls	nutmeg
breadcrumbs	½ teaspoonful pepper

Peel the potatoes and boil them. Slice and fry onion and garlic in 1 tablespoonful

margarine for about 2 minutes. Mash the potatoes, mix with the fried onions, garlic and minced meat, egg and rest of the seasoning. Spread the breadcrumbs and ½ tablespoonful margarine in a fireproof pie-dish and add the mixture. Heat well in moderate oven. Serve hot.

Roast Chicken (Ajam panggang) (for 4)

1 small roasting	¼ teaspoonful
chicken	coriander
2 cloves of garlic	1 lb. shallots
2 almonds	1 teaspoonful
1 tablespoonful	granulated sugar
margarine	2 tomatoes
½ lb. desiccated coc-	2 bay leaves
nut or coconut milk	

Clean and wash the chicken. Melt the margarine. Put all the other ingredients, except the bay leaves and tomatoes, through a mincer and fry the mixed ingredients. Add the chicken and cook for about 3 minutes. Add about 2 teacupfuls of coconut milk (made with the desiccated coconut, see Yellow Rice recipe) and cook until it thickens. Place the cooked chicken in the grill pan and grill for about 5 minutes.

Grilled Lamb (Sate kambing) (for 4)

1 lb. lamb	¾ teaspoonful
1 onion	coriander
Salt and pepper to	1 clove of garlic
taste	Lemon juice
For the sauce	
1 teacupful peanuts	½ teaspoonful ground
3 red chillies	ginger
1 clove garlic	1 onion
Lemon juice	

Cut the meat into squares of about 1 in. Mince the coriander, onion and garlic, mix this with the meat, pepper, salt and lemon juice. Thread on skewers, about four or five pieces to each, and grill. Serve with fried onion rings, a little vinegar and sauce made as follows: Put the peanuts through a mincer, fry with chopped onion, garlic, chillies and ginger, and add a little water. Finally, add lemon juice.

VEGETABLE DISHES

French Beans (Sambel goreng boontjes)

½ lb. meat or 1 pint	2 onions
shelled prawns	Salt
½ lb. desiccated	1 lb. French beans
coconut	3 chillies
1 bay leaf	Fat for frying

Mix the coconut with 6 or 7 teacupfuls of water, squash well and sieve. Cut up the meat into pieces about 1 in. square. Fry the onions a light brown, add the rest of the seasoning and the meat or prawns, fry, add the beans and the coconut milk. Bring to the boil and cook for a few minutes.

Urap (for 4)

Vegetables

¼ lb. French beans	¼ lb. soya bean
¼ lb. cabbage	sprouts
2 carrots	¼ lb. spinach
Cos lettuce	

NOTE: To obtain bean sprouts, put a cupful of soya beans in a damp sack in a damp atmosphere for 3 days and 3 nights. They should then be sprouting well and ready for use.

Seasoning

¼ lb. desiccated	1 teaspoonful sugar
coconut	4 red chillies
¼ onion	2 cloves of garlic
1 bay leaf	Salt

Wash the vegetables, cut into pieces about 1 in. long, except carrots, which are cut into slices, and the spinach. Steam vegetables together until three-quarters cooked. Put all seasoning through mincer, except coconut. Fry coconut in a little oil and then mix it with the minced seasoning and steamed vegetables and put in a fireproof dish. Heat through in a moderate oven. This dish is eaten as a savoury after the main course.

Mixed Vegetable Salad (Gado-gado) (for 4)

2 or 3 cabbage leaves	¼ lb. bean sprouts
2 tomatoes	(see Urap recipe)
2 boiled potatoes	½ cucumber
½ lettuce	2 onions
Prawn crackers	2 hard-boiled eggs
A little margarine	

For the sauce

½ jar peanut butter	1½ tablespoonfuls
2 tablespoonfuls sugar	lemon juice
1 teaspoonful	1½ teacupfuls water
chilli powder	Salt to taste
½ tablespoonful margarine	

Wash and cut up cabbage. Cook it and bean sprouts separately. Slice tomatoes, cucumber, washed lettuce, boiled potatoes and eggs. Fry prawn crackers and sliced

A favourite Indonesian meat dish is Abon, made by first boiling beef until it is so soft it falls apart, and then frying it

onion separately. Arrange as follows. First put the cabbage on a plate, and on it the lettuce and bean sprouts, cucumber, potatoes, tomatoes, eggs, prawn crackers and fried onions. To make the sauce, fry chilli powder in margarine, add 1 teacupful of water, mix in sugar, salt and peanut butter, and stir until well mixed. Add ½ teacupful water with lemon juice. Boil for a few minutes.

HOT DISHES (containing Chilli)
Hot Tomato Dish

¼ onion	2 tomatoes
2 chillies	1½ tablespoonfuls
Juice of 1 lemon	water
Salt	

Slice onion, tomatoes and chillies very finely. Mix, add salt, lemon juice and water. Serve with rice, meat and a vegetable dish, and eat in *very* small quantities.

Hot Fried Tomato Dish

½ onion	4 red chillies
2 tomatoes	2 tablespoonfuls
Salt	margarine

Fry the sliced onion a golden brown in the margarine and add the finely sliced chillies. Add the sliced tomatoes and salt and fry for about 7 minutes.

EGG DISHES
Stuffed Omelet (for 4)

1½ lb. minced meat	2 cloves of garlic
1 onion	4 eggs
Pepper and salt	Margarine for frying

For the stuffing.—Slice onion and garlic and fry till golden brown in margarine, add pepper and salt. Put the minced meat in with the fried onions, etc., and keep frying until meat is cooked.

For the omelet.—Beat up the eggs with a pinch of salt. Melt a little fat in frying pan and pour in just enough of the beaten eggs to cover the bottom of pan. Cook until set, then toss over on to other side and spread with a portion of the filling and roll up. Repeat until eggs and filling are used.

Fried Eggs (for 4)

4 hard-boiled eggs	2 tablespoonfuls
1 onion	chillies
Margarine	3 tomatoes
Salt	

Peel the eggs and cut each egg in two. Slice onion, chillies and tomatoes, and fry in melted margarine, add the eggs and salt, and fry till vegetables are done.

Boiled-egg Dish (Sambel goreng telor) (for 4)

4 hard-boiled eggs	1 clove of garlic
2 tomatoes	½ onion
2 teacupfuls coconut	1 bay leaf
milk (see Yellow	½ teaspoonful sugar
Rice)	Salt
3 chillies	Margarine

Put the onion, garlic and chillies through the mincer and fry in a little margarine. Slice tomatoes into the frying pan, add seasoning and coconut milk, bring to the boil and cook until it thickens. Keep stirring to prevent curdling. Add the hard-boiled eggs and cook for about 2 minutes.

Egg Dish (Tjeploh asem) (for 4)

4 eggs	Salt and pepper
1 teaspoonful chilli	4 sliced tomatoes
powder	½ teaspoonful sugar
3 tablespoonfuls	3 tablespoonfuls
sliced onions	margarine
2 cloves of garlic	½ teacupful water

Fry the eggs in 1 tablespoonful of margarine. Add salt and pepper.
For the sauce.—Fry the sliced onion and garlic in 2 tablespoonfuls of margarine. Add chilli, tomatoes, water and sugar. Pour this sauce over the fried eggs.

MISCELLANEOUS
Fried Corn Fritters (Prekedel djagung) (for 4)

1 large can sweet	Salt and pepper to
corn	taste
5 stalks of spring	2 eggs
onions	2 tablespoonfuls
2 tablespoonfuls	sliced onions
margarine	Celery

Beat the eggs and mix with salt, pepper, onions, chopped spring onions, sliced celery and corn. Fry as for fritters.

Soya Bean Drink (Katjang idjo)

½ lb. soya beans	2 teacupfuls thick
½ teaspoonful ground	coconut milk (see
ginger	Yellow Rice)
A pinch of salt	4 tablespoonfuls
	sugar

Soak the soya beans for 1 hour in 3 teacupfuls of water. In the same water bring to the boil. Add sugar, salt and ginger, cook until thick. Add the coconut milk and stir to prevent curdling. Cook for about 10 minutes and serve hot.

Sosaties are generally eaten at a braaivleis, a kind of night-time picnic, cooked over an open fire

SOUTH AFRICA

Including dishes of Afrikaans origin and others brought from Malaya, described by Mrs. Wrightson, author of "The Royal Hostess"

Sosaties

1 *small fat leg of lamb or 2 lb. cut from fatty leg*	1 *tablespoonful curry powder*
1 *teaspoonful salt*	1 *tablespoonful sugar*
¼ *teaspoonful pepper*	2 *cupfuls vinegar*
2 *medium-sized chopped onions*	1 *tablespoonful fruit chutney*
2 *or 3 tablespoonfuls dripping*	1 *cupful cold water*
	6 *lemon or orange leaves coarsely chopped*

Cut the meat into small squares, season with salt and pepper, and put on to small wooden skewers, alternating meat and fat. Prepare a marinade as follows: Slice and chop the onions and brown them in a pan with dripping. Sprinkle in the curry powder and stir. Add the sugar, salt, pepper, vinegar, fruit chutney, water and lemon or orange leaves. Stir well. Put the skewered meat into a deep bowl and pour over it the marinade. Stand overnight, or longer, and stir so that all the meat is impregnated with the sauce. Remove the meat from the marinade and drain it. Grill over a hot fire (barbecue) or under an electric or gas grill for 10–15 minutes. The sauce should be heated, strained and served as gravy.

Robotie

A dish brought to South Africa by the Malays, who settled in the Cape in the early days.

2 *medium-sized sliced onions*	1 *teaspoonful salt*
2 *tablespoonfuls butter or dripping*	1 *tablespoonful vinegar*
1 *tablespoonful curry powder*	1 *lb. minced cooked beef or mutton*
1 *dessertspoonful sugar*	1 *thick slice bread*
	½ *pint milk*
	2 *eggs*

Fry the sliced onions in the butter or dripping until lightly browned. Sprinkle the curry powder over the onions, add salt, sugar, vinegar and meat, and mix well together. Soak the bread in the milk, then drain off the milk, mash the bread with a fork and add it to the meat mixture, to-

429

gether with 1 beaten egg. Turn into a buttered pie dish. Add sufficient milk to the milk drained from the bread to make up to ¾ cupful. Beat the remaining egg and mix it with the milk. Season with salt and pepper, and pour this over the meat mixture in the pie dish. Dot with small pieces of butter and stand the pie dish in a pan of water. Bake in a moderate oven for 30–40 minutes.

Pork with Sweet-Sour Sauce

1½ lb. belly of pork	Apples
Spinach	Pineapple
Tomatoes	Cucumber
Green peppers	Spring onions (or
Garlic and chillies to	other onions)
taste	Fat for frying

For the batter

2 eggs	3 tablespoonfuls flour

Cut the pork into ¾-in. squares, dip in batter made with the eggs and flour (do not use any water or milk), and fry in deep hot fat until dark golden brown; drain and place on a large meat dish. Chop up coarsely all the vegetables and fruit, and put into a pan with about 2 tablespoonfuls of hot fat and cook for about 4 minutes; then pour over the meat. Finally, pour over the whole dish sauce made as follows:

1 tablespoonful corn-flour	1 tablespoonful sugar
1 tablespoonful malt vinegar	1 tablespoonful soya sauce (dark)
1½ cupfuls water	1 tablespoonful tomato sauce

Place all the ingredients except the tomato sauce in a pan and cook over a slow heat, stirring all the time, until the sauce has the consistency of treacle; add the tomato sauce.

NOTE: The sauce can be made first and reheated when needed.

Mos-bolletjies

These were originally made from fermented grape juice (mos) and are still fairly common in the wine-growing districts of the Western Cape. Because fermented grape juice is not easy to come by, raisins have been substituted.

¼ lb. raisins stoned and chopped finely	2 teacupfuls milk, scalded and cooled to blood tempera-ture
2 cupfuls warm water (blood tempera-ture)	1 teaspoonful cinna-mon
1 cake yeast	
5 lb. flour	1 tablespoonful aniseed or grated nutmeg
6 oz. lard or good dripping	
1 tablespoonful salt	6 oz. butter
3 eggs	1 cupful sugar

Put the chopped raisins into a quart screw-topped jar, together with warm water. Cream the yeast cake with 1 tablespoonful of the sugar and add this to the raisins and water. Screw on the lid and place the jar in a warm place overnight for the mixture to ferment. Next morning, strain the yeast (which should be well risen) into a warmed bowl and add 1½–2 cupfuls of flour, beating into a smooth batter. Cover this sponge and stand in a warm place until bubbly and light. Mix the spices, salt and sugar with the remaining flour, and rub in the butter and lard finely. (All butter can be used if preferred.) When the sponge is nice and light, add the well-beaten eggs. Mix, and gradually add the flour mixture alternately with the scalded and cooled milk to blend into soft dough. A little more warm water can be added if necessary. Knead the dough for 10 minutes, cover and stand in a warm place until more than doubled in bulk. Turn on to a floured board, cut small pieces and form into balls. Place the bolletjies on a greased baking tin, close together, greasing lightly between them with a little cooking oil so that they will break apart easily when baked. Leave to rise in a warm place until very light, and bake in a hot oven for 20–25 minutes.

Koeksusters

1 lb. flour	4 teaspoonfuls baking powder
¼ teaspoonful salt	
Deep hot oil or fat for cooking	2 beaten eggs
	¼ lb. butter

A little milk

For the syrup

4 cupfuls sugar	3 cupfuls water

The syrup should be prepared a few hours before using and chilled thoroughly in a refrigerator.

Bring the sugar and water to the boil in a saucepan, stirring until the sugar is dissolved. Cool, then chill in refrigerator. The syrup can be flavoured with 1 teaspoonful cinnamon or 1 teaspoonful lemon essence if desired.

Sift the flour, salt and baking powder into a bowl, rub in the butter finely, then add the beaten eggs with a little milk to blend into a stiff dough. Roll out to ¼ in. thick and cut into strips approximately 4 by 2 in. Divide the strips into three tails, leaving the dough joined at one end. Plait the strips and press to join at the ends. Drop a few of the *koeksusters* at a time into the hot oil or fat, and cook until lightly browned and puffed. Lift out of the fat and drain for 1 minute on crumpled grease-proof paper, then drop at once into the chilled syrup. Turn over in the syrup, then lift out and drain on a sieve until dry. Store in a tin.

Melktert

For the pastry

¾ lb. flour	3 tablespoonfuls
¼ teaspoonful salt	castor sugar
2 teaspoonfuls baking powder	6 oz. butter or mixed shortening
¼ teacupful milk	1 egg
½ teaspoonful vanilla essence (optional)	

For the filling

1 tablespoonful flour	3 tablespoonfuls
1 tablespoonful corn-flour	sugar
4 eggs (separated)	1 teaspoonful cinnamon
2 pints milk	

Sift the flour, salt and baking powder into a bowl; add the sugar and rub in the shortening until the mixture is the consistency of fine breadcrumbs. Beat the egg and mix with the milk; add vanilla essence if desired. Pour the liquid gradually into the dry mixture, stirring with a fork to blend it to a soft dough. The texture of the dough must be firm enough to roll out, but not dry.

For the filling.—Blend the flour and corn-flour into a thin paste with a little of the milk, then put the remaining milk on to boil with the sugar. Separate the eggs, beating the yolks well and adding them to the flour and cornflour mixture. Pour the hot milk on to this mixture, stirring vigorously all the time, then return to the pan and cook, stirring constantly, until thickened. Remove from heat and cool a little. Beat the egg-whites until stiff and fold them into the mixture.

Lightly grease two deep tart-plates and line them with the pastry rolled out to ¼ in. thick. Pour in the cooked filling and bake in a moderate oven for about 20–25 minutes. Sprinkle the cinnamon over the tarts just before baking.

Photo: Royal Baking Powder

It is said that Melktert (the Afrikaans for milk tart) was a favourite of Queen Elizabeth, the Queen Mother, during the Royal Tour of South Africa

AUSTRALIA

*A fascinating cuisine full of exciting flavour contrasts
that will appeal to all lovers of good food,
described by Nancy Gepp*

FISH

FISH is plentiful in Australian waters, but of different varieties from those found in the sea surrounding the United Kingdom. Some of the salt-water fish are as follows:

Whiting—has a very delicate flavour and is one of the more expensive fish.

Mullet—similar in shape and texture to whiting, but not so delicate in flavour.

Flounder—can be found in the shallows of the bay beaches and is often caught by spearing. On a summer's night it is quite usual to see bathers with a torch attached to a stick walking along at the edge of the water. The light attracts the flounder and then it is speared. It is a flat fish somewhat similar in shape to plaice.

Schnapper—is a larger fish with a distinctive flavour and is very popular, usually sold in cutlets.

Flathead—as its name suggests, has a flat head. It has a very nice flavour and is often baked.

Bream—has a slightly coarser flesh than whiting and is usually baked whole, coated in breadcrumbs and stuffed.

Garfish—is a small thin fish with a long, hard, pointed nose. It is usually coated in flour, egg and breadcrumbs after the nose has been pushed into the tail, forming a circle. Shallow-frying is the usual method of cooking.

Turbot—is similar in size to schnapper and is also mainly sold in cutlets.

Pike—is a large fish with a pointed nose and may be cooked whole or in cutlets.

Other fish include: Kingfish, Barracouta, Barramundi, Trumpeter, Nannygai or Pearl Perch, John Dory, Gummy Shank, Perch, Jackass Fish, Tuna, Mackerel.

Crayfish—vary from lobster in that they have a long fat tail with a lot of flesh in it, but the claws are small in comparison.

Oysters.—These are commercially "grown" in some places around the Australian coast. They are quite large and juicy and much cheaper than in Britain.

Freshwater Fish

Murray Cod—is found only in the Murray River, which is over 1,000 miles long and is Australia's longest river. Some have been caught weighing up to 100 lb. For eating they must be over 18 in. long.

Rainbow and Spotted Trout—are caught mainly by amateur fishermen and rarely appear in the shops. They can be caught only in the appropriate season. The flesh is white and the skin is either spotted or multi-coloured.

Salmon Trout—are also seasonal and have pale pink flesh.

Fish Puff (for 6)

6 slices of stale bread, buttered and cut into cubes	4 oz. finely grated cheese
2 eggs	8 oz. flaked, cooked fish
½ teaspoonful Worcester sauce	Salt and Cayenne pepper
½ pint milk	

Place layers of bread cubes, cheese and fish alternately in a greased dish, the top layer being bread. Beat the eggs, add milk, sauce and seasonings, and strain over the contents of dish. Bake in a slow oven for 1 hour.

Oyster Pie (for 6)

½ pint thick white sauce (see Sauces chapter)	1 teaspoonful lemon juice
1 tablespoonful white wine (Chablis or Sauternes)	8 oz. rough puff pastry
1 dozen oysters	Salt and Cayenne pepper

Beard and blanch the oysters, then add them to the white sauce with the lemon juice, seasonings and wine. Allow the mixture to get cold. Roll out half the pastry and line a deep 7-in. tart plate. Add the filling and cover with remainder of pastry. Make a slit in the top, brush with egg glaze and bake in a hot oven for 30–35 minutes.

Schnapper with Mushroom Sauce (for 6)

6 schnapper cutlets
Salt and pepper
½ pint milk
Sprigs of parsley

For the sauce
1 oz. butter
½ pint water
2 tablespoonfuls
    cream
Salt and pepper
¼ lb. mushrooms
1 tablespoonful corn-
    flour
½ gill sherry

Wash the cutlets and place in a baking dish with the milk, seasoning and parsley. Bake gently for 40 minutes, turning the fish over after 20 minutes. Melt the butter in a pan, and add the peeled and chopped mushrooms. Cook for 5 minutes. Blend the corn-flour with a little of the water and add the rest to the mushrooms with the sherry. Cover the pan and cook gently until the mushrooms are tender. Pour some of the boiling liquid on to the corn-flour, return to the pan and stir until boiling. Cook for 2 minutes. Season well, add the cream and do not allow the sauce to boil. Lift on to a hot dish and add the sauce.

For a main meal Garden Salad with slices of luncheon meat and home-made mayonnaise in the centre

MEAT DISHES

Crown Roast of Lamb with Accompaniments (for 6–8)

A loin of lamb con-
    sisting of about 12
    chops
1 lb. potatoes
Gravy

2 tablespoonfuls fat
1 lb. new carrots
1 lb. peas
12 1-in. cubes of
    bread

Trim the fat from the meat and scrape the flesh from the top 2-in. of the bones. Bend the joint round to form a circle, having the skin side inwards. Secure with skewers and string. Place a bread cube over each bone. Weigh the meat and calculate cooking time. Roast until tender, adding the potatoes ¾ hour before serving.

Cook carrots and peas separately. When joint is cooked, remove string and bread, and place on hot serving dish. Fill the centre with some of the carrots and peas (serve the rest separately), put the potatoes round the meat and place a cutlet frill on each chop bone. Serve gravy separately.

Inside-out Pie (for 6–8)

For the case

1 lb. minced steak
1 tablespoonful
    chopped parsley
Tomato halves

1 egg
2 oz. soft white
    breadcrumbs
Bacon rolls

Salt and pepper

For the filling

½ pint medium white
    sauce (see Sauces
    chapter)
¼ cupful cooked peas

4-oz can sweet corn
    kernels
½ cupful cooked diced
    carrots

Mix the steak, crumbs, parsley, seasonings and egg together and press it evenly on to the bottom and sides of a deep 8-in. diameter oven-ware plate. Combine the sauce and vegetables, season well and put into the uncooked meat case. Cover with a piece of greased paper and bake in a moderate oven for 30 minutes. Garnish with grilled tomatoes and bacon.

Liver Patties with Pineapple (for 6)

1 lb. calf's liver	1 can pineapple slices
½ level teaspoonful salt	(6 rings)
	4 oz. soft white
1 egg or 3 table-	breadcrumbs
spoonfuls milk	6 bacon rashers
A little pepper	½ oz. fat

For the garnish

Green peas	Brown gravy made
Potato purée	with pineapple
	juice

Wash and dry the liver, then pass it through the mincer. Mix in the breadcrumbs, salt, pepper and egg or milk. Form into 6 patties, wrap a piece of bacon round each and secure with a cocktail stick. Stand a patty on each pineapple ring. Heat the fat in a baking tin and bake the patties for ½ hour in a moderate oven. Serve with vegetables and gravy.

Pork and Prune Casserole (for 6)

1 lb. pork fillets	4 oz. cooked prunes
Salt and pepper	1 oz. flour
1 large onion, peeled	1 oz. fat
and cut into rings	1 lb. potatoes, peeled
Green vegetables in	and sliced, or tiny
season	new potatoes
½ pint prune juice	

Cut the meat into neat pieces. Add the seasonings to the flour and toss the meat in it. Melt the fat and fry the meat until browned. Place a layer of potatoes in a casserole, then onion, pork, prunes, onion and finish with potatoes. Season each layer. Pour in the prune liquor. Put the lid on tightly and cook in a moderate oven for 1–1¼ hours. Serve green vegetables separately.

VEGETABLE DISHES

Cauliflower Pie

1 large cauliflower	1 large onion
2 oz. cheese (grated)	Salt and pepper
1 dessertspoonful	4 tablespoonfuls
chopped parsley	milk
2 oz. butter or mar-	1 lb. tomatoes
garine	1 lb. potatoes, boiled

Cook the cauliflower until tender, then beat it until creamy with the butter, cheese, seasonings, parsley and half the milk. Line a deep casserole with the mixture and place on top the peeled, sliced tomatoes, and peeled and finely chopped onion with seasoning. Mash the potatoes with the rest of the milk and spread on top. Mark the top with a fork, dot with butter and bake for 20–30 minutes in a moderate oven.

Vegetable Cheese Shortcake

For the shortcake

8 oz. self-raising flour	½ teaspoonful salt
¼ teaspoonful dry	Pinch of Cayenne
mustard	pepper
2 oz. butter	3 oz. finely grated
1 egg	cheese
4 oz. milk (approx.)	

For the filling

½ pint medium white	Salt
sauce (see Sauces	1 onion, diced and
chapter)	cooked without
½ cupful cooked peas	browning
½ cupful cooked	½ cupful tomato pulp
diced carrots	Cayenne pepper

For the garnish: Bacon rolls

Sift the flour and seasonings together. Rub in the butter, add the cheese and mix to a soft dough with the beaten egg and as much milk as is necessary to obtain the correct consistency. Knead on a lightly floured board. Roll out to ½ in. thickness and cut with a 3-in. round plain cutter. Brush the surface with milk and bake in a hot oven for 10–12 minutes. Combine the vegetables with the white sauce and season well. Slit each shortcake in half. Put some of the filling on the base, cover with the top, and spoon extra filling over. Serve with grilled bacon rolls.

If desired, the shortcake can be made by baking the dough in two greased 7-in. sandwich tins, then sandwiching the cakes together with filling, and pouring the remainder of the filling on top.

Another variation is to use fish or meat fillings.

SALADS

Apple, Celery and Walnut Salad (for 6)

3 eating apples	1 lettuce
2 oz. chopped	2 tablespoonfuls
walnuts	salad cream or
Salt and pepper	mayonnaise
6 stalks of celery	

"Peaches" made from Queen Cake mixture baked in gem irons. Two cakes are put together with butter cream, brushed with warmed apricot jam and tossed in pink-coloured granulated sugar

Wash the apples and celery and cut them into small dice, leaving the rosy skin on the apples. Mix with the walnuts, salad cream and seasonings. Spoon into lettuce shells to serve.

This salad makes a nice accompaniment to cold meat.

For a variation, cut a slice from the top of the apples and scoop out the flesh. Make the salad and stuff the apples with the mixture, replacing the tops.

Garden Salad

In Australia this salad is varied according to taste, adding fruits as well as vegetables to the dish. It may be made up from the following selection, arranged attractively on a large platter:

Vegetables

Grated raw carrot	Cooked potato
Grated raw beetroot	Grated raw turnip
Radish roses	Celery curls
Spring onions	Lettuce
Sliced cucumber	Spiced beetroot slices
Cooked cauliflower sprigs	Raw tomato halves or slices
Cooked sweet corn kernels	Cooked French beans
	Cooked asparagus
Cooked garden peas	

Fruits

Apricot halves	Peach halves
Pineapple slices	Banana
Grated apple	Grapefruit sections
Orange slices	Grapes

The dressing to accompany these salad platters is often made with cream as a base and thinned down with juice from either the pineapples, apples, cucumbers or oranges. This gives an added "bite" to the salad.

Dressing for a Garden Salad

3 tablespoonfuls whipped cream	1 dessertspoonful white vinegar
Salt and pepper	1 tablespoonful fruit or cucumber juice
1 teaspoonful sugar	
Mustard	

Mix the seasonings, sugar and vinegar together, then stir them into the cream. Add the fruit juice and leave to stand for a while before serving. A tablespoonful of finely diced fruit or cucumber may also be added if liked.

Pineapple and Cheese Slouch Hats (for 6)

6 slices of pineapple (fresh or canned)	Salt and Cayenne pepper
2 tablespoonfuls mayonnaise	Thin strips of red pepper or tomato skin for the hatbands
Lettuce leaves	
4 oz. grated cheese	

435

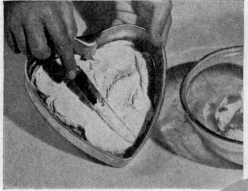

Upside-down Dessert can be made with various fruits and nuts. Above, the butter and sugar mixture is spread into the greased tin

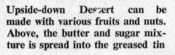

The fruit is arranged in patterns. Dates and walnuts are used here

Add the mayonnaise and seasonings to the cheese; divide into six portions and shape each to form the crown of a slouch hat. Place a "crown" on each piece of pineapple and finish with the red strip to form the hatband. Serve on a lettuce leaf.

This salad may be served on its own or as an accompaniment to cold cooked pork or other meat.

Stuffed Tomato Salad (for 6)

6 large round tomatoes	½ cupful cooked peas
¼ cupful cooked diced carrots	½ cupful diced cucumber
Salt and pepper	2 tablespoonfuls mayonnaise
1 lettuce	Parsley sprigs

Wash the tomatoes and remove a slice from the stem end of each. Scoop out the flesh and cut it into dice. Turn the tomato cases upside down to drain. Mix the drained tomato pulp with the other vegetables, seasonings and mayonnaise. Spoon the mixture into the tomatoes, replace "caps" and serve on lettuce leaves garnished with parsley.

Summer Salad (for 6)

1 packet lemon table jelly	1 small lettuce
½ cupful finely diced cucumber	1 tablespoonful vinegar
½ cupful cooked peas	½ cupful finely grated carrot
½ cupful finely diced green pepper or celery	½ cupful drained crushed pineapple
4 oz. large cream crackers	½ teaspoonful salt
	4 oz. packet cream cheese triangles
¼ teaspoonful pepper	

This is a very good dish for picnics or suppers on a hot evening.

Make the jelly, using the vinegar made up to 1 pint with hot water. Allow to cool until it begins to set, then add the vegetables and pineapple and season to taste. Pour into a plain mould and leave until firm. Turn out on to a bed of lettuce leaves, stand cheese wedges round the base and serve biscuits separately.

Triple Salad (for 6)

1 large Spanish onion	Sugar
1 lb. tomatoes	Salt and pepper
1 apple cucumber or ½ a long cucumber	2 tablespoonfuls white vinegar

Peel the vegetables and cut them all into very thin slices. Arrange them in a dish, keeping them separate. Sprinkle all with salt and pepper, and the tomatoes with a little sugar. Pour the vinegar over and allow to stand for at least 1 hour before serving.

HOT DESSERTS

Bananas in Raisin Sauce (for 6)

6 *bananas*	*Juice of 1 lemon*
3 *oz. seedless raisins*	2 *level tablespoonfuls*
3 *level tablespoonfuls*	*cornflour*
honey	½ *oz. butter*
	½ *pint water*

Peel the bananas, cut them in half lengthwise, then across. Melt the butter in an oven-ware dish and place the bananas in it. Boil the raisins in ¼ pint water for 5 minutes, then add the honey and lemon juice. Blend the cornflour with ¼ pint water, add some of the raisin mixture, return all to the pan and stir until boiling. Cook for 2 minutes until the mixture clears. Pour it over the bananas and bake for 20 minutes in a moderate oven.

sugar gradually, leaving 1 teaspoonful until later. Pile the meringue on top of the apples, decorate with cherries and angelica, sprinkle the teaspoonful of sugar over and bake in a cool oven for 10 minutes until the meringue is a golden brown.

The remainder of the batter is spread on top (top right); the cake is turned out upside down (above) and decorated with whipped cream and more walnuts before cutting (right)

Hot Fruit Trifle

1 *7-in. round of fat-*	2 *tablespoonfuls*
less sponge cake	*sherry*
2 *egg-whites*	1 *cupful stewed*
3 *oz. castor sugar*	*apple*
Angelica	*Pinch of salt*
2 *glacé cherries*	

Stand the sponge in an 8-in. oven-ware pie plate and pour the sherry over. Spread the apple on top. Add salt to the egg-whites and beat them until stiff. Add the

This recipe may be varied by using any of the following fruits: 1 cupful drained stewed rhubarb; 1 cupful crushed pine-apple; 1 cupful drained sliced peaches; 1 cupful drained preserved apricots; 1 cupful drained preserved or fresh mashed pears.

Peach Caramel Crumble (for 8)

1-lb. can sliced peaches	½ pint milk
2 oz. moist brown sugar	1 oz. butter
	1 oz. flour
	1 egg

For the crumble topping

2 oz. self-raising flour	1 oz. butter
1 oz. moist brown sugar	Pinch of salt
	2 oz. cake crumbs
1 oz. coconut	

Strain the liquid from the fruit and put the peaches into an oven-ware dish. Melt the butter in a pan, add the sugar and stir for 1 minute. Stir in the flour, cook for 1 minute, then add the milk and cook over the flame until the mixture boils. Allow to stand a little, then stir in the egg-yolk and cook, but do not boil. Beat the egg-white stiffly, then fold it in. Pour the sauce over the peaches.

Sift the flour and salt, rub in the butter, mix in remainder of the ingredients and sprinkle on top. Bake for 20 minutes in a moderate oven.

If the peach juice is thickened with a little cornflour, it can be used as an accompanying sauce.

Pineapple Upside-down Dessert (for 8)

2 oz. butter	2 oz. moist brown sugar
6 rings canned pine-apple	A few walnut halves

For the batter

2 oz. butter	A little milk
Vanilla essence	3 oz. castor sugar
6 oz. self-raising flour	1 egg
Pinch of salt	

Melt the butter in a pan, add the sugar and cook for 1 minute. Spread it into a greased oblong tin 6 in. × 8 in. Drain the juice from the pineapple and place the rings on to the caramel mixture, putting the walnuts between. Cream the butter and sugar with the vanilla. Add the egg gradually and beat well. Fold in the sifted flour and salt alternately with the milk so as to keep the mixture the correct consistency. Spread the batter over the pineapple and bake for 35 minutes in a moderately cool oven. Turn out with the pineaple on top.

This recipe can be used hot as a dessert, or allowed to cool and served as a cake. It can also be made with other fruits—see photographs on previous page.

Pumpkin Pie (for 6)

½ pint pumpkin pulp	Shortcrust pastry
½ pint milk	made with 6 oz.
¼ teaspoonful grated nutmeg or mace	flour (see Pastry chapter)
2 oz. sugar	2 eggs

To prepare the pulp.—Cut a ripe pumpkin into thick slices. Pare off the skin and remove seeds. Cook gently with very little water until tender, then pass through a fine sieve and measure the pulp.

Separate the egg-yolks from the whites, beat the yolks and sugar together, add the spice, then the pumpkin pulp and milk. Fold in the stiffly beaten egg-whites. Roll out the pastry and cut a 1-in. strip to line the edge of the pie dish. Pour in the filling; cover with the pastry. Cut a slit in the top; glaze with milk and bake in a moderately hot oven for 20–30 minutes.

COLD DESSERTS

Apple Blossom Pie (for 8)

(This recipe won first prize as Australia's National Pie in a nation-wide competition held by *Woman's Day*.)

7-in. baked sweet pastry case.

1st layer

2 or 3 cooking apples	2 oz. sugar
½ cupful water	2 passionfruit

2nd layer

½ can sweetened condensed milk	1 egg-yolk
	Juice of 1 lemon

3rd layer

1 level dessertspoonful gelatine	1 egg-white
	Juice from the cooked apples
½ teaspoonful lemon essence	made up to ¼ cupful with water
Sweetened whipped cream	Red colouring

Peel, core and slice the apples. Place in a pan with sugar and water and cook until soft. Drain off the syrup and keep for third layer. Add the passionfruit pulp. Cool the mixture and put into pastry case.

Combine condensed milk with egg-yolk and lemon juice and beat until well mixed. Spread over the apple layer. Soak gelatine well in the cold apple syrup, then dissolve it over hot water, add the lemon essence and a few drops of red colouring. Allow to cool and become partly set. Beat until it becomes light and fluffy, then fold in the stiffly beaten egg-white. Pile on top of pie. Decorate with the cream by using a piping bag and tube.

Melon or Pineapple Fruit Salad

1 *large canteloup or*	*A bunch of mixed*
honeydew melon or	*flowers or leaves*
1 *large pineapple*	1-*lb. can Australian*
	tropical fruit salad

Wash and dry the fruit. Cut a slice from the stem end of the melon or from the top of the pineapple. Remove the pulp, discarding the seeds or the hard core. Cut the fruit into dice and mix it with the fruit salad. Return the fruit salad to the case and replace the cap. Stand it on a glass platter and arrange the flowers or leaves round its base. Chill before serving.

This makes a very attractive centre-piece for the table, and the top is removed when the fruit salad is required.

Passionfruit Flummery (for 6–8)

3 *eggs*	3 *passionfruit*
Juice of 1 *lemon*	1 *dessertspoonful*
1 *cupful water*	*gelatine*
½ *cupful sugar*	¾ *cupful milk*

Separate the egg-whites from the yolks and put the yolks in a large bowl with the passionfruit pulp, lemon juice, milk and sugar. Soak the gelatine in the water for 10 minutes, then dissolve it over hot water and add to the other ingredients. Leave to become quite cold, then beat it to a froth. Fold in the stiffly beaten egg-whites and transfer to a glass serving dish to set.

Passionfruit Pavlova (for 8–10)

4 *egg-whites*	1 *level teaspoonful*
8 *oz. castor sugar*	*cornflour*
1 *level teaspoonful*	1 *level teaspoonful*
vanilla	*vinegar*
A pinch of salt	

For the decoration

3 *passionfruit*	¼ *pint whipped cream*

Add the salt to the egg-whites and beat them until stiff and fluffy. Gradually beat in half the sugar, then fold in the rest

Apple Blossom Pie, the first prize-winner as Australia's National Pie in a nation-wide competition held by "Woman's Day," has a three-layer filling

Next sift the cornflour over the surface and add the vanilla and vinegar. Fold these in, then transfer the mixture to an 8-in. well-buttered oven-ware dish. Bake in a cool oven for 1¼ hours. Turn out and, when cold, spread the underside with the cream. Cut passionfruit in half, scoop out pulp and put on top of the cream.

Peach Marshmallows (for 6)

6 rounds of fatless sponge cake	3 tablespoonfuls sherry
6 canned peach halves	¼ pint red table jelly

For the marshmallow

2 level teaspoonfuls gelatine	¾ cupful cold water
4 oz. castor sugar	½ teaspoonful vanilla essence
2 egg-whites	

For the decoration

3 glacé cherries   Angelica

Sprinkle a dessertspoonful of sherry over each piece of sponge. Set a little jelly in the hollows of the peach halves, then place them, cut side down, on the sponge. Dry the rounded side of each peach with a soft cloth (this prevents the marshmallow from sliding off). Soak the gelatine in the cold water, then dissolve it over hot water. Beat the egg-whites stiffly and gradually beat in the gelatine, then the sugar and vanilla. Pour the marshmallow smoothly over each peach, completely covering the sponge as well. Decorate with a half-cherry and leaves cut from angelica.

Pineapple Whip (for 6)

1-lb. can crushed pineapple	1 level tablespoonful gelatine
A small strip of angelica	2 glacé cherries Whipped cream

Strain the juice from the pineapple and make the liquid up to ½ pint with water. Soak the gelatine in a little cold water, then dissolve it over hot water. Place the pineapple pulp, liquid and gelatine in a bowl and put in a very cold place until it begins to set. Whisk until it becomes light and frothy. Leave to set, then pile it into a serving dish. Decorate with whipped cream, cherry slices and thin strips of angelica.

SAVOURIES

Apple Bites (for about 48 savouries)

2 eating apples	1 oz. soft cream cheese
1 tablespoonful mayonnaise	1 oz. finely chopped walnuts
48 cocktail sticks	

Wash and dry the apples, leaving the skin on, and cut each into 24 cubes. Dry them well. Soften the cream cheese and mix in mayonnaise. Cover each apple cube with the cheese mixture, toss in the walnuts and roll into a ball. Impale each "bite" on a cocktail stick to serve.

Cheddar Cheesettes (for 24 savouries)

24 ½-in. cubes of fresh bread	2 oz. finely grated dry Cheddar cheese
1 oz. butter (melted)	1 egg
Salt and pepper	

Beat the egg well, add the butter and seasonings. Dip each bread cube into the egg mixture, drain off any excess, then toss in the cheese. Stand on a greased baking tray and cook for 10 minutes in a hot oven. Serve hot.

Curried Pineapple Titbits (for about 48 savouries)

1-lb. can of pine-apple cubes or rings	4 oz. plain flour Pinch of salt
1 level teaspoonful curry powder	2 tablespoonfuls salad oil A little tepid water
1 egg-white	Fat for deep frying

Drain the liquid from the pineapple and dry each portion. If pineapple rings are used, cut each one into eight. Sift the flour, salt and curry powder together. Add the oil and stir it in, then add the water, keeping the batter fairly stiff. Allow it to stand for ½ hour. Fold in the stiffly beaten egg-white. Dip each piece of pineapple into the batter and deep-fry a golden brown. Serve hot. These savouries may be cooked before they are required and reheated.

Devilled Almond Croûtes (for 12 savouries)

2 oz. butter	12 rounds of bread
2 oz. finely grated cheese	1½ in. in diameter
1 heaped tablespoon-ful sweet chutney	2 oz. finely chopped almonds or almond nibs
1 dessertspoonful chopped parsley	Salt and Cayenne pepper

Melt the butter in a pan and brush one side of the bread with it. Sprinkle this side with some of the cheese and brown under a grill. Add the almonds to the remainder of the butter and cook to a golden brown. Add the cheese, chutney, seasonings and parsley, and heat until the cheese starts to melt. Spread on to the untoasted side of the croûtes. These savouries may be served hot or cold.

Open Sandwich Grill (for 4, or 16 pieces)

4 slices stale bread
4 small tomatoes
Salt, pepper

4 oz. bacon rashers
2 oz. sliced processed
cheese
Parsley sprigs

Toast the bread on one side only. Cut the rind from the bacon and place the bacon on the untoasted side of the bread. Cook under the grill until the bacon fat is clear. Skin and slice the tomatoes and put them on top of the bacon, season well and cover with the cheese slices. Return to the grill until the cheese is brown and bubbly. Serve hot, garnished with sprigs of parsley.

This savoury may be served whole as an after-theatre snack, or cut into finger lengths for a buffet supper, etc.

SCONES, BISCUITS, CAKES

Anzac Biscuits (for 24 biscuits)

2 oz. butter
½ level teaspoonful
  bicarbonate of soda
1 teaspoonful Golden
  Syrup
4 oz. castor sugar
1 tablespoonful
  boiling water
3 oz. plain flour
4 oz. rolled oats

Melt the butter and Golden Syrup in a pan. Dissolve the soda in the water and add to the butter and syrup. Stir into the dry ingredients and mix well. Put on to a greased tray in small heaps, allowing room for the mixture to spread. Bake for 10 minutes in a cool oven. Lift on to a cooling tray before they become set.

Apricot and Walnut Loaves (for 2 loaves)

4 oz. dried apricots
Pinch of salt
2 oz. butter
1 egg
8 oz. self-raising flour
4 oz. castor sugar
2 oz. chopped walnuts
¼ pint milk

Wash the apricots and soak them for 1 hour. Drain and dry them, and cut into small pieces. Sift the flour, salt and sugar together.

Rub in the butter. Add the apricots and walnuts, and mix to a soft dough with the beaten egg and milk. Half-fill two nut-loaf tins; put the lids tightly on and cook in an upright position for 40 minutes in a moderately hot oven. Remove the loaves from the tins to cool and next day serve them sliced and spread with butter.

The mixture can be baked in two 1 lb. cocoa or baking-powder tins or in open loaf tins.

Date Slice (for 32 fingers)

12 oz. stoned dates
1 teaspoonful
  bicarbonate of soda
Pinch of salt

5 oz. butter
1 teacupful water
8 oz. flaked oats
6 oz. self-raising flour
4 oz. castor sugar

Place the dates, water and soda in a pan,

Gem irons—used here to make Gem Scones—can also be used for Snowballs and other fancy cakes

and cook until the dates are soft. Mash them well and keep the mixture warm. Sift the flour, salt and sugar together, add the oats. Rub in the butter. Press half into a greased baking tray 10 in. × 9 in. Spread the date mixture over, then sprinkle on and press down the remainder of the oats mixture. Bake for 25 minutes in a moderate oven. Allow to cool a little, then cut into finger lengths and leave until quite cold before storing.

Eggless Spicy Apple Cake

4 oz. butter	6 oz. self-raising flour
¾ cupful stewed apple	4 oz. sugar
¼ level teaspoonful ground nutmeg	1 level teaspoonful bicarbonate of soda
½ level teaspoonful ground cinnamon	1 level teaspoonful cocoa
3 oz. seedless raisins	

Cream the butter and sugar. Add the warm apple with the soda mixed in. Stir in the sifted flour, cocoa and spices mixed with the fruit. Transfer to a lined 7-in cake tin. Bake for 1 hour in a cool oven. Remove from tin and, when cold, ice with lemon water icing and dust the surface with ground cinnamon.

Gem Scones (for 24 scones)

2 oz. butter	3 oz. milk (approx.)
Vanilla essence	3 oz. castor sugar
8 oz. self-raising flour	1 egg
Pinch of salt	

A gem iron is a set of twelve deep semi-circles joined together. As the cake batter rises to a dome, a round cake is the result. Deep bun tins are the next best thing to use.

Put the greased gem irons to heat. Cream the butter and sugar with the vanilla added. Add the egg gradually and beat well. Fold in the sifted flour and salt alternately with the milk to make a very soft mixture, similar in consistency to a cake batter. Quickly half-fill each container of the gem irons. Return to the hot oven and bake for 12–15 minutes. Turn out to cool and, when quite cold, serve slit in half and buttered.

In Australia the gem irons are also used for the baking of cake batters to be made into snowballs, peaches (like those made from Queen Cake mixture and shown on page 435) and other fancy cakes.

Jelly Biscuits (for 24 biscuits)

4 oz. butter	2 oz. cornflour
A little lemon essence	1 oz. castor sugar
1 packet (4 oz.) strawberry or raspberry jelly crystals	1 small egg
	2 oz. coconut
	4 oz. self-raising flour
Pinch of salt	

Cream the butter and sugar with the lemon essence. Add the egg gradually and beat well. Stir in the jelly crystals and coconut, then the sifted flour, cornflour and salt. Roll into 24 balls, place on a greased tray and flatten with the blade of a knife. Bake in a cool oven for 15 minutes. Allow to get quite cool before storing.

Lamingtons (for 12 or 16 cakes)

These are a favourite with Australians.

For the cake batter

4 oz. butter	A little milk
Vanilla essence	6 oz. castor sugar
10 oz. self-raising flour	2 eggs
	Pinch of salt
Raspberry jam	

For the coating

7 oz. sifted icing sugar	1 oz. cocoa
3 tablespoonfuls boiling water	4 oz. desiccated coconut

Cream the butter and sugar with the vanilla. Add the eggs gradually and beat well. Fold in the sifted flour and salt alternately with the milk to keep the mixture the correct consistency. Spread it into a prepared 8-in. square or 6-in. × 8-in oblong cake tin and bake for 50–60 minutes in a moderately cool oven.

Next day, slit the cake through the centre and spread with the raspberry jam. Place the two layers together again and cut into 2-in. squares.

Put the icing sugar in a bowl, make a well in the centre and add the cocoa. Pour the boiling water slowly on to the cocoa and at the same time stir with a wooden spoon, gradually working in the icing sugar. Add more water if necessary. Keep the icing thin by standing it over a bowl of hot water.

Put a square of cake on the prongs of a fork and dip it into the chocolate icing. Allow any excess to drip off, then toss the cake into the coconut.

When quite set, store in an airtight tin.

A national favourite, Lamingtons are coated with chocolate icing and desiccated coconut

Puffed Wheat Cookies (for 36 biscuits)

4 oz. butter	Pinch of salt
Vanilla essence	3 oz. castor sugar
5 oz. plain flour	1 egg
3 oz. puffed wheat	

Cream the butter and sugar with the vanilla. Add the egg gradually and beat well. Stir in the sifted flour and salt, then the puffed wheat. Place in dessertspoonfuls fairly well spaced apart on a greased baking tray. Bake for 10 minutes in a moderately cool oven, when they should be golden and crisp.

Pumpkin Sultana Cake (Eggless)

3 oz. butter	⅔ cupful castor sugar
Vanilla essence	1 cupful cooked
2 cupfuls self-raising	mashed pumpkin
flour	Pinch of salt
½ cupful milk	½ cupful sultanas

Cream the butter and sugar with the vanilla added. Stir in the pumpkin and mix well. Fold in the sifted flour and salt alternately with the milk, to keep the mixture the correct consistency. Lastly, fold in the sultanas. Transfer to an 8-in. square papered tin and bake in a cool oven for 1½ hours. Allow to stand for 15 minutes before turning out. When quite cold, ice with lemon butter icing (see chapter on Icings for method) and top with chopped peel.

Raisin-and-Walnut Slice

4 oz. butter	8 oz. plain flour
3 oz. castor sugar	Pinch of salt
1 egg	1 level teaspoonful
4 oz. raisins	baking powder
2 oz. chopped walnuts	2 tablespoonfuls milk

Cream the butter and sugar, add the egg and beat well. Stir in the raisins and walnuts, then the sifted flour, salt and baking powder, adding sufficient milk to make a soft mixture. Spread into a greased tin 8½ in. by 11 in., and bake for 25 minutes in a moderate oven. Allow to cool a little, then cut into 24 pieces. Leave in the tin to become cold before storing in an airtight tin.

NEW ZEALAND

Cake-making is a special national skill, and recipes brought out by pioneering ancestors are still used

THE New Zealand woman is a very skilled cake-maker. She can be ranked as an equal with the famous Belgian *pâtissiers*.

It is at tea and supper parties that she displays her special skill. A New Zealand tea table is something very special. It will include such items as scones made with butter and spread thickly with it; a homemade fruit or nut loaf also spread with butter; sandwiches such as oyster and brown bread, and asparagus rolls; pikelets or drop scones made with butter and spread with it, and biscuits and large cakes in great variety.

Women vie with each other in the quality and variety of food provided at these teas, and this is probably responsible for the development of a number of their excellent recipes. While many of these have been invented by present-day New Zealanders, others are treasured family recipes brought out by pioneer grandmothers and great-grandmothers over a hundred years ago.

The most popular cake of all is a light sponge made with fresh eggs and butter and filled with a mixture of whipped cream and passionfruit pulp or with a butter cream.

Nuts and dried fruits are used liberally in New Zealand cakes, and much wholemeal flour, giving variety in flavour and texture. The combination of flavours when butter and nuts or butter and brown sugar are used together is particularly pleasant.

The following typical New Zealand recipes are supplied by the Butter Information Council.

Anzac Nutties (enough for 24 small biscuits)

2 oz. wholemeal flour	2 oz. butter
4 oz. brown sugar	2 oz. white flour
2 oz. desiccated coconut	1 level tablespoonful Golden Syrup
1 tablespoonful hot water	½ level teaspoonful bicarbonate of soda
1 oz. chopped nuts	

Mix all the dry ingredients in a bowl. Melt the butter and syrup until hot but not boiling. Mix the water and soda and add both liquids to the dry ingredients. Mix well. Roll in small balls and place on baking trays, leaving plenty of room for spreading. Bake in a moderate oven for about 20 minutes. Leave on the trays to cool, when they will become quite crisp.

Fudge Fingers (no baking needed)

½ lb. sweet biscuits	4 oz. butter
4 oz. granulated sugar	3 level tablespoonfuls cocoa
Pinch of salt	2 tablespoonfuls milk
4 oz. chopped walnuts	Vanilla essence or rum or brandy
Chocolate icing	Desiccated coconut

Put the biscuits through the mincer or crush them to coarse crumbs with a rolling pin. Put butter, sugar, cocoa, salt and milk in a saucepan and bring to the boil. Add walnuts and flavouring, mix well and press into a greased tin about 9 in. × 6 in. Leave to set. Ice the top with chocolate icing and sprinkle with desiccated coconut. Cut in fingers to serve.

Shortbread Biscuits

4 oz. butter	Glacé cherries
6 oz. plain flour	2 oz. icing sugar
Pinch of salt	1 oz. cornflour
	Vanilla essence

Cream the butter and icing sugar until light and soft. Gradually work in the flour and cornflour with the salt and a few drops of essence. Knead well until quite smooth. Roll out about a quarter of an inch thick and cut in rounds or fancy shapes. Place a small piece of cherry in the centre of each. Bake on trays in a moderate oven for about 20 minutes. They should not be allowed to brown.

The following recipes are by Catherine Macfarlane, Lecturer (Foods) at the University of Otago, Dunedin, New Zealand.

Kiwi Crisps (yields about 2 dozen biscuits)

4 oz. butter
6 oz. flour
2 tablespoonfuls sweetened condensed milk
4 oz. dark chocolate (broken into small pieces)
1 teaspoonful baking powder
2 oz. sugar

Cream the butter and sugar. Add the flour sifted with the baking powder alternately with the condensed milk. Add the chocolate. Shape the mixture into small balls; place them on oven trays, flatten the tops and bake in a moderate oven for 15–20 minutes.

Lemon Chiffon Pie
(for 4–6)

Crumb pastry
1 cup finely crushed wine biscuits
3 oz. butter

Lemon filling
1 tablespoonful gelatine
½ cupful lemon juice
8 oz. sugar
4 eggs (separated)
1 teaspoonful grated lemon rind
¼ cupful cold water
½ teaspoonful salt

Soften the butter and stir in the biscuit crumbs. Press the buttered crumbs evenly over the bottom and sides of a pie plate to make a layer ⅛-in. thick. Chill until firm.

For the filling, soak the gelatine in the cold water for 5 minutes. Add the lemon juice, egg-yolks, half the sugar and the salt. Cook over hot water, stirring constantly until the gelatine has dissolved and the mixture has thickened. Add the lemon rind and cool. When the mixture is beginning to stiffen, beat the egg-whites until stiff; add the remaining sugar gradually; fold in the lemon mixture. Place in the prepared crumb lining and chill. Garnish with cream.

FRUIT with LAMB

RIGHT, New Zealand lamb cutlets simmered in juice of 2 oranges, the liquid then made into sauce with 1 orange rind, ⅕ pint water, 1 tablespoonful flour. Below, boned shoulder of New Zealand lamb stuffed with a breadcrumb stuffing (see Poultry and Game chapter), containing chopped dried apricots. Delicious and different!

Scalloped Seafood

2 tablespoonfuls butter
8 oz. liquid (fish stock or milk)
1 dozen oysters
1 cupful flaked cooked fish
½ teaspoonful salt
½ cupful buttered breadcrumbs
2 tablespoonfuls flour
1 cupful chopped crayfish
2 teaspoonfuls lemon juice

Melt the butter in a saucepan, stir in the flour and salt and cook for a few seconds. Remove from the heat. Blend in the liquid and reheat until thick. Cook for 1 or 2 minutes; season with lemon juice. Butter individual heat-proof dishes. Place alternate layers of fish and sauce in the dishes, finishing with a layer of sauce. Sprinkle buttered crumbs over the top. Reheat in a moderate oven until the food is very hot and the crumbs are golden brown. Garnish with parsley and lemon. Serve very hot.

UNITED STATES

Barbecued meats with pineapple *slices . . . golden corn made into*
exciting dishes . . . unusual ice *creams—American food is full*
of new ideas and combinations

MAIN DISHES

American Pot Roast

Joint of beef (allow   Salt and pepper
½ lb. per person)   1 cup hot water
Salad oil or fat for frying

Melt the fat in a deep saucepan and brown the meat on all sides in it. Season with pepper and salt, add the hot water. Lift meat on to a rack, cover pan and simmer gently until tender, adding a little more water if necessary. A pot roast for six or more persons will take from 3–4 hours, according to size.

For Beef Pot Roast and Vegetables: Slice and brown 2 carrots, ½ turnip and 1 small onion per person, with several small potatoes, and add to the meat 1 hour before cooking time is completed.

Baked Ham with Pineapple (for 4)

1½ lb. smoked ham,   4 slices canned pine-
cut about ⅜ in.   apple
thick   ½ cupful pineapple
1-in. piece stick cinna-   syrup
mon   1 pint cold water
½ cupful light brown   Parsley or watercress
sugar   to garnish
4 glacé cherries

Cover ham with cold water and bring to boil to remove any excess salt. Drain. Place in fireproof dish, pour pint of water over, add cinnamon and bake in moderate oven until tender—about 1 hour or longer. Baste frequently with the liquid in the pan; turn over when half cooked. Drain, place the slices of pineapple on the ham, cover with the sugar and pour the pineapple syrup over the top. Bake 15 minutes longer, basting several times. Serve on hot dish, decorated with a cherry in the centre of each pineapple slice, and garnish with parsley or watercress.

Boston Baked Beans (for 4)

2 cupfuls haricot   ½ teaspoonful dry
beans   mustard
1½ teaspoonfuls salt   2 tablespoonfuls
2 tablespoonfuls   finely chopped
brown sugar   onion
¼ cupful molasses   Salt pork (about
1 cupful boiling water   ¼ lb.)
1 bay leaf

Wash beans; cover with cold water and leave overnight to soak. Drain. Cover well with boiling salted water and simmer gently for 1 hour; drain well. Mix together salt, sugar, molasses, bay leaf, dry mustard, chopped onion and cup of boiling water. Place all together with pork in covered pan and bake in slow oven for 4 hours, or until beans are tender. Remove cover of pan for last ½ hour.

Cover with a little additional boiling water if necessary during cooking.

Pan-broiled Porterhouse Steak

Grilling steak between   Fat
¾ in.–1½ in. thick   Salt
(allow ½ lb. per   Pepper
person)

Melt fat in a heavy saucepan and, when smoking, brown steak quickly on both sides. Reduce heat and cook slowly until done, pouring off fat if necessary; sprinkle with salt and pepper to suit taste.

Broiled Steak

Grilling steak at least   2 tablespoonfuls
1 in. thick (allow ½   melted butter
lb. per person)   Salt and pepper

First get the grill really hot so that the meat is seared quickly, or it may be tough and dry. Grease the meat rack and brush steak lightly with melted butter. If steak

A favourite American dish is Fried Chicken—at its best with dishes of piping hot skillet corn and strawberry sundaes to follow

is 1–1¾ in. thick, it should be about 2 in. below the heat.

Allow 7–8 minutes for a rare red steak; 8–9 minutes for medium done, and 10–12 minutes for well-done steak, if meat is 1 in. thick. For 1½ in. meat, allow 8–9 minutes for rare steak; 10–12 medium, and 12–15 well done.

Turn meat, seasoning with salt and pepper to taste, when half cooking time is completed.

Barbecued Ham

1 slice gammon per person	Fat or salad oil
3 tablespoonfuls Worcester sauce	2 tablespoonfuls sugar
2 tablespoonfuls vinegar	½ cupful ketchup
	1 clove garlic
	1 medium-sized onion
	¼ teaspoonful tabasco

Melt fat in frying pan and cook gammon gently, without browning. Mix together Worcester sauce, vinegar, sugar, ketchup and tabasco. Mash clove of garlic and chop onion; tie in muslin and add to sauce. Put gammon in deep pan or casserole, cover with sauce and cook for 1 hour. Remove muslin bag with onion and garlic before serving.

Corned Beef Hash (for 4)

2 cupfuls corned beef chopped into cubes	Fat
3 tablespoonfuls finely chopped onion	3 cupfuls cold cooked potatoes, chopped
	½ cupful milk
	Salt and pepper

Mix together corned beef, potatoes, onion and milk. Season with salt and pepper. Melt fat and cook mixture until well browned, turning frequently.

Fried Chicken

Jointed chicken	Salt
A little flour	Pepper
Fat	

Wash the jointed chicken and dry well. Roll in flour seasoned with salt and pepper. Melt fat (it should be about ¾–1 in. deep) and, when smoking, put in the chicken. Cover and cook slowly for about 45 minutes, turning frequently.

Hamburgers

1 lb. finely minced beef (allow ¼ lb. per person)
½ teaspoonful salt
¼ teaspoonful pepper
2 tablespoonfuls finely chopped onion
2 tablespoonfuls butter, or salad oil

Blend together meat, seasoning and finely chopped onion, mixing thoroughly, and shape into cakes. Melt the fat in a frying pan and cook for 10 minutes, turning carefully to brown both sides. The onion may, if liked, be cooked separately, and a little placed on top of each hamburger before serving.

Lobster Newburg (for 4)

2 lb. cooked lobster
¼ cupful butter
1 tablespoonful flour
1 cupful cream (top of milk can be used)
3 egg-yolks
2 tablespoonfuls sherry
Salt
A little paprika

Remove lobster meat from shell and dice it. Melt butter, add flour and seasoning and, when smooth, gradually blend in the cream, stirring well all the time. Bring to boiling point and stir in lobster meat. When this is thoroughly heated, add the beaten egg-yolks and the sherry. Transfer to a double saucepan and allow to cook gently until it thickens; it must not be allowed to boil.

Serve on toast.

Lobster Thermidor (for 4)

1½ lb. cooked lobster
2 tablespoonfuls flour
2 tablespoonfuls butter
⅓ cupful white wine
1 tablespoonful minced parsley
1 cupful thin cream
1 teaspoonful dry mustard
¼ teaspoonful salt
Dash of Cayenne pepper
Grated Parmesan cheese

Cube the lobster meat and sauté in the butter for 5–7 minutes, then add the flour, salt, Cayenne, mustard, parsley and the cream, stirring continually while the mixture is heating. Add the wine; return the mixture to the lobster shells, sprinkle with the cheese and bake for about 10 minutes in a hot oven, or brown under a grill.

Shrimps á la Creole (for 4)

1 pint shrimps
1½ cupfuls stewed (or canned) tomatoes
1½ level tablespoonfuls flour
1 teaspoonful grated onion
1 bay leaf
2 level tablespoonfuls butter
Salt and pepper to taste

Melt the butter, add onion and flour and stir until smooth; add the seasonings, tomatoes and bay leaf, and bring to the boil, stirring all the time. Prepare the shrimps and add them to the sauce, stirring from time to time while they heat (about 7 minutes).

Boiled rice may be served as an accompaniment to this dish.

Southern-style Hash (for 4)

1 lb. minced veal
2 onions
2 cupfuls canned (or cooked) tomatoes
½ cupful rice
3 tablespoonfuls fat
1 teaspoonful salt
Pepper
1 teaspoonful chilli powder

Melt the fat in a deep saucepan, slice the onions and fry until golden brown. Add the meat and brown, then the tomatoes, rice, chilli powder, salt and pepper. Cover and cook for 35–40 minutes, or until the rice is tender, stirring from time to time.

Roast Stuffed Turkey with Cranberry Sauce

Turkey
Salt
2–4 oz. melted butter or margarine

For the stuffing

12 cupfuls bread-crumbs
¾ cupful finely minced onion
1 cupful bacon fat, margarine, or clarified dripping
1½ cupfuls finely chopped celery
1 small level teaspoonful pepper
1 heaped table-spoonful mixed herbs
1 lb. pork sausage meat
Hot water as required
2 teaspoonfuls salt

To make the stuffing.—Melt the fat and cook the minced onion over a gentle heat until golden brown. Add some of the bread-crumbs, stirring well to prevent burning. Turn into a large bowl and add the rest of the ingredients, with the sausage meat browned lightly over a gentle heat. Mix in just enough hot water to moisten sufficiently. Allow to cool before using.

Wash the prepared bird inside and out, drying well. Rub over inside with salt. Stuff bird, and brush well with melted fat. If cooking on rack in pan, place on one side, so that it roasts evenly, and can be turned when half cooked; cover with well-greased paper.

For a bird from 8–10 lb. allow 3–3½ hours
For a bird from 10–14 lb. allow 3½–4 hours
For a bird from 14–18 lb. allow 4½–6 hours

For the cranberry sauce

2 *cupfuls sugar*   2 *cupfuls water*
    4 *cupfuls cranberries*

Boil sugar and water briskly for 5 minutes. Add cranberries and continue boiling for a further 5–10 minutes, or until the berries are cooked.

When Buying Duck

Allow at least ¾–1 lb. drawn duck per person. An easy way to tell if a duck is young or old is to pinch its windpipe. If it is rubbery, it is a young bird. If it cracks, it is too old.

Roasting Duck

The best results are obtained by placing the duck on a wire rack in a roasting pan. Do not prick, or brush with oil. Roast until thigh joint of bird moves easily. Another test is to press the drumstick meat between the fingers. If it is soft, the bird is done. The skin should be crisp.

When Buying Goose

Allow 1¼–1½ lb. drawn goose per person.

Roasting Goose

After stuffing goose, prick with fork through fat layers over back, around tail and into body around wings and legs. This helps draw out fat. Do not brush with fat or oil. Roast as for duck.

Roast Duckling (for 4)

1 *5-lb. duck*   *Hot water and butter*
Fruit stuffing   *for basting*
2 *oz. flour*   *Salt and pepper*

Wash bird and cut off neck. Fill cavity with apple stuffing. Fasten opening with skewers or sew it up with thick thread. Roast duck in very hot oven for 15 minutes. Reduce oven to moderate heat and continue roasting, basting often with hot water and butter. Remove excess fat as it accumulates in the pan. Season with salt and pepper when duck is half-cooked (25 minutes per lb.).

Pineapple is a popular accompaniment to many meat and poultry dishes. Here it is served grilled with chicken. It also goes with baked ham

Meanwhile, simmer neck and giblets for 45–50 minutes in sufficient water to cover, with one small onion and two or three sticks of celery.

To make gravy, drain stock from giblets and put on one side. Chop giblets and brown in 4 tablespoonfuls of fat from pan in which duck has been roasted. Add the flour. Stir till smooth and brown. Add 2 cupfuls of giblet stock and stir until thick. Cook for 5 minutes, season and strain.

Apple Stuffing (Suitable for duck or goose)

2 oz. butter or margarine	Salt and pepper
1 slice onion	4 oz. breadcrumbs
4 oz. chopped celery	4 oz. peeled chopped tart apples

Melt the butter or margarine and brown the onion. Add remainder of the ingredients, seasoning to taste and mix thoroughly. Heat through. Stuff the bird as directed. This is a sufficient quantity for a 5-lb. duck.

Goose with Prunes

1 goose	Clear stock
1 small onion, minced	Salt and black pepper
1 oz. goose fat	Pinch of sage
8 oz. soft breadcrumbs	1 tablespoonful minced parsley
½ lb. sausage meat	1 tablespoonful minced onion
1 egg, beaten	1 teaspoonful brandy
3 dozen small prunes, stoned	

Brown the onion in the goose fat. Add crumbs, sausage meat and beaten egg, and mix thoroughly over low flame. Soak the prunes for 3 hours in enough clear stock to cover. Add minced onion and seasonings. Mix well and add to crumbs and sausage meat mixture. Stuff goose and skewer or sew up. Baste frequently with fat from pan. Allow 25–30 minutes per lb.

Remove all fat from roasting pan and add 1½ pints clear stock, or meat essence melted in hot water. Cook until reduced to ½ pint. Add brandy and serve with goose.

Cantonese Duck

2 tablespoonfuls soy sauce	1 oz. cornflour
1 tablespoonful sherry	½ teaspoonful salt
1 chopped shallot	4 tablespoonfuls water
Breast and leg of duck	3 oz. lard or 3 tablespoonfuls vegetable oil
2 eggs	

Mix the soy sauce, sherry and chopped shallot. Put in the breast and leg of the duck and leave to marinate for 1 hour. Make a paste with the cornflour, eggs, salt and water. Remove the duck from sauce and roll in paste. Heat lard or vegetable oil in a large frying pan. Fry duck for 2 minutes on each side. Turn. Fry for further 2 minutes, then turn and fry for 10 minutes on each side or until skin is crisp. Serve the duck cut in ½-in. slices, accompanied by little bowls of 3 tablespoonfuls salt and ½ tablespoonful pepper mixed together.

Blade Duck

1 duck	2–4 oranges
Salt and pepper to taste	Juice of 1 orange
	½ lb. redcurrant jelly

Place duck in shallow roasting tin. Sprinkle with salt and pepper. Put in very hot oven and roast for 20 minutes. Reduce to moderate heat and cook until tender (25 minutes to the lb.). When the duck has cooked for a quarter of the allotted time, pour off most of the fat and add the juice of one large orange and the jelly. Cut remaining oranges into thick slices and place round the duck in the sauce. Baste frequently.

Duckling in Cranberry Sauce (for 4)

1 5–6-lb. duckling (whole or cut)	1 lb. fresh cranberries
4 cupfuls bread stuffing (optional)	¼ pint water
½ oz. cornflour	¼ pint orange juice
4 oz. sugar	1 unpeeled orange, cut in 6 wedges

Stuff duckling, if desired. Roast in moderate oven for about 2 hours or until skin is light brown. Meanwhile, make sauce. Mix the cornflour and sugar in a saucepan, add the cranberries, water and orange juice and bring to the boil quickly, stirring constantly. Cook over moderate heat for 5 minutes or till liquid is syrupy and clear. Remove from flame and add orange. Take the duck out of the oven, put into a deep casserole, pour sauce over it and cover casserole. Return to oven for about 20 minutes or until the duck is tender when pricked with a fork. Baste the duck, or, if cut up, turn pieces once during the cooking.

Veal Orloff (for 6–8)

3 lb. shoulder of veal, boned and rolled	1 lb. chopped mushrooms, canned or fresh
2 oz. butter or margarine	4 oz. minced onion
1½ teaspoonfuls salt	

Succotash made from sweet corn and beans goes perfectly with America's traditional Thanksgiving Day turkey

For the Mornay sauce

6 oz. butter or mar-	¾ pint milk
garine	¼ pint roast veal juice
4 oz. flour	3 egg-yolks, beaten
½ teaspoonful salt	4 oz. shredded
Pinch of pepper	Gruyère cheese

If the veal is very lean, cover with bacon rashers. Roast in moderate oven, allowing 40 minutes to the lb. Remove from the oven and leave for about 15 minutes. Then slice in ½-in. slices almost, but not quite through. Keep hot. Save juice which flows during slicing.

The Stuffing should be made while the meat is cooking. Melt the butter in a large frying pan. Add mushrooms, onion and salt and cook for 7 minutes uncovered if canned mushrooms are used. If fresh mushrooms are used, simmer 10 minutes with pan covered. Take lid off and cook for a further 5 minutes.

The Mornay sauce can be made only when meat is roasted. Melt the butter in a pan, stir in flour, salt and pepper. Add milk and veal juice from slices gradually. Continue cooking until thickened, stirring constantly. Mix egg-yolks with 2 or 3 tablespoonfuls of hot sauce, then stir slowly back into remainder of sauce. Simmer for about 3 minutes, stirring all the time. Remove pan from the flame. Stir in cheese.

To finish.—Mix about 4 tablespoonfuls of the sauce with the stuffing. Spread between the slices of veal. Remove string from around the meat and tie back into oblong shape if necessary. Put the meat on serving dish, pour sauce over it and garnish with tomato decorations (see below) and parsley.

Tomato decorations.—Firm medium-sized tomatoes must be used. Peel each one as you would an apple, with a sharp knife, beginning at the flower end, peel round and round to stem end. Do not break peel. Wind the peel round finger. Place it down on stem end and fasten with cocktail stick or toothpick.

Steak Superb (for 6)

4 oz. soft butter or margarine	4 egg-yolks
1 tablespoonful lemon juice	1 tablespoonful Tarragon vinegar
¼ teaspoonful grated onion	¼ teaspoonful dried Tarragon
½ teaspoonful minced parsley	Dash of Cayenne pepper
Dash of paprika	6 fillets of beef, 1–1½ in. thick
6 rounds of toast	

First, make the Béarnaise sauce. Melt butter in the top of a double boiler over hot, but not boiling, water. Beat the egg-yolks, stir in lemon juice, vinegar, seasonings. Add to the butter. Stir constantly until the sauce is as thick as mayonnaise. This will take about 10 minutes. Remove from the hot water at once and place over lukewarm water whilst you prepare the steaks. Grill meat, allowing 5 minutes each side for under-done steaks, 6 minutes each side for medium and 8 minutes each side for well-done steaks. Place each steak on a round of toast, top with a spoonful of the Béarnaise sauce.

Pretzel Stuffing (for Turkey) (Sufficient for a 6–8-lb. bird)

¾ lb. coarsely crumbled pretzels	8 oz. diced celery
1 large onion, chopped	Pinch of pepper
1 teaspoonful mixed herbs	½ pint milk
	6 oz. butter or margarine, melted
	1 gill water

Mix the pretzel crumbs, celery, mixed herbs, onion and pepper in a bowl. Stir in the butter or margarine, milk and water. Mix well and stuff the turkey.

Barley Pilaff (for 4)

2 medium onions	14 oz. barley
½ lb. mushrooms	1½ pints clear or chicken stock
2 oz. butter	
Salt and pepper	

Heat oven to moderate. Chop onions coarsely and slice mushrooms thinly. Melt butter in a frying pan and cook the mushrooms and onions for about 5 minutes. Remove from pan. Put barley into fat in pan. Cook over medium heat until brown, turning frequently. Add mushrooms, onions and half the stock. Cover closely, put in oven and cook for ½ hour. Take off lid.

Add seasoning and remainder of stock. Cook for further ½ hour and, if the barley looks dry, add a little more stock. Bake for 10–20 minutes longer, until barley is cooked. Serve with roast duck or goose, or as a supper dish on its own.

Apple Ham Rolls (for 6)

8 oz. shredded raw apple	1 teaspoonful sugar
4 oz. fine or dry breadcrumbs	2 oz. melted butter or margarine
Pinch of salt	6 slices of cooked ham
Pepper	12 cloves
1 teaspoonful dry mustard	6 whole canned apricots

Mix the apple, crumbs, salt, pepper, mustard, sugar and butter in a bowl. Spread each slice of ham with a spoonful of this mixture and roll up. Fasten with cocktail sticks and put into a shallow casserole or pie dish. Pour syrup glaze (see below) over them. Bake in a hot oven for ½ hour, basting several times; 5 minutes before the rolls are done, push 2 cloves into each half apricot and put them round the ham.

Syrup Glaze.—Mix ¼ pint light corn syrup, 3 tablespoonfuls water, ⅛ pint cider vinegar, 2 teaspoonfuls grated orange rind, 6 whole cloves and a stick of cinnamon in a saucepan. Bring to the boil and simmer for 5 minutes.

Cucumbers with Tuna Fish (for 4)

4 cucumbers about 6 in. long	1 can of tuna fish, flaked
2 teaspoonfuls grated onion	2 oz. chopped celery
6 tablespoonfuls mayonnaise	6 oz. white breadcrumbs
2 tablespoonfuls lemon juice	½ teaspoonful salt
	2 oz. butter or margarine
Pinch of pepper	

Cut a thin slice from one side of each cucumber lengthwise. Boil cucumbers in sufficient salted water to cover for 10 minutes, then remove carefully from the water. Cool for a few minutes. Scoop out pulp and save, being careful not to break the shells. Drain and sprinkle inside with salt. Chop cucumber pulp and drain off liquid. Mix pulp with salt, pepper, lemon juice, mayonnaise, two-thirds of breadcrumbs, celery, onion and tuna fish. Put the mixture into the shells and sprinkle with rest of the breadcrumbs. Dot with butter. Bake in shallow dish with a little water in moderately hot oven until browned.

VEGETABLES

Orange Curry Cabbage

1 medium-sized cabbage	¼ teaspoonful curry powder
3 oz. butter	Grated rind and juice of 1 orange
1 teaspoonful chutney	

Shred cabbage and cook for 4 minutes in 1 quart salted boiling water. Drain well. Brown the butter and add chutney, curry powder, orange rind and juice. Pour over the cabbage, cover and leave to stand 10 minutes before serving.

Stuffed Egg-plant (for 2–3)

1 large egg plant or 2 or 3 smaller ones	Dash of Cayenne
1 clove garlic, finely chopped (optional)	3 oz. butter or margarine
4 oz. green pepper	4 oz. onion, chopped
Small can tomato purée	¾ lb. cooked rice
	1 teaspoonful salt

Cut off the top quarter of the egg-plant. Scoop out, leaving shells about ½ in. thick. Chop the pulp roughly. Melt the butter in a frying pan, add egg-plant pulp, onion, sliced green pepper and garlic (if liked). Cook until soft, then add rice, tomato purée, salt and Cayenne. Fill egg-plant shells with this mixture and bake in a hot oven for about 15 minutes.

Stuffed Turnips (for 4)

4 medium-size turnips	8 oz. cooked peas
1 tablespoonful chopped parsley	2 oz. butter or margarine
Pinch of salt and pepper	

Peel the turnips and cook whole in boiling salted water until tender. Drain and scoop out centres, leaving shells about ½ in. thick. Keep these warm while making filling. Mix remaining ingredients in a saucepan. Heat until the butter melts and the peas are hot. Fill the turnip shells with the mixture.

Mint Potato Custard (for 4)

4 medium-size potatoes	½ cupful mint leaves, chopped
1 small onion, minced	1¼ pints milk
3 eggs	2 oz. butter
1½ teaspoonfuls salt	

Hamburgers topped with creamed mashed potato and grilled tomatoes, garnished with onion rings and parsley. These, the Devil's Food Cake and the Lemon Meringue Pie were specially made and photographed at the Spry Cookery Centre

Heat oven to moderate. Meantime peel, dice and boil the potatoes till tender but not too soft. Bring milk just to the boil. Remove from heat and add butter, salt and minced onion. Stir lightly beaten eggs into milk very slowly, a little at a time. Mix the chopped mint with the potatoes and add to milk and egg. Pour into casserole and place in a pan of warm water. Bake for 45 minutes.

CHOWDERS

Corn Chowder (for 4)

1 cupful water	4 cupfuls milk
1 small onion	1½ cupfuls canned
3 potatoes	(whole kernel) corn
¼ cupful margarine	Salt and pepper
Chives (optional)	

Peel and dice potatoes; peel and grate onion; add water and margarine and simmer gently until tender. Add corn and milk to this mixture and simmer a further 15 minutes. Season to taste with salt and pepper.

This dish may be garnished with finely chopped chives, if liked.

Manhattan Fish Chowder (for 3–4)

1 onion	1 cupful cooked,
1 potato	flaked cod
2 tablespoonfuls fat	Salt and pepper
1 cupful diced celery	1 slice bread per
1 cupful cooked	person
tomatoes	2 heaped tablespoon-
1 cupful (whole	fuls grated cheese
kernel) canned corn	

Chop onion very finely and cook in fat. Peel and dice potato. Add with celery, tomatoes, pepper and salt and simmer for 15 minutes. Mix in the corn and flaked fish, and heat well. Toast bread, or fry crisply in shallow fat. Place small slice or triangle on each portion and serve sprinkled with cheese.

Clam Chowder (for 4)

¼ cupful chopped	2 cupfuls boiling
onion	water
1 cupful diced potato	2 tablespoonfuls mar-
(raw)	garine
2 tablespoonfuls	1 cupful chopped
minced green	clams
peppers	1 cupful clam liquor
3 tablespoonfuls	Pinch of thyme
chopped celery	Salt and pepper
1 cupful canned tomatoes	

Melt margarine and brown onion and green pepper; then add celery, potato, and water, cover and cook for 15 minutes, when potato should be tender. Now add toma-

toes, clams, and liquor, and salt, pepper and thyme.

Cover, simmer gently for a further 20 minutes to ½ hour, and serve.

SALADS

Waldorf Surprise Salad

2 cupfuls red-skinned,	¼ cupful chopped
apples (unpeeled),	celery
cut in cubes	¼ cupful chopped
½ cupful chopped	walnuts
stoned dates	1 lettuce
	Mayonnaise

Mix together apples, dates, celery and nuts, and serve on prepared lettuce, with mayonnaise dressing (see Salads chapter).

Slaw Royal

½ cupful sliced apple	1 banana
(peeled)	½ cupful chopped
1½ cupfuls shredded	celery
red cabbage	Salad dressing to taste

Mix together salad dressing and slices of apple, and add sliced banana; mix in shredded cabbage and chopped celery.

Tomato and Lima Bean Salad

4 large tomatoes	1 small onion
1½ cupfuls cooked (or	1 cupful mixed nuts
canned) Lima	2 tablespoonfuls
beans	finely chopped
2 dessertspoonfuls	celery
finely chopped	Salt and pepper
parsley	Mayonnaise

Chop the nuts finely; grate the onion. Cut a slice from the top of each tomato and remove the pulp. Add celery, nuts, onion, parsley, salt and pepper to the beans, which should be well drained and cut in halves if large, and mix in a little mayonnaise.

Fill the scooped-out tomatoes with the mixture, and top with a little mayonnaise when serving.

Cheese and Grapefruit Salad

1 lettuce	Tomatoes
1 can grapefruit	½ cupful chopped wal-
3 large tablespoonfuls	nuts
cream cheese	Radishes to garnish
Mayonnaise or salad cream	

Mix chopped nuts into cream cheese, adding a little mayonnaise or salad cream, if necessary. Keep aside several nuts as garnish. Drain grapefruit, peel and slice tomatoes. Prepare lettuce. Arrange grapefruit, sliced tomatoes, and cheese on bed of lettuce. Garnish with radishes and the remaining walnuts. Serve with mayonnaise or salad cream.

Celeriac Salad

1 *small celeriac*	6 *walnuts*
1 *teaspoonful honey*	1 *sweet apple*
½ *cupful soaked sultanas*	1 *cup yoghourt*
	Pepper and salt

Peel and grate the raw celeriac and apple (or chop very finely). Drain the previously soaked sultanas and dry well. Chop the walnuts. Mix the honey with the apple and add to the grated celeriac. Finally, mix all together with the yoghourt and serve.

Coleslaw

3 *cupfuls shredded raw cabbage*	*Paprika to season*
	½ *cupful salad dressing*

For the salad dressing

2 *tablespoonfuls flour*
1 *tablespoonful salt*
¾ *tablespoonful dry mustard*
1 *tablespoonful sugar*
Pepper
Paprika
1 *egg*
1 *cupful milk*
¼ *cupful vinegar*
2 *tablespoonfuls margarine or butter*

To make the dressing mix together flour, salt, mustard, pepper, paprika and sugar. Beat the egg well and add, then gradually mix in the milk. Cook in a double pan over boiling water, stirring all the time until it thickens; add the vinegar very gradually and then the butter or margarine. Cover and allow to cool.

Mix the shredded cabbage with the dressing and sprinkle with a few grains of paprika. Serve at once.

Autumn Soufflé Salad (for 4–6)

1 *packet lime or lemon jelly*	2 *oz. chopped walnuts*
¼ *pint cold water*	½ *pint hot water*
¼ *pint mayonnaise*	2 *tablespoonfuls lemon juice*
6 *oz. seeded black grapes*	8 *oz. diced peeled apples*
	Pinch of salt

Dissolve jelly in hot water, then add mayonnaise, lemon juice, salt and cold water. Beat with egg whisk. Pour into freezing tray of refrigerator and freeze for 15–20 minutes or until firm at the edge but soft in the centre. Turn into a bowl and whip until fluffy. Fold in apples, grapes, and walnuts, and pour into a quart jelly mould or individual small moulds. Chill in the refrigerator, or leave overnight. Turn out and serve, garnished with fruit as desired.

Pepper Salad Jelly (for 4–6)

1 *packet lemon jelly*	¼ *pint hot water*
1 *tablespoonful vinegar*	¼ *pint cold water*
1 *teaspoonful salt*	6 *oz. finely diced celery*
2 *oz. finely diced green peppers*	4 *oz. shredded or finely sliced carrots*

Dissolve jelly in hot water and add vinegar, cold water and half the salt. Mix thoroughly. Chill in the refrigerator until slightly thickened. Sprinkle remaining salt over vegetables and fold into jelly. Put into a quart mould or individual small moulds. Chill until firm or leave overnight. Turn out and decorate with tomatoes or other salad. Serve with lettuce and mayonnaise.

Fruit and Celery Jelly (for 8)

	1 *packet lime jelly*
	1 *pint hot water*
	1½ *bananas, diced*
	3 *oz. diced celery*
	1 *packet lemon jelly*
4 *oz. diced unpeeled apples*	4 *tablespoonfuls lemon juice*
1 *pint cold water*	1 *teaspoonful salt*

Dissolve lime and lemon jellies in hot water. Add lemon juice, salt and cold water. Chill in refrigerator until slightly thickened. Fold in celery, bananas and apples. Pour into 1½-quart mould or individual moulds. Chill in refrigerator until firm or leave overnight. Turn out and serve on lettuce with mayonnaise (optional).

CORN DISHES

Boiled Corn on the Cob

Prepare ears of corn by husking and removing silk. Cover the corn with salted boiling water and boil in a covered pan for 5–8 minutes.

Drain well and serve with melted butter, salt and pepper.

COOK'S TIP
STICKING CAKE

It won't stick to the tin if you stand the tin for a few minutes on a damp cloth when it comes out of the oven.

Sautéed Corn

1 *ear of cooked corn per person*	¼ *cupful cream*
2 *tablespoonfuls butter*	*Salt*
	A little sugar
	Pepper to taste

Remove corn kernels from cob, using sharp knife. Melt butter in saucepan and brown kernels lightly. Add cream, salt, pepper and sugar, and heat all together gently over a low heat until ready to serve.

Corn Fritters (1) (for 4)

4 *level tablespoonfuls flour*	½ *cupful milk*
2 *eggs*	1½ *cupfuls cooked or canned whole*
½ *teaspoonful salt*	*kernel corn*
Fat for frying	

Mix the well-beaten egg-yolks with the milk and add to the flour and salt to make a batter; beat until very smooth. Beat the egg-whites until fairly stiff and fold gently into the batter.

Melt the fat and, when very hot, drop in a little batter, pour a spoonful of the corn on to it before it sets, and press firmly down. Fry to a crisp golden brown, lift out on to a hot dish, and repeat until both batter and corn are all used.

Corn Fritters (2) (for 4)

1 *cupful cooked or canned whole kernel corn*	½ *teaspoonful baking powder*
2 *eggs*	½ *level teaspoonful salt*
½ *cupful flour*	*Pepper to taste*
Fat for frying	

Place corn in bowl with well-beaten eggs; sift and add dry ingredients and beat until smooth. Melt fat and drop mixture into it, one or two tablespoonfuls at a time. Dry on soft crumpled paper and serve piping hot.

Corn fritters are an ideal accompaniment to fried chicken, and may be served in place of potatoes.

Green Bean Succotash (for 4)

1½ *cupfuls cooked or canned green beans*	1½ *cupfuls cooked or canned whole*
½ *cupful cream*	*kernel corn*
Pepper and salt	

Mix together the beans and the corn, add the cream and season to taste with pepper and salt. Heat for about 10 minutes, stirring constantly.

Sage Succotash (for 4)

2 *cupfuls cooked or canned lima beans*	½ *cupful thin cream or top of milk*
1½ *cupfuls cooked or canned whole kernel corn*	½ *teaspoonful salt*
	2 *tablespoonfuls margarine*
½ *eggspoonful sage*	

Drain the beans well. Mix together with the corn, add sage, salt, cream or milk and the margarine. Heat for 10–15 minutes, stirring constantly.

WAFFLES

Plain Waffles

2 *cupfuls sifted flour*	½ *teaspoonful salt*
2 *eggs*	1¼ *cupfuls milk*
6 *tablespoonfuls melted margarine*	2 *teaspoonfuls baking powder*

Separate the whites from the yolks of the eggs. Mix the dry ingredients together and make into a batter with the milk, beaten egg-yolks and melted fat. Beat the egg-whites until stiff, and fold lightly in.

Well grease the waffle iron, and cook the waffles on the preheated irons for 3 minutes.

Banana Waffles

2 *cupfuls sifted flour*	½ *cupful thin sliced banana*
2 *eggs*	2 *teaspoonfuls baking powder*
6 *tablespoonfuls melted margarine*	¼ *teaspoonful salt*
1¼ *cupfuls milk*	

Prepare and mix waffles as above, adding the sliced banana to the batter *before* folding in the egg-whites.

Nut Waffles

¾ *cupful mixed finely chopped nuts*	2 *eggs*
2 *cupfuls sifted flour*	2 *teaspoonfuls baking powder*
1¼ *cupfuls milk*	¼ *teaspoonful salt*
6 *tablespoonfuls melted margarine*	

Prepare and mix waffles as for plain waffles above, adding the finely chopped nuts to the batter *before* folding in the egg-whites.

Chocolate Waffles

2 *cupfuls sifted flour*	2 *teaspoonfuls baking powder*
3 *tablespoonfuls cocoa*	6 *tablespoonfuls melted margarine*
1¼ *cupfuls milk* less ⅓ *cup (replaced by black coffee)*	2 *eggs*
	¼ *teaspoonful salt*

Mix and prepare as for plain waffles, substituting 3 tablespoonfuls of cocoa for 3

Add the egg-yolks to the milk and beat well together, mixing gradually with the dry ingredients. Add flavouring essence. Beat the egg-whites until stiff, and fold lightly in.

Cook on preheated waffle irons, which have been well greased, until a crisp golden brown and serve at once with honey or Maple Syrup.

ICE CREAM DISHES
Vanilla Ice Cream

½ cupful condensed milk (sweetened)
½ cupful water
½ cupful cream
1 teaspoonful vanilla essence
Pinch of salt

Mix together all ingredients except the cream, and chill well. Whip cream slightly and fold into the mixture. Place in a refrigerator and freeze to a mush. Now turn out into a

Waffles come in all varieties—plain with maple syrup (above); or savoury, topped with grilled kidneys (right) or sausages (below)

tablespoonfuls of the flour when making the batter, and replacing ⅓ cupful of milk by strong, freshly made black coffee.

Coconut Waffles

2 cupfuls flour
2 large eggs
2 tablespoonfuls sugar
½ cup desiccated coconut
½ level teaspoonful salt
1¼ cupfuls milk
6 tablespoonfuls melted fat

Sift together flour, sugar, salt, and add coconut. Beat the egg-yolks and add to the milk, gradually mixing in the dry ingredients, and beat until smooth; add melted fat. Beat the egg-whites until stiff and fold them in gently.

Cook in well-greased waffle irons, which have been previously heated, until crisp and golden brown. Serve with melted butter and thin honey or maple syrup.

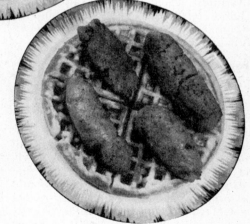

previously chilled bowl and beat well. Return to refrigerator and freeze firm.

This ice cream can be served with any sauce to suit individual taste.

Chocolate Ice Cream

1 oz. unsweetened chocolate
½ cupful sweetened condensed milk
½ cupful water
Pinch of salt
1 teaspoonful vanilla essence
½ cupful cream

Oaten Waffles

1 cupful Quick porridge oats
1 cupful wholemeal flour
1 cupful milk
½ level teaspoonful salt
2 eggs
1 teaspoonful vanilla essence

Mix together the flour, oats and salt.

Devil's Food, a rich dark chocolate cake with a crisp white icing, used on top and as a filling in the centre

Hot Chocolate Sauce

(To serve with ice cream)

> 3 oz. (unsweetened) chocolate
> ¼ cupful sugar
> Pinch of salt
> ¼ teaspoonful coffee essence (optional)
> ½ cupful water

Break up chocolate, add the water and heat together, stirring continually, until the chocolate is melted; then add the sugar, stirring well until it is dissolved. Remove from heat, add pinch of salt and coffee essence, if desired. Serve hot with ice cream.

Melt the chocolate in a double saucepan and add the condensed milk. Cook gently for about 5 minutes, or until thick, stirring continually. Gradually add the water and a pinch of salt; chill. Whip cream lightly and fold into mixture, adding the vanilla essence. Place in refrigerator and freeze to a mush. Then turn out into a previously chilled bowl and beat until smooth. Return to refrigerator tray and freeze until firm and ready to serve.

Banana Ice Cream

> 2 egg-yolks
> ⅔ cupful sugar
> 1½ cupfuls milk
> ½ cupful cream
> Pinch of salt
> 2 egg-whites
> ¼ cupful water
> 2 tablespoonfuls light corn syrup
> 1 teaspoonful vanilla essence
> 1 sieved banana

Beat the egg-yolks well and add to half sugar, milk and pinch of salt. Cook slowly in a double saucepan until mixture thickens. Cool and set in refrigerator until it forms a mush. Meanwhile, boil together water, remainder of sugar and corn syrup until small quantity dropped from spoon forms a long thread. Beat egg-whites until stiff and add syrup gradually, beating all the time, and then the vanilla essence.

Turn out the mixture into a previously chilled bowl, and beat well until perfectly smooth, lightly folding in the two egg-whites and syrup mixture. Whip the cream and fold in together with the sieved banana pulp. Return to refrigerator and freeze till ready to serve.

Butterscotch Walnut Ice Cream

> 2 eggs
> ⅔ cupful brown sugar
> Pinch of salt
> 1½ cupfuls milk
> ¼ cupful water
> ½ cupful cream
> 1 teaspoonful vanilla essence
> ½ cupful shelled chopped walnuts
> 2 tablespoonfuls light corn syrup

Separate the whites and yolks of eggs; beat the yolks, adding half the sugar, milk, pinch of salt. Cook in a double saucepan, stirring well all the time, until mixture thickens. Cool, add chopped walnuts and set in freezing tray of refrigerator until mixture is mushy. Meanwhile, boil together water, remaining half of brown sugar and corn syrup, until mixture forms long thread when dropped from tip of spoon. Beat egg-whites stiffly, add syrup gradually, beating well all the time, then vanilla essence. Allow to cool; then turn first mixture out into previously chilled bowl, beat well until smooth and fold in egg-white mixture. Whip cream and fold in lightly. Return the completed mixture to refrigerator and freeze until firm and ready to serve.

HOT SANDWICHES

Hot sandwiches, which are more in the nature of quick hot "snacks" than sandwiches, are an important feature of American life. Here are some of the most popular:

Toasted Meat Rolls (for 4)

4 round soft rolls	4 eggs
3 tablespoonfuls margarine	1 cupful minced cooked meat
1½ tablespoonfuls minced onion	Salt and pepper to taste
Grated cheese (optional)	

Cut thin slices from tops of rolls and scoop out centres, making these into bread-crumbs. Melt 2 tablespoonfuls of mar-garine and brown onion, then add bread-crumbs and minced meat. Season with salt and pepper.

Melt remaining margarine and brush on to top of rolls, heat them for 10 minutes in hot oven; fill with hot meat mixture. Poach eggs and place one on top of each roll.

A little grated cheese may be sprinkled over, if liked.

Hot Roast Beef Sandwiches

1 slice of bread per person	A little gravy or horseradish sauce
Slices hot cooked roast beef	Salt and pepper

Toast the slices of bread, and top each one with slices of hot meat, sufficient to cover. Season with salt and pepper and cover with a little hot gravy, or garnish with horseradish sauce.

Hot Ham Sandwiches (for 4)

1 cupful finely minced cooked ham	2 tablespoonfuls margarine
2 tablespoonfuls sweet pickle or chutney	½ cupful milk
	1 egg
	2 slices of bread per person
3 tablespoonfuls ketchup	

Mix together the minced ham, sweet pickle and the ketchup, and spread on slices of bread to make sandwiches. Beat the egg well and add the milk. Dip each sandwich in the egg-and-milk mixture and brown quickly in the melted margarine. Serve hot.

Hot Cheese, Tomato and Bacon Sand-wiches

1 slice streaky bacon per person	1 tomato per sandwich
1 slice bread per person	Parsley or watercress to garnish
Cheese	

Slice the cheese and place on the bread. Peel tomatoes by plunging in boiling water, then in cold, so that skin is easily removed, slice and place on the cheese Cut each piece of bacon in half (lengthwise) and lay on top of the cheese and tomato.

Grill until bacon is cooked, turning it after a few minutes. Serve hot. Mustard may be put on the cheese under the bacon, if liked. Garnish with chopped parsley or a little watercress.

SWEET DISHES

Apple Mince Pie (for 4)

½ lb. flour	Hard-sauce apple rings (see below)
Water to mix	
1¼ lb. mincemeat	6 oz. butter, margarine or lard
2 medium-size tart cooking apples	Pinch of salt

Rub the butter or other fat into the flour and salt until the mixture resembles fine breadcrumbs. Mix to a soft dough with water. Roll out on floured pastry board to a round 12 in. in diameter. Cover 9-in. flan tin or plate with this. Trim until there is about ½-in. overlap. Turn this under flan so that it is flush with the edge. Decorate edge with knife or fork. Peel, core and finely chop the apples. Mix mincemeat and apples and put into pre-pared pastry. Spread evenly. Bake in hot

Angel Food Cake—as airy and light as its name suggests—is made in a specially shaped ring tin

oven for 30 minutes or until filling is bubbly and pastry is golden brown. Top with hard-sauce apple rings, put hard-sauce balls in their centres and serve.

Hard-sauce Apple Rings

2 medium-size apples
½ teaspoonful cornflour
2 oz. sugar
Few drops of red vegetable colouring
1½ teaspoonfuls sugar dissolved in ½ gill water

Peel and core the apples, slice each into four rings. Mix the sugar, cornflour and sugar syrup in a frying pan and add enough red colouring to make the mixture deep red. Cook over medium heat, stirring occasionally until sugar is dissolved. Put the apple rings in the syrup and simmer for 10 minutes or until tender, turning frequently. Drain and cool.

Hard-sauce Balls

4½ oz. butter or margarine
¾ lb. sifted icing sugar
½ teaspoonful vanilla

Cream the butter or margarine, adding the sugar gradually and beating until soft and fluffy. Stir in the vanilla. Form with butter pats or fingers into eight large balls, chill in refrigerator and serve in the centre of hard-sauce apple rings.

Special Apple Pie (for 6)

2 lb. cooking apples
1 tablespoonful lemon juice
½ teaspoonful nutmeg
½ lb. flour
Water to mix
1 teaspoonful grated lemon rind
2 oz. butter or margarine (for filling)
6 oz. butter, margarine, lard or a mixture (for pastry)
Pinch of salt
¾ cupful sugar

Peel, core and slice apples. Put them in a buttered pie dish. Sprinkle with lemon rind, juice, sugar and nutmeg. Dot with butter or margarine. Top with pastry made from the butter or other fat, flour, salt and water. Bake in a very hot oven for 10 minutes, reduce to moderate and bake for 30–40 minutes until crust is golden brown and apples tender.

Apple Pandowdy (for 6)

For the pastry

¾ lb. sifted flour
4 tablespoonfuls water
4 oz. butter, margarine or shortening
¼ teaspoonful salt

For the fruit mixture

8 medium-size cooking apples
2 oz. sugar
¼ teaspoonful cinnamon
⅛ pint molasses
⅛ pint water
¼ teaspoonful salt
Pinch of nutmeg
2 tablespoonfuls melted butter or margarine
2 tablespoonfuls milk

Make the pastry and then peel, core and cut apples into ½-in. wedges. Put in a shallow buttered pie dish and sprinkle with salt, cinnamon, nutmeg and sugar. Mix the molasses, melted butter or margarine and water, and pour over apples.

Cover completely with the rolled out pastry. Press edges down and brush with milk. Bake in hot oven for 10 minutes. Remove pudding from the oven and chop the crust into the apples until some pieces of crust stand on end. Reduce oven heat to warm and return pie to oven. Bake 1 hour or until the apples are tender.

Apple Chewies (for 8)

For the pastry

8 oz. sifted flour
2¼ oz. shortening, butter or margarine
2–3 tablespoonfuls water
¼ teaspoonful salt
Grated rind of half lemon

For the filling

4 medium-sized cooking apples
Pinch of cinnamon
1 oz. butter or margarine
Pinch of salt
2 oz. brown sugar
6 oz. shredded coconut
2 oz. granulated sugar
2 tablespoonfuls double cream
1 egg, slightly beaten

Rub shortening, butter or margarine into sifted flour and salt until mixture resembles breadcrumbs. Add grated lemon rind. Mix to stiff dough with water. Roll out on lightly floured board to fit baking tin about 13 in. by 9 in. by 2 in. Line bottom of pan with the pastry. Peel, core and slice the apples. Arrange in overlapping rows on pastry. Mix brown sugar and cinnamon. Sprinkle over apples. Dot with margarine or butter. Bake in a hot oven for 25 minutes. Remove from the oven. Reduce oven temperature to moderate. Mix coconut, granulated sugar, beaten egg, salt and whipped cream. Spread over apples and return to oven. Bake for about 15 minutes until the apples are tender and the topping is crisp.

Probably the most famous of all American sweet dishes — Lemon Meringue Pie is surprisingly quick and easy to make and always wins praise for a hostess from her guests

Apple Macaroon
(for 6)

4 medium-size
  cooking apples
8 oz. sugar
2 eggs
8 oz. flour
½ teaspoonful
  cinnamon
4 oz. chopped pecan
  nuts
4 oz. butter or
  margarine, melted

Peel, core and slice the apples. Fill a 9-in. flan tin or pie plate with apple slices. Mix half the sugar, cinnamon and chopped pecan nuts and sprinkle over the apples. Beat the eggs well and add remaining sugar, flour and melted butter or margarine. Beat until smooth and pour over apples. Bake in cool oven for 1¼ hours or until apples are tender and top crisp.

Lemon Meringue Pie (for 8)

1 oz. flour or corn-
  flour
½ lb. sugar
8 oz. boiling water
  Short-pastry flan case

2 eggs (separated)
½ oz. butter
Rind and juice of 1
  lemon

Mix sugar and flour in pan, add boiling water slowly and boil until clear, stirring all the time with a wooden spoon. Add butter gradually and the egg-yolks, lightly beaten. Still stirring, cook over boiling water until it holds its shape. Remove from heat and add lemon juice and rind. When cool, pour into baked short-pastry flan case, about 8 in. diameter (see Pastry chapter). Cover with meringue made by beating egg-whites stiff with 4 dessertspoonfuls sugar. Put in very cool oven until meringue is delicately browned in peaks, about 15 minutes.

Pumpkin Pie

2 cupfuls steamed
  pumpkin
1 cupful sugar
½ level teaspoonful
  salt
2 eggs

Uncooked pastry shell
1 level teaspoonful
  ginger
1 level teaspoonful
  cinnamon
½ teaspoonful nutmeg
¾ pint scalded milk

Rub the pumpkin through a sieve, and add to it the sugar, spices, salt, milk and the well-beaten eggs. Allow to cool. Fill the uncooked pastry case with this mixture and bake in a moderate oven for 40–45 minutes.

CAKES

Angel Food Cake

1 cupful fine white
  flour
1½ cupfuls sugar
10 egg-whites
  ¼ teaspoonful salt

1¼ teaspoonfuls
  cream of tartar
1 teaspoonful vanilla
  essence

Sift the flour and ⅓ cupful sugar three times. Beat the egg-whites until foamy, and add the cream of tartar and the salt; beat until the mixture is stiff, but not dry. Sift the remaining sugar three times and gradually fold into the egg-white mixture, 2 tablespoonfuls at a time. Add the vanilla essence. Sift ¼ cupful flour and fold in lightly, continuing until all the flour is used. Pour into an ungreased border cake tin and bake in a moderate oven for 1¼ hours. Remove from oven and turn cake tin upside down on wire cake rack until cold—about 1 hour—before turning out cake.

Boston Favourite

4 oz. butter or mar-
  garine
3 egg-yolks
2 egg-whites
8 oz. sugar
  14 oz. flour

1 gill milk
2½ teaspoonfuls
  baking powder
Flavouring or shelled
  walnuts

Cream butter and sugar, add well-beaten egg-yolks. Mix and sift flour and baking powder, and add alternately with milk. Then add egg-whites, beaten stiff, nuts or essence, and bake in moderate oven for 45–50 minutes. Top with Boiled Frosting.

Boiled Frosting

8 *oz. sugar*	*Flavouring—tea-*
1 *gill boiling water*	*spoonful vanilla or*
1 *egg-white*	*as liked*

Boil sugar and water together until it threads with a little stirring. Pour syrup over beaten egg-white and beat until it reaches spreading consistency. Add flavouring, pour over cake and crease with knife.

Bride's Cake

8 *oz. butter*	8 *oz. cornflour*
1 *lb. flour*	5 *egg-whites*
1 *lb. sugar*	½ *teaspoonful almond*
1 *tablespoonful*	*essence*
baking powder	1 *gill milk*

Well cream butter and sugar together; sift dry ingredients and add, mixing thoroughly, alternately with the milk. Fold in stiffly beaten egg-whites and flavouring, divide between two sandwich tins and bake in moderate oven for about 25–30 minutes. Put together when cool with butter filling (see Icings chapter) or whipped cream flavoured to taste, ice with Boiled or Nut Caramel Frosting.

Nut Caramel Frosting

10 *oz. brown sugar*	2 *egg-whites*
2 *oz. white sugar*	1 *teaspoonful vanilla*
1 *gill water*	*essence*
4 *oz. chopped walnuts*	

Boil sugar and water until it threads, then pour, while beating, on to stiffly beaten egg-whites. Beat until lukewarm. Stand pan in larger pan of boiling water over heat and stir constantly until it becomes granular round the edges. Remove, and beat in with spoon the chopped walnuts and vanilla. Pour over cake, spread roughly.

Buckwheat Cakes

1 *cupful buckwheat*	1¾ *cupfuls milk*
flour	4 *level teaspoonfuls*
1 *cupful white flour*	*baking powder*
1 *egg*	2 *tablespoonfuls*
1 *level teaspoonful*	*molasses (optional)*
salt	

Sift together the buckwheat flour, plain flour, salt and baking powder. Beat the egg well, and stir it in gradually with the milk. Beat thoroughly to remove any lumps and cook at once on a hot, greased griddle.

If desired, two tablespoonfuls of molasses may be added to the mixture before cooking. This helps to brown the cakes as well as to sweeten them.

Corn Bread

1 *cupful plain white*	½ *teaspoonful salt*
flour	1 *egg*
1 *cupful corn meal*	1 *cupful milk*
3 *teaspoonfuls baking*	¼ *cupful melted fat,*
powder	*or salad oil*

Sift together the flour, corn meal, baking powder and salt. Beat the egg, and mix with the milk and melted fat. Add to dry ingredients. Pour into a greased pan and bake in a hot oven for ½ hour.

Cream Sponge

4 *eggs*	1½ *tablespoonfuls*
8 *oz. sugar*	*cornflour*
3 *tablespoonfuls cold*	8 *oz. flour*
water	1½ *teaspoonfuls*
1 *teaspoonful lemon*	*baking powder*
essence	¼ *teaspoonful salt*

Separate egg-yolks from whites, beat yolks until thick, add the sugar gradually, then water and essence. Mix and sift flour and cornflour with baking powder and salt, and add to egg-yolk mixture. Beat egg-whites until stiff and fold into the dough. Divide into two sandwich tins and bake in a fairly quick oven for 25–30 minutes. When cold, put together with whipped cream, sweetened and flavoured to taste.

Devil's Food Cake

2 *eggs*	1 *teaspoonful bicar-*
1 *lb. brown sugar*	*bonate of soda*
4 *oz. melted butter*	1 *gill of boiling water*
4 *oz. plain chocolate,*	1 *lb. flour*
grated	*Vanilla essence to*
1 *gill sour milk*	*flavour*

Dissolve chocolate in boiling water. Add sugar and melted butter, stir soda into milk and add with beaten eggs to chocolate mixture. Mix in sifted flour, add vanilla, beat well, divide between two sandwich tins and bake in moderate oven. When cold, put together and top with Boiled Frosting.

CANADA

Original salads and fish dishes, crisp and crunchy cookies, clever
ways with beans—they are all to be found in Canadian cookery

SOUPS

Bean Soup (for 4)

1 pint black beans	1 teaspoonful meat
3 oz. butter	extract
⅛ teaspoonful paprika	Salt to season
2 tablespoonfuls	Hard-boiled egg
sherry	2 slices white bread
1 lemon	A little milk

Soak the beans in cold water for 12 hours. Drain, cover with fresh cold water, bring to the boil and cook for about 1 hour, or until soft. Pass through sieve or fine strainer, stir in salt, paprika and meat extract. Add butter. Remove from the heat and stir in the bread, broken into small pieces and without the crust. If soup is too thick, add milk as necessary, and let it simmer gently for about 15 minutes, stirring well.

Stir in the sherry just before serving, and garnish each bowl with a thin slice of hard-boiled egg resting on a thin slice of lemon.

Crab Soup (for 4)

1½ pints milk	1½ oz. cornflour
½ pint water	14 oz. cooked crab
½ teaspoonful	meat
Worcester sauce	1½ oz. butter
1 teaspoonful curry	4 hard-boiled eggs
powder	1 gill sherry
2 sticks celery	(optional)
⅛ teaspoonful mace	Twist of lemon peel

Wash and trim celery stalks, cut into small lengths (about ¾ in.) and boil for 10 minutes in well-salted water. Drain. Mix the cornflour with enough cold milk to make a smooth paste; heat the rest of 1 pint and, when boiling, pour on to the paste, stirring well so that the mixture is smooth and free from lumps. Add the celery and allow to simmer very gently for a further 5 minutes, adding butter. Separate yolks and whites of hard-boiled eggs; chop whites finely and add to the soup, together with the Worcester sauce, mace, curry powder and crab meat. Remove from heat and gradually add the rest of the milk

mixed with the ½ pint of water, as necessary; you may not need to use quite all of it. Allow to simmer gently for a further 10 minutes, stirring from time to time.

Crumble the egg-yolks over the top of the soup after it has been put into individual bowls, just before serving.

If sherry is to accompany this soup, it should be well heated and handed round separately, with two thin coils of lemon peel in it, so that guests may help themselves, according to their taste.

French Canadian Chestnut Soup (for 4)

1 lb. chestnuts	2 oz. fresh butter
1 onion	1 quart stock
3 tablespoonfuls	½ teaspoonful celery
cream (optional)	salt
	¼ teaspoonful pepper

Boil the chestnuts for 20 minutes, then peel them and put them into a saucepan with the stock and the onion, peeled and chopped. Boil together for 20 minutes, then rub through a hair sieve.

Add the butter, celery salt and pepper and, if available, the cream.

FISH

Canadian-style Poached Fish (for 4)

1 slice lemon	1½ lb. fresh haddock
2 teaspoonfuls salt	Few sprigs of green
1 bay leaf	celery top
¼ teaspoonful whole	Tablespoonful
black peppers	chopped parsley
2 slices onion	2 oz. melted butter
1 pint water	

Put the lemon, salt, bay leaf, peppers, onion slices and celery sprigs into the water and boil for 10 minutes. Add the fish and simmer gently for 10 minutes, or until the fish flakes easily with a fork (time depends on its thickness).

Drain and serve hot with the melted butter poured over; garnish with the chopped parsley.

Montreal Tuna Fish Fritters (for 3 or 4)

6 oz. tuna fish	¼ teaspoonful pepper
2 eggs	4 oz. rice
⅛ pint milk	2 rounded table-
1 teaspoonful salt	spoonfuls flour
	Salad oil for frying

Bring the rice to the boil in a saucepan with ¾ pint of well-salted water. Cover and cook gently over a low heat for 15 minutes, then remove from the heat.

Separate the whites and yolks of the eggs; mix together the fish, milk, egg-yolks, flour and pepper and add to the rice, mixing well together.

Beat the egg-whites until stiff, and fold gently into the rice and fish mixture. Drop from a tablespoon into hot deep fat and fry until a crisp golden brown.

Oyster Stew (for 4)

1 pint oysters	1½ oz. margarine
Sprig of parsley	1½ tablespoonfuls
1 bay leaf	flour
1 slice onion	Salt and Cayenne
1 pint milk	pepper

Prepare the oysters, strain the liquor through a cheese cloth, cut the oysters in half and cook in the liquor for 3–5 minutes, or until the edges curl.

Add the parsley, bay leaf and onion to the milk and bring to the boil; strain. Melt the margarine and blend in the flour; add the milk gradually, and cook until slightly thickened, stirring all the time. Add the oysters and season with the salt and Cayenne pepper. Serve at once

Tuna Chow Mein (for 4)

3 sticks celery	4 oz. cooked mush-
1 chopped onion	rooms
½ green pepper	6 oz. cooked or
1 oz. margarine	canned tuna fish
4 teaspoonfuls soy	1 tablespoonful corn-
sauce	flour
Salt and pepper to	4 oz. noodles
taste	2 teaspoonfuls lemon
⅛ pint mixed milk	juice
and water	

Chop the washed celery into short match-stick lengths, and cook in the margarine with the onion and finely chopped green pepper. Add mushrooms, cut into halves or quarters, soy sauce and fish; season with salt and pepper and mix in the milk and water. Bring to boil, cover and cook for 15–20 minutes.

Mix the cornflour to a smooth paste with cold water, add to the mixture, stirring in carefully, and cook until it thickens; stir continually so that no lumps form.

Cook the noodles in boiling salted water for 15 minutes, or until tender; drain well.

Stir the lemon juice into the fish mixture, and turn out on to the noodles before serving.

MEAT AND POULTRY

Braised Pork Chops with Mushroom Gravy (for 6)

6 loin pork chops	1 bay leaf
1½ oz. bacon fat or	½ pint milk
margarine	Salt and pepper and a
¼ lb. mushrooms	little flour for chops
	1 tablespoonful flour

Wipe the chops and trim away any excess fat. Sprinkle with salt and pepper, and roll in flour. Melt fat or margarine and brown chops lightly on both sides. Remove from the pan and keep hot. Prepare mushrooms and cut into quarters, cooking in the same fat. Season with salt and pepper.

When they are done, mix the flour to a smooth paste, using sufficient milk from the ½ pint, gradually add the rest of the milk, stirring all the time; pour over the mushrooms and bring all together to the boil; add bay leaf and simmer for 5 minutes, stirring from time to time.

Place the chops in a fireproof dish and pour the mushroom gravy over; cover closely and bake in a moderate oven for 45 minutes, turning the chops occasionally.

Cheeseburgers (for 4)

1 lb. finely minced	Fat for frying
beef	1 large or 2 small soft
Seasoning and	rolls per person
chopped onion	

For the Cheese Topping

¼ lb. grated Cheddar	2 tablespoonfuls
cheese or cheese	prepared mustard
spread	1 teaspoonful lemon
2 tablespoonfuls	juice
mayonnaise	½ teaspoonful celery
	salt

Mix the meat, onion and seasoning thoroughly, shape into cakes to fit the rolls, then fry in melted fat until cooked to individual liking, either " rare," medium or well done. Split the rolls and put a hamburger into each, then top with:

Small roast turkey is served with Chestnut Dressing. Simmer coarsely chopped cooked chestnuts with a little chopped onion and sliced apple, salt and sage, in butter for 10 minutes. Mix with breadcrumbs and pack lightly into the bird

Cheese Topping

Blend all ingredients thoroughly, spread cooked hamburgers with this and put under a hot grill until the cheese begins to bubble and brown slightly.

Chicken and Dumplings (for 4)

12 oz. cold cooked chicken	2 oz. margarine Tablespoonful
1 oz. flour	chopped parsley
1½ pints stock	

For the dumplings

1 egg	4 oz. flour
¼ teaspoonful salt	⅛ pint milk

Melt the margarine in a saucepan and blend the flour in carefully; add the stock gradually and cook until it thickens, stirring constantly. Add the pieces of chicken and bring the mixture gradually to the boil.

For the dumplings.—Beat the egg well and add the milk. Mix together the salt and flour, and sift into the liquid; beat until smooth. Drop the dumpling mixture into the chicken soup by tablespoonfuls. Cover and simmer for 10–12 minutes.

Sprinkle with the chopped parsley and serve.

Ham and Mushroom Casserole (for 4)

4 oz. macaroni	1 tablespoonful flour
8 oz. ham	6 oz. grated cheese
1 tablespoonful minced onion	½ pint milk
	2 oz. margarine
Salt and pepper	4 oz. mushrooms

Cook the macaroni in boiling salted water until tender, drain and set aside. Melt the margarine in a frying pan and gently cook the mushrooms; when they are done, remove from pan, blend in flour with the fat and pour in the milk and about ⅛ pint of cold water. Bring gently to the boil, stirring all the time, and allow to simmer for 5 minutes.

Mix together the macaroni, ham, cheese, mushrooms and liquid from the pan, together with the minced onion. Season well with salt and pepper. Turn into a greased dish and bake in a medium oven for ½ hour.

Potatoes au Bœuf (for 4)

1 lb. minced beef	4 large potatoes
2 teaspoonfuls mixed herbs (thyme, marjoram, parsley)	1 oz. margarine
	¼ teaspoonful paprika
Salt and pepper to season	½ pint milk

Scrub potatoes, prick once or twice with

a fork and bake in a fairly hot oven for between 1 and 1½ hours, according to size.

Melt fat in frying pan and brown the beef lightly, stirring with a fork, mix in the herbs, salt and pepper.

When potatoes are done, cut off the tops and scoop out the inside. Keep the skins. Whip up the potato, season with salt and pepper, and add enough hot milk to make the mixture light and fluffy. Fold the meat into the potato, and fill the skins with the mixture.

Sprinkle each potato with a little paprika and put under the grill until they are heated through and lightly browned on top.

Stuffed Shoulder of Mutton

Shoulder of mutton   Salad oil
    Salt and pepper

For the stuffing

1 small egg
2 teaspoonfuls finely chopped mint
2 heaped tablespoonfuls breadcrumbs
Seasoning

Wipe the meat over with a damp cloth, and remove skin, using a sharp knife. Next, remove bone (or you can ask for this to be done at the butcher's).

Rub meat well with salt and pepper, and then with salad oil.

Mix together the breadcrumbs, minced or finely chopped mint, and salt and pepper. Beat up the egg and use just enough to bind the breadcrumb mixture. Insert the stuffing into the pocket left by the bone, and sew up.

Put into a hot oven for 10 minutes; then lower heat to moderate and cook till done, allowing 20 minutes for each pound and 20 minutes over for any remaining part of a pound.

VEGETABLE DISHES

Asparagus with Eggs (Asperges aux Œufs) (for 4)

1 bundle asparagus
3 oz. grated cheese (Parmesan or Gruyère)
4 slices toast
4 eggs
2 tablespoonfuls salad oil
Salt and pepper to taste
Small clove of garlic

Wash the asparagus well and cook in boiling salted water for 10–15 minutes, or until barely tender; drain and put aside to keep hot.

Heat the oil, add the garlic and cook for about 1 minute, remove garlic, then fry eggs gently in a covered pan for about 3 minutes. Season with salt and pepper.

Divide the asparagus into four portions, top each with an egg and pour over a little of the hot oil. Sprinkle well with the grated cheese and serve with the toast cut into triangles.

Canadian Beans and Rice (for 4)

½ lb. lean salt pork or bacon
6 oz. rice
6 oz. red kidney beans
1 clove of garlic
2 teaspoonfuls parsley, finely chopped
Salt and pepper to taste

Wash the beans and boil in well salted water for 20 minutes, or until tender; drain and set aside. Cook the rice in boiling salted water until done; drain and set aside. Dice and fry the pork or bacon until brown and crisp. Remove from the pan, and cook the minced clove of garlic gently for about 2 minutes.

Add the rice and beans, salt and pepper, and mix well together, heating thoroughly.

Turn into a pre-heated dish, top with the diced pork cubes and sprinkle with the chopped parsley before serving.

Scalloped Asparagus (for 4)

1 bundle asparagus
3 oz. margarine
4 tablespoonfuls flour
¾ teaspoonful salt
¼ teaspoonful pepper
3 oz. soft breadcrumbs
1 dessertspoonful finely chopped parsley
1 pint milk
2 oz. grated cheese (Cheddar or Gruyère)
½ teaspoonful paprika
½ teaspoonful Worcester sauce
2 tablespoonfuls sliced stuffed olives

Wash and cut the asparagus into 2-in. lengths. Cook in salted water until barely tender—about 10–15 minutes; drain carefully and put in shallow fireproof baking dish.

Melt the margarine in top of double saucepan; take out a third (1 oz.) and mix with the breadcrumbs. Blend flour and seasonings carefully with the remaining margarine. Add the milk and cook over boiling water until the mixture thickens, stirring all the time. Add the cheese and cook until it melts, then the sliced olives. Pour the mixture over the asparagus and top with the margarined crumbs.

Bake in a moderate oven for 15 minutes —or slightly more—until the crumbs are golden brown. Garnish with finely chopped parsley.

Vegetable Hot-pot (for 4)

1½ oz. margarine
6 peeled potatoes
8 small carrots
6 spring onions
6 oz. shelled fresh
   peas
¼ lb. runner beans
2 tomatoes
1 tablespoonful
   chopped parsley
1 teaspoonful mixed
   herbs
Salt and pepper

Heat margarine in saucepan and prepare vegetables. Cut potatoes in half and brown in heated fat. Add carrots, sprinkle with salt and pepper, cover and cook for 5–7 minutes. Add onions, peas, beans, herbs and ½ pint of water; cover and allow to simmer gently for 30 minutes. Halve tomatoes and place them, cut side uppermost, on top of the other vegetables, cooking for a further 5–10 minutes.

Garnish with the chopped parsley and serve.

Cheeseburgers, hot and sizzling, are an ideal supper dish. Serve them with spring onions and radish roses

SALADS

Canadian-style Country Salad

1 cucumber
4 tomatoes
Tarragon or herb
   vinegar
1 green pepper
2 sticks celery

Salt and pepper
1 tablespoonful
   minced or finely
   chopped onion
1 diced, unpeeled red
   apple, if liked

Wash and slice the tomatoes, peel and slice the cucumber; chop the green pepper and the celery into small pieces. Dice the apple and mix all together with the chopped or minced onion.

Season with salt and pepper to taste, and add the vinegar.

Canadian Tomato Salad

6 tomatoes
1 large clove garlic
1 tablespoonful
   chopped chives
2½ tablespoonfuls
   mayonnaise

1 tablespoonful finely
   chopped parsley
1 teaspoonful salt
1 teaspoonful mixed
   dried herbs
Pepper to taste

Wash the tomatoes and cut into large pieces, sprinkle the salt over and mix together lightly. Leave for 5 minutes, then drain.

Mix together the remaining ingredients and the garlic, cut into halves. Add this to the tomatoes and toss lightly. Cover and store in the refrigerator for 2–3 hours, if possible, before serving.

Montreal Chicken Salad

6 oz. cold cooked
   chicken
6 heaped tablespoon-
   fuls chopped celery
2 tablespoonfuls
   finely chopped
   green peppers

Lettuce
4 tomatoes
2 tablespoonfuls
   almonds
1 hard-boiled egg
Juice of ½ lemon
A few radishes
¼ pint mayonnaise

Chop the chicken into small pieces. Wash the lettuce. Blanch the almonds. Just slit the tomatoes into six portions, which remain joined together underneath. Prepare radishes.

Mix the chicken well with the celery, green peppers, blanched almonds and half the mayonnaise. Set the tomatoes out on a bed of lettuce, and fill each with the mixture; moisten with a little lemon juice and garnish with slices of hard-boiled egg and slices of radish.

Pile the remaining chicken mayonnaise in the centre of the dish and top with the rest of the mayonnaise.

Pear and Peanut Salad

1 lettuce	4 heaped tablespoonfuls diced celery
2 ripe eating pears	
2 dessertspoonfuls salted peanuts	2 tablespoonfuls capers
½ lemon	Paprika to taste
	Mayonnaise

Peel and core the pears and cut them into dice. Add lemon juice and mix well; then stir in the celery, peanuts, capers and enough mayonnaise to moisten. Arrange on a bed of crisp, washed and thoroughly dried lettuce, and sprinkle lightly with paprika.

This salad is improved if the mixture is chilled in a refrigerator before it is placed on the lettuce.

Salade aux Olives

4 oz. olives	½ pint (10 oz.) frozen or fresh peas (cooked)
1 spring onion	
2 heaped tablespoonfuls finely chopped green pepper	½ lemon
	Salt and pepper
6 heaped tablespoonfuls finely chopped celery	Dash of paprika
	½ teaspoonful made mustard
¼ pint mayonnaise	½ teaspoonful Worcester sauce
6 oz. processed cheese	

Mix together the olives, finely chopped, the chopped onion, green pepper, celery, peas and cheese cut into dice. Mix together the mayonnaise, lemon juice, mustard and Worcester sauce and combine with first mixture, seasoning with salt and pepper. (Chill at this point, if possible.)

Sprinkle over very lightly with paprika before serving.

SWEETS, COOKIES, Etc.

Butter Fruit Tartlets (for 4)

2 eggs	6 oz. seedless raisins and sultanas mixed
8 oz. light brown sugar	1 oz. chopped walnuts
2 tablespoonfuls vinegar	Short pastry (see Pastry chapter)
4 oz. butter	1 teaspoonful vanilla essence

Beat eggs lightly, just sufficiently to blend yolks and whites. Add sugar, vinegar and vanilla essence. Stir in melted butter and add fruit and nuts.

Line tartlet tins with pastry and fill each case about two-thirds full with the fruit and butter mixture. Bake in a hot oven for first 7 minutes; then reduce heat to moderate for balance of baking time—about 20–25 minutes, or until filling is firm.

Coconut Pie (for 4)

2 eggs	4 oz. sugar
Pinch of salt	4 oz. desiccated coconut
Short pastry (see Pastry chapter)	

Line a flan ring or tin with pastry. Beat eggs, add sugar, pinch of salt and coconut, stirring well in.

Pour into pastry-shell and bake in moderate oven for about 25–30 minutes, or until mixture is firm and a golden brown.

Coconut and Walnut Cookies

4 oz. butter or margarine	6 oz. flour
	2 oz. brown sugar
For the nut mixture	
8 oz. brown sugar	3 oz. desiccated coconut
3 tablespoonfuls flour	
½ teaspoonful vanilla essence	3 oz. finely chopped walnuts
2 egg-whites	

Rub the butter or margarine lightly into the flour. Add the sifted brown sugar and mix well. Pat this mixture well into a pan about 14 × 7 in. Bake in a moderate oven until a delicate golden brown, setting on a fairly high shelf so that it does not brown unduly on the bottom. Allow to cool.

For the nut mixture.—Mix together the flour and brown sugar, well sifted, and add the mixture gradually to the stiffly beaten egg-whites. Add the vanilla essence, and lightly fold in the coconut and walnuts.

Spread this mixture gently over the baked crumble crust, and return tin to oven, cooking in a slow oven until the nut méringue is delicately browned.

Remove from oven and, while still warm, cut into finger strips. Allow these to cool in the tin before removing.

Oatmeal Lace Cookies

7 oz. sugar	½ lb. flour
2 eggs	½ lb. quick-cooking porridge oats
1 teaspoonful powdered cinnamon	
	2 oz. chopped nuts
4 oz. seedless raisins	6 oz. mixed pure lard and margarine
½ pint water	Pinch of salt

468

Stew the raisins in the water and set aside.

Cream the sugar and fats together, and add the well-beaten eggs. Fold in the flour, salt and cinnamon. Add porridge oats, nuts and stewed raisins. Use sufficient of the liquid in which the raisins were cooked to make a dough which will drop from a spoon.

Drop the mixture in spoonfuls on to a greased baking sheet and cook in a hot oven for about 10 minutes.

Party Sandwich Loaf (for 8–10)

1 *unsliced sandwich loaf, one day old*	*Cheese frosting*
	Cheese spread
Radishes	*Parsley*
Watercress	*Tomatoes*

Chicken Salad Filling:

½ *cupful chopped cooked or canned chicken or turkey*	½ *teaspoonful salt*
	Grated rind of ½ *lemon*
¼ *cupful minced celery*	2 *tablespoonfuls mayonnaise*

Egg Salad Filling:

2 *hard-boiled eggs, finely chopped*	½ *teaspoonful prepared mustard*
2 *tablespoonfuls minced olives*	⅛ *teaspoonful curry powder*
½ *teaspoonful salt*	2 *tablespoonfuls mustard*

To make the fillings, combine the ingredients and chill until ready to use.

Cheese Frosting:

8 *oz. soft cream cheese*	¼ *lb. grated Cheddar Single cream*

Beat cream cheese until light and fluffy. Gradually blend in grated cheese with enough cream to make mixture light, fluffy and a good consistency for spreading.

Trim crusts from loaf and slice lengthwise into ½ in. slices. Spread alternate slices with different fillings. Frost top and sides of sandwich loaf with cheese frosting, garnish with sliced radishes, parsley and watercress.

The loaf will cut more easily and be easier to serve if prepared 6–12 hours in advance and stored in a refrigerator in a covered container.

No, not an iced cake but a party sandwich made by slicing a large loaf lengthwise, spreading with various savoury fillings and frosting all over with cream cheese

THE VERSATILE PASTA FAMILY

How to recognise good quality and how to cook the many varieties so that they are tasty, nourishing—and not fattening

MARCO POLO, it is rumoured, first introduced noodles to the Western world after one of his visits to China. True or not, it is a fact that pasta has now become the staple diet of the Italians, as well as being accepted all over the world as an economical and nutritious food.

Dozens of different kinds of pasta are to be bought in London's Soho, and the best are made from the same basic ingredient, durum wheat. This is a hard, glutinous wheat which is washed and then finely ground to meal, the husk and other rough parts being removed. Most important in the production of pasta is the selection of the finest wheat and the drying of the paste, which ensures that the finished product will be of the right colour and consistency when cooked.

Among the types most popular in the U.K. are macaroni, spaghetti, vermicelli, noodles, shells, bows, macaroni alphabets, and even animal shapes for children's soup. Incidentally, all these varieties are actually made in Britain, and since the finest-quality wheats are in many cases Empire-grown, these products have many advantages over their imported counterparts. The longer varieties should not break when being lifted from the pot after cooking, and other types should retain their shape.

The characteristics of a first-class macaroni or spaghetti are that it should be a creamy pale amber in colour, of a smooth appearance, and free from mottled specks or similar discolorations. It should break with a clean snap, leaving fresh glossy ends, and when cooked should be firm, non-sticky and have retained its shape.

Right Cooking Method

The most readily available type of paste product in the U.K. is macaroni, which may be used in any dish where pasta is required. It has a high protein content and is rich in energy-giving carbohydrates. Its low fibre content makes it readily assimi-lated without any irritating effects on the digestive system, and it is thus suitable for both children and invalids.

An excellent standby in the kitchen, easily and quickly prepared, pasta should not be spoiled by bad cooking. It should always be plunged into plenty of salted, fast-boiling water, and removed while still firm, and not after it has been stewed to a pulp. Time of cooking varies with individual products—about 8 minutes for quick-cooking varieties, and 15–25 minutes for stick or thicker types.

Many people steer clear of pasta because they believe it to be "fattening," but, in fact, most of the free starch is removed after cooking, by placing the pasta in a colander and running hot water through it. This rinsing is essential for perfection of taste and texture if the pasta is being served with a sauce and not being cooked in with the main ingredients.

Need Not Boil Over

A useful hint in the cooking of pasta is to add a spoonful of olive oil or a knob of margarine to the cooking water to prevent it from boiling over. To give your spaghetti or macaroni a glossy appearance, toss it in a little fat after cooking. This also helps to drive off excess water.

Pasta, and particularly macaroni, is the most versatile of foods, and can be served with meat, fish or cheese as a main dish; as an accompaniment to the main dish; in soups and in sweets. Cold macaroni, blended with a sauce, can make a substantial addition to salads.

The recipes that follow give some idea of the uses to which pasta may be put. Spaghetti or noodles can often be substituted for macaroni, if so desired.

SOUPS

A Hint for all Soups . . .

Cook a handful of macaroni, drain well, toss in 1 oz. melted fat and leave to become

These are some of the innumerable varieties of Pasta now obtainable quite easily in London's Soho and in many other parts of the world as well, where the virtues of the Italian's national dish are now being discovered

cold. Add to soup before serving, and it will be found that the delicious nutty flavour of the pasta is retained and the texture remains firm.

Noodle Soup—Spanish Style (for 4)

1 pint stock	1 dessertspoonful
4 oz. cooked noodles	flour
1 small onion	Salt and pepper to
1 small can pimento	taste
Fat for frying	

Chop onion finely, fry golden brown in fat. Stir in flour, cook for 5 minutes over low heat, stirring all the time. Add stock and noodles, and boil for 5 minutes. Chop pimento coarsely, add to the soup with salt and pepper and boil for 1 minute.

Shrimp and Macaroni Soup (for 4)

1 pint shrimps	½ pint stock
4 oz. macaroni	1 small onion
½ pint cider	chopped
1 teaspoonful	1 teaspoonful
Worcester sauce	chopped parsley
Salt and pepper to	2 oz. margarine or
taste	butter

Cook onion in margarine until soft, add shrimps and parsley, cook for 5 minutes, add cider and stock. Bring to the boil, add macaroni, season and boil until cooked. A teaspoonful of Worcester sauce may be added before serving.

Genoese Soup (for 4–6)

8 oz. macaroni or	2 bay leaves or
noodles	marjoram leaves
1 quart stock, or 1	2 tablespoonfuls
quart water and 3	grated cheese
meat cubes	Salt and pepper to
1 egg	taste

Bring the stock, or water and meat cubes, to the boil and add the bay or marjoram leaves and the macaroni. Cook for 5 minutes. Mix the egg with 2 tablespoonfuls of the soup, season and boil for 1 minute, remove the herbs, sprinkle cheese on top and serve at once.

MEAT AND FISH DISHES

Oxtail Suprême

½ lb. macaroni or	1 chopped carrot
noodles	1 cupful beer or
1 oxtail	cider
2 oz. fat from oxtail	Salt and pepper
½ lb. tomatoes	2 bay leaves
1 teaspoonful paprika	1 small can processed
2 onions	peas

Cut oxtail into pieces, removing surplus fat. Fry in the fat until browned, stir in paprika, fry for another 5 minutes. Add sliced tomatoes, sliced onions and carrot. Stir well, add beer or cider, salt and pepper and bay leaves. Simmer in oven or on hot plate for 2 hours. Cook macaroni or noodles in plenty of well-salted boiling water (only 7 minutes if quick-cooking variety) and drain well. Toss in a little butter or margarine, mix with the peas, arrange round edge of large warmed serving dish, pour oxtail mixture into centre, then warm through in oven.

Sausage and Tomato Macaroni (for 4–6)

8 oz. macaroni	¼ pint thick tomato
½ lb. sausages	sauce or purée
2 medium-sized	6 chopped olives
onions	(optional)
½ saltspoonful pepper	1 teaspoonful salt
Fat for frying	

Put macaroni on to cook. Cut the sausages into 1-in. pieces and fry. Remove from pan and fry the chopped onions in the fat until a delicate brown. Return sausages to pan, add the tomato sauce or purée and the chopped olives, if used. Drain the macaroni and fold in the sausages, onions, etc., and season with salt and pepper. Place in a greased pie dish and bake in a slow oven for 15–20 minutes.

Spaghetti Italienne (for 4)

This is a basic recipe which can be used for any type of pasta.

½ lb. spaghetti (or	2 tablespoonfuls
other pasta)	tomato purée
1 tablespoonful flour	1 onion
½ pint water	Tomato sauce
4 oz. grated cheese	Fat for frying

Cook spaghetti for 15 minutes (if quick macaroni is used, cook for 8 minutes). Blend flour with a little cold water from ½ pint. Boil rest of water, add to flour, stirring constantly. Re-boil, add tomato purée. Season and simmer for 3 minutes. Cook chopped onion gently in fat. Add tomato sauce, grated cheese and spaghetti, well drained. Serve with grated cheese served separately.

Macaroni and Fish in Scallop Shells (for 4)

4 deep scallop shells	1 cupful cooked fish,
1 cupful cooked	lobster or shrimps
macaroni	½ cupful white sauce
2 tablespoonfuls	(see Sauces chapter)
butter	1 lightly beaten egg
2 tablespoonfuls grated cheese	
(½-pint cups used throughout)	

Sausage and Tomato Macaroni is a tasty and satisfying lunch or supper dish—particularly good if garnished, as here, with stuffed olives

Butter the four shells. Mix the hot macaroni with the butter and cheese, and partly fill each shell with this mixture. Place the fish, shredded, on the bed of macaroni, cover with the white sauce mixed with the egg, sprinkle with a little cheese and bake for 10 minutes in a hot oven.

Macaroni Fish Loaf
(for 5–6)

6 oz. quick macaroni
1 lb. white fish, flaked
   and boned
1 dessertspoonful
   lemon juice
1 teaspoonful grated
   onion
½ pint milk
2 eggs
Salt and pepper
Slices of cucumber
2 slices lemon
2 tablespoonfuls
   breadcrumbs

Macaroni Fish Loaf is both cool and decorative for a summer meal—and ideal for a picnic, with its fresh garnish of sliced cucumber and ornamental lemon slices

Cook macaroni for 8 minutes. Drain. Mix with milk, fish, lemon juice, grated onion and eggs, lightly beaten. Season to taste. Grease loaf tin, sprinkle with breadcrumbs and bake for 40 minutes in a moderate oven. Cool, turn out of tin and garnish with slices of cucumber and rounds of lemon peel.

SAVOURY DISHES

Macaroni Cheese (for 4)

Cheese and pasta are often combined in cooking, and of the many dishes known in the U.K., perhaps macaroni cheese is the most popular. There are many variations of this dish, and the following are two basic recipes which can be amended according to taste.

4 oz. quick macaroni	¼ teaspoonful paprika
2 oz. cornflour	3–4 oz. grated cheese
½ pint milk	Dash Yorkshire
¼ teaspoonful	relish
mustard powder	Pinch salt
Knob of margarine	Breadcrumbs

Cook macaroni until tender. Drain, keeping liquor. Blend the cornflour with a little milk taken from ½ pint, add rest of milk to ½ pint macaroni liquor and boil. Stir into blended cornflour, return to pan, simmer for 3 minutes, stirring constantly. Add margarine, mustard powder and paprika, Yorkshire relish and salt. Add grated cheese. Stir, add macaroni, reheat gently without overcooking cheese. Pour into fireproof dish, sprinkle with mixed breadcrumbs and grated cheese, dot with margarine and brown under grill. Garnish with chopped parsley and triangles of toast, if desired.

Savoury Cheese Macaroni (for 4)

8 oz. macaroni	3 eggs
½ oz. butter or	1 teaspoonful salt
margarine	Pinch Cayenne
4 oz. bacon	pepper
4 oz. grated cheese	

Cook macaroni in plenty of boiling, salted water. Drain and turn into a heated dish. Dot with butter or margarine and keep warm. Cut the bacon across into thin strips, add the beaten eggs and seasoning, and scramble until the mixture begins to thicken. Add to the macaroni with the 4 oz. grated cheese, and give the macaroni a good stir. Garnish and serve at once. Serve a bowl of grated cheese separately.

Macaroni with Chestnuts (for 4)

4 oz. macaroni	3 tablespoonfuls
8 oz. chestnuts	cream or top of
Salt and pepper	milk
2 oz. grated cheese	2 oz. margarine

Cook the macaroni and drain well. Slit skins of chestnuts and boil for 20 minutes, remove outer and inner skins and chop roughly. Mix chestnuts and macaroni, season with salt and pepper, and put in a greased baking dish. Sprinkle with grated cheese and dot with margarine. Add the cream or top of milk and bake in a moderate oven for 20 minutes.

DESSERTS

Apricot Macaroni Meringue (for 4–5)

2 oz. macaroni	1 small can of apricots
6 eggs	½ pint milk
1 dessertspoonful	1 dessertspoonful
cornflour	sugar

Cook macaroni until tender, and strain. Chop apricots and fold through macaroni. Make a custard by beating the egg-yolks, then stirring into the heated milk, blended with the cornflour. Cook gently without boiling until mixture thickens. When thick, fold into macaroni. Beat the egg-whites until very stiff, adding sugar. Pile on top of mixture and cook in hot oven until meringue is set and just turned in colour. About 15 minutes. Serve hot.

Noodle Omelet

3 tablespoonfuls milk	3 eggs, lightly beaten
½ teaspoonful salt	3 cupfuls cooked
3 tablespoonfuls	noodles
butter or margarine	Fat for frying
	Sugar

Add milk and seasoning to eggs. Sauté the noodles in butter or margarine until lightly browned, then pour in egg mixture and mix. Heat a little fat in omelet pan, pour in noodle mixture and when set fold in half. Dust with sugar and serve immediately.

Noodles with Cream Cheese (for 4)

½ lb. noodles	6 oz. cream or cottage
2 tablespoonfuls	cheese
warm water	3 dessertspoonfuls
½ teaspoonful	sugar
cinnamon	3 oz. sultanas

Add noodles to plenty of salted boiling water and cook until tender. Soak sultanas in boiling water for 15 minutes. Mix cheese with warm water, sugar and cinnamon.

Macaroni Cheese may not sound exciting but there are many variations; here is a delicious one, crisp and brown on top, served with triangles of toast

Add to drained noodles, together with sultanas, previously dried in a cloth.

Macaroni and Date Charlotte (for 4)

3 oz. macaroni	1 pint milk
1 tablespoonful sugar	2 eggs
	4 oz. chopped dates

For sprinkling

2 oz. margarine	1 teaspoonful sugar
2 oz. breadcrumbs	Grated nutmeg

Cook the macaroni and drain well. Add the sugar and milk, and simmer for 5 minutes. Remove from the heat and add the slightly beaten eggs, stirring well. Put the chopped dates in a well-greased pie dish; pour in the macaroni mixture. Melt the margarine in a saucepan, add the crumbs, teaspoonful of sugar and the grated nutmeg. Stir until the margarine has been absorbed by the crumbs, then spread on top of the macaroni. Bake for 20 minutes in a hot oven, or until the top is browned.

SALAD SAUCES

Here are three basic sauces for use with cold macaroni in salads.

Tomato-Onion Sauce

Simmer 1 large, coarsely chopped onion in 1 cupful of water, with salt, pepper and a dash of sugar. When tender, add 1 small can tomato purée. Blend 1 heaped teaspoonful flour with a little water and thicken sauce. Mix well with macaroni. Serve cold.

Creamy Cheese Sauce

Blend 1 teaspoonful cornflour with 1 cupful evaporated milk. Put in saucepan with 1 cupful grated sharp cheese, salt and pepper. Simmer until cheese is melted, stirring constantly. Add some finely chopped spring onions and mix with macaroni. Serve cold.

Celery Cheese Sauce

Drain the macaroni and keep hot. Mix 1 large cupful grated cheese with $\frac{1}{2}$ cupful macaroni water. Bring to the boil, season with pepper and a teaspoonful of celery salt. Mix with hot macaroni. Cool before serving.

THE DECORATION OF FOOD

*Dyed Easter eggs . . . tomato men . . . a sandwich tower . . .
rainbow-hued jellies and heraldic gingerbread, all described*

and illustrated by NINA DE YORKE

THERE are two important principles to be considered in cooking: pleasing the palate and pleasing the eye. One achieves the first by means of the second. Not nearly enough attention is paid to the presentation of food.

It is so easy to make even the dullest dish look attractive. For example, fish is in itself very decorative, yet *steamed plaice* has, for many of us, the most unpleasant associations. But try this way of presenting it: Before cooking, rub the white sides of the fish with lemon to bleach them. Lightly steam the fillets, leaving them in their black skins. Lay them alternately on your dish—one black, one white, etc., so that you get a pattern of light and dark which compels interest. Choose brightly coloured vegetables and arrange them round the fish.

Use of Colour

We have certain inherent feelings towards colour in food which are most important when considering its presentation. Dark colours are often associated unconsciously in our minds with dirt, and we hardly ever colour food blue or green. Green is the colour of nature, but it is also the colour of poison.

Always try to include at least one example of naturally decorative food, such as sliced tomatoes or fried egg, when arranging each meal. Keep a bunch of parsley at hand. It looks more interesting in its natural state. Chives are also a useful decoration, and a sprinkling of chopped watercress is to be thoroughly recommended on almost any type of unsweetened dish. It adds a most distinctive flavour and

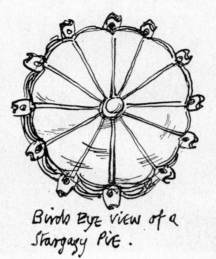

Birds Eye view of a
Stargazy Pie.

an attractive dash of dark green to any dish. A subtle visual effect can also be achieved by using Cayenne pepper instead of the ordinary kind.

Pies are the easiest dishes to decorate. The reason for their particular shapes is usually very practical. A Cornish Pasty has a join along the top because it was considered less likely to spill the gravy that way when it was baked in the old Cornish hearth ovens. Certain pie fillings have traditional decorations. Apple pies, for example, are traditionally covered with wide strips of lattice which should be "nailed" together with cloves.

Stargazy Pie is an interesting-looking dish for a Buffet Supper. It is an old recipe and was originally made from pilchards, but any fish of a similar shape will do, and even sprats could be used as a filling for tiny individual pies. It was considered wasteful to cover the fish-heads with pastry, but if they were cut off, the rich oil would be lost. So the fish were laid, tails together, heads outwards like the spokes of a wheel, on a round dish and covered with a circle of pastry, leaving their heads bare. You can add your own decoration by cutting the remainder of the pastry into thin strips and laying them on the pastry cover to form the spokes of the wheel.

Decorating with Pastry

Pastry lends itself very well to all sorts of designs and patterns. You can plait and twist to your heart's content. Try decorating your next pie with enormous pastry flowers. Cut out of the remains of the pie pastry three sets of petals, each set a little larger than the previous one. For a medium-sized pie, the largest petals should be 3 in. long. Arrange the petals to form a flower, working in layers inwards and curving the petals slightly to make them look natural. Make several flowers for a large pie.

Decorated Easter eggs are easily made by drawing an original design on a hard-boiled egg with a piece of sharpened candle wax. Dip the egg into cochineal or some other harmless dye and the wax will form a white pattern on the coloured ground. This is the Czechoslovakian method. The Caucasian way is to tie the hard-boiled eggs in different coloured scraps of material and boil them again for a few minutes. Remove from the saucepan and unwrap them when they have cooled and you will discover the most beautiful multi-coloured marbled eggs. Finally, polish them with goose fat to make them glow.

Salad Ideas

Here are a few ideas to help with salads: Chop your lettuce into long thin slices. It looks more unusual, and it goes farther too. Serve a small plate of lettuce salad with the main dish as they do on the Continent. To keep it from becoming limp and discoloured, always cut lettuce with a steel knife. Leave the rind on the cucumber; it is easier to digest and looks much more at-

Radishes and a Tomato Man.

An Easter Egg.

tractive. Cut patterns on radishes; this is easier to do than it looks. Sprinkle capers and slices of raw pimento over your salad.

Making tomato men is a good way of keeping children busy. Choose a few very large firm tomatoes and slice off the tops. Scoop out enough of the inside to allow a hard-boiled egg to sit firmly on each tomato. Fix the remainder of the tomato on each egg to make a hat and secure with a cocktail stick. Mark out the face and hair with black peppers and make legs and arms with celery stalks.

Celery in a jug on the table looks more attractive if the ends are curled. This you can do by drawing the point of a skewer through, from the top, dividing the celery into strips for about 5 in.

Open sandwiches provide a great many

opportunities for ingenuity. Cut with a pastry cutter into various shapes or roll them up and secure with cocktail sticks. Cut the crusts neatly off and sink them trellis-wise in extra rich sandwich spread. Make squares, Battenberg fashion, of closed or open sandwiches.

A good idea for parties is a Sandwich Tower. Buy a cylindrical loaf and carefully cut the whole into sandwiches with different-coloured fillings. Cut each sandwich in half and then build up the tower—one sandwich on top of another. Pass a wide ribbon underneath and tie at the top with a huge bow.

Although Chaudfroid of Chicken looks complicated, it is in actual fact quite easy to make at home. It was discovered accidentally by the Mareschal of Luxembourg, who was called away from table for some time. When he returned, he ate the food which had got cold and was so delighted with its taste that he had it served that way in future. It is made by cooking a chicken and making $\frac{3}{4}$ pint of white sauce and $\frac{1}{4}$ pint of aspic jelly. Cut the white flesh of the chicken into large pieces and lay them on a rack. Add the aspic jelly to the sauce, and when it is smooth but not set, pour over the chicken; decorate with slices of hard-boiled egg, ham, tomatoes, cucumber, etc., cut into shapes. When the chicken has set, coat each portion with liquid aspic jelly and arrange on a bed of the remainder of the chicken (boned), mixed with a salad and seasoned.

Choosing the right china in which to present your dishes is equally important. Dark colours and over-patterned dishes rarely show the food to advantage. Contemporary china is excellent for casual decoration, but traditionally decorative foods look their best on silver dishes; so do jellies and sweets, which also look very attractive served in cut-glass bowls or individual dishes.

Old Jelly Moulds

It is sad that the use of moulds has declined. If you have any old-fashioned ones in good condition, do use them. They were made in much more interesting shapes then than they are to-day. To get the best results for multi-coloured jellies, cut a piece of cardboard to fit the middle of the mould very closely and pour different-coloured jellies down the sides. Wait for them to set, remove the cardboard and fill the remainder with yet another colour.

Make cakes and puddings in moulds which should be well buttered before filling. Here is a delicious recipe which should be made in a Continental-type mould with a hole in the centre:

Take $\frac{1}{2}$ lb. shelled walnuts, 8 tablespoonfuls of castor sugar, 8 eggs and 3 tablespoonfuls home-made bread-crumbs, vanilla and a little rum or brandy. Beat the egg-yolks and the sugar to a white creamy consistency and add the walnuts, breadcrumbs and vanilla and mix thoroughly. Whip the egg-whites until stiff, add to the mixture and pour into the mould. Bake in a cool oven for about $\frac{3}{4}$ hour. Dilute a sherry glass of rum or brandy with a tumbler of water, add sugar to taste and bring to the boil. While both the cake and the rum are still hot, pour slowly over the cake.

Old fashioned Jelly moulds and an Orange Basket.

Flower Pie and Curled Celery.

Just before serving, whip double cream with sugar and fill the hole and surround the cake, sprinkle with cinnamon and decorate with roasted walnut halves.

Now that so many people have electric mixers, it is much easier to make the complicated sweets that used to take hours to whisk by hand. Here is a beautiful-looking one: Pulp and sweeten ½ dozen apples. Whisk six egg-whites and add two tablespoonfuls of sugar. Mix the two together until stiff. To make the outside crisp, put in the oven for 2 minutes to harden. Garnish with tarragon leaves and slices of sugared fruit.

Try arranging fresh fruit with moss and tiny fern leaves as a centrepiece for the table. Orange baskets are great favourites with children. Mark out, on half of each orange, a diamond pattern. On the other half mark the handle, which should be ½ in. wide and include the stalk end of the fruit. Scoop out the inside and cut your pattern with a sharp-pointed knife and push out the unwanted pieces from the inside with the flat end of a spoon. Fill the baskets with jelly and garnish with glacé cherries and angelica speared on cocktail sticks.

Here is an American recipe for Gingerbread. Warm ½ lb. of treacle and stir in ¼ lb. of butter. Mix and sift together 4 tablespoonfuls of sugar, a pinch of mixed spice, 3 teaspoonfuls of ginger, finely sliced lemon rind and 1 lb. of flour and stir into the treacle and butter. Dissolve 1 teaspoonful of bicarbonate of soda in a tablespoonful of warm cream, add to the mixture and stir well. Roll out about ½ in. thick and cut into large heraldic and fleur-de-lys shapes. Lay them on a greased tin and bake for 15 minutes in a moderate oven. Decorate with cloves.

Given at Tournaments

The oldest gingerbread was not a cake, but a solid slab of honey, baked flour and ginger. In medieval days it was a popular gift, rather like expensive chocolates to-day. It was given at tournaments and appropriately it seems to have been designed to imitate armour, being coloured a deep tawny brown shade, polished with egg-white and decorated with clusters of six small box leaves to form a fleur-de-lys and gilt-headed cloves driven in like nails. A wonderful chance to revive, even if only in gingerbread, the glory of pageantry.

For a decorative summer drink, peel a pineapple, cut into thin slices, place in a bowl, cover with castor sugar and leave for a few hours. Bring the peel to the boil in a little water, skim and pour over pineapple. Add 6 oz. sugar and a bottle of wine and chill. Just before drinking add a bottle of soda water or—for the millionaire touch—champagne.

COOKING WITH WINE

It need not be in the least exotic or extravagant,
but what a difference it makes to the simplest food

LET'S first put it out of our heads that cooking with wine is (*a*) exotic, and (*b*) reserved for Continental types or the very rich. It can, of course, be exotic, but so can steak and kidney pudding with a dozen or so oysters added—you ask any connoisseur of this English classic. As for expense, you can buy extremely good wines for 5*s.* to 6*s.* a bottle, and since one uses it mostly by the tablespoonful, a bottle of wine will go a long way.

If you intend to try cooking with wine off your own bat, adding wine to your favourite dishes, remember that, generally speaking, fish and white wine go together, and meat usually calls for red wine. This is much too simple a division, but it is a good starting point.

You might also like to remember that lobster and crayfish have an affinity for sherry—and an even greater one for sherry and cream. And here is an "after the cinema" dish which has the double virtue of being made in about 10 minutes and tasting quite delicious.

QUICK DISHES

For two people you need one good-sized crayfish tail (out of season you can buy frozen ones), which the fishmonger will split for you, so that scooping it out of its shell is easy. You can use it either in its two halves or cut into smaller pieces. Make your very best white sauce (much nicer made with butter), add the crayfish, and then a glass of sherry, and let it get good and hot without reaching the boil. If there is a tablespoonful of thick cream available, or even the top of the milk, stir it in at the last moment. The cream is not essential, but it does add that touch. Dish up sprinkled with parsley and eat it piping hot with, or without, some crisp thin toast.

Alternatively, toast some thin bread on one side only, butter the untoasted side,

spread with Parmesan cheese (which *must* be the powdered kind) mixed to a paste with vermouth, clap two pieces together—and eat. Good for parties, too.

SAUCES

Perhaps the most familiar method of cooking with wine is the making of sauces. One of the best known is Sauce Espagnole, a sauce that was equally well known in France and England some three hundred years ago—and the only thing Spanish about it is its name.

Sauce Espagnole

Chop 2 oz. of bacon into tiny pieces and fry in 1 oz. of butter, adding a few sliced mushrooms, a carrot and an onion, both chopped. When the vegetables begin to brown, stir in 1 oz. of flour and cook till smooth, then add a gill of stock (the best stock for this sauce is made from veal bones), salt and pepper, and simmer very gently for half an hour. Then add 2 tomatoes cut into small pieces, 2 tablespoonfuls of sherry and cook for a further 10 minutes.

You can, if you wish, use Burgundy or Madeira for this sauce, or, if you feel that way about it, Champagne. With rather less stock added, it makes an excellent filling for omelets.

Madeira Sauce is another classic, and is particularly good with baked or grilled ham.

Begin by making a roux, using water instead of milk, and 1 oz. of butter to a tablespoonful of flour. To this add a wineglass of Madeira and one of a good meat stock, and, of course, salt and pepper. The Madeira should be added gradually.

White Sauce—the only sauce the English can make, according to the French—*can* be so dull if it is badly made, but it can be very good, particularly when "dressed up." Our old friend parsley sauce, for instance, takes very happily to the addition of chopped chives, in small quantity, and a dessert-spoonful of white wine. To go with fish, try adding a few shrimps or prawns, or some coarsely chopped hard-boiled eggs, with some grated lemon and a dessert-spoonful of white wine, preferably Chablis.

Hungarian Sauce—so useful because it goes with every kind of meat.

Brown 1 lb. of chopped onions in butter or lard (or, better still, kidney fat), add a large pinch of paprika, a glass of white wine, a pint of sour cream, bring it all to the boil, and serve. For variation, add chopped tomato too.

Old English Sauce is designed to mate with venison, but it goes equally well with mutton.

Boil 1 oz. of currants in water for a few minutes; add 3 tablespoonfuls of grated bread, a walnut-sized piece of butter, 4 cloves and a glass of port, and stir till it boils. Serve hot.

Sherry Sauce—for puddings, but equally happy with a lemon soufflé.

Put 2 egg-yolks, 5 tablespoonfuls of sherry and a teaspoonful of castor sugar into a double boiler (or a basin over a pan of boiling water) and beat until the mixture thickens, but do not boil. Remove from the stove and stir in 1 tablespoonful of thick cream.

SOUPS

The canning of soups has been brought to such a high art that it is no longer a heinous offence to own a can opener. But, good as they are (particularly when glorified a little by the cook), some proud

Any fairly large fresh- or sea-water fish is excellent stuffed with savoury rice or a vegetable mixture and cooked in wine

hostesses like to show that they can still make their own. Have a care, though, in adding wine to your soups: increasing the quantity recommended in a recipe does not necessarily improve the flavour. But for fun—*and* good flavour—let's start with a soup that comes from Belgium and is nearly all wine.

Wine Soup

Boil equal quantities of red wine and sweetened water with a stick of cinnamon. Pour it over toasted bread (or biscuits, if you prefer them), and there's your soup.

Mussel Soup (which sounds much more grandiose if you call it Moules Marinière).

Put 1½ pints of fish stock (or water with lots of fish bones) into a pan with 3 tablespoonfuls of white wine, and add a bouquet garni and a clove of garlic. Bring to the boil and simmer for 20 minutes. Make a thickening of 1 oz. of butter with flour and seasoning, and when smooth add to the stock. Stir till it boils, then simmer for 15 minutes.

Wash and scrub the mussels, and put them into another pan, with 3 tablespoonfuls of wine. Cover and bring to the boil, then shake over the heat for 2 or 3 minutes, and strain the liquor into the soup. Beard the mussels, but leave them in a half shell, and put them into the soup with some finely chopped parsley. Simmer for 5 minutes, add 2 tablespoonfuls of cream and serve.

Shrimp Soup

You need 1 onion, 1 leek, 1 carrot, cut into thin slices; put them into a pan with a bunch of mixed herbs and a clove and 2 wineglassfuls of white wine and bring to the boil. Then throw in the unshelled shrimps and cook for 10 minutes. Remove the shrimps and shell just a few of them, cutting up the flesh into small pieces. Grind the remainder into a paste (yes, the shells too) and return it to the pan with 1½ pints of fish stock (or water), 2 oz. of rice and 2 tablespoonfuls of tomato purée. Cook on a fairly low heat, with a cover on, for 1 hour. Then pass it through a sieve, forcing through with a wooden spoon any lumps of shrimp or vegetable, season, bring almost to the boil; add the cut-up pieces of shrimp and serve really hot.

Bean Soup

Soak ½ lb. dried haricot or butter beans overnight and cook them the next day in the same water until they are mushy, and beat them until smooth. Brown 2 oz. flour in 1 oz. of butter, mix with the beans and add 2 pints of white stock (or a mixture of water and milk), season and simmer for an hour. Add a gill of sour cream, 3 oz. grated cheese and a wineglassful of white wine. Reheat, but do not boil, and serve, preferably with croûtons.

Potato Cream Soup

Cook in 1 oz. of butter, 1 lb. of cubed old potatoes and some diced celery—do not brown. Add 1½ pints of stock and simmer till potatoes are cooked, then rub through a sieve and add an onion (into which you have stuck several cloves), and a quart of fresh milk, and return to stove. Cook slowly for an hour, remove the onion and thicken with 3 oz. of flour, blended into a smooth paste before adding. Finally, add a gill of evaporated milk and 2 wineglassfuls of white wine and stir well.

Clear Game Soup

Simmer 2 rashers of diced bacon, 1 onion and a stick of celery, chopped, in about 2 oz. of butter with the giblets and carcase of any game bird. Broil all together briskly, add a quart of stock, stirring all the time, then simmer for a further half-hour. Add a few cooked peas, some small pieces of game if available, reheat and add a glass of sherry.

FISH

Take a look at the wondrous displays of fish on almost any fishmonger's slab in the U.K.—and think what a sorry sight it makes when it appears on so many family tables—slightly grey and almost invariably accompanied by a solid white sauce. We have some of the world's best fish, and we should treat it with the respect it deserves. Choose your sauces to enhance, and not to mask, the flavour of the fish itself, and at all costs avoid that soiled-looking pink dab which goes by the name of anchovy sauce.

There is a recipe which is usually given for the cooking of sole or plaice fillets, but it is especially good for the unfairly despised cod. Put pieces of cod (the pieces should be serving size) into a flat casserole with a good sprinkling of finely shaved onions and sliced mushrooms, pepper and salt, a generous glassful of white wine and a dab or two of butter. Cook in the oven until tender, and serve with a sauce made from the usual butter and flour, cooked with the liquid from the fish and thinned with milk, to which you should add shrimps or more mushrooms. Pour the sauce round, not on, the fish, and remember a touch of green—chopped parsley, or a few sprigs of watercress.

Sole Normande

Make a white roux with a dessertspoonful of flour, a tablespoonful of butter, half a glass of water, and a glass of white wine. Let it bubble a minute or two, then put in the prepared sole, and let it poach gently

Poached fish steaks are particularly good served with Sherry Sauce. Here the steaks are seen "sandwiched" together in pairs with savoury stuffing

for about 20 minutes. Clean a dozen mussels, cook them and remove from their shells, then put them to keep warm, saving the liquor from their cooking. Shell half a pound of shrimps. Cook in butter half a pound of mushrooms. *Now*, strain the sauce, very carefully, off the sole, add to it the liquor from the mussels and from the mushrooms, reducing a little if necessary —then add, away from the fire, the beaten yolks of 2 eggs and 3 dessertspoonfuls of double cream. Serve the sole surrounded with the shrimps, mushrooms and mussels and mask with the sauce. This sounds a great deal more complex than it really is, but the flavour is well worth any amount of trouble.

Baked Fish

This recipe is ideal for any large freshwater fish, but can be very happily used for fresh haddock or cod. Chop finely a large onion, a stick of celery and a carrot and fry them lightly in olive oil or butter, adding when they are just getting tender a handful of finely chopped parsley and some peeled, chopped tomatoes. Stuff the cleaned fish (if you have a nice fishmonger, he will take out the backbone, which makes it very

much easier) with the vegetable mixture; put the fish into a fireproof dish, dot with butter, add the liquid from the vegetables, cover with red or white wine and simmer gently until it is cooked through.

A variation on this theme is to stuff the fish with a savoury rice—that is, rice (already cooked) mixed with chopped fried mushrooms, a very small quantity of herbs and an even smaller quantity of tarragon. If you are too generous with the tarragon, it covers every other flavour. For this dish dot with butter and allow to cook for a little while before adding the wine—white for preference. Bream is ideal for this method.

Poached Fish with Sherry Sauce

Make a sherry sauce by blending 1 oz. of melted butter with 1 oz. of flour and adding $\frac{1}{4}$ pint of fish stock and a tablespoonful of sherry. Stir all the time until it reaches boiling point, then add a bay leaf and a small shallot and reduce by simmering. Add 1 egg-yolk mixed with a tablespoonful of cream, and then a dessertspoonful of lemon juice, a little salt and some Cayenne pepper.

Serve the sauce with any white fish, preferably the kind you buy in steaks, such

483

as turbot, which has been poached in boiling water with a teaspoonful of lemon juice and seasoning. Garnish with parsley.

MEAT

Recipes for cooking every kind of meat, poultry and game with wine are legion, but with a little experience a good cook will find her own moments for the addition of wine to a favoured dish. One small tip—if you are roasting wild duck, teal or widgeon, make the gravy (before you remove the bird) by pouring off most of the fat, leaving the delicious juices and adding a wineglassful of red wine. Put the dish back in the oven for a few minutes, and at the last squeeze just a few drops of lemon juice into it. Another tip is to add a glass of port to our old friend steak and kidney pudding (with a funnel inserted under the top crust) just before it is served.

Pork with Red or White Wine

Take 1 pork chop for each person, and even if they are quite fat, dot them with butter (though not lavishly), sprinkle with mixed herbs, add a tablespoonful or so of water and a glass of white wine. Cover the fireproof dish with greaseproof paper and put into a really hot oven for about 15 minutes, then reduce the heat and let the chops cook very slowly for at least 1½ hours. About half an hour before they are ready, add some small mushrooms, which you should push *under* the meat, and just before you serve, take off the superfluous fat, but not all of it, add a little more wine and one gherkin to each person. The gherkins look prettier and heat through in the sauce more quickly if you slice them, like a fan, down to the stalk.

If you are using red wine instead of white, add when putting in the mushrooms. When properly cooked, you will find the meat is so tender that your greatest difficulty is serving it. It is wise, therefore, to cook it in a dish which can be taken to the table.

To vary this dish you can put in onions and/or tomatoes when the meat first goes in the oven, or use different herbs.

Beef Olives

These take quite a long time to prepare, but your reward comes with the appreciation of your guests.

Each olive requires a piece of really good stewing beef about 3 in. square, and you should allow 4 or 5 to each person. A good butcher will prepare the pieces for you, but see that they are *really* thin, something like ¼ in. Make a stuffing of herbs (as distinct from sage) and onions, as one does for pork, adding chopped hard-boiled egg if you like, and spread a little over each piece of beef. Then roll each piece up and secure with very fine string or thread, which must be removed before serving. Roll in seasoned flour and fry in a good beef dripping until they are a tempting brown, then put them either into a casserole or a good thick saucepan with meat stock or water and a generous glass of red wine. The liquid should cover them by about an inch. Simmer them for a minimum of 2 hours, but longer if possible.

Bœuf Bourguignon

Cut 1 lb. stewing beef into fairly small pieces and chop 2 or 3 rashers of bacon, and brown them in ½ oz. butter with about 6 small onions. Drain off the butter, sprinkle a little flour into the pan and add two very finely chopped cloves of garlic. Pour in ½ pint of red wine and a little water —just enough to cover the contents of the pan, and add salt and pepper. Cover the pan and simmer for 2 hours, but half an hour before the end add 4 oz. mushrooms cut into thin slices.

German Veal à la Minute

Cut some thin slices of veal about 4 in. long, pepper and salt them and lay them in a deep dish with nearly ½ pint of white wine. Let it stand for 3 hours. Cover the bottom of a stewpan with butter, sprinkle both sides of the veal with flour, add a little more wine and enough white stock to cover it, together with the juice of a lemon. Simmer then for 5 to 10 minutes and serve.

Spanish Steak Stew

You need a thick piece of rump steak larded with fat bacon, and anchovies if you like them. Put it into a dish lined with fat smoked bacon, mixed herbs and spices to taste (*no salt*), 2 cloves of garlic, 2 shallots and a glass of white wine, and simmer very slowly for 5 to 6 hours. Strain the sauce, add a lump of butter with a little flour and some capers, thicken it over the stove and pour it round the steak.

Bœuf en Daube (for 4)

Cut up into small cubes about 1½ lb. of stewing steak, carefully removing the fat. Melt 1 oz. of lard or dripping in a large strong pan, add a couple of diced bacon rashers, two sliced onions, two sliced tomatoes and a calf's foot or pig's trotter cut in half (this is optional, but you will find it vastly improves the dish). Brown all these ingredients and the cut-up steak very gently. Then add mixed herbs, a bay leaf, two cloves of garlic, pepper and salt, a good wineglassful of red wine and sufficient stock (or, if you have none, water strengthened with a little Marmite) to cover the meat completely. Cover the pan and cook in a slow oven for about 5 hours.

Baked Chicken

Cut up a chicken and fry it in oil with some bacon, then lay it in a saucepan and on each piece place a slice of bacon and a slice of tomato. Season with salt and pepper, pour over the oil in which the chicken was cooked, add a little garlic, rosemary and parsley finely chopped, with a glass of white wine, and bake for half an hour in a moderate oven.

Braised Rabbit (or Chicken)

Joint the rabbit, roll each piece in seasoned flour, then put into a casserole or a thick saucepan with a tight-fitting lid. Cover with a good stock and a wineglassful of sauterne, and allow to simmer gently for about 2 hours. One can add vegetables, but they should be fried with the rabbit. Onions, sliced carrot or small new carrots left whole are the best, but you could also use celery.

SWEETS

Everyone knows about sherry and trifles, kirsch with pineapple, and maraschino with fresh strawberries—but the West Indians cook bananas with brown sugar, sherry and a dab of butter. Choose fairly firm bananas, and blanch them with boiling

Add a glass of port to a steak and kidney pudding just before serving—and taste the difference

water, so that they will keep their colour; but this is not vital. Put the dish low down in the oven (which should be medium hot) when you are dishing up the first course, and they'll be ready when you are.

A wineless variation (though it need not be) is to slice the bananas lengthwise, insert jam between the slices, put them in a dish with two or three tablespoonfuls of water (or a soft white wine) and a dab or two of butter, cover with greaseproof paper and cook for about 20 minutes. This is usually served with thick cream, and it is so good that no one seems to mind the richness.

Melon with Brandy is easy to prepare. Just cut out a small square, pour in a little brandy and chill for a couple of hours before serving.

Peaches in Claret for Impressive Occasions

You can use a cheap claret, but in this instance the better the wine, the more rewarding the dish. Allow about 1½ peaches to each person, according to size of peaches, skin and stone them and cut them into what the Americans call "bite-size" pieces. Put them into fairly deep drinking glasses (not shallow dessert dishes), sprinkle liberally with sugar and more than cover with claret. Do this some time before you need them, preferably a few hours, so that the wine and the peaches take on something of each other's flavour. The best guests abandon their spoons with the last of the peach and drink the remaining nectar.

Brandy Pudding

One of the joys of this dish is that you can make it hours before you need it and have it well out of the way in the refrigerator while you are preparing the rest of the dinner.

Begin by whipping ½ pint of cream. Then slice some sponge cake and lay it in brandy, after which you add a small glass of kirsch or maraschino. Over this put another layer of brandy-flavoured sponge, dabbed over with apricot jam, covered with a layer of cream, more sponge and finally another layer of cream—and freeze it for a minimum of 4 hours.

Stuffed Apples

Peel and core 4 medium cooking apples, and stuff the centres with a mixture of sultanas, currants and mixed peel moistened with a little sherry. Put them into a fireproof dish and pour over them 1 tablespoonful of melted honey. Add the rind and the juice of 1 lemon and about 4 tablespoonfuls of white wine (or just enough to cover the bottom of the dish). Bake in a moderate oven, basting well, and serve hot.

MADE WITH LIQUID APPLES

Now some dishes using the unfermented non-alcoholic juice of English apples, prepared by a famous Swiss process, instead of white wine

IN "Shloer" liquid apples, the natural fruit sugars are preserved and not converted into alcohol, as in cider. It is therefore excellent for children, and may be served, preferably cold, in a wineglass as a table drink or for breakfast, or used to make any of the following delicious dishes:

Apple Zabaione (Egg-punch) or
Sauce Cheaudeau

This should be served in large wine glasses, hot or cold, and eaten with a spoon.

1 *whole egg and* 2 *egg-yolks*	½ *pint "Shloer" liquid apples*
1½ *oz. sugar*	

Put the whole egg, yolks and sugar in a basin. Beat till the mixture is almost white and very light.

Add the "Shloer" and mix thoroughly. Pour into a saucepan and put on a quick fire, beating incessantly, without allowing the mixture to boil or thicken. As soon as it begins to rise, remove from fire. Pour into glasses, and if to be served cold, keep in a cool place until required. Can also be used as a sauce for puddings or tinned fruit.

Apple Jelly

1 *pint "Shloer" liquid apples* (20-*oz. bottle*)	½ *to* 1 *oz. powdered gelatine* 1 *oz. sugar*
Few drops lemon juice	

Heat to just below boiling point. Put in a cold place to set. When serving, top with a glacé cherry or cream.

Apple Blanc-mange

2 tablespoonfuls custard powder	3–4 tablespoonfuls sugar
1 pint bottle "Shloer" liquid apples	1 or 2 eggs
A few drops of lemon juice	

Mix the custard powder with 6 table-spoonfuls "Shloer" to a smooth paste, and then pour in the rest of the bottle. Bring the liquid slowly to the boil, stirring all the time. Add sugar and a few drops of lemon. Take it from the heat and beat into the mixture the egg-yolks and the stiffly beaten whites.

Mix well and pour into a water-rinsed mould. Serve very cold.

Here are some excellent drinks, both alcoholic and non-alcoholic, made from "Shloer" liquid apples, to add to the drinks in our chapter on Cocktails, Cups and Punches.

NON-ALCOHOLIC DRINKS

Safety First

¾ "Shloer"	A few drops of lemon
¼ ginger ale	juice, twist of
Pineapple juice to taste (optional)	lemon peel Seasonal fruits
Mint	

Mix all the ingredients together, put a twist of lemon peel on top, adding pineapple juice, if desired. Serve ice cold.

Mulled Liquid Apples

1 pint "Shloer"	A few drops of lemon
A few cloves	juice, some slices
A little sugar	of lemon

Heat the "Shloer" slowly, add the sugar and lemon juice to taste. Remove from the fire just before it reaches boiling point, garnish with cloves and lemon slices. Serve immediately while piping hot.

ALCOHOLIC DRINKS

Liquid Apple Hot Toddy (an excellent cold cure)

Make exactly the same as Mulled Liquid Apples (see recipe above under Non-Alcoholic Drinks), but add rum as required.

Hock Cup

⅔ Hock	Some drops of lemon
⅓ "Shloer"	juice and slices of
Sugar to taste	lemon or cucumber

Melon with brandy makes a wonderful sweet. You just cut out a small square, pour in a little brandy and chill

Mix hock and "Shloer" together with a little sugar and the lemon juice, add the lemon or cucumber slices on the top and serve ice cold.

Champagne Cup

⅔ Champagne	⅓ "Shloer"
A few slices of lemon	

Chill the champagne and ice the "Shloer," mix, adding the lemon slices on the top.

Ace Cooler

Measure of gin	"Shloer" to fill
Measure of Dubonnet	Sliced apple and
Dash of cherry brandy	cucumber rind Cracked ice

Mix the gin, Dubonnet and cherry brandy, then fill up with "Shloer," garnish with sliced apples and cucumber rind. Add cracked ice.

Liquid Apple Highball

2 oz. gin, brandy or rum	8 oz. "Shloer" Lemon peel, mint and
Cracked ice	borage

Pour the gin, brandy, or rum into a 10-oz. glass with cracked ice. Fill up with "Shloer" and stir. Garnish with lemon peel, mint and borage.

SIMPLE HOME-MADE CHEESES

Three tested recipes that are easy to follow

by GILBERT HARRIS, M.R.S.

FEW housewives consider making cheese until they find themselves with a bottle of sour milk on their hands. Yet it can be made with very simple equipment.

First of all a little "starter" will have to be made. This is done by warming a cupful of milk to about 95° F. Into this, shred a piece of ripe crumbly cheese about the size of a walnut. Any kind of cheese will do except the processed kinds (the ones wrapped in foil). Cover the cup with a piece of butter muslin and stand in the airing cupboard or other warm spot for at least 24 hours.

Pot Cheese.—This is a firm cheese. When you have some starter ready, heat 2 quarts of milk to 95° F. and add 2 teaspoonfuls of starter and ten drops of cheese rennet (not the variety used for making junket). Stir the starter and the rennet well into the milk for at least 1 minute. Now stand the container on a piece of wood and wrap it in two or three thicknesses of woollen or blanket cloth to retain the heat. Leave until a thick curd has formed. This will take 5–12 hours.

When the curd has formed, re-heat the whole lot—curd and whey—very, very slowly, until it reaches a temperature of 120° F. Next, pour off as much of the whey as possible without losing any of the curd. Do not throw the whey away; you will want this for the third recipe.

Now turn the sliced curd out into a double thickness of fine butter muslin, and hang up in an airy place, but out of direct sunlight, to drain. Place a bowl underneath to catch the whey and add it to what you already have.

When the whey has finished dripping, sprinkle over the curd a teaspoonful of salt and work the curd together with the hands to get the salt well distributed. A variation in flavour can be obtained by adding a heaped teaspoonful of celery seeds as well.

When the curd has been well worked with the hands, take a loose-bottomed cake tin, line with greaseproof paper, pile in the curd, place a pastry- or bread-board over the top and turn the whole thing upside down. Press down the bottom of the cake tin. Place the tin and board in a cool place and put on some weights to act as a press.

Leave for 2 days, then remove the weight and press on the bottom of the tin to push out the finished cheese. Remove the waxed papers, and the cheese is then ready for use. A pot cheese will keep for up to two weeks if it is stored on the bottom shelf of a refrigerator or well covered in a cool pantry.

Cream Cheese

To make this delicious spreading cheese, use either two 6-oz. cans of cream or ¾ pint of fresh double cream. Heat very slowly to 70° F., stirring occasionally until the required temperature is reached. Now add 1 level teaspoonful of starter and eight drops of cheese rennet. Cover with butter muslin and leave in a warm place for 16 hours. Pour off what little whey there is and work in salt to taste.

Tie the curd up in a tight bag. Put the bag on to a board and place another on top of it. Weight the top board and leave in a cool place for 2 days. Keep in the refrigerator without actually freezing or store in a cool spot.

Mysost—Whey Cheese

This is a type of cheese little known in the U.K. It is a Scandinavian speciality made from the whey saved when preparing other types of cheese.

The whey should be poured into a scrupulously clean meat tin and put on to a very low flame to evaporate until it reaches the consistency of thick treacle. It should then be cooled rapidly. Stand the tin in the sink and then run in sufficient cold water to reach almost to the lip of the tin. Scrape out the smooth paste and put into small glass jars. It should be a deep honey colour and have the consistency of butter.

It is best eaten either spread on buttered cheese biscuits or new crusty rolls. It will keep for months and is highly nutritious, containing the bulk of the proteins from the milk.

HAYBOX COOKERY

It saves fuel and labour—and even the toughest meat comes out beautifully tender

THE haybox is an invention of the Norwegian peasants and it is used all over Europe. The principle is the same as that of a Thermos—conservation of heat by insulation. There are many advantages in haybox cookery: it saves gas or electricity, and a good deal of labour, since the food needs no attention while cooking. Besides this, if you are out the whole day, you can still come home to a ready-cooked meal. Even the toughest meat will be tender by then.

HOW TO MAKE A HAYBOX

A haybox is simple to make. You can use a strong packing-case with no wide cracks in it, a tin box or an old trunk. For insulating material, wood shavings are preferable to hay, but there are even people who have made a good job using newspapers, torn up and made into balls. Whatever you use, it must be packed in very tightly. In addition, you need a few yards of cotton or linen material for the lining and cushion.

A very good haybox was made as follows: A wooden case was used, 16 in. × 30 in. × 16 in. deep. These measurements need not be taken too literally, as the only important thing is the width of the space between pot and wood. This must not be less than 4 in.

This particular haybox was made to hold two pots, therefore it had to be fairly long. Apart from the space needed for the two pots there was a 4 in. space between them and 4 in. to spare each side.

The up-to-date version of the old-fashioned haybox uses the newest insulating material. It was specially made and photographed by Gordon McLeish

MATERIALS NEEDED

1. A good wooden box from the grocer or wine merchant, approximately 16 in. × 12 in. × 10 in. deep.
2. A lid made of ply the same size as top of box.
3. Pair of hinges approximately $\frac{1}{2}$ in. × $1\frac{1}{2}$ in. with flat-headed screws.
4. A simple snap clip to keep lid shut.
5. Food jars with clip-down sealing lids (obtainable from Benjamin Edgington, 69 Great Queen Street, London, W.C.2).
6. A bag of Micafil, from any builder's merchants.
7. A large sheet of stiff white card.
8. A sharp-pointed knife, a pencil and a roll of Sellotape.
9. Half an old pillow case to make top cushion.

Having fixed the plywood lid to the long edge of the box with the hinges and fitted the snap clip so that it keeps the lid tight, prepare the food containers

1

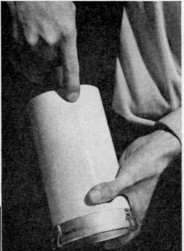

Cut a piece of white card about 7 in. × 14 in. and test for size (1 left), then wrap the card loosely round the food jar and fasten the join with Sellotape to make a cylinder (2)

Cut another piece of card the exact size of the inside of the box, mark round the bottom of the food jars, then cut round the pencil lines (3 left), and make sure the jars will slide easily through the holes. Keep the discs

2

Now lay the strip of card with the holes cut out for the food containers on the bottom of the box (4) and mark the outline of the circles on the bottom of the box in pencil

4

3

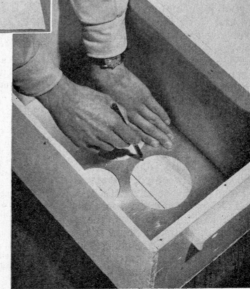

The lid, overhanging the box on three sides, was fixed along the fourth side with two hinges. To make it absolutely tight, a hasp lock was fixed at the front. A cushion was fitted inside the lid, and this, too, was 4 in. deep and tightly stuffed.

To prepare the nests for the two pots, covers were made which fitted the bottom and sides of each pot. A piece of material was then taken, large enough to cover the surface of the box, two holes were cut in this and the nests inserted. With the empty pots in place, the insulating material was stuffed tightly around them, so as to get it well into the four corners, and the cover fixed with nails or drawing pins along all four sides.

A more ambitious design is shown on

these pages with step-by-step instructions for making.

FOOD MUST BE BOILING

The best type of pot to use in a haybox is the one with either no handles or very short ones and a tight-fitting lid.

Some important points to remember, when you are using the haybox, are: Food must be taken off the cooker while still at boiling point and must be put into the hay-box as quickly as possible. There it must be covered by the cushion and the lid closed immediately. If you are preparing a dish which would take a long time to cook in the normal way, allow three times as much for its cooking in the haybox. Fowl or really tough meat should be cooked for the first $\frac{1}{2}$ hour on the stove before being

5

7

Now (5) place the card cylinders to coincide exactly with the circles on the bottom of the box. Fix in position with several tabs of Sellotape

Pour Micafil into the box to fill all the space around the cylinders and fill the bottom of each cylinder (6). Shake down the Micafil to pack it really tight

6

Lay the card with the holes cut out of it on the top and fix with Sellotape. Then drop in the discs to finish the container (7) and put in food jars

Finally, pour enough Micafil into the pillow case to fill up the remaining space in the top of the box (8). When it is patted down, the lid should only just close

8

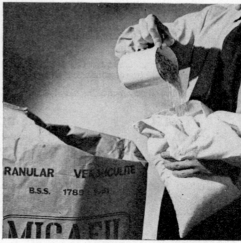

RANULAR — VERMICULITE
B.S.S. 1789

MICAFIL

transferred to the haybox. Porridge or rice, on the other hand, must only be brought to the boil. Porridge can then be cooked overnight; rice for 2½ hours or potatoes for 1½ to 2 hours.

The pots should always be fairly full, and dishes such as stews, soups, pulses or dried fruit give the best results when done by this slow, gentle method.

The following recipes will give four good-sized helpings.

Pot-au-Feu

2 lb. brisket beef without bone. (Do not buy a rolled-up piece, as there is usually some fat hidden in the centre)	A bone (preferably marrow)
	1 onion
	1 turnip
	1 parsnip
	2 bay leaves
	5 peppercorns
2 carrots	Salt

Peel or scrub the vegetables and cut them into big chunks. Bring 3–4 pints of salted water to the boil. Add the meat and simmer for ½ hour. Add all the other ingredients, boil for another few minutes and transfer to the haybox. Allow between 6 and 8 hours there. Serve with boiled potatoes and all the vegetables.

Hungarian Goulash of Beef

2 lb. stewing steak	2–3 tomatoes
1½ lb. onions	1 dessertspoonful of paprika
2 potatoes	
2 oz. fat	Salt

Cut the meat into pieces as for stew. Slice the onions thinly, and peel and cut the potatoes. Melt fat and cook the onions till golden. Then add meat, salt and cook, well covered, for ½ hour. Add tomatoes and potatoes. Have ready less than a pint of boiling water. Add this and put the Goulash into the haybox for about 4 hours. Before serving, add the paprika dissolved in a tablespoonful of hot water. Serve with boiled potatoes. (The 2 potatoes cooked with the meat serve only to make the sauce creamy.)

Stewed Dried Fruit

1 lb. of dried prunes or ¾ lb. dried apricots
(For the prunes a stick of cinnamon, for apricots a few blanched almonds)
2 tablespoonfuls brown sugar

Wash the dried fruit and soak for some hours. Bring to the boil in the water in which it has been soaked. Add another pint of boiling water and the sugar. Allow 4–5 hours of cooking in the haybox.

Steamed Sunday Pudding

2 oz. dried bread-crumbs soaked in coffee	2 oz. sugar
	2 oz. chocolate
	2 oz. groundnuts
2 oz. butter or margarine	3 eggs

Melt chocolate, cream fat, egg-yolks and sugar. Whisk the whites until very stiff. Mix all the ingredients but fold in the whites at the end. Put the mixture into a greased, floured pudding basin and cook this in the pot which you use for the haybox for 20 minutes. Move it into the haybox and allow 4 hours there. Serve the pudding hot with either whipped cream or custard.

☆ ☆ ☆ ☆ ☆ ☆ ☆ **HAYBOX COOKING TIME TABLE** ☆ ☆ ☆ ☆ ☆ ☆ ☆

Always fill containers to the top and bring the contents to the boil just before the lid is clipped on. Place them in the box immediately and cover with the top cushion.

Most foods will go on cooking slowly for hours, so the contents need only be partly cooked before they are put in.

DISH	PRE-COOK ON STOVE	IN HAYBOX
Vegetable Soup	¾ hour	4 hours
Irish Stew	½ hour meat—5 mins. potatoes	1½ hours
Beef Stew and Vegetables	¾ hour	3 hours
Potatoes	5 mins.	1½ hours
Boiled Rice	2–3 mins. boiling	2½ hours
Stewed Apples	2–3 mins. boiling	1½ hours
Boiled Bacon	45 mins.	4–5 hours

☆ ☆

VEGETABLES IN THE NEW ENGLAND MANNER

Some good old American ways with sprouts, corn and beans,
described by ELENE FOSTER

IN New England, sprouts are an autumn vegetable, and we have a way of combining them with chestnuts and serving them in rich white sauce. The sprouts are boiled, the chestnuts baked, peeled and halved, and both are heated in the white sauce.

Green corn is another popular vegetable in America which goes a-begging in the U.K. because few housewives know how to cook it (see chapter on Vegetables).

There is also the succulent American dish called "succotash," which consists of the corn kernels combined with flat butter beans (see also Cookery in the United States). Corn meal is extensively used for delicious muffins, and "corn mash" is a popular breakfast dish, fried in bacon fat and served with maple syrup.

Boston baked beans, accompanied by sausages or fishballs and hot steamed brown bread, followed by freshly fried doughnuts and coffee, comprise Sunday morning breakfast in New England.

Boston baked beans are made by cooking 1 lb. of small white beans (which we call "pea beans") and adding a good big piece of fat salt pork in a special way. The beans are soaked overnight, the water drained off in the morning and the beans parboiled until they are fairly soft, then placed in a stone crock with a lid. The pork is placed on the top and over this goes a tablespoonful of molasses and another of sugar, and pepper and salt. The pot is then filled up with water and put in a slow oven to bake for several hours. As the water boils away, more is added. When the pork rind, which, by the way, has been slit in strips, is a golden brown, the dish is ready to serve.

On Sundays the bean pot, piping hot, is wrapped in heavy paper, placed in the bundle-handkerchief and given the place of honour on the breakfast table. A pyramid of steamed brown bread is brought in with the sausages or fluffy, feather-weight fishballs. Following this come the hot doughnuts, not the tough, doughy cakes of the English bakeries, but light, puffy, crispy rounds with a hole in the middle and a sprinkling of powdered sugar on the top.

After such a meal, the family was fortified for the long church service and the long-winded sermon.

☆ ☆ ☆ ☆ ☆ ☆ ☆ ☆

MAKE THE BEST OF CHRISTMAS HOLLY

Variegated holly should not be neglected at Christmas. It will lighten other evergreens and produce the same kind of effect obtained sometimes by sparkling or painted branches. Here it is simply arranged in a porcelain mug.

DRY AND WET ROT IN TIMBER

Hints on how to recognise the arch-enemies of woodwork in buildings and how to deal with them

Even a newly built house may be affected by fungi and insects. Any piece of damp, untreated timber will eventually be attacked by some form of fungus

DRY ROT

MERULIUS LACRYMANS is the fungus which is responsible for most of the destruction of woodwork in buildings—Dry Rot. Normally it attacks softwood only.

Propagation is caused by means of contact with wood already infected or by microscopic airborne spores which can drift for long distances until they find conditions suitable for their purpose—namely, sufficient moisture and a favourable temperature. In fact, spores have been trapped in aircraft at an altitude of several miles above the earth.

If these conditions are found and the fungus develops and reaches maturity, it forms, after a period of two years or more, what is known as a fruiting body which can be several square feet in extent. The function of the fruiting body is to propagate spores *which it can discharge at the rate of 50,000,000 per minute for every square yard of its area over a period lasting several days.*

Some idea of the widespread nature of fungal propagation is given by the fact that *any* piece of damp, untreated timber will eventually be attacked by one or more of the various types of fungi.

In many cases the wood is attacked first by fungi (not necessarily Merulius lacrymans) and then by wood-boring insects, some of which, notably the Death Watch Beetle, obviously prefer wood which has been previously attacked by fungi.

The Conditions Needed

In order for "dry" rot or other fungi to develop in timber, a certain amount of moisture must be present; at least 20 per cent. for Merulius lacrymans and more than 30 per cent. for "wet" rot. Timber in buildings normally contains from 12 per cent. to 18 per cent. of moisture (just barely safe) but a dripping tap in the cellar, a leaking pipe or a damaged damp course can easily increase the moisture content to the danger level. In addition to this moisture content, a stagnant, unventilated atmosphere with a temperature of between 68° and 86° F. favours the development of the fungi.

Given these primary conditions, the bill for repairs within a few short months can easily be several hundred pounds.

The trouble is that once the Merulius lacrymans has established itself, it spreads to sound, dry timber. This is because, in the process of its growth, it actually produces sufficient moisture to make dry timber wet enough to attack (experiments have shown that a culture of Merulius lacrymans in a small flask containing sawdust will produce nearly half a pint of water in one month).

Where to Look

Nor is "dry" rot confined to timber. In its search for fresh wood to attack, the strands of the mycelium can easily penetrate through the joints of brick walls and even infect large areas of brickwork. It

Left, some typical examples of dry rot in timber, showing different kinds of damage

An unusual instance of infection—the suitcase (below) had been left in a cellar in which dry rot had taken hold

has been known to travel along metal-work.

Since fungi thrive upon damp conditions, "dry" rot generally takes hold in the lower part of the house or building where ventilation may be poor and moisture is present.

What to Look For

Check for signs of unexplained warping or cracking in the ground-floor skirting boards. Wood which has been affected by dry rot is similar in character to that which has been subjected to prolonged heat, being excessively brittle, light in weight and cracked both along and across the grain into rough, rectangular blocks. It can be crumbled into powder between the fingers (hence *dry* rot).

A simple test is to press a penknife blade or gimlet into it. If the wood has been attacked, it will offer no resistance. The presence of dry rot is generally indicated by a musty smell like that of mushrooms, and timber which is in process of being attacked will show signs of thin, grey, threadlike strands with occasional white, fluffy cottonwool-like growths and matted grey festoons.

Assessing the Damage

Quite often a fruiting body may be seen (it has a most unpleasant smell). The fruiting body of Merulius lacrymans has a characteristic rusty red centre with white edges. The presence of such a fruiting body would indicate that the trouble is of a long-standing nature.

In cases of serious dry rot, householders would be advised to seek professional help.

Having opened up the area, determine the extent of the rot, bearing in mind that once the fungus has taken hold it will spread to dry timber. The outside limits of the rot can be tested superficially with a knife blade or gimlet as already suggested. If the timber resists the blade, there are two further tests that can be made.

Try to prise up a long splinter of wood. If you are successful, this is a healthy sign because decayed timber invariably breaks off short. As a final check, a test drilling may be made; the sound waste wood which comes from the drill hole should have a warm, pleasantly resinous smell.

If the timber affected is in contact with brickwork, as is often the case, remove any plaster which appears to be loose or crumbly and then examine the exposed bricks carefully for any signs of the grey threads and strands with which the fungus spreads. Look particularly for crumbly mortar in the joints and the musty smell which is generally present.

All timber that has been badly affected must be burnt immediately. (This is often required by local bylaw. Such timber is incapable of supporting weight and liable to crumble without warning, as well as being highly infectious.) The cause of dampness must then be cured.

Treatment

Where bearers or joists have only been partially attacked and are still mechanically sound (having four-fifths of their original dimensions intact) removal is not necessary and treatment may be given as below, providing the wood is freely accessible.

Where Timber is Accessible

1 lb. of Xylamon E.C. diluted in 2 parts water should be applied by brush to cover 50 sq. ft. of timber. Two coats should be applied. A long flowing stroke with a well filled brush is advised.

It does not matter if the wood to be treated is damp, or even wet as a result of further leakage. The effectiveness of Xylamon will not be impaired although its penetration will be reduced.

Where Timber is Inaccessible

A solution of 1 part Xylamon and 1 part water should be made up and the bore-hole method used. In this method, staggered bore holes $\frac{1}{2}$–1 in. wide are drilled downwards into the wood at a distance from 12–16 in.

apart. Their depth should equal about three-quarters of the thickness of the beam. These holes should then be "topped up" two or three times with the Xylamon E.C. solution and plugged with wood or a cork.

Staggered drilling does not reduce the mechanical strength of the beam.

Infected Brickwork

This can be treated as for accessible timber, but if the trouble is deep-seated, the bore-hole method should be employed. In all cases the cement and plaster rendering should be removed and the loose mortar raked out from between the courses. Spraying is preferable to brushing in this instance and, after it has been allowed to soak in, a further spray coat should be given.

With regard to the bore-hole method, it should be stressed that it is a job for ex-

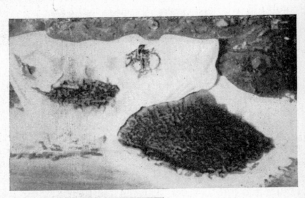

The fruiting body of dry rot (above) can discharge spores at the rate of 50,000,000 per minute for every square yard of its area

Left, flooring joists badly attacked by dry rot. Wood so affected crumbles into powder in the fingers

perts. The method employed is as follows: Inclined, staggered holes are drilled to a depth of two-thirds of the wall's thickness. The 1–1 solution is poured into the holes, but the degree of saturation is judged by the amount of seepage into the lower line of holes from the upper line. After some days have elapsed, the brick may be rendered over again. Apart from sterilising the affected area, certain additives present in Xylamon have the effect of hardening cement and plaster.

Above, Xylamon is applied by brush in two coats to easily accessible wood only partially affected by dry rot and still mechanically sound ,four-fifths being intact

CELLAR OR WET ROT FUNGUS

Although the Merulius lacrymans is the most virulent of fungal attackers, there are also a number of others. First among these and second only in importance to Merulius lacrymans is Cellar Fungus (Coniophora cerebella), and these two together probably account for as much as 95 per cent. of all fungal decay of timber in the U.K.

This is a very common fungus and is hardier than the Merulius lacrymans in that it can exist in the open on decaying timber lying on the ground. Fortunately, however, it cannot spread to dry timber as can the former, and is restricted to damp areas only, but despite this it can cause serious damage.

Where the affected timber is inaccessible, the bore-hole method is used, the holes being topped up two or three times with Xylamon solution and plugged with wood or a cork

Where to Look

Sometimes referred to as "wet" rot fungus, the Coniophora cerebella requires moister conditions than dry rot. This fungus has a fluffy blackish-brown mycelium; its fruiting body is also of dark colour and covered with small pimply or papillary growths. Decay is indicated by a darkening of the wood and by pronounced fissures along and across the grain.

Look for this fungus in cellars where very damp or wet conditions exist; wet, untreated timber lying in the open; solid floors laid directly on cement or rooms which are not provided with a cellar.

Treatment

This is the same as for dry rot but probably more localised. Timber should be tested internally, since this fungus can attack the centre of a board or beam and leave the outside apparently sound. Proper removal of the causes of dampness will generally prevent recurrence. Decayed timber must, of course, be removed. Both hard- and softwood can be affected.

OTHER FUNGI WHICH ATTACK TIMBER IN BUILDINGS

Mine Fungus (Poria vaillantii and other species of Poria)

So called because it causes extensive damage to timber in mines, this fungus also attacks timber in houses. Rather similar in appearance to dry rot insofar as decay is concerned. Is confined to damp areas. Fruiting bodies are generally white and covered with small round holes. The mycelium is also white.

Phellinus Megalaporus

Attacks oak timbers of old buildings.

Lentinus Lepideus

Can be regarded as a form of wet rot. Might cause heart-wood rot on timber in the open.

Treatment.—As has been described.

Footnote.—The discovery of small fungi of the nature of toadstools, while not themselves dangerous, should serve as an indication of dampness which might lead to dry rot.

HINTS FOR HOUSEHOLDERS

Generally speaking, reasonable care will ensure that your house is kept free from timber decay. Fortunately, in the case of fungi at least, a warm, dry house is the best safeguard. Where insect attack is concerned, be wary of unexplained presence of small heaps of "sawdust" beside furniture. It may only be the result of a tight drawer chafing against a runner, but it will put you on your guard. Inspect the roofing timber for signs of Furniture Beetle attack.

The following simple rules will help:

Things to Avoid

Things in a house which cause dampness make trouble. Leaky gutters, blocked downpipes, bad pointing, faulty damp courses. Have them attended to as quickly as you can. The cost of such repairs is generally trifling in comparison with the bill you may get otherwise. Have gutters and downpipes cleared regularly, preferably after the leaves have fallen in the autumn.

Never allow the ventilation bricks outside the house to become clogged with earth and on no account block them deliberately with the idea of preventing draughts. A current of air must move about under the floor boards of a suspended floor, if the house is to be healthy. Never lay impervious types of floor coverings over floors which show signs of dampness. Cure the dampness first.

After Flooding

If you have been unfortunate enough to be flooded, even if only for a very short while, you might be advised to increase the passage of air beneath the house by lifting up floorboards in the ground-floor rooms. Two or three in each room will do, and leave them up for a day or so. Make sure, too, that the ventilating bricks have not been silted up. Houses after flooding are very prone to fungal attack.

Inspect Regularly

Timber pests obtain the hold they do because generally they are not noticed quickly enough—so be on your guard. Inspect the attic and the cellar at least twice a year.

The Xylamon Advice Bureau has been established to give expert guidance on matters arising out of the problems of timber preservation and the use of Xylamon.

Advice and guidance are free. The address is: The Xylamon Advice Bureau, Silexine Paints Limited, Richford Street, London, W.6.

The fruiting body of the Cellar Fungus (Coniophora cerebella), which flourishes in moister conditions than Dry Rot

HOW TO MEND A FUSE

A simple repair iob which everyone should be able to do in an emergency

PRACTICALLY everyone living in a house with electric lighting is liable at some time to be faced with a blown fuse, so it is as well to know in advance how to mend it.

Fuses are simple but most effective little devices that form the "safety valves" of the electrical system. Elementary in design (though with many variations), the same principle applies in all cases.

The fuse wire—a slender, short length of fusible alloy—is of a type which rapidly melts if the wiring circuit carries too large a load. Thus, before the wiring can attain that degree of heat sufficient to cause a fire, the thin fuse wire melts and collapses. This breaks the circuit and immediately cuts the current.

The first thing to do when you set about mending a fuse (or doing any other electrical work) is to **turn off the current at the main.**

Then, with the main switch safely off, open the fuse box. Inside you will find several porcelain fuse blocks. Gently ease them out one at a time from their grips and inspect each one carefully until you find the one with the broken wire. This is the blown fuse.

Remove all wire from the defective fuse and replace it with a fresh length of fuse wire long enough to extend and to be fastened to the terminals

(or screws) at each end of the block. Give the wire a turn or two round each terminal before it is tightened down.

Avoid fitting a taut wire, and snip off any surplus fuse wire close to the terminal.

For household lighting, use 5 amp. fuse wire; for heating, 10 amp.; and for power, 15 amp. A card of each should be kept always at hand and close to the fuse box, so that it can be found in the dark.

The position of the fuse boxes should be noted. The company supplying the electricity install a fuse box which is sealed with a lead seal. *This fuse box must never be disturbed*—it is the company's responsibility.

The fuse box to which the householder has access can normally be found close to the meter, and there may well be another fitted elsewhere on the premises.

Scout around the house before the necessity of fitting a new fuse arises, to locate the fuse boxes. It is much easier than groping around to find them with a torch after the house is plunged into darkness.

The fuse block with the broken wire (left) is the blown one. Attach a fresh length of fuse wire to each terminal (above). Equipment needed for the job—pliers, penknife, card of fuse wire

AMATEUR HANDYWORK ADDS
£500 TO VALUE OF A HOME

*With hardboard, the most versatile of materials, the
face of a house has been changed—for less than £100*

by Patric J. Baker

MR. ROBERT WARD, a Post Office engineer, has brought the business of home-brightening to a fine art. During the war, he spent nearly four years in Japanese prison camps, where he kept himself sane by planning how he would decorate his home if and when he saw it again. After release, he set to work at once and has already added about £500 to the value of his property, though his total outlay in materials is well under £100.

When the Wards bought their house at Wembley, Middlesex, the kitchen was virtually non-existent. It contained one tap, a broken earthenware sink and a decaying shelf or two. The walls were chipped and peeling and half the floor tiles were missing. It would have cost Mr. Ward a great deal of money to have the place reconditioned professionally, so he set to work and did the whole job himself.

A Dream Kitchen for £30

First of all he cleaned the room thoroughly; that took a week-end. Then he set to work on a new sink unit. Timber battens, 1 in. × 2 in., were used for the framework and ⅛-in. standard hardboard

for the panelling. All the joints were of simple overlap type secured by screws. Special cupboards and drawers, designed and made by Mr. Ward, were incorporated in the unit to house the various items of cutlery and household equipment. In addition, he made a neat pull-out breadboard of oak. For the doors, panelled on both sides with hardboard, an overlapping, contemporary style was chosen, and the cupboard section, also panelled in hardboard, was topped by a one-piece plastic sink.

Neat plastic fittings were added and the whole unit was finished in an attractive shade of pastel blue. Four coats were applied after the hardboard had been carefully sealed and primed. The whole job took about three weeks of spare time.

The next task was to make a large kitchen cabinet which would occupy nearly

How an old-fashioned panel door (left) was "flushed up" into a modern one (above) with a sheet of hardboard, easily applied with panel pins and adhesive without removing the door from its hinges

500

the whole of one wall. Using the same technique and materials, he built a really de luxe unit in matching style. This has separate compartments for food, crockery, cleaning materials and coats, etc. There is also a central hatch which drops down to form a baking table. This is lined with plastic-faced hardboard to make a durable working surface. Beneath this is a small larder, complete with door ventilators. The compartments above are fitted with frosted-glass panels which help to break up the massive but pleasing appearance of the cabinet. The unit was then finished in the same pastel shade as the sink, and very smart they both look.

Mr. Ward then turned his attention to the walls, which were replastered and given several coats of emulsion paint. After this he applied a composition floor covering. An

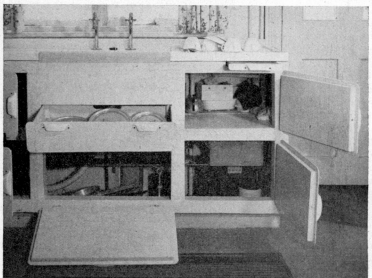

This capacious kitchen cabinet, with shelves for everything (even coats and hats) was made by an amateur with simple timber framing and standard ⅛-in. hardboard. It is finished in pastel blue

The handyman who made the sink unit (left) had no previous experience of carpentry. The sink is plastic and drawers and cupboards are fitted with neat plastic handles. Above the cupboards on the right is a pull-out oak breadboard, and there are compartments for pots, pans and cleaning materials

501

An alcove in an old-fashioned room is fitted with a cupboard made from hardboard by Mr. Robert Ward, who has entirely re-made the inside of his home

have one thing in common—the use of hardboard in brightening up the home.

FIBREBOARD FOR INTERIOR CONVERSIONS

Fibreboards are becoming increasingly popular for conversion purposes in all types of interiors. This is due not only to their low cost and ease of application, but also to the wide range of surface finishes in which they are available. Furthermore, the home converter is now able to use adhesives as an alternative to pinning and screwing, which saves a lot of time.

On the home front, hardboard is ideal for brightening up old-fashioned kitchens and bathrooms and for modernising living rooms, halls and bedrooms which have that out-dated look. Much can be achieved for very little, and it is surprising what a difference can be made to the atmosphere of a house by repanelling ugly doors or laying a neat surround in a lounge or sitting room.

What is Fibreboard?

Fibreboard is a general name for rigid-sheet building materials; it is wood in a reconstituted form, possessing all the advantages but without such disadvantages as knots, grains, etc.

attractive hardboard pelmet was then fitted over the window and the fireplace and hearth were retiled. This transformation has changed a primitive wash-house into a contemporary dream kitchen any woman would be proud to work in. Yet it only cost about £30 in materials.

From this stage on, there was no stopping Robert Ward. He built a bathroom and lavatory out of an extended coal store and did all the plumbing himself, panelling walls and enclosing the bath with hardboard.

Then flush cupboards were built in the ugly recesses beside the sitting-room fireplace, old-fashioned panelled doors were "flushed-up" with neat hardboard panels and more pelmets made for the bedrooms.

At the moment, Robert Ward is contemplating making a suite of hanging cupboards for his wife and himself. But that will have to wait for a while, as he is now engaged in installing a central-heating system and acting as "handyman-consultant" to his neighbours.

Some of the pictures we took of Mr. Ward's work are reproduced here. None of the jobs is professional—all were done by the householders themselves. They

Showing how simple it is to apply fibre insulating board to wood walls. Here the system is pinning, but you get just as good results with adhesives

Fibreboard gives a room a contemporary look. The left-hand wall is of ½ in. insulating board, the right-hand one of reeded hardboard, both fixed with adhesives and finished in different pastel shades of matt surfaced paint

The fibre building board family has two main roots—hardboard and softboard.

The hardboard section—most widely used by handymen—is divided into standard, super and medium grades, which vary only in strength and surface texture. These are suitable, among other things, for partitioning, furniture, built-in cupboards and units, floors, model-making and carving.

Varieties of Hardboard

A range of hardboards is also produced for specialised purposes. For example, buy enamelled hardboard for coloured bathroom panelling and tiling; veneered fluted and reeded boards for dadoes, room or hall panelling; leatherboard for general decorative use, or the newly developed plastic-faced hardboard for shelving and working surfaces. Also available is perforated hardboard—"pegboard"—which is rapidly gaining favour for contemporary decoration and—supplied with special fittings—as a novel base on which to hang toilet requisites or kitchen utensils.

Insulating Board

The second branch of the fibre building board family tree is insulating board, which has special properties of insulation and acoustic control. This type of board is softer and less dense than hardboard and is widely used for lining walls and ceilings. Statistics show that the use of insulating board produces an improvement in thermal insulation of up to 77 per cent.

Fixing techniques are quite simple and well within the capabilities of the advanced worker.

How you buy it

Generally speaking, standard hardboard, ⅛ in. thick, is the most suitable board for the handyman. It comes in sheets, 4 ft. × 6 ft. and so on, up to 18 ft., or cut in sizes. The retail price starts at about sixpence a square foot, which is not high for a first-class sheet material combining lightness in weight and flexibility with structural strength and long-wearing life. The surface of hardboard has a naturally attractive appearance, varying from a deep brown to a light buff colour and is quite smooth and snag-free. This means that there is no danger of laddering nylons or damaging delicate fabrics when working with it.

Fibreboard can be easily worked with ordinary household tools—saw, hammer, screwdriver, bradawl. It cuts quickly and cleanly, can be fixed by pinning, screwing or by adhesive and requires no special skill of any kind. From the handyman's angle, adhesion is probably the most satisfactory fixing method for the majority of household jobs, and a number of proprietary firms now produce types of adhesives designed specially for use with fibre boards. Most of these are of the impact variety and set almost at once. This does away with the necessity for strutting the job or, on horizontal surfaces, applying weights to give adhesion.

Provided that a hardboard sealer is first applied and an undercoat, as recommended by the manufacturers, any of the decorative finishes suitable for wood may be used on hardboard. These include oil paints and varnishes, emulsion paints, enamels, cellulose stains, French and wax polishes. Wood veneers and certain types of wallpaper may also be applied.

THE RIGHT FIBREBOARD FOR THE JOB

This table will help you to find the correct board type for your purpose.

Under the columns headed thicknesses and sheet sizes, and against each type of board, are three figures. These indicate, respectively, the smallest size, the most commonly stocked size and the maximum which may be obtained.

HARDBOARD

Type of Board	Uses	Thicknesses	Sheet sizes
Standard	Building construction generally, including exterior work; floor tiles; display panels; furniture and door panels; temporary concrete shuttering, and most general carpentry purposes.	$\frac{1}{16}$ in. $\frac{1}{8}$ in. $\frac{1}{4}$ in.	Small offcuts 8 ft. × 4 ft. 6 ft. 6 in. × 14 ft.
Super	As standard hardboard, and in circumstances where a particularly hard or moisture-resisting surface is required, e.g. flooring, concrete form work, exterior work, bath panels, vehicle bodies.	$\frac{1}{16}$ in. $\frac{1}{8}$ in. $\frac{1}{2}$ in.	Small offcuts 4 ft. × 8 ft. 6 ft. 6 in. × 14 ft.
Medium	Building construction generally, including some exterior work; wall and ceiling panelling; underlay for floor coverings; motor-car, caravan and railway coach work; shipbuilding; signs; some varieties for pin-up boards and chalk boards.	$\frac{1}{4}$ in. $\frac{1}{4}$ in. $\frac{1}{2}$ in.	Small offcuts 4 ft. × 8 ft.
Perforated	Interior decoration; shopfitting, display; vent covers; surfacing to acoustic material.	$\frac{1}{16}$ in. $\frac{1}{8}$ in. $\frac{1}{4}$ in.	Small offcuts 4 ft. × 8 ft. 4 ft. × 14 ft.
Surfaced	Panelling to walls, doors and furniture; splashbacks; table and cupboard tops, and in all circumstances where a decorative, washable, hard-wearing surface sheet material is required.	Usually $\frac{1}{8}$ in.	Small offcuts Usually as standard hardboard

A MODERN LOOK
FOR YOUR HOME

PANELLED doors may be converted into modern flush or single-panel doors (see left) by facing them with a suitable type of fibre building board.

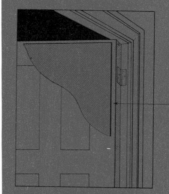

Margin between hardboard and edge of doors allows door to close without need for re-siting hinges on door-stop

New Doors for Old

PREPARING THE HARDBOARD

The door panels, which have first been cut to size, should be moistened on the back with water, and then placed back-to-back on a flat base and stored in a cool place at least 48 hours before fixing.

FIXING THE HARDBOARD

The panels may be secured with a suitable contact adhesive which immediately becomes firmly fixed, so mark out the precise position first. Use a few panel pins even with the adhesive, and for external doors both adhesive and pins.

If fixing with adhesive, the door surfaces should first be scraped or sandpapered.

The board may be fixed by panel pins 3 in. apart round the edges and at approximately 6 in. centres at the intermediate fixing points. Work from centre out.

REMOVING FIXTURES

Remove fixtures which may protrude beyond the door face. It is generally more satisfactory to take the door down before fixing the hardboard.

MEASURING AND CUTTING

Carefully measure the door and cut the board with face upwards, true to size, using a medium-toothed saw. Or cut a pattern in brown paper the required size, and then cut the fibre board from the pattern. The board should be set back a little from the edges of the door in order to protect the edge of the board and obviate the necessity for adjusting the door stops. The margin which can conveniently be allowed between the edge of the hardboard and the edge of the door may be $\frac{1}{4}$ in. to about 3 in.

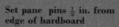

Temporary guide pins at lower edges of hardboard (left) serve as a support for the hardboard when placing in position and ensure correct centring

Draw guide line for panel pins $\frac{1}{2}$ in. from edge of hardboard by running pencil along, using finger as a stop

Set pane pins $\frac{1}{2}$ in. from edge of hardboard

Panel pins at 3-in. intervals at outer edges of hardboard

Panel pins at 6-in. intervals elsewhere

DECORATIVE EDGES

The edges of the panel should be cleaned up with sandpaper, and if desired a bevelled or rounded edge can be produced. If a decorative edge is required, a small wood moulding may be applied.

A MODERN LOOK FOR YOUR HOME

Fresh walls, a sink splash-back and plenty of built-in cupboards all easily made from hardboard

THE kitchen is often the "Cinderella" of the house. If your kitchen is dull and awkward to work in, try bringing it up to date at a cost well within your reach.

All the improvements shown on these pages were carried out with hardboard, obtainable in a number of thicknesses, ¼ in. being the most commonly used. It is easily worked with ordinary carpenter's tools, can be sawn or drilled, and may be fixed by pinning, screwing or bonding.

WALLS

One of the best ways of brightening your walls is by covering them with enamelled hardboard. This cheery material is available in a variety of colours. You can buy it with a plain surface or in tile pattern, or with horizontal lines. Your local timber merchant, or builders' merchant or ironmonger will have a selection. Enamelled hardboard has a hard glossy finish which can be easily wiped down and needs no hard rubbing. In tiled pattern it achieves the same effect as ceramic tiling with the minimum of time and expense.

When cutting enamelled hardboard, use a straight-edge (such as a ruler) and an awl to score the surface. This has the same effect as a diamond for marking glass and will help to prevent the enamelled edge from getting chipped. Follow the awl mark with a fine-toothed wood saw and then finish off with fine sandpaper. Always give the finished edges two coats of paint (in surface shade) before fixing.

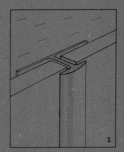

Enamelled hardboard may be fixed in the following ways:
(1) by pinning to timber battens 1 in. by ½ in. set vertically at 16 in. centres, not forgetting to provide a nailing base for all edges;
(2) by using metal moulding strip which also covers the joint;
(3) by bonding direct with adhesive to the plaster after sand-papering surface.
Your wallboard supplier can help you to select a suitable adhesive. Be sure to follow the adhesive manufacturer's instructions.

CUPBOARDS AND FITMENTS

Standard hardboard is ideal for making "built-in" or removable kitchen fitments of every description. Mounted on a timber frame-work by means of pins, screws, or again, adhesive, hardboard panels give a good-looking result. Provided a suitable sealer is first applied, any type of paint can be used. Complete the job with matching accessories of contemporary style.

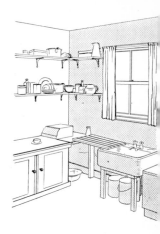

Brighten up your Kitchen

SINK SPLASH-BACKS

A particularly attractive touch can be given to your kitchen by fitting a hardboard splash-back above the sink. Use off-cuts of enamelled hardboard or obtain a panel cut to size. Bonding by adhesives is generally the best method of fixing, but the board can also be screwed into place, using dome-headed chromium - plated screws for the purpose.

FLOORS AND CEILINGS

Some handymen like to leave no stone unturned when doing a conversion job. For them we offer two extra kitchen ideas.

The ceiling can be covered with ¼ in. insulating board, or a more decorative effect can be obtained by using the insulating board in, for example, small squares, with bevelled edges. Nail through to the joists or bond to the plaster, using the same method as for walls. The insulating board will help reduce condensation.

The floor can be re-surfaced with tempered hardboard in the form of sheets, strips or tiles. Pin or bond to surface.

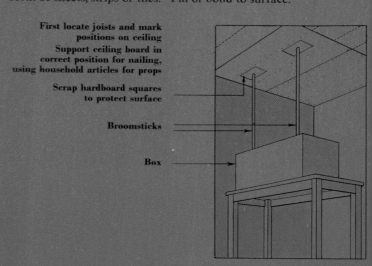

First locate joists and mark positions on ceiling

Support ceiling board in correct position for nailing, using household articles for props

Scrap hardboard squares to protect surface

Broomsticks

Box

POINTS TO REMEMBER

For table tops it is advisable to use one of the plastic-surfaced sheet materials, and not standard enamelled hardboard.

All hardboards should be conditioned before fixing. This is done by moistening the backs of the boards 48 hours before use.

Modernise your Bathroom

Even the most old-fashioned baths and basins can be brought up to date

BATHROOM WALLS

A tiled or plain enamelled hardboard which can be finished off at dado height or taken right up to the ceiling is recommended

The cost can be reduced by using a standard, untreated, hardboard and painting the surface.

Fixed either by a suitable adhesive—provided the surface is true and smooth—or to 2 in. by ¾ in. battens plugged to the wall. Finish with mouldings as desired.

Adhesive manufacturer's instructions must be followed. Do not use a water-soluble glue in the bathroom.

Wood framework 2 in. by 1 in.

Maximum distance between uprights: 12 in.

Dome-headed screws

ENCLOSING THE BATH

Prepare wood framework of 2 in. by 1 in. battens. Fix securely to the floor and walls at each end. Uprights must be fixed at each end and at intervals of not more than 12 in. along the front. Keep the whole framework back about ¼ in. from the outer edge of the bath.

Cut and fix the hardboard with 1 in. dome-headed chromium-plated screws at 12 in. intervals. Panel is removable for access to pipes and wastes.

A MODERN LOOK FOR YOUR HOME

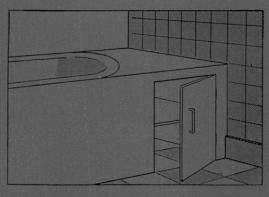

Utilise any space between end of bath and wall by extending bath-panelling and fitting cupboard door

USEFUL CUPBOARD

With round-ended baths the framework may be continued to support a filler piece of hardboard at the round end (shown as above) to make a useful cupboard underneath, using 1½ in. by ¾ in. timber as a frame for the door, which should be covered on both sides with hardboard.

Similarly, the space under the wash basin can be enclosed to form another cupboard.

Light framework of wood for bathroom cupboard

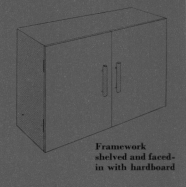

Framework shelved and faced-in with hardboard

BATHROOM CABINET

A useful bathroom cabinet can be made from a framing of 1 in. by ¾ in. timber covered with hardboard, fixed by a suitable adhesive and/or panel pins.

SPLASH-BACK

Odd pieces of board can be used as a splash-back above the wash-basin. If this is not enamelled board, it should be painted. The exposed edges of any board should be sealed with paint. Bonding by adhesives is the best method of fixing, or screw into place, using dome - headed chromium-plated screws.

UNSIGHTLY PIPES

These can be concealed by framing with light timber and boxing-in with either hardboard or enamelled board to match the other wall surfaces. Note (left) removable panel for access to main tap if necessary.

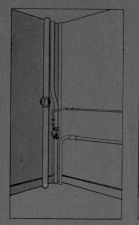
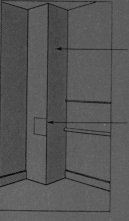

Unsightly pipes concealed by hardboard covering

Removable panel for access to main tap

SIMPLE GUIDE FOR THE HOME HANDYMAN

Practical hints on some of the common tasks and some useful advice about the choice and care of tools

USING PLASTIC WOOD

ONE of the handyman's (or woman's) greatest stand-bys is a tin of plastic wood. As a filler to remedy defects in timber—cracks or knot-holes; for covering up misdirected whacks with a hammer or slips from a screwdriver—it is first rate.

It can also be used to conceal screw heads or nails and so permit an unmarked surface of wood for polishing, painting or staining.

Plastic wood filler is simple enough to apply; just remember to press it firmly home, and allow for shrinkage by leaving it proud of the surface. When thoroughly dried out, it can be chiselled off level or sandpapered down.

If, however, you have a large hole to fill, cut down expense by almost filling it with a shaped wooden plug, leaving only a comparatively small surface layer to be covered with the plastic filler.

On occasion a defect filled in by this filler seems to stand out against the surrounding grain of the wood, especially in rather open-grained timber such as oak. A simple and useful tip to make the filler blend is to trace across it, from the grain of the surrounding wood, with a small knife. This is best carried out after the filler has set.

If it is intended to use a fair quantity of the filler, say, for making up a damaged section of moulding, use the preparation in a series of built-up layers, allowing each layer to dry out before applying the next. Never blob it all on at once; the chances are you will damage the filling when trying to shape it to match the adjoining moulding.

Knife Handles

Plastic filling is a useful remedy, too, for kitchen knives whose handles have become loose.

Remove the blade from the handle and wad in the hole an ample charge of the

Plaster board is easily cut with a Stanley trimming knife, which also prunes trees, cuts paper, linoleum, wall boards, etc., and carries four spare blades in the handle

filler. Leave it to set for a short time then, before it dries, push the tang of the blade well into the plastic-filled hole in the handle. Insert the tang with one firm push; don't wiggle it about during the push, or once it is bedded down. Leave to harden thoroughly before putting the knife into use.

In Crumbling Walls

If you have difficulty in getting hooks or brackets to stay put in crumbling plaster walls, a little "plastic surgery" will make a firm base to take the screws. Remove the bracket from the wall, scrape away any loose plaster (don't overdo this scraping, though), and then plug the holes in the plaster with a firm packing of plastic filler.

Allow the preparation to harden a little and then with care screw in the wood-screws to cut their own thread. Remove

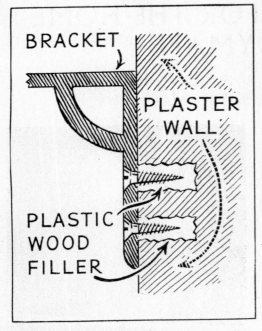

BRACKET

PLASTER WALL

PLASTIC WOOD FILLER

To make a bracket stay put in a crumbling wall, plug the holes with plastic filler

the screws and let the filler harden off. When it is dry, the bracket can be fixed to the wall by screwing into the pre-threaded holes. Be firm, but not forceful with the screwdriver.

Plastic wood filler soon dries hard when exposed to the air, so make a point of keeping the lid firmly fixed to the tin when not in use.

HITTING THE NAIL ON THE HEAD

HAMMERING nails into a piece of wood should be one of the simplest of jobs. A couple of pieces of stout timber, some sharp nails, a well-balanced hammer, and you are well away. But even this elementary method of joining has a snag—splitting.

There are three main causes. First, the nail may have been driven in too close to the end of the plank; second, the nail may have been placed too near the side of the board; and third, displacement of the grain by two or more nails placed directly in line with each other. In the latter case, the first nail acts as a wedge and subsequent nails

open the gap still wider until the wood splits.

The obvious way to avoid mishaps Nos. 1 and 2 is to bring the nail farther in from either the end or the side of the board. If that cannot be done, it is advisable to make a guide for the nail by boring through the timber with a bradawl.

Easy, gentle pressure on a sharp awl will quickly bore through the wood; but it is imperative that the blade of the bradawl is held so as to cut *across* the grain of the timber. Failure to take this precaution will result in splitting.

Stagger the Holes

Where two or more nails are to be driven into the same piece of timber, and comparatively close to each other, the safest method is to stagger the holes. Not only does this prevent splitting, but it gives added security to the joint. Another worthwhile expedient is to blunt slightly the point of the nail before entering it into the wood.

The handyman must bear in mind that although nails are, perhaps, the easiest method of uniting a couple of pieces of wood, their security cannot always be guaranteed. In heavy out-of-door jobs they are apt to work loose, even free themselves from the wood. This tendency can largely be overcome by driving the nails in on the slant—an angle of approximately 30 degrees is about right—the nails sloping alternately to the right and to the left.

For heavy constructive work, or where looks do not matter, it is advisable to use nails long enough to protrude a fair distance, and then to hammer them over with a stapling effect on the opposite side.

If possible, try to avoid drilling holes to take nails. Admittedly this will practically eliminate splitting, but it also reduces the gripping area. The drill expels a lot of the "grip" in the form of wood-dust; a bradawl does not, it merely parts the wood fibres.

GETTING IT STRAIGHT WITH RULE AND PENCIL

IN woodwork, "marking out" demands, as in other handicrafts, considerable accuracy.

Pencil is excellent for marking out most

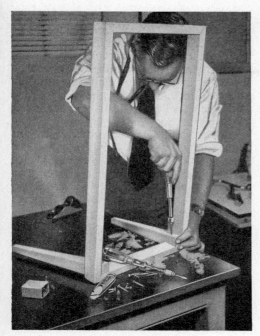

Drilling holes in hard-to-get-at corners is easy with a Stanley "Yankee" Handyman Push Drill (above), an easily handled tool that bores holes in wood, plaster and plastics, and drills without splitting wood

marks are to be of equal distance, a pair of dividers, correctly set, is ideal. Those with a fine adjustment screw are even better.

Simple to Use

Two kinds of gauge are usually in demand by the woodworker: the marking gauge and the cutting gauge. The former has a plain, nail-like point which marks the surface and is suitable for running a mark parallel with the grain. If used across the grain, it has a tendency to make a jagged scratch.

The cutting gauge is perhaps the best all-round tool; the knife-like cutter marks equally well across and parallel with the grain. It is simple to use and the depth of the mark can be set by adjusting the cutter, which is held in position by a wedge.

A "must" for any woodworking hobbyist is a try-square. With the blade and the butt (bottom plane) set at an accurate 90 degrees, the handyman cannot go wrong in marking up right angles.

jobs. But particularly fine work calls for a chisel, and at other times marking can best be done by a gauge.

Unless you are going to rip a long length of timber, in which case precision does not matter, always place the folding rule so that its *edge* comes into contact with the surface to be marked, i.e. the divisions on the rule are brought into contact with the timber. Avoid using the flat of the rule—it can prove a hit-or-miss method.

The pencil should be sharpened to a fine point for a fine line; but for a "hair" line a chisel is best and should be so held that the bevelled edge is against the try-square.

For repeat measurements, guides for drillings, positioning screws, nails, etc., where the

The Stanley "Yankee" Handyman Spiral Ratchet Screwdriver (above) is simply placed on the screw head, a lever is flicked and the screw goes in—or out—in a second. Can be used also to drill holes and countersink

On the Spot

An important point is to ensure that the surface of the wood against which the butt rests is perfectly straight, otherwise the angle is thrown out. Another useful tip when using a try-square is to measure off the distance to be ruled. Place the point of the pencil on the spot, and then slide the blade along to meet the pencil.

Then we have a cousin to the try-square —the set mitre. Instead of the blade being set at 90 degrees, this one is positioned at 45 degrees with the butt. An extremely useful tool for marking out work to be joined at right angles—picture frames and the like.

The flexible steel rule, which can be extended to several feet, although handy for measuring-off purposes, should rank second in importance to the folding rule where marking is concerned.

CHOOSING AND USING A SAW

NEXT to a hammer, the most useful piece of equipment in the handyman's tool kit is a saw.

The two saws in general use are the handsaw and the tenon saw. The former is the maid-of-all-work and, when starting to make up his kit, the amateur would be wise to select a saw having six or seven teeth to the inch. This enables him to make a neat cut across the grain, yet at the same time does not make the job of sawing with the grain a tedious task. If funds run to it, the saw for running with the grain is a ripsaw with teeth that are larger and set wider.

For general bench work, cutting small pieces of wood, joints and the odd jobs calling for fine cuts, the saws in demand are the tenon and the dovetail. The dovetail saw is comparatively small and the teeth are of a finer gauge than the tenon, thus leaving a narrower cut with the minimum of waste. Here again, with an eye on his pocket, the home handyman can select a saw combining, to a certain extent, the merits of both.

Other types available include the bow saw, keyhole saw, compass saw, bead saw; but of these, the bow saw and the keyhole saw best fit into the amateur's range of activities.

For cutting curves the bow saw is perhaps the best; its one disadvantage being that the cut is limited by the distance from the blade to the frame of the saw.

Its advantage is that the blade can be turned at any angle to the frame and will still cut effectively. With the blade turned at right angles there is no limit to the length of the cut.

Last on the list of practical saws for the home carpenter is the keyhole saw—also used for curves, but more generally for cutting out holes larger in diameter than the drill can cope with. Not a good saw, because it has a habit of "whipping" and the teeth are set rather coarse. If a fretsaw can be used, it makes a far neater and cleaner cut.

Useful Gadget

An extremely useful accessory when using the tenon or dovetail saw is the bench hook, which the handyman can make at a trifling cost (see diagram A opposite). It enables the work to be steadied against the bench and the timber kept in position while the saw does its job.

It is not difficult to acquire the knack of easy sawing. Do not force the saw through the wood; it will not cut any quicker and is unnecessarily hard work. If a saw is kept sharp—and clean—its own weight more or less takes it through the wood, with but little pressure. Even, steady strokes are the secret, with a nice easy rhythm.

GLUE: HOT OR COLD

"ALL I have to do now is glue it together!" It is a great day when the handyman can say that. But some thought for the preparation and use of glue is most important.

Nowadays quite a few amateur carpenters have taken to a "cold" glue; squeezed from a tube or taken from a tin, it calls for little preparation.

Scotch Glue still Holds

Without detracting from the merits of such glue, it is interesting to note that the professional joiner, cabinet and furniture maker still stick to Scotch glue. When prepared and applied in the correct way, it certainly holds. And it is comparatively cheap.

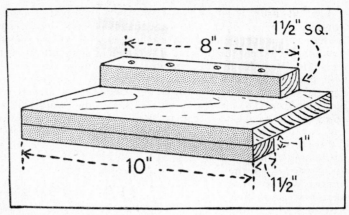

Diagram A: The Bench Hook, which can be made at trifling cost, keeps the timber in position while sawing—a boon to the handyman

When buying a cake of Scotch glue, see that it is clear and light in colour —almost amber. Fight shy of the dark and cloudy kind, and do not buy a cake that is at all soft. It should be hard and brittle.

Before hammering the cake into the desired small pieces, place it in a piece of sacking or other strong material; this saves splinters of glue cake flying about the place. A glue pot is needed, of course, but the glue chips can be put in a watertight tin, and this in turn placed in an old saucepan. Sufficient water just to cover the glue should be poured into the tin, and the vessel holding the tin partly filled with clean water, the water-level being about two-thirds of the way up the outside of the tin. For added efficiency the best method is to allow the chips to soak overnight in cold water. Surplus water can be drained off before heating.

Use Hot

Place the saucepan over the gas and stir the glue frequently with a stick, lifting it up and letting it flow back into the tin. The glue is ready for use when it flows off the stick in a steady, continuous stream; not being lumpy or breaking off into drops. The glue must be really hot before making the test—warm glue invariably appears thick and is therefore deceptive.

If at all possible, warm the joints before applying glue. Glue quickly cools off against cold timber, and consequently is apt to lose some of its grip.

Speed is the keynote of the operation, so don't glue too much at one time. Do the job in sections so that the glue can sink into the warm pores of the wood before they cool off.

Be careful not to overdo the application of glue; the less that is needed in a joint the better, so make certain that the prepared joints are a snug fit. Wipe off any surplus glue before it sets. This is easier than trying to chip it off after it has hardened.

Keep an eye on the water-level in the saucepan; it soon boils away and burnt glue is not of much use.

After heavy sanding jobs, sweep the wood dust into a jar. Mixed with glue, as required, it makes a first-rate and inexpensive filler.

THE ART OF SOLDERING

THE majority of metals met with in and around the house and garage—lead, zinc, tinplate, mild steel, bronze, etc.—can be effectively joined with tinman's solder. Do not tackle cast iron, however.

One of the more important points in the process of soldering is thoroughly to clean up the surfaces to be united. All traces of dirt and grease must be removed, and that goes for rust, too. It is no use tackling the job half-heartedly.

Knack soon Comes

To assist the flow of the solder you will need to buy flux, obtainable at the local ironmonger's, a tin of which lasts a long time.

Now for the soldering iron. These are made in a number of sizes, and naturally the size of the iron used will depend upon the job to be tackled. It is not so much a question of the size of the iron as the size and weight of the copper bit inserted in the iron—for this is the part that does the work. A small bit will not retain the heat long enough to "run" a long strip of soldering.

The bit itself must be kept properly "tinned"; i.e. all four sides adequately coated with solder. A simple method of doing this is to heat the bit until it will melt the solder, then dip it into some flux along with some small blobs of solder. By easing the sides of the bit on the solder, tinning will form. This requires a little experience, but the knack soon comes. Wipe off any surplus flux while the iron is warm.

Care is necessary in the heating of the iron for, if overheated, the tinning will eat into the copper and cause erosion. Heat the bit until it will just melt the solder. Practice is necessary to gauge the right temperature, but a useful guide is to heat the bit until it colours quickly, after wiping it with a piece of clean rag. Apply the flame just above the point of the copper bit—and do not use a coal fire for the heating.

The next step is the actual soldering. Having ensured that the surfaces are clean, apply flux to them. For a small job, take the solder from the stick by way of the tinned surfaces of the heated bit. The bit is then brought into contact with the joint and held there for a moment to allow it to warm up. If the joint is really clean, the solder will run from the tip of the bit on to the job; it can then be "wiped" over with the bit to make a clean face.

For a join of any length, run the iron and the solder along the seam, keeping the bit flat on the metal and slightly in advance of the solder. Do not lift the bit from the work while soldering a seam.

DOVETAILING MAKES A GOOD JOINT

BY far the strongest method of joining boards at right angles—e.g. for boxes, drawers, frames, etc.—is to dovetail the ends, yet many amateurs shrink from this method. True, it entails a little more work, but the result is very rewarding.

No dovetailed joint falls apart, and the neat pattern of interlocking pieces certainly improves the job.

The joint, for practical purposes, is made up of tapered pins (or pegs) and sockets; the number of pins depends upon the width of the board. For appearance's sake, small pins are better; but they must be strong enough to hold up against the strain at the joint. Softwood naturally needs a larger pin than hardwood.

Tackle the pins first, after seeing that the ends of the boards are trimmed square before marking. Set a gauge to the thickness of the timber and use this to mark both ends of each board. The two end pins are marked out first, the remainder distanced out evenly between them.

Outside Always

Having marked out the pegs (for $\frac{1}{2}$ in. boards, say, $\frac{1}{2}$ in. wide tapering down to $\frac{1}{4}$ in.) at the end of the board, continue the pencil marks down both faces of the wood to the gauge mark, using a try-square. The wide part of the peg is *always* on the outside of the board.

To cut the pegs, saw down the pencil guides to the gauge mark, then with a chisel cut out the waste, taking pains to see that the shoulders are straight and square. To avoid splintering, remove half the waste from one side, reverse the wood and complete the chiselling from the other side.

In for Good

Now for the sockets. The best method is to place the *inside* of the board with the pins to the gauge line of the board selected for the sockets. Holding this guide firmly in position, with a sharp pencil mark out the position of the sockets. As with the pins, a saw and chisel are used to cut the sockets.

TIPS ABOUT TOOLS

1 Keep a full set of screwdrivers, or at least a 3 in., 6 in., and 8 in., with perhaps a " stubby," blade length 1¼ in., for working on awkward places. Then you will be equipped to tackle any screw in the house.

2 Always wipe your screwdrivers over with an oily rag before putting them away after use.

3 you have only a small cupboard for your tools, screw clips for the tools on the inside of the door. This will leave almost the entire cupboard free for timber off-cuts, trestle, etc.

Having fashioned both pegs and sockets, fit the joint together and test for firmness and angle. Make a practice of fitting the socket piece to the pins—not vice versa. A piece of wood placed over the sockets and gently tapped should enable the board to slip into place without the ends of the sockets being splintered by the entry of the pins.

Having satisfied yourself as to firmness, all that remains is to glue the joint together, squaring up before the glue sets.

Dovetailing may take up a little more time and involve more precision; but the finished job pays dividends. If the joint is correctly made, it is there for keeps.

Some practice may be necessary, of course; start with a couple of pieces of off-cuts until you master the knack.

GIVING PLYWOOD A GOOD FINISH

THE amateur woodworker's usual choice of wood for panelling, cabinets and odd items of furniture is plywood. He often makes a good job of the construction, but spoils the look of his work by an indifferent finish.

The reason is that plywood calls for treatment before any polish, stain or varnish can be satisfactorily applied. Yet it is not difficult to give it a really good top surface.

First of all, apply a coating of size; after it has dried, follow on by rubbing down with a fine sandpaper. Brush off all dust and apply another coat of size. Allow it to dry out again, dust off, and the surface is then ready to take a good polish.

Edges of plywood, if not covered by beading or moulding, present a snag. If you do not happen to have any wood filler handy, the answer is whiting mixed to a paste with glue, and the mixture rubbed well into the grain. Let it set, then clean up with fine sandpaper.

Staining plywood may prove rather disappointing unless the article is made from one sheet and cut off as required. If you buy odd pieces of ply, it invariably happens that the finished job is made up in varying grades of wood, each taking the stain differently. The result is an uneven overall colour.

When staining plywood, stick to an oil or turps stain, as little or no raising of the grain results (it is the raising of the grain in this type of wood that produces such a poor finish).

After the stain has dried, lightly rub the surface down with fine sandpaper. A good plan is to rub a couple of sheets of fine sandpaper together to obtain the desired smoothness. The job is now ready for the final varnishing or polishing.

When varnishing, make a point of keeping the brush well supplied but not overloaded, and apply it lightly. Too energetic use of the brush produces tiny bubbles, or "tears," in the varnished surface which eventually dry, burst and produce ugly pinpricks. Work the brush in all directions, but try not to "paint" the varnish on —varnish evens itself out. Make a practice of starting at the highest point of the work and varnishing downwards.

Do your varnishing in a warm, dry room or workshop. A simple point, but a worthwhile one. The disfiguring "bloom" that appears on varnished surfaces is generally due to dampness affecting the varnish while it is soft, and becoming trapped in it while it hardens; so watch out for draughts from doors and windows.

In some cases the bloom can be cured by rubbing over the surface with a mixture of oil and vinegar, afterwards rubbing the work clean with a dry, soft duster. If this does not effect a cure, the only answer is to strip the work completely and re-varnish.

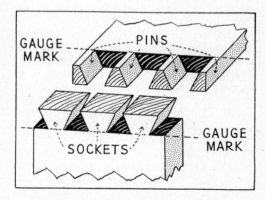

A dovetailed joint, made up of tapered pins and sockets, never falls apart and gives a job a most professional look

A STRONG TRAY FOR ELEVENSES

*It can be made cheaply and easily by
even the most inexperienced woodworker*

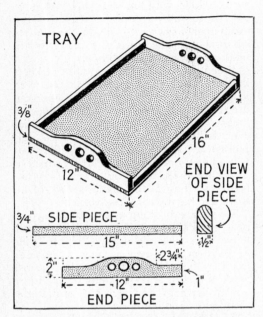

TRAY

3/8"

16"

12"

END VIEW
OF SIDE
PIECE

3/4" SIDE PIECE

15"

1/2"

2"

2¾"

12"

1"

END PIECE

Showing the dimensions of the various component parts and how the tray is assembled

A NEAT and serviceable tray, just right for tea and biscuits, can be made cheaply and easily, even by the most inexperienced woodworker. The materials needed can very likely be found in the "off-cuts" bin in the shed.

The base of the tray can be either five-ply, or ⅜-in. board, 12 in. wide and 16 in. long. For choice, the five-ply; the chances are that you will have to join a couple of boards to get a width of 12 in., and a join down the centre, however well made, spoils the "clean" look of the finished article.

Two pieces of hardwood are needed for the sides, each 15 in. long, ¾ in. wide and ½ in. thick. The ends are fashioned from two pieces of the same hardwood, each being 12 in. long, 2 in. wide and ½ in. thick.

So much for the materials required. Square and clean up the plywood base of

the tray, taking it easy at the corners, for plywood has a great tendency to split. The two sides call next for attention. Ensure that the ends are absolutely square, and that one of the surfaces along the length is perfectly flat. This will be the edge fitted to the base, so no "rocking" can be permitted. The uppermost edge of the side piece is rounded off. This can be carried out with a plane, followed by sanding with a coarse paper, finishing off with a fine grade.

The two end pieces require a little more work to comply with the design; but by following the pattern shown in the diagram the job should not prove difficult.

Three holes drilled in the end pieces provide a convenient means of holding the tray, and it is advisable to bore these out before cutting the wood to shape.

Boring Bit

The centre hole should be 1¼ in. in diameter, and the holes either side 1 in. bore. Run a pencil line along the centre of the side pieces. Exactly in the middle of these lines, i.e. 6 in. from either end, will be the spot for the large hole to be drilled out. Make another pencil mark 1⅜ in. to either side of this spot to take the tip of the bit for the smaller holes.

After the holes have been drilled, lightly sandpaper the edges to remove any roughness— a piece of sandpaper wrapped round a pencil comes in handy here.

The sides and ends of the tray are glued and screwed to the base. Sixteen slender ¾-in. screws, countersunk and screwed home from the base—four screws to each side of the tray—finish the construction. Have a preliminary fitting before using screws and glue.

The tray can then be stained or painted. If the wood looks attractive in its natural state, a thin coating of wax well rubbed in, followed by a vigorous polish with a soft cloth, will be sufficient.

MAKE YOUR OWN IRONING BOARD

*It is the right height to reduce fatigue and backache to
a minimum and is strong enough to stand up to its job*

HERE'S a useful piece of work for the handyman: a folding ironing board made to stand up to its job, and of a height to reduce ironing fatigue and backache.

The diagrams are more or less self-explanatory; close attention should be given to the marking out, which is not at all difficult if undertaken with a strict eye to the drawings.

The timber used is $\frac{7}{8}$ in. thick deal boarding, cut and shaped to the sizes specified, plus three small lengths of $\frac{1}{2}$ in. dowelling used as pivots—one piece 8 in. long and two shorter ones, each 2 in. in length. The 8 in. dowel passes through the two brackets B and holes drilled at the top of the outer legs to form an "axle." When the dowel is in position it is held secure by a thin nail driven through the bracket into it. The smaller dowels pivot the two pairs of legs together, and again the dowels are secured by a nail driven through from the underside of the outer legs into the peg.

So far as the legs are concerned, drill the holes and cut out the mortises *before* cutting angles. The dotted lines shown on the ironing board itself indicate positions of the brackets holding the 8 in. dowel rod, and the outer legs are fitted *inside* these. Brackets are screwed into place.

The "stop" C is recessed to take the top platform of the inner legs A. Some care is necessary in shaping the platform. This is fashioned from a small block of wood $2\frac{3}{4}$ in. long and $2\frac{3}{8}$ in. wide and angled as shown. When shaped, the platform fits flush between the top of the inner legs and is secured by two screws (countersunk), thus providing a firm rest for the board when it is unfolded for use.

Allow a Little Extra

Accuracy is necessary when marking out the bracing struts which fit between the legs. Allow a little extra on the tenons so that these may later be sawn off level with the legs to make a neat joint.

At the squared end of the ironing board is fitted a piece of asbestos (or some other

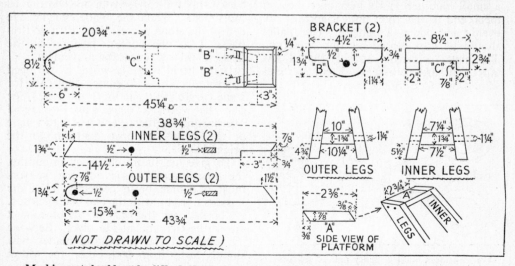

(*NOT DRAWN TO SCALE*)

**Marking out should not be difficult if strict attention is paid to these drawings. Timber used is $\frac{7}{8}$ in.
thick deal boarding cut to sizes specified, plus three small lengths of $\frac{1}{2}$-in. dowelling**

heat-resisting substance), 7⅞ in. by 4⅞ in., and kept in place by a mitred frame of ⅜ in. beading, or a metal strip surround.

Assembly is easy enough and needs no further explanation, but carry this out before covering. The board is first covered by a layer of white felt (or blanket if you have a spare piece) which ends at the asbestos plate, and is cut so that it can be pinned tightly (but not stretched) in position along the edge by small upholstery nails

which should be inserted at 6-in. intervals. Over the felt is a double thickness of linen, which can be removed for washing when it becomes grubby.

Prevents Tearing

The linen is also nailed to the board, but a length of ½ in. wide tape fitted along the edge of the material before entering the pins will prevent the linen tearing and also facilitate its removal for washing.

SHARPENING SCISSORS

*No need for a blunt pair anywhere in the house if you test
them for efficiency regularly and repair damage promptly*

IT is surprising the number of faulty pairs of scissors to be found in most houses that merely need a little simple maintenance to make them work efficiently.

One of the results of constant use is that the pivot becomes loose, which makes cutting an annoying task. Test for excessive looseness by opening the blades to their fullest extent and working them against each other. If the pivot is loose, it must be tightened.

Blades are usually held together by a screw-headed pivot, so give the head a slight tightening turn with a screwdriver. Now reverse the scissors and rest the head of the pivot on a flat metal surface. With a small hammer gently burr over the soft metal end of the pivot until it spreads out evenly and makes a tight fit. The blades should be kept closed for this operation. The metal is usually so soft that a few taps only are necessary. Frequent tests should be made for tightness.

Maybe the blades of the scissors have become blunt and the cutting edges need attention. To make a good job of sharpening the blades, the best plan is to separate them. This means removing the pivot. Carefully file off the burred edge and the rivet can be removed quite easily.

Care at the Grindstone

Use an oilstone for the sharpening. After placing two or three drops of oil on the stone, grip the blade by the tip and the heel and place it on the oilstone so that the *bevelled edge only* lies perfectly flat on the stone. Now draw the blade from end to end of the stone diagonally. Do not work backwards and forwards in one continuous movement. When the blade reaches the end of the stone nearest you, lift it and replace it in the correct position at the farthest end and repeat the movement.

If the bevel is badly worn, it will need renewing before sharpening. This calls for some careful work at the grindstone. See that the wheel revolves slowly to avoid overheating the metal, and watch the angle of the bevel—it must conform to the original angle.

To give maximum efficiency in cutting, the reassembled blades of the scissors must, of course, be set correctly. Hold the scissors upright, with the two blades closed. If correctly set, the only points of contact are at the tips and at the pivot. Between the tips and the pivot, the blades bow slightly away from each other, the widest part of the bow—which must not be excessive—being half-way along the blades.

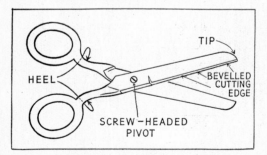

You can often make a faulty pair of scissors work again simply by tightening the screw-headed pivot—or sharpening with an oilstone

A BATH TRAY TO MAKE

Large enough to hold soap, face flannels and nail brushes for the family, it can be enamelled to match the bathroom colour scheme

A USEFUL bathroom accessory for the handyman to make is an easily constructed rack to hold soap, face flannels and nail brushes.

The materials needed are not expensive. Two pieces of $\frac{1}{2}$ in. dowelling, 2 ft. 3 in. in length, are required for the rack supports which rest on the sides of the bath. For the rack (or tray) itself, eight 1 ft. $2\frac{3}{4}$ in. lengths of $\frac{3}{8}$ in. dowelling will be wanted. The four ends of the supports are sleeved with thin, corrugated rubber hose, each piece being 4 in. long and having an inside diameter of $\frac{1}{2}$ in. (white for preference).

The two ends are fashioned from $\frac{1}{2}$ in. board, each measuring $9\frac{1}{2}$ in. by $2\frac{1}{2}$ in.

The dowelling should be "squared" up at the ends and, if it is rough, finely sandpapered.

The two ends forming the pattern of the tray demand the most attention. Plane and square up the ends and test the angles with a try-square. Determine which shall be the top and bottom edges. Mark off 1 in. along the upper edge from each corner, and a further pencil mark 1 in. down from the same corners (see diagram). With a compass, link the pencil marks with a curved line. Chisel off the waste wood (a fretwork saw will make the job cleaner and neater).

Now for the lower edge. Two pencil marks are made, each $1\frac{1}{2}$ in. distant from the right and left corners respectively. These pencil marks are linked up in a more gradual curve with the 1 in. marks previously made. Remove the waste wood. A fine sandpapering will take off any "edges" from the curves.

Draw the Line

A pencilled line drawn across the face of the end pieces from the 1-in. marks will provide a guide for drilling the holes for the two supporting rods. Having drawn the line, mark off a spot $\frac{3}{4}$ in. from either end. The spot will be the centre of the $\frac{1}{2}$-in. hole to be drilled out.

Another pencilled line drawn $\frac{3}{8}$ in. from the lower edge of the end-pieces, and

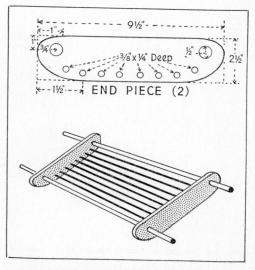

The end pieces, which form the pattern of the tray, demand the greatest care in construction, but the diagram (top) shows how to do this—and here is the finished article

parallel to it, is the guide for the tray rod drillings. The eight drillings are marked off at equal distances along this line and bored with a $\frac{3}{8}$-in. bit to a depth of $\frac{1}{4}$ in. —*not* right through the wood.

Coats of Enamel

That completes the construction. The assembly is a simple matter. Fit and glue the tray dowellings into one of the end pieces first, then tackle the other. Slide the outer supporting rods through their respective holes, ensuring that equal lengths protrude. Secure these in position by a thin panel pin driven through the end pieces into the rods and concealed.

A couple of coats of enamel—to match the bathroom colour scheme—finish the job, apart from the final fitting of the rubber sleeves when the enamel has dried out.

NOTE: The length of the supporting rods may need to be modified slightly, so before cutting these, measure the width of the bath.

A FOLDING STOOL FOR THE GARDEN OR FOR FISHING

It takes up little storage space either in the home or in transit

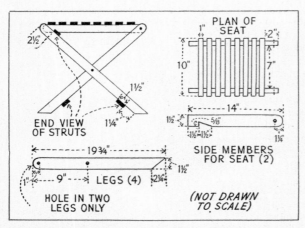

Showing the correct measurements of the various parts and where to drill holes, etc. The seat is made of eight slats

HERE is an ideal folding stool for fishing, picnicking, or just sitting in the garden. Compact and strong, it occupies little storage space.

Choose one of the harder woods for the stool. Four pieces of timber, each 19¾ in. long, 1½ in. wide and ¾ in. thick, are needed for the legs. Angles at the foot of the legs are made by marking off 2¼ in. from one end, pencilling to the opposite corner and sawing off the waste (see diagram).

Guides for Drilling

The tops of the legs are slightly rounded. On all four legs measure off 9 in. from the top, and on two of the legs make a further mark 1 in. away from the top. These marks are guides for drilling ¼ in. holes.

Three leg-bracing struts are needed: two for the outer legs, each measuring 11¾ in. by 1½ in. by ½ in., and a third, 10 in. by 1½ in. by ½ in.

Two side members are required for the seat, each measuring 14 in. by 1½ in. by ¾ in. Round off one end of each side member and then mark off 1¼ in. With this mark acting as a guide, drill a ¼-in. hole

through each. Working from the squared end, pencil off 1½ in. Use a try-square to make a ⅝ in. vertical line. Link the top of this line with another mark pencilled 1½ in. from the base of the line (see diagram). This is for the "hook" which rests in the top bracing strut of the outer legs, and can be sawn out.

The seat itself is made of eight slats, each 10 in. long, 1 in. wide and ¼ in. thick. These slats are screwed to the two side members (two ⅝ in. slender screws each end of the slat, and countersunk). Inside width between the side members should be 7 in. and, after allowing a clear space of 2 in. from the drilled end, evenly space out the slats.

The longer leg-bracing struts are fitted to the outer legs. Screw the lower strut beneath the leg 1¼ in. from the angle; the upper bracing strut is screwed above the leg and 2½ in. from the rounded end. Four 1½-in. slender screws (countersunk) to each strut.

Scissor-fashion

The shorter and remaining strut is screwed across and beneath the two inner legs, 1¼ in. from the angle.

The two pairs of legs are hinged, scissor-fashion, by two 1½ in. by ¼ in. wood bolts inserted in the holes already drilled. A circular recess, just sufficient to take the nuts, should be drilled on the inside of the inner legs. One washer to each nut is advisable.

Two further wood bolts, same dimensions, are needed to hinge the seat to the legs —again the nuts and washers are recessed.

When the stool is assembled, note where the "hooks" in the side members of the seat rest against the top strut, then chamfer away just sufficient of the strut to make a good seating for the "hook" without weakening the cross-member.

CONTEMPORARY CIRCULAR TABLE

A strong and serviceable one suitable for occasional
use or to take a radio can be made by the handyman

AN occasional table is always useful, and quite a strong, contemporary one can be turned out by the handyman.

The four legs are each constructed from 4 in. by 1 in. by 16 in. boards, and the two cross-pieces to support the table-top each from 3½ in. by 1 in. by 12 in. boards. The top itself can be designed according to personal taste—oblong, oval or a patterned shape. The size of the top best suited to the leg dimensions is 22 in. by 24 in., and the thickness from ½ in. to 1 in. If the table is intended to carry any weight—such as a radio set—then 1 in. is desirable.

The sketches set out clearly the shaping of the legs, cross-supports and general construction. Dowelling makes a neat and effective job of fixing the legs to the cross-pieces. Dowel holes should be drilled ⅜ in. in diameter, two dowels to each leg—and ensure that the dowels themselves are a good, tight fit before glueing up. Length of the dowels, 2 in.: 1 in. in the leg and 1 in. in the cross-piece. When drilling the holes to take the pegs, make certain that they are straight and at right angles to the surface.

Cross-members are slotted together and glued. The slots, 1 in. wide and 1¾ in. deep, and exactly in the centre, are sawn and chiselled out. A snug, tight fit is called for. Legs and cross-pieces when dowelled and glued should be clamped firmly until the glue sets. A length of stout cord, used

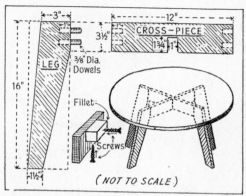

Showing the shaping of the legs, cross-supports and general construction of the table

Spanish windlass fashion, is an excellent substitute for clamps, but protect the edges of the wood where the cord bites.

If desired, moulding or beading can be glued or pinned (with panel pins) round the edges of the table-top—but their use is a matter of taste. Too much ornamentation is apt to spoil the lines of the table.

The top may be fixed to the cross-members by fillets of wood glued or screwed to the top and the cross-pieces. If screws are used to give additional strength, see that they do not protrude above the surface. Small, metal angle brackets will also serve the purpose.

The finished job can be treated for staining or polishing.

THREE-LEGGED STOOL

No complicated carpentry is needed to make this neat
piece of furniture for the bathroom or kitchen

A VERY handy three-legged stool, suitable for the bathroom, or for occasional use in the kitchen, can be constructed at small cost and without complicated carpentry.

The seat, circular in shape and 14 in. in diameter, is made from ¾-in. thick timber,

or a heavy ply. The legs, each 14 in. long and 1 in. in diameter, can be sawn from a long broom, garden rake or hoe handle; for strength, use one of the harder woods such as beech or birch.

For additional support, the legs are fixed at an angle to the seat—a splayed effect

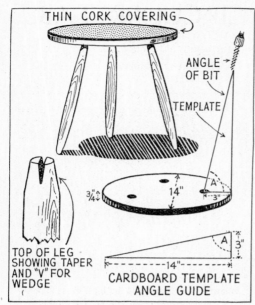

THIN CORK COVERING

ANGLE OF BIT

TEMPLATE

3/4"   14"   A'   3"

TOP OF LEG SHOWING TAPER AND "V" FOR WEDGE

A   3"

14"

CARDBOARD TEMPLATE ANGLE GUIDE

The seat can be neatly covered with cork glued on and trimmed to fit. Note how the legs are fixed at an angle to the seat

that will make the stool less likely to topple.

Choose which side of the seat is to be the underside and pencil a circle 3 in. inside and parallel to the rim of the seat. On this inner circle mark out the positions of the three legs the same distance apart.

Having marked where the seat is to be drilled to take the legs, the next step is to bore a hole, using a $\frac{3}{4}$-in. bit. The correct angle for the hole is shown in the diagram.

When cutting the legs, leave them oversize—say, about 16 in. in length. The top of the leg, i.e. the part let into the seat, is tapered off to make a tight fit into the hole, and about $\frac{1}{8}$ in. proud at the top of the seat. Having satisfied yourself that the leg really is a tight fit, remove it from the hole and saw a V-shaped niche down the centre from the top—$\frac{3}{16}$ in. wide and $\frac{5}{8}$ in. deep. Some wooden wedges to fit the Vs need to be shaped, allowing the top of the wedge to protrude $\frac{1}{4}$ in. above the top of the leg.

Cork Seat

Glue the legs (see p. 508) into their respective sockets, driving them well home from the bottom. Rest the stool on a firm base and tap the glued wedges tightly into position without disturbing the setting of the legs.

Give the glue ample time to set and harden off, then clean away any surplus that may have oozed out. The tops of the legs, including wedges, can be carefully chiselled off flush with the seat.

Measure the length of the legs by placing a rule hard up against the underside of the seat and measuring off 14 in. Cut to size. See that there are no odd chips of glue still adhering to the joints, otherwise the rule will not go home; the result will be legs of varying lengths.

☆ ☆ ☆ ☆ ☆ ☆ ☆ ☆ ☆ ☆ ☆ ☆

STRAW LAMPSHADE

Materials: 1 *lampshade frame—drum shape*; 2 *or* 3 *straw wine-bottle sleeves; raffia*; 1 *medium-sized crochet hook; trimming.*

SELECT widest pieces of straw, remove the fibre and wipe with a cloth. Attach to top and bottom of the frame with raffia. This is done with chain-stitch crochet, one stitch above the wire, the next below, zig-zag fashion. To keep the work under control, attach about 20 straws to both upper and lower rings before continuing. When complete, crochet a line of stitches round the centre. To finish, cut the straw so that it overlaps the frame by 1 in. at the top and $1\frac{1}{2}$ in. at the base.

Add trimming. The shade illustrated is decorated with artificial cherries and rose leaves.

RESURFACING FURNITURE

*Without skilled assistance, you can give kitchen
tables, trolleys, etc., wipe-clean, stainless tops*

LAMINATED PLASTICS

ONE of science's biggest contributions to the modern, labour-saving kitchen beautiful is the stainless, heat-resisting, wipe-clean veneer made of laminated plastics. It is suitable for all hard-worked surfaces, from sink counters to tables and trolleys, needs the minimum of upkeep and looks decorative into the bargain. A special attraction is that it can be applied without expert knowledge, provided meticulous attention is paid to the instructions and due care given to detail.

The new laminated plastic surfaces are just as good in dining rooms as in kitchens and nurseries. Above, table and storage unit tops and sliding doors are veneered in Formica in blue, pink or primrose. Furniture is by Kandya Ltd.

VARIOUS KINDS AND HOW THEY DIFFER

A variety of laminated plastics veneers are on sale to the home handy man and woman. Most straightforward both to buy and use are the standard size panels, ranging from 3 ft. by 2 ft. upwards in most brands and from 1 ft. 6 in. by 2 ft. upwards in one type that is proportionately somewhat cheaper. Three popular branded makes are Formica, Warerite and Klingdecor. All look very similar, and the first two differ little except in one important particular—the method of application. Klingdecor has an asbestos sheeting foundation that makes it cigarette proof but rather more brittle.

There are two kinds of standard size panel—bonded and unbonded. The former are simple veneer sheets, incorporating various plastic substances, of from $\frac{1}{16}$–$\frac{1}{8}$-in. thickness. The surface to which they are stuck or bonded must be perfectly even, level and rigid. Pre-bonded panels have a backing of thin ply or foundation board to which they have already been stuck. They cost a little more, but less surface preparation is necessary before fixing them.

METHODS OF FIXING

Fixing depends largely upon the adhesive used. Some makers specify an impact adhesive (a synthetic rubber glue), others prescribe the use of a resin cement. The latter takes some hours to dry, and during the process must be subjected to heavy, even pressure. It is advisable to buy the adhesive expressly recommended for the particular make of panel. Others of the same type may not give quite such good results.

Prior preparation of the surface to be covered: Ensure that it is clean, grease- and paint-free, and dry. This holds good

After the table top has been cleaned down with sandpaper to ensure that no grease or dirt remain on the surface to be covered, apply the special adhesive provided, quickly and thinly to the back of the Formica panel, then leave on one side to dry for 15 minutes

Next apply the adhesive to the surface of the table (which must be thoroughly dried if it has been washed) thinly but evenly with the spreader supplied. It is important that the edges and corners of both table and panel should be well covered with adhesive

whether the thin veneers or the pre-bonded panels are being used. Additional preparation for unbonded veneers is sandpapering the surface to be covered and, in some cases, roughening the back of the veneer itself.

An impact, rubber-type adhesive is spread, with special applicator or a piece of stick, both on to the reverse side of the panel and on to the surface to be covered. This is a longer job than might be anticipated, as both surfaces must be evenly coated and the adhesive is rather sticky and does not flow. After a short interval (15 minutes) for drying, one corner and one edge of the panel are carefully lined up with one edge of the surface to be covered. It is essential to get the positioning accurate before the main part of the panel is let down on the surface because it sticks instantly and no sliding or alteration is possible. Maximum pressure should be used to see that the veneer adheres evenly.

With **resin cements** of the approved type, one surface is covered with the cement and the other with a special acid hardener supplied with it. This kind of adhesive is quicker to apply as it does not set at once. The veneer can be slid or eased into position as required. As soon as it is well smoothed down, so that all air is excluded, a really heavy continuous weight must rest on top throughout the drying period of up

to 6 hours. Suitable weights are pails of water (for tables that can be placed upside down on the floor) or large heavy books of the encyclopædia type.

FINISH

A coat of paint to cover the raw edges where veneer and surface join is simple and effective. More elaborate alternatives are wooden beading, put on with tiny tacks or a special metal edging.

Points to watch are that all necessary tools, as prescribed in the instructions supplied with each panel, are to hand. Also that adequate time is allowed, the work being more finicky in practice than it sounds when described. Wearing a pair of old gloves is a useful precaution because the rubber-type adhesives are difficult to remove and the acid hardener used with the resin cements can be injurious to the skin.

Veneers can be cut to size with a tenon saw or hacksaw and then filed smooth after fixing. This requires some skill, especially if a long length has to be cut, and should be avoided as far as possible if the handy man or woman is not expert. The unbonded panels are easier to saw than the bonded ones but crack or break at corners more easily. Relatively small size panels are safest for the amateur to tackle initially.

Having first applied adhesive to table and panel (opposite), you now fix drawing pins into the edge of the table on two sides for accurate positioning. After fifteen minutes, the two surfaces should be tacky enough for bonding together. One edge and one corner are lined up

Above, roll down the Formica panel so that any remaining air will be pressed out. Then, working from the drawing-pinned end, thump with your fists hard all over the new top and along the edges to make sure the joint really meets

Above, should there be too much Formica overlap to remove conveniently with a file, cut it off with a handsaw with medium or fine teeth, using quick downward strokes, then smooth the sharp edges and round away with sandpaper or pot-scouring steel wool

Step-by-step method of resurfacing a kitchen table, using "instant impact" adhesive

Edging with Formica is work for an expert, but you can finish off the job effectively by painting the edges with several thin coats of paint to match or contrast. And finally, you have your gay, stainless, spongeable table top ready for use

Remember: these modern glues have "impact adhesion" and stick instantly. You cannot slide the two parts into correct relation. Once the Formica panel has made contact with the table top, it is almost impossible to remove it. So position it accurately at the start for good results

SASH WINDOW
FAULTS AND REMEDIES

How to fit a new sash cord and maintain your windows in
good working order without outside help

A BADLY fitting window sash or a broken sash cord are constant causes of annoyance to the householder. Broken sash cords are positively dangerous. A sash will, no doubt, hang for a long time by one cord, but when that cord breaks, results are often startling and sometimes painful. Every householder should therefore see that all sashes are in good order and carrying their full equipment of cords.

Before anyone can replace a broken sash cord the construction of the window frame and the workings of the sashes must be understood.

How a Sash Window Works

Sashes are balanced on each side by heavy weights. The weights are attached to the cords that pass over the pulleys, and a special cavity is constructed in the window frame to allow these weights to move up or down, according to the position of the sashes.

Fig. 1 shows the cords and weights as they appear in a view from behind the frame. The piece marked *A* is known as a parting slip. Its special purpose is to prevent the weights from banging and clanging together when the sashes are moved up or down in the frame.

Broken Sash Cord in Lower Sash

When the broken cord is one attached to the lower sash, the upright beading should be prised off on the side on which the cord is broken.

In doing so it is not necessary to spoil the paint and make unsightly bruises. A broad wood chisel should be inserted in the joint formed by the window frame and the beading, somewhere about the middle, and gently tapped with a mallet, using a prising motion at the same time. When the beading has been prised off slightly, the nails that hold it will be visible. Always prise near the nails to reduce the danger of snap-

ping the beading. When the beading has been prised off until it forms an arch, as shown by the dotted outline in Fig. 2, it will easily spring out of position.

Where only one cord is broken, the unbroken one should be examined and tested. If there is the slightest doubt about its condition, renew it at the same time. Having removed the upright beading, lift the sash clear of the horizontal bead fixed to the bottom bar or sill. If both cords need renewing, lift the sash out entirely, but where only one cord is broken, the free end only of the sash is lifted clear and rested on something suitable, such as a pair of steps, so that it is clear for further operations.

On examining the channel of the window frame, in which the sash works, a small trap will be noticed, as shown in Fig. 1. In some cases this trap is held by a screw which may be well hidden by several coats of paint. Remove the screw and the trap can be prised out of position with a chisel. The weight will then be seen lying in the recess, when it can be lifted out.

The two pieces of broken cord are now taken in hand, one piece from the sash, the other from the weight. Notice how the knot has been tied at the weight end so that you can copy it.

Ordinary rope is of no use for sashes; it would soon stretch and become unserviceable. Strong cord made specially for sashes is obtainable at the ironmonger's, as also are the clout nails for nailing the cord to the sash. These nails are a special length so that the point does not damage the glass.

Having measured and cut to length a piece of new cord, using as a measure the two old broken pieces, take a thin piece of string and attach to one end a small, comparatively weighty object—a piece of chain, such as that to which wash-basin plugs are attached, is very useful for this purpose, or a "mouse," constructed as shown in Fig. 3, can be used.

Pass this weight over the pulley and allow it to pull the string until the weight is visible at the trap opening. Then tie one end of the string to the piece of prepared sash cord, and by this means pull the cord over the pulley and down into the weight cavity until finally one end can be passed through the trap opening. Having pulled through a sufficient length of cord, thread through the eye of the weight, tie the knot and hammer well into the groove of the eye.

The free end of the cord now remains to be fixed to the sash. Take hold of the cord and pull the weight to the top of the weight cavity and fix it there temporarily by driving a nail through the strands of the cord into the window frame; this leaves the end of the cord free and further operations are unhampered.

The free end of the cord is now taken in hand and nailed with one clout nail in the specially prepared grooves shown in Fig. 3. The position of this nail should be such that the distance from it to the top of the sash is not greater than the distance from the centre of the pulley to the top of the window frame.

Now return the cord to its proper position and test the cord by moving the sash up and down. If the sash will not go to the bottom, the cord is too short. If the cord bulges out at the top when the sash is shut, the cord is too long. In this case the weight is, of course, resting on the bottom of the cavity. If the sash will not go high enough, care has not been taken in fixing the position of the clout nail.

Having found the correct position for the first nail, two or three more may be driven in carefully below. The sash can then be returned to its place, the trap refixed and the beading nailed into position.

Replacing a Cord in an Upper Sash

When replacing a cord in an upper sash, it is necessary first to remove the bottom sash. The beading is taken out and one cord released by prising out the clout nails that hold it. Having released this cord, a knot should be tied in it immediately to prevent the loose end from slipping over the pulley. The bottom sash, when taken out, should either be rested on something suitable or held by an assistant, so that it does not hinder your movements.

There is still a centre beading holding the top sash in place, and this beading must be carefully

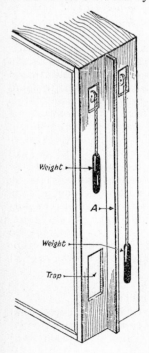

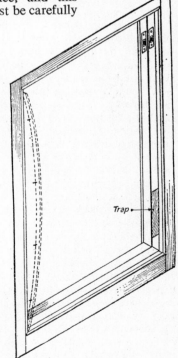

Weight

A

Weight

Trap

Trap

Fig. 1 (left): A view of the weight cavity from behind. Note that the trap has been removed to enable the weight in the recess to be lifted out. The parting strip (A), which prevents the weights from banging when the sashes are pulled up and down, is in position

Fig. 2 (right): How the frame appears when both sashes have been taken out, showing again the position of the trap. The dotted outline indicates how the beading is prised off until it forms an arch and will easily spring out of position

prised out of position on one side of the frame. This bead will be held by very few nails.

In order to obtain the weight of an upper sash, it will be necessary to push aside the parting slip, marked *A* in Fig. 1. Use the screwdriver to push it out of position and by careful manipulation to replace it afterwards. From then on the work proceeds as already described for a bottom sash.

Examine the Pulleys

When renewing cords in window frames that have been in position a good many years, the pulleys should be examined. Quite often the edges become rough and thin through corrosion and will soon cut their way through even a new cord. Pulleys are easily replaced, as they are simply fixed by two screws and, being of standard size, new ones will fit straight into the place from which the old ones have been taken.

Replacing Beads

Care is necessary when replacing the beads to avoid damaging the paint. If there are nails in the parting beads, they need not be disturbed as they can be inserted in the old holes and the bead gently tapped into the groove.

With the guard beads it is best to break off the top and bottom nails at the back of the bead by giving the nail a sharp turn with the pincers close to the wood. Now place the bottom mitre of the bead in position, bend the bead outwards at the middle and force the top mitre in position; guide the old nails into the old nail-holes and tap the bead into position. If this method is adopted, it is only necessary to insert two new nails, one at the top and one at the bottom, thus doing the minimum of damage to the paint.

Sashes Too Tight or Too Loose

Trouble with window sashes is, however, often experienced even when all the cords are in good condition. The sashes, for example, may be too tight in the frame, or so slack that they rattle. After painting especially, one often finds that the sashes have become bound by the paint which may have run at various points between the sashes and the beading.

To loosen stubborn sashes, first bang them vigorously and simultaneously with both hands, underneath the top rail of the bottom sash, the full force of the blow being taken with the base of the hand. This method will often prove successful when the sashes are held only by small patches of paint. Having opened the bottom sash, the top one can often be pulled down if a vigorous shaking motion is used at the same time.

When sashes still refuse to be opened by the hands, sterner methods have to be applied. First of all, insert a thin putty knife between the beading and the sashes in the spots which appear to be stuck. Then place a piece of three-ply or thin board under the top rail of the bottom sash and tap smartly with the hammer, taking care to give a direct upward blow in order to avoid damaging the glass. The wood, of course, is merely to prevent the hammer from marking the sash and bruising the paint work. Perseverance with these methods will eventually open the most obstinate sashes. When releasing the top sash by means of the board and hammer, the bottom sash should be closed and the board should, of course, be narrow enough to avoid resting on the top rail of the bottom sash.

In extreme cases, when all other methods have failed, it may be necessary to take out the beadings before the sashes can be made to work freely.

Having released the sashes, all parts showing signs of being paint-bound should be scraped with the putty knife and rubbed with glasspaper, care being taken to avoid disfiguring any part of the sash that is always exposed to view. If disfigurement is unavoidable, the disfigured places should be carefully touched in afterwards.

A sparing application of tallow will greatly facilitate the movement of the sashes and a small quantity smeared on the cords will keep them flexible and prolong their usefulness. Sash cord can also be purchased specially impregnated with wax. The pulley wheels and axle should also be oiled in moderation occasionally to prevent the window squeaking when being opened and shut.

Other Causes of Faulty Sashes

There are, of course, other causes that prevent the sashes from working properly. The outer beading may have been fixed

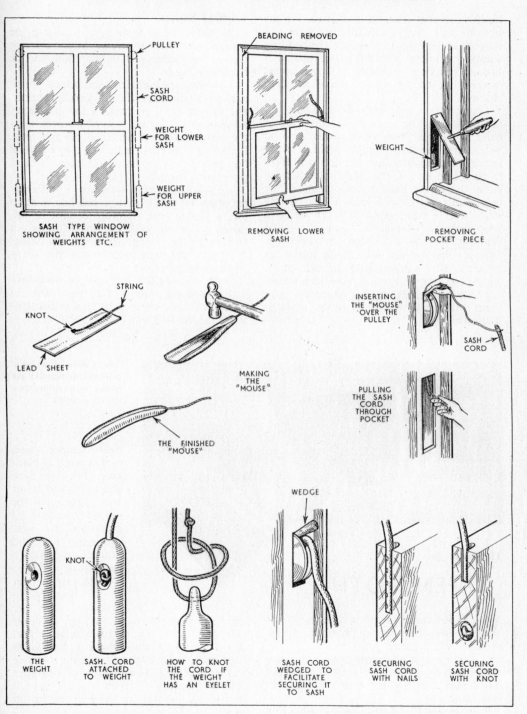

PULLEY

SASH CORD

WEIGHT FOR LOWER SASH

WEIGHT FOR UPPER SASH

SASH TYPE WINDOW SHOWING ARRANGEMENT OF WEIGHTS ETC.

BEADING REMOVED

REMOVING LOWER SASH

WEIGHT

REMOVING POCKET PIECE

STRING

KNOT

LEAD SHEET

MAKING THE "MOUSE"

THE FINISHED "MOUSE"

INSERTING THE "MOUSE" OVER THE PULLEY

SASH CORD

PULLING THE SASH CORD THROUGH POCKET

WEDGE

THE WEIGHT

KNOT

SASH. CORD ATTACHED TO WEIGHT

HOW TO KNOT THE CORD IF THE WEIGHT HAS AN EYELET

SASH CORD WEDGED TO FACILITATE SECURING IT TO SASH

SECURING SASH CORD WITH NAILS

SECURING SASH CORD WITH KNOT

Fig. 3: Step by step stages in the repairing of a broken sash cord, showing how to make a "Mouse" and how to knot and secure the cord in position

faultily, so that it leaves a channel for the bottom sash that gradually becomes too narrow at the top. In this case the beading should be taken off and either planed a little to reduce it in width, or it can be set farther out at the top to make an even channel.

One of the cords may have slipped off the pulley, or the end of the cord that is fixed to the sash may have turned up and be causing the sash to jam, perhaps every few inches. In this case the sash will have to be taken out and the offending cord end either cut off or fixed by clout nails. The best plan is to have a look at the parting strip, which may either be worn or have been incorrectly replaced. Again, the guard beading may be too loose; it sometimes happens that the nail holes in the frame become slightly enlarged after the nails holding the beading in position have been prised out. In such cases, it is advisable to plug them with small sticks of wood (matchsticks are ideal).

Rattling Sashes

A badly fitting sash can, of course, be wedged to prevent rattling. Small wooden wedges or, better still, rubber ones can be bought or made.

The best treatment for such sashes, which are, no doubt, badly fitting through shrinkage of timber, is to make a few necessary adjustments. In the case of a lower sash, the beading should be taken off and fixed farther in, thereby reducing the width of the channel. This is usually successful in preventing the rattle.

An ill-fitting top sash is a different proposition, as the middle beading is fitted into a rebate and therefore cannot be adjusted. The top sash should be taken out and made the proper thickness by fixing, with glue and panel pins, some thin strips on the inside face of the stiles.

Some adjustment will also be necessary to the meeting rails of the two sashes in order to make them thoroughly draughtproof for the winter.

* * * * * * * * * * * * * * * * * *

Just a strip of material padded with blanket and bound in a contrasting colour

Make a gay

OVENCLOTH

MATERIALS: strip of canvas, thick linen or other strong material 42 in. by 8 in. and 2 pieces 8 in. by 7 in., 3 yd. bias binding in contrasting colour, a skein of embroidery cotton to suit colour scheme, and 2 pieces of blanket 8 in. by 6 in. for interlining.

Prepare a strip of required length. For heat-resisting parts tack a piece of blanket 7 in. from each short end and cover with one of the small pieces of material, with $\frac{1}{2}$-in. turnings top and bottom to make a neat finish.

Turn strip over and, turning in material on top side, stitch down bias binding at short edge and again $1\frac{1}{2}$ in. from edge. Bind long edges with bias binding, fold over short ends from edge of padding to make pockets, joining down sides. Embroider edges of binding in chain stitch. Make a loop of bias binding for hanging and sew in place.

* * * * * * * * * * * * * * * * * *

HOW TO TILE YOUR OWN WALLS

The ideal surface for bathrooms, sink surrounds and larders,
tiles suitable for easy home use come in four types

TILING, the ideal treatment for all larder, bathroom and kitchen walls, will last almost indefinitely, though initial costs are fairly high. There are four types of tiling suitable for installation by amateurs and all quite simple to do.

RIGID TILES

1. **Ceramic tiles,** costing from about 6d. each, are the most attractive of all and are fixed with a special adhesive, the joins then being filled in with grouting cement.

2. **Rigid plastic tiles** are straightforward for the inexperienced housewife, to cope with and the handyman, or even give very good results. They are fixed in position by a special mastic. Although they come in various sizes and shapes, including angles, they can be cut or drilled to fit against switches, pipes and similar projections. Under normal usage, they will not crack or chip, once in position.

Plastic tiles are not affected by grease (or bathroom steam, soap or mild heat, though they should not be used for tiling a fireplace). They are easily cleaned with a damp cloth. Abrasives and chemical cleaning fluids are not advisable.

Fixing is done in three stages. First comes surface preparation. Any flaking distemper or blistered wallpaper must be scraped away. A wooden surface must be dry and clean. Small irregularities in the surface do not matter but if the walls are uneven, choose wider-bevelled tiles. With them, a fraction more space is allowed between the surface and the tile.

An elegant modern bathroom tiled by an amateur with rigid plastic tiles, easily handled and quite simple to install. See next page for step-by-step guide

First, draw a base line that is quite even and to mark the spot where the first tile should go. Adhesive is applied to each tile singly, instructions with the tiles stating just where (it varies according to make). Finally, each tile is held carefully in one hand, about $\frac{1}{2}$ in. away from where it should go, then slid into position, and pressed firmly in place. Any adhesive is removed by a little paraffin on a cloth. Tiles can be cut with a small tenon saw or a hacksaw and the edge smoothed with a file. Holes, to take screws for a fixture, are easily bored with a drill.

FLEXIBLE TILES

3. **Thermoplastic wall tiles** do not look quite so realistic, as they are flat instead of having the depth given by the bevelled edge. But they have other advantages. The adhesive is either spread evenly over

the surface to be tiled, or the adhesive may be already on the backs of the tiles themselves, which only need to be immersed in hot water to remove a protective film. Once in position, they are immovable. These flexible tiles can be moulded round curved surfaces or scored on the back so they can be put on a right-angle bend. Beading and angle strip are also obtainable.

INSTALLING RIGID TILES IN 6 STEPS

1. First scrape off old wallpaper (above), flaked plaster and paint. Wash wall with warm soapy water, rinse with clean, cold water and dry thoroughly

2 (left). Lay out base line, drawing it parallel with the floor unless there is a sink top or bath edge, in which case check it *is* horizontal

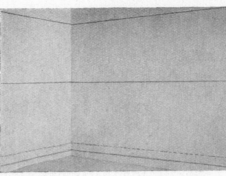

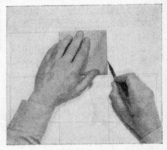

3 (right). Using a tile as a set square, mark out with a pencil the area to be tiled and the number of tiles required; no spaces need to be allowed between tiles

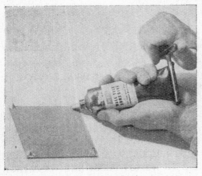

4 (above). Place tile face down on a clean flat surface, squeeze about $\frac{1}{4}''$ of adhesive on to a spot about $\frac{1}{2}''$ from each corner and the centre, keeping cement from face of tile

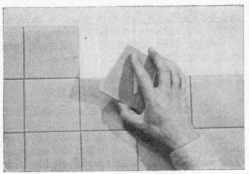

5 (above). Place first tile $\frac{1}{4}''$ from base line in left-hand corner, then slide it gently into position and press firmly

6 (left). Repeat with further tiles, placing them from left to right along base line. To clean, just wipe with warm soapy water

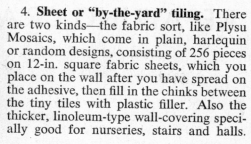

4. Sheet or "by-the-yard" tiling. There are two kinds—the fabric sort, like Plysu Mosaics, which come in plain, harlequin or random designs, consisting of 256 pieces on 12-in. square fabric sheets, which you place on the wall after you have spread on the adhesive, then fill in the chinks between the tiny tiles with plastic filler. Also the thicker, linoleum-type wall-covering specially good for nurseries, stairs and halls.

HOW TO APPLY MURAPLAS PLASTIC
WALL TILES

1 (above). To remove the transparent film which protects the adhesive on the back of each tile, immerse the tile in hot water for about 30 seconds

2 (left). Remove tile from water, shake well and peel off crinkled backing paper, drying adhesive face with a clean non-fluffy cloth

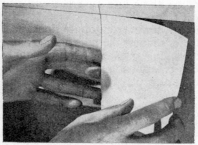

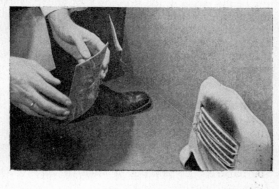

3 (above). Handling and fixing the tile. It should be put straight into position without sliding, as it cannot be moved once in place. Press well into position

4 (above). If a curved surface is to be dealt with, gently warm the tile, as shown, in front of an electric or gas fire, turning the glazed side towards the heat

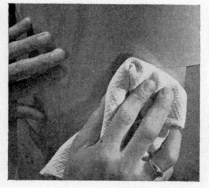

5 (above). The tile is pressed well home on a curved surface with a dry cloth and held in position until cold and rigid

6 (right). For a right-angle bend, first score the tile on the back (more heavily for an outward than an inward bend), then put into place as shown

REPAIRING CRACKS IN PLASTER

Many and varied are the causes, but this is a job which
should always be done before starting any decorations

CRACKS in plaster arise from various causes. Minor cracks are usually the result of the shrinkage of the wood which the plaster surrounds. In a ceiling, the drying out of the beams and the laths generally results in a number of small cracks. These are not serious if the ceiling has been properly plastered in the first place but, when the ceiling is so bad that it is divided into small areas, complete replastering may be necessary.

Cracks radiating from door and window frames are common. These are caused by the wood shrinking or swelling with changing atmospheric conditions. Another kind of crack is found over fireplaces. The heat rising in the chimney breast assists the drying of the wood in the floor or roof above, and this causes cracks to appear at the junction of the ceiling and the wall over the fireplace. Cracks caused by the subsidence of a wall are beyond the scope of ordinary repairs, because this involves underpinning the foundations.

Before Redecorating

Repairs to plaster walls and ceilings should be undertaken immediately before redecorating so that a proper finish may be given to the surface. After stripping a wall for papering or painting, it must be carefully examined for cracks and holes.

The first step in repairing a crack is to examine the soundness of the plaster immediately surrounding it. All loose plaster round the crack must be broken away or the mend will be unsatisfactory. If the crack is over a doorway, it is probable that a similar crack may be on the other side of the wall but may have passed unnoticed because of a picture or other hanging.

If the crack is long and thin, cut away some of the existing sound plaster on either side of it to enable the new cement to be worked into the cleft. If the crack is not opened out in this way, the filling will not penetrate sufficiently to hold securely in place.

Cut away the old plaster on either side of the crack with a straight thin steel knife for about $\frac{1}{4}$ in. on either side. The more experienced may prefer to chip out the plaster with a broad thin chisel. On ceilings, great care must be taken when using the chisel or you may start other cracks in the plaster.

Undercutting the Crack

When the crack has been cut, it is undercut so as to form a dovetail-shaped ridge for the new plaster. This provides a method of keying the filling into the crack and also prevents it from falling out.

No repair, however carefully done, will be satisfactory unless the hole or crack and the surrounding plaster are thoroughly wetted before applying the filling. However wet the new plaster may be, it will not adhere to the old plaster unless the old plaster is first properly wet. Moisten the crack to be repaired before mixing the plaster and again after mixing it, immediately before putting in the filling. Water the crack twice because most of the water first applied soaks right into the surrounding plaster. A distemper or whitewash brush is most effective for wetting the crack. With this, the water can be thrown well into the crack as well as brushed in.

The material for filling is Keene's cement. This is very pale pink in colour. A mixture of equal parts of plaster of Paris and Keene's cement produces a whiter mixture, but is more difficult to handle, because it sets more quickly. Do not attempt to use plaster of Paris alone. This sets very rapidly; in fact, it is sometimes impossible to mix it properly before it has set. A stronger and slower setting mixture, used for setting tiles and pointing glazed brickwork, is made of a mixture of equal parts of Portland and Keene's cements.

Mixing the Plaster

If a large amount of plastering is to be done, do not mix enough for the whole lot at once, but only as much as you think you can use up in five minutes. The portion of plaster for mixing is heaped on a board,

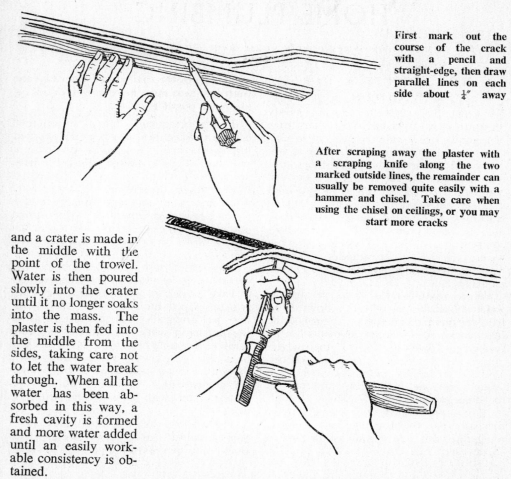

First mark out the course of the crack with a pencil and straight-edge, then draw parallel lines on each side about $\frac{1}{4}''$ away

After scraping away the plaster with a scraping knife along the two marked outside lines, the remainder can usually be removed quite easily with a hammer and chisel. Take care when using the chisel on ceilings, or you may start more cracks

and a crater is made in the middle with the point of the trowel. Water is then poured slowly into the crater until it no longer soaks into the mass. The plaster is then fed into the middle from the sides, taking care not to let the water break through. When all the water has been absorbed in this way, a fresh cavity is formed and more water added until an easily workable consistency is obtained.

If the mixture is too wet at first, add more plaster and mix again. It must be mixed quickly and used at once, before it hardens. No more water may be added after the mixture begins to harden during the application. As soon as the plaster on the board becomes too stiff to apply easily, make a fresh lot.

Filling the Crack

The best tool for applying the Keene's cement is a small, pointed trowel, like that used by bricklayers for pointing work. The plaster is taken from the board in small quantities, on the underside of the tip of the trowel, and worked into the crack. If the hole is large or deep, two applications may be necessary to complete the filling. This is quite safe if done while the first part

of the plaster is still wet. It is important to work the plaster into the base of the crack before filling it flush with the wall or ceiling. If you attempt to fill a deep hole with a single application of the trowel, an air-pocket will be formed which will prevent the plaster from keying properly to the sides of the crack.

Finishing the Surface

When the crack has been filled, smooth off as evenly as possible with the trowel, then quickly clean off plaster and wet it. The surface of the damp plaster is now brushed with water and the trowel again used to even up the surface. Repeat this process until the repaired portion is level with the surrounding surface.

HOME PLUMBING

How to tackle emergency repairs to the domestic water system and drains

HOW TO FIT A TAP WASHER

IF a water tap drips, the reason is pretty certainly a worn washer. First obtain three or four washers of different sizes. The half-inch size is most frequently used, but as you cannot be certain of the exact dimensions until the water is cut off and the tap dismantled, it is just as well to be prepared with alternative washers measuring $\frac{3}{8}$–$\frac{3}{4}$ in. Red fibre and treated leather washers are used for cold water taps, whilst rubber composition washers are essential for hot water taps. Do not attempt to make washers; they can be purchased at any ironmonger's.

Before anything is done to the tap, the water should be cut off. If it flows direct from the main, it is necessary to turn off the main cock and wait a few moments for the connecting pipes to empty themselves. Sometimes this cock is near the kitchen sink, but frequently there is no other main cock except one in the front garden or in the street pavement,

If the supply comes from a tank, shut off the ball valve by lifting the ball arm and tying it up, and then waiting for the tank to empty itself.

NOTE: In the case of hot water taps the source of heat must be removed, or an explosion is possible.

Taps are frequently difficult to unscrew, especially when they have been undisturbed for some time. In the absence of a plumber's wrench, a large adjustable spanner is the most suitable tool. The essential thing is to turn the spanner the correct way. Some taps have right-hand threads—that is to say, they undo when the cap is turned anti-clockwise, as seen from the top of the tap. A larger proportion of taps have left-hand threads. If you do not know whether a tap is left or right handed, try both ways before using too much force on the spanner.

Take extra care when unscrewing a tap which is wiped into a lead pipe, or the joint may be damaged. Hold the tap firmly in the left hand while the spanner is being turned. Similarly, when the tap is backed by a tiled wall, always unscrew away from the wall so that a sudden slip of the spanner will not damage it. Basin and bath taps are easiest to deal with because their seating is firmer.

The majority of taps fitted these days have a domed "easy-clean" shield. This shield must be unscrewed in order to get to

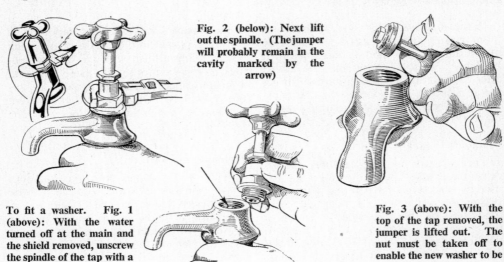

To fit a washer. Fig. 1 (above): With the water turned off at the main and the shield removed, unscrew the spindle of the tap with a spanner

Fig. 2 (below): Next lift out the spindle. (The jumper will probably remain in the cavity marked by the arrow)

Fig. 3 (above): With the top of the tap removed, the jumper is lifted out. The nut must be taken off to enable the new washer to be put on the body nut, and the body nut unscrewed to get to the washer. It should only be necessary to unscrew the dome and lift it to get to the body nut. However, there is seldom sufficient of the body nut exposed to enable one to get a grip on it with a spanner, because the top of the easy-clean shield, even when completely unscrewed, comes up hard under the handle of the tap.

The answer is to undo the small grub-screw set in the tap handle and which holds the handle firmly fixed to the spindle. When this screw is slackened off, the handle may be eased up and off the spindle; this in turn enables the dome to be removed and the body nut fully exposed to view.

NOTE: It is a good plan to fit the plug into the sink or wash basin before loosening off the grub-screw. These screws are comparatively small and headless, and they take a fiendish delight in slipping away down the waste pipe.

Although the easy-clean shield should be just hand-tight, it often happens that if undisturbed over any lengthy period (say, between washer renewals), the shield has a tendency to stick at the thread. Successive applications of a soft cloth steeped in hot water and applied to the dome should loosen the corrosion and do the trick.

When the nut has been loosened (Fig. 1), the upper part of the tap can be lifted off the fixed body, revealing the jumper (Fig.

2). This is the portion of the tap to which the washer is fixed. Its object is to prevent the rotation of the washer when the tap is turned. If the washer were to rotate with the tap, it would soon wear out on the seating. Some taps are made with the jumper separate from the cap of the tap; others are separate because the retaining pin has broken. When the jumper remains in the tap when the cap is lifted off, it should then be possible to lift it out (Fig. 3). If the jumper will not lift out easily, grip the spindle strongly in a pair of pliers with a protecting piece of leather in their jaws. The jumper is then forced out with the old washer attached. Care must be taken not to damage the jumper spindle; it is made of copper and is easily scored with the pliers. The washer is held on to the jumper with a small nut (Fig. 4). This unscrews anti-clockwise, looking down on the nut. If the washer nut is very tight, it may be necessary to grip the flange of the jumper in a second pair of pliers to unscrew it.

When the new washer has been fitted to the jumper (Fig. 5), examine the washer which provides a watertight joint between the cap and the body of the tap. This washer is renewed if necessary and is made of leather. Fibre should not be used, because it is liable to fray when the tap is screwed up. Do not put any paint or red lead on the cap thread with the object of making the joint watertight, because this will contaminate the water supply. Make sure that the jumper rotates freely in the cap of the tap before putting the tap together again (Fig. 6).

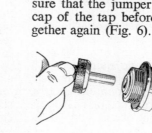

Fig. 4 (above): The new washer is then fitted on to the jumper. (If the jumper is a fixed one, it will come away with the top of the tap)

Fig. 5 (right): Of the two jumpers shown, one is fitted with a new washer; the other with a worn one

Fig. 6 (above): Put the tap together again, the barrel of the jumper fitting into the tube running through the centre of the spindle

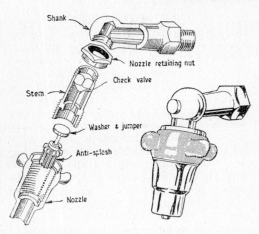

Shank
Nozzle retaining nut
Check valve
Stem
Washer & jumper
Anti-splash
Nozzle

Washer-changing on the up-to-date Supatap is simple, and it is not necessary to turn off the water at the main. The sketch above shows the components and method of assembly

If, when the water supply is turned on, the tap is no better than it was before, the reason is that (1) the washer has not been properly fitted, (2) the washer is not the right size—probably too small, or (3) the tap is worn out and needs to be replaced.

BURST PIPES

Every responsible householder should make a point, as soon as he moves into new premises, of finding out where the stop-cock and the water cistern are and, if they are not in his part of the premises, how, in an emergency, to contact those who have access to them. It is too late to start looking for these vital points when water is cascading down walls and staircases.

In most cases of burst pipe, drastic emergency methods are required immediately to prevent the flooding of a ceiling or swamping of a room. Adopt one or both of the following methods:

(1) Turn off the main stop-cock either inside or outside the house immediately. This will not, however, prevent whatever water there is in the cistern from flooding the ceiling.

(2) Plug the pipe at the bottom of the cistern with an old broomstick, pointed stick or something of the kind.

In very cold weather it is worth remem-

bering that a pipe bursts when it freezes and not when it thaws; therefore, if there are any places specially exposed it is worth looking at them before the thaw sets in, so that they can be repaired before any damage ensues. The ice will be seen glistening in the slit. Any places where there are bends in the pipes or where a draught of cold air can play on them should be suspected.

A very satisfactory repair can be carried out by means of rubber hose, ensuring that the inside diameter of the hose makes a tight fit with the outside diameter of the water pipe.

Assuming that the burst is in a pipe in a corner or close up to a wall, the first thing is to pull the pipe out carefully, removing some of the wall hooks if necessary. Do not use a sharp instrument, but prise the pipe out with a piece of board about 2–3 in. wide. Then cut out the length of damaged pipe with a hacksaw or even an old knife with a notched blade. Cut the pipe away as square as possible and make sure the whole length of damaged pipe is removed. If the burst pipe is a cold-water one running from the cistern, obtain a length of canvas-covered radiator hose from a garage or indiarubber stores. In order to get hose the right size, take along a piece of the pipe that has been cut out. The hose should be 6–8 in. longer than the damaged piece of pipe so that it will extend 3–4 in. at each end. If possible, obtain also two good hose clips of the correct size.

Before putting the hose on, make sure that there are no rough edges to the lead pipes and that the ends are clean. Also make a mark with a pencil roughly 3 in. from one of the ends of the pipe. Rub soft soap over the ends of the pipe if the hose is a tight fit or, if a permanent job is intended, use rubber puncture solution. Now slip the hose on one end of the pipe far enough for it to be got on the other end, work it back until it is level with the pencil mark. Next, put on the hose clips and tighten up, push the pipe back into place and refix in position if necessary.

As an alternative to hose clips, which may not be available, tightly wire (with a "soft" wire) the hose to the pipe. The hose should project at least 4 in. either side of the fracture to permit of half a dozen turns of the wire each side, as close as possible to the break, and a further half-dozen turns at each end of the hose.

This emergency measure will seal off the leak and enable the householder to use the taps until a plumber can effect a permanent repair. After any temporary repair it is advisable to turn the stop-cock to half-pressure to ease off the force of water from the main water supply to the pipes in the house.

CLEARING STOPPED-UP DRAINS

By far the greatest number of drain stoppages occur in the "U"-bend of the pipe fitted between sink basin and the waste pipe. Water is always present in these "U" bends, finding its own level. Odd pieces of undissolvable waste find their way into the bed and remain there until an accumulation builds up into a compact mass sufficient to block the pipe.

When water drains away slowly, it shows that foreign matter has accumulated. Fortunately, the "U"-bend is easy of access and easy to clear. At the bottom of the "U" is fitted a drain plug, the removal of which enables one to clear the stoppage (Fig. 7).

First, place a bowl or bucket immediately underneath the plug to catch any water and waste matter. Then remove the plug, which is fitted with two projecting lips against which the handle of a spanner, blade of a file or some similar object can be levered to turn the plug on its thread. Before unscrewing the plug, place a stout piece of wood (a hammer or brush handle or even a short length of broom-handle) between the "U" bend to take up the strain as the plug itself is unscrewed. This is necessary because the plug, which has to be a tight fit to prevent water seeping through, will call for a certain amount of strain being imposed to unthread it. Unless this strain is counteracted in the "U" bend, the result may be a loosening of the joint between pipe and sink fitting, bringing inevitably more repair work and expense.

If the cause of the blockage does not immediately come away when the plug is removed, a cane should be pushed up to force any solid matter in the pipe back into the sink and to remove any solid deposit from the walls of the pipe.

OUTSIDE GUTTERS

The commonest blockages are due to leaves, pieces of paper blown to rest by the wind, and odd sticks and twigs brought to a prospective nesting site by birds. The best way of preventing trouble is to make a point of thoroughly cleaning out the gutters at least twice yearly.

Remember not to prop the ladder against the guttering but to rest the top against the wall. Equipment needed is simple: an old bucket and a meat hook (or a piece of stout wire shaped "S" fashion). One end of the hook can be slipped over a rung of the ladder, the bucket can be suspended from the other, thus leaving both hands free to work. After the guttering has been cleared out, a thorough inspection should also be made of the guttering joints—i.e. where the lengths meet. Unless these are kept watertight, the rain will drip through and down the brickwork of the house. If there are any gaps between lengths through which water can trickle, they can be closed quite effectively with putty, making a smooth and well-sealed joint.

To prevent sludge, twigs, paper, etc., from getting washed along the guttering to the outlet pipe with the risk of choking it, lightly "ball" a piece of 1-in. wire mesh and insert not quite half the ball into the outlet pipe, making sure it is a tight fit and will not get washed down the pipe. The mesh will trap all the unwanted material, but will only be effective if removed and cleaned at intervals.

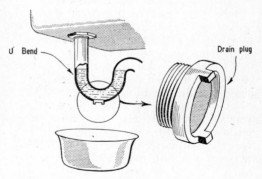

Fig. 7: To clear a stopped drain, unscrew the drain plug at the "U" bend, having first put a basin or bucket underneath, ready to catch any water and waste matter (1) turn the plug on its thread with a spanner

535

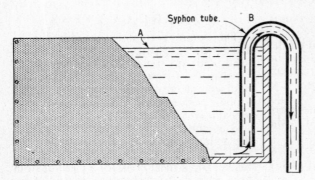

Fig. 8: This diagram illustrates the siphon principle on which nearly all flushing systems work

Once the siphonic action has started, the cistern will continue to empty until air is drawn in at the bottom edge of the bell, when the siphonic action ceases. As the level of water falls, the ball valve goes down with it, so admitting water to refill the cistern.

This type of cistern is almost trouble-free, and if it does not work properly, the cause is seldom anything more serious than

REPAIR OF FLUSHING CISTERNS

The commonest kind of cistern is that known as the bell type. In practically all systems the cistern works on the siphon principle, illustrated in Fig. 8, which shows a tank filled to the level *A* and a tube *B* over the side of the tank, the end of which is lower than that on the inside. If the pipe is full of water, the fact that the water in the tank is at a higher level than the bottom of the pipe outside will cause a flow of water through the pipe, and this flow will continue until the water-level reaches the bottom of the pipe inside the tank. This siphon action would not take place if there were any air in the pipe to begin with.

Now consider Fig. 9, which shows a typical bell-type installation. When the handle is pulled downwards, the loose bell in the cistern is raised. Water flows into the well to take the place of the iron rim that has been lifted out, but nothing else happens while the handle is still held.

As soon as the handle is released, the weight of the bell causes it to drop. The effect is to trap the water within the well, so that it rises up inside the bell and falls down the standpipe with sufficient force to thrust out the air, fill the pipe with falling water and so start a siphonic action. In effect, this means that the stand pipe with attached flush pipe forms the long limb of the tube shown in the first illustration, and the inside of the bell forms the short limb.

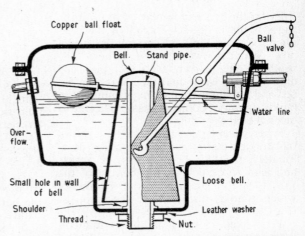

Fig. 9: The same principle in the form of a typical bell-type installation. This is the commonest kind of flushing cistern and is practically trouble-free

the need for a new hard rubber washer.

The modern trend is, however, towards low flush cisterns. The principle is practically the same, but the siphon action is modified, a plunger replacing the bell and with a fixed head connected to the flushing pipe. This type of cistern seldom gives trouble, either, and, if it does, it can usually be traced to lock-nuts or collars on the handle shifting and causing it to stick down. Re-alignment is all that is required, and this is not difficult for the handyman with common sense and patience. Trouble can usually be prevented if it is remembered that the handle of this type only needs to be gently pulled down to its limit, never tugged as is common practice with the chain variety.

On all flushing cisterns, some form of ball valve is incorporated which stops the flow of the water into the cistern when it has reached a certain level. Details of a typical ball valve are shown in Fig. 10. *A* is the body of the valve, *B* the plunger valve which has a washer *C* kept in place by nut *D*. The ball is attached to a lever pivoting *on* the fulcrum pin *E*. The illustration shows how the plunger *B* is withdrawn by the short arm of the lever when the cistern is empty. As the ball rises, this plunger is pushed inwards and forces the valve washer *C* against the nozzle, so that any further flow of water is stopped.

Before attempting any repairs to the flushing cistern, it is always advisable to cover the W.C. basin and seat with a board to prevent damage should any tools be dropped down.

If the pan becomes empty instead of containing water, the best remedy is repeated flushings or working a wire brush under the trap. If this fails, the wisest plan is to call in an expert. The sudden pouring of a bucket of water into the pan will often

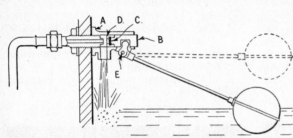

Fig. 10: Details of a typical ball valve. This stops the flow of water into the tank when water has reached the desired level

cause it to empty suddenly. Flushing in the normal way should quickly put this right.

Sometimes the handle has to be pulled several times before the water will start. Two very likely causes of this trouble are: (1) water line in cistern not high enough and (2) bell fits too tightly.

Water line in cistern not high enough may be due to the rubber washer in the ball valve swelling and cutting the water off too soon. The simplest method of curing this is to bend the lever attached to the copper float slightly in an upward direction. This must be done carefully with an adjustable spanner, holding the lever firmly in the

right hand and bending it with the left (Fig. 11). On no account attempt to bend the lever by pulling the ball itself. Alternatively, shut the water off and replace the washer with one slightly thinner.

Bell fits too tightly: remove the bell and scrape all rust from the inside of the well. The edge of the bell should also be slightly filed to make it smooth.

If these emergency measures fail to cure the trouble, more complicated repairs may be required and it is advisable to call in a skilled plumber.

Water Dripping from Overflow Pipe which may Freeze

This is an indication of a faulty ball-cock and should be dealt with promptly, especially in cold weather when there is danger of the overflow pipe becoming frozen and flooding. The most likely cause is one of the following: bent ball lever, ball punctured or faulty washer.

If the ball lever is bent, the water will rise to the overflow pipe before the valve closes. Bend the lever to bring the ball slightly lower into the tank. A punctured ball can be remedied by soldering, after first removing any water inside the ball. If the cause is a faulty washer, it is a simple enough task to replace with a new one.

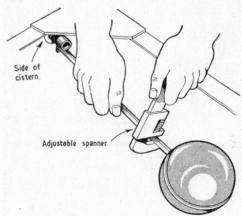

Fig. 11: To raise the cistern water line, bend the lever attached to the copper float slightly in an upward direction, using an adjustable spanner

CARE OF ELECTRICAL EQUIPMENT

Follow these practical and simple rules for efficiency and safety
by N. F. CUDDY, *National Institute of Houseworkers, Ltd.*

A CLEAN, well-run home depends not only on the skill and knowledge of the housewife, but to a large extent upon the equipment available.

The efficiency of your equipment in turn will depend upon the care you give it. No matter how expensive it is, or what the manufacturers claim for it, no equipment will work perfectly or give entire satisfaction unless you look after it.

When buying such things as vacuum cleaners, electric polishers, or washing machines, buy those carrying a guarantee, and for which spare parts are readily obtainable. Manufacturers nearly always give instructions for care and maintenance of their wares; you will be wise to study these. If you are buying a piece of equipment which is entirely new to you, ask for a demonstration. Most manufacturers are willing to let you try out their goods in your own home.

Here are a few hints on the care of some of the electrical equipment found in the home.

Electric Washing Machines

(1) Before using, check to see that the electrical details on the base of the machine correspond with your electricity supply.

(2) Be sure to put in sufficient water.

(3) Do *not* put in too many articles at once.

(4) Always thoroughly rinse and wipe dry the machine and wringer.

(5) Remove any fluff and bits from the drain and clean under the agitator.

(6) Avoid the use of harsh abrasives which may damage the surface.

Electric Refrigerators

(1) Wipe the outsides with a cloth wrung out in ammonia or detergent and water to remove finger marks.

(2) Defrost according to maker's instructions—generally once in ten days or so is sufficient.

(3) Wash the insides with borax and water (one teaspoonful to one pint), if possible avoiding the use of an abrasive. Wipe dry.

Flex must be treated with care. Never tie it up tightly, as shown here (left), or the inner strands will break and eventually cause a fuse. The correct way is to roll it as shown here (right), so that there are no sharp bends to cause cracks

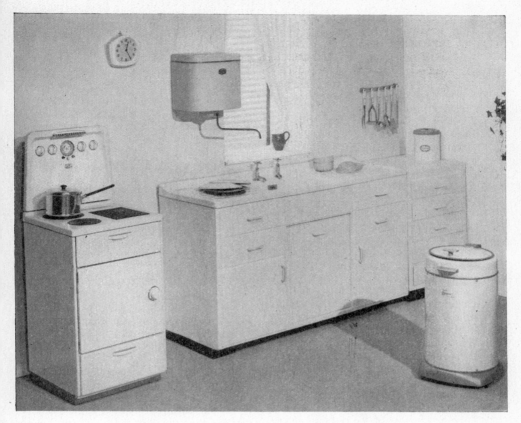

This labour-saving kitchen with matching electrical appliances deserves the proper maintenance you can only provide if you understand your equipment. Cooker, spin dryer and over-the-sink water heater are all Creda models

(4) Wash all the removable parts and the ice trays, remembering to dry their undersides before putting them back.

(5) Don't open the door more than is necessary and never put hot foods into a refrigerator.

Electric Cookers

(1) Do not let spilt food burn on to the hot-plates or floor of the oven. Always wipe up straight away anything spilt on the hot-plates or in the oven.

(2) Wash enamel parts with hot soapy water, using a mild abrasive, if necessary, for obstinate stains.

(3) Rub solid hot-plates with scourer or steel wool.

(4) Remove and wash metal saucers from under radiant hot-plates, using scouring powder or steel wool if necessary.

(5) Wash the oven with hot soapy water, using an abrasive if needed. If the oven is always wiped out while still warm from cooking, drastic cleaning will not be necessary. Take out all removable parts and wash them in the sink. Remove stubborn grease with Oven-stick.

(6) *Never* put the elements in water or get them wet.

(7) Always switch off at the main when cooking is finished and before cleaning.

Vacuum Cleaners

These are of two types, the cylinder and

CARE OF ELECTRICAL EQUIPMENT

upright models, the underlying principle in both being practically identical.

(1) Be sure that your electricity voltage is within the range marked on the name-plate of the cleaner and that the correct plug is used.

(2) Always switch off the current before making adjustments.

(3) See that the cleaner is correctly adjusted to the thickness of the carpet.

(4) Do not use a vacuum cleaner on a new carpet.

(5) Inspect hoses and tubes from time to time to see that they are not clogged with dust.

(6) Remove fluff and bits from brushes.

(7) Empty dust-bags frequently.

(8) Do not pull or strain the flex, and when disconnecting the machine from the wall socket take hold of the plug, *not* the flex.

(9) Use the correct attachment for the particular type of cleaning you are doing, and be sure you know how to fit them in properly.

(10) Wash brushes occasionally, rinsing them in cold salt water (one table-spoonful to one quart) to restore the stiffness.

(11) Do not oil the cleaner unless told to do so by the makers.

(12) Take advantage of the regular servicing facilities that most manufacturers provide.

(13) Replace worn-out brushes and other attachments as necessary.

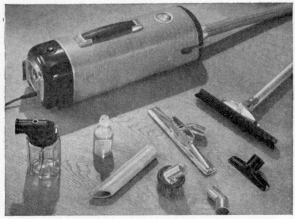

To keep your vacuum in good order, use the correct attachment for the job, keep brushes free from fluff and have it serviced regularly

Electric Polishers

(1) Put the polish on by hand, or, if you use a liquid polish, sprinkle it on the floor. This prevents clogging the brushes with polish.

(2) Clean the brushes occasionally by rubbing them over with a turpentine-soaked rag to remove soiled wax.

(3) To get the best from your polisher, use it evenly and smoothly and do not move too quickly over the floor.

Electric Kettles

(1) If you live in a district where the water is "hard," use a fur-collecting shell or pad, which prevents the formation of "fur" inside the kettle. Lime in hard water forms a coating on the inside of the kettle and water takes longer to heat up.

(2) Always put in sufficient water to cover the heating ring.

(3) Never pull out the plug by the flex.

(4) Always switch off the electricity before pouring water from the kettle.

Electric Irons

(1) Always switch off before connecting or disconnecting flex.

(2) Do not wind flex tightly round the iron when putting it away.

(3) See that the flex does not rub against the edge of the ironing board and become frayed.

(4) Don't overheat the iron.

Electric Fires

(1) Disconnect fire, or switch off, and dust with a duster or brush to remove surface dust, being very careful not to damage the element.

(2) Keep the reflectors well polished to ensure getting the maximum heat.

(3) Don't have a trailing flex where people may trip over it, and *never* have an electric fire in a bathroom unless fixed high up on the wall, out of reach of wet hands.

(4) Replace old or broken elements.

One word of warning. If you do your own minor repairs, switch off the current first.

KEEP A CARE AND REPAIR CUPBOARD

Lots of odd jobs crop up around the house that can easily be attended to if the necessary equipment is on hand in one place. Here are suggestions for useful preparations, tools and so on, and the uses to which they can be put

ADHESIVES

Uses for: sticking rubber to metal, leather and leather-cloth to metal and wood (example, Bostik); fabric to fabric and other uses (example, Jiffytex); earthenware and china repairs (example, Durofix). Also adhesive tape for many purposes.

ANGLE BRACKETS

Uses for: backless bookshelves that begin to lean with the weight of books can be made firm with an angle bracket screwed into each corner.

Wobbling chair legs can often be made firm by screwing a short bracket to top of leg and under edge of seat. Buy from ironmonger.

BINDING, iron-on

Uses for: splits in carpets; frayed edges of carpets, rugs and coco-matting; splits in pillow and mattress tickings; these are some of the household repairs effectively carried out with this type of adhesive binding, ironed-on flat, or as a binding. Buy from haberdashery counters.

CEMENT AND SAND

Uses for: filling between crazy paving when original filling begins to wear; filling up holes between outside bricks where nails have been knocked in for tying up climbing plants; filling cracks in concrete floors, etc. A mixture of dry cement and sand can be bought in handy packets from Woolworths. A little can be used at a time, water added to form a soft but not wet-looking mixture. The area to be repaired should be dust- and grease-free, and well wetted, otherwise the new cement will shrink and the repair be inefficient.

FILLERS, various

Uses for: a packet of the white, dry plaster-like type (Alabastine, etc.) is an excellent stand-by for repairs on interior walls. It is almost always essential for filling purposes before redecoration, but a crack can appear in a ceiling at any time, or a nail, lifted out of a wall may bring plaster with it. Such defects need immediate attention, if greater damage is to be prevented, and this type of filler is very simple to use.

A small tin of plastic wood is handy for filling in

When mending cups and plates, first put the pieces together with china cement, then stick with adhesive tape to hold in place while drying

541

has been previously used, and for repairing new breaks. For example, the front rod of a chair sometimes snaps in the middle. The break should be glued, surfaces brought together and strapped with string, and the legs held in position with a loop of string, twisted in the middle with a short stick, to tighten on tourniquet lines. Pad the chair legs under the string to prevent damage.

GLUE POT

Uses for: necessary for carpenter's glue, which is bought from an ironmonger in hard pieces. The glue is put into the inner pan and covered with water. The outer pan is filled with water to come half-way up inner pan, and set to boil gently until

To repair a trolley (above) first apply glue; then stick firmly with adhesive tape to hold in position until the glue has hardened

No household can run smoothly without oil—and remember to give doorkeys a good oiling occasionally, especially those not often used. And drop a little oil in the locks too, from a feather

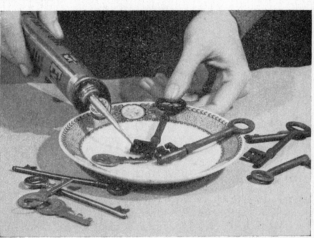

holes where nails and screws have been removed; for filling in cracks in wood and gaps between floorboards and for repairing accidents to furniture.

Seelastik, in a trouble-saving applicator tube, is another filler with many uses; for gaps between sink and wall, floor and wall, and so on, it has an expanding action, does not set hard, but develops a surface film that takes paint after 24 hours.

GIMLET

Uses for: starting the holes when cup hooks are to be screwed in position, and for starting holes for screws and the rings for expanding curtain wire hooks to catch over. Small or medium size.

GLUE, carpenter's

Uses for: repairing loose chair backs, legs, or any furniture joint for which glue

glue melts. This is a particularly strong glue to stand the wear and tear on furniture.

INSULATING TAPE

Uses for: safety measures of electrical equipment; flex of all kinds should be examined regularly for fray, either in the length or where it enters plugs. Bind the worn part with a length of tape until a professional repair can be made.

NEEDLES, household

Uses for: stitching carpets, upholstery, canvas and similar cloth. Cards of assorted household needles for various purposes can be bought from Woolworths or at haberdashery counters.

OIL, machine

Uses for: oiling locks, squeaking hinges, sewing machines, typewriters, scissors, keys and garden shears, and for oiling round an obstinate screw or bolt to ease the job. Examples: Singer Sewing Machine Oil; "3-in-One" oil.

PAINT BRUSHES, artist's

Uses for: very handy for brushing out narrow cracks before filling, for applying a delicate touch of oil or glue, for getting insecticide down woodworm holes when no applicator is available; in fact, there are many household jobs made easier with the help of a paint brush. Choose those sold for children's use; one fine, one medium and one thick, should cover most jobs.

PALETTE KNIFE, artist's

Uses for: although these might shock the artist, such a knife is streets ahead of an old kitchen knife for applying the wall and wood fillers already described. It is smaller and more pliable, enables you to press home the filler efficiently, and altogether effect a good job. Buy from an art shop.

PINCERS

Uses for: withdrawing nails and tacks; grip the head of the nail with the pincers upright, then roll them back on the curved side, and the nail is forced out. For a long nail, raise the pincers on a small block of wood to finish off the drawing-out process. Pincers are often successful in loosening an obstinate screw, driven in crookedly with head protruding; and they are quite handy for nipping through wire.

PLANE

Uses for: shaving off that necessary fraction from cupboard doors and windows when warped; preparing floors before staining (see chapter on *How to Stain Floors*); smoothing table tops before applying a topping such as Formica (see chapter on Resurfacing Furniture); for finishing any wood that has become splintery. Buy a plane from a first-class ironmonger, choosing one that fits your hand comfortably and is not too heavy.

PLATES, metal

Uses for: these are as handy for repair purposes as angle brackets; various sizes can be bought, together with angle brackets, from ironmongers or Woolworths. These plates are flat and bored with screw-holes. If you lay in a small stock, buy enough of the right-sized screws at the same time. If a shelf "gives" through lack of underneath support, or splits along

Always rub down white wood with sandpaper to clean it or before painting

the grain, metal plates screwed across the danger area will give it the necessary strength. A four-sided chair cross-bar that splits can be strengthened with a plate screwed to the underside.

PLIERS

Uses for: unloosening nuts, small size; twisting and untwisting wire, bending and straightening out sheet tin. Another type, known as a set of footprints, has an adjustable toothed head that can be closed or opened to fit any sized nut; invaluable when changing tap washers and for loosening the screw at the bottom of the U-bend when clearing blocked drains.

SANDPAPER

Uses for: a sheet or two of fine, No. 0 or

1, is handy for rubbing down white wood and cork-topped stools, to clean them. Medium sandpaper is needed for rubbing down paint before repainting, scoring the soles of new shoes and gripping stubborn caps on bottles. It is also good for rubbing up rusted steel scissors and knives and garden tools.

SAW, coping

Uses for: this looks like a fretsaw and does similar jobs, including cutting metal curtain rods to the length needed.

SCREWDRIVER

Uses for: a small one with insulated handle is needed for the tiny screws in fuses, electric plugs and so on. For any other screwing jobs, keep handy a medium size with long shaft, about 10 in. total length.

TACKS

Uses for: the very necessary job of keeping carpets, lino, etc., firmly anchored to the floor. Tacks have a way of working out, and if accidents are to be prevented, they should be replaced immediately. A box each of $\frac{1}{2}$-in. and $\frac{3}{4}$-in. should meet all replacement needs, if the length of tack is chosen according to the thickness of the floor covering.

UPHOLSTERY: canvas, tacks, twine, webbing

Uses for: sagging chair seats, as these are usually due to a spring that has come unstitched and fallen sideways, or webbing that has split and dropped the springs. If the damage is no more than this, it is a repair to do at home, as follows: turn chair upside down and take off canvas covering by prising up the tacks with the screwdriver. Put all usable tacks into one saucer, and damaged ones into a second saucer. If canvas is in good condition, set aside; if it has stretched and split in places, it is best to renew it. Now take a look at webbing and springs and you will see that each spring is stitched to the webbing to keep it upright. If the webbing is firm and looks strong and it is merely a matter of re-stitching one or more springs in place, take a suitable household needle and length of upholstery twine, and stitch them to webbing as the others are stitched.

If the webbing has broken, cut the twine holding the springs and remove it. Now ease out the tacks holding the outside back-to-front strip of webbing, noting how the tacks are placed, usually two under the fold and three outside. Cut a similar length of webbing from your new roll and attach one end to the back of the chair with tacks. Now pull the other end as tight as possible. Repeat with the rest of the strips, then renew the side-to-side strips, remembering to thread them over and under the top-to-bottom strips. When all are fastened securely, stitch springs to webbing, carrying thread from spring to spring in a continuous run. Finally replace canvas.

WALL PLUGS

Uses for: anything heavier than a light picture, to be hung on a plaster wall, should be screwed into plugs for safety; otherwise mirror, cupboard, shelf, etc., may suddenly fall, bringing away a lot of plaster with it. Rawlplug put up handy kits.

WASHERS

Uses for: home replacement (see chapter on Home Plumbing). Keep an assortment of $\frac{1}{2}$-in. and $\frac{3}{4}$-in hot and cold tap washers, or better still, a nylon reconditioning set, which provides a new seating for the tap as well as a washer. No more difficult to put on than a washer, it should last as long as the tap.

WIRE, fuse

Uses for: home replacement. Keep a couple of cards of 5-amp. wire, and a card of 10-amp. and 15-amp. in your cupboard. When a fuse blows, shut off *all* electricity for safety. Open main fuse box and examine each carrier until you reach the one with sooty marks and broken wire. If the carrier does not indicate the size of wire to be used (5, 10 or 15 amp.), match a piece of the old wire to the new and cut a fresh length. (See How to Mend a Fuse.)

An open window arouses the suspicions of a policeman—but not before your home has been ransacked and your valuables stolen

BEAT THE BURGLAR

Better be safe than sorry—it is wiser to pit your brains against the criminal beforehand than regret his visit afterwards

IT would make a startling record if the daily newspaper one day contained no mention of robbery. As it is, reports of petty theft make us cluck with indignation, and burglary on a large scale is a matter for wonderment as to "how they get away with it." But how often do you check up on your own immunity?

The fact is that householders could make the effort and put burglars out of business, if only they gave the matter due thought before, instead of after, the event.

Thieves are astute and patient. Breaking-in to occupied premises is invariably a matter of careful planning and diligent watching beforehand. Police records show that small premises—houses, flats and shops—are entered far more often than larger houses and business premises.

You may open the door to a well-groomed salesman one day; for all you know, he may, while you talk, run expert eyes over your safety precautions, if you have them. If you have not, and later you are burgled, that salesman may well be the one who did the job. Ask any policeman, and he will confirm the fact that the burglar prefers to enter through the front door, and is more likely to do so in daylight than after dark.

Don't Advertise

Many burglars are provided with tempting invitations by too trusting or just thoughtless householders. The family who decide in a hurry that it is going to be a glorious week-end, and dash off to the country on Friday evening, for instance. On Saturday and Sunday milk and papers accumulate on the doorstep. If there is a housebreaker in the vicinity, he is not going to miss an opportunity like that. And it takes a thief a very short time to go through every room in the place.

Some householders have been known to leave notes pinned to the outer door, telling their tradesmen they will be away from home for several days. Others pop out for a packet of cigarettes and leave the front door on the latch. Housewives go off to do a bit of quick shopping, leaving doors shut but windows open.

Again, there are those, setting off for a holiday, who do remember to stop regular deliveries but insist on drawing all the curtains or closing shutters across windows before they go. This is just as much an advertisement that furnished premises are unoccupied as a collection of milk bottles and papers.

Apart from advertising your absence from home, there are other ways of unwittingly encouraging the burglar. A garage with a lock that is easily picked or forced gives him access, not only to your car and anything left in it, but to ladders if you house them there.

Leaving the outer door key under the mat or attached to string and pushed through the letter box is a practice that may easily let you down one day. The thief knows these tricks as well as you do, so carry keys with you when you go out. And when you go on holiday, write to your local police station and let them know that the house will be empty.

Precautionary Measures

It is not only good sense to safeguard property of all kinds; it is also good civic sense, because any effort to reduce crime benefits the community as a whole.

Insurance is a natural precaution, and most owners of houses, flats and business premises hold a policy covering them against theft or a comprehensive policy that covers other risks as well. Such a policy should be read carefully, because it does not follow that, should you be burgled, the Insurance Company will meet your claim in full. If you have not provided adequate safety measures, your claim will be assessed accordingly (see also chapter on Insurance).

Windows and doors can be made safe. Police and Insurance Companies advise mortice deadlocks and a bolt on outer doors.

Your front door may be fitted with glass panels. If you are burgled and these panels have no protective backing, and only a snap lock on the door, it will almost certainly tell against your claim. When snap locks are used, the door should also have a bolt at top or bottom.

A further useful device is the door chain. This is a sensible precaution, apart from being anti-burglar, if you are much alone during the day. So is the "seeing eye," a neat little gadget easily fitted to a front door, through which you can see who is outside, without the caller seeing in.

All types of window can be provided with safe fastenings. Sash windows can be fitted with bolts through the thickness of the frames, or stops that allow the window to be raised to a certain height and no farther. Centre catches may be bought that cannot be opened by slipping a knife between the frames, a simple method practised by the experienced housebreaker.

Metal windows and wood-framed windows of the casement type have also been catered for, and a visit to a reputable ironmonger will provide the information and appliances you need to protect them.

Burglar Alarms

Here there is a wide choice and a price range to suit everyone and all purposes. At the top of the scale there are soundless electronic devices, almost uncanny in their efficiency, which no burglar could discover or put out of action before they had given him away and silently summoned help.

Then there are all manner of indoor and outdoor systems of alarm bell, loud enough to wake the heaviest sleeper, or summon outside help.

There are firms throughout the country specialising in burglar alarms, most of whom have experts who will advise and estimate. Your first call is best made at your local police station, where an officer will give you information on police-approved alarms, and how to get them.

And Remember: Television viewing time is proving another boon to the thief, when occupants are gathered in one room, oblivious of what goes on elsewhere on the premises.

So lock up before you begin looking in. Lock inside doors as well as windows and outer doors before you go to bed, thus isolating any breaker-in. A convenient escape route is as important to the burglar as his means of entry; to be locked in is as bad for him as to be kept out. Take all reasonable precautions and you will help to prevent crime, as well as guarding yourself and your family from loss and alarm.

The police view is that it is best to have nothing in the home worth stealing. This, of course, is not always easy. Most homes hold at least a few prized possessions in the way of portable silverware, valuable china pieces, personal jewellery and so on, that are in more or less constant use. The best plan is to limit the number of such articles as much as possible and arrange that your insurance policy covers specially valuable pieces. If you inherit a family heirloom that you wish to use all the time, your insurance company will adjust the policy to include the item by name and allow for its value in the coverage. You may have to pay a slightly higher premium, but that would be worth while.

Valuables

All valuables not in use should be put into safe keeping outside your home, either in a safe deposit or at the bank. It is asking for trouble and extra damage to lock them up in desks, cupboards or drawers. The thief will simply force the locks and probably break up the furniture.

Home safes do not necessarily give the security we might expect; burglars are quite capable of loading one on a trolley and removing it. They are extremely bright at blowing open safes with the minimum of noise, or getting hold of an impression of the key. They are not nearly so successful with the safe that can be sunk into

Many families advertise their absence by forgetting to cancel milk and papers

British official photos from the C.O.I. film, "Help Yourself"

the wall in a surround of concrete, a free-standing type that can be bolted to a wall or set into a concrete base.

Reliable safe deposit companies are fairly widespread, and a recommendation from your police or insurance company should be sought if you need information.

Finally, one of the most effective measures you can take is to buy a good house dog. Intruders clear off quickly when a dog barks.

This sort of note pinned to the door gives a burglar just the information he requires

SUCCESSFUL HOME DYEING

How to guard against the commoner hazards
and thus stand the best chance of good results

THE best approach to home dyeing is to accept it as a hazard; it can be so successful that the risk is well worth taking, but you need also to acquire a philosophical view that you may not care for the results. The following notes take the job to pieces as minutely as possible, for the more you know the less likely you are to hate the sight of your "transformed" garment.

KINDS OF DYE

Those we buy for home use can be brought to the boil, used in hot water, or in cold or lukewarm water. Some must not be used on "Celanese" or other acetate fabrics (to test as such, apply a match to a small piece of spare rayon—if an acetate, it will melt, bubble and blacken).

According to their composition, all home dyes differ in their application to the various fabrics. In some cases the dye may be boiled into wool. In the main, the dye bath for wool, silk, cotton, rayon and nylon should be brought only to simmering point. It may be advisable to boil dye into Terylene, Orlon, etc.

All dyes may be used for tinting only, the dye being first prepared in the usual way and added to the right amount of very warm, lukewarm or cold water, according to the brand.

Cold-water dyes in pastel shades can safely be used in the bath, washing machine or a plastic bowl and will neither stain the container nor your hands. They should only be used on cotton, linen or silks; not wool, rayon or synthetic fibres.

The different makes of home dyes, between them, cover all familiar fabrics—cotton, linen, rayon, wool, pure silk, nylon, Terylene, Orlon, and so on.

COLOURS

A simple rule is: any colour may be dyed BLACK; white, cream and pastels may be dyed ANY COLOUR.

Beyond this, colours are best related for good results, as follows:

REDS are best dyed Maroon, Nigger, Navy, Purple.
PALE GREENS are best dyed Medium Greens, Darker Greens, Nigger, Navy.
MEDIUM GREENS are best dyed Dark Greens, Nigger, Navy.
YELLOWS are best dyed Greens, Tangerine, Red, Maroon, Brown, Navy.
OATMEAL, FAWN, PALE BEIGE, STONE are best dyed shades of Red and Brown, Dark Green, Navy.
PALE BLUES are best dyed Medium Blues, Dark Blues, Navy, Crimson, Dark Brown, Dark Green.
MEDIUM BLUES are best dyed Dark Blues, Navy, Crimson, Dark Brown, Dark Green.

So much for light shades into darker shades. The reverse was at one time not possible. Now, with the aid of colour removers, you can strip out dark colour and re-dye any shade you wish. Again, a precautionary measure is to read the instructions that accompany the different makes, choosing the one that will suit your fabric.

Except where fine-textured, delicate fabrics are concerned, it is a good plan to strip out old colour, even if pale, before re-dyeing, because strippers have the virtue of being stain removers also.

PATTERNED FABRICS

Here even the professional dyer and cleaner may not be successful.

In textile dyeing there are at least six main types of dye used, each giving varying degrees of colour fastness under different conditions. Two or more such dyes may have been used to make up the pattern of your fabric, meaning that some of the colours will be faster than others. Therefore, when you attempt to dye a patterned fabric, the dye may obliterate some of the original colours but not others, and an indefinite pattern will still remain; nor would a stripper necessarily remove all the dyes. If you have bought a fabric under a guarantee of fast colour, a stripper will not touch it, but if it is a light colour it can be dyed a darker shade.

THE THINGS THAT GO WRONG

Grease stains must be entirely removed, otherwise the dye will cling and be absorbed to a greater depth

Dylon cold-water dyes, in lovely pastel shades, can be used in the bath without staining it—or your hands

than in the surrounding fabric, and show up as a dark splodge.

Fade from sunlight is almost certain to produce a patchy effect, in the main because the faded fibres absorb more dye than the unfaded areas. A uniform, all-over fade is usually safe for re-dyeing.

Dressing.—If a fabric is dyed before it has been washed several times, a certain amount of dressing may remain in the fibres and cause unevenness in dyeing.

Streaks on wool may appear if alkali from soap has collected in the parts that are the last to dry in the garment. If you have always been careful to rinse woollens thoroughly after washing, or if the woollens have always been washed in detergent liquid or powder, this should not arise.

Other causes of unevenness in home dyeing: (*a*) Lack of cleanliness. The fabric must be newly and very thoroughly washed and rinsed and stains removed. (*b*) Lack of uniformity of dampness. If the garment to be dyed has been washed and left to rough-dry, it must be uniformly damp all over. The best plan is to wash, rinse, squeeze off excess moisture and put the fabric straight into the dye bath.

EQUIPMENT

For ordinary hot-water dyeing, keep a set of dye equipment for this purpose. A large zinc or enamel bowl or bath; a length of clothes line, a few pegs and several bamboo sticks or unpolished, wooden coat-hangers and a couple of thick, perfectly smooth wooden sticks for lifting and stirring. Also you will be wise to keep a pair of well-fitting rubber gloves and long plastic apron for this job, for dyed hands and dye-spotted clothes are no fun to get right afterwards.

THE JOB ITSELF

It cannot be too strongly stressed that the maker's instructions should be faithfully carried out word by word.

Quantities of dye per dry weight of material are clearly given and should be worked out accurately.

The instruction to keep the garment moving in the dye bath is most important as a factor in obtaining even colour.

Water temperatures must be noted and the quantities of water needed, and both must be exactly as advised. If you are in the least doubtful whether all the dye has dissolved, strain it into the dye bath through very fine linen. Any undissolved particles in the water will bed themselves into the fabric fibres and appear as dark specks or small spots of darker colour.

Take particular note when salt or vinegar is to be added to the dye bath. They are advised in certain cases to ensure that the dye penetrates the fibres.

It is important to rinse until the water is clear, and then to hang the dyed item straight out on the line to drip—on a hanger if a garment, by the edges if a cloth or curtains.

Carpets, rugs and thick, fixed upholstery on chairs and settees can be treated with the carpet dyes now on the market. All that has already been said should be borne out when tackling this kind of dyeing, and it is wise to experiment, either on a small separate piece of carpet if available, or a part of the carpet that is hidden under a piece of furniture. If you tackle this job, add a brush to equipment.

HOW TO STAIN FLOORS

*Whether your house is old or new, shining
polished boards give it a cared-for appearance*

IT is not always enough to sweep the dust
off the boards and apply a coat of floor
stain. To achieve a lasting, good-looking
job, be prepared to give it the time and
patience it needs.

The new floor in a new or recently built
house should need little preparation. If the
house has been well built, the floors should
have been carefully laid, closely fitting and
planed smooth. Dust, perhaps a mark or
two, should be the main items with which
you have to deal.

An old floor may need much more preparation after years of wear and tear and
previous staining, and perhaps polishing or
varnishing.

PREPARATION BEFORE STAINING

New Floor

Examine the whole carefully for any
slightly raised nail heads and hammer
these home. See the chapter on Stain Removal for dealing with drops of paint or
distemper. Next, sweep the floor and, finally, wash all over with plain water. This
only should be necessary unless cement and
plaster dust have been trodden in by the
builders, and in this case scrub with warm,
soapy water, rinse in clean water and swab
as dry as possible.

Old Floor

This may need quite a lot done to it.
Look again for upraised nails and even
missing nails, as these can work out. The
latter are often the cause of a squeaking
floorboard, where the nail has worked
loose from the joist underneath and the
board is no longer held firmly in place.

Nails attended to, look next for rough
patches and plane smooth. Fill gaps between boards with plastic wood applied
with an old knife, and smooth level with
the floor. Wide cracks are best filled with
pieces of lath, hammered between the
boards and planed off level. Some of the
boards themselves may need filling and

Use a fairly wide brush and apply floor
stain the way of the grain—working always
towards the door

levelling with plastic wood, especially
those of old oak, from which the knots
sometimes loosen and come out.

If the floor has been covered with a
fitted carpet, there may be no stains and
you can give it its scrubbing next; soap and
water, followed by plain water rinsing, as
dust is almost bound to be ingrained. Pay
particular attention to corners, clearing
them of caked dust with a skewer.

When the floor is dry, rub down the entire surface with glasspaper tied over a
thick pad.

An old floor that has been previously
coloured may need stripping before fresh
stain is applied if it is to look good, and
this is best done before filling. If it is
stained and varnished, the colour good and
the varnish worn, you may simply need to
rub down the old varnish with glasspaper
and apply a fresh coat.

If the colour is worn and patchy, it is
better to remove it. This is a longish job,
needing care, but it is worth the effort. You
will need a solution of 1 lb. caustic soda
dissolved in 3 quarts of water, and an *old*

paint brush. Apply several coats at longish intervals, until you judge the stain and any varnish have softened. Next, scrub with as hot water as you can bear until the floor is clear. Rinse and wash down with vinegar to counteract the action of any remaining soda water.

NOTE: The solution should not touch the skin, and for safety wear strong rubber gloves.

STAINS TO USE

You can treat your floor in one of the following ways:

(a) dye it, afterwards shining it with floor polish;

(b) treat it with oil stain followed by floor varnish;

(c) use a varnish stain which includes the colouring matter.

Where (a) and (b) are concerned, the colour penetrates deeper into the wood and the job lasts longer; (c) is the quickest method but may need renewing more often.

There are recognised means of preparing home-made stains, useful when a number of floors are to be stained and economy is important.

A warm nut brown: Dissolve 1½ oz. permanganate of potash crystals in 1 gallon boiling water. When cold, apply with an old brush, stirring occasionally to keep colour even. When quite dry, polish or varnish.

A darker brown comes from mixing 2 oz. vandyke brown pigment (from a paint shop) with 1 oz. liquid ammonia and dissolving the paste in 1 pint boiling water.

A very dark brown, almost black, can be made by diluting Japan black (also from a paint shop) with turpentine to the required shade, experimenting on a piece of wood first, to get the depth needed.

For economy's sake, when buying proprietary stains and varnish, choose the well-tried brands, for instance: Ronuk Ltd. (Colron wood dyes and floor polishes); Solignum Ltd. (floor stain, matt or glossy); Colthurst & Harding, Ltd. (Darkaline high gloss stains); Goodlass, Wall & Co. Ltd. (Valspar 2–4-hour varnish and high gloss stains).

APPLICATION

Allow one coat of matt stain or dye and two of varnish, or two coats of stain if you are following up with floor polish. Two coats of varnish stain are usually necessary. You can reckon that 1 pint covers approximately 8 square yards.

These quantities apply to unstained or stripped floors. If the floor is already stained and in reasonably good condition, one coat of fresh stain should be enough.

Use a fairly wide brush and apply stain the way of the grain, and don't forget to work towards the door.

Make this
DUSTER GLOVE

Materials: Yellow duster, scrap of material for "hand," a bead for ring.

Put your hand flat on piece of paper and draw its outline. Allow ½ in. all round for turnings. Using this as a pattern, cut out "hand" in material. Tack edges and embroider ring, with bead as stone. Put "hand" in position and sew on to duster.

FIRST IMPRESSIONS

The front door, the gate, the porch, the door mat—should
all extend a welcome to those arriving at your house

An open door, a lighted hall and a thick mat,
made by blind workers at the Royal School for
the Blind, invite you into this house

THE main door is often the most conspicuous feature of a house; its design and fittings can make a great difference to the appearance of a dwelling as well as to the convenience and safety of its inhabitants.

The size and shape of the door itself are, of course, part of the architectural design of the building. There are still country cottages with doorways sometimes less than 5 ft. high, through which you creep after lifting a primitive latch. There are early Tudor houses (and imitation ones) with oaken, iron-studded doors, stoutly barred, whose main function is quite clearly to keep out the unwelcome. The doors of the Regency type of house, given dignity and importance by elegant fanlights and porticoes, are welcoming with their bright paint and gleaming brass knockers. Modern houses more often have doors that are strictly functional in character, combining strength and security with lightness in weight and cheerful colour. They are often flush surfaced—with perhaps a wired glass panel, or strips of glass blocks at the sides to give light in the hall. Their fittings are shaped for ease in handling. Their claim to beauty depends upon their suitability, their good line and proportions, rather than on ornamentation.

EXTERNAL DOORS

Door "furniture" is made in a great variety of materials to-day. As well as the wrought iron, bronze, brass and cast iron of earlier periods, fittings come in mild or stainless steel, alloys of copper and zinc, with a variety of finishes to give an attractive and durable surface. (Aluminium is not suitable for external doors, as it may be injured by air pollution. Glass and china fittings, because they are breakable, are best used on internal doors.)

There are to-day so many varieties of material available, and so many types of fittings, electrical and otherwise, in so many period styles, that it is easy for a doorway and porch to look a hotch-potch. Though there is no need to be severely regimented into one period, the fittings should be in harmony with the door and the whole house, and door handle, knocker and letter plate should preferably have the same finish. Sets of fittings are obtainable from specialists in door furniture and through ironmongery and department stores.

Finishes which need little cleaning are obviously worth consideration. They are often damaged, however, by incorrect cleaning with metal polishes and abrasives, which should not be used on them. Soap and water—and a rub with a soft cloth—are quite sufficient. Treatment with a little fine oil is recommended for chromium and stainless steel, provided this is not allowed to collect damaging dust. A rub with a *wax* furniture polish keeps bronze finishes gleaming.

The following are the main items of external door fittings and accessories arranged alphabetically.

Bells

There is the old-style non-electric bell with the knob or handle of iron, steel, bronze or brass which is pulled to set up a resounding ting-a-ling within. Perhaps more common now is the electric bell, worked by a push button made of metal or plastic (avoid a very modern plastic bell

Glass panelling makes the entrance hall of this modern bungalow pleasantly light. The door surround consists of glass blocks, the inside door on the right and the panel in the front door are glazed

Below, the Pushlite electrically illuminated combined bell push and name plate even lights the keyhole and helps you find your key in the dark

Above, Morphy-Richards battery operated door chimes have mellow, clear notes

push on a period door). In order to be seen clearly, the push button should contrast in colour with its body—a light-coloured button on a dark body or vice versa. Bell pushes come in a wide variety of shapes.

The electrically illuminated push button is convenient and welcoming. At a negligible cost in current, a ring of light can outline the bell push, lighting the keyhole at the same time. One useful unit fitting illuminates both a push button and a card for name, house name or number.

The bell itself, in the hall, is complete in one unit with either a battery or a transformer. Bells can be obtained with a power booster. There is also a type which includes in one unit a bell for the front door and a buzzer for the back.

Chimes hanging in the hall and electrically operated by a push button on the doorway are decorative as well as melodious, with from two to eight or more notes.

An ordinary electric bell can be converted into a burglar alarm at night with a simple adjustment.

There is also a fitment available, manufactured by the General Electric Company,

It is automatically bolted when the door is shut and released when it is opened (used when extra security is required, it helps to prevent the door being *battered* down).

Door Chains

These give added security. The type illustrated enables you to open the door partially while checking on the caller. It is useful particularly on rear and side doors.

Door Holders and Door Stops

Various types of spring catch can be placed on the wall behind to hold the door back.

Rubber door stoppers fixed to the floor are easy to fall over: it is preferable to fix them on the wall.

Door Speakers

A metal "door speaker" attached to the door is of particular convenience to doctors, enabling them to talk with night callers from their bedside. The night bell is connected with a wall receiver in the bedroom. When this rings, the doctor can pick up the receiver and talk directly with the caller outside.

The Sterdy Porter System incorporates a type of door speaker with an electric lock (see page 556), and is designed for the convenience of flat-dwellers. A plate on the main door includes push buttons, name plates, a luminous strip— and a set of louvres. The caller presses the button, which rings a small telephone in the flat. The owner picks this up and speaks to the caller, the voice coming through the louvres. The caller replies through the louvres, and the person upstairs can then press a button to release the lock on the door and so admit the caller.

A turn of the key on leaving the premises deadlocks the bolt and the handle on the inside of the Chubb Mortice Locking Latch (above)

The Acorn Sash Stop (right) is an excellent fitting for securing sliding sash windows so that they can still be opened enough for ventilation. Chains on a similar principle allow a front door to be partially opened

which is useful for a deaf person. A lamp unit can be wired in parallel with the bell, so that the button operates not only a bell, but a small visual signal which can be placed in any room and remains on until cancelled.

Another fitment connected with a bell is the door speaker (see next column).

Bolts

There are many varieties and sizes, both barrel type and flush, to be fixed inside a door, and in common use. Of the more elaborate types, the "Cremone" bolt extends the length of the door; by turning a handle, the top part moves up into a catch and the lower part moves downwards. The "Espagnolette" bolt follows this principle and also pulls the door tight. The "Dog" bolt is attached to the hinge side of a door.

Handles and Door Knobs

These should be of a comfortable size and shape to grip; round knobs should preferably be not less than 2 in. in diameter. The modern lever handles are usually shaped for easy gripping and should have smooth, rounded edges.

Hinges

These are sometimes ornamented, but on modern doors are usually inconspicuous. There are a number of types. With one kind the door can be easily lifted off if necessary; with a rising and falling butt hinge, the door is raised slightly when opened, so clearing a mat or carpet, and then dropped again when closed to prevent a draught.

Above, the name of your house in attractive painted lettering on an oak board

House-name Signs

These can be decorative without losing clarity. They can have, for example, letters of metal or plastic mounted on oak boards, or can be hand-carved on wood and decorated in colour, or with gold or white relief decoration. The boards themselves can be plain squared blocks or decorative in shape, fixed to the wall or door, or obtainable with

Above, an oak board with applied plastic lettering, giving a most unusual raised effect

Gold bevelled lettering incised and gilded on teak board (above). All three designs by The Lettering Centre, London

A variety of hand-made, hand-painted house name boards in wood hanging from wrought-iron brackets made by the House Names & Lantern Company, Chislehurst, Kent

posts and wrought-iron brackets and chains for hanging.

Knockers

These are often highly ornamental, particularly on period doors. They should be easy to handle and in proportion to the size of the door.

Latches

The old-fashioned thumb latches (used

chiefly on rear doors, sheds and gates) are preferably galvanised to withstand exposed conditions. When a pull handle is fitted beneath the latch, sufficient space should be left for the fingers (often it is not, and fingers get pinched).

Letter Cages

Made of enamelled metal, with or without locks, for attachment behind the letter-plate aperture, these should be adequate in size.

Letter Plates

These are usually in brass, bronze or plated finishes, horizontal or vertical, with or without postal knockers attached, and in a style to match the other fittings. A combined postal set with space for the keyhole or name plate can be obtained.

The aperture should be adequate in size: the postal authorities recommend a size of 8 in. by $1\frac{3}{4}$ in. The flap usually closes by a spring, or it can be by a dead weight. For draughty apertures, the "Netador" draught preventer—a metal plate with a flap—could be fitted on the inside of the door.

A good-looking and serviceable letter cage, enamelled in white, cream or gold, with lock, by Contemporary Products, from the Army & Navy Stores, London

Locks

It is obviously important to have a secure lock. The lock you choose may, in fact, affect the insurance on the house. The type in general use on an exterior door is the cylinder night latch, with which a door can be closed by slamming and opened with a key from the outside and a knob from the inside. Police authorities recommend that, in addition to this, a mortice deadlock should be used; the latter is fitted into the thickness of the door and is locked and unlocked by turning a key which operates a bolt.

Having two locks means, of course, carrying two keys for one door; but there are a number of locks on the market which combine the advantages of both types and are designed to baffle a burglar. One lock on the door is then quite sufficient. With the Chubb Front Door Mortice Locking Latch, for example, the door is closed by slamming; then, by inserting and turning the key on the outside, both the bolt *and* the lever handle on the inside are deadlocked and immobilised. This is especially advantageous where there is a glass panel in the door, through which a burglar might be tempted to break, to reach the handle inside. (A similar lock can be obtained, locking from both sides of the door.) A cylinder night latch type can also, in a patent lock (e.g. the Sidleen Cylinder Night Latch) have this feature—i.e. of deadlocking the bolt and lever handle inside by a reverse turn of the key from outside.

Electric Locks

These are designed for the electrical release of a door from a remote position by means of a bell push or other contact, and are worked in conjunction with the normal cylinder locks which can still be operated in the usual way with a key or by the knob inside. The electric lock is found chiefly on the outside doors of blocks of flats. The flat-dweller, instead of toiling up and down the stairs in response to the bell, can admit a caller into the hall by pressing a push button in the flat. The lock is released and the door can be pushed open. As soon as it is shut, the door is automatically relocked.

The bell push and lock could also be attached to an outside gate, enabling it to be unlocked from within the house.

Padlocks

If you use a padlock (more likely on the garage door or gate than on the house door), it is well to make sure that it is a really strong type.

Mats

Mats for use outside or inside an external door are usually of coconut fibre or of rubber and can be obtained in sizes to fit any permanent "well," so that they lie flush with the floor. Most coconut mats are imported from India; those woven in the U.K.

Dust, dirt and moisture drop off the shoes, through the Typrod doormat, into the portable well below, whence it is easy to remove them without the usual dirty job of shaking dust-laden mats

Porch light (above) in muffled glass on a black wrought-iron bracket, gives just enough illumination for safety and a friendly welcome.
General Electric

Instead of having "Welcome" on your doormat, why not your name? Blind workers at the London factory of the Royal School for the Blind wove the one on the left, and will make mats to order

are often made by blind people (e.g. in the London factory of the Royal School for the Blind), who make long-wearing mats to any shape or size ordered. They will also weave in to order any name, word or design required.

The Typrod "Beatall" mat, made of strong fabric reinforced by rubber strips, is of linked construction to act as a non-slip wiper. The dust, etc., falls through to the permanent well, or into the portable well which can be supplied with it.

Name Plates and Numbering

Clearness and durability are essential here. Names and numbers can be engraved on metal or carved on wood or painted. Individual letters and numbers can be obtained in many kinds of metal and plastic in various styles and sizes, with enamelled and other decorative finishes of

Nothing gives a house a more delightfully Continental air than a sunblind. The Sopra blind (above) is in many gay colours and designs with painted wood and metalwork

flush - surface door — which may even be made entirely of glass.

Door Closers

A self-closing door is sometimes desirable. Some door closers, which are fitted at the top of the door, are rather large and conspicuous for use in a private house. Preferably, the closing is operated by a floor spring mechanism, as this is concealed in the floor.

Draught Preventers

Special metal strips can any colour. They can be fixed to wood by pins at the back, or to tiles, metal plates, etc., by adhesive, or to brick by means of threaded lugs, nuts and washers.

Porch Lights

A porch light is not only a great convenience, but is decorative and welcoming. The fittings should be durable and weatherproof and are available in great variety, to be suspended or attached to the wall or porch ceiling. Wrought-iron lanterns are effective in many suitable settings.

Sun Blinds

A colourful canvas blind gives gaiety as well as protection. It may be a simple ringed curtain running on a rod over the door, an awning on extending arms over an entrance or French casement doorway, mounted to an automatic spring roller and operated by a pole and hook (or by a side cord).

INTERNAL DOORS

The choice of fittings naturally depends on the style of door as well as on the style of room. A highly ornamental door knob, which would give charm to a panelled door, would look out of place on a modern

Particularly attractive in a contemporary home is this charming "Armourcast" door, consisting of a single sheet of shock-resisting glass, by Pilkington Bros.

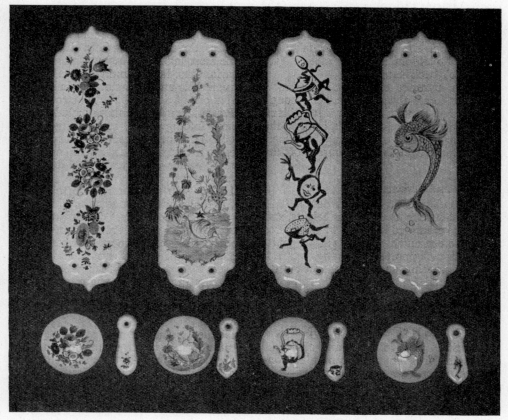

Door furniture—matching finger plates, door knobs and keyhole tabs—in hand-painted china by Richard Quinnell—in designs suitable for the sitting-room, kitchen, bathroom or nursery

be attached to the door edges. If there is a wide gap under the door, the most useful fitting is one with a sealing strip which drops when the door is closed and automatically rises (to pass over a carpet) when it is opened.

Handles; Fingerplates

Lever handles are common on modern doors. Knobs can be of metal, plastic, china or glass, in a great variety of designs. Fingerplates, if any, usually match the handles.

A clear-glass fingerplate and matching door knob or a simple set in gleaming metal can look well on most types of door.

The charming sets available of fingerplates, door knobs and keyhole tabs in decorated china can give a colourful finishing touch to a room. The designs are usually floral—but not always: appro-priate designs can be had for kitchen, bathroom and nursery doors. Special subjects or designs can be carried out to order by one firm.

Gates

Whether of wood or metal, the garden gate should bear some relation to the fencing or railing and to the style of the house door and porch. The highly decorative wrought-iron gates are increasingly popular. If the gate is at an appreciable distance from the house door, it should carry the name board or house number.

Latches and hinges are important because there is nothing so self-destructive as a gate swinging in the wind. Weak latches are usually the cause, but sometimes tradesmen's messengers are to blame.

Malleable iron latches are on the market in various designs, but the best is a pattern sold with a bevelled catch over which the latch slips smoothly into a fixed position. Hinges should be very strong to stand the constant slamming, or to take the weight of children swinging on the gate when one's back is turned.

As an entrance to a small garden, a simple oak gate always looks well, though a painted gate, hung between brick pillars, gives more intimacy. Wrought iron, on the other hand, means security against dogs, yet allows passers-by a glimpse of the garden.

Trellises and Screens

Diamond trellis of common deal laths is sold in 12-ft. lengths of various heights, and should be creosoted before using. It makes a good screen and can also be used against ugly walls to support self-clinging climbers.

Screen fencing should harmonise with the gate, and for this wattle hurdles are popular. They are sold, with stakes to suit, by the dozen, in various sizes.

GARDEN FURNISHINGS

Almost as wide in range and choice as household furnishings, these may be considered under two main headings—permanent and portable.

Urns are good to flank long, otherwise unattractive cement paths. On the pillars here are traditional figures called the "The Dish Dancers"

Permanent garden furniture consists of such articles as hardwood seats, cement tables and seats cast in moulds, summer houses, dovecotes, sundials, bird baths, stone mermaids, stone herons (fishing), stone dwarfs, urns, Italian antiques; the range is innumerable and covers everything that remains out of doors all the year round.

Portable garden furniture includes deckchairs, folding stools, sun-bathing chairs, couch hammocks, beach mattresses, umbrellas, awnings, tables; also a range becoming wider each year with designers' inventiveness.

Under "portable" it is wise to include such articles as hardwood seats which have no wrought-iron legs. Other attractive types of seat made from timber taken from world-famous liners and battleships are obtainable, and these should be removed to a dry shed during the winter, otherwise the legs soon begin to rot.

The same heading might cover such ornaments as hanging baskets and tubs of flowers.

Neither permanent nor portable garden furniture is essential to the charm of a garden, but each—if tastefully chosen— can make an exciting contribution to its attractions.

Perhaps here a word of warning might be appropriate. It is as easy to overfurnish a garden as it is to overcrowd a room with furniture. Many Italian gardens look like cemeteries for that reason—the stone work is so abundant.

Garden furniture of a permanent kind should be collected piece by piece, with no apprehension that the antique will clash with the modern. A stone figure of an "apple boy," for example, is a fitting introduction to an orchard or fruit garden. This figure is moulded in large quantities to meet popular demand, as also are urns supported by standards, with figures entitled "The Dish Dancers."

Urns are delightful to flank long, unattractive cement paths. They can be filled with bulbs for spring flowering, and replanted with geraniums or bright-coloured plants afterwards.

For those who like formal ornaments, wooden pillars supporting miniature Japanese gardens are attractive. Flowers massed round the base of the pillars add to the charm.

Photo: Peter Sowerby

TURN A BRIGHT FACE TO THE SUN

FOR happy summer lounging on terrace, balcony or in the garden, choose chairs that are comfortable and practical. The gay red-and-white striped furniture shown above is covered in Lionide, a plastic-coated material resistant both to dirt and scratches, and comes from Maples, London. And even if you have no garden, you can still have a gay front door and welcoming windows.

Colour transforms the entrance below. Left, a simply constructed plain metal canopy on tubular steel supports makes a smart porch. Note strong contrast of white and yellow paint

Above, an old-fashioned panelled door gets a new look with a two-colour paint treatment. Twin metal wall brackets hold pot plants

TO GLADDEN THE HEARTS OF THE YOUNG

These quickly made toys are easy enough for the children to make themselves

Designed and described by
SHEILA WEBB

No Christmas tree is complete without a fairy on top and no nursery ever had too many animal inhabitants. On the opposite page are simple instructions for dressing the fairy doll in all her tinsel finery. The Sea Animals (below) and the cute long-legged foal (right) will all come to life in no time—instructions and diagrams for making them and other animals in felt on the following pages.

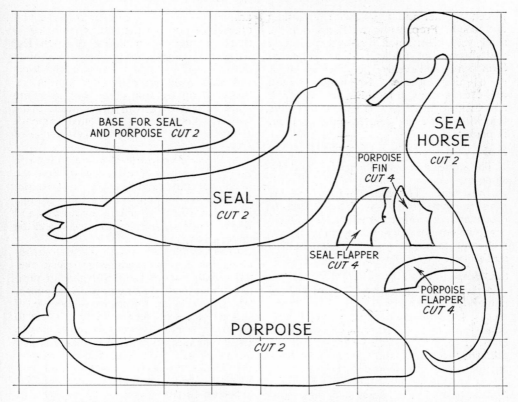

BASE FOR SEAL AND PORPOISE *CUT 2*

SEAL *CUT 2*

SEA HORSE *CUT 2*

PORPOISE FIN *CUT 4*

SEAL FLAPPER *CUT 4*

PORPOISE FLAPPER *CUT 4*

PORPOISE *CUT 2*

The diagrams for the Sea Animals, shown in colour opposite, are half-scale. To make your animals the full size, each square should equal one inch. Draw them on paper first, then cut out pieces in felt

CHRISTMAS TREE FAIRY

Materials Required: A baby doll about 6 in. tall.

For the frock: one piece of white net 3 in. by 22 in., one piece 6 in. by 40 in.; tinsel; narrow coloured ribbon for sash.

For the foundation: two pieces of white taffeta each 4 in. by 7 in.

To Make Up: Seam together the 4-in. sides of the taffeta pieces, leaving a small opening in each seam near the top for armholes. Neaten armholes, hem bottom edge and make a ¼-in. turn on to the wrong side along top edge. Run a gathering thread round top edge, slip foundation on to doll and draw up round neck. Fasten off firmly.

Next fold the two net strips in half lengthwise and run gathering threads along each fold. Draw up narrow strip round doll's neck, and the wider strip round the waist. Catch skirt and neck frill here and

there to foundation if too bouffant. Finish with ribbon sash and drape tinsel prettily over frock, using a short length as a circlet for the head.

SEA ANIMALS
Porpoise

Materials Required: One 9-in. square of coloured felt; embroidery thread to match; small piece of cardboard; kapok for stuffing; scraps of black and white felt.

To Make: Draw out diagrams on squared paper (one large square equals one inch), following those shown. From the felt cut out the necessary number of pieces indicated on diagrams. Place the two body pieces together, edges level, and oversew with matching thread. Leave 1½ in. open along top of back for stuffing, and before oversewing base into position glue a piece of cardboard to inside of base, cut to shape but slightly smaller. Oversew two fin pieces together and repeat with remaining two pieces. Prepare the two flappers in the same way, then stitch fins to top of body and flappers to under part as in photo. Stuff firmly and evenly, then oversew edges of opening together. Embroider mouth and eyes or draw in mouth with Indian ink and make eyes from small pieces of white felt with black felt centres, glueing them in place.

Seal

The same quantity of materials and the same instructions should be used for making the seal. The ball balanced on his nose is made from two circles, 1 in. in diameter, cut from contrasting felt. Oversew together, leave a small opening, lightly stuff and complete sewing. Stitch ball to seal's nose.

Sea Horse

Again use the same quantity of materials. After cutting out the two body pieces, you will also need to cut two strips, one $6\frac{1}{2}$ in. long, the other $8\frac{1}{2}$ in. long, and both strips $\frac{3}{4}$ in. wide. Trim the ends of each strip to points, and start by sandwiching the shorter one between the two body pieces, starting at tip of tail and coming up front of animal. The longer strip runs from tip of tail up back of animal. Saddle-stitch strips into place. Continue to make up as for seal and porpoise, but "stuff" the snout with a sliver of matchstick to give it a good shape and prevent it curling.

FELT FOAL

Materials Required: One piece of black felt 20 in. by 15 in.; small pieces of yellow and red felt; one hank yellow embroidery wool for tail; kapok for stuffing; matching embroidery threads.

To Make Up: Using squared paper, draw the pattern pieces shown half-scale in the diagram. Cut out carefully, then place the body, under-body, and ear-pieces on the black felt, pin in position and cut out the required number (see diagram). Cut out mane and back and front hooves from yellow felt, and mouth from red felt, again following the number of pieces required as shown on diagram.

Next place under-body pieces together, edges even, and oversew along top edges for about 1 in. in from each end, leaving centre opening through which to stuff the animal. Now stitch ears in position and oversew a hoof to the end of each leg so that stitching is on inside of each leg. Sandwich under-body between body pieces, edges even, pin in position and oversew edges together, from outer point of one hind leg, up leg and along back to where mane is joined; at this point insert mane between body-pieces, and either glue or saddle-stitch in position. Oversew rest of edges.

Next cut four ovals of yellow felt to fit into the bottom of each leg so that the horse will stand, and oversew into position. Stuff reasonably firmly and evenly, using a long-pointed pencil or knitting needle, and when completed oversew the opening in the under-body.

Oversew the two mouth-pieces together along the nearly-straight edge, place over the mouth part of head and glue in position. Paint in an eye or cut out from yellow felt and glue on. Remove a couple of strands of embroidery wool from skein to tie round horse's neck, trim remainder to about 6 in. and stitch to back where marked on diagram. Cover joins between hooves and legs with narrow strips of red felt, edges "pinked," and glue or stitch in place.

Biscuit cutters in various shapes, weights from the kitchen scales and other household items are used to make the patterns for the pets that follow.

KITTY-CAT
(Shown on page 564)

To make pattern.—Place 2 lb. scale weight on paper and draw round. Next place $\frac{1}{2}$ lb. weight on top and slightly overlapping; draw round this. Draw on the pointed ears and cut out round outline (see page 564).

To make up.—Cut out the pattern twice from felt. On one piece draw in a face with ink, or use scraps of felt for eyes, nose and mouth and glue in position. Now place the two pieces together evenly and oversew the edges, leaving an opening at the bottom. Push in the stuffing with a pointed pencil, distributing it evenly and not too tightly. Finally, oversew the opening.

NOTE.—If a piece is cut off across the bottom, the sides and top oversewn together and the shape left unstuffed, Kitty-Cat becomes an amusing egg cosy.

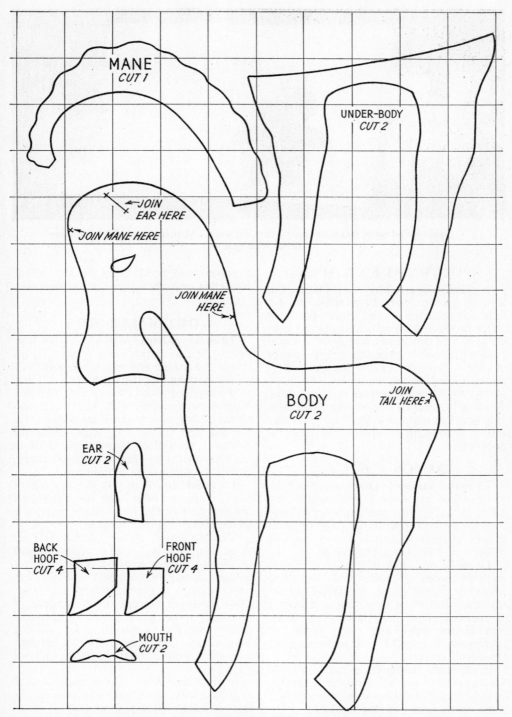

Diagram, drawn half-scale, showing the pieces required to make the little foal pictured on the colour page facing page 561. Note: to make him full-size, draw out on paper with one-inch squares

A plastic biscuit cutter makes the pattern for Gingerbread Man, and Kitty-Cat is cut from kitchen scale weights

GINGERBREAD MAN

A plastic biscuit cutter is used here. Cut a paper pattern first, if preferred, or, if a light coloured felt is used, draw round the shape on the felt, using a well-pointed pencil. Cut out two pieces and draw in facial features on one or make them from scraps of felt. Oversew pieces together, stuff through head, oversew opening. To make up the toy even more quickly, use saddle-stitching instead of oversewing. (See also chapter "Let's Make a Toy" for more detailed information about the general principles).

QUICK-CHICK

To make pattern.—Draw round a 2 lb. weight, then place the $\frac{1}{2}$ lb. weight a little down to the left this time, and not straight over the top as for Kitty-Cat. Draw round smaller weight (no ears wanted in this pattern) and cut out round outline.

To make up.—Cut two. Draw in eyes on both pieces, or make from black and white felt circles, glued in position. Oversew and stuff. For beak, cut a diamond of red felt, 1 in. long and $\frac{1}{2}$ in. wide, fold across width and catch centre of fold firmly to edge of head with matching thread.

If you want the chick to stand, cut two 1-in. squares of red felt, sandwich a smaller square of cardboard between, oversew and catch centre firmly to base of chick.

Again you could make some tiny felt chicks, unstuffed, leaving the lower edges unsewn—and perch them on top of the breakfast eggs on Easter Sunday morning.

DRUMMER BOY

To make pattern.—HEAD: $2\frac{1}{2}$ in. long and $1\frac{1}{2}$ in. across at widest point. Draw round the handle end of a tablespoon as a guide, curving out the sides with a pencil to the required width if necessary. BODY: Rule a vertical line 4 in. high; with this as the centre, rule a line 3 in. wide across the top, and a line 1 in. wide across the bottom. Rule lines between the ends of the two horizontal lines to complete shape, BASE: A circle 2 in. in diameter.

To make up.—Cut two pieces each of head, body and base. For the busby, use the top half of the head shape, cutting a shade wider to fit over head.

Oversew busby pieces together and set aside until doll is finished. Draw in face on one head piece, oversew both pieces together, leaving neck open. Stuff through neck, lightly and evenly, and set aside. Glue three felt buttons down top half of one body piece, place pieces together and oversew sides and across shoulders, leaving bottom open and a centre opening between shoulders wide enough to take neck of head piece.

Prepare base next. Cut a circle of card slightly smaller than base and glue to one half of base. Glue a short cork, 1 in. in diameter, to centre of card. Cut a central hole, 1 in. in diameter, in remaining half of

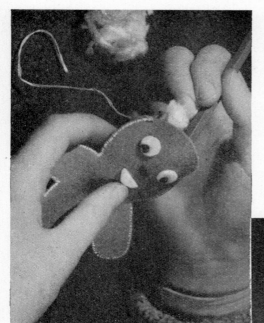

base and lay on top of card. Oversew base pieces together, coat sides of cork with glue, fit narrow end of body piece over it and press in position. Leave till glue dries, then stuff body through neck opening, insert neck of head piece in the opening and stitch head into opening, taking needle through from back to front, catching neck opening to neck of head as you go. Finish with a narrow felt strip round middle.

PIERROT
(Shown on page 566)

The same body piece as for Drummer Boy is used, in reverse. After oversewing

To make up Ginger-bread Man, oversew back and front together (right). Push stuffing in firmly with a pencil (above)

Quick-Chick (below) is designed by drawing round two kitchen weights

the sides, oversew the wide end round a 2-in. circle of felt interlined with cardboard. Cut two 2-in. circles for the head, adding a short neck piece to each circle. Oversew together, stuff through neck opening. Stuff body through neck opening, insert neck of head into this opening and stitch in place as for the Drummer Boy. Finish with felt buttons, ribbon neck frill and felt cap.

Cap and base look pleasant in contrast felt, and help to use up scraps left from Drummer Boy or other toys.

HUMPTY-DUMPTY
(Shown on page 566)

An individual pie dish, 5½ in. long by 4 in. wide, inspired this nursery favourite. Draw out pattern and cut two pieces. On the top half of one piece draw in the face

(Tenniel's Humpty in *Alice* was used as a guide in this case). Oversew or saddle-stitch the two pieces together, leaving opening for stuffing. Close opening after stuffing. Make two legs from plaited black wool, each about 2½ in. long, and stitch to body. Finish with a strip of felt about ¾ in. wide for the collar, holding the turned-back points with a black wool bow.

NOTE.—Humpty's shape, cut in half, would make two egg cosies. One could be decorated with his, or any, face, and the other with small circles of contrast felt glued on here and there.

Plastic biscuit cutters can be used to cut out all sorts of animals, two pieces of felt then being sewn together with saddle-stitching, which is rather quicker than oversewing.

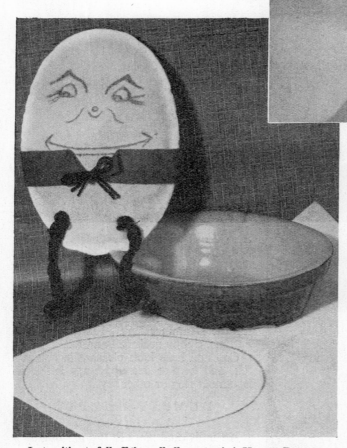

Pierrot can be turned into Drummer Boy by making upside down! It's the placing and colour of the neck frill, buttons, etc., that makes the difference

Just waiting to fall off the wall all over again is Humpty Dumpty —designed from a one-person pie dish, with legs of plaited wool and a very smart felt collar

OTHER NOTIONS

When household goods cease to provide ideas, it is often possible to take one or two patterns from a child's painting book in which are plain, bold outlines. These can be traced on to greaseproof paper and cut as patterns.

One or two good butterfly shapes, gained in this way, and made up as already described, could be utilised as a pram toy. Make, say, six in pastel colours and sew on to silk cord, long enough to tie to either side of the pram hood.

MAKING *in* MINIATURE

There is a special fascination about tiny things, particularly when they are exact reproductions, like these

Animal Fair (above)

THE frame to hold the little animals is simple to make.

It is 15 in. by 15 by 3½ in. deep.

Materials Required

Four pieces hardwood 15 in. by 3½ in. by ⅜ in.; 2 3-ft. lengths ⅜ in. D beading; 9 yd. covered bell wire; 3 glass shelves 15 in. by 3¼ in. (20 oz.); 8 1-in. wire nails; thin ⅝ in. panel pins; glue and adhesive tape.

To Assemble

Mark position of shelves on two of the boards and insert two nails for each shelf support. Bind nails with adhesive tape to protect glass. Glue and nail boards in form of box with the two side pieces outside top and base. Add triangles of thin wood to the back of corners to make frame rigid.

Sandpaper and enamel in your chosen colour. When dry, the wire and the beading can be added. Mitre beading by laying it on the edge of the box and marking the corner cuts. Cut wire into four lengths. Lightly pin beading on to one edge (a pin either end will do) and slide loops of wire under it, twelve loops to each edge. Arrange wire and tap down beading alternately to get a regular loop form.

Finally, insert two or three more pins along the length of beading and hammer home to hold wire rigid. Repeat with each edge in turn. Insert ends of wire under adjacent ends of beading on each corner. When nailing hardwood, drill small pilot holes first to avoid splitting.

The Animals

The little china ones are Wade's "Whimsies," obtainable in sets of five (there are four different sets) from the Civil Service Stores, Strand, London, W.C.2, who also stock the glass animals. The pottery animals are from Kynance Galleries, Kynance Place, London, S.W.7.

Rose Garden (shown on next page)

Cover the bottom of the bowl with 1 in. of coarse gravel, fill up with loamy soil and press down. Water the soil well and plan your garden before planting. Put in the arches and steps first. The arches are of plaited rush with wire laced through. Make the pool with a small glass dish; for the steps leading down to the pool, use flat stones. Border them with silver saxifrage. Build up the soil slightly so that the steps lead down to the sunken pool.

There are 18 rose bushes in the garden; pink roses called Sweet Fairy, Little Princess, Rosa Roulettii, the smallest of all roses; red roses, Peon, Maid Marion, and Lawrenciana Oakington for training

567

Rose Garden

over the arches; a white rose called Cinderella.

Remove the roses from the pots and tease out the roots before planting.

Give the roses a lot of fresh air and a little rain water from time to time. During their flowering period feed them once a week with a good plant food, and deal immediately with any sign of pests.

The miniature rose plants may be obtained from the Bozenham Gardens, Ashton, near Northampton.

Water Garden (opposite)

Materials: Aquarium sand, shells and the following water plants: Ambulia (feathery plant), Elodea densa (similar to Ambulia but thicker), Sagittaria (straight leaves), Hygrophila (small paired leaves on stalk), Oko Fern.

Water plants may be obtained from all good pet and aquarium shops or, alternatively, from Harrods Ltd., Brompton Road, London, S.W.1, or Gamages Ltd., High Holborn, London, E.C.1.

Wash sand well and put into bowl, add shells and fill bowl with cold water. Allow to settle and put in plants and water snails.

The water garden entails no work once it has been prepared. The water is kept sweet by the plants, and has only to be changed about once or twice a year. Additional water must, however, be added now and then to keep it up to same level.

Tree Island (opposite)

Fill the bottom of a container with crocks, then build a landscape with soil suitable for alpine plants.

Remember the container must have at least one hole to allow for drainage.

Gather up coloured pebbles from the beach or garden and sprinkle them in a winding path up to the trees.

A mixture of the following trees was used to make the Tree Island photographed here: Shipaku (Japanese), Juniper Hibernica Compressa, Japanese larch and Cupressus Ellwoodii.

Miniature trees obtainable through the Mini-Tree Guild, 31/32 King Street, Covent Garden, London, W.C.2.

Water
Garden
(*Above*)

Tree
Island
(*Left*)

MAKING NEW HOMES OUT OF OLD PROPERTY

Your local Council may be able to help with a cash grant towards modernising or converting premises

PERHAPS you own an old house, well enough built, but lacking in modern amenities for your own convenience or that of tenants; or it may be too large for you, and you have thought of converting it into two or more separate flats; or you own a building which could be converted into a dwelling house or flats. Perhaps you have hesitated to have the improvements or conversion made because of the expense.

It is worth enquiring into the money grants available through local Councils for works of this kind in the U.K. The grants fall into two categories: Standard Grants and Discretionary Grants. Standard grants you can claim as a right because in certain circumstances the local authority cannot refuse your application. But you must get your application approved before you start work. These standard grants are made for installing a bath or shower, a wash-hand basin, a water closet, a hot water supply, and a food store.

If you need to put in all five improvements, you will get £155, or half the cost of the work if it is less than that. If you do not need to put in all five improvements because some are already there, the grant of £155 is reduced in proportion.

Discretionary grants are made to help house owners to modernise houses by carrying out more extensive work than can be covered by standard grants, or by converting into flats a large house. These grants are made by the local Council—but only if they wish.

The total sum granted under the scheme is £400, but if you have already been granted the £155 under the standard grant, you will get only £245 of discretionary grant.

Any owner, or leaseholder with at least 15 years to run, may qualify for a grant, without regard to his financial position. Normal repairs, mere replacements and decoration cannot count as qualifying for a grant. The purpose of these grants,

made under the Housing Act, 1949, and the Housing Repairs and Rent Act, 1954, is to save and bring up to modern standards the older houses in the U.K., which, if attended to now, will last a long time yet, but, if neglected, will sink beyond repair and have to be replaced by costly new houses, built at public expense. Tenants, owners—and taxpayers—it is considered, will all benefit.

If you are interested, write to your local Council, giving them details of what you propose to do and what you think it will cost. To qualify for the grant, the estimated cost of the proposed work must be at least £100 per house or flat. If the application is approved you may need to produce plans and specifications. (It is best to have professional help in preparing these. The fees can be included in the cost of the improvement or conversion, and so half of them may be covered by the grant.)

The Council's decision to approve your scheme for a grant will depend on their being satisfied that the dwelling, when the work is done on it, will be satisfactory for at least 15 years more and will be in good repair, free from damp, properly lighted and ventilated, with adequate water supply indoors, satisfactory means of supplying hot water, have an inside or easily accessible lavatory and a fixed bath or shower, preferably in a separate room, have a sink or sinks, with suitable arrangements for disposal of waste water, have a proper drainage system, be provided in each room with adequate points for gas or electric lighting (where available), have adequate facilities for heating and for storing, preparing and cooking food, and have proper provision for fuel storage.

The improvements qualifying for a grant will be those undertaken to comply with these standards, though there may be some relaxation or adjustment in special circumstances. A conversion can include these improvements plus any struc-

Below, the sitting room in a Victorian villa in Leeds as it was. Right, the same room modernised and transformed out of all recognition during the conversion into maisonettes, the dreary brown paint and ugly wallpaper removed and a modern fireplace installed

British official photographs: Crown copyright reserved

Right, the bedroom as it was—a dark, cheerless attic with a sloping ceiling. Below, as it looks to-day, with a new window in the rear wall, the old-fashioned fireplace removed, an all-over fitted carpet to give an illusion of space, colourful curtains and light decorations

tural work required. If the house is let, a rent increase can be made to give a return on the money the owner spends—but limited, because public money has also been used. The local Council usually fixes a maximum rent to replace the previous controlled rent, if any. Where the rent has been already fixed by a Rent Tribunal, the owner has the right to increase the rent figure by 8 per cent. of the money he has spent out of his own

Before: **The sordid entrance passage, with dark stairway, peeling wallpaper and chipped paint**

After: **The passage (left) transformed into a small but bright and well-equipped kitchen**

pocket on improvements or conversion. Owners are advised to indicate, in the preliminary talks with the Council, the rent they propose to charge, and enquire whether this is likely to be approved by the Council.

The tenant's agreement must be obtained before the work is begun, and he can refuse to give it if he does not think the improvements worth the extra rent.

The following are the conditions attached to a grant: the dwelling must be used only as a private house and must be occupied by the owner or a member of his family, or must be let at a rent not exceeding the maximum fixed by the Council. These conditions will apply for ten years after completion of the improvements. You may not sell your house to a new owner for his own occupation (unless he is a member of your family) within a period of three years from the completion of the improvements for which you have been given the grant.

A further point is that if the owner cannot meet his share of the cost, he can borrow money for the purpose from the Council at a low rate of interest. The Council may also lend him money to pay for repairs not covered by the grant.

A free leaflet, "Improve Your House With A Grant," giving further details, can be obtained from your local Town Hall or Council Offices. For more information and examples, with plans, you can obtain "New Grants For Better Homes" from H.M. Stationery Office (price 1*s.* 6*d.*).

To encourage the purchase of older houses, arrangements have been made between the Government and various building societies to lend up to 95 per cent. of the value or purchase price of older houses in appropriate cases. These arrangements can help you if you are thinking of buying a house built before 1940 and costing not more than £3,000 in London and the Home Counties, and £2,500 elsewhere in the United Kingdom.

Before: **The bathroom, if such an old-fashioned inconvenient horror was worthy of the name**

After: **The same room when modernised— shining white, hygienic, easily kept clean**

WATCH YOUR BULBS GROW!

Just put the bulb in the top of a special glass filled with water (left), cover with a paper cap (above) and the roots will soon begin to appear

HYACINTHS are usually sold in "collections" of four, six or twelve. These are suitable for pots, bowls, or simply to grow in water. The latter process demands no horticultural skill; indeed, it may be a very happy hobby for children.

The flower is cultivated in water in glasses sold for the purpose. Not only does it provide decorative value, but there is great interest in watching the entire plant through its normal process of development.

Darkness retards top growth, but does not delay the root production, and the original technique was to place the bulbs in a dark cupboard for a few weeks, then take them out to rush into flower. But that is unnecessary now. Little caps can be bought, or easily made out of brown paper at home, which serve the same purpose, and the plants can be kept in view all the time. The temperature, however, should be uniform night and day, and the water must be kept pure and bright.

On no account should the water be allowed to touch the bulb or the latter will rot and, as hyacinth flowers are big and heavy, they should be supported by wires.

The mantelshelf is a most unsuitable place to keep bulbs in glasses, because of the fluctuations in temperature.

Our pictures show the process from start to bloom, and the ease with which a hyacinth can be flowered. It is not recommended that any stimulating substance should be used in the water, but the glasses must always be kept full, as the bulbs are very thirsty and use it up in their growth.

Varieties recommended are: King of the Blues, Jan Bos, Myosotis, Princess Margaret, Orange King, La Victoire, Lord Balfour, Ostara and Anne Marie. Such a collection will provide a whole range of different colours; and the average price of the bulbs from the best growers is about a shilling each.

A simple method of indoor flower cultivation in which the children can share

SIMPLE PATCHWORK

You can have a quilt to rival great-grandmother's—and the making will give you many happy hours, cost very little

THE fascination of Grandmother's Patchwork Quilt remains, although now it is more often Great-Grandmother's work or even that of Great-Great-Grandmother. But there is no reason at all why this art should die out. Anyone can possess a quilt, cushions, work-bags, aprons, skirts, even bigger garments made of patchwork.

There are various forms of patchwork, but the two main kinds are Appliqué and Pieced. Again, under these two headings there are various methods which the more experienced may want to try.

MATERIALS

In either case, the first thing to do is to assemble as many oddments of material as possible. The family scrap bag will probably yield a good hoard of cuttings from dressmaking, chair covering and other work. Friends and neighbours must be enlisted into the collecting, and it is surprising how quickly the number of scraps grows.

Any kind of silk, rayon, cotton, chintz, velvet, brocade, etc., is suitable, but when planning the work, do not mix cotton and linen with silk. Velvet, stiff silks and brocades do not go well with the more delicate silks, because their weight pulls the finished work out of shape. Do not turn down any offers, however. Once started on patchwork, a silk cushion cover will almost certainly be followed by a cotton skirt or quilt. Just keep the various types of material separate.

APPLIQUÉ PATCHWORK

This may consist either of pieces of materials of all shapes and sizes, known as

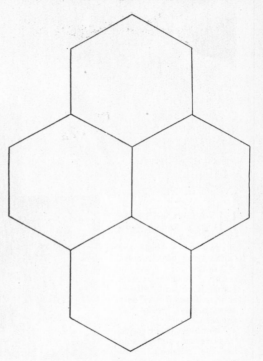

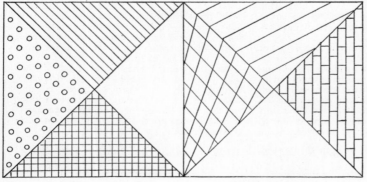

For Pieced Patchwork you cut the pieces from a master pattern. The hexagon is a useful shape; (above) four hexagons joined together. Regular Appliqué is often made up of triangles and squares —like the 3-in. squares divided into four triangles (left)

The old-fashioned patchwork quilt, laboriously made perhaps by a great-grandmother, is a prized possession to-day, only rivalled by the work of modern enthusiasts

crazy patchwork, or of specially shaped pieces, triangles, rectangles, squares, and more elaborate shapes which must be cut from patterns.

To deal with the more simple forms of this:

For appliqué patchwork you require a piece of material, such as linen, poplin, or strong cotton, for the base. The finished work has to be lined and, though the foundation must be strong, it should not be too solid.

Cut your material for the foundation to the size and shape you want, allowing good turnings.

Crazy Patchwork.—Cut your patches into any sizes and shapes you like and tack the first pattern in place on the base, beginning at the top right-hand corner of the work. Thereafter, turn under the edges of each patch, overlapping the previous one until the entire base is covered. Though you are not working to any design, you may nevertheless want to make changes when you see all the pieces tacked into place. Do this before you start the final stitching.

It is largely a matter of taste what stitch you use for the finished work. In many old quilts feather stitch is used, but with very elaborate patterned patches an invisible slip stitch is infinitely preferable. Other simple embroidery stitches, such as chain, couching, etc., are equally effective.

"Regular" Appliqué.—A very simple form of this kind of work is that made up of triangles, squares, etc. It is worked in exactly the same way as Crazy Patchwork, except that the pieces must all be exactly the same, or they will not fit. Quarter-inch turnings should be allowed, and the overlap of the patches on one another should not exceed this. If preferred, a number of patches may be tacked together before being sewn on to the foundation.

PIECED PATCHWORK

Materials.—For this you need a master pattern from which to cut the pieces. These vary in shape and size, but the hexagon is effective and used a great deal. Metal or plastic "templates," as they are called, can be bought at good needlework shops and, although they can be made at home from stout cardboard, plywood, etc., it is well worth the few pence they cost to get a good one which will last indefinitely.

In addition to the template, you require a good supply of thick paper or thin cardboard, tacking thread and good cotton or silk for the final sewing.

Method.—First cut a large number of paper or cardboard patterns, using your template and being careful to be very exact. There are various methods of doing this, i.e. tracing the shape of the template on to the paper or cardboard and then cutting with a sharp pair of scissors; holding the template firmly on the paper or cardboard and cutting direct; or laying your paper or cardboard on some solid surface (a chopping board is ideal), putting your template on top, holding it down firmly and cutting round it with a very sharp penknife or razor blade.

Having cut your patterns, cut your material very roughly by the template, allowing $\frac{3}{8}$-in. turnings all round. Very thin materials should have a lining of cotton or some other strong material to hold them in shape.

Now you are ready to start. Put your paper or cardboard pattern on the wrong side of your material in the centre and turn under allowances, being careful to keep the material absolutely taut without pulling it out of shape. Tack with large stitches.

Continue in this way until you have a good supply of patches in all the various materials you are using.

In pieced patchwork it is most important that the patches should blend and, until you have laid them out next to one another you will not know whether they do, for they can be most deceptive.

When you are ready to sew them together, put the first two patches together, right sides facing, and oversew one side with small strong stitches, being careful not to take up the cardboard or paper, which will later be slipped out and kept for use again. Sew the next one to another side of the hexagon, and continue in this way, building round your original hexagon.

With a big piece of work it is best to plan and make it in sections 12 or 16 in. square, joining the whole together afterwards. Each section must, however, be carefully planned. If you are making a quilt and intend to build round a central square, then the surrounding sections must be complementary to it and in no way dominate this centre piece.

Many quilts have plain borders, which throw up the work most attractively.

All patchwork should be lined. When the main work is completed, turn under all round and tack. Cut lining to fit. Turn under edges and tack to patchwork. Stitch invisibly all round.

In pieced patchwork, it is most important that every piece should be absolutely accurate in size and shape. So do not begrudge the extra minutes spent in cutting the patterns. If carefully handled, they can be used again and again. The accuracy with which you cut them will alone ensure the success of your patchwork.

The pleasure one gets from this work is indescribable, and the only way to share in it is to have a go yourself. Patchwork grows quickly, can be picked up at odd moments, and gives very real satisfaction to the artistic sense.

Six petals around a centrepiece make a charming patchwork flower with many uses. Try making a number, then appliqué them round the hem of a skirt; or mount them on heat-resistant material and use as dinner mats.

AN ANCIENT ART AND AN UP-TO-DATE IDEA

Old-fashioned patchwork is a fascinating hobby

There are **2,040** pieces of brightly coloured material in the patchwork quilt at the top of the page. Each small section has six sides, each larger grouping the same number, the border being additional and the corners filled in to fit. If this is too big for you to tackle, why not make a patchwork border for a plain bedspread?

A clever conversion for the nursery

An old trolley, bought at a second-hand shop and painted with hard gloss enamel, makes an ideal travelling wardrobe for a baby. If doors can be fitted to the lower shelf and a towel rail to one end, it is particularly practical and can be wheeled from nursery to bathroom with the minimum of effort with everything for baby's toilet.

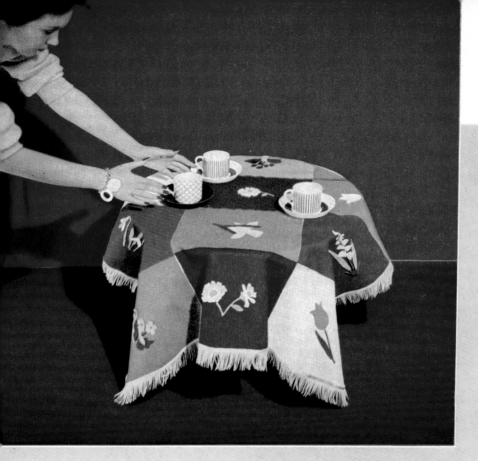

CUT FLOWERS FOR YOUR TABLE

You can make this original and colourful cloth without sewing a stitch

THE tablecloth itself consists of 12 pieces of felt—those used for the original shown in the colour photograph here were each 8 in. by 12 in., but they could be any size you like. Felt comes in 42 beautiful, glowing shades and one 12 in. square costs about 1s. 3d. To put the pieces of felt together, use Copydex and tape stuck on the underside—or, if you prefer, you can of course sew it together.

Then scatter your colourful table-cloth with spring flowers cut out of other pieces of contrasting felt, or from any pieces you have left over. On the opposite page are the flower outlines in diagram form, together with indications of the colours used; you can either trace them off as they are and cut the felt from the tracings, or enlarge them according to taste and the size of the cloth you are decorating. Remember to use a heat-proof adhesive to fix the flowers on to the cloth.

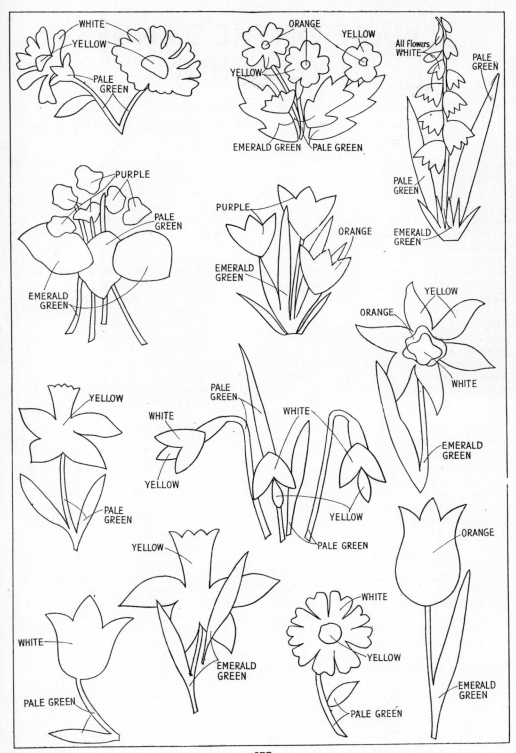

BEWARE OF THE DANGERS IN YOUR HOME

Far more—old people in particular—have serious accidents indoors
than out on the roads, and most of these tragedies could be prevented

MORE than 7,000 people in England and Wales die each year as the result of accidents which occur in and around their homes. Nearly a million more are injured there. These far outnumber those killed and hurt on the roads—a fact not realised by many people. Indeed, 24 men, women and children lose their lives every day in home accidents, compared with a daily death roll of 14 in motoring accidents.

Nearly every one of those home tragedies, like all accidents, *could* have been prevented. None of them *need* have happened, if someone had used a little more thought, had a little more knowledge, taken a little more care. That someone is usually the housewife and mother.

Everyone with old people or children in their homes should watch with special care the many lurking dangers about the house. By far the greatest number of home accident fatalities are people of over 65, closely followed by children under 5.

Here are the chief dangers, together with practical advice on how to prevent accidents. For the appropriate treatment if an accident does happen, see chapter on First Aid.

FALLS

Falls are the commonest cause of all accidents.

(1) **Staircases** can be very dangerous places, particularly for the old or the very young. Always repair immediately any loose stair rods, brass treads or broken bannisters. While waiting for bannisters to be mended, or if the staircase is dark, put up a strong rope which can be held by those going up or down. Painting the edges of the stairs white will give more light. When stair carpet gets worn, shift it so that the thin patches are against the risers,

not on the steps. Stairs should be well and clearly lighted, with a two-way switch top and bottom. Never leave cleaning materials or let children leave toys on the stairs, even for a moment; before you come back, someone may easily fall over them. Children should never be allowed to play on the stairs, which are much safer "barred" to toddlers by safety gates.

(2) **Floors.**—Too highly polished floors are dangerous: never polish under loose rugs or make nursery floors slippery. Rugs are safer if fixed with non-slip pads or drugget pins. Encourage tidiness in the home and teach children to put toys away. Be sure to wipe up spilled grease immediately.

(3) **Domestic Cleaning.**—Never climb on to a step-ladder unless it has a strong rope joining the two halves; and do not try to reach things by standing on a rickety chair or table. Never climb on to the outside of a high window to clean it—or for any other reason. Bar windows in children's rooms.

BURNS AND SCALDS

Children under 5, and people over 65, are particularly susceptible to this kind of home accident. More girls get badly burned than boys, and the reason is simple: they wear long nightdresses (sometimes made of flannelette or winceyette) and party frocks made of net. Those materials are dangerously inflammable unless treated with the new Proban anti-flame finish and excepting nylon net. The merest flick of a skirt against an inadequately guarded fire and the wearer can in a moment be in flames.

(1) **Keep all fires guarded.**—You are bound by Act of Parliament to have a fireguard wherever there are children under 12 years old. You should also protect fires with a small-mesh guard

within children's reach.

(4) **Keep electric wiring in good condition** and do not tamper with it. In case of difficulty, call an expert. Be sure to switch off current and remove hot iron to a safe place when you have finished.

(5) **When cooking,** keep boiling liquids, teapots, kettles, etc., out of the way of children, turning the spouts and handles *inwards,* so that they cannot be reached. Never carry hot

Someone thoughtlessly left a saucepan handle sticking out, so this little boy was badly scalded. (Right) A sensible mother puts pots and pans away from a toddler's prying hands and turns back her tablecloth

where there are old people, who may lose their balance and fall.

(2) **Never use inflammable materials.**— These include flannelette and winceyette (unless impregnated with Proban) and net (other than nylon), celluloid toys, etc., cotton-wool party decorations, paraffin, petrol-containing substances, such as cleaning fluids, etc. Pure nylon net is safe. When subjected to intense heat, it will smoulder but never flame. So insist, when buying net, that it should be pure nylon and that winceyette has the anti-flame finish.

(3) **Take care with matches, cigarettes, naked lights and hot ashes.**—Ashtrays and hot ashes should be emptied only into metal bins. Never leave matches

liquids unnecessarily; when you must, make sure the way is clear first. Keep the top of the stove and oven free from grease. Always have a good thick cloth handy for holding hot dishes. Take special care when handling hot fat or boiling sugar.

(6) **Avoid long, overhanging tablecloths which are a great temptation to a small child.**—Many children have been badly scalded as a result of pulling a

hot teapot or other vessel off the table. The best precaution is to secure the cloth to the table with clips, or use a smaller one which does not overhang. Failing that, fold the edges back under the cloth, rather than let them dangle.

(7) **When bathing a baby,** put the cold water in first so that there is no danger if it gets upset or you have to leave the room for a moment. Test the temperature of the water with your elbow before putting the baby in.

(8) **Never leave buckets of water uncovered** where there are young children.

(9) **Never use paraffin** to make a fire burn.

MISUSE OF ELECTRICAL EQUIPMENT AND GAS FITTINGS

(1) The flex of portable electric equipment (fires, kettles, irons, etc.) should be examined at regular intervals. If the outer covering is wearing or fraying, exposing the wiring, it may cause a dangerous shock.

(2) Never attempt even the simplest repairs to electrical equipment without first switching off the current at the main.

(3) All bathroom electric fittings must be specially insulated. **It is highly dangerous to take a portable electric fire, hair drier or reading lamp into a bathroom. The shock you receive from faulty wiring is increased well above danger level if you have damp hands or are standing on a wet floor.**

(4) If you suspect a leak of gas, carefully inspect pipes and especially junctions between pipes and report the fault to the gas company as soon as possible. In the meantime, turn off the gas at the main.

(5) Do not search for a gas leak with a match or lighted candle. Remember that a cooking jet turned down low can blow out in a draught and is then capable of producing quite a nasty explosion when a match is lighted in the vicinity.

(6) Choose equipment with adequate safety devices and devote a reasonable time to mastering these before you start using them. This applies particularly to geysers, pressure cookers, etc. See that electric equipment is fitted with three-pin plugs and properly earthed.

(7) Make sure that the gas taps on your cooker are so constructed that a small child cannot turn them on.

(8) Switch off the current before you fill or empty an electric kettle or clean an electric cooker.

(9) Electric and gas switches and plugs must all be out of reach of small children. The safest method is to cover the whole fireplace with a large guard.

POISONING

(1) Bring up children never to eat anything without permission—especially strange berries out of doors and unusual tablets indoors.

(2) Keep poisonous cleaning materials well out of children's reach.

(3) Store drugs and medicines in a locked cupboard, keeping those for external use on a separate shelf from those to be taken internally, marking drugs and poisons accordingly—and never turn the contents of a chemist's special poison bottle into any other container. They are specially made of dark glass with a ridged surface that *feels* different even in the dark.

SUFFOCATION

This is the cause of many serious accidents to children.

(1) A pillow should never be used for a baby.

(2) Babies should always sleep in a separate bed, not with grown-ups. One can be made, in emergency, out of a drawer or clothes basket.

(3) Precautions should be taken to keep small articles such as beads, buttons, etc, out of reach of small children, who often put such objects into their ears, nose or mouth, with disastrous results.

(4) Use a pram net to protect a child from cats, etc.

MISCELLANEOUS

(1) Keep sharp knives, scissors, etc., where children cannot easily find them.

(2) Whatever you are doing, avoid muddle and confusion. Accidents are much

BEWARE OF THE DANGERS IN YOUR HOME

On her way to a party, she glanced into the mirror over the fireplace and her dress caught fire. In such a case, smother the flames with a rug wrapped tightly round the person (right)

Photographs: Central Office of Information

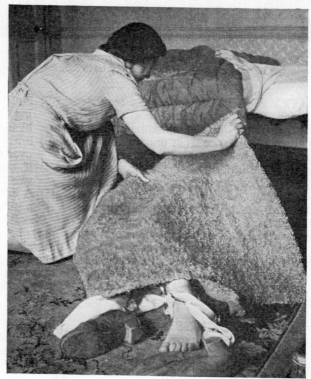

less liable to happen if you have plenty of clear space to put down hot dishes when cooking, and room for easy movement whatever work you are doing.

(3) Good lighting is vital, particularly in the cooking area.

(4) Never hang a mirror over a mantelpiece where there is a fire. It is an invitation to people to stand too close to the flame or element.

(5) Provide old people with a rubber mat on the bottom of the bath and a hand-rail or a bell-pull which they can easily reach.

FIRST AID IN ACCIDENTS

Whatever the emergency, keep calm yourself and be sure to comfort and reassure the patient – often the best treatment of all

Someone falls downstairs in your house, perhaps breaking a leg or spraining an ankle—would you know what to do and what not to?

BITES—see Dog, Insect, Snake, etc.

BLEEDING—see Cuts, Internal Hæmorrhage, Nose Bleeding, Tooth Socket (Bleeding from)

BURNS AND SCALDS

Prompt first aid is essential because the loss of tissue fluid caused by extensive burning can prove fatal. If 5 per cent. of the body area is burned, the patient needs prompt hospital treatment; if 10 per cent., a transfusion of blood or fluid should be given within an hour.

First-aid Treatment

(1) Send for a doctor or call an ambulance, stating clearly that it is a case of burning.

ACCIDENTS occur in the best regulated families. They are met most efficiently by the person who has taken the trouble to find out in advance what practical steps to take—or who can always turn to a reliable guide without losing her head in an emergency. Once you know what first-aid treatment may—and just as important, what may *not*—be given in the commoner contingencies, it is easier to keep calm and so reassure the patient and those around you.

Here, in brief form to which you can easily and quickly refer in emergencies, are the chief Do's and Don't's in dealing with the kind of accidents likely to occur at some time or another in any family.

AIR SICKNESS—see Travel Sickness

APOPLEXY—see Fits

(2) Put the patient to bed, *without* removing his clothes, but cover him with blankets and keep him warm.

(3) Put a piece of clean, dry linen or cotton over the exposed portions of the burn.

(4) If the patient can swallow, give hot sweet drinks.

(5) A burned arm or leg may be raised on a pillow.

Small burns (such as those on the hands) may be covered with small Elastoplast dressings or plain bandage. They should, however, be seen by a doctor, as they sometimes need professional dressing, can be very painful and may turn septic if neglected.

Do not apply any liquid or ointment to burns. The only exception is in cases where there is going to be long delay in getting the patient to hospital or before the doctor arrives. A baking-soda paste may then be applied. Mix sufficient baking soda with water (first boiled, then cooled) to make a thin paste, spread it on gauze, lint or a clean handkerchief and apply to the burned surface.

CAR SICKNESS—see Travel Sickness

CONCUSSION

If unconscious, treat as described under Unconsciousness. Whether conscious or not, send for a doctor and keep perfectly quiet and lying down in a darkened room. Do not attempt to rouse.

CONVULSIONS—see Fits

CUTS

Treatment for Small Simple Cuts
(1) Bathe gently round the wound with a *very mild* antiseptic lotion.
(2) Apply a clean dressing and Elastoplast, putting the Elastoplast on so as to bring the edges of the wound as closely together as possible.

Treatment if Bleeding is Severe
(1) If the above treatment does not stop the bleeding, raise the affected part of the body, if a leg, arm or hand.
(2) Apply pressure with your hand over a firm, clean pad (a folded white handkerchief will do) placed on the wound.

(3) Replace later with a firm bandage; if blood soaks through that, apply more bandages *over* the first one.

Arterial Hæmorrhage, recognisable by the bright scarlet colour of the blood which spurts out, is very serious and must be stopped without delay.

Treatment
(1) Raise the limb and apply pressure (as above). If this fails:
(2) Pressure must be exerted on the appropriate pressure point (see next page) and/or a tourniquet applied—subject to the important warnings below.

Pressure Points.—The arteries are the tubes through which the heart pumps pure arterial blood to the organs and tissues all over the body. In each main artery there is at least one spot (the pressure point) at which the application of sufficient pressure will stop the flow of blood through the artery almost entirely. One way to stop arterial bleeding is therefore to exert pressure on the appropriate point immediately *above* (or nearer the heart) than the injury.

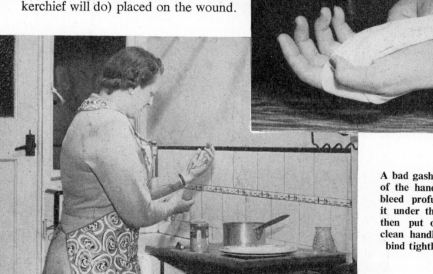

A bad gash on the palm of the hand (left) may bleed profusely. Hold it under the cold tap, then put on a folded clean handkerchief and bind tightly, as above

CHART OF PRESSURE POINTS

Site of injury	Pressure point	How to apply pressure
Arm or hand	* Subclavian (behind collar bone)	Press down behind clavicle against 1st rib, the arm being held down.
Arm or hand	* Brachial (in upper arm)	Press outwards against shaft of humerus.
Hand	Radial or Ulnar (both at wrist)	Press against the bone.
Hand	Palmar Arch (in palm of hand)	Flex fingers tightly over hard round pad.
Leg or foot	* Femoral (in groin)	Press backwards against haunch bone.
Leg or foot	Femoral (in middle of thigh)	Press outwards and backwards against the femur.
Leg or foot	Popliteal (at back of knee)	Press forwards against the bone, pad in popliteal space and flex knee.
Foot	Anterior tibial (in middle of foot in front)	Press backwards against the bone.
Head and neck	* Carotid (left or right at side of neck)	With the thumb, press inwards and backwards on one side only against the spine below and outside the bottom of the Adam's apple. (*Take care not to press on the windpipe.*)
Face below the eye	Facial (on the jaw)	With thumb, press against lower jaw 1 in. in front of angle of jaw. (Pressure to both facial arteries may be needed for lip hæmorrhage.)
Scalp and side of head	Temporal (in the temples)	Press against bone 1 in. in front of ear hole and a little above.
Back of scalp	Occipital (back of head)	Press the thumb where head and neck join, about four fingers' breadth behind rim of ear.

* = Most practical and frequently used.

A Tourniquet is an apparatus designed to stop the blood flowing through the main artery and consists of a band round the limb which can be tightened so as to press on the artery and obstruct the flow of blood. It should be used by the amateur only in cases of very severe arterial hæmorrhage when all other methods of treatment have failed, and then only with the utmost care.

(1) Put a narrow bandage or any piece of material round the raised limb, over a towel or handkerchief, tie in a half-knot on outer side of limb.

(2) Insert a pencil or short stick into the knot and then tie it off in a reef-knot.

(3) Twist the pencil or stick to tighten the bandage and put pressure on the artery.

(4) With another bandage, fix the stick in this position.

(5) At 10-minute intervals, the stick *must* be loosened. If bleeding starts again, tighten the tourniquet but loosen it again *without fail* in 10 minutes at most. If there is no more bleeding, leave it loose.

Remember, more harm than good can

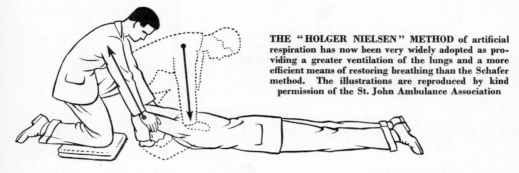

THE "HOLGER NIELSEN" METHOD of artificial respiration has now been very widely adopted as providing a greater ventilation of the lungs and a more efficient means of restoring breathing than the Schafer method. The illustrations are reproduced by kind permission of the St. John Ambulance Association

be done if a tourniquet is not used with the greatest care. If, for instance, it is not loosened at 10-minute intervals, the blood supply to the limb may be permanently cut off and the limb will become gangrenous. If it is applied too tightly, a main nerve may be compressed and paralysis result.

A tourniquet can only be used on the arm or thigh. It should be applied to the arm half-way between elbow and armpit, or in the middle of the thigh.

DOG BITE

Treatment.—Wash wound well with a mild, warm, antiseptic solution and encourage it to bleed freely. See a doctor.

DROWNING

Treatment of the Apparently Drowned
(1) Lay patient face downwards.
(2) Loosen all clothing, allow plenty of air.
(3) Clear air passages (mouth and nose) of any foreign matter and froth, using the finger covered with a handkerchief.
(4) Pull tongue forward. It must never fall back and obstruct air passages.
(5) Apply artificial respiration immediately. The "Holger Nielsen" is the approved method.
(6) Send for an ambulance and doctor.
(7) Keep the patient warm with dry rugs.

The "Holger Nielsen" Method of Artificial Respiration

Position of Patient

Lay the patient in the prone position on a flat surface.

Place the patient's hands one over the other, under his forehead. If this is insufficient to keep the nose and mouth from the ground, the head must be turned slightly to one side. The nose and mouth must be unobstructed.

Turning

If the patient is lying on his back, turn him to the prone position as follows. Go down on the right knee opposite the patient's head. Place the left foot on the ground, but to the side. Place the patient's arms carefully above his head and keep them there during the turn. Grasp the patient's left upper arm and turn him over, protecting his face with the right hand. Adjust the position of the patient's hands as previously instructed.

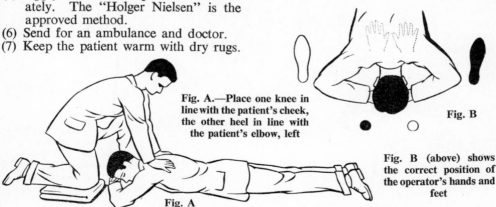

Fig. A.—Place one knee in line with the patient's cheek, the other heel in line with the patient's elbow, left

Fig. A

Fig. B

Fig. B (above) shows the correct position of the operator's hands and feet

Fig. C

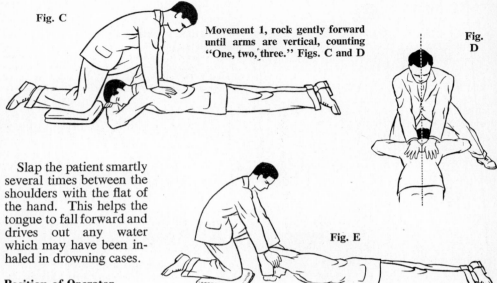

Movement 1, rock gently forward until arms are vertical, counting "One, two, three." Figs. C and D

Fig. D

Slap the patient smartly several times between the shoulders with the flat of the hand. This helps the tongue to fall forward and drives out any water which may have been inhaled in drowning cases.

Fig. E

Position of Operator

Place one knee with the inner side in line with the patient's cheek 6 to 12 in. from the top of the patient's head.

Place the other foot with the heel in line with the patient's elbow.

Place the hands on the patient's back with the palms resting on the shoulder-blades, the thumbs on the spine and the fingers pointing to the patient's feet (Figs. A and B).

Movement 1.—Keeping the arms straight, rock gently forward until the arms are vertical, using no special force. The movement takes $2\frac{1}{2}$ seconds, counting "One, two, three." This pressure causes expiration (Figs. C and D).

Movement 2. — The operator now rocks back, counting "Four," and slides his hands past the patient's shoulders until they can grasp his upper arms near the elbows. He raises and pulls on the

Movement 2, rock back, counting "Four" and sliding hands to grasp patient above the elbows, then raise and pull on the arms, counting "Five, six, seven." Figs E and F

Fig. F

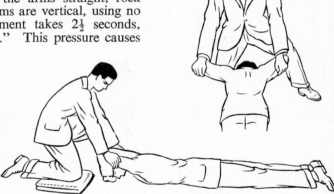

Fig. G

When the patient begins to show signs of breathing, continue with Movement 2, counting "One, two, three" for inspiration, "Four, five, six" for expiration. Figs. G and H

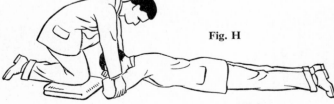

Fig. H

arms for a period of 2½ seconds, counting "Five, six, seven." (Figs. E and F.)

This movement causes inspiration. The arms should remain straight for the whole period.

Counting "Eight," the operator lowers the patient's arms to the ground and glides his hands back to the original position.

The whole operation should be rhythmic in character and should be continued until breathing starts again.

When the patient begins to show signs of breathing, the operator should continue with Movement 2 only, raising and lowering the arms alternately, counting "One, two, three" (2½ seconds) for inspiration and "Four, five, six (2½ seconds) for expiration. This will now give a rate of 12 times per minute (Figs. G and H).

Children

Children over 5 should be treated in the same way, except that the pressure on the shoulder blades should be considerably reduced and applied with the fingertips only. The rate should be 12 times per minute. For children under 5, lay the arms by the sides and place a support under the head, then grasp the shoulders with the fingers underneath and the thumbs on top. Lift the shoulders steadily with the fingers to expand the chest; lower the shoulders and with the thumbs press gently on the shoulder blades. The rate should be 2 seconds inspiration and 2 seconds expiration, or 15 times per minute. This may be done with the patient on a table and the operator standing.

Injury to Upper Limb

When the upper limb is injured, the patient should be laid on his face with his arms by his sides. The operator should be nearer the patient, and after pressing on the shoulder blades for expiration (Movement 1) should place his hands under the shoulders and raise them for inspiration (Movement 2). He should then lower them and continue with Movement 1 at the standard rate of 8 to 9 times per minute.

EARS (Foreign Bodies in)—see Foreign Bodies

ELECTRIC SHOCK

(1) *Turn off the current* before attempting to move the patient or you may well become a victim yourself. If it is for any reason impossible to turn off the current at the main, the rescuer must protect himself by standing on insulating material (the best is rubber, so if a rubber mat is available, this will do very well) and using gloves made of insulating material (rubber again) before touching the patient. The crook of a *wooden* (not metal) walking stick or a rope may be used to move the patient, but electric cable or wiring must *never on any account* be cut with knife or scissors.

(2) Having removed the patient from contact with the current, treat the asphyxia with artificial respiration (see under treatment of the Apparently Drowned for method to be used).

(3) When breathing normally, treat the burns (see Burns).

When an accident occurs at a power station or as a result of a cable falling and someone is electrocuted, *no attempt at rescue* must be made except by experts. With such a high voltage there is not the slightest hope that the victim is still alive, and the rescuer will only get killed himself.

EPILEPSY—see Fits

EYES (Foreign Bodies in)—see Foreign Bodies

FAINTING

To treat a simple faint due to shock, fright, pain, etc.:

(1) Lower the head either between the knees or lying flat.

(2) Give all the fresh air possible, opening windows, loosening tight clothing and keeping away crowds.

(3) When the patient has recovered sensibility, give a warm, sweet drink, such as a cup of tea, keep warm and reassure.

FITS

Apoplectic Fit (Stroke)

The patient, who is usually elderly, is often found unconscious or quite suddenly and without warning loses consciousness. Other symptoms are puffing and blowing, redness of face. After a time he may regain consciousness but be unable to speak; or there may be paralysis down one side or part of one side (the face, arm and/or leg).

Treatment
(1) If unconscious, treat as described under Unconsciousness.
(2) Keep very quiet and warm in a darkened room.
(3) Send for the doctor.

Major Epileptic Fits

These fits are totally different from Apoplexy, and occur most frequently in younger people and follow a quite definite form. The first sign is usually that the sufferer gives a cry (though this does not always happen), starts twitching violently and falls down, then goes blue in the face, possibly foaming at the mouth, after which consciousness is gradually regained. At any time during the fit he may soil himself.

Treatment.—Prevent the patient from banging himself or falling where he may get hurt (near a fire, for instance). If possible, insert a ruler or small strong stick wrapped in a clean handkerchief in the mouth to prevent the tongue getting bitten. When the fit has passed, put the patient to bed and allow to sleep.

Minor Epileptic Fits

Usually the patient stays quite still for a moment or two, sometimes rolling the eyes, then recovers and goes on as if nothing had happened.

Treatment.—See that the patient does not hurt himself. Otherwise, ignore the fit entirely.

Hysteria

This is produced by shock or mental stress and sometimes *looks* to the uninitiated rather like an epileptic fit, but there are marked differences which the first-aider should look for. There may be convulsions, though only if there is an audience present, and, even then, they are unlike real epileptic fits—the tongue is not bitten, there is no incontinence and never complete unconsciousness. Commoner symptoms of hysteria are alternate laughing and crying, perhaps with tearing at the hair and clothes, clutching at other people.

Treatment.—Do *not* sympathise with the patient. Be firm and, if necessary, leave alone in a room, when the symptoms will very soon stop.

Infantile Convulsions

These occur sometimes with teething, at the start of an illness or for no apparent reason.

Signs.—General twitching and tremor. Pallor of face, later becoming blue. Rolling of the eyes, holding the breath and sometimes frothing at the mouth.

Treatment
(1) Hold child with its head on one side and the chin raised to prevent the tongue from falling back and obstructing the air passages.
(2) Put child into a warm bath (body temperature) and sponge forehead with cool water.
(3) Dry and wrap in a warm blanket but keep the head cool.
(4) Always call the doctor.

FOREIGN BODIES IN EARS

It is much safer to get foreign bodies removed from the ear by a doctor or at a hospital. If the inexperienced person tries to get them out, there is always the danger of pushing them still farther in.

An insect in the ear can be removed by filling the ear with liquid paraffin or olive oil; the insect will then float to the surface.

FOREIGN BODIES IN EYES

(1) To remove from (*a*) corner of eye or lower lid, use the corner of a clean handkerchief and a *very light touch*; (*b*) under upper lid, pull the lid down over the lower lid or blink the eye under water. (Some people can roll the upper lid back over a match-stick, but this requires considerable practice.)
(2) After trying to remove a foreign body from the eye, always bathe in an eye-bath containing salt and water (1 teaspoonful salt to 1 large tumblerful of water).

If the foreign body is on the eyeball and is movable, bathe the eye in an eyebath. If embedded in the eye, only a doctor should attempt to remove it.

FOREIGN BODIES IN NOSE, THROAT, ABDOMEN

These are cases for a doctor or hospital. No attempt should be made to remove them at home.

FRACTURES

A bone that is broken or cracked will cause pain at the site of injury; swelling round it; inability to use the limb or injured part normally. There may also be deformity of the part. If there is any doubt as to whether an injury is a sprain or a fracture, it is safer to treat it as a fracture until a doctor has seen it.

Treatment

(1) Keep the limb still until professional help comes. Often a pillow to rest it on is sufficient; a sling will rest an arm. Do not move the patient if it can be avoided. It is of the utmost importance to prevent further injury, which can easily occur if the fractured bone moves, possibly tearing other tissues. A patient with a fractured leg, who must be moved, should be moved only on a stretcher. A door or hurdle makes an improvised stretcher; tie the patient's legs together at the ankles and also above and below the knees.

(2) Keep the patient warm and comfortable with rugs or blankets.

Do not attempt to move a patient whom you suspect of having a fractured skull or spine.

GAS POISONING

(1) Remove patient from gas-contaminated atmosphere into the fresh air, opening or breaking down doors and windows, if necessary.

(2) Apply artificial respiration (see Treatment of the Apparently Drowned).

(3) Send for an ambulance.

HYSTERIA—see Fits

INFANTILE CONVULSIONS
—see Fits

INSECT BITES

(1) Extract the sting if present (as in wasp and bee stings) by squeezing the part firmly or preferably with a pair of tweezers.

(2) Apply sal volatile, weak ammonia, soda bicarbonate solution, washing soda or a blue bag to the spot.

(3) If the bite is infected, in which case it appears red and feels hot, the best treatment is a hot bath followed later by hot fomentations to the spot.

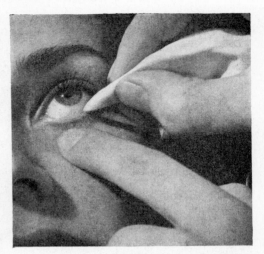

To remove a foreign body from the corner of the eye or lower lid (above), use the corner of a clean handkerchief and a very light touch. Never rub the eye

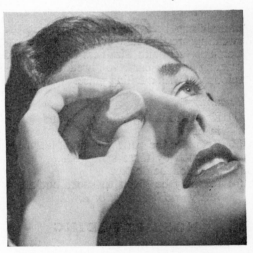

After removing a foreign body or when the eyes are sore or red, bathe with a warm salt and water solution in an eye-bath

To treat an insect bite in the mouth—use a mouthwash made from 2 teaspoonfuls soda bicarbonate to a pint of water.

INTERNAL HÆMORRHAGE

Although there may be no visible loss of blood, internal hæmorrhage can be recognised by the following signs and symptoms: pallor, first visible on the lips; pulse rapid and soft; temperature sub-normal; deep

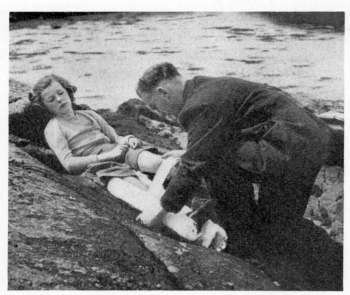

British European Airways photo

Swallowed Poisons

(3) If patient is conscious, without signs of burning or blistering of lips, induce vomiting by tickling the back of the patient's throat with two fingers or, if this fails, give an emetic (1 tumblerful of water containing 2 tablespoonfuls salt).

NOTE: If the patient is unconscious or the lips and mouth appear burned or blistered, do *not* induce vomiting.

(4) Except in case of unconscious patient or where mouth or lips are burned or blistered, give an antidote—(*a*) a pint of milk or, if milk is not available, (*b*) a pint of water, which will dilute the poison, or, where the nature of the poison is known and its antidote available, (*c*) a special antidote.

Special Antidotes

For corrosive acids (sulphuric acid, hydrochloric acid, etc.)—2 tablespoonfuls magnesia powder in 1 pint water. Chalk or soapy water may also be used.

For corrosive alkalis (caustic soda, ammonia, caustic potash)—2 tablespoonfuls vinegar in 1 pint water.

For carbolic acid (carbolic-smelling disinfectants, Phenol, Lysol, etc.)—2 tablespoonfuls Epsom salts in 1 pint water or 8 tablespoonfuls medicinal liquid paraffin.

For oxalic acid and oxalates (salts of lemon, etc.)—2 tablespoonfuls powdered magnesia or chalk in 1 pint water.

For iodine—1 pint thin starch.

For aspirin—2 teaspoonfuls soda bicarbonate in a tumblerful of water.

For lead salts—2 teaspoonfuls Epsom salts to a tumblerful of water.

For morphine—Potassium permanganate (strong pink solution).

NOTE: For children from 2 to 8 years,

---

and sighing breathing; faintness; profuse sweating; restlessness and thirst; the extremities feel cold; dizziness of vision and buzzing in the ears, followed by unconsciousness with a failing pulse.

Treatment

(1) Keep absolutely still, quiet and warm in bed.
(2) Reassure the patient, who is naturally alarmed by these symptoms.
(3) Send for the doctor.
(4) Ice may be given to suck, but absolutely *nothing to eat or drink*.

NOSE BLEEDING

Treatment

(1) Sit up, well propped up with pillows, so that the blood is not swallowed (which leads to vomiting) or inhaled.
(2) Apply cold compresses to the bridge of the nose and nape of the neck.
(3) Reassure the patient.
(4) Send for a doctor if the bleeding does not yield to treatment as sedation, and/or plugging may be required.

POISONS

Treatment for all Forms of Poisoning

(1) Send for a doctor or take to hospital.
(2) Preserve any vomit, etc.

halve the quantities. For children under 2, quarter the quantities.

SEASICKNESS—see Travel Sickness

SHOCK

Shock may result from emotional stress, injury or illness. Its typical characteristics are: Pallor, rapid pulse and respirations and other signs of collapse, or it may produce an excited state. It is always advisable to treat a person for shock before anything else (except external hæmorrhage) if there is any reason to suppose that it may occur—following an accident or after great mental strain, for instance.

Treatment
(1) If there is external hæmorrhage (see Cuts), treat that first, as delay may result in the patient's death in a very short time.
(2) Reassure and calm the patient.
(3) Make him lie down, with head lowered and legs raised—*provided* this is practicable in view of other injuries (for instance, there should be no unnecessary moving if a bone is fractured and the head must not be lowered if the nose is bleeding). Common sense must be used. Loosen tight clothing.
(4) Keep patient warm with blankets and *covered* hot water bottles (uncovered ones are dangerous in such cases and may burn the patient).
(5) If the patient is conscious and there is *nothing* to suggest internal hæmorrhage, give warm, very sweet tea to drink.

SNAKE BITE

A bite from a poisonous snake endangers the patient's life, so treat as follows:
(1) Send for an ambulance or go straight to hospital.
(2) Keep the limb or body absolutely still—movement causes

A little girl falls and cuts her elbow —she needs comfort, reassurance and a clean bandage tied firmly over the wound

All photos in this chapter except the one on page 590 from Central Office of Information

the venom to flow into the body.
(3) Wash the venom away from the site of the bite.
(4) Apply a tight ligature—braces, a necktie, any strip of cloth—round the upper arm or thigh (if the bite is on a limb) and *be sure* to loosen this every 10 minutes till the limb becomes pink.

NOTE: If you fail to loosen the tourniquet regularly, the damage done may be more serious than that caused by the snake bite.

SPRAINS

A sprain occurs when muscles and ligaments are overstretched and perhaps torn as a result of severe exertion or a sudden twist. There is a sudden sharp pain at the site of injury, usually followed by swelling and inability to use the limb or joint. It is difficult or impossible to continue using the injured part. It is advisable to get a doctor's advice.

Treatment
(1) Rest the injured part, raising it if possible.
(2) If treating immediately after injury, apply a cold compress; if there is a lapse of time before treatment can take place, apply a hot compress.

STROKE—see Fits (Apoplectic)

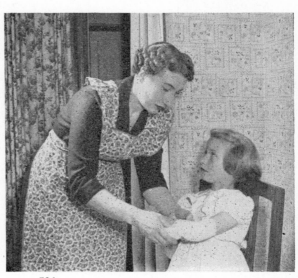

SUFFOCATION BY SMOKE
(as in fires)

Treat as for Gas Poisoning.

The rescuer must enter the room with a wet towel tied over mouth and nose to avoid suffocation from smoke himself.

If the patient's clothes are on fire, roll in a carpet or rug to smother the flames.

SUNSTROKE

The results of excessive exposure to hot sun are headache, accompanied by a rise in temperature.

Treatment

(1) Remove from the heat into a cool place —preferably a bed in a cool room.
(2) Sponge down with a cool sponge and apply ice bag to head and back of neck.
(3) Take 2 aspirins.

Treatment of patient unconscious from sunstroke

(1) Move into a cool place, strip to waist and fan vigorously.
(2) Apply ice bags to head and spine, and cool sponge elsewhere.
(3) Take to hospital.

TOOTH SOCKET (Bleeding from)

(1) Sit up to prevent the blood being swallowed.
(2) Reassure the patient.
(3) Keep warm.

(4) Give large roll of bandage to bite on.
(5) Keep still for at least 1 hour. Moving the bandage or much movement of the head or body will start the bleeding again.

TRAVEL SICKNESS (Air, Sea or Car)

Travel sickness can very often be prevented by taking Avomine or Kwells tablets before a journey.

If it does occur, give sips of fluid (slightly warm glucose drinks are best), keep quiet and warm.

Treatment for shock may be required afterwards.

UNCONSCIOUSNESS

General rules for the treatment of insensibility:

(1) Turn patient on back with head to one side and, if necessary, press forward the angle of the jaw so that the tongue does not fall back and impede breathing.
(2) Undo all tight clothing, particularly about chest, neck and waist.
(3) Ensure plenty of fresh air and quiet.
(4) Give no food or fluids by mouth.
(5) Send for the doctor or ambulance and *stay with the patient* till some responsible person arrives to take charge.
(6) Keep patient warm with blankets and covered hot water bottles.

☆ ☆ ☆ ☆ ☆ ☆ **RULES FOR FIRST-AIDERS** ☆ ☆ ☆ ☆ ☆ ☆

1. *Never try to do without a doctor—or to do a doctor's job.*

2. *Remember your aim is only to do what you can to prevent the patient's condition from becoming worse and to make him as comfortable as possible until medical attention is available.*

3. *Treat a person, not a broken limb—and remember that calm reassurance and comfort are often more valuable than splints or bandages.*

4. *Waste no time in stopping profuse bleeding, treating for shock or applying artificial respiration—otherwise stop and think before you take action.*

5. *Give artificial respiration even when breathing has stopped.*

6. *Do not remove clothes or move the patient unnecessarily.*

7. *Keep calm yourself.*

HOME TREATMENT FOR MINOR AILMENTS

Listed alphabetically, here are some of the commoner illnesses, with advice on how to relieve or cure them

BOILS

BOILS are deep-seated infections of the hair follicles and sebaceous glands below the surface of the skin. They are especially prevalent in adolescence, when these glands tend to be over-active. A sufferer from persistent boils should consult a doctor, as they may be a symptom of something requiring special treatment. Only a qualified medical practitioner can prescribe penicillin or one of the various vaccines now used to treat some cases of recurrent boils.

Local Home Treatment for Boils

(1) In the early stages, pus formation and the resultant scarring may be prevented by the application of a ring of Elastoplast fitting round the outside of the swelling; cover both ring and boil with a large piece of Elastoplast.

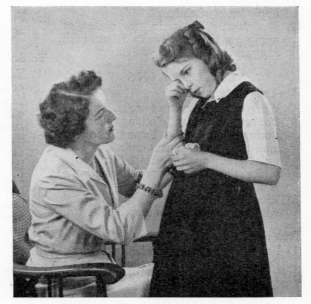

Headache, irritability and depression may be symptoms of constipation, particularly if there is also discomfort in the abdomen and blown-up feeling

(2) Paint round the outside of the boil with a 1 per cent. solution of gentian violet (obtainable from chemists) to prevent re-infection.

(3) If there are any hairs near the spot, shave them off.

(4) Treat with hot fomentations—boracic (pink) lint steeped in boiling water and applied, smooth side to the skin, as hot as it can be borne.

(5) Rest—the affected part if it is a limb; the whole body, otherwise.

General Treatment

(1) A daily bath with sufficient potassium permanganate crystals to tint the water pale pink.

(2) Take plenty of rest.

(3) Increase the vitamins in the diet, eating plenty of fresh fruit, vegetables and green salads; and/or take vitamin tablets.

Additional for Adolescent Sufferers

(4) Cut down on starchy foods (cakes, bread, potatoes, pastry, heavy puddings), fried and highly seasoned dishes.

(5) Take iron in tablet form.

(6) Never use on the skin ointments or any cosmetics containing oil.

(7) Wash nightly with hot water and sulphur soap. Apply and leave on all night a mild sulphur lotion (the chemist will make one up on request).

To Prevent Re-infection

(1) Always keep boils covered.

(2) Wash your hands every time you dress a boil and take great care not to let clothing, towels or handkerchiefs come into contact with one. Burn all dressings immediately.

BRUISES

Treatment

(1) Immediately: Bathe in cold water, apply ice or witch hazel.

(2) If delayed: Bathe in hot water or apply hot fomentations to disperse the congealed blood in the tissues.

CHILBLAINS

Preventive Measures

(1) Wear warm gloves and socks, shoes or boots, and warm clothing generally during cold weather. Exposure to cold and draughts produces chilblains very quickly, so guard against those gaps under the doors through which the wind whistles in winter.

(2) Vitamins A, D and C, plus a good wholesome diet, to tone up the system.

Treatment

(1) For irritating but unbroken chilblains, Snowfire cream relieves the irritation.

(2) To broken chilblains, apply a mild antiseptic cream and bandage.

(3) Drugs which dilate the blood vessels in the skin prevent chilblains in some people and may be prescribed by a doctor.

COLDS

Nearly everyone catches a cold sometimes; some people seem to have one most of the time. At least we now know how we get colds—not from standing in the cold, getting our feet wet or sitting in a draught (though these will all aggravate a cold when we have one), but by direct contact with someone who already has a cold.

To Cure a Cold and also avoid spreading it:

(1) Stay away from other people—children should not go to school or play with their friends when they have colds; mother can avoid passing the infection on by wearing a gauze mask over her mouth and nose while in contact with the children; those who must go out among other people should equip themselves with plenty of large handkerchiefs to trap the germs.

(2) Go to bed and keep warm.

(3) Take two aspirins, a light diet and plenty of hot drinks.

(4) Inhalations (one teaspoonful friars balsam or a few grains of menthol to a pint of boiling water) will generally relieve sore throat, loss of voice and "stuffed up" sensation in the head.

(5) For a cough, a simple linctus or hot fruit drinks (lemon or blackcurrant).

To Build Up Resistance to Colds

(1) Take vitamins A and D—two cod-liver or halibut-liver oil capsules or tablets a day—and vitamin C (in oranges and other fresh fruits, rose hip syrup or in tablets).

(2) Have a good, well-balanced, nourishing diet and regular meals.

(3) Be sure clothes are warm and shoes keep out the damp.

(4) Avoid crowded, stuffy places where there is likely to be a lot of infection about and get out into the fresh air instead.

Those who suffer from excessive colds should consult their doctor about the possibility of preventive injections. These are usually given during the spring and summer, and some people, though not by any means all, derive great benefit from them. It is also occasionally possible to prevent a cold from developing at the outset by taking two 200 mg. Ascorbic Acid (vitamin C) tablets every two hours, day and night, until the symptoms disappear. It is important to start this treatment at the very first signs of a cold, and even then it does not work with everybody.

CONSTIPATION

Many people worry quite unnecessarily about what they imagine to be constipation and so make it worse. A daily motion is not in itself essential to health and well-being; one every two days suffices for many.

Symptoms requiring treatment are:

(1) Discomfort in the abdomen with blown-up feeling.

(2) Headache.

(3) General irritability.

Immediate Treatment

This is the time (and not as a regular habit) to take a laxative. Recommended are (*a*) senna pods—steep between 5 and 8 in cold water all day and drink the liquid at night, varying the quantity according to requirements. (*b*) Epsom salts. (*c*) Compounds of liquid paraffin and agar.

Long-term Treatment

(1) Rearrange your diet to get plenty of foods containing roughage (fruit, brown bread, fresh vegetables and salads, etc.), lots of liquids (especially hot drinks first thing in the morning) and cutting out white bread, pastry, cakes, sweets, all fried and rich foods. Your aim should be from 4 to 6 pints of tea, coffee, fruit juices, etc., a day.

(2) Increase the exercise you take every day.

(3) Take a good stiff dose of whatever laxative you decide upon until your bowels become accustomed to a daily motion, then gradually reduce the size of the dose.

(4) Avoid worrying about constipation and try to relax as much as possible.

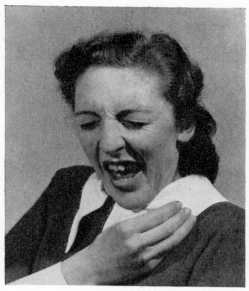

Keep a cold like that to yourself. You will get better quickly and avoid infecting others if you stay at home. When sneezing or coughing, trap the germs in a handkerchief

DIARRHŒA AND/OR VOMITING

Treatment

(1) Rest and warmth in bed.

(2) Give frequent sips of fluid (lemon drinks, barley water, etc.), with glucose in generous quantities.

(3) A bismuth mixture or chlorodyne will help.

(4) Gradually reintroduce food, starting with dry biscuits, then sweet ones, one or two at a time. Omit all fats, including milk, from the diet until the patient's tummy is less queasy.

FIBROSITIS

Pain and tenderness in the muscles which causes a marked restriction of movement, such as stiff neck or shoulder, lumbago, etc., is generally due to muscular rheumatism.

Treatment

(1) Warmth—apply a hot-water bottle to the spot.

(2) Rest, in bed or in whatever position is comfortable.

(3) Relieve the pain with analgesic drugs—aspirin, codeine, etc.

The best way to prevent chilblains is to keep the hands, feet and the whole body well covered in cold weather

(4) As the pain goes, movement of the affected part and gentle massage will both help to loosen up the muscles.

(5) Creams and lotions which bring the blood to the surface and dull the pain may also be prescribed by your doctor.

HAY FEVER

To Prevent

The most important thing is to find out what causes your attacks of Hay Fever— it may be primulas, grass seed, almost any kind of flower or pollen—and then, if at all possible, avoid going near it.

Treatment

The antihistamine drugs, which can be prescribed by your doctor, cure the condition temporarily in most cases. So, in a bad attack, it is advisable to consult the doctor promptly.

HICCOUGHS

Caused by a spasm of the diaphragmatic muscle, hiccoughs may be brought on by an over-full tummy or by alcohol. They generally respond to a drink of cold water, eating a lump of sugar or holding the breath while slowly counting ten. If they are persistent, the doctor should be called, as they can be very exhausting.

INDIGESTION

Symptoms

Indigestion has many, varied symptoms, but these are the commonest:

(1) Pain or discomfort in the abdomen or part of it, before or after meals.

(2) Flatulence (wind) and a sensation of being full.

(3) Heartburn (bitter taste).

(4) Vomiting or nausea.

(5) Tummy rumblings.

(6) Headache and spots before the eyes.

(7) Backache and pain in the shoulder.

(8) Appetite poor, erratic, excessive or non-existent.

The indigestion sufferer may have any one or more of these symptoms. Most important is, of course, to try to track down the cause. An occasional mild bout of indigestion, the cause of which can be traced without much difficulty, may safely be treated at home. Chronic indigestion and attacks with any of the following symptoms are matters for a doctor:

(1) Pain coming on within an hour of a meal, occurring regularly for some weeks or more and then disappearing until another attack starts.

(2) Pain just before meals and at night (hunger pain relieved only by food).

(3) Pain that follows eating fatty foods.

(4) Any indigestion symptoms accompanied by loss of weight, particularly in people of forty and over.

Treatment for a Mild Attack of Indigestion

(1) Drink large quantities of fluids—plain water, soda water, tea or fruit drinks containing glucose.

(2) If possible, induce vomiting.

(3) Take a dose of Milk of Magnesia or soda bicarbonate and, if there is also headache, two aspirins.

(4) Stick to a very light diet for at least a day.

Preventive Measures

Indigestion is very often due to a psychological cause, the tummy being remarkably sensitive to emotional upheavals. The important thing in curing the indigestion, therefore, is to track down the anxiety and face it. Jealousy, money worries, unrequited love, family quarrels—they can all cause tummy troubles.

A heavy meal should never be taken when one is tired out. No tummy can cope with it when exhausted, and some stomachs react so violently that they cannot digest anything when tired or overwrought. Take a milk drink or a very light dish and delay eating a proper meal until partly rested and relaxed.

Watch posture, and regularity of habits, too, in connection with indigestion, particularly sitting hunched up over a typewriter or crouched over a car steering wheel for hours at a time without exercise or regular meals.

Check up on teeth (visit the dentist twice a year), see that the diet is well-balanced (with plenty of fresh fruit, salads and green vegetables) and guard against constipation, but without taking strong purges.

Finally, if experience proves that a certain food or drink causes indigestion, the obvious and only sensible remedy is to avoid it.

Never take alcohol on an empty

Treatment for styes: wrap a wooden spoon in cotton wool, tie a clean handkerchief on top, dip into boiling water and bring as near to the eye as possible, right

stomach. Drink a glass of milk before a party.

INGROWING TOE NAIL

Treatment

(1) If inflammation is present, bathe in hot water or apply hot fomentations.
(2) Cut the toe nail straight across, or better still, down in the centre in a V.
(3) Avoid pressure from shoes.

JAUNDICE

This is a serious complaint, and the patient should be put to bed and the doctor called promptly.

NEURALGIA

The pain can be relieved with aspirin or codeine. If the pain is muscular, warmth (from a hot-water bottle) will help to ease it; but not if it is due to inflammation of a nerve.

Rest as much as possible and see the doctor.

PYORRHŒA

Treatment is perfectly possible and most effective, especially if started in the early stages. It is now seldom necessary to remove all the teeth. At the first signs of gum recession and bleeding, see the dentist.

RHEUMATISM

(1) **See Fibrositis** (muscular rheumatism).
(2) **Pain in the Joints.**—If persistent, see a doctor. Treat temporarily with aspirin, warmth and rest.

SCIATICA

This causes pain down the leg.

Treatment

(1) Rest the leg completely.
(2) Do *not* apply warmth.

(3) Relieve the pain with aspirin or codeine and take vitamin B. (in Marmite, for instance).
(4) See the doctor if it does not clear up quickly.

STYES

Treatment

Wrap an ordinary wooden cooking spoon in cotton wool, tie a scrupulously clean handkerchief or piece of linen firmly over the wool, then dip the covered spoon in boiling water and bring it as near to the stye as you can bear it.

If styes are persistent, consult a doctor, who may prescribe penicillin ointment.

Prevention

Build up resistance and thus help prevent the recurrence of styes by taking plenty of rest and vitamins in your diet (see general treatment for Boils).

TOOTHACHE

Emergency Treatment

(1) Aspirin or codeine to relieve.
(2) Apply warmth to the cheek—by a covered hot-water bottle.
(3) Apply oil of cloves or brandy to the tooth. Go to the dentist as soon as possible—even if the pain stops temporarily—because it will inevitably start again.

AN INVALID IN THE HOUSE

Some practical hints on how to be a good nurse—
and how to get your patient better quickly

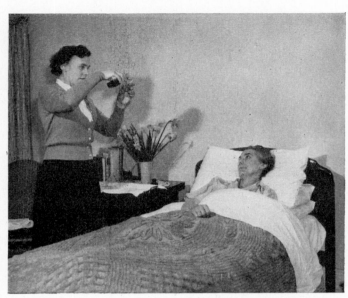

When pouring out the medicine, shake the bottle well, check the
dose with the instructions on the label—and pour on the side away
from the label, to avoid staining it

WHEN someone in the family falls ill, a
bedroom has to be quickly adapted for
use as a sickroom. If there is any choice in
the matter, a reasonably large room with a
good window is best. It should also have
some convenient form of heating, whether
by gas, electricity or solid fuel.

Large furniture, such as wardrobes, need
not be moved, but anything unnecessary,
such as ornaments and knick-knacks that
will collect dust, get in the way and require
keeping clean, is better out of the way.

A single bed is more convenient than a
double one and should not be too low, if
nursing is not to be a back-breaking business. Have plenty of soft (and some firm)
pillows available to prop up the patient
when sitting up in bed.

Other essential equipment for the sickroom includes:

(1) Bedside table and chair.
(2) One light over the bed or on the bedside table.

(3) A second light for the
nurse's use, particu-
larly during the night,
when it should be
dimmed and placed
so that it does not
shine in the patient's
eyes.
(4) Table and chair for
the nurse.

A commode by the side
of the bed can be most
useful and can be hired
from most chemists.

The sickroom should
be thoroughly cleaned
and dusted once every day
with the minimum of fuss,
a damp duster being used
to take up dust. Carpets
may be cleaned with a
vacuum cleaner, but lino-
leum or polished wood
floors are easier to keep
clean, particularly if there
are rugs which can be
taken out of the room for shaking and/or
vacuum cleaning.

Everything should be done to keep the
room looking as attractive and smelling as
sweet and fresh as possible. One of the
liquid or solid deodorants or a perfumed
spray will help freshen up the atmosphere.

GENERAL PRINCIPLES OF SIMPLE NURSING

Routine

It pays to have a daily routine and to
stick to it when nursing a sick person at
home. The patient then knows what is
coming next and also gets the full necessary
quota of rest, usually the most important
part of any treatment. Here is a suggested
routine which can be adapted to suit individual circumstances:

6 *a.m.* Wash, take temperature, etc. Early
cup of tea.
8 *a.m.* Breakfast. Tidy room and make
bed. Rest.

10 *a.m.* "Elevenses." Rest.

12.30 *p.m.* Lunch. Rest (the most important rest of the day).

2.30 *p.m.* Visitors.

3.30 *p.m.* Tea.

6.30 *p.m.* Wash, take temperature, etc.

7 *p.m.* Supper.

8 *p.m.* Settle for the night.

Visitors

It is most important to be firm about too many visitors. Never allow more than three visiting hours a day, say between 11 a.m. and 12 noon; 3 and 4 p.m. and 6 and 7 p.m. Dropping in at odd times should not be permitted.

Bed-making

The bed should be made carefully at least once each day, more often if the patient is restless and uncomfortable. If the patient is confined to bed and heavy, be sure to get adequate help before attempting to make the bed.

Bed-pans and Commodes must be emptied and thoroughly cleansed immediately after use. Disinfect with Dettol.

Meals should be punctual, small, varied and attractively served (see chapter on Invalid Cookery). Never attempt to force a sick person to eat.

Occupation

A patient who is getting better and not inclined to sleep all day should be provided with some kind of recreation—radio, TV, books and magazines, crossword or jigsaw puzzles—but not worried to do anything if disinclined. Women patients particularly must not be allowed to wear themselves out the moment they begin to feel better, with too much knitting or sewing. A bed table is always convenient and quite indispensable when the patient is a child.

The Nurse must have her time off duty. An hour or two away from the sickroom every day is absolutely essential, even for the most devoted mother, who cannot go on nursing even her own child night and day without making herself ill and bad-tempered.

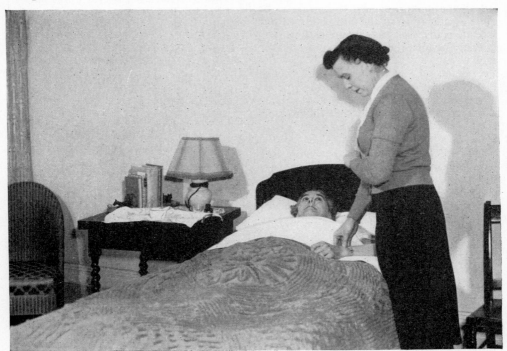

Photos: Central Office of Information

Everyone should learn how to take the pulse and temperature—and equally important, how to shake down the thermometer

INFECTIOUS DISEASES

*A quick guide to the all-important Incubation, Isolation
and Quarantine Periods*

TO prevent the spread of infectious diseases, it is as well to know:
(1) **The Incubation Period (I.P.):** the time between picking up the infection and the onset of the disease.
(2) **The Isolation Period (Is.P.):** the time from the onset of the disease till the patient is free from infection.
(3) **The Quarantine Period (Q.P.):** the time during which those in contact with the patient may develop the disease.

Isolation.—Even with the milder infectious diseases, it should not be assumed that, because one member of the family has it, the other children will inevitably get it—or "might as well have it at the same time." Every effort should be made to keep the incidence to one.

Call the doctor, even if it appears to be quite a mild form of the complaint. Some infectious diseases have complications, and to guard against these the doctor should see each case.

Contacts who have already had Chicken Pox, Smallpox or Measles can safely be regarded as immune from a further attack. This probably applies also to other infectious diseases but is not definitely established as a fact.

Special care should be taken with contacts who may be infectious though not yet showing definite signs of the disease. A child incubating Measles and only (as yet) showing signs of a running nose can easily spread the disease among dozens of other children.

CHICKEN POX

The rash is often the first sign; it looks like small blisters and commonly starts on the hair line. The blisters form scabs and are very irritating. If scratched, may leave permanent scars. Every effort, therefore, must be made to prevent scratching. A good soothing application is calamine lotion. The patient does not generally feel particularly ill in himself with Chicken Pox.

I.P.: 12 to 21 days.
Is.P.: till last crust has separated.
Q.P.: 21 days.

DIPHTHERIA

This used to be one of the most dreaded diseases of childhood. Now it has almost entirely disappeared, due to the number of children rendered immune to infection by the highly efficient inoculations available. It is advisable for all babies to be inoculated against diphtheria at about 6 to 8 months of age.

Signs and Symptoms.—Fever, sore throat, blood-stained nasal discharge, enlargement of cervical glands (which also feel tender) and of a membrane over the throat, which can cause suffocation.

A doctor should be called immediately.

I.P.: 2 to 7 days.
Is.P.: 4 weeks or till all discharges have ceased.
Q.P.: 7 days.

GERMAN MEASLES

This is generally a mild disease. The patient appears to have a cold, and a rash develops on the face and limbs, generally without any fever or other symptoms.

I.P.: 15 to 21 days.
Is.P.: 7 days from appearance of rash.
Q.P.: 21 days.

MEASLES

This can be a severe disease and should be nursed very carefully.

Signs and Symptoms.—Running nose and eyes, fever, cough. Rash appears on face, trunk and limbs on the third or fourth day.

Nursing.—It is advisable to nurse the patient in a darkened room to prevent eye complications until all signs of redness round the eyes or of discharge have disappeared.

I.P.: 7 to 14 days.
Is.P.: 15 days from onset.
Q.P.: 14 days.

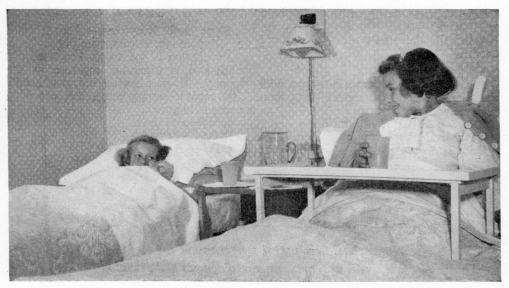

When one child in a family has an infectious disease, the others should not be put in the same room on the theory that "they might as well all have it together"

MUMPS

This starts with a fever, followed by pain on chewing and swelling of the parotid glands on one or both sides of the face and neck. The patient should be kept on a light diet and *must rest* for at least a week.

I.P.: 17 to 26 days.

Is.P.: 1 week after subsidence of swelling.

Q.P.: 28 days.

PARATYPHOID FEVER

see under TYPHOID AND PARATYPHOID FEVER (A & B)

ANTERIOR POLIOMYELITIS

This starts with a fever, which may be followed by paralysis to a greater or lesser degree of part of the body.

I.P.: 10 to 14 days.

Is.P.: 4 weeks.

Q.P.: 14 days.

SCARLET FEVER

Signs and Symptoms.—Sore throat, vomiting, fever, "strawberry" tongue, a ring of pallor round the mouth, rash. It may be a mild disease or take a very severe form.

I.P.: 2 to 5 days.

Is.P.: 4 to 6 weeks.

Q.P.: 8 days.

SMALLPOX

This is a rare disease in the Western hemisphere, but more common than it was on account of air travel. The best protection against it is for every child to be vaccinated at the age of about 4 months. A person coming into contact with Smallpox years later will have it very much more lightly—if at all—so long as he has been vaccinated at least once.

The Onset of Smallpox is sudden, with headache and pain in the back. On the third to fifth day a rash develops in the form of blisters which may contain pus. Scabs form later which leave scars if scratched.

I.P.: 5 to 15 days.

Is.P.: 4 weeks if discharges absent.

Q.P.: 17 days.

TYPHOID AND PARATYPHOID FEVER (A & B)

Typhoid.—This has an *insidious* onset, with headache, continuous fever, bronchitis, "rose" spots, "peasoup" stools and intestinal hæmorrhage.

I.P.: 10 to 14 days generally, can be 5 to 21 days.

Is.P.: till the stools clear of typhoid bacillus.

Q.P.: 21 days.

Paratyphoid.—The onset is *abrupt*, with vomiting, diarrhœa, very variable temperature and profuse rash.

I.P.: 7 to 21 days.

Is.P.: till declared free by doctor.

Q.P.: 21 days.

WHOOPING COUGH

Signs and Symptoms.—Catarrh, paroxysmal cough, whoop, vomiting.

Inoculation of infants at 6 to 8 months confers a considerable measure of immunity. Even when an inoculated child does catch whooping cough, it is invariably a very mild attack.

I.P.: 7 to 14 days.

Is.P.: 6 weeks.

Q.P.: 16 days.

FOR THESE SYMPTOMS,

CONSULT THE DOCTOR

Some conditions may be aggravated by unskilled treatment or require prompt diagnosis and attention

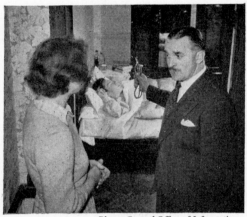

Photo: Central Office of Information

A raised temperature for more than 24 hours means that a doctor should be called to see the patient without delay

MANY of the ills the flesh is heir to can perfectly well be treated at home and do not necessitate taking up the time of a busy doctor. Practical home treatments for such minor ailments are described on p. 593.

There are also certain conditions which can very easily be aggravated by unskilled treatment or which may prove more difficult to cure if medical advice is not obtained promptly.

Though it is obviously quite impossible to list all such conditions, here are some of the commoner symptoms about which a doctor should be consulted without delay.

Raised temperature if it persists for more than 24 hours.

Pain of any kind and in any part of the body is a danger signal. It is therefore much more important to discover its cause than to alleviate it. If it persists or recurs and its cause cannot easily be explained, medical advice is required.

Loss or increase of weight.

Skin affections should always be seen by a doctor. They may be infective (with the danger of spreading to other people and other parts of the body), due to an allergy that needs to be traced if you are to avoid it in future, or they may be symptoms of a more general illness.

Moles in parts of the body where they are subject to irritation.

Irregular or painful menstruation, including flooding and blood clots, the loss of more or less blood than is normal, or abdominal pain that really interferes with normal life (as opposed to the comparatively mild inconvenience and discomfort suffered at some time by all women).

Coughs that last for more than three weeks.

Lumps, particularly on the breasts in women, whether they are painful or not.

Headaches, if persistent or recurrent.

Constipation that does not yield to normal treatment or becomes chronic.

THE FAMILY MEDICINE CUPBOARD

If it contains the real essentials—and no left-overs or unnecessary extras—it will prove a standby in time of trouble

MOST family medicine cupboards contain a weird assortment of left-over relics collected through the years—a few drops of cough syrup, a scrap of penicillin ointment, some crumbling aspirin tablets, one or two rather sticky vitamin capsules and the dregs of a tonic that put you on your feet after 'flu last year. They are treasured against the day when they will "come in useful."

Unhappily, however, many of them will never be of any use. Some may even be actually harmful. For medicines and drugs are not everlasting. They deteriorate with time and also with exposure to light, damp and heat. (The bathroom, where most medicine cupboards are housed, is therefore one of the worst places in the house for keeping them.) They can undergo chemical changes in time, entirely lose their effectiveness or even turn rancid.

Your medicine cupboard, if it is to enable you to deal with emergencies and minor ailments quickly and competently, needs to be turned out, its contents checked and replacements made, just as much as your food store cupboard.

These are some of the items which you should never attempt to keep beyond the time stated:

Penicillin solution (such as eye-drops) or *penicillin cream* lasts only for the time stated on the container.

All medicines prescribed by a doctor for a specific purpose should be used for that purpose only and then thrown away, as they are not intended to last. Chemical reaction is particularly liable to occur in prescription cough mixtures. Tonics often contain alkaloids similar to strychnine, which settle at the bottom of the bottle with time. The last few doses therefore tend to contain excessive quantities of these alkaloids and may be dangerous.

Most solutions (such as boric acid solution) evaporate, with the result that, after a time, the concentration becomes gradually higher. Destroy within a month.

Belladonna, digitalis, cascara and

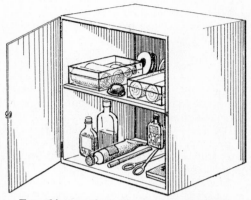

Everything must be neatly arranged—medicines being kept separate from ointments for external use—so that what is wanted can be found without delay in a hurry

spirits of nitre all deteriorate in warmth, light or both. Their effectiveness cannot be trusted longer than four or five weeks.

Nasal drops, many of which contain one of the sulpha drugs, lose their potency in about a month. Since the droppers also tend to become contaminated by germs from the air, there is always the danger of infecting with a more severe virus.

Eye-drops easily develop a kind of mould which may prove harmful to the eye. Do not keep beyond a few weeks.

Hydrogen peroxide rapidly turns to water. If it is stored for more than three or four weeks, it is probably quite useless.

Iodine dries up and, like the other solutions, becomes so strong that it can be highly irritant to the skin. Keep only four to six weeks.

Those are all candidates for immediate destruction if they have been in stock longer than the times mentioned. Now for the bottles, jars and pill boxes which can be kept, *provided* you check them at regular intervals—and particularly before use—for signs of deterioration.

Aspirin should not be taken if the tablets are broken and powdery. They can then set up stomach irritation.

Cod-liver and vitamin oils deteriorate in contact with the air—i.e. if the bottle is not firmly stoppered.

Castor oil should not be used if it smells at all rancid.

All tablets should be regarded as suspect when they begin to crumble. They have probably lost all their effectiveness.

Capsules, whose base is a jelly, deteriorate in contact with damp, warmth or air. Discard them when they become sticky.

Medicines that leave a sediment after shaking, that turn from clear to cloudy, change colour or have affected the cork in the bottle, have obviously been affected by time and should not be used.

Adhesive tape is better discarded when it gets dry and is no longer adhesive. It will only waste your time when an emergency arises.

Medicated bandages, even those packed in Cellophane containers, lose their medicated qualities in a few months unless carefully stored, and should be replaced by new ones.

To provide the best possible conditions for keeping essential remedies always at hand, a medicine cupboard should be in a cool, dark place, as far away as possible from hot, steamy atmospheres. Many drugs are very sensitive to light, and those which are supplied in dark-coloured bottles should never be transferred to ordinary containers. Screw-topped jars or pots are best for storing lotions, ointments, vitamins and tablets, and much better than corked bottles or cardboard boxes, both of which allow the air to get in. The screw-topped jars in which honey, preserves or face creams have been bought can safely be used, so long as they are first sterilised by boiling.

Remember that people are at their most harassed and anxious and usually in a hurry when they use the medicine or first-aid chest. So it should be easy for every member of the family to find what is required. That means that every item on the shelves must be clearly and accurately labelled—with the name of the substance, the date on which it was bought or prescribed, the dose to be given and its purpose.

Only by keeping the contents down to a minimum and ruthlessly destroying all "left-overs", can your medicine cupboard provide essentials quickly.

Keep ointments, lotions and all products for external use on one shelf; tablets, capsules and liquids to be taken on another. Never under any circumstances transfer the contents of a poison bottle—which is so coloured, shaped and often ridged so that it even *feels* different—into an ordinary one, or vice versa.

Before pouring out a dose of medicine, shake it thoroughly and always check with what it says on the label, measure the dose accurately, either into a medicine glass or according to the measurements on the side of the bottle. If it is not shaken well, the first doses will be relatively weak and the later ones excessively strong—and therefore possibly dangerous.

Generally speaking, it is wiser and, in the long run, more economical, to buy medical requirements in small quantities.

At least once a year spring-clean the medicine chest thoroughly and ruthlessly discard anything about whose efficacy there is the slightest doubt. As a guide, hang a list of contents on the inside of the door—then lock the cupboard door and put the key somewhere where every adult in the house knows where to find it.

It is most important that the medicine cupboard should be out of reach of children. There are far too many tragic cases of toddlers being poisoned by eating medicinal tablets that look pretty and taste pleasant, such as the sugar-coated, coloured iron tablets. It is a measure of the seriousness of this danger that many manufacturers deliberately put drugs into large (and very unappetising-looking) capsules and omit the sugar or chocolate coating from tablets.

What Stores to Keep

A well-equipped family medicine cupboard ready for most contingencies should contain the following:

(1) Bottle of aspirin or codeine tablets— for headaches, temperatures and rheumatic pains.

(2) Bottle of friar's balsam or menthol crystals for inhalations in throat and chest troubles.

(3) Bottle of camphorated oil (but use with care; some skins find it intensely irritant).

(4) Some kind of laxative, such as fluid magnesia for babies and children

and senna pods for adults. (Dose 8 to 10 senna pods for an adult, 4 to 6 or less for children; reduce the dose after the first).

(5) A thermometer: learn how to shake it down.

(6) Bicarbonate of soda or anti-acid powder for mild attacks of indigestion. A teaspoonful of bicarbonate of soda to a tumbler of water is good for insect bites and bicarbonate paste may occasionally be used for burns, when medical aid is not available for some hours.

(7) Bottle of sal volatile for fainting and a stick of solid eau de Cologne for bad headaches and feverish conditions.

Whatever room in the house you choose to keep the medicine cupboard in, put it high up—well out of reach of small children, who have a taste for coloured tablets—and keep it locked

(8) Bandages: several 2-in. and 3-in. wide; one 3-in. crêpe bandage (about the only kind that really stays on a knee). One triangular for use as a sling.

(9) Roll of cotton wool.

(10) Boric (pink) lint and white lint (apply smooth side to the skin; store them wrapped up in a clean handkerchief). Gauze.

(11) One or two sterile dressings in sealed packets for severe burns and wounds.

(12) Adhesive plaster in a roll; also box of little adhesive dressing strips.

(13) Bottle of antiseptic (such as 1 or 2 per cent. gentian violet solution or acriflavine—*not* in spirit, which will evaporate.

(14) Vaseline or zinc and castor oil ointment for skin irritations.

(15) Bottle of witch hazel (good for bruises).

(16) Pair of sharp scissors.

THE CARE OF OLD PEOPLE

*Most families today have an elderly relative to care for, so it is
important to know about the special needs and problems of old age*

MORE and more people are living to a ripe old age. As a result, there are few families without at least one grandparent, and some knowledge of the way to care for the old is of very real concern to everyone.

This greater expectation of life has led to the development in recent years of a new branch of medical science—Geriatrics, the study and care of the aged. The experts in this subject all agree on two main points— that it is essential to preserve an old person's independence for as long as possible; and that, however aged, they *must* continue to be treated as individuals, which makes it hard to lay down more than broad general lines for their care.

Preserving Independence

Younger members of the family should not try to persuade elderly relatives to leave their own homes, even if they live alone, so long as they are physically able to manage on their own and are happy. You will do much more to boost their morale by visiting them often and regularly, thus making them feel wanted, than by trying to uproot them against their will. Quite often it is the necessity to do things for themselves that keeps the old active and well. If you remove that incentive, however good your intentions, you may be taking away all that remains of the will to live. It is quite common for an old person who has been forced to give up living alone to become bedridden, not because of any particular illness, but simply because the urge to get up and carry on has been removed.

When the time eventually comes that they can no longer fend for themselves, then an elderly person will be happier living in the family circle. Usually, this means a parent moving in with a married son or daughter, but not necessarily. In those unfortunate cases where there is a real clash of personalities between, say, a mother-in-law and her son-in-law—or where there simply is not room to take in an aged parent—the solution may well be to make a home with a strange family. A surprising number of people, who genuinely love the elderly and get real satisfaction out of caring for them, take them into their homes at prices that seldom compensate them for the time and labour expended. Some local authorities in the U.K. have lists of such families, but there are at the time of writing not nearly enough for the old people wanting such homes.

Making the Old Happy

Should you take an elderly person into your home—whether your own relative or a stranger—remember to make them feel a part of the family circle, allocating them little household jobs or responsibilities within their capabilities and strength, and finding the time each day for a little chat, to pass on bits of family news that will interest them, and so prevent them from feeling "out of everything." Loneliness is one of the greatest tragedies of old age, and it can easily happen in a house full of people, particularly if the old person is a little deaf and forgetful and the younger folk are busy with their own affairs.

Old people tend to live in the past among their happiest memories. For that reason they cling to their familiar pieces of furniture, their favourite pictures and little ornaments. It adds enormously to their general happiness if you allow them to furnish their own rooms just as *they* like —however much you may hate the sight of some of their things.

Minor Maladies

Warmth in the home, important at all ages, is absolutely essential for the health and comfort of old people, whose rooms may well need some kind of heating both night and day to maintain a good even temperature. They should wear plenty of warm, light clothing, but this alone is not sufficient, unless the room is adequately heated and draughts kept out.

Most of the minor ailments and disabilities of the aged are, of course, manifestations of the effect of wear and tear on

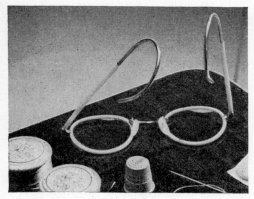

Never put glasses down like this: the lenses will get scratched, especially if plastic. Keep them in their case when not in use

mind and body. The family doctor should be consulted about them, and should, if possible, see his aged patients fairly often, as this may prevent difficulties in case of sudden death.

The problem of deafness, which so often cuts off the old from contact with others, can sometimes be overcome by speaking clearly and slowly and close to the better ear. The elderly who are hard of hearing nearly always hear better with one ear than the other. Much stress, strain, loneliness and anxiety can be eliminated by taking the trouble to find out from which side contact can most easily be made. Although it is often difficult to persuade them, old people will often benefit from a hearing aid.

In most cases there is no need for them to struggle along with failing sight, when cataracts can be simply removed and glasses are obtainable in the U.K. through the National Health Service. Younger members of the family are well advised to try to talk their elderly relatives into taking full advantage of these facilities. Old eyes usually benefit from two pairs of spectacles, one for reading, the other for long vision. To prevent glasses from being constantly mislaid, they should be firmly fixed round the owner's neck on a long, strong cord and never put face down on a table.

Constipation is, to some degree, inevitable in the elderly, but a morbid preoccupation with the subject should be discouraged. Plenty of fruit and fluids will help to alleviate the condition, and a good aperient will probably be necessary and

should be taken in sufficient dosage to be really effective. It is important to see that dentures fit properly—and are worn—as ill-fitting ones may result in indigestion.

It is of the utmost importance from all points of view to try to prevent the elderly from becoming bedridden. Eating and reading in bed are most uncomfortable. There is the danger of bed sores developing, and the elderly patient tends to become miserable and querulous if kept in bed, thus adding to his (or her) own troubles and making things much more trying for those in charge.

Getting Them Up

The most modern theory of Geriatrics is that the old are better nursed out of bed for part at least of the day, even when quite seriously ill. Get your patient up and sit him in a straight-backed chair with a cushion *behind the neck*, not the buttocks, thus encouraging him to sit up and a little forward. It is comparatively easy to get even quite a heavy man from bed to chair, provided you first help him into a sitting position in the bed by putting one hand at the base of his skull or between the shoulders. With the other hand, move the legs over the edge of the bed. Then, using your own foot as a foot-stop for the patient's feet, turn his trunk and raise him to an upright position, then lower into a chair placed parallel with the bed.

When sitting up in this position, day clothing may be worn or a warm dressing-gown, preferably with socks or stockings

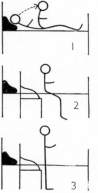

To get a patient from bed to chair: (1) help him into sitting position in bed; (2) move legs over edge of bed; (3) turn his trunk and raise him upright; (4) lower into chair parallel with bed. Sit upright, cushion behind neck (5), not the buttocks (6)

and leather shoes, the wearing of which will help prevent sores from developing on the heels. One of the great advantages of getting your patient up every day is that the position is different from that in bed during the night, and the change of pressure reduces the danger of sores developing. Also a patient sitting up in a chair finds it much more comfortable to eat a meal, do some knitting, writing or reading, and needs much less attention. An old person quite unable to walk should use a wheel chair equipped with a brake.

Going to Hospital

There are, of course, occasions when it is essential for an elderly person to go to hospital, and it is important not to delay, as the old deteriorate very quickly if treatment is not given promptly. The decision between home nursing or hospital must, naturally, rest first and foremost with your family doctor, who alone can judge the particular case on all its merits.

Need for Patience

Great patience and understanding are needed in caring for the old, who often require as much looking after as a small child,

maybe more. Hardening of the arteries may cause a slow and gradual deterioration of the faculties and an increasing stubbornness. An old person often does not hear what you want him to hear, but picks up snatches of conversation not intended for his ears. There is a tendency to ask the same question or make the same remark over and over again, which can be most irritating. Remember, however, that no old person *wants* to be a nuisance, and that even those who are quite trying may only be bitterly resenting the loss of their independence and fighting uselessly against it. Try not to write them off as useless members of society, but make them a necessary and valued part of the family, however limited their contribution may be.

It is worth recalling that, as children, we ourselves taxed the patience and devotion of our parents, sometimes, no doubt, to breaking point. That being so, we should be able to exercise the same kind of patience with our parents and other elderly people when, at the end of their lives, they need it most. Besides, old age is something that, all being equal, will one day come to us all; we shall then look to younger people for kindness, understanding and patience.

Illustrations reproduced by permission of the Editors from an article by Dr. Marjory Warren on The Home Nursing of the Aged Sick in "The Practitioner"

THE RIGHT DIET FOR THE ELDERLY

Information supplied by the Medical Director of the Nutrition Information Centre, Vitamins Ltd.

IT has been said that "Youth is not a time of life; it is a state of mind." With the increasing population of older people, it is essential that all possible steps should be taken to keep them in good health, physical and mental.

Unfortunately, many old people live alone and tend to eat a very limited range of foods, chiefly bread and butter and tea, soup or broth with bread or potatoes. On grounds of expense or because they cannot be bothered to prepare them for themselves, they neglect fresh fruit and vegetables. Even among those old people living with young relatives, cheese is often discarded as indigestible, as are "fat" fish and sometimes even meat. The result is that

their diet is sadly lacking in essential protein foods and vitamins.

Contrary to popular belief, their *need* of these constituents is actually increased with age. Extra vitamins are needed if the various parts of the body are to be adequately supplied by a less adequate circulation. When people seem older than their years, it is worth while examining their diet. Inadequacy may be due to many causes, including poverty, loneliness, loss of appetite and lack of knowledge.

THE FOODS NEEDED

Metabolism is reduced in older people and, in general, their diminished physical activities demand a lowered intake of calories. Small meals, taken more frequently, are better than larger meals taken at longer intervals. Unless, however, the smaller meals are well chosen, there is a tendency for such vital constituents as protein, calcium and some of the vitamins to be in short supply.

Protein.—Some adults have a mistaken idea that, having finished growing, they need very little protein. The fact is that body tissues are constantly being broken down and need replacement, and that plasma proteins play a particularly important part during sickness, infection and convalescence.

Calcium. — Calcium absorption and utilisation seem to become less efficient in old age. The diet should provide at least 1 g. daily, because when the blood calcium is low, this element is withdrawn from the bones, weakening their structure. Vitamin D is also important in this connection. It is often assumed that this vitamin is necessary only during the period of bone development and growth, but some vitamin D should be taken during the whole of adult life to prevent bone decalcification. Pains in the back arise from this cause, and the frequency of fractures—for example, of the femur—in old people is evidence of bone fragility.

Iron.—A moderate degree of anæmia is not uncommon in old age and may be partly responsible for lethargy and weakness.

Vitamins.—All investigations indicate that a higher rather than a lower vitamin intake is needed in old age. The vitamin B_1 of the blood is in many cases lower than normal. Complaints which have been shown to respond favourably to additional B complex vitamins are general fatigue, swollen ankles, weakness, tenderness of the calves, soreness of the tongue, constipation and poor appetite. Thickening of the conjunctiva and inflammation of the eyelids improve with extra vitamin A, and vitamins C and B are thought to be of value in increasing vitality and vigour.

An old person will be happy and contented and much healthier if made to feel a part of the family circle, with her own household responsibilities

SUPPLYING THE NEEDS

A deficient diet is often the result of such circumstances as poor cooking facilities, inadequate dentures or lack of interest. Yet appetising, interesting, varied and easily digested meals can be prepared with very little equipment and trouble.

A saucepan with a steamer over it can, for instance, be used to prepare a complete meal. Meat or liver can be cooked in the saucepan with very little water and the vegetables over it, and custard or apple cooked in a basin in the steamer. If an oven is available, meat and vegetables can be cooked in a casserole.

In age, as in infancy, milk is an excellent food. If milk drinks are disliked, milk can be taken in the form of junket, jelly cream, egg custard or milk pudding, all of which are easily made. Semolina might be used to replace arrowroot or sago, which are pure carbohydrate with no protective value. Ice cream is a pleasant way of taking milk and is a good source of riboflavin.

The addition of Bemax to cereals, milk puddings or other foods after cooking provides extra protein as well as iron and a good supply of vitamin B complex.

Cheese is most easily digested when grated. It can be made into an appetising "spread" if mixed with a very little milk and flavoured with chopped parsley, grated apple, chopped date or paprika.

Vitamin C is often deficient. If salads cannot be eaten, freshly cooked potatoes, carrots and cabbage (cooked in very little water—see Vegetable chapter) will provide enough. There is a mistaken idea among old people that citrus fruits are "acid-forming." This is not so, and they should be encouraged to take them. If no fruit is eaten, blackcurrant purée is an excellent substitute taken in small amounts.

Syrup (costing 1d. or 2d. a day) is a pleasant way of ensuring both vitamin D and the three other important vitamins.

If, during the day, ½ pint of milk is taken (including that taken in tea), 8 oz. of bread (6–8 slices) and 1 oz. of butter, this will provide $\frac{2}{5}$ of the protein, $\frac{3}{4}$ of the calcium, $\frac{1}{3}$ of the iron, $\frac{1}{2}$ of the vitamin A, $\frac{1}{2}$ of the vitamin B₁, $\frac{1}{4}-\frac{1}{3}$ of the riboflavin, $\frac{1}{5}$ of the nicotinic acid, and $\frac{1}{9}$ of the vitamin C, needed by an adult. The remainder must be supplied by other foods. It is not essential that each meal should, by itself, be fully protective, providing that its deficiencies are made up at some other time during the day.

The table shows the proportions of the day's needs supplied by different meals.

Old people confined to bed for long

	Pro-tein	Cal-cium	Iron	Vit. A	Vit. B₁	Ribo-flavin	Niacin	Vit. C	Vit. D
Scrambled egg (1) on toast with margarine	$\frac{1}{6}$	$\frac{1}{8}$	$\frac{1}{5}$	$\frac{1}{3}$	$\frac{1}{7}$	$\frac{1}{5}$	small amount	small amount	some
Pot roast with cabbage and potatoes (3 oz. meat, 4 oz. cabbage, 4 oz. potatoes)	$\frac{1}{4}$	$\frac{1}{9}$	$\frac{1}{2}$	$\frac{1}{5}$	$\frac{1}{4}$	$\frac{1}{4}$	$\frac{1}{2}$	all	—
Steamed fish with carrots and potatoes (4 oz. fish, 1 oz. margarine, 3 oz. carrots, 4 oz. potatoes)	$\frac{1}{3}$	$\frac{1}{10}$	$\frac{1}{5}$	all	$\frac{1}{4}$	$\frac{1}{6}$	$\frac{1}{3}$	all	some
Liver casserole with carrots, turnips and potatoes (3 oz. liver, 3 oz. root vegetables, 4 oz. potatoes)	$\frac{1}{4}$	$\frac{1}{13}$	all	all	$\frac{1}{2}$	all	all	all	—
Egg custard (10 oz. milk, 1 egg)	$\frac{1}{4}$	$\frac{1}{3}$	$\frac{1}{7}$	$\frac{1}{3}$	$\frac{1}{5}$	$\frac{1}{2}$	—	$\frac{1}{7}$	—
Semolina pudding (5 oz. milk, ½ oz. semolina) with ½ oz. blackcurrant purée	$\frac{1}{11}$	$\frac{1}{5}$	some	$\frac{1}{16}$	$\frac{1}{15}$	$\frac{1}{7}$	small amount	$\frac{1}{2}$	—
½ oz. Bemax with 5 oz. milk	$\frac{1}{8}$	$\frac{1}{6}$	$\frac{1}{9}$	$\frac{1}{16}$	$\frac{1}{4}$	$\frac{1}{5}$	$\frac{1}{11}$	small amount	some
1 oz. grated cheese, 1 oz. tomato, ½ oz. margarine, 1 oz. bread	$\frac{1}{7}$	$\frac{1}{4}$	$\frac{1}{16}$	$\frac{2}{5}$	$\frac{1}{13}$	$\frac{1}{9}$	some	$\frac{1}{3}$	some

It should be remembered that margarine is a good source of vitamin D and should be eaten by people who do not take the fat fish (herrings, sardines and salmon), which are the other good sources of this vitamin. If fat fish are not easily digested, Vitavel periods are in particular danger of dietary deficiencies. It is most important to see that their meals include plenty of proteins (eggs, fish, digestible meat), plus dairy products, fruit and vegetables rather than starchy foods.

BEAUTY ROUND THE HOUSE

Even the roughest of chores need—and
indeed must—not spoil your appearance

A DASH of lipstick, a hasty dab of powder—how often that sums up a whole day's beauty care for the busy housewife!

"But I haven't time! " she will protest; or: "I can't afford fancy creams," or even: "What does it matter, anyway? There's only the milkman to see me!"

No one leads a busier life than the housewife, but the great secret about beauty for the busy is to be methodical. Try to make each thing you do a beauty treatment in itself, a sure way to save both time and money, so that even if you are a busy housewife, you can be a well-groomed woman as well.

So many beauty chores can be worked into the normal day's programme. There need be no hard and fast rules about when and where. Whether you are at the sink or making the beds, you can be adding to your good looks. Plan your beauty to fit into whatever tasks the day may bring.

For instance, give yourself a manicure just after you have done some washing; your hands will then be soft and clean and ready to work on. And skinfood does not necessarily have to be applied at night to achieve results. Pat in a layer and let it sink in while you do the ironing or peel the vegetables or, better still, while you are in the bath. The steam opens the pores and allows the cream to penetrate. A steamy atmosphere is good for waves and curls, too, so give yourself a quick set by pinning your hair up in a net beforehand.

You want to keep your figure, but you have no time for a daily dozen? You can even fit that into your daily routine. Here, for the housewife who wants to keep her figure slim and supple, are three "round the house" exercises:

(1) **While you are at the sink:** Swing the right leg out from the hip and point as high as you can. Do this six times, then repeat, swinging the leg backwards. Turn with your back to the sink, and swing the leg forwards. Repeat all this with the other leg; it is

Actress Zena Marshall, starring here in the film, "My Wife's Family," proves she can look charming even in the midst of a batch of ironing

grand for keeping that "hippy" look at bay.

(2) **While you are dusting:** Choose a clear wall, and stand with your back to it. Leave the hands dangling loosely in front. Now slowly stretch, lifting the arms high above the head. As you do it, you will feel your diaphragm lift, your tummy stretch.

(3) **While you are making the beds:** Keeping your tummy flat and your knees straight, breathe in as you bend down from the waist to tuck the clothes in; breathe slowly out as you straighten up again. Simple, but just the thing for keeping a trim waist and flat tummy.

(See also chapter on "Housework for the Figure.")

Relaxation

Just as important as your daily dozen is your daily relaxation. If, at the end of the day you feel "all in," with aching back, throbbing feet and frayed nerves, the answer is probably that you have not, for one single minute, really "let go." Once again, it may be a question of time. But, once you have learned the art of complete relaxation, you will realise that time is not such an important factor after all: ten minutes' real relaxation is worth half an hour of vague "resting." And, as with your exercises, it is something that can be fitted into your daily routine as it suits you best.

One of the quickest and simplest ways to relax is to *stretch*. You can do this at any odd time during the day. Draw yourself up and stretch your hands right above your head until you can feel a long pull through your body.

First thing in the morning, when you wake up, is another good time to stretch, and you can do it while still in bed. Lying on your back, stretch your body to its utmost. Then try to touch the corners at the head and foot of the bed with your toes and fingers. Between times, let your arms and legs relax and lie loosely. Make sure your breathing is slow and rhythmical throughout this exercise.

One of the most effective, and certainly the most beautifying ways of relaxing is the filmstar way. Once a day, for five, ten or fifteen minutes, get yourself into the Hollywood Body Slant. This means lying completely flat on your back, with your feet raised above your head. Then, eyes closed, mind a complete blank, body limp, let yourself go. After only five minutes you will feel a new woman—lines of fatigue will be smoothed away, your skin will be clearer, your feet and back will have lost that tired, dragging feeling. The best way to achieve the Body Slant position is to lie on a flat board: the Relaxaboard is made specially for the purpose, or you can make do by propping one end of an ironing-board on a low stool or chair. Start with five minutes the first day, and work gradually up to twenty whenever you can manage it. Turn also to chapter, "Learn to Relax and Vanquish Worry" for more information about the medical aspects of relaxation.

Massage

Massage, too, as you know, has a wonderfully relaxing effect on taut nerves and stiff muscles, and is a real beautifier. Few housewives can spare the time or money for regular professional massage treatments, but with one of the new, featherlight electric vibro-massagers, such as the Vibrette, you can give yourself a treatment every day. This massager has three separate attachments—for face, scalp and body massage. Besides giving yourself a luxury "facial" whenever you feel like it, it is a boon for toning slack muscles and reducing puffy ankles. The scalp massage attachment will help to clear up dandruff, and improves impoverished, out-of-condition hair.

Happy Feet

Do you ever complain, "I'm on my feet from morning till night"? Then ask yourself: *Is it really necessary?* So many jobs that are done through force of habit standing up can quite easily be done sitting down. Make a rule to sit whenever you

You can massage face, scalp and body and also give yourself a luxurious facial with the Vibrette electric massager

can; while doing the vegetables, cleaning the silver, even when ironing. And, while you *are* sitting, tone up your feet and guard against dropped arches with this simple exercise: Cross your legs and with your free foot, pointing your toe and keeping your heel steady, circle it round and round (clockwise with the right foot, anti-clockwise with the left). Repeat with the other foot.

And remember, happy feet give better service, so keep yours in good trim. When you are in your bath, scrub your feet with a soft nailbrush to stimulate circulation and flake off hard skin. Remove any callouses with pumice stone. Always dry your feet briskly, concentrating between the toes and round cuticles. Then, working up from the toes towards the ankles, massage in a soothing foot cream.

A quick reviver for end-of-day feet is to

Painting and gardening are not too hard on the hands for Hollywood star Ann Blyth. You too can protect yours from damage by using barrier creams

plunge them alternately into contrast foot baths of hot and cold water. Or soak them in a bowl of hot water containing a dessertspoonful of salt.

Care for Hard-worked Hands

"How can I keep my hands nice?" is another common problem of the housewife. Well, prevention is better than cure, and even if your hands are in and out of water all day and busy with endless chores, there is no need for them to suffer.

Keep a jar of hand cream by the sink—and use it. In Vienna, by the way, housewives always keep a jar of sugar by the sink; they swear by it for keeping hands satin smooth. To remove ingrained

Phyllis Calvert doesn't look in the least hot and bothered while cooking—either in real life or before the cameras. Here she plays a housewife in "It's Never Too Late"

dirt, try soaking your hands for a few minutes in olive oil, then rub sugar well into them. Rinse thoroughly and finish off with a dollop of nourishing hand cream.

Rubber gloves are, of course, excellent protection against wear and tear on the hands, but if you are one of those people who like to have the hands free, a pair of "invisible" gloves in the form of barrier cream will do just as good a job. "Gauntlet" has the advantage of protecting against both wet and dry dirt. You simply work a little into your hands to form a protective film. When you finish work, you wash your hands and they are soft and white, looking as though they had never heard of housework or gardening.

For hands that are already suffering from neglect, try this rejuvenating treatment once or twice a week: Warm a dessertspoonful of olive oil, soak some cotton wool in it and smooth over your hands and nails, easing back the cuticles with an orange stick. Then go to bed wearing an old pair of cotton gloves.

A tip, too, for "housework" knees and elbows; mix one teaspoonful of olive oil with half a teaspoonful of kitchen salt and rub into the skin, then remove with cleansing cream.

Red hands are usually a sign of faulty circulation. A brisk daily walk and warm clothing will help. So will holding your hands limply from the wrists and flapping them about vigorously.

To remove stubborn vegetable stains, rub with pumice stone (but not so hard as to make the skin red), then dab on peroxide as a bleach. Or there is an effective cream called Bantol, specially for removing all kinds of stains, that works like a charm.

Never, never throw away a squeezed-out lemon: keep it for rubbing your hands to whiten and smooth them, and to remove odd stains. Excellent for cleaning your nails, too.

Bedtime Beauty

Now, what about that important bedtime beauty care? It will only take a matter of minutes, but without it no woman can reasonably expect to keep her looks for long.

However tired you are, never skip thorough night-time cleansing. Double-cleanse with a penetrating cleansing cream or lotion, swirling it in little circles all over face and neck, to remove every speck of the day's dust and grime and every trace of make-up. (See following pages for diagrams showing how to massage and cleanse your face.) Finish by patting your face with skin tonic applied on a pad of cotton wool that has been wrung out in cold water. Finally, with light upward and outward strokes, pat in your night cream.

For real busy-bodies, there is a cream called Late Night Final which does double duty: use it first as a cleanser, then smooth on again to nourish while you sleep.

Young and normal skins can take a light night cream, but dry and over-thirty skins need extra nourishment. The various vitamin creams are excellent for dull, parched skins. There are, too, revitalising emollients, such as Captive Beauty, or the lanolin liquid formula, Revelotion.

Choose your skinfood with care, according to your skin type, and it will be money well and wisely spent. A little of the right preparation will do far more for you than a whole row of unsuitable preparations.

Up in the Morning Early

Your morning beauty routine need only take a minute. Splash your face with cool water (or wash if it is the oily type), then smooth on an all-in-one powder-foundation. Apply your lipstick, comb out your curls, and you are ready for whatever the day may bring.

But what about those special occasions when a really glamorous make-up is needed, when you want to look your loveliest in the shortest possible time?

Quick Beauty Treatment

Start your preparations with a warm bath, spiced with pine essence or bath Cologne to give you that walking-on-air feeling. Before you step into it, damp your hair with wave set or eau de Cologne, and pin it in pin curls.

Cleanse your face, and smooth on a film of skinfood to do its work while you bath. Before you start cleaning operations let your body relax in the warm water to relieve any tension.

After drying with a rough Turkish towel, have a quick rub down with toilet

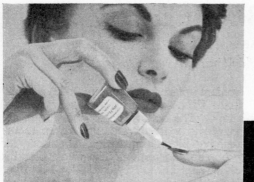

Long, well-shaped, elegant nails are varnished to match your lipstick for a party—the finishing touch in a special-occasion make-up

You'll always be ready for a party if you wear rubber gloves for all the washing and dirty chores. You hardly know you're wearing the latest gloves, like Marigold, which slide on easily and are nonslip

but evenly to make a thin film of colour over your face. Then a touch of cream rouge, blended in lightly over the cushions your cheeks make when you smile. Next, press in generously powder one shade lighter than your foundation—this gives your skin a lovely translucent look—then brush off any surplus with a soft com-

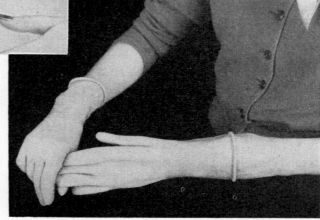

water (or there are perfumed deodorant Colognes that leave you tingling-fresh); apply your usual anti-perspirant, and dust with talc.

Remove any surplus skinfood, then apply your face-pack—the quickest way to a sparkling skin.

If there's no time to buy a mask, here's a good substitute. Just paint the white of an egg all over your face with a fine camel-hair brush and allow to dry thoroughly. Or you can mix a tablespoonful of toilet oatmeal with rose water, or with warm almond or olive oil. This makes an excellent mask for a dry skin.

Lie down for from ten to twenty minutes, pads of cotton wool soaked in warm milk over your eyes. Then remove your mask carefully with warm water and you are ready for your make-up.

If your skin is greasy, pat with astringent before applying your powder base, for a longer-lasting make-up. If it is inclined to be dry, then smooth in a little moisture-retaining cream, or skinfood.

Choose a flatteringly tinted foundation for evenings out. Smooth it on sparingly

plexion brush or a ball of clean cotton wool.

Now your lipstick. Outline the lips first, following their natural shape, then fill in with colour. Blot with a tissue, then apply a final layer, letting it "set." Remember to choose a deeper, richer shade of lipstick for night to stand up to artificial lighting. Revlon have solved the problem with two versions of their Kissing Pink lipstick—one shade for day, a deeper one for night.

Eyes next. Flatter them with a touch of eyeshadow applied to the outer half of the eyelid only, blending it upwards and outwards towards the temples. A pretty trick is to put a thin, emphatic line of colour immediately above the eyelashes. Choose your shadow to echo the colour of your eyes, or try the more exotic gold or silver for evenings.

Use mascara on upper eyelashes only—two thin applications—then with your brush, feather in little strokes along the natural line of your eyebrows.

Brush out your set, spray with lacquer; then a last touch of perfume . . . and no one would dream you had spent most of the day in the kitchen.

WE CAN ALL BE LIFE-SAVERS

*As well as knowing all about First Aid and Home Nursing, we
can give our blood—painlessly and without harm to ourselves*

THE BLOOD TRANSFUSION SERVICE

As a result of discoveries during and since the Second World War, there has been a great increase in the number of cases treated by blood transfusion and also in the amount of blood given to individual cases.

Transfusions may be necessary as part of the treatment of accidents, hæmorrhage, burns, anæmia and after childbirth and operations. There is, as yet, no substitute for blood. Since transfusion has become part of everyday medical treatment, the National Blood Transfusion Service must expand steadily if it is to keep ahead of the rising demands of the hospitals and ensure that no one who needs a transfusion will have to go without one.

In order to avoid the necessity of calling upon donors more than twice a year, another 125,000 volunteers are needed, making a total of over 600,000 regular donors in the U.K. This is because hospitals are now using about 70 times as much blood as before the war; more than one donation for every minute of each day and night throughout the year.

Donors Needed

Donors are wanted between the ages of 18 and 65, those of the younger generation being most urgently wanted to safeguard the future of the Service. People who have had jaundice should not volunteer, as this condition may be passed on with their blood.

The National Blood Transfusion Service is administered by the Regional Hospital Boards under the National Health Service, with 12 regional centres in England and Wales. Each regional centre is at a university town: Newcastle, Leeds, Sheffield, Cambridge, London (two regions), Oxford, Bristol, Cardiff, Birmingham, Liverpool and Manchester. At each of these centres an organisation is maintained for collecting blood within the region, including the arrangement of bleeding sessions at convenient places throughout the regional area. Each donor gives just under a pint of blood. The bottles of blood collected are placed in a refrigerator and taken to the regional blood transfusion laboratory for grouping and testing. The whole blood is either kept in the Regional Blood Bank or issued to Area Blood Banks maintained at large general hospitals. Each of the principal hospitals holds a supply of blood sufficient not only for its own needs, but also for the smaller hospitals, nursing homes and general practitioners in its district. This supply is replenished every week, or oftener if the need arises.

Preserving Blood

Since red cells cannot be preserved for longer than 21 days outside the body, blood which has been issued but not used within 21 days is returned to the Regional Transfusion Centre, where the spent red cells are removed. The straw-coloured fluid which remains (plasma) is then sent to the Blood Products Laboratory to be dried. Blood plasma in this dried state can be stored indefinitely and given to patients of any blood group. It is also a valuable adjunct to whole blood, being particularly valuable in cases of severe hæmorrhage, for maintaining life until supplies of blood of a suitable group can be obtained. For this reason, small hospitals, especially in remote parts of the country, carry a supply of dried plasma for emergency use.

For normally healthy people between 18 and 65, giving blood is perfectly harmless and quite painless. The bleeding sessions are presided over by a doctor assisted by skilled nurses; regular tests are made to ensure that donors are not themselves anæmic; there are no ill effects or inconvenience and, to make quite certain of this, every donor is given a cup of tea and a biscuit and rested for at least ten minutes after giving blood.

A quarter of an hour thus spent once every six months is a very small price to pay for the knowledge that your blood may be saving a life.

MODERN GLASSES CAN IMPROVE A FACE

Gone are the days when a woman who had to wear spectacles gave up thinking of her appearance. Now they emphasise good points and minimise bad

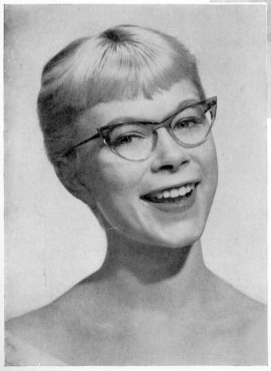

WHEN a short-sighted but pretty girl gets married, she does not risk stumbling blindly up the aisle. Instead, she chooses glasses worthy of the occasion—in a hand-made frame of clear plastic inset with silver leaves and pearls. Note how the width at the temple and the lower rim curving in towards the cheekbones (above) combine to soften the square jawline.

FOR the very youthful merry little face of Zoe Newton, famous photographic model, a simple, unobtrusive type of frame has been chosen. It is slightly upswept and has clear lower rims, which always suit a young face. The "keyhole" bridge is specially good because it has the effect of lengthening her rather pert little nose.

Styles for work and play, for differing colourings and contours

IF you wear glasses, don't on any account be ashamed of them. As well as giving you that priceless gift—good sight—they should add to your appearance. Choose them, then, with an eye to your facial contours, your colouring, your dress colours and the occasion, for what is right for the office won't do for a dance or look right on the golf course.

THE delicate look of the frame (above) is achieved by the absence of lower rims, the lenses being held in by a tiny nylon thread which is almost invisible. Lilac plastic inset with gold tinsel is very becoming to the model, Yvonne Nightingale, with her beautiful auburn hair.

NOT too showy for day wear, yet ornamental enough for an evening party, this frame is in bright red plastic with gold eyebrow and temple motifs. Note how cleverly the top rim complements the sweep of the model's eyebrow, following it almost exactly. Remember to link what you wear with the colour of your spectacle frames.

THE unusual and decorative frame (above) is slightly reminiscent of the Venetian mask and looks most attractive for evening wear. It also subtly draws attention to the wearer's good profile by means of its ornamented sides. The eyes need careful make-up to go with glasses, so mascara the top lashes, brushing upwards, apply eye shadow to outer half of lid, blending up and out, and define the brows with feather strokes from an eyebrow pencil.

CHERRY plastic inset with gold tinsel flatters the oval face with its upswept line and lower rims softly curving to the tip of the browline. Glasses for this shape of face must emphasise the width of forehead and cheekbones, the jaw and chin tapering in perfect symmetry.

TAKE CARE OF YOUR HAIR

As with all beauty, cleanliness is the keynote, so shampoo your hair once a week; and brush it daily—lying flat on your bed, with your hair hanging over the edge. Combat dryness and brittleness by massaging with oil before shampooing; avoid drying in front of a fire.

NEVER have a perm when you have a cold or are otherwise off-colour. Solve the problem of between-perm limp ends, wisps and straggles with Richard Hudnut's End Curl, specially designed as a pick-up home perm. Gay Pretender, the attractive hairstyle shown both back and front view on this page, was achieved with only 14 curlers and a half bottle of End Curl.

THE MENOPAUSE

Dr. Mary Lymington explains what can be expected—and what need not be feared—at this quite natural time of change in every woman's life

THE forties are a time of life with advantages of their own for women. The worst struggles lie behind and life tends to assume a calmer, more gracious rhythm, until one becomes reluctantly aware that one of the womanly qualities—and a key one at that—is gradually slipping away. Common sense demands that every woman face up to the inevitable. Some time between, say 45 and, at latest, 55, the menopause will take place. The true facts need to be sorted out from the welter of old wives' tales that have somehow grown up around this subject.

All that actually happens during the menopause is that the womb gradually contracts and goes out of action, its function being no longer required, while the action of the ovaries gradually slows down and finally ceases altogether. It is the ovaries that produce during the child-bearing years the ova or female eggs and also the mysterious but all-important hormones.

Ignore Alarmist Talk

Translated into its effects on a normal, healthy woman, the menopause will probably begin with a hardly noticeable irregularity of the normal periods. It may be a steady lessening both in frequency and in the loss of blood, or an alternate "heavy" and "light" period. Different people are affected in different ways, so it is impossible to lay down hard and fast rules. But in any case it should not seriously affect anyone's way of life or cause any real inconvenience. A woman who, because of fibroids or for some other reason, has had a Hysterectomy (operation for the removal of the womb) before the onset of the Menopause, will not of course have this sign to guide her, as her periods have already been ended by the operation. In every other respect, however, she is likely to have exactly the same experiences as any other woman at this time of life. Apart from a tendency to an occasional sudden hot flush—such as could happen at any time in a hot atmosphere or after hurrying—and perhaps a slight sensation of dizziness, this should be the only physical symptom experienced.

Pay no attention to any gruesome stories. The vast majority of women who have sailed successfully through this experience with a minimum of trouble are not the ones who talk about it. Those who wax most voluble about what they describe in hushed whispers as "the change" are invariably those who have failed to keep this perfectly natural process in proportion.

Excessive flooding, for instance, is not a normal occurrence at this or at any time. If it does occur, medical advice should be sought. Equally, if the hot flushes cause acute embarrassment or there are any other symptoms, a doctor can prescribe treatment that really helps, so it is well worth a visit.

Some people tend to feel overwhelmed, emotionally, by the depressing finality of the menopause. That is only because Nature, always efficient at her job, has linked our emotions so closely with the functioning of our reproductive organs. Even women with grown-up children, who would shudder at the thought of starting another family at this stage, have been known to rebel instinctively at the prospect that they will soon be incapable of further child-bearing.

No Loss of Femininity

But the ability to have a baby is the one and only aspect of the menopause which *is* final. There is not the *slightest* cause to fear that, while the process is going on or after it is complete, one becomes in any other respect less feminine, attractive, desirable or capable of sexual desire and fulfilment. It is simply a transition to the third stage of woman's natural development. After childhood and the child-bearing years comes the age of maturity, when looks, character and personality achieve their ultimate, most radiant fulfilment. For proof, try making a list of the most glamorous and successful actresses with their ages. It will be a revelation.

The menopause should be thought of as a bodily readjustment very much like puberty, though infinitely less drastic. Most women survived that physical, mental and emotional upheaval years before, without practical experience of life to guide them, and when they were a prey to all sorts of nameless doubts, fears and uncertainties. At this second period of adjustment they have their philosophy and experience, perhaps a loving husband and family, friends, outside interests, a quieter, better organised way of life. A woman in the forties is infinitely better qualified to deal with a very much simpler problem than the one she coped with as a teenager.

Yet some are tempted to sit back and rest more, to withdraw from some of their more active pursuits, either because they feel a little sorry for themselves or are embarrassed in public by the fear of hot flushes. Whatever the reason, this is a temptation to be resisted. The line must be drawn rigidly between normal rest, which is good, and the slightest tendency to mollycoddling, which can be disastrous. Remember, because you are going through the menopause, you are not ill. Neither are you old or losing your looks. But you can very easily turn yourself into a nervous wreck—and a trial to live with—if you once give way to self-pity.

Avoid Self-pity

Label self-pity Public Enemy Number One and remember it is an expert at infiltration tactics. It is responsible for most of the women who go to pieces at this time. Quite unfounded worry about losing their looks and their husband's love makes them sorry for themselves. They sit at home and brood, instead of getting out and about. Because they are always thinking about it, they flush more and become nervy, bad-tempered and "difficult." When the unfortunate husband loses patience and snaps back, their worst fears are immediately confirmed. If he tries to make amends, they resist his advances and so convince themselves that they have already turned into frigid women. Before they know where they are, they have resigned themselves to semi-invalidism, wailing to their few remaining friends about the miseries of "the change."

Watch out, too, for another vicious circle. Once a woman starts slacking off, particularly in the forties and over, she tends to grow lazy and then bored. Boredom leads to eating more (to pass the time) and that in turn makes her lazier, so that she puts on more weight. The heavier she gets, the less inclined she is to take exercise —and so on *ad infinitum*.

Excessive slimming, on the other hand, can make the skin baggy and haggard. Extremes should be avoided, a normal amount of exercise kept up and diet regulated without starvation.

In ninety-nine cases out of a hundred, modern women get through the menopause without any visible signs of inconvenience at all. That is one of the good things woman's emancipation has achieved, making her far too busy and too determined to make the best of her appearance to mope over something that is inevitable.

It's Up to You

Of all the fallacies connected with this subject, one of the most dangerous is the idea that men also undergo a modified "change of life" some time in the forties. They do not. The husband who in middle life suddenly starts seeking solace outside his home, has usually been driven to it— by a "good" wife. She is often the kind who wears herself out working for her home and children. By the time she reaches the forties, she is always too tired to care about her appearance or to respond to the advances she once welcomed from her husband. The final crash usually comes when the children leave home and the last bond is removed. Years of drifting apart, of boredom and physical and emotional frustration eventually drive the husband into the arms of another woman— which is hard on a wife who has sacrificed everything to her family. But it cannot be blamed on to the menopause. The fault lies fair and square at her own door.

The menopause comes sooner or later to every woman. Whether it brings emotional strain and anxiety or passes by, hardly noticed, is up to the individual alone. Face it the right way and you can be like a certain highly successful businesswoman who ran a job, a home and brought up two children. One day this very charming and attractive woman realised, to her own amazement, that she had had the menopause and not even known it. That is how it should be.

CHOSEN FOR MODERN COLLECTORS

From the Royal Doulton Potteries come these unique heirlooms of to-morrow

The choir boy (right) is an angelic little figure in his red cassock and white surplice

Top o' the Hill, this gay little damsel wears either green, red or pink, according to taste, and is 7 in. high

Giselle is one of the popular Ladies of the Ballet, a dainty ballerina only $7\frac{1}{4}$ in. high in pastel colourings

Autumn Breezes (below) stands $7\frac{1}{2}$ in. high. The full skirt and bonnet are pale yellow, the muff ermine

A Gypsy Dance (above), a captivating little lady full of gay movement

Left, a swaggering, immensely rotund Falstaff, $7\frac{1}{4}$ in. high

THE LAW AND YOUR HOME

Because of the many differences in legal systems, it is only possible to describe the law as it applies in England and Wales

THERE is much more to the law than going to court or being taken there. All our formal transactions with others are regulated by the law of the land, and we should all have some idea of the nature of our rights and of the obligations which we owe to neighbours and other persons.

It is not possible here to give more than an outline of some of the legal matters which may crop up in home and family life. If you are in any doubt or difficulty on a legal point, you should take proper advice just as promptly as you would in a medical matter. No two cases are exactly alike, and for this reason it is essential to tell your solicitor without reserve all the facts bearing on your particular problem.

HOME OWNERSHIP

Let us first consider the place where you make your home—your house or flat and the plot of land on which it stands.

Freehold and Leasehold

It may be that you have set up home in a house of your own, or that you intend to do so. You may "own" a house in two different capacities—as a freeholder or leaseholder. "Freehold" does not always mean that there are no restrictions on the way the property may be used. Freehold land is often subject to agreements about maintaining fences, the type of buildings allowed and other matters. These will be set out in the deeds. If the agreements are broken, there may be an action for damages or an injunction, but the right to hold the land will not cease. The freeholder remains entitled absolutely to the property until he sells it or until on his death it passes to his successor. The right he possesses and can pass on is of a perpetual kind.

A leasehold interest in property may also be sold, and it also passes as part of a deceased leaseholder's estate. Where it differs from a freehold interest is in having a limited overall duration. The whole in-terest is always scheduled to come completely to an end at some future date, when the property will go back to the lessor or ground landlord unless the person who is then the leaseholder can obtain from him a new lease of it. And even before that, a breach of the covenants may cause the lease to be forfeited.

Dilapidations

One frequently sees short "remainders" of leases advertised for sale—that is to say, the last few unexpired years (ten, or even less) of a longer term. The immediate price is often attractive, but there will usually be a liability for dilapidations to be met by the purchaser when the lease expires, and that may be heavy.

Protection of Ground Lessees

A leaseholder of a house which was in 1939 of rateable value not exceeding £100 in London or £75 elsewhere who himself occupies it under a lease which was originally for more than 21 years cannot be made to leave the house except under a court order. At the end of the term of the lease the lessor may serve a notice under the Act, and it is then important for the lessee, if he wishes to stay on, to write at once and so inform the lessor. The lessor may propose a new lease on fresh terms, or may on certain grounds apply to the court for possession. The court may grant possession or, on the other hand, may decide on the terms of a new lease. A booklet on the Landlord and Tenant Act, 1954, which is obtainable for 6d. from the Stationery Office, gives a useful explanation of the rights of both parties in regard to this new security of tenure. The lessee's liability for dilapidations is much less stringent where this Act applies than otherwise, but the conditions of obtaining a new lease may bind him to pay the lessor (usually by instalments) the cost of putting the property into good repair in so far as it has become dilapidated by any breach of the repairing covenants in the old lease.

If you think of buying the "fag-end" of a lease, you should find out as nearly as possible what the repair bill is likely to be when the date of expiry arrives.

It is as well to take advice on the value of any property you are buying, and best to go to a reputable surveyor or estate agent who is not also acting for the person selling and who will therefore be able to give you an independent opinion.

You may "own" the house you occupy in two different capacities—as a freeholder or leaseholder—and there may be restrictions on the way such property can be used

"Subject to Contract"

When you find a house that suits you, you will probably be asked to pay a deposit and to sign an agreement to purchase. It is a wise precaution for a purchaser to make his contract at this stage provisional, for with house property so many hidden snags may exist. Your solicitor will want to make enquiries into the nature of the title and the plans of the local authority for future development and into any unusual charges or outgoings there may be. If money has to be borrowed to buy the house, you will also want to make sure that the building society or other lender will accept it as security.

A convenient way to provide an opportunity for this before you become irrevocably bound to purchase is to see that any document you sign or any receipt you are given contains the magic phrase "subject to contract." No vendor or agent should object to this nowadays unless the sale is by auction, in which case the "particulars and conditions of sale" are published in advance, and you should always read these carefully and understand them before you bid.

TENANCIES

Suppose you do not buy a house, but decide to set up home as a tenant in a rented house or flat, or in rooms in someone else's house. Unlike a paying guest or lodger, a tenant has, by his agreement with his landlord (which need not be in writing if the tenancy is for three years or less), the right to the exclusive use and occupation of the principal part of the premises, though he may in addition have to share some rooms —kitchen, bathroom, etc.—with another tenant or with the landlord.

Furnished and Unfurnished

The premises may be furnished or unfurnished, or—a device frequently adopted by landlords—the letting may include a little furniture, whether the tenant needs it or not.

The idea of this is to prevent the tenancy from being protected by the Rent Acts. Tenants should understand that if the amount of the furniture (or the value of any services provided—cleaning or the use of a lift, for example) is such that a fair hire-payment for it represents a substantial portion of the total rent, the landlord will not be restricted by the Rent Acts in the amount he can ask for the premises, and will also be able to require the tenant to leave as soon as the agreement for the tenancy comes to an end or is brought to an end by a proper notice to quit given in accordance with its terms. In other words, a furnished tenancy is unprotected. Unfortunately, there is no accurate measure of a "substantial portion," but a modern rule of thumb which a county court judge has employed in the case of furniture is to assess the capital value of the furniture and not to hold the tenancy to be a furnished one unless that value is equivalent to at least a year's total rent.

Rent Control

A furnished tenant of premises rated at £40 or under in London (£30 elsewhere) can apply to a Rent Tribunal to approve or reduce his rent. So can a tenant who shares some essential living accommodation with his landlord. A kitchen is living accommodation for this purpose, but not a bathroom or lavatory. Local authorities keep a register of rents so fixed. The tribunal can also protect such a tenant from being turned out by granting him a guaranteed continuance of his tenancy for short periods at a time.

RENT RESTRICTION

By a series of Acts of Parliament dating from the time of the First World War, unfurnished tenancies of certain dwelling-houses are controlled and the tenants protected both as regards the maximum rent which may be charged and the conditions on which the landlord can regain possession. "Dwelling-house" here includes one or more rooms in a house, provided that no essential living accommodation is shared *with the landlord*, but it does not include a new house or conversion completed after August 30th, 1954, unless its erection or the conversion was subsidised by a Housing Act grant. Nor does the protection attach if the rent is less than two-thirds of the rateable value, or if the landlord is a local authority, a New Town Development Corporation or an approved Housing Association or Trust.

Until a few years ago the upper limits of rateable value which determined whether or not a dwelling-house was controlled were £100 in the London Metropolitan Police District, and £75 elsewhere. The Rent Act, 1957, however, removed the full protection of the Acts from houses of which the rateable value on 7th November, 1956, was over £40 in London or £30 in the rest of England and Wales. Certain notices had to be given by the landlord to bring about decontrol, and if the tenant remained on after those notices expired the landlord cannot generally recover possession before the 31st July, 1961, without applying to the court for an order. The 1957 Act also brought about a complete decontrol of all dwelling-houses, whatever their rateable value, on their being let after the 6th July, 1957, to new tenants. But premiums cannot lawfully be charged on any letting or assignment made after that date, and before July, 1960, of premises which were previously controlled, nor can more than one periodic payment of rent be demanded in advance.

As regards houses remaining within the protection of the Acts, the permissible rent is no longer based on the standard rent ascertained from the letting history of the property. It varies, according to the responsibility for repairs, between a figure one-and-a-third times the gross annual value of the premises and two-and-a-third times that value. Increases are allowed for rates, if the landlord pays them, and for any services or furniture provided. The gross value is the amount of the rating valuation of the property before deducting the statutory repairs allowance, and can be found by enquiry at the local council offices. (The values used in deciding whether the property is controlled are the net values, i.e., gross less the repairs allowance.)

The landlord under a tenancy which remains controlled can only regain possession of the property, notwithstanding that the agreement has expired or has been terminated by notice to quit, if he can persuade the court that it is reasonable for him to do so, and that certain other conditions are fulfilled. For instance, he may be able to show that alternative accommodation suitable to the tenant's needs is available, or that he requires the premises for occupation by himself or by his adult son or a parent of his. But a landlord cannot avail himself of this last reason if he has bought the property after 6th November, 1956, and the court in any case will not make the order if the tenant can satisfy the judge that it would work greater hardship to him to order possession than to the landlord if it were refused.

On the death of a tenant, a member of his family who has lived with him in the house may enjoy the protection of the Acts.

The interpretation of the Rent Acts is a complicated study owing to the wide variety of circumstances which may occur, and anyone affected by a problem arising under them can hardly afford not to take expert advice. A booklet is on sale at the Stationery Office for 6d. giving information about the Acts, and particularly about ascertaining maximum rents.

NOTICE TO QUIT

Quite apart from the Rent Acts, a landlord cannot sue for possession (so long as the tenant fulfils all his agreements) until the contractual tenancy between them expires or is brought to an end. A tenancy by contract may be for a fixed term (a year or, commonly, three years) or it may be periodical (by the week, month, quarter or year). Unless there is an express agreement, the period of the tenancy will be taken to follow the interval at which the rent is to be paid. Thus a letting at 30s. a week is considered to be a weekly tenancy. A weekly tenancy of any dwelling now requires for its determination at least four weeks' notice to quit or, if given by the tenant, of intention to quit, and the notice must expire on a day of the week corresponding to that on which the tenancy began, Monday to the fourth Monday afterwards for example. The notice must be in writing, addressed to the other party and expressed in definite terms. It is necessary to see that he receives it before the required period of notice begins to run. A monthly tenancy requires a calendar month's notice, and a quarterly tenancy a quarter's notice; but a yearly tenancy may be brought to an end by six months' notice expiring at the end of the tenancy year.

OBLIGATIONS OF LANDLORD AND TENANT

Repairs

The responsibility for repairs and decorations depends upon the agreement between the landlord and tenant. A usual arrangement in the case of a yearly or quarterly tenancy is that the landlord shall do structural repairs and external decoration and the tenant shall keep the inside repaired and decorated. A weekly tenant does not usually undertake to do any repairs or decoration. In any case, unless it is so agreed when the tenancy begins, there is no liability on either party to repair so long as the landlord, in the case of small property, sees that it is fit for human habitation (a requirement that is interpreted fairly generously to him) and so long as the tenant makes good any actual damage to the property or to its decorations, fixtures and fittings committed by him or by his family or guests.

If a tenant considers that the state of the property is insanitary, and he is not liable for the want of repair which makes it so, it is open to him to complain to the local authority, who may then take steps to compel the landlord to put it right. And if the tenancy is protected by the Rent Acts, the local authority may be able to give a certificate which will enable the tenant to withhold part of the rent

A furnished tenant of property of small rateable value can apply to a Rent Tribunal to approve or reduce his rent. Here the members of a tribunal inspect a kitchen

until the repairs are done.

Tenancy agreements which provide for repairs sometimes use the words "fair wear and tear excepted." This exception is now interpreted rather narrowly. The burden is on the party concerned to show that any defect is in fact due to reasonable use and the ordinary operation of natural forces. The words would not excuse neglect to do any repairs at all.

Rates and Taxes

A tenant of a whole house is usually responsible to the Inland Revenue for income tax at the full standard rate (Schedule "A" or Landlord's Property Tax) on the net annual value of the house. He can ordinarily recover the whole of this by deducting it from his next payment of rent. In rare cases where the rent is less than the annual value the tenant has to bear the tax on the difference, unless his taxation allowances are not all absorbed by his ordinary income. The local Inspector of Taxes will deal with this on being informed of the full circumstances (see also chapter on Income Tax).

Rates are payable to the local authority by the occupier of property. Whether they are borne by the landlord or the tenant depends on the agreement between them. If the landlord is to bear them, he may arrange to pay rates direct to the council. They are calculated on a poundage (fixed for the year) on the net annual value and are usually collected half-yearly in advance. Water rate is also based on the annual value, but there are additional charges if a hose is used for watering the garden or cleaning a car.

Assigning and Subletting

The tenant may assign his tenancy, or may sublet the whole or part of the premises, provided that his agreement does not specifically prohibit him from doing so. But if he assigns or sublets the whole premises without the landlord's consent, the assignee or subtenant will not have the benefit of the Rent Acts. A person who proposes to take a subtenancy or an assignment should in any case always see that the landlord's consent is obtained, if the tenant's agreement renders this necessary. Another point is that the original tenant does not, by assigning or subletting, get rid of his liability to the landlord for due fulfilment of the agreement, including the payment of rent. He remains so liable throughout the term of the tenancy in addition to the person who occupies the premises for the time being.

Payment of Rent

Although most landlords arrange for the rent to be collected as it falls due, they are under no compulsion to do so. It is the tenant's duty to take or send the rent to the landlord or his authorised agent. He should see that he gets a receipt (stamped with a twopenny stamp if the amount is £2 or more) either separately or in a rent book.

Tenant's Default

What happens if a tenant falls into arrear with his rent? The landlord can distrain—that is, he can put in the bailiff to seize furniture or other goods. He needs the leave of the court if the premises are protected. Or he can sue the tenant for the rent, or for possession of the premises. Should the tenancy not be a protected one, he can technically, instead of going to court, evict the tenant himself. But this form of self-help is not to be recommended to landlords because of the difficulty of carrying it out without infringing some right of the tenant. In any case, the landlord would commit a criminal offence if he made a forcible entry.

If the tenant should fail to perform any other agreement he has entered into (such as a covenant to repair the premises or not to sublet or assign them), the landlord may proceed to forfeit the tenancy. However, in the case of a controlled tenancy, he can only do so through the court, and in almost all other cases he must first serve a notice which gives the tenant the right to apply to the court for relief.

HOUSEHOLDER'S OBLIGATIONS

Nuisances, etc.

Owners and occupiers of property ought to see that neither its condition nor anything that is done on the premises constitutes a nuisance or annoyance to neighbours or to members of the public. As regards things that are inherently dangerous (such as explosives), the man who

You are responsible if a bonfire in your garden causes damage to neighbours' property

brings them on to his property (or who starts a bonfire, to give another instance) is absolutely liable if they escape from the land and do damage. But apparently innocuous things can become nuisances if neglected or mishandled. Dangerous fences and excessive noise from radios are common examples. Again, trees should not be allowed to overhang or their roots to protrude into the property of others. If this happens and damage results (and tree roots have been known to unsettle the structure of substantial houses) the occupier will be liable. A neighbour may cut down overhanging branches or sever roots which undermine his land, but the roots and branches do not become his property, and he must, for instance, restore any fruit that an overhanging branch may bear.

Safety of Premises

An occupier of a house should see that the premises, particularly the entrance, front path, staircases and passages, are not in a condition likely to cause injury to people who visit him. He must not set a trap to hurt anybody, even technically a burglar. As regards people who come to do business with him or as his guests, he is liable if they are injured because of his lack of reasonable care for their safety. If dangerous features, such as a defective step in a dark place, cannot for the moment be remedied, at least the householder should warn visitors of them. A common source of danger is linoleum which has been polished under a mat. One cannot foresee all the accidents which may happen in the home, and the financial side of this risk may be covered by insurance (see

chapter on Insurance). The prudent householder will, however, take care to see that his premises are not likely to cause anyone to fall or otherwise hurt themselves.

A landlord who is responsible to his tenant for repairs is also liable to his tenant's visitors for injury from dangers arising from his failure to observe his agreement.

FAMILY LAW

Let us now turn to consider the personal relationships of the people in the home. The law enters into their lives, too. Rights and obligations are ugly words in a purely domestic context. Yet even in the case of a normal smooth marriage the partners will sometimes want to know how they stand about property and other matters.

Husband's and Wife's Property

Both husband and wife can now freely hold and deal with property of their own. Though a wife cannot generally sue her husband except in the matrimonial courts, she has access to the ordinary courts in matters concerning her separate property, and also (which is frequently important) in connection with her share of property bought by or given to husband and wife jointly.

There is now no presumption that wedding presents are joint property. In a recent case the court inferred that those that came from the wife's side were intended as gifts to her and vice versa. But an article for the home given by a "mutual friend" may belong jointly to the spouses; and so may a gift which the party receiving it has treated as a joint possession. Sometimes the funds to buy a house or the instalments to pay off a building society mortgage are provided partly by the wife and partly by the husband; or the wife may pay the instalments even though the property is held in the husband's name alone. If she does this out of the general housekeeping money, it does not affect the position, for the wife has no title to keep any balance of a housekeeping, as distinct from a personal, allowance. But even if she pays out of her own money, it is very rarely that any strict account is kept of the state of things, though it perhaps should be. The ruling question in such cases is the intention of the parties at the time the money was spent, but the recent tendency of the courts in these, as in joint banking account cases, is to regard the property as owned in equal shares where accounts cannot be disentangled.

Right and Duty of Support

A husband is responsible for providing the necessities of life for his wife and for the children of the marriage up to the age of sixteen years. If he does not do this, the wife may obtain necessary goods from tradesmen and others and have the bills sent to him, but he is not otherwise liable for any debts she may incur without his authority. Provided he does meet his obligations so far as necessaries are concerned, he may prevent her from making him responsible for her debts on the footing that she has his authority, if he gives notice to the particular tradesman or creditor that he will not be so responsible. One occasionally sees notices in newspapers disclaiming responsibility generally, but though these may be effective in practice, they are not legally relevant to any particular claim against the husband unless he can show that the creditor in question actually saw the advertisement.

Apart from pledging his credit in this way, a wife whose husband neglects to maintain her according to his station in life may apply to the magistrates for maintenance to be awarded for her support and that of his children, whether or not she is living apart from him. The amount awarded may be up to £5 per week for the wife and £1 10s. for each child under sixteen. (A Bill now before Parliament proposes alterations in these limits and other reforms in the matrimonial jurisdiction of magistrates.)

A wife loses her rights to support, to pledge credit, and to apply for maintenance if she commits adultery, unless and until her husband with full knowledge has forgiven her and taken her back.

DIVORCE AND SEPARATION

The fact that the vast majority of marriages are basically happy should not deter us from considering the position in case "unhappy differences," in the legal phrase, should arise to an irreconcilable extent.

Making it Up

The first thought should always be of the possibility of reconciliation. However strongly either party feels, and however much they may regard the quarrel as a personal affair not to be intruded on by strangers, neither should neglect the good offices nowadays provided willingly by doctors, ministers of religion and welfare workers generally in negotiating a settlement of marital differences. The matrimonial law should be regarded as a last resort.

Separation

If all else fails, that law provides the possibility of a separation agreement by which the spouses agree to live apart and under which agreed maintenance payments may be enforced. The courts can also grant judicial separation or dissolution of the marriage.

Divorce

But these drastic remedies in court are possible only if a matrimonial offence has been committed by the party against whom the relief is sought—adultery, cruelty, continuous desertion for the past three years, and some others of less common occurrence.

Nullity

A marriage may also be annulled for incapacity on either side to consummate it, or for wilful refusal to consummate.

Desertion

A party may be held to have deserted the other notwithstanding that it was that other who actually left the home. Whether or not desertion has occurred, and the course of conduct that should be pursued by a wife or husband whose partner has left home, are questions frequently calling for expert advice. One thing worth remembering is that if the parties have agreed to separate, or if the wife has obtained a *separation* order from the magistrates (as she may do on the ground of adultery or persistent cruelty, provided that she is herself innocent of adultery), that will stop desertion running, but this does not now necessarily apply to agreements made before 1938. An order merely for maintenance does not interrupt desertion.

Cruelty

By cruelty is meant deliberate conduct or neglect which causes bodily or mental ill-health.

Condonation

A matrimonial offence cannot be made the foundation of a petition for divorce if it has been condoned—that is, if the wronged party, knowing of it, forgives and reinstates the offender as his or her spouse, but its efficacy may be revived by a fresh offence

Maintenance and Custody

When dissolving or annulling a marriage or granting judicial separation, the courts may order maintenance to be paid or secured, and may also say which of the parties is to have the custody of the children. Generally speaking, the courts may not make a final decree until satisfied that the best arrangement possible in the circumstances has been made for all children under sixteen. The children's welfare, and not the guilt or innocence of the parents, is the criterion which the courts must adopt in regard to custody and similar matters. Maintenance is settled according to the parties' means, the broad aim being to ensure that the total income available to the wife is not less than one-third of the combined incomes of the husband and the wife, with an additional sum for any children of whom she has the custody.

Costs and Legal Aid and Advice

The husband is, as a rule, liable for all the costs of the proceedings whoever may bring the petition. In matrimonial proceedings, as in other litigation in the High Court or a county court, it is possible to obtain State-subsidised legal aid if the litigant's yearly income after deducting certain outgoings is under £420 and his disposable capital not more than £500. Application should be made in the first place to one of the Law Society's local advisory committees. The figures stated are now under review by Parliament.

In addition, it is now possible for persons of very small means to obtain legal advice at an oral interview with a solicitor at a charge of 2s. 6d., or free if they are on

Photo : Crown copyright

The aw insists that a fireguard be used in any room where there is a child under the age of 12. The owners of the room (above) are risking prosecution in case of accident

national assistance. A panel of solicitors is maintained in each of twelve areas covering England and Wales. *Anyone* can have an interview for £1 under a voluntary scheme. Names and addresses of the solicitors who are available are kept at the Citizen's Advice Bureaux.

OTHER MATTERS

But enough of matrimonial troubles. Here are a few miscellaneous ways in which legal matters may become relevant in a trouble-free home.

Adoption

Many couples wish to adopt a child. This may be done under an order of the court, which always hears such matters in private. The best method of approach is to write to one of the registered adoption societies. Their officers will put intending adopters into touch with a suitable child (though there is usually a waiting list of adopters) and explain the formalities and the safeguards which the law requires to be observed in the interests both of the child and of its natural parents. A legal adoption has the effect of putting the child in the position, as regards status and succession to property, of the adopter's own child, and of removing it altogether from the control and responsibility of its natural parents. Their consent is therefore always a necessary condition, unless the court for certain reasons dispenses with it. A probationary period of three months' residence with the proposing adopters is now required in every case, and the local authority must be notified at the beginning of this period.

Registration of Birth

If you are fortunate enough to have a child of your own, the law will require you to see to the registration of its birth. This must be done with the local Registrar of Births and Deaths within forty-two days, and the information may be given by the father or mother, by a person present at the birth, or by the occupier of the house where the child was born. Buy a copy of the certificate of registration at the time and keep it safely.

Care of Children

The care and upbringing of children is an anxious as well as a joyous task. Though kindness is the best method, it is neither necessary nor desirable to indulge a child's every whim to the point of spoiling. Recognising this, the law allows a parent to chastise his child, but it must be done with moderation or a summons for assault may follow. Abandonment or physical neglect in any manner likely to cause suffering or ill health may also lead to an appearance before the magistrates. Another measure of protection which Parliament has enacted is that which insists on the use of a fireguard in any room where a child under the age of twelve years is allowed to be, and there is a proposal to extend this provision to older children.

Incidentally, if a chimney in an urban area catches fire even accidentally, the occupier of the house is liable to a fine unless he can show that the incident was not due to his neglect.

Education

Parents must arrange for their children of school age (from five years until the end of the school term in which the child becomes fifteen) to receive proper education. Private tutors are out of the question for most people now, so that this usually means attendance at a school maintained or approved by the Education Authority. A parent is liable to prosecution if a child is kept away without good excuse.

Private schools, which charge fees, usually insist on a parent entering into an agreement which binds him to give a term's notice of withdrawal or to pay a term's fees in lieu of notice. Such an obligation may be implied even without written agreement if it is brought to the parent's attention by words printed on the school bill or other literature. If there is no such condition, the parent may still be liable to repay to the proprietor any profit lost to him by the failure to give notice.

No general liability for one's children's acts

Some children get into mischief to an unusual degree, so as to need special control, and in these cases a parent will wish to see that they do not do damage to other persons or their property. So far as legal liability is concerned, however, a parent is not responsible for wrongs (nor, for that

628

matter, breaches of contract) committed by his child either civilly or criminally, unless he has ordered or encouraged the child to commit them.

Permission to Marry

Sooner or later in the course of family life the young people of the home may want to marry. The age at which marriage is legally possible in the U.K. is sixteen, subject to the consent of the parents or guardian if the intending bride or bridegroom is under twenty-one. But a parent's objection may be overridden by the magistrates on application being made by the young people. Naturally, the parent has a right to put before the court his reasons for the objection.

Wills and Intestacy

Recognising his obligation to make provision, so far as he is able, for the dependants he may leave behind him, the homemaker (and, indeed, any other member of the family who owns any property of substance) will want to consider the question of making a will. The first thing to take into account is the position which would arise if he died intestate—that is, without leaving a will. These are, shortly, the people who would then benefit: (1) *A surviving spouse* would take the household furniture and other "personal chattels" and all the rest of the property up to £5,000 if there is issue (i.e. children or grandchildren and so on), or £20,000 otherwise. The matrimonial home may be appropriated as part of this sum, subject to certain conditions. As to any surplus, the spouse is entitled to the income for life of half of it if there is issue; to half the remainder outright if there is no issue but the deceased left one or more of the relatives mentioned in (3) below; and to all the remainder otherwise. (2) *Surviving children* and the issue of any who have died before the intestate take between them on reaching twenty-one the remainder of the property absolutely including the capital of the spouse's life interest on her death. (3) Only if there is no issue do (i) parents, (ii) brothers and sisters, (iii) half-brothers and half-sisters, (iv) grandparents, and uncles and aunts of (v) the whole blood and (vi) half blood take any benefit. Their entitlement is in the order indicated by our num-

The owner is always liable for any damage his dog may do to cattle, horses, sheep, pigs or chickens—even if he did not know the dog was fierce or destructive

bering, and if one class is available those we have numbered afterwards take no benefit. The class that does benefit gets half the remainder of the property after the spouse's £20,000 if there is a surviving spouse, and the whole of the estate otherwise. If neither a spouse nor any of the relatives we have mentioned survives the deceased, the whole estate goes to the Crown. Land and houses no longer descend differently from personal property unless under a prior settlement.

If a person is not content that his property shall be applied in this order of succession, he must make a will. By making a will he may also appoint an executor of his choice to wind up his affairs and to see that his debts are paid and the property passed on to those who become entitled to it. The Public Trustee or one of the big banks or insurance companies will act if desired, though many people prefer to appoint a friend if a knowledgeable one is available and willing to act.

Making a Will

Home-made wills are dangerous, and you are far less likely to put a lot of money into the pockets of lawyers if you have your will drawn by a solicitor in accordance with your instructions than if you try your own prentice hand at it and produce a document which is capable of leading to long wrangles in court. In any case where any complicated provision is desired, such as beneficiaries sharing an item of property or enjoying it in succession, or when a house or land is likely to form part of the estate, it is foolish not to have the will prepared expertly.

In an emergency it may not be possible to get in a solicitor. The real answer is not to leave making a will until the emergency arises. But if you do have to tackle such a task on your own, the great thing to remember is to use simple straightforward language and to avoid any term you do not understand. " I leave all my property [do not say 'money' unless cash only is meant] to my sister Ellen [or as the case may be] and appoint her my executrix" is relatively safe. Gifts of particular sums of money and specific items should be mentioned first (e.g. "I give the sum of £100 to my cousin John Jones and my oak roll-topped desk to Stephen Smith of 488 Smith Lane London") and in this case the final gift should be of "all the remainder of my property" to the desired beneficiary

Execution

A will must be signed by the testator or by someone for him in his presence if he is physically unable to sign for himself. Mental incapacity may mean that a valid will cannot be made at all. The testator's signature must be made or acknowledged by him as such in the presence of two witnesses, both present at the same time. The witnesses then sign as such *in the testator's presence.* An executor may be a witness, but neither a witness nor the husband or wife of a witness may take any benefit under the will.

A will is of no effect until the testator dies and the executor (or some other person appointed by the court if no executor is available or willing) proves it in the court registry. Thus it does not in any way restrict the freedom of the testator to dispose of his property during his lifetime; the will operates on whatever estate he actually leaves behind him.

Family Provision

Generally speaking, a person may by his will leave his property exactly as he desires. It is possible now, however, for the widow or widower, infant or disabled son, or unmarried or disabled daughter of a deceased person, if he or she considers that insufficient provision has been made for him or her by the will or by the law of intestacy, to apply to the court for a more reasonable provision. But if a testator has good reasons for disinheriting someone who might so apply, he may leave a statement of those reasons either in his will or separately, and the court will take them into account.

MISCELLANEOUS

Licences

Among routine duties under the law which will fall periodically on the person running a home there may be mentioned the completion by householders of electoral returns in accordance with notices which the local officials will bring or send to the house; obtaining annual licences for wireless and television, and for dogs. A dog licence is necessary for each dog over six months old.

Animals

A word about domestic animals. Unlike wild animals, which count as inherently dangerous things, animals of a tame species do not automatically subject their owners to liability for any injury they may cause, unless the owner knows of a vicious propensity in the particular animal. This is what is meant by saying that a dog is allowed its first bite. Yet in another respect the case of a dog is exceptional. The owner is always liable for any damage the dog may do to cattle, horses, sheep, pigs or chickens. And irrespective of any knowledge on the part of the owner of any animal of its ferocity or destructiveness, the owner would be responsible if he were negligent in its control, or, as regards animals other than a dog or a cat, for the consequences of its trespassing on someone else's property.

Cleaner's and Laundry's Conditions

Questions sometimes arise in connection with laundry losses. The general rule is that a cleaner or repairer must replace or pay for any article which is lost or damaged while in his custody. But laundrymen and dry cleaners often try to modify this liability by special contract, with the object either of excluding their responsibility altogether or of setting a maximum upon the amount which they can be called upon to pay. Now the special contract may be expressed in conditions printed on the receipt handed out for the goods or on a notice hung in the shop. The wise person always reads these conditions, as, indeed, everyone ought to read any business document which affects him (particularly one that he is asked to sign). However, whether he reads the conditions or not, he will be bound by them if the tradesman has taken reasonable steps to bring them to his notice.

Unclaimed Goods

Do not leave goods uncollected at a repairer's or cleaner's shop for too long. By a modern statute such traders may now put themselves in a position to sell articles that are left with them for more than a year after they are ready. To obtain this facility they must display a notice at their premises when the goods are accepted, and must also give notice by post to the owner when the goods are ready for collection and again when the twelve months are up. At no time can a cleaner or repairer be compelled to deliver out the goods until his agreed or reasonable charges have been paid.

Incidentally, it is worth going to a reputable repairer if things go wrong with an expensive piece of equipment, such as a television set, and to insist on an estimate before any repairs or replacements are carried out. It may be possible to have television tubes reconditioned rather than buying new ones, and the saving is considerable. Old parts are the owner's property unless he has been charged only on an exchange basis.

Domestics

Some households are still fortunate enough to have the assistance of servants. By custom a full-time domestic servant is entitled to a month's notice of termination of her service (except for misconduct) and must give a month's notice if she wants to leave. If a servant, even a "daily," works for more than eight hours a week for any one employer, she counts as an employed person under the National Insurance Acts, and the first employer during the week must see to the payment of the contributions. Moreover, if an employer pays her (or any other employee) more than £3 15s. per week or £15 10s. per month, he is bound also to deduct the appropriate amounts of income tax from her wages and pay them over to the Collector of Taxes. Full details from the local offices of the Ministry of Pensions and National Insurance and the Inspector of Taxes.

When a servant leaves, she may ask for a reference or "character," or a person proposing to engage her may write or telephone for the former employer's opinion. There is no obligation at all to give a reference or to answer any questions, but if answers are given they must be honest and truthful. Needless to say, an employer will not allow himself to be actuated by spite, however badly the servant may have behaved. But if the servant, for instance, is positively known to have been guilty of pilfering, it would be quite wrong to give her a clean character out of any misplaced compassion, and to do so might lead to an action by anyone who was deceived. On the other hand, if an unjustifiably bad picture is painted, the servant may sue for libel or slander. However, so long as the employer is not actuated by malice, he can say anything that is relevant without fear.

Defamation Generally

For an employer giving a reference enjoys a privilege in the law of defamation which can be destroyed only if he acts with an indirect motive or says something not relevant. Other communications, for instance what is said over the garden wall reflecting on the honesty of one of the local shopkeepers, may not be so protected. The only true safeguard against the unpleasantness which is bound to follow carelessness in matters of this kind, whether in the shape of proceedings for slander or libel or of an unneighbourly atmosphere, is never to say or write anything damaging about others unless you feel it to be absolutely your duty to do so, and then not unless you are certain that your information is accurate.

On a well-known residential site near Exeter, run by the Pathfinder Caravan Co., caravanners live amidst idyllic surroundings, with every modern facility near at hand

CARAVANS AS HOMES–OR FOR HOLIDAYS

Streamlined, modern, made of the newest materials, everything is planned for comfort and convenience in a small space

by W. M. WHITEMAN, M.A. (Cantab), Editor of *The Caravan*
and *The Caravan Manual*

NO one can go far these days in the U.K. without seeing a caravan. It is a far cry from the time when a caravan, drawn slowly along by a horse, was a picturesque rarity, the hobby of some eccentric nobleman or enthusiast for the open-air life, or the home of some gypsy.

Now there are perhaps a quarter of a million caravans in the U.K., the home of private caravanning. There is a flourishing industry which exports caravans to more than half Europe and many other countries. The eagerness of the public for caravans outstrips the nervous local authorities trying to adjust old frameworks and patterns to a new phenomenon, which has become for so many people an enrichment of life, and for many thousands of families an actual way of life.

For the trailer caravan, exploiting the mobility which the motor car has brought, has proved equally valuable as a mobile home and as a holiday dwelling, while an exciting story could be written of the part that "special purpose" caravans have come to play in the life of the community— mobile banks, shops, surgeries, dental clinics, cinemas, showrooms, workshops, laboratories, photographic darkrooms and so on.

CARAVANS AS HOMES

A good caravan planned as a home has been recognised by many knowledgeable people outside the industry as a notable piece of functional design. There is no space to waste. Thanks to various proprietary materials, such as glass fibre, kapok blanket, reflecting foil or honey-

Clothing and bedding are kept well aired, and damp is unknown, unless the occupiers manage their heating and ventilation so badly that condensation forms on the walls, as in overheated railway carriages. Condensation may also be found if one lives through the winter in a van meant only for summer holiday use, or one in which insulation has been scamped for cheapness. In a real "living van," to use the trade's term for a caravan meant

Photo: " The Caravan"

How to live in perfect **r u r a l** surroundings—a residential caravan beautifully situated at Fleet, Hants (above). Right, the exterior of the Fairholme Housemaster 32ft. caravan, which is almost as spacious as a modern bungalow.

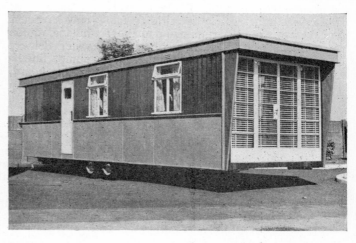

comb plastics, a wall only $1\frac{1}{2}$ in. thick provides as much insulation as a brick and cavity wall in a house. In the average house, ventilation is left mainly to chance and to the traditional British open fire and its chimney. In the smaller space of a caravan, the ventilation has to be planned. In a typical system, fresh air is brought in through the floor, warmed by a solid fuel stove and distributed about the van. Windows and doors fit better than in houses, so that there are fewer draughts, but this means that, to prevent a dangerous situation arising if the occupants try to "raise a fug" by shutting off fresh oxygen, there must be some minimum ventilation not under their control.

When the heating stove has been on for two or three days, the whole structure and air space of the van are thoroughly warm.

as a home, comfort, convenience and health reach high standards.

The Right Size

Such a caravan should, at least, be built to the maximum dimensions permitted for a vehicle to be towed along British roads—22 ft. long and 7 ft. 6 in. wide, including all projecting parts except the drawbar (the steel nose extending from the body and carrying the coupling for the car). It is sometimes made smaller than this, either to get the price down, or because some buyers want something lighter which they can tow about more easily.

Since the war, there has been a great increase in the number of people who live in caravans because they need a kind of home which can move. Commercial travellers, variety artists and, of course, the travelling showmen or fairground folks have used caravans for many years. Now caravan homes are favoured also by executives and workmen employed by the big public works contractors; by inspectors employed by the Ministry of Education, the health services and commercial concerns; by technicians and consultants of many kinds, officials of voluntary organisations, authors and artists, research workers, etc. Service men, especially those in the R.A.F., are extensive users of caravan homes because of the frequency with which they are sent to new posts.

Cheapness or mobility, therefore, may dictate something smaller than the maximum, but even for two people 16–18 ft. should be the minimum. Where mobility and lowest price are not over-riding factors, the oversize vans, running up to about 40 ft. in length and 10 ft. in width, should be considered. "Oversize" means that they cannot be towed as trailers and must be transported on special vehicles.

Apart from the extra space, these models approach much closer to a house. They may have movable house-type furniture in the sitting and bedrooms, and main services may be laid on to the van—electricity, water, waste water outlet, and even flush sanitation.

Another idea is the twin caravan, which comprises two parts, say 17 ft. long, made to be towed separately on the road but to join up on the site and make a kind of movable bungalow 34 ft. long. Then, again, there are caravans with extending ends or sides which give extra accommodation while keeping to the legal limits on the road.

Workable Kitchens

The great majority of living vans have a separate kitchen at one end, usually the rear. It is equipped with a butane gas cooker similar to, but a little smaller than, those used on coal gas in houses; also with a sink and drainer, and a variety of cupboards and lockers, some of them ventilated. Thanks to clever planning, such a caravan kitchen is very workable. It also eliminates the considerable walking to and fro which is all too common in a house kitchen.

More expensive and elaborate kitchens may have a refrigerator, also operated on butane, running hot and cold water, or else water delivered to the sink by a hand pump, fitted china cupboards, a folding ironing board, a cutlery drawer, etc.

The Usual Offices

Alongside the kitchen, in one corner, there is usually a lavatory with a chemical closet, i.e. a special type of pail with seat. The contents are kept inoffensive and safe by means of chemicals and are tipped when necessary into the disposal point provided on the site, or in isolated positions can be buried. Sometimes this little room is made large enough to accommodate also a small bath or a shower bath.

The rest of the van is usually planned as one big lounge, but at night time it can be divided into two rooms by means of folding partitions, sliding doors, or a double leaf door fitted to the main wardrobe. This big room contains the beds for four persons, which also form most of

Photo: "The Caravan"

As comfortable as any luxurious sitting room, the interior of the Pathfinder 32 ft. Tenwide, with its smart contemporary styling and furnishings

CARAVANS AS HOMES—OR FOR HOLIDAYS

A Venetian blind forms a serving hatch-way from kitchen to lounge—the interior of the Beverley Marathon 22 ft. model, with its well-equipped kitchen

Everything for storing clothes, crockery, cooking utensils, etc. is cleverly built in to allow the utmost space in the Normandie Flamingo Mk. 111 22 ft. van

All aboard and away on the open road! Here you see the Paladin Toreador holiday van on the road

Photo: " The Caravan "

the seating, with one, two or three wardrobes, a sideboard, dining table and/or other furniture. Here also is the heating stove, generally for solid fuel, but sometimes burning butane or paraffin. It is built-in with wardrobes near, to benefit from the warm air, and in most vans there is an airing cupboard round the stack pipe.

In the oversize vans, central heating or all-electric heating are possible luxuries, also a house-type bath, washing machine and spin dryer. All the over-size vans and some of the 22-footers have one or more bedrooms with permanent partitions.

Though most caravans have four berths, there are a few with five or six, and it is often possible to fit a fifth into a standard four-berth model by placing an extra bed above another, bunk style.

Beds and Mattresses

Caravan beds are either double or single, and most caravans have one double and two singles, or (where the layout fits more furniture into limited space) two doubles. The double bed may be of the type which has a one-piece mattress which folds away, complete with its bedding, made up ready

635

for the night, into a wall cupboard; or it may make a settee by day; or it may be an arrangement called a dinette, like the seating in a Pullman railway car, with a table hooked on to a wall and a seat for two persons each side. By night this makes up into a double bed, the mattress being in four transverse sections. Mattresses in caravans have to be of good quality, since they usually rest on locker tops and not on spring bedsteads. Spring interior types and foamed rubber or plastic are both found.

Types of Fuel

Living vans are often wired for mains electricity, and radio receivers, television, electric irons, electric shavers, and other equipment are frequently used by caravanners, but only rarely electric cookers and fires, because few sites have wiring stout enough to carry the heavy current these items of equipment consume.

Butane gas, which is the caravanner's main fuel, whether for residential or holiday purposes, is a by-product of refining petrol and comes, compressed into a liquid, in steel cylinders. In this way, a caravan can carry or store enough gas to last about a month. The distributors of the two main proprietary forms of butane—Calor Gas and Bottogas—both have chains of agents covering the country, so that when a cylinder is empty it can be changed for a full cylinder, the caravanner paying merely for the gas contents. The gas is quite safe—in fact, safer than town gas—and the only accidents that occur are due to the users doing foolish things like changing the cylinder without shutting off the valve, looking for a leak with a match, or shutting off all incoming oxygen, as already discussed in connection with ventilation.

Paraffin is sometimes used for supplementary heating in separate bedrooms. A convector heater should be chosen, and placed where it cannot be knocked over, while adequate ventilation is vital.

HOLIDAY CARAVANS

The caravan meant to be moved frequently, whether for holidays or as the home of a man whose business takes him about the country, differs in several ways from the living van. It has to be light enough to be pulled by normal private cars, whereas living vans are often moved to order by specialist towing contractors using heavy vehicles. If it is of medium or small size, it can be towed without anxiety even on crowded roads, and manœuvred more easily on and off the sites. A holiday caravan may have proportionately more window space, to make the most of the sun and because insulation is not so important. It does not need so many cupboards for clothing, etc., and the weight distribution is important, because a caravan in which the designer has not overcome the problem of combining a good practical layout with a good weight distribution gives the caravanner an uncomfortable time on the road; the caravan may not ride steadily above 20 or 25 miles per hour, and may try to take charge going downhill. So here again, skilful design is called for.

Holiday caravans may be of any size from 8 or 9 ft. long up to the maximum 22 ft. The smaller sizes are commonly called touring vans, because they are often bought by sporting caravanners and Caravan Club members, who like to make long tours in Scotland or on the Continent, and want caravans that can be pulled up steep hills, that always ride very steadily, and that do not spoil the pleasure of motoring on long distances. In the best touring vans, great care has been given by the makers to steadiness on the road, and some of them have been pulled at speeds up to 70 miles per hour or more on the great Continental motor roads.

Living in Confined Space

Vans may, of course, be made small for cheapness, because the materials account for the main part of the cost. Where three or four berths are fitted into vans about 12 ft. long, either for cheapness or for light weight, the art of living in this confined space takes a little learning. Getting the family up in the morning is an example. Everyone must be tidy. There must be a place for everything, and it must be kept strictly in its place. But families used to tent camping, or boats, will have no difficulty, and this is all part of the character training which caravan holidays provide. To talk about it to the family may make the holiday sound less enjoyable, but it is true that team spirit, self-discipline and qualities of initiative and resourcefulness

"Photo:" The Caravan"

The special two-berth layout for the manufacturers' managing director in the Willerby 15 ft. Veritas still leaves plenty of space to move around

are taught by caravanning. Husbands and children who try to shirk their share of the household chores at home will cheerfully do them in a caravan. It is part of the fun.

One of the best things about caravan touring is its freedom. No need for advance planning, hotel reservations or worrying over meal times or whether there will be accommodation in the next town. Except that the right maps may not be in the car, it really matters little if the family does not decide until the morning of the start whether to go to Scotland or Cornwall. Another advantage is the way in which a town family can get to know the country folk much more intimately than is possible in hotels, whether in the U.K. or abroad.

A neat little fold-away table for meals—bench seats with storage space underneath—cupboards and shelves everywhere, these are features of the Bluebird Skylark 8 ft. 6 in. four-berth van

Photo: " The Caravan"

The Caravan on the Road

The business of driving a car towing a caravan need cause no anxiety provided too heavy a van has not been chosen. While it is not possible to lay down any rigid formula, a useful rule is that there should not be more than 1¼ cwt. of total caravan weight to 100 c.c. of car engine, or ¾ cwt. of caravan to 1 cwt. of total car weight, whichever is the less. These limits can sometimes be exceeded for mere point-to-point transportation by selected routes, but not for real touring. Incidentally, owing to an ambiguity in the law, the weights marked on caravans are often unhelpful, and it is wise to ask for the "ex works weight" (complete as the caravan comes from the factory) in writing.

A trailer caravan does not cut corners to any serious extent, and two or three hours suffice to put a motorist at his ease, making allowance for the greater weight and width. Learning the art of reversing, which may be needed on a difficult site, or if a turning is missed, takes longer. The secret of hill climbing is to estimate the lowest gear likely to be needed, get into that gear at the start, and go up with the engine turning confidently without racing.

Choosing the Site

One has only to look round the U.K. to see that touring is not by any means the only form, or even the most common form, of the caravan holiday. Caravans in much larger numbers are kept more or less stationary, sometimes on private secluded country sites, where they are used like week-end cottages, or more usually on commercial sites, especially by the sea. Enormous numbers of caravans are to be found along the coasts. There are places where several thousand caravans can be seen from one viewpoint. That sort of mass holiday-making does not appeal to everyone, but it has helped millions of people to take healthy and enjoyable holidays. The secluded private site anywhere near the sea is now very hard indeed to find, even in such distant counties as Cornwall.

A great many of these stationary caravans are not kept simply for the owners' pleasure. They are let as a business, for the most part not by the site owners but by private owners doing some letting as a sideline. In the spring and summer, caravans for hire in every holiday county are advertised in the caravan magazines and in newspapers.

Charges range mostly from about 7 to 14 guineas in July and August, and drop somewhat for the less popular months. For caravans to be towed away by the customer the charges are generally similar, but in that case the customer has to pay his own site fees and insurance, and, of course, must have a suitable attachment, called a towing bracket, fitted to his car. For all popular cars, prefabricated brackets can be bought from specialist firms and fitted by any competent mechanic. For other cars, brackets must be specially designed and made by hand, a task for only the experienced caravan dealers and the garages that sometimes work in collaboration with them.

BUYING A CARAVAN

Many people hire a caravan first to find out if they will like it before buying. Those who are certain they want one of their own —and there is an extraordinary "bug" about caravanning which gets people of all kinds—should be clear in their minds as to what sort of caravan they need. It is a costly mistake to buy a model which proves to be too large or too small, too heavy or insufficiently comfortable. The problem is analysed fully in the popular handbook, *The Caravan Manual*. Alternatively, talk it over with an experienced dealer. To start looking at vans without these preliminaries leads to bewilderment, because the choice is very large.

When choosing a dealer, it is safest to look for good premises, with an accessory shop, a proper service department, etc.— i.e. something more than an undeveloped bomb site or a piece of open field. A caravan should not be bought like a pound of apples from a market stall.

Prices and Points

Prices range from under £200 for the smallest touring vans to more than £1,500 for big luxury vans which in materials and workmanship rival the rich man's yacht. Without going into the luxury class, a fair price to pay for a holiday four-berth about 14 ft. long is between £300 and £400, and for a living van between £500 and £800,

Photo: "The Caravan"

A riverside caravan site at Houghton Bridge, Amberley, Sussex. There are many holiday sites in peaceful rural settings like this, as well as the more popular ones at seaside resorts

"All mod. cons." including bath and Elsan in this pleasant toilet room in a 22 ft. Thomson living van

although there are cheaper vans which are sound.

It is not necessary to understand a lot about the construction of a caravan to buy a good one. Careful inspection of the workmanship and finish, especially of the paint and the body joints, will show whether rain is likely to find its way in after a time. Comparison of different vans will show which makers have put value into the basic structure, and which have concentrated mostly on dressing up the interior to impress the inexperienced buyer. If the tyre size looks small for the body in comparison with other makes, it is probable that some other things have been stinted also.

National Caravan Council Transfer

Most caravans made today carry the National Caravan Council's transfer reading "A" for approved. This means that the Council, which is the principal trade body, has investigated and approved the manufacturer's works, business record, resources, typical products and after-sales service. Approved makers have to conform to certain standards covering the safety, health and welfare of the occupants.

Aluminium is the material normally used for panelling the walls and roof of a modern caravan, but a few makes have sections of the body, for example the roof or bay window ends, moulded in glass fibre reinforced plastic. The technique is more expensive than aluminium construction, but has attractions for makers not in the largest output class.

SITES

Even excluding the casual sites which the touring caravanner finds for himself on farm land—of course, with the permission of the farmer—there is an enormous variety in sites, and an almost equal variety of opinion on what makes a good site.

Commercial sites may be little more than open fields with a water tap and some primitive sanitation. They may be beautiful parks formerly belonging to wealthy families, with woodland, a lake, fishing, shooting and wonderful views as the chief attractions. Or they may be expensively developed businesses with an office, a shop, clubroom with television, etc., flush lavatories, baths or showers, a laundry with electric irons for hire, and other sophisticated amenities.

The average site is not lavishly equipped and many are poor. Some are a disgrace. That is because the enormous growth of caravanning has tended to outrun the supply of sites, and there has not been enough competition. But the best sites are very good, and often in very privileged situations. The right ones are worth looking for, and the caravan and camping clubs and the motoring organisations publish lists for their members.

Residential sites near London and a few other big cities with severe housing problems are hard to find, so are vacant pitches on sites at the most popular seaside resorts. Charges range from about 10s. to £2 a week according to the amenities. On the popular holiday coasts £1 a week is fairly normal, with a big reduction by the season, while residential sites run mostly from 12s. to 25s. Rates and water rate are paid by the site owner, so there are no other charges for the caravanner except his outlay on butane gas and the maintenance and insurance of the caravan.

LAW

Caravan law is quite impossible to explain both briefly and authoritatively, because it contains numerous ambiguities which have not yet been resolved by the courts. Uncertainty is aggravated by the fact that the law does not speak of caravans, but of "trailers" in the context of road law and "movable dwellings" in the context of public health and planning.

Fortunately, the caravanner need not trouble much about it. Most caravans are kept on commercial sites, with which may be included the municipal sites, and the obligations fall on the site operators. The touring caravanner stops either on commercial sites or finds his own casual sites on private land.

In the first case, he has no legal worries; in the second he will find it helpful to join the Caravan Club or the Camping Club, which have obtained certain privileges from Parliament and have a reputation for good behaviour which weighs with landowners.

Only if the caravanner wishes to stop more or less permanently on a private site —i.e. on a farm or other private land which has no other caravans—will he need to concern himself with the two permissions which (in England and Wales) are required —planning permission and a licence.

Application is made for these to the local council. They are free but may not be granted and, if granted, will be subject to conditions: they are required even if the caravanner himself owns the land.

In rural areas where caravans are not numerous enough to present problems, there is rarely any difficulty, but near big towns, especially where the housing shortage has driven many families into caravans, as round London and Birmingham, it has become difficult to obtain the planning permission.

Given planning permission, securing the licence is mainly a matter of satisfying the local council over the sanitation, water, supply, etc.

Within easy range of most big towns— that is, within the sort of distance a man would be willing to travel to work—it is really necessary to look to commercial sites.

When the caravanner buys his caravan, the dealer, if he knows his job, will instruct him on insurance, etc.

The chief point of road law for the caravanner is that he is limited to 30 miles per hour *everywhere* and not only in "30 limit" areas.

SIMPLE CAR MAINTENANCE

*Without being a skilled mechanic, you can give your car the
routine care and attention it needs to keep it running smoothly*

By D. O. SYMES, *Editor*, The Austin Magazine

A MOTOR car is a fairly complex collection of machinery, and no matter what the age or condition of yours, it will need a certain amount of care and attention to keep it running day after day with the maximum of safety, economy and reliability, three factors which contribute so much to the pleasure of motoring under present-day conditions.

If you are able to attend to the simpler items of routine maintenance yourself, you will not only help quite substantially to keep your running costs down, but you will also take a far more personal interest in your vehicle's well-being than if everything is left to the local garage.

It is not necessary to be a skilled mechanic in order to do many of these day-to-day tasks, but it is helpful to know roughly how the car functions.

A second and absolutely essential requi-

site is time, as, to be most effective, your attentions should be frequent and regular—a couple of hours each week is far more beneficial to the car than half a day when the mood takes you.

What makes the Wheels go round

First, then, a very brief and general idea of what makes the wheels go round.

The engine is, of course, the source of power, and this consists basically of a number of cylinders inside which pistons are driven up and down. These pistons are connected to a crankshaft which transforms their vertical movement into a rotary one in much the same way as a cyclist's legs drive the pedals, and so the wheels, of a bicycle.

The pistons are driven by the rapid expansion of gases following the ignition of a mixture of petrol vapour and air in the

A four-cylinder overhead valve Austin engine: 1. Lifting brackets. 2. Oil filler cap. 3. Dynamo. 4. Connection for water temperature gauge. 5. Oil filter. 6. Oil-level dipstick. 7. Oil sump drain plug. 8. Distributor. 9. Cylinder block drain tap. 10. Oil pressure warning light switch. 11. Distributor vacuum pipe

tops of the cylinders, and this mixture is produced in the carburettor.

Petrol is fed to the carburettor from the tank through a system of pipes, usually with the assistance of a pump.

The petrol and air mixture is ignited by an electric spark, the result of a high-voltage charge jumping across the points or electrodes of the sparking plugs, one of which is fitted to each cylinder.

Electricity for this spark is generated by the dynamo at a pressure of either six or twelve volts, which is then increased by the coil to several thousand volts and dis-

tributed to each sparking plug at the appropriate time by the distributor.

A battery stores the surplus electricity generated when the engine is running, and can be used to operate the starter and the lights when the car is parked. The ignition process already described generates considerable heat which has to be dissipated if the engine is to run satisfactorily for any length of time.

Most car engines are water-cooled, which means that water is circulated from a radiator through passages surrounding the cylinder walls and back to the radiator, where the water is in turn cooled by air being drawn through a fine honeycomb of copper pipes by the fan. On most modern cars this water circulation is pump assisted. Lubrication by the engine oil which is pumped from the sump to the moving parts also plays a large part in

Right, the radiator header tank with filler cap removed. The water-level in the radiator should be checked daily

keeping engine temperature down.

The power produced by the engine is transmitted through a gearbox and propeller shaft to one of the axles, usually the rear, and thus to the road wheels.

This description of the "works" is the merest outline and is given only so that some of the maintenance tasks now to be explained will be more easily understood.

Check Water and Oil

Two of the simplest yet most important items, which should be attended to daily and which take only a few moments, are checking the levels of water in the radiator and oil in the sump.

In the case of the radiator, re-move the filler cap in the top, or header tank and ensure that water is up to the base of the filler opening. Rainwater or other soft water should be used, as this minimises "furring" up inside. To keep the system clear of rust and other foreign matter, the water should occasionally be drained off and renewed. A drain tap will be found in the lower radiator tank, and on some cars an additional tap is situated low down in the

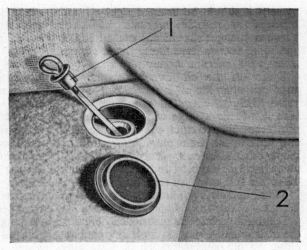

To check the gearbox oil-level, it is necessary to roll back the front carpet to reveal: 1. Gearbox filler plug and dipstick. 2. Rubber cover. The oil should be changed after about 6,000 miles

cylinder block of the engine.

The sump oil-level is checked by means of a dipstick, and to take a reading, this should first be withdrawn and wiped clean. The oil-level should not be allowed to fall below the mark on the dipstick. Use only the grade and brands of oil recommended by the maker of the car and, when topping up, use the same brand as that which is already in the sump. Do not mix oils if this can be avoided, and never use cheap oil, which is very false economy.

The oil in the sump is pumped around to various parts of the engine and back to the sump again, and in this process it collects all kinds of impurities and may become diluted with petrol seeping past the pistons. It is for these

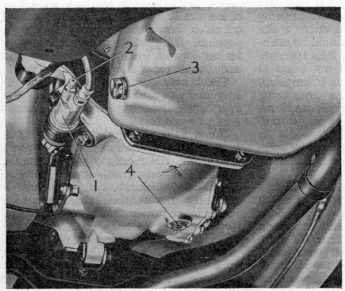

An underneath view of an engine sump and gearbox showing: 1. Clutch operating cylinder. 2. Clutch cylinder bleed nipple. 3. Engine sump drain plug. 4. Gearbox drain plug

reasons it should be drained right off and renewed at regular intervals. Mileage between changes should not exceed 3,000, and some owners have found that a change every 1,000 miles is money well spent.

Drain off the oil immediately after a good run when the oil is warm, as it is then more likely to carry all impurities away with it. Place a large wide container beneath the sump to catch the discharged oil, and remove the drain plug. After allowing plenty of time for every drop of oil to come away, replace the plug and refill with clean oil to the full mark on the dipstick.

Water and oil levels should, of course, be checked when the engine is not running.

It should perhaps be mentioned here that the instrument panels on most cars include either an oil pressure gauge or a warning light, and some include a thermometer which registers water temperature. If, at any time during a run, the oil pressure falls below normal or the water temperature starts soaring, the engine should be stopped at once and the reason investigated.

Maintain Oil Level in the Gearbox

Whilst on the subject of lubrication, it is also very important that correct oil levels are maintained in the gearbox and the driving axle. However, these should not need checking so frequently as the engine and oil changes in these units need only be carried out at intervals of 6,000 miles.

To check the gearbox level you will probably have to remove the floor covering from the front of the car and, unless a dipstick is fitted, the oil level should be maintained up to the base of the filler aperture.

Dealing with the axle is not quite so simple, as it is usually difficult to introduce oil into the filler aperture without using some form of pressure feed. It can, however, be done with an ordinary oil gun and, as with the gearbox, the level should be maintained up to the base of the filler aperture. Once again, use only recommended grades and brands of oil.

Other levels which should be checked every 1,000 miles are the brake and clutch fluid reservoirs on those cars which have hydraulically operated brakes or clutch. Top up only with the recommended fluid.

Before cleaning the oil off your hands and discarding your overalls, a word about chassis lubrication. All the places on a car where one moving surface contacts another need lubrication; for example, steering and brake rod joints, spring shackles and "prop" shaft bearings.

With the aid of a hand oil gun and a lubrication chart for your particular model, this is not a very difficult service to carry out.

A chart showing the various points which need attention will be found in your car handbook. If you have no handbook, you can usually obtain such a chart from the car's maker or from one of the well-known oil companies on request. The various points where lubrication is needed are fitted with oiling nipples on to which the oil gun fits. By applying pressure to the gun, oil or grease is forced into the place where it is needed. Always clean each nipple carefully before applying the gun.

A good deal of space has been devoted to this business of lubrication as it is so vital to the satisfactory functioning of any car.

Electrical maintenance is also important and, although much of this is work for the expert, it is possible, by adopting a regular routine of inspection, to minimise those annoying hold-ups on the road which are so often the result of some minor electrical fault.

If your car is fitted with an ammeter on the instrument panel, make a habit of glancing at it often.

Under normal running conditions the needle should, unless you have a number of electrically operated accessories switched on, either show a charge or be in the neutral position. If it starts to register a discharge for no apparent reason, get someone who understands these things to find out why.

Check over electrical connections regularly to make sure that all terminals are kept tight and that the insulation on cables is in good condition.

Remove the sparking plugs every 3,000 to 4,000 miles and clean the points with a wire brush; then check the gap between the points. This is done with a feeler gauge of the required thickness, and adjustment is made by moving the outside electrode nearer to or farther from the centre one. Never attempt to move the centre electrode, or you will damage the plug.

Incidentally, before disconnecting the leads from their respective plugs prior to removing the latter, make sure that these

Right, a propeller shaft universal joint, one of the places on a car where one moving surface contacts another and lubrication is therefore required.   A indicates the joint lubricating nipple

A rear spring shackle with the arrow A indicating the lubricating nipple. This also should be oiled regularly for good maintenance

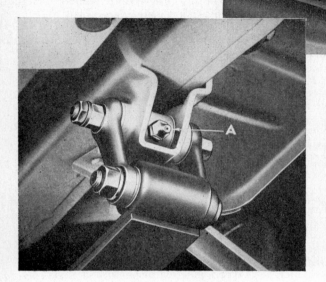

remove stones and other sharp objects from tyre treads frequently, and change wheels from front to rear and near side to off-side every 2,000 miles, so that tyre wear is even all round. The spare should be brought into this cycle.

Bodywork and Upholstery

Finally, a few words about preserving bodywork and upholstery. The best treatment for paintwork, whether it be cellulose or the synthetic enamels which are now used so widely, is

are marked, so that they can be returned to their correct positions.

The battery consists of a series of metal plates immersed in a solution of acid and distilled water, known as the electrolyte. This electrolyte should just cover the plates and, as it evaporates, especially in hot weather, it has to be topped up frequently and regularly with distilled water. It is now possible to obtain patent battery fillers which simplify this little job, but in any case don't splash the electrolyte about and do not try to ascertain its level with the aid of a naked flame.

Take Care of the Tyres

Tyres are now an expensive item, so that it is well worth while to take some trouble to prolong their lives.

There are three simple attentions which help a lot in this direction: always maintain correct pressures—this will also increase the safety and comfort of your motoring;

frequent washing and leathering. This will save much use of patent cleaners and polishers, which are only necessary when the car's glossy finish becomes dulled by in-grained dirt.

Chromium plating, too, should be washed and dried off or cleaned with a petrol-moistened cloth as often as possible and not be allowed to remain stained or wet for any length of time if this can possibly be avoided.

Leather or leather cloth upholstery should be cleaned with a weak detergent solution and protected with a good leather polish. Fabric upholstery and carpets benefit from frequent brushing and vacuum cleaning.

The foregoing suggestions are not, of course, intended to replace an occasional check-over by a skilled mechanic but, if carried out regularly and conscientiously, they will save many minor repair bills.

FOR SAFE CYCLING TAKE GOOD CARE OF YOUR MACHINE

A rusty, ill-adjusted bicycle is no fun, but a potential
danger to yourself and everybody else on the roads

CYCLING can be one of the safest, healthiest and most pleasurable forms of exercise; and it is certainly one of the most economic forms of transport. But if you and your children are to get the best out of cycling, you must look after the efficiency of your bicycle.

Not even the most careless individual would dream of dragging a watch on a piece of string down the gutter, yet many people have no regard for the care of a bicycle—in its way just as delicate a piece of mechanism.

A rusty, ill-adjusted machine will not only spoil the fun of cycling but will cause endless trouble and may be a potential source of road danger to others.

Making a Cycle Road-worthy

What is necessary to keep your machine in first-class order? Your dealer from whom you buy your bicycle will see that it is correctly adjusted and fit for the road. He will adjust the saddle and handlebars to give the most comfortable riding position. This is most important; to be safe on a cycle you must be comfortable. A sound rule is that you should just be able to touch the ground with your toes whilst seated in the saddle. Then the following nuts and bolts are tightened:

Expander bolt;
Head nuts;
Seat pillar nut;
Saddle nuts;
Mudguard stay bolt and nuts;
Front and rear axle nuts;
Cotter pin nuts.

The dealer then sets brakes and tightens all brake nuts, sets the front and rear wheels correctly and adjusts the chain. He pumps up the tyres, tightens the valve tube nuts and lightly lubricates all bearings and moving parts.

Regular Maintenance

Now that your bicycle is road-worthy, how should you keep it in condition? Here are some tips given by a man who should know all about cycling, Reg Harris, the Raleigh professional rider and four times world professional sprint champion. Here is his five-point maintenance plan:

(1) Once a fortnight lightly lubricate the bearings. Don't *bathe* them in oil, which is wasteful and unnecessary and in any case runs out of the bearings and accumulates dust.

(2) Once a fortnight check your brakes.

(3) Give the bicycle a thorough clean with a damp rag; this prevents dust and mud from scratching the enamel. Then go over it again with a dry rag. Enamel may be treated with a wax-type polish applied with a soft rag. It is only necessary to apply wax about every three months. Chromium can be wiped over with a soft rag with just a trace of oil. It needs no other treatment, and metal polishes, etc., should be avoided.

(4) Regarding saddles, if the top is leather, periodic treatment with a good preservative is recommended, as this keeps the leather in first-class pliable condition. Saddles with a Rexine type of top need only be cleaned with warm water and soap.

(5) Tyres need very special attention and frequently their proper inflation is neglected. Bicycles are too often ridden with tyres under-inflated. This seriously accelerates tyre-wear in so far as the walls may be split long before the tread is finished. In under-inflated condition, tyres pick up nails, tacks, sharp stones, etc., which cause punctures.

Under-inflated tyres also affect the steering and general control of the bicycle, and can make hard work of what should normally be a pleasure.

Inner tubes have considerable life but they, too, must have proper attention by careful use of tyre-levers when needed.

Tubes can be ruined through too much

lubrication of the hub, when oil runs down the spokes by the nipple and washers on to the rim tape and tube. The action of oil on rubber is to destroy its nature.

Care of Tyres

To sum up, these are the rules to be observed to get correct and safe service from tyres:

(1) Inflate reasonably hard, minimum being to allow for not more than 25 per cent. cover deflection.

(2) Avoid fierce braking and deliberate skidding.

(3) Remove flints which may become embedded in the cover.

(4) When replacing tubes, see that they are correctly fitted.

Another important point which has direct bearing on tyre-wear is to avoid over-loading the bicycle. Remember it is not only dangerous, but also illegal, to carry another person on a bicycle unless it is fitted with proper fixings for this purpose. As tyres are inflated normally to carry the weight of one person only, this can be a cause of

The joy of the open road and the countryside is yours for the asking in your leisure hours with a cycle

serious tyre damage. Fuller advice on how to keep your bicycle in good repair will be found in the Raleigh handbook on maintenance, a 72-page publication given free to every purchaser of a Raleigh bicycle. Raleigh also have an organisation for road safety amongst youngsters owning tricyles, and a school of cycling to teach young cyclists everything there is to be known about efficient and safe riding.

Service Facilities

Should any unusual conditions develop with your bicycle, such as a squeak in the bearings which oiling will not cure, it is best to consult the dealer from whom the bicycle was bought. He has experience and service facilities to enable him to correct the trouble quickly.

If these points are carefully watched, your bicycle should give you years of satisfactory, trouble-free running and will pay for itself in pleasure and cheapness of transport many times over.

Many children develop a taste for riding with their first baby tricycle. This one has a collapsible safety handle fitted into the back shaft—ideal for controlling young children when taking them out on busy roads

MAKING THE BEST OF YOUR LOOKS

A simple course of home beauty treatment
suitable for women of all ages and skin types

BASIC BEAUTY ROUTINE

HERE is a basic beauty routine for good skin care. We used Richard Hudnut Cleansing Cream, Skin Freshener, Bloom cream rouge and two shades of Flatter-glo fluid foundation and powder. One should be a little darker, the other a shade lighter than your skin tone. Use the light foundation and powder by day, the dark at night. And remember, never mix up different makes of cosmetics, or you won't get the best out of any of them. Choose one range that suits your skin and stick to it.

a. Once a day, cleanse your face thoroughly with cleansing cream. Tie your hair out of the way in a headband, then smooth on the cream generously all over your face and neck, with an upward and outward motion. Never encourage downward lines, which make the face droop, add years and are the worst enemies of good looks.

b. Now, having massaged your cheeks, work upward and outward along both jaw lines, up from your brows to your hairline (eliminating frown lines on the way) and up your neck under the chin. Remove the cleansing cream with face tissues, using the same movements, then apply Skin Freshener in the same way.

c. Now (left) for special cleansing, say once a month. For this you need a face pack (there are many good paste ones on the market). Spread it all over your face and neck, except round eyes and lips, leave it on for about 15 minutes, till it sets like a mask and feels tight and stiff. Wash completely off with cold water.

The Neck

a. It will keep its youthful contours and the skin will not get crêpey, if you massage your neck regularly with both hands, working from the chest up to the chin with firm, gentle motions.

b. To brace the back of the neck, place fingers of both hands at centre of hairline. Glide down, pressing firmly at the base of the neck, swing out to shoulder muscles and up on each side of the neck, repeating the whole circular movement three times.

a

b

The Face

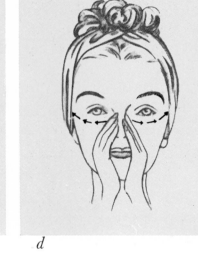

c. Place tips of fingers of both hands on the chin, circle round the mouth in upward direction, lift fingers when they are under nostrils and return them to the chin to start the whole movement again.

d. Close your hands gently over your face, fingers on sides of nose, and then very gently swing upward and outward, smoothing right along the tops of your cheek bones with the tips of the fingers.

c

d

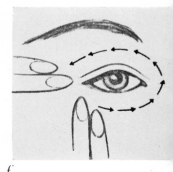

f

The Nose and Forehead

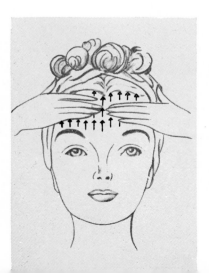

d. While the fingers are over the nose, work your cream well into the sides of both nostrils, particularly the crease where dust tends to accumulate and black-heads quite often form.

e. Now smooth gently but firmly upwards from eyebrows to hairline across the forehead to smooth and iron out creases.

The Eyes

f. Hold the skin on the temple with two fingers, then with the two middle fingers of the other hand start at the outer corner of the eye and work in under the eyes towards the nose, then right round, up and over the lid, very gently without exerting pressure.

e

POWDER MAGIC

*Use two shades—
one dark, one light*

■ Is yours the square face?

If so, make the width of those jaws less obvious by applying your darker shade of powder diagonally from each cheekbone to the point of the chin. Darker powder has the effect of diminishing, the lighter shade of emphasising.

● Is yours the round face?

Then you must always add an extra application of the darker powder right down the outside of the cheeks, so as to tone down and diminish their fullness. Be sure to blend the two powder shades in carefully.

▼ Is your face triangular this way?

Use the lighter powder on your jaws on each side of the chin, to broaden your jawline and help balance the width above. Now a touch of the darker shade to the chin to make it look less pointed and to round out the angular jawline.

▌ Is yours the oblong face?

This being your problem, powder your face normally all over, then add an extra application of a darker shade on the whole of the lower part of face and chin, to minimise any long, lantern-jawed look.

▲ Is your face triangular?

You must powder, not merely the jawline, but also the lower part of the cheeks with darker powder, in order to make less obvious that full-blown look in the cheeks.

ROUGE FOR TRICKS

It will change the shape of your features

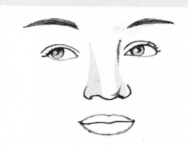

A nose that is too long can be discreetly foreshortened with the tiniest dot of cream rouge blended underneath the tip, like this. Then powder right over so that rouge disappears from view completely.

Nostrils that are too wide and full will cease to be so noticeable if you blend the merest scrap of cream rouge on either side, working it carefully out on to the lobes—then softly powdering out of sight.

A double chin is best overcome by attention to posture. Meanwhile, disguise it with a wee spot of rouge blended under the chin like this, from below one ear behind the jawline, then right round to the other ear.

Eyelids too deeply sunk? Try the tiniest scrap of cream rouge—just enough to give a warm glow, not a tint—blended in just below the eyebrows. It will help very deep-set eyes to shine more brightly.

Use cream rouge to play up good features, distract attention from bad ones. Always apply it before powdering. Here's how:

1. Touch your finger tip in your cream rouge and then, as lightly as a feather, touch the upper and outer part of your cheek four times.

2. Now blend it over the cheekbone into the shadow of the cheek and back towards the hair-line. Be sure to apply the rouge very sparingly and to fade it gently into the skin, avoiding hard lines.

Eyebrow Tips.

It is neither smart nor beautiful to pluck your brows to a fine line and pencil them in. They should be fairly thick and well-defined, natural-looking but controlled

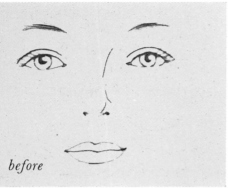

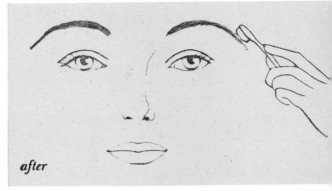

before

after

DO your eyebrows grow fairly well half-way and then peter out into nothing but fair fuzz? If so, do not attempt to pencil on top of the existing eyebrows, just extending the line out on to the skin; the result will be ugly and most unnatural.

INSTEAD, tint those tiny hairs in the sparse fuzz very carefully with mascara. It's amazing what a number of minute hairs you will find when you look for them in a bright light; they only fail to show because they are fair. In the total absence of any fuzz, use well-pointed eyebrow pencil and draw in little feathery strokes.

Hair to Suit the Face

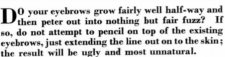

 With an oblong face, you should avoid long, straight hair styles. Shorten your whole face with soft curls over the forehead or widen it with waves brushed out softly at the temples and away from the cheekbones. The hair should only just cover the ear lobes.

If yours is a square face, the last thing for you is a boxy hair style. Instead, counteract the squareness by drawing your hair back and up off the forehead, wearing it smooth and close to the head at the sides, high on top, with soft, fairly long curls at the neck.

The fortunate few who are the lucky possessors of perfect oval faces should never spoil that classic shape with fussy curls. Accentuate good contours with a smooth style, parted in the centre, softly rolled under at the ends and worn fairly long on to the nape of the neck.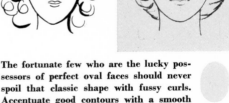

Round-faced girls should never, never wear fat ringlets. The style for you is dressed high to give added length to your face, with soft waves over forehead and temples. Wear your hair fairly long and not too curly, to add length and reduce the look of width.

MADE FROM MIRROR GLASS

Here are some charming and highly original ornaments you can make for your own home or as gifts for someone else's, designed by ZITA DUNDAS

MANY attractive ornaments can be made of flexible mirror, which is sold in sheets 18 in. by 24 in., each individual piece being ½ in. by 2 in. The mirror is backed with a flannel-like fabric and should be cut into the required measurements by drawing a razor blade down the joints. To cut a piece 1 in. by ½ in., simply scratch the surface with a glass-cutter and snap the glass—cutting through the fabric afterwards.

When glueing the mirror to the foundation, the fabric is bound to take up a fraction of space, so allow for this.

Wood, smaller in size than required, may be built up with layers of cardboard glued together. This was done in the lamp stem.

Place-mats

Materials: *One piece of hardboard 10 in. by 9 in. for the larger mat, one 4 in. square for the glass mat.*

2 areas of mirror 10 in. by 9 in. and 4 in. by 4 in.

Glue

To make the mats, simply stick the areas of mirror on to the board with strong glue or adhesive, leaving plenty of time to dry completely and stick firmly. Any rough edges should be filed or sandpapered smooth. Additional mats of other sizes may be added to complete a set as desired.

The light from your lamps or candles will be reflected brilliantly in these pretty table mats with matching candlesticks made from mirror glass

Candle-holder

Materials: *15 in. of 2 in. by 2 in. by ½ in. battening*
Two 2-in. squares of felt.
4 corrugated nails
Flexible mirror

The foundations of the candle-holder shown with place-mats (above) are built up from 2 in. by ½ in. battening (see diagrams left), the pieces being glued together. The corrugated nails should be hammered home before the 1-in by ½ in. pieces are stuck in place.

Cover the sides and top surfaces with mirror and stick a square of felt on the base so that it will not scratch the table. Four of these pretty, squat little candle-holders look charming as a centre piece or at the four corners of a dinner-table.

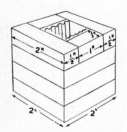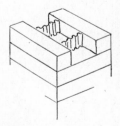

Showing how the foundations of the candle-holder are built up from 2 in. by ½ in. battening, the pieces being glued together. Hammer home corrugated nails before sticking

The mirror glass table lamp has a smart contemporary shade covered with cellulose tape. To complete the set, make the cigarette box too

Cellulose Tape Lampshade

Materials: 1 *drum- or semi-drum-shaped frame, 10 in. deep*
2 *sheets of coloured tissue paper—that sold for model aeroplanes is best*
1 *reel of ½-in. cellulose tape*
Transparent cellulose glue

Stick the tissue paper to the top and base rings of the frame and to the half-way struts only—not to the intervening struts. Trim away surplus paper.

Rotate the reel of cellulose tape on a piece of wood or finger, and draw off about 20 yd. at a time. Cut tape and rewind on to a wad of folded paper—for easier handling. Stick one end of the tape to the top rim of the shade and start to bind, from top to bottom, overlapping each piece by half. When joining tape and finishing off, simply glue ends together with transparent adhesive.

Table Lamp

Materials: 1 *piece of wood for stem 10 in. by 1½ in. by 1½ in.*
1 *piece of wood for base 5½ in. by 5½ in. by 1 in.*
4 *yd. of flex*
4 *rubber studs*
2 *pieces of white felt 1½ in. square*
1 *piece of white felt 5½ in. square*
2 *screws 2 in. long*
Glue and normal electric fixtures

To make the lamp (shown left), gouge a trough the depth of the flex being used down one side of the stem. If it is necessary to build up the girth to fit the glass, stick on layers of cardboard (diagram 1). Put the flex in position, knotting it at the top, and stick the mirror round the stem.

Next, drill three holes in the base, two for the screws, one for the flex (diagram 2); also cut corresponding holes in one of the squares of felt. Then cover the base with mirror and screw it to the stem, firmly but not too tightly, with the piece of felt between to act as a cushion (diagram 1). Run the flex through the base before screwing,

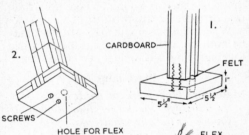

and through a corresponding hole in the 5½ in. square piece of felt. Stick the felt to the base and carefully knock a rubber stud into each corner. Now cut a hole in the centre of the other small felt square, lead the top of the flex through it, and stick it to the top of the stem. Screw on rose and lamp-holder, etc., to complete (diagram 3).

Cigarette Box

Materials: 1 *piece of 3-ply wood 6 in. by 4 in. for top*
1 *piece of 3-ply wood 6 in. by 4 in., less thickness of sides, for base; approx. 20 in. by 1 in. by ¼ in. for sides of box; approx. 20 in. by ¼ in. by ¼ in. for sides of top*
2½-*in. hinges*
Pin nails
Glue
1 *piece of felt 6 in. by 4 in.*

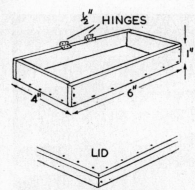

½" HINGES

4" 6" 1"

LID

Detail of box
lining

View from back,
showing hinge
setting

Detail of lid

Completed cedar
lining

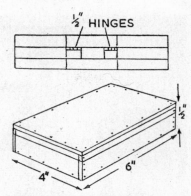

½" HINGES

½"

4" 6"

Cedar-wood veneer for lining
2 pieces of narrow red ribbon 3½ in.
long
Flexible mirror

The thickness of the wood used for the cigarette box shown in the photograph with the lamp is immaterial, provided the outside measurements of the box are correct.

Follow the diagrams for the construction of the box. The hinges are countersunk into the lower part only. All joins should be glued first, then nailed. Line the box throughout with cedar-wood veneer. This may be bought quite cheaply from wood or hobby shops.

To finish, nail piece of ribbon to lid and box to prevent the lid from falling back. Stick piece of felt to base.

☆ ☆

MAKE YOUR FLOWERS LOOK A REAL PICTURE

*Display them, not in an ordinary
container, but a frame*

In nearly every home there is an old picture frame
just waiting for a new use—get it out, treat it to a
fresh coat of paint and a simple construction job and
just wait for the admiring comments

Materials required:
1 *picture frame*
Battening, 2¼ *in.*
wide, ¼ *in. thick*
Glue
Small pin nails
Paint

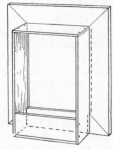

*Showing recess for
water container*

FLOWER-HOLDER framework is fitted into recess made for glass, picture and backing. Battening is fixed at right angles behind inside edge of frame, with sides extending to base of entire frame. Battening fixed across extension—top level with bottom of aperture—forms a well to hold water-container. Construction is as shown in diagram, all joints being glued and nailed. Complete framework is then glued and nailed into recess, and painted if desired.

Start with a Room Divider Bookshelf unit, mahogany veneered, create your own design and build it up gradually. You do not even need a screwdriver to assemble these strong, well-made Brianco shelves

MAKE YOUR OWN FURNITURE

You have simply to fit together the factory-made parts—the only tools needed are a hammer and screwdriver

"DO It Yourself" has become a familiar phrase. Few of us now are unable to "do something" ourselves. Consequently home-making is much more exciting. The large number of reasonably skilled amateur painters, decorators, carpenters, plumbers, and electricians—at least one in most families—are out to welcome any new, practical, money-saving scheme.

"Make-It-Yourself" furniture therefore makes an instant appeal to the imagination and common sense of most homemakers.

How it is Made

There are literally no snags. The reading of descriptive pamphlets on this type of furniture, one must agree, makes it sound too simple to be true. For once, such simplicity *is* the truth. The most you will need are a hammer and a screwdriver; the least, a screwdriver.

All the arduous, messy, and highly skilled work is already done. In modern factories, precision machines cut out and prepare the parts. Joints, tongues, grooves,

and screwholes are all there. Your work is to fit one part into another (and they do, with the smoothness of silk), apply glue (when necessary) and run home the screws.

Apart from all the necessary parts to make the chosen piece, every accessory is included. Glue and sandpaper, the right number and size of screws, door catches, hinges, curtain rails are some examples of accessories; whatever is needed to complete the job is there, and nothing beyond a hammer or screwdriver has to be provided.

Assembly is, in many cases, simply a matter of attaching legs to tables with the screws included, and applying what finish you wish if this is necessary. Where larger pieces are concerned, the parts are fitted together first, but this is no jig-saw puzzle and, in all cases, clear instruction leaflets are enclosed.

Finishes

You can choose from solid oak, walnut, mahogany and beech. Veneers include sycamore and ebony as well as mahogany,

Assembling a Furni-Kit needlework cabinet made of solid oak is child's play for anyone—the only tools you need are a hammer and a screwdriver

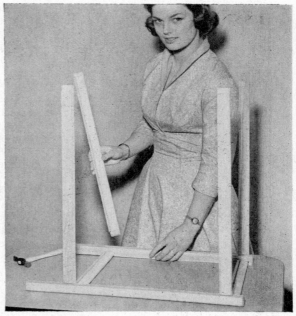

oak and walnut. Where it is considered more suitable, mainly for bathroom and kitchen furniture, strong laminated wood is used, and some table tops are available in "Warerite." A recent addition is melawis, an Indo-Malayan timber with the look and durability of oak, but less expensive.

Legs available for use with tables and chairs come in solid wood or metal. The latter, when single, are rubber-footed; the double kind, known as the Hairpin type, looks just like its name, and there is the Tri-pin leg. All legs are splayed to 12 degrees, and there are lengths and types to suit all weights and sizes of table or chair tops.

Some manufacturers supply woods in their natural colours, ready for staining or painting, or simply polishing if the natural colour is preferred. In other cases the wood is already finished. "Warerite" tops are usually in red, green, blue or bird's-eye maple. Steel legs can be had in colours, stove enamelled in black, white, cream or red.

Several manufacturers offer finishing kits suitable for different woods. These are useful and reasonable, comprising exclusively prepared stain and polish, a specially fine rubbing-down paper and instructions.

What you can Make

The choice is wide, from a bathroom stool to a wardrobe or kitchen cabinet. Everyone's choice of table can be met from among the many designs offered. In addition, most hardware and turnery stores now supply tapering legs with brass ends in several lengths, together with the necessary fitments for screwing on to chair or table.

Furni - Kit furniture, awarded the Good Housekeeping Institute Seal, includes a roomy, well-planned kitchen cabinet in

Make the Brianco dining table (left) with metal or wooden legs the shape and length required—then add chairs to match—and all your own work

This immensely strong yet easily put together gramophone record cabinet by Furni-Kit is in striped walnut. Both sections have sliding doors, the top ones glazed. The entire range is available either with plinths or legs, in oak, walnut or mahogany

a simple, good design. Their furniture covers a very wide range and includes a 9-piece kitchen unit with "Formica" tops. The parts just click together and, when assembled, your dream kitchen comes true. You can buy one unit at a time or the complete set.

The increasingly popular room divider is available in the Brianco range, and this is merely a matter of screwing top caps on to the shelf supports. Tables of every description, chairs, a TV table, record cabinet, shelf brackets and a delightful plant-holder are other items in this range. Steel or wooden legs are supplied, according to the type of table top chosen.

Another manufacturer going in for this type of furniture in a big way is Homeworthy—"You buy it in a carton factory fresh." The range includes a most attractive and reasonably priced round coffee table with a laminated "Elegon" top in red, blue, yellow, white, bird's-eye maple, or figured walnut wood grain. This top needs cleaning only with a damp cloth and resists heat, scratches and staining.

A dual purpose stool by Homeworthy has a tapestry-covered, foam-filled

Plank tables—long and low with simple lines—are a popular feature of contemporary furnishing. This one by Brianco can be had in mahogany, light oak, sycamore or ebony for home assembly

cushion and is perfect for dressing-table, piano or as an occasional seat when entertaining guests. Take away the cushion and it is a table suitable for any purpose and especially handy as a TV table.

Others of the wide Homeworthy range are an original telephone table and a smartly-designed record cabinet finished in walnut, mahogany or oak, holding approximately 250 records. The interior is lined with mahogany and includes a small drawer.

Homeworthy also do a cocktail cabinet with elegant ebonised legs. It is lined with stainless bird's-eye maple "Elegon," is equipped with cocktail accessories and has ample space for bottles and glasses. A luxury item for the home at a very modest price.

Much of the design of this furniture is tip-top contemporary, some is simpler and more sedate, but all

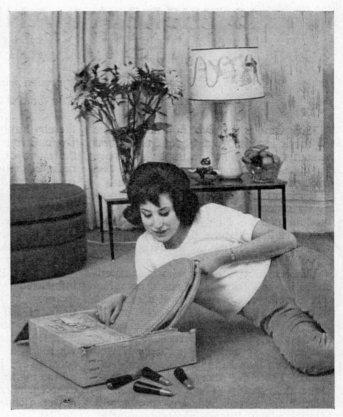

The Puffin, a novel inflatable pouffe, is assembled with the minimum of effort to accommodate that unexpected guest. It is made of strong, washable vinyl in an embossed pattern and in four different colours

This Homeworthy plant stand is available in walnut, mahogany and light or medium oak. It is 22″ high and measures 10″ × 31″

is good and adaptable. Some of the firms arrange hire-purchase terms and most welcome export orders. This scheme is money-saving, for the final assembly is done at home, and not in the factory by paid staff.

How to choose your Furniture

All manufacturing firms supply catalogues on request. As new ones are constantly making their appearance, the best plan is to watch advertisements in the daily press and the magazines with a home-making bias, or those catering for handicrafts, and to send for catalogues.

IS THERE A PIANIST IN
THE FAMILY?

*If so, skill and experience are needed when you choose
an instrument, which must also be looked after with care*

THE piano is the pivot in a home where music is regarded as a social or cultural amenity. It is therefore important, when buying an instrument, to choose one that will benefit the family as a whole.

It requires over 10,000 parts and about eighty different pairs of hands to make a modern piano. This illustrates the complexity of the instrument. The products of various manufacturers differ in appearance as well as sound.

The prospective buyer who is inexperienced in the intricacies of piano manufacture should seek the advice of a musician who is familiar with the different makes and types of piano. A reputable dealer would also provide expert advice. The service of a specialist is particularly welcome when negotiating for a second-hand piano. There are many available of first-rate craftsmanship. There are others, however, with a polished and presentable exterior which disguise a shoddy interior. An ornate exterior usually betrays age, but age in itself should not be a barrier, provided the mechanics are sound.

Here are some points that a buyer might observe when considering a piano, new or second-hand. He should ensure that the keys are properly aligned and that they respond quickly to the touch. A well-made piano will have a good repetition action; when a key is struck several times in rapid succession, the hammer will react immediately. Each note of the key-board should be tested by a rapid chromatic scale. This will reveal any tendency to unevenness in touch. The high treble notes should be brilliant, but not harsh. The lower notes should be sonorous, but not muffled. Brittle and dull sounds are common faults in inferior pianos.

A cast-iron frame is of the utmost importance, for it enables the strings to be drawn to a maximum tension. It is an acknowledged fact that the more highly tensed the strings, the more harmonics they give out,

thereby improving the quality of the tone. By removing the lower panel, the inside of the piano can be examined. It is wise to make this request to confirm that the frame is of iron and not of wood. It is necessary to emphasise the need for such precautions. Although the wooden frame has been superseded by the iron frame, many wooden frames are still to be found in older pianos, and sometimes they are camouflaged by modern exteriors.

The size of the piano will naturally be influenced by space, and modern manufacturers have taken the restricted conditions of flat-dwellers into consideration when designing their streamlined instruments. Miniature pianos, which enjoyed a vogue in the 1920s, are still attracting patrons. They have the advantage of taking up the minimum of space. But one cannot expect a miniature instrument to have the power, richness of tone and beauty of inflexion of a larger instrument of good manufacture. It is therefore wise to remember these limitations if the piano is intended to contribute greatly to home music-making.

Grand or Upright?

What of the grand piano? Both size and cost put the grand piano out of reach of most households. The baby grand, however, does not require so much space and it adds grace to the drawing room. But, when considering the sound produced, it has no advantage over the good upright. There is little difference in construction. The iron frame over which the strings are stretched (forming the base of the grand) is placed vertically in the upright. It will be observed on examination that the baby grand has 3 ft. 3–4 in. of string and the upright 4 ft. (with a correspondingly larger sound-board). As the larger sound-board and longer strings produce a better tone, it is evident that a good upright is preferable to a baby grand.

To sum up: An upright piano, with iron frame, an underdamper action (which wears better and ensures good damping and silencing of strings) and overstrung (the strings fitted diagonally instead of from top to bottom increases the length and better tone results), is a good investment when obtained from a reliable source.

It is a fallacy to assume that anything is "good enough for a beginner." On the contrary, if beginners are to derive the greatest benefit from their studies, they require an instrument in the best condition at the outset of their training. It is a handicap if, in the initial stages, they are confronted with sticky notes, prolonged vibrations, mysterious rattles and creaky pedals. The beginner will either tend to ignore these noisy intrusions (and thereby lose musical sensitivity) or become restless and discouraged. These reactions are not conducive to successful development. It is better to wait a year or two until the cost of a better piano is available than compromise with an instrument which has serious defects.

With care, a good piano will last upwards of a hundred years. But to obtain a long life from the instrument, regular tuning and maintenance are necessary. Tuning should be carried out from three to four times a year by an expert tuner, preferably one holding the certificate of the Institute of Musical Instrument Technology. Regular tuning improves the tone and should be carried out even if the piano is not in constant use. If tuning is neglected, the strings slacken and the tone suffers. To restore the pitch, tunings at frequent intervals would be necessary.

Position in the Room

Of utmost importance in ensuring a long life for a piano is the position that it occupies in a room. Excessive heat and cold,

A small upright piano takes up little space, but it should be a good one, even for a beginner to practise on

dryness and dampness, can all have an injurious effect on the instrument. Therefore, a piano should not be placed near a damp wall, a fire or radiator. Heat affects the tension of the strings and makes the pitch unreliable. Generally, an inside wall is the best position, and a certain amount of space should be left at the back of the piano so that air can circulate. Exposure to sunlight should also be avoided, as the polish will suffer, especially if the casework is rosewood. If there is no alternative to a sunny position, the piano should be covered when the sun's rays are striking directly on it, with a rug or some other thick material.

The internal works of the piano should be cleaned only by an expert. Unskilful adjustments can easily disturb the delicate mechanism and the ensuing repairs may prove costly. The action, in particular, should not be removed by a novice.

The frequency with which a piano should be cleaned depends on several factors. If the room in which it stands is occupied a great deal, or if the house is in an industrial area, a certain amount of grit will penetrate the instrument. In such cases a thorough cleaning by an expert, once a year, is advisable.

Superficial dust can be removed by the

cautious use of a vacuum cleaner. When releasing the panel to do this, remember not to tamper with the mechanism.

The case work can be cleaned with a dry duster or chamois leather. Furniture polish should not be used on modern instruments. The keys can be wiped clean with a damp cloth, but care must be taken not to let moisture get between the keys. The use of warm milk for this purpose is quite superfluous.

Discoloured Keys

The only remedy for discoloured keys is to have them scraped and polished. Although celluloid and plastics are used on many modern pianos, ivory is still in demand and will be found on most second-hand instruments. The yellow discoloration to which ivory is subject is merely the substance reverting to its natural colour. Keeping the lid of the piano open and exposed to the light helps to retain the bleach. There is another advantage in having an open lid; air is thereby allowed to circulate through to the action and so counteract the effect of heat and damp and reduce the tendency of the keys to stick.

Moths are a continual menace, and once they have laid their eggs inside, complete re-felting may be entailed. To avoid this expensive repair, place a small amount of Paradichlorbenzine crystals in two bags (similar to those used for lavender). They should be tacked at each side of the piano away from the movement of the hammers. The crystals evaporate rapidly and will need frequent renewal.

If vases of flowers are placed on the piano for decorative purposes, they should be removed during a performance. As the keys are struck, any object on the piano will cause rattling and will be an impediment to the player. Not infrequently when a party is being held, the piano becomes a repository for glasses containing spirits, cups of hot beverages, plates of sandwiches or pastries. Stains can disfigure the surface because of this, and if a drop of spirit contacts the strings—especially the bass strings, which are usually overspun or wound with fine copper—the metal will corrode. It is therefore a wise precaution to cover the piano with a cloth when offering refreshments.

Piano stools should be firm. A solid dining-room chair is a good substitute if the traditional adjustable piano stool is not available. The use of cushions (preferably covered with a woven or woollen fabric) could help to raise young students to the required level. A chair that is not well balanced is distracting to the player. As the study of music requires aural, visual, mental and physical co-ordination, every mechanical deficiency becomes a handicap to efficient work.

Music cabinets are necessary as well as decorative. Music that is left in a pile causes loss of time and frayed pages. It is wise to instil into the young student the advantages of classifying music. As the repertoire grows, it is an asset to be able to find any volume easily. Shelves that are shallow are ideal for this purpose. A filing cabinet with a curtain matching cushions or window curtains is effective.

For a young child who cannot reach the pedal with comfort, a thick wooden board placed beneath the pedal will be of assistance.

If several members of the family are musical, the violin, 'cello, recorder, etc., increase the attraction of music-making in ensemble. These instruments have the advantage of being inexpensive and mobile. They can be practised in the bedroom and will thereby avoid competition for the use of the piano.

The Music Teachers' Association, The Incorporated Society of Musicians and The Society of Women Musicians are organisations which would recommend qualified teachers.

Silencing the Piano

Fear of the complaints of neighbours is familiar to all students needing to practise. Some, indeed, are so intimidated that they hesitate to pursue their hobby. The *celeste* (or piano mute) is an innovation which comes as a relief to flat-dwellers, or those who do not want to disturb invalids and children. It consists of a strip of felt fastened to a rail which fits inside the piano just above the hammers. By manipulating a lever on one side, the felt is brought into position between the hammers and the strings, thus effectively damping the sound. This device is fitted into the piano by Larg & Sons, High Holborn, London.

CONTRAST IN TABLES

Traditional damask cloth or modern place mats?

The beautiful traditional tablecloth, left, in Acanthus scroll patterned Irish linen damask, makes a perfect setting for fine china, gleaming silver and sparkling glass

Colourful modern place mats, below, look charming on a highly polished table. They are Irish linen, specially designed to match Susie Cooper's spot pattern china in shades of Fern Green, Aqua, Terra-cotta, Kingfisher and Sèvres blue

SPACE-SAVERS...TIME-SAVERS...

*Some economy ideas for those living in cramped quarters
—and those with no time to spare or money to waste*

HANG YOUR BOOKS AND SAVE WALL SPACE (below). Just a couple of hooks screwed firmly into the wall and you can hang the top shelf, adding lower ones as your library increases. Shelves, seen at the Council of Industrial Design, have a gay plastic surface that can be wiped clean and looks fresh

YOU NEED A DISAPPEARING KITCHEN? So do many people in cramped quarters or living in one room. The Sissons Cabinette sink unit, seen at Froys, with its round Swedish bowl sink and stainless steel drainer, hides under a lid when not in use, has good cupboard and shelf space below

OCCASIONAL TABLE THAT RISES TO ANY OCCASION. Folded in half (right), it takes up little space, melts unobtrusively into a sitting-room décor; open its swivel top full-out and you can give a dinner party with ease. It comes from the Neil Morris Cumbrae range in walnut, oak and mahogany

"Why ever didn't I think of that long ago?" We all say it sometimes, when our own particular domestic problem is solved. Perhaps you will find here just what you've always wanted. . . .

TEA FOR TWO IN TWO MINUTES. Quick, convenient and economical, the Swan Brand Siren electric kettle, below, whistles when it boils, so it's almost impossible to forget it. Even if you do, their's a safety device which ejects the connector if the kettle boils dry or is accidentally switched on without water. It will boil the water for 50 cups of tea on one unit of electricity

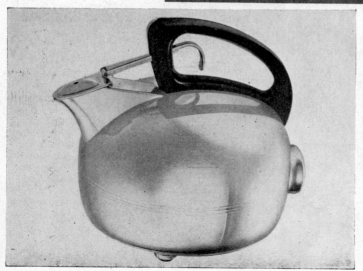

ONE PERSON CAN PAPER A CEILING using the Ashley Ceilingmaster, above. No planks or trestles are needed; just a chair or pair of steps to stand on will do. The Ceilingmaster holds the paper for you, leaving both hands free to hang and adjust it quickly, without trouble

DUAL PURPOSE FURNITURE SOLVES SMALL HOUSE PROBLEMS. Designer William Perring, himself a TV addict, found his friends always phoned at the wrong moment. So he created his Teletable (below) with a compartment for the telephone, pullout writing flap and stool. Now he can view and phone too!

DOUBLE-DUTY TABLE AND WASHABLE RUG (above). There'll be more room at your fireside with this two-tier table in walnut finish, whose lower tier swings out. The gay striped Norwegian rug is cotton and washable. Furniture and furnishings from William Perring of Kensington

COOKING WITHOUT A COOKER—What could be more time-, space- and labour-saving than the Sunbeam controlled heat automatic frypan (left)? Cooking temperatures are listed on the handle. You just set the switch to the heat for the dish to be cooked, plug the pan into an electric point—and sit back while it cooks to perfection

662

Scotties take life seriously even at an early age

A DOG ABOUT THE HOUSE

*How to choose him and how to train him
whether you live in town or country*

by T. A. LOWE

NOTHING in the world is quite so charming as the companionship of a child and a puppy. After both have grown up, the happy devotion remains until the animal's span is complete. This should be many years, provided the child and its parents know how to care for the puppy.

By far the best plan is to start with a puppy of two or three months old. Train him yourself and let the children help. He will always love the people who taught him to be civilised. No dog need be a nuisance in or out of doors if he is properly trained, sufficiently exercised and groomed enough to keep him healthy.

Elementary Training

The first thing to teach a puppy is to be clean in the house. Begin by putting his nose into a puddle he has just made, and then taking him straight out of doors. By your voice let him know you are displeased, or smack him if he won't learn quickly.

Very soon the puppy will go to the door and "ask," and when this happens, let him out at once. Normally he should go out after every meal, and if a grass plot is available for him to visit, so much the better.

The next most important thing to teach him is to "sit." He can learn this either at

your word or when you raise your hand. He must be gently pushed down and kept there until you tell him he may get up. After this, teach him to go to his own particular place in the room, his "basket," or "mat" or just "place."

If the word "basket" is used, stick to it; it is the simplest, since his basket is his bed. Begin by putting him into it, saying "basket," and make him stay there until you tell him he may come out. Always make him stay there during your own meal-times. Never give him titbits at the table, for that means he will become a begging and pestering nuisance.

Puppies are sensitive creatures and nothing gets on their nerves so much as continual confinement, so do not overdo the "basket" training. The dog is an active animal which requires plenty of opportunity to work off his superfluous energy. Deprive him of that and you create bad temper.

Out of Doors

Training out of doors is just as important as it is indoors. One of the early necessities is the wearing of a collar, a human imposition backed by the Law so that the animal may be identified if it is lost. Collars invariably have metal plates on which the

663

name and address of the owner *should* always be engraved. Owners forget this sometimes.

Puppies hate collars at first. They appear to be entanglements which must be shed; and some are extremely clever in ridding themselves of their collars. Instruction is therefore necessary in short spells, until the dog becomes accustomed to his collar and quite unconscious of its presence. Then it is possible to attach a lead, and for a few minutes at a time let him play with this new form of restraint. At the first attempts to make him follow at the end of the lead, he will pull back or sit down. Here the tone of voice is once again important. Talk cheerfully to the puppy, and he will soon discover that it is better to follow than to indulge in strangulation. If the lessons are brief, it will not be long before he is walking out at heel.

The traditional word 'Heel" must now be taught, for on his first walks the puppy will be greatly interested in the sights and smells he meets for the first time. He will dash to wag his tail at other dogs; each time he must be gently pulled back, with the word "Heel."

A time will now quickly arrive when the puppy will, when off the lead, return to his master's or mistress's side when he hears the word. He should be patted and encouraged to do so.

Road Safety

Some dogs are more traffic conscious than others, but they must all be taught road safety, since more road accidents are due to dogs than to any other cause.

Probably the best thing that can happen to a dog is a "near miss" by a motor vehicle early in life, for after this he will look out before leaving the footpath. But one cannot expect motorists to find much fun in training a dog this way, so owners must help. Keep the dog on the lead, say "No" or "Go" as the time is appropriate. Town dogs do learn, and it is wonderful to see some of them when on their own, stop on the kerb and look both ways before crossing the road, even selecting a zebra crossing or a policeman's stand at a crossroad. Country dogs, on the other hand, are not so good. Except on a lead, they should not be allowed near a road at all.

Our "dog about the house" may also be trained as a useful guard; or he may need no training at all, for in some breeds the guardian instinct is strongly developed. Barking is the usual form this takes.

It can be a great nuisance, of course, to neighbours if barking is unrestrained, so a puppy must be taught to stop making a noise when his owner tells him.

Training is best achieved with the reward of titbits and by the tone of voice, but certain breeds are aggressive by nature and will single out the postman or some tradesmen as objects of frenzy and hate. My own plan is to effect "introductions," by bringing the dog on a lead to meet the persons he appears to dislike. After a good sniff round, they usually become firm friends.

Burglar Problems

The problem remains: if the dog is restrained in his dislike of strangers, how is he to discriminate between them and a possible burglar? The truth is, he cannot; and all the best burglars know this and have developed an uncanny knack of making friends with the dog before starting the job.

A lot, too, depends on where the dog sleeps. If indoors in his basket, he is more likely to alarm the household if strange noises are heard than he would if sleeping in an outside kennel where he is often disturbed by the nightly antics of cats. Here a strange freak of sex is of interest. Farmers have a saying, "When a dog barks you can turn over and go to sleep again, but when a bitch barks—get up! " There is much evidence to support the theory that bitches are far better burglar alarms than are dogs.

Few householders can train their pets to be happy and companionable about the home and be "police dogs" as well. The latter live in kennels and are never allowed in a house; they are trained for fierce action. My conclusion, therefore, is that you cannot have it both ways. Leave it to the instinct of the animal which you have civilised to do his stuff if an emergency arises. It is amazing how often he does.

Dogs for Town

Environment means much to a puppy, so in selecting a breed this should be noted. It is cruel to keep a large dog in a town house or a flat, and give it no more exercise than is needed by a peke, a pom or a poodle. He will not have enough outlet for his energies, and may become obstreperous in the house.

The small terriers adapt themselves quickly to town life, but if in doubt, you cannot do better than compromise with a Cocker spaniel, especially where children are concerned. He can be taken out with the pram without getting mixed up in fights, he is friendly with everyone, his affection for his own people unfailing, he is not excitable and he always seems to be happy. Except when—and this point must be emphasised about spaniels in particular, though it applies to all breeds—he is overfed and undergroomed. A Cocker with a dirty coat and dilated belly is the very picture of misery. Yet, even in spite of this neglect, he will keep on thumping his tail.

Dogs for the Country

All dogs prefer to live in the country. Scent means so much to them, and they are by nature hunters for their own food, so the chance of catching a rat is always a possibility.

Country dwellers who are contemplating buying a pup should, however, be careful about one thing. The bigger the dog, the more it eats. They should ask themselves the question—can I afford to keep a St. Bernard or a Great Dane? Dogs of this size must have at least 3 lb. of meat per day, and large quantities of meal and biscuits. An Alsatian needs 1 lb. of meat per day, and so does a Boxer; and if you do not feed and exercise dogs of this size properly they may become dangerous.

Working Dogs

The ideal country dog is a setter or a retriever. They are excellent guards without being yappers. They need little grooming; and if you ride a bicycle to and from the village shop, as so many country people do, they learn quickly to stay to "heel" (or rather "wheel"), and do not go off hunting on their own. But, of course, they are *working* dogs and much prefer to be trained to the gun than as house-dogs. The same applies to all breeds of sheepdogs. They enjoy the warmth of the kitchen fire in the evening, but work is their life and they can't bear being indoors if Master is out in the fields.

The general feeding rule for puppies is—four meals a day up to three months, three meals up to six months, after which they are classed as adults and have only two meals a day, morning and evening.

What sort of meals? Fresh meat for the principal one, if you can afford it, or the cheaper meat labelled "unfit for human use," which must be washed before cooking, and some green vegetables added.

No hard-and-fast rules about vegetables can be made. Dogs are exactly like humans in their tastes; one puppy will clear up his dinner with relish, while another will show his displeasure by covering his food up in his bedding.

Like most dogs, the Cocker Spaniel, one of the most popular of all breeds, is happiest in the country

The family soon gets to know what their "dog about the house" enjoys most, but one form of food he must not have is soggy, soaked meal and too much gravy. Some experts scald the meal and leave it to soak before feeding, but a better plan, from my experience, is to measure out the meal each time, put it in a bowl, pour on a little stock or soup, cut up the meat (preferably raw).

Bones

Large bones serve a dual purpose: first, they provide strong work for the teeth, and then become playthings to be hidden in the garden and dug up again for recreation. But always give a dog his bone raw, never cooked. Cooking causes a change in the composition of the bone marrow which can produce very serious illness.

Chicken bones should not be given unless they have been stewed for long enough to make them soft. If fed to a dog in the form of table scraps, these or other small bones splinter and may pierce the intestines. In fact, if you observe your dog pawing his mouth at any time, examine him immediately to see if something has got wedged between his teeth. This may be a piece of wood, or a feather, or a small bone, and if left can cause septic sores. Don't be nervous about opening a dog's mouth and putting your fingers to his teeth; he is just as anxious to get rid of the obstruction as you are, and will never snap.

Dogs eat grass when they are out, but they do not like it to be mixed up for them in their regular meals. Grass is a sort of corrective for their insides, and they are happy to choose their own variety and know exactly how much they require.

At all times have a bowl of fresh water available; and if you have a dog with you in a car for a long motor journey, always ask at garages for water when you pull in. One of the major cruelties perpetrated by ignorant humans is to leave a dog shut up in a car with all the windows closed on a hot day. The police are taking action about this at parking places now, and careless owners may find themselves charged in court with cruelty.

Grooming

Keep a brush and comb for your dog, because every breed, rough-haired or smooth, needs daily grooming. For the rough-haired varieties this is an arduous business because knots have to be combed out, sometimes a painful proceeding for the dog.

This is not the place to explain the technique of stripping, trimming and preparing a dog for show purposes; for that, it is better to take him to a professional. Have it done according to the show standard laid down for the breed, for this will gain him many points. But for a rough-haired *house*-dog, not designed for shows, stripping need only be done when he appears to be uncomfortable in hot weather; *never* in cold weather, or he will get a chill.

Baths

Baths? Some people assert that dogs should not have baths, but they cannot have kept spaniels which sometimes delight in rolling in filth. So do other breeds, and you cannot escape the fact that a dog which comes home filthy *must* be bathed. Apart from that, all dogs like a bath now and then. The water should be tepid, and diluted with some good strong disinfectant that gets rid of fleas (if any). Shampoo the coat with soap, and rinse it well out afterwards before drying. Then give the dog a good combing, and his coat will be a walking advertisement for the care his owner gives him.

Where the Vet. Comes In

A dog's health during his entire life depends greatly upon the start he gets as a pup. After six months he may never have to see a vet. at all, provided certain essentials were attended to by the breeder.

These concern immunisation against distemper and the dreaded "hard pad." No one should dream of buying a pup that has not had these injections; it is an accepted routine, like vaccination for a baby.

Also, the dewclaws of many puppies are amputated now as a matter of course, a few days after they are born. These claws are found quite high up on the forelegs, and they are of even less use to a dog than the appendix to a human, If they are not cut out, they may get caught and broken afterwards, and cause the animal a lot of pain, besides being unsightly.

Veterinary authorities do not always agree on the subject of worming puppies. Some believe that all puppies are born with worms, which should be cleared out

Boxers are very gentle with children, but they are also excellent guards and highly intelligent

when the animal is very young, or the puppy's health and growth may be affected. The majority, however, advise against any action unless there are definite signs that the puppy has worms, in which case take him to the vet.

Adult dogs suffer sometimes from tapeworm. The vet. is not required for treatment in this case. Ask the chemist for *arecoline-acetarsol*, which is also sold under various trade titles with instructions on the label about use. The great thing is that it requires no preliminary fast, but watch out for the evacuations because these must be burnt, as they are bags containing millions of eggs capable of reinfestation later on.

The vet. should therefore only be needed in case of accidents. So far as the dog's general health is concerned, there should never be anything wrong with him at all. A dose of castor oil will cure constipation, a malady suffered by dogs when they are fed too many bones.

The Final Routine

The address of the Kennel Club is 84 Piccadilly, London, W.1, and this is mentioned because every thoroughbred puppy should have been registered there before sale. A prospective buyer may say, "But I only want a dog about the house, a companion for my child, and a friend for the family," but the point is he may afterwards be sorry that he has not also insisted on getting a pedigree. Like that of a thoroughbred horse, a dog's pedigree looks awesome, going back to G.G.G.G.-parents.

The value of it only comes in later on when some casual acquaintance may say, "I would love to mate my bitch with your dog"; or, and this is another common happening, when an expert stops you in the road and says, "That's a fine-looking dog, have you ever shown him?" Then the first thing that springs to mind is, "I wish I had asked for that pedigree."

Another valuable service provided by the Kennel Club is the "Transfer Certificate." If an owner is going abroad, for instance, or is forced for some reason to dispose of his dog, the new owner will demand this certificate. It is a guarantee of what he is getting, because the Kennel Club will inform him where and by whom the dog was bred, his age and, in fact, his history.

On Selecting a Breed

The name of the late Mr. Charles Cruft became a hallmark in the dog world for two reasons. His aim in life was (a) to improve pedigree stock in dogs, and (b) to encourage the public to keep better dogs And he attained both these objectives. Moreover, he was a great showman, and he knew how to bring people to his dog shows; and always there would be some special attraction for those who wanted something different.

One year it would be Pomeranians, another Griffons or Schipperkes; or perhaps Italian greyhounds, Chows, Japanese spaniels—or Elkhounds from Afghanistan, Lion dogs from Rhodesia or Llassa terriers. Some of us remember the Basenji, or "barkless" dog, which produced soft little yodelling noises to express pleasure, but otherwise made no sounds.

Useful Lectures

But always the British breeds dominated, as they still do, at Cruft's shows, and the fashion started for judges to give little lectures about the breed they had been handling and how the points allotted to the winners were arrived at. This idea was greatly appreciated and has now been extended to TV programmes, and very popular events they are, especially for those selecting a breed. Dog fights, previously very common at dog shows, have almost disappeared owing to good feeding and management, but accidents happened, even at Cruft's, to make headlines in the papers.

On one occasion during the judging of Russian wolfhounds, a man strolled into the ring with a Japanese spaniel on a leash. A Borzoi who had not forgotten the disgrace of the Russo-Japanese War, pounced on the unsuspecting Oriental, and with one shake broke his neck. Conversely, a clipped French poodle, when called a "sissy" by an Irish terrier, nearly tore the Hibernian limb from limb. This fight caused a sensation, and British people began to look at poodles in a different way. But not even Mr. Cruft could have guessed that by the 1950's the poodle would have become the most popular dog in Britain.

On the subject of selecting a breed, therefore, we must discuss him first.

The Poodle. The breed is divided into two classes: the large, or standard, size, and the miniature, which should not be over 15 in. Intelligence is exceptional, a poodle can be trained to anything. The French use the standard size as gun-dogs. They are very good in water and at nosing out lost birds. They love showing off and that is what started the clipping fashion in France. The reason why poodles are so often seen clipped with bracelets on the ankles and ruffs round the neck is that they can be perfect clowns; and this curious pattern is supposed to represent the clown's costume. Don't be sorry for a poodle when you see him togged up that way; he likes it. And he is a wonderful performer in a circus.

Only a small proportion of British poodles are clipped in this manner, and when the miniatures became favourites, it was for reasons other than entertainment—they were discovered to be the perfect house-dogs.

Dog-lovers who live in flats are confined to a limited number of breeds, and the miniature poodle proved himself to be the ideal house-dog for a *flat*. He fits in anywhere, eats very little, is exceptionally obedient, sensible in traffic and avoids trouble with other dogs, though he can also be an excellent guard dog in emergency. His loyalty and devotion are manifest.

Prices are high, because of this popularity, for both the standard and miniature varieties, especially those animals which conform to the Poodle Club's points. Colour must be either all black, all white, all brown or all blue.

Since the late King George VI took a fancy to the breed in 1933, Welsh Corgis have been royal favourites

The white poodle should have dark eyes, black nose, lips and toe-nails. The brown poodle dark amber eyes, dark liver nose, lips and toe-nails. The blue poodle should be of even colour and have dark eyes, lips and toe-nails.

Under the heading of "General Appearance," the Club lays down that the poodle must be "a very active, intelligent and elegant dog, well built and carrying himself proudly."

The miniature should be in every respect a complete replica of the standard poodle, except that his height at shoulder should be under 15 in.

If poodles are expensive (to buy, not to keep), the same cannot be said about the next breed to be considered—

The Spaniel. There are several varieties such as the Clumber, the Field and the Springer, all of which make fine housedogs, preferably in the country, but there can be no doubt that it is the Cocker spaniel which has established himself as the friend of the family in so many homes, anywhere and everywhere.

This is easy to explain. He is a dog of moderate size, very adaptable to environment, of a placid and merry temperament that makes him the ideal companion for a child. He is always alert, and will give warning in no measured tones of the approach of strangers or undesirables. Yet he rarely goes the whole hog and causes unpleasantness by attacking. He has a hardy constitution and can stand all weathers and temperatures; he is healthy and easily managed. He thrives on a common-sense diet, such as we have described; he is not only a thing of great beauty but a first-class, all-round utility dog as well. What more is there to say?

At Cruft's Show one year there were over 700 Cocker spaniels entered, yet the judges managed to pick out one, not only as champion of his own breed, but also as the best dog in the show, of all breeds.

But what most of us want for a dog about the house is not a champion, and fortunately there are hundreds of well-bred, good-looking spaniels to be had from the breeders at very reasonable prices. They are extensively advertised in the weekly papers devoted to dogs.

Next on the popularity list of breeds comes—

The Alsatian, a breed which was rare in

Britain before the War of 1914–18, where it was much admired by our troops on the Continent. The dogs were employed by the French to carry messages and Red Cross supplies to wounded, and this was an entirely new idea then, but was developed greatly in the Second World War.

The Alsatian is first of all a sheep-dog in character, which explains why he is best as a one-man dog and is suspicious of strangers until they have been accepted in the home. He is also an ideal companion for children, and very gentle. In addition, the Guide Dogs for the Blind Association, which does such magnificent work in training suitable dogs to help the blind, have found the Alsatian to be excellent for this purpose, as the dog is really "shepherding" his disabled master.

The standard of points laid down for the breed is high, but the following quotation concerns the heading of "General Appearance" only. It is an excellent guide to those who are weighing up carefully the problem of selecting a breed.

"The Alsatian is a well-proportioned dog showing great suppleness of limb, neither massive nor heavy, but free from any suggestion of weediness. Height not less than 24 in. in dogs (22 for bitches), and not more than 26 in either sex. Its method of locomotion is a tireless, long striding gait, and all its movements should be entirely free from stiltiness. The whole dog and its expression give the impression of perpetual vigilance, strong fidelity, lively and ever watchful, alert to every sight and sound, nothing escaping its attention, showing no fear. Three of its most outstanding traits are its incorruptibility, its discernment and its ability to think for itself."

All of which may sound like a counsel of perfection, but Alsatian owners everywhere would vouch for its truth. A word of warning is, however, necessary. To own an Alsatian means a very great responsibility, in that he simply *cannot* be neglected. You may go away for a holiday and leave a poodle or a spaniel to be cared for by a neighbour, but you must not do that with an Alsatian. He might become restless, homesick and wild in your absence, which leads to endless trouble. This is a factor which should be carefully thought out before buying.

Also high in popularity comes—

The Boxer. Another large-size dog, compact, and should weigh about 55 lb.; originally a native of Germany. The body is square, with a deep back, a broad and deep chest, well muscled, small cat-like feet, the tail set high and docked close.

The coat is short and smooth, and brindles, fawns and reds are the principal colours. The head is convex with attractive wrinkles running down each side of the face, the ears are set high; the muzzle is square, with powerful jaws and slightly undershot teeth.

The Boxer has leaped into favour in this country since the last war, mainly because of his record in it and, again, the fact that so many troops met the breed for the first time. One animal, employed in the guarding of a very secret radar station, actually arrested fifty-seven intruders on as many different occasions, some of them armed. Yet he did not bite one of them.

Boxers are very gentle with children, and have been found to be excellent pram guards for babies while mistress is shopping. Certainly no one could kidnap a baby that has a Boxer in attendance. But the warning about owner's responsibility must be repeated—an ideal dog for the home when under supervision.

Welsh Corgis have been popular with the Royal Family, ever since the late King George VI took a fancy to the breed in 1933. The Queen and Princess Margaret, as well as Prince Charles and Princess Anne, grew up with corgis.

They were originally cattle-dogs, employed in Wales for that purpose because they could nip the heels of the cattle and evade the retaliatory kick; the Welsh word "curgies" means—to watch over.

General appearance and expression, to be as foxy as possible; alertness essential, the body to measure about 36 in. from point of nose to tip of tail.

A very good dog to have about the house or flat, but naturally vociferous and apt to disturb the neighbours unless trained to keep his mouth shut on command. Very hardy, easy to feed and groom.

The Pekingese. Volumes have been written about this amazing animal, whose ancestry goes back for hundreds of years. A Peke is an aristocrat, an Imperialist, a creature of privilege, who regards the world through eyes filled with disdain for normal human beings. He lives behind the doggy "iron curtain."

But he forgets all this when you get to know him; or rather, perhaps, when he gets to know you, and the fact that over 4,000 highly distinguished members of the breed are registered on the Kennel Club books proves how well he adapts himself to English life. In truth, the Pekingese is an attractive little dog of handy size, unique character and with a full capacity for companionship.

He has a memory like an elephant. The writer was rapturously greeted after an absence of at least two years by a Peke with whom he had been on friendly terms, and the sincerity of the greeting was striking because he was by no means a sociable dog.

Retrievers are the ideal dogs for country life, as we have already established.

The flat-coated retriever is a fine utility dog for retrieving game, a fact much appreciated by sportsmen. To him the handsome golden retriever is very closely related. The big family includes the Labrador, whose capacity for faithfulness and devotion, and his utter adoration and obedience, are among the marvels of the canine race.

Stories abound concerning the sagacity of these lovely dogs, and together with the English and Irish setters they are excellent house-dogs too, but they mope without plenty of outdoor work. Fetching the morning newspapers from the shop round the corner is not enough; they want moorland, and a master who can pick up a gun.

Dachshunds, long-haired, smooth-haired and wire-haired, each have their devoted admirers; and latterly we have miniatures, very attractive little things which go well with a fur coat, though this is deceptive as they have hearts like lions and enjoy being rude to large dogs.

They are all hounds, and were kept by the noble families of Germany and Austria purely for sporting purposes. They should be long, low, with a compact and well-muscled body. They must have a bold, defiant carriage of head and an intelligent expression.

All dachshunds adapt themselves to life in towns quite happily; and the smooth-haired variety is very easy to keep clean and in good condition.

Cairn Terriers and Scotties are much alike in character.

When the Duke of Windsor was Prince of Wales, he always had a Cairn around with him, and they became very fashionable at that time. Very intelligent, but not always merry. Handy.

The Wire-haired Fox-terrier is much

Alert, intelligent and a devoted companion, the Dachshund, although originally bred for sporting purposes, adapts itself easily to town life

loved but a terrific fighter. Otherwise I would describe him as "everyman's dog," but not necessarily every woman's.

Apart from the ten most popular breeds of pedigree dogs in the British Isles, there are at least another hundred breeds. Papillons, Pomeranians, Pugs, Yorkshire and Welsh Terriers, Griffons, Black and White Terriers—all have a huge following. So have Bulldogs, Bull-terriers, Sealyhams, Shetland sheep-dogs, and that charming member of the community—the Old English sheep-dog, who was found in this country when the Romans came.

About this dog a breeder told us, "I know no animal more sensitive to praise or blame. I know no animal more sagacious in its day-to-day relations with the human family. I know no breed that shows such comprehension of human speech."

That is how it is with dog-lovers everywhere, the breed they live with is always the best.

Buying an Old Dog

But what about the family with only a few shillings to spend who are longing to have a dog about the house?

Our advice here is simple—go to a dogs' home and have a look round, or if there is not one in your neighbourhood, write to the Secretary of the Battersea Dog's Home and tell him what you want. *He* wants to find *good homes* for his dogs.

It may be an old dog when it arrives, and for the first few months you may discover the truth of the adage: "You can't teach an old dog new tricks."

Or can you? A personal experience proves that you can. The writer saw an advertisement, "Good home wanted for pedigree Welsh terrier, owner going abroad," and acquired the dog for nothing—a very beautiful-looking black and tan, belonging to that handy breed which, for some reason, you don't see much outside Wales.

The immediate sequel was almost tragic. So devoted was she to her former master, that she almost died of grief at being parted from him. She wouldn't eat, she wouldn't sleep, she just moped herself into a skeleton. It took us six months of very patient, tactful handling to get her back to life, if that is not an understatement of the ball of fun, mischief and Celtic exuberance she is now.

Which brings us to another question: whether to choose a dog or a bitch. The answer is simple—if you can look after her, a bitch every time. Bitches are more intelligent than dogs; they learn more quickly, are infinitely more loyal and affectionate; and they are the solution to the burglar problem, for you cannot fool a bitch the way you might a dog. But twice a year, for three weeks, a bitch comes into season and must be protected from the usually most unwelcome attentions of all the dogs in the neighbourhood.

This need not be difficult, even in towns, provided her owner is prepared to take a little trouble on her behalf. If she is let out to run in her own garden, it *must* be strongly fenced or walled. Take her out in the park or street only at times when other dogs are unlikely to be out for their exercise—before breakfast or quite late at night—and, before going out, give her a regular dose of the chlorophyll tablets specially made for this purpose and obtainable from all good chemists. Be careful not to let her off the lead. Most of the time a bitch will snap at strange dogs that attempt to follow her, but there is always the danger that she too may go wild and run away with one of her admirers.

This, however, is a very small price to pay for owning a bitch. Besides, a dog, however well trained, can *never* be relied upon not to go off after somebody else's bitch; a bitch of your own is only a problem six weeks in a year.

You *can* teach an old dog new tricks, but it is simpler to start with a puppy. He is a member of the family, for a good dog about the house is beloved by all.

ON KEEPING A CAT

How to make a good companion for the family out of this popular pet

"IT is enough to make a cat laugh" is a common expression—and a cat might well laugh, since she reigns supreme in five and a half million homes in the U.K. and countless more in other countries. Why this is so nobody knows. It could be that, for most of us, C-A-T is the first word we learn to spell, or perhaps it is that none can resist the appeal of a fluffy, bright-eyed kitten.

Anyhow, the chances are about three to one that you have—or soon will have—a cat, so a few hints should be useful.

Choosing a Kitten

If you have the opportunity to choose a kitten from a litter, look for the liveliest—the one that is "ruling the roost"—for it will almost certainly be the healthiest also. If it is a blue-blooded aristocrat you want, there is a varied choice. Siamese, Persian, Abyssinian, British Short Hair—there are a score or more breeds to choose from. All have their band of zealous followers and any will make a good pet. A pedigree kitten will cost anything up to £5. For the rest—the unknowns—if you cannot get one from your neighbour, a few shillings will purchase you the "pick of the litter" at any pet stores. Look for the kitten with bright eyes, firm legs, a clean mouth and no discharge from ears, eyes or nose.

Once in the home she should quickly be taught "house manners." Provide her with a sanitary pan—an ordinary baking tin will do—and fill it with earth, sand, or peat moss. Put her in at the first signs of scratching the floor or crying. She will soon learn and will go there herself, provided the box is always kept in the same

A common or garden tabby will become just as valued a member of the household as a pedigree Persian

place. As soon as she is old enough to go out, the pan can be dispensed with.

Sleeping Quarters

A cat should have its own bed and bedding. To allow her to sleep on your best armchair is to encourage dirt and vermin. A basket or plastic bed can be obtained very cheaply, and an old blanket or cushion will provide adequate bedding. Give her a quiet corner of her own and do not disturb her when she is there.

Brushing and combing will be necessary now and again but, broadly speaking, a cat is well able to keep itself clean without human aid. If it is necessary to remove any "unwelcome guests" from her coat, take her outside and give her a good dusting with pyrethrum powder, followed by a good brushing.

Feeding

Food and its preparation are most important factors in maintaining a cat's health. Raw meat is unsuitable food for cats, and the kind sold for animal consumption is sometimes infected, and so should not be handled, particularly by the housewife in her kitchen. Modern methods of preparation ensure that canned foods provide your pet with a balanced meal, wholesome and safe, cooked and ready to serve.

Sensible cats like liver or fish as a change from cooked meat, but not too much fish, please. A cat cannot be healthy on fish alone.

Nearly all cats like milk, but it is no substitute for fresh clean water, which should always be available.

The Prowler

Tom cats which are not "doctored" spend much of their time fighting and straying away for days, or even weeks on end. They will return from these amorous expeditions battle-scarred, dirty and smelling to high heaven—a situation liable to try the patience of the most ardent animal lover.

A simple operation, performed by a veterinary surgeon when the kitten is a few months old will free you, and the cat, from all such problems. And pay no attention to those well-meaning neighbours who tell you a doctored cat will get fat and lazy. There is no evidence of this. In fact, some of the most active "mousers" are those who have no other outlet for their excess energy.

Fortunate are the cats whose owners put their faith in wholesome food rather than the medicine chest. But despite this, there will occasionally be times when your pet is "off colour." A condition powder, obtainable from the chemist, will sometimes help, but if she persistently shows signs of being unwell, consult a veterinary surgeon. Don't try to treat her yourself. A little expert advice is always better than a lot of needless worry.

Cats make splendid playmates for children, particularly if human and animal young grow up together from early youth

**Children's Pets described
by Alfred Leutscher**

SMALL RODENTS

*Fancy mice and rats, hamsters
and dormice, kept in clean
surroundings, all make charming
additions to the family*

The habits of the dormouse are somewhat squirrel-
like—it is fond of climbing, builds its nest above
ground and relishes hazel-nuts or walnuts

RODENTS are animals which gnaw their food, and are provided with prominent incisor teeth for this purpose. These front teeth are shaped like chisels and make very effective cutting instruments. Since they never stop growing, they are in constant use, not because the owner is necessarily hungry, but because it needs to wear down and shape its teeth to the proper level.

Before starting to keep a rodent as a pet, it is useful to understand their characteristics.

Firstly, because of their nibbling habits, their homes should always be made of stout material. Many a pet rodent has gnawed its way out of its box. A wire cage is the best kind of hutch or, failing this, a strong wooden one lined on the inside with tin sheeting.

Secondly, rodents do not have very clean and regular sanitary habits, and their droppings and urine are left anywhere. The cage floor should therefore be covered with a good layer of absorbent material, such as sawdust, sand or dry earth. This is cleared away and replaced at regular intervals.

Thirdly, rodents are rather "messy" feeders, carrying and dropping uneaten food all over the place. Food should therefore be given sparingly and often, a little at a time.

Fourthly, a rodent's fertility rate is high, with large and frequent families. This may be controlled by keeping the sexes apart until an increase in the family is required.

Lastly, if any of the above points are disregarded, then these little animals will make themselves unpopular in the house-

hold. Boys and girls must therefore be told from the very start that to keep such pets in a clean and healthy state they must look after them properly themselves.

Mice and Rats

Two rodents which have been domesticated from wild ancestors are the mouse and rat. The Fancy Mouse comes from the wild House Mouse, and the Fancy Rat from the wild Common or Brown Rat, which lives in sewers, rubbish dumps, farms and along rivers. Both the domestic kinds may be coloured white, black, piebald and various shades of grey or brown. In both there is an albino with pink eyes.

Their general care is the same, except that the rat requires a bigger cage. Being social animals, rats or mice can live in small separate colonies in well-ventilated cages. Provide a nest box which is closed in, apart from a small entrance hole, since these animals like to sleep and rear families in the dark. A variety of clean nesting material—dry hay or straw, paper, cloth or cotton wool—should be placed in the run. It is better to let these pets make their own nests, and the process is fascinating to watch. Unless a family is on the way, or is actually being reared, the nest material should be cleaned out about once a fortnight.

Food is placed in feeding trays morning and night, in small quantities, and all surplus must be removed before it goes bad. Mice and rats will eat almost any seed, grain or nut, soft fruit or greenstuff, also table scraps, such as cheese and bacon rind, porridge oats, biscuits and potato peel.

Clean drinking water must always be available. Rodents soon foul their drinking bowls, so a "drip-feed" is advised. This consists of an inverted bottle with a length of narrow glass tubing running through the cork.

It is sometimes possible to catch and tame wild rodents, especially in the country. I have managed to tame and even breed from the wild Wood Mouse and the Field Vole. These charming little creatures were kept in small colonies in their separate cages. The floors were heavily spread with loose earth and leaves to resemble a woodland floor, and flat pieces of raised bark acted as roofs for their nest. Although they did not enjoy being handled, they took food from the fingers and frequently sat on the hand and rarely bit. Voles, incidentally, are cousins of mice and rats with small ears, blunt faces and short tails.

Hamster History

A vole-like little creature with short tail, which has now become a world-famous children's pet, is the Golden Hamster. It has an interesting history. The first specimen ever found came from the Mount Aleppo region in Syria, in 1839. No further hamsters were seen for nearly one hundred years. Then, in 1930, in almost the same place, a female and her twelve young turned up in a burrow. They took kindly to captivity and the many descendants were soon in demand by scientific laboratories all over the world. Gradually, as more and more hamsters appeared, they found a ready market in the pet trade. By careful breeding, a golden form was produced—and so the Golden Hamster was born. The many thousands of hamsters in laboratories and homes to-day are the descendants of the original family found in Syria. Since 1930 no further wild specimens have been found.

This clean and friendly little rodent makes an ideal pet. Provided it is kept in a clean hutch, it may even live in the drawing room. There is no smell. Hamsters have charming habits, such as stuffing their cheek pouches with

A piebald hamster—like all the hamsters in the Western world, a direct descendant of one family of thirteen found in 1930 in Syria

Photo: Mustograph

676

Photo: John Markham

Rodents do not always drink as politely as this tame albino rat and it is usually advisable to provide drinking water in an inverted bottle from which they can lick up the drips

food, rolling on their backs to be stroked, and lying about in all sorts of amusing positions when asleep.

Hamsters eat much the same food as mice. Here again, their sleeping quarters should be closed in except for the doorway, as in nature they appear to live in burrows in the dark. This is important from the breeding point of view. Here a word of warning is not out of place. Hamster litters may number up to twenty young, the babies become fertile in one month and families may occur every six weeks. This high breeding rate compensates for the hamster's short life of only eighteen months to two years. The females are in breeding condition every fortnight, and at these times may become a little short-tempered and inclined to bite.

Don't Disturb a Sleeping Dormouse

One of the most attractive rodent pets is the Dormouse. This plump little creature has a rich, reddish coat, big, black eyes and a furry tail. In habits it is rather squirrel-like, being fond of climbing. It also builds its nest above ground.

Its cage should be tall rather than broad, and fitted out with small branches. If pro-

vided with dried grass or loose hair, it may build a ball-like nest in the branches. If not, this should be made for it and placed on a shelf fixed near the top of the cage. A suitable home can be made out of a stout wooden box turned up on end, and fitted with a glass front and a small doorway.

Dormice eat almost any kind of seed, nut or fruit, and occasionally small insects. Hazel nuts and walnuts are greatly relished, and are usually carried up into the branches to be eaten. A nut is opened by nibbling a neat hole through the shell.

In nature, dormice retire to special nests below ground to hibernate from October to about March, but a pet one will only do this if its cage is placed in a cold room or shed. During this winter sleep, it is tightly curled into a ball and should on no account be disturbed.

Rodents as pets will give much pleasure to the owner, provided they are treated kindly and handled gently, and, above all, kept in clean surroundings. Should they ever bite, the wound must be washed and disinfected at once. A rodent bite causes a deep, puncture-like wound and may carry germs into the blood-stream.

RABBITS AND GUINEA PIGS

*Favourites with children, these delightful little animals are not
much trouble to care for and should live to a ripe old age*

THESE two popular animals are among the larger rodents kept as pets by many children.

The rabbit originally came from Southwest Europe, probably Spain, and was imported during Norman times. All through the Middle Ages it was kept as a food animal and for its fur, in special places known as warrens. Later it spread to all parts of the country, becoming a serious nuisance to farmers, and various attempts have been made to keep it under control. The latest way has been to introduce a virus disease, called myxomatosis. This was deliberately started in France and Australia, and possibly in the U.K. as well. At all events, millions of rabbits died in these countries

as a result. So far the pet rabbit seems to have escaped, probably because the disease carrier, a flea, does not reach the hutches of domestic rabbits.

All domestic breeds, such as the black-and-white Dutch, the Blue Beverin, the short-haired Rex varieties and the Flemish Giant are descended from the Spanish wild rabbit. Their general care is the same. The home should be a hutch made from stout wood and chicken wire, consisting of a suitable-sized run and covered-in sleeping quarters. In making such a hutch, two important factors must be borne in mind. Although rabbits can withstand severe cold, they must not be exposed to rain or draughts. The sleeping quarters, especially, should therefore be made of strong, well-protected wood with a waterproofed roof, preferably a sloping one with overhanging ledges. A cover to the run is also helpful in keeping off rain.

A hutch placed outside should be sheltered from wind, close to a wall or fence and raised off the ground. Some owners simply make a hutch frame which is placed directly on the earth or grass. This is usually satisfactory in the drier summer, but during wet, wintery spells can become very damp and draughty. If a ground run is used, then some chicken wire should be buried below it, a foot or so underground, in order to discourage digging. Keep a wooden run covered with fresh sawdust or dry earth, and provide the sleeping quarters with hay or straw.

Many Varieties of Colour

Guinea pigs may be kept in a similar way. Like rabbits, they are now bred in many colour varieties, and have their own albino form as well as an Angora breed with long, silky hair. The wild ancestor is a South American Cavy, and long before Europeans went to the New World it had become domesticated in countries like Peru, Ecuador and Colombia. The guinea pig was then bred for its meat and skin, and this practice continued for some time

Photo: Neave Parker

"Cold I can stand—but rain and draughts, no!
And please don't dangle a rabbit by its ears—
it hurts! And may make me scratch you !"

Photo: Mustograph

after it was brought back to Europe by explorers.

Both rabbits and guinea pigs breed three or four times a year in captivity. The baby rabbit is naked, blind and helpless at birth, and not really able to look after itself until about four weeks old. The baby guinea pig, on the other hand, is sometimes out and about with its parents an hour or two after birth, fully clothed and eyes wide open.

Both these pets are vegetarian and eat quantities of fresh grass, to which may be added greenstuff, carrots and certain wild plants, such as dandelion and dock leaves. A daily dish of moistened bran and oats is included in their diet, together with occasional fruit and peelings. You can tell whether the diet is satisfactory by the state of the droppings. When these are loose and discoloured, more "body" and less greenstuff are required; when dry and hard, more fruit and greens are needed.

There is a correct way to handle these gentle creatures. The legs, especially of rabbits, should always be supported on the hand. It is cruel to dangle them by the ears alone. They can easily be cradled in the arms against the body. Rabbits show displeasure by growling and kicking or scratching. Guinea pigs give a high-pitched whistle, especially when hungry. They show pleasure and contentment with a curious chattering sound.

Provided they are well looked after, these pets need never become ill, and will live to a ripe old age of from ten to twelve years or more. Colds and digestive complaints are their main troubles.

Photo: Zoological Society of London

TORTOISES

Describing the likes, dislikes and habits of this
hardy pet which may well out live its owner!

THE choice of a pet is usually governed by the demands on its owner's time and pocket. A cautious adult need have no qualms in selecting a tortoise—the ideal pet for even the youngest child. It is clean and slow-moving, rarely, if ever, bites, and with care will outlive its young owner.

The common tortoise of the pet trade is called the Algerian tortoise. In its native home along the Mediterranean seaboard this tortoise lives in semi-desert surroundings, spending the day in feeding on low-lying vegetation and fallen fruit, or basking in the sun. At night it retires under bushes or rocks, and usually hides during poor weather.

Wild Ancestry

The winter sleep, or hibernation, is profound and lasts throughout the winter months, from about October to March. The tortoise hides itself completely, digging into the earth or under rocks, and lies dormant with the head and limbs pulled inside the shell. The best home for a pet tortoise is in the garden, where it can live an open-air life. As, however, it may damage plants or wander away through a gap (some of these pets are great roamers), some restriction is necessary. A low square frame of wood and wire netting, which is shaped after the fashion of a baby's play-pen, is quite suitable. Painted in colours to match the surroundings, it will not look out of place on the lawn. From time to time its position should be changed. Alternatively, a corner of the garden may be divided off with a low wall.

Whatever type of pen is chosen, tortoises must have access to water and shelter. A flat dish sunk in the ground at earth level should contain a permanent supply of clean drinking water. A shelter, such as a box with a doorway, or a low roof supported on uprights, will provide cover from rain and strong sunshine, both of which a tortoise avoids. Exposure to long spells of hot sun or rain can be harmful. A bed of dry leaves or hay in the shelter will give the pet something in which to burrow at night. A patch of sand in the enclosure will serve as a sunning spot. The tortoise will sprawl on this to receive a beneficial warmth from the sun, and here, too, the female can bury her eggs.

Food and Water

Food need present no difficulties. A variety of greenstuff may be given, such as lettuce and young cabbage, dandelion, rose and clover leaves, also soft fruit, husks of peas, sliced tomato and young carrot. Some tortoises show a special preference for one of these. Occasionally, bread soaked in jam may also be tried.

Food should be placed in the same spot so that the tortoise will get into the habit of finding it without difficulty. These pets often display a regular routine in their daily activities. My own tortoises begin their day as soon as the sun reaches their shelter, and wander over to have an early breakfast. The morning, weather permitting, is spent in basking on the sand patch. At midday they retire for a siesta, either in the shelter or under one of the low bushes in the enclosure, where burrows have been dug over the course of years. Further exercise is taken in the late afternoon when the hot sunshine is diminishing. Shortly after the second meal at teatime, and well before sunset, they retire for the night. They are quick to sense weather changes and will often go into hiding an hour or two before a storm.

Tortoises will sometimes enjoy an occasional bath in the warm weather. They can be placed in a shallow bowl of warm water for half an hour, and allowed to soak themselves thoroughly. This is a useful tip for getting a shy tortoise to feed. Afterwards the pet must be dried with a cloth. To keep the shell clean and bright give it an occasional rub with olive oil. Grated cuttle-fish bone and some cod-liver oil mixed with the pet's food will assist in proper shell growth and will provide extra vitamins, a lack of which may produce a kind of rickets.

Tortoise ailments are few, but one

should watch for the signs, as they can lead to more serious trouble. Froth at the nose and mouth and a wheezy breath mean a chill, which can easily lead to pneumonia. Warmth is necessary (indoors by the fire in bad weather), and the tortoise should be encouraged to drink water. Slime and blood in the excreta indicate intestinal trouble. Olive oil and a small quantity of mild purgative should be added to the food. Worms may sometimes be found in the droppings. In such cases, administer a little worm-powder with the food.

Parasites

Parasites on tortoises are few. The harmless tortoise-tick is one. Because it looks unsightly—an oval, greyish object attached to a fold of skin on the neck or leg —it should be removed with tweezers. Soften the skin first with a little vegetable oil, otherwise the skin may be torn and the tick's claws left in. This may cause an open wound with a risk of infection to follow. Cases of blindness should be carefully watched, especially after hibernation. The eyes remain closed, often sealed with a matter which in some cases is a parasitic fungus. It may attack the eye, causing permanent blindness, even death when, in the final stages, it penetrates the brain. A few drops of an eye-lotion, given about three times at two-day intervals, should clear up this trouble. A preparation called Protargol (5 per cent. solution), obtainable from a chemist, is recommended.

With the approach of winter the tortoise becomes more and more sluggish and less inclined to move about or feed, and by mid-October has usually begun its winter sleep. In the garden it may have dug itself into some retreat and, provided that this is draught- and damp-free, may be left where it is. For absolute safety it is advisable to pack it away in a box containing dry leaves or hay, which is covered with sacking and placed in a cold, dry spot at outdoor temperature. Either a garden shed or garage, sheltered porch or conservatory will do. The winter surroundings must be cold. Many tortoises spend unhappy winters roaming about the house or cellar, or struggling inside the box, because they are not cold enough to hibernate, yet not lively enough to take an interest in food. They usually die.

Determining Sex

When selecting a tortoise, choose a specimen which is firm and lively, and pulls in its head quickly when touched. Avoid listless ones and those with damaged shells or sores on the skin. The sex may be determined by the shape of the shell. In the male it is less rounded and there is a hollow in the under-shell. The shield just above the tail is flat in the female; in the male it is curved and slightly hooked. The popular belief that the number of rings indicates the tortoise's age is a fallacy.

Age in this animal is indeterminable unless its history is known. There are records of these pets living to be over a hundred years old. Gilbert White's famous Timothy lived for fifty-four years, and its shell, about a foot long, is on exhibition in the reptile gallery of the Natural History Museum in London.

Photo: Zoological Society of London

When selecting a tortoise, choose one that is firm and lively—like this active family—but pulls in its head quickly when touched

CAGE BIRDS

Canaries, budgerigars, various kinds of finches and doves, all take happily to life in a human home

If a canary gets really dirty, you can bath it with a shaving brush, soap flakes and warm water, drying it thoroughly afterwards

THE large number of birds which are kept these days as cage pets may be divided into two classes—those which have been domesticated and those which are still wild, but have been found and tamed. The true, domesticated cage birds include parrots and budgerigars, canaries and other finches, and doves. Of these, the canaries and budgerigars are probably the most popular.

The canary is a greyish-brown finch in the wild state, found in the Canary Islands and Madeira. It was first domesticated in Italy, and now occurs in many varieties. There are also a number of hybrids, or mules, which are the sterile offspring of birds resulting from crossing canaries with other finches, such as the goldfinch, greenfinch, linnet and siskin. There is, incidentally, a wild race of canary found in North Africa and Europe, called the serin. It occasionally turns up in Britain.

Canaries are bred for their shape, colour and song. Some of the finest singers come from the Hartz Mountains in Germany and, since the canary readily imitates other birds, it is possible to train it to imitate the nightingale from gramophone records.

In nature the canary pairs, but in captivity the cock is polygamous. The hens may produce up to four broods of about six eggs each year. The hen usually builds the nest and broods the eggs, then the cock takes over in feeding the nestlings. Given suitable surroundings and proper food, canaries will readily breed in roomy cages. A single indoor pet will make a delightful addition to the household and gives little trouble. The cock fills the air with its sweet, clear music.

The Budgerigar from Australia

The budgerigar (a word meaning "good bird") is a small parakeet which is found in most parts of Australia. It lives and travels about in flocks, feeding on grass seeds and nesting in the hollows of gum trees. The wild colour is a pale, greenish yellow with dark brown cross-bars, and from this have now been fixed a number of colour strains in different shades of grey, blue, yellow and green, also white and black.

This hardy bird, like some canaries, lives quite well out of doors, provided it is sheltered from damp and draught. It can be kept in small flocks, and will breed if provided with proper nest boxes.

Budgerigars are largely seed eaters, but will also take small nuts and fruit. Like its larger cousins, the parrots and cockatoos, it uses its beak for feeding and climbing. Cockatoos, incidentally, are the crested variety which occur only in Australia.

Apart from their use in climbing, the parrot's feet are used like hands to hold such food as nuts and fruit. Generally speaking, the more gaudy parrots look, the more raucous are their vocal efforts. The brilliant macaws can make ear-splitting screams, but it is the sombre-coloured Grey Parrot of Africa which excels as a talker and imitator.

Concern is sometimes expressed about the possibility of catching psittacosis from the bite of an infected bird. For this reason

A pair of pet budgerigars make a home for Sooty, an orphan sparrow (above) that fell down a chimney, fortunately into the home of a young animal-lover

The budgerigar, left, is so tame that he always helps his owner with her school homework, sometimes even sitting on her pen

A handsome rose-crested cockatoo can make plenty of noise when he's in the mood — generally, the gawdier the feathers, the louder the parrot screeches

there have been bans on imports of parrots from time to time, but the risk is now known to be only very slight, and the disease can be caught from other sources. A diseased parrot is very quickly detected by its condition and listless manner, and any pet in this state should immediately be taken to a qualified animal clinic.

Another kind of cage bird is the Barbary Dove, which comes from North Africa, and must not be confused with the other breeds of doves seen living around a dove cote, or in large cages. Such birds are hardened to the climate and are really native, having been originally domesticated from the wild Rock Dove, which can still be seen nesting on some of the rocky coasts of Scotland. Some well-known examples are the Carrier Pigeon, the Fantail, Tumbler and Pouter. The so-called London Pigeon is an escaped "mongrel" from private collections.

The Barbary Dove is smaller and neater-looking, and coloured a creamy brown with a black necklace. It does well in an average cage indoors, especially in pairs, which often show great affection for one another. The food consists mainly of grain and greenstuff.

There are many other cage birds in existence, but we must now consider the genuine wild birds which, for one reason or another, end up as house pets. This is usually the result of an injured bird being found or a young bird picked up in a misguided attempt to save its life.

"Rescued" Wild Birds

The word "misguided" is deliberately used. During the spring months many young birds, such as thrushes, blackbirds and starlings, are to be seen in our gardens, and it is often too readily assumed that they are lost, or in danger from cats. Usually they are safe in the branches and the parents not far away. It is much better to leave the young thrush alone than to try to rear it on bread and milk, the usual dish. These youngsters need plenty of insects and worms. If children would only realise this, many a heartbreak would be saved, since these babies almost invariably die when kept by young humans.

The following examples of wild birds have, however, been successfully kept as pets. A baby Tawny Owl was found soaked to the skin under a bush on a stormy day. The parents were nowhere to be found, so the baby was taken home. It lived and thrived on a diet of dead mice, odd birds and pieces of raw meat, and was even taught to fly.

We learned a lot from this interesting pet, in particular the way an owl will dispose of unwanted food. Small pellets which contain the remains of meals, such as bones, fur and feathers, were coughed up from the stomach and found lying on the floor of the garden toolshed where it spent most of its life. When fully grown and able to fend for itself, our owl was released. For some weeks it remained in the area, roosting by day in a nearby tree.

On another occasion we found during a seaside holiday a guillemot covered in oil. This was bathed and cleaned with soapy water and powder, and kept for some weeks as a family pet. It became quite tame but, being a voracious fish-eater, set a problem in housekeeping.

The latest to join our menagerie is a jackdaw. At the time of writing, this delightful but inquisitive pet is not yet one year old. It will spend hours trying to open a tin, or will attempt to unravel a knotted watch-chain. Anything bright is a great attraction. Being somewhat destructive and also a blatant thief, it must remain in its roomy cage when nobody is about. It has a varied appetite, and will take grain, fruit, bread, dog biscuit, insects and milk. Its wings are clipped and are best kept like this, since a tame jackdaw at large can be a nuisance to neighbours. It is a good match for any cat, since its gentle, exploring beak can become a vicious, stabbing weapon when necessary.

THE GOLDFISH

*Treat him nicely, feed him well and he will soon
be tame enough to take food from your fingers*

GOLDFISH have been kept in garden ponds and aquariums for so long that it may come as a surprise to learn that there is a wild ancestor which is not gold at all. This is a kind of carp, native to Eastern Asia, which is coloured a deep olive-brown. It was the Ancient Chinese, and later the Japanese, who carefully bred from this fish.

There is the Common Goldfish, which retains the ancestral shape, but is coloured a rich reddish gold. The Shubunkin has a variegated colour pattern of gold, white, blue and black. The Veiltail is an attractive breed with a plump body and high, dorsal crest, with a trailing double tail-fin. The Celestial Goldfish has upturned eyes, and the Bramblehead has a curious swollen and lumpy head, and is without the dorsal fin.

These are the aristocrats among goldfish and may be seen at aquarium shows. Most goldfish owners are content to keep a specimen or two which would never win a prize and might be called the "mongrels" of the goldfish world, since their colours and shapes do not conform to the required standards. However, they are just as hardy and interesting as their thoroughbred cousins.

In purchasing such a pet for a child it is well to pick out a healthy specimen which shows no signs of sores or torn fins. Look out especially for traces of fungus, a whitish growth looking like cotton wool. The fish should be swimming about in a lively manner, not sulking in a corner or gasping at the surface. It is a very good sign if the dorsal fin is carried erect in the water.

Far better than the old-fashioned goldfish bowl is a rectangular aquarium containing gravel and water plants. The goldfish, above, have been visited by a budgerigar with an unusual love of water

Preparing the Home

The new home should be prepared beforehand. The old-fashioned goldfish bowl is not recommended, since the restricted neck cuts down the oxygen supply from the air above. Also, the curved sides distort the view. The rectangular aquarium made of angle iron or in one entire piece of glass is the best container. Well-washed gravel or aquarium sand should be placed on the bottom, banked up towards the back, and in this, various water plants firmly secured with small stones as anchors. These help to keep the water fresh and will supply oxygen as well. Two very good oxygenators are the Italian Waterweed (*Vallisneria*) and the Canadian Pondweed (*Elodea*), both of which can usually be obtained from aquarium shops.

Place the aquarium in its permanent home on a firm stand or shelf near a window, then slowly fill it with tap-water, and add a cupful or two of pond-water. Leave the aquarium to settle down for a week before putting in the fish. About one inch of fish to every gallon of water is about the correct population; an aquarium should never be overcrowded.

Being carp, the goldfish will feed on soft water plants and small water animals, such as the water flea (*Daphnia*) and the little red worm, called *Tubifex*. Both these foods can usually be bought. Small garden worms make a useful addition to the diet, as do the various prepared fish foods. The latter should be given sparingly, as any surplus will quickly pollute the water and kill the fish. The so-called dried "ants' eggs" are useless.

A common mistake among new goldfish keepers is to keep on changing the water because it turns cloudy or green. This is quite unnecessary. Provided the water does not smell bad, there is no need to change it and the condition should right itself after a few days.

Don't Tap on the Glass

Goldfish should never be alarmed by tapping the glass or by rough handling. Always use a net when transferring fish, and make sure that the water is the same temperature.

These pets live for many years and become very tame. They will take food from the fingers and are not aggressive in any way.

POND-LIFE FOR THE AQUARIUM

Tadpoles, sticklebacks, newts, etc., can all be reared successfully indoors if the right conditions are provided

Smooth Newts are about four inches long and are the commonest and best-known kind. In the water they look like miniature soft-skinned crocodiles

THE fascination of a pond for a child, and indeed for many adults, is understandable. Its mysteries lure the curious to the water's edge each year and the spoils are taken home in jars and tins, in many cases, unfortunately, to die untimely deaths through lack of proper care.

Tadpoles

Ever popular are the wriggling tadpoles which swarm in the ponds in early summer. Either frogspawn, or a long strip of toad's eggs may be taken home and reared with little trouble. It should be put into shallow water in a dish or aquarium and encouraged to hatch by placing it in sunlight whenever possible.

The baby tadpoles, once free of the jelly, which dissolves after about a week, will need feeding on the clumps of soft, green plant life called algæ, which float at the pond's edge and can be lifted out with a stick. They will feed ravenously on this and also on lightly boiled lettuce and spinach. Later, when legs begin to appear, they change their vegetarian habits and will eat any small, dead creature, including other tadpoles, and also raw meat.

As the tadpole becomes more frog-like, it begins to rise to the surface to breathe. Some sort of landing place on to which the baby frog can climb, such as a sloping bank of sand or a heap of stones, should then be built up in the water. They will climb out long before their tails have gone. Finally, after about six weeks from the time of hatching, the full metamorphosis (from tadpole to frog) is complete.

For a while no food is taken, but now as miniature frogs they change to an entirely carnivorous diet of insects and other small creatures. As such food is difficult to find, it is perhaps wisest to free the youngsters near a pond or ditch. However, with care and individual attention, a few can be reared on greenfly and small white worms called *Enchytræus*.

The Stickleback

Another creature of the pond is the stickleback, whose young hatch from a nest built by the father. The breeding experiment is well worth trying. A layer of well-washed sand is first placed in a tank and planted with pond weeds, such as the Canadian Pondweed, which grows well and releases abundant oxygen. It should be set out in small clumps of three or four sprays, anchored in the sand with stones. It will soon root and take a firm hold.

The tank should be placed where it gets good light but not direct sunlight, and then carefully filled with tap-water to which a little natural pond- or rain-water is added. Next, allow it to settle for about a week. The water may turn green, which is a good sign, as it means the microscopic life is multiplying. After a day or so it should return to its former clearness, and is now said to be "matured."

The aquarium is then ready for the male stickleback. From April onwards the males can be recognised by the bright red on the throat. There is a good chance that the male will choose a spot in his new home and begin to build a nest by collecting bits of plant matter and debris which he carries in his mouth. When this is ready, two or three females (much duller in colour and swollen with eggs) can be put in the tank. After much chasing and pushing, the male will entice each in turn to enter the nest and lay eggs, which he now guards jealously by chasing away all intruders, even the females.

In about three weeks' time the young hatch out and hover near the nest in a shoal of fifty or so. They soon begin feeding on water creatures, and later will thrive on the same food as their parents. This should consist of pond fleas, small earthworms and bits of raw meat.

Newts

Newts will also live in the same kind of aquarium, but it needs a landing platform, made from a flat stone or piece of slate supported on two upright stones so that it rests just clear of the water. In the water, newts look rather like miniature, softskinned crocodiles, and can be caught in a net as they rise to breathe. The males have a crest running along the back and tail, and are a much brighter colour than the females. In the aquarium they will feed on small water creatures, tadpoles, earthworms and bits of raw meat.

The Smooth Newt, about four inches long, is the commonest and best-known British newt. In some ponds may also be found the almost black Great Crested newt, which grows to six inches. This should always be kept by itself, as it may attack and devour smaller newts.

Breeding in Captivity

Newts often breed in captivity. The female climbs among the plants, and lays her eggs in the leaves (Canadian Pondweed is good for this). The eggs are best removed by cutting away the plants, since the parents may eat them. They should be placed in a shallow dish of water. They will hatch into newt tadpoles, with gills, and will feed on minute water creatures scooped out of a pond with a fine-meshed net. In from two to three months they grow lungs, and are able to crawl out of the water. They can be reared on worms, slugs and small white worms.

Photos: A. R. Thompson

These young frogs, still possessing tails, come to the surface to breathe and will climb out of the water. In six weeks from hatching, the tadpole becomes an adult frog

START AN "ANIMAL GARDEN"

A miniature glasshouse full of ferns makes an ideal home for toads,
salamanders, reptiles, lizards or insects—all fascinating to watch

FOR the pet lover who likes something out of the ordinary, there are many strange yet fascinating animals which do well in small homes called vivariums. Unlike the water-filled aquarium suitable for fishes and pond-life, or the sawdust-lined hutch occupied by rabbits or mice, a vivarium is made to take living plants, either growing in open soil or in their own pots.

A vivarium might be described as an "animal garden." It consists, simply, of a shallow, watertight tray, either of metal, or of wood lined with tin sheeting, over which is erected a kind of miniature glasshouse. The popular plant case of Victorian days, known as the Fernery, makes an ideal vivarium.

The tray is first lined with some loose rubble or stones. Over this is laid a sheet of perforated zinc or narrow-meshed wire-netting. On top goes a generous layer of rich, loose, loamy soil. In this soil can be planted a variety of small ferns and other kinds of house plants, especially those many attractive evergreens which are now so popular as house decorations. If preferred, these plants can be placed in the tray in their pots, the spaces between being filled in with further soil or small stones.

Pieces of bark and small branches on which moss is growing can be added, so as to give the atmosphere of a miniature woodland.

The glass cage will require a doorway and a small amount of ventilation in the form of one or two small "windows" of perforated zinc. One should aim at creating a dampish atmosphere inside the cage, as this will help to keep the mosses and ferns fresh and healthy.

Toad Hall

Such a vivarium makes a perfect home for those small creatures known as amphibians. Having naked skins, they avoid sunshine and exposed places, preferring to live in damp, shady surroundings. One well-known amphibian is the toad. This fat, warty little animal could never claim a beauty prize, but makes up for its ugliness with its gentle and docile manners. Toads like to sit about under shelters, which can be provided by using strips of bark raised on stones. A flower-pot split lengthwise and placed on its side makes a very good "Toad Hall."

It is interesting to watch a toad catch its food. It will feed on almost any kind of insect or worm, and any small, moving object nearby will attract its attention. There is a sudden flick of the tongue and the meal disappears. A pet toad becomes very tame and may even take a meal out of the owner's hand, but it will only catch live or moving prey.

Frogs are sometimes kept in captivity, but are not such a success, as they scare very easily and may dash about madly inside the cage, doing themselves harm. They are much more lively, and may be distinguished from toads by their smooth, moist skins, longer legs and pointed snouts.

Photo:
Zoological Society
of London

The Malay horned bull toad—these amphibians make up for their ugliness with their gentle and docile manners

An even stranger amphibian is the bright yellow and black salamander which occurs all over Europe. It hides in rocks and undergrowth by day, coming out after rain or in the evening time. This harmless little animal has a notorious history. Many people still believe that it is deadly poisonous, and there is a legend that it can live in fire. All this is nonsense, and it can quite safely be handled. Safely, that is, from the human's point of view, if not the salamander's. Handling is not recommended, because a salamander's skin is soft and sensitive and can easily be damaged.

Sometimes a family is born, and this is the only time a salamander enters water. Unlike frogs and toads, there is no egg stage and the mother produces large living families of gilled babies. These take about three months to develop lungs before leaving the water. They can be easily reared by feeding on tiny water creatures.

Reptiles Love the Sun

Reptiles, such as snakes and lizards, require a somewhat different treatment. These scaly creatures prefer dry and warm surroundings and are fond of basking. The vivarium tray should be filled with dry, sandy earth, with "caves" of rockwork and curved strips of bark provided as hiding places. These should contain nests of dry grass or moss. A drinking dish must be placed in a corner. If plants are to be included, these should be buried in their pots so that when they are watered the rest of the vivarium remains reasonably dry. Plants to choose include succulents, cacti and rock plants which enjoy warm and dry places. The reason for these dry conditions is that snakes and lizards regularly shed or slough their outer skins and it is important that these should come away cleanly. Health is impaired if the skin is always moist, as this tends to encourage fungus growths.

A favourite pet snake is the grass-snake, which may be purchased or caught wild. In catching a snake, it is important to know the difference between the grass-snake and the venomous adder. The former is usually larger, more slender, and has bright patches of yellow behind the head. The adder is more thick-set, sluggish in movement and has a dark zig-zag stripe along the back.

The Soft and Silky Grass-snake

Handling or stroking a grass-snake comes as a revelation to many people. They discover that it is not wet and slimy, but soft and silky to the touch. The tongue is not a "sting" but a soft, delicate organ of touch and smell. Also, the grass-snake rarely, if ever, bites. It feeds on frogs, toads and newts, also freshwater fish, being an excellent swimmer. The prey is swallowed alive, but a tame pet can usually be made to take a freshly killed meal.

Lizards make lively and interesting pets. A popular species seen in pet shops is the Green Lizard from South Europe. It lives quite well in groups of three or four, even with a grass-snake for company, since this snake does not eat lizards. The lizards will feed on many kinds of insects, spiders and worms. A useful, bought food is the mealworm, really a larval beetle which is bred as animal food.

A reptile vivarium should be placed in a sunny spot near a window, or even outdoors, so long as it is sheltered from rain. In dull weather an electric-light bulb suspended in the cage roof can be switched on. This should hang a few inches above a flat stone or some bark which will be used by the pets as a sunning spot.

Many naturalists and pet lovers keep and rear insects such as caterpillars. One can learn so much about their habits and life histories this way. As the plants are liable to be eaten away, the vivarium or insect cage should be tall, with a false bottom fitted about six inches from the floor. Small, round holes are drilled into this, and bottles full of water placed in the compartment underneath. Sprays of the food plant are then collected, and pushed through the holes into the bottles below. In this way they will keep fresh for many days until it is necessary to replace them.

Caterpillars vary in their food habits. When fully grown, after their skins are shed a number of times, the caterpillar changes into a pupa or chrysalis, then eventually emerges as a moth or butterfly. Some caterpillars spin a cocoon before pupating, others dig into the soil. It is as well to know about this beforehand.

A famous caterpillar which weaves a

Photo: A. R. Thompson

The common lizard, seen left with young, lives well in groups of three or four, even with a grass-snake for company, and eats insects, spiders and worms

Handling or stroking a grass-snake (below) comes as a revelation —it is not wet and slimy but soft and silky to the touch

silken cocoon is the larva of the silkworm moth. It is possible to rear these interesting caterpillars on an open tray which holds the food plant, even without the use of a cage, since they never leave their food. Mulberry leaves are mainly eaten.

Stick insects make curious pets for the insect cage. They seem to breed and grow up indefinitely on a diet of privet or laurel leaves. They can do this in the absence of males, producing a number of eggs which all hatch into females. Drinking water should be supplied but, as insects drown easily, the dish should contain a wad of cotton wool soaked in water.

There is no end to the curious but interesting pets one can keep in the vivarium. It is a good way of studying small creatures, and a valuable education for children, which helps to teach observation and responsibility, tolerance and kindness towards wild things. In spite of what is often written and said, one quickly learns that the "creepy-crawlies" of Nature are not all necessarily vicious and harmful, ever ready to pounce and sting or bite.

A vivid experience comes to mind. I once kept a particularly large and hairy, tropical spider, popularly known as a tarantula. It turned out to be the gentlest creature in my collection. It did not bite once, and would allow itself to be stroked with the finger-tips, even crawling on to my bare skin as if to enjoy the warmth.

Photos: Zoological Society of London

Frogs, like the Marsh Frog (above), are sometimes kept in captivity but dash madly about in the cage and hurt themselves

690

BUILDING YOUR OWN HOUSE

This is a momentous decision to make, so be sure you have first weighed up all the pros and cons, then consider the various ways of doing it

MUCH thought has to go into the decision to build a house and even more into weighing up what kind and where. A house will absorb a great deal of money, and you are going to be comfortable—or uncomfortable—in it probably for years to come. If you wish to sell it later, obviously the way it is built now, and where it is built, will affect its market value then.

Advantages of Building

The advantages are that one can choose where one lives, and have a house adapted to one's individual needs and taste in size, design and equipment, within the limits of one's financial resources. If you buy an existing house, it is probably because it is the price you can afford to pay and you like, say, the large sunny sitting room so much that you are prepared to put up with the dark passages and the former owner's taste in mantelpieces. If you build, you have the satisfaction of a home that is an expression of your own individuality, incorporating only the features you desire; and you can ensure, by taking care, that it is well constructed, however simple it may be. Moreover, you have a new house, with everything in it new—no half-perished gutters, no corroded boiler system. Once it has got over any minor "teething" troubles, it should cause no worry, given proper maintenance, for about twenty-five years.

Probably you first think of building because you want to live in a certain place— to be near your work, or your friends, or because you are attracted to a particular locality. It is as well to make quite certain that one really does know the locality. The spot that seemed so charming when visited in high summer may prove intolerable in winter. Consider also whether the district will retain its residential character. Do not be in too great a hurry to settle down in a particular place. If possible, live in it temporarily for a while—to find out what it is like. This will also give you a chance of discovering the opportunities there: whether there is, after all, an existing house that would suit you well, what the local builders are doing, what sites may be available. Temporary residence may enable you to carry out the preliminary enquiries more adequately.

Alternative Methods

You may decide to buy a site and build with the help of an architect, or build on your own land but relying mainly on a local builder, or have a house built on a builder's estate. You may even decide to build it with your own hands in the company of other house-seekers.

The steps involved in each case are considered here; also the cost and how to cover it—whichever method is adopted.

BUILDING WITH AN ARCHITECT

He will become your agent and general adviser and will supervise the work

SHOULD I employ an architect? Probably most people ask themselves this question when faced with the problem of building a house: in what follows the advantages of using an architect are set out, and a description given of how exactly, if you call on his services, he will be able to help you.

Firstly he will design a house for you which will be a unique answer to your individual problems. He will ask you exactly what you want in the way of accommodation—number of bedrooms, living rooms, etc.; he will discuss with you and advise on the subject of heating and similar problems; he will explore all the possibilities of

House A: View from south-east, showing large living and dining area window

the site (when this has been chosen with his assistance), and then, with all these considerations in mind, he will make a house that will work well, look well and as nearly as possible fit the needs of your family.

The architect becomes your agent and general adviser in the intricacies of building. He will negotiate with the Local Authorities and obtain the necessary permissions, and he will help to choose a builder as well as supervise the work when building starts. His knowledge of builders in a particular locality is useful here.

An architect has up-to-the-minute knowledge of the latest building techniques and of the associated sciences of heating and lighting. He will also be glad to let you have his advice on the choice of any new furniture you may contemplate buying,

the interior decoration of the house and the layout of the garden.

An architect, with his expert knowledge, working in your interests, may well in the long run save you more than the cost of his fee. Finally, it should be remembered that an architect-designed house, wherever it is located and whatever its size, always has a higher market value should you decide to sell at a later date.

Choosing the Architect

It may be that your

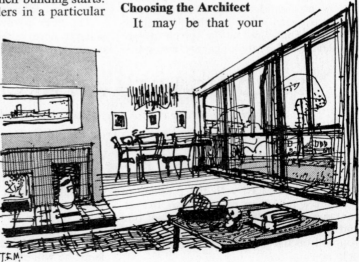

View across the living room towards the dining area

E ELEVATION   S. ELEVATION

House A has the square type of plan considered to be very economical. Entrance is on
the side, heating is by continuous slow-burning
fire in living room with warm air duct to main
bedroom. The roof is of brown interlocking
pantiles set at a 35° slope

friends can recommend one, or you may
see some work that pleases you and ask for
the name of the architect. Alternatively,
the Royal Institute of British Architects,
66 Portland Place, London, W.1, would be
glad to let you have a list of architects in
your district who would be suitable for
your requirements. Also the local Chapter
of Architects (the regional group of members of the Royal Institute of British Architects) would provide you with a list of local
architects.

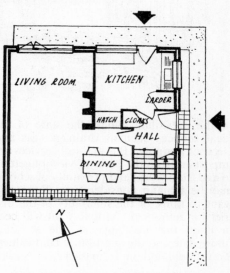

The ground floor plan (above); living and
dining areas look out south to the road running
past the site

Architect's Fees

These will be in accordance with a scale
laid down by the Royal Institute of British
Architects. You will be given a copy of this
scale: briefly, the fees are calculated as a
percentage of the total cost of the building
on a sliding scale which begins at 10 per
cent. for new work costing up to £500,
falling to 6 per cent. for new work costing
£4,000 and over.

Preliminary Investigations

If the site has not already been chosen,
your architect will be able to give you valuable help in choosing one. Some of the factors to be taken into consideration are its
position in respect to the sun, the direction

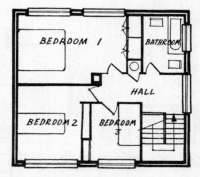

The upper floor with main bedroom, two
smaller bedrooms and bathroom

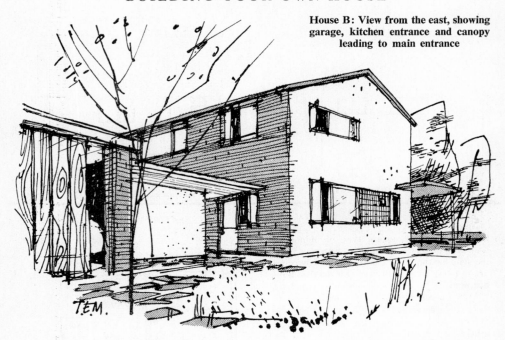

House B: View from the east, showing garage, kitchen entrance and canopy leading to main entrance

of the prevailing winds, the state of the local services such as drainage, gas and electricity supply. Bus and rail services are important from the point of view of getting to and from work, and proximity of schools may be a major consideration. Some will want to think of the suitability of the district for retirement; probably all will bear in mind the possibility of sale at some future date and the question of land values. You should find out from the Local Autho-

rity whether the surroundings are likely to be involved in any development scheme and, if so, what form it is likely to take. Soil is important—it can make a lot of difference to the price of a house, if special foundations are needed.

During these preliminaries, you will have been sorting out your notions of what your requirements are. The ideal client is one who has a fairly clear idea of the size and type of accommodation required, coupled with an open mind on how it can best be provided. Before the first talks with his architect, the client must have made up his mind on the following points: how much he can afford to spend, whether or not the house is to be built with a view to future extension, the number and type of rooms required, type of equipment for the bathroom and kitchen, and, perhaps most important of

Looking across living room towards kitchen; stair screen on the left

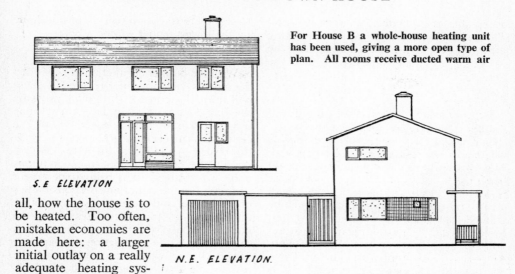

For House B a whole-house heating unit has been used, giving a more open type of plan. All rooms receive ducted warm air

S.E ELEVATION

N.E. ELEVATION.

all, how the house is to be heated. Too often, mistaken economies are made here: a larger initial outlay on a really adequate heating system will be money well invested.

When it comes to deciding what the house is to be built of, your architect will be able to suggest the use of new materials as well as the traditional ones, and to strike a balance with what already exists in the neighbourhood.

Sketch Scheme

When all these points have been discussed, the architect is ready to work out a preliminary or sketch scheme. The name "sketch scheme" is probably misleading because it is at this point that the architect

has to perform his hardest task, that of producing a coherent and good-looking solution to the problem that is presented by the client's requirements. Probably one or two answers will suggest themselves—these the architect will explain to you. When with his advice you have chosen the scheme that suits you best, you must be quite sure that all the important issues have been settled; any major changes from now on would lead to a confused plan and extra expense.

Working Drawings

Assuming that his estimate of the cost is

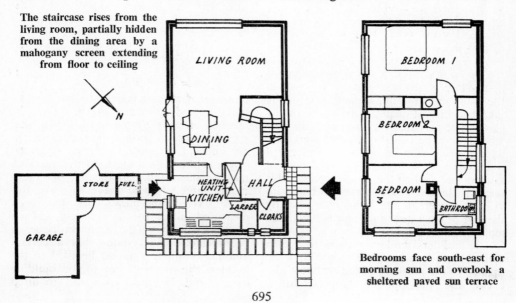

The staircase rises from the living room, partially hidden from the dining area by a mahogany screen extending from floor to ceiling

Bedrooms face south-east for morning sun and overlook a sheltered paved sun terrace

acceptable, the architect can now go ahead with what are known as the "working drawings" for the house. These show the work in great detail and are, in fact, the drawings which the builder eventually uses.

Permissions

At this stage, in the U.K. the Local Authority require certain information about the proposed house so that they can decide whether or not to approve its construction. They will want to know what materials are being used, details of drainage, how it is to be set on the site and its relationship with nearby properties. Two approvals must be granted: (1) the proposed house must conform to local bylaws as regards construction and drainage, etc., and (2) the County Authority must approve it under Town Planning Regulations.

Your architect will be familiar with these negotiations.

Selecting the Builder

Now comes the question of a builder. It may be that a particular builder of known repute has already been singled out. If not, a selected number of reputable firms who are interested in doing the work will be invited by the architect to tender. To each of these will be sent a set of working drawings, together with a "Specification," which is a document describing exactly what has to be done, and in what way. It will contain a general section covering the whole work, and then go on to describe the scope and standard of the work. If the house is going to cost more than £3,000, a further document is sent to the builders invited to tender: this is a Bill of Quantities, which is a schedule of the materials to be used in the building, describing them and giving the quantities of each involved. Normally this will be prepared by a quantity surveyor who is an expert in this type of work and has an up-to-date knowledge of prices, of materials and building operatives' current rates of pay. When the builder receives his copy of the bill of quantities on being invited to tender, he fills in his own price by the side of each item and returns it with his tender.

The builders tendering have to return their tenders by a specified time. They are opened in the presence of the architect, the client and the builders' representative.

Unless there is a good reason for not doing so, the lowest tender will be accepted.

Contract Documents

With the builder decided on, the contract documents can now be prepared. These will normally consist of a set of working drawings, a specification and, if it is being used, a bill of quantities, together with the contract form itself, which will usually be that issued by the Royal Institute of British Architects. This sets out the conditions under which the work is being undertaken, and specifies the duties and responsibilities of the builder and the client. Among other things, the contract stipulates when the builder will take over the site, when work is to commence, the completion date and the period during which the builder will be responsible for making good defects. A sum is also agreed which the builder will have to pay as a forfeit for every week that the work remains incomplete after the agreed completion date.

All the contract documents have to be available in duplicate and are signed by the parties to the contract, the client, and the builder. The architect prepares these documents and usually witnesses the signing.

Under Construction

From start to finish, the architect makes frequent visits to the site to examine and supervise the work in progress. He makes sure that the builder does all that the drawings and specification indicate, and if he is not satisfied with any part of the work he may require that it be taken down and rebuilt to his satisfaction.

Payments to the Builder

As the work progresses, the builder will require some payment from the owner, the manner of payment having already been specified in the contract. For a house it is not unusual to make payments at agreed stages of the work: alternatively, the work may be measured periodically, say every month, and payment made to cover this work. When the new work has been measured, either by the architect or by a quantity surveyor, the architect issues a "certificate" which states that a certain amount of money should be paid to the builder; this is then sent to the building owner and he must pay the required amount to the builder within a given period. As each certificate is issued, an agreed percentage is retained from each; half of the total retained sum is payable on virtual completion of the work and the remainder on the expiry of the defects maintenance period. When this stage is reached, the accounts are balanced, taking into consideration any extra work that may have been ordered or any omissions.

The work is then virtually complete.

Payments to the Architect

The architect's fees are paid in instalments as the work proceeds: one-sixth becomes due on completion of the sketch design and a total of two-thirds on completion of the working drawings. The remaining one-third is payable as the work proceeds.

BUILDING WITHOUT AN ARCHITECT

*You may decide to call in an estate developer or
builder—or to lay the bricks with your own hands*

by P. M. DONAHUE

ON A BUILDING ESTATE

AN estate developer may be at work on land available for building in the locality you have chosen. He will have bought the land and divided it into building plots. Some houses on the estate may be completed and occupied, or perhaps built ready for sale; others may be in course of construction. Sites for houses will be vacant and advertised.

If you consider having a house on one of the vacant plots, you can be shown at the estate office the types of houses that can be built there: the estate developer has five or six designs, possibly more. You can perhaps view houses built to these designs. You may be given a choice as to details—e.g. a "through-type lounge" (open drawing room and dining room instead of separate rooms). Most estate builders are prepared to offer optional extras—e.g. parquet floors, full tiling for bathroom and kitchen—but would not be likely to agree to major modifications. Such items as facing bricks and roofing tiles he buys in quantity, and he may be unwilling to cater for individual tastes in these matters.

If you acquire a house on a building estate, you pay a set price for an agreed type of house. The developer will have handled any problems connected with the site and will have secured the necessary permissions. After you have moved in, you have the garden to make up, and for a time you may have the disadvantage of an unmade road and of construction on other houses going on around you. But within a year these things will probably have been cleared up. You may well have good value for your money. The developer has brought the costing of a house to a fine art, and through buying in quantity and reproduction can keep the price down.

BUILDING AN INDIVIDUAL HOUSE

If you decide on free choice of design and a house built for you individually, you are likely to need expert advice on handling the negotiations and seeing the project through the various stages. If you decide against employing an architect, it is essential that you select a reputable firm of builders, as the success of the project will depend on their ability to supervise and build your house.

Points which should be watched with particular care if you are acting without an architect are detailed below.

Choice of Builder

A good builder is of vital importance. Unfortunately, the jerry-builder is not yet extinct, so, if you are not employing an architect to guard your interests, you are strongly advised to write to: The Registrar, The National House-Builders Registration Council, 58 Portland Place, London, W.1, asking for a list of house-builders in your area who are registered with them, which will be sent free of charge. This Council is a non-profit-making body, formed with the official approval of the Ministry of Housing and Local Government and recognised by Statute, whose principal object is to maintain and improve housing standards. Builders registered with them are pledged to conform to the standards of quality prescribed by the Council's specifications. A house being built by a registered house-builder is inspected at several (normally five or more) stages of construction by a N.H.B.R.C. inspector, and on completion a certificate is given that it conforms to the prescribed standards. You are thus given valuable protection from jerry-building. This certificate will be passed to you by the builder; its possession will increase the value of the house should you wish to sell later. The builder will complete an agreement with you which covers the house against all structural defects arising within two years through non-compliance with the Council's standards. The Council will also appoint an arbitrator in the event of any dispute between the builder and yourself.

The N.H.B.R.C.'s fee is three guineas, covering their complete service, which is payable in the first instance by the builder.

You may have chosen your builder at an early stage, through recommendation, or because you are taking a site bought by a builder for building purposes. You will then have his help as regards the site, drawing up plans and getting permissions. Otherwise, when you have reached the stage of having detailed plans and specifications, you can send out copies to tender and obtain building services at a competitive price, as is done by an architect.

Site

This may be on a builder's plot, or chosen and bought by you from the original owner (here you will probably call upon a solicitor's help). A surveyor or builder would advise you as to its suitability. Its nearness to shops, schools, main roads and public transport will doubtless be factors of importance. The type of soil and whether the site would need much levelling will naturally affect the total cost of your house, and so would the availability of main water and main drainage. If it is in an isolated spot, you may need to have a cesspool made and a well sunk (the builder would see to this). Choose the site before you decide in detail on the type of house you wish to have.

Plans

A builder will produce plans for your inspection. Books of designs can be obtained from firms specialising in them. The site will condition your choice: a plan for a house facing north cannot be simply turned round to fit a site facing south. Your chosen plan can then be modified according to your own ideas—and to how much you are prepared to spend. But outlay in some directions may be a good investment. At this stage reckon up how many electric points you require for single-purpose use and how many for plugging-in portable appliances. It is also well worth considering the advantages of the various modern methods of warming the house, such as electrical under-floor heating, gas warm-air ducted heating, and oil-fired central heating. You may also wish to have extra insulation, for instance, in the roof, or have doors and windows draught-proofed, or have double glazing on the north side. Do not begrudge time spent in making sketches and in discussion of detail. Decide as far as possible on even minor matters before construction begins.

Your preliminary enquiries, making of draft plans and final decisions may take months—but the resulting house is going to last for years.

Materials

It is worth investigating the great variety and latest development in materials and equipment available. At the Building Centre, Store Street, Tottenham Court Road, London, W.C.1, manufacturers are enabled to exhibit objects and materials used in the erection and equipping of buildings. It is open, free, to architects, builders and members of the public.

Permissions

When your plans are completed, copies must be sent to the Local Council and Town and Country Planning authorities before starting to build in the U.K. There are a number of formalities to be gone through and, as indicated previously, it is advisable to have expert help. It may take a few months to get your plans passed.

Builder's Contract

This is drawn up once the plans are officially approved, and here it is best to have assistance from a firm of solicitors, who would also make sure that the builder's contract includes every item—including road development charges (the builder must place a deposit with the Local Authorities to guarantee these), drainage, solicitor's and transfer fees. It is depressing to be faced with a load of extras later on, and you would pay more in the long run.

It is preferable for the contract to include a maintenance period. During the first year small defects tend to appear, chiefly owing to the drying out of the house. Doors may

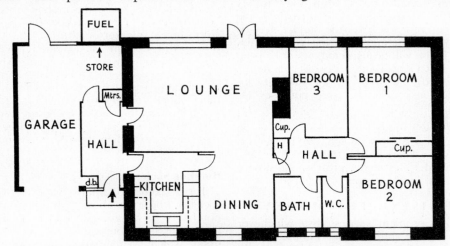

Plan of the Renway (Type C/6) Bungalow, with good built-in cupboards in the bedrooms, planned kitchen, garage, and store

The Renway (Type C/6) Bungalow built by Renway Construction Co. Ltd., on their estate at Edgcumbe Park, Crowthorne, Berks, has warm-air central heating, first-class insulation, including "dry lining" and double glazing

stick through the shrinkage of the wood, cracks appear in the plaster and pipes may drip. If his contract provides for maintenance for a certain period, the builder will rectify this. Otherwise, they would have to be dealt with in the course of redecoration, and might cost you £50 more.

Construction

This usually takes from four to six months. Progress will depend partly on the weather and how busy the builder may be on other buildings. During construction your house will be inspected, not only by an N.H.B.R.C. inspector (if your builder is registered), but by a Local Authority inspector, inspecting for bylaw purposes.

Cost

By now you are in a position to know, at least roughly, how much the house will cost you. There will be the cost of the site, the builder's estimate, professional advice fees, and legal charges.

RAISING THE MONEY

This problem arises by whichever method one builds one's house. Most people would find it impossible or would not choose (preferring to invest the money) to pay down the total sum to cover the whole cost. They therefore seek to raise a loan on mortgage from the Local Authority or a Building Society or an Insurance Company. It is worth obtaining details of the facilities all can offer and comparing them before deciding which to apply for. Your bank manager can also advise you.

It is normally possible to obtain a loan of up to about 90 per cent., provided you can give evidence of being able to repay over a period. Nevertheless, do not assume that almost the whole of your outlay can be covered by a mortgage. Whoever is considering granting you a loan will have an independent valuation made of your house, and the offer is based on whichever is the lower figure—this valuation or the actual cost.

Copies of your plans and specifications will have to be submitted with your application for a loan.

In the brief notes below, the terms mentioned may be subject to alteration.

Local Councils

Under the Housing Acts, Local Authorities are enabled to make loans on mortgage. The facilities offered vary from place to place. If you come under an Urban District Council where the scheme does not operate, the County Council would probably consider your application.

To quote an example: the London County Council is prepared to advance up to 100 per cent. of what the Council's surveyor estimates to be the market price of your property. The interest rate varies with current market conditions; the 1960 rate is $6\frac{1}{4}$ per cent. on a loan repayable over a period of not more than twenty years. If necessary, advances will be made by instalment as the building proceeds, the Council's surveyor having visited the site. The fee for the survey ranges from £4 to £8 10s. with an additional charge for each inspection when the advance is made by instalments.

Building Societies

Terms and conditions vary between societies (there are about 750), but you are not likely to be granted a loan of more than three times your annual income or one upon which the monthly instalment is greater than your weekly income. The surveyor of a Building Society to which you have applied will inspect on completion of your house and make his valuation, though he will inspect at an earlier stage if you wish to borrow money in advance to pay the builder's instalments before completion. Normally a loan will be up to 90 per cent., and the interest rate, which varies, may be from 6 to $6\frac{1}{2}$ per cent. The repayments, usually monthly, may be able to be spread over a longer period with a Building Society than with some Local Councils. An insurance policy, giving security to dependents as regards the mortgage in the event of your death, can be included in a Combined Scheme.

Insurance Companies

Here again, terms and conditions vary. The following particulars are of one of the largest insurance societies: Loans are made normally of 75 per cent. (but rising to a maximum of 90 per cent.) on properties of not less than £2,000 market value (as estimated by the Society's valuer, who will visit the site, with your plans and specifications before him. The house will be sub-

Some of the fourteen houses the Isis Housing Association built with their own hands in Oxford, with little experience of building. Houses cost about £1,800 each; market value is much higher

ject to a final inspection by the valuer on completion to ascertain that it is, in fact, completed properly.) In this Insurance Society, advances during the course of construction are not made. The rate of interest charged is $5\frac{1}{2}$ per cent.

Repayment is made by means of an Endowment Insurance Policy on the life of the borrower, the sum insured being equal to the amount of the loan and maturing in a specified period, usually twenty years. The loan is thus fully paid off on maturity of the policy or on the death of the insured person, whichever event first occurs (the borrower's dependants thus gain valuable protection). The borrower will, of course, have to satisfy the Insurance Society as to his eligibility (e.g. on medical grounds) to be a life policy holder.

BUILDING WITH YOUR OWN HANDS

In 1949 a group of ex-Servicemen in Brighton set about building homes for themselves with their own hands, and since then over 200 groups have been doing likewise in their leisure time and holidays. The Self Build Housing Society movement has had a great success, and new groups are still being formed.

The members of a group work together until each has a completed house—the undertaking usually takes about two and a half years. Generally, three-bedroomed semi-detached houses and bungalows are built.

The National Federation of Housing Societies, 12 Suffolk Street, Pall Mall, London, S.W.1, acts as an advisory body to help self-help building groups in their approach to the Local Authorities and on financial matters. It advises them to register as legal entities and as duly constituted Housing Associations or Societies, under the Industrial and Provident Societies Acts—so gaining status to enter into contracts and become eligible for facilities —e.g. mortgage loans—under the Housing Acts. It also advises their engaging a surveyor when buying the land and securing the services of an architect.

The Federation recommends that the original contribution of each member for preliminary expenses and working capital should be about £50. As a recognised Housing Association, it is possible for a group to borrow almost 100 per cent. of its further costs from the Local Authority (provided the latter is willing to co-operate) or from a Building Society.

INSURANCE AND THE FAMILY

A comprehensive guide to the various forms of cover
available for your protection, in and out of the home

THE United Kingdom provides one of the finest insurance services in the world, and nowhere is the quality of British insurance better exemplified than in the many forms of cover provided for the personal protection of private householders.

To begin with, there is the householder's comprehensive policy itself. For a few shillings a year per £100 of value, this policy covers the contents of your home against all sorts of risks. Among the main ones are fire, explosion and lightning; storm, tempest and flood; burst pipes and overflowing tanks; and burglary, housebreaking and theft. The same policy provides similar protection for the possessions of domestic servants, and also covers many possessions of yourself and your family while temporarily removed from the home. A case in point is the clothes you stand up in, which might be burnt on a bus or train by someone's cigarette.

Tenants and Owners

There are, by the way, two types of householder's comprehensive policies. One type is for those who rent a house or flat and who, therefore, usually have a limited responsibility for damage to the actual property. The other type gives wider cover on the building and is for those who own their home.

All comprehensive policies, however, indemnify you in respect of your legal liability to members of the general public who suffer personal injury or damage to their property while on your premises. If that sounds a bit complicated, suppose the milkman broke his ankle by missing his footing on one of your steps that was in a bad state of repair, or Mrs. Jones from next door slipped on your highly polished floor and broke her arm. The milkman or Mrs. Jones might then very well take legal action and succeed in obtaining damages against you. There are many proceedings of this sort in our courts every year, so do not imagine that provision of cover against

such incidents is merely "window-dressing" the policy. Like other forms of insurance, it exists to fulfil a definite need.

A further benefit of the comprehensive policy, and one that often escapes notice, is the death cover on the life of the policyholder. This provides a capital sum in the event of the policyholder's death in his or her home due to fire or burglars or housebreakers.

The Value of Possessions

However, the point about insurance of the home which is most frequently overlooked is the necessity of insuring possessions for their full value. Without this simple precaution you may well find that, if one day you lose everything in a fire, the amount you receive from the insurance company will not be enough to buy replacements. So as soon as you have time to spare, go from room to room listing all that you possess—and all means everything from the children's toys to kitchen utensils, not just the more obvious items of furniture. Then work out what it would cost to replace the things on your list at present-day values. The total which you arrive at is the proper amount for which you should insure. What is more, you will probably be pleasantly surprised to discover how much you have belonging to you.

Should you have any difficulty in deciding on the correct figure, seek the help of your insurance company. Though naturally they cannot undertake a valuation of your possessions, they will be pleased to give advice born of very long and very practical experience. And it costs you nothing. Similarly, they are always prepared to give free advice on ways of reducing the risk of fire and burglary. In case you are prompted to think that the taking of proper precautions doesn't matter when you are adequately insured, it is as well to bear in mind these two points: first, no amount of insurance can recompense you for all the inconvenience a bad fire or burglary causes; second, it is a cardinal

It might have been your home (left), its roof gutted by fire and furniture ruined. It pays to insure adequately against such contingencies

A common cause of fire (below): timber beams under the hearth smouldered for days, undetected, then caught fire when the householder was out

principle of the contract between you and the insurance company that at all times you act with the same care as you would if you were not insured.

It should be realised, too, that householder's comprehensive insurance does not give cover against mere loss of an article. For protection against this hazard, and that of accidental damage, a separate "all risks" policy is required. As its name implies, "all risks" insurance covers the articles specified in the policy against almost every mishap, whether in the home or not. The kind of possessions needing "all risks" protection are valuables you take about with you: jewellery, furs, watches, rings, portable typewriters. The standard "all risks" policy is for the U.K. only, but for a small extra premium can be extended to include other countries. For those who travel a great deal there is a special "all risks" insurance designed to cover everyday personal effects, while for the photographer, both amateur and professional, there are inexpensive "all risks" camera policies.

Household Removals

Two other insurances very much concerned with the home are the "household removals" policy and the "television and wireless" policy. The household removals policy protects your possessions during moving against loss or damage caused by fire, theft, pilfering and accident. Here the word "accident" denotes everything from a collision involving the furniture van to the removals men dropping a crate of your best china. Cover under the policy is effective from the moment moving is begun at the old home until it is finished at the new one, where, of course, your goods are immediately covered by the ordinary householder's comprehensive policy. In effect, what happens is that the insurance people co-ordinate the various insurances so that your things are not left even momentarily without adequate protection. Incidentally, if you are buying your new home, the insurance on the house itself should start as soon as you pay your deposit, for that is when your insurable interest in the property begins.

Television and wireless insurance, which also covers radiograms and high fidelity amplifiers, includes loss or damage to the set resulting from fire, lightning, explosion, theft and what are called "accidental external means." Not covered are ordinary electrical breakdowns caused by wear and tear. On the other hand, you are protected against damage to property (your own or your family's, or for which you are responsible) caused by the equipment. Likewise, protection is given in respect of your legal liability for injury to other people and damage to *their* property—though, of course, injury or damage would have to be caused by the TV or radio apparatus insured. Commonest source of such third party claims are aerials carried away in gales.

Sporting Policies

So from TV's passive entertainment to one's own sporting activities. Here three types of cover are inexpensively combined under one policy: personal accident, public liability, and insurance on the sports equipment itself to guard against damage by fire and accident and loss by theft.

Main provisions of the personal accident part of the cover are for a capital sum for the loss of an eye or limb, or for accidental death, or weekly compensation for temporary total disablement resulting from an injury. Naturally, to qualify for benefit you have to suffer injury while actually taking part in the sport for which you are insured. The same principle applies to the public liability section of a sporting policy. Thus a golfer's policy would pay the legal damages and costs awarded against you because, during a game of golf, you had unfortunately driven the ball into someone's face or through a window of a house. But clearly, the golfer's policy would not cover you against the consequences of those or other misfortunes caused while you were playing cricket, say, or tennis.

Like the golfer's insurance, most sporting policies available to amateurs cost only 10s. each a year; some are a few shillings more. Cover for more than one sport

brings a reduction of up to a third of the total premium.

Holiday Insurance

Another worthwhile investment to ensure leisure-time peace of mind is holiday insurance. This, for a few shillings per person per week of holiday, provides for payment of doctors' fees and hospital costs arising out of any injury that comes your way on holiday. Equally important, provision is made for the payment of extra hotel and travelling expenses which such injury causes through postponement of the return journey. Covered, too, are the costs of X-ray and other specialist treatment, ambulance journeys and surgical appliances. Death cover which, if you die as a result of an accident, brings your dependants a capital sum can be added to the holiday policy for a small additional premium. This extension, however, is not normally required by those who already have a personal accident or life assurance policy.

Holiday insurance is doubly reassuring when taking holidays abroad where you get the medical attention you pay for. We in Britain are dangerously inclined to overlook the fact that medical, hospital and other treatment is *not* free in many other countries of the world. These are some of the reasons why one of the most popular forms of holiday insurance is the accident cover specially written for winter sports enthusiasts.

Luggage and Rain

Whenever you are travelling with a fair amount of luggage, either on holiday or business, it is always advisable to safeguard your belongings with baggage insurance. It costs very little and is virtually an "all risks" policy on your luggage, safeguarding it against such familiar hazards as straightforward loss, damage or total loss by fire, accident, theft, flood.

Admittedly less essential, but certainly very comforting at holiday time, is rain insurance. Few things are calculated to fray the nerves more than hour upon hour spent within the four walls of an hotel, one eye cocked permanently at rain-beaten windows for a break in the weather, the other keeping wary watch on what-the-children-are-up-to-now. And all you wanted was peace and quiet and a place in the sun. What a consolation, then, the thought of financial recompense from your rain insurers! Besides, there is always the chance that most of the stipulated rainfall will come at night—in which event you have your holiday weather and the pay-out from the rain insurance people, too.

Compensation paid by the usual rain insurance is either seven or eight times the weekly premium; it depends on the time of year. A premium of £3 in July and August would bring compensation of £21; in March, April, May, June and September, £24. At all places on the rain insurers' "official" list you have a claim if (a) ·20 of an inch of rain falls on each of three or more days in a week, or (b) during a week there is enough rain to make up a total of 1½ in. Minimum premium is 5s. a week, but the top limit is up to you. For districts not on the standard rain insurance list,

If a burglar steals your jewellery, you may never be able to replace it—but it is some consolation to be covered by insurance

most rain insurers readily quote premium rates and rainfall levels by request. They also quote rates for short-term rain insurance on specific events. Examples: cricket matches, garden parties, outdoor wedding receptions.

Caravan Cover

For people who go holidaying in their own caravans the right insurance is advisable on a number of counts, two of the most important being the cost of replacing these vehicles and making good accidental damage, and the fact that they often contain at various times a goodly proportion of their owners' valuables. And, of course, when it comes to living permanently in a caravan, suitable insurance on one's home is just as important as it is for the house or flat dweller.

To whichever of the two uses the caravan is put, the insurance policy is the same. Its protection is three-fold. First, loss of, or damage to, the caravan and its equipment. Second, similar cover in respect of your luggage and personal belongings— and those of your family—while *actually* in the caravan or the car by which the caravan is being drawn. To clarify that last point, the insurance people don't mean that your luggage and possessions and those of your family which are in the car are not covered unless car and caravan are on the move. What they do mean is that, in general, they are not covered by the

How it's done—the burglar is disturbed, so he grabs the "swag," jumps out the window and is off to a waiting car

caravan insurance if you unhook the car and drive off to the nearest market town for food supplies or a visit to the cinema. A further qualification to have in mind is that equipment, as well as luggage and personal effects in the caravan, are not covered in most respects unless the caravan is locked-up when you leave it unattended. The only exceptions to this ruling are when the loss or damage is caused by fire or accidental collision. Remember also that if ever you rent your caravan to other people you need special insurance. The ordinary policy, while valid when non-paying relatives and friends use the caravan, ceases to cover you the moment you hire out the vehicle for reward.

The third form of protection provided by caravan insurance covers you against your legal liability—that is, your financial liability at law—for death or injury to other people, or damage to their property caused by the caravan. Here it is important to understand that this public liability section gives no cover in respect of third party claims arising out of accidents caused by the motor car drawing the vehicle. You should, therefore, make quite sure that your motor insurance policy allows you to use your car with a trailer. If it does not, ask your motor insurer to amend it accordingly. Otherwise you may find yourself breaking the law, which lays it down that *valid* third party insurance is compulsory for every motor car on the road.

Motor Insurance

As to motor insurance itself, a great many people are necessarily familiar with this class of cover in one form or another. However, since it comes in several different forms in the U.K. it is as well to describe them briefly here. To begin with, there is what insurance men call "Act" only insurance. The Act referred to is the Road Traffic Act of 1930 which, along with subsequent legislation, requires that every driver of a motor vehicle—motor car, motor cycle or motorised bicycle—must be insured to cover his or her legal liability for death or injury to third parties. Before third-party insurance became compulsory, it sometimes happened that the motorist was quite unable to pay the amount of the damages awarded against him. Thus the victims of the accident received little

or no financial compensation. To-day all types of motor vehicle insurance include proper cover against the third party risk; but the "Act" only policy is limited to insurance of this risk and no other.

Cheap though it is, comparatively few people rely on the very limited "Act" only protection. The more usual form of basic motor vehicle insurance is the "full" third party policy, which adds to third party death and injury protection, cover against third party claims in respect of damage to property. Though third party property damage insurance is not compulsory, it has an obvious advantage: your motor insurers and not you as a driver pay the cost of the damage to other people's property for which you are found legally liable. Without such cover you might one day emerge from court to find yourself responsible for several hundred—or thousand—pounds' worth of damage to someone else's property. This would cause most people some hardship; for many it would mean financial ruin.

Next in the scale of motor insurance is the policy which provides full third party protection, plus cover on your own vehicle in respect of theft and fire. Finally, there is the comprehensive policy, which is by far the best type of insurance safeguard for the motoring public. As well as full third party protection, there is fire, theft and accidental damage cover (including frost damage) on the vehicle itself, and personal accident insurance on the driver against injury or death. In addition, most comprehensive motor car policies pay up to a certain sum for medical expenses incurred by driver and passengers through injuries received on the road. Up to a certain amount is also payable on rugs, coats and luggage damaged accidentally in the car, or lost because of fire or theft. For a slight extra premium the comprehensive policy can be extended to include the third party liability of motor-car passengers, the most likely source of such claims being the careless opening of car doors and the consequent knocking down of pedestrians and cyclists.

Obtainable for a somewhat larger additional premium is personal accident cover for passengers, i.e. a capital sum in the event of death or the loss of one or more eyes and limbs, or so much per week up to 26 weeks in cases of temporary total disablement. This extra personal accident cover for your passengers has nothing to do with any legal claims they might take against you for injuries—in respect of which contingency you are already adequately protected by the full third party cover of the standard comprehensive policy. If, incidentally, you have one of the "Act" only policies already described, then you are not normally covered against third party claims by passengers. For except in a few special circumstances, passengers do not qualify as third parties within the meaning of the Road Traffic Acts.

For Motor Cyclists

Another case in which you are not normally covered against third party injury claims by a passenger is when he or she is riding pillion on a motor cycle which you are driving. Nor can you get for that passenger insurance providing personal injury benefits.

Among other respects in which motor cycle comprehensive insurance differs from comprehensive car cover are the exclusion of frost damage to the engine and personal injury insurance for the driver. This last,

however, is usually obtainable as an extra —as are personal accident insurance on sidecar passengers, and cover for your third party liability to them. Just one more point concerning sidecars; for those who always use a motor cycle with sidecar attached most companies halve the premium for the basic policy—but not that for the extras mentioned above.

Much the same as motor cycle insurance are the policies available for auto-cycles, power-assisted pedal cycles and ordinary bicycles: according to your needs, you can choose one of several insurances ranging from fully comprehensive to third party only. For instance, comprehensive cover—including personal injury benefits —on a bicycle valued at £15 costs less than £1 a year.

In discussing the different insurances for motor vehicles the assumption has been that use of the vehicle is confined to what is called "class one" usage. Intended primarily for "social, domestic and pleasure purposes only," most policies in this classification nevertheless allow certain limited forms of business use. But very often the business use in question is outside the scope of the "class one" policy, so a policy giving wider protection is then needed. Since practice in this matter varies between

Whenever you travel with a fair amount of luggage, you can safeguard it against all the familiar hazards with a special baggage insurance

companies, the best thing is always to talk it over with the motor insurers of your choice. In that way you can be quite sure of having the right policy, and therefore the proper cover at all times.

Whatever sort of motor insurance you have, it is important to realise that "proper cover at all times" means you must have a current road fund licence and a current driving licence. If either of these is out of date, you not only break the law by taking your car or motor cycle on the road, you also invalidate your insurance.

Personal Liability

Now a brief word or two about personal liability insurance. Its purpose is to provide you with cover against your legal liability to members of the general public as you go about daily life in your private capacity—and not in some special capacity such as that of motorist or householder, for which, as was shown earlier, legal liability cover is included already in your motor insurance and your householder's comprehensive insurance. But, you say, how does this affect me? Here are some ways in which it has affected other people. A man running for a bus knocked down a woman shopping; she sued him; the court found in her favour and he had to pay her £1,300 in damages. A woman stepped off the pavement without looking, caused a car to swerve and kill a man crossing the road. After a court action the woman had to pay £2,500 to the dead man's dependants.

A light-hearted example is that of the city business man who, returning home in a rush-hour train, accidentally spilt a pot of paint over a fellow traveller. Being insurance-conscious, our spiller-of-paint already had a personal liability policy; otherwise the cost of his carelessness—£40—would have had to come out of his own pocket.

Like many another, that policyholder thinks personal liability cover at 10s. a year is right out of the insurance market's bargain basement. And indeed it is. Because for this 10s. you get more than legal liability protection for yourself; you get it for your wife and children and any other members of your household, too. This is a comforting thought for parents who cannot always tell what their children will be up to next. According to the insurance records, there was one father who had no

idea that his young son was going to fill a balloon with hydrogen in his back garden. But he did. And a few feet up the balloon exploded and shattered dozens of neighbouring windows. Father, of course, got the bill for the damage.

Fortunately that particular incident injured no one. But the fact that it might have done leads automatically to the more serious topic of personal accident insurance. This is one of the most inexpensive forms of cover designed to safeguard your personal welfare as opposed to the protection of your property and your legal responsibilities to others. At the cost of a few pounds a year, it ensures that if you are laid up as a result of an accident, you receive a regular weekly income for up to two years. Provision is also made for capital sum payments should you lose one or more eyes or limbs, while accidental death brings the benefit of a lump sum to your dependants.

Some P.A. policies, as they are called, pay weekly benefits only in respect of "*temporary total* disablement." Others also pay reduced benefit for "*temporary partial* disablement"; in any event, those that do not can always be extended to include this extra safeguard if you think you may have need of it. In the unfortunate circumstance of "*permanent total* disablement," some policies provide a regular income up to a certain maximum period, others a single capital payment.

Personal Sickness

On similar lines to personal accident insurance are personal sickness policies. They provide much the same benefits in cases of sickness as the other type does in cases of accident. In fact, for all-round protection many people take out a combined personal accident and sickness policy. Either way, the sickness cover can be had on specified diseases only or on most of the ills we humans are heir to. Whichever type of policy you decide is best for you—personal accident or sickness or the two combined—you should always make sure that the weekly income payable in the event of a claim would be sufficient to meet all your regular household expenses. For some of us £5 a week would be enough; others would need £20 a week.

Without insurance against third party property damage, a motorist can easily find himself responsible for hundreds of pounds' worth of damage (above). But without third party cover against death and injury (right), he is also breaking the law

You can usually obtain cover more cheaply if you agree that no weekly benefits shall be payable during the first month, say, of sickness or accidental disability. Generally, this money-saving concession has especial appeal for those who know that when they are laid up they will continue to receive their full wage or salary for some definite period.

The cheapest of all forms of annual personal accident insurance is the policy which provides cover restricted to rail and road accidents. One well-known road and rail accident policy on the market costs £1 a year and pays £6 a week for up to 52 weeks for temporary total disablement. Capital sums are £1,000 on death, or on the loss of two limbs or eyes or one limb and one eye; and £500 for the loss of one limb or eye. To avoid any misunderstanding as to when you would qualify for any of these benefits, the precise terms of the policy are—accidental death or injury caused by: (1) an accident to a train in which you are travelling as fare-paying

passenger; (2) an accident to any road vehicle (except a motor cycle) in which you are travelling or driving; (3) the impact of a train or any road vehicle while you are a pedestrian. As well as covering you against such misfortunes all the year round, it covers you in all parts of the world, too.

Finally, if you do not want world-wide, year-round protection, or if you want to increase your P.A. protection for a particular journey, there is always the short-term policy which for a shilling or two covers you against disaster on a specified train or aeroplane trip.

Life Assurance

Though the popularity of personal accident cover has for long been on the increase, the form of personal insurance protection best known to-day is life assurance. And for good reason—namely, that it can be used to the advantage of one's financial security in so many different ways. But before looking at the most important of these ways, it is a help to distinguish between two branches of life assurance business. One is referred to as "industrial" life assurance, the other as "ordinary" life assurance. The first thing to make clear is that the name "industrial" has nothing to do with industry; it is purely historical in origin, and derives from the fact that this branch of life assurance was first brought into being to serve the limited needs of the industrial population of Victorian times.

To-day, the most easily discernible difference between it and "ordinary" life assurance is in the method of collecting the premiums. "Ordinary" life premiums are paid annually, six-monthly or quarterly—sometimes monthly—by cheque or by banker's order. "Industrial" life premiums, on the other hand, are collected at regular and frequent intervals—usually weekly or fortnightly or monthly—by life assurance agents calling on policyholders at their homes. That is why the "industrial" branch is becoming increasingly known as "home service" life assurance. That, too, is one reason why it is so popular as a method of making financial provision for the future; the agent's regular visits so conveniently gear the life assurance savings habit to the budgeting routine of the average family.

Two Life Branches

Another difference between the two life branches is that, generally, the individual sums assured under "ordinary" life policies are bigger than those under "home service" policies. One very practical aspect of this difference is that the buying of a house by means of a life policy, which usually involves assurance for a substantial amount, is always done through the "ordinary" life branch. That, however, is no cause for concern for the holder of a "home service" policy who is also a prospective house purchaser, for almost every "home service" agent transacts "ordinary" life business also.

Though tailor-made, as it were, to meet individual needs in the way of personal and family security, life assurance policies of all kinds divide up into roughly two main classes of cover. These are "whole life" assurance and "endowment" assurance. "Whole life" assurance has as its single purpose the provision of a capital sum for the dependants of the person assured in the event of his or her death. As the most inexpensive form of permanent life cover available, it is particularly suited to someone whose first thought must be for the welfare of others in case of the insured's early death. An everyday example is the young man of modest means who is newly married or who is the sole support, say, of a widowed parent. However, "whole life" policies, which may be taken out for any desired sum, are also frequently used concurrently with endowment assurance, the idea being that when the endowment matures the whole life cover ensures continuing protection for one's dependants.

Endowment Policies

This second type of life assurance, endowment assurance, is essentially a method of saving now for your financial security in the future. It runs for an agreed period of years—15 or 20, for instance—or else is designed to mature at some pre-determined age of the life assured: at 60 or 65, say. When the policy matures, you receive either a capital sum there and then or regular pension payments over the years.

During the term of the endowment policy—and "term" is merely a convenient way of saying "from the time it is taken out until the time it matures"—life cover is included for the protection of your dependants. Thus if you took out an endowment policy designed to pay you £1,000 at the end of 20 years and you died before the 20 years was up, then your wife and children would immediately receive the £1,000.

Both endowment and whole life assurance can be had in the form of a "with-" or "without-profits" policy. Premiums for the "with-profits" policy are slightly more expensive, but have the advantage of enabling you to share in the profits of the life assurance office concerned with your policy. The life offices declare the profits due to holders of "with-profits" policies regularly every few years; normally, these profits take the form of a valuable bonus addition to policyholders' benefits which can be drawn as these become due or added on to the total.

And talking of benefits in a wider sense, life assurance has the advantage over most other forms of saving in that the Government allows valuable income-tax relief on the money you set aside for premiums for whole life or endowment cover on your own life or that of your wife. Furthermore, the money which you invest in life assurance is always a useful source of ready cash in case of urgent need, for your bank or life office will loan you up to 90 per cent. of the surrender value of your policy. Some life policies acquire a surrender value after one year; most after two years.

Children's Education

That endowment assurance is a method of helping to ensure a suitable standard of living in retirement and old age is well known. Less well known is the fact that you can also use it as a very practical means of assisting to-morrow's generation to make the best of *their* future. Take the

very important matter of your children's education. Most of us want to give our children the best education we can afford, because we know what a good start in life it gives them. To this end, the life assurance people have produced special education endowment assurance.

In the event of Death

This is how it works. An endowment policy is taken out on the life of one of the parents, usually the father, when the child is about 2 years old. Assuming that the child is a boy and that he will be going to a public school at 13, and that the school fees will be £300 a year, the father takes out a policy which, in 11 years, pays £300 a year for 5 years. For the convenience of the parents, the annual benefit payable over the 5 years is normally paid in quarterly or termly instalments. Against the death of the father or the child there are a number of important safeguards.

If the child dies during the 11-year endowment period, the policy may be handed in to the life office, who pay you the ap-

Parents cannot always tell what their children will be up to next—or if that ball is going to injure someone or break a window. Personal liability insurance covers parents against such liabilities

propriate surrender value for the number of years the endowment has been in force. If, however, the child dies during the 5-year benefit period, our hypothetical £300 a year continues to be paid until the end of that time. Should the father die before the 11-year term of the endowment is up, the policy immediately pays the remaining parent (or guardian) £300 a year for the next 5 years. The income payable under such an education policy is not conditional on its being used to pay the child's school fees, so were the father to die, the mother would be quite free to decide to use the income to meet more pressing needs.

Child Endowment Policies

Also available for your children's future well-being is the child endowment policy. It is taken out on the life of the child, not that of a parent, as soon after birth as possible. The policy matures when the child comes of age at 21, at which time he or she may either elect to receive a capital sum or convert the child policy into an ordinary whole life or endowment assurance at a considerably lower rate of premium than would otherwise be possible. Should the child die before reaching 21, the parents receive a capital sum equivalent to the premiums paid.

From all that has been said, it is readily understandable that life assurance is so firmly linked in the mind with predominantly manly responsibilities and with the family, that many young single women tend to think it is of little use to them. Their thoughts, certainly, are with manly responsibilities and the family, but they take quite another direction. Yet it is precisely in this other direction that life cover can be of value to the bachelor girl, for whom there is what is known as the "single woman's policy." It is to be had either in the form of whole life cover or of an endowment assurance. And its three special features all hinge on the probability of marriage. When that happens she can trade in the policy for a lump sum, which makes a useful dowry. Or she can transfer the policy to her husband's life without his being required to undergo the usual life office medical examination, which strengthens the financial aspect of the marriage. Or she can decide to keep the policy in force on her own life, which she

might well do for a number of reasons, such as ensuring the future welfare of a dependent relative.

House Purchase

As to their future life together, our erstwhile bachelor girl and her husband will inevitably want a house of their own. There are several ways in which life assurance can help them—and you—to achieve this ambition. One way is to borrow the money from a life office, with whom you take out an endowment assurance equivalent to the amount of the house purchase loan. The sum assured under the policy is payable at the end of an agreed term of years or in the event of your previous death. In both cases the life office use the sum assured to repay the money which you borrowed from them. Then the house immediately becomes your own property or that of your legal heir.

The amount of money which a life office is prepared to lend a prospective house purchaser is generally 75 to 80 per cent. of the purchase price or of the surveyor's valuation, whichever is less. The actual amount must depend on the age and condition of the house, sometimes on its situation, and always on whether it is freehold or leasehold. In common with the building societies, life assurance offices prefer to deal in freehold properties.

"Decreasing Term" Policies

Should you for any reason prefer to borrow the money from a building society, you can normally protect the amount of the loan with an endowment policy in the same way as when borrowing direct from a life office. All that happens is that you pay both the life assurance premiums and the interest payments on the loan to the building society. They pass the assurance premiums on to a life office, and when the policy matures, or if you die within the term of the policy, the sum assured goes to the building society in repayment of their loan to you.

Alternatively, the building society loan may be covered by a "decreasing term" life policy. Under this arrangement, you actually repay the loan by means of regular instalments to the building society. Therefore, as long as you go on paying

A very common and often tragic fire hazard, it is now an offence to leave a child in a room with a fire that is not adequately guarded

your instalments, the amount which you owe is growing smaller and smaller—in other words, decreasing. And were you to die, the amount of the loan or mortgage outstanding at that time would be the amount the building society would receive under the "decreasing term" assurance. Such assurances as these are popularly called in the business world "mortgage protection" policies.

Mortgage Protection

When using this method of house purchase, it is customary for the building society to pay for the mortgage protection policy in one lump premium, so to speak. A sum equal to this premium is then added to your loan, which means that you automatically reimburse the building society for the cost of the life cover as you pay the instalments on the mortgage.

A house purchase loan from a building society may also be linked to one of the increasingly popular "family income policies." To mention just one of these—and it is a very attractive one—there is the kind made up of a mortgage protection assurance, which safeguards your dependants, and a number of short-term endowment assurances. These endowments are designed to mature at regular intervals during the period of the mortgage, thereby providing you with a useful capital sum every so often. Typical benefits would be £100 every 5 years of a 20-year period. You can spend these sums just as you please, but the wise course is to use them for the purpose for which they are really intended—that is, to help you meet the constant and recurring cost of the upkeep on your home.

From all this, it can be seen that the insurance companies are prepared for most contingencies. If however you have any special insurance problem, either connected with your home, your work or play, they will always be ready to help and advise you.

MANAGING THE MONEY

*Good budgeting means a pattern of spending that
gives the best return in happy living for the whole family*

BUDGETING

GOOD budgeting is something more than
living within income, vital though this
is. It means a pattern of spending that
gives, for the particular people and circumstances concerned, the biggest possible return in happy living.

Although we are used to thinking of budgeting as having solely to do with money,
one cannot draw up a satisfactory budget
without taking into consideration both time
and effort involved. For example, when
both husband and wife have paid jobs
which take the greater part of their energies, it may be better budgeting to spend
more on ready-to-serve foodstuffs than to
buy less expensive ones which demand a lot
of preparation. Similarly, conserving the
strength of an over-taxed mother by having paid help should take preference over
most other expenditure.

In the same way, though the custom is to
draw up an annual budget to apportion *income, capital* expenditure needs to be taken
into account, too. For example, instead of
allowing 13s. weekly for boiler fuel, it may
be far sounder to buy a modern boiler for
£30 that will cut in half the amount spent
each week on keeping it going. The new
boiler may have to be financed out of income (by means of hire purchase), with the
result that the weekly expenditure on water
heating (hire purchase instalment plus fuel)
will rise sharply until it is paid off. On the
other hand, if the boiler can be bought out
of savings or other capital, expenditure
from income under the same heading will
be reduced.

Drawing Up a Budget

Ideally, a preliminary plan, at least,
should be made before *any* commitments
are entered into. For instance, the young
couple about to set up home could well
begin when they find a possible flat or
house. The question of whether the rent
can be afforded can only be decided when
the estimated cost of all the necessaries is
written down too. It is at this stage that

decisions as to the amount of life assurance
that can be carried, how much hire purchase would be safe, whether a telephone
can be managed, and so on, should be
made. Expenditure of this kind, once entered into, cannot easily be altered for
some time ahead at least, so any contracts
should be on the cautious side. Amounts
spent on entertainments, clothes and even
food can be cut back from week to week if
necessary, though it is not good budgeting
to depend on this. The inexperienced
should also guard against omitting or
underestimating everyday items such as
household cleaning materials, minor household renewals and repairs, and the cost of
fuel. It is prudent to allow some margin
for price increases, too.

Who Pays for What?

When a first budget is being talked over,
thought must be given to the question: who
shall pay for what? The wife may be sole
Chancellor of the Exchequer. The husband's and any other wage packets are
handed direct to her. She returns an agreed
sum for pocket money, fares or other expenses, and herself pays for everything that
the household needs. Where the income is
not very large and the wife is a good
manager, it is doubtful whether a better
method can be devised. An alternative
arrangement is for the husband to give the
wife a housekeeping allowance and possibly a separate personal allowance, and
himself to pay such things as rent or mortgage repayments, rates, life assurance and
house insurance, car expenses and school
fees (if any) and certain regular bills, such
as for light, heat and telephone. The husband would then probably pay his own personal expenses and pocket money, and perhaps also buy his own clothes (instead
of drawing on a family clothes allowance)
and pay for holidays.

This kind of spending pattern works well
when there is complete frankness as to the
family income and it is all budgeted. It
will be less successful if the husband does

not like to divulge all his earnings and keeps back an unspecified and overgenerous sum for his personal expenditure. If in these circumstances the housekeeping allowance has to be unduly stretched or the wife has no separate allocation for her personal spending, frictions can arise that place a serious strain on the marriage.

What should "Housekeeping" Comprise?

A housekeeping allowance may be meant to pay the cost of food, household cleaning materials, laundry, daily papers and household help, or to cover practically everything except the husband's pocket money. The sovereign rule is that both parties concerned must be absolutely clear as to what it does embrace. Generally speaking, it is better for separate sums to be allocated for clothes (for the wife alone or for the whole family) and for the wife's pocket money. Admittedly, when the total income is slender there are difficulties about this; however, it is bad budgeting for the husband and not the wife to have free spending money.

There is no need to have any technical knowledge of bookkeeping to keep a workable record of family income and expenditure

What Proportion of Income to Various Expenses?

Are there any rules that the inexperienced can follow when working out the amounts to be allocated under the different headings? Frankly, none that are very reliable. It used to be thought that the most to be spent on rent (or its equivalent in Schedule A) and rates or mortgage repayment and rates, should not exceed one-fifth of the total income. Owing to today's housing shortage, there is sometimes no alternative to exceeding this proportion, though it still remains undesirable to do so. This does not apply to furnished accommodation, which can legitimately take a larger share of the total.

One-third of a modest, middle-class family's income for housekeeping, to include food, cleaning materials, small household repairs and renewals, heat and light, is an approximate average. Again, circumstances may greatly alter the case. The smaller the income, the higher proportionately will be the amount spent on food. When total resources are very small, food and warmth will absorb the lion's share of what is left after the cost of shelter and, when necessary, of travelling to work has been paid.

Each Family has its own Priorities

Next in the budget come fixed expenses. These comprise insurance (including life assurance), professional association subscriptions or trade union dues, education costs (if there are children), and any hire purchase commitments. Clothes and household renewals will probably be ranked next, with amenities and luxuries in the last group. These include personal allowances and pocket money, entertainment, cost of running a car if not used mainly for business, telephone charges in the same circumstances, other-than-business subscriptions, emergencies and savings.

In just what order these should rank is a matter for the individual family. In fact, the only sound way to determine it is to draw up a provisional budget on paper. On one side should be put the total *net* income (after income tax has been deducted) of the family available for distribution. If some part of the income is reserved for a special purpose—e.g. a wife's income kept aside as a personal dress allowance, or Family Allowances for the children banked for their future education—it should, of course, not be included.

On the other side, all the various calls on the income, known or carefully estimated, should be itemised. If, as is only too likely, the expenditure column totals more than income, each item must be considered to see where cuts can be made.

It is in deciding what can—and what must not—be whittled that the art of budgeting lies. Hard and fast rules cannot apply, for we all have our own priorities. To some people a warm house and plenty of hot water means infinitely more than outings of any kind. One family would sacrifice almost anything for a slap-up holiday. Another would rather dispense with going away and find more satisfaction in spending on the garden and on books or magazines. Clothes matter to some, and putting by something regularly against a rainy day ranks high with others. Working out a spending plan for a single person is fairly straightforward. With a family budget, the aim must be to use what is available so that the family, both corporately and individually, receive the utmost possible benefit.

HOUSEHOLD ACCOUNTS

The thought of keeping accounts is terrifying to some people, but there is no need to have any technical knowledge of bookkeeping to keep a workable record of family expenditure. The golden rule, especially important for the inexperienced, is *to write everything down*.

Keeping Simple "Books"

Purely for convenience, it is a good idea for the new housewife to have two record books. The first, a little notebook small enough to go into her handbag, is best kept in the form of a "day book." *Everything* spent is entered under each day's heading as it is spent. The second, a rather larger

book, should be divided into sections to correspond with the items in the expenditure column of the budget. At the top of each section should be written the yearly, quarterly, monthly or weekly figure allowed, or estimated.

This book would have, for example, sections headed Rent, Insurance, Light and Heat, Housekeeping, Telephone, Entertainment, Clothes, Savings, etc. Once a week the total spent on food, etc., should be entered under "Housekeeping," and other sums disbursed transferred from the day book to the appropriate page in the big book. By this means it will soon be seen if too much is being spent in one direction. Retrenchment or readjustment is then possible before things have gone too far. Admittedly, all this does take a certain amount of time, but until sound budgeting and financial habits have been formed, there is no other check so straightforward and valuable. The keeping of the day book, with its record of cash spending, is also helpful in the actual balancing of the cash account.

Shopping Methods—Cash or Credit?

Personal shopping and immediate payment in cash is the surest way of disciplining one's spending. The less money one has, the more meticulous it is necessary to be in sticking closely to the practice of buying only what can be immediately paid for in cash. When tradesmen deliver, as in the case of milk or bread, they usually prefer a weekly payment. On no account should this be allowed to run longer than a week. Indeed, if retrenchment is necessary, it is better to cut out all deliveries and pay for every small item bought. It is surprising how this will obviate any wastage and pare down consumption without undue effort.

The "Envelope System"

A simple and effective way of seeing that the budget is not exceeded when shopping is to parcel out the money as received. For instance, the weekly "housekeeping" might be divided up between groceries, meat, fish, milk, bread, cleaning materials, newspapers, laundry and dry cleaning. The sum allowed for each would be put in a separate envelope. These envelopes are then taken out when shopping or used for paying the milkman, etc., at the door. If the contents of any of them is getting dangerously low, that is a signal to hold back and economise or do without. Naturally, a certain amount of borrowing and paying back from one envelope to another is practised, but one is constantly reminded of the limits imposed and that the wherewithal for spending is fast disappearing.

Monthly Credit Accounts

Credit shopping has its uses and advantages, but it holds great risks for those who are pressed for money or who are not strong-minded about living within their means. *A sound rule to follow is never to shop by credit (i.e. to run approved monthly accounts) if you cannot pay cash.* When there is money in the current account that can rightly be expended on such shopping, payment by a monthly cheque is often convenient and sensible. It therefore follows that the inexperienced housewife will do better to start on a strictly cash basis and graduate to a certain amount of credit shopping when she "knows her way round" in managing her housekeeping and other allowances.

Payment out of Income

While perishables such as food are expected to be paid for either by immediate cash or on the weekly or monthly account, a large number of comparatively long-lasting goods such as all kinds of furnishings and equipment are now offered by retailers on a payment-out-of-income or hire-purchase basis. As is explained in the article on Hire Purchase, goods bought by this method do not legally become the property of the purchaser until the last instalment is paid. Until then they are loaned to the purchaser, the shopkeeper (or lender) remaining their legal owner. Quite apart from the disadvantages arising from this, buying goods out of income should not be lightly undertaken. First, such goods cost more because of the interest charges included in the price. Secondly, it is insidiously easy to undertake bigger commitments of this kind than can be easily, or safely, borne. That is why hire purchase is an item needing serious thought when a budget is being worked out. As far as *shopping* (or the actual payment of hire purchase instalments) is concerned, the

When buying furniture or equipment on hire purchase, it is wise to put the necessary amount on one side each week or month before making other purchases

Tradesmen who deliver, such as the milkman, usually prefer a weekly payment; on no account let such bills run longer than a week

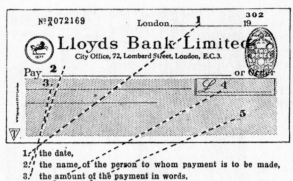

№ R 072169   London, _____1_____ 19___   302

Lloyds Bank Limited
City Office, 72, Lombard Street, London, E.C.3.

Pay **2**
_____ or Order

3
_____ £ **4**

5

1. the date,
2. the name of the person to whom payment is to be made,
3. the amount of the payment in words,
4. and figures,
5. and the signature of the drawer.

How to fill in a cheque form. The twopenny stamp impressed on the cheque is an Inland Revenue charge

to be an adequate balance in *relation to the amount of work entailed* is not kept, the bank makes a charge. This varies according to the bank and the account, but 2-3 guineas per annum would be quite normal for a small private account not involving much work.

How to Open a Current Account

From the foregoing it is clear that, before opening an account, one must be prepared to pay in a sum that will not be drawn against almost completely. Banks welcome new account holders and their Managers are happy to see intending customers. A courteous reception is given to all enquirers and no obligation is entailed.

Sometimes a married couple decide to open a *joint account*. Each of the parties can pay in or draw cheques, one or both signatures being necessary, according to arrangement. This has its advantages, but its dangers, too, especially when one signature only is necessary. Unless there is complete confidence between the joint account holders, and usually prior consultation as to expenditure, it is far too easy to overdraw. Also there may not always be complete agreement as to the necessity or otherwise of drawing a cheque

However, in some circumstances, such as when a husband places a sum to the credit of the account each month and the wife draws on it for housekeeping purposes, the arrangement works very well. It is worth noting that on the death of one of the parties to a joint account any credit balance is payable to the survivor, but if the balance of the joint account is £300 or more it is subject to apportionment for purposes of Estate Duty.

Crossed Cheques.—A crossed cheque has two parallel lines drawn across it and the words "and Co." written between them. The bank upon which a crossed cheque is drawn will not pay out cash against it across the counter. The cheque must be paid into a banking account to which it can be traced. It is therefore wise to use a

sensible course is to put the necessary amount on one side each week or month before any other purchases are made.

A BANKING ACCOUNT

When money is received largely in the form of cheques, it becomes convenient to open a current account at one of the Joint Stock banks. The largest in England and Wales are: Barclays, Lloyds, Midland, National Provincial and Westminster, but there are also Martins, District and some other smaller ones. Cheques, warrants, money orders, postal orders and cash can be paid into the account, and cheques drawn on it to the extent of the credit balance. The cheques may be drawn in favour of third parties—say, for payment of bills—or can be used for withdrawing cash from the account.

A current account obviates the need for carrying round large sums of money when shopping or paying bills. Also, by means of the counterfoils in cheque books and paying-in books (both are supplied free by the bank, the cheque book stamps being an Inland Revenue charge), the account holder can keep a handy record of transactions. Statements of the account, sent to the holder periodically, supply this record in a more concise and lasting form.

Obviously banks could not offer such services (as well as various others to be described later in this chapter) without some return. They make their profit by lending money at interest, so they will be adequately paid only if there is a sufficiently large sum (or balance) permanently in the account. When what is considered

crossed cheque when paying bills and accounts. A customer possessing a book of crossed cheques who herself wishes to draw out money across the counter will be asked by the cashier to "open" the cheque by writing "pay cash" and signing her name between the crossing lines.

To sum up, a crossed cheque can be collected only through a bank; on the other hand, an uncrossed cheque can be cashed when presented at the branch on which it is drawn.

Endorsements.—A cheque made out to a particular person must be endorsed on the back by the person concerned; that is, she must write her name in the same form as on the front of the cheque, but omitting courtesy titles or ranks. Thus a cheque made payable to Miss Alice Jones or Dr. Alice Jones is endorsed Alice Jones; one made payable to Mrs. John Jones is endorsed Alice Jones, wife of John Jones.

Special Banking Services

In addition to maintaining current accounts, the banks provide a number of special services. For some of these facilities no specific charge is made.

(1) **Standing Orders.** — The bank will, on request, undertake to pay on behalf of a customer insurance premiums, subscriptions, Building Society repayments, instalments under hire purchase agreements and other regularly recurring payments as they become due.

(2) **Cashing Cheques at Other Branches and Banks.**—By previous arrangement, an account holder can cash cheques up to an agreed specified limit, at another branch or even another bank.

(3) **The Custody of Valuables.**—Customers may have a deed box stored in the bank vaults in which papers, jewellery, etc., may be kept, or they may entrust securities, documents, etc., to the bank for safe keeping.

(4) **Foreign Travel.**—Customers may obtain up-to-date information and advice on Exchange Control formalities, monetary arrangements, passports and visas. Subject to the requirements of the Exchange Control, the bank can provide foreign currency, travellers' cheques and letters of credit.

(5) **References.**—The bank's name may be given as a reference.

(6) **Income Tax.**—The preparation of returns for the assessment of income tax and surtax, and claims for the repayment of tax are undertaken by the bank for private customers. Charges are reasonable, depending upon the amount of work involved and, when appropriate, the amount of money recovered.

(7) **Stock Exchange Transactions.**—Banks can obtain the suggestions of leading Stockbrokers regarding investments and can arrange for the purchase and sale of all classes of stocks and shares. When the Brokers' commission is shared with the bank, no extra payment is involved.

(8) **Executor and Trustee Business.**—Most banks will act as executors or trustees for customers and have special departments for this work. Charges depend upon the size of the estate and work involved, and a scale of charges is usually available on request.

Advances.—It is a function of the banks to make advances to customers for legitimate personal and business purposes— normally against approved security. A customer wishing to overdraw her account should first discuss the matter with the Manager.

Bank Savings Facilities

No interest is paid on current accounts, but the Joint Stock Banks provide facilities for those who wish to save.

A Deposit Account is often opened by current account holders for the saving of money that is not required for immediate use. Should a current account balance become larger than is economic, a sum can be transferred to the deposit account where it will earn interest which usually varies with the Bank rate. Withdrawals from deposit accounts are subject to notice.

A Savings Bank Account is intended for the accumulation of genuine small savings. Such an account is frequently opened by banks' customers for their children, the attraction being that a Home Safe (a money box) may be had on loan from the bank to encourage savings in the home. Withdrawals up to £5 can usually be made at any branch of the bank concerned, or they may be effected through the post.

SAVINGS ACCOUNTS

The most popular type of savings account in the U.K. is that operated by the Post Office. The money is held in safety by the Government and a fixed rate of interest (2½ per cent. per annum) paid. Money may be withdrawn or the account closed at any time. Once an account is opened, sums may be paid in, or withdrawn, at the great majority of the post offices in Great Britain and Northern Ireland, and in the Channel Islands and the Isle of Man. Withdrawals may also be made in the Irish Republic. Up to £10 may be withdrawn "on demand." For larger sums a written application to the Savings Bank headquarters (details given in bank book) has to be made.

Opening a Post Office Account

An account may be opened at any Post Office Savings Bank with as little as 5s. by simply filling up a form and furnishing a specimen signature. A bank book is then supplied by the Post Office. Further deposits are accepted of a minimum of 1s. and upwards. To aid home saving, National Savings Stamps in denominations of 6d. and 2s. 6d. are sold. The stamps may be paid into a savings account or used for the purchase of National Savings Certificates (see below) when sufficient are accumulated.

Depositors' Qualifications

Anyone over the age of seven years may become a depositor, and accounts may also be opened on behalf of, and in the names of, children under the age of seven. Money so deposited is not withdrawable until the child reaches the age of seven, and is then payable on his or her signature only.

Accounts may be opened by two or more persons jointly on their own behalf. Such an account can be held in addition to an account standing in the sole name of any or all of the parties to the joint account.

Maximum Deposits

Post Office Savings Accounts are meant mainly for small savers, as the terms are considered favourable owing to the high degree of safety and the ease of withdrawal. A limit is placed on the total amount that may be deposited in a Post Office Savings Account. This has been raised to £5,000. Income Tax is payable on interest exceeding £15 in any year.

Established by local groups of citizens to encourage thrift, Trustee Savings Banks, of which there are over eight hundred in the U.K., are subject to Government supervision. They offer interest on deposits at rates comparable with the Post Office Savings Bank.

SAVINGS CERTIFICATES

These also offer a popular form of saving. Certificates may be bought in various denominations at most post offices or banks or through national savings groups. Certificates of the present Tenth Issue cost 15s. and, if left to maturity in 7 years, increase in value to £1. This represents compound interest at about 4·2 per cent. per annum and is free of income tax. If need be, a certificate may be encashed with any interest due at any time after purchase. The maximum holding of this issue is £900 (1,200 certificates) in addition to any existing holdings of previous issues.

PREMIUM SAVINGS BONDS

Premium Savings Bonds are a Government security with the essential difference that, instead of earning interest like other forms of saving, they carry a chance of winning a tax-free prize.

Bonds cost £1 and may be purchased through most post offices or banks to a maximum of £800. Each bond gives the holder one chance in each monthly draw for which it is eligible. A Bond becomes eligible after being held for 3 months. The prizes range from £5,000 to £25. A Bond may be repaid at face value at any time on application.

5 PER CENT. DEFENCE BONDS

Five per cent. Defence Bonds (Second Issue) are sold at most post offices or banks in multiples of £5 to a limit of £5,000. This limit is in addition to Defence Bonds of previous issues. The Bonds are redeemable after 7 years at the rate of £103 for £100 of bonds, but they may also be encashed before maturity at par by giving 6 months' notice or immediately subject to a deduction equivalent to 6 months' interest. Dividends are paid on 15th June and December.

HIRE PURCHASE

How this system of trading operates and what happens
if you fall into arrears or wish to end the agreement

SO much household equipment is acquired by hire purchase that it is worth considering what the system is and what obligations and rights a householder has.

What does hire purchase mean? The term is sometimes vaguely thought to cover all forms of instalment credit. Strictly speaking, hire purchase is only one form: it is a method of trading whereby a trader hires goods he owns to a customer and at the same time gives the customer an option of purchasing them. The customer cannot, in fact, be compelled to buy the goods he has hired. He pays a hire rent weekly or monthly for an agreed length of time, and if and when the total amount he has paid equals the total hire-purchase price of the goods, they become his. Until then, though the customer has the use of the goods, they remain the property of the trader or owner. Usually the agreement will provide that the customer must keep them at the address notified to the trader and that the customer is responsible for maintaining them in good condition and for loss or damage (fair wear and tear excepted).

Choose a Reputable Firm

Hire purchase is a long-established practice, and nearly all the transactions in which the general public are concerned (chiefly for the acquisition of domestic goods) operate under the Hire Purchase Acts of 1938 and 1954, which cover transactions up to £300 (except for livestock) and provide for the protection of both customer and trader. Properly used, it can be of great assistance, particularly, of course, to a young couple setting up house, whose prospects are good but who might not be able to meet at the outset the full cost down of necessary but expensive items—furniture, cooker, sink unit, and so on. It is a system which can, however, be abused. Hardship can follow hire-purchase commitments undertaken without due care.

If you decide to acquire goods on hire purchase, make sure first that you are dealing with a trader of good repute. Most traders are prepared to meet your request for hire-purchase arrangements—provided they are assured that you are a customer of good credit standing. They are entitled in their own interests to check on your likely capacity to keep up the payments and may ask to be given evidence in this regard.

The Credit Charge

Then make certain that you know the correct cash price of the goods you want. The trader is legally obliged to declare this to you—but not all customers pay attention. An over-reaching trader who wanted to charge more for his credit facilities than he wished to show could do this by inflating the cash price on which it is reckoned. It is better to ascertain what the price is and to compare it with the cash price asked for elsewhere.

The next step is to find out from the trader how much the hire-purchase facilities will cost. The amount of this credit charge will vary according to the work, expense and risk in which your agreement involves the trader. It will depend on the length of the agreement (e.g. two years will cost more than six months), the number of rentals to be paid, whether weekly or monthly (it is to your advantage to pay monthly), and how they are paid (if you are willing to pay by banker's order the trader may be able to lower the credit charge). As it costs the trader as much to collect a small rental as a large one, the percentage will be higher on the small one.

Most traders will expect a substantial down payment. The Hire Purchase Trade Association have always maintained that the taking of a substantial deposit is one of the essentials of sound hire-purchase trading. For one thing, the fact that you can pay a fair amount down gives the trader some assurance and indication of your financial reserves. And it is to the customer's advantage to pay as much deposit as he can, since the charge is calculated only on the remainder of the cash price.

The cash price, less the deposit and plus the credit charge, is divided into the number of weeks or months the agreement is to run, and you will thus know the amount of each rental you will have to pay.

By way of a simple illustration, let us suppose you are arranging to buy £100 worth of goods on hire purchase. You arrange to pay 20 per cent. deposit; so the balance left is £80, and it is on this figure that the credit charge is calculated. If you are to pay by twelve monthly instalments, the credit charge might well be 5 per cent. on £80—i.e. £4. So you will have to pay £84 by twelve equal payments—i.e. £7 per month. (The hire-purchase price of the article is, of course, £100 plus £4—i.e. £104.)

At this point it would be as well to consider whether the regular payment to be made is really within your scope. Customers tend sometimes to be over-optimistic, especially young couples, and find that what is easily paid at first becomes a crippling burden in a year's time. It depends naturally on your reserves and other commitments.

If you decide that the proposed arrangements are satisfactory and that your resources over a period are likely to be sufficient to meet the payments, the trader makes out the formal agreement. If (as is probable) the transaction comes under the Hire Purchase Acts, the trader is under legal obligation to give you a copy of the agreement within seven days of its being made and signed by him. The terms will be stated here and also the measures designed for the protection both of yourself and the trader. So read the agreement carefully before you sign it yourself and make sure that you know the conditions and do, in fact, agree to the terms.

If You cannot Pay

You will probably find in the agreement a clause stating that you are responsible for loss of or damage to the goods delivered to you. They are *hired* on the risk of the hirer. Take a look, therefore, at your insurance cover, and see whether it is adequate.

But just suppose an emergency arises and you find you cannot maintain the payments. Do not lurk at home worrying in silence, ignoring all reminders from the trader. Get in touch with him—go and see him if possible—and tell him of the position. You will, in all probability, get consideration. He will adjust the transaction to meet the difficulty.

If you do not notify the trader or respond to reminders, and have paid so far less than one-third of the total hire-purchase price of the goods, the trader is entitled to remove his goods from your house with or without your consent. But if you have paid one-third, he cannot (under the Hire Purchase Acts) do this without your consent unless he has obtained an order of the Court. If he applies to the Court for such an order, the Court may empower him to remove his goods—or may allow you to keep the goods on condition that the balance of the price is paid in the way ordered by the Court, or to keep some of the goods according to what has been already paid.

Returning the Goods

If you wish to terminate the agreement, you should do so in writing and return the goods (at your own cost). If this happens —or if the goods are recovered by the trader without your consent—you will have to pay the trader all arrears of rent together with the difference, if any, between the total amount paid (including arrears) and half of the hire purchase price. In addition, if you have failed to take proper care of the goods you may have to pay to have them repaired.

Finally, what happens to a hire-purchase agreement if the hirer dies? In this case, the rights the hirer has acquired under the agreement pass to his estate and his executors deal with the matter. They can do one of three things. Supposing 90 per cent. has been paid off on £100 worth of goods. The executors then have the valuable right of paying the odd £10—the estate so acquiring £100 worth of, say, furniture, which can be distributed according to the will. Or, they can terminate the hiring and return the goods to the trader. Or, the executors can continue making the already agreed payments until the end of the period.

The immense scale of hire-purchase trading, conducted under legal safeguard, indicates its usefulness to the public. Used with discretion, it is a valuable service.

HINTS ON INCOME TAX

*Showing how it is assessed in the U.K. and some of
the allowances and reliefs which reduce total liability*

INCOME Tax is an extremely complex
subject and any attempt even to sum-
marize its legislation and practice would
take up more space than is available in this
entire volume. This chapter will, however,
help to overcome some of the snags en-
countered by the layman when preparing
his annual Income Tax Return and will
answer many of the questions which more
frequently arise. As it does not concern
the average taxpayer, Profits Tax has been
ignored.

THE RETURN FORM

It must be remembered that the onus of
making a Return of total income rests with
the taxpayer. Where the Revenue believe
that a taxpayer's only income arises from
salary or wages, they may dispense with
the issue of a Return Form, but nevertheless, it is up to the individual to notify his
Tax Inspector of other income sources,
even if a Return Form is not sent to
him.

The Return Form is designed to segre-
gate the various classes of income and it
contains a separate section to cover
charges paid by the taxpayer, such as
Ground Rent, Overdraft, Loan, Mortgage
and Building Society interest and National
Insurance Contributions. A further section is provided in which to furnish details
of the allowances which a taxpayer may
claim to set off against his total income.

It is essential to disclose income from all
sources and (except where a separate
assessment is claimed) a married man must
include his wife's income also.

Where investment income has been
taxed at source, the gross amount prior to
tax deduction must be shown on the
form. All items of untaxed interest, however small, arising from or accruing on
Bank Deposits, Savings Banks and Government Securities, etc., should be shown.
Post Office Savings Bank interest should
also be declared, although the first £15

carries exemption and will not be charged
to Income Tax.

Overseas income is returnable and taxable and its precise nature and source
should be stated. Any foreign tax suffered
should be indicated so that the Revenue
can calculate credit for Double Tax Relief,
where due.

Every income section of the Return
should be completed. Where no income
arises from a particular source, the word
"none" should be inserted, as failure to do
this may result in the form being returned
for full completion. It will be appreciated
that if a particular section is left blank,
the Inspector cannot tell whether income
has arisen from that source or not, or
whether the section has been merely overlooked.

Equal care should be taken in completing the claim for allowances to ensure that
liability is minimised and the insert notes
provided with all Returns will be found
helpful in this direction. The values of the
various allowances are revised from time
to time but their general nature and scope
are as follows:

ALLOWANCES AND RELIEFS

(1) The single person's allowance, available to all individuals except married
women.

(2) The additional personal allowance,
available to a married man for his wife,
living with, and maintained by him.

(3) Relief for earned income (including
pensions).

(4) Similar relief for small unearned
income and incomes of persons over 65
(subject to restriction on account of total
income).

(5) Old age exemption relief on small
incomes of persons over 65.

(6) Relief for children under 16 or, if
over 16, receiving full-time educational or

professional training, provided the child's income from sources other than scholarships does not exceed £100 in the year of claim. The allowances vary according to the child's age.

(7) For aged or infirm relatives, resident with or maintained by the taxpayer (subject to possible restriction on account of the dependent's total income).

(8) For a daughter kept at home to care for the taxpayer or his wife by reason of their old age or infirmity.

(9) The housekeeper allowance in respect of a female relative or, if none is available, any employed female, resident with a widow or widower for purpose of housekeeping or of looking after children for whom Child Allowance is claimed. A similar allowance is claimable by a single taxpayer having the care or charge of a child resident with him and for whom he claims Child Allowance.

(10) Allowance to a widow or widower having the care of children eligible for Child Allowance, but who does not employ a housekeeper.

(11) For maintaining his widowed mother or other female relative for purpose of looking after his dependent brothers or sisters, an unmarried man may claim relief.

(12) Relief for premiums on life or endowment insurance policies secured on the life of the taxpayer or his wife. Except in the case of policies taken up before 22nd June, 1916, the allowances are as follows:

(i) The total premiums paid, if under £10.

(ii) £10, if the premiums total more than £10 but less than £25.

(iii) 2/5ths of premiums over £25.

In all cases, premiums are restricted to 7 per cent. of the capital sum assured at death and to 1/6th of the taxpayer's total income.

For pre-1916 policies, relief is given on the premiums at:

(a) 3s. 6d. in the £ when total income does not exceed £1,000.

(b) 5s. 3d. in the £ when total income does not exceed £2,000.

(c) 7s. in the £ when total income exceeds £2,000.

(13) Reduced rates of taxation, applicable to the first £360 of taxable income (i.e. total income less allowances).

(14) Relief on the *earned* income of a married woman, equivalent but additional to (1) and (3), with the benefit of separate reduced rate reliefs (13).

The Income Tax year ends on the 5th April and this is the date to be borne in mind when completing the Tax Return. For example, a Return for the assessment year 1961/62 would be issued in April 1961 and would be completed with income details for the year to the 5th April, 1961, and include an advance claim for allowances for the ensuing year.

Where personal circumstances alter during the year, for example, on marriage, an additional child, further life assurance policies, etc., the Revenue should be notified so that the correct allowances can be given in computing the taxpayer's liability.

THE P.A.Y.E. SCHEME

P.A.Y.E. (Pay As You Earn) is a scheme of tax collection, operated by the employer under direction of the Revenue Department, whereby the tax liability of employed persons is deducted from their wages and salaries on a weekly or monthly basis. The employee's tax allowances are expressed as a code number, which the employer applies to a series of tax tables, designed to spread the allowances and reduced rate reliefs week by week or month by month throughout the tax year. Despite fluctuations in weekly or monthly earnings, the approximately correct tax deduction is taken from each payment and at the end of the year it will be found that the total deductions closely correspond with the employee's individual liability.

At the year end the employee should receive a certificate from his employer, showing his total earnings and tax deducted, details of which the employer also submits to the Revenue Department.

The Revenue check the employer's figures and compare the P.A.Y.E. tax deductions against their computations of the taxpayer's liability, based on his total income, less the allowances and reliefs claimed. If the deductions are correct to the nearest £ or so, no further action is taken, but if there is a larger under- or over-payment, a statement will be sent to the employee showing how this is computed.

On application by the taxpayer an over-payment will be refunded. Unless there are reasons why it cannot be recovered in a later year, any under-payment will be carried forward and liquidated by increased P.A.Y.E. deductions from future earnings.

Beyond ensuring that he makes a claim for all his tax allowances and checks the coding notice issued to him by the Revenue, the wage or salary earner need not concern himself with the technicalities of P.A.Y.E., but if he feels that incorrect tax deductions are being taken from his earnings, he should certainly query the position with the Local Tax Office.

SURTAX

Surtax is additional to Income Tax and is chargeable on incomes which exceed £2,000 after deducting charges and allowances. Most of the Income Tax allowances are also available against Surtax, the exceptions being the Single Personal Allowance, Earned Income and Wife's Earned Income Reliefs, and relief on Life Assurance premiums.

Surtax is charged on a sliding scale slab system and is payable on 1st January following the assessment year.

*

Out of the many hundreds of questions which must come into the minds of taxpayers generally. the following is a random selection which may help to answer the reader's particular problem.

1. (Q) Can I claim relief for premiums which I pay on life assurance policies secured on the lives of my children?
   (A) No. You can only claim where the life assured is that of yourself or your wife.

2. (Q) Interest received from my Building Society investment is described as "tax paid." Why must I show it on my Return?
   (A) This interest is exempt from further Income Tax because tax has already been borne by the Society. When considering age relief, small income relief and surtax liability, however, the Revenue need to know the taxpayer's total income, including Building Society interest, and it is for this reason that it must be disclosed.

3. (Q) With my landlord's consent I have let half of my house furnished. What allowances should

A Sweet Victorian Posy

This unusual Victorian vase is only a small container, but it can produce the effect of quite a good-sized flower arrangement. Here it contains lamb's ears and white sweet peas. The rather narrow porcelain tubes need to be well filled with water.

I claim against the rent received?

(A) You may claim one-half of your rent, general and water rates, and household contents insurance, plus the cost of renewing soft furnishings, utensils, etc., in addition to 1 per cent. of the rent received to cover wear and tear of hard furniture. If you incurred expenses on advertising the letting, or employed an agent or solicitor, you should claim these costs also. If you owned the house, you could claim one-half of the gross Schedule "A" value in lieu of rent paid.

4. (Q) You say that the joint income of a married couple is treated as the husband's income for tax purposes. If my wife takes a job, am I liable to tax on her wages?

(A) No. The earned income of a married woman carries separate allowances and reliefs (similar to those of a single person) and in practice any tax due on salary is recovered from the wife by the employer under the P.A.Y.E. scheme.

5. (Q) My wife employs a part-time domestic help whose insurance contribution she shares with two neighbours. Can I claim tax relief for this insurance payment?

(A) Yes. You and your neighbours can claim one-third of the total employer's contribution, the allowance being approximately £5 to each of you.

6. (Q) The treasurer of my Church has invited me to sign a Deed of Covenant by which I would undertake to make an annual subscription to the Church for seven years. What are the advantages or otherwise from my point of view?

(A) If you pay tax at the full standard rate on a sufficient part of your income, there is no disadvantage to you. You will make a net annual subscription to the Church and the Trustees will be able to recover the tax which you are deemed to deduct from the gross equivalent of your subscrip-

tion. On the other hand, if you pay tax at less than the standard rate, or pay no tax at all, you will have to make good to the Revenue the amount of tax which the Church can recover.

7. (Q) I borrowed £500 from a relative at 5 per cent. interest and understand I should deduct tax at standard rate from my interest payments. Why is this?

(A) You are required by law to deduct tax and, if you fail to do so, the Revenue will ignore the fact that you have paid the interest gross. You will thus get no relief for the interest paid, and if you are not otherwise liable to standard rate tax on your income, the Revenue may claim from you the balance of tax which you should have deducted.

8. (Q) I own a house which I have let rent free to my widowed mother who has no income other than retirement pension. Am I chargeable with Schedule "A" tax on the property?

(A) As your mother pays no rent, she is regarded as the beneficial occupant and the Schedule "A" assessment will be treated as part of her income. As her only other income is the retirement pension, neither of you will be required to pay Schedule "A" tax.

9. (Q) Can I claim the cost of replacing and laundering overalls required for my job?

(A) Yes. If a fixed allowance has not been agreed between the Revenue and your Union, send details to your Tax Inspector with your annual Return.

10. (Q) I own my house on which I pay interest to a Building Society. Am I liable to tax on the property?

(A) Yes, but you can claim relief on the interest you pay. For example, if your house has a net annual value of £30 and you pay £30 interest, the tax liability is cancelled. If you pay, say £35, the £5 excess will be relieved against other income sources.

11a. (Q) Can I claim tax relief for repairing and decorating the house which I own and occupy?

(A) Yes, provided the average annual cost over five years exceeds the repairs allowance already given in arriving at the net assessment on the property. Ask your local Tax Office for a Property Maintenance claim form, which contains directions for its completion. Remember to preserve the receipted repair bills as the Revenue will not admit relief without them, and include your fire insurance premium on the building.

11b. (Q) But I have just bought my house and have incurred expenses on re-decorating and essential repairs. Must I wait five years before claiming property maintenance relief?

(A) Although maintenance relief is normally given by reference to average expenditure over the five preceding years, the Revenue will accept a claim by new owners based on actual expenditure for each of the first five full years of ownership, after which the average basis applies. Where there is exceptionally heavy expenditure in the first couple of years, however, it is unwise to claim on "actual" basis as relief is restricted to the annual value of the property and any unrelieved expenditure cannot be carried forward. If the previous owner claimed relief and consents to you utilising his expenditure figures, your claim can be put on the five-year average basis from the outset, if this is advantageous.

12. (Q) My wife receives dividends from which tax is deducted at source. Can she claim repayment of this tax?

(A) For tax purposes your wife's income is treated as your own so that entitlement to repayment will depend on your personal rate of liability. Dividends suffer tax at the highest (standard) rate, so that if your other income has not exhausted your reduced rate reliefs, there will be some repayment. Send the deduction vouchers to the Inspector with your Tax Return.

13. (Q) Are the following State Benefits treated as income for tax purposes?

(A) (a) Unemployment, Sickness and Industrial Injury Benefits. No.
(b) Maternity Benefits and Allowances. No.
(c) Family Allowances. Yes.

Peonies in all their glory

In a porcelain basket peonies are used with their own leaves but without any other flowers. Peonies are most obliging and come in a great variety of colours. Two or three add distinction to a mixed bowl or, as here, look lovely alone.

(*d*) Widows' Pensions, Benefits and Allowances. **Yes.**

(*e*) War Widows' Pensions. **No.** (Except for childrens' allowances if included).

(*f*) Retirement Pension. **Yes.**

14. (Q) My employer is deducting excessive P.A.Y.E. tax from my wages on what he calls an "Emergency" coding. Why is this and what should I do to correct it?

(A) This is because you have not put in a claim for allowances. Ask your Local Tax Office for a pink form (P.1), complete and return it, and the Revenue will revise your coding. Any excess tax previously deducted will then be repaid automatically through your employer.

15. (Q) Why must I include "tips" on my Tax Return?

(A) Although these are in the nature of gifts, they arise directly from your employment and are treated as part of your remuneration. A reasonable estimate will be sufficient if you have not kept a complete record.

16. (Q) Can I claim the cost of rail fares between my home and place of employment?

(A) No, except for any additional expenses incurred owing to a change in your place of residence brought about by the last war. The Revenue regard the choice of one's residence as a personal matter, and in no other circumstances will relief be allowed.

17. (Q) I am separated from my husband, from whom I receive a voluntary allowance. Is this taxable?

(A) A voluntary allowance is not taxable and need not be shown on your Return.

18. (Q) I am separated from my wife. Am I still liable to include her income on my Return?

(A) No, as she is not living with you, she must make her own Return, but you of course will forfeit the Higher Personal Allowance.

19. (Q) As a newly-wed, am I liable to return my wife's income received immediately before our marriage?

(A) No. Your wife is personally liable on such income.

20. (Q) I pay maintenance of £4 weekly to my wife under a Court Order. Should I deduct tax from this?

(A) No. Payments not exceeding £5 per week can be made gross.

PENALTIES

Touching on the question of penalties, these are heavy and can even involve imprisonment. Failure to make a Return without reasonable excuse, making a deliberately incorrect or incomplete Return or fraudulently claiming allowances, are all acts which are liable to penalty proceedings.

Innocent omissions and mistakes will not attract penalties, but where these have occurred and are subsequently discovered by the taxpayer, he should at once notify his local Tax Inspector.

Where there is doubt as to liability on a particular item of income or a claim for an allowance, it is advisable to discuss the matter with the Tax Office when submitting the Return to avoid possible misunderstanding later on.

Finally, study the Return Form thoroughly before completion, and carefully read through the declaration before signing it.

HOLIDAYS ABROAD

By KAY VERNON

*All about passports, currency, tipping in
foreign countries, travel by sea and air*

The magnificent Jungfrau, snow-capped in the sunshine, is one
of the most beautiful and unforgettable sights to be seen on a
holiday in Switzerland

GOING abroad—especially if it is for the first time—is a thrilling experience. It's good to see how others live. New sights, new sounds—there are few joys to be compared with your first glimpse of a strange country and the pleasure is repeated on every subsequent visit.

But, like most things, it has its snags and certain preparations must be made well in advance if happy anticipation is not to be overshadowed by anxiety and panic.

Passports

First get your passport. This can be obtained from the Passport Office, Clive House, Petty France, London, S.W.1 or through your nearest office of the Ministry of Labour and National Service.

The fee for a passport is 30s. and to obtain it birth and (if married) marriage certificates must be produced, together with two copies of a recent photograph. This can be an amateur snapshot provided it is clear, full front view, and head and shoulders only, unmounted and not more than 2½ in. by 2 in. Upon enquiry at your local Employment Exchange you will receive all details and the necessary application form. This must be signed by a Member of Parliament, a Justice of the Peace, a minister of religion, a bank officer, a medical or legal practitioner, an established civil servant, a police officer or any person of similar standing who has been acquainted with the applicant for at least two years. A member of the applicant's family is not acceptable.

Passports are valid for five years in the first instance, but may be renewed for further consecutive periods of one to five years. The fee for each year of renewal is 2s. They are not valid beyond ten years from the original date of issue. After this period a new passport must be obtained. If you already hold a passport, check the date of its expiry well in advance of your holiday in order that you may renew it if necessary. Complications might arise should it expire during your holiday.

One passport will serve for husband and wife if they travel together. The husband can use it if he travels alone, but his wife cannot. Should she want to go abroad without her husband, she must obtain a separate passport. Children under the age of sixteen can be entered on the passport of their parent or parents. On reaching sixteen, each child must have a separate passport.

A visa must be obtained for certain countries. This will be explained at the Employment Exchange, and you will be told exactly what you have to do. Each adult should keep his passport in his own possession—it is a valuable document.

Getting There

Buy your travel tickets in advance. You can book your passage right through to any destination in Europe by writing to British Railways, Continental Booking Office, Victoria, London, S.W.1 or through a local travel agency. But many people prefer to use the services of one of the travel agencies, such as Thomas Cook's, Global Tours or the Workers' Travel Association. Such agencies can, in fact, save you the bother and uncertainty of booking accommodation abroad because they will do it all for you and, moreover, provide a courier to meet you at your destination and take you by car to your hotel or *pension*.

The Workers' Travel Association have branches in Manchester, Birmingham, Bristol and Glasgow and nearly 500 agents throughout the country. For friendly party holidays their "packaged tours" are hard to beat and include travel reservations and excursions to places of interest round and about the place at which you choose to stay. The WTA also run a number of international holiday camps on the Continent.

Your holiday can be paid for by instalments spread over twelve months through such organisations as Voyagers, Limited. No entrance fee is payable and you decide for yourself the amount you want to put aside each month. Having paid three subscriptions, you can take your holiday at any time, the amount of money available being in proportion to your total subscription. Having had your holiday you continue your monthly subscription to complete the twelve-month period.

Money

It is a good idea to become accustomed beforehand with the currency of the country you are to visit. You can change British currency into foreign money at your bank or at the travel agency, but your passport must be produced.

The basic travel allowance to persons resident in the United Kingdom is up to £250 per head during any travel year. Applications for exchange facilities in excess of this figure should be submitted to the Bank of England. Each person must make a separate application for the travel allowance. Not more than £50 in English money may be taken out of the country.

It is advisable to take about £5 of your allowance in the currency of the country or countries you intend to visit, to cover initial expenses, and the rest in travellers' cheques cashable in any of those countries. Most foreign hotels will now accept travellers' cheques, or they can be cashed by your travel agency or at any office of Cook's. Any travellers' cheques you don't use, can be returned to your bank or agency at the end of your holiday and your English money will be refunded, minus a modest percentage for expenses. Take your passport with you.

Foreign coins of small denominations are not worth changing back into English money. Boxes at British airports and railway termini invite returning travellers to deposit their spare coins for the benefit of charitable organisations.

Tipping

This worries a good many inexperienced travellers quite needlessly. In most Continental countries 10 to 15 per cent. is automatically added to all hotel, restaurant and café bills, and you can be sure the waiter will tell you if this is not so. But in cafés it is customary to leave the loose change from your bill in spite of the service charge.

The average tip for room maids and hall porters at hotels is 1s. 6d. for a night, 5s. for a week's stay. Railway porters are usually satisfied with 1s. for each piece of luggage, but Dutch railway porters should be tipped 25 cents (roughly 6d.) in addition to a charge of 50 cents for the first bag, 25 cents for each of the others. Belgian porters have a fixed price of 20 francs (about 3s. 3d.) for each bag. In Switzerland there is little tipping above the 10 to 15 per cent. service charge, and

730

café waiters and washroom attendants are content with 6d. Swiss porters expect 60 centimes (about 1s. 3d.) for the first bag, 40 centimes for each of the others. If you have booked with one of the holiday organisations these expenses are taken care of for you.

In France it is important to remember that theatre and cinema ushers must be tipped for showing you to your seat (usually the equivalent of 1s.) and cloakroom attendants expect up to 2s.

Language No Barrier

Lack of knowledge of the language need be no bar to your enjoyment of a holiday abroad. English is an almost universal language and it is astonishing how often you will find someone who speaks it a little, even in remote areas of the Continent. In any case, making yourself understood is a large part of the fun.

A phrase book giving the simple, everyday things you are likely to want to ask, will be found useful and a pocket dictionary will enable you to point to the word you mean if, when shopping, you find you cannot make your request understood. If something you want to buy has no price ticket on it and you cannot understand the price when spoken in a foreign tongue, indicate by signs that you wish the figure to be written down and the shopkeeper will certainly comply.

Be careful not to "over-shop". Remember that everything bought abroad is subject to duty or Purchase Tax by British Customs. You are permitted to bring home half a pound of tobacco or 200 cigarettes, half a bottle of spirits, a bottle of wine and a $\frac{1}{4}$-pint of perfume and $\frac{1}{4}$-pint of toilet water. These are allowed in duty-free as a concession—not as a right. Be co-operative and frank about what you have to declare and you will find the Customs officials understanding and reasonable. The best way is to write down everything and hand the list to the Customs official.

Try to accustom yourself to thinking in terms of twenty-four-hour time, which is standard on the Continent. It will help you with time-tables if you begin to think of "four o'clock" as "sixteen hours".

Animals should not be taken abroad. Restrictions are many and when you return you may have to part with your pet for six months' quarantine.

Sufferers from certain diseases, such as diabetes and coronary artery disease, should take with them a letter from their doctor giving details of any treatment they are having. Most Continental doctors will

Riva del Sole on the Mediterranean coast of Italy is a modern holiday village—you can take a flat for four (exterior and interior views shown here) or stay in the hotel. Bookings through the Workers' Travel Association

understand a letter of this kind written in English. It is also advisable to take a supply of the preparation the patient normally uses in the case of a sudden attack of illness.

Going By Air

If you decide to travel by air, you can book through any of the travel agencies. Unless you are travelling with a party, you will have to find your own way to the London air terminals, but from there you will be taken by coach to the Airport, where you will find everything taken care of for you.

Taking The Car

If you propose to take your car abroad, you should book your cross-Channel passage as early in the year as possible, particularly if you want to travel between the middle of July and the middle of September. Have the car "vetted" by a good garage about a week beforehand. If you are a member of the Automobile Association or the Royal Automobile Club, they will make arrangements for getting the car across the Channel and provide you with all necessary papers and documents, travel routes and tickets. The AA also arrange for you to pay for your car and passenger tickets over a period of twelve months, if this is more convenient to you.

If you wish to travel independently of these organisations, the principal cross-Channel services are:

BY SEA

Cargo or passenger boats. Loading and unloading by crane

Newhaven–Dieppe　Southampton–
　　　　　　　　　　　　Le Havre
Southampton–　　　Dover–Calais
　St. Malo
Folkestone–Calais　Folkestone–Boulogne
　　　　　Dover–Ostend

Special car ferry. Drive on and off
Dover–Boulogne　Dover–Calais
Dover–Ostend　　Dover–Dunkirk

British Railways operate a car-sleeper service twice weekly, May–September, from Newcastle, York and Manchester direct to Boulogne via Dover.

BY AIR
Lydd to Le Touquet, Calais and Ostend
Bournemouth (Hurn) to Cherbourg and
　Deauville

Southend to Calais, Ostend and Rotterdam
Manston to Ostend

Costs are according to overall measurements of car.

The AA and RAC, in addition to their other services, will send spare parts by air in case of need and will get the car home if it breaks down. They will provide routes and maps free of charge and will, if desired, plan a tour according to individual requirements.

Be sure you have the log book of the car, your driving licence (no one is allowed to drive under the age of 18 on the Continent) and an International Insurance Certificate (called the Green Card) which will avoid the payment of premiums at ports and frontiers. Contact your insurance company in good time and inform them that you are taking your car abroad. Be sure to let them know if you are also taking a caravan or trailer, so that the vehicle is covered by the Green Card. Make Cross-Channel bookings for caravans in January for July or August.

Ask your dealer for a kit of spare parts. The cost of any parts not used is refunded on your return. Give relatives two or three addresses on the Continent (*poste restante* if you haven't booked accommodation) and the latest date at which you intend being in each place.

Everywhere on the Continent, with the exception of Sweden, you drive on the right. In many countries it is an offence to park on the left, so get into the habit of always parking on the right wherever you may be. This will not only eliminate any risk of committing an offence but will also tend to prevent you from absent-mindedly driving off on the wrong side when you move away again. In most built-up areas, traffic coming from the right has priority.

Camping

Europe is a camping paradise and this is the answer for the family who want to go abroad as cheaply as possible. Well-run camps are plentiful and most countries have tourist agencies in London where excellent brochures and other information, including maps of camping sites, can be obtained free of charge.

Whether touring or camping, one word of warning—don't leave litter. Regulations about this are stringently enforced.

INDEX

Acanthus, **199**
Accidents, 504
Acne, 506
Adam, Robert, **227**
Adolescence, 506
Adoption, **627–8**
Adult education, 748
Afternoon tea, 549, **256, 263, 268**
Agapanthus, **200**
Age allowance, **723**
Air sickness, **592**
Air travel, **252–3, 732**
All-electric water heaters, **118–20**
"All risks" insurance, **703**
Almond milk soup, 348
Almond pudding, **291, 303**
Alsatians, **669–70**
Aluminium plates, 322
Aluminium saucepans, 437
Amaranthus, **200**
Ambulance services, **250, 252**
Analgesia, 476
Anchovy, 16–17, 175
Anemones, **219**
Angelica, **282**
"Animal gardens," **688–90**
Animal owner's liability, **630**
Ante-natal care, 476–8
Antique collecting, **230–2**
Ants, 446
Anxiety, 730–1
Anzac Nutties, **444**
Aperitifs, 304
Apple drinks, **487**
Apple Florentine pie, **288**
Apple pasty, **290**
Apple pudding, **297–8**
Apple snow, 346
Apple trees, 585–6
Apples, 116–18, 131, 152, 156, 346
Apricots, 588
Aquarium, **686–7**
Architect, **691–7**
Arrowroot, 261
Art, **723, 747**
Artichokes, 97, **320**
Artificial sunlight, 617
Artists International Association, 746
Arts Council of Great Britain, 745–6

Arundel mullets, **303–4**
Asparagus, 97
Asphalt floors, **70**
Aspic, 77, 110, 237, 289, 350
Aspidistras, **223**
Astrantia, **199**
"At home," **241**
Atholl Brose, **314**
Atomic power, **4–6**
Aubergine (egg-plant), 98
Australian cookery, **432–43**
Austrian cookery, **382–7**
Avocado pears, **279**
Awnings, **214**

Baby bedding, 486
Baby care, 489–98
Baby clothes, 406
Baby foods, 288, 491–4, **258**
Baby toys, 517–18
Back boilers, **56, 57**
Backstone cakes, **298**
Bacon, 55, 64, 70, 171, 172, 176, 179
Bacon pudding, **288**
Baked apples and caraway comfits, **304**
Baked fruit, 152, 156
Bakewell tart, **292**
Baking powder, 116, 184, 186
Ball-making, 516
Balm, **282**
Balm wine, 610
Bamboo, **184–5**
Bananas, 98, 105, 112, 119, 152, 153
Banbury apple pie, **301**
Bank overdraft, **719–20**
Banking accounts, **718–20**
Bara-brith, **315–16**
Barfi, **416**
Barley pilaff, **452**
Barley water, 262
Bath buns, **302**
Bath mats, **125–6**
Bathroom colour schemes, **15–16**
Bathroom equipment, **29, 127**
Bathroom heating, **63, 68**
Baths, **122–3**
Batter, 123, 124
Bay leaves, **282**
Beans, 253, 254, 598–600

Beauty treatment, **611–15, 648**
Bed-bugs, 446
Bedcovers, 674, **112–14, 158, 159**
Bed jackets, 675
Bed lighting, **96**
Bedroom colour schemes, **14–15**
Bedroom furniture, **27–8**
Bedroom stools, 675
Beds, **27, 104–14**
Bed-settees, **29**
Bedspreads, 674, **112–14, 158–9**
Bed warmer, 474
Beef, 54, 58–62, 81, 276
Beef tea, 259
Beehives, 622–3
Beekeeping, 621–4
Beetroot, 98, 239
Belgian cookery, **406–12**
Belladonna, **285**
Bells, **553**
Berberis, 571–2, **200**
Bernerplatte, **344–5**
"Best man," 714
Bias, 635–6, 652
Bicarbonate of soda, 116, 185, 477
Bicycles, **646–7**
Biffins, **298**
Bircher muesli, 245
Bird baths, 577
Birthday cake, 205
Birth marks, 498
Biscuits, 144, 214–20, 513, **441–3**
Blackberries, 587
Blackberry wine, 608
Blackcurrants, 584–5
Blackcurrant wine, 611
Blankets, **109–10**
Blinds, **558**
Blinys, **369–70**
Bloaters, 44
Blood transfusion, **616**
Bluebottles, 446
Board games, 521, 523
Body odour, 458
Boilers, 433, **43–4, 52–6, 115–16**
Boiling meat, 56
Boils, **593–4**
Bolsters, **109**

Figures in bold type refer to Volume II

Figures in bold type refer to Volume II

INDEX

Figures in bold type refer to Volume II

INDEX

Figures in bold type refer to Volume II

INDEX

Figures in bold type refer to Volume II

Figures in bold type refer to Volume II

Figures in bold type refer to Volume II

Figures in bold type refer to Volume II

Figures in bold type refer to Volume II

Figures in bold type refer to Volume II

Figures in bold type refer to Volume II

INDEX TO COLOUR PLATES

Figures in bold type refer to Volume II

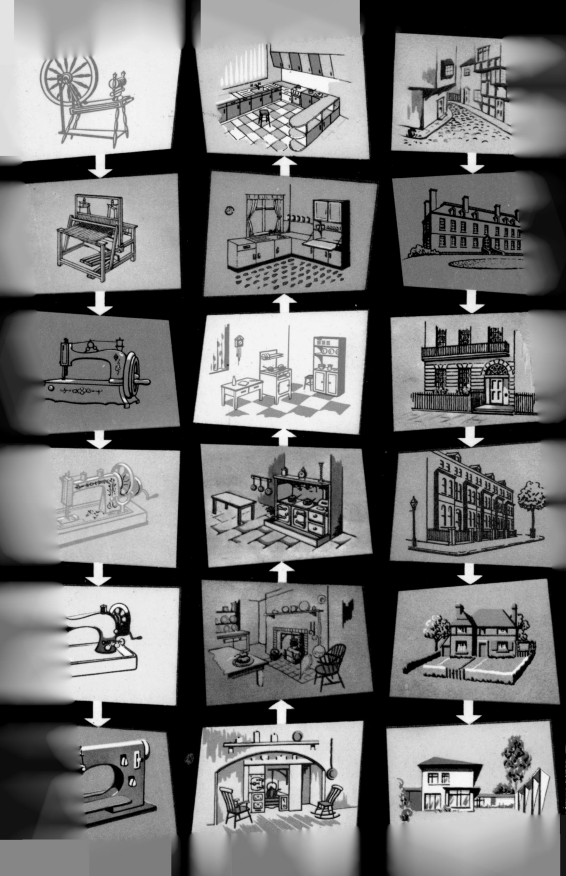